Mastering
HTML and XHTML

Mastering™
HTML and XHTML

Deborah S. Ray

Eric J. Ray

SYBEX®   San Francisco   Paris   Düsseldorf   Soest   London

Associate Publisher: Dan Brodnitz

Acquisitions and Developmental Editor: Willem Knibbe

Editor: Liz Welch

Production Editor: Erica Yee

Technical Editor: Martin Reid

Book Designer: Franz Baumhackl

Electronic Publishing Specialist: Franz Baumhackl

Proofreaders: Emily Hsuan, Laurie O'Connell, Nancy Riddiough, Yariv Rabinovitch

Indexer: Ted Laux

Cover Designer: Design Site

Cover Illustrator: Jack D. Meyers

To Ashleigh and Alex,
who have taught us what's important in life.

Acknowledgements

WE'D LIKE TO THANK the many folks who helped bring this book together. First, a big thanks to Dan Brodnitz, with whom we were fortunate enough to work again on this edition as we were on the book's very first edition some years ago. Excellent working with you again, Dan. Thank you.

We were also fortunate to work with Willem Knibbe, whose excellent guidance, quick turnaround, and attention to quality helped shape this book and its content. Thanks also to Erica Yee for keeping the process moving along smoothly.

We'd also like to thank the behind-the-scenes team at Sybex who brought this book together. Thanks to Martin Reid for helping make this book as accurate as possible. Thanks also to Liz Welch for her excellent editing, comments, and suggestions. And to Franz Baumhackl, Emily Hsuan, Laurie O'Connell, Nancy Riddiough, Yariv Rabinovitch, and Ted Laux. You folks rock, and we thank you!

Contents at a Glance

Contents

Introduction

WELCOME TO *Mastering HTML and XHTML, Premium Edition*—your one-stop comprehensive guide to the Hypertext Markup Language (HTML) and Extensible Hypertext Markup Language (XHTML)! In this book, you'll find the following features:

- Plain English explanations of what HTML and XHTML are, what the differences are between the two, and which one is right for your needs.

- Easy-to-follow instructions that help you build HTML and XHTML documents one step at a time, or to convert documents from HTML to XHTML.

- Easy-to-understand descriptions of how to apply HTML and XHTML elements to create features you want.

- Tips, advice, examples, and explanations of how to develop Web sites with users' needs in mind.

- Examples of how you can enhance your Web pages with various technologies, including JavaScript and multimedia.

- Design guidelines to help you use HTML and XHTML properly and effectively.

- Thorough coverage of XML uses, applications, and structure, along with information about how to integrate XHTML and XML documents.

- Thorough coverage of advanced HTML and XHTML topics, such as generating HTML or XHTML from a database and creating searchable HTML or XHTML.

- Useful information and advice about choosing tools that meet your Web page creation, management, and publishing needs.

- A comprehensive reference on HTML, XHTML, style sheets, JavaScript, special characters, browser-safe colors, and the XML specification.

We developed this book so that any Web content developer—whether a newbie or a seasoned professional—can learn and use HTML and XHTML effectively. For example, if you're new to HTML or XHTML, you can start at the beginning and work your way forward as you improve and expand upon your skills. You'll find the step-by-step instructions and examples easy to follow and understand. However, if you're already up to speed on authoring in HTML, you can thumb through later chapters to learn about new topics (including XHTML and XML) and develop new skills, use the Master's Reference to find the information you seek, or jump straight to the sections on XML or converting from HTML to XHTML to see where the future lies. So, if you're involved in any way with creating documents for the Web, you'll find this book an invaluable reference.

What's in This Book?

This book contains nine parts, including the Master's Reference. Here's what to expect:

Part 1: Getting Started

In this part, you'll learn about HTML and XHTML code, develop your first HTML or XHTML document—including all the common page elements and even a few relatively advanced features, such as links, adding images, and working with fancy formatting controls.

Part 2: Advancing Your Skills

In this part, you'll move on to some of the more sophisticated and interesting HTML and XHTML effects, such as working with tables, frames, and forms. You'll also learn how to convert HTML files into their XHTML equivalents, including some cool tools to help automate this otherwise time-consuming and tedious task.

Part 3: Moving Beyond Pure XHTML

In this part, you'll learn how to use Cascading Style Sheets to manage how Web documents appear inside your users' browsers with verve and precision. You'll also learn about incorporating interactivity and flexible controls with JavaScript, and how to include multimedia effects in your Web pages. Armed with this information, you should be able to create HTML and XHTML pages with great power and eye appeal!

Part 4: Developing Web Sites

In this part, you'll learn the ins and outs of developing and managing highly functional Web sites that your users will want to keep coming back to visit. Here, you'll learn many aspects you'll need to consider in planning, developing, and testing your site, and you'll find tips and tricks to help you develop specific types of Web sites—including public, personal, and intranet sites—with ease and panache. These chapters show you how to develop and design your pages and sites according to how they'll be used and to meet your users' needs.

Part 5: Applying HTML and XHTML to Advanced Applications

In this part, you'll learn about some more sophisticated HTML and XHTML applications. First, you'll find out how to apply what you've already learned about style sheets and JavaScript to create dynamic HTML or XHTML pages. Next, you'll discover how publishing HTML or XHTML directly from a database can ease your workload and help you keep your site entirely up-to-date. Finally, a chapter on creating and managing searchable HTML or XHTML gives you the tools you need to let people search your Web site easily and effectively.

Part 6: XHTML Development Tools

In this part, you'll survey the ever-changing landscape of Web development tools, including those that work with HTML, XHTML, and XML. You'll learn about some of the capabilities that high-end authoring tools have to offer, as well as explore the value and confidence that validation tools can confer. Next, you'll find out the secrets and importance of validating your XHTML documents.

Part 7: XHTML: A Bridge to XML

In this part, you'll examine the interesting and powerful relationship between XML and XHTML (the "X" in XHTML stands for extensible, after all). First, you'll tackle a review of XML's capabilities and characteristics. Then, you'll find an in-depth discussion of the many and various relationships that it's possible to create between XHTML and other XML applications, with a particular emphasis on how to extend documents beyond XHTML's built-in markup and semantics.

The next two chapters cover the ins and outs of working with the formal definitions of XML markup called Document Type Definitions (DTDs); here, you'll learn how to define and use you own customized markup! Finally, you'll examine the details behind the W3C's efforts to break XHTML into a series of interrelated subsets called *modules* (which is why this effort is called "modularization") so that certain XHTML documents need only incorporate those components of the markup language that they actually use. (Thus, a cell phone with XHTML support does not have to incorporate support for tables, frames, or graphics, because it's not likely they will be used on the itty-bitty screen so typical on such a device.)

Part 8: The XML Family of Applications

In this part, you'll get a sense of what the XML fuss is all about, as you look at important ways to use XML-based markup languages to manage and present XML-based documents and data. Starting with an examination of the Extensible Stylesheet Language Transformations (XSLT), you'll learn how to turn XML into HTML or XHTML on the fly for delivery to older Web browsers (or for maximum backward compatibility). After that, you'll get a chance to see what XML's Synchronized Multimedia Integration Language (SMIL) can do to help you coordinate voice, text, and multimedia effects in your Web pages. Next, you learn how to navigate, interrogate, and access the contents of parsed XML documents (including XHTML) using easy programming tools and techniques. Finally, you learn about XML Schemas, another method for defining XML documents that's particularly well suited to capture complex data types and for screening input and output values.

Part 9: Master's Reference

The Master's Reference includes five sections:

HTML and XHTML Elements and Attributes   A comprehensive list of HTML and XHTML elements and attributes, with definitions, explanations, and examples of proper usage.

Cascading Style Sheets Reference   A comprehensive explanation of style sheet markup, with a list of related markup elements and attributes, plus examples of proper usage.

Scripting Reference   A comprehensive list of JavaScript objects, properties, methods, and functions with examples of how to use them.

HTML and XHTML Special Characters   A collection of pointers to the numerous variants of the ISO-8859 Character sets (also known as ISO-Latin character sets) and to the ISO 10646 Character sets (also known as Unicode).

Color Codes   A list of pointers to color descriptions and equivalent numeric RGB code values.

Conventions in This Book

Throughout this book, we've employed several conventions intended to help you find and use the information it contains more easily.

Text Conventions

The following text conventions will help you easily identify new words, show you how to follow along with the examples, and help you use menu commands.

The first time a new word is used, it appears in *italics* and is followed by a brief definition or example. For example, we explain that *markup* is the formal term used to describe the text that denotes XHTML elements within a document.

Examples of HTML and XHTML markup appear in a special font `like this`, and usually appear within a line of copy, or on one or more lines that stand by themselves. If an example requires that you type in new markup for each step, the new markup you enter appears in bold, like this:

```
<p>A line of markup from a previous step.</p>
<p>Another line of markup from a previous step.</p>
<p>New markup to enter in the current step!</p>
```

Finally, instructions for using a menu command appear like this:

1. Choose File ➤ Save As to open the Save As dialog box, and then choose Options.

This sequence means you should go to the File menu, and choose Save As from the drop-down list of entries. The Save As dialog box appears, from which you should choose the Options entry.

Icon Conventions

The following icons indicate helpful tips and warnings. They're flagged to get your attention, and are usually worth reading for that very reason!

TIP   *Tips include time-saving information to help you make your HTML and XHTML authoring easier and faster.*

WARNING   *Warnings flag potential trouble spots (or potential sources of trouble, anyway). Ignore them at your own risk!*

Examples Used in this Book

Throughout this book, we've included a slew of examples to accompany descriptions, explanations, and step-by-step instructions:

The TECHWR-L Web site (a RayComm, Inc. Resource) This is our Web site, an online magazine and resource for technical writers. Established in 1997, this site is significant a source of firsthand information, tips, and advice we share in this book. At the time of writing, the site serves an average of 700,000 page views to 60,000 unique visitors per month.

ASR Outfitters This is a fictitious company and Web site that we developed for the first edition of this book. Although ASR Outfitters' Web site design is a bit dated (in that the current site designs favor smaller links and text, for example), this sample site illustrates current applications for HTML and XHTML code.

Michael Jantze's "The Norm" In Chapter 11, you'll see how Michael Jantze used HTML and JavaScript-based effects to present information on his "The Norm" Web site (`www.thenorm.com`), and then used Flash to present the same content more effectively. Then, in Chapter 12, "The Norm" site shows how text, graphics, and color can be combined into effective navigation.

WAMMI, Inc. Another fictitious company, the WAMMI examples help guide you through planning your Web site in Chapter 12.

Exploring Additional Resources

Throughout this book, we point you to lots of Web sites—some show you examples of how companies apply HTML and XHTML code to meet their needs, some offer software for you to download, and some are information resources to help you keep up-to-date on HTML, XHTML, and related topics, tools, and technologies. Remember that Web content changes frequently so you may not find everything exactly as described in this book, or in the location we say it resides. Although we verified everything immediately before this book went to press, we can't guarantee specific content at specific addresses, given the rate and scope of change on the Web.

Contact Us

We're glad you chose *Mastering HTML and XHTML* as your one-stop HTML and XHTML resource and reference. Please let us know how it goes—we're always glad to read your comments, ponder your suggestions, and respond to your questions. You can contact us at `MasteringHTMLandXHTML@raycomm.com`. We look forward to hearing from you!

Part 1

Getting Started

WHERE DID HTML AND XHTML COME FROM?

The roots of *HTML* (which is the predecessor to XHTML) go back to the late 1980s and early 1990s. That's when Tim Berners-Lee first developed HTML to provide a simple way for scientists at CERN (a particle physics laboratory in Geneva, Switzerland) to exchange reports and research results on the Web. HTML is based on a formal definition created using a powerful *meta-language*—a language used to create other languages—called the *Standard Generalized Markup Language (SGML)*. SGML is an International Organization for Standardization (ISO) standard tool designed to create markup languages of many kinds.

By the early 1990s, the power and reach of the World Wide Web was becoming well known, and CERN released HTML for unrestricted public use. CERN eventually turned HTML over to an industry group called the World Wide Web Consortium (W3C), which continues to govern HTML and related markup-language specifications. Public release of HTML (and its companion protocol, the *Hypertext Transfer Protocol, or HTTP*, which is what browsers use to request Web pages, and what Web servers use to respond to such requests) launched the Web revolution that has changed the face of computing and the Internet forever.

In the years since HTML became a public standard, HTML has been the focus of great interest, attention, and use. The original definition of HTML provided a way for us to identify and mark up *content*—specific information judged to be of sufficient importance to deliver online—without worrying too much about how that information looked, or how it was presented and formatted on the user's computer display. But as commercial interest in the Web exploded, graphic designers and typographers involved in Web design found themselves wishing for the kind of presentation and layout controls that they received from software such as PageMaker and QuarkXPress. HTML was never designed as a full-fledged presentation tool, but it was being pulled strongly in that direction, often by browser vendors, such as Microsoft and Netscape, who sought market share for their software by accommodating the desires of their audience.

Unfortunately, these browser-specific implementations resulted in variations in the HTML language definitions that weren't supported by all browsers and resulted in functionality that wasn't part of any official HTML language definition. Web designers found themselves in a pickle—forced either to build Web pages for the lowest common denominator that all browsers could support, or to build Web pages that targeted specific browsers that not all users could necessarily view or appreciate.

Basically, XHTML was created as a means to address this discrepancy. XHTML provides a way to take advantage of a newer, more compact underlying meta-language called XML (Extensible Markup Language) that is inherently extensible and, therefore, open-ended. More important, XHTML helps rationalize and consolidate a Web markup landscape that had become highly fragmented (a result of different and incompatible implementations of HTML). There are many other good reasons for using standard-compliant HTML or XHTML, and you'll learn more about them later in this chapter and throughout this book.

The HTML and XHTML specifications—all versions, revisions, and updates—are maintained by the W3C and can be found at www.w3.org. Taking a tour through the W3C Web pages can be quite useful, in terms of learning what issues are considered most pressing or least important to the people making the specifications. In addition, you can find out if your personal concerns are being addressed.

Continued on next page

WHERE DID HTML AND XHTML COME FROM? *(continued)*

At the time this book was written, the primary issues being addressed by the HTML Working Group were pushing XHTML in the direction of modularization (Chapter 25) and toward use of Schemas (Chapter 29, on the Web). Both of these issues reflect the importance of moving HTML toward standards that are:

◆ Compatible with existing browsers and tools

◆ Flexible enough to accommodate non-traditional browsers, like handheld computers and Web-enabled cell phones

◆ Consistent and predictable enough to be readily parsed and processed by Web servers and other programs to provide tailored content

That said, you do not need to worry about the future of HTML as you know it. No plans are under way to make any changes or improvements to HTML 4.01, and XHTML 1.0 is explicitly defined as being a "reformulation" of HTML 4.01 in XML; therefore, your investment of time and effort in learning HTML or XHTML won't be wasted. In our opinion, given the number of Web pages out there, there's virtually no possibility that HTML 4.01 or XHTML will change substantially or cease to exist in the next several years—high-end Web sites and information delivery systems will evolve to take advantage of the new features that the W3C defines, but all of the basics (for example, everything in this book) will continue to work for the foreseeable future.

You'll find more history about markup languages in Chapter 21, which discusses XML in the context of how it fits into HTML and SGML (Standard Generalized Markup Language).

What Tools Do You Need?

Whether you're planning to develop HTML or XHTML documents, you'll need three basic tools:

◆ A plain-vanilla text editor, which you will use to create and save your documents. The "HTML and XHTML Editors" sidebar provides more information about some of the editors that are available; however, keep in mind that we highly recommend using a plain-text editor for developing HTML and XHTML documents—at least when you're learning to use these markup languages.

◆ A Web browser, which you will use to view and test your documents. In fact, you should have multiple Web browsers available so that you can see how your documents look when viewed in these different browsers.

◆ A validator, which you will use to verify that your HTML or XHTML documents are developed and coded correctly. We recommend using a validator if you're developing HTML documents; however, because browsers can often display HTML code that's a bit sloppy or not completely "standard," validating your HTML documents isn't an absolute must. If you're developing XHTML documents, however, you *must* use a validator as part of your document-development and publishing process. The XHTML standard has specific rules to follow, and if you want to use XHTML, you must ensure that your XHTML code is applied correctly.

Let's take a more in-depth look at these necessary tools.

Text Editors

Text editors force you to *hand-code*, meaning that you, not the software, enter the code. Hand-coding helps you learn HTML and XHTML elements, attributes, and structures, and it lets you see exactly where you've made mistakes. Also, with hand-coding, you can easily include the newest enhancements in your documents, whereas WYSIWYG editors don't have those enhancements available until updated product versions are released.

Some basic text editors are:

◆ Notepad for all Windows versions

◆ vi or pico (command line), or GEdit or Kate (GUI) for Linux/Unix

◆ TeachText or SimpleText for Macintosh

WARNING   *Using a word processing program such as Word, StarOffice, or even WordPad to create HTML documents often inadvertently introduces unwanted formatting and control characters, which can cause problems. HTML and XHTML require plain text, so either make a special effort to save all documents as plain text within such applications, or take our advice and use a text editor instead.*

HTML AND XHTML EDITORS

In general, editors fall into two categories:

Text- or code-based editors, which show you the HTML or XHTML code as you're creating documents   A variety of code-based HTML and XHTML editors exist for Windows, Macintosh, and Linux/Unix, and most of them are fairly easy to use (and create HTML code just as you wrote it). That said, as we write this chapter, few editors are available that produce XHTML code (or rigorously standard-compliant HTML code, for that matter).

However, it's possible to use an HTML editor or a simple text editor to create an initial version of your XHTML documents and then to make use of a special-purpose tool, such as HTML Tidy or HTML-Kit, to transform your HTML into equivalent, properly formatted XHTML. Because this requires a bit more savvy than we assume from our general readership, this material is aimed only at those more experienced readers to whom this kind of approach makes sense.

WYSIWYG ("What You See Is What You Get") editors, which show the results of code, similar to the way it will appear in a browser, as you're formatting your document   Simple WYSIWYG editors, such as Netscape Composer and Microsoft FrontPage Express, are good for quickly generating HTML documents. These editors give you a close approximation of page layout, design, and colors, and are good for viewing the general arrangement of features. However, they do not give you as much control over the final appearance of your document as code-based editors do. Additionally, although there have been improvements over the last couple of years, WYSIWYG editors notoriously introduce unneeded elements, non-compliant code, and other characteristics that purists object to.

After you've developed a few HTML documents and understand basic HTML principles, you may choose to use both a WYSIWYG editor and a code-based editor. For example, you can get a good start on your document using a WYSIWYG HTML editor and then polish it (or fix it) using a code-based one. Others prefer Web editing/publishing tools like Dreamweaver, which offers a combined approach with both WYSIWYG and code-based modes.

For now, though, we recommend that you hand-code HTML and XHTML using a plain-text editor.

Web Browsers

The most common browsers are Microsoft Internet Explorer (IE) and Netscape Navigator; however, many other browsers are also available for virtually all computer platforms and online services. (AOL's browser is based on IE and functionally nearly the same.) We're especially fond of Opera (available free at `www.opera.com`) and Amaya (available free at `www.w3.org/Amaya/`) because they often support advanced features and functions better and sooner than the more popular IE and Netscape browsers do.

As you're developing HTML or XHTML documents, keep in mind that exactly how your documents appear varies from browser to browser and from computer to computer. For example, most browsers in use today are *graphical browsers*: they can display elements other than text. A *text-only* browser can display—you guessed it—only text. How your documents appear in each of these types of browsers differs significantly, as shown in Figures 1.1 and 1.2.

FIGURE 1.1

An HTML document displayed in Netscape Navigator

Even graphical browsers tend to display things a bit differently. For example, one browser might display a first-level heading as 15-point Times New Roman bold, whereas another might display the same heading as 14-point Arial italic. In both cases, the browser displays the heading bigger and more emphasized than regular text, but the specific text characteristics vary. Figures 1.3 and 1.4 show how two other browsers display the same XHTML document.

FIGURE 1.2

The same HTML
document viewed in
Lynx, a text-only
browser

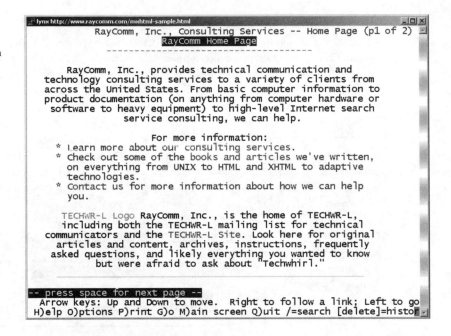

FIGURE 1.2

The same HTML
document viewed in
Lynx, a text-only
browser

FIGURE 1.3

The W3C Amaya
browser has its own
unique look and feel

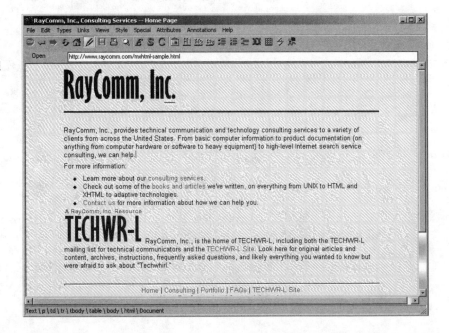

FIGURE 1.4

The Opera browser shows the same document with slightly different formatting

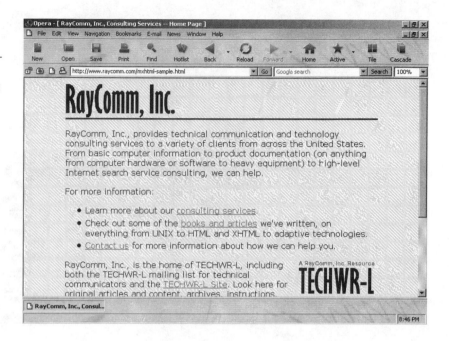

TIP   Finally, your user's computer settings can also make a big difference in how your HTML or XHTML documents appear. For example, the computer's resolution and specific browser settings can alter a document's appearance.

So, as you're developing and viewing your documents, remember that what you see may look a bit different to your users. Test your documents in as many different browsers as possible, at as many different resolutions and color settings as possible, on as many different computers as possible. You won't be able to test for all variations, but you should be able to get a good idea of what your users might see.

The W3C Validator

You should also use an HTML or XHTML *validator*, which is a tool that examines your documents and verifies that the documents follow the rules for applying code and document structure.

Although a number of validators exist, the W3C Validator is the most definitive, because it's developed by the same folks who developed the HTML and XHTML specification. To use it, first open your browser. Then:

1. Go to `http://validator.w3.org/file-upload.html`.

2. Browse your local hard disk, and upload the file you want using the validator's interface.

If you're in luck, what you get back looks like what's shown in Figure 1.5. If you're not in luck, you will need to find out how to read and interpret the validator's sometimes-cryptic error messages. Because this interpretation is a substantial chore, we've devoted Chapter 20 to this topic; you may want to read it through before your first encounter with the validator.

FIGURE 1.5

When the W3C validator finds no errors, its output is both short and very sweet!

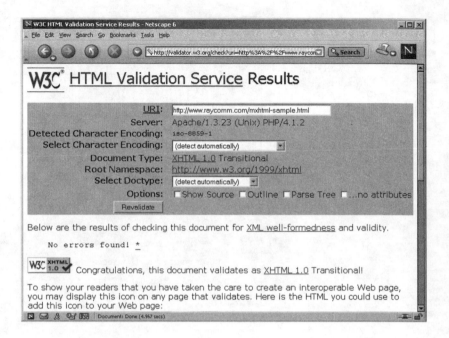

You should make validation part of your standard authoring process. That way, you'll get the best possible guarantee that most browsers will be able to view and display the contents of your documents.

NOTE   Remember, validating your XHTML is necessary to ensure that it really is compliant with the XHTML standards.

What Does HTML and XHTML Code Look Like?

As Figure 1.6 shows, HTML and XHTML documents are plain-text files. They contain no images, no sounds, no videos, and no animations; however, they can include *pointers*, or links, to these file types, which is how Web pages end up looking as if they contain non-text elements.

As you can see, HTML and XHTML documents look nothing like the Web pages you view in your browser. Instead, documents are made up of *elements* and *attributes* that work together to identify document parts and tell browsers how to display them. Listing 1.1 shows the elements and attributes that create the Web page shown in Figures 1.1 through 1.4.

FIGURE 1.6

HTML and XHTML documents are just text files, containing the code and content you provide

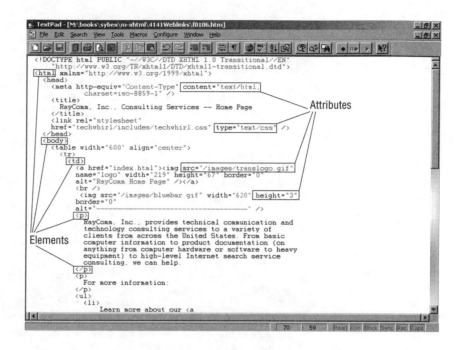

LISTING 1.1: HTML AND XHTML CODE INCLUDES CONTEXT, ELEMENTS, ATTRIBUTES, AND LINKS THAT FORM A WEB PAGE

```
<!DOCTYPE html PUBLIC "-//W3C//DTD XHTML 1.0 Transitional//EN"
    "http://www.w3.org/TR/xhtml1/DTD/xhtml1-transitional.dtd">
<html xmlns="http://www.w3.org/1999/xhtml">
  <head>
    <meta http-equiv="Content-Type" content="text/html;
          charset=iso-8859-1" />
    <title>
      RayComm, Inc., Consulting Services -- Home Page
    </title>
    <link rel="stylesheet"
    href="techwhirl/includes/techwhirl.css" type="text/css" />
  </head>
  <body>
    <table width="600" align="center">
      <tr>
        <td>
          <a href="index.html"><img src="/images/translogo.gif"
          name="logo" width="219" height="67" border="0"
          alt="RayComm Home Page" /></a>
          <br />
           <img src="/images/bluebar.gif" width="620"
```

```
height="3" border="0"
alt="-------------------------------------" />
<p>
RayComm, Inc., provides technical communication and
technology consulting services to a variety of
clients from across the United States. From basic
computer information to product documentation (on
anything from computer hardware or software to heavy
equipment) to high-level Internet search service
consulting, we can help.
</p>
<p>
  For more information:
</p>
<ul>
  <li>
    Learn more about our <a
    href="consulting.html">consulting services</a>.
  </li>
  <li>
    Check out some of the <a href="books.html">books
    and articles</a> we've written, on everything
    from UNIX to HTML and XHTML to adaptive
    technologies.
  </li>
  <li>
    <a href="contact.html">Contact us</a>
      for more information about how we can help you.
  </li>
</ul>
<p>
<img src="/techwhirl/images/techwhirllogo.gif"
alt="TECHWR-L Logo" align="right" /> RayComm, Inc.,
is the home of TECHWR-L, including both the TECHWR-L
mailing list for technical communicators and the <a
href="/techwhirl/">TECHWR-L Site</a>. Look here for
original articles and content, archives,
instructions, frequently asked questions, and likely
everything you wanted to know but were afraid to ask
about "Techwhirl."
</p>
<br clear="all" />
<hr />
<p class="centered">
  <a href="index.html">Home</a> | <a
  href="consulting.html">Consulting</a> | <a
  href="portfolio.html">Portfolio</a> | <a
  href="faqs.html">FAQs</a> | <a
```

```
           href="/techwhirl/index.html">TECHWR-L Site</a>
           <br />
           <a href="aboutraycomm.html">About RayComm, Inc.</a>
           | <a href="contact.html">Contact Information</a>
        </p>
        <p class="centered">
           Last modified on 1 April, 2002
           <br />
           Site contents Copyright &copy; 1997 - 2002 RayComm,
           Inc.
           <br />
            Send comments to <a
           href="mailto:webmaster@raycomm.com">webmaster@raycomm.com</a>.
           <br />
        </p>
      </td>
    </tr>
  </table>
  </body>
</html>
```

TIP *Throughout this book, we use the term* users *to describe the people who view and use the HTML and XHTML documents you develop.*

Understanding Elements

HTML and XHTML elements serve two primary functions. First, they identify *logical document parts*—that is, major structural components in documents, such as headings (h1, a heading level 1, for example), numbered lists (o1, also called ordered lists), and paragraphs (p). For example, if you want to include a paragraph component in an HTML or XHTML document, you type the text and apply the appropriate elements (<p> to the beginning of the paragraph and </p> at the end) to that text, as this snippet from Listing 1.1 shows:

```
<p>
   RayComm, Inc., provides technical communication and
   technology consulting services to a variety of
   clients from across the United States. From basic
   computer information to product documentation (on
   anything from computer hardware or software to heavy
   equipment) to high-level Internet search service
   consulting, we can help.
</p>
```

And, voila, the paragraph element (<p>...</p>) marks that document part to be a paragraph.

Second, some elements refer to other things that are not included in the HTML or XHTML document itself. Whereas the <p> and <h1> elements just mentioned refer to paragraph and heading components within the document itself, elements can also mark *pointers*—essentially just links—to other documents, images, sound files, video files, multimedia applications, animations, applets, and so on. For example, if you want to include an image of your company's product in your document, rather than pasting an image directly into the document (as you might in a word processing file), you include an element that points to the file location of that image, as shown here:

```
<img src="logo.gif" alt="logo" />
```

In this example, the img (image) element points to a logo file (logo.gif) that the browser should display. This illustrates that browsers rely on information within the HTML or XHTML document to tell them what to display, as well as how to display it.

Understanding Attributes

Some HTML and XHTML elements take modifying values called *attributes*, which provide additional information about the elements, such as:

◆ What other files should be accessed, such as an image file

◆ What alternative text should be associated with the element

◆ Which style classes should be used to format the element

Let's assume you want to center a heading 1 in the browser window. You'd start with your heading and elements, like this:

```
<h1>A heading goes here</h1>
```

Next, you'd add the style and type attributes to the opening element, like this:

```
<h1 style="text-align:center">A centered heading goes here</h1>
```

In this example, the heading level one element includes attributes that specify the style to be aligned in the center. As you can see, attributes normally have two parts: the attribute name (style=, in this example) and the value ("text-align:center"). The value *should* appear in quotes in HTML and *must* appear in quotes in XHTML.

ABOUT COMMON ATTRIBUTES

In HTML and XHTML, there are several attributes that can be applied to nearly all elements; these are known as the *common* attributes. They include:

id="name"   Assigns a unique name to an element within a document.

style="style"   Allows the author of the document to use Cascading Style Sheets (CSS) as attribute values or to define the presentation parameters for that specific element. You can use the style attribute with all elements except html, head, title, meta, style, script, param, base, and basefont.

class="name"   Assigns a class or a set of classes to an element. This attribute is frequently used with CSS to establish the display properties for a particular subset of elements.

Continued on next page

ABOUT COMMON ATTRIBUTES *(continued)*

lang="language code"   Specifies the language of the content contained by the element. For example, `lang="en"` declares that English is the language used.

dir="ltr | rtl"   Specifies the direction text should be displayed. This doesn't seem like an important attribute unless you remember that many of the world's languages are not read from left to right. Yes, `ltr` means "left to right," and `rtl` means "right to left."

title="text"   Functions in a manner similar to the `title` element but applies only to a specific element instead of an entire document. Caveat: The attribute's *behavior* is not defined by the HTML or XHTML specification. Instead, the way that behavior is rendered is left up to the browser, and the content is usually presented as a pop-up tooltip when readers hover the mouse pointer over the text. This attribute is currently most useful on sites or documents that the author knows will be viewed by users of Internet Explorer 5, Opera 6, or Netscape 6 (or later) browsers. The `title` attribute cannot be used with the following elements: `html`, `head`, `meta`, `title`, `script`, `param`, `base`, and `basefont`.

Typing Elements and Attributes Correctly

As our examples so far should illustrate, elements and attributes are reasonably intuitive. Although markup can occasionally be cryptic, you can generally get some idea of an element or attribute function from its name.

Before we get started on typing elements and attributes, be aware that entering elements and attributes varies *slightly* depending on whether you're using HTML or XHTML. Remember that we mentioned XHTML is a bit pickier? Well, entering XHTML markup is where that pickiness comes into play. Again, though, XHTML is not harder; you'll just have to pay a bit more attention as you're learning to use it. In the next sections, we'll do the following:

- Describe general guidelines for typing HTML and XHTML elements and attributes
- Show you how to *nest* elements (apply more than one element to a document part)
- Explain specific rules for typing XHTML elements and attributes
- Help you improve readability of your HTML and XHTML documents

TYPING ELEMENTS AND ATTRIBUTES IN EITHER HTML OR XHTML (GENERAL INFORMATION)

To begin, all elements are composed of *element names* that are contained within *angle brackets* (< >). The angle brackets simply tell browsers that the text between them represents HTML or XHTML markup rather than ordinary text content. Some sample elements look like these:

- `<h2>` (for heading level 2)
- `<p>` (for document paragraph)
- `<strong>` (to emphasize a particular section of content)

TIP   *You'll learn more about these elements and their uses in Chapter 2.*

Second, many elements are designed to contain content; they use a pair of tags, where actual content occurs between the *opening tag* (for example, `<h1>`) and the corresponding *closing tag* (`</h1>`). Both tags look alike, except the closing tag includes a forward slash (/) to denote the end of the element container. To apply tags to something in your document, place an opening tag before the content that should be associated with the element you want to use, and place the closing tag after it, as these examples show:

```
<h1>Information to which the tags apply</h1>
```

or

```
<title>Correctly Formed Title</title>
```

When typing elements, be particularly careful *not* to include extra spaces within the tag itself, as in this erroneous example:

```
< title >Incorrectly Formed Title< /title >
```

If you include spaces within the elements, browsers may not recognize the element and may not display the content correctly (or at all). Sometimes, a browser might display the markup itself because it's unable to distinguish improperly formed markup from normal element content.

TIP *When creating HTML or XHTML markup by hand, enter both the opening and closing tags at the same time. That way, you won't forget the closing tag.*

Keep in mind that you'll also use the occasional *empty elements*, which do not include a closing tag. Some empty elements include the line break element (`<br />`) and the image element (`<img />`), which do not require the closing element but include a space and a forward slash (/)after the element name. This example shows the break element (`<br />`), which would put in a line break after each line:

```
<p>
   RayComm, Inc., provides technical communication and<br />
   technology consulting services to a variety of<br />
   clients from across the United States. From basic<br />
   computer information to product documentation (on<br />
   anything from computer hardware or software to heavy<br />
   equipment) to high-level Internet search service<br />
   consulting, we can help.
</p>
```

We'll point out these empty elements throughout this book and show you how to use them correctly.

NOTE *Empty elements in HTML—as opposed to XHTML—do not require the closing / character. However, the extra / causes no problems in HTML, so we customarily use it in both HTML and XHTML.*

As we discussed, elements don't usually appear by themselves; often you'll also include attributes that provide supporting information about the element. The `style=` attribute in this example indicates that the heading level 1 should be centered:

```
<h1 style="text-align:center">A centered heading goes here</h1>
```

As you enter attributes, remember these guidelines:

◆ Include the attribute within the element after the element name, as in `<h1 style="text-align:center">`.

◆ Use spaces to separate attributes from other attributes and the element itself, as in `<h1 id="5325a" style="text-align:center">`.

◆ Enclose attribute values in quotes, as in `style="text-align:center"`. The quotes are required in XHTML and part of developing "correct" HTML. Learning to include them now will help you in the future, when newer specs are released that insist on this convention.

Finally, be aware that:

◆ HTML allows you to type in elements (and attributes) using uppercase, lowercase, or a combination of both. It's not picky, and browsers will display HTML code using whichever capitalization choice you make.

◆ XHTML requires that elements and attributes—with a few exceptions—must be typed using all lowercase. We'll point out exceptions throughout this book; however, we recommend that you use lowercase for both HTML (for good practice, should you ever move to XHTML in the future) and XHTML (because lowercase is required). The examples in this book will all be lowercase.

APPLYING MORE THAN ONE ELEMENT TO A DOCUMENT COMPONENT (NESTING ELEMENTS)

In the preceding examples, you saw how you apply elements around the text to which they apply. Suppose, though, that you need to apply more than one element to a document component. For example, say you have a paragraph that also includes a few words that you want to emphasize. To apply more than one element to a particular piece of content, you nest the tags. *Nesting* means placing one set of tags inside another set. For example, to apply strong emphasis to a word within a paragraph, you nest the `strong` element within the paragraph `p` element, as follows:

```
<p>The <strong>right</strong> way to use strong emphasis is to
   enclose only those words you want to emphasize inside a
   strong element.</p>
```

When you nest elements, the first opening tag must be matched by a corresponding closing tag at the end of the related block of content, and the second opening tag must be closed with a corresponding closing tag immediately after its related content block. XHTML is quite insistent that you nest tags in the right order. Therefore, a block of text like this:

```
<p>The last word gets strong <strong>emphasis.</p></strong>
```

is invalid because it closes the outside `p` element before closing the nested (or inside) `strong` element. It's also technically incorrect for HTML, but such issues *usually* don't cause problems in HTML.

TYPING XHTML ELEMENTS AND ATTRIBUTES

With the general information and guidelines for typing elements and attributes established, we'll now take a look at the specific rules you'll need to follow for developing XHTML documents. Although

Elements Must Be Nested Correctly

In the previous section, we described the concept of nesting, where you apply one or more elements within another element. For example, the following markup defines a `title` element that is nested with the `head` element:

```
<head>
   <title>Document title</title>
</head>
```

This may seem straightforward; however, there are cases where people make mistakes. For example, can you spot the mistake in the following markup?

```
<p>You can bold a <b>word</p></b>
```

The problem is that the tags are overlapping; no one element is nested within the other. The golden rule is "what you open first, you close last." To correct this syntax, you would write:

```
<p>You can bold a <b>word</b></p>
```

Notice how the b element is nested completely within the p element.

TIP   When referring to an element that is nested within another element, we call the nested element a child of the container element; the container is the parent element. Throughout this book we refer to nested elements as "children of a parent element."

There are a few other XHTML-specific rules that apply to certain elements and attributes. We'll mention these as we come to them in this book. The XHTML rules described here are the ones you will need to know as you're getting started.

IMPROVING DOCUMENT READABILITY

Throughout the book, because of the width limits of the printed page, we wrap and indent code lines that are meant to be written all on one line. This doesn't mean you have to wrap or indent the code you develop, but we do recommend using hard returns in your code to help make the lines a bit shorter and easier to read. Doing so does not affect how browsers display your documents (unless you inadvertently put in a space between an angle bracket and an element name); it just makes that document easier for you and others who may have to maintain the code to read when you're editing its contents.

For example, take a look at this code:

```
<!DOCTYPE html PUBLIC "-//W3C//DTD XHTML 1.0 Transitional//EN"
"http://www.w3.org/TR/xhtml1/DTD/xhtml1-transitional.dtd">
<html xmlns="http://www.w3.org/1999/xhtml"><head><title>
Mastering HTML Document Title</title></head><body>Mastering
HTML Document Body</body></html>
```

Although we've included line breaks so that the code won't run off the book's page, we could improve the readability by separating some of the code a bit, like this:

```
<!DOCTYPE html PUBLIC "-//W3C//DTD XHTML 1.0 Transitional//EN"
    "http://www.w3.org/TR/xhtml1/DTD/xhtml1-transitional.dtd">
```

```
<html xmlns="http://www.w3.org/1999/xhtml">
    <head>
        <title>Mastering HTML Document Title</title>
    </head>
    <body>
        Mastering HTML Document Body
    </body>
</html>
```

No question which one's easier to read or follow, right?

What Other Resources Can Help?

In addition to this book, you can find information, resources, and specifications on the Web. In particular, the W3C site, as well as several product-specific Web sites, will help you learn, use, and keep up with changes in HTML (unlikely to change) and XHTML (somewhat more likely to change).

Visit the W3C

The W3C was created in 1994 at the Massachusetts Institute of Technology (MIT) to oversee the development of Web standards, eventually including the XHTML standard. This consortium defines and publishes HTML, XHTML, and numerous other Web-related standards, along with information about the elements and attributes that may legally appear within HTML or XHTML documents. So, an excellent way to monitor changes is to visit the W3C site at www.w3.org/MarkUp. There you'll find new releases of XHTML standards and information about HTML standards.

For more information on proposed standards and other developments in Web-related specifications, such as Cascading Style Sheets (CSS) and XML specifications, visit the W3C's home page at www.w3.org.

Can you use new elements and attributes as they become available? For the most part, yes. By the time many popular elements and attributes become part of a standard, they already work with many or most browsers. However, some elements and attributes (including some that were introduced with HTML 4) did not have wide or stable browser support when that specification was released and, to this day, do not have nearly the breadth of support that some other elements and attributes enjoy. We'll point these out throughout this book and show you how they differ from previous versions of HTML.

Monitor Netscape and Microsoft Sites

When HTML was the prevailing Web markup standard, each time Netscape or Microsoft released a new browser version, it would also add new markup *extensions*, which are browser-specific, nonstandard elements and attributes. Some of these extensions were useful, some less so. However, as a whole, any nonstandard elements introduced into HTML caused problems both for Web developers and for users. Fortunately, far fewer extensions seem to be introduced now that XHTML has made the scene, but you should still be aware of what's added with each new browser release, if only to know what progress the browsers have made in supporting the elements and styles that are already defined.

If you're considering using extensions in your XHTML documents, keep in mind that they're not standard and that the W3C validator will not recognize or validate nonstandard markup. Also, extensions that are specific to a particular browser (for example, Netscape) will probably not work in other browsers (such as IE or Opera). For this reason, we strongly recommend that you refrain from using extensions and use only standard HTML or XHTML elements and attributes. This way, you'll not only be able to validate your documents to make sure they're syntactically correct, but you can also be reasonably sure that all your users can access the information you provide therein.

You can find Netscape's elements and attributes at

```
http://developer.netscape.com/docs/manuals/htmlguid/index.htm
```

And you will find Microsoft's elements and attributes at

```
http://msdn.microsoft.com/library/
```

under the Web Development, HTML subsections. (Note that these pages move frequently, so you may need to browse a little to get there.)

Monitor Other Sites

Although definitive information comes from the W3C, you should also check other reliable resources for information about HTML and XHTML. Here's a list of sites to check regularly.

Organization	URL
Web Design Group	www.htmlhelp.com
Web Developer's Virtual Library	www.wdvl.com
HTML Writer's Guild	www.hwg.org
WebMonkey	www.webmonkey.com
CNET's Builder.com	www.builder.com
Oasis	www.oasis-open.org
Zvon	www.zvon.org
Google Web Directory	http://directory.google.com/Top/Computers/Data_Formats/Markup_Languages/HTML/References/
WebReference.com	www.webreference.com/

Where to Go from Here

This chapter gave you a brief overview of HTML and XHTML—what they are, what they're used for, how to enter their tags and attributes correctly, and what supplemental resources might be helpful to you. Although you haven't done any HTML or XHTML coding yet, you should now possess a good foundation of basic concepts and terminology.

From here, we suggest you proceed to Chapter 2, where you'll learn more details about XHTML document syntax and structure and will create your first HTML or XHTML document. You might also browse Part IV, "Developing Web Sites," to learn about the HTML and XHTML document life cycle as well as about developing and publishing Web sites.

Chapter 2

Creating Your First HTML or XHTML Document

IF YOU'RE READY TO create your first HTML or XHTML document, you're in the right chapter! Here, we'll help you start a new HTML or XHTML document and save it using the appropriate file formats, show you how to add document structure elements (which help browsers identify your document), and show you how to apply some common formatting elements.

If you're new to HTML or XHTML (or rusty at hand-coding), you might want to review the element and attribute information in Chapter 1. Before starting this chapter, you should be familiar with elements and attributes, as well as how to apply them to your content.

Throughout this chapter, we provide lots of code samples and figures to help guide you and to show you what your results should look like. You can substitute your own text if you prefer, or you can duplicate the examples in the chapter. The step-by-step instructions will work regardless of the specific content you use. After you work through this chapter, you'll have developed your first document, complete with text, headings, horizontal rules, and even some character-level formatting.

In this chapter, you'll learn the following markup skills:

◆ Creating, saving, and viewing documents

◆ Including structure elements

◆ Applying common elements and attributes

◆ Including fancier formatting

Creating, Saving, and Viewing Documents

Exactly how you start a new document depends on which operating system and editor you're using. In general, you'll find that starting a new document is similar to starting other documents you've created. You'll make your new document an official HTML or XHTML document by saving it as such, which is discussed next.

Before you begin hand-coding HTML or XHTML, be aware that you should frequently save and view your work so you can see your progress. By doing so, you can make sure that things appear as you expect them to and catch mistakes within a few new lines of code. For example, we typically add a few new lines of code, save the document, then view it... then add a few more lines of code, save the document, then view it.... Exactly how often you save and view your documents depends on your preference. Chances are that at the beginning, you'll probably save it frequently.

You create an HTML or XHTML document in much the same way that you create any plain-text document. Here's the general process:

1. Open your text editor.

2. Start a new document. If you're using Windows, Macintosh, or Linux/Unix GUI applications, choose File ➤ New. If you're using Unix, type **vi** or **pico** to start a text-based editor.

3. Enter the code and text you want to include. (You'll have plenty of practice in this chapter.)

TIP   We recommend that you practice using HTML or XHTML by completing the examples throughout this and other chapters.

4. Save your document. If you're using Windows, Macintosh, or Linux/Unix GUI applications, choose File ➤ Save or File ➤ Save As. Otherwise, use the commands required by your editing program.

GUIDELINES FOR SAVING FILES

As you work your way through this chapter, keep these saving and viewing guidelines in mind:

◆ Name the file with an htm or html extension (yes, even if you're creating an XHTML document). Windows 3.*x* doesn't recognize four-character extensions, so you're limited to htm on that platform.

◆ If you aren't using a text-only editor such as Notepad or TeachText, verify that the file type is set to Text or ASCII. If you use word-processing programs to create HTML or XHTML documents (and remember our caveat about this from Chapter 1), save your documents as Text Only, ASCII, DOS Text, or Text With Line Breaks. The specific options will vary depending on the word processor you use.

◆ Use only letters, numbers, hyphens (-), underscores (_), and periods (.) in your filename. Most browsers also accept spaces in filenames; however, spaces often make creating links difficult, as you will see in Chapter 4.

◆ Save the document and any other documents and files associated with a particular project all in one folder. You'll find that this makes using links, images, and other advanced technologies easier.

◆ Double-check after you've saved your files to be sure that they really have an htm or html extension. Depending on Windows Explorer settings (Hide Extensions For Known File Types), it might look like filename.htm, but really be filename.htm.txt because of some unneeded help from Windows.

Viewing the HTML or XHTML documents that you develop is as simple as opening them from your local hard drive in your browser. If you're working with an open document in your editor, remember to save your latest changes and then follow these steps in your browser:

1. Choose File ➤ Open, and type the local filename or browse your hard drive until you find the file you want to open. Your particular menu command might be File ➤ Open Page, or Open File, but it's all the same thing.

2. Select the file and click OK to open it in your browser.

ALTERNATIVE WAYS TO VIEW FILES

Most browsers provide some clever features that can make developing HTML and XHTML files easier.

You can easily see your editing changes in a file by reloading it. For example, after you view a document and then save some editing changes, you can reload the document and see the latest changes. You'll probably find that clicking a Reload button is much easier than going back through the File ➤ Open and browse sequence. Generally, you reload documents by clicking a Refresh or Reload button or by choosing a similar option from the View menu. (If you make an editing change but it does not seem to show up in your browser, make sure you've saved it in your text editor, then try holding down the Shift key and clicking Refresh or Reload to force it to reload your latest changes.)

In addition, you can open a file by selecting it from a list of "bookmarks" or "favorites." *Bookmarking* a file means adding a pointer to the file so you can open the file quickly, just as a bookmark makes it easier to open a book to a specific page. Creating bookmarks, or favorites, is as easy as clicking a menu option (or even just typing a keyboard shortcut) while viewing a page. Whenever you want to go back to that page, simply click the bookmark rather than choosing File ➤ Open and selecting the file. Most browsers have bookmark options; just look for a button or a menu command.

Applying Document Structure Elements

After you create a new document, your first task is to include *document structure elements*, which provide browsers with information about document characteristics. For example, document structure elements identify the version of HTML or XHTML used, provide introductory information about the document, and include the title, among other similar things. Most document structure elements, although part of the HTML or XHTML document, do not appear in the browser window. Instead, document structure elements work behind the scenes and tell the browser which elements to include and how to display them. Although these elements do not directly produce the snazzy results you see in Web pages or help files, they are essential.

TIP   Most browsers, including Netscape Navigator and Microsoft Internet Explorer, correctly display documents that do not include document structure elements. However, there's no guarantee that future versions will continue to do so or that your results will be consistent. We strongly suggest that you use the document structure elements because they're required by the HTML and XHTML specifications.

All HTML documents should include five document structure elements, nested and ordered as in the following sample markup:

```
<!DOCTYPE HTML PUBLIC "-//W3C//DTD HTML 4.01 Transitional//EN"
        "http://www.w3.org/TR/html4/loose.dtd">
<html>
  <head>
    <title>Title That Summarizes the Document's Content</title>
  </head>
  <body>
    HTML Document Body
  </body>
</html>
```

All XHTML documents should include five document structure elements, nested and ordered as in the following sample markup:

```
<!DOCTYPE HTML PUBLIC "-//W3C//DTD XHTML 1.0 Transitional//EN"
    "http://www.w3.org/TR/xhtml1/DTD/xhtml1-transitional.dtd">
<html xmlns="http://www.w3.org/1999/xhtml">
  <head>
    <title>Title That Summarizes the Document's Content</title>
  </head>
  <body>
    XHTML Document Body
  </body>
</html>
```

TIP   You can save time when creating future HTML or XHTML documents by saving document structure elements in a template document. That way, you can easily reuse them in subsequent documents, rather than retyping them time after time. If you use an HTML or XHTML authoring program, such as Macromedia's Homesite, this markup (or something similar to it) is usually the base of a new document.

The *DOCTYPE* Declaration

The DOCTYPE declaration tells browsers and validation services which version of HTML or XHTML the document complies with. The important part of the DOCTYPE declaration is the DTD (Document Type Definition) attribute, which specifics the DTD your document follows. In brief, your HTML and XHTML documents need to comply with some basic rules—rules about what the documents can include and not include and some guidelines about how you need to structure the documents. These rules are outlined in DTDs.

NOTE   A DTD serves two purposes: to specify which elements and attributes you can use to develop markup language documents, and to specify the document structure and rules you must adhere to while developing markup language documents. Chapter 23, "Getting Started with DTDs," describes DTDs in more detail.

Both HTML and XHTML DOCTYPE declarations comes in three varieties: Strict, Transitional (Loose), and Frameset. Exactly what these declarations include depends on whether you're developing HTML or XHTML documents.

IF YOU'RE DEVELOPING HTML DOCUMENTS

Strict   This version prohibits everything except "pure" HTML, and you're not likely to use it unless you're writing HTML documents that use no formatting elements and that rely only on style sheets to make them look good. To indicate that your document complies with the Strict specification, use:

```
<!DOCTYPE HTML PUBLIC "-//W3C//DTD HTML 4.01//EN"
    "http://www.w3.org/TR/html4/strict.dtd">
```

Transitional   This version is the most flexible for accommodating deprecated elements and attributes (ones that are still useful but that may be phased out in favor of newer or different ones). In most cases, you'll want to use the Transitional DOCTYPE element. To indicate that your document complies with the Transitional specification, use:

```
<!DOCTYPE HTML PUBLIC "-//W3C//DTD HTML 4.01 Transitional//EN"
    "http://www.w3.org/TR/html4/loose.dtd">
```

Frameset   This version is similar to the Transitional specification, but it also supports the elements and attributes needed to use frames:

```
<!DOCTYPE HTML PUBLIC "-//W3C//DTD HTML 4.01 Frameset//EN"
    "http://www.w3.org/TR/html4/frameset.dtd">
```

TIP   For both HTML and XHTML documents, we recommend using the Transitional DOCTYPE element for most of your HTML document needs, unless you are planning to use frames, as discussed in Chapter 7. The Strict DTD is generally too restrictive to be useful, except in fairly unusual situations.

IF YOU'RE DEVELOPING XHTML DOCUMENTS

XHTML document DOCTYPE declarations are similar to those of HTML declarations, except that they specify different DTDs.

Strict   This version prohibits everything except "pure" XHTML, and you're not likely to use it unless you're writing HTML documents that use no formatting elements and that rely exclusively on style sheets to make them look good. To indicate that your document complies with the Strict specification, use:

```
<!DOCTYPE html PUBLIC "-//W3C//DTD XHTML 1.0 Strict//EN"
    "http://www.w3.org/TR/xhtml1/DTD/xhtml1-strict.dtd">
```

Transitional   This version is the most flexible for accommodating deprecated elements and attributes (ones that are still useful but that may be phased out in favor of newer or different ones). In most cases, you'll want to use the Transitional DOCTYPE element. To indicate that your document complies with the Transitional specification, use:

```
<!DOCTYPE html PUBLIC "-//W3C//DTD XHTML 1.0 Transitional//EN"
    "http://www.w3.org/TR/xhtml1/DTD/xhtml1-transitional.dtd">
```

TIP   We recommend using the Transitional DOCTYPE element for most of your XHTML document needs, unless you are planning to use frames, as discussed in Chapter 7.

Frameset   This version is similar to the Transitional specification, but it also supports the elements and attributes needed to use frames:

```
<!DOCTYPE html PUBLIC "-//W3C//DTD XHTML 1.0 Frameset//EN"
    "http://www.w3.org/TR/xhtml1/DTD/xhtml1-frameset.dtd">
```

The *html* Element

The html element identifies the document as an HTML or XHTML document. But wait. Didn't the DOCTYPE element just specify this? Yes, but the html element, enclosing the entire document, is still a required component in both the HTML and XHTML specifications.

If you're developing an HTML document, you add just the html element below the DOCTYPE declaration, like this:

```
<!DOCTYPE HTML PUBLIC "-//W3C//DTD HTML 4.01//EN">
<html>
</html>
```

If you're developing an XHTML document, you should also add the xmlns namespace to the html element. As discussed in Chapter 22, "Extending XHTML with Namespaces," a *namespace* uniquely identifies a set of elements that belong to a given document type, and it ensures that there are no element name conflicts. Remember that XHTML is a subset of XML (Extensible Markup Language), so the specification calls for using the xmlns namespace attribute in the html element, like this:

```
<!DOCTYPE html PUBLIC "-//W3C//DTD XHTML 1.0 Transitional//EN"
    "http://www.w3.org/TR/xhtml1/DTD/xhtml1-transitional.dtd">
<html xmlns="http://www.w3.org/1999/xhtml">
</html>
```

The *head* Element

Required in every HTML and XHTML document, the head element contains information about the document, including its title, scripts used, style definitions, and document descriptions. Additionally, the head element can contain other elements that have information for search engines and indexing programs.

Few browsers actually require this element, but most browsers expect to find any available additional information about the document within the head element. To add the head element in either an HTML or XHTML document, enter it between the html opening and closing elements, as in this incomplete XHTML document (the next several sections will show how additional elements fit into place to complete an HTML or XHTML document):

```
<!DOCTYPE html PUBLIC "-//W3C//DTD XHTML 1.0 Transitional//EN"
    "http://www.w3.org/TR/xhtml1/DTD/xhtml1-transitional.dtd">
<html xmlns="http://www.w3.org/1999/xhtml">
    <head>

    </head>
</html>
```

TIP   Don't confuse this document **head** *element, which is a structure element, with* heading *elements, such as* **h1**, *which create heading text in a document body. We discuss heading elements later in this chapter in the "Creating Headings" section.*

The `head` element must contain other child elements (that is, other elements that nest within the head element), including the `title` and `meta` elements, along with a few less commonly used elements. Let's take a look.

THE *title* ELEMENT

The `title` element, which both HTML and XHTML specifications require, contains the document title. The title does not appear within the browser window, although it's usually visible in the browser's title bar (often the blue bar at the top of your screen). To use the `title` element, enter it between the opening and closing `head` elements, as shown in this sample XHTML document:

```
<!DOCTYPE html PUBLIC "-//W3C//DTD XHTML 1.0 Transitional//EN"
    "http://www.w3.org/TR/xhtml1/DTD/xhtml1-transitional.dtd">
<html xmlns="http://www.w3.org/1999/xhtml">
    <head>
        <title>
            Title That Summarizes the Document's Content
        </title>
    </head>
</html>
```

Because the title bar has limited space, take care to ensure the title briefly summarizes your document's content and keeps key words at the beginning of the title. Titles should represent the document, even if the document is taken out of context. Some good titles include the following:

- Sample XHTML Code
- Learning to Ride a Bicycle
- Television Viewing for Fun and Profit

Less useful titles, particularly taken out of context, include the following:

- Examples
- Chapter 2
- Continued

WARNING   Watch out for the default titles produced by WYSIWYG editors. Always be sure to put in your own title.

THE *meta* ELEMENT

The `meta` element is used to embed document meta-information. *Meta-information* contains information about the contents of the document, such as keywords, author information, and a description of the document. The primary advantage to including `meta` elements in your HTML and XHTML document is that these elements make it possible for search engine robots and spiders to identify, catalog, and find the information in your document.

For both HTML and XHTML documents, you can include author information, keywords, and a description of the document contents using the empty meta element in combination with name= and content= attributes. Here's an example of some meta information in an XHTML document:

```
<!DOCTYPE html PUBLIC "-//W3C//DTD XHTML 1.0 Transitional//EN"
    "http://www.w3.org/TR/xhtml1/DTD/xhtml1-transitional.dtd">
<html xmlns="http://www.w3.org/1999/xhtml">
    <head>
        <meta name="author" content="Your name" />
        <meta name="keywords" content="A keyword,a keyword,a
            keyword" />
        <meta name="description" content="This is the Home Page
            of the Web site of Your Name. " />
        <title>
            Title That Summarizes the Document's Content
        </title>
    </head>
</html>
```

TIP   *When using the* meta *element in XHTML, remember to close it with a space and a slash before the final angle bracket (/>) because it's an empty element. In HTML, you may omit the / symbol.*

OTHER CHILDREN OF THE *head* ELEMENT

In addition to the title and meta elements, the head element may contain the following child elements:

script   Instructs the browser that the enclosed content is part of a scripting language such as JavaScript (also called JScript or ECMAScript) or VBScript. See Chapter 10 for more information about scripting.

style   Contains internal Cascading Style Sheets (CSS) information. See Chapter 9 for more information about style sheets.

link   Defines a link. This element functions somewhat like the anchor (a) element (discussed in detail in Chapter 3). The link element is most commonly used to link external CSS style sheets to a document.

base   Defines a document's base Uniform Resource Locator (URL) using the href attribute. It must occur as a child of the head element, and it establishes a base URL for all relative references. This element is often used in conjunction with anchors to enable navigation within a single document or within documents in a single directory or folder.

TIP   *A URL is a type of Uniform Resource Identifier (URI). The value of the* href *attribute can be any type of URI, such as a Uniform Resource Name (URN).*

The *body* Element

The body element encloses all the elements, attributes, and information that you want a user's browser to display. Almost everything else we talk about in this book takes place between the opening and closing body elements (unless you're creating a framed document—see Chapter 7 for more information). To use the body element, enter it below the closing head element and above the closing html element, like this:

```
<!DOCTYPE html PUBLIC "-//W3C//DTD XHTML 1.0 Transitional//EN"
    "http://www.w3.org/TR/xhtml1/DTD/xhtml1-transitional.dtd">
<html xmlns="http://www.w3.org/1999/xhtml">
    <head>
        <title>
            Title That Summarizes the Document's Content
        </title>
    </head>
    <body>
        All the elements, attributes, and information in the
        document body go here.
    </body>
</html>
```

TIP   Throughout this book, we'll provide examples for you that won't include these structural elements. This doesn't mean you shouldn't include them; it just means that we're focusing on the immediate topic.

If you've been following along, save your document, view it in a browser, and compare it with Figure 2.1 to confirm that you're on the right track. The title appears in the title bar, and some text appears in the document window.

FIGURE 2.1

Your first XHTML (or HTML) document, including all structure elements

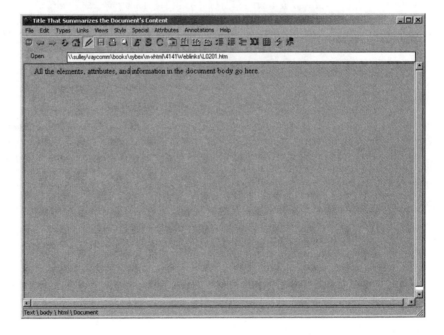

Applying Basic Elements

After you include the structure elements, you're ready to start placing basic content in the document body. The following sections show you how to include paragraphs, headings, lists, and rules (horizontal lines). These elements constitute the basic HTML and XHTML document components and, unlike the structure elements, do appear in the browser window. Learning to apply these basic elements and attributes will prepare you to apply practically any element or attribute.

As you create your content, keep in mind that its exact appearance will vary from browser to browser. As we said in Chapter 1, two browsers will both display a heading bigger and bolder than body text, but the specific font, size, and emphasis will vary. In addition, the user may have specific browser settings on his or her machine that will affect the display of the document.

Finally, in several places, we've included information on how to change the appearance of some elements—for example, how to right-align a heading or how to change a paragraph's text color. As you're working through this chapter, note that many of these formatting-level elements have been *deprecated* in HTML 4.01 (and thus also in the XHTML specification)—meaning that technically they're still available and most browsers will still interpret and display them, but the HTML and XHTML specifications are now using new elements (or, in most cases, style sheets) to create the same effects. On a more practical level, this means that, while you can use these formatting elements and attributes, you should strongly consider specifying formatting-related information using style sheets, which are covered in Chapter 9. The sidebar "Deprecated Elements" specifies which elements have been deprecated, and lists reasons not to use deprecated elements in general.

TIP *Throughout the rest of this chapter, we primarily use XHTML sample code; however, keep in mind that these examples will work in either HTML or XHTML. You'll find detailed information about the (slight) differences between HTML and XHTML code in Chapter 1.*

DEPRECATED ELEMENTS

One of the original goals of markup languages in general is to separate document structure from presentation—although HTML 3.2 and browser support have veered a long way from this goal. In an effort to get back on track, the presentational elements in HTML (and thus XHTML) have been "deprecated." *Deprecated elements* are elements that may be phased out of the next version of HTML (even though there may not be a *next* version). They're more likely to disappear from future versions and revisions to XHTML.

Although the HTML 4.01 and XHTML 1.0 Transitional DTDs permit the use of many of these deprecated elements, it's really better to think toward the future and avoid their use altogether in favor of other elements or other options, such as CSS (explained in Chapter 9). Why? Well, consider the long-term publication of your documents. Right now, browsers support these elements, but it's hard to say which browsers will support them in the future. Also, consider the difficulties of using these elements now and then changing to using CSS in the future. While developing a style sheet and then applying it to your documents isn't that big of a deal, *removing* all the character-level formatting *is* a big deal. And that character-level formatting overrides formatting specified in the style sheet, so you would likely need to remove the character-level formatting in order for style sheet formatting to be visible. Removing character-level formatting from more than just a few documents is very tedious and time-consuming, to say the least.

Continued on next page

DEPRECATED ELEMENTS *(continued)*

These HTML elements have been deprecated in HTML 4.01 and XHTML 1:

font   Local change to font. Deprecated in favor of CSS.

center   Shorthand for `div align="center"`. Deprecated in favor of CSS.

s or **strike**   Strikethrough text. Deprecated in favor of CSS.

u   Underlined text. Deprecated in favor of CSS.

applet   Java applet. Deprecated in favor of the `object` element.

basefont   Base font size. Deprecated in favor of CSS.

dir   Directory list. Deprecated in favor of unordered lists (the `ul` element).

isindex   Single-line prompt. Deprecated in favor of the use of `input` to create text input controls.

menu   Menu list. Deprecated in favor of unordered lists (the `ul` element).

Additionally, virtually all attributes that specify appearance or formatting are deprecated.

When we show you how to apply these elements throughout this chapter, we note that they are deprecated and give alternatives where possible.

Creating Paragraphs

One of the most common elements you'll use is the paragraph element, **p**, which is appropriate for regular body text. In HTML, you could use just the opening **p** element to mark your paragraphs. However, in XHTML, the paragraph element must be paired—use the opening element `<p>` where you want to start a paragraph and the closing element `</p>` to end the paragraph. It's easier to identify where the element begins and ends if you use both opening and closing elements.

To use the paragraph element, enter the opening and closing elements around the text you want to format as a paragraph, like this:

```
<p>
A whole paragraph goes right here.
</p>
```

TIP   You don't have to type an element's content on a separate line; `<p>Paragraph goes here.</p>` is also valid. We do this just to make the sample code easier to read.

Figure 2.2 shows a few sample paragraphs.

FIGURE 2.2

Paragraph text is the most common text in HTML and XHTML documents

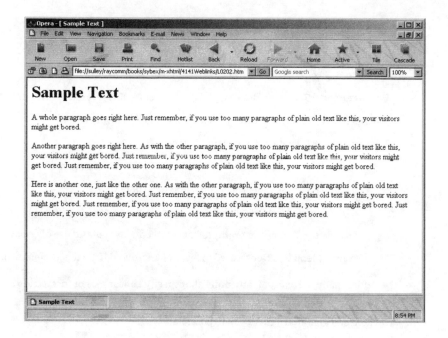

You can also use the `align` attribute with the paragraph element, which has values of `left`, `center`, `right`, or `justify`. To apply this attribute, include it in the opening paragraph element, like this:

```
<p align="center">
Paragraph of information goes here.
</p>
```

NOTE   Note that the `align` attribute is deprecated, so we suggest using style sheets to achieve the same effect.

You can also apply other paragraph-level (or block-level) elements instead of the `p` element to achieve some slightly different effects, as explained in Table 2.1.

TABLE 2.1: OTHER PARAGRAPH-FORMATTING ELEMENTS

ELEMENT	EFFECT
address	Used for address and contact information. Often appears in italics and is sometimes used as a footer.
blockquote	Used for formatting a quotation. Usually appears indented from both sides and with less space between lines than a regular paragraph.
pre	Effective for formatting program code or similar information (short for *preformatted*). Usually appears in a fixed-width font (such as Courier) with even space between words and letters.

Figure 2.3 shows how the `address` and `pre` elements appear in Internet Explorer.

FIGURE 2.3

Special paragraph-
level elements make
information
stand out

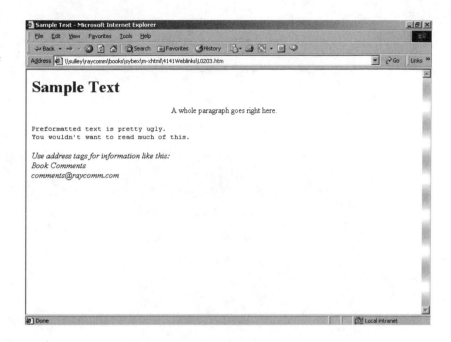

Creating Headings

Headings break up large areas of text, announce topics to follow, and arrange information according to a logical hierarchy. In HTML and XHTML, you can use up to six levels of headings; h1 is the largest of the headings, and h6 is the smallest. The paired elements look like this:

```
<h1>...</h1>
<h2>...</h2>
<h3>...</h3>
<h4>...</h4>
<h5>...</h5>
<h6>...</h6>
```

TIP   For most documents, limit yourself to two or three heading levels. After three heading levels, many users begin to lose track of your hierarchy. If you find that you're using several heading levels, consider reorganizing your document or dividing it into multiple documents—too many heading levels often indicates a larger organizational problem.

Here's an example of how to use the heading elements:

```
<!DOCTYPE html PUBLIC "-//W3C//DTD XHTML 1.0 Transitional//EN"
   "http://www.w3.org/TR/xhtml1/DTD/xhtml1-transitional.dtd">
<html xmlns="http://www.w3.org/1999/xhtml">
   <head>
      <title>Sample Headings</title>
   </head>
```

```
<body>
    <h1>First Level Heading</h1>
    <h2>Second Level Heading</h2>
    <h3>Third Level Heading</h3>
</body>
</html>
```

Figure 2.4 shows how Netscape 6 displays a few heading levels.

FIGURE 2.4

Heading levels provide users with a hierarchy of information

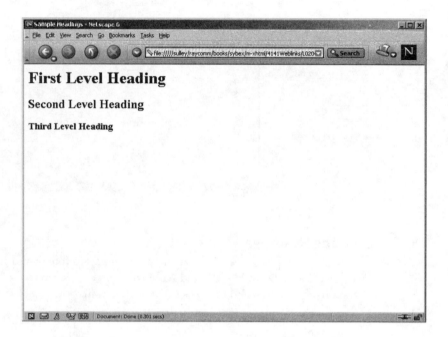

In general, you should use heading elements only for document headings—that is, don't use heading elements for figure captions or to emphasize information within text. Why? First, you don't always know how browsers will display the heading. It might not create the visual effect you intended. Second, some indexing and editing programs use headings to generate tables of contents and other information about your document. These programs won't exclude headings from the table of contents or other information just because you used them as figure captions, for example.

By default, all browsers align headings on the left. However, most browsers support the align attribute, which also lets you right-align, center, and justify headings. To use the align attribute, include it in the heading elements, like this:

```
<h1 align="left">Left-aligned Heading</h1>
<h1 align="center">Centered Heading</h1>
<h1 align="right">Right-aligned Heading</h1>
```

Figure 2.5 shows headings aligned left, center, and right.

FIGURE 2.5

Headings aligned
left, center, and right

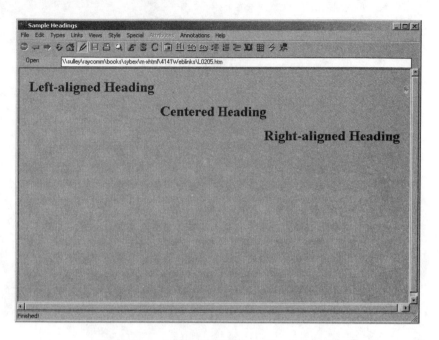

TIP   The HTML and XHTML specifications deprecate (strongly discourage) the use of the `align` *attribute. Therefore, although this attribute is still supported at this time, if your users will be using current browsers, you should consider using CSS for your formatting needs. You'll find how-to information about CSS in Chapter 9 and a comprehensive list of CSS options in Master's Reference Part 2.*

TIP   If you're writing for a wide audience, some of whom might be using older browsers, nest the element that has the `align="center"` *attribute inside a* `center` *element to ensure that the text actually appears centered. The markup would look similar to this:* `<center><h1 align="center">Centered Heading</h1></center>`.

Creating Lists

Lists are a great way to provide information in a structured, easy-to-read format. They help your users easily spot information, and they draw attention to important information. A list is also a good format for a procedure. Figure 2.6 shows the same content formatted as both a paragraph and a list.

Lists come in two varieties: numbered (called *ordered* lists) and bulleted (called *unordered* lists). To create either kind of list, you first specify that you want information to appear as a list, and then you identify each line item in the list. Table 2.2 shows the list and line item elements.

FIGURE 2.6

Lists are often easier to read than paragraphs

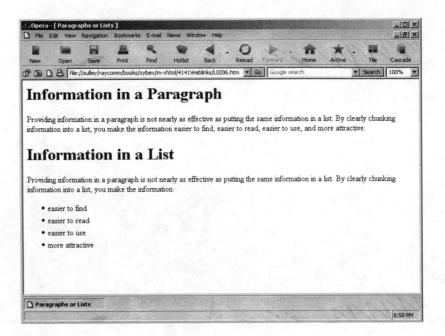

TABLE 2.2: LIST AND LINE ITEM ELEMENTS

ELEMENT	EFFECT
ol	Specifies that the information appear as an ordered (numbered) list. Ordered lists are appropriate for listing steps or information that needs to be presented or completed in a specific order.
ul	Specifies that the information appear as an unordered (bulleted) list. Unordered lists are appropriate for drawing attention to bits of information that do not need to be presented or completed in a specific order.
li	Specifies a line item in either ordered or unordered lists.

The following steps show you how to create a bulleted list; use the same steps to create a numbered list but use the ol element instead of the ul element.

1. Start with text you want to format as a list, such as the following:

```
Lions
Tigers
Bears
Oh, My!
```

2. Insert the ul elements around the list text.

```
<ul>
Lions
```

```
Tigers
Bears
Oh, My!
</ul>
```

3. Put the li opening element and closing element around each list item.

```
<ul>
<li>Lions</li>
<li>Tigers</li>
<li>Bears</li>
<li>Oh, My!</li>
</ul>
```

The resulting list, viewed in a browser, looks similar to that shown in Figure 2.7.

FIGURE 2.7

Bulleted lists make information easy to spot on the page and can draw attention to important points

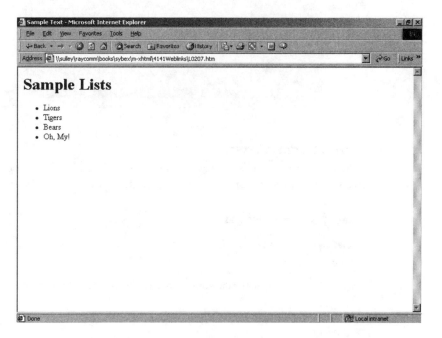

To change your list from unordered (bulleted) to ordered (numbered), change the ul element to ol. The resulting numbered list is shown in Figure 2.8.

TIP   Other, less commonly used and deprecated list elements include dir, *to create a directory list, and* menu, *to create a menu list. You use these elements just as you use the* ul *and* ol *elements.*

FIGURE 2.8

Numbered lists provide sequential information

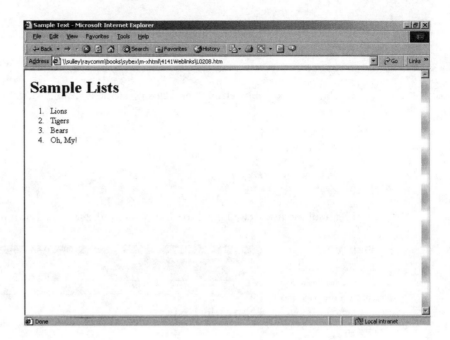

SETTING LIST APPEARANCE

By default, numbered lists use Arabic numerals, and bulleted lists use small, round bullets. You can change the appearance of these by using the attributes listed in Table 2.3.

TABLE 2.3: LIST ATTRIBUTES

ELEMENT	EFFECT
For numbered lists:	
type="A"	Specifies the number (or letter) with which the list should start: A, a, I, i, or 1 (default).
type="a"	
type="I"	
type="i"	
type="1"	
For bulleted lists:	
type="disc"	Specifies the bullet shape.
type="square"	
type="circle"	

To use any of these attributes, include them in the opening `ol` or `ul` element or in the opening `li` element, like this:

```
<ol type="A">
<li>Outlines use sequential lists with letters.</li>
<li>So do some (unpopular) numbering schemes for
    documentation.</li>
</ol>
```

Or like this:

```
<ul type="square">
<li>Use bullets for non-sequential items.</li>
<li>Use numbers for sequential items.</li>
</ul>
```

Or this:

```
<ul>
<li type="circle"> Use bullets for non-sequential items.</li>
<li type="square"> Use different bullets for visual
    interest.</li>
</ul>
```

Figure 2.9 shows how these attributes appear in a browser.

FIGURE 2.9

You can change the appearance of numbers and bullets by using list attributes

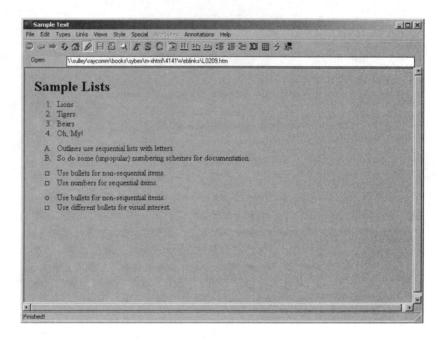

TIP *You can add the* `compact` *attribute in opening* `ol` *or* `ul` *elements to tell browsers to display the list as compactly as possible. Generally, this setting will make little difference, because most browsers render lists this way by default. This attribute is deprecated.*

TIP *The* type *attribute for unordered lists is currently supported by many (but by no means all) browsers; it is also deprecated in favor of using style sheets to accomplish the same thing.*

MORE OPTIONS FOR ORDERED LISTS

Ordered lists have additional attributes that you can use to specify the first number in the list, as well as to create hierarchical information.

First, you can start a numbered list with a value other than 1 (or A, a, I, or i). Simply include the start attribute in the initial ol element, as in <ol start="51">, to start the list at 51. Or you can even change specific numbers within a list by using the value attribute in the li element, as in <li value="7">.

TIP *Both the* start *and* value *attributes are deprecated.*

To use these attributes, include them in the ol element, like this:

```
<ol start="51">
   <li>This is the fifty-first item.</li>
   <li>This is the fifty-second.</li>
   <li type="i" value="7">This item was renumbered to be the
      seventh, using lowercase roman numerals,
      just because we can.</li>
</ol>
```

Figure 2.10 shows how this code appears in a browser.

FIGURE 2.10

Attributes let you
customize ordered
lists in several ways

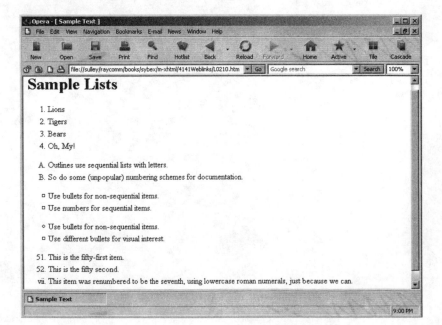

Second, you can use nested ordered lists and different `type` attributes to create outlines. The numbering continues past each lower-level section without the need to manually renumber with a `value` attribute. Here's an example of what the code looks like:

```
<ol type="I">
    <li>Top Level Item</li>
    <li>Another Top Level Item</li>
    <ol type="A">
        <li>A Second Level Item</li>
        <li>Another Second Level Item</li>
        <ol type="1">
            <li>A Third Level Item</li>
            <li>Another Third Level Item</li>
        </ol>
        <li>Another Second Level Item</li>
    </ol>
    <li>A Top Level Item</li>
</ol>
```

As you can see, to nest a list within another one, you just include the opening element, line items, and closing element within part of the main list's code. The results are shown in Figure 2.11.

FIGURE 2.11

Ordered lists are even flexible enough to format outlines

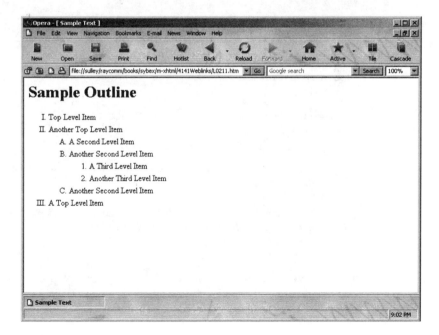

USING DEFINITION LISTS

Finally, one special list variant, *definition lists*, can be useful for providing two levels of information. You can think of definition lists as dictionary entries—they have two levels of information: the entry and a definition. You can use these lists to provide glossary-type information, or you can use them to provide two-level lists. Table 2.4 lists the elements and their effects.

TABLE 2.4: DEFINITION LIST AND ITEM ELEMENTS

ELEMENT	EFFECT
dl	Specifies that the information appear as a definition list.
dt	Child of dl; identifies definition terms.
dd	Child of dl; identifies definitions.

To create a definition list, as shown in Figure 2.12, follow these steps:

1. Enter the dl opening and closing elements to start the definition list.

   ```
   <dl>
   </dl>
   ```

2. Add the dt opening and closing elements around the definition terms.

   ```
   <dl>
   <dt>XHTML</dt>
   <dt>Maestro</dt>
   </dl>
   ```

3. Add the dd element to identify individual definitions.

   ```
   <dl>
   <dt>XHTML</dt>
   <dd>Extensible Hypertext Markup Language is used to create
       Web pages.</dd>
   <dt>Maestro</dt>
   <dd>An expert in some field. See "Readers of <i>Mastering
       HTML and XHTML</i>" for examples.</dd>
   </dl>
   ```

TIP   A great way to apply definition lists is in "What's New" lists—a special page that tells people what's new and exciting on your site or at your organization. Try putting the dates in the dt element (maybe with boldface and italics) and the information in the dd element.

FIGURE 2.12

Definition lists are a formatting option that is useful when presenting dictionary-like information.

Definition List

XHTML
    Extensible Hypertext Markup Language is used to create Web pages.
Maestro
    An expert in some field. See "Readers of *Mastering HTML and XHTML*" for examples.

Applying Bold, Italic, and Other Emphases

In addition to creating paragraphs, headings, and lists, you can apply formatting to individual letters and words. For example, you can make a word appear *italic*, **bold**, <u>underlined</u>, or superscript, as in H^2O. You use these character-level formatting elements only within paragraph-level elements—that is, you can't put a p element within a character-level element such as b. You have to close the character-level formatting before you close the paragraph-level formatting.

Correct:

```
<p><b>This is the end of a paragraph that also uses boldface.
   </b></p>
<p>This is the beginning of the following paragraph.</p>
```

Incorrect:

```
<p>This text <b>is boldface.</p>
<p>As is this.</b></p>
```

Although many character-formatting elements are available, you'll probably use b (for **boldface**) and i (for *italic*) most often. Table 2.5 lists the most common character-formatting elements.

TABLE 2.5: COMMON CHARACTER-FORMATTING ELEMENTS

ELEMENT	EFFECT
b	Applies boldface.
blink	A proprietary Netscape element that makes text blink; usually considered highly unprofessional. Not supported in some current browsers.
cite	Indicates citations or references.
code	Displays program code; similar to the pre element.
em	Applies emphasis; usually displayed as italics.
i	Applies italics.
s or strike	Apply strikethrough to text; deprecated.
strong	Applies stronger emphasis; usually displayed as bold text.
sub	Formats text as subscript.
sup	Formats text as superscript.
tt	Applies a fixed-width font.
u	Applies underline; deprecated.
var	Displays variables or arguments.

To use these elements, enter them around the individual letters or words you want to emphasize, like this:

```
Making some text <b>bold</b> or <i>italic</i> is a useful
technique, more so than <strike>strikethrough</strike> or
<blink>blinking</blink>.
```

Figure 2.13 shows some sample character formatting.

TIP   Spend a few minutes trying out these character-formatting elements to see how they work and how they look in your favorite browser.

CONSIDER CSS INSTEAD OF FORMATTING ELEMENTS

The HTML and XHTML specifications strongly encourage using CSS for your formatting needs. Although the specification still supports many deprecated individual formatting elements, the use of CSS is the recommended way to include formatting in your XHTML and HTML documents. Using CSS, you can apply the following:

◆ Character-level formatting, such as strikethrough and underline

◆ Paragraph-level formatting, such as indents and margins

◆ Other formatting, such as background colors and images

See Chapter 9 and Master's Reference Part 2 for CSS information.

FIGURE 2.13

Character formatting helps you emphasize words or letters

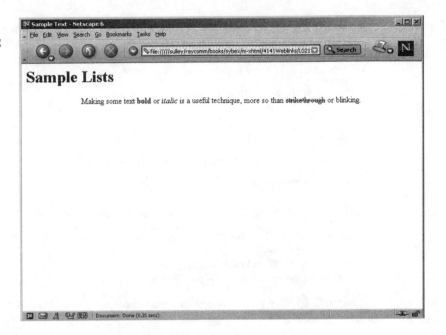

Including Horizontal Rules

Horizontal rules are lines that break up long sections of text, indicate a shift in information, or help improve the overall document design. To use a horizontal rule, which is an empty element, include the hr element where you want the rule to appear, like this:

```
<p>Long passages of text should often be broken into sections
    with headings and, optionally, horizontal rules.</p>
<hr />
<h3>A Heading Also Breaks Up Text</h3>
<p>A new long passage can continue here.</p>
```

By default, horizontal rules appear shaded, span the width of the browser window, and are a few pixels high. You can change a rule's shading, width, height, and alignment by including the appropriate attributes. Note that all horizontal rule attributes have been deprecated in favor of the use of CSS. Table 2.6 shows horizontal rule attributes.

TIP   Pixels are the little dots on your screen that produce images; pixel is an abbreviation for picture element. If your display is set to 800 × 600, you have 800 pixels horizontally and 600 pixels vertically.

TABLE 2.6: ATTRIBUTES OF THE HORIZONTAL RULE (**hr**) ELEMENT (ALL DEPRECATED)

ATTRIBUTE	SPECIFIES
align="…"	Alignment to left, center, or right
noshade="noshade"	That the rule has no shading
size="n"	Rule height measured in pixels
width="n"	Rule width (length) measured in pixels
width="n%"	Rule width (length) measured as a percentage of the document width

To use any of these attributes, include them in the hr element, like this:

```
<hr width="80%" size="8" />
<hr width="50%" />
<hr width="400" align="right" />
<hr noshade="noshade" align="center" width="200" />
```

Figure 2.14 shows some sample horizontal rules with height, width, alignment, and shading attributes added.

FIGURE 2.14

Horizontal rules can help separate information, improve page design, and simply add visual interest to the page

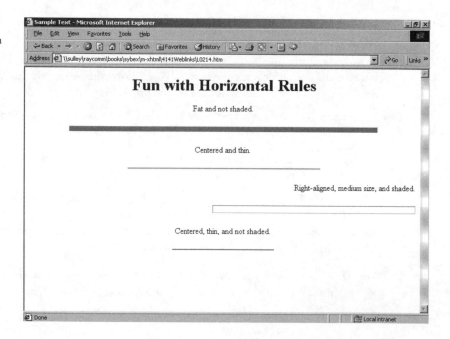

Specifying Line Breaks

Sometimes you need to break a line in a specific place, but you don't want to start a new paragraph (with the extra spacing). For example, you might not want lines of poetry text to go all the way across the document; instead, you might want to break them into several shorter lines. You can easily break paragraph lines by inserting the empty element br where you want the lines to break, like this:

```
<p>
There was an XHTML writer<br />
Who tried to make paragraphs wider<br />
He found with a shock<br />
All the elements did mock<br />
The attempt to move that text outside-r.<br />
Mercifully Anonymous
</p>
```

Including Fancier Formatting

Now that you have a firm grip on using common document elements, you can dive into some of the fancier formatting effects. In the following sections, we'll show you how to add colors and specify fonts and sizes.

Note that most of the elements in the following sections have been deprecated in favor of style sheets. While you can use these formatting elements and attributes, you should strongly consider specifying formatting-related information using style sheets, which we cover in Chapter 9 and Master's Reference Part 2. See also the sidebar "Deprecated Elements" earlier in this chapter for a list of deprecated elements and a brief discussion of why we shouldn't use them.

Adding Colors

One of the easiest ways to jazz up your documents is to add colors to the background or text. You can liven up an otherwise dull Web page with a splash of color or an entire color scheme. For example, add a background color and change the text colors to coordinate with the background. Or highlight a word or two with color and make the words leap off the page. Or, if you're developing a corporate site, adhere to the company's color scheme to ensure a consistent look.

WARNING You can also make your pages completely unusable with a poorly selected color scheme, or make it very difficult for users with vision problems to access your pages. See Chapter 13 for more information about accessibility issues.

TIP As you'll see in Chapter 14, developing a color scheme is a great way to help unite your pages into a cohesive Web site.

The drawback to setting colors is that you really don't have control over what your users see. Users might set their browsers to display colors they like, or they might be using a text-only browser, which generally displays only black, white, and gray.

You specify colors using hexadecimal numbers, which combine proportions of red, green, and blue—called *RGB numbers*. RGB numbers use six digits, two for each proportion of red, green, and blue. As you're choosing colors, remember that not all RGB numbers display well in browsers; some colors *dither*, meaning that they appear spotty or splotchy. We recommend that you select RGB values that are appropriate for Web-page use, as listed in Table 2.7, which illustrates that R, G, and B can each take on the values 00, 33, 66, 99, CC, or FF—giving you 256 possible combinations. Although you'll most likely never go wrong with these "safe" colors, it's most important to use these colors in page backgrounds or in places with large patches of color, where dithering may occur if you don't use these number combinations.

TABLE 2.7: RECOMMENDED RGB VALUES

R	G	B
00	00	00
33	33	33
66	66	66
99	99	99
CC	CC	CC
FF	FF	FF

To create an RGB number from the values in this table, simply start with a pound sign (#) to indicate the hexadecimal system and then select one option from each column. For example, choose FF from the Red column, 00 from the Green column, and 00 from the Blue column to create the RGB number #FF0000, which has the largest possible red component but no blue and no green; it therefore appears as a pure, bright red. See Master's Reference Part 5 for pointers to complete lists of the appropriate RGB numbers and corresponding descriptions.

NOTE   *Note that the color values are not case sensitive in either HTML or XHTML.*

SETTING BACKGROUND COLORS

Using a *background color*, which is simply a color that fills the entire browser window, is a great way to add flair to your Web pages. By default, browsers display a white or gray background color, which may be adequate if you're developing pages for an intranet site where flashy elements aren't essential. However, if you're developing a public or personal site, you'll probably want to make your site more interesting and visually appealing. For example, if you're developing a public corporate Web site, you might want to use your company's standard colors—ones that appear on letterhead, logos, or marketing materials. Or you might want to use your favorite color if you're developing a personal site. In either case, using a background color can improve the overall page appearance and help develop a theme among pages.

TIP   *Check out Chapters 13 and 14 for tips and information about developing coherent Web sites and for specific tips about public, personal, and intranet sites.*

As you'll see in the following section, pay careful attention to how text contrasts with the background color. If you specify a dark background color, use a light text color. Conversely, if you specify a light background color, use a dark text color. Contrast is key for ensuring that users can read information on your pages.

To specify a background color for your documents, include the `bgcolor` attribute in the opening body element, like this:

```
<body bgcolor="#FFFFFF">...</body>
```

SETTING TEXT COLORS

Similar to background colors, text colors can enhance your Web pages. In particular, you can specify the color of the following:

◆ Body text, which appears throughout the document body

◆ Unvisited links, which are links not yet followed

◆ Active links, which are links as they're being selected (clicked)

◆ Visited links, which are links previously followed

Changing body text is sometimes essential—for example, if you've added a background color or an image. If you've added a dark background color, the default black body text color won't adequately contrast with the background, making the text difficult or impossible to read. In this case, you'd want to change the text color to one that's lighter so that it contrasts with the background sufficiently.

Changing link colors helps keep your color scheme intact—for unvisited as well as visited links. Set the visited and unvisited links to different colors to help users know which links they've followed and which ones they haven't. That said, remember that users expect that links they've not yet visited are blue and underlined, while others are a different shade. Be sure that any changes you make help—rather than thwart—your users.

To change body text and link colors, simply add the attributes listed in Table 2.8 to the opening body element.

TABLE 2.8: TEXT AND LINK COLOR ATTRIBUTES (ALL DEPRECATED)	
ATTRIBUTE	**SETS COLOR FOR**
`text="..."`	All text within the document, with a color name or a #RRGGBB value
`alink="..."`	Active links, which are the links at the time the user clicks them, with a color name or a #RRGGBB value
`link="..."`	Unvisited links, with a color name or a #RRGGBB value
`vlink="..."`	Links the user has recently followed (how recently depends on the browser settings), with a color name or a #RRGGBB value

TIP   We recommend setting all Web page colors at one time—that way, you can see how background, text, and link colors appear as a unit.

To change text and link colors, follow these steps:

1. Within the body element, add the `text` attribute to set the color for text within the document. This example makes the text black:

```
<body text="#000000">
```

TIP   When setting text colors, using a "safe" color is less important for text than for backgrounds. Dithering is less apparent in small areas, such as text.

2. Add the `link` attribute to set the link color. This example uses blue (#0000FF) for the links:

```
<body text="#000000" link="#0000FF">
```

3. Add the `vlink` attribute to set the color for visited links. If you set the `vlink` attribute to the same as the link, links will not change colors even after users follow them. This could be confusing, but also serves to make it look like there is always new material available. This example sets the visited link to a different shade of blue:

```
<body text="#000000" link="#0000FF" vlink="#000099">
```

4. Finally, set the `alink`, or active link, color. This is the color of a link while users are clicking it and will not necessarily be visible in Internet Explorer 4, depending on the viewer's settings. This example sets `alink` to red:

```
<body text="#000000" link="#0000FF" vlink="#000099"
    alink="#FF0000">
```

TIP   Specify fonts and increase font sizes to improve readability with dark backgrounds and light-colored text.

Specifying Fonts and Font Sizes

You can use the `font` element to specify font characteristics for your document, including color, size, and typeface. However, it's worth noting that the `font` element and its attributes have been deprecated in favor of CSS. We suggest you check out the font properties in CSS and use them instead of the `font` element. Table 2.9 describes the elements and attributes you'll use to set font characteristics.

TABLE 2.9: FONT CHARACTERISTICS (ALL DEPRECATED)

ITEM	TYPE	DESCRIPTION
font	Element	Sets font characteristics for text.
color="..."	Attribute of font element	Specifies font color in #RRGGBB numbers or with color names. This color applies only to the text surrounded by the font elements.
face="..."	Attribute of font element	Specifies possible typefaces as a list, in order of preference, separated by commas—for example, "Verdana, Arial, Helvetica".
size="n"	Attribute of font element	Specifies font size on a scale of 1 through 7; the default or normal size is 3. You can also specify a relative size by using + or − (for example, +2).
basefont	Element	Sets the default characteristics for text that is not formatted using the font element or CSS.

As you're determining which font face to use, keep in mind that the font must be available on your users' computers for them to view the fonts you specify. For example, if you specify the Technical font and your users do not have it, their computers will substitute a font—possibly one you'd consider unacceptable. As a partial way of overcoming this problem, you can list multiple faces in order of preference; the machine displays the first available. For example, a list of `"Comic Sans MS, Technical, Tekton, Times, Arial"` will display Comic Sans MS if available, then try Technical, then Tekton, and so forth.

So, which fonts should you choose? Table 2.10 lists fonts that are commonly available on Windows, Mac, and Unix platforms.

TABLE 2.10: COMMONLY AVAILABLE FONTS

WINDOWS	MACINTOSH	LINUX/UNIX
Arial	Helvetica	Helvetica
Courier New	Courier	Courier
Times New Roman	Times	Times

TIP   You might check out Microsoft's selection of downloadable fonts (`www.microsoft.com/typography/free.htm`). These fonts are available to users who have specifically downloaded the fonts to their computers, or who are using Internet Explorer 4 or newer, or Windows 98 or newer.

To specify font characteristics, follow these steps. You can set some or all of the characteristics used in this example.

1. Identify the text to format with the `font` element.

   `<font>``Look at this!`**`</font>`**

2. Select a specific font using the `face` attribute. See Table 2.10 for a list of commonly available fonts.

   ```
   <font face="Verdana, 'Times New Roman', Times">
      Look at this!</font>
   ```

3. Change the font size using the `size` attribute. You set the size of text on a scale from 1 to 7; the default size is 3. Either set the size absolutely, with a number from 1 to 7, or relatively, with + or − the numbers of levels you want to change. Almost all browsers support `size` to set font size. The only significant downside to setting the font size is that your user might already have increased or decreased the default font size, so your size change might have more of an effect than you expected.

   ```
   <font face="Technical, 'Times New Roman', Times" size="+2">
      Look at this!</font>
   ```

4. Add a `color` attribute to set the color, using a color name or a `#RRGGBB` value.

```
<font face="Technical, 'Times New Roman', Times" size="+2"
    color="#FF0000">Look at this!</font>
```

Figure 2.15 shows the result.

FIGURE 2.15

Setting font characteristics can spiff up your pages and help you achieve the visual effect you want

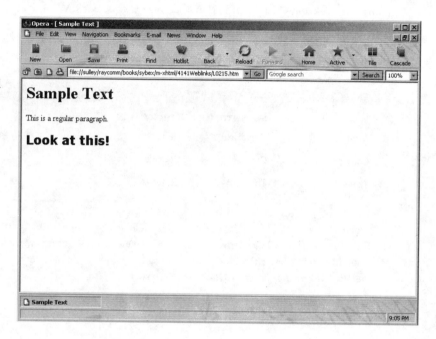

Where to Go from Here

Congratulations! You've just learned to apply HTML and XHTML code, and you even learned some of the most common elements and attributes. From here, you can jump to just about any chapter in the book. Here are a few suggestions:

- If you've just created your first page during this chapter, check out Chapter 3 to learn how to link your page to documents.

- See Chapter 9 to learn about the recommended way of applying formatting commands to your documents.

- If you want to include images in your documents, go to Chapter 4.

- If you want to add some advanced document features, such as tables, forms, and frames, check out Part II.

- To learn more about the document development and publishing process, peruse Part IV, specifically Chapters 12 and 15.

Chapter 3

Linking Your Documents

LINKS ARE THE "HYPER" part of hypertext—the part that you use to jump from one document to another. They connect your HTML or XHTML documents to each other to create a unified Web site, and they connect your documents to other information on the Internet.

In this chapter, we'll show you how to include various kinds of links in your HTML or XHTML documents. Through the examples and instructions, you'll see that links are made up of nothing more than Web addresses and a few HTML or XHTML elements, which are easy to include in your Web pages. Specifically, you'll learn to link to pages within your site, to pages at other sites, and to specific places within pages. You'll also learn how to include e-mail links.

This chapter covers the following topics:

◆ Understanding types of URLs

◆ Looking at link anatomy

◆ Constructing link anchors

◆ Linking to a specific place in a document

◆ Inserting e-mail links

URL Anatomy

The most common type of address used in hypertext links is a *URL* (usually pronounced yoo-arr-ell; it stands for Uniform Resource Locator), which is an address of a document on the Web or, more accurately, on the Internet. Although a URL can look complex and long, it generally consists of four basic parts—protocol, hostname, folder name, and filename—each of which has a specific function.

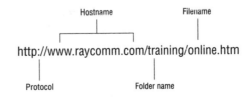

URL, URI, URN—WHAT'S THE DIFFERENCE?

As you spend more time developing Web documents (and, in particular, if you check out the HTML or XHTML specifications), you'll see a muddle of terms that all seem mostly the same. URL seems to be interchangeable with URI, which seems interchangeable with URN. Here's the scoop:

URI (Uniform Resource Indicator)   The address of a document (or file, or image, or whatever) on the Internet.

URL (Uniform Resource Locator)   The address of a document (or file, or image, or whatever) on the Internet; customarily used in conjunction with the common protocol schemes discussed in this chapter. This less-precise term is most commonly used in casual conversation, but is no longer used in technical specifications.

URN (Uniform Resource Name)   A URI from an organization that commits to maintaining live (everlasting) links. As Web sites evolve, pages are removed or moved. If links to the original pages result in a "Page not found" error, the original URLs were not URNs. If, however, links to the original pages are redirected to the new page, then you know those were URNs. In other words, URL and URI are technical descriptions, while URN describes both location and development or business practices on the part of the organization publishing information on the Internet. A `urn:` is also a protocol scheme, but is not implemented in common browser software.

Protocol

The *protocol* specifies the computer language used to transfer information. Specifically, a protocol tells the browser where the information is located. For example, the information can be located on a Web server, FTP (File Transfer Protocol) server, local hard drive, and so on. The protocol also tells the browser what to expect from the document-retrieval process—for example, whether logon is required, what information about the document will be provided by the server, and so on.

NOTE   *Throughout this chapter,* originating document *refers to the document that is linked* from *and contains the* anchor element, *and* linked document *refers to the document that is linked* to.

The protocol you use in your links depends on where the destination file is. The most common protocol you'll use in links is HTTP, or *Hypertext Transfer Protocol*, which indicates that information is located somewhere on the World Wide Web. Likewise, if you're linking to a document in a specific location on your local computer, you'd use `file:///` (with the third slash a substitute for the hostname) as the protocol indicator to specify that a browser should look for the file on its local computer. Or, if you want to link to information located on an FTP server, you'd use `ftp://` as the protocol indicator.

Table 3.1 lists some of the more common protocols you can use in links within your documents.

TABLE 3.1: COMMON PROTOCOLS

PROTOCOL INDICATOR	USE
`http://`	For documents on the Web, including XHTML documents and associated files.
`file:///`	For documents on the local hard drive. The third slash replaces the hostname, so you can simply type the folder and filename.
`ftp://`	For documents on an FTP server.
`gopher://`	For documents on a gopher server.
`telnet://`	To open a telnet connection to a specific host. Good for connecting to library catalogs. However, linking with this protocol indicator is chancy unless you're certain that telnet applications are installed or configured on the user's end.
`mailto:`	To open a mail message window in which users can send e-mail messages to the specified address. Most browsers support `mailto:`, although it is not a standard or an officially accepted protocol. This indicator does not include `//`.
`news:`	To connect to a newsgroup or a specific article in a group. Such a link is not guaranteed, because you don't know to which newsgroups your users have access. Also, before using the `news:` protocol, consider that articles periodically expire and disappear from the server. This indicator does not include `//`.

Hostname

The *hostname* is the name of the server that holds HTML or XHTML documents and related files. Each server has a specific address, and all documents stored on the server share the same hostname. For example, if your ISP's server name is raycomm, your hostname might be something like `www.raycomm.com`.

Folder Name

Folder names are the next chunk of information in a URL, indicating the folder (or directory) in which files are located. You might think of folders as containers for the documents you create. Just as you might use a manila folder to organize paper documents in your file drawer, you use folders/ directories to organize your materials on the computer.

TIP   The terms folder *and* directory *are interchangeable.* Folder *is more commonly used in the context of current desktop computers;* directory *is more common for older versions of Windows and for Linux or Unix.*

Filename

Filenames are the names of specific documents (and other resources) and consist of two pieces of information:

◆ A name, which identifies the file to display

◆ A file extension, which specifies the file type—an HTML or XHTML document, an image, a text file, and so on

If you're creating links to other documents and other locations on the Internet, you might use a wide range of filenames. Some will be short and cryptic—`frntmter.htm`, `mynewhmp.htm`—as a result of developer preference, developer habit, or software that automatically creates the documents from some other format. However, you will more likely see much longer and more descriptive filenames.

WARNING   We suggest that you don't use spaces in your filenames even though some systems allow them. They can cause problems when you link to the documents.

When you're including links in your documents, you might not include a filename at all. For example, if you're pointing to a Web site, you may use a URL such as

```
http://www.yahoo.com/
```

that includes only the protocol and the hostname. The specific filename (and folder name, in this case) is not necessary; users click that link, and the Yahoo! server displays the home page by default because of the specific server settings.

WARNING   When using URLs in your links, enter them exactly as they're given to you, including the same capitalization, or the link won't work.

Types of URLs

URLs vary depending on the location of the document to which you're linking. For example, a URL will be longer and include more information if the file is on the World Wide Web. A URL will be shorter and include less information if the file is on your local computer or server. Basically, URLs fall into two categories:

◆ An *absolute URL* contains all the information necessary to identify files on the Internet.

◆ A *relative URL* points to files in the same folder or on the same server. In other words, the file linked to is relative to the originating document.

Figure 3.1 illustrates absolute and relative URLs, which are discussed in the next two sections.

FIGURE 3.1

Relative URLs point
only to documents
near the originating
document, and
absolute URLs point
to documents on
other machines

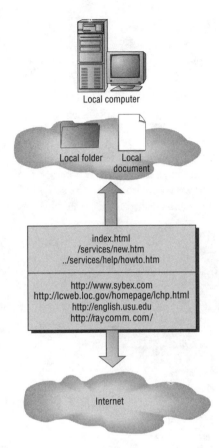

Local computer

Local folder | Local document

index.html
/services/new.htm
../services/help/howto.htm

http://www.sybex.com
http://lcweb.loc.gov/homepage/lchp.html
http://english.usu.edu
http://raycomm.com/

Internet

Absolute URLs

You can think of absolute URLs as being similar to official postal service addresses, which include a name, street address, apartment number (if applicable), city, state, and postal code. All this information is necessary for your letter to Aunt Cindy to arrive at her house, and if any piece of information is missing (such as the street address or apartment number), the letter might arrive late, arrive at someone else's house, or not arrive at all.

Likewise, an absolute URL contains the protocol, hostname, folder name, and filename, which are all essential for linking to Web sites. To link to another Web site, you have to provide all these tidbits of information so that the correct server, folder, and document can be found.

Here are some sample absolute URLs:

```
http://www.raycomm.com/books/errata/default.htm
http://www.raycomm.com/techwhirl/index.html
http://www.google.com
ftp://ftp.w3.org/pub/
```

TIP *Remember from our discussion in the "Filename" section that specific filenames are sometimes not necessary because they're set by default on the Web server.*

Relative URLs

A relative URL usually contains *only* the folder name and filename, or even just the filename. You can use these partial URLs when you're pointing to a file that's located in the same folder or on the same server as the originating file. In these cases, a browser doesn't need the server name or protocol indicator, because it assumes the files are in a folder or on a server that's relative to the originating document.

Using a relative URL is similar to instructing someone to look "next door" for a piece of information. In this case, next door is relative to where you are; it's accurate and complete only if you originate the request from a place that has a next-door neighbor with the correct information.

You can use relative URLs to refer to documents in relation to the originating document (called a *document-relative URL*) or to the server on which the originating document resides (called a *server-relative URL*). Figure 3.2 illustrates how relative folders and files relate.

FIGURE 3.2

You can indicate each of these locations with a relative URL when linking from other nearby documents

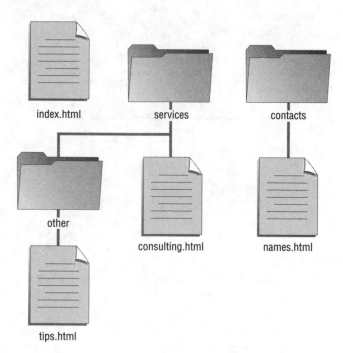

index.html   services   contacts

other

consulting.html   names.html

tips.html

DOCUMENT-RELATIVE URLS

You'll often use a document-relative URL when you're developing or testing a set of XHTML documents. As we developed examples for this book, we used document-relative URLs and put all the files in a single folder. In fact, in most cases, we included only the filename. For example, when linking from the `index.html` document in Figure 3.2, we use these document-relative URLs:

```
services/consulting.html
services/other/tips.html
```

Notice that these URLs include only the folder names and filenames. The protocols and host-names are not necessary because both these documents are relative to the originating `index.html` document. However, when linking between these two documents, you have to include the folder names, because these documents are in different folders. If `consulting.html` and `tips.html` were both in the `services` folder, you could link them by *just* their filenames.

If you're familiar with the Linux/Unix and DOS convention of using two periods (`..`) to move up a directory in the hierarchy, you can also use that to link to documents in other folders. For example, to link from `consulting.html` to `names.html`, you could use a link similar to this:

```
<a href="../contacts/names.html">link text</a>
```

The address indicates moving up a level (the `..` part), then into the `contacts` folder, and then to the `names.html` document. Likewise, a link within `tips.html` to the `names.html` file would look like this:

```
<a href="../../contacts/names.html">link text</a>
```

Nested folders that lie deep within the server hierarchy or sets of folders that might be used and moved as a unit can benefit from these links. These relative URLs can link all the documents within the unit, and then you can move the unit to other servers or even to other locations within the specific server hierarchy. All the links among the documents will continue to work.

SERVER-RELATIVE URLS

A server-relative URL is relative to the *server root*—that is, relative to the hostname part of the URL. Figure 3.3 illustrates how documents and folders relate to servers.

Server-relative URLs have a forward slash (`/`) at the beginning of the filename, which indicates that you interpret the path of the document from the top of the current server (the server root), rather than from the current document location. For example, from anywhere in our site, we could use a server-relative URL to display our home page with a link to `/index.html`, which would display the `index.html` file right under the top of the server. Some server-relative URLs are:

```
/index.html
/contacts/names.html
```

Likewise, you can link to folders and filenames with a server-relative URL. From the `tips.html` document, you can link to the `names.html` document within the `contacts` folder with a link to a URL like the preceding example.

Server-relative URLs are useful when you're linking to a specific location on the server (such as contact information) that isn't likely to change and that isn't clearly relative to the current document. For example, you might use a server-relative URL if you're working on a document that does not yet have a specific home on the server but still links to specific pages, such as the home page. If you don't use a server-relative URL, you'd have to code the server name into the URL, and then if you had to change servers or move the documents to a different server, the links would no longer work (in other words, the links would "break").

TIP   Use relative URLs whenever possible, because they let you move your documents around without breaking too many links. If you link all your documents with absolute URLs, you'll break all those links each time you move the documents around on a server or move them to a different server.

FIGURE 3.3

The same set of files as in Figure 3.2, positioned in relation to the server

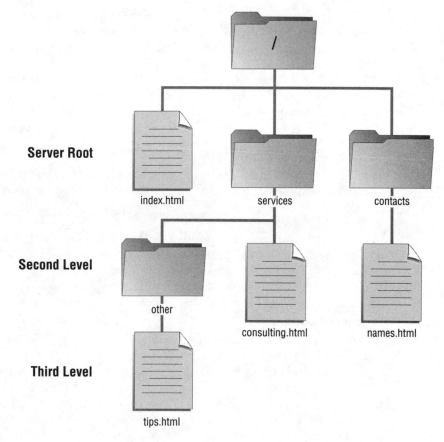

Server Root

index.html   services   contacts

Second Level

other

consulting.html   names.html

Third Level

tips.html

SETTING THE BASE LOCATION FOR A DOCUMENT

A lot of times, you'll develop documents and put them in one folder, only to later move some of the documents to a different folder. When you move documents to new folders, all the document-relative links will be broken. Rather than changing all the relative URLs, you can use the base empty element with the href attribute in the head element to specify what the relative URLs are relative to.

For example, suppose you want to move a document called www.raycomm.com/books/index.html out of the books folder into the server root. Rather than editing all the links, you can just add the base element within the head element, like this:

```
<head>
    <title>Document Title</title>
    <base href="http://www.raycomm.com/books/index.html" />
</head>
```

Including the base element with the href attribute in the head element resets all relative links in the document so that all relative URLs point correctly to the real locations of the documents. Without base and href, all relative URLs from the default.htm document would point to nonexistent documents.

Link Anatomy

Links, also called anchors, mark text or images as elements that point to other HTML or XHTML documents, images, applets, multimedia effects, or specific places within an HTML or XHTML document. Links are made up of three parts:

- Opening and closing anchor elements, `<a>...</a>`, which mark the text or image as a link.

- An attribute, `href`, which is located within the opening anchor element, as in `<a href="...">...</a>`.

- An address—the value of `href`—that tells browsers the file to link to, identifying a file location on the Web or on your local hard drive. These addresses can be markup-language (such as HTML, XHTML, and XML) documents or elements referenced by documents, such as images, applets, scripts, and other files. The address is always enclosed in quotes—for example, `"address.html"`.

NOTE   *HTML anchors and XHTML anchors are identical, so the instructions in this chapter will be appropriate for any kind of HTML or XHTML document you create.*

Put these together, and a basic link looks like this:

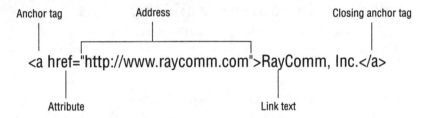

As you can see, the "link text"—the text that appears between the opening and closing tags—actually appears in the document. Text links usually display as blue and underlined text, but this depends on your user's computer and browser settings and how you specify link formatting. Image links generally appear in a border. Figure 3.4 shows text and images used as links.

TIP   *See Chapter 2 for information about setting link colors, or see Chapter 9 for information about doing so using style sheets.*

All links include opening and closing anchor tags, an attribute, and an address. However, the specific address you use depends on where the documents you link to are located.

FIGURE 3.4

Text links usually appear underlined; image links usually have a border around them

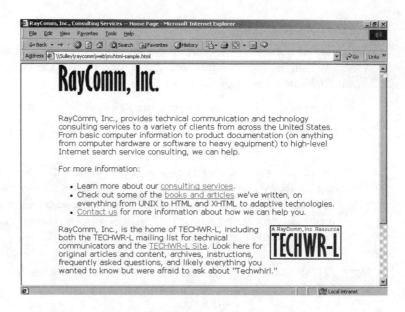

Linking to Documents and Web Sites

Link anchors are the glue that holds the Web together. Fortunately, they are simple to construct—they require only a single element and careful use of the URL. In this section, we'll look at how to link to documents in the same folder, in different folders, and on different servers (other Web sites).

Linking to Documents in the Same Folder

The basic link connects one document to another file in the same folder. Figure 3.5 shows two documents within the same folder.

FIGURE 3.5

`DocumentA.html` and `DocumentB.html` both reside in a folder called `FatFolder`

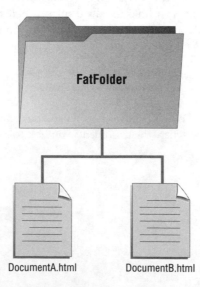

To create a link from `DocumentA.html` to `DocumentB.html`, you include the anchor element (`a`), the `href` attribute, and a URL that points to the filename of Document B. In this case, the link from the originating document (Document A) might look like this:

```
<a href="DocumentB.html">link text goes here</a>
```

When linking to documents within the same folder, you need to include only the filename. Without additional information, browsers will look in the same folder as the originating document. In this sense, the locations of Document A and Document B are both indicated relative to the folder in which they reside.

Linking to Documents in a Different Folder

Commonly, you'll link two documents that reside in different folders, as Figure 3.6 shows. To create a link from `aboutus.html` to `consulting.html`, you include the folder and filename, as in:

```
<a href="services/consulting.html">link text</a>
```

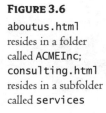

FIGURE 3.6

`aboutus.html` resides in a folder called `ACMEInc`; `consulting.html` resides in a subfolder called `services`

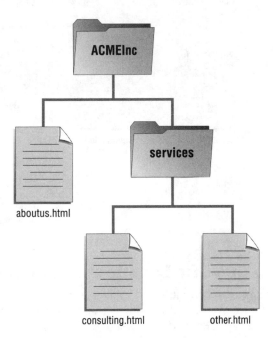

The folder (`services`) and filename (`consulting.html`) are separated by a forward slash (`/`), which indicates the end of the folder name and the beginning of the filename.

Linking to Documents on the Web

When you link from one document to another document on the Web, the documents likely reside on different servers. Figure 3.7 shows an originating document, `acmeinfo.html`, with a link to a document on a different server on the Web. Remember that linking to documents on another server requires an absolute URL so that the correct host, folder, and file can be found. Therefore, to link to the `futile.html` file in the `attempts` folder on the `www.coyote.org` Web site, you need to include an absolute URL, similar to this one:

```
http://www.coyote.org/attempts/futile.html
```

The full link would look like this:

```
<a href="http://www.coyote.org/attempts/futile.html">
   Last Try</a>
```

FIGURE 3.7

The `acmeinfo` `.html` file resides on a server called `www.acme.com`; `futile.html` resides on a server called `www.coyote` `.org` in the `attempts` folder

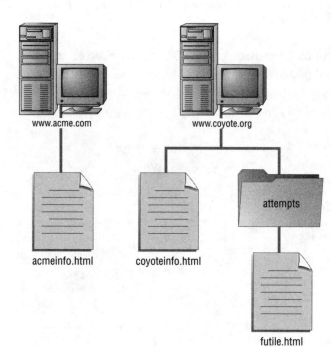

Linking to a Specific Location in a Document

In addition to linking to a document, you can link to a specific place within a document. For example, rather than linking to the Web-Based Training document, you can link to a subheading called Class Schedule within that document. By doing so, you can let your users move directly to the information they seek, rather than having them reach a document and scroll to the tidbit of information.

You link to specific places within documents with the help of a *name anchor*, which marks the targeted link location. In this example, you'd put the name anchor at the Class Schedule subheading and then link directly to that anchor from another document. Very cool... and efficient for your users.

Forming Name Anchors

Name anchors are made up of three parts:

- Opening and closing anchor tags, `<a>...</a>`, which mark the text or the location within a document as a target

- An attribute, `name`, which identifies the anchor as a name anchor

- A name, enclosed in quotes, which identifies the specific location

Put these together, and a basic name anchor looks like this:

```
<a name="location">Document content goes here</a>
```

The text between the opening and closing anchor tags is visible in your document, but, unlike link anchors, it's not highlighted, nor is any other specific visual indicator associated with it. It's simply the place (text) in the document to which you want to link. If you prefer, you can leave out the text and just insert the link, as follows: `<a name="location"></a>`. You can use the `name` attribute with the a element with other elements in your document.

Here's a sample process for creating a name anchor:

1. Start with a subheading:

   ```
   <h2>Class Schedule</h2>
   ```

2. Add the anchor element:

   ```
   <h2><a>Class Schedule</a></h2>
   ```

3. Add the `name` attribute. Use something specific that you'll be able to remember:

   ```
   <h2><a name="schedule">Class Schedule</a></h2>
   ```

That's all there is to it. You will see nothing different in your document when you view it with your browser, but you have just provided the tools necessary to link directly to a subsection of your document, as described in the following section.

Linking to Name Anchors

After you create a name anchor, you can link to it by using the "pound sign" (or in the U.K., the "hash sign": #). To continue with our example, the Class Schedule section is in a document that has the filename `online.htm`, which is in the `training` folder on the `www.raycomm.com` server.

A link to that document looks like this:

```
<a href="http://www.raycomm.com/training/online.htm">Link</a>
```

A link to the Class Schedule section, using an absolute URL, looks like this:

```
<a href="http://www.raycomm.com/training/online.htm#schedule">
   Link</a>
```

Notice the `#schedule` addition in the targeted link, which is what tells the browser to link to that heading. How much information you include in a targeted link and what it looks like depends on where the linked document is located, as shown by the following examples:

Link to the same document:

```
<a href="#schedule">…</a>
```

Link to a different document in the same folder:

```
<a href="online.htm#schedule">...</a>
```

Link to the same server (different folder and document, server-relative URL):

```
<a href="/training/online.htm#schedule">...</a>
```

Link to a different server:

```
<a href="http://www.raycomm.com/train/online.htm#sched">...</a>
```

TIP   You can't link to name *anchors that don't exist. To ensure that users can link to specific places within your documents, include* name *anchors in places likely to be visited.*

Inserting E-mail Links

Another handy link you can use is an *e-mail link,* which takes your users from the Web page to an already-addressed blank e-mail message in their e-mail program. By including e-mail links in your Web pages, for example, you can let users easily contact you.

To create an e-mail link, simply add an anchor link with the `mailto:` protocol indicator and the e-mail address. For example, you might include a link to send the authors of this book e-mail with a link like this:

```
<a href="mailto:info@raycomm.com">Send Feedback</a>
```

TIP   As we mentioned in Table 3.1, the `mailto:` *protocol is not an XHTML standard, but it's widely used and recognized.*

HELPING USERS WITH LINK DESCRIPTIONS

The HTML 4 (and therefore XHTML 1) specification introduced a feature that allows you to add link descriptions that pop up on the screen when users move their mouse over the link, as shown here:

To add pop-up descriptions, sometimes called tooltips, to your links, simply include the `title` attribute in the a element, like this:

```
<a href="http://www.raycomm.com" title="RayComm, Inc., home of TECHWR-L">
    RayComm, Inc.</a>
```

This feature doesn't work in all browsers; but it does works in Internet Explorer 4 and higher, Opera 3 and higher, and Netscape 6 and higher, so most of your readers will likely be able to see your tooltips.

Where to Go from Here

In this chapter, you learned about the various flavors of URLs and how to use them to construct links. You also learned how to label locations within your documents with name anchors and link to those locations. Armed with this information, you're now ready to tackle just about any HTML or XHTML task.

- In Chapter 4, you'll learn how to include images in your documents.

- See Chapter 12 for information about publishing documents on a Web server.

- See Part II, starting with Chapter 5, for information about adding tables, forms, and frames, as well as how to convert your HTML documents to XHTML.

- Visit Part IV for handy tips and advice for developing a coherent Web site, as well as specific techniques for developing public, personal, and intranet sites.

Chapter 4

Including Images

YOUR NEXT STEP TOWARD becoming an HTML or XHTML pro is including images, which can add pizzazz to your Web pages, help provide information, serve as navigational aids, or just add a splash of color. The key to including images is to do so wisely—that is, choose graphics with a purpose, use appropriate file formats, and employ graphics that help you design your pages effectively. In other words, if the image exists to convey information, use it; if it does not, reconsider using it. By taking the time to use images well, you can maximize their effectiveness for your users.

In this chapter, we'll show you how to select appropriate images, choose appropriate file formats, use images for different purposes, and develop image maps (those clickable images with multiple links).

This chapter covers the following topics:

- ◆ Selecting appropriate file size, physical size, and image format
- ◆ Adding images to HTML or XHTML documents
- ◆ Specifying image characteristics: height, width, alignment, and borders
- ◆ Using images as links
- ◆ Creating image maps
- ◆ Using images as backgrounds

Developing Images

Although images add life to your Web pages, they can become a liability if they are not developed properly. For example, images can seemingly take F-O-R-E-V-E-R to load, becoming an obstacle for your users. Likewise, images can unnecessarily waste page space or disk space, perhaps obscuring or overshadowing important content. So, your goal in using images is to develop them properly by considering three things:

- ◆ File size
- ◆ Physical dimensions
- ◆ File format

Determining File Size

Think of image files as being three-dimensional, having height and width as well as many colors. For example, a 16-color image not only has height and width, which you can see on the screen, but it also has 16 *layers*, one for each color; this is called the *color depth*. An image's basic file size equals width × height × color depth.

With the following techniques, you can reduce file size and, therefore, make your images as efficient as possible:

Reduce the number of colors.   This technique is particularly useful for Graphics Interchange Format (GIF) images. You'll find more information on the number of colors in GIFs in the section "Understanding GIFs," later in this chapter.

Reduce the image's physical dimensions.   For example, you can reduce an image from 600 × 400 pixels to 300 × 200 pixels. The resulting smaller image usually includes the details and clarity of the larger one, yet it occupies significantly less storage space, takes less download time, and uses less screen real estate. You'll find guidelines for sizing images in the next section.

Use a format that compresses the file to cram more data into less space.   You'll find more details about suitable image formats in the section "Understanding Image Formats," later in this chapter.

TIP   Every time you reduce file size, you make it easier for users to download and view your page. But always keep an eye on image quality—if your graphic is too small or too compressed, you might lose the effect of it completely.

Dealing with Physical Dimensions

The physical size (dimensions) of an image is its height and width; this affects not only how the image appears in a browser, but also how quickly it loads. Just how big should images be? Well, that depends. Many sites use itty-bitty images, such as buttons and icons, that effectively add color or dimension to a Web page. Other sites use larger graphics for logos or button bars, which are also effective. There's no "right" size for images; instead, the key is to consider the following:

◆   The image's purpose

◆   The overall page design

◆   Your users' computer settings and connection speed

◆   The total size of the page and all the images it requires

CONSIDER IMAGE PURPOSE

Every time you add an image to a page, you need a good reason for doing so—to illustrate a point, to show a person or a location, to show a product, to outline a process, to make navigation easier and clearer, or simply to add some color and zest to an otherwise hum-drum document. Be sure that every image enhances content, design, or both.

When determining the dimensions of an image, consider its importance. For example, if your users need an image to understand a concept, the image should be larger. On the other hand, an image that merely adds a splash of color should probably be a bit smaller. If you're not sure how important an image is, lean toward smaller. Remember, images are the major contributor to the total file size of a page, and therefore to the loading time of the page, so they can affect how easily a user can access your pages.

CONSIDER PAGE DESIGN

Images are visually "weighty" objects—that is, they attract attention faster than other page elements. Images that are too large often overwhelm page contents and obscure the message. When determining image size, in particular, consider how the image will appear relative to other page elements. Here are some questions to ask yourself:

◆ Will the page include multiple graphics?

◆ Will the page incorporate borders and shading, which are also weightier than text?

◆ Will the page contain a substantive amount of text or only a few words? Text can make up in volume what it lacks in visual weight. A lot of text balances a graphic more effectively than a small amount of text.

CONSIDER USERS' COMPUTER SETTINGS

Your users' computer settings also affect how images appear on screen. An image that's 600×400 pixels will take up almost the entire browser window on Windows computers using the lowest screen resolution of 640×480 pixels (even allowing for most browser interface elements), so that's a good standard for a maximum image size. The most common screen resolution is currently 800×600, and many users use a resolution of 1024×768 or higher; that same 600×400 image will take up much less screen space on their computers. Check your pages at several screen resolutions to make sure that the images and content remain clear at different settings. And, of course, if you can make images smaller, do so to help speed loading time.

TIP   To convey content adequately, few images need to be larger than 600×400. Something in the range of 300×200 pixels is usually a good size for photographs, and buttons are generally 50×50 pixels or smaller.

CONSIDER TOTAL FILE SIZE OF THE PAGE

By adding up the size of all files associated with a page, you can calculate the total file size of a page and estimate the download time for that page. We will walk you through an example to show you how to do this. For this example, we will use a hypothetical page, `index.html`; the values for this page are shown in Table 4.1.

TABLE 4.1: FILE SIZE VALUES FOR index.html

FILENAME	FILE SIZE
index.html	4 KB
header.gif	17 KB
logo.gif	5 KB
navbar.jpg	13 KB
styles.css	1 KB
Total	40 KB

1. Write down the size of all the files associated with a page and add them.

2. Take the total file size in kilobytes (KB) and multiply by 8 to convert to kilobits (Kb; 1 byte = 8 bits).

3. Divide by the bandwidth (connection speed) of the user to estimate the actual download time for the page.

NOTE *Modem speed (as opposed to the speed of a reader with a DSL connection or a cable modem) will be the lowest value and therefore of most concern to you. A page that works well over slow connections will be great over faster ones.*

In this example, a user using a 28.8-Kbps (kilobits per second) modem would be able to completely download the page index.html in about 11 seconds (using the values in Table 4.1, 40 KB × 8 = 320 kilobits; 320 kilobits/28.8 Kbps = 11.1 seconds).

WARNING *Don't mix up kilobytes (used for file size and abbreviated KB) and kilobits (used for download rate and abbreviated Kb). Many people use just K for both; they refer to 56K modems and also to file sizes such as 56K. But a 56-Kbps modem doesn't download a 56-KB file in one second! (It takes about eight seconds.)*

A good rule of thumb is to keep the total file size of a page between 30 and 50 KB so download time is reasonable for all users.

Understanding Image Formats

When developing images, you should also consider your format options. Basically, you can use Graphics Interchange Format (GIF), Joint Photographic Experts Group (JPEG), or Portable Network Graphics (PNG) format, depending on what you want to do.

UNDERSTANDING GIFS

The most common image format is Graphics Interchange Format (GIF), developed by CompuServe for online use. If you check out your image-editing software's Save As options, you might have a choice between two versions of GIF: 87a and 89a. You want to choose version 89a; whether it's called GIF-89a or just GIF, this format includes the following features:

◆ Transparency

◆ Animation

◆ Progressive rendering

◆ Lossless compression

GIF Supports Transparency

GIF supports *transparency*. This means that you can make part of a GIF image transparent so that what is underneath the image shows through the transparent areas. In most cases, this will be the background color of the page. For example, in the ASR Outfitters logo image, the corner areas are a different color and set to be transparent. Figure 4.1 shows this image as it appears in Paint Shop Pro, an image-editing program; even if you set the background as transparent, you can still see it. Figure 4.2 shows the same image as it appears in Internet Explorer.

FIGURE 4.1

Viewed in an image-editing program, the transparent background is still visible

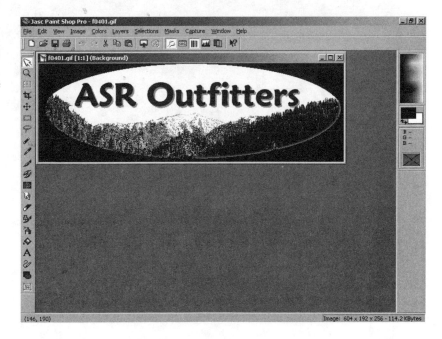

It's sometimes not necessary to use transparency to achieve this effect. If you set the background color of the image to the exact same color as the background color of the page (which is set in the body element—for example, `<body bgcolor="#ffffff">` for a white background—or in an associated style sheet), the image background will sometimes blend seamlessly with the page background. This is called *pseudo-transparency* or *fake transparency*. However, sometimes browsers render images with vaguely different color than the rest of the page contents, so the image backgrounds are not really quite transparent.

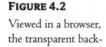

FIGURE 4.2

Viewed in a browser, the transparent background is not visible

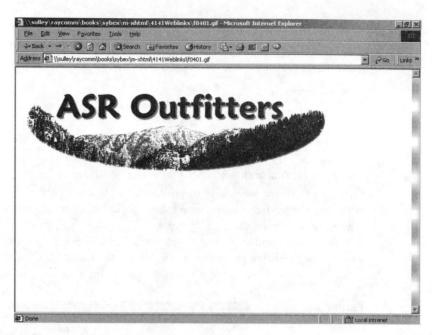

GIF Supports Animation

Some image-editing programs and specialized image-processing or Web-design programs can combine several GIF images into a single file, which then displays each image or panel in turn. The effect is similar to the effect found in cartoon-flip books—you flip the pages and see the illusion of motion, that is, animation.

Not all browsers display animated GIFs, although almost all commonly used browsers today support them. Browsers that don't support animated GIFs include text-only browsers and browsers that use text-to-speech software.

Using animated GIFs is a simple way to provide animation without resorting to Java applets or to more sophisticated plug-ins such as Shockwave or Flash. You'll find more information about animated GIFs in Chapter 11.

TIP   *Animated GIFs are much larger than nonanimated ones because they contain the equivalent of an additional image for each panel (frame) of animation.*

GIF Supports Progressive Rendering

Progressive rendering is also known as *interlacing* and refers to how an image is displayed on the screen while it downloads. A browser displays a noninterlaced image line by line, as it's received over the network or loaded off a disk. The complete image is not visible until it has been completely loaded. A browser displays interlaced images in passes, filling in every eighth line until the entire image is displayed.

The effects of interlacing vary from browser to browser. Some browsers display the download-ing image as slowly coming into focus. Other browsers display it like Venetian blinds that are slowly opened until the entire image is displayed. Either way, interlaced images begin to appear on the screen faster than noninterlaced images and allow users who are familiar with the image to get the gist before the whole image appears. Interlaced images also help reassure the user that the image download is progressing.

GIF Supports Lossless Compression

Lossless compression is an efficient way to save files without losing image details. When GIFs are saved, they are compressed to take less space on the disk and less time to download. With lossless compres-sion, the compression algorithm notices broad expanses of single colors, and instead of recording the color for each pixel, it indicates the color and the number of times to repeat the color. The image is not changed; it's simply saved more efficiently.

GIFs can include up to 256 colors. However, if your image does not have this many colors, a smaller file size can be created by limiting the number of colors in the GIF to only as many as you actually need. Therefore, when you save an image as a GIF in an image-editing program, save it with only as many colors as necessary. This will decrease the file size and the download time.

TIP *Because GIFs can only include 256 colors, they're not sufficient for true photographic quality. GIF images are best used for line art, icons, and drawings with a limited number of colors. You will probably want to use the JPEG or PNG file formats for images requiring higher quality.*

UNDERSTANDING JPEGS

JPEG, which is pronounced *jay-peg*, is an acronym formed from Joint Photographic Experts Group (it's sometimes written as JPG because that's a common file extension). JPEG is the second most popular format for images on the Web. As a whole, JPEG images are less flexible than GIF images, and most important, they do not support the variety of rendering options that GIFs support.

The most significant advantage of JPEG is that it supports millions of colors, thereby providing much more realistic photographic reproduction. JPEG images use a *lossy* compression algorithm. Lossy compression discards some details of the image to decrease the file size. JPEG images are best for photographs because the loss of detail is less noticeable with photographs than with line art; in addition, the compression ratio and resulting quality are much better with photographs.

Setting JPEG options in your image-editing program helps control both the eventual file size and the quality. In many programs, you can set the resolution, or number of pixels per inch (ppi), and the level of JPEG compression. If the images are for Web use only—that is, they won't be used for print publications—a resolution of 100 is more than adequate. Screen resolution is only 72 ppi for Mac monitors and 96 ppi for PC monitors; therefore, using a resolution higher than 100 uselessly increases an image's file size. Depending on the image, the application, and the eventual purpose of the image, you can often increase the compression substantially without losing much detail. If the same image is going to be used both on the Web and in print, save one version as a JPEG for the Web and another version as a higher resolution TIFF for print.

WARNING *Although JPEG supports progressive rendering, older browsers do not support this feature and will display a broken image icon when you use a JPEG with progressive rendering. If using progressive rendering is important, consider using the GIF file format.*

UNDERSTANDING PNGS

The latest development in Web image file formats is *PNG*, pronounced *ping*, which stands for Portable Network Graphics. This format is only supported by relatively recent browser versions (Microsoft Internet Explorer 4 or later and Netscape Navigator 4.04 or later). PNG images combine most of the advantages of GIF, including transparency and interlacing, plus the ability to accommodate millions of colors and a tight, lossless compression technique.

WHICH IMAGE FORMAT IS RIGHT FOR YOU?

The image format you choose depends on the features you want to include. Table 4.2 compares the features of the three graphic formats examined.

TABLE 4.2: FEATURES OF GIF, JPEG, AND PNG

FEATURES	GIF	JPEG	PNG
Transparency	Yes	No	Yes
Interlacing/progressive rendering	Yes	Yes	Yes
Millions of colors	No	Yes	Yes
Lossless compression	Yes	No	Yes
Good for line art	Yes	No	Yes
Good for photographs	No	Yes	Yes
Accepted on most browsers	Yes	Yes	Yes

As you can see, GIF and JPEG have complementary advantages and disadvantages. However, as more browsers support PNG, it is becoming the first choice.

XML OPPORTUNITIES

The W3C is currently finalizing the Scalable Vector Graphics (SVG) 1.0 specification (which is a W3C Recommendation). SVG is an XML language used to describe two-dimensional graphics. The W3C defines vector graphics as "paths consisting of straight lines and curves." Find out more about SVG at www.w3.org/Graphics/SVG/Overview.htm8.

Adding Images

In this section, we're going to create some Web pages for ASR Outfitters, a mountaineering and hiking supply company that is a mythical, mini-version of REI, the recreation equipment retailer. In the process, you'll learn how to include images in an HTML or XHTML document. Although this may seem like putting the cart before the horse, knowing how to include images makes learning to develop them easier.

NOTE *In this section, the examples show how to add images using XHTML. Using HTML would be just the same, except that the* img *element would not require a / before the closing >.*

Table 4.3 shows the main image element and its attributes, which are used to insert images in Web pages.

TABLE 4.3: MAIN ELEMENT AND ATTRIBUTES OF IMAGES

ITEM	TYPE	SPECIFIES
img	Empty element	Marks an image within an XHTML or HTML document.
align="…"	Attribute of img	Image alignment as top, middle, bottom, left, or right; deprecated.
alt="…"	Attribute of img	Alternative text to display if an image is not displayed (necessary for accessibility reasons); required.
border="n"	Attribute of img	The width of a border around an image in pixels; deprecated.
height="n"	Attribute of img	The final height of an image in pixels.
src="url"	Attribute of img	An image file and location (URL) to include; required.
width="n"	Attribute of img	The final width of an image in pixels.

Adding an Image

Adding an image is similar to adding the elements and attributes you've already used. You use the img element, which specifies an image, plus the src attribute to specify the image filename and location (URL). For example, if you're including an image that's located within the same folder as your document (a relative URL), your code might look like this:

```
<img src="logo.gif  />
```

Or, if you're including an image located on another server, you could include an absolute URL, like this:

```
<img src="http://www.asroutfitters.com/gifs/asrlogo.gif" />
```

TIP *The* img *element is classified as an empty element; it uses a space and a slash (/) before the closing >.*

A URL used in the `src` attribute is called a *remote reference*. Referencing logos and images remotely has certain advantages and some significant drawbacks. One advantage is that remote references to images ensure that you're always using the current logo. For example, if ASR Outfitters hires a graphic design company to change its corporate image, a franchisee's site that uses remote references to the main site will reflect the changes as soon as the main site changes. Additionally, remote references lighten the load on your server and reduce the number of files you must manage and manipulate.

On the downside, changes that are out of your control can easily break links from your site. If the ASR Outfitters Webmaster decides to move the images from the `gifs` subdirectory into an `images` subdirectory, the franchisee's images will no longer work, because the `src` attribute points to the sub-directory that no longer contains the image files. From the user's perspective, the franchisee simply has a nonfunctional site—the user really doesn't know or care why.

Additionally, network glitches or server problems can also render your images inoperative if you link to them remotely. If the load on your own site is significant and you use remote images, the other site may be swamped with the demand and not even know why. Overall, you're probably better off copying the images to your server, rather than relying on remote servers.

WARNING *Be careful about linking to or copying remote images, because those images may be copyrighted material. For example, if Bad Karma Hiking Equipment decided that the ASR Outfitters images were cool and incorporated those cool images in a site design by using them without permission, Bad Karma would be infringing on ASR Outfitter's copyrighted material. This also applies to background images (covered later in this chapter) and any other document content. So, be careful!*

To add images to your document, start with a basic HTML or XHTML document that, along with content, includes the following:

- The `DOCTYPE` declaration
- The `html` element with the XHTML namespace
- The `head` element
- The `body` element

We used the basic document in Listing 4.1 for ASR Outfitters.

LISTING 4.1: THE ASR OUTFITTERS BASIC PAGE

```
<!DOCTYPE html PUBLIC ".//W3C/DTD XHTML 1.0 Transitional//EN"
   "http://www.w3.org/TR/xhtml1/DTD/xhtml1-transitional.dtd">
<html xmlns="http://www.w3.org/1999/xhtml">
   <head>
      <title>ASR Outfitters</title>
   </head>
<body>
      <h1 align="center">ASR Outfitters</h1>
      <p>We provide mountaineering and hiking equipment
         nationwide via mail order as well as through our
         stores in the Rocky Mountains.</p>
```

```
    <hr width="70%" size="8" noshade="noshade" />
    <p>Please select from the following links:</p>
    <ul>
        <li><a href="camping.html">Camping News</a></li>
        <li><a href="catalog.html">Catalog</a></li>
        <li><a href="clubs.html">Clubs</a></li>
        <li><a href="contact.html">Contact Us</a></li>
        <li><a href="weather.html">Check Weather</a></li>
    </ul>
    <hr width="70%" size="8" noshade="noshade" />
    <center>
        <address>ASR Outfitters<br />
            <a href="mailto:info@asroutfitters.com">
                info@asroutfitters.com</a><br />
            4700 N. Center<br />
            South Logan, UT 87654<br />
            801-555-3422<br />
        </address>
    </center>
</body>
</html>
```

WARNING *Attribute–value pairs should be written in full; for example,* noshade="noshade" *in Listing 4.1. In HTML, an attribute name can sometimes be specified without an attribute value (e.g., the attribute* checked *for a* form *element). In XHTML, the value must be specified—even in cases such as this where the name and the value are the same. Specifying the value is good practice, in any event.*

To add an image to this basic document, follow these steps:

1. Insert an <img /> element where you want the image to appear:

```
<h1 align="center">ASR Outfitters</h1>
<img />
<p>We provide mountaineering and hiking equipment
    nationwide via mail order as well as through our
    stores in the Rocky Mountains.</p>
```

2. Add the src attribute that points to the image filename and location. In this example, the filename is asrlogo.gif, and it's in the same folder as the document; so that's all that's required.

```
<img src="asrlogo.gif" />
```

3. In this case, add a line break element <br /> after the <img /> element so that the following text starts on the next line (and not in any available space behind or on either side of the image).

```
<img src="asrlogo.gif" /><br />
```

4. Because the image duplicates the content of the first-level heading (`<h1 align="center">ASR Outfitters</h1>`), consider removing the first-level heading.

5. The first-level heading was centered, so add the `center` element around the logo to center it as well.

`<center><img src="asrlogo.gif" /><br /></center>`

TIP   The `img` element supports the `align` attribute with a value of `top`, `middle`, `bottom`, `left`, or `right`, but it does not support horizontal centering. If you want to use horizontal centering, use the `center` element. However, note that the `center` element is deprecated in favor of using style sheets. See the "Aligning the Image" section later in this chapter for more information.

You can see the resulting image in the ASR Web page shown in Figure 4.3.

FIGURE 4.3

An image in the ASR Web page

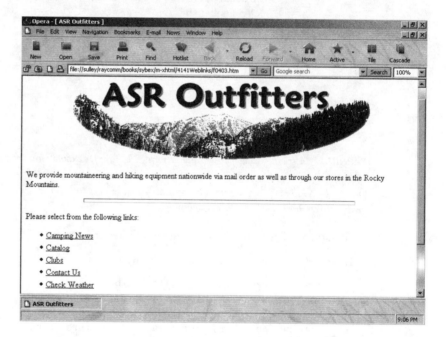

Including Alternative Text

Alternative text describes an image you've used in your Web page. You should include alternative text for the following reasons:

◆ The XHTML 1 specification requires the `alt` attribute for many elements, including `img`. Your documents won't be valid without it, which will mean extra work for you to update them in the future.

◆ Some of your users may be using text-only browsers.

◆ Some of your users may be visually impaired and using text-to-speech converters that can't render graphics.

◆ A user may have turned off images so that files will load faster.

◆ Sometimes browsers don't display images correctly.

◆ Sometimes images don't display because the links aren't working properly.

◆ Sometimes browsers display alternative text while images load.

◆ Search engines may use alternative text as the only source of information on image content.

Alternative text should be clear and concise, and should provide your users with enough information so they can understand the image content without viewing it. Alternative text for a logo can be as simple as the company name and the word *logo*. Even text as brief as "ASR sample photograph" or "ASR content-free image" is helpful to users. If they see only the word *Image* (which they would if you omit the alt attribute), they'll have to load the images to see the content.

To add alternative text to your images, simply add the alt attribute to the img element, like this:

```
<img src="asrlogo.gif" alt="ASR Outfitters Logo" />
```

The resulting alternative text is shown in Figure 4.4.

FIGURE 4.4

Alternative text provides information about the image

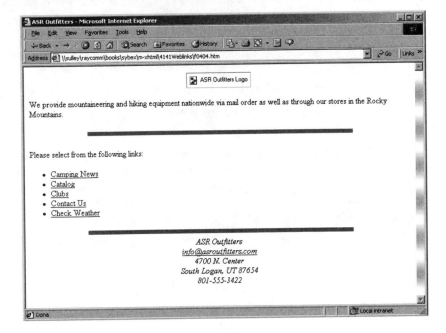

Specifying Height and Width

You can speed up the loading time of images by specifying an image's height and width. As the browser loads the page, it notes the `height` and `width` attributes and leaves that much space for the image. Next, it lays out the remaining text, then it goes back and fills in the image. If you do not include these attributes, the browser has to download enough of the image to get the dimensions before it can lay out the rest of the text, thereby slowing the display of other page elements.

To specify image height and width, add the `height` and `width` attributes in the `img` element, like this:

```
<img src="asrlogo.gif" alt="ASR Outfitters Logo" width="604"
    height="192" />
```

As a rule, use the actual height and width of the image. To get the dimensions, open the image in an image-editing program and use the program's option for finding pixel measurements (usually a properties page, status bar, or Image Size command). You will see something like $604 \times 192 \times 256$, which indicates, in this example, that the `asrlogo.gif` image is 604 pixels wide, 192 pixels high, and 256 colors deep. With this information, you can then add the `width` (604) and `height` (192) attributes to the `img` element.

WARNING   *Reducing these attributes doesn't reduce download times; the same image file still has to load. See the section "Creating Thumbnails" later in this chapter for a technique to include smaller images that are also less memory intensive.*

Aligning the Image

HTML and XHTML provide several image-alignment options:

- Three vertical options align the image with respect to a line of text.

- Two options align the image to the left or to the right of the window (with corresponding text wrap).

The alignment options within the `img` element override other alignment settings within the document, such as `<center>...</center>` tags surrounding the `img` element.

By default, images align on the left, with a single line of accompanying text appearing on the same line; however, long text wraps to the following line. To ensure that accompanying text appears beside the image, specify `align="left"` in the `img` element, like this:

```
<img src="asrlogo.gif" alt="ASR Outfitters Logo" width="604"
    height="192" align="left" />
```

The text appears to the right of the left-aligned image, as shown in Figure 4.5.

TIP   *Remember that all attribute values must be quoted in XHTML, and should be quoted in HTML (although that is not mandatory). For example,* `align="left"` *is valid code, and* `align=left` *is not valid code.*

You can create attractive effects by combining image alignment and text alignment. For example, setting an image to `align="right"` and then setting the accompanying text to `align="right"` forces the text to be flush against the image with a ragged left margin, as shown in Figure 4.6.

FIGURE 4.5

Specifying left alignment for an image ensures that accompanying text appears to the right of the image

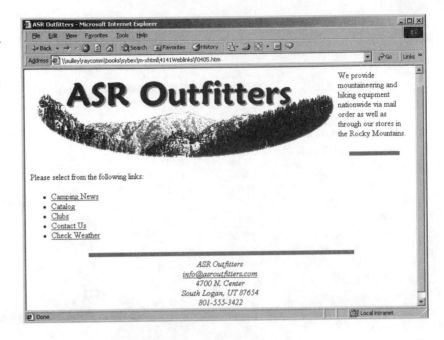

FIGURE 4.6

Specifying right alignment for the image and text produces appealing results

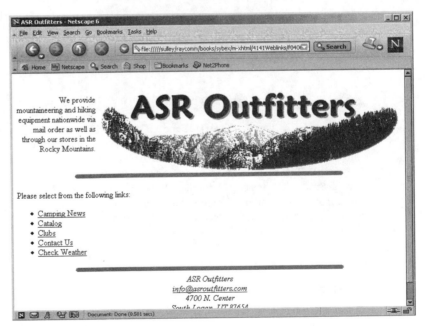

The remaining alignment options—top, middle, and bottom—can be used to align the image within the text. For example, using align="top" aligns the top of the image with the top of the surrounding text, and the remainder of the image hangs below the text line. Using align="middle" places the

middle of an image at the baseline of surrounding text. Similarly, using `align="bottom"` places the bottom of an image on the same line as the text, and the remainder of the image extends considerably higher than the surrounding text. The effect of these options is shown in Figure 4.7.

FIGURE 4.7

Top, middle, and bottom alignment float the image differently in relationship to the surrounding text

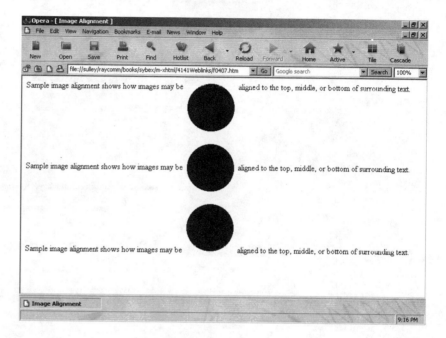

STYLE SHEET OPPORTUNITIES

As mentioned in Chapter 2, the HTML and XHTML specifications deprecate presentational markup in favor of style sheets. The `align` attribute and the `center` element are presentational, which means they provide information about the display of a document. Presentational elements and attributes can be used in HTML or XHTML documents as long as the documents use the Transitional DTD. However, if you want to use the Strict DTD, any alignment must be specified in a style sheet. (See Chapter 23 for further information about DTDs, Chapter 2 for more about presentational attributes and elements, and Chapter 9 and Master's Reference Part 2 for details on using style sheets to set alignment and other presentational properties.)

Controlling the Border

You control the border around an image with the `border` attribute. In most browsers, by default, the border is visible only on images that are used as links. To turn the border off for an image, add the `border="0"` attribute to the `img` element, resulting in a complete image element like this:

```
<img src="asrlogo.gif" alt="ASR Outfitters Logo" width="604"
    height="192" border="0" />
```

Likewise, you can increase the border width around an image by increasing the value of the border attribute, like this:

```
<img src="asrlogo.gif" alt="ASR Outfitters Logo" width="604"
    height="192" border="7" />
```

The resulting border looks like the one in Figure 4.8.

FIGURE 4.8

Setting a large border width frames your images

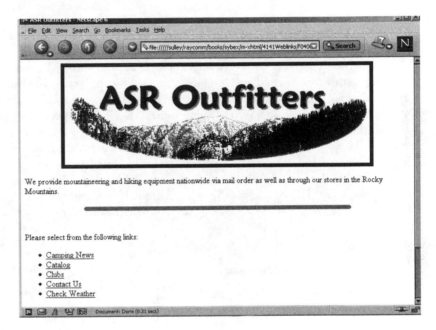

Choosing Suitable Colors

When creating your own images—or choosing colors for Web page or table backgrounds—you want to choose colors that look good in most browsers, most of the time. If you're selecting colors for text or for small swatches, choose anything that appeals to you. However, if you're selecting a background color or a color that will appear in broad expanses of your documents, be careful.

If you select a color that is not available on a user's system, the browser will dither the color to approximate its appearance. *Dithering* is the technical term for substituting other colors, partially or wholly, to minimize the impact of not having the correct color. Dithering in photographs or small images is rarely noticeable, but dithering in large single-color areas results in blotchy or mottled appearances.

In the past, personal computers only supported 8-bit color, or 256 (2 to the power of 8) colors at a time. The three major operating systems (Macintosh, Unix, and Windows) each used different sets of colors for system functions, and those colors—up to 40—are taken from the available 256, leaving only 216 colors for general use. If you choose one of these 216 colors (also called *Web-safe colors*), you can be certain that the colors will look as good as they can in all browsers on all platforms. These remaining 216 colors are evenly distributed over the color spectrum, giving you a wide range of colors from which to choose.

Today, most personal computers support not only 8-bit color but also 15-bit or 16-bit color (also called *high color*), and many computers support 24-bit color (also called *true color* or *millions of colors*). If your computer is set to display 24-bit color, it can display 16,776,216 colors. However, despite the fact that most users have more than 256 possible colors available, color display is still not completely uniform in different browsers and different platforms.

TIP *If you would like to learn more about Web-safe color, including the pros and cons of using the Web-safe color palette, see the article "Death of the Websafe Color Palette?" by David Lehn and Hadley Stern at* `http://hotwired.lycos` `.com/webmonkey/00/37/index2a.html`*.*

Monitor colors are represented as proportions of their red, green, and blue components, which together form an *RGB value*. In most image-editing programs, you can choose component levels in decimal (base 10) numbers, on a scale of 0–255 for a 256-color system. However, when you're specifying colors within a Web page, the most common format is hexadecimal (base 16) numbers. The "hex" digits are 0123456789ABCDEF, so the hexadecimal version of 0–255 is 00–FF.

If you limit yourself to 216 total colors, you can build a color's RGB value from the numbers in Table 4.4 for each color component. To create a safe (nondithering) color, choose a system (hexadecimal or decimal) and choose one value from each column. For example, a Web-safe "sky blue" color might be 51, 204, 255 for the red, green, and blue components. The corresponding hexadecimal numbers would be 33, CC, FF. (Hex digits aren't case sensitive, so ff is the same as FF.)

TABLE 4.4: PREFERRED RGB VALUES

HEXADECIMAL			DECIMAL		
Red	Green	Blue	Red	Green	Blue
00	00	00	0	0	0
33	33	33	51	51	51
66	66	66	102	102	102
99	99	99	153	153	153
CC	CC	CC	204	204	204
FF	FF	FF	255	255	255

You signal, in your code, that you're using a hexadecimal color value by placing a pound sign (#) before the six digits for the color code; for example, `<body bgcolor="#33CCFF">`. Decimal color values (which are less common in XHTML) are defined in parentheses: `<body bgcolor="rgb(51,204,255)">`.

TIP *For 16 predefined colors, rather than specify a number for the color value, you can use a keyword. These keywords are listed in Master's Reference Part 5. You'd use them as attribute values in place of the hex code—for example,* `<body bgcolor="teal">`*.*

As a rule, colors that are close to the 256 colors built from Table 4.4 will also not dither, but there's no hard and fast rule on how "close" is close enough. For example, we tried #000001 and found that it didn't visibly dither on our computers… this time.

TIP   Visit Chapter 13 for information about using colors to help create a coherent Web site. Also, you'll find more on browser-safe colors in Master's Reference Part 5.

Using Images as Links

Using images as links offers two distinct advantages to both you and your users. First, images really can be as good as a thousand words. Often, including an image link can replace several words or lines of text, leaving valuable space for other page elements and content. Second, you can also use *thumbnails*, which are smaller images that link to larger ones. By doing so, you can let users get the gist of an image and choose whether they want to load the larger version. (You'll find details about thumbnails in an upcoming section, "Creating Thumbnails.")

Creating Image Links

To add an image as a link, start by adding the `img` element. In this example, we are adding a fancy button to the ASR Outfitters page to replace the more prosaic Camping News bulleted list item. The name of the image is `camping.gif`, and the file it should link to is `camping.html`.

TIP   When you use images as links, alternative text is critical. If clicking the image is the only way users can connect to the other page, the alternative text is their only clue when the image is not displayed (whether because of technical difficulties, because they've turned off images, because they have text-only browsers, or because they use a screen-reading program for the visually impaired).

TIP   Consider using images as links at some points within your page design, and text for the same links elsewhere (perhaps at the bottom). By providing both, you increase the chances that your readers will find and be able to use the links you provide.

Here are the steps for adding an image link:

1. Add an `img` element and an `src` attribute with the name of the image file as the value to the document.

   ```
   <img src="camping.gif" />
   ```

2. Include alternative text using the `alt` attribute:

   ```
   <img src="camping.gif" alt="Camping News" />
   ```

3. Add any other attributes you want to include, such as the `height`, `width`, and `border` attributes. If you choose to use `border="0"` to turn off the border completely, be sure that the image is visually identified as a link. Otherwise, your users might not know it's a link unless they pass their mouse over it and see the pointing-hand cursor.

   ```
   <img src="camping.gif" width="300" height="82" border="0"
       alt="Camping News" />
   ```

4. Add the link anchor opening element (`<a>`) before and the closing element (`</a>`) at the end of the image element:

```
<a><img src="camping.gif" width="300" height="82"
   border="0" alt="Camping News" /></a>
```

5. Add the `href` attribute to the opening anchor element (`<a>`) to specify the image filename and location:

```
<a href="camping.html"><img src="camping.gif" width="300"
   height="82" border="0" alt="Camping News" /></a>
```

Now you have an image that acts as a link to the `camping.html` file. After adding a couple more images and surrounding them all with the `center` element, the ASR Outfitters page is similar to Figure 4.9.

NOTE *Today's Web site designs generally favor text-based links or small image-based links; however, throughout this chapter, we've used some larger images to help illustrate concepts. In designing images and image-based links for your site, develop ones that meet your users' expectations and needs. See Chapters 12, 13, and 14 for additional information about determining and accommodating user needs.*

FIGURE 4.9

Image links can make a page much more attractive (and slower to load)

Creating Thumbnails

As we mentioned earlier, a thumbnail is a smaller version of an image, but it's also a link to the larger version. Thumbnails can also link to multimedia files or to other content that is time-consuming to download or not universally accessible.

For example, ASR Outfitters included a thumbnail of the original photograph that inspired its logo. This thumbnail links to the original photograph, which is a larger image.

To add a thumbnail image, start by having both images—the thumbnail and the larger version—available. Make a thumbnail by starting with the full-size version (scanned from your private collection or from another source—remember the copyright rules). Use your image-editing software to resize or resample the image to a much smaller size—as small as possible while still retaining the gist of the image. Save this second image under a different name and follow these steps:

1. Include the thumbnail image in your document the way you'd include any other image. For example, the code might look like this:

```
<img src="photo-thumbnail.jpg" height="78" width="193"
    align="right" border="1" alt="Thumbnail of original
    photo" />
```

2. Add a link from the thumbnail to the larger image.

```
<a href="photo.jpg"><img src="photo-thumbnail.jpg"
    height="78" width="193" align="right" border="1"
    alt="Thumbnail of original photo" /></a>
```

If you set the border to 0, be sure that the supporting text or other cues in the document make it clear that the image is, in fact, a link to a larger photograph. Alternatively, do as we did and simply set border="1" to make it clear that an image is a link. Here's the result from the bottom corner of the ASR Outfitters home page:

Although you can achieve the same visual effect in your document by using the original image and setting a smaller display size with the height and width attributes, this technique defeats the purpose of thumbnails. Even if you reset the display size with smaller values for height and width, the entire full-size image will have to be downloaded to your computer. The trick to effective thumbnails is to reduce both the dimensions and the actual file size to the smallest possible value so the page will load quickly.

Creating Image Maps

An image map, also called a *clickable image*, is a single image that contains multiple links. In your Web travels, you may have used image maps without knowing it. Clicking a portion of an image map takes you to the link connected with that part of the visual presentation. For example, a health-information Web site might present an image map of the human body to a patient, with instructions for the patient to "click where it hurts." Another good use replaces individual images (which browsers could realign depending on the window width) with a single *graphical menu*. Figure 4.10 shows a sample image map from the ASR Outfitter's Web site. Users can click each area for weather conditions—weather at the high peaks and lower elevations—and even the ultraviolet index.

FIGURE 4.10

Image maps are single images with multiple links to other information or graphics

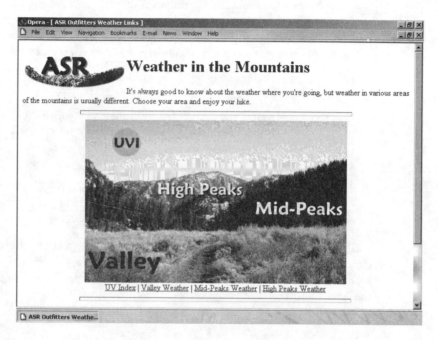

In the past, image maps were processed on the server—called *server-side image maps*. That is, when somebody clicked part of the image map, the server where the image map resided received the coordinates that were clicked and then figured out which linked document to display. In the past few years, though, server-side image maps have increasingly been replaced by *client-side image maps*, which are ones that are processed by users' browsers. This trend toward client-side image maps has happened for several reasons.

To start with, they're faster (because there's no need for back-and-forth communication between client and server to process the map) and more reliable for those browsers that support client-side maps (and most do). For example, if a document with a client-side image map comes from Server A and points to a document on Server B, the client can do the calculations and request the document directly from Server B.

Client-side image maps are more user-friendly than server-side image maps. When a user moves the cursor over an image-map link within a document, the status bar generally displays the URL of the link. Newer browsers, including the latest versions of Netscape Navigator and Internet Explorer, also show information about the link in a small pop-up window. In contrast, when a user places the cursor over a server-side image-map link, the status bar displays only the coordinates of the cursor.

Finally, client-side image maps are better for you, the Web author, because you can use and test them before you put the image map on the server. In contrast, server-side maps do not work until they have been installed on the server, making testing much more difficult.

So, for these reasons, client-side image maps have become the norm. Although you could develop a server-side image map, we recommend developing a client-side image map instead, as discussed in the remainder of this chapter.

MAKING APPROPRIATE IMAGE MAPS

Poorly constructed or carelessly selected image maps can be much worse than no image map at all. The inherent disadvantages of images (for example, their download time and their inaccessibility for text-only browsers) apply in spades to image maps. When determining whether an image map is appropriate for your needs, ask the following questions:

Is the image map linking to a stable navigational structure?   If the links will be changing or if the overall site navigation structure isn't completely worked out, it's not time for an image map. Revising image maps is possible, but generally a real hassle. It's often easier to completely redo an image map than to update it.

Is the image final?   If the image hasn't passed all levels of review and isn't polished, you're not ready to make an image map. Changes as trivial as cropping the image slightly or rescaling the image by a few percentage points can completely break your map.

Is the image function appropriate to an image map?   Flashy images on a home page are good candidates for image maps, particularly if the design reflects the corporate image. In many cases, an intricate design must be a single image anyway—browsers cannot always accurately assemble individual images into the arrangement the designer intends—so adding image-map navigation is just using the image more efficiently. However, pages buried within an intranet site or that have a technical and practical focus are less likely to benefit from an image map.

Is the image content appropriate to an image map?   Artificial or gratuitous use of image maps can be a real drawback to otherwise fine Web pages. Is clicking certain spots in an image really the best way for your users to link to the information they need? For example, in a Web site about automobile repair and diagnosis for the layperson, a picture of a car and the instructions to click where the funny sound seems to originate is completely appropriate. In a site directed at experienced mechanics, however, a list of parts (hood, trunk, dashboard, tire) would be much faster and more appropriate.

Does the function or content merit an image map?   If both do, that's great. If one does, you can probably proceed with an image map. However, if the links on a page don't need to be flashy and the content is not substantially clarified with an image map, omit the image map entirely. Don't forget that image files add substantially to the download time of a page, so use them wisely.

Can the image map be completely reused?   If you are planning to use an image map on several pages (you will use exactly the same image and code), its value increases. In this case, it's more likely to be worth the download time than if it's only being used once.

If you answered no to one or more of these questions, consider using traditional, individual images or navigation aids. For example, if you can easily break the content or image into multiple smaller images with no significant problems, strongly consider doing so. Remember that image maps are time-consuming to develop and may not be available to all your users, so be sure an image map is right for your needs before developing one.

SELECTING AN IMAGE

When you select a suitable image to use as an image map, follow the same guidelines as you would for choosing other images:

◆ Be sure that the image supports the content.

◆ Be sure that the physical size is as small as possible, but large enough to convey the content.

◆ Be sure that the file size is as small as possible.

◆ Photos are usually not good choices for image maps. It's hard for the user to know where to click in a photo unless it also includes text that clearly points out the clickable areas.

For example, if you are creating an auto-repair image map for laypersons, use a simple drawing or schematic. At the other extreme is the ASR Outfitters image map, which is primarily a visual attraction with only a tangential function. The image map shown in Figure 4.10, earlier in this chapter, is part of a localized weather page. Users can click an area to get the weather for that region.

SETTING ALTERNATE NAVIGATION

Unless you know beyond a doubt that *all* your users have graphical browsers and will choose to view images, you must provide alternate navigation options. Those who don't see the images—for whatever reason—won't be able to link to the information via your image, so provide text-based alternatives. An easy solution is to create a list of links. For example, alternate navigation for the image shown in Figure 4.10 might look like the following code:

```
<br />
<a href="uvi.html">UV Index</a> |
<a href="valley.html">Valley Weather</a> |
<a href="midpeaks.html">Mid-Peaks Weather</a> |
<a href="highpeaks.html">High Peaks Weather</a>
```

In this code, the vertical line or "pipe" character (|) separates the links and creates the menu effect, as shown at the bottom of Figure 4.10.

TIP   Creating the alternate navigation before you develop the image map helps remind you of the links to include in the image map.

Creating Client-Side Image Maps

Creating a client-side image map involves three steps:

1. Define the image area.

2. Create the image map.

3. Activate the image map.

DEFINING IMAGE AREAS

All image maps are simply a combination of three shapes:

◆ Circles

◆ Rectangles

◆ Polygons (any shapes other than circles and rectangles)

You can create almost any image by combining these shapes. Figure 4.11 shows the ASR Outfitters image map from within a map-editing program. The UVI link is a circle, the valley temperatures link is a rectangle, and the mid- and high-peak links are polygons.

FIGURE 4.11

This image map includes a circle, a rectangle, and two polygons

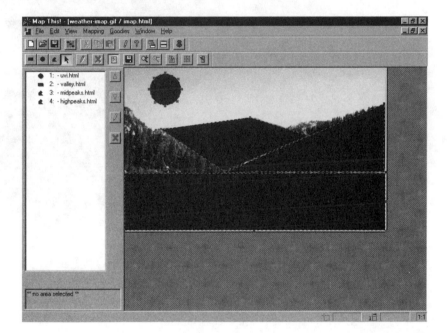

TIP   You don't have to be precise with most map definitions. You can assume that most users will click somewhere in the middle of the link area; if not, they're likely to try again.

The following three sections show you how to define these three shapes manually. Before you get started, open an image in an image-editing or -mapping program, such as Paint Shop Pro.

TIP   If you'll be developing several image maps, we recommend installing and using image-mapping software, which is available on the Internet. However, if you're creating simple maps or if you're only doing a few, creating them manually is almost as easy. Most WYSIWYG editors include image-map tools that are very easy to use. See the Chapter 1 sidebar "HTML and XHTML Editors" for more information about WYSIWYG editors.

Defining Circles

To define a circle, follow these steps:

1. Identify the center and the radius. Use the pointer tool to point at the center of the circle and note the coordinates in the status bar of your paint program. For example, in Paint Shop Pro (as shown in Figure 4.12), the pointer tool looks like a magnifying glass, and the x,y coordinates are at the bottom of the window. The x is the number of pixels from the left edge of the image, and the y is the number of pixels from the top.

FIGURE 4.12

Use your cursor to find the coordinates of various points, such as the center of a circle or corner of a polygon

2. Move the cursor horizontally to the edge of the circle, and note the coordinates.

3. Subtract the first x coordinate from the second x coordinate to get the radius of the circle.

4. Make a note of these coordinates.

Defining Rectangles

To define a rectangle, follow these steps:

1. Identify the upper-left corner and the lower-right corner. Point your mouse at the upper-left corner of the rectangle and record the coordinates; then point at the lower right and record the coordinates.

2. Make a note of these coordinates.

Defining Polygons

To define a polygon, follow these steps:

1. Identify each point on the shape, moving in order around the shape. You can start at any point on the perimeter and proceed clockwise or counterclockwise, as long as you don't skip points.

For example, in the ASR Outfitters map, the Mid-Peaks area can be defined with three points—making a right triangle with the long side running between the Mid-Peaks and High Peaks areas. The High Peaks area might include several points across the top of the mountains, or it might be as simple as another triangle.

2. Make a note of these coordinates.

CREATING THE IMAGE MAP

When you create an image map, you include elements and attributes that tell a browser what to do when a user clicks the defined map areas. You can include this information within the XHTML document that contains the image map, or you can include it in a separate document. The first is more common, but if you'll be using the image map (say, as a navigation aid) in several documents, consider storing it in a separate file and referencing it from each of the documents.

You can place the map definition block anywhere within the body of your XHTML document, but it's easier to update and maintain if you place it either immediately after the opening <body> element or immediately before the closing </body> element. Table 4.5 explains the most common image-map elements and attributes.

TABLE 4.5: MAIN IMAGE-MAP ELEMENTS AND ATTRIBUTES

ITEM	TYPE	USE
img	Element	Indicates inclusion of an image map.
ismap="ismap"	Attribute of img	Specifies that the image uses a server-side image map.
usemap="…"	Attribute of img	Names the client-side map definition to use.
map	Element	Marks the map definition block within the XHTML document.
id="…"	Attribute of map	Provides an identifier for the map definition block; required attribute.
name="…"	Attribute of map	Provides a name for the map definition block; deprecated.
area	Empty element	Defines an area within the map.
alt="…"	Attribute of area	Provides alternate text (or pop-up text) describing each link; required attribute.
coords="x1,y1,x2,y2…"	Attribute of area	Identifies the shape of an area.
href="url"	Attribute of area	Specifies a link for the area. A click in the area links to this URL.
nohref="nohref"	Attribute of area	Specifies that a click in this area will not link anywhere.
shape="…"	Attribute of area	Identifies the shape of an area as a rectangle (rect), circle (circle), or polygon (poly).

WARNING   *In HTML and XHTML, the* name *attribute for the elements* a, applet, form, frame, iframe, img, *and* map *is deprecated. XHTML documents should use the* id *attribute rather than the* name *attribute. To ensure maximum compatibility, use both the* name *and* id *attributes with identical values; for example,* <map name="navmap" id="navmap">.

To include a client-side image map, follow these steps (we'll use the ASR Outfitters page in this example):

1. Within your XHTML document, add opening and closing map elements:

    ```
    <body>
    <map>
    </map>
    </body>
    ```

2. Give the map a clear, descriptive name with name and id attributes. (See the previous warning.) The values used for the name and ID must be exactly the same, and these values may be used only once in the same document. They provide an internal anchor of sorts that you can link to either from the same document or from other documents.

    ```
    <map name="weather_zones" id="weather_zones">
    </map>
    ```

3. Add an area empty element for one of the shapes.

    ```
    <map name="weather_zones" id="weather_zones">
    <area />
    </map>
    ```

4. Add a shape attribute to the area element. In this example, circle represents the UVI area in the ASR example map.

    ```
    <area shape="circle" />
    ```

5. Add the coords attribute with the *x,y* coordinates of the center of the circle and with the radius of the circle.

    ```
    <area shape="circle" coords="82,43,30" />
    ```

6. Add an href attribute pointing to the target file. You can use relative or absolute URLs in client-side image maps, but, as with other links, using relative URLs is a good idea. In this case, the area links to a file called uvi.html in the same folder.

    ```
    <area shape="circle" coords="82,43,30" href="uvi.html" />
    ```

7. Add the alt attribute describing the link for use in pop-ups.

    ```
    <area shape="circle" coords="82,43,30" href="uvi.html"
        alt="UV Index" />
    ```

TIP   *As you add areas, some may overlap others. The first area defined overrides overlapping areas.*

8. Add additional `area` elements, one at a time. In this example, the next `area` element is for the Valley area, so it is a `rect` (for rectangle). The coordinates for the top left and lower right are required to link to `valley.html`.

```
<area shape="circle" coords="82,43,30" href="uvi.html"
   alt="UV Index" />
<area shape="rect" coords="1,209,516,320"
   href="valley.html" alt="Valley Weather" />
```

9. For the Mid-Peaks area, a triangle will suffice to define the area, so the shape is a `poly` (polygon) with three pairs of coordinates. This links to `midpeaks.html`.

```
<area shape="circle" coords="82,43,30" href="uvi.html"
   alt="UV Index" />
<area shape="rect" coords="1,209,516,320"
   href="valley.html" alt="Valley Weather" />
<area shape="poly" coords="199,207,513,205,514,71"
   href="midpeaks.html" alt="Mid-Peaks Weather" />
```

10. The High Peaks area is easily defined with a figure containing four corners—vaguely diamond-shaped, as in the following example:

```
<area shape="circle" coords="82,43,30" href="uvi.html"
   alt="UV Index" />
<area shape="rect" coords="1,209,516,320"
   href="valley.html" alt="Valley Weather" />
<area shape="poly" coords="199,207,513,205,514,71"
   href="midpeaks.html" alt="Mid-Peaks Weather" />
<area shape="poly"
   coords="63,123,251,98,365,134,198,204"
   href="highpeaks.html" alt="High Peaks Weather" />
```

Refer to Figure 4.11 for a reminder of what this shape looks like.

11. Set the `href` attribute for the remaining areas. You could set the remaining area so that nothing at all will happen when a user clicks there by using the `nohref` attribute. However, you must specify both a name and a value for this attribute, even though both are the same.

That's all there is to it. The final map looks something like the code in Listing 4.2. (We'll come back to this code block when we build server-side maps later in this chapter.)

LISTING 4.2: THE ASR OUTFITTERS IMAGE MAP

```
<map name="weather_zones" id="weather_zones">
<area shape="circle" coords="82,43,30" href="uvi.html"
   alt="UV Index" />
<area shape="rect" coords="1,209,516,320" href="valley.html"
   alt="Valley Weather" />
<area shape="poly" coords="199,207,513,205,514,71"
   href="midpeaks.html" alt="Mid-Peaks Weather" />
```

```
<area shape="poly"
   coords="63,123,251,98,365,134,198,204"
   href="highpeaks.html" alt="High Peaks Weather" />
<area shape="default" nohref="nohref" />
</map>
```

ACTIVATING THE MAP

Before you can activate the map, you must place the map image in your document. The img element (in a new document from the ASR site), looks like this:

```
<img src="weather-imap.gif" width="516" height="320" border="0"
   alt="Weather Zones in the Mountains" />
```

To connect the image to the map definition created in the previous section, simply add the usemap attribute, as in the following example:

```
<img src="weather-imap.gif" width="516" height="320" border="0"
   alt="Weather Zones in the Mountains"
   usemap="#weather_zones" />
```

TIP   *The* usemap *attribute requires a pound sign (#) in the value to indicate that the link goes to a place within a document.*

If you want to link to a map definition in another document, add an absolute URL to the usemap attribute. If you do this, test thoroughly because not all browsers support this feature. The final map is shown in Figure 4.13.

FIGURE 4.13

The ASR Outfitters image map

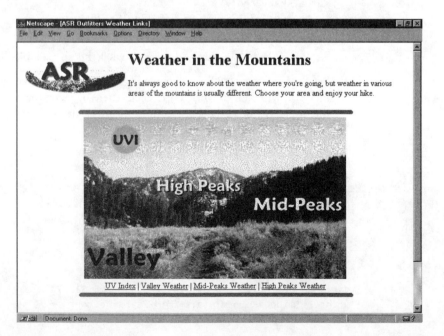

Using Background Images

Most browsers support background images, the patterns or images behind the text in XHTML documents. As a rule, background images are *tiled* throughout the available space, meaning that they are multiple copies of one image placed side by side both horizontally and vertically to fill the screen.

Tiling offers two main advantages. First, you can produce a *seamless background*, meaning that the casual user cannot see where individual images start and stop. Figure 4.14 shows a seamless background.

FIGURE 4.14

In seamless backgrounds, the tiled images blend together

Second, you can develop more visually interesting backgrounds by making background images that are most likely to tile only horizontally or only vertically. For example, an image that is only 10 pixels high and 1280 pixels wide is as wide or wider than most current browser windows. Therefore, the image will most likely repeat vertically but not horizontally. This can produce a vertical band, as shown in Figure 4.15.

WARNING *Many users are currently using at least 17-inch monitors, and 19- and 21-inch monitors are becoming more common. Whereas a large monitor does not necessarily mean that the user will open the browser window to any particular size, it's important to remember that, in general, you can't control the size of the user's browser window or the resolution of the user's monitor. Keep this in mind if you're using a large background image, especially if you made the image large to prevent tiling.*

Similarly, you can use a tall image to produce a tiled horizontal band, as shown in Figure 4.16. Pay careful attention to the image height. If the image height is less than the window height the user is using, the background will tile. Another good technique is to make the image fade into the background color of the document.

FIGURE 4.15

Wide images usually
tile only vertically

FIGURE 4.16

A horizontal band
looks like this in a
browser

TIP   *Always specify a background color, even if you're using a background image. The color will load faster than the image, so it will be visible while the image is loading. Also, if the image does not load, the background color will still be visible behind the other elements on the page.*

To set the background image and color of your page, use the attributes in Table 4.6 in the opening body element, as shown here:

```
<body background="asrback.jpg" bgcolor="#000000">
```

TABLE 4.6: BACKGROUND ATTRIBUTES OF THE **body** ELEMENT

ATTRIBUTE	USE
background="…"	Uses a URL to identify the name and location of an image for the background of an HTML or XHTML document; deprecated.
bgcolor="…"	Sets a background color for the page; deprecated.

TIP   *Both of these attributes are deprecated, and style sheets can be used to prevent background images from tiling, or to make them tile only horizontally or vertically. You can also use style sheets to include background images or background color behind individual page elements, rather than behind the entire page. See Chapter 10 for more information on backgrounds.*

Where to Go from Here

In this chapter, you learned how to select appropriate images, include them in your HTML and XHTML documents, and format them to make them appear as you want. You also learned about image maps, which give you a useful way to provide multiple links from a single image.

From here, you could move on to one of several chapters, but here are a few suggestions:

◆ See Chapter 1 for details on well-formed and valid HTML and XHTML documents.

◆ Check out Chapter 2 for more HTML and XHTML formatting information.

◆ See Chapter 5 to see how to include images in tables.

◆ See Chapter 9 and Master's Reference Part 2 for information about style sheets.

Part 2

Advancing Your Skills

Chapter 5

Developing Tables

THIS CHAPTER INTRODUCES *TABLES*, which are grids made up of rows and columns. These rows and columns create individual *cells* that can contain text and images. A table is an effective design element that allows you to communicate information visually, yet in a way that is most likely to be presented by a user's browser in the manner that you intended. The material in this chapter will walk you through the effective use of tables.

This chapter covers the following topics:

◆ Creating basic tables

◆ Adding and deleting rows and columns

◆ Spanning rows and columns

◆ Adding captions

◆ Formatting tables

◆ Using advanced table features

Using Tables Effectively

Tables serve two functions. First, they help present complex data in a readable format. Traditionally, you use tables when information can more effectively be portrayed visually than described in paragraph form.

Second, you can use tables to incorporate more sophisticated design elements into Web pages. The effect of using tables for page layout is similar to that of using frames (discussed in detail in Chapter 7); however, if you use tables for page layout, users can still bookmark a specific page on your Web site, which they can't do as accurately with frames. Figure 5.1 shows an example of a Web site formatted using tables. Do note that the HTML and XHTML specifications and many accessibility guidelines recommend using CSS (Chapter 9) for formatting, rather than tables.

FIGURE 5.1

Tables help you
develop interesting
page designs

TABLES AND THEIR EFFECTS ON ADAPTIVE TECHNOLOGIES FOR THE VISUALLY IMPAIRED

As useful as tables are for developing interesting designs, be aware of how tables affect *adaptive technologies* that help visually impaired people access the information your Web site provides. In particular, screen-reader technologies read Web page text aloud, moving from left to right, line by line throughout the screen. So, if you develop a page using plain headings and paragraphs, like this brief example:

UNDERSTANDING SCREEN ENLARGERS

Screen-enlarger technologies, used by people with various degrees of low vision, help people more easily access and use on-screen content. Essentially, screen enlargers magnify a small portion of the screen, enlarging the content by a factor users choose according to the software's capabilities. For example, users can enlarge an entire screen, specified screen portions (such as a single line), or just the area around the mouse.

The screen reader would read, *"Understanding screen enlargers…screen enlarger technologies, used by people with various degrees of low vision, help people more easily access and use on-screen content…."* And so on, just as it's intended to be read.

Continued on next page

TABLES AND THEIR EFFECTS ON ADAPTIVE TECHNOLOGIES FOR THE VISUALLY IMPAIRED *(continued)*

However, suppose you decided to use tables to format this information—say, as a dictionary-like listing, definition, and example:

Screen Enlargers

Used by people with low vision   They can enlarge an entire screen, specified screen portions (such as a single line), or just the area around the mouse.

In this case, the screen reader would read the text like this:

"Screen enlargers they can enlarge an entire screen specified used by people with low vision screen portions (such as a single line), or just an area around the mouse."

Although tables are commonly used in Web publications to present information more clearly and effectively, be aware that tables in particular cause problems for those who use adaptive technologies. For more information about developing Web sites with these readers in mind, see Chapter 12.

TIP *If some of your users don't have browsers that fully support HTML and XHTML as well as style sheets, using tables for formatting is a good way to go. However, as you'll see in many places throughout this chapter, the HTML 4.01 and XHTML 1 specifications move away from using this formatting technique in favor of style sheets. Find out how to develop style sheets in Chapter 9, and a complete style sheet reference is in Master's Reference Part 2.*

Not all browsers that support tables support all table features. For example, Netscape 6 supports tables, but does not support extended features such as table footers. Table 5.1 lists the browsers that support tables as well as extended table features.

TABLE 5.1: BROWSER SUPPORT FOR STANDARD TABLES AND HTML 4.01 TABLES

BROWSER	STANDARD TABLES	HTML 4.01 TABLES
Netscape Navigator	Yes	Yes (in Netscape 6)
Internet Explorer	Yes	Yes (in IE 4 and later versions)
Lynx	No	No
Opera	Yes	No

Generally, before including tables in a document, be sure your users use a graphical browser. If they don't, the table will not appear properly, if at all.

TIP *Table features commonly not supported are noted throughout this chapter.*

Creating Basic Tables

Creating tables is a two-step process:

1. Create the table structure—that is, enter the `table` element, specify rows and columns, and specify column headings.

2. Enter the data in table cells.

TIP   You may want to sketch a diagram of your table before you begin coding. This will help you ensure that you have all the necessary components for your table before you start coding it.

By first creating the table structure and then entering the data, you can avoid errors. Most commonly, Web authors forget the closing `</table>` element or omit an entire paired element. These errors result in an odd-looking table or no table at all. Ensuring that the basic table structure is in place before you start adding text can help you troubleshoot problems. Table 5.2 describes the basic table elements.

TIP   Table elements become complex quickly! Be sure that you open and close tags as needed, that you don't omit elements, and that you properly nest elements. Debugging problems in a table can be tedious and very frustrating.

TABLE 5.2: BASIC TABLE ELEMENTS

ELEMENT	MARKS
table	A table within a document
tr	A row within a table
td	A cell (table data) within a row
th	A heading cell within a row

TIP   Closing tags are optional in HTML 4.01 but are required in XHTML. They also help you see where one element ends and another begins, so you should plan to use them in either case.

The following steps show you how to build a table and enter information into it. In the examples throughout this section, we show how to build tables according to XHTML requirements, but they'll work equally well within an HTML document. The sample table in Figure 5.2 represents a product summary on a fictitious corporate Web site.

1. Start with a functional document that contains the appropriate structure elements (the DOC-TYPE declaration, `html`, `head`, `title`, and `body` elements) and any additional information you want to include.

2. Add the `table` element where you want the table boundaries to appear:

```
<table>
</table>
```

TIP   *For accessibility reasons, you can use a* `summary` *attribute in the* `table` *element to describe your table's content; its value tells users what the table contains. This is not required by the specification, but it's a good idea to make your Web pages as readable as possible to as many people as you can.*

3. Add a `tr` element for each row, between the `table` elements. The sample table includes four `tr` elements, one for each row.

```
<table>
<tr>
</tr>
<tr>
</tr>
<tr>
</tr>
<tr>
</tr>
</table>
```

4. Add `th` elements in the first row where you want to include table headings. The sample table includes two `th` elements. You might include some spaces to set off the table heading (and data) elements so you can easily see which text is associated with each row and cell.

```
<table>
<tr>
    <th></th>
    <th></th>
</tr>
<tr>
</tr>
<tr>
</tr>
<tr>
</tr>
</table>
```

5. Add `td` elements to create individual cells in which to include information. The sample table includes six data cells, two in each row.

```
<table>
<tr>
    <th></th>
    <th></th>
</tr>
<tr>
    <td></td>
    <td></td>
</tr>
<tr>
    <td></td>
```

```
      <td></td>
   </tr>
   <tr>
      <td></td>
      <td></td>
   </tr>
</table>
```

6. Add the content for each cell. Place table heading information between the opening and closing th elements, and enter data between the opening and closing td elements:

```
<table>
<tr>
   <th>Product</th>
   <th>Purpose</th>
</tr>
<tr>
   <td>Binder 1.0</td>
   <td>Join multiple objects.</td>
</tr>
<tr>
   <td>Organizer 2.2</td>
   <td>Join multiple objects for easy access and
      changing.</td>
</tr>
</table>
<tr>
   <td>Splitter 3.2</td>
   <td>Divide single object into multiple smaller
      objects.</td>
</tr>
```

This code produces the results shown in Figure 5.2. Notice that the content is present but that the table does not include any formatting or borders.

FIGURE 5.2

A basic table includes content, but it does not include formatting or borders—yet

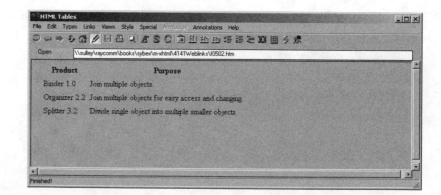

Adding or Removing Rows and Columns

After you create a table, you can easily add and delete elements as your information changes. The following sections show you how to add and remove rows and columns. The example results in a table that has one more column and one more row than the previous sample.

Adding Rows

To add a row to your table, insert additional `tr` and `td` elements where you want the new row to appear. For example, you can add a new row in the middle of a table like this:

```
<table>
<tr>
    <th>Product</th>
    <th>Purpose</th>
</tr>
<tr>
    <td>Binder 1.0</td>
    <td>Join multiple objects.</td>
</tr>
<tr>
    <td>Organizer 2.2</td>
    <td>Join multiple objects for easy access and changing.</td>
</tr>
<tr>
    <td>Combiner 0.9</td>
    <td>Join multiple objects at the edges.</td>
</tr>
<tr>
    <td>Splitter 3.2</td>
    <td>Divide single object into multiple smaller objects.</td>
</tr>
</table>
```

The table now looks like the one shown in Figure 5.3.

FIGURE 5.3

The sample table now has four rows

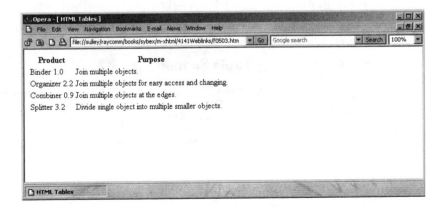

Adding Columns

Adding columns is somewhat more difficult than adding rows because you have to add a cell to each row. However, the general process is the same: You insert the elements where you want the new column to appear, either to the left or to the right of existing columns or somewhere in between.

For example, you can add a new column to the right side of the sample table by adding another th element to the top row and a td element to each of the other rows. The sample code would look like this:

```
<table>
<tr>
    <th>Product</th>
    <th>Purpose</th>
    <th>Industry standard term</th>
</tr>
<tr>
    <td>Binder 1.0</td>
    <td>Join multiple objects.</td>
    <td>Stapler</td>
</tr>
<tr>
    <td>Organizer 2.2</td>
    <td>Join multiple objects for easy access and changing.</td>
    <td>Ring binder</td>
</tr>
<tr>
    <td>Combiner 0.9</td>
    <td>Join multiple objects at the edges.</td>
    <td>Tape</td>
</tr>
<tr>
    <td>Splitter 3.2</td>
    <td>Divide single object into multiple smaller objects.</td>
    <td>Scissors</td>
</tr>
</table>
```

The resulting table looks like that shown in Figure 5.4.

FIGURE 5.4

Adding columns allows you to provide additional information

Table Sample

Product	Purpose	Industry standard term
Binder 1.0	Join multiple objects.	Stapler
Organizer 2.2	Join multiple objects for easy access and changing.	Ring binder
Combiner 0.9	Join multiple objects at the edges.	Tape
Splitter 3.2	Divide single object into multiple smaller objects.	Scissors

Deleting Rows and Columns

Deleting rows and columns is easier than adding them. However, you have to be careful and make sure you delete all the elements associated with a row or a column:

◆ When deleting a row, be sure to delete the `tr` opening and closing elements and the `td` elements and other information they surround.

◆ When deleting a column, be sure to delete the `th` and `td` opening and closing elements (and any other information within them) from each row.

For example, to delete the *bottom row* in the sample table, you delete the elements in strikethrough in the following code:

```
<table>
<tr>
   <th>Product</th>
   <th>Purpose</th>
   <th>Industry standard term</th>
</tr>
<tr>
   <td>Binder 1.0</td>
   <td>Join multiple objects.</td>
   <td>Stapler</td>
</tr>
<tr>
   <td>Organizer 2.2</td>
   <td>Join multiple objects for easy access and changing.</td>
   <td>Ring binder</td>
</tr>
<tr>
   <td>Combiner 0.9</td>
   <td>Join multiple objects at the edges.</td>
   <td>Tape</td>
</tr>
</table>
```

To delete the *final column* in the sample table, delete the last `td` element from each table row, like this:

```
<table>
<tr>
   <th>Product</th>
   <th>Purpose</th>
   <th>Industry standard term</th>
</tr>
<tr>
   <td>Binder 1.0</td>
   <td>Join multiple objects.</td>
   <td>Stapler</td>
</tr>
<tr>
   <td>Organizer 2.2</td>
```

```
      <td>Join multiple objects for easy access and changing.</td>
      <td>Ring binder</td>
   </tr>
   <tr>
      <td>Combiner 0.9</td>
      <td>Join multiple objects at the edges.</td>
      <td>Tape</td>
   </tr>
   <tr>
      <td>Splitter 3.2</td>
      <td>Divide single object into multiple smaller objects.</td>
      <td>Scissors</td>
   </tr>
</table>
```

WARNING *If you delete the final cell from each row, your revised table will look just fine. If you delete a random cell from each row, your table will still look just fine, but the data will be inaccurate. Be careful to delete the elements and content consistently from each row.*

Spanning Rows and Columns

Spanning refers to stretching a cell over multiple rows or columns. Figure 5.5 shows a sample table in which the cells labeled Merchandise and Descriptive Information span two columns each, indicating that they apply to the multiple columns they span. The Joining Tools cell spans three rows to show which rows apply to that category. To specify column and row spans, use the attributes listed in Table 5.3.

FIGURE 5.5

This sample table features a cell (Joining Tools) that spans three rows

Table Sample

Merchandise		Descriptive Information	
Type	Product	Purpose	Industry standard term
	Binder 1.0	Join multiple objects.	Stapler.
Joining Tools	Organizer 2.2	Join multiple objects for easy access and changing.	Ring binder.
	Combiner 0.9	Join multiple objects at the edges.	Tape.
Dividing Tools	Splitter 3.2	Divide single object into multiple smaller objects.	Scissors.

TABLE 5.3: TABLE ROW AND COLUMN SPAN ATTRIBUTES

ATTRIBUTE	USE
rowspan="n"	Used in th or td elements, rowspan indicates how many rows the cell should span. For example, rowspan="3" spans three rows.
colspan="n"	Used in either the th or td elements, colspan indicates how many columns the cell should cover. For example, colspan="3" spans three columns.

Spanning Rows

You can span rows using either the th or td element, depending on whether you're spanning a table heading or table data. The following example shows you how to span one cell over three rows, as in the Joining Tools cell in Figure 5.5, earlier in this chapter:

1. Add a new column for the tool categories, as shown in Figure 5.5. Place the category text **Type** in the top-left cell with a th element. Place **Joining Tools** in the second cell (with a td element), which will eventually span three rows. Place **Dividing Tools** in the third cell but in the fifth (bottom) row with a td element.

```
<table>
<tr>
   <th>Type</th>
   <th>Product</th>
   <th>Purpose</th>
   <th>Industry standard term</th>
</tr>
<tr>
   <td>Joining Tools</td>
   <td>Binder 1.0</td>
   <td>Join multiple objects.</td>
   <td>Stapler.</td>
</tr>
<tr>
   <td>Organizer 2.2</td>
   <td>Join multiple objects for easy access and
       changing.</td>
   <td>Ring binder.</td>
</tr>
<tr>
   <td>Combiner 0.9</td>
   <td>Join multiple objects at the edges.</td>
   <td>Tape.</td>
</tr>
<tr>
   <td>Dividing Tools</td>
   <td>Splitter 3.2</td>
   <td>Divide single object into multiple smaller
       objects.</td>
   <td>Scissors.</td>
</tr>
</table>
```

TIP *Three of the rows now have too many cells. If you display the table in a browser at this stage, you'll see that the cells appear out of alignment.*

2. Add the rowspan attribute to the th or td element that affects the cell you want to span. In the sample table, add the rowspan="3" attribute to the Joining Tools td element (which should affect rows 2 through 4), like this:

```
<td rowspan="3">Joining Tools</td>
```

The resulting table now includes a spanned row, which looks like the Joining Tools row shown in Figure 5.5.

Spanning Columns

You can span columns using either the th or td element, depending on whether you're spanning a table heading or a table cell. The following example shows how to add two cells that each span two columns. Start with the code from the previous section, which includes the spanned row:

1. Add a tr element for the new row:

```
<table>
<tr>
</tr>
<tr>
    <th>Type</th>
    <th>Product</th>
    <th>Purpose</th>
    <th>Industry standard term</th>
</tr>
```

2. Add th or td cells that you want to span. In the sample table, add two th cells—one with the word **Merchandise** and one with the phrase **Descriptive Information**.

```
<table>
<tr>
    <th>Merchandise</th>
    <th>Descriptive Information</th>
</tr>
<tr>
    <th>Type</th>
    <th>Product</th>
    <th>Purpose</th>
    <th>Industry standard term</th>
</tr>
```

3. Add the colspan attribute to the th or td element that affects the cell you want to span. In the sample table, add colspan="2" to both the th elements, because each cell should span two columns.

```
<tr>
    <th colspan="2">Merchandise</th>
    <th colspan="2">Descriptive Information</th>
</tr>
```

The resulting table, complete with a row span and a column span, should now look like the one in Figure 5.5.

You can include both the rowspan *and* colspan attributes in one th or td element. For example, a large or complex table might have two heading rows and two columns with descriptive information, such as the following:

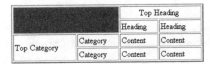

The first cell in the table spans two columns (colspan="2") to cover both category columns. It simultaneously spans two rows (rowspan="2") to cover both heading rows. No content necessarily fits in this area of the table, so you might use a logo or some sort of graphic to fill the space attractively.

Adding Captions

A *caption* is explanatory or descriptive text that usually appears above the table. You use captions for two purposes:

♦ To summarize table contents

♦ To provide at-a-glance information about table contents

You should position the caption above the table to ensure that your user sees it. If a table is more than one screen tall, a user might not scroll down to read the caption.

Place the caption element right after the opening table tag. Only one caption element is allowed per table.

You can locate the caption in relation to the table visually by adding the align attribute. The caption can be aligned at the top, bottom, left, or right of the table. (Note that the align attribute is deprecated.) To add a caption to the sample table, follow these steps:

1. Add the caption element between the opening and closing table tags. In the sample table, place the caption element below the opening table tag.

```
<table>
<caption>
</caption>
```

2. Add caption text, like this:

```
<caption>
Office Product Merchandise and Category Information
</caption>
```

3. Specify whether the caption should appear above or below the table by using the `align="top"` or `align="bottom"` attribute, like this:

```
<caption align="top">
Office Product Merchandise and Category Information
</caption>
```

4. Optionally, add character-level formatting elements to the caption. (See Chapter 2 for a review of character-level formatting.) Without boldface or italics, the caption is often hard to identify in the table.

```
<caption align="top">
<b>Office Product Merchandise and Category Information</b>
</caption>
```

The resulting caption looks like Figure 5.6.

FIGURE 5.6

Table captions provide an at-a-glance summary of table contents, in browsers that support them

Table Sample

Office Product Merchandise and Category Information

Merchandise		Descriptive Information	
Type	Product	Purpose	Industry standard term
	Binder 1.0	Join multiple objects.	Stapler.
Joining Tools	Organizer 2.2	Join multiple objects for easy access and changing.	Ring binder.
	Combiner 0.9	Join multiple objects at the edges.	Tape.
Dividing Tools	Splitter 3.2	Divide single object into multiple smaller objects.	Scissors.

Formatting Tables

After you set up a table, you can add formatting options that improve its overall appearance. In particular, you can do the following:

- Add borders
- Include background colors and images
- Adjust cell spacing and padding
- Adjust cell alignment
- Specify cell size
- Specify table alignment

As you'll see in the next several sections in this chapter, you can add a lot of formatting to tables—backgrounds, borders, colors, alignment, and so on. Keep in mind that many of these options are not standard XHTML or HTML and that not all browsers support them. Additionally, HTML 4.01 and XHTML 1 strongly encourage you to use style sheets—instead of these elements and attributes—to apply formatting options, because most of these attributes are deprecated.

If your users use browsers that support HTML 4.01 table elements, strongly consider using style sheets to format your tables. Style sheets, which are supported by the HTML 4.01 and XHTML 1 specifications, are the preferred way to apply styles throughout your documents—tables included! See Chapter 9 and Master's Reference Part 2 to learn to use style sheets.

Adding and Formatting Borders

Borders are the lines that enclose tables and that clearly separate rows, columns, and cells. By default, most browsers display tables without borders; however, tables that have borders are much easier to read and more attractive. For example, the sample tables shown thus far in this chapter have not had borders and have been rather difficult to read—it's hard to tell where one cell stops and the next begins. Without borders, the cells visually run together, and the columns and rows are somewhat obscured, as you can see back in Figure 5.6.

CREATING TABLE BORDERS

You specify table borders using an attribute and a number, measured in pixels, that tell browsers the width of the border. As shown in Figure 5.7, most browsers display borders as lines with a 3D effect. Table 5.4 lists the table border attributes.

FIGURE 5.7

A 2-pixel border added around table cells

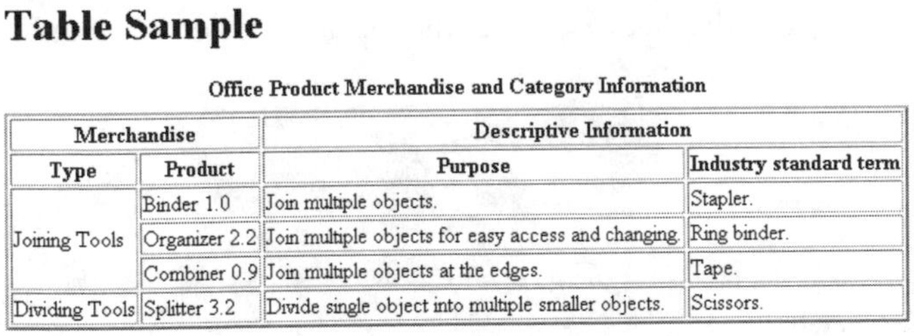

Table Sample

Office Product Merchandise and Category Information

Merchandise		Descriptive Information		
Type	**Product**	**Purpose**	**Industry standard term**
Joining Tools	Binder 1.0	Join multiple objects.	Stapler.
	Organizer 2.2	Join multiple objects for easy access and changing.	Ring binder.
	Combiner 0.9	Join multiple objects at the edges.	Tape.
Dividing Tools	Splitter 3.2	Divide single object into multiple smaller objects.	Scissors.

TABLE 5.4: TABLE BORDER ATTRIBUTES

ATTRIBUTE	SPECIFIES
`border="n"`	A table border width, in pixels. The larger the number, the wider the border. `border="0"` removes borders (generally also the default setting).
`bordercolor="…"`	A color for the table border, as `#rrggbb` number or color name. Supported by newer versions of Netscape Navigator and Internet Explorer; however, it's not part of the HTML or XHTML specifications.

To create a table border and specify its color, follow these steps:

1. Add the `border` attribute to the opening table element:

   ```
   <table border="2">
   ```

2. Specify the border color using the `bordercolor` attribute and either an RGB number or an accepted color name. Specifying the border color is not essential—the border will be wider because of the `border="2"` attribute, and the color is simply another formatting characteristic that you can add if you choose.

   ```
   <table border="2" bordercolor="#FF0000">
   ```

Figure 5.7 shows the results of using `border="2"` in the `table` element.

TIP   *See Chapter 4 for more information about RGB color values.*

SPECIFYING NO TABLE BORDERS

Although most browsers display tables without borders by default, you can specify no borders to ensure that no borders display. For example, if you're using tables for advanced formatting such as columns, side headings, or juxtaposed text and graphics, you want to ensure that the table appears without borders. Figures 5.2 through 5.6 are all examples of tables that have no visible borders. To specify no table borders, set the `border` attribute to zero (0), like this:

```
<table border="0">
```

USING INTERNET EXPLORER–SPECIFIC BORDER ATTRIBUTES

Microsoft has implemented two additional elements in Internet Explorer to control border color. In many browsers, the table borders are presented in 3D—that is, a darker color at the bottom and right edges, with a lighter color at the top and left, as shown in Figure 5.8.

FIGURE 5.8

Internet Explorer allows you to set different colors for the bevel or shadow effect in table borders 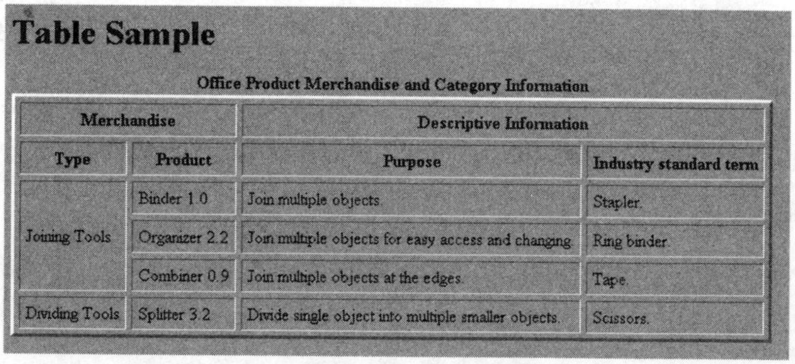

Internet Explorer recognizes attributes to set the darker and lighter color of the 3D effect. Table 5.5 lists these attributes.

WARNING   *These attributes are not part of the XHTML specification. They are proprietary Internet Explorer attributes that may not render correctly in other browsers.*

TABLE 5.5: INTERNET EXPLORER TABLE BORDER ATTRIBUTES

ATTRIBUTE	SPECIFIES
bordercolorlight="…"	A light border color (in #rrggbb format) for 3D effect on tables.
bordercolordark="…"	A dark border color (in #rrggbb format) for 3D effect on tables.

To apply these attributes, insert them in the opening `table` element, just as you insert standard border attributes, separately or together. These are all well formed:

```
<table bordercolorlight="#CCCCCC">…</table>
<table bordercolordark="#33FF33">…</table>
<table bordercolorlight="#CCCCCC"
    bordercolordark="#33FF33">…</table>
```

TIP   If you have specific border color needs and you know that your users will be using Internet Explorer, you can further customize border colors by applying the same attributes to individual table cells.

Setting Table Background Options

In addition to specifying border color, you can specify that the table background appear as a particular color or image. Using a background color or image enhances table appearance, makes the table more interesting, provides a place for corporate logos, and helps contrast text and image colors.

TIP   Although these background options will still work in Netscape Navigator and Internet Explorer, consider setting table background colors using style sheets because the HTML 4.01 and XHTML specifications deprecate table background options.

SETTING A TABLE BACKGROUND COLOR

Old versions of Netscape Navigator and Internet Explorer do not support table background colors, but most current browsers fully support these features. At any rate, you can provide table background colors and images with no adverse effects on those who use other browsers. For example, Figure 5.9 shows a table that uses a background color viewed in Netscape Navigator. If you display this table in an older browser, the background color will be the same as the background color of the browser.

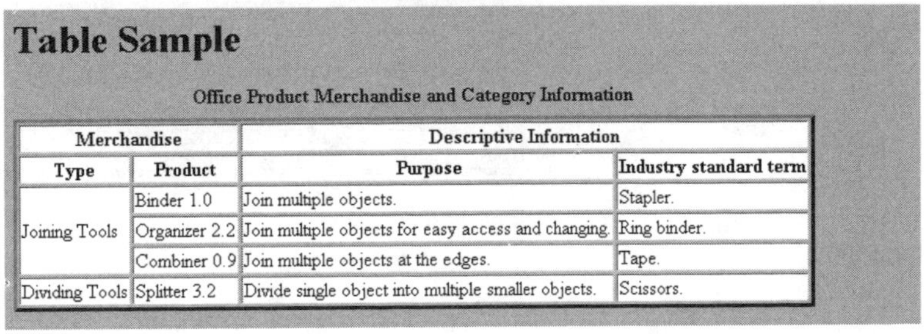

FIGURE 5.9

A color background can enhance a table's appearance when viewed in a browser that supports background colors

For background colors to be effective, they must adequately contrast with text color(s); otherwise, the text becomes virtually unreadable, as you can see in Figure 5.10.

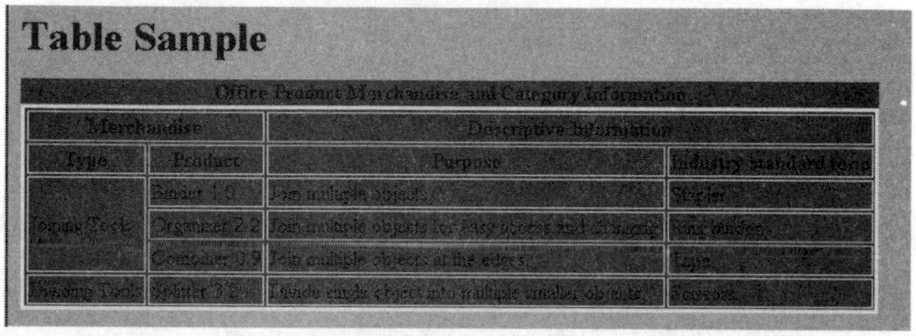

FIGURE 5.10

Consider your page's text colors when choosing table background colors

To ensure that your table background color(s) are effective, follow these guidelines:

◆ Choose a light background color if your text is dark; choose a dark background color if your text is light.

◆ Choose colors that are aesthetically pleasing and suit the purpose of your document. For example, if your topic is fast-paced and you know your audience won't mind, choose bright, readable colors; if your topic is slower-paced, choose paler colors.

◆ View your documents in a few different browsers.

◆ Choose from one of the 216 nondithering colors.

TIP   *As we detailed in Chapter 4, nondithering colors appear solid (not splotchy or spotted) in browsers.*

The table background color attribute is `bgcolor="#rrggbb"`, and it's used in the opening `table` element. To use a color throughout the background of the table, add `bgcolor` followed by the RGB number or color name, as in the following:

```
<table bgcolor="#CCFFFF">
```

The table background (not including the borders) will be colored, as in Figure 5.11. 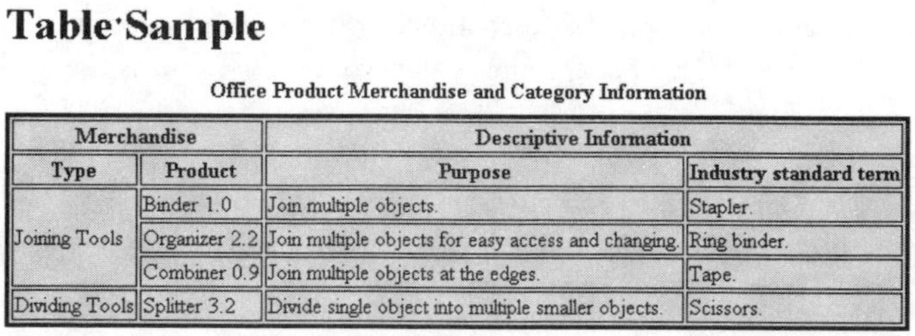

FIGURE 5.11

The resulting table background color

Table·Sample

Office Product Merchandise and Category Information

Merchandise		Descriptive Information		
Type	Product	Purpose	Industry standard term
Joining Tools	Binder 1.0	Join multiple objects.	Stapler.
	Organizer 2.2	Join multiple objects for easy access and changing.	Ring binder.
	Combiner 0.9	Join multiple objects at the edges.	Tape.
Dividing Tools	Splitter 3.2	Divide single object into multiple smaller objects.	Scissors.

SETTING A TABLE BACKGROUND IMAGE

Not all browsers support table background images, although most newer browsers do. Other browsers display the browser's default background color instead of the background image.

TIP   To accommodate users with browsers that do not support background images and users who have image options turned off, use background colors even with background images. Users can then view a table enhanced with color, rather than one that uses the browser's default background color.

Table background images are tiled—that is, they are repeated on the screen until the available background space is filled. Not all browsers tile images in the same way. For example, Figures 5.12 and 5.13 show how some versions of Netscape Navigator and Internet Explorer display a table that uses a small pair of scissors as the background image.

FIGURE 5.12

A table background image viewed in Netscape Navigator

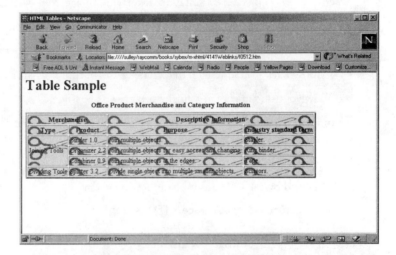

FIGURE 5.13

A table background image viewed in Internet Explorer

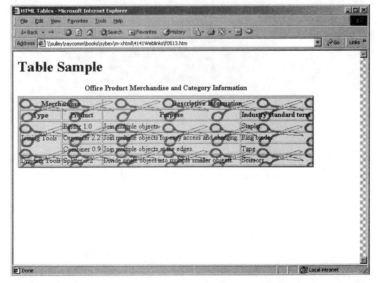

Although the image is inappropriately dark and the text is unreadable, the overall effect is quite different in each browser. In Figure 5.12, the tiling restarts at the upper-left corner of *each cell*, and the caption is not considered part of the table for the purpose of background. In Figure 5.13, however, the image is rendered slightly larger and is tiled throughout the table without consideration for individual cells. These differences are not as noticeable in the most recent versions of the browsers (Netscape 6 and Internet Explorer 5.5).

TIP   *To ensure that the whole image is visible in a table cell (and only once), include the* img *element in the table cell, not as a background image for the table or for the cell.*

Also, as Figures 5.12 and 5.13 show, table background images can easily overpower table content if you use too many shapes, patterns, or colors. The resulting text becomes virtually unreadable.

To ensure that you choose a suitable background image, follow these guidelines:

◆ Choose small, subtle images that are not essential for conveying information.

◆ Choose simple background images—ones with few shapes, patterns, or colors.

◆ Choose background images that enhance the purpose of the document.

◆ View your documents in as many browsers as possible.

To indicate a background image in a table, you use the background image attribute.

Most browsers support these elements on individual cells as well as for the table as a whole. Add the attribute to the td or th element, just as you would add it to the table element.

Figure 5.14 shows an effective background image. To use a table background image, add background followed by the URL, as in the following code:

```
<table background="coolimage.gif">…</table>
```

FIGURE 5.14

An effective table background image enhances the table content

Table Sample

Office Product Merchandise and Category Information

Merchandise		Descriptive Information		
Type	Product	Purpose	Industry standard term
Joining Tools	Binder 1.0	Join multiple objects.	Stapler.
	Organizer 2.2	Join multiple objects for easy access and changing	Ring binder.
	Combiner 0.9	Join multiple objects at the edges.	Tape.
Dividing Tools	Splitter 3.2	Divide single object into multiple smaller objects.	Scissors.

Specifying Cell Alignment

Cell alignment refers to the horizontal or vertical alignment of cell contents. Most browsers have the following default cell alignment settings:

◆ Table *headings* are aligned in the center (horizontally and vertically) in the cell.

◆ Table *contents* are aligned on the left (horizontally) and center (vertically) in the cell.

Using the attributes described in Table 5.6, you can change the default horizontal and vertical alignment in table cells.

TABLE 5.6: TABLE CELL ALIGNMENT ATTRIBUTES	
ATTRIBUTE	**SPECIFIES**
align="…"	Horizontal alignment of cell contents, as left, center, or right.
valign="…"	Vertical alignment of cell contents, as top, middle, bottom, or baseline.

To use these alignment attributes, include them within any tr, td, or th element, as these three examples show:

```
<tr align="right">…</tr>
<td valign="top">…</td>
<th align="center" valign="middle">…</th>
```

TIP   *You can save some typing by setting the alignment for a row in the tr element, rather than in each individual cell. If you set the alignment in the tr element, you can override it on a cell-by-cell basis in the td or th element.*

Specifying Cell Size

Most browsers make cells as large as necessary to hold the contents and wrap text to a new line only after the table is as wide as the browser window and table width settings permit. You can specify cell size to keep the text from wrapping to a new line or to make content easier to read.

TIP   *Specifying all cell widths decreases perceived download time by allowing some browsers to lay out the table as it arrives, rather than waiting for the whole table to download. The table still takes the same time to download; however, it appears to load faster because it arrives gradually, rather than in one big chunk.*

You can specify cell size in two ways:

◆   As a percentage of the table width

◆   As a specific size, measured in pixels

Although most browsers support alignment attributes, how they display attributes depends on the table size and other table or cell settings. For example, a cell size that is 50 percent of the table will be wider or narrower, depending on the screen resolution and on the size of the browser window. Likewise, if you set cell width to 100 pixels, it will be exactly that wide in browsers that support cell width elements, regardless of what that does to the overall page layout.

TIP   *If you can avoid setting specific cell widths in your tables, do so. The more restrictive the table formatting, the less leeway the browser has to reformat the table to fit and the more unpredictable the results.*

Use the attributes in Table 5.7 in either the th or td element to control the table width and text wrap.

TABLE 5.7: TABLE WIDTH AND TEXT WRAP ATTRIBUTES

ATTRIBUTE	USE
width="n"	Specifies the width of a cell in either pixels or as a percentage of table width; deprecated.
nowrap="nowrap"	Prohibits text wrapping within the cell, thus requiring all text to appear on one line; deprecated.

WARNING   The width *and* nowrap *attributes are deprecated in favor of using style sheets. See Chapter 9 for more information on style sheets.*

SPECIFYING CELL WIDTH

To specify cell width, simply add the width="n" attribute to the td or th elements. For example, you can specify that a header cell (and, therefore, the cells below it) occupy 15 percent of the table width, like this:

```
<tr>
    <th>Type</th>
    <th>Product</th>
    <th>Purpose</th>
    <th width="15%">Industry standard term</th>
</tr>
```

If you set the width in a cell with a colspan attribute, similar to the Descriptive Information cell shown in Figure 5.15, the attributes affect individual columns below proportionately.

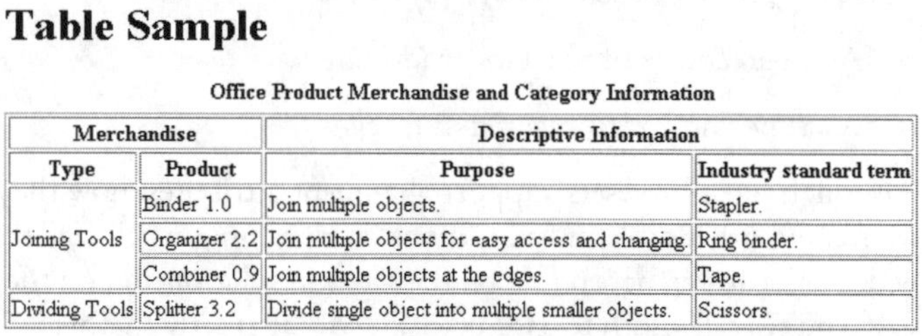

FIGURE 5.15

The browser determined the sizes of the cells in this table automatically.

Table Sample

Office Product Merchandise and Category Information

Merchandise		Descriptive Information		
Type	Product	Purpose	Industry standard term
Joining Tools	Binder 1.0	Join multiple objects.	Stapler.
	Organizer 2.2	Join multiple objects for easy access and changing.	Ring binder.
	Combiner 0.9	Join multiple objects at the edges.	Tape.
Dividing Tools	Splitter 3.2	Divide single object into multiple smaller objects.	Scissors.

For example, if you add width="50%" to the Descriptive Information cell, the browser attempts to make the columns starting with Purpose and with Industry Standard Term together total approximately 50 percent.

```
<tr>
    <th colspan="2">Merchandise</th>
    <th colspan="2" width="50%">Descriptive Information</th>
</tr>
```

Figure 5.16 shows the resulting table.

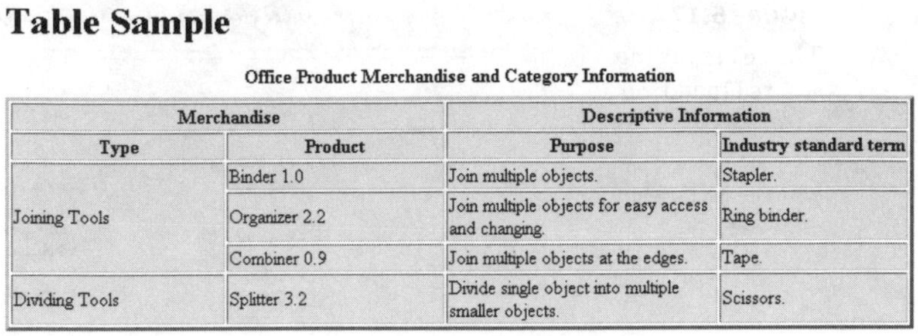

FIGURE 5.16

Combine cell size and column span attributes to customize your tables

Table Sample

Office Product Merchandise and Category Information

Merchandise		Descriptive Information	
Type	Product	Purpose	Industry standard term
Joining Tools	Binder 1.0	Join multiple objects.	Stapler.
	Organizer 2.2	Join multiple objects for easy access and changing.	Ring binder.
	Combiner 0.9	Join multiple objects at the edges.	Tape.
Dividing Tools	Splitter 3.2	Divide single object into multiple smaller objects.	Scissors.

SPECIFYING NO TEXT WRAPS

If you reset the width of certain cells, you may want to ensure that the contents do not wrap to multiple lines. Note that nowrap is also a stand-alone attribute and, as such, it must be set equal to itself as indicated in the XHTML specification. (Or just use nowrap by itself if you're using plain HTML.) Add the nowrap attribute, as in the following example, to encourage the browser not to break the line:

```
<th colspan="2" width="30%" nowrap="nowrap">Descriptive
    Information</th>
```

To set a minimum size for a cell, smaller than which it cannot be displayed, use a transparent GIF image 1 pixel × 1 pixel in size with height and width attributes set to the necessary size. This process is technically an ugly workaround, but it's also quite effective.

Adding Cell Spacing and Padding

Cell spacing and padding refer to how much white space appears in a table. In particular, *cell spacing* refers to the spacing between cells, and *cell padding* refers to spacing between cell contents and cell borders.

For many tables, open space around cell contents makes the table much easier to read and more aesthetically pleasing. Table 5.8 describes cell spacing and cell padding attributes.

TABLE 5.8: TABLE CELL SPACING AND PADDING ATTRIBUTES

ATTRIBUTE	SPECIFIES
cellspacing="n"	Amount of space between cells, in pixels.
cellpadding="n"	Amount of space between cell contents and cell borders, in pixels.

TIP   If the table has a border, the cellspacing *attribute enlarges the rule between cells. If there is no border, the space between adjacent cells will simply be somewhat larger.*

To add cell spacing and padding, include the attributes in the table element, like this:

```
<table cellspacing="5" cellpadding="5" border="3">...</table>
```

The resulting table will look like Figure 5.17. As you can see, there is more white space around the text.

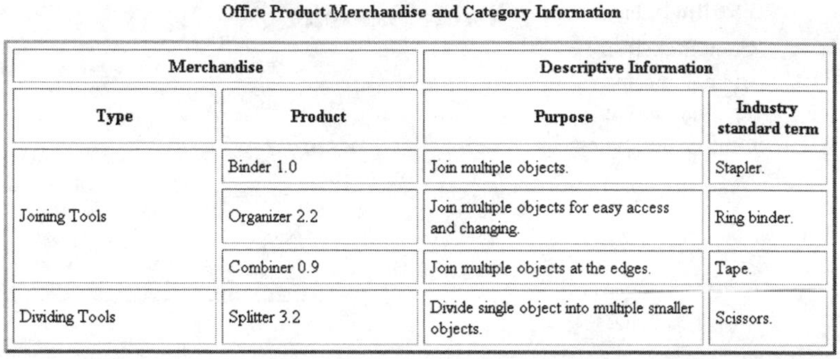

FIGURE 5.17

The `cellspacing` and `cellpadding` attributes can increase space between and within table cells

Office Product Merchandise and Category Information

Merchandise		Descriptive Information	
Type	**Product**	**Purpose**	**Industry standard term**
Joining Tools	Binder 1.0	Join multiple objects.	Stapler.
	Organizer 2.2	Join multiple objects for easy access and changing.	Ring binder.
	Combiner 0.9	Join multiple objects at the edges.	Tape.
Dividing Tools	Splitter 3.2	Divide single object into multiple smaller objects.	Scissors.

Specifying Table Alignment, Width, and Text Wrap

So far in this chapter, most of the elements and attributes have specified the relationship of the table contents to each other or to other table components. However, table width, alignment, and wrap settings specify how the table fits into the document as a whole.

These settings are important for two reasons:

◆ Browser and computer settings vary significantly from computer to computer. By using width, alignment, and wrap attributes, you help ensure that your users can easily view your tables.

◆ By default, text that surrounds tables does not wrap—it stops above the table and starts below the table. The table itself takes up the full browser width. These attributes narrow the space that the table uses and allow the text to wrap around the table.

Table 5.9 describes the table width, alignment, and wrap attributes.

WARNING *The* `align` *and* `clear` *attributes are deprecated in favor of using style sheets. See Chapter 9 for more information on using style sheets.*

TABLE 5.9: TABLE WIDTH, ALIGNMENT, AND WRAP ATTRIBUTES

ATTRIBUTE	USE
`width="n"`	Specifies table width, in pixels or as a percentage of the window width.
`align="…"`	Specifies table alignment, as `left`, `center`, `right`, and, for Internet Explorer only, `bleedleft`, `bleedright`, and `justify`; deprecated.
`clear="…"`	Specifies that new text following the table should appear below the table, when the `left`, `right`, `all`, or no margins are clear (unobstructed by the table); deprecated.

To use any of these attributes, insert them in the opening `table` element. The following code uses the `width` attribute to set the table width to 600 pixels:

```
<table border="3" width="600">…</table>
```

However, as a rule, setting your table width to a percentage of the browser window—not to a fixed number of pixels—results in a more reliable display. For example, if you set the table width to a size wider than users have available, the table could easily run off the edge of the browser window and require them to scroll horizontally.

To restrict the width of the table (for example, to allow text to wrap around it), use percentages, as in the following example:

```
<table border="3" width="70%">…</table>
```

Aligning the table to the left, right, or center is as easy as adding another attribute to the table, as in the following:

```
<table border="3" width="70%" align="right">…</table>
```

When you use these attributes and make the table substantially narrower than the window, you may also have to contend with unwanted text wrapping. For example, the preceding line of code causes text following the table to wind up on the left of the right-aligned table, as in Figure 5.18.

FIGURE 5.18

Text wrapping sometimes causes unusual effects

Table Sample

The accompanying table provides basic information about our products. If you have any questions, please contact us and we'll be happy to provide more information.

Office Product Merchandise and Category Information				
Merchandise			**Descriptive Information**	
Type	**Product**		**Purpose**	**Industry standard term**
Joining Tools	Binder 1.0		Join multiple objects.	Stapler.
	Organizer 2.2		Join multiple objects for easy access and changing.	Ring binder.
	Combiner 0.9		Join multiple objects at the edges.	Tape.
Dividing Tools	Splitter 3.2		Divide single object into multiple smaller objects.	Scissors.

Using Advanced Table Features

The table features discussed in this section were introduced with HTML 4 and have carried over into XHTML. These features give you added control over formatting tables. Instead of formatting the table as a whole, you can format specific table parts, such as the table head, body, footer, and column groups. You can also format tables using style sheets, which we recommend.

You can use these table elements to format portions of the table separately—as sections, rather than as individual cells. For example, you can do the following:

◆ Group similar areas of tables and add borders around the areas.

◆ Add lines or text formatting to table headings.

◆ Include a table footer, which is handy if a table has totals at the bottom of the columns.

◆ Use these additional elements as hooks for style sheets to get into more sophisticated formatting. All style elements can be used with these elements.

TIP   *See Chapter 9 for more about style sheets.*

For example, Figure 5.19 uses table elements and attributes to create two main columns (Merchandise and Descriptive Information) that group the other columns (Type, Product, Purpose, Industry standard term), and to include two rows of headers.

These table elements work in conjunction with standard table elements—that is, you develop tables using the standard elements, and then you add the advanced table elements and attributes. The result is that users using the newest browsers can view the complete set of effects and users of other browsers can still view the basic table.

To apply these table elements and attributes, follow these general steps, which are described in detail in the next two sections:

1. Identify table sections.

2. Apply borders and rules to table sections.

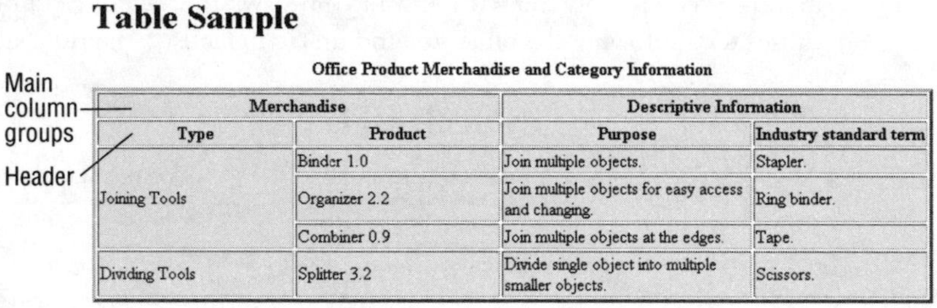

FIGURE 5.19

You can use advanced table elements to group table parts

Table Sample

Identifying Table Sections

The first step in using advanced table features is identifying table sections by grouping similar table parts and identifying each part as being part of the table heading, body, footer, or columns. Using these elements can, but won't necessarily, speed display of your tables. As always, it depends on the browser. Table 5.10 describes advanced table elements.

TABLE 5.10: ADVANCED TABLE ELEMENTS

ELEMENT	USE
thead	Labels the header area of a table.
tbody	Labels the body area of table.
tfoot	Labels the footer area of table.
colgroup	Identifies column groups within a table.
col	Identifies columns in a table within a column group. This is an empty element.

IDENTIFYING ROW GROUPS

Row groups include parts such as the header, body, and footer—the table parts that contain table rows. To identify row groups, start with the standard table elements and then include the table elements around them. Take a look at the following code, which nests the standard table elements within the table header element (<thead>...</thead>):

```
<thead>
<tr>
    <th colspan="2">Merchandise</th>
    <th colspan="2">Descriptive Information</th>
</tr>
<tr>
    <th>Type</th>
    <th>Product</th>
    <th>Purpose</th>
    <th>Industry standard term</th>
</tr>
</thead>
```

You can also identify table body parts by using the **tbody** element, like this:

```
<tbody>
<tr>
    <td rowspan="3">Joining Tools</td>
    <td>Binder 1.0</td>
    <td>Join multiple objects.</td>
    <td>Stapler.</td>
</tr>
<tr>
    <td>Organizer 2.2</td>
    <td>Join multiple objects for easy access and changing.</td>
    <td>Ring binder.</td>
</tr>
<tr>
    <td>Combiner 0.9</td>
    <td>Join multiple objects at the edges.</td>
    <td>Tape.</td>
</tr>
<tr>
    <td>Dividing Tools</td>
    <td>Splitter 3.2</td>
    <td>Divide single object into multiple smaller objects.</td>
    <td>Scissors.</td>
</tr>
</tbody>
```

Finally, you can identify a table footer by using the `tfoot` element in the same way. The `tfoot` element must follow the `thead` element and *precede* the `tbody` element.

```
<tfoot>
<tr>
   <td>Tool Combo</td>
   <td>All</td>
   <td>Use for all office needs.</td>
   <td>N/A</td>
</tr>
</tfoot>
```

At this point, the advanced table won't look any different from the standard table. After you've tagged your table with these additional table elements, you can either identify column groups or format the tagged parts with the advanced formatting elements.

IDENTIFYING COLUMN GROUPS

In addition to identifying table headers, body, and footers, you can identify column groups. The `colgroup` element, which is used in conjunction with the `span` attribute, is located at the beginning of the table and announces the columns to which it applies. You can also use the `width`, `align`, `char`, `charoff`, and `valign` attributes with the `colgroup` element.

The table shown in Figure 5.7, earlier in this chapter, contains two distinct groups of columns, with two columns in each. Therefore, there will be two `colgroup` elements with `span="2"` attributes in each. We also want all these columns to align to the left, as shown in the following example:

```
<caption align="top"><b>Office Product Merchandise and Category
    Information</b></caption>
<colgroup span="2" align="left"></colgroup>
<colgroup span="2" align="left"></colgroup>
<thead>…</thead>
```

IDENTIFYING COLUMNS WITHIN *colgroups*

The `col` empty element allows you to apply formatting to individual columns in a column group (`colgroup`). For example, in the previous example, we have two `colgroups` of two columns each all aligned to the left. Let's say we want the first column in the first group to be centered and the second column to be aligned to the left. The markup would look like this:

```
<colgroup>
<col align="center" />
<col align="left" />
</colgroup>
<colgroup span="2" align="left">…</colgroup>
```

Table Borders

You can use special formatting capabilities to create custom table borders—called *rules*—which apply to specified sections of the table. Rather than applying borders to an entire table, which is all you can do with standard table capabilities, you can apply borders just to the table heading, body, footer, or specific columns. Table 5.11 describes the advanced table formatting attributes.

WARNING *These formatting attributes are deprecated in favor of using style sheets. See Chapter 9 for more information on using style sheets.*

TABLE 5.11: ADVANCED TABLE FORMATTING ATTRIBUTES

ATTRIBUTE	USE
frame="…"	Specifies the outside edges of the table that will have a border. Possible choices include border (the default), void (no borders), above, below, hsides (top and bottom), lhs (left-hand side), rhs (right-hand side), vsides (left and right), and box (all sides).
rules="…"	Specifies which internal borders of the table are displayed. none, groups (rules between table groups such as thead, tbody, tfoot, colgroup), rows (rules between table rows), cols (rules between table columns), all.
cols="…"	Specifies the number of columns in the table.

To format the identified table parts, include these attributes in the **table** element by following these general steps:

1. Add an outside border (the frame) by adding the frame attribute to the **table** element, like this:

```
<table frame="box">…</table>
```

TIP *You can still control the border width with the* **border** *attribute, covered earlier in this chapter. For example, to set the outside border to 3 pixels wide, the opening* **table** *element would look like this:* <table frame="box" border="3">. *The* **border** *attribute in the* **table** *element affects only the width of the outside border, not the width of the internal rules.*

2. Add inside borders (called rules) by adding the rules attribute to the **table** element, like this:

```
<table frame="hsides" rules="none" border="3">…</table>
```

The resulting table, when viewed in Internet Explorer, looks like Figure 5.20. If you look carefully at Figure 5.20, you'll notice a thin line above the table footer—that's part of the footer formatting, just as the boldface is part of the th formatting.

FIGURE 5.20

You use advanced tables to be creative with table design and rules

Table Sample

Office Product Merchandise and Category Information

Merchandise		Descriptive Information	
Type	Product	Purpose	Industry standard term
	Binder 1.0	Join multiple objects.	Stapler.
Joining Tools	Organizer 2.2	Join multiple objects for easy access and changing.	Ring binder.
	Combiner 0.9	Join multiple objects at the edges.	Tape.
Dividing Tools	Splitter 3.2	Divide single object into multiple smaller objects.	Scissors.
Tool Combo	All	Use for all office needs.	N/A

The accompanying table provides basic information about our products. If you have any questions, please contact us and we'll be happy to provide more information.

TIP *To insert a rule between the groups you defined in the table, add* `rules="groups"`. *This is an effective technique, as is* `rules="rows"`.

Additionally, you can specify the number of columns in the table to decrease the perceived download and redraw time. Doing so has no effect on the visual appearance of the table, but still allows the browser to lay out the table more quickly. To use this trick, add the `cols` attribute to the `table` element, like this:

```
<table cols="4">…</table>
```

TIP *Because tables are laid out as soon as the whole table is downloaded to the browser (rather than line by line as with regular text), using multiple, smaller tables will improve the perceived download time.*

DESIGN WORKSHOP: CREATING NEWSPAPER-STYLE HEADINGS

Here's a handy formatting trick. Use tables to set up a heading with several columns of text below it—like a newspaper:

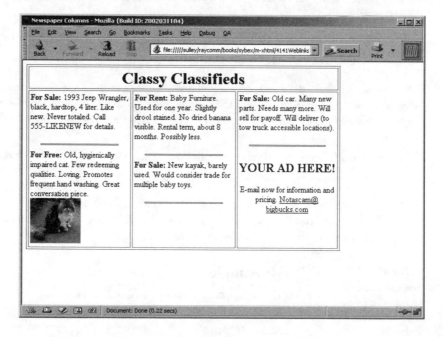

The code that produces this effect follows:

```
<!DOCTYPE html PUBLIC "-//W3C//DTD XHTML 1.0 Transitional//EN"
    "http://www.w3.org/TR/xhtml1/DTD/xhtml1-transitional.dtd">
<html xmlns="http://www.w3.org/1999/xhtml">
```

Continued on next page

DESIGN WORKSHOP: CREATING NEWSPAPER-STYLE HEADINGS *(continued)*

```
<head><title>Newspaper Columns</title></head>
<body bgcolor="FFFFFF" text="000000" link="0000FF"
    vlink="800080" alink="FF0000">
<table cellpadding="3" cellspacing="3" border="1" width="80%">
<tr><td valign="middle" align="center" colspan="3">
    <h1>Classy Classifieds</h1></td></tr>
<tr><td valign="top" width="120"><b>For Sale:</b> 1993 Jeep
    Wrangler, black, hardtop, 4 liter. Like new. Never
    totaled. Call 555-LIKENEW for details.<br />
<hr width="80%" />
<b>For Free: </b>Old, hygienically impaired cat. Few redeeming
    qualities. Loving. Promotes frequent hand washing. Great
    conversation piece.
<img src="winthumb.gif" align="left" width="100" height="88"
    border="0" alt="Winchester" /></td>
<td valign="top" width="120"><b>For Rent:</b> Baby Furniture.
    Used for one year. Slightly drool stained. No dried
    banana visible. Rental term, about 8 months. Possibly less.
    <br />
<hr width="80%" />
<b>For Sale:</b> New kayak, barely used. Would consider trade
    for multiple baby toys. <br />
<hr width="80%" /></td>
<td valign="top" width="120"><b>For Sale:</b> Old car. Many
    new parts. Needs many more. Will sell for payoff. Will
    deliver (to tow truck accessible locations). <br />
<hr width="80%" />
<center><h2>YOUR AD HERE!</h2>
    E-mail now for information and pricing.
<a href="mailto:Notascam@bigbucks.com">
    Notascam@bigbucks.com</a></center>
</tr></td>
</table>
</body>
</html>
```

Feel free to take this example and adapt it for your own needs. It contains many of the elements and concepts discussed in this chapter.

Where to Go from Here

This chapter showed you how to develop and format standard HTML tables plus tables built with advanced elements and attributes. If you know how to develop tables, you can effectively present complex data and create interesting page layouts. From here, check out these chapters:

- Check out Chapter 2 for general formatting and design topics.
- See Chapter 9 and Master's Reference Part 2 for complete information about creating and applying style sheets.
- Look at Chapter 4 to see how to include images and use colors wisely.
- See Chapter 7 to see how to create frames.
- See Master's Reference Part 1 for more table options.

Chapter 6

Developing Forms

WHEN YOU SUBMIT CREDIT card information to purchase something online, search the Web with Google or Excite, participate in a Web-based chat room, or even select a line from a Web-page drop-down menu, you're using a form. Within the scope of plain HTML or XHTML—as opposed to extensions such as JavaScript, Java applets, and other embedded programs—forms are the only method of two-way communication between Web browsers and Web servers.

Perhaps because of the name, Web developers tend to assume that forms are just for collecting pages of data. In fact, you can use forms to get any kind of information from users without giving them the feeling of "filling out a form." A form is often as simple as a blank entry field and a Submit button.

In this chapter, we'll look at how to develop forms using standard elements and attributes, which virtually all browsers support. We'll develop a form piece by piece, including the following essential tasks in using forms effectively:

- Determining the form content

- Starting a form

- Adding Submit and Reset buttons

- Including check boxes, radio buttons, and other input fields

- Using text areas and select fields

- Processing forms

Determining Form Content

The first step in developing a form is determining which information to include and how to present it—that is, how to break it into manageable pieces. You then need to ensure that users can easily provide the information you want from them, which means that your form needs to be both functional and visually appealing.

Information Issues

When deciding which information to include and how to break it down, consider your purposes for creating the form. You might begin by answering these questions:

◆ What information do I want? Customer contact information? Only e-mail addresses so I can contact users later? Opinions about the site?

◆ Why will users access the form? To order something online? To request information? To submit comments or questions about products or services?

◆ What information can users readily provide? Contact information? Description of their product use? Previous purchases?

◆ How much time are users willing to spend filling out the form? Would they be willing to describe something in a paragraph or two, or would they just want to select from a list?

After determining what information you want and what information your users are willing to provide, break the information into the smallest chunks possible. For example, if you want users to provide contact information, divide contact information into name, street address, and city/state/postal code. You could even go a step further and collect the city, state, and postal code as separate items so you can sort data according to customers in a particular area, for example. If you don't collect these items separately, you won't be able to sort on them individually.

TIP   Although it's possible to go back and change forms after you implement them, careful planning will save a lot of trouble and work later. For example, if you complete and implement a form and then discover that you forgot to request key information, the initial responses to the form will be less useful or skew the resulting data. Fixing the form takes nearly as much time as doing it carefully at first.

Our site, TECHWR-L ("tech-whirl"), might hypothetically include a form to collect targeted addresses for future product and sale announcements. Although one could just as easily (but not as cheaply) use regular mailings by purchasing mailing lists, a Web site form avoids the cost of traditional mailings, collects information from specifically interested users (respecting their privacy, of course, and also addressing any governmental regulations regarding data collection and use), and keeps the Internet-based company focused on the Web.

Because filling out a Web page form takes some time, TECHWR-L created a form, shown in Figure 6.1, that includes only the essentials.

FIGURE 6.1 TECHWR-L's form collects only basic demographic and marketing information

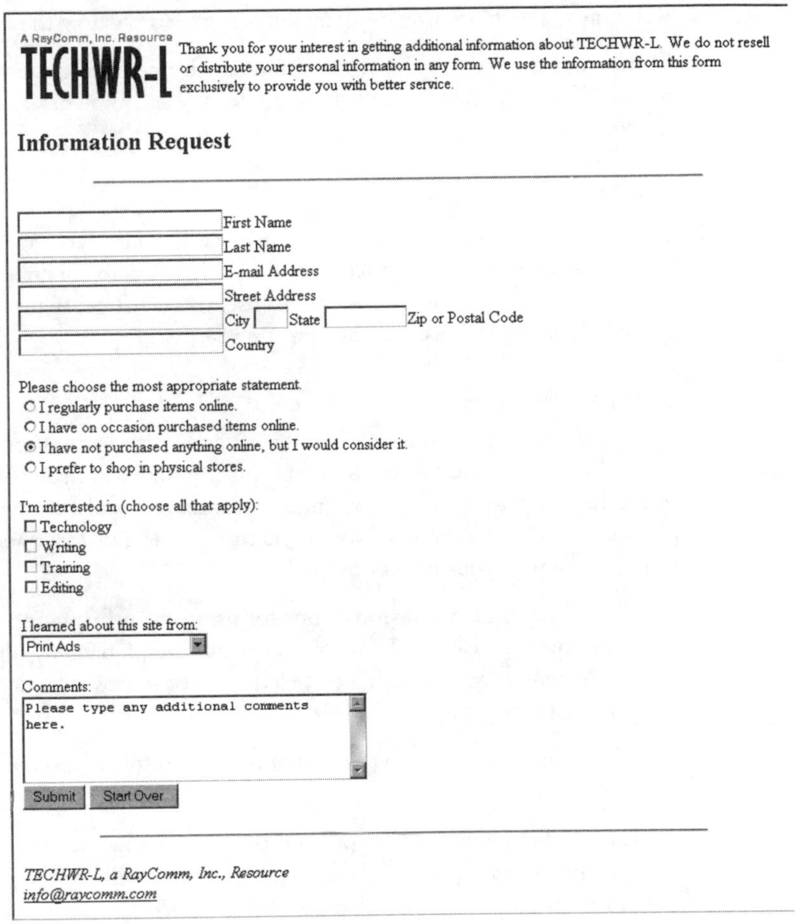
A RayComm, Inc. Resource
TECHWR-L
Thank you for your interest in getting additional information about TECHWR-L. We do not resell or distribute your personal information in any form. We use the information from this form exclusively to provide you with better service.

Information Request

First Name
Last Name
E-mail Address
Street Address
City State Zip or Postal Code
Country

Please choose the most appropriate statement.
- I regularly purchase items online.
- I have on occasion purchased items online.
- I have not purchased anything online, but I would consider it.
- I prefer to shop in physical stores.

I'm interested in (choose all that apply):
- Technology
- Writing
- Training
- Editing

I learned about this site from:
Print Ads

Comments:
Please type any additional comments here.

Submit Start Over

TECHWR-L, a RayComm, Inc., Resource
info@raycomm.com

In this case, a little demographic information is needed:

First name This is necessary to help personalize responses.

Last name This is also necessary to help personalize responses.

E-mail address Collecting this information is the main purpose of the form.

Street address, city, state, postal code These are all necessary for future snail-mailings and demographic analysis. Collecting the address, even with no immediate intent to use it, is probably a wise move, because it would be difficult to ask customers for more information later.

Online purchasing habits TECHWR-L wants to learn about the possible acceptance rate for taking orders over the Web.

Areas of interest TECHWR-L wants to find out about the customer's interests to determine areas in which to expand its online offerings.

Referral   The marketing department wants to know how the audience found the Web site.

Other comments   It's always important to give users an opportunity to provide additional information. You may want to limit the space for these comments, so the person who has to read them doesn't have to read a novel's worth of information.

Usability Issues

Usability, as it applies to forms, refers to how easily your users can answer your questions. Most online forms require some user action and usually offer no concrete benefit or reward for the users' efforts. Therefore, if forms are not easy to use, you won't get many (or any) responses. Here are some usability guidelines to consider when creating forms.

ADDRESS PRIVACY FIRST

Because of the floods of spam on the Internet and ongoing questions about what happens to personal data after Web sites collect it, you should explicitly state what you plan to do with the data you collect as well as link to privacy policies or similar information available on your site. By including a statement or privacy policy, you indicate to your users that you acknowledge and care about their concerns, and you inform them of your intentions:

- Take time to plan your intentions for using the information after it's collected, and ensure your company can live by the policy it outlines. Changing a privacy policy after its been implemented would be difficult to do, if not impossible, depending on what the original policy states.

- Make sure that the people receiving or using information collected know the details of the privacy policy.

- Ensure that people across your company also know the uses for the information collected. For example, if your policy says that your company will use the information for product shipping purposes only, make sure that product developers and the marketing team know that the user information is not for their purposes.

- Consult an attorney to ensure the policy is adequate for both your company's needs as well as your users' needs.

GROUP SIMILAR CATEGORIES

When you group similar categories, as shown in Figure 6.1, the form appears less daunting, and users are more likely to fill it out and submit it. TECHWR-L can group the information it's soliciting from users into three main categories:

- Contact information
- Purchasing habits and areas of interest
- Referrals and other information

MAKE THE FORM EASY

If you've ever completed a long form, you know how tedious it can be. Think of a tax form for an example of how *not* to do it. Although the specifics depend greatly on the information you'll be collecting, the following principles remain constant:

◆ Whenever possible, provide a list from which users can choose one or more items. Lists are easy to use, and they result in easy-to-process information.

◆ If you can't provide a list, ask users to fill in only a small amount of text. Again, this takes minimal time, and it provides you with data that is fairly easy to process.

◆ Only ask users to fill in large areas of text if it's absolutely necessary, because large blocks of text take a lot of time to enter for the user and for you to process. Additionally, many users are likely to ignore a request that requires them to enter a great deal of information.

TIP *For more information about how to create lists and areas to fill in, see the section "Creating Forms," later in this chapter.*

PROVIDE INCENTIVES

Provide users with incentives to fill out the form and submit it. Offer them something, even if its value is marginal. Studies show that a penny or a stamp included in mailed surveys often significantly improves the response rate. Consider offering a chance in a drawing for a free product, an e-mailed list of tips and tricks, or a discount on services.

TECHWR-L could have offered anything from a free tote bag, to an e-mailed collection of tips, to a discount on the next purchase, but chose to settle for a small giveaway book.

WARNING   *Most drawings and giveaways are legally binding in some way, and you need to be sure of their legal standing.*

Design Issues

Perhaps because of the need to address all the technical issues, Web authors often neglect design issues. However, a well-designed form encourages users to give you the information you want.

TIP   *For how to incorporate sound Web design on your site, check out* Effective Web Design, *by Ann Navarro (Sybex, 2001).*

What constitutes good form design? Good form design is something visually appealing, graphically helpful, and consistent with the remainder of the site. A form at an intranet site that has a white background and minimal graphics and that is managed by conservative supervisors would likely have a simple, vertical design and be none the worse for it. However, a visually interesting or highly graphical Web site calls for a form in keeping with the overall theme.

Although the visual interest of the form should not overwhelm the rest of the page, you'll want to make judicious use of color, alignment, small images, and font characteristics. Here are some guidelines:

◆ Use headings to announce each new group of information. This helps users move easily through the form.

◆ Be sure to visually separate groups. This makes the forms easier to use because sections become shorter and easier to wade through. You can use horizontal rules or the `fieldset` element to do this.

- Use text emphases to draw the audience to important information. Use emphases sparingly; emphasize only a few words so that they stand out on the page.

- Specify how users should move through the form. Don't make your users scroll horizontally to access information. Consider making a narrow, longer form rather than a wider, shorter form to accommodate users who have lower monitor resolution. If your survey is in multiple columns, make different categories visually obvious.

- Use arrows to help users move through the page in a specified order.

- Be sure that it's clear which check boxes and fields go with the associated descriptive information. For example, if you have a long row of check boxes and labels, users may be have a hard time figuring out whether the check box goes with the text on the right or the text on the left. Use line breaks and spacing to clearly differentiate.

- Specify which fields are optional and which are required:

  - Lump all required fields together under a "Required" heading and optional ones together under an "Optional" heading, or put "Required" beside each required field.

  - Put asterisks (*) by optional fields, with a note indicating that asterisks indicate optional fields.

  - Put the word "optional" in parentheses next to each optional field.

  Regardless of how you indicate what's required and what's optional, understand that some processing programs reject incorrectly filled out or incomplete forms, which can cause frustration for you and your users.

- Use a background image. Forms with some texture tend to be less form-ish and friendlier. However, be sure that the image doesn't outweigh the content and that the text adequately contrasts with the image so the text is not difficult to read.

- Make all the text-entry fields the same width and put them on the left if you have a vertical column of name and address information. This allows all the text to align vertically and looks much better. If the text labels go on the left, the fields will not (cannot) align vertically and, therefore, will look more random and less professional.

TIP *Check out Master's Reference Part 1 for a comprehensive list of form elements and attributes.*

Creating Forms

Forms have two basic parts:

- The part you can see, which a user fills out

- The part you can't see, which specifies how the server should process the information

In this section, we'll show you how to create the part that you can see. We'll show you how to create the other part later in the section "Processing Forms."

Understanding Widgets

Forms consist of several types of widgets, also called *controls*, which are fields you can use to collect data, including:

Submit and Reset buttons   send the form information to the server for processing and return the form to its original settings.

Text fields   are areas for brief text input. Use these for several-word responses, such as names, search terms, or addresses.

Select lists   are sets from which users can choose one or more items. Use them to present a long but finite list of choices—for example, choosing a state or province from a list, or choosing one of 17 options.

Check boxes   allow users to select none, one, or several items from a list. Use them to elicit multiple answers. For example, TECHWR-L used check boxes to get information about the activities of its customers.

Radio buttons   give users an opportunity to choose only one item—for example, gender, a preference, or anything else that can be only one way or one value from a group.

Text areas   are areas for lengthy text input, as in open-ended comments or free-form responses. Figure 6.2 shows a sample form that includes these widgets.

FIGURE 6.2

Forms give users different ways of entering information

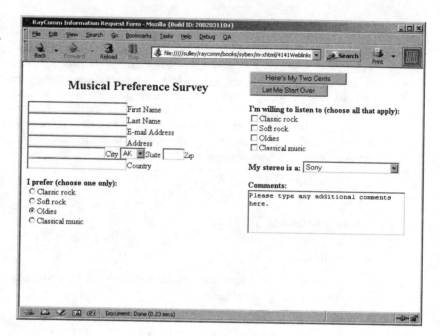

Creating a Form and Adding Submit and Reset Buttons

The first step in creating a form is to insert the form element and add Submit and Reset buttons. Submit and Reset buttons are essential components because they allow users to submit information and, if necessary, clear selections. Although you must add other form fields before the form will do anything worthwhile, the Submit button is the key that makes the form go somewhere.

TIP Forms require two form element attributes (action and method) to specify what happens to the form results and which program on the server will process them. We'll look at these attributes in the section "Processing Forms," later in this chapter.

Table 6.1 lists and describes the basic form button elements. (See Table 6.2 for more attributes to use with the input element.)

TABLE 6.1: BASIC ELEMENTS FOR FORM BUTTONS

ELEMENT	PROVIDES
`<input type="submit" value="…" />`	A Submit button for a form. The value attribute produces text on the button.
`<input type="image" name="…" src="urlv />`	A graphical Submit button. The src attribute indicates the image source file.
`<input type="reset" value="…" />`	A Reset button for a form. The value attribute produces text on the button.

In the following example, we'll create a form for the TECHWR-L site as we show you how to start a form and then add Submit and Reset buttons. The code in Listing 6.1 produces the page shown in Figure 6.3.

NOTE   *The examples in this chapter strictly use XHTML, rather than HTML, because, as in other chapters, XHTML examples work well in all cases, while HTML examples do not constitute valid XHTML.*

FIGURE 6.3

The TECHWR-L
form page, sans form

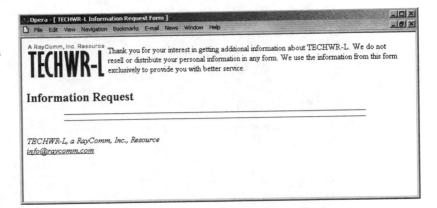

LISTING 6.1: THE TECHWR-L INFORMATION PAGE, WITHOUT FORM

```
<!DOCTYPE html PUBLIC "-//W3C//DTD XHTML 1.0 Transitional//EN"
"http://www.w3.org/TR/xhtml1/DTD/xhtml1-transitional.dtd">
<?xml version="1.0" encoding="iso-8859-1" ?>
<html xmlns="http://www.w3.org/1999/xhtml">
  <head>
    <title>TECHWR-L Information Request Form</title>
  </head>
  <body>
    <table>
      <tr>
        <td valign="top"><img src="techwhirllogo.gif" alt=
          "TECHWR-L Logo" border="0" />
        </td>
        <td>
          <p>
          Thank you for your interest in getting additional
          information about TECHWR-L. We do not resell or
          distribute your personal information in any form. We use
          the information from this form exclusively to provide
          you with better service.
          </p>
        </td>
      </tr>
```

```
        </table>
        <h2>Information Request</h2>
        <hr width="80%" />

        <hr width="80%" />
        <address>
          <br />
            TECHWR-L, a RayComm, Inc., Resource<br />
            <a href="mailto:info@raycomm.com">info@raycomm.com</a><br />
        </address>
      </body>
</html>
```

To add a form to the page, follow these steps:

1. Add the `form` element where you want the form. We're going to put ours between the horizontal rules.

```
<hr />
<form>
</form>
<hr />
```

TIP *You can avoid problems with your forms by properly nesting your form within other elements in the form. Be careful to place the form outside paragraphs, lists, and other structural elements. For example, you do not want to open a table within the form and close it after the end of the form. Also, be sure to test your forms carefully.*

2. Create a Submit button by adding the `input` empty element, the `type="submit"` attribute, and the `value` attribute. Although the Submit button traditionally goes at the bottom of the form (immediately above the closing `form` tag), it can go anywhere in the form. You can set the text on the face of the Submit button to any text you want—simply substitute your text for the text in the `value` attribute (just be sure it's still obvious that this button submits something).

```
<form>
<input type="submit" value="Submit" />
</form>
```

3. Create a Reset button by adding the `input` empty element, the `type="reset"` attribute, and the `value` attribute. Again, although the Reset button traditionally goes at the bottom of the form with the Submit button, immediately above the closing `form` tag, it can go anywhere in the form. The Reset button can have any text on its face, based on the `value` attribute. The following example has "Start Over" on the face.

```
<form>
<input type="submit" value="Submit" />
<input type="reset" value="Start Over" />
</form>
```

Figure 6.4 shows what the buttons look like in a completed form.

FIGURE 6.4

The Submit and Reset (Start Over) buttons are added to the form

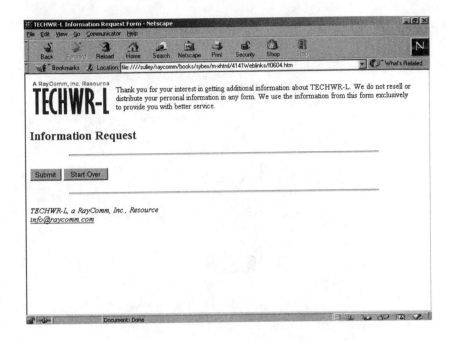

TIP *You cannot control button size directly; the length of the text displayed on the button determines the size of the button.*

If the appearance of your form is extremely important to you, consider using a graphical Submit button. However, be sure that your users are using browsers that can handle these buttons.

WARNING *If you use something other than a Submit button (one that says Submit on it), be sure it's obvious what it's supposed to be. Most users are familiar with "Submit" and may not readily understand other text you choose.*

If you want to use an image for your Submit button, substitute the following code for the Submit button (substituting your own image for `submitbutton.gif`):

```
<input type="image" name="submitbutton" src="submitbutton.gif" />
```

The `type="image"` attribute specifies that an image is used to submit the form when clicked. The `name="point"` attribute specifies that the *x,y* coordinates where the mouse is located will be returned to the server when the image is clicked. Finally, the `src` attribute works just as it does with regular images.

Figure 6.5 shows the complete TECHWR-L form with a graphical Submit button.

WARNING *XHTML makes no direct provision for a Reset button with an image; therefore, if you want to use an image for your Submit button, you might choose to dispense with a Reset button. If you don't, you'll have to deal with the potentially poor combination of an image and a standard Reset button.*

FIGURE 6.5

Graphical Submit buttons can make your form more interesting

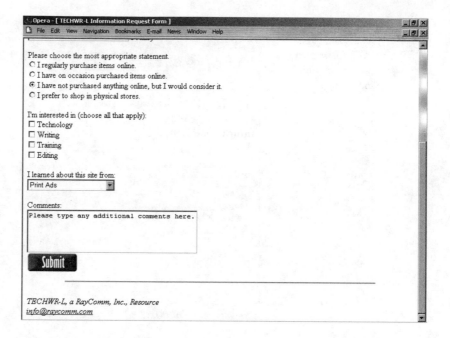

OPPORTUNITIES

Assuming that your users are using browsers that comply with HTML 4.01 and later versions (and they probably are, for the most part), you can use the button element to create a button that you can include instead of or in conjunction with Submit and Reset buttons. Buttons created with the button element have no specific action associated with them, as the Submit and Reset buttons do. However, if you're so inclined, you can link the button to JavaScript. Doing so gives you all sorts of functional and flashy possibilities (see Chapter 10).

To provide a Submit button using the button element, use code similar to the following:

```
<button type="submit" value="submit" name="submit">
    Click to Submit Form
</button>
```

To provide a graphical Reset button using the button element, use code similar to the following:

```
<button type="reset" value="reset" name="reset">
    <img src="gifs/resetbuttonnew.gif" alt="Reset button" />
</button>
```

If you want to use a button element to call a script that, for example, verifies a form's contents, you might use something like this:

```
<button type="button" value="verify" name="verify"
    onclick="verify(this.form)">
    Click to Verify Form
</button>
```

Including General Input Fields

You can also develop other types of input fields using various attributes in the `input` element, an empty element that sets an area in a form for user input. Table 6.2 shows the most frequently used attributes of the `input` element. (See Master's Reference Part 1 for a complete listing of attributes you can use with the `input` empty element.)

TABLE 6.2: MOST COMMON INPUT FIELD ATTRIBUTES

ATTRIBUTE	USE
`accept="…"`	Specifies the acceptable MIME types, in a comma-separated list, for file uploads. Wildcards are acceptable, as in `accept="image/*"`.
`maxlength="n"`	Sets the maximum number of characters that can be submitted. Use this attribute with text fields.
`name="…"`	Specifies the name of the field for the program that processes form results.
`selected="selected"`	Indicates the default selection to be presented when the form is initially loaded or reset.
`size="n"`	Sets the visible size for a field. The number *n* equals characters with text input fields and pixels in other fields.
`type="…"`	Sets the type of input field. Possible values are `text`, `password`, `checkbox`, `radio`, `file`, `hidden`, `image`, `submit`, `button`, and `reset`.
`value="…"`	Provides content associated with `name="…"`. Use this attribute with radio buttons and check boxes because they do not accept other input. You can also use this attribute with text fields to provide initial input.

TEXT FIELDS

A text field is a blank area within a form and is the place for user-supplied information. As you can see, text fields are commonly used for a name, an e-mail address, and so on:

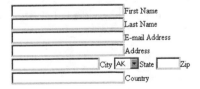

To add a text field to an existing form, follow these steps:

1. Add an `input` element where you want the field:

```
<form>
<input />
</form>
```

2. Specify the type of input field. In this case, use `type="text"`.

```
<form>
<input type="text" />
</form>
```

3. Add the `name` attribute to label the content. For example, one of the first fields in the TECHWR-L form is for the first name of a user; therefore, the field name is `firstname`.

```
<input type="text" name="firstname" />
```

TIP *The values for* `name` *should be unique within the form. Multiple forms on the same site (or even on the same page) can share values, but if different fields share the same* `name` *value, the results will be unpredictable.*

4. Specify the size of the field in the form by including the `size` attribute. Although this is optional, you can ensure your user has ample space and can make similar text fields the same size. For example, 30 is a generous size for a name, but still not overwhelmingly large, even on a low-resolution monitor.

```
<input type="text" name="firstname" size="30" />
```

5. Add the `maxlength` attribute if you want to limit the number of characters your users can provide (for example, if the field passes into an existing database with length restrictions). Keep in mind that `maxlength` settings should not be less than the `size` attribute; otherwise, your users will be confused when they can't continue typing to the end of the field.

```
<input type="text" name="firstname" size="30"
   maxlength="30" />
```

6. Add text outside the `input` field to indicate the information your user should provide. Remember that the name of the field is not visible in the browser; up to this point, you've created a blank area within the form, but you have not labeled that area in any way. You may also want to add a `br` element because the `input` element doesn't insert line breaks.

```
<input type="text" name="firstname" size="30"
   maxlength="30" />First Name<br />
```

Figure 6.6 shows the resulting text field in the context of the form. Use the same process to add other text fields with the name to the right of the element.

FIGURE 6.6

Users can enter information in text fields

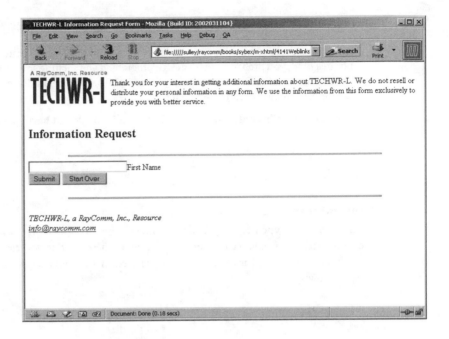

As a rule, forms are much more attractive if the fields are aligned. If they're nearly, but not exactly, aligned, the form looks sloppy, just as a misaligned paper form looks sloppy.

Here are some guidelines to follow when you include multiple text fields in your form:

◆ Place the fields at the left margin of your page, followed by the descriptive text. If you place the descriptive text (such as "First Name" or "Last Name") to the left of the fields, the fields will not line up vertically. Alternatively, consider putting your form fields and descriptive text in a table so you can ensure that the rows and columns are evenly aligned. Set the text fields to the same size, when appropriate. Of course, you wouldn't set the field for entering an official state abbreviation to 30 characters, but there's no reason that first name, last name, and company name couldn't all be the same length.

◆ As you add descriptive labels, remember to also add line breaks (`<br />` or `<p>...</p>`) in appropriate places. None of the form elements forces a line break, so your form elements will all run together on a single line if you do not include additional elements. In some cases, this is fine, but it can also look a little odd.

◆ Optionally, you can add a `value` attribute to the text input element to "seed" the field with a value or to provide an example of the content you want. For example, you could add `value="First Name Here"` to the input field used for the first name to let your users know what information to type.

Continued on next page

GUIDELINES FOR INCLUDING MULTIPLE TEXT FIELDS *(continued)*

If you're taking a survey, seeding a field is of questionable value. If your users can't figure out what to put in a field, you probably have a design problem. If you include some text, your users are more likely not to complete the field (and submit your sample) or to accidentally leave part of your sample text in the field, thereby corrupting your data.

The best—possibly only—time to seed a field is if you do not have space on the form for descriptive labels.

RADIO BUTTONS

A *radio button* is a type of input field that allows users to choose one option from a list. Radio buttons are so named because you can choose only one of them, just as you can select only one button (one station) at a time on your car radio. When viewed in a browser, radio buttons are usually small circles, as shown here:

> **I prefer (choose one only):**
> ○ Classic rock
> ○ Soft rock
> ◉ Oldies
> ○ Classical music

In the TECHWR-L questionnaire, we wanted to find out if users were inclined to make purchases online; the choices range from refusing to purchase to regularly purchasing online. Each choice is mutually exclusive—choosing one excludes the remainder. Radio buttons were our obvious choice.
To add radio buttons to a form, follow these steps:

1. Add any introductory text to lead into the buttons, at the point where the buttons should appear. Also add descriptive text and formatting commands as appropriate. The text of the TECHWR-L example looks like the following:

   ```
   <p>
   Please choose the most appropriate statement.<br />
      I regularly purchase items online.<br />
      I have on occasion purchased items online.<br />
      I have not purchased anything online, but I would
      consider it.<br />
      I prefer to shop in physical stores.<br />
   </p>
   ```

2. Add the input element where the first radio button will go:

   ```
   <input />I regularly purchase items online.<br />
   ```

3. Add the type="radio" attribute:

   ```
   <input type="radio" />I regularly purchase items
      online.<br />
   ```

4. Add the `name` attribute. The name applies to the collection of buttons, not just to this item (all the radio buttons of a given set repeat the same `name` attribute value), so be sure the value is generic enough to apply to all items in the set.

```
<input type="radio" name="buying" />I regularly purchase
    items online.<br />
```

5. Add the `value` attribute. In text input areas, the value is what the user types; however, you must supply the value for radio buttons (and check boxes). Choose highly descriptive, preferably single-word values (such as "regular" rather than "yes" or "of course").

```
<input type="radio" name="buying" value="regular" />
    I regularly purchase items online.<br />
```

6. If desired, add the attribute `checked` to one of the items to indicate the default selection. Remember that only one radio button can be selected, so only one button can carry the `checked` attribute.

```
<input type="radio" name="buying" value="regular"
    checked="checked" />I regularly purchase items
    online.<br />
```

TIP   *In general, make the most likely choice the default option, both to make a user's job easier and to minimize the impact of their not checking and verifying the entry for that question. Although adding the* checked *attribute is optional, it ensures that the list records a response.*

7. Add the remaining radio buttons.

Use the same `name` attribute for all radio buttons in a set. Browsers use the `name` attribute on radio buttons to specify which buttons are related and, therefore, which ones are set and unset as a group. Different sets of radio buttons within a page use different `name` attributes.

The completed set of radio buttons for the TECHWR-L form looks like the following:

```
<p>
Please choose the most appropriate statement.<br />
    <input type="radio" name="buying" value="regular" />
        I regularly purchase items online.<br />
    <input type="radio" name="buying" value="sometimes" />
        I have on occasion purchased items online.<br />
    <input type="radio" name="buying" value="might"
        checked="checked" />I have not purchased anything online,
        but I would consider it.<br />
    <input type="radio" name="buying" value="willnot" />
        I prefer to shop in physical stores.<br />
</p>
```

When viewed in a browser, the radio buttons look like those in Figure 6.7.

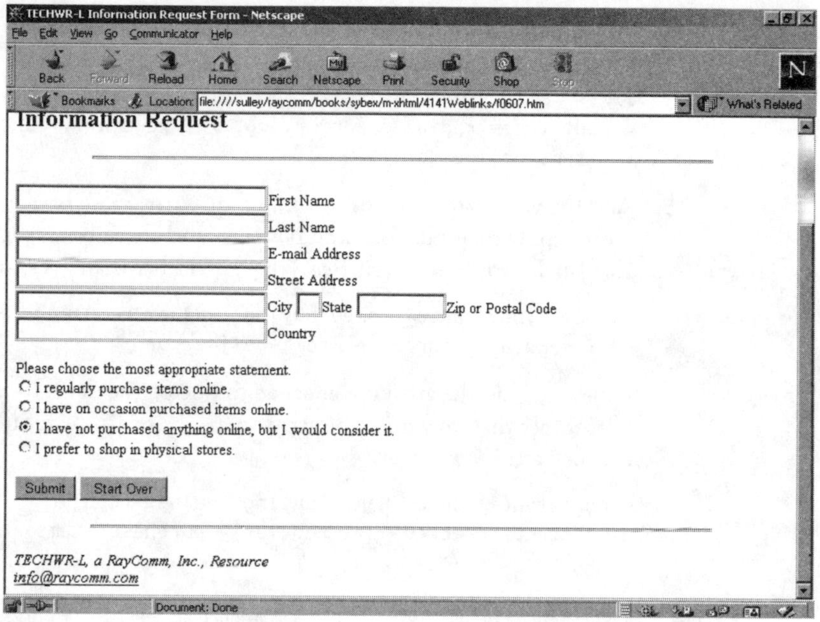

FIGURE 6.7

A user can select a radio button to choose an item from a list

USING *fieldset* TO GROUP ELEMENTS

XHTML lets you easily group related items using the fieldset element. For example, in the TECHWR-L form, several fields collect personal information, and you could group them within a fieldset element, like this:

```
<fieldset>
...various input fields for personal information go here...
</fieldset>
```

Additionally, by adding legend elements (aligned to the top, bottom, left, or right), you can clearly label content:

```
<fieldset>
<legend align="top">Personal Information</legend>
...various input fields for personal information go here...
</fieldset>
```

Continued on next page

USING *fieldset* TO GROUP ELEMENTS *(continued)*

A `fieldset` element with a `legend` element can look quite sophisticated, as shown here:

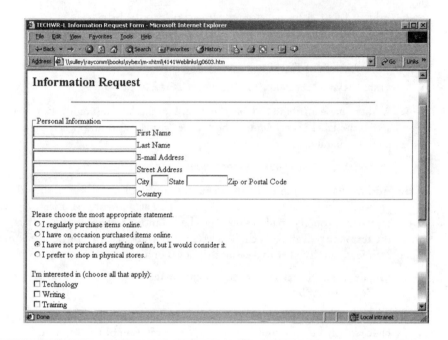

CHECK BOXES

Users can also use *check boxes* to select an item from a list. Each check box works independently from the others; users can select or deselect any combination of check boxes. Using check boxes is appropriate for open questions or questions that have more than one "correct" answer.

In most browsers, check boxes appear as little squares that contain a check mark when selected:

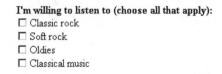

The TECHWR-L form is designed to find out about activities that interest customers. Any combination of answers, from none to all, might be possible, so this is a good place to use check boxes.

To add check boxes to your form, follow these steps:

1. Enter the lead-in text and textual cues for each item, as in the following code sample:

```
<p>I'm interested in (choose all that apply):<br />
   Technology<br />
   Writing<br />
```

```
        Training<br />
        Editing<br />
</p>
```

2. Add an `input` element before the first choice in the list:

    `<input />Technology<br />`

3. Add the `type="checkbox"` attribute to set the input field as a check box:

    `<input type="checkbox" />Technology<br />`

4. Add the `name` attribute to label the item. For check boxes, unlike radio buttons, each item has a separate label. Although the check boxes visually appear as a set, logically the items are completely separate.

    `<input type="checkbox" name="tech" />Technology<br />`

5. Add the `value` attribute for the item. In the TECHWR-L form, the value could be `yes` or `no`—indicating that technology is or is not an area of interest. However, when the form is returned through e-mail, it's useful to have a more descriptive value. If the value here is `tech`, the term *tech* returns for a check mark, and nothing returns for no check mark. The e-mail recipient can decipher this easier than a yes or a no.

    ```
    <input type="checkbox" name="tech" value="tech" />
        Technology<br />
    ```

6. Add a `checked` attribute to specify default selections. With check boxes, you can include a `checked` attribute for multiple items, but be careful not to overdo it. Each `checked` attribute that you include is an additional possible false positive response to a question.

    ```
    <input type="checkbox" name="tech" value="tech"
        checked="checked" />Technology<br />
    ```

7. Repeat this process for each of the remaining check boxes, remembering to use different `name` attributes for each one (unlike radio buttons).

In the TECHWR-L form, the final code looks like this:

```
<p>I'm interested in (choose all that apply):<br />
<input type="checkbox" name="tech" value="tech" />
Technology<br />
<input type="checkbox" name="writing" value="writing" />
Writing<br />
<input type="checkbox" name="training" value="training" />
Training<br />
<input type="checkbox" name="editing" value="editing" />
Editing
</p>
```

When viewed in a browser, the check boxes look like those in Figure 6.8.

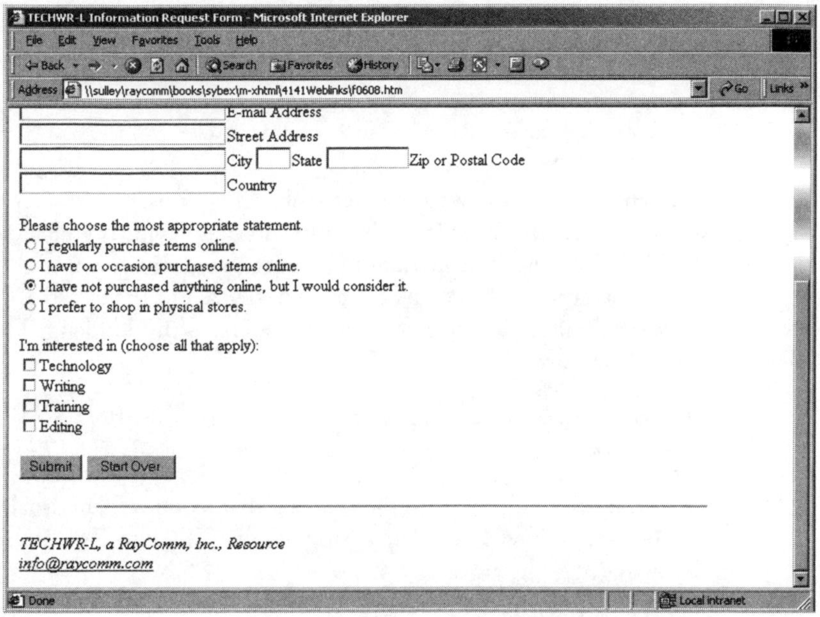

FIGURE 6.8

Users can use check
boxes to choose
multiple items
from a list

PASSWORD FIELDS

Password fields are similar to text fields, except the contents of the field are not visible on the screen. (They're not encrypted or otherwise secured, but are hidden from casual eyes.) Password fields are appropriate whenever the content of the field is confidential—as in passwords, Social Security numbers, or the mother's maiden name. For example, if a site is accessed from a public place and requires confidential information, a user will appreciate your using a password field. Of course, because your users cannot see the text they type, the error rate and problems with the data rise dramatically.

To establish a password field, follow these steps:

1. Add the `input` field:

   `<input />`

2. Set the `type="password"` attribute:

   `<input type="password" />`

3. Add the `name` attribute:

   `<input type="password" name="newpass" />`

4. Specify the visible size and, if appropriate, the maximum size for the input text by using the `maxlength` attribute:

   ```
   <input type="password" name="newpass" size="10"
       maxlength="10" />
   ```

Viewed in the browser, each typed character appears as an asterisk (*), like this:

 Password

HIDDEN FIELDS

Hidden fields are—obviously—not visible to your users. However, they are recognized by the program receiving the input from the form and can provide useful additional information. For example, TECHWR-L uses the program cgiemail to process its form, which includes a hidden field that essentially says, "When this form is submitted, show the user the Thanks page." Therefore, when the form is submitted by the user, cgiemail recognizes this hidden field and renders the Thanks page shown in Figure 6.9.

TIP   The cgiemail program, which is software for a Linux/Unix Web server to return form results with e-mail, is discussed at length in the final section of this chapter, "One Solution: Processing Results with cgiemail."

If you need hidden fields, the program that requires them usually includes specific documentation for the exact values. The cgiemail program that TECHWR-L uses requires a hidden field such as the following:

```
<input type="hidden" name="success"
    value="http://www.example.com/techwhirl/techwhirl-mail-thanks.html" />
```

The `type="hidden"` attribute keeps it from being shown, and the `name` and `value` attributes provide the information that cgiemail expects.

Hidden fields can go anywhere in your form, but it's usually best to place them at the top, immediately after the opening `form` tag, so they aren't misplaced or accidentally deleted when you edit the form.

FIGURE 6.9

A hidden field can tell the server to send a reference page (like this one) to the user, or pass other information to the server

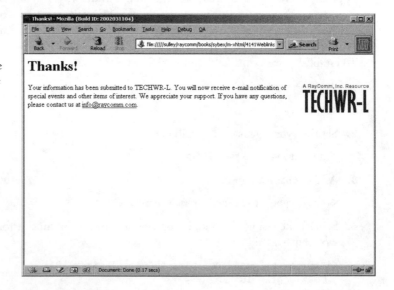

FILE FIELDS

HTML and XHTML also support a special input field, a *file field*, to allow users to upload files. For example, if you want users to submit a picture, a scanned document, a spreadsheet, or a word-processed document, they can use this field to simply upload the files without the hassle of using FTP or e-mailing the file.

This feature must be implemented both in the Web browser and in the Web server, because of the additional processing involved in uploading and manipulating uploaded files. After verifying that the server on which you'll process your form supports file uploads, you can implement this feature by following these steps:

1. Add the appropriate lead-in text to your XHTML document:

```
Upload this picture:
```

2. Add an `input` field:

```
Upload this picture:
<input />
```

3. Add the `type="file"` attribute:

```
Upload this picture:
<input type="file" />
```

4. Add an appropriate `name` attribute to label the field:

```
Upload this picture:
<input type="file" name="filenew" />
```

5. Optionally, specify the field's visible and maximum lengths with the `size` and `maxlength` attributes:

```
Upload this picture:
<input type="file" name="filenew" size="30"
   maxlength="256" />
```

6. Optionally, specify which file types can be uploaded by using the `accept` attribute. For example, add `accept="image/*"` to accept any image file:

```
Upload this picture:
<input type="file" name="filenew" size="30"
   maxlength="256" accept="image/*" />
```

The values for the `accept` attribute are MIME types. If you accept only a specific type, such as `image/gif`, you can specify that. If you'll take any image file, but no other files, you could use `image/*`, as TECHWR-L did. Finally, if you will accept only a few types, you can provide a list of possible types, separated by commas:

```
<input type="file" name="filenew" size="30"
   maxlength="256" accept="image/gif, image/jpeg" />
```

TIP   *To download a complete list of MIME types, visit* `ftp://ftp.isi.edu/in-notes/iana/assignments/` `media-types/`.

When rendered in most browsers, this code results in a text area plus a button that allows users to browse to a file, as shown in Figure 6.10.

FIGURE 6.10

You can use file fields to upload files

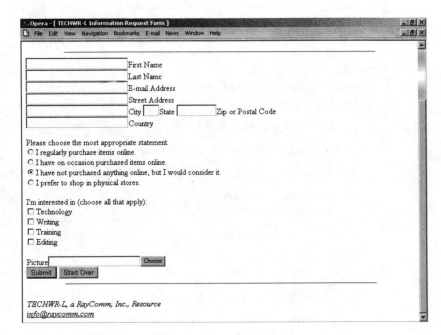

Including Text Areas

Text areas are places within a form for extensive text input. One of the primary uses for text areas is to solicit comments or free-form feedback from users, as shown here:

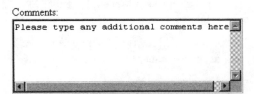

The `textarea` element sets an area in a form for lengthy user input. Initial content for the text area goes between its opening and closing elements. Table 6.3 lists and describes the chief attributes used for text areas within forms.

TABLE 6.3: MAJOR ATTRIBUTES OF THE `textarea` ELEMENT

ATTRIBUTE	USE
`cols="n"`	Sets the number of columns (in characters) for the visible field.
`name="…"`	Establishes a label for an input field. The name attribute is used for form processing.
`rows="n"`	Sets the number of rows (lines of type) for the visible field.

TIP *Don't confuse text fields with text areas. Text fields are appropriate for shorter input;* text areas *are appropriate for longer input.*

To include a text area in a form, follow these steps:

1. Enter any lead-in text to set up the text area wherever you want it to appear:

   ```
   <p>Comments:</p>
   ```

2. Add the opening and closing `textarea` elements:

   ```
   <p>Comments:</p>
   <textarea></textarea>
   ```

3. Add a `name` attribute to label the field:

   ```
   <textarea name="comments"></textarea>
   ```

4. Add `rows` and `cols` attributes to set the dimensions of the text area. The `rows` attribute sets the height of the text area in rows, and `cols` sets the width of the text area in characters.

   ```
   <textarea name="comments" rows="5" cols="40"></textarea>
   ```

5. Enter some sample information to let your users know what to type by adding the text between the opening and closing `textarea` tags.

   ```
   <textarea name="comments" cols="40" rows="5">
   Please type any additional comments here.</textarea>
   ```

This `textarea` markup produces a text area field in the XHTML document similar to the one shown in Figure 6.11.

FIGURE 6.11

A user can type comments in a text area

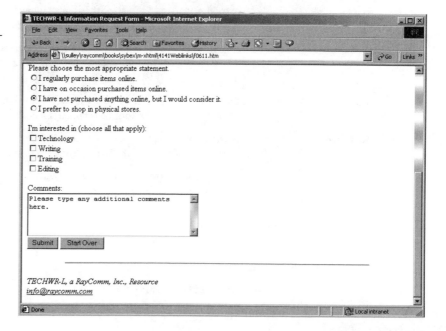

Including Select Fields

Select fields are some of the most flexible fields used in developing forms because you can let users select single and multiple responses. For example, suppose you need users to tell you the state or province in which they live. You could list the regions as a series of radio buttons, but that would take up tons of page space. You could also provide a text field, but users could make a typing mistake or spelling error.

Your best bet is to use a select field, which lets you list, for example, all 50 U.S. states in a minimal amount of space. Users simply select a state from the list without introducing spelling errors or typos.

Select fields, such as the one shown here, can either provide a long (visible) list of items or a highly compact listing, similar to the fonts drop-down list in a word-processing program.

 State

The `select` element defines an area in a form for a select field. Table 6.4 lists and describes the elements and attributes used to create select fields.

TABLE 6.4: IMPORTANT SELECT FIELD ELEMENTS AND ATTRIBUTES

ITEM	TYPE	USE
select	Element	Sets an area in a form for a select field that can look like a drop-down list or a larger select field.
multiple="multiple"	Attribute of select	Sets the select field to accept more than one selection. Use this attribute along with the size attribute to set to a number as large as the maximum number of likely selections.
name="…"	Attribute of select	Establishes a label for an input field. The name attribute is used for form processing.
size="n"	Attribute of select	Sets the visible size for the select field. The default (1) creates a drop-down list. You can change the default (to 2 or higher) if you want more options to be visible.
option	Element	Marks the items included in the select field. You'll have an option element for each item you include.
selected="selected"	Attribute of option	Lets you specify a default selection, which will appear when the form is loaded or reset.
value="…"	Attribute of option	Provides the content associated with the name attribute.

Use a select field any time you need to list many items or ensure that users don't make spelling or typing errors. To include a select field in a form, follow these steps:

1. Enter the lead-in text for the select field:

```
I learned about this site from:<br />
```

2. Add the opening and closing `select` elements:

```
I learned about this site from:<br />
<select>
</select>
```

3. Enter a `name` attribute to label the select field:

```
<select name="referral">
</select>
```

4. Add the choices that your users should see. Because the select field and `option` element inserts line breaks and other formatting, do not include any line-break elements.

```
I learned about this site from:<br />
<select name="referral">
  Print Ads
  In-Store Visit
  Friend's Recommendation
  Sources on the Internet
  Other
</select>
```

5. Add the opening and closing `option` elements for each possible selection:

```
<select name="referral">
  <option>Print Ads</option>
  <option>In-Store Visit</option>
  <option>Friend's Recommendation</option>
  <option>Sources on the Internet</option>
  <option>Other</option>
</select>
```

6. Provide a `value` attribute for each `option` element. These values are what you will see when the form is submitted, so make them as logical and descriptive as possible.

```
I learned about this site from:<br />
<select name="referral">
  <option value="print">Print Ads</option>
  <option value="visit">In-Store Visit</option>
  <option value="rec">Friend's Recommendation</option>
  <option value="internet">Sources on the Internet</option>
  <option value="other">Other</option>
</select>
```

7. Optionally, let users select multiple items from the list by including the `multiple` attribute in the opening `select` element:

```
<select name="referral" multiple="multiple">
```

TIP *If you choose to include* `multiple`, *your user can select one or all options; you cannot restrict the choices to only, say, two of four items.*

8. Optionally, add the `selected` attribute to the option element to specify a default selection. You can offer more than one default setting if you used the `multiple` attribute.

```
<option value="print" selected="selected">
```

With this, the basic select field is complete. Browsers display this select field as a drop-down list, as in Figure 6.12.

FIGURE 6.12

Select fields let you provide many choices in a compact format

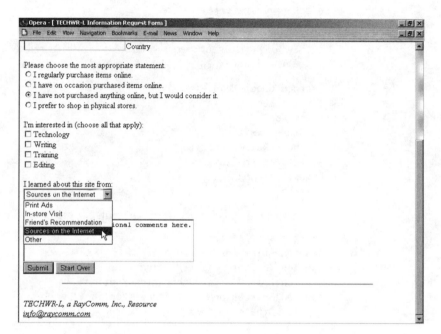

When developing particularly long select fields—ones that include many items—be sure to make the area as easy to use as possible. Here are some guidelines:

◆ Be sure that the select field appears within one screen; don't make users scroll to see the entire select field.

◆ Add a `size` attribute to the opening `select` element to expand the drop-down list to a list box, like this:

```
<select name="referral" multiple="multiple" size="5">
```

The list box can have a vertical scroll bar, if necessary, to provide access to all items, as shown here:

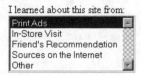

Select boxes are horizontally fixed, meaning that they cannot scroll horizontally.

TIP *You can use JavaScript to validate form input. For example, you can ensure that users fill out contact information or credit card numbers you need to process their information or requests. See Chapter 10 for details.*

Processing Forms

In general, after a user clicks the Submit button on a form, the information is sent to the Web server and to the program indicated by the `action` attribute in the form. What that program then does with the data is up to you. In this section, we'll look at some, but not nearly all, of your options. The server can

◆ Send the information to you via e-mail

◆ Enter the information into a database

◆ Post the information to a newsgroup or a Web page

◆ Use the input to search a database

When you're working out what to do with the data you collect or if you're just checking out what others have done in order to get some inspiration, your first stop should always be your Web server administrator. In particular, ask which programs are installed to process form input. Depending on what's available, you might be able to take advantage of those capabilities.

Regardless of how you want the information processed, you include specific attributes in the opening `form` element, as explained in Table 6.5.

TABLE 6.5: PROCESSING ATTRIBUTES FOR THE `form` ELEMENT

ATTRIBUTE	USE
`action="…"`	Indicates the program on the HTTP server that will process the output from the form.
`method="…"`	Tells the browser how to send the data to the server, with either the `post` or the `get` method.

The `action` and `method` attributes depend on the server-side program that processes the form.

In general, the documentation that came with your form-processing script or with your Web server will tell you what to use for `post` and `get`. For example, TECHWR-L's Internet service provider (ISP), `www.example.com`, publishes information on its Web site about how to set up a form to mail the results (using a CGI script called cgiemail, discussed later in this chapter). In this case, the proper opening `form` element is as follows:

```
<form method="post" action="http://www.example.com/cgi-bin/
    cgiemail/~user/user-mail.txt">
```

WARNING *Remember that we have to break long lines, like this one, in print. You should type this all on one line, because including hard returns in attribute values can lead to unpredictable browser behavior.*

Of course, the attributes you use depend on the program processing the information. By changing the attributes, you can also specify a different program. Because this single line of code within a form determines how the information is processed, you can change what happens to the data without significantly changing the form itself.

Why would you want to change what happens to the data? You'd do so primarily because you discover better ways to manipulate the data. For example, if you want feedback about your company's new product, you want the quickest way to collect the data, which is probably to have it e-mailed to you. Later, you could investigate ways to have the data written directly to an automated database—which isn't as speedy to set up as e-mail, but could save you some work.

Some Web servers have built-in scripts or commands to process form results; others, particularly Linux/Unix servers, require additional programs.

In the following sections, we discuss your form-processing options—sending with e-mail, writing to a database, posting to a Web page, and other possibilities. Because your ISP's particular setup can vary significantly, we've provided general information that you can apply to your specific situation—probably with the help of your server administrator. The final section in this chapter gives you a specific example of setting up an e-mail return—an option you're likely to use.

TIP   To learn your form-processing options, check with your server administrator or visit your ISP's Web site.

ABOUT USING FORM DATA

Getting a good response rate is the single biggest challenge to survey takers. Using a form to collect information puts you in a similar role, with the added complication that your users must find your Web site to complete it. After you get the data, you need to use it wisely. Here are some guidelines:

- Tell your users how you're going to use the information. For example, if you ask for users' e-mail addresses, let them know if you plan on sending them e-mail about your product. Better yet, ask them whether they want information sent to them. See the "Usability Issues" section earlier in this chapter for more information about including privacy policy information.

- Carefully consider the source, and don't read more into the data than you should. It's quite tempting to assume that the available information is representative of what you might collect from an entire population (customers, users, and so on).

- Take the time to analyze your data carefully, determining what it does and doesn't tell you.

For example, after TECHWR-L implements its form and receives a few hundred responses, it will have a general idea of how many customers are willing to make purchases online, how many are located in specific areas, how many have certain interests, and even how many use online services. Much of this information was not previously available to TECHWR-L, and it is tempting to assume that the data is representative of all TECHWR-L customers.

The results of TECHWR-L's online survey reflect only the preferences and opinions of that small set of customers who use the Internet, and visited the site, and took the time to fill out the survey. Even if 95 percent of the people who complete the survey express interest in technology, that might not reflect the interests of the overall TECHWR-L customer base.

PROCESSING FORMS VIA E-MAIL

Having the server return form results to you via e-mail isn't always ideal (although it can be depending on your situation); however, it's often useful, nearly always expedient, and cheap. Using e-mail to accept form responses simply sends the information the user submits to you (or someone you designate) in an e-mail message. At that point, you have the information and can enter it (manually) in a database, send a response (manually), or do anything else you want with the data.

If you're collecting open comments from a relatively small number of people, receiving the results via e-mail is a reasonable, long-term solution. That is, it's a reasonable solution if you—or whoever gets the e-mail—can easily address the volume of form responses. E-mail is also a good solution if you do not know what level of response to expect. If the volume turns out to be manageable, continue. If the volume is high, consider other solutions, such as databases.

DATABASE PROCESSING

Writing the information that respondents submit into a database is a good solution to a potentially enormous data management problem. If you're collecting information about current or potential customers or clients, for example, you probably want to quickly call up these lists and send letters or e-mail, or provide demographic information about your customers to potential Web site advertisers. To do that, you'll want to use a database.

Although the specifics of putting form data into a database depend on the server and the software, we can make some generalizations. If you work in a fairly large company that has its own Web server on site, you'll encounter fewer problems with tasks such as putting form results directly into a database or sending automatic responses via e-mail. If you represent a small company and rely on an ISP for Web hosting, you may have more of a challenge.

If your Web server uses the same platform on which you work—for instance, if you use Windows 2000 and your Web server is a Windows 2000 Web server—feeding the form results directly into a database is manageable. However, if your Web server is, for example, on a Linux/Unix platform and you work on a Windows machine, you may face some additional challenges getting the information from a form into a readily usable database.

POSTING TO A WEB PAGE

Depending on the information you're collecting, you might want to post the responses to a Web page or to a discussion group. For example, if TECHWR-L sets up a form to collect information, the natural output might be a Web page.

OTHER OPTIONS

If you find that the options available on your system do not meet your needs, check out Matt's Script Archive at www.worldwidemart.com/scripts, HotScripts at www.hotscripts.com, or Extropia's scripts at www.extropia.com.

These scripts offer a starting point, for either you or your server administrator, to handle form processing effectively. In particular, the form-processing script from Selena's archive offers everything from database logging to giving audiences the opportunity to verify the accuracy of the data they enter.

Keep in mind, if you choose to install and set up these scripts yourself, that the installation and debugging of a server-side script is considerably more complex and time consuming than installing a new Windows program. Not that it isn't impossible for the novice to do it, and do it successfully, but set aside some time.

If you choose to download and use scripts from the Web, be sure that you get them from a reliable source and that you or your server administrator scan the scripts for possible security holes. Form-processing programs must take some special steps to ensure that malicious users don't use forms to crash the server, to send spam, or worse. Without your taking precautions, forms can pass commands directly to the server, which will then execute them, with potentially disastrous results.

One Solution: Processing Results with cgiemail

Because you'll likely choose—at least initially—to have form results e-mailed to you, we'll walk you through a form-to-e-mail program. The cgiemail program is produced and distributed for free by MIT, but it's only available for Linux/Unix servers. Check out

```
http://web.mit.edu/wwwdev/cgiemail/index.html
```

for the latest news about cgiemail (yes, it looks old, but it works very well and is currently widely used across the Web). This program is a good example because many ISPs offer access to it and because it's also commonly found on corporate Internet and intranet servers.

TIP   *You can find a comparable program for Windows 95/98/NT/2000, MailPost for Windows 32-bit Web, at* www.mcenter.com/mailpost.

Here is the general process for using cgiemail:

1. Start with a complete form—the one developed earlier in this chapter or a different one. Without a functional form, you cannot get the results sent to you via e-mail.

2. Add the `action` and `method` attributes with values you get from your server administrator. (See the "Processing Forms" section, earlier in this chapter, for more information about the `action` and `method` attributes.)

3. Develop a template for the e-mail message to you. This template includes the names of each of your fields and basic e-mail addressing information.

4. Develop a response page that the user sees after completing the form.

Now, let's look at how TECHWR-L can use cgiemail to implement its form.

1. THE FORM

You don't need to do anything special to forms to use them with cgiemail. You have the option of requiring some fields to be completed, but that's not essential. For example, because the purpose of the TECHWR-L form is to collect e-mail addresses, TECHWR-L should make the e-mail address required.

The solution? Rename the `name` field from `emailaddr` to `required-emailaddr`. The cgiemail program will then check the form and reject it if that field is not complete. The actual code for that line of the form looks like this:

```
<br /><input type="text" name="required-emailaddr" size="30" />
    E-mail Address
```

Optionally, add `required-` to each field name that must be completed.

2. THE *action* AND *method* ATTRIBUTES

The server administrator provided TECHWR-L with the `action` and `method` attributes shown in the following code:

```
<form method="post" action="http://www.example.com/cgi-bin/
    cgiemail/techwhirl/techwhirl-mail.txt">
```

The file referenced in the `action` line is the template for an e-mail message. In this case, the `http://www.example.com/cgi-bin/cgiemail` part of the `action` line points to the program itself, and the following part (`/techwhirl/techwhirl-mail.txt`) is the server-relative path to the file. (With a server-relative path, you can add the name of the server to the front of the path and open the document in a Web browser.)

3. THE TEMPLATE

The plain-text template includes the bare essentials for an e-mail message, fields in square brackets for the form field values, and any line breaks or spacing needed to make it easier to read.

In general, you can be flexible when setting up the template, but you must set up the e-mail headers exactly as shown here. Don't use leading spaces, but do capitalize and use colons as shown. The parts after the colons are fields for the `From` e-mail address, your e-mail address (in both the `To:` line and in the `Errors-To:` line), and any subject field you choose:

```
From: [emailaddr]
To: Webmaster <webmaster@raycomm.com>
Subject: Web Form Submission
Errors-To: Webmaster <webmaster@raycomm.com>
```

Format the rest of the template as you choose—within the constraints of plain-text files. If you want to include information from the form, put in a field name (the content of a `name` attribute). The resulting e-mail will contain the value of that field (either what a user enters, or the `value` attribute you specify in the case of check boxes and radio buttons).

Be liberal with line breaks, and enter descriptive values as you set up the template. E-mail generated by forms may make sense when you're up to your ears in developing the form, but later it's likely to be so cryptic that you can't understand it.

Following is the complete content of the `techwhirl-mail.txt` file:

```
From: [emailaddr]
To: Webmaster <webmaster@raycomm.com>
Subject: Web Form Submission
Errors-To: Webmaster <webmaster@raycomm.com>
Results from Information Request Web Form:
[firstname] [lastname]
[emailaddr]
[address]
[city], [state] [zip]
[country]
Online Purchasing:
```

```
[buying]
Interested In:
[tech]
[writing]
[training]
[editing]
Referral:
[referral]
Comments:
[comments]
```

The cgiemail program completes this template with the values from the form, resulting in an e-mail message similar to the following:

```
Return-path: <www@krunk1.example.com>
Delivery-date: Sat, 25 May 2002 10:03:55 -0600
Date: Sat, 25 May 2002 10:03:51 -0600 (MDT)
X-Template: /home/users/e/public_html/techwhirl/techwhirl-mail.txt
From: mjones@example.com
To: Webmaster <webmaster@raycomm.com>
Subject: Web Form Submission
Errors-To: Webmaster <webmaster@raycomm.com>
Results from Information Request Web Form:
Molly Jones
mjones@example.com
402 E 4th
South Logan, UT 84341
USA
Online Purchasing:
might
Interested In:
tech
writing
Referral:
rec
Comments:
I'd also like information about online help.
Thanks!
```

4. SUCCESS PAGE

The only remaining step is to set up a success page—a document that is returned to the user indicating that the form has been received. Although a success page is optional, we recommend that you use one. In the form code, a "success" field is actually a hidden input field that looks like this:

```
<input type="hidden" name="success"
  value="http://www.example.com/techwhirl/techwhirl-mail-thanks.html" />
```

A success page can contain any content you choose. If you want, you can point the success page back to your home page or to any other page on your site. On the other hand, many developers use the success page as a place to thank the user for taking the time to fill out the form, to offer an opportunity to ask questions or make comments, or to confirm what the user submitted.

WARNING *A less-robust way of returning forms is to use a* `mailto` *URL in the* `action` *line, as in* `action=` `"mailto:webmaster@raycomm.com"`. *This solution, however, does not consistently and reliably deliver form results. A much better solution, unless you can closely control the browsers your users use, is a server-based e-mail program, which can process, validate, and help control the data you collect.*

Where to Go from Here

In this chapter, you learned how to determine what information to include in forms and to develop them using a variety of widgets. Additionally, you learned about the different ways to process forms and to get the data back.

What now? Following is a list of chapters that include related topics:

◆ For more information about WYSIWYG editors, see Chapter 1.

◆ For more information about using JavaScript to help control forms, see Chapter 10.

◆ For more information about planning XHTML documents, check out Chapter 12.

Chapter 7

Creating Frames

FRAMES DIVIDE BROWSER WINDOWS into several independent sections, each containing a separate HTML or XHTML document. Subdividing browser windows can dramatically improve both the appearance and the usability of a site. For example, because frames group information, users can more easily find what they want. Frames can, however, make navigation difficult. For example, if followed links seem to appear randomly in different frames, your users will become confused.

In this chapter, we'll discuss framing principles, create a framed site, and look at navigation issues that arise when you use frames. We'll also discuss inline frames, an HTML 4.01 and XHTML Frameset specification option supported by many, but far from all, current Web browsers.

This chapter covers the following topics:

◆ Understanding frames

◆ Deciding to use frames

◆ Creating frames

◆ Enabling effective navigation

◆ Creating inline frames

Understanding Frames

Throughout this chapter, we use a few terms you should become familiar with:

Framed pages or framed sites are HTML or XHTML documents that use frames.

Frameset specifies the layout for frames, including the locations and characteristics of the frames. The frameset acts as a holder for frame information.

Nonframed pages or nonframed sites   are documents that do not use frames.

Nonframed browsers   are browsers that do not support frames.

Parent documents   are documents that contain frames.

Frames are an HTML 4.01 (and therefore XHTML) standard. Framed sites use a combination of documents, displayed together in a browser window. Most commonly, frames divide the window into two or more sections, with one larger section containing content and the smaller section(s) containing a logo, navigation links, or both. Figure 7.1 shows a framed site; one section contains content, and the other contains a logo and navigation links.

FIGURE 7.1

Frames usually contain either the main content or peripheral content such as a navigation menu or a logo

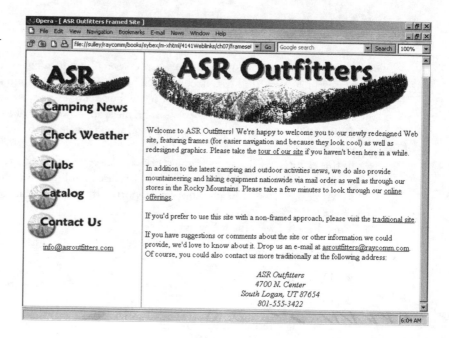

The appearance of frames depends on how you design them. For example, the frames in Figure 7.1 are vertical frames, which means that the border between them runs vertically in the window. You can also create horizontal frames, in which the border runs horizontally, as shown in Figure 7.2.

TIP   Because of the limited space in most browser windows—the result of limited screen resolution—using more than two or three frames is typically not a good choice. Use additional frames only if they're small and unobtrusive.

FIGURE 7.2

This horizontal frame divides the window into top and bottom sections

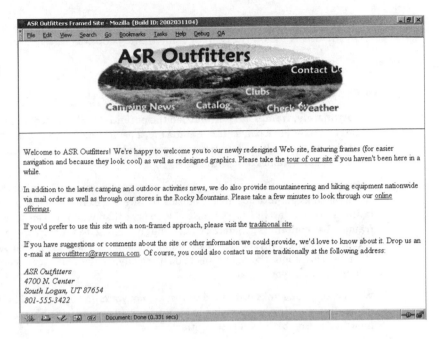

Deciding to Use Frames

The decision to frame your site will have long-range implications, particularly in terms of development effort. When deciding whether to use frames, consider both the advantages and disadvantages of doing so. Let's take a look....

Some Advantages of Using Frames

Frames are widely supported by popular browsers, and offer several advantages, both to users and developers, such as:

◆ Frames can be implemented so your pages also accommodate browsers that can't display frames, so if you're willing to take the time and effort, you can effectively serve all users to your site.

◆ Frames reduce download time. When using frames, users can download only the content pages. The static elements, such as logos and navigation menus, are already downloaded when the user first loads the site.

◆ Frames can improve site usability. Navigation remains visible as content changes in a separate frame.

◆ Because frames separate content from navigation elements and structural elements, you can easily and quickly update pages and provide new content. For example, if a framed site uses a top banner and a bottom banner, with scrolling content in the middle, you can replace the content—and only the content—without compromising appearance or navigation. That said, if this is the only reason for using frames, consider alternatives, such as templates or server-side includes.

A CAUTION ABOUT LINKING TO OUTSIDE SITES

Unfortunately, frames have introduced the potential for legal problems. A standard framed site, for example, might use a banner frame at the top, a navigation frame on the left, and a content frame on the right. A user clicks a link in the left frame and views the content in the right frame—the top (banner) and left (navigation) frames remain the same.

This layout works well as long as the links all point to documents within your site. However, problems occur when the links point to documents outside the site. For example, a company could use this type of frame layout and include a link to a CNN News Web page that, when clicked, loads the CNN page into the right frame. That content is generated by CNN but not labeled as such. This "borrowed" content appears to belong to the company, not to CNN. A number of lawsuits have been filed over this kind of issue, with no clear decision about the right thing to do. Basically, do not make it appear that someone else's content belongs to you or your organization.

When you include links to documents that are not yours and not created by you, you need to clearly identify the information as belonging to an outside source (and possibly obtain permission to display that information), or, better still, use nonframed pages.

Some Disadvantages of Using Frames

As a result of early implementation problems and site design issues, some drawbacks are associated with using frames.

Frames have an inconsistent usability record. For the first several months after frames were introduced, the Back button in some browsers returned to the last nonframed page, even if the user had been browsing through multiple pages within a framed site. This inability to move backward through visited pages was frustrating and caused many users to completely reject framed sites. Although this problem is infrequent as more people use much newer browsers, you should still accommodate all users by providing a highly visible link, possibly at the top of your site, that will take users to an equivalent, nonframed site. Alternatively, start your users at a nonframed site and then allow them to choose the framed site if they want it.

Creating a parallel nonframed site can require significant effort to develop and maintain. If you create a framed site, you may also need to create a parallel nonframed site to accommodate users who have browsers that are not frames-compatible. Of course, if you develop both framed and nonframed versions, you'll also need to maintain them both, which requires more time and resources—essentially like maintaining two separate sites, even though the content is theoretically identical.

Frame navigation can be a mystery. Even several years after frames were introduced, frame navigation continues to be a mystery to many. When users visit a nonframed site, they click a link, and the link takes them to a new page. In using a framed site, however, linked pages are often displayed in the same window (simply replacing the previous content), or linked pages can appear in a different frame. While these options sound cool, consider that they're different from how other site navigation works and require the user to figure out how the navigation works before being able to use the site efficiently. You need to ensure that your users can easily find what they want.

Frames pose substantial accessibility issues.   Back in Chapter 5, we mentioned that tables pose usability problems for users who rely on screen readers. Because content appears in different frames (or different cells, in tables), these adaptive technologies are not effective in differentiating content in different frames and, therefore, reads the content—often jumbled—as if it were in all one frame or window, or cannot access the content at all. See Chapter 12 for more information about accessibility issues.

Frames take up a lot of screen space.   Frames may take up a lot of screen space—often more space than they are worth. For example, the ASR Outfitters framed site was designed specifically for 800 × 600 or better resolution (assuming the browser window takes the whole screen) and looks good in Figure 7.1, at the intended resolution. However, when the site is viewed at 640 × 480, as shown in Figure 7.3, appearance degrades drastically. Not only do the graphics appear improperly, but the scroll bars also obscure more of the page. Granted, many people have better resolution than that, but many also choose to use the Web with a browser that doesn't use their whole screen.

FIGURE 7.3

Lower resolution in browsers can wreak havoc on framed sites

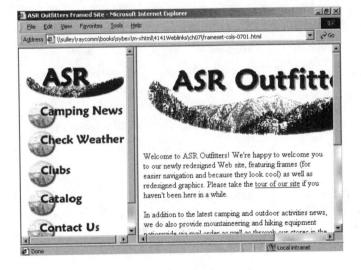

NOTE   Today's Web site designs generally favor small images (to speed download time, for example); however, throughout this chapter, we've used some larger images to help illustrate concepts. In designing images for your site, develop ones that meet your users' expectations and needs. See Chapters 12, 13, and 14 for additional information about determining and accommodating user needs.

Most browsers support frames, but give frames careful consideration before you implement them on your site.

Creating Frames

Creating frames requires relatively few steps:

1. Create a frameset (or layout) document that determines the location and characteristics of the frames.

2. Designate the frames and their contents.

3. Format the frames.

4. Make provisions for frames when viewed in nonframed browsers.

Table 7.1 lists and describes the frame elements and attributes used to create frames.

TABLE 7.1: FRAMESET ELEMENTS AND ATTRIBUTES

ITEM	TYPE	USE
frameset	Element	Establishes frames within a document.
rows="n1, n2, …"	Attribute of frameset	Sets the size for rows—horizontal frames—in pixels, as a percentage, or as "all remaining space" with "*".
cols="n1, n2, …"	Attribute of frameset	Sets the size for columns—vertical frames—in pixels, as a percentage, or as "all remaining space" with "*".
frame	Empty element	Identifies frame characteristics and initial content.
src="url"	Attribute of frame	Identifies the source for the frame content, as a standard URI.
name="…"	Attribute of frame	Labels a frame so it can be targeted or referred to from other frames or windows.
noframes	Element	Sets a section of a document to be visible to nonframed browsers (and invisible to framed browsers).

Determining Frame Size

As with all HTML and XHTML documents, frames render differently on various operating systems and browser combinations, with various display settings. Therefore, as you make decisions about how to frame your site, keep in mind size and scaling of the frames.

DETERMINING SIZE

The size at which frames display depends on the resolution of your user's monitor and the size at which the browser window is displayed. If a site is designed for a high-resolution monitor, it will be hard to use on a low-resolution monitor even if it has only a couple of frames.

For example, suppose you have two columns. The first is set to a width of 200 pixels for your logo and navigation buttons; the other column fills the remaining space (indicated by an asterisk in the cols attribute). At high resolution, you have a potentially attractive page. At 800 × 600, your logo will take about 25 percent of the window width, and at 1024 × 768 it will take about 20 percent. Not really a problem. However, at 640 × 480, your logo will fill 30 percent of the window width, leaving too little space for your content. Figure 7.3, earlier in this chapter, shows a two-frame page viewed at 640 × 480 resolution.

You can improve this page by setting the columns to 25 percent each, but then the logo column will require horizontal scrolling at lower resolutions. The only real solution is to think small (or no frames at all), particularly if you do much of your development at a high resolution. Test extensively at lower resolutions, and provide links that visitors can use to break out of the frames into a full-screen view.

DETERMINING SCALING

Scaling refers to how different screen resolutions and the size of browser windows affect the display of frames. By default, frames are resizable and automatically appear with scroll bars as needed to allow a user to view everything in the frame.

Depending on the layout, however, some frames might be more effective if they cannot be scrolled or resized. In particular, if frames contain only images—either image maps or regular images—set them to a fixed size and disable scroll bars and resizing. Doing so forces frames to accommodate the images and prevents users from resizing them. Your layout is thus preserved.

In general, simpler frames and sizes are better than fancy ones. Just because two frames are good doesn't mean that four frames are twice as good. Besides being ugly, the use of more than two frames leads to frames that are so small that even audiences using a high-resolution monitor must scroll both horizontally and vertically to read the content. Figure 7.4 shows a page with too many frames.

FIGURE 7.4

When you use too many frames, your Web pages become busy, confusing, and often difficult to read

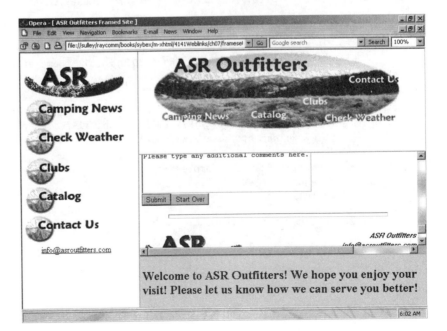

Creating a Frameset

A frameset is the foundation for individual frames and their content, in which you specify the general frame layout—either vertical (using columns) or horizontal (using rows). The basic frameset document is very similar to a standard HTML or XHTML document; however, it uses the Frameset DTD instead of either the Strict or Transitional DTD, and the `frameset` element instead of the `body` element.

The following example sets up a basic frameset document with two columns. Other examples in this section will develop this sample document further.

Before you start, prepare several HTML or XHTML documents with minimal content, but possibly different background colors. This will allow you to easily experiment with and view various frameset combinations.

TIP   The source documents in these examples are virtually blank documents, containing different colored backgrounds to make it easier to see different frames.

Follow these steps to start your frameset document:

1. Start with a basic HTML or XHTML document, including the `DOCTYPE` declaration, the `html`, `head`, and `title` elements, and the `meta` elements of your choice.

As you may recall from Chapter 2, there are three DTDs for HTML 4.01 and three for XHTML 1.0. One of each set is used specifically for frameset documents: the Frameset DTD. Therefore, the first line of your HTML 4.01 frameset document should be as follows:

```
<!DOCTYPE HTML PUBLIC "-//W3C//DTD HTML 4.01 Frameset//EN"
        "http://www.w3.org/TR/html4/frameset.dtd">
```

Your XHTML 1.0 document would include this `doctype` declaration:

```
<!DOCTYPE html PUBLIC "-//W3C//DTD XHTML 1.0 Frameset//EN"
    "http://www.w3.org/TR/xhtml1/DTD/xhtml1-frameset.dtd">
```

The basic starting document for an XHTML document might look like this:

```
<!DOCTYPE html PUBLIC "-//W3C//DTD XHTML 1.0 Frameset//EN"
    "http://www.w3.org/TR/xhtml1/DTD/xhtml1-frameset.dtd">
<html xmlns="http://www.w3.org/1999/xhtml">
<head>
    <title>Frameset Samples</title>
</head>
</html>
```

2. Add the `frameset` element to establish the frameset:

```
<html xmlns="http://www.w3.org/1999/xhtml">
<head>
    <title>Frameset Samples</title>
</head>
<frameset>
</frameset>
</html>
```

3. Add a `cols` or `rows` attribute, depending on whether you want vertical or horizontal frames. We used the `cols` attribute with values of **50%** and * to get two columns, one at 50 percent and one filling the remaining space (the * is a wildcard character):

```
<frameset cols="50%, *">
</frameset>
```

We could also use 50% for the second column in this case, because we know how much space remains, but using the * is a better choice because we can add columns without changing the existing values. If you change the first 50% value here, you don't have to make any other changes. If you specify all values, you must then change all values when you want to add columns.

TIP   If you view the document at this point, you won't see anything because you haven't specified any content. That comes when you add frames.

Within a frameset, you can specify either rows or columns, but not both. To divide your browser window into columns and then subdivide each column into rows, you nest `frameset` elements, like this:

```
<frameset cols="200,50%,*">
    <frameset rows="100,* ">
    </frameset>
</frameset>
```

JUST HOW ARE FRAME SIZES CALCULATED?

When you specify frame sizes within your frameset, the user's browser must accommodate both your specifications and the browser size and resolution. The browser calculates the actual sizes as shown here:

◆ Browsers apply percentages, which indicate a percentage of the entire browser window, first, if specified in the frameset.

◆ Browsers apply pixel values, which specify an exact size, second, if specified in the frameset.

◆ Browsers use wildcard (*) settings to fill the remaining space.

In general, you can use the * to set up proportional columns or rows. For example, the following frameset element has three values after `cols`; therefore, the space is divided into three parts. To allocate those proportionately (evenly), use an * as shown here:

```
<frameset cols="*, *, *">
```

To make the middle frame twice as large as the other two, add a 2 to the *, as in the following:

```
<frameset cols="*, 2*, *">
```

Continued on next page

JUST HOW ARE FRAME SIZES CALCULATED? *(continued)*

The middle frame fills half the space, and the other two columns fill one-quarter each. If you add a 2 to the third space, the first column fills one-fifth and the remaining two fill two-fifths each, as shown in the following illustration.

```
<frameset cols="*, 2*, 2*">
```

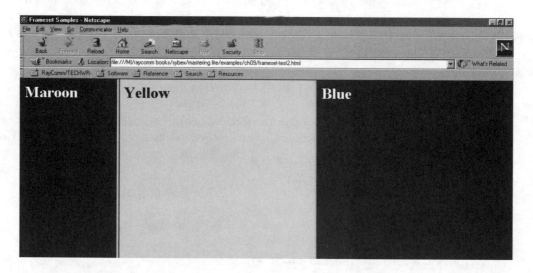

As we mentioned earlier, you can specify frame width in percentages, in pixels, or as a proportion of the remaining space. You can also combine these specifications. For example, a frameset might require one section that is 100 pixels wide, another that is 50 percent of the window, another that fills two parts of the remaining space, and a final section that is one part of the remaining space. That code, including the frame elements (remember that the frame element is an empty element), looks like this:

```
<frameset cols="100, 50%, 2*, *">
   <frame name="first" src="z-maroon.html" />
   <frame name="second" src="z-yellow.html" />
   <frame name="third" src="z-blue.html" />
   <frame name="fourth" src="z-green.html" />
</frameset>
```

Continued on next page

JUST HOW ARE FRAME SIZES CALCULATED? *(continued)*

This code results in the following frames:

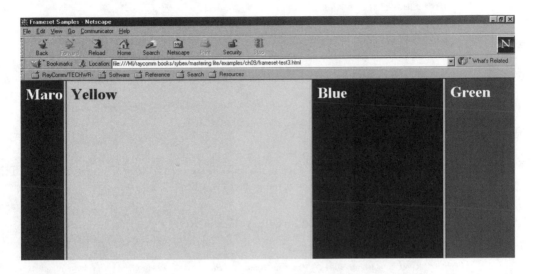

Adding Frames

Adding frames to an existing frameset document is straightforward. You add a frame element for each column or row in the frameset document, specify the content for each frame, and then name each frame.

In the following example, we're going to add vertical frames. The process for adding horizontal frames is the same except for the rows or cols attribute in the frameset element.

We'll start with the frameset document that we created in the last section, and then we'll add two frame elements and the content for each frame. The starting document looks like this:

```
<!DOCTYPE html PUBLIC "-//W3C//DTD XHTML 1.0 Frameset//EN"
    "http://www.w3.org/TR/xhtml1/DTD/xhtml1-frameset.dtd">
<html xmlns="http://www.w3.org/1999/xhtml">
<head>
    <title>Frameset Samples</title>
</head>
<frameset cols="50%, *">
</frameset>
</html>
```

Now, follow these steps:

1. Add a frame element between the opening and closing frameset elements:

```
<frameset cols="50%, *">
    <frame />
</frameset>
```

2. Add the name attribute to label the frame. Because browsers fill frames from left to right and top to bottom, this frame name is for the left frame. The second frame name is for the right frame.

```
<frameset cols="50%, *">
    <frame name="first" />
</frameset>
```

3. Add the src attribute to specify the HTML or XHTML document that will fill the frame. The document filling this frame is z-yellow.html.

```
<frameset cols="50%, *">
    <frame name="first" src="z-yellow.html" />
</frameset>
```

TIP *The URL you use depends on where the file is located. If you're using a file in the same folder as the frameset document or in an adjacent folder, you can use a relative URL, as we do here. If the file is located elsewhere, you need to adjust the URL accordingly.*

4. Add the second frame element, with the name second and source of z-blue.html:

```
<frameset cols="50%, *">
    <frame name="first" src="z-yellow.html" />
    <frame name="second" src="z-blue.html" />
</frameset>
```

This step completes the frameset document. The frames, which include the yellow and blue documents, look like those in Figure 7.5.

TIP *As you test your documents, you may find that reloading framed documents looks a little random—sometimes the whole document reloads, while at other times only a certain frame reloads. The easiest way to control how browsers reload is to ensure that the item you want to reload is active. To reload a single frame, click inside the frame and then click the Reload (or Refresh) button. To reload the entire frameset, click in the location line or in the address line (depending on the browser you use), and then click the Reload (or Refresh) button.*

To add another column, alter your frameset to make space and then add another frame element. The current frameset looks like this:

```
<frameset cols="50%, *">...</frameset>
```

FIGURE 7.5

Two frames, each with a separate document

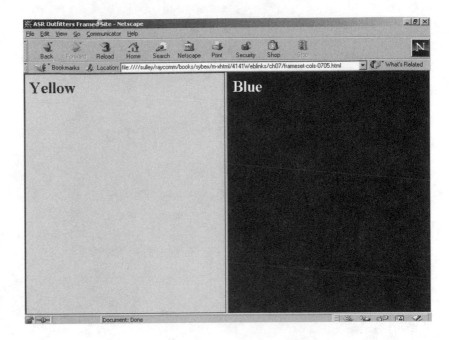

The 50% specifies that the first column fill 50 percent of the window. The * specifies that the second column fill the remaining space.

To add an additional column, follow these steps:

1. Specify the amount of space for the additional column. For example, if you add a 200-pixel column after the 50% column, the frameset element looks like this:

    ```
    <frameset cols="50%, 200, *">…</frameset>
    ```

2. Add another frame element. If you add the frame element *before* the two existing elements, the new frame appears on the left, and the other two appear in the center and on the right. If you add the frame element *after* the two existing elements, the new frame appears on the right, and the other two appear on the left and in the center. The frame columns fill in the order they appear in your code, from left to right in the browser window. If you add the new frame element at the beginning, the code looks like this:

    ```
    <frameset cols="50%, 200, *">
        <frame name="third" src="z-maroon.html" />
        <frame name="first" src="z-yellow.html" />
        <frame name="second" src="z-blue.html" />
    </frameset>
    ```

The framed page looks like that shown in Figure 7.6.

TIP   *You can follow these same steps to add horizontal frames (except you use the* rows *attribute).*

FIGURE 7.6

Multiple vertical frames get a little busy

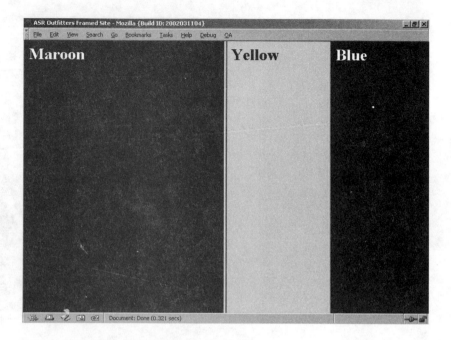

COMBINING HORIZONTAL AND VERTICAL FRAMESETS

Although many of your framing needs probably require only a pair of horizontal or vertical frames, you can easily nest frameset elements to combine vertical and horizontal frames within a single document. Each frame area in a `frameset` element can contain either a `frame` element, as in the preceding examples, or another `frameset` element.

In the next example, we set up a simple frameset with two columns and then divide the columns into two rows each. Follow these steps:

1. Start with a blank document, similar to the following:

```
<!DOCTYPE html PUBLIC "-//W3C//DTD XHTML 1.0 Frameset//EN"
    "http://www.w3.org/TR/xhtml1/DTD/xhtml1-frameset.dtd">
<html xmlns="http://www.w3.org/1999/xhtml">
<head>
    <title>Frameset Samples</title>
</head>
</html>
```

2. Add the `frameset` element:

```
<html xmlns="http://www.w3.org/1999/xhtml">
<head>
    <title>Frameset Samples</title>
</head>
<frameset>
</frameset>
</html>
```

3. Create two columns by adding the `cols` attribute. In this example, one column fills 30 percent of the window, and the other fills the remaining space.

```
<frameset cols="30%, *">
</frameset>
```

4. Add a second `frameset` element pair, for two rows, each at 50 percent of the window, as shown in the following code. Within the first `frameset` element pair, you could place two frames, two framesets, or one frame and one frameset (as this example shows):

```
<frameset cols="30%, *">
   <frameset rows="50%, 50%">
   </frameset>
</frameset>
```

5. Add the three necessary `frame` elements so you can view your document. The second frameset requires two `frame` elements, and the primary `frameset` element requires only one (because the second frameset is taking one of the two available columns). Be sure to include both the `name` and `src` attributes with the `frame` elements. Your code should look like the following:

```
<frameset cols="30%, *">
   <frameset rows="50%, 50%">
      <frame name="topleft" src="z-maroon.html" />
      <frame name="lowerleft" src="z-blue.html" />
   </frameset>
   <frame name="right" src="z-white.html" />
</frameset>
```

Your frames should look like those in Figure 7.7.

FIGURE 7.7

A combination of horizontal and vertical frames is often effective

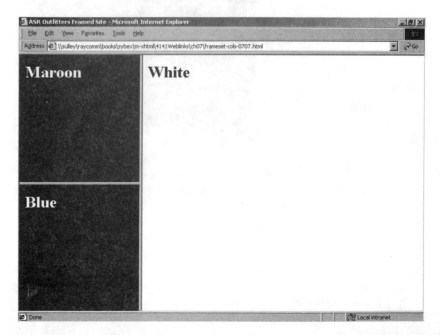

To set a second pair of frames on the right side, replace the final frame element with an additional frameset element, as well as two frame elements to fill it. The final code looks like this:

```
<frameset cols="30%, *">
    <frameset rows="50%, 50%">
        <frame name="topleft" src="z-maroon.html" />
        <frame name="lowerleft" src="z-blue.html" />
    </frameset>
    <frameset rows="100, *">
        <frame name="topright" src="z-yellow.html" />
        <frame name="lowerright" src="z-white.html" />
    </frameset>
</frameset>
```

When you view the results of this code in a browser, you'll see the frames as shown in Figure 7.8.

FIGURE 7.8

Four frames are easy to create, but visually a little much

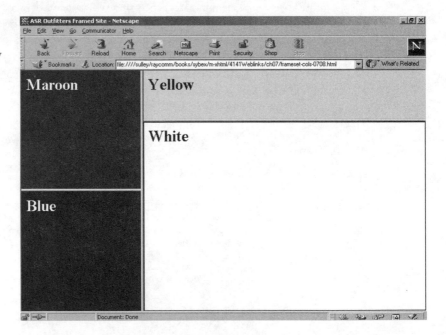

TIP If your document does not appear in the browser, double-check that you have the correct number of frames and that every frameset *element that you opened has a closing tag. An omitted closing* frameset *tag is usually the villain, particularly if you're nesting multiple framesets.*

Formatting Frames

Formatting a frame primarily involves changing its borders and adjusting its margins. You use the attributes shown in Table 7.2 to do so. According to the specifications, these attributes apply to the frame elements within a frameset. However, various browsers support the use of these attributes in the frameset element.

TABLE 7.2: FRAME FORMATTING ATTRIBUTES

ATTRIBUTE	USE
frameborder="…"	Sets or removes the border around a frame. For uniform results in all browsers, use in conjunction with the border attribute. Possible values are 1 (on) and 0 (off), for IE and the specification. For Netscape, the values can be either 1 or 0, or Yes or No. The default is 1.
border="n"	A proprietary Netscape 4.x attribute (that also works in IE 4 and higher and in other browsers) that sets or removes the border around a frame. For uniform results in all browsers, use in conjunction with the frameborder attribute. Possible values are 0 for off, or the number of pixels.
noresize="noresize"	Prohibits users from resizing a frame. In the absence of this attribute, users can click and drag the mouse to move the frame borders.
scrolling="…"	Prohibits scroll bars (with a value of no), requires scroll bars (yes), or lets the browser provide scroll bars if required (auto, the default).
marginheight="n"	Sets the number of pixels of the margin above and below the content of the frame.
marginwidth="n"	Sets the number of pixels of the margin to the left and the right of frame content.
bordercolor="…"	Sets the color of the frame border as either a #rrggbb value or a color name.

TIP These options apply to actual frames, not to the content of the frames. Remember that frame content is simply a standard document and is formatted accordingly.

REMOVING BORDERS

By default, all frames have borders. However, you can remove them to give your pages a more streamlined appearance. To remove borders from your frames, follow these steps:

1. Start with a functional frameset document, such as the following.

```
<!DOCTYPE html PUBLIC "-//W3C//DTD XHTML 1.0 Frameset//EN"
    "http://www.w3.org/TR/xhtml1/DTD/xhtml1-frameset.dtd">
<html xmlns="http://www.w3.org/1999/xhtml">
<head>
    <title>Frameset Samples</title>
</head>
<frameset cols="30%, *">
    <frameset rows="50%, 50%">
        <frame name="topleft" src="z-maroon.html" />
        <frame name="lowerleft" src="z-blue.html" />
    </frameset>
    <frameset rows="100, *">
        <frame name="topright" src="z-yellow.html" />
        <frame name="lowerright" src="z-white.html" />
```

```
        </frameset>
    </frameset>
</html>
```

2. To remove all borders from your frames, add both `border="0"` and `frameborder="0"` to each frame element:

```
<frameset cols="30%, *">
    <frameset rows="50%, 50%">
        <frame name="topleft" src="z-maroon.html" border="0"
            frameborder="0" />
        <frame name="lowerleft" src="z-blue.html" border="0"
            frameborder="0" />
    </frameset>
    <frameset rows="100, *">
        <frame name="topright" src="z-yellow.html"
            border="0" frameborder="0" />
        <frame name="lowerright" src="z-white.html"
            border="0" frameborder="0" />
    </frameset>
</frameset>
```

These attributes result in the document shown in Figure 7.9.

FIGURE 7.9

Frames without borders often look more attractive than bordered frames

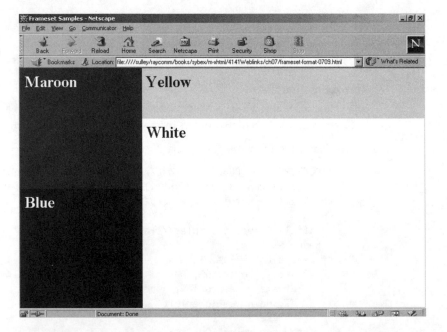

TIP   Because of the conflicting elements proposed and supported by Microsoft and Netscape, you must use both the `border` *and the* `frameborder` *attributes to turn off borders in all browsers. However, if you're on an intranet and all your users use Netscape browsers exclusively, you could use only the* `border` *attribute. If your users use Internet Explorer exclusively, you could use only the* `frameborder` *attribute.*

WARNING *If you remove or set borders in individual frames, remember that the borders that frames share must* both *be set to* 0 *to completely remove the border. If one frame is set to no borders and an adjacent frame has borders, you will see borders in the browser.*

SPECIFYING BORDER WIDTH

Adding borders of a specific size gets a little more complex because of the conflicting attributes supported by the HTML 4.01 specification, Internet Explorer, and different versions of Netscape Navigator and other browsers. To turn on borders, set `frameborder="1"` (for Internet Explorer) and `border="1"` (for Netscape Navigator). To set the border width, increase the value of the `border` for both browsers.

TIP *The HTML 4.01 (hence the XHTML) specification does not support the* `border` *attribute. In addition, the specification does not support the use of the* `frameborder` *attribute in the* `frameset` *element.*

For example, to turn on borders at the default value, use the following:

```
<frameset cols="30%, *" border="1" frameborder="1">
```

To set the borders to a width of 20 pixels (excessively wide, but easy to see if you're following the example), use this:

```
<frameset cols="30%, *" border="20" frameborder="1">
```

The resulting screen looks like that shown in Figure 7.10.

TIP *Internet Explorer supports a* `framespacing="n"` *attribute, which should increase the space between frames (in addition to the border width). However, because of Netscape's lack of support for this attribute and because this attribute is not included in the current frame specifications, we don't recommend using it.*

FIGURE 7.10

A 20-pixel width is excessive, but it makes the change in border width apparent

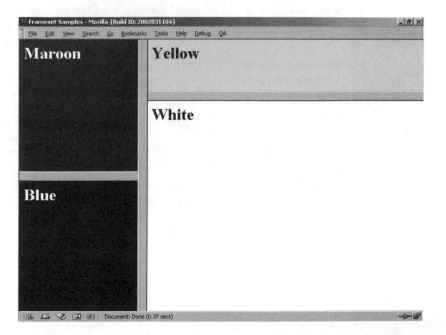

SPECIFYING BORDER COLOR

Colored borders can enhance or complement the color schemes of the documents in the frames. However, only the latest versions of Netscape Navigator and Internet Explorer support them, and they're not part of the current frame specifications.

To color frame borders, add the `bordercolor` attribute to the `frameset` or (better) `frame` element, as in this example:

```
<frame name="left" src="navbar.html" border="2" frameborder="2"
    bordercolor="#008000" />
```

When coloring borders, add the color to the individual frames for more consistent results. Although you can often add colors to `frameset` elements, not all browsers consistently support that usage.

Controlling Frames

Depending on your layout, you might want to exercise a little extra control over how frames appear. In particular, you can:

◆ Prevent users from resizing the frame

◆ Determine whether scroll bars appear on framed pages

◆ Set frame margins

Controlling these aspects will help keep your site predictable and thus more usable for your users.

CONTROLLING FRAME SIZE

If you have content of a known size, you might want to establish a fixed size for a frame and choose not to let users resize it. For example, if a frame encloses an image map that is used for site-wide navigation, you would probably size the frame to the image map. If the image map is 390 pixels wide and 90 pixels high, you might set the frame to 400 × 100 pixels with the following code:

```
<frameset cols="400, *">
    <frameset rows="100, *">...</frameset>
</frameset>
```

You know the exact size of only the first (top-left) frame: It will be 400 pixels wide and 100 pixels high. All other frames on the page will be resized according to the size of the browser window. If the browser window is set to 800 × 600, the second (variable) column will be about 400 pixels wide. If the browser window is 1024 × 768, however, the variable column will be about 600 pixels wide.

You can also set a frame to `noresize` to prevent users from resizing it. Although many Web surfers do not know that they can resize frames by simply clicking and dragging the borders, some do and will rearrange the borders to suit themselves. However, if users resize a frameset to avoid scrolling, they might obscure some content without realizing it. To avoid this, simply add the `noresize` attribute to the `frame` element, like this:

```
<frame name="menu" src="imagemap.html" noresize="noresize" />
```

TIP The `noresize` *attribute is set equal to itself. Setting one frame to* `noresize` *also prohibits other adjacent frames from resizing. For example, if the Maroon frame in Figure 7.10 is set to* `noresize`*, users cannot horizontally resize the Yellow frame or vertically resize the Blue frame.*

CONTROLLING SCROLL BARS

Although scroll bars are essential so users can see all the content in frames, they can be superfluous and visually distracting. Depending on the margin that a browser inserts around an image, scroll bars might appear in some browsers on some platforms and not in others. For example, if the entire image map fits within the frame, little scrolling is necessary, and scroll bars would probably obscure more of the image map than what would be lost through the margins. Therefore, you might set this frame to `scrolling="no"` to prohibit scroll bars, like this:

```
<frame name="menu" src="imagemap.html" scrolling="no"
    noresize="noresize" />
```

TIP Set `scrolling="no"` *only if the frame contains an image or an object of a known size. Because browser settings, available fonts, and monitor resolution vary, you cannot reliably predict what text might or might not fit within a frame.*

Conversely, you might also set `scrolling="yes"` in some cases. For example, if you have a contents page that contains most of the links from your navigation frame, you might set scrolling to yes so the frame always has a scroll bar. If you have shorter documents, the scroll bar will be nonfunctional, but it will appear consistently and make your site look just a wee bit more professional. If you set scrolling to auto (the default), some pages may have a scroll bar and some may not, which can be distracting to a user.

SETTING FRAME MARGINS

A frame margin is the space between the edge of the frame and the visible content of the document. Adjusting the frame margin affects the framed document itself and keeps documents from appearing to touch each other; in other words, adjusting the frame margins gives your documents a little "breathing room."

To set frame margins, add the `marginheight` (for vertical margins) and `marginwidth` (for horizontal margins) attributes to the `frame` element, as shown in the following code:

```
<frame name="topleft" src="z-maroon.html" marginwidth="100"
    marginheight="100" />
```

This code moves the document 100 pixels from the top and left margins, as illustrated in Figure 7.11.

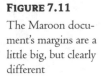

FIGURE 7.11

The Maroon document's margins are a little big, but clearly different

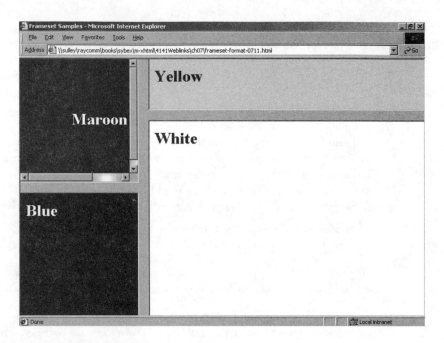

Accommodating Nonframed Browsers

As mentioned earlier, not all browsers support frames. If a user to your framed site has a nonframed browser, what does he or she see? Nothing. Because that's the last thing you want, you need to accommodate users who are using nonframed browsers. This usually means supplying text that replicates the information in the framed document.

TIP   While traditional Web browsers that do not support frames are pretty rare, the same techniques are also required to support aural browsers (for visually impaired visitors), text-only browsers like Lynx, Web crawlers (which find pages for inclusion in Google and other Web search services), and other nontraditional browsers.

If you're developing a Web site for general use, you need to give careful thought to how you will supply information to visitors using nonframed browsers. Here are some guidelines:

Provide some amount of nonframed information.   Even if you decide not to accommodate nonframed browsers, display a courtesy message stating (positively) that your site requires that browsers support frames and that it's inaccessible with other browsers. (This is technically an option, but isn't recommended.)

Use a browser-detection script that automatically redirects nonframed browsers to the nonframed pages.   This option requires more work than the preceding guideline; however, it makes you and the Web browser do the work, not the visitor.

Include alternate text within the `noframes` section.   If you do this carefully, your users may not even know that your site has other content. This option increases your workload substantially. You must often maintain two complete documents—the content within the frames and the content within the `noframes` section.

Create your home page using frames, but provide a link to the nonframed version. Users thus have the option to use frames, but they aren't forced to do so. This option also doubles your work.

Develop your home page without frames, and then provide links to the framed version. Again, this is a double-your-work option.

At one time (in 1997, actually), the RayComm Web site (real, not hypothetical) used this last solution, as shown in Figure 7.12. The home page looked like a framed site, but was actually a fancy background and a table to separate the navigation features from the content. A link ("Try the High-Tech Site") went to a roughly parallel page that looked the same but used frames.

NOTE   It's interesting to recall what we regarded as "high-tech" in 1997. Keeping old versions of your Web sites is often useful for surprising reasons—consider it.

TIPS FOR MAINTAINING FRAMED AND NONFRAMED DOCUMENTS

One way to lighten your workload is to make extensive use of "server-side includes" (code that tells the server to automatically include specified information or functionality in your pages) so your content and presentation are essentially separate. You include the content in framed pages. In the nonframed pages, you include the content and another document that has navigation links. Check your server documentation for more information about using server-side include capabilities.

Another alternative is to include the navigation links in your document and then use JavaScript to hide the links from framed browsers. This is not an elegant solution, but it works. Almost all browsers that support JavaScript also support frames, and vice versa (unless the user has disabled either frames or JavaScript).

FIGURE 7.12

A table can masquerade as a set of framed documents

ARE TABLES OR FRAMES BETTER FOR YOUR DESIGN NEEDS?

You can use both tables and frames to create interesting page layouts and work around the limitations of HTML and XHTML. For example, you can place navigation information beside the text of a document or array two columns of text side by side, using either tables or frames.

So how do you decide which to use? The advantages of tables include the following:

◆ Tables are more widely recognized by browsers than frames.

◆ Tables create fewer site navigation difficulties than frames.

◆ Tables create fewer accessibility challenges.

◆ Tables are standard HTML 3.2 or 4.01 and XHTML, according to all versions of the DTD.

The advantages of frames include the following:

◆ Frames are easier to update and maintain because the individual documents are shorter and simpler.

◆ Framed pages tend to download faster because information doesn't have to be downloaded repeatedly.

◆ Frames are more flexible for complex layouts. For example, they allow you to have information across the top of a page and scroll other information under that banner.

◆ Frames offer some useful bells and whistles, such as being able to call up a document in a specific part of the browser window—an effect that can be simulated with tables only at the cost of incredible effort.

◆ Frames are standard HTML 4.01 and XHTML, according to specific versions of the DTD.

For more information about tables, see Chapter 5.

PROVIDING NONFRAMED CONTENT

To accommodate users using nonframed browsers, use the `noframes` element and include the alternate text. Start with an existing frameset document such as the following:

```
<!DOCTYPE html PUBLIC "-//W3C//DTD XHTML 1.0 Frameset//EN"
    "http://www.w3.org/TR/xhtml1/DTD/xhtml1-frameset.dtd">
<html xmlns="http://www.w3.org/1999/xhtml">
<head>
    <title>Frameset Samples</title>
</head>
<frameset cols="30%, *" border="0" frameborder="0"
    bordercolor="#008000">
    <frameset rows="50%, 50%">
        <frame name="topleft" src="z-maroon.html" />
        <frame name="lowerleft" src="z-blue.html" />
```

```
   </frameset>
   <frameset rows="100, *">
      <frame name="topright" src="z-yellow.html" />
      <frame name="lowerright" src="z-white.html" />
   </frameset>
</frameset>
</html>
```

Now, follow these steps:

1. Add the `noframes` tag pair somewhere in the document between the `frameset` tags. The best choice—for ease of development—is either at the beginning, immediately following the first `frameset` tag, or at the end, just before the closing `frameset` tag.

```
   ...
       <noframes>
          <body>
          </body>
       </noframes>
      </frameset>
   </html>
```

TIP   The body *element is required in the* noframes *element according to the Frameset DTD. Therefore, if you're going to validate your frameset documents, you should include the* body *element in the* noframes *element.*

2. Add any appropriate content within the `noframes` elements. The approach you take, as mentioned previously, will vary. For an intranet site for a company that has standardized on the latest version of Internet Explorer, you might choose something like the following:

```
<noframes>
   <body>
      <h1 align="center">Intranet Access Problem</h1>
      <p>WAMMI, Inc., has standardized on the newest version of Internet
      Explorer. You seem to be using an older version or a different browser
      entirely. Please see your network administrator or check with the Help
      Desk to get the proper browser. With the newest browser, you will be able
      to access the corporate intranet.</p>
   </body>
</noframes>
```

When viewed in a nonframed browser such as Lynx, this page looks like Figure 7.13.

TIP   Some nonframed browsers support only a limited set of formatting elements. Keep this in mind if you're tempted to get fancy with your nonframes formatting.

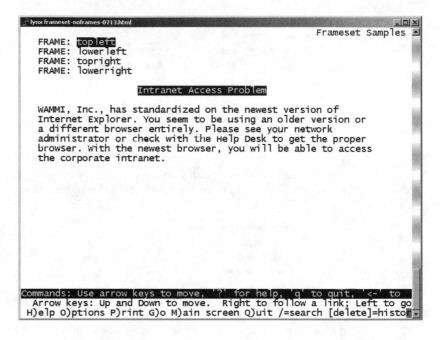

Enabling Effective Navigation

Designing with frames and helping your users navigate your site effectively requires moderation and simplicity. The following sections explain the navigation types and show you how to implement navigation.

Choosing Navigation Types

You can design frames so users can navigate in two ways:

◆ Users can click in one frame and view the resulting document in another frame (as shown in Figure 7.14).

◆ Users can click in one frame and view the resulting document in that same frame.

When you use the first option, navigation tools remain visible at all times in one frame, and the content appears and changes in another frame. In Figure 7.14, clicking a link on the left changes the content in the frame on the right.

When you use the second option, clicking a link changes the content in the frame that contains the link. For example, in Figure 7.14, clicking a link in the frame on the right changes the content of that frame.

You normally use the second option when content is logically cross-referenced to other documents at the site. However, all frames can contain links, whether they are navigation links or cross-references.

FIGURE 7.14

Navigation links can lead to a document in the same frame or in another frame

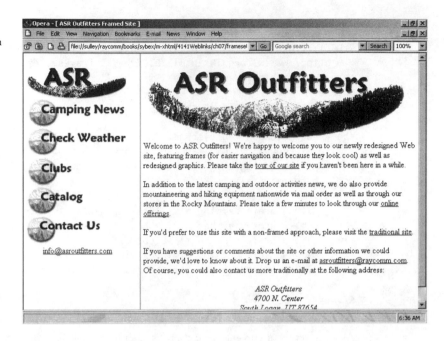

Implementing Navigation

Linking to specific frames requires only one new attribute, `target`. When used in an anchor (a) element, this attribute directs the content of the link into a different frame.

The frameset document for Figure 7.14 looks like this:

```
<!DOCTYPE html PUBLIC "-//W3C//DTD XHTML 1.0 Frameset//EN"
    "http://www.w3.org/TR/xhtml1/DTD/xhtml1-frameset.dtd">
<html xmlns="http://www.w3.org/1999/xhtml">
<head>
    <title>ASR Outfitters Framed Site</title>
</head>
<frameset cols="230, *">
    <frame name="left" src="lefttoc1.html" />
    <frame name="main" src="content.html" />
    <noframes>
      <body>
        <p>If you can see this, your browser is not capable
            of displaying frames.</p>
      </body>
    </noframes>
</frameset>
</html>
```

The first (left) `frame` element carries the attribute `name="left"`, and the other frame has the attribute `name="main"`. These attributes allow the frames to be specifically addressed.

The basic code for the left frame is as follows:

```
<!DOCTYPE html PUBLIC "-//W3C//DTD XHTML 1.0 Frameset//EN"
    "http://www.w3.org/TR/xhtml1/DTD/xhtml1-frameset.dtd">
<html xmlns="http://www.w3.org/1999/xhtml">
<head>
    <title>ASR Outfitters</title>
</head>
<body background="" bgcolor="#ffffff" text="#000000"
    link="#0000ff" vlink="#800080" alink="#ff0000">
    <img src="asrlogosm.gif" align="" width="200" height="84"
        border="0" alt="ASR Logo" />
    <ul>
        <li><a href="camping.html">Camping News</a></li>
        <li><a href="weather.html">Check Weather</a></li>
        <li><a href="clubs.html">Clubs</a></li>
        <li><a href="catalog.html">Catalog</a></li>
        <li><a href="contact.html">Contact Us</a></li>
    </ul>
</body>
</html>
```

As the document currently stands, clicking a link—say, Camping News—in the left frame displays the new document in the left (same) frame, because frame links, by default, land in the same frame. If you want the linked document to appear in the right frame, follow these steps:

1. Add the `target` attribute to the a element:

```
<li><a href="camping.html" target="">Camping News
    </a></li>
```

2. Add the name of the frame to which you want to link. The initial frameset names the frame on the right `main`, so that's the name you use.

```
<li><a href="camping.html" target="main">Camping News
    </a></li>
```

Now when you click the Camping News link, the file appears in the right frame, as shown in Figure 7.15.

Of course, in this particular scenario, each link from this document should open in the main frame. To save time and reduce the possibility of error, you can add the `target="main"` attribute to the `base` element and force it to affect the entire document.

The `base` element goes in the document head and sets the rules for the whole document. To set all links from the document in the left frame to open in the main frame, add the element and attribute to the document head as in the following example:

```
<!DOCTYPE html PUBLIC "-//W3C//DTD XHTML 1.0 Frameset//EN"
    "http://www.w3.org/TR/xhtml1/DTD/xhtml1-frameset.dtd">
<html xmlns="http://www.w3.org/1999/xhtml">
<head>
```

```
        <title>ASR Outfitters</title>
        <base target="main" />
</head>
```

FIGURE 7.15

The `target` attribute controls which frame receives the content of a link. The Camping News link was directed into the "main" frame

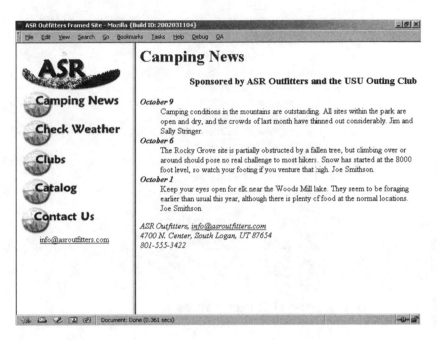

With the base target defined, you only need the `target` attributes to link to other locations. The following section discusses some special target locations and names.

USING IMAGE MAPS AS NAVIGATION TOOLS IN FRAMED DOCUMENTS

The `target` attribute works in all contexts where links occur. For example, you can use an image map in a frame to provide navigation for an entire site. The following code and example show how to include an image map in a framed page:

```
<map name="frame-imagemap">
<area shape="rect" coords="4,4,190,51" href="camping.html"
    alt="Camping" />
<area shape="rect" coords="5,57,191,110" href="weather.html"
    alt="Weather" />
<area shape="rect" coords="4,112,191,165" href="clubs.html"
    alt="Clubs" />
<area shape="rect" coords="3,167,191,220" href="catalog.html"
    alt="Catalog" />
<area shape="rect" coords="3,222,191,277" href="contact.html"
    alt="Contact" />
```

Continued on next page

USING IMAGE MAPS AS NAVIGATION TOOLS IN FRAMED DOCUMENTS *(continued)*

```
<area shape="default" href="lefttoc1.html" alt="Contents" />
</map>
```

To force each area, except the last, to open in the main frame, add the `target="main"` attribute to each one, as in the following code:

```
<map name="frame-imagemap">
<area shape="rect" coords="4,4,190,51" href="camping.html"
   alt="Camping" target="main" />
<area shape="rect" coords="5,57,191,110" href="weather.html"
   alt="Weather" target="main" />
<area shape="rect" coords="4,112,191,165" href="clubs.html"
   alt="Clubs" target="main" />
<area shape="rect" coords="3,167,191,220" href="catalog.html"
   alt="Catalog" target="main" />
<area shape="rect" coords="3,222,191,277" href="contact.html"    alt="Contact"
   target="main" />
<area shape="default" href="lefttoc1.html" alt="Contents" />
</map>
```

Using Special Target Names

In addition to the target names that you define in `frame` elements within the frameset document, you can use other, special target names in all elements that link documents, such as `a`, `form`, and `area`. Table 7.3 explains these target names and their functions.

TABLE 7.3: SPECIAL TARGET NAMES

ATTRIBUTE VALUE	USE
target="…"	Sets the link to open in the frame named between the quotes.
target="_self"	Sets the link to open in the current frame.
target="_blank"	Sets the link to open in a new window.
target="_parent"	Sets the link to open in the parent frameset of the current document. If only one frameset is present, this removes the frameset.
target="_top"	Sets the link to open in the browser window, breaking out of all frames.

By using these special `target` attribute values, in any context, you control where the linked file appears. In general, you can keep the targets predictable and usable by following these guidelines:

◆ Keep your pages together. If you're linking a closely related page from your site, direct the link into an adjacent frame, not into a separate window, so your site remains visually cohesive.

◆ Keep your navigation content and regular content in a consistent location. If your navigation links appear in a frame that spans the top of the browser window, the content to which the objects in that frame link should appear in a different frame. Similarly, if a link within your Web content displays related content, use `target="_self"` to ensure that the link appears in the same window, because your users will expect content in that particular frame.

◆ Link to nonframed pages using `target="_top"` to ensure that your nonframed documents really aren't framed.

◆ Keep your pages visible. If you link to another site, use `target="_blank"` to open a new browser window for the other site, while keeping your window open and visible. That way, if your user tires of the other site, your site is still easily accessible.

◆ Don't frame other pages. By setting `target="_blank"` or `target="_top"` for external links, you can ensure that other people's content doesn't appear within your frames. Why? First, if you display content on your site that was created by someone else, that's potentially misleading at best, and copyright infringement at worst. Second, you don't necessarily want your site associated with content from another site. (See the sidebar "A Caution About Linking to Outside Sites" earlier in this chapter for more information.)

TIP *See Chapter 10 to learn how to keep your site from being framed by other sites.*

◆ Don't frame yourself. If your framed site includes an active link to the home page (likely the frameset document for the site), be sure that the link includes `target="_top"`. If you accidentally point the link to your main frameset into a frame within the site, your home page will appear within your home page within your home page and so on. See Figure 7.16 for an example.

FIGURE 7.16

Framing your own site, even accidentally, can look odd at best and completely silly at worst

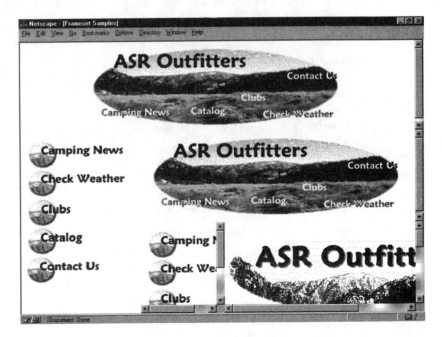

TIP A little creativity in `target` *attributes is a good thing, but a lot of creativity will either scare off users or entice them to click every link you have just to see where it goes.*

THE ORDER OF *target* ATTRIBUTES

If `target` attributes appear in more than one place—or don't appear at all—the order of precedence is as follows:

◆ No `target` attributes means that the link will appear in the same frame.

◆ Attributes in the base element apply to all links in the document.

◆ Attributes in a elements override the base element.

Creating Inline Frames

Inline frames, often called *floating frames,* appear as part of a document in much the same way that images appear in a document. They allow you to insert an HTML or XHTML document into an area within another document. In this sense, inline frames blend traditional documents with framed documents. At the time of writing, Internet Explorer 3 and higher, Netscape 6, Mozilla, and recent versions of Opera supported inline frames, which are part of the HTML 4 specification. Figure 7.17 shows a sample inline frame from an ASR Outfitters page.

The basic element you use for your inline frames is the `iframe` element, which identifies a floating frame's characteristics and initial content. Its attributes are listed and explained in Table 7.4.

TABLE 7.4: ATTRIBUTES OF THE `iframe` ELEMENT

ATTRIBUTE	DESCRIPTION
`src="url"`	Identifies the source for the frame content as a standard URL.
`name="…"`	Labels the frame so it can be targeted or referred to from other frames or windows.
`frameborder="n"`	Sets or removes borders around the frame.
`scrolling="…"`	Prohibits scroll bars (no), requires scroll bars (yes), or lets the browser provide scroll bars if required (auto, the default).
`marginheight="n"`	Sets the number of pixels in the margin above and below the content of the frame.
`marginwidth="n"`	Sets the number of pixels in the margin to the left and right of the frame.
`height="n"`	Specifies the height of an inline frame in pixels.
`width="n"`	Specifies the width of an inline frame in pixels.
`align="…"`	Specifies the alignment as left, middle, right, top, or bottom.

FIGURE 7.17

Inline frames can contain any HTML or XHTML document and can float within another document

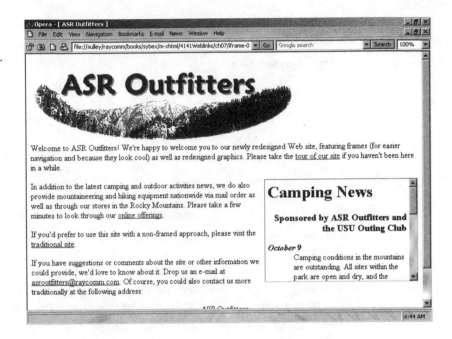

To add an inline frame to your document, start with a functional document:

```
<!DOCTYPE html PUBLIC "-//W3C//DTD XHTML 1.0 Frameset//EN"
    "http://www.w3.org/TR/xhtml1/DTD/xhtml1-frameset.dtd">
<html xmlns="http://www.w3.org/1999/xhtml">
<head>
    <title>Floating Frame Samples</title>
</head>
<body background="" bgcolor="FFFFFF" text="000000"
    link="0000FF" vlink="800080" alink="FF0000">
    <h1>Floating Frames</h1>
</body>
</html>
```

Now, follow these steps:

1. Add an iframe element pair:

```
<body background="" bgcolor="FFFFFF" text="000000"
    link="0000FF" vlink="800080" alink="FF0000">
    <h1>Floating Frames</h1>
    <iframe>
    </iframe>
</body>
```

2. Add the `name` attribute to the `iframe` element. Just as with traditional frames, the `name` attribute labels the frame so it can be targeted by links.

```
<iframe name="float1">
</iframe>
```

3. Add the `src` attribute to specify the document that will fill the frame. Technically, an image could also fill a frame, but that would rather defeat the purpose of a floating frame where a document can be placed.

```
<iframe src="z-maroon.html" name="float1">
</iframe>
```

4. Include the `height` and `width` attributes to specify the dimensions of the floating frame in pixels. These values are analogous to the `height` and `width` attributes for an image.

```
<iframe src="z-maroon.html" name="float1" height="200"
    width="300">
</iframe>
```

5. Provide alternate text to accommodate users using browsers that do not support inline frames. This text is similar to the `alt` text from images, except that you do not use an attribute–value pair here; just enter the alternate text between the `iframe` elements.

```
<iframe src="z-maroon.html" name="float1" height="200"
    width="300">
    Users of browsers without iframe support get to see this message.
</iframe>
```

6. Optionally, add an alignment attribute. Generally, you'll use either `left` or `right`, but any alignment attribute that you'd use with images will also work with floating frames.

```
<iframe src="z-maroon.html" name="float1" height="200"
    width="300" align="right">
    Users of browsers without iframe support get to see this message.
</iframe>
```

If you're using a browser that supports inline frames, you'll see something like Figure 7.18.

Because floating frames closely resemble images in the way they are implemented and manipulated within the parent document, you can often treat floating frames in similar ways. For example, you can arrange them within table cells to force a specific layout scheme. You can also wrap text around the floating frame just as you wrap text around an image, as ASR Outfitters did in Figure 7.17, earlier in this chapter.

Navigating in and among floating frames is similar to navigating in regular frames. The `name` and `target` attributes serve the same purposes, and you use them the same way whether you're dealing with inline frames or regular frames. For example, use the following code to force a document to appear in a floating frame:

```
<a href="z-blue" target="float1">Click to put the blue document
    in the floating frame.</a>
```

FIGURE 7.18

Floating frames can be visually interesting and make pages more attractive

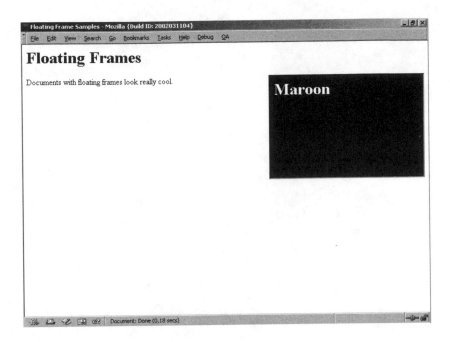

Where to Go from Here

In this chapter, you learned about frames—their uses, advantages, and disadvantages—and about how to include them in your documents. Keep in mind that not all browsers support frames, so use the guidelines throughout this chapter to determine when and how to include them effectively.

Also in this chapter, you learned how frames relate to other components. Following is a list of related information you might find useful:

- For information about computer and browser settings, see Chapter 1.

- For information about keeping up with standards, also refer to Chapter 1.

- For more information about URLs, see Chapter 3.

- To find out more about images and image maps, see Chapter 4.

- To read more about tables, see Chapter 5.

- To read more about accessibility and site usability issues, see Chapter 12.

Chapter 8

Converting HTML to XHTML

THE ODDS ARE THAT you already have a few (or many) HTML documents lying around. It may be that you want to do what we did: update your entire HTML site to XHTML. That doesn't mean that you have to start over from scratch.

Remember that XHTML uses the exact same elements and attributes as HTML (with the exception of adding the XHTML namespace, discussed in Chapter 22). This means that you don't have to change your vocabulary much; all you need to do is update your syntax. There are two ways you can do this: by hand or with the help of a tool.

This chapter covers the following topics:

◆ Understanding why you should convert your documents

◆ Converting your HTML documents by hand

◆ Converting your HTML documents using HTML Tidy

Why Convert Your Documents?

This seems to be the first question that comes out of a Web developer's mouth: "Why should I convert to XHTML?" Because the two languages use the same element set, and they should function the same in a browser, why would you want to take the time to convert them? Here are just a few of the reasons:

◆ Because XHTML is an application of XML, an XML processor can process XHTML.

◆ XHTML can be extended to include other document models (or vocabularies), including Scalable Vector Graphics (SVG), Synchronized Multimedia Integration Language (SMIL), Mathematical Markup Language (MathML), or even your own XML vocabulary.

◆ XHTML encourages the separation of style from structure, which can enable you to focus on content and design issues separately.

◆ XHTML promotes cleaner markup that will be easier for both a processor and a human to read.

♦ XHTML allows traditional HTML content developers and Web designers to continue using what they know, albeit in the framework of a more structured markup environment.

♦ Although many tool vendors have not yet caught on, most experts think it's just a matter of time before vendors big and small make mechanical validation part of their built-in editing processes.

♦ Current efforts on XHTML modularization (which breaks markup into categories, and lets each category be used independently of the others in documents) and related forms of XML-based markup—for instance, the work on XForms that's currently under way—promise to give XHTML documents access to capabilities that HTML does not (and will never) have. Over time, improved functionality will move the market simply because content developers will need the capabilities that other XML applications can deliver.

♦ More history and experience with XHTML and with the XHTML–XML connection are likely to demonstrate lower costs of ownership, maintenance, and development. If realized, these benefits will move the market inexorably in that direction.

♦ HTML won't be developed any further by the W3C except as new versions of XHTML; therefore, it's unlikely to be taken any further by browser vendors. (Browser vendors will most likely continue support for HTML, but they just won't develop additional support for new features.)

♦ Newer technologies will likely require XHTML, not HTML. For example, the wireless Internet industry requires XHTML and does not support HTML.

WARNING   *To reuse a bad cliché: If it ain't broke, don't fix it. If you have no direct benefits to be gained from converting to XHTML, and do not have a roadmap outlining how and why you need to change, don't. Perhaps make a point of developing XHTML documents in the future, but do not convert legacy documents just for the sake of converting.*

Converting Documents by Hand

If you're updating only a few documents, and you want to get some XHTML practice, you might choose to convert your HTML page to XHTML by hand. But you probably won't do more than one. There's no need to, because there's a wonderful free tool (HTML Tidy, discussed in the "Working with Tidy" section) that will do it for you in a jiffy. However, it's a good idea to understand what the tool is doing, so you can take advantage of its capabilities.

To understand what the tool is doing, let's take a look at what's involved in manual conversion.

Backward Compatibility

XHTML is backward compatible with browsers, meaning that it includes all the functionality that previous browsers accommodated. Keeping in mind that XHTML uses HTML's vocabulary, the only real obstacle that would prevent XHTML from compatibility with older browsers would be syntactic conventions. Lucky for us, XML syntax is close enough to SGML (and therefore HTML, because HTML was derived from SGML) that the syntactic differences are small.

TIP   See Chapter 21 for a broad discussion of many of the XML terms and concepts mentioned in this chapter.

In Chapter 1, you learned all the rules your XHTML document must follow, most of which were already defined by HTML. A few additions, such as closing all elements and adhering to an empty-element syntax, are new to XHTML. Whereas older browsers have very few problems processing XHTML documents, you need to abide by a few rules to avoid any problems, as you'll see in the next section.

The Rules

As an application of XML, XHTML requires that you follow XML's syntax requirements. These syntax requirements are similar to those followed by HTML and should be easy to get a handle on.

Although we discussed several of these rules in Chapter 1 (in the context of learning to type elements and attributes correctly), we'll discuss those and other rules here in the context of converting your HTML code to XHTML.

Terminate all elements.   All elements must be balanced with a closing element, or if considered empty, they should follow XML's empty-element syntax.

Use proper empty-element syntax.   Empty elements must also be terminated; however, as the document author, you have two options. You could add a closing end tag to balance the empty element; for example, `<br></br>`. However, because adding a closing tag doesn't seem logical, a shortened syntax was also defined—adding a trailing forward slash to the opening tag; for example, `<br />`. If you use the empty-element syntax (`<br />`), you have to add a white-space character before the trailing forward slash, for backward compatibility reasons.

Quote all attribute values.   All your attributes' values must be in quotation marks.

Give values for all attributes.   HTML allows for a handful of attributes that function as Boolean attributes, which stand alone, without a value. When one of these is present, it turns a function on. When the attribute is omitted, the function is not activated. Because XHTML follows XML's syntax rules, all attributes must have values, so the stand-alone attributes (formally known as examples of "attribute minimization") are no longer valid. The alternative is to set the attribute equal to itself, as in:

```
<input type="checkbox" checked="checked" />
```

Lowercase element and attribute names because XHTML is case sensitive.   The XML specification requires that XML documents obey the rules of an associated DTD, including naming conventions for elements and attributes. If the DTD defines all element and attribute names in lowercase, as developers we have to abide by that rule. Therefore, all XHTML elements and attributes must be lowercased, because the DTD defines them as lowercase. We also lowercase case-insensitive attribute values to be consistent.

Nest elements correctly.   Nesting elements correctly wasn't critical to HTML; however, it's a strict requirement for XHTML. Because elements must be balanced with an opening tag and a closing tag, it's necessary to be careful with nesting; it establishes element hierarchy and relationships.

TIP   There's an easy way to remember your nesting principles: What you open first, you must close last. Repeat that to yourself over and over and you will never forget how to nest again.

Include a DOCTYPE declaration. If you're adhering to one of the XHTML 1 DTDs, you can't use an HTML 4.01 DTD reference. When you're converting your document from HTML to XHTML, make sure that you're using the correct `DOCTYPE` declaration. For a listing of the three XHTML DTDs, see Chapter 2.

Add the XHTML namespace. XHTML makes use of XML namespaces to help uniquely identify its collection of elements and attributes. This is especially handy if you plan on mixing (embedding) other XML vocabularies. Namespaces are covered in Chapter 22; be sure to read more about namespaces if you haven't already. According to the XHTML specification, all XHTML documents must use the default XHTML namespace (`xmlns="http://www.w3.org/1999/xhtml"`). This namespace is required and must be defined within the `html` start element.

Use external style sheets and scripts. Use external style sheet or script documents, rather than embedding them in the head of your XHTML document. If you must use embedded scripts or style sheets, be sure that the internal syntax does not contain `<`, `&`, `]]>`, or `--`. See Chapters 9 and 10 for information about embedding style sheets and scripts in the document head, respectively.

Use white space carefully. Do not add line breaks or multiple white-space characters within attribute values. Many XML developers use line breaks to aid document readability, but browsers handle white space inconsistently, and multiple white-space characters can translate into problems when rendering XHTML documents. If you're going to use white space for readability, be sure you include it only between elements.

Mark internal references carefully. Use both the `name` and `id` attributes when referring to a document location that you use as an internal anchor (`#location`). The `name` attribute was originally used to refer to named anchors; however, HTML 4 deprecated this attribute and introduced the `id` attribute to replace it as a way to uniquely identify a given element. For future compatibility, you want to use the `id` attribute; however, because many current and older browsers don't support this attribute, you use the `name` attribute as well. For example:

```
<a name="one" id="one">…</a>
```

Summing It Up

Listing 8.1 is not a well-formed XHTML document, and we're going to make it one.

LISTING 8.1: SLOPPY HTML DOCUMENT

```
<HTML>
<HEAD>
<TITLE>Sloppy HTML</TITLE>
</HEAD>
<BODY>
<H1>Element Rules</H1>
<P><FONT COLOR=RED>Elements provide the structure that holds your document
together.</FONT>
<BR>
<OL COMPACT>
```

```
<LI>Close all elements.
<LI>Empty elements should follow empty-element syntax, and be sure to add the white
space for backward compatibility.
<LI>Convert all stand-alone attributes to attributes with values.
<LI>Add quotation marks to all attribute values.
<LI>Convert all uppercase element and attribute names to lowercase.
<LI>Use the appropriate DOCTYPE declaration.
<LI>Add the XHTML namespace to the html start tag.
<LI>Make sure you comply with any backward-compatible steps defined in the section
"Backward Compatibility."
</OL>
</BODY>
</HTML>
```

Follow these steps to make the document well formed:

1. Close all elements. Notice that the p element and none of the list item (1i) elements have closing tags, so add the closing p and 1i tags.

   ```
   <P><FONT COLOR=RED>Elements provide the structure that
   holds your document together.</FONT></P>
   <BR>
   <OL COMPACT>
   <LI>Close all elements.</LI>
   <LI>Empty elements should follow empty-element syntax.</LI>
   <LI>Convert all stand-alone attributes to attributes with
   values.</LI>
   <LI>Add quotation marks to all attribute values.</LI>
   <LI>Convert all uppercase element and attribute names to
   lowercase.</LI>
   <LI>Use the appropriate DOCTYPE declaration.</LI>
   <LI>Add the XHTML namespace to the html start tag.</LI>
   <LI>Make sure you comply with any backward-compatible steps
   defined in the section "Backward
   Compatibility."</LI>
   </OL>
   ```

2. Empty elements should follow empty-element syntax, and be sure to add the white space for backward compatibility. The BR element is the only empty element in this document. Change it to <BR />.

3. Convert all stand-alone attributes to attributes with values. Change COMPACT to COMPACT=COMPACT.

4. Add quotation marks to all attribute values:

   ```
   <P><FONT COLOR="RED">Elements provide the structure that
   holds your document together.</FONT></P>
   <BR>
   <OL COMPACT="COMPACT">
   ```

5. Convert all uppercase element and attribute names (and attribute values) to lowercase:

```
<html>
<head>
<title>Sloppy HTML</title>
</head>
<body>
<h1>Element Rules</h1>
<p><font color="red">Elements provide the structure that
holds your document together.</font></p>
<br />
<ol compact="compact">
<li>Close all elements.</li>
<li>Empty elements should follow empty-element syntax.</li>
<li>Convert all stand-alone attributes to attributes with
values.</li>...
```

6. Use the appropriate DOCTYPE declaration. We're going to use the Transitional DTD:

```
<!DOCTYPE html
 PUBLIC "-//W3C//DTD XHTML 1.0 Transitional//EN"
 "http://www.w3.org/TR/xhtml1/DTD/xhtml1-transitional.dtd">
```

7. Add the XHTML namespace to the html start element:

```
<html xmlns="http://www.w3.org/1999/xhtml">
```

8. Make sure you comply with any backward-compatible steps defined in the section "Backward Compatibility." Our document doesn't need any adjustments here.

TIP *To avoid browser confusion, use external script and style sheets when possible.*

Your resulting code should look like Listing 8.2.

LISTING 8.2: CLEAN XHTML DOCUMENT

```
<!DOCTYPE html PUBLIC "-//W3C//DTD XHTML 1.0 Transitional//EN"
   "http://www.w3.org/TR/xhtml1/DTD/xhtml1-transitional.dtd">
<html xmlns="http://www.w3.org/1999/xhtml">
  <head>
    <title>Sloppy HTML</title>
  </head>
  <body>
    <h1>Element Rules</h1>
    <p><font color="red">Elements provide the structure that
      holds your document together.</font></p>
    <br />
    <ol compact="compact">
      <li>Close all elements.</li>
      <li>Empty elements should follow empty-element syntax, and
```

```
      be sure to add the white space for backward
      compatibility.</li>
    <li>Convert all stand-alone attributes to attributes with
      values.</li>
    <li>Add quotation marks to all attribute values.</li>
    <li>Convert all uppercase element and attribute names to
      lowercase.</li>
    <li>Use the appropriate DOCTYPE declaration.</li>
    <li>Add the XHTML namespace to the html start tag.</li>
    <li>Make sure you comply with any backward-compatible
      steps defined in the section "Backward Compatibility."
      </li>
  </ol>
 </body>
</html>
```

In this listing, you'll notice that we indented the markup. We do this to make the markup easier to read.

WARNING *We don't recommend using the* font *element to define presentation. We recommend using Cascading Style Sheets (CSS) to define presentation style rules for your document. If your target audience uses Internet Explorer 5 or higher, we recommend you opt for CSS style rules. See Chapter 9 for more information about style sheets.*

Working with Tidy

HTML Tidy, a tool created by David Raggett, is the answer to any Web developer's problem in converting HTML to XHTML. Tidy, which has been around for a while, converts HTML documents into clean XHTML in a matter of seconds. In the beginning, it was designed to clean up HTML markup. Now, Tidy is included as a plug-in with most major HTML editors. In addition, Tidy comes in a version you can run from the command prompt and a GUI version (TidyGUI).

So, what exactly can Tidy do? Here are some examples:

Detects mismatched end tags   In most cases, Tidy will locate mismatched end tags and make the appropriate corrections.

Corrects incorrectly nested elements   In most cases, Tidy will correct nesting errors.

Locates misplaced elements   Tidy will alert the document author if an element is misused—for example, if the td element is nested within a form element.

Lowercases element and attribute names   Tidy will correct any uppercase element names and attribute names automatically.

Adds quotation marks to attribute values   Tidy will add double or single quotation marks around all attribute values (you can specify which).

Of course, these are just some examples of how Tidy can make the conversion process easier—much easier! You can also customize Tidy to do just about anything relating to the conversion process. For example, you can control whether the modified version uses indentation for nested elements, or you can request that Tidy invoke only some, but not all, of the rules. To learn more about HTML Tidy's many, many abilities and options, visit www.w3.org/People/Raggett/Tidy.

The markup shown in Listing 8.3 is the sloppy.htm document that we'll convert to clean XHTML. The clean markup that's produced by all methods discussed in the following sections is shown in Listing 8.4.

LISTING 8.3: SLOPPY HTML DOCUMENT

```
<HEAD>
<TITLE> RayComm, Inc., Consulting Services -- Home Page </TITLE>
<LINK REL=stylesheet HREF=techwhirl/includes/techwhirl.css type=text/css > </HEAD>
<BODY>
<A HREF=index.html><IMG SRC=http://www.raycomm.com/images/translogo.gif
NAME=logo WIDTH=219 HEIGHT=67 BORDER=0
ALT="RayComm Home Page" ></a>
<P> <IMG SRC=/images/bluebar.gif WIDTH=620 HEIGHT=3
    BORDER=0 ALT=------------------------------------- >
RayComm, Inc., provides technical communication and
technology consulting services to a variety of
clients from across the United States. From basic
computer information to product documentation (on
anything from computer hardware or software to heavy
equipment) to high-level Internet search service
consulting, we can help.
<P>
For more information:
<UL><LI> Learn more about our <A
HREF=consulting.html>consulting services</a>.
<LI> Check out some of the <A HREF=books.html>books
and articles</a> we've written, on everything
from UNIX to HTML and XHTML to adaptive
technologies.
<LI> <A HREF=contact.html>Contact us</a>
for more information about how we can help you.
</UL>
<P> <IMG BORDER=2
    SRC=http://www.raycomm.com/techwhirl/images/techwhirllogo.gif
    ALT="TECHWR-L Logo" align=right > RayComm, Inc.,
is the home of TECHWR-L, including both the TECHWR-L
mailing list for technical communicators and the <A
HREF=/techwhirl/>TECHWR-L Site</a>. Look here for
original articles and content, archives,
instructions, frequently asked questions, and likely
everything you wanted to know but were afraid to ask
about Techwhirl.
```

```
</P>
<BR clear=all> <HR> <P class=centered>
<A HREF=index.html>Home</a> | <A HREF=consulting.html>Consulting</a> |
   <A HREF=portfolio.html>Portfolio</a> | <A HREF=faqs.html>FAQs</a> |
   <A HREF=/techwhirl/index.html>TECHWR-L Site</a>
<BR>
 <A HREF=aboutraycomm.html>About RayComm, Inc.</a>
| <A HREF=contact.html>Contact Information</a>
</P>
<P class=centered>
Last modified on 1 April, 2002
<BR>
 Site contents Copyright &copy; 1997 - 2002 RayComm,
Inc.
<BR>
 Send comments to <A
HREF=mailto:webmaster@raycomm.com>webmaster@raycomm.com</a>.
</P>

</BODY>
</HTML>
```

LISTING 8.4: CLEAN XHTML VERSION PRODUCED BY HTML TIDY

```
<!DOCTYPE html PUBLIC "-//W3C//DTD XHTML 1.0 Transitional//EN"
    "http://www.w3.org/TR/xhtml1/DTD/xhtml1-transitional.dtd">
<html xmlns="http://www.w3.org/1999/xhtml">
  <head>
    <title>RayComm, Inc., Consulting Services -- Home
    Page</title>
    <link rel="stylesheet"
    href="techwhirl/includes/techwhirl.css" type="text/css" />
  </head>

  <body>
        <a href="index.html"><img
         src="http://www.raycomm.com/images/translogo.gif"
         name="logo" width="219" height="67" border="0"
         alt="RayComm" /></a>
        <p><img src="/images/bluebar.gif" width="620"
         height="3" border="0"
         alt="------------------------------------" /> RayComm,
         Inc., provides technical communication and technology
         consulting services to a variety of clients from across
         the United States. From basic computer information to
```

```
product documentation (on anything from computer
hardware or software to heavy equipment) to high-level
Internet search service consulting, we can help.</p>

<p>For more information:</p>

<ul>
  <li>
    <p>Learn more about our <a
    href="consulting.html">consulting services</a>.</p>
  </li>

  <li>
    <p>Check out some of the <a href="books.html">books
    and articles</a> we've written, on everything from
    UNIX to HTML and XHTML to adaptive
    technologies.</p>
  </li>

  <li>
    <a href="contact.html">Contact us</a>
    <p>for more information about how we can help
    you.</p>
  </li>
</ul>

<p><img border="2"
 src="/techwhirl/images/techwhirllogo.gif"
 alt="TECHWR-L" align="right" /> RayComm,
Inc., is the home of TECHWR-L, including both the
TECHWR-L mailing list for technical communicators and
the <a href="/techwhirl/">TECHWR-L Site</a>. Look here
for original articles and content, archives,
instructions, frequently asked questions, and likely
everything you wanted to know but were afraid to ask
about Techwhirl.</p>

<br clear="all" />
<hr />

<p class="centered"><a href="index.html">Home</a> | <a
href="consulting.html">Consulting</a> | <a
href="portfolio.html">Portfolio</a> | <a
href="faqs.html">FAQs</a> | <a
href="/techwhirl/index.html">TECHWR-L Site</a>
<br />
 <a href="aboutraycomm.html">About RayComm, Inc.</a> |
<a href="contact.html">Contact Information</a></p>
<p class="centered">Last modified on 1 April, 2002
```

```
      <br />
       Site contents Copyright &copy; 1997 - 2002 RayComm,
      Inc.
      <br />
       Send comments to <a href="mailto:webmaster@raycomm.com">
       webmaster@raycomm.com</a>.</p>
  </body>
</html>
```

To help you learn how to work with Tidy, we've included three final sections in this chapter. Determine which computing environment you're using, then skip to the appropriate section:

Working Via	Read This Section
Command line (Windows or Linux/Unix)	"Using Tidy from the Command Prompt"
Windows	"Using TidyGUI" or "Using Tidy in HTML-Kit"
Macintosh	"Using Tidy on the Mac"

Using Tidy from the Command Prompt

If you are a Linux/Unix user, you may be comfortable using Tidy as a stand-alone tool at the command prompt. Windows users who want a traditional Windows interface should skip forward to the sections "Using TidyGUI" or "Using Tidy in HTML-Kit." Macintosh users need to jump ahead to the "Using Tidy on the Mac" section.

Before we get started with this mini tutorial, download the appropriate version of HTML Tidy from the Web, if necessary, at `tidy.sourceforge.net`.

TIP   If you want to use the Windows/DOS command-line version of Tidy, you'll have to download it. If you use Linux/Unix, it might already be installed as `/usr/bin/tidy` or `/usr/local/bin/tidy`.

Select the appropriate version for your environment. After you have Tidy on your system (you'll probably have to unzip the files after you download them, using whatever tools you customarily use), you're ready to begin:

TIP   To fire up the DOS prompt, select Start ➤ Programs ➤ Command Prompt or MS-DOS Prompt, depending on your version of Windows. (You might need to go to Start ➤ Programs ➤ Accessories ➤ Command Prompt or MS-DOS Prompt.)

Tidy allows you to point to an HTML document and use commands to convert the document. To do this, you need an HTML document to work with. We'll use the document shown in Listing 8.3, and we'll assume the document to be converted has a filename of `sloppy.htm`.

To convert your document to XHTML using Tidy, follow these steps:

1. If you're using Windows, you might enter the following command at the Windows command prompt:

   ```
   c:\tidy\tidy -asxhtml c:\XHTML\sloppy.htm > c:\XHTML\clean.htm
   ```

The above command breaks down as follows:

`tidy`	Calls the Tidy program from its location in the `tidy` folder on drive C.
`-asxhtml`	Tells Tidy to convert the HTML document to XHTML.
`-i`	Tells Tidy to indent the output so it is easier to read.
`c:\XHTML\sloppy.htm`	Specifies the location of the sloppy HTML document that needs to be converted. (Substitute whatever drive, path, and folder your document is in.)
`c:\XHTML\clean.htm`	Specifies the location of the clean HTML document to be created. (Substitute whatever drive, path, and folder your new document should be in.)

2. If you're using Linux/Unix (including a MacOS X shell prompt), you might enter something like the following command:

`/usr/local/bin/tidy -asxhtml /home/jdoe/sloppy.htm > /home/jdoe/clean.htm`

The above command breaks down as follows:

`/usr/local/bin/tidy`	Calls the Tidy program.
`-asxhtml`	Tells Tidy to convert the HTML document to XHTML.
`-i`	Tells Tidy to indent the output so it is easier to read.
`/home/jdoe/sloppy.htm`	Defines the location of the sloppy HTML document that needs to be converted. (Substitute whatever path your document is currently in.)
`/home/jdoe/clean.htm`	Specifies the location of the clean HTML document to be created. (Substitute whatever path your new document should be in.)

3. After you enter this command, the `sloppy.htm` document will be replaced with a cleaner XHTML version. The cleaned-up version of our example document is shown in Listing 8.4.

TIP   Add `-m` after the Tidy command (as in `c:\tidy\tidy.exe -m` or `/usr/local/bin/tidy -m`) to tell Tidy to convert the document in its current location and therefore modify the original document rather than save the clean version into a separate file. Make sure you have a backup before you do this—the results aren't always perfect.

TIP   Check out the documentation and instructions on the Tidy Web pages to see what else you can do with Tidy at the command line. With little effort, you can customize the formatting of your clean file and make other changes as well.

Using TidyGUI

Many of you might not be inspired by the command prompt. In fact, you may want to run from it. And some of you may not want to download another text editor. If you're interested in using a GUI interface for Tidy but don't want a full text editor attached, André Blavier has created a version that you just might get along with.

This GUI version of Tidy is easy to use. Take a look at the TidyGUI interface shown in Figure 8.1.

FIGURE 8.1

The TidyGUI main window, configuration settings, and output

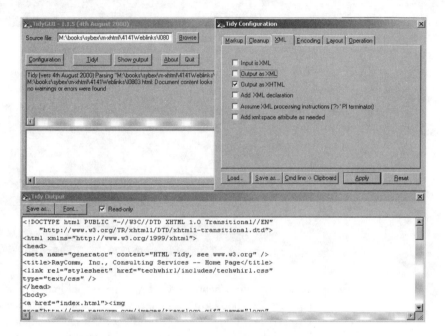

You simply browse for the file you want to Tidy by clicking the Browse button and then click the Tidy! button. After that, you click the Show Output button and save the Tidied output to a new document to save it as your own. To read more about this version, visit `http://perso.wanadoo.fr/ablavier/TidyGUI/`.

Using Tidy in HTML-Kit

Windows users who don't like to work from the command prompt can also use HTML Tidy in a GUI interface, as a part of HTML-Kit. HTML-Kit is a free text editor that allows you to use predefined templates for HTML documents, and it can do anything a snazzy text editor can do. However, in addition to helping you create HTML documents, it uses HTML Tidy to convert HTML documents to XHTML. There's no extra download needed; all you have to do is download HTML-Kit (from `www.chami.com/html-kit/`) and Tidy comes as a part of the package.

NOTE *The download size of HTML-Kit is significantly larger than the download size of both* `tidy.exe` *and TidyGUI.*

After you've downloaded and installed HTML-Kit, open it to see what its interface looks like. Figure 8.2 shows the main HTML-Kit interface (with a new document open).

FIGURE 8.2

HTML-Kit's interface

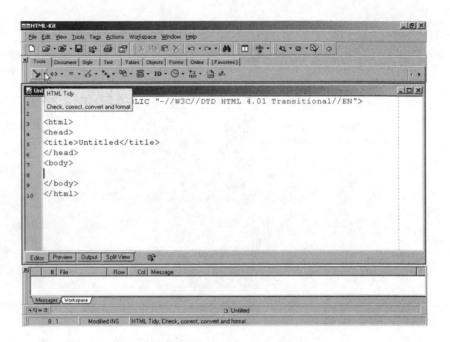

To convert all your documents to XHTML, you should customize the conversion options. Select Edit ➤ Preferences and choose the Tidy tab shown in Figure 8.3. Make sure the Output says XHTML, and feel free to browse through and adjust other options as well (we like having Tidy indent the output for better legibility). After you customize the conversion options, you just click the HTML Tidy icon (the little broom-like icon at the top-left corner of the window) and your document will be converted to XHTML.

FIGURE 8.3

The Tidy tab of the HTML-Kit Preferences

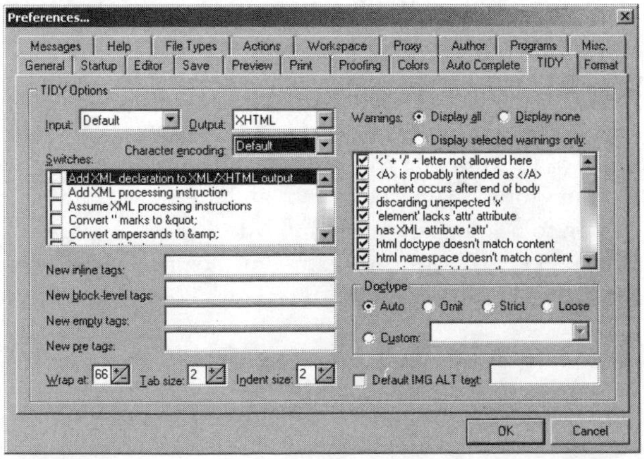

Now, let's convert a document (for example, Listing 8.3) to XHTML using HTML-Kit. Follow these steps:

1. Select File ➤ Open File and find the document.

2. Click the HTML Tidy icon. Alternatively, you could select the down arrow next to the HTML Tidy icon shown in Figure 8.2 and select Convert To XHTML from the drop-down menu. The new output (Listing 8.4) appears on the right side of the screen, and any errors found in the document appear at the bottom of the screen (see Figure 8.4).

FIGURE 8.4

Tidy has cleaned up this document, all within HTML-Kit

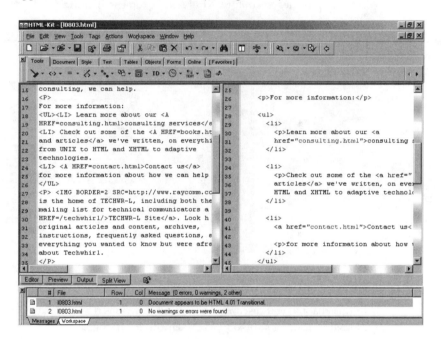

3. If you want to replace the old HTML document with the new XHTML document, right-click in the right window and select Copy Output To Editor from the shortcut menu.

4. Select File ➤ Save, and click the Editor tab at the bottom of the window to continue modifying your document, or just to see the XHTML in all its glory.

Using Tidy on the Mac

Tidy support for the Mac has been around for a while. There are several options for Mac users, all of which are described and available for download at the Tidy for Mac OS site:

www.geocities.com/SiliconValley/1057/tidy.html

One of the possibilities is comparable to the TidyGUI application for Windows: It's called MacTidy. In fact, TidyGUI was based on MacTidy. However, the most common way to use Tidy with the Mac is to download a plug-in for BBEdit.

TIP   *BBEdit is one of the premier text editors for Macintosh Web developers and can be found at* www.barebones.com.

Download the HTML Tidy plug-in from the Tidy for Mac OS page listed earlier. After you've downloaded the StuffIt file that contains the plug-in, copy the BBTidy plug-in to the BBEdit Plug-ins folder. After the installation is complete, you can convert your first XHTML document.

To start the conversion process, make sure you have an HTML document (Listing 8.3, for example) open in BBEdit, select Tools ➤ Tidy HTML, and BBEdit will begin to work its magic (see Figure 8.5). You will be presented with two documents, one that documents the errors and warning messages and one that provides the output XHTML document (Listing 8.4, for example).

FIGURE 8.5

Selecting HTML
Tidy from the
BBEdit Tools menu

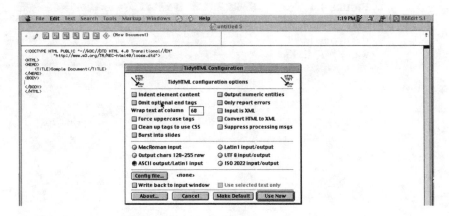

Where to Go from Here

In this chapter, you discovered the possible reasons that you may want or need to convert existing HTML documents to XHTML. Remember, of course, that if you don't have a specific reason to convert your documents, don't. Instead, try your hand at using XHTML in subsequent documents you create.

From here, you might visit these other parts and chapters:

- Review Chapters 1 and 2 for information about correctly typing and applying HTML and XHTML elements and attributes.

- Move on to Part III to find out about using style sheets, using JavaScript, and including multimedia.

- See Part IV for extensive information, guidelines, and advice for using HTML and XHTML to develop Web sites.

- See Part VI for information about XML.

- See Chapter 22 for information about namespaces and to learn how to use them to extend your XHTML documents.

Part 3

Moving Beyond Pure HTML and XHTML

Chapter 9

Using Style Sheets

USING CASCADING STYLE Sheets (CSS) is one of the best ways to format HTML and XHTML documents easily and consistently. Style sheets are a major step toward separating presentation from content, allowing the document to specify structure and content, yet giving you almost total control over page presentation. The latest CSS recommendation adds even more control, including aural style sheets for screen-reading software, more options for formatting printed documents from the Web, and options for relative and absolute positioning.

Are style sheets here to stay? Yes. In fact, the HTML 4.01 and XHTML 1.0 specifications deprecate formatting elements and attributes (such as the `font` element and the `align` attribute) in favor of style sheets, as we've noted in many places throughout this book.

In this chapter, you'll see how style sheets enhance the effectiveness of HTML and XHTML and how you can benefit from using them. We'll discuss the advantages and limitations of style sheets to help you decide whether they're right for your needs. And, of course, you'll find out how to implement them. To give you a solid foundation in the use of style sheets, we'll discuss the following topics in this chapter; see Master's Reference Part 2 for a complete reference of style sheet options:

◆ Understanding style sheets

◆ Applying style sheets to documents

◆ Developing style sheets

◆ Setting properties: type, box, color, background, lists

◆ Setting properties: aural, printing, positioning

How Do Style Sheets Work?

As we mentioned in Chapter 1, HTML and XHTML are markup languages that you use to identify structural elements in a document. For example, you can specify that one element is a first-level heading, one is a bullet point, one is a block quotation, and so on, by manually inserting formatting elements and attributes. Inserting these elements every place they occur can quickly become a tedious process. With style sheets, however, you specify formatting once, and it's applied throughout the document. If you've used styles in a word processor, you're familiar with this concept.

Style sheets—formally known as the World Wide Web Consortium (W3C) *Cascading Style Sheets Recommendations*—promise to give you layout and format control similar to what you may be accustomed to in programs such as PageMaker or Quark. You can control how page elements look, where they appear, their color and size, the fonts they use, and so on, and do so without awkward workarounds. Now, you can determine page appearance to a far greater extent than was possible before.

WARNING *Before you decide to use style sheets, keep in mind that the newest browsers support most of the features of CSS level 1 and that the existing support for CSS level 2 is sketchy. Current versions of Microsoft Internet Explorer (5 and later), Netscape Navigator (6 and later), and Opera (5 and later) browsers offer very good style sheet support (CSS level 1); however, many style sheet features do not work consistently or at all in earlier browser versions. Version 6 browsers generally offer support for many, but not all, features of CSS2.*

WARNING *Regardless of style sheet support, remember that your users can override your settings at any time and use their own style sheets. HTML or XHTML, in any form, cannot ensure that your visitors see exactly what you want them to see. For that, you will have to use Adobe Acrobat PDF (Portable Document Format) files (***www.adobe.com***), which maintain the document formatting you set.*

BROWSERS, USERS, AND STYLE SHEETS

Style sheets were introduced in Internet Explorer 3, Netscape Navigator 4, and Opera 3. In the very unlikely event that you have visitors using these browsers or even older ones, they may experience unexpected formatting glitches, or, in the case of older browsers, see just plain documents that include little more than the logical formatting elements, such as headings, paragraphs, tables, and lists. Very few people use browsers without good style sheet support (at least CSS level 1), however.

The latest browsers (IE 6, Netscape 6, and Opera 5) all come close to supporting Web standards, including CSS1 and some elements of CSS2. Support for Web standards allows Web developers more potential for a consistent appearance of Web pages in different browsers and on different platforms.

Also, your users still have final control over the document appearance, regardless of the formatting you supply in the style sheet. They can disable style sheets or override them with their personal preferences for colors and fonts. This rarely happens, but it is possible. CSS2 offers additional support for users, including the capability for users to override the designer's style sheets. This is a very important part of making the Web more accessible to users with disabilities, and we can expect more emphasis on users' needs as CSS and the Web develop. See Chapter 12 for more information about making your documents accessible to people with visual impairments.

Some Advantages of Using Style Sheets

In addition to giving you more control over how your documents appear to users, style sheets let you manage documents more easily than if they were filled with formatting elements. When you place formatting markup in the style sheet, your HTML or XHTML document is less cluttered.

Style sheets also reduce the time you spend developing and maintaining documents. Rather than manually formatting paragraphs of text, you simply change the style definition in one place—the style sheet—and the style sheet applies the definition to all occurrences in the document. No muss, no fuss.

Finally, style sheets give you flexibility from document to document within a Web site. Even if you set up a style sheet that applies to all pages in the site, you can set up individual style sheets to apply to individual documents. The individual style sheet overrides the global one. In addition, you can further tweak individual style sheets to accommodate special text formatting, such as a document in which certain paragraphs should appear in a different color.

Cascading Style Sheets Level 1

Cascading Style Sheets level 1 (CSS1) introduced extensive style properties for many features of page layout and text presentation. The CSS1 Recommendation was adopted by the W3C in December 1996 and revised in January 1999. The CSS1 style properties include the following:

- Font properties, including expanded options for setting font size and other font features

- Text properties, including text alignment and decoration

- Box properties, such as margins, padding, borders, and floating elements

- Color and background properties, including background repeat options and background color for elements

- Classification properties, including styles for displaying lists

All of these properties are covered in detail in various sections in this chapter.

TIP   *The W3C CSS1 recommendation is available online at* **www.w3.org/TR/REC-CSS1**.

Cascading Style Sheets Level 2

The *CSS2* recommendation was adopted in May 1998. This recommendation builds on the features included in CSS1 and adds new style properties, including the following:

- Media types and properties, including aural style sheets and printed media

- Positioning properties, such as absolute, relative, and fixed positioning

- Downloadable fonts

- Table style properties

- Additional box properties, including new box types

- Visual formatting model, including properties for overflow, clipping, and visibility

- Generated content, used to import content from another Web location

- Text shadows

- System colors

- Cursor styles

The only features of CSS2 that have widespread support as of this writing (and only in newer browsers) are the positioning properties and some of the changes in CSS selectors. (For more on selectors, see "Developing a Style Sheet" later in this chapter.) Aural style sheets and printed media properties (even though they're not yet supported), and CSS positioning are discussed in detail later in this chapter.

TIP   The W3C CSS2 recommendation is available online at www.w3.org/TR/REC-CSS2.

Cascading Style Sheets Level 3 and Beyond

Although CSS2 has very limited support in current browsers, CSS3 is being developed. Unlike previous versions of CSS, CSS3 is being developed as individual modules (much as XHTML is evolving into a modularized approach, as we discuss in Chapter 25). This will make it easier for browsers to support CSS3 on a module-by-module basis, easier for updates in individual modules, and easier for users, Web designers, and Web developers to easily figure out which modules are supported in a particular browser. While there will be more modules to manage with this approach, each module will provide a specific kind of functionality, and (presumably) browsers will use some intelligence in their handling of the various modules.

CSS3 is still in Working Draft form, but some of the modules currently being developed are:

◆ User-interface enhancements for dynamic and interactive features

◆ Scalable Vector Graphics (SVG)

◆ Behavioral extensions (adding the ability to attach dynamic script actions to elements)

◆ Expanded accessibility features

◆ International layout properties

◆ Multicolumn layout

Future additions to CSS will most likely include further accessibility properties, enhanced multimedia support, and expanded dynamic and interactive capabilities.

TIP   For information on all the types of style sheets, including the advanced Extensible Stylesheet Language (XSL), check out the W3C's style site at www.w3.org/Style.

Implementing Style Sheets

As you're perusing the rest of this chapter, remember that your documents and the associated style sheets work as a team. HTML or XHTML documents carry the content, and style sheets carry the formatting information. As you'll see, developing style sheets is a two-part process:

1. You associate (or connect) a style sheet with the document.

2. You develop a style sheet's contents, complete with all the formatting information.

TIP   After you become familiar with creating style sheets, you may create the style sheet first and then associate it with an XHTML document. However, for instructing purposes, it makes more sense for us to tell you how to associate the (as yet nonexistent) style sheet first, so you can test the style sheet as you develop it later in the chapter.

Associating Style Sheets with Documents

You can associate style sheets with your HTML or XHTML documents in four ways:

◆ You can embed the style sheet in the document by defining it between the opening and closing head elements.

◆ You can store the style sheet in a separate document and either link to it or import it.

◆ You can apply style definitions to specified parts of the document.

◆ You can use inline style definitions.

Embedding the Style Sheet in the Document

Embedding the style sheet is the easiest of the four methods of associating it with your HTML or XHTML documents. To embed a style sheet, you use the style element, along with style information, between the opening and closing head elements.

Embedding style sheets makes developing styles easy because you have to work with only one document—instead of working with a style sheet document and an HTML or XHTML document. You simply open the document and adjust the style sheet code. If you're working with multiple documents or documents that you update frequently, however, you have to adjust the style sheet in every document if you use the internal style sheet. We recommend using the external style sheet method instead unless a specific document has formatting that applies only to it.

TIP   After you develop an embedded style sheet, consider moving the style definitions to a different file and using an external style sheet. This will make it easier to apply the same styles to multiple documents.

To embed a style sheet in a document, you'll apply the items shown in Table 9.1 between the opening and closing head elements.

TABLE 9.1: STYLE SHEET CODE COMPONENTS

ITEM	TYPE	DESCRIPTION
style	Element	Specifies the style sheet area within a document. Within this section, you can define or import formatting.
<!--…-->	Comment markup	Hides style sheet contents from non-style-capable browsers.
type="text/css"	Attribute of style	Specifies the type of style sheet; required.

To embed a minimal style sheet in an existing document, follow these steps:

1. Start with a functional document header.

```
<!DOCTYPE html PUBLIC "-//W3C//DTD XHTML 1.0 Strict//EN"
    "http://www.w3.org/TR/xhtml1/DTD/xhtml1-strict.dtd">
<html xmlns="http://www.w3.org/1999/xhtml">
<head>
    <title>Embedded Style</title>
</head>
</html>
```

> *TIP* *Choose an appropriate DTD for your document, just as you usually would. Theoretically, you could use the Strict DTD in a document that contains style sheets, because the Transitional DTD allows formatting elements and the purpose of style sheets is to avoid using them. However, realistically, the Transitional DTD will meet most needs well.*

2. Add opening and closing `style` elements as well as the `type` attribute:

```
<head>
   <title>Embedded Style</title>
   <style type="text/css">
   </style>
</head>
```

3. Add the comment markup (`<!--...-->`), within the `style` element, to hide the contents from non–style-capable browsers.

```
<head>
   <title>Embedded Style</title>
   <style type="text/css">
      <!--
      -->
   </style>
</head>
```

Browsers that do not support style sheets ignore the `style` element but display the text that appears between them. Adding comment markup within the `style` elements ensures that the styles will not appear as content in older or less-capable browsers.

4. Add style definitions within the comment markup. In this (minimal) example, we specify that the paragraph text is red.

```
<head>
   <title>ASR Outfitters</title>
   <style type="text/css">
      <!--
         p {color: red}
      -->
   </style>
</head>
```

5. Add a `body` element, a `p` element, and content for the `p` element, and you're ready to test your embedded style.

```
<!DOCTYPE html PUBLIC "-//W3C/DTD XHTML 1.0 Strict//EN"
   "http://www.w3.org/TR/xhtml1/DTD/xhtml1-strict.dtd">
<html xmlns="http://www.w3.org/1999/xhtml">
<head>
   <title>Embedded Style</title>
   <style type="text/css">
      <!--
         p {color: red}
      -->
```

```
        </style>
    </head>
    <body>
        <p>This paragraph uses an embedded style.</p>
    </body>
</html>
```

That's it! To test your embedded style sheet, save this markup, and open the document in your favorite browser.

Storing Style Sheets Separately

A separate style sheet (an *external style sheet*) is simply a plain-text file, saved with a `.css` file extension, that includes style definitions. You should develop an external style sheet any time you're working with several documents that share some similar formatting. In this case, you develop a single style sheet and apply it to all the documents, as shown in Figure 9.1. You can then make formatting changes in all the documents simultaneously by simply changing the external style sheet.

FIGURE 9.1

When you develop a separate style-sheet, you can easily apply styles to many XHTML documents

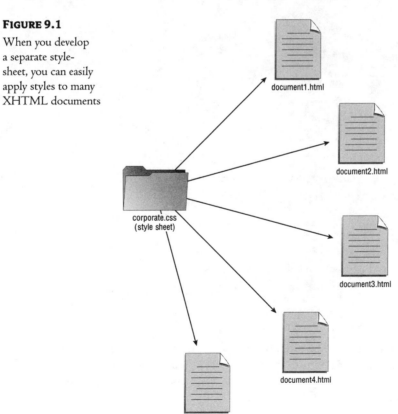

TIP   *Even if you're only working with a few documents, consider developing an external style sheet. You never know how many documents your site will eventually include.*

After you develop the external style sheet document, you associate it with the document(s) using one of two methods: importing or linking.

IMPORTING A STYLE SHEET

This method is handy when you're developing multiple style sheets, each with a particular function. For example, as illustrated in Figure 9.2, you can develop a page that applies corporate styles, one that applies styles for your department, and another that specifies particular document formatting. Rather than wading through a 10-page style sheet, you work with multiple smaller ones.

TIP   *Importing style sheets only works well in some browsers. To find out which browsers currently support importing (as well as other CSS properties), check the most current version of the style sheet Reference Guide Master Grid at* `www.webreview.com/style/css1/charts/mastergrid.shtml`.

FIGURE 9.2

Importing allows you to easily maintain a detailed style sheet

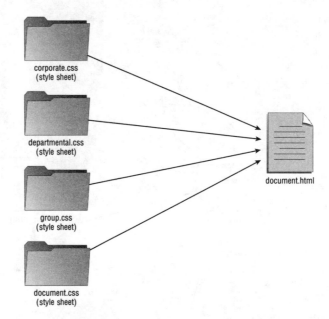

You import a style sheet by inserting an `@import` statement within the `style` element inside the comment delimiters. The syntax for these imports is `@import url(…)`, with the URL of the imported style sheet inside the parentheses.

To import a style sheet, follow these steps:

1. Start with a complete style block, such as the following code:

```
<!DOCTYPE html PUBLIC "-//W3C/DTD XHTML 1.0 Strict//EN"
    "http://www.w3.org/TR/xhtml1/DTD/xhtml1-strict.dtd">
```

```
<html xmlns="http://www.w3.org/1999/xhtml">
<head>
   <title>Imported Style</title>
   <style type="text/css">
      <!--
      -->
   </style>
</head>
```

2. Within a style block or style sheet, add a line similar to the following (substitute the name of your CSS file for red.css):

```
<style type="text/css">
   <!--
      @import url(red.css);
   -->
</style>
```

WARNING   *If you're using* @import *in addition to other embedded style properties,* @import *must always be the first style declaration listed, followed by any additional* @import *declarations, and then followed by the additional style declarations.*

A complete style block that does nothing but import two style sheets (red.css and blue.css) would look like the following:

```
<style type="text/css">
   <!--
      @import url(red.css);
      @import url(blue.css);
   -->
</style>
```

WARNING   *Currently,* @import *offers no advantages over the link method, which is explained in the following section and is supported in almost all browsers that support style sheets. Therefore, we recommend the link method.*

LINKING A STYLE SHEET

This method has a distinct advantage over the other methods: it gives users a choice of style sheets to use for a specific page. For example, you can link one style sheet to a page for users who will read on screen and link a different style sheet to the same page for users who will print, as shown in Figure 9.3. Theoretically, you could even develop a style sheet (since browsers implement this functionality) optimized for aural presentation.

Although you can import a style sheet, linking the style sheet is a better long-term choice because future browser versions should offer users more flexibility in handling style sheets, including the option to select from multiple style sheets. Importing offers no choices—it just loads the style sheet. Table 9.2 explains the elements and attributes you use to link style sheets to documents.

FIGURE 9.3

Linking lets you apply style sheets for specific uses

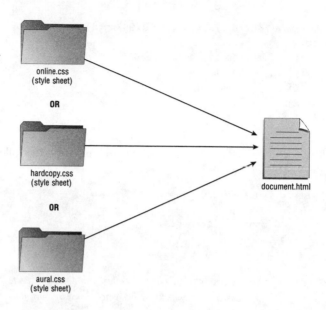

online.css
(style sheet)

OR

hardcopy.css
(style sheet)

OR

aural.css
(style sheet)

document.html

TABLE 9.2: ELEMENTS AND ATTRIBUTES FOR LINKING STYLE SHEETS

ITEM	TYPE	DESCRIPTION
link	Empty element	References a style sheet.
href="url"	Attribute of link	Identifies the style sheet source as a standard URL.
rel="stylesheet"	Attribute of link	Specifies that the referenced file is a style sheet.
title="…"	Attribute of link	Names the style sheet. Unnamed style sheets are always applied; named style sheets are applied by default or provided as options, depending on the rel attribute used.
type="text/css"	Attribute of link	Specifies the type of the style sheet.

To link a style sheet to a document, follow these steps:

1. Start with a complete head section, such as the following code:

```
<!DOCTYPE html PUBLIC "-//W3C/DTD XHTML 1.0 Strict//EN"
    "http://www.w3.org/TR/xhtml1/DTD/xhtml1-strict.dtd">
<html xmlns="http://www.w3.org/1999/xhtml">
<head>
    <title>Linked Style</title>
</head>
```

2. Add the link empty element:

```
<head>
    <title>Linked Style</title>
```

```
    <link />
</head>
```

3. Specify the `rel` and `type` values of `stylesheet` and `text/css`, respectively, to link to a standard style sheet:

```
<link rel="stylesheet" type="text/css" />
```

4. Specify the address of the style sheet with the `href` attribute. Specify either a relative URL, as in the sample code, or an absolute URL.

```
<link rel="stylesheet" href="blue.css" type="text/css" />
```

There you go! To link your document to more than one style sheet, simply include multiple `link` elements, complete with each of the style sheets to which they link. For example, you might link a document to a generic style sheet that contains basic style definitions and then also link it to a more specific style sheet that contains definitions suitable to a particular style of document—instructions, marketing, and so on. If you link to multiple style sheets, all take effect. However, if you define the same element in multiple sheets, the later links override the previous links.

The HTML and XHTML specifications indicate that you can also link your documents to optional style sheets using the `rel="alternate stylesheet"` attribute so that users can choose which styles to use. Theoretically, you can provide optional style sheets that, for instance, let users choose a low-bandwidth style for viewing over a modem connection or a high-bandwidth style with lots of cool images for viewing over a high-speed connection. Or you can present choices for high-resolution and high-color-depth monitors and provide alternatives for standard monitors at lower color depths. However, at the time of writing, no browsers support optional style sheets.

Applying Style Sheets to Parts of Documents

So far, you've seen how to apply style sheets to entire documents. You can also apply styles included in a style sheet to specific parts of documents, as shown in Figure 9.4. This is called applying *style classes*, which you define in your style sheet. For example, suppose you specify in a style sheet that the first line of all paragraphs should be indented. You may find that paragraphs after a bulleted list should not be indented because they continue the information from the paragraph before the list. To address this issue, you can manually format the paragraph for this occurrence. However, a better solution is to set up a new paragraph element class within your style definition, called, for example, `continue`. You can use this new paragraph class whenever the first line of a paragraph should not be indented. Table 9.3 describes the elements and attributes you use to apply classes.

FIGURE 9.4

Applying style classes, you can specify how parts of XHTML documents appear.

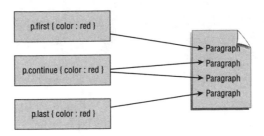

TABLE 9.3: ELEMENTS AND ATTRIBUTES FOR APPLYING CLASSES

ITEM	TYPE	DESCRIPTION
div	Element	Holds style attributes and applies them to the code between the opening and closing elements. Surround paragraphs or other block-level elements with these.
span	Element	Holds style attributes and applies them to the code between the opening and closing elements. Surround letters, words, and other inline elements with these elements.
class="…"	Attribute of various elements	References a style class to apply to a specified part of a document.
id="…"	Attribute of various elements	Specifies a unique name associated with a specific style definition. You can use this only once within a style sheet.

You can apply a class to an existing HTML or XHTML element, or you can use the div and span elements to specify that the class applies to other elements—such as specific letters or words—not individually specified by an HTML or XHTML element.

APPLYING CLASSES TO AN ELEMENT

You apply a class to an existing element—such as p, h1, ul, and so on—to specify formatting for a group of items. To apply classes within an HTML or XHTML document, follow these steps:

1. Start with an existing paragraph within a document.

```
<p>Many people buy ASR products despite the higher
    cost.</p>
```

2. Add the class attribute to the opening p element, like this:

```
<p class="">Many people buy ASR products despite the higher
    cost.</p>
```

3. Add the name of the paragraph class. (You'll see how to define and name classes when you develop the style sheet later in this chapter.)

```
<p class="continue">Many people buy ASR products despite
    the higher cost.</p>
```

That's it!

If you have a specific unique formatting need—a one-time per document need—you can define a style ID and then apply the id attribute in place of the class attribute in the preceding example. You would end up with something like this:

```
<p id="538fv1">Many people buy ASR products despite the higher
    cost.</p>
```

APPLYING CLASSES TO OTHER DOCUMENT PARTS

You can also apply classes to specific parts of a document that do not have existing elements. For example, suppose you want to make the first few lines in the document body a different color. Because no specific element exists to designate the first few lines, you must specify the paragraph or text to which the style applies.

To apply classes to specific parts of a document, use the div and span elements, described earlier in Table 9.3. These elements provide a place to apply class formatting when there's no existing formatting.

You use the div element to apply classes to block-level sections of a document—areas where you need the class to apply to more content than just one element. Here are the steps to apply the div class margin, which is defined elsewhere to, say, set the left margin to 40 percent:

1. Start with a section of an existing document:

   ```
   <p>Many people buy ASR products despite the higher
      cost.</p>
   <blockquote>"We sell only the highest quality outdoor
      equipment."</blockquote>
   ```

2. Add the div elements around the section:

   ```
   <div>
   <p>Many people buy ASR products despite the higher
      cost.</p>
   <blockquote>"We sell only the highest quality outdoor
      equipment. "</blockquote>
   </div>
   ```

3. Add the appropriate class attribute:

   ```
   <div class="margin">
   <p>Many people buy ASR products despite the higher
      cost.</p>
   <blockquote>"We sell only the highest quality outdoor
      equipment. "</blockquote>
   </div>
   ```

The margin class will now apply to both the p and blockquote elements.

Use the span element to apply classes to characters or words—any stretch of content that's *less* than a full, regular element. For example, to apply the firstuse class (that you define elsewhere) to a word, follow these steps:

1. Start with an existing element—for example, a p element:

   ```
   <p>Many people buy ASR products despite the higher
      cost.</p>
   ```

2. Add the span opening and closing elements:

   ```
   <p>Many people buy <span>ASR products</span> despite the
      higher cost.</p>
   ```

3. Add the appropriate class attribute:

   ```
   <p>Many people buy <span class="firstuse">ASR
      products</span> despite the higher cost.</p>
   ```

TIP You might use classes in conjunction with tables (covered in Chapter 5). Table elements accept class *attributes to apply formatting—either to the table sections you specify, to individual cells, rows, and columns, or to the table, cells, rows, or columns as a whole. (See the section "Applying Classes to an Element" earlier in this chapter.)*

Applying Inline Style Definitions

Applying inline style definitions throughout a document is similar to adding formatting attributes. For example, just as you can apply an `align` attribute to a paragraph, you can apply a style definition within the `p` element. Of course, with style sheets you have far more formatting possibilities than with traditional HTML or XHTML formatting commands.

The technique is simple: add the `style="..."` attribute to any element. Provide the style definition within quotes (and if there are quoted items within the `style` attribute, put them in single quotes). For that element, then, these values will override any other style definitions that are defined, imported, or linked into the document.

Although you wouldn't use this method to apply styles throughout a document—it's extremely time-consuming and defeats the purpose of having style sheets—you could use it in special cases for a specific instance in an existing style sheet. For example, your style sheet might specify that paragraphs appear in blue text. You can then apply an inline style to specify that one particular paragraph appears in red text.

To add a style definition to an existing element, follow these steps:

1. Start with an existing element—for example, the `p` element:

   ```
   <p>Many people buy ASR products despite the higher
      cost.</p>
   ```

2. Add the `style` attribute:

   ```
   <p style="">Many people buy ASR products despite the higher
      cost.</p>
   ```

3. Add the style definition(s), separated by semicolons. Substitute single quotes for double quotes within the attribute; otherwise, you'll close the attribute prematurely.

   ```
   <p style="color: red; font-family: 'Times New Roman',
      serif"> Many people buy ASR products despite the higher
      cost.</p>
   ```

TIP Notice that Times New Roman *is quoted and* serif *is not. This is because Times New Roman contains white space and, as such, must be quoted. However, serif does not contain white space; therefore, it does not need to be quoted.*

WARNING Using style sheets in this manner negates many of the advantages of style sheets. If you need to apply styles to a specific element in a specific case, use classes or ID attributes, as discussed in the previous section.

What Is Cascading?

As you have seen in the preceding sections, there are several ways to specify styles for a document: external style sheets, embedded styles, and inline styles. Conflicts may exist between these styles; for example, the external style sheet specifies all text in the document is red, and the embedded style specifies blue text for paragraphs. The browser resolves these conflicting style definitions by applying the precedence rules for style sheets; these rules are called *the cascade*.

The two general cascading rules are:

1. The most specific style rule will be applied—that is, a style that applies only to paragraphs is more specific than a style that applies to all the document text.

2. If two style rules are equally specific, the style rule that occurs *later* is considered more specific and will be the one applied. If you have two different style definitions for paragraph color, for example,

```
p {color:green}
p {color:blue}
```

the second definition would take precedence; therefore, the paragraph text is displayed in blue.

Style definitions declared in an external style sheet come before style definitions embedded in a document, and these come before inline style declarations. Therefore, the precedence order, from lowest to highest, is:

3. External style sheet

2. Embedded styles, including `@import` (if any, override external style sheet)

1. Inline styles (if any, override others)

Developing a Style Sheet

In the previous sections, you learned how to associate a style sheet with a document. Your goal now is to develop the style sheet—that is, to specify the style definitions you want to include. A *style definition* (also called a *style rule*) specifies formatting characteristics.

You can choose from any combination of the eight categories of style properties. We'll cover each of these in its own section later in this chapter.

Font properties   Specify character-level (inline) formatting, such as the typeface.

Text properties   Specify display characteristics for text, such as alignment or letter spacing.

Box properties   Specify characteristics for sections of text, at the paragraph (or block) level.

Color and background properties   Specify color, background color, and images at both the inline and block levels.

Classification properties   Specify display characteristics of lists and elements (such as `p` or `h1`) as inline or block level.

Aural style sheet properties   Control the presentation of documents by sound (CSS2 only).

Printed style sheet properties   Add features specifically to control printed output of documents (CSS2 only).

Positioning properties   Add features to precisely control the placement of elements on the display (CSS2 only).

You can easily get carried away with formatting options, but start simple. Look through the style sheet information in Master's Reference Part 2 to get an idea of the vast number of options. As you might guess, using even some of these options can quickly get complex.

Before we dive into developing a style sheet, let's take a look at some style sheet code:

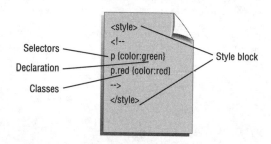

Here's what each part does:

The style block This includes style elements and comment markup, plus style definitions (or rules).

Selectors These are HTML or XHTML elements. In this example, the p—as in a paragraph element—is a selector.

Declarations These are the properties of the elements, such as color, background, alignment, and font. In this example, `color:green` and `color:red` are the declarations. Declarations consist of two parts, a property and a value, separated by a colon. In the second example, `color` is the property and `red` is the value. The property/value combination is enclosed within curly brackets, or braces—{}.

Classes These specify an additional style definition associated with specific occurrences of an element. For example, paragraphs tagged with `<p class="red">` use this style class.

Each style definition can define the formatting associated with a specific HTML or XHTML element, with a specific `class`, or with a specific `id`. The formatting associated with elements appears in the document without any special action on your part (aside from referencing or including the style sheet in your document). Style definitions for classes or IDs also require that you add the `class` or `id` attribute to the appropriate document section before the formatting can appear in the document.

To add these elements in an internal style sheet, follow these steps:

1. Be sure the style block is in place, like this:

```
<style type="text/css">
   <!--
   -->
</style>
```

2. Add a selector and braces, as shown here:

```
<style type="text/css">
   <!--
      p { }
```

```
    -->
  </style>
```

3. Add the declaration between the braces.

```
<style type="text/css">
  <!--
     p { color: aqua }
  -->
</style>
```

STYLE SHEET TIPS

As you're building a style sheet, the process will be easier and the results more readable if you follow these guidelines:

◆ To include multiple selectors, place them on separate lines, like this:

```
<style type="text/css">
  <!--
     p {color: red}
     h1 {color: blue}
     blockquote {color: green}
  -->
</style>
```

◆ To provide multiple declarations for a single selector, group the declarations within the braces, separated by semicolons. In addition, you might find the style definitions easier to read if you space them out somewhat, and put only one declaration on a single line. For example, to define p as red text with a yellow background, use the following markup:

```
<style type="text/css">
  <!--
     p { color: red;
         background: yellow; }
  -->
</style>
```

◆ Start at the highest level—the most general level—within your document, which is probably the body. Format the body as you want most of the document to appear, and then use more specific style rules to override the body settings.

◆ White space within style definitions and rules is ignored; each of the following lines of code produces the same result:

```
p{color:red}
p {color:red}
p {color: red}
p { color:red}
p { color:red }
```

In addition, become familiar with ways to specify measurements and values, which are discussed in the following two sections.

Specifying Measurements

When specifying locations of elements, you might also want to specify their size. For example, when specifying that the first line of a paragraph is indented, you can also specify the size of the indention. In general, provide measurements in the units shown in Table 9.4. You can also express most measurements as a percentage of the browser window.

Your measurement might look like one of the following lines:

```
p { text-indent: 2px }
p { text-indent: 1em }
```

TABLE 9.4: UNITS OF MEASURE IN STYLE SHEETS

UNIT	WHAT IT IS	DESCRIPTION
cm	Centimeter	The measurement in centimeters.
em	Em space	In typography, an em is the width of a capital M in the typeface being used. In CSS, 1 em is equal to the font size—for example, if the font size is 12 pt, the size of 1 em is equal to 12 points.
ex	x-height	The height of a lowercase letter x in the typeface being used.
in	Inch	The measurement in inches.
mm	Millimeter	The measurement in millimeters.
pc	Pica	A typographic measurement that equals 1/6 inch.
pt	Point	A typographic measurement that equals 1/72 inch.
px	Pixel	An individual screen dot.

Relative units such as em are usually preferred to absolute units such as pt when specifying font size, because relative units are scalable by the user. For example, users with visual disabilities may set their browser preferences to "larger" text. If the font size is specified in ems, all of the text will be scaled proportionately; the same text layout relationships exist, just at a larger size.

Specifying Colors in Style Rules

When using style sheets, you can specify colors in the standard HTML or XHTML ways (as #rrggbb values or as color names), as well as in two other ways, which use a slightly different approach to specify proportions of red, green, and blue. The following four lines show how to specify red in each method.

Method	Example
Hex Code	p{color: #ff0000}
Color Name	p{color: red}
Decimal	p{color: rgb(255,0,0)}
Percentage	p{color: rgb(100%,0%,0%)}

TIP   Although each of these is equally easy to use, we recommend using the #rrggbb option; it's likely to be more familiar, because it matches HTML or XHTML color statements, as described in Chapter 4.

In the following sections, we'll show you how to develop an embedded style sheet. After you complete an embedded style sheet, you can move it to a separate document and import it or link it.

To follow along with the example, have a document with the complete structure elements ready, or use Listing 9.1.

LISTING 9.1: A DOCUMENT WITH THE COMPLETE STRUCTURE ELEMENTS

```
<!DOCTYPE html PUBLIC "-//W3C/DTD XHTML 1.0 Transitional//EN"
  "http://www.w3.org/TR/xhtml1/DTD/xhtml1-transitional.dtd">
<html xmlns="http://www.w3.org/1999/xhtml">
<head>
  <title>ASR Outfitters</title>
</head>
<body>
  <h1>Welcome to ASR Outfitters!</h1>
  <p>We're happy to welcome you to our newly redesigned Web
site, featuring <b>styles</b> (because they look cool) as well
as redesigned graphics. Please take the <a href="tour.html">
tour of our site</a> if you haven't been here in a while. In
particular, you may appreciate the now automatically updated
camping news, as well as the new weather imagemap. Additionally,
we've been getting some nice kudos from frequent and occasional
visitors.</p>
  <blockquote>Your site always provides timely and useful
  information. Keep up the good work.<br />
  Jim Smith
  </blockquote>
  <hr />
  <h2>What's Here</h2>
  <ul>
    <li><a href="camping.html">Camping News</a> provides the
      latest comments from the trails.</li>
    <li><a href="weather.html">Check Weather</a> offers weather
      updates from a variety of sources.</li>
    <li><a href="clubs.html">Clubs</a> gives local hiking and
      mountaineering clubs a place to provide information about
      their activities. </li>
    <li><a href="catalog.html">Catalog</a> presents our entire
      inventory, including announcements of the latest sales.
      </li>
    <li><a href="contact.html">Contact Us</a> links to a page
      with a contact form, e-mail addresses, snail mail
      addresses, and phone numbers. If it isn't here, you can't
      find us.</li>
```

```
</ul>
<h2>What We Do</h2>
<p>In addition to providing the latest camping and outdoor
activities news, we also provide mountaineering and hiking
equipment nationwide via mail order as well as through our
stores in the Rocky Mountains. Please take a few minutes to
look through our <a href="catalog.html">online offerings</a>.
</p>
<h2>Other Issues</h2>
<ul>
    <li>As you may know, our URL was misprinted in the latest
      <i>Hiking News</i>. Please tell your hiking friends that
      the correct URL is <tt>http://www.asroutfitters.com/</tt>.
      </li>
    <li>To collect a $1000 reward, turn in the name of the
      person who set the fire in the Bear Lake area last
      weekend.
        <ol>
            <li>Call 888-555-1212.</li>
            <li>Leave the name on the recording.</li>
            <li>Provide contact information so we can send you the
              reward.</li>
        </ol>
    </li>
</ul>
<h2>What Would You Like To See?</h2>
<p>If you have suggestions or comments about the site or other
information we could provide, we'd love to know about it. Drop
us an e-mail at <a href="mailto:asroutfitters@example.com">
asroutfitters@example.com</a>. Of course, you could also
contact us more traditionally at the following address:</p>
<address>ASR Outfitters<br />
    4700 N. Center<br />
    South Logan, UT 87654<br />
    801-555-3422
</address>
</body>
</html>
```

Without any styles or formatting other than the standard browser defaults, the document from Listing 9.1 looks something like Figure 9.5.

FIGURE 9.5

An XHTML document without any special formatting or style sheets

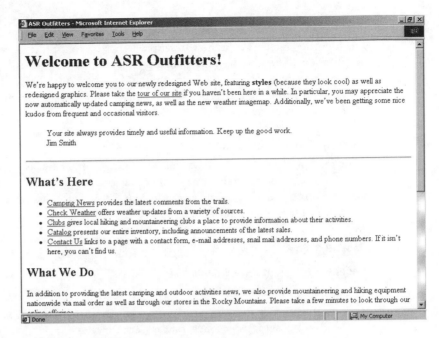

To add a style block to the document, follow these steps:

1. Add a pair of opening and closing `style` elements within the document head, as shown in the following code.

```
<!DOCTYPE html PUBLIC
    "-//W3C/DTD XHTML 1.0 Transitional//EN"
 "http://www.w3.org/TR/xhtml1/DTD/xhtml1-transitional.dtd">
<html xmlns="http://www.w3.org/1999/xhtml">
<head>
    <title>ASR Outfitters</title>
    <style type="text/css">
    </style>
</head>
```

2. Add the comment markup (`<!-- -->`) within the `style` elements, as shown here:

```
<style type="text/css">
    <!--
    -->
</style>
```

After the `style` element and comment markup are in place, define the style sheet. You specify style properties, such as fonts, text, boxes, colors, backgrounds, and classifications, as discussed in the next section. Think of defining styles as specifying rules for what each element should look like. For example, specify that you want all text blue, all bullets indented, all headings centered, and so on.

Setting Style Sheet Properties

The following sections cover how to set properties for fonts, text, boxes, colors, backgrounds, and classifications. The sections do not build on one another; instead, they show you how to set each of the properties separately, based on the sample ASR Outfitters page. Through these examples, you'll see *some* of the style sheet effects you can achieve. For a more complete list of style sheet options, see Master's Reference Part 2.

Setting Font Properties

If the fonts you specify are not available on a user's computer, the browser will display text in a font that is available. To ensure that one of your preferred fonts is used, choose multiple font families and common fonts, and, in addition, always include a generic font family choice. Table 9.5 shows some of the basic font properties and values.

TABLE 9.5: FONT PROPERTIES

PROPERTY	POSSIBLE VALUES
font	Any or all of the following font properties can be set within this combination font property.
font-family	Font names, such as Times New Roman or Arial, or generic font families, such as serif, sans-serif, monospace, fantasy, and cursive
font-size	xx-small, x-small, small, medium, large, x-large, xx-large, or size measurement in length or percentage
font-style	normal, italic, oblique
font-variant	normal, small-caps
font-weight	normal, bold, bolder, lighter, 100, 200, 300, 400, 500, 600, 700, 800, 900

The following example sets a basic font for the whole document—everything between the opening and closing body elements. It sets the basic font for a document to Comic Sans MS, with Technical and Times New Roman as other choices and with a generic serif font as the last choice.

1. Within the style block, add a body selector and braces to hold its properties:

```
<style type="text/css">
  <!--
     body {}
  -->
</style>
```

2. Add the property. To set only the typeface, use font-family:

```
<style type="text/css">
  <!--
     body { font-family }
  -->
</style>
```

3. Add a colon to separate the property from the value:

```
<style type="text/css">
   <!--
      body { font-family: }
   -->
</style>
```

4. Add the value "Comic Sans MS" (the first-choice typeface). (If the font family name contains a space, put the name in quotes. Otherwise, quotes are optional.)

```
<style type="text/css">
   <!--
      body { font-family: "Comic Sans MS" }
   -->
</style>
```

5. Add additional values, as you choose, separated by commas. Conclude your list of fonts with either a serif or sans-serif font that's likely to match a font on the user's computer.

```
<style type="text/css">
   <!--
      body { font-family: "Comic Sans MS", Technical,
             "Times New Roman", serif }
   -->
</style>
```

Figure 9.6 is the resulting page, complete with the new font for the document body.

FIGURE 9.6

We've converted our whole page to a new font, without having to insert font elements in the document!

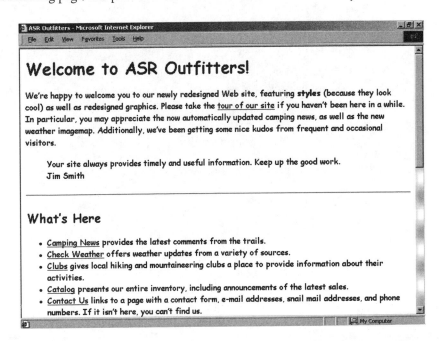

TIP *Newer browsers support three additional choices for generic font families. In addition to* `serif` *and* `sans-serif`, *the three additional generic font families are* `cursive`, `fantasy`, *and* `monospace`.

SETTING LINK CHARACTERISTICS

You use three special style classes (also known as *anchor pseudo-classes*) along with font style rules to control the colors of links in your document:

- `a:link`
- `a:active`
- `a:visited`

Use these within your style sheet definition to specify the rules that apply to links, active links, and visited links. For example, to set unvisited links to blue, active links to red, and visited links to magenta, your style block would look like this:

```
<style type="text/css">
  <!--
    a:link { color: blue }
    a:active { color: red }
    a:visited { color: magenta }
  -->
</style>
```

You can also define additional text styles within the document. For example, to set all headings to Arial italic, follow these steps:

1. Add a comma-separated list of all headings to the existing style block, as selectors. The comma-separated list specifies that the style rule applies to each selector individually.

```
<style type="text/css">
  <!--
    body { font-family: "Comic Sans MS", Technical,
                        "Times New Roman", serif }
    h1, h2, h3, h4, h5, h6
  -->
</style>
```

2. Add braces:

```
h1, h2, h3, h4, h5, h6 { }
```

3. Add the `font-family` property, with Arial as the first choice, Helvetica as the second choice, and sans-serif as the third choice:

```
h1, h2, h3, h4, h5, h6 { font-family: Arial,
                                      Helvetica,
                                      sans-serif }
```

4. After the font-family values, add a semicolon and a new line so that you can easily enter (and read) the font style rule:

```
h1, h2, h3, h4, h5, h6 { font-family: Arial,
                                     Helvetica,
                                     sans-serif;
                       }
```

5. Add the font-style property, a colon, and the italic value:

```
h1, h2, h3, h4, h5, h6 { font-family: Arial,
                                     Helvetica,
                                     sans-serif;
                       font-style: italic }
```

6. Continue adding font properties, separated by semicolons, if you want to define other aspects, such as font size or weight. The following lines of code show the headings set to a larger size and weight than usual. You'll see the results in Figure 9.7.

```
<style type="text/css">
<!--
     body { font-family: "Comic Sans MS", Technical,
                         "Times New Roman", serif }
     h1, h2, h3, h4, h5, h6 { font-family: Arial,
                                          Helvetica,
                                          sans-serif;
                            font-style: italic;
                            font-size: x-large;
                            font-weight: bolder; }
-->
</style>
```

FIGURE 9.7

The results of setting the font-family, style, size, and weight for headings

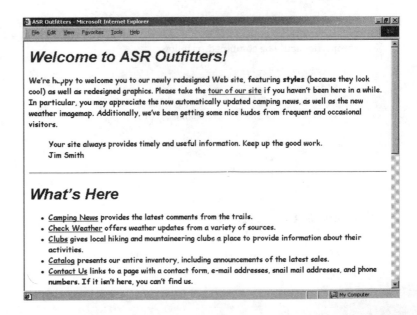

COMBINING FONT PROPERTIES

If you use the special, combination font property to set several different font properties at once, the properties must be specified in a certain order or they won't display correctly in a browser.

♦ The first are font-style, font-weight, and font-variant. They can be in any order, but must come before other font properties. Any of these three properties can be omitted and default values will be used.

♦ Next is font-size, which is required if you use the combination font property.

♦ You can follow font-size by a slash (/) and a line-height value, which specifies how far apart the lines in a paragraph are:

```
p { font-size: 12pt/14.4pt }
```

Line height can also be set as a separate font property—for example:

```
p { font-size: 12pt; line-height: 14.4pt }
```

(See "Setting Text Properties," the next section in this chapter.)

♦ Last is font-family, which is also required if you use the combination font property.

For example, rather than specifying each font property separately, as in the following code sample:

```
<style type="text/css">
    <!--
    body {font-style: italic;
          font-weight: bold;
          font-variant: normal;
          font-size: 1em;
          line-height: 1.2em;
          font-family: "Zapf Renaissance", "Snell Roundhand",
                        cursive}
    -->
</style>
```

The properties could be combined, as follows:

```
<style type="text/css"
    <!--
    body {font: italic bold 1em/1.2em "Zapf Renaissance",
                "Snell Roundhand", cursive}
    -->
</style>
```

Setting Text Properties

Text properties specify the characteristics of *text blocks* (sections of text, not individual characters). Table 9.6 shows some of the most common text properties.

TABLE 9.6: TEXT PROPERTIES

PROPERTY	POSSIBLE VALUES
letter-spacing	Measurement
line-height	Number, measurement, or percentage
text-align	left, right, center, justify
text-decoration	none, underline, overline, line-through, blink
text-indent	Measurement or percentage
text-transform	none, capitalize, uppercase, lowercase
vertical-align	baseline, super, sub, top, text-top, middle, bottom, text-bottom, or a percentage
word-spacing	Measurement

You apply these properties to selectors in the same way you apply font-level properties. To indent paragraphs and set up a special, nonindented paragraph class, follow these steps:

1. Within the style block, add a p selector and braces:

```
<style type="text/css">
  <!--
     p { }
  -->
</style>
```

2. Add the text-indent property, with a value of 5% to indent all regular paragraphs by 5 percent of the total window width:

```
<style type="text/css">
  <!--
     p { text-indent: 5% }
  -->
</style>
```

3. Add the p.noindent selector (and braces) on a new line within the style block. Using a standard selection, in conjunction with a descriptive term that you make up, you create a new style class within the style sheet:

```
<style type="text/css">
  <!--
     p { text-indent: 5% }
     p.noindent { }
  -->
</style>
```

4. Add the `text-indent` property, with a value of `0%` to specify no indent:

```
<style type="text/css">
   <!--
      p { text-indent: 5% }
      p.noindent { text-indent: 0% }
   -->
</style>
```

5. To specify which text should be formatted without an indent, add a new p element with a `class="noindent"` attribute, as shown here:

```
<p>We're happy to welcome you to our newly redesigned Web
   site, featuring <b>styles</b> (because they look cool)
   as well as redesigned graphics. Please take the
   <a href="tour.html">tour of our site</a> if you haven't
   been here in a while. In particular, you may appreciate
   the now automatically updated camping news as well as
   the new weather imagemap.</p>
<p class="noindent">Additionally, we've been getting some
   nice kudos from frequent and occasional visitors.</p>
```

Figure 9.8 shows the results. All text tagged with p in the document is indented by 5 percent of the window width, and special formatting, set up with the class attribute, does not indent.

FIGURE 9.8

Setting text properties lets you customize your documents—the second paragraph is not indented, while the first one is, because of a style class

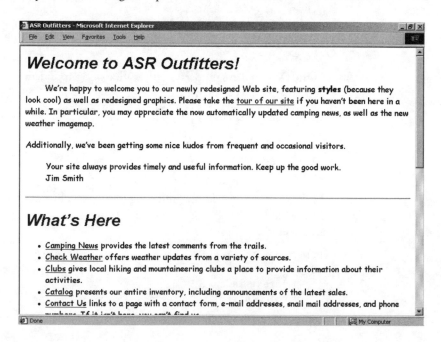

SPECIFYING GENERIC STYLE CLASSES

You can also specify a class without a selector, as in the following style block:

```
<style type="text/css">
   <!--
      .red { color: #ff0000 }
   -->
</style>
```

You can use a *generic class*, such as red in this example, with any elements in your document. However, if you specify an element with a class (p.red, for example), you can use that class only with p elements.

You can also use text properties to apply special formatting to headings. To format all headings with a line below them, centered, and with extra spacing between the letters, follow these steps:

1. Add the list of heading selectors you want to format to your basic style sheet. To apply these formats to headings 1 through 3, for example, list h1, h2, h3, with braces following the list:

```
        <style type="text/css">
   <!--
      h1, h2, h3 { }
   -->
</style>
```

2. To place a line below each heading, add the text-decoration property with underline as the value:

```
        <style type="text/css">
   <!--
      h1, h2, h3 { text-decoration: underline }
   -->
</style>
```

3. Add a semicolon to separate the rules, and add the text-align property with a value of center to center the headings:

```
        <style type="text/css">
   <!--
      h1, h2, h3 { text-decoration: underline;
                   text-align: center }
   -->
</style>
```

4. Finally, add another separation semicolon and the letter-spacing property with a value of 5px (5 pixels):

```
        <style type="text/css">
   <!--
      h1, h2, h3 { text-decoration: underline;
                   text-align: center;
```

```
                                        letter-spacing: 5px }
                -->
            </style>
```

The sample page looks like Figure 9.9.

FIGURE 9.9

You can apply text properties to several elements at once— for example, centering all headings

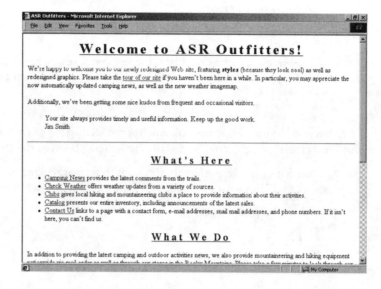

SPECIFYING STYLE IDS

You can specify an id for a one-time use—for example, if you're developing a Dynamic HTML or XHTML document and want to format specific elements in specific contexts. Use a # at the beginning of the id selector, as in the following style block:

```
<style type="text/css">
    <!--
        #firstusered { color: red }
    -->
</style>
```

You can use an id, such as firstusered in this example, with any single id attribute in your document. If you specify an element with the id attribute (<p id="firstusered">, for example), you can only use that id once in the document.

Sometimes you may want to set links without underlines. You can use the anchor pseudo-classes and set the text-decoration property to a value of none, as in the following example:

```
<style type="text/css">
    <!--
        a:link, a:visited, a:active {text-decoration: none}
    -->
</style>
```

Just be sure to make it obvious from your page design that these are links!

Setting Box Properties

You use box properties to create box designs—a feature that's not available in standard HTML or XHTML. You can box text, such as cautions or contact information, to call attention to it. You can adjust the margins to control how close text is to the border, and you can also remove the border to create floating text. Table 9.7 lists some commonly used box properties.

TABLE 9.7: BOX PROPERTIES

PROPERTY	POSSIBLE VALUES
border	Any or all of the following border- attributes
border-color	#rrggbb
border-style	none, dotted, dashed, solid, double, groove, ridge, inset, outset
border-width	Measurement, thick, medium, thin
clear	right, left, none, both
float	right, left, none
height	Measurement or auto
margin	Measurement, or percentage of parent
margin-bottom	Measurement, or percentage of parent
margin-left	Measurement, or percentage of parent
margin-right	Measurement, or percentage of parent
margin-top	Measurement, or percentage of parent
width	Measurement, percentage, or auto

TIP   At the time of writing, Internet Explorer and Netscape Navigator support box properties differently—in particular, the relationship between the surrounding text and the box, the size of the box around text, and the interpretation of the width *value are quite inconsistent.*

To create a box, apply these box-level characteristics to existing text in a document, including paragraphs, block quotes, and headings. The following steps show you how to create a box using an existing block quote. This box will float close to the right margin with a 2-pixel border and will occupy only 50 percent of the window width.

1. Within the style block, add a `blockquote` selector and braces:

```
<style type="text/css">
  <!--
     blockquote { }
  -->
</style>
```

As shown in the following steps, you can tile the background image either vertically or horizontally:

1. To add a background image to the document body, add the `background-image` property, separated from the previous property with a semicolon:

```
<style type="text/css">
    <!--
        body { background-color: #ffffcc;
                background-image: }
    -->
</style>
```

2. Add the value for the background image as `url(pattern.gif)`. Use any absolute or relative URL in the parentheses:

```
<style type="text/css">
    <!--
        body { background-color: #ffffcc;
                background-image: url(pattern.gif) }
    -->
</style>
```

3. Add `background-repeat: repeat-x` to specify that the background image repeat horizontally (in the direction of the x axis). To repeat only vertically, use `repeat-y`; use `no-repeat` if you don't want a repeat.

```
<style type="text/css">
    <!--
        body { background-color: #ffffcc;
                background-image: url(pattern.gif);
                background-repeat: repeat-x; }
    -->
</style>
```

Setting Classification Properties

You use classification properties to change specific elements from inline (such as i or b) to block elements with line breaks before and after (such as p and h1), as well as to control the display of lists. Table 9.9 lists some classification properties and their values.

TABLE 9.9: CLASSIFICATION PROPERTIES

PROPERTY	POSSIBLE VALUES
display	inline, block, list-item
list-style-image	url(http://example.com/image.gif)
list-style-type	disc, circle, square, decimal, lower-roman, upper-roman, lower-alpha, upper-alpha, none

To specify that an unordered list use square bullets, follow these steps:

1. Within the style block, add a ul selector followed immediately by an li selector on the same line. By combining these, the style rule will apply only to an li element within a ul element. If you set a rule for only the li element, it would affect all numbered and bulleted lists in your document, not just those within ul elements.

```
<style type="text/css">
  <!--
    ul li
  -->
</style>
```

2. Add braces:

```
<style type="text/css">
  <!--
    ul li {}
  -->
</style>
```

3. Add a list-style-type property with the value of square:

```
<style type="text/css">
  <!--
    ul li { list-style-type: square }
  -->
</style>
```

You can also set a specific image for use as a bullet by using list-style-image: url(figure.gif), as shown here:

```
<style type="text/css">
  <!--
    ul li { list-style-image: url(figure.gif) }
  -->
</style>
```

TIP *If you specify a* list-style-image *property, it's a good idea to also include a* list-style-type *property in case the image is not displayed (that is, if the browser is unable to download or display the image). The image will be used if available, but if not,* list-style-type *will be used instead.*

By changing the display property, you can change a list from displaying as a vertical list, as is customary, to an inline list in which each item appears within a line of text. To do so, use the following style rule:

```
<style type="text/css">
  <!--
    ul li { display: inline }
  -->
</style>
```

WARNING *Display properties are supported only in recent browsers: Netscape 6, IE 5.5, and Opera 4 and later.*

See Listing 9.2 for an example of a document with a link to an external style sheet and the code needed to apply these style definitions. Listing 9.3 details the external style sheet code.

LISTING 9.2: AN XHTML DOCUMENT LINKED TO AN EXTERNAL STYLE SHEET

```
<!DOCTYPE html PUBLIC "-//W3C/DTD XHTML 1.0 Transitional//EN"
   "http://www.w3.org/TR/xhtml1/DTD/xhtml1-transitional.dtd">
<html xmlns="http://www.w3.org/1999/xhtml">
<head>
  <title>ASR Outfitters</title>
  <link rel="stylesheet" type="text/css" href="0903.css">
</head>
<body>
  <h1>Welcome to ASR Outfitters!</h1>
  <p>We're happy to welcome you to our newly redesigned Web
  site, featuring <span class="emph">styles</span> (because
  they look cool) as well as redesigned graphics. Please take
  the <a href="tour.html">tour of our site</a> if you haven't
  been here in a while. In particular, you may appreciate the
  now automatically updated camping news, as well as the new
  weather imagemap. Additionally, we've been getting some nice
  kudos from frequent and occasional visitors.</p>
    <blockquote>Your site always provides timely and useful
    information. Keep up the good work.<br />
    Jim Smith</blockquote>
  <hr />
  <h2>What's Here</h2>
  <div class="text"><ul>
    <li><a href="camping.html">Camping News</a> provides the
      latest comments from the trails.</li>
    <li><a href="weather.html">Check Weather</a> offers
      weather updates from a variety of sources.</li>
    <li><a href="clubs.html">Clubs</a> gives local hiking and
      mountaineering clubs a place to provide information
      about their activities.</li>
    <li><a href="catalog.html">Catalog</a> presents our entire
      inventory, including announcements of the latest sales.
      </li>
    <li><a href="contact.html">Contact Us</a> links to a page
      with a contact form, e-mail addresses, snail mail
      addresses, and phone numbers. If it isn't here, you
      can't find us.</li>
    </ul></div>
  <h2>What We Do</h2>
  <p>In addition to providing the latest camping and outdoor
  activities news, we also provide mountaineering and hiking
  equipment nationwide via mail order as well as through our
  stores in the Rocky Mountains. Please take a few minutes to
  look through our <a href="catalog.html">online offerings</a>.
```

```
    </p>
    <h2>Other Issues</h2>
    <div class="text"><ul>
      <li>As you may know, our URL was misprinted in the latest
        <span class="ital">Hiking News</span>. Please tell your
        hiking friends that the correct URL is <span
        class="inlineurl">http://www.asroutfitters.com/</span>.
      </li>
      <li>To collect a $1000 reward, turn in the name of the
        person who set the fire in the Bear Lake area last
        weekend.
        <ol>
          <li>Call 888-555-1212.</li>
          <li>Leave the name on the recording.</li>
          <li>Provide contact information so we can send you the
            reward.</li>
        </ol>
      </li>
    </ul></div>
    <h2>What Would You Like To See?</h2>
    <p class="diff">If you have suggestions or comments about the
    site or other information we could provide, we'd love to know
    about it. Drop us an e-mail at <a
    href="mailto:asroutfitters@raycommexample.com">
    asroutfitters@raycommexample.com</a>. Of course, you could
    also contact us more traditionally at the following address:
    </p>
    <div class="text"><address>ASR Outfitters<br />
      4700 N. Center<br />
      South Logan, UT 87654<br />
      801-555-3422
    </address></div>
  </body>
</html>
```

LISTING 9.3: AN EXTERNAL STYLE SHEET

```
body
{background-color: #ffffcc;
 margin: 5%;
 font-style: normal;
 font-family: "Comic Sans MS", Verdana, Arial, Helvetica,
              sans-serif;
 font-size: 12pt;
 line-height: 16.5pt}

h1, h2
{font-family: "Comic Sans MS", Verdana, Arial, Helvetica,
              sans-serif}
```

```
p
{font-style: normal;
 font-family: "Comic Sans MS", Verdana, Arial, Helvetica,
             sans-serif;
 font-size: 12pt;
 line-height: 16.5pt}

blockquote
{color: red;
 font-family: "Comic Sans MS", Verdana, Arial, Helvetica,
             sans-serif;
 font-size: 11pt;
 line-height: 15pt;
 margin-left: 15%;
 width: 300px}

li
{list-style-type: disc;
 font: bold 12pt/16.5pt "Comic Sans MS", Verdana, Arial,
       Helvetica, sans-serif}

li li
{list-style-type: circle}

address
{font-style: normal;
 font-weight: bold;
 font-size: 13pt;
 line-height: 17.5pt}

.emph
{font-weight: bolder}

.ital
{font-style: italic}

.inlineurl
{font-family: Courier, monospace;
 font-size: 10pt}

.diff
{color: red}

.text
{font-style: normal;
 font-family: "Comic Sans MS", Verdana, Arial, Helvetica,
             sans-serif;
 font-size: 12pt;
 line-height: 16.5pt}
```

Setting Aural Style Sheet Properties

One of the more recent additions to style sheet capabilities is aural properties, which allow you to set properties for documents that will be read aloud by a device. Visually impaired users use these properties; you could use them as supplements to visual presentations or in situations in which reading is not possible—for example, in the car. Aural style sheet properties let you specify that documents be read aloud, specify sound characteristics, and specify other auditory options.

WARNING   *At this time, most browsers do not yet support aural style sheets. One exception is Emacspeak* (`www.cs.cornell.edu/Info/People/raman/emacspeak/emacspeak.html`), *which you can use for testing these style sheets.*

Table 9.10 lists some aural style sheet properties and their values. Visit Master's Reference Part 2 for additional properties and values.

TABLE 9.10: AURAL STYLE SHEET PROPERTIES

PROPERTY	POSSIBLE VALUES
pause	Time, percentage
pitch-range	Value
speech-rate	Value, x-slow, slow, medium, fast, x-fast, faster, slower
volume	Value, percentage, silent, x-soft, soft, medium, loud, x-loud

To specify that the document be read aloud with loud volume and fast speech (for efficiency), follow these steps:

1. In a new style block, provide a body selector to make your settings apply to the entire document, followed by braces:

```
<style type="text/css">
  <!--
    body { }
  -->
</style>
```

2. Add a volume property with the value of loud:

```
<style type="text/css">
  <!--
    body { volume: loud; }
  -->
</style>
```

3. Add a speech-rate property with the value of fast:

```
<style type="text/css">
  <!--
    body { volume: loud; speech-rate: fast;}
  -->
</style>
```

Aural style sheets are part of the CSS2 specification and are not currently supported by browsers. Check the W3C's Accessibility Features of CSS (www.w3.org/TR/CSS-access) for the latest on these features. You can also check Webreview.com's Style Sheet Reference Guide at www.webreview.com/style/index.shtml. Note that although the most recent major browsers do not support these features, there are some specialized browsers that render these style rules appropriately.

Setting Printed-Media Properties

Printed-media properties can help you accommodate users who print your documents rather than read them online. These CSS2 properties let you set values for the page box, which you might think of as the area of your printout. For example, in hardcopy, your page box might be the 8.5" × 11" piece of paper; the page box includes the content, margins, and edges. Table 9.11 lists some of the more common printed-media properties and their values. Master's Reference Part 2 provides additional information.

TABLE 9.11: PRINTED-MEDIA STYLE SHEET PROPERTIES

PROPERTY	POSSIBLE VALUES
margin	Length, percentage, auto
marks	crop, cross, none
orphans	Value
page-break-after	auto, always, avoid, left, right
page-break-before	auto, always, avoid, left, right
page-break-before	auto, always, avoid, left, right
page-break-inside	auto, always, avoid, left, right
size	Value, auto, portrait, landscape
widows	Value

WARNING *Like aural style sheets, printed-media properties are part of the CSS2 specification and are not currently supported by browsers.*

To specify a page break before all h1 elements in a printed version of your document, follow these steps:

1. In a style block, provide an h1 selector and braces to apply your settings to all first-level headings in the entire document:

```
<style type="text/css">
  <!--
     h1 { }
  -->
</style>
```

2. Add a `page-break-before` property with the value of `always`:

```
<style>
  <!--
      h1 { page-break-before: always; }
  -->
</style>
```

See the Web sites listed in the previous section for more on CSS2 features. Although the most recent browsers do not support these features, there may be specialized equipment that renders these style rules appropriately.

Setting Positioning Properties

Using positioning, you can add properties to style rules to control element positioning. For example, you can identify specific locations for elements, as well as specify locations that are relative to other elements. Positioning properties are part of the CSS2 specification, and only the newer browser versions support them. Table 9.12 lists some positioning properties and their values.

TABLE 9.12: POSITIONING PROPERTIES

PROPERTY	POSSIBLE VALUES
float	left, right, none
overflow	visible, scroll, hidden, auto
position	static, absolute, relative, fixed
top, bottom, left, and right	Length, percentage, auto

Let's look at an example of how positioning properties work. To specify that the `.warning` classes in the document float to the left with text wrapping around to the right, and that the `p.logo` class sits at the bottom of the window, follow these steps:

1. In a new style block, provide a `.warning` selector and braces to hold its properties:

```
<style type="text/css">
  <!--
      .warning { }
  -->
</style>
```

2. Add a `float` property with the value of `left`:

```
<style type="text/css">
  <!--
      .warning { float: left }
  -->
</style>
```

3. Add a `p.logo` selector and braces:

```
<style type="text/css">
   <!--
      .warning { float: left }
      p.logo { }
   -->
</style>
```

4. Add a `position` property and `fixed` value:

```
<style type="text/css">
   <!--
      .warning { float: left }
      p.logo { position: fixed }
   -->
</style>
```

5. Add `bottom` and `right` properties and length of `0` (use any units) for each value:

```
<style type="text/css">
   <!--
      .warning { float: left }
      p.logo { position: fixed; bottom: 0px; right: 0px }
   -->
</style>
```

Positioning properties are a part of the CSS2 specification that is supported by newer browsers. However, relative positioning is supported more fully than absolute positioning at the present.

THE FUTURE OF STYLE SHEETS

It seems likely that *external* style sheets will be the preferred way to use styles with HTML and XHTML documents in the future. Embedded and inline styles options are available in XHTML 1.0; however, XHTML 1.1 requires the use of the style sheet module in order to use the `style` element. Using CSS with XML is only possible with external style sheets. External style sheets offer ways to use all of the features of both embedded and inline styles through specifying classes and IDs as well as XHTML element selectors.

In addition, if you're going to venture more into XML, you should check out the Extensible Stylesheet Language (XSL) and XSL Transformations (XSLT). You can find out more at www.w3.org/Style/XSL.

Where to Go from Here

In this chapter, you learned how style sheets and HTML or XHTML documents relate and how to develop style sheets for your own needs. As you can see, style sheets are certainly more comprehensive than any formatting option previously available.

Next, you might check out some of these chapters:

◆ See Chapter 2 for more information about standard HTML and XHTML elements and formatting options.

◆ See Chapter 12 for more information about accessibility issues for users with visual impairments.

◆ See Chapter 5 to find out more about tables.

◆ Check out Chapter 7 to learn about frames.

◆ See Part VI for information about XML.

Chapter 10

Adding JavaScript

USING JAVASCRIPT, YOU CAN add some pizzazz to your pages, taking them from ho-hum pages to ones that react to user actions, process and check information that users provide, and even deliver information appropriate to each user. With the increasingly sophisticated nature of the Web, you often need these kinds of attractions to hold users' attention and to keep them coming back. What's more, JavaScript allows you to include some useful capabilities, such as tracking users' visits and keeping other sites from "framing" your material. (Chapter 7 discusses frames and being "framed.")

In this chapter, we'll look at what JavaScript is and how to use it, and, with some examples, we'll show you how to include JavaScript in your HTML and XHTML documents. We'll start with simple scripts and then build on them. We'll concentrate on basic JavaScript capabilities (JavaScript 1.1 and some of 1.2 and 1.3), which is a good compromise between high functionality and broad browser acceptance.

This chapter covers the following topics:

- ◆ What is JavaScript?
- ◆ Adding JavaScript to your document
- ◆ Adding event handlers
- ◆ Keeping your Web site from being "framed"
- ◆ Tracking users using cookies

What Is JavaScript?

Created by Netscape, JavaScript is a scripting language that vaguely resembles Sun's Java programming language. Most popular browsers, starting with Netscape Navigator 2 and Internet Explorer (IE) 3, support JavaScript. Microsoft's JScript and the international standard, ECMAScript, are very similar to JavaScript. For our purposes, we'll just refer to all these scripting languages as JavaScript.

Table 10.1 shows which browsers support which versions of JavaScript.

TABLE 10.1: BROWSER SUPPORT FOR JAVASCRIPT

JAVASCRIPT VERSION	NETSCAPE NAVIGATOR	OPERA	INTERNET EXPLORER
JavaScript 1.0, JScript 1.0	2.0 and higher	3.0 and higher	3.0 and higher
JavaScript 1.1	3.0 and higher		
JavaScript 1.2, JScript 3.0	4.0 – 4.05		4.0 and higher
JavaScript 1.3	4.06 – 4.75	4.0 and higher	
JavaScript 1.4, JScript 5.0	5.0*	5.0 and higher	5.0 and higher
JavaScript 1.5	6.0		

JavaScript 1.4 was part of Netscape Navigator 5, which was not released.

TIP *Microsoft also supports VBScript, a competing scripting approach. We recommend JavaScript (or the Microsoft equivalent, JScript) for most purposes because JavaScript is much more widely supported.*

TIP *You'll find lots of scripts available for public use on the Web. For starters, go to* http://javascript.internet.com. *You could also search for "JavaScript" at* www.yahoo.com, www.google.com, *or other search services, or visit* www.javascript.com.

JavaScript is powerful enough to be truly useful, even though it isn't a full-fledged programming language. What's more, JavaScript is relatively easy and fun to use. Be careful, though, because Java-Script can cause problems with accessibility for visually impaired visitors, and its use can irritate visitors. For example, the event handlers, discussed later in this chapter, often violate visitor expectations and make the visitor's experience less predictable, which can often have negative effects.

JavaScript is simpler and less sophisticated (therefore less complex) than a "real" programming language. To work with JavaScript, you need to be familiar with the following terms and concepts:

Object An *object* is a thing—a check box on a form, the form itself, an image, a document, a link, or even a browser window. Some objects are built into JavaScript and are not necessarily part of your Web page. For example, the `Date` object provides a wide range of date information. You can think of objects as the "nouns" in the JavaScript language.

Property A *property* describes an object. Properties can be anything from the color to the number of items, such as radio buttons, within an object. When users select an item in a form, they change the form's properties. You can think of properties as the "adjectives" in the JavaScript language.

Method A *method* is an instruction. The methods available for each object describe what you can do with the object. For example, using a method, you can convert text in an object to all upper-case or all lowercase letters. Every object has a collection of methods that act on that object, and every method belongs to at least one object. You can think of methods as the "verbs" in the JavaScript language.

Statement A *statement* is a JavaScript language "sentence." Statements combine the objects, properties, and methods (nouns, adjectives, and verbs). Many of the statements for JavaScript are remarkably natural in their structure and terminology.

Function   A *function* is a collection of statements that performs an action or actions. Functions contain one or more statements and can therefore be considered the "paragraphs" of the Java-Script language.

Event   An *event* occurs when something happens on your page, such as the page being loaded, a user submitting a form, or the mouse cursor being moved over an object.

Event handler   An *event handler* waits for something to happen—such as the mouse moving over a link—and then launches a script based on that event. For example, the onmouseover event handler performs an action when the user moves the mouse pointer over the object. You can think of an event handler as posing questions or directing the action of a story.

Variable   A *variable* stores data temporarily (usually until the user closes the page or moves to a new page). Each variable is given a name so that you can refer to it in your code.

Before we get started, let's take a look at some JavaScript code. Once you can identify the pieces, JavaScript is as easy to read as HTML or XHTML code:

```
<!DOCTYPE html PUBLIC ".//W3C/DTD XHTML 1.0 Transitional//EN"
    "http://www.w3.org/TR/xhtml1/DTD/xhtml1-transitional.dtd">
<html xmlns="http://www.w3.org/1999/xhtml">
<head>
    <title>The Basic Page</title>
</head>
<body>
    <h1>Welcome!</h1>
    <a href="http://www.raycomm.com/"
        onmouseover="window.status='Check us out!'; return true; "
        onmouseout="window.status=''; return true;">
        Visit our site</a>
</body>
</html>
```

In the preceding code, note the following JavaScript elements:

Object	window is a JavaScript object.
Property	status is a JavaScript property.
Statement	return true is a JavaScript statement.
Event handler	onmouseover and onmouseout are both JavaScript event handlers.

WARNING   *Although we often use extra spaces, indents, and line breaks for readability in our printed code, do not insert any additional spaces or line returns in your JavaScript code. Make sure that each JavaScript statement is on a single line, and allow the text to wrap without a line return. JavaScript sees line returns as JavaScript characters and adds them to your code (which will often make the code nonfunctional). It's fine to use line returns at the actual end of a line of code, before you start the next line, but not in the middle of a line of code.*

TIP   Master's Reference Part 3 includes a comprehensive guide to JavaScript, which you can use to expand on the basics in this chapter.

If you test the previous code in a browser, you'll see the message "Check us out!" appear in the status bar at the bottom of the browser window when you roll the mouse cursor over the "Visit our site" link, and disappear when you roll the mouse cursor off the link.

TIP   The JavaScript discussed in this chapter is exclusively client-side JavaScript. This simply means that the user's browser does the work and the server is not involved. Although server-side JavaScript exists, it is outside the scope of this book.

TIP   For more information about JavaScript, see Mastering JavaScript Premium Edition, *by James Jaworski and published by Sybex.*

Adding JavaScript to Your Document

You can add JavaScript to your page in three ways:

◆ Embed the JavaScript in the page.

◆ Place the JavaScript in the document head.

◆ Link to JavaScript stored in another file.

TIP   The options for placing JavaScript closely resemble the options for placing style sheets, discussed in Chapter 9.

Table 10.2 describes the elements and attributes you use to add JavaScript to your documents.

TABLE 10.2: ELEMENTS AND ATTRIBUTES USED TO ADD JAVASCRIPT

ITEM	TYPE	DESCRIPTION
`script`	Element	Identifies the script section in the document.
`language="javascript"`	Attribute of `script`	Specifies the scripting language (and, optionally, version).
`src="url"`	Attribute of `script`	Optionally specifies the location of an external script.
`type="text/javascript"`	Attribute of `script`	Provides the script MIME type; required.
`noscript`	Element	Provides content for non-script-capable browsers.
`<!-- //-->`	Comment markup	Hides the contents of the script from non-script-capable browsers. Note that this differs from comment markup used for style sheets.

Embedding JavaScript

If you're adding a fairly short JavaScript, your best bet is to embed it in the HTML or XHTML document in the code that the JavaScript affects. For example, JavaScript that adds the current date to your document is a few lines long, so you can easily embed the script in your document.

Embedding works like this: When users open your page, their browsers "read" your source document line by line. If your code includes JavaScript within the document body, the browser performs the actions as it reads the page. For example, if the body element includes JavaScript, the first task the browser completes is running the script. Or, if you include JavaScript in the first actual text of the document, the browser runs the script as soon as it gets to the text.

Let's embed a JavaScript that prints the current time and date as the page loads. The JavaScript statement—in this case, the whole script—is `document.write(Date())`. Here are the steps:

TIP *As in other chapters, we're using XHTML as the sample code; however, the examples and steps would work just as well if you used HTML.*

1. Start with the following XHTML code:

```
<!DOCTYPE html PUBLIC
    "-//W3C/DTD XHTML 1.0 Transitional//EN"
  "http://www.w3.org/TR/xhtml1/DTD/xhtml1-transitional.dtd">
<html xmlns="http://www.w3.org/1999/xhtml">
<head>
    <title>The Date Page</title>
</head>
<body>
    <h1>Welcome!</h1>
</body>
</html>
```

2. Add an introductory sentence, like this:

```
<body>
    <h1>Welcome!</h1>
    <p>Today's date is:    </p>
</body>
```

3. Add `script` tags where you want the script:

```
    <p>Today's date is:
        <script>
        </script>
    </p>
```

4. Add the `type` attribute to specify the script's MIME type, and the `language` attribute to specify that the scripting language is JavaScript:

```
    <p>Today's date is:
        <script type="text/javascript" language="javascript">
        </script>
    </p>
```

5. Add comment lines to hide the script from browsers that do not recognize scripting. Include standard comment markup (`<!--` and `-->`), and preface the closing comment markup with `//`

to hide the comment close from the JavaScript interpreter; if you don't, you'll get an error. The complete comment looks like this:

```
<p>Today's date is:
   <script type="text/javascript" language="javascript">
       <!--
       // -->
   </script>
</p>
```

6. Add the actual JavaScript statement:

```
<script type="text/javascript" language="javascript">
    <!--
        document.write(Date());
    // -->
</script>
```

That's it! The resulting page looks like this:

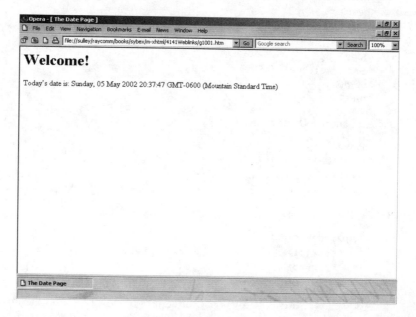

Using this method, the initial "Today's date is" text appears in all browsers, regardless of whether they support JavaScript. Browsers that don't support JavaScript display *Today's date is* and a blank. To hide the text from browsers that don't support JavaScript, simply remove the text from the **p** element and replace the JavaScript statement as shown in the following code:

```
<script type="text/javascript" language="javascript">
   <!--
      document.write("Today\'s date is: " + Date());
   // -->
</script>
```

This way, users will either see the JavaScript or won't see it, but they won't see a lead-in with an unfulfilled promise. You get the same effect in JavaScript-capable browsers and nothing at all in non-JavaScript browsers.

TIP *JavaScript, like all programming languages, has its own punctuation rules, vocabulary, and terminology. Most of that is beyond the scope of this book, but we'll point out the specifics where we can. In the preceding code, notice that the single quote in* Today's *has a backslash in front; that's the "escape character" that tells JavaScript, "Treat this single quote as a text character, not programming punctuation."*

You're not restricted to a single JavaScript statement, and you can embed several statements through the page source. The additional statements in the following code display information about the user's browser in the document:

```
<body>
    <h1>Welcome!</h1>
    <p><script type="text/javascript" language="javascript">
    <!--
        document.write("Today\'s date is: " + Date());

        // -->
    </script></p>
    <p><script type="text/javascript" language="javascript">
        <!--
            document.write("You appear to be using " +
                navigator.appName + " version " +
                navigator.appVersion + ".")
        // -->
    </script></p>
</body>
```

In this script, the JavaScript is interpreted line by line as it appears in the source. In the new statement, the text strings, such as *You appear to be using*, are combined with properties of the navigator object—that is, with characteristics of the browser—to display the line shown. See Master's Reference Part 3 for a full rundown of objects, including the navigator object, and their properties. The resulting page from this example looks like this (see next page):

NOTE *The title bar says Opera, but the JavaScript claims Internet Explorer. Chapter 16 provides both an explanation and examples of how to address this.*

Embedding is a great way to start adding JavaScript to your page. You can use this technique alone or combine it with others.

TIP *If you choose to embed the JavaScript, you'll need to provide for older browsers that don't support it, or, more likely, for visitors who have chosen to disable it. See the section "Providing for Older Browsers" later in this chapter.*

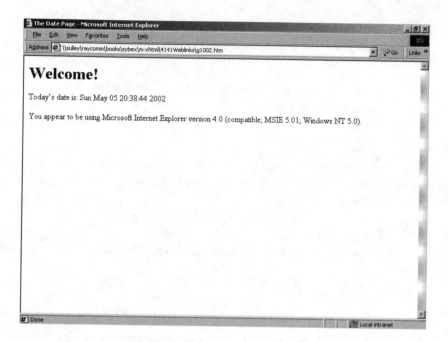

Adding a JavaScript Function in the Head

If you repeatedly use specific JavaScript procedures within documents, consider placing a JavaScript function in the document head element. Collecting individual statements in one place creates a function; creating functions in the head element is convenient and easier to troubleshoot, and it reduces the amount of code to manage and download to users' browsers.

In the following examples, we'll show you how to add JavaScript statements to the document head. Here's the code to start with:

```
<!DOCTYPE html PUBLIC "-//W3C/DTD XHTML 1.0 Transitional//EN"
    "http://www.w3.org/TR/xhtml1/DTD/xhtml1-transitional.dtd">
<html xmlns="http://www.w3.org/1999/xhtml">
<head>
    <title>The Date Page</title>
</head>
<body>
    <h1>Welcome!</h1>
    <p>
    </p>
</body>
</html>
```

This document will include two JavaScript sections. One displays the current date and time, and the other displays the name and version number of the user's browser—the same actions we demonstrated earlier within the body of the document. You include the JavaScript function command in the document **head** element and then run the function from the document body by calling just its name. Here are the steps:

1. Add the **script** tags to the document **head** element, like this:

```
<head>
    <title>The Date Page</title>
    <script>
    </script>
</head>
```

2. Add the **type** attribute to specify that the script is a JavaScript, and the **language** attribute to specify that the scripting language is JavaScript:

```
<head>
    <title>The Date Page</title>
    <script type="text/javascript" language="javascript">
    </script>
</head>
```

3. Add comment markup (<!-- //-->) to hide the script from other browsers. Don't forget the slashes.

```
<head>
    <title>The Date Page</title>
    <script type="text/javascript" language="javascript">
      <!--
      // -->
    </script>
</head>
```

Remember, we're putting the script in the document head, so by itself it will not display anything in the browser window. You have to place instructions within the document body to do anything with the script.

4. To make a function out of the JavaScript statement that displays the date, you name the statement and place it in inside "curly brackets" (a.k.a. *braces*: { }). In this example, the name is **printDate**. Add the keyword **function**, the function name (including a set of parentheses), and the braces.

```
<head>
    <title>The Date Page</title>
    <script type="text/javascript" language="javascript">
      <!--
      function printDate() {  }
      // -->
    </script>
</head>
```

TIP   *If a function needs parameter values, they're usually inserted in these parentheses. For consistency, even functions without parameters, like this one, include these parentheses in their names.*

5. Add the JavaScript statement within the braces. Use the same code we used within the document body a few pages ago. (Remember, we have to wrap lines to fit them on the printed page; you should type the JavaScript function all on one line.)

```
<head>
   <title>The Date Page</title>
   <script type="text/javascript" language="javascript">
      <!--
         function printDate() {
            document.write("Today\'s date is: " + Date());}
      // -->
   </script>
</head>
```

6. To "call" (which means to activate or run) the function from the document body, add another set of script tags within the body tags, as shown here:

```
<body>
   <h1>Welcome!</h1>
   <p>
      <script type="text/javascript" language="javascript">
         <!--
         // -->
      </script>
   </p>
</body>
```

7. Add printDate(), which is the name you gave the function, within the tags:

```
<body>
   <h1>Welcome!</h1>
   <p>
      <script type="text/javascript" language="javascript">
         <!--
            printDate()
         // -->
      </script>
   </p>
</body>
```

Now our code looks like Listing 10.1.

LISTING 10.1: INCLUDING JAVASCRIPT IN THE *head* ELEMENT

```
<!DOCTYPE html PUBLIC "-//W3C/DTD XHTML 1.0 Transitional//EN"
    "http://www.w3.org/TR/xhtml1/DTD/xhtml1-transitional.dtd">
<html xmlns="http://www.w3.org/1999/xhtml">
<head>
    <title>The Date Page</title>
    <script type="text/javascript" language="javascript">
      <!--
          function printDate() {
              document.write("Today\'s date is: " + Date()); }
      // -->
    </script>
</head>
<body>
    <h1>Welcome!</h1>
    <p><script type="text/javascript" language="javascript">
      <!--
          printDate()
      // -->
    </script></p>
</body>
</html>
```

TIP   *If you separate the JavaScript into its own section, enclose it within comment markup: <!-- and //-->. Not all browsers can interpret JavaScript, and the comment markup instructs these browsers to ignore the JavaScript section. JavaScript-enabled browsers will see past the comments and recognize the* script *element.*

COMMENTS MAY NOT WORK IN XHTML IN THE FUTURE

The traditional practice of using the comment element (`<!-- -->!>`) to "hide" scripts from browsers that do not support JavaScript may not work in the future in XHTML, because XML parsers may silently remove the contents of comments—i.e., your script!

There are two possible solutions to this:

1. Use external scripts (which is recommended for XHTML). (See the section "Linking JavaScript.")

2. Wrap the content of the script within a CDATA-marked section, which defines the content of the script as data that an XML parser will not parse. For example:

```
<script>
  <![CDATA[
    ...script content ...
  ]]>
</script>
```

At the time this book is being written, no browsers know how to handle XML CDATA sections. However, further support for XML is very likely in the next versions of browsers. See Part VI for more information about XML. The comment element used in HTML documents should not be affected.

Linking JavaScript

If you plan to use script functions in several documents, consider placing them in a separate file and referring to that file from your document. You can build, test, and store working JavaScript code in one location and use it in several Web pages. You can also share this code with others who can link it into their documents.

TIP   Linking JavaScript is preferable, if possible, because it eases management issues and helps you reuse the code effectively.

The linked document is simply a text file that includes all your variable definitions and functions. You can even copy the functions from the headers of your existing documents if you want. If this document also includes variables and functions that you don't need for the Web page, the browser uses what it needs as the variables and functions are called by the JavaScript code in the document.

To continue with our date example, you can create a `functions.js` document that contains the following text:

```
function printDate() { document.write(Date()) }
```

This linked document does not require any special headings or elements—so it doesn't need comment markup or script tags. An external JavaScript file is a text document whose only content is JavaScript code (similar to an external style sheet, which is a text document with only style definitions). It doesn't require any HTML or XHTML code, but simply includes the definitions for the variables and functions. You can then link to the script with the following code from the document `head` element (including all the surrounding tags):

```
<head>
   <title>The Date Page</title>
   <script src="functions.js" type="text/javascript"
      language="javascript">
   </script>
</head>
```

Now, by including this reference to your external script document, using the appropriate URL for the `src` attribute, you can access any functions included in this external script from any document you create simply by using the same function call that you would have used if the script had been embedded.

You can include as many functions or variable definitions within your external script document as you like. Alternatively, you can reference multiple external scripts by including additional `script` elements.

Providing for Older Browsers

As you add JavaScript to your pages, you must accommodate browsers in which JavaScript is disabled or unavailable, as well as older browsers that cannot interpret JavaScript. If you include JavaScript in the `head` element or if you link the JavaScript from a separate document, you've already provided for older browsers because these don't show up in the document body.

However, if you embed the JavaScript, you must make sure the script doesn't show up. The best way to accommodate older browsers is to make sure that text that is dependent on the JavaScript (such as "Today's date is") is part of the JavaScript statement. You might recall from Listing 10.1 that the embedded code looks like this:

```
<script type="text/javascript" language="javascript">
   <!--
      document.write("Today\'s date is: " + Date());
   // -->
</script>
```

However, if you want to give additional information to non-JavaScript browsers (rather than just hiding information from them), you can also use the noscript element and include alternative text. For example, if you have a form that uses JavaScript to validate input, you might add a statement to the top of the form, within a noscript element, that warns users of non-JavaScript browsers that their responses won't be validated and that they should be particularly careful to proofread their responses; for example:

```
<h2>Personal Information Form</h2>
<noscript>
   <p>Please be very careful to proofread your responses.
      If any information is incorrect (particularly your
      e-mail address), we won't be able to contact you.</p>
</noscript>
Please enter your name and address below:<br />
```

In this example, the JavaScript-enabled browser displays only the *Personal Information Form* heading, followed by "Please enter your name and address below:". Other browsers will *also* display the "Please be very careful" text.

For a small amount of JavaScript or for JavaScript that isn't essential to the content of your document, using the noscript element is a convenient way to deal with both situations. If you have more complex JavaScript applications on your page, you'll need to identify users' browsers and automatically direct them to the correct page. In that case, instead of putting content within the noscript tags, a separate page is created for users without JavaScript. To do this, you need a script to perform browser detection, and at least two different versions of the page (one for users with JavaScript enabled and one for users without JavaScript).

TIP *See HotScripts on the Web at* www.hotscripts.com *for server-side means of identifying browsers and redirecting them appropriately, or see Chapter 16 for a client-side version of browser detection using JavaScript.*

Adding Event Handlers

JavaScript relies heavily on event handlers, which react to users' actions by running statements or calling JavaScript functions. Event handlers react to what is happening (the page loading into the browser, for example) or what a visitor is doing on the page—moving the mouse, clicking a button, or selecting options on a form—and then do whatever you tell them to do in each instance. For example, with the onmouseover and onmouseout event handlers, you can change the information in your status bar, flash an alert box, or change an illustration.

TIP *JavaScript provides a variety of event handlers that can react to users' actions. In this chapter, we discuss only a couple of them, but the principles used for these apply to all event handlers. Master's Reference Part 3 explains all of them.*

WARNING *The examples in this chapter are—relatively speaking—easy to implement, easy to understand, and easy to test. However, they are not necessarily appropriate for your users and could, in fact, confuse or irritate them. The key information for you to bring away from this section is how to use event handlers, not necessarily how to cause your user's browser to gyrate whenever the mouse is moved. See Part IV for information about developing a Web site with your users' needs in mind.*

Using *onmouseover* and *onmouseout* Events

You commonly use an onmouseover event with the anchor element (a) to provide additional information about the link. The onmouseout event, then, generally undoes what the onmouseover event does.

Using these event handlers, you can, among other things, implement timed status bar events, swap images, and alert users. We'll show you how in the next few sections. But first, let's look at how to add the onmouseover and onmouseout event handlers.

TIP *Neither IE 3 or earlier nor Netscape Navigator 2 or earlier recognizes the onmouseout event. If your visitors use these browsers (which is pretty unlikely anymore), consider using a separate function (described later) to clear the status bar. According to statistics derived from the users of* **www.thecounter.com**, *only 7 percent of people use a 4.0 or older browser.*

Let's add the onmouseover and onmouseout event handlers to display a new message in the status bar and then remove it. This is handy for displaying information in the status bar that is more descriptive than the URL that the browser automatically displays there. Here are the steps:

1. Start with a document that includes a link, like this:

```
<!DOCTYPE html PUBLIC
   "-//W3C/DTD XHTML 1.0 Transitional//EN"
 "http://www.w3.org/TR/xhtml1/DTD/xhtml1-transitional.dtd">
<html xmlns="http://www.w3.org/1999/xhtml">
<head>
   <title>Status Bar</title>
</head>
<body>
   <h1>Welcome!</h1>
   <a href="http://www.raycomm.com/">
      Visit the Raycomm, Inc. site.</a>
</body>
</html>
```

2. Add the onmouseover event handler to the a element:

```
<a href="http://www.raycomm.com/" onmouseover="">
   Visit the RayComm, Inc. site.</a>
```

3. Add `window.status=` to the event handler. The `window.status` property specifies what appears in the status bar.

```
<a href="http://www.raycomm.com/"
   onmouseover="window.status=">
   Visit the RayComm, Inc. site.</a>
```

4. Add the text that will appear in the status bar, enclosed in single quotes (' '). You use single quotes because the `window.status` statement itself is enclosed in double quotes, and you must nest unlike quotes within each other.

```
<a href="http://www.raycomm.com/"
   onmouseover="window.status='Check us out!'">
   Visit the RayComm, Inc. site.</a>
```

5. Add a semicolon (to indicate the end of the statement), and add `return true` to the end (just before the closing quotes). This essentially tells the JavaScript interpreter that the action is complete and to do it.

```
<a href="http://www.raycomm.com/"
   onmouseover="window.status='Check us out!'; return
   true;">
   Visit the RayComm, Inc. site.</a>
```

If you try this, you'll see that the "Check us out!" statement appears in the browser status bar after you move the cursor over the link. The statement stays in the status bar, which probably isn't what you want.

To restore the status bar after the cursor moves away from the link, add the `onmouseout` event handler, like this:

```
<a href="http://www.raycomm.com/"
   onmouseover="window.status='Check us out!'; return true"
   onmouseout="window.status=''; return true;">
   Visit the RayComm, Inc. site.</a>
```

COMMENTS IN JAVASCRIPT

Add comments (actual notes to yourself, not just comment markup) to your JavaScript to track what the script does. This is useful for future reference and helpful to people with whom you share your JavaScript functions. Comments in JavaScript are preceded by two forward slashes, //. You need to add these slashes at the beginning of each comment line, as in the following code segment: `<script type="text/javascript" language="javascript">`

```
<!--
function checkOut() {
    // The following loop rejects the survey if any
    // fields were not filled out
    for (x = 0; x < document.survey.elements.length; x++) {
        if (document.survey.elements[x].value == "") {
```

Continued on next page

COMMENTS IN JAVASCRIPT *(continued)*

```
            alert("Sorry, you forgot one of the required
                fields. Please try again.")
            break;  }  }
     return false;
     if (document.survey.firstname.value.length <= 2) {
        alert("Please enter your full first name.")
        return false;  }  }
   //-->
</script>
```

ADDING A LITTLE EXCITEMENT TO THE PAGE LOAD

Just as events can respond to a user's mouse actions, events can occur when the page loads or unloads. However, anything time consuming (such as playing a sound) or intrusive (such as displaying a welcome alert) can irritate users far more than impressing them with your technical skills.

We suggest that you perform actions with onload or onunload event handlers only if users will expect it in the context of the page or for other reasons, such as the example of breaking out of frames, later in this chapter.

See Chapter 11 for more information about adding sounds.

SWAPPING IMAGES

You can use the onmouseover and onmouseout event handlers to change linked images when the mouse cursor moves over them. These are often called *rollovers*.

WARNING   *This technique works only with Netscape Navigator 3 or later and IE 4 or later. Older browsers don't recognize images as objects.*

To change an image when the mouse moves over it, you need an anchor element (<a href="url">) and two versions of the image: one is the standard presentation, and the other is the highlighted presentation. When the page initially loads, the standard image is visible. Then, when the mouse moves over the image, the highlighted image replaces the standard image. Finally, when the mouse cursor moves away again, the images change back. Conceptually, the process is the same as changing the status bar text in the preceding example; however, instead of changing the status bar, you swap images.

To set up images to swap, you first need a pair of images that are precisely the same size but visually different. (If the images are different sizes, the process works but looks pretty bad to users.)

Next, you need a link using an image in your document. The img element must also have a name attribute so the JavaScript can identify and refer to it. We'll use the following sample document:

```
<!DOCTYPE html PUBLIC "-//W3C/DTD XHTML 1.0 Transitional//EN"
   "http://www.w3.org/TR/xhtml1/DTD/xhtml1-transitional.dtd">
<html xmlns="http://www.w3.org/1999/xhtml">
```

```
<head>
   <title>Image Swap</title>
</head>
<body bgcolor="ffffff" text="000000" link="0000ff"
   vlink="800080" alink="ff0000">
   <center>
      <a href="http://www.example.com/">
         <img src="image1.gif" width="50" height="10" border="0"
            name="catbtn" id="catbtn" alt="catbtn" /></a>
   </center>
</body>
</html>
```

Two images, cleverly titled `image1.gif` and `image2.gif`, are available to swap within the `img` element. To identify the image, you refer to it by name (here, `catbtn`) and `src`, which is a property of the `catbtn` image object. For example, to change the image (but not change it back), you can use a statement such as the following:

```
onmouseover="catbtn.src='image2.gif'; return true;"
```

In the context of the img element set to `image1.gif`, the `onmouseover` statement looks like this:

```
<a href="http://www.example.com/"
   onmouseover="catbtn.src='image2.gif'; return true; ">
<img src="image1.gif" width="50" height="10" border="0"
   name="catbtn" id="catbtn" alt="catbtn" /></a>
```

Triggering this statement changes the source (`src`) property of the object named `catbtn` to `image2.gif`.
Similarly, to change the image back when the cursor moves away, use an `onmouseout` statement with the opposite image setting, as shown here:

```
<a href="http://www.example.com/"
   onmouseover="catbtn.src='image2.gif'; return true;"
   onmouseout="catbtn.src='image1.gif'; return true;">
<img src="image1.gif" width="50" height="10" border="0"
   name="catbtn" id="catbtn" alt="catbtn" /></a>
```

The complete code for simple image swapping with two images is shown in Listing 10.2. Note that this is just a contrived example. If you enter this code in a text editor, it will work only if you have two images titled `image1.gif` and `image2.gif`.

LISTING 10.2: SIMPLE IMAGE SWAPPING WITH TWO IMAGES

```
<!DOCTYPE html PUBLIC "-//W3C/DTD XHTML 1.0 Transitional//EN"
   "http://www.w3.org/TR/xhtml1/DTD/xhtml1-transitional.dtd">
<html xmlns="http://www.w3.org/1999/xhtml">
<head>
   <title>Image Swap</title>
</head>
<body bgcolor="ffffff" text="000000" link="0000ff"
```

```
        vlink="800080" alink="ff0000">
  <center>
    <a href="http://www.example.com/"
        onmouseover="catbtn.src='image2.gif'; return true; "
        onmouseout="catbtn.src='image1.gif'; return true; ">
    <img src="image1.gif" width="50" height="10" border="0"
        name="catbtn" id="catbtn" alt="catbtn" /></a>
  </center>
</body>
</html>
```

For a series of images, you use a series of `if` statements in a function to make the changes. Using `if` statements keeps your code easier to read and makes it easier to change your script later. You can add more statements to reshuffle images in different contexts by adding a function like this in the head section of your document:

```
function imagereplacer(place) {
    if (place==1) document.catbtn.src="image2.gif";
    if (place==2) document.catbtn.src="image1.gif";  }
```

The `if` statements check for the value of `place` and changes the image accordingly. You call this function from the body of your document. Instead of writing the full `imagereplacer` function in the a element, you put just the function name in the attribute value, with the desired setting for `place` in the parameter parentheses, as shown here:

```
<a href="http://www.example.com/">
    <img src="image1.gif" width="50" height="10" border="0"
        onmouseover="imagereplacer(1)" alt="catbtn" name="catbtn"
        id="catbtn" onmouseout="imagereplacer(2)" />
</a>
```

If you want to do more—such as change the image *and* change the status bar, or if you have several different cases that you want to handle without writing `if` statement after `if` statement—you can use a special JavaScript keyword, `switch`, as shown here:

```
function imagereplacer(place) {
    switch (place) {
        case(1): document.catbtn.src="image2.gif";
            window.status="Second Image";
            break;
        case(2): document.catbtn.src="image1.gif";
            window.status="First Image";
            break;  }  }
```

Using this technique, you can list all the options. Similar to the previous `if` statements, the `switch` statement lists each option and the action to take, but with `switch` it's easier to perform multiple or complex actions. In a `switch` statement, each option is a `case`.

In this example, the first line calls the function and includes the number for the variable place. You use place in the switch statement, which has two cases. If place is equal to one, use case(1), which sets the source property for the image named catbtn (catbtn.src) to image2.gif.

TIP *If you're using objects, methods, properties, or event handlers from early versions of JavaScript, you don't need to add the version to the* language *attribute. However, if you're using expanded capabilities from later versions—as we're going to do with the* switch *statement here—and functions are defined in the document, include the version number within the attribute, for example,* language="javascript1.2".

The change from the if-statement imagereplacer function to the case-statement version requires no changes within your document body. When you put JavaScript functions in the document head, you can make changes without editing all the elements in your code.

WARNING *It's very important to test your JavaScript code in as many browsers as possible. The code in Listing 10.2 works in both Netscape Navigator 3 and later and IE 4 and later. However, the code using the* switch *statement works in IE 4 and later, but only in Netscape Navigator 6.*

Using *onclick* and *onchange* Event Handlers

In addition to onmouseover and onmouseout event handlers, you can use onclick and onchange event handlers, which are activated when users click an object or a button or change a form field, respectively. Including these event handlers is similar to using the onmouseover and onmouseout event handlers. You can use the onchange or onclick event handler to set link destinations in forms, among other things.

ALERTING USERS WITH *onclick*

A handy use for the onclick event is an alert box, which is a small dialog box that contains a message and an OK button. For example, an alert could be an expanded note about the object, such as "Come to this page for more news on this year's programs!"

At its simplest, you can combine an event handler (to start the process) with an alert, like this:

```
<img src="infolink.jpg" alt="link"
   onclick="alert('Visit RayComm!'); return true;" />
```

Users see the accompanying dialog box and must click OK to proceed. Alerts can be quite irritating, however, so use them with great care and careful thought. For example, you can combine the alert with form-validation information and base the alert box on the user's form responses.

SETTING LINK DESTINATIONS IN FORMS

One of the handiest JavaScript functions is setting link destinations in forms to direct users to information based on their selections in the form. For example, if a form contains a Course Offered selection list, users can choose courses that interest them, and you can programmatically set the destination of a jump to meet the needs of the selections. You can also use JavaScript to set destinations so that when a user clicks buttons or performs other actions on the page, the script opens new pages—just as traditional links would. This technique can add visual interest to your pages as well as let you interactively produce new pages for your users.

Minimally, to set destinations and activate links, use the `onclick` event handler, as shown here:

```
<form>
    <input type="radio" name="lesson" value="Lesson 1"
        onclick="self.location='lesson1.htm'" />
    Lesson 1: Getting Started
</form>
```

The `self.location='lesson1.htm'` entry opens the file `lesson1.htm` in the same window when a user clicks the radio button. If you want the document to open in a separate window, the process is similar. For example, to open `lesson1.htm` in another frame, called `main`, you can use the following:

```
<input type="radio" name="lesson" value="Lesson 1"
    onclick="parent.main.location='lesson1.htm'" />
    Lesson 1: Getting Started
```

TIP *The* `parent.main.location` *object name refers to the parent document. In this example, that would be the frameset document; this name then refers to the* `main` *object (frame) within the frameset, then the* `location` *property of the frame.*

A single jump can also lead to a variable destination—the document opened depends on the user's selection from a list. Say your document contains catalog information, such as pictures, product descriptions, and prices. A user clicks a category to open the correct page of your catalog. Users might also select activities from a list such as this:

```
<form>
    <select name="Activity"
            onchange="setLink(this.selectedIndex)">
        <option>Hiking</option>
        <option>Camping</option>
        <option selected="selected">Mountain</option>
        <option>Sailing</option>
        <option>Winter</option>
    </select>
</form>
```

The `onchange` event handler passes information to a function called `setLink`. The `selectedIndex` property is the position in the list (starting with zero of the current selection in the list. So, `this.selectedIndex` is the numeric value that represents the position in the current list of the value selected.

A relatively simple function `setLink`, located in the document head, assigns the final URL to the page properties and loads the new URL:

```
<script type="text/javascript" language="javascript">
    <!--
    function setLink(num) {
        if (num = 0) { self.location="hiking.html"   }
        if (num = 1) { self.location="camping.html"  }
        if (num = 2) { self.location="mountain.html" }
        if (num = 3) { self.location="sailing.html"  }
        if (num = 4) { self.location="winter.html"   }  }
    //-->
</script>
```

With this type of scripting, it's easier to figure out what's going on, to make changes later, and to accommodate unique, nonsequential names, such as `newmountainbikes.html` or `augustactivities.html`.

Using the *onsubmit* Event Handler

One of the most common uses for the `onsubmit` event handler is to validate form input. You can verify that users fill in required fields, that they make required selections, or that they fill in an appropriate combination of fields. Suppose you provide a form that lets users purchase T-shirts. You can use JavaScript to verify that users include their mailing address, provide a credit card number, and specify a color. If you lack any of this input from users, you won't be able to complete the order.

The following examples, based on the TECHWR-L general information form, show a couple of approaches to form validation. These examples assume a form with `name="survey"`. If your form is named differently, please adjust accordingly. You can also substitute `form[0]` for the name of the first form within your page.

You can use the following generic script to loop through your form and check for forgotten or omitted values:

```
<script type="text/javascript" language="javascript">
    <!--
    function checkOut() {
        for (x = 0; x < document.survey.elements.length; x++) {
            if (document.survey.elements[x].value == "") {
                alert("Sorry, you forgot one of the required
                      fields. Please try again.")
                break;   }   }
        return false;   }
    //-->
</script>
```

To check your form, use `onsubmit="checkOut(this.form)"` in your `form` element. The script looks through each of the fields in your form to see whether any are completely empty, and if there's an empty field, an alert appears with the "Sorry..." text and then the function completes.

TIP   *For a more sophisticated (and user-friendly) solution, consider making the script report back to the user which field was not completed. Your users will thank you.*

If some fields need to be filled and some don't, or if you need to check specific values, you can handle these situations. For example, to ensure that the first name field (called `firstname`) is filled out and not too short (fewer than two characters), add the following `if` statement to the script:

```
if (document.survey.firstname.value.length <= 2) {
    alert("Please enter your full first name.")
    return false;   }
```

The complete script would then look like this:

```
<script type="text/javascript" language="javascript">
    <!--
```

```
        function checkOut() {
            for (x = 0; x < document.survey.elements.length; x++) {
                if (document.survey.elements[x].value == "") {
                    alert("Sorry, you forgot one of the required
                            fields. Please try again.")
                    break;  }  }
            return false;
            if (document.survey.firstname.value.length <= 2) {
                alert("Please enter your full first name.")
                return false;  }  }
    //-->
</script>
```

You can continue adding other conditions in the same way.

One of the more complex validation problems involves e-mail addresses. Although more complex scripts are available, you'll probably find that a basic check to ensure that the address includes something, an @ sign, and something else (like kelly@somewhere) will suffice:

```
<script type="text/javascript" language="javascript">
    <!--
    function checkOut() {
        for (x = 0; x < document.survey.elements.length; x++){
            if (document.survey.elements[x].value == "") {
                alert("Sorry, you forgot one of the required
                        fields. Please try again.")
                break;  }  }
        return false;
        if (document.survey.firstname.value.length <= 2){
            alert("Please enter your full first name.")
            return false  }
        if (document.survey.emailaddr.value.indexOf('@') == -1 ) {
            alert("Please correct your email address. It should
                    look like you@domain.com")
        return false  }  }
    //-->
</script>
```

This addition verifies that the address contains an @ and that something after the @ exists. If you need more comprehensive validation, check out the scripts at the following Netscape site:

`http://developer.netscape.com/library/examples/javascript/formval/overview.html`
or look for form validation scripts at `javascript.internet.com/forms/`.

Using the *onload* Event Handler

The `onload` event handler is activated when a document loads in a Web browser. After a user clicks a link (or follows a bookmark, or whatever), the new page is transferred from the server and loaded into the browser. The `onload` event handler is activated as soon as the necessary functions and the opening body element load.

You can use this event handler to play a sound file or to launch those annoying pop-up ads, but you can also use it for more practical purposes. For example, if you have a Web site that does not use frames, you might want to use an `onload` event handler to ensure that your pages are not loaded into frames. In other words, if you are in charge of the Yahoo! Web site, you would not want to be "framed," as shown in Figure 10.1.

FIGURE 10.1

You can use event handlers to keep from being "framed," as Yahoo! is here

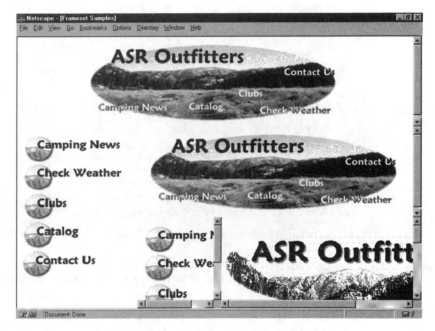

TIP   See Chapter 7 for more information about why you don't want other sites framing your site.

In this example, we first check the `location` property of the `window` object to see whether it is `top`, meaning that it is not embedded in a frameset. If the property is not `top`, the JavaScript function resets the `location` property to make it `top`.

To use an `onload` event handler, you must do two things:

◆   Create the function you want to use.

◆   Add the `onload` event handler to the opening `body` element.

As we have done previously, we create the script in the document head. Here's how:

1.   In an HTML or XHTML document, add the `script` element and comment lines in the document head:

```
<!DOCTYPE html PUBLIC
    "-//W3C/DTD XHTML 1.0 Transitional//EN"
"http://www.w3.org/TR/xhtml1/DTD/xhtml1-transitional.dtd">
<html xmlns="http://www.w3.org/1999/xhtml">
```

```
<head>
   <title>Framed Document</title>
   <script type="text/javascript" language="javascript">
      <!--
      //-->
   </script>
</head>
<body>
   <h1>Framed Document</h1>
   <p>Content goes here</p>
</body>
</html>
```

2. Name the function `breakFrames` and add the needed braces:

```
<script type="text/javascript" language="javascript">
   <!--
   function breakFrames() {  }
   //-->
</script>
```

3. Add the `if` statement to determine whether the document is within a frameset:

```
<script type="text/javascript" language="javascript">
   <!--
   function breakFrames() {
      if (window.top.location != window.self.location ) {}
   //-->
</script>
```

4. Add the action to be performed when the `if` statement is true (that is, when the document is included in frames):

```
<script type="text/javascript" language="javascript">
   <!--
   function breakFrames() {
      if (window.top.location != window.self.location )
{ window.top.location = window.self.location }
   //-->
</script>
```

5. Add a `return true` statement. Again, this serves to tell the JavaScript interpreter that the function is done.

```
<script type="text/javascript" language="javascript">
   <!--
   function breakFrames() {
      if (window.top.location != window.self.location )
{ window.top.location = window.self.location }
      return true;  }
   //-->
</script>
```

6. With this `breakFrames` script in the document head, now you need to call the script from within the `body` element to execute the entire function. Add an `onload` statement to the `body` element:

```
<body onload="breakFrames()">
```

Listing 10.3 shows the complete code.

LISTING 10.3: JAVASCRIPT USING A `onload` **EVENT HANDLER**

```
<!DOCTYPE html PUBLIC
    "-//W3C/DTD XHTML 1.0 Transitional//EN"
  "http://www.w3.org/TR/xhtml1/DTD/xhtml1-transitional.dtd">
<html xmlns="http://www.w3.org/1999/xhtml">
<head>
    <title>Framed Document</title>
    <script type="text/javascript" language="javascript">
      <!--
    function breakFrames() {
        if (window.top.location != window.self.location )
{ window.top.location = window.self.location }
        return true;  }
        //-->
    </script>
</head>
<body onload="breakFrames()">
    <h1>Framed Document</h1>
    <p>Content goes here</p>
</body>
</html>
```

With the event handler and script in place, your document will break out of any frameset it appears in (including your own, of course).

Tracking Users Using Cookies

Cookies are objects you can use to store information about users of your site, and that you can access with JavaScript. You can think of cookies as being high-tech name tags that identify your browser and pass along a little other information to a server computer. For example, if you visit the Amazon.com Web site using your Opera browser and purchase a book there, the Amazon.com server deposits a cookie on your computer. Then, the next time you visit that site with that browser, the server looks for the cookie so it can identify you. The cookie on your computer is then matched to information about you that is stored on the server, such as the information you provided and the books you purchased. In this case, cookies can help make subsequent visits easier because users don't have to reenter information.

Although the security risk to users is minor, many people are (understandably) a little sensitive about having information stored about them and read by other computers. For that reason, browsers now offer users a lot of control over how cookies are handled. Early versions of Netscape Navigator simply accepted all cookies. Now, most browsers that recognize cookies have an option to warn users when a cookie is created and give users the option to accept or reject individual cookies, or to reject cookies that are not coming from the same site you are browsing.

TIP *Most browsers include options for handling cookies. In Netscape Navigator, select Edit ➤ Preferences ➤ Advanced to specify how you want the browser to handle cookies. In IE, go to Tools ➤ Internet Options ➤ Security ➤ Custom for cookie options. The default in both browsers is to enable cookies, so you need to change the options only if you want to disable cookies, or if you want to receive a message before allowing a cookie to be placed in your computer.*

Either way, the cookie information is not public property; the cookie stores information for you only, and not for public broadcast. Additionally, the cookie generally just contains information to identify you to the server, and then the server associates that information ("aha, it's Jane Doe back for more books") with your address, credit card, and book purchasing history, for example. Additionally, when the server asks your browser for the cookie, it can only see and read the cookie it deposited, not other cookies, files, or information.

If you want to track users to your Web site, you can, using two types of cookies:

◆ Session cookies, which endure only until a user closes the browser

◆ Persistent cookies, which endure until the expiration date you set

Session Cookies

Suppose you want to keep some information about a user's browsing session, such as the pages browsed or the products viewed. You can do so using *session cookies*. This JavaScript not only records the user's session information, but also sends a message to the user when he or she arrives at and exits your site.

TIP *This example shows some of the capabilities and power of cookies. It's also likely to irritate many users. Even if they know that cookies can be set and used, they likely don't want to be reminded of it overtly.*

To implement session cookies, first create an empty cookie when the page loads. Start with a functional document, such as the following:

```
<!DOCTYPE html PUBLIC "-//W3C/DTD XHTML 1.0 Transitional//EN"
    "http://www.w3.org/TR/xhtml1/DTD/xhtml1-transitional.dtd">
<html xmlns="http://www.w3.org/1999/xhtml">
<head>
    <title>ASR Outfitters Cookie Form</title>
</head>
<body>
    Cookie Bearing Document
</body>
</html>
```

Now, follow these steps:

1. Add a function to the document head element that sets the document cookie to the local time and date:

```
<script type="text/javascript" language="javascript">
  <!--
  function homeMadeCookies() {
      var gotHere = new Date();
      document.cookie = gotHere.toLocaleString()  }
  // -->
</script>
```

2. Initialize the cookie from the onload event handler, like this:

```
<body onload="homeMadeCookies()">
```

The onload event handler starts the function called homeMadeCookies, which creates and places a value into the variable gotHere. From that information, the next line converts the GMT time to local time and stores that in document.cookie.

By setting up a second function, you can display a message when the user leaves. The fareWell function looks like this:

```
function fareWell() {
    var timedVisit = new Date();
    var tempTime = timedVisit.toLocaleString();
    alert("You got here at: " + document.cookie +
          " and now it's: " + tempTime + ".  " +
          "Thank you for visiting our site.");  }
```

Then, by adding an onunload event handler to the body element, you can display the farewell message:

```
<body onload="homeMadeCookies()" onunload="fareWell()">
```

The fareWell entry uses an alert to display a brief—cookie-based—message thanking the user, as shown in Figure 10.2.

FIGURE 10.2

You can use cookies to produce alerts specific to the user's situation

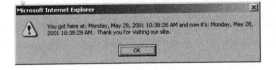

Persistent Cookies

You can also store information in cookies for a period of time. You use *persistent cookies* when you want to store information and use it in the future. For example, if a user fills out a form that includes his or her name and other personal information, you'd want to keep that information and use it when the user visits in the future. This is, for example, how the Amazon.com site tracks your visits and seems to know things about you during subsequent visits.

Here are some facts you should know about persistent cookies:

◆ A browser retains a limited number of cookies. Older cookies are discarded to make room for new ones.

◆ A cookie cannot be larger than 4 KB.

◆ You can have only 20 cookies per domain. If you're working from a large ISP, you might not be able to set cookies for all users.

These restrictions may not seem limiting at first, but they become so when the demand for feedback increases. Unlike session cookies, persistent cookies need an expiration date. After the cookie expires, a former user is treated as a new user.

TIP   *Matt's Script Archive includes a section titled "HTTP Cookie Lib" that provides an excellent overview of the subject, pointers to many important resources, and a helpful list of FAQs. You'll find all this material online at* `www.worldwidemart.com/scripts/faq/cookielib.shtml`. *The material looks dated, but it is still accurate. Also see* `www.cookiecentral.com/faq/` *for lots of good information.*

Where to Go from Here

In this chapter, we introduced you to JavaScript and showed you some of the most basic (and useful!) JavaScript functions. As you can see, JavaScript offers a variety of useful applications and can help you create cutting-edge documents.

From here, you can wander to several chapters. Here's what we recommend:

◆ See Chapter 11 to learn about including multimedia in your XHTML documents.

◆ See Chapter 12 to plan a Web site that meets your users' needs.

◆ Visit Chapter 15 to learn about publishing your XHTML documents.

◆ See Master's Reference Part 3 for a comprehensive guide to JavaScript.

◆ See Chapter 7 for information about frames.

◆ See Chapter 9 for information about style sheets. (The methods for associating style sheets with documents is similar to how you associate JavaScript with documents.)

Chapter 11

Including Multimedia

IN RECENT YEARS, WEB surfers have seen text-only pages transform into pages that bounce, shimmy, sing, and gyrate. Developers of public sites, in particular, are using flair and excitement in an effort to attract users and to keep them coming back again and again. Flashy elements don't always attract, however. Some users find them such a distraction that they don't continue to browse the site, nor do they return to it. The key is to use glitz wisely and to carefully weigh its benefits and liabilities—and only use it if it adds to the overall value of the page.

In this chapter, we'll show you how to include special effects—animated Graphics Interchange Format (GIF) files, sounds, videos, Flash animations, Java applets, and ActiveX controls—collectively known as multimedia. (In this book, we define multimedia as anything you can include in a Web page other than basic HTML or XHTML code and static images.) We'll look at the pros and cons of various elements and discuss how to include them effectively, if you do choose to include them. This chapter covers the following topics:

◆ Deciding to include multimedia

◆ Using animated GIFs

◆ Adding sounds

◆ Adding video

◆ Adding Java applets

◆ Adding Flash animations

◆ Adding multimedia

Deciding to Include Multimedia

Animated images, sounds, and video can make your pages come alive. Done correctly, multimedia can also give Web pages that "up with technology" look and feel. However, before you run off to gather multimedia elements, take heed: Multimedia poses several challenges, both for users and for the developer.

TIP *The principles for including these effects apply to other elements you might discover. For example, if the engineers at your company want to publish their AutoCAD files on your corporate intranet, you can include them in Web pages, following the principles outlined in the "Adding Multimedia" section in this chapter.*

The Challenges for Users

Multimedia can bring your pages to a virtual halt as users sit and wait (and wait!) for the effects to download. Although some multimedia effects, such as animated GIFs, can be as small as 2 KB, other effects, such as video, can easily grow to 5 MB or more. Even though many of your users may have fast Internet connections that would make multimedia usable and useful, many will likely have much slower connections.

TIP *Of all the various multimedia formats available, Macromedia's Flash (*`www.macromedia.com/software/`
`flashplayer`*) is the most widely available on all browsers and operating systems. Therefore, it is the least likely to inconvenience your users.*

In addition, some multimedia effects require *plug-ins* (which are programs used to view effects that may not come with browsers). In the past, users had to download and install a separate plug-in for each multimedia effect and for each format that created the effect (for example, one plug-in for one video format, another for a different kind of video, and so on). However, in newer browsers, support for many multimedia elements is part of the basic browser installation package, including support for *streaming* audio and video (which can be listened to and/or viewed as the download is occurring) and QuickTime video playback, as well as 3D animation and the *Virtual Reality Markup Language* (VRML). (VRML is one way to provide 3D simulations on the Web.)

Internet Explorer (3.0 and higher) can download plug-ins automatically if a user needs a feature that's not already installed. The user still has to wait to view the effect, though. Netscape Navigator users, however, may click to view the effect and then (in one vividly memorable example):

1. Be informed that they don't have the right plug-in.

2. Be taken to the Netscape Web page to get it.

3. Click to download the plug-in.

4. Fill out a form with personal information (name, address, type of business).

5. Submit the form.

6. Be taken back to the original site (a different page).

7. Choose to download the plug-in.

8. Specify where it should be saved.

9. Wait for it to download.

10. Browse to the downloaded file on the local hard drive.

11. Double-click the installation program to run it.

12. Accept the license agreement.

13. Approve the installation location.

14. Wait for the installation to finish.

15. Exit Netscape Navigator.

16. Restart Netscape Navigator.

17. Browse back to the original site.

18. View the effect (finally).

Eighteen steps and many minutes later, they get to see the multimedia effect, which may not even be worth the time and effort it took.

Luckily, this happens rarely with the newer versions of Netscape, which include many multimedia features as part of the basic installation. Of course, the user can always choose *not* to install a plug-in or to view a particular multimedia element on a page.

TIP   Netscape Navigator also includes another feature for multimedia users. If you go to the Help menu and choose About Plug-ins, you'll find out which plug-ins are currently installed, the version number, and what type of multimedia files they support.

MULTIMEDIA DEVELOPERS

Some multimedia software companies offer integrated packages of free software (you can also purchase expanded versions), which support almost all multimedia file formats available on the Web. If you download and install one or more of these programs, you will be able to view multimedia on the Web with few hassles, but remember that your users would have to do the same to get the same capabilities. These software programs include:

◆ RealPlayer, which supports RealAudio and RealVideo, as well as several other media types available as plug-ins. Currently, plug-ins are available for RealText, RealPix, WAV, Audio Video Interleave (AVI), Be Here iVideo, RealText 3D, Liquid Music Player, Screenwatch, Learnkey's RealCBT, NetPodium Quickcast, Moving Picture Experts Group (MPEG) Video (Layer 1), GIF, JPEG, MP3 Audio & Playlist (Layer 1), and Musical Instrument Digital Interface (MIDI) formats. Download RealPlayer at:

   www.real.com

◆ QuickTime, which supports more than 200 types of digital media, including MP3, MIDI, AVI, AVR, streaming media, and digital video. Download QuickTime at:

   www.apple.com/quicktime

◆ Windows Media Player, which includes seven features in a single application: CD player, audio and video player, media jukebox, media guide, Internet radio, portable device music file transfer, and an audio CD burner. It's available for both PCs and Macintosh computers. Download Windows Media Player at:

   www.microsoft.com/windows/windowsmedia/EN/default.asp

The Challenges for Developers

In addition to these resounding indictments of carefree multimedia use in Web pages, it gets worse. For you, the developer, obtaining relevant and useful multimedia objects is often difficult. Your first option is to create the effects yourself, which requires both raw materials (such as photographs, sounds, and video clips) and often special software that you must both purchase and learn to use. In addition, even if you're familiar with the software, developing effective multimedia objects can be time consuming.

You can also browse the Web for multimedia elements, which is a less expensive and less time-consuming option, but you may not find exactly what you want. Although tons of multimedia elements are available on the Web, they're likely to be inappropriate or not freely available for you to use.

Your goal is to carefully consider the advantages and disadvantages of each multimedia element *before* you include it. Start by asking these questions:

- ◆ Does the multimedia element add content that I cannot otherwise provide?

- ◆ Does the multimedia element clearly enhance or complement content?

- ◆ Do the users have browsers that support these elements?

- ◆ Do the users have fast Internet connections?

- ◆ Are the users likely to have the appropriate plug-ins or the time, inclination, and technical wherewithal to get and install them?

- ◆ Do I have the time, skills, and resources to develop or find multimedia elements?

If you answer yes to some or all these questions and you opt to include multimedia, the rest of this chapter is for you.

TIP *Throughout this chapter, we point out that you can find multimedia elements on the Web. However, remember that much of what you find is not available for public use. Before you take a file and use it as your own, be sure that it's clearly labeled "for public use" and that the licensing agreement is compatible with your intended use. For example, many multimedia effects are available for non-commercial use on private Web pages, but not for a business application. If something is not clearly labeled, you should assume that it's not for you to take and use, or just send the Webmaster an e-mail and ask for permission. Nothing ventured, nothing gained.*

CONSIDERING MULTIMEDIA USABILITY

Before you commit to fully multimedia enhanced pages—or even to a single animated GIF on your home page—consider carefully what including multimedia will do to your site's usability. User Interface Engineering (`http://world.std.com/~uieweb/surprise.htm`) presents some alarming findings about the usability of Web pages that incorporate multimedia elements.

In their pilot study, these authors found that "animation did seem to cause delays in the users' performance" and support that finding with observational research in which Web site visitors sat and waited through several cycles of an animation in order for the page to finish displaying—which of course it never did, since the animation continued to cycle.

Continued on next page

Developing and Using Animated GIFs

Perhaps the easiest multimedia element to include is an animated GIF, which is a file that, more or less, includes a bunch of images stacked together to give the illusion of movement. Animated GIFs are similar to those little cartoon booklets or "flip books" you had as a kid. When you quickly whirred through the pages, the cartoon seemed to move. Of course, the illusion of movement was nothing more than each drawing being slightly different. Animated GIFs work the same way.

The uses for animated GIFs vary considerably, from flashing commercial messages, to elaborate mini-movies, to small bullets or arrows that appear to grow or move. Animated GIFs are commonly used to help attract users' attention to a specific element.

Developing Animated GIFs

If you're interested in developing your own animated GIFs, we recommend software such as Animation Shop from JASC (maker of Paint Shop Pro, `www.jasc.com`) or GifBuilder for the Macintosh (`homepage.mac.com/piguet/gif.html`). These packages provide the tools to combine individual images into an animated GIF; however, you can also develop animated GIFs by developing a set of individual images with any software that can create GIF images, including Photoshop, Paint Shop Pro, Image-Ready, Gimp, Illustrator, and Fireworks. If you want to see what's available on the Web, go to `www.yahoo.com` or `www.google.com` and search on "gif animation" (be sure to use the quotes). You will find lots of information, software, and software reviews.

Developing an animated GIF often takes more time and effort than you expect. The process can become tedious, especially if you're working with longer animations or animations in which the illusion of smooth motion is needed (rather than simply presenting discrete panes of information, as in ad banners).

The first step is to generate the individual images that will eventually be each panel within the animated GIF. For a basic animated bullet—that appears to move from left to right—you might create a set of images similar to those shown in Figure 11.1.

The easiest way to get smooth animation is to create a single image, select the object that changes or moves, move it into each successive position, and then save the image with each new object position. In this example, after creating the small ball, we selected the ball, moved it two pixels to the right, saved the image, moved it again, and so forth. The more pixels between images, the jerkier the motion; the fewer pixels between images, the smoother the motion.

After you create the images, use a GIF animation program, such as JASC Animation Shop (Figure 11.2) or any of the graphics programs mentioned earlier, to sequence the images and to set animation properties, such as how often to loop through the animation and how to redraw the images as the animation proceeds.

After you insert each of the frames and preview the image to your satisfaction, simply save it as a GIF file.

FIGURE 11.1

Creating a bullet that slides right, in Paint Shop Pro

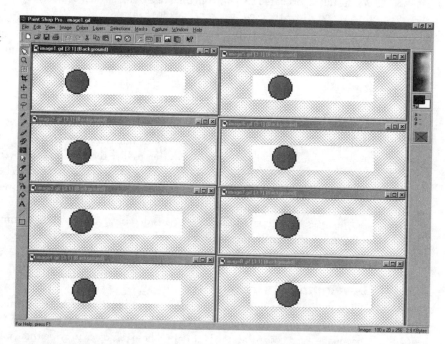

FIGURE 11.2

Animating the bullet, in JASC Animation Shop

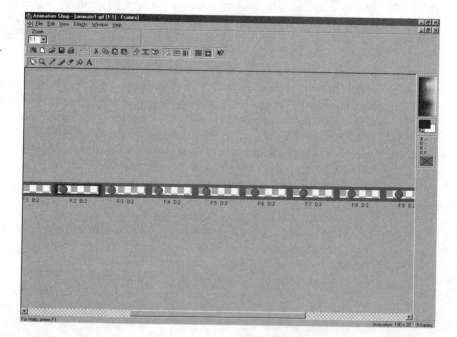

Incorporating Animated GIFs into HTML and XHTML Documents

Table 11.1 lists and describes the elements and attributes you use to include animated GIFs in your XHTML documents. You can treat animated GIFs just like any other images. (See Chapter 4 for more information on images.)

TABLE 11.1: MAIN ELEMENTS AND ATTRIBUTES OF ANIMATED GIFs

ITEM	TYPE	DESCRIPTION
`img`	Empty element	Inserts an image in a document.
`src="url"`	Attribute of `img`	Specifies the location of the image file; required.
`alt="…"`	Attribute of `img`	Provides alternate text for users who don't view the image; required.

To include an animated GIF in your Web page, follow these steps:

1. Find or create an appropriate animated GIF image.

2. Place the image in your HTML or XHTML document, with the regular image elements. Your code could look similar to the following:

```
<img src="animate2.gif" width="99" height="16" border="0"
    alt="animated gif" />
<a href="camping.html">Camping News</a> provides the latest
    comments from the trails.<br />
```

3. Enjoy the experience!

TESTING MULTIMEDIA

If you're testing your pages either locally or over a direct Internet connection—for example, through your network at the office, connected to the Internet with a dedicated line—take the time to test them with the slowest dial-up connection your users will be using. Check out what happens with 56 Kbps (and possibly slower) modems. What's tolerable with a direct connection can seem interminable over a dial-up connection.

In ideal circumstances, a user with a 56-Kbps modem can download a maximum of 7 KB per second. In real life, that number decreases dramatically, depending on network traffic and a variety of intangibles. If your page contains 2 KB of text, a 4-KB bullet image, a 20-KB photograph, and a 9-KB logo, you're already talking about at least a 5-second download. Add a 60-KB animation or sound file, and you've just bumped that to 15 seconds—best-case scenario. At this point, the user has likely moved on to another site.

However, this is becoming less of an issue as more users obtain faster Internet connections, such as cable modems and Digital Subscriber Line (DSL) service. As always, have an idea of what your users will have, and cater to the lowest common denominator. At the very least, be aware of what portion of your potential users may not wait for your multimedia elements to download.

Adding Sounds

Adding audio can produce some fun effects, but if you surf the Web looking for sound, you'll find little of practical use. Generally speaking, Web page sounds come in three varieties:

◆ Sounds that play when users access the page

◆ Sounds that play when users click something

◆ Sounds that are part of a multimedia file, such as a Flash animation or a video file

Sounds that play when users access a page are called *background sounds* and can be a short tune or one that plays the entire time a user is at the page. These mooing, beeping, crescendo-ing background sounds usually do nothing more than entertain (or irritate). Figure 11.3 includes a control box that users can click to play a sound.

TIP   Our take on the "it-plays-the-whole-time-you're-visiting" background sounds is that if we want music to play while we're surfing the Web, we'll put a CD in the computer.

Although sounds accessed in this way are primarily for entertainment purposes, they could be of practical use—for example:

◆ If your car sounds like this *rumble*, you need a new muffler.

◆ If your car sounds like this *choke*, you might have bad gasoline.

◆ If your car sounds like this *kaCHUNK* when you shift gears, your transmission is going out.

You get the idea. In lieu of adding the whole control box, however, you could just link directly to an audio file, which might well keep readers happier as well.

FIGURE 11.3

The control box lets users choose whether to play the sound

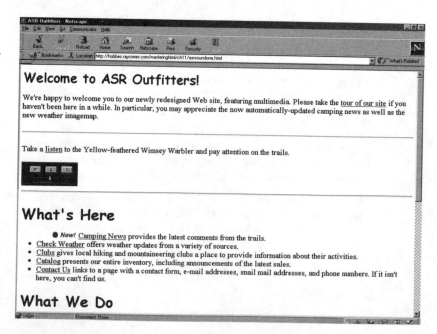

Some Disadvantages of Sounds

Many of the disadvantages associated with using multimedia elements in general are also associated with using sounds:

◆ Sound files are usually large and load slowly.

◆ Users in a corporate environment might not welcome a loud greeting from their computer.

When choosing to add sound to your page, apply the guidelines we mentioned earlier about using multimedia elements in general. If an audio element does not enhance your message or provide content that is not possible in any other way, you're probably better off not using it.

Sound File Formats

If you do decide to include a sound in your Web page, all you have to do is find a sound file in one of six formats (other formats are available, but are less common):

MIDI (Musical Instrument Digital Interface)   A MIDI file contains synthesized music. If you can find or create one that meets your needs, MIDI is a great choice because the files are small. If you have a MIDI-capable musical instrument (such as an electronic keyboard) and a little skill, you can create your own MIDI files.

AIFF (Audio Interchange File Format)   An AIFF file contains a recorded sound sample, which can be music or a sound effect. This format is most common on Macintosh and usable on most other systems.

AU (or basic AUdio)   An AU file also provides acceptable—but not great—quality sampled sound. These files are accessible on the widest range of browsers and computer systems.

WAV (as in WAVe)   A WAV file provides very good quality sampled sound, but is usable almost exclusively on Windows computers.

RAM or RA (RealMedia)   A RAM or RA file provides high-quality streaming sound, but requires the use of RealPlayer software.

MP3   An MP3 file provides outstanding (nearly CD-quality) sound, but it's usable only through browser plug-ins. (The name *MP3* is actually derived from Moving Picture Experts Group, or MPEG, Audio Layer 3.)

If you have a sound card and a microphone, you can record your own sounds. And, of course, you can find thousands if not millions of sounds and samples on the Web.

TIP   There are many sources for sound files on the Web. Do a search at www.yahoo.com *or* www.google.com *for "audio files", or use Comparisonics' search engine for sound effects on the Web at* www.findsounds.com. *Many of the sound files on the Web are not public domain, which means you can borrow them to experiment with and learn from, but not to publish as your own.*

To include sound files in the easiest and most user-friendly way, link to them. You add a link to a sound file in the same way that you add a link to an image. The code looks like this:

```
<p>Take a <a href="weirdbrd.aif">listen</a> to the Yellow-
feathered Wimsey Warbler and pay attention on the trails.</p>
```

If you use this option, users can choose whether to hear the sound, which is accessible from most browsers.

If you want to give users additional control over the sound, including volume level, pause, and play, you need to use the **object** element to add the sound file and to create a viewable sound control box on the page. See "Adding Multimedia" later in this chapter for details on using the **object** element, including a table of supported attributes.

Adding Video

You'll find that video—in the right situation—is perhaps the most practical multimedia element. In one quick video clip, you can *show* users a concept or a process, rather than describing it in lengthy paragraphs or steps.

Video files can be huge, however, so you must be sure that a large video file is essential enough to your presentation to ask a user to wait for it to download. Video technology is continuing to develop, and movie clips of reasonable size are increasingly available. Many news and entertainment sites, such as www.cnn.com/videoselect and www.comedycentral.com, offer short movie clips that download quickly.

Newer versions of Internet Explorer support video streaming, MPEG video, and QuickTime movie playback in the basic installation. Netscape Navigator support of video playback and video streaming is more limited, and Netscape requires a plug-in for QuickTime movies. Opera includes some video support directly, but requires a plug-in for QuickTime.

Video File Formats

You can create your own video files or find them on the Web. Look for files in the following formats:

AVI (Audio Video Interleave)　This format, originally a Windows standard, is now somewhat more widely available. It's a good choice if your users will almost exclusively be using Windows.

MPEG (Moving Picture Experts Group)　This format is the most widely supported, and viewers are available for most platforms. Because it's highly compressed and usable, MPEG is the best universal choice.

QuickTime　This format, originally a Macintosh standard, is now available for Windows as well. It provides good quality, but users must have the plug-in to view these files in Netscape Navigator or Opera. (QuickTime movie playback is a basic feature of later versions of Internet Explorer.)

We recommend linking to video files, rather than directly placing them in a Web page. When video files are linked, users can choose whether to view them. The code to do this would look similar to this:

```
<p>Take a <a href="weirdbrd.mpg">look at video</a> of the
Yellow-feathered Wimsey Warbler.</p>
```

If you want to add a video file directly on your page, rather than linking to it, you need to use the object element to add a video file and to create a viewable movie control box on the page. See "Adding Multimedia" later in this chapter.

Adding Java Applets

Applets, developed with the Java programming language, are mini-programs that enable you to animate objects, scroll text, or add interactive components to your Web pages. Figure 11.4 shows a TicTacToe applet, and Figure 11.5 shows an applet that scrolls a welcome message across the top of a Web page.

FIGURE 11.4

Even a simple applet adds interest and interactivity to a Web page

TicTacToe Applet

FIGURE 11.5

The "Welcome" message scrolling across the top of the page is animated by an applet

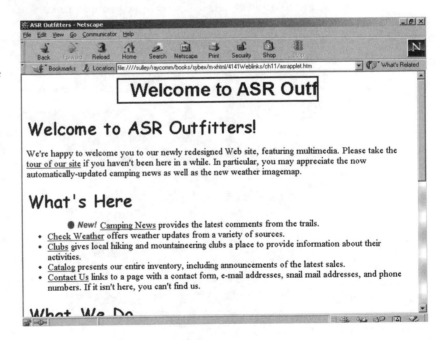

Java applets have the .class filename extension. In the simplest cases, you need only the name of the applet to use it—for example, TicTacToe.class. With more complex applets, you must also provide *parameters*. You'll have to get the exact information to include in the parameter from the documentation that comes with applets.

The software that enables you to program in Java, available at www.sun.com, includes tools for developing applets. Unless you're a programmer or have some time on your hands, you'll be better off using prepackaged applets or tools that develop applets on the fly. (Search for "applet" at software archives such as www.shareware.com, www.hotscripts.com, or softwaredev.earthweb.com/java to find these tools.)

Applet files, like video files, are big and take up to a couple of minutes to download. On the positive side, though, users with most versions of Netscape Navigator or Internet Explorer can use applets without additional software, and the plug-ins for other browsers are easy to come by from java.sun.com.

Adding Flash Animations

Flash animations are created in Macromedia Flash, which is a vector-based animation program. Because they're vector graphics, Flash files can be small enough in size to be reasonable for use on many Web sites. And it's possible to develop Flash animations that provide additional capabilities and functionality for a Web site—not just Flash for its own sake. Figure 11.6 shows a page from Michael Jantze's "The Norm" comic strip's Web site (with HTML and JavaScript-based effects), while Figure 11.7 shows the same content presented (more effectively) with Flash. For more information on Flash, visit Macromedia's site at www.macromedia.com.

FIGURE 11.6

Providing additional information through JavaScript and pop-up windows is a little awkward, at best

FIGURE 11.7

A Flash animation (complete with text that fades in over the picture) provides the same information in a flashier format, which can enhance the user experience

Adding Multimedia

The future of developing multimedia elements for the Web is clear: instead of using several elements and attributes, you'll simply include the `object` element and choose from attributes that support this element. Previously, you needed the `applet`, `embed`, and `object` elements, among others, to provide multimedia to your users. In this respect, the HTML 4.01 and XHTML 1.0 Recommendations accommodate any kind of multimedia element, and most common browsers also support this single element. Wow! You don't need to specify that you're including a sound, a video, an applet, or whatever; you simply specify that you're including an object. And, you use only the `object` element and its attributes, listed in Table 11.2. You no longer need to code separately for both Netscape Navigator and Internet Explorer to use multimedia files on your pages.

TABLE 11.2: OBJECT ELEMENTS AND ATTRIBUTES

ITEM	TYPE	DESCRIPTION
object	Element	Embeds a software object into a document.
align="…"	Attribute of object	Indicates how the object lines up relative to the edges of the browser window and/or other elements within the window. Possible values are left, right, bottom, middle, or top.

Continued on next page

TABLE 11.2: OBJECT ELEMENTS AND ATTRIBUTES *(continued)*

ITEM	TYPE	DESCRIPTION
archive= "url url url…"	Attribute of object	Specifies a space-separated list of addresses for archives containing resources relevant to the object, which may include the resources specified by the classid and data attributes. Preloading archives generally results in reduced load times for objects.
border="n"	Attribute of object	Indicates the width (in pixels) of a border around the object. border="0" indicates no border.
class="…"	Attribute of object	Assigns a class name or set of class names to an object.
codebase="url"	Attribute of object	Specifies the absolute or relative location of the base directory in which the browser will look for data and other implementation files.
codetype="…"	Attribute of object	Specifies the MIME type for the object's code.
class="…"	Attribute of object	Indicates which style class applies to the element.
classid="…"	Attribute of object	Specifies the location of an object resource, such as a Java applet. Use classid= "java:appletname.class" for Java applets.
data="url"	Attribute of object	Specifies the absolute or relative location of the object's data.
height="n"	Attribute of object	Specifies the vertical dimension (in pixels) of the object.
hspace="n"	Attribute of object	Specifies the size of the margins (in pixels) to the left and right of the object.
id="…"	Attribute of object	Indicates an identifier to associate with the object.
	Attribute of object	Specifies the name of the object.
standby="…"	Attribute of object	Specifies a message that the browser displays while the object is loading.
style="…"	Attribute of object	Specifies style information.
title="…"	Attribute of object	Specifies a label assigned to the element.
type="…"	Attribute of object	Indicates the MIME type of the object.
vspace="n"	Attribute of object	Specifies the size of the margin (in pixels) at the top and bottom of the object.
width="n"	Attribute of object	Indicates the horizontal dimension (in pixels) of the object.

TIP   Table 11.2 includes the most common attributes of the object element, but there are many additional attributes for special circumstances. For more information about these additional attributes, see the HTML 4.01 Specification and the XHTML 1.0 Recommendation at www.w3.org. Another excellent source of information is the XHTML 1.0 Reference at www.zvon.org/xxl/xhtmlReference/ Output/index.html.

When objects require more information—for example, a Java applet usually needs specific settings to run—you pass data to the object with the param element. Table 11.3 lists and describes the param elements and attributes.

TABLE 11.3: PARAMETER ELEMENTS AND ATTRIBUTES

ITEM	TYPE	DESCRIPTION
param	Empty element	Specifies parameters passed to an object. Use the param element within the object or applet element.
id="…"	Attribute of param	Assigns the object an ID so other items in the document can identify it.
name="…"	Attribute of param	Indicates the name of the parameter passed to the object; required.
type="…"	Attribute of param	Specifies the MIME type of the data found at the specified URL.
value="…"	Attribute of param	Specifies the value associated with the parameter passed to the object.
valuetype="…"	Attribute of param	Indicates the kind of value passed to the object. Possible values are data, ref, and object.

You can use the object element to include almost any kind of object. Let's start with the Java TicTacToe applet shown in Figure 11.4.

To add an applet using the object element, follow these steps.

1. Start with a basic document, like this:

```
<!DOCTYPE html
  PUBLIC "-//W3C//DTD XHTML 1.0 Transitional//EN"
  "http://www.w3.org/TR/xhtml1/DTD/xhtml1-transitional.dtd">
<html xmlns="http://www.w3.org/1999/xhtml">
<head>
    <title>TicTacToe</title>
</head>
<body>
    <h1>TicTacToe Applet </h1>
</body>
</html>
```

2. Add the object elements:

```
<h1>TicTacToe Applet </h1>
<object>
</object>
```

3. Add alternate text between the object elements:

```
<h1>TicTacToe Applet </h1>
<object>
    If your browser supported Java and objects, you could be
    playing TicTacToe right now.
</object>
```

4. Add the `classid` attribute to indicate the name of the Java class file (program file). You use `classid` to incorporate programs, such as applets or ActiveX controls.

```
<h1>TicTacToe Applet </h1>
<object classid="java:TicTacToe.class">
   If your browser supported Java and objects, you could be
   playing TicTacToe right now.
</object>
```

5. Add the `width` and `height` attributes. A square that is 120×120 pixels should be sufficient.

```
<h1>TicTacToe Applet </h1>
<object classid="java:TicTacToe.class" width="120"
   height="120">
   If your browser supported Java and objects, you could
   be playing TicTacToe right now.
</object>
```

6. If you had the `TicTacToe.class` file, and you saved and tested your document, you'd see something similar to the following:

TicTacToe Object

Users using browsers that don't support the `object` element or don't support Java will see something similar to the following:

TicTacToe Object

Unknown Media T〉

If your browser supported Java and objects, you could be playing TicTacToe right now.

TIP　See Chapter 16 for tips on handling missing capabilities more cleanly.

The process for adding video and sound is similar. The only difference is that you use the `data` attribute instead of the `classid` attribute. Also, you add a `type` attribute to show the MIME type of the object. (You don't need the `type` when you're adding an applet because `java:` precedes the name of the applet, making it clear what kind of object it is.)

MAKING IT SOUND EASY

If you're embedding sounds in your pages, consider using a regular link to the sound file rather than using the object element to embed it. The only real advantage to using the object element is a neat little widget in the Web page that users can use to play the sound as if they were using a VCR. However, those neat little widgets aren't the same size in Internet Explorer and Netscape Navigator, so you end up with either a truncated object or one with loads of extra space around it.

We recommend using an icon or a text link to the sound file—it's much easier. Anyway, if the sound takes so long to play that the users have time to click Stop or Pause, the sound file is probably too big.

To add a sound using the object element, follow these steps:

1. Start with a document.

2. Add the object elements:

```
<object>
</object>
```

3. Add the data attribute along with the filename:

```
<object data="weirdbrd.aif">
</object>
```

4. Add the type attribute to specify the type of multimedia:

```
<object data="weirdbrd.aif" type="audio/aiff">
</object>
```

5. Add the height and width attributes to specify the object's size:

```
<object data="weirdbrd.aif" type="audio/aiff" height="50"
   width="100">
</object>
```

There you go! If you had the weirdbrd.aif file, your document would now look like Figure 11.3, shown earlier in this chapter.

INCLUDING ACTIVEX CONTROLS

ActiveX controls are similar to Java applets—they're little programs that provide enhanced functionality to a Web page. For example, ActiveX controls can provide pop-up menus, the ability to view a Word document through a Web page, and almost all the pieces needed for Microsoft's HTML Help. These controls—developed by Microsoft and implemented with Internet Explorer 3—are powerful but Windows-centric. Although you can get a plug-in to view ActiveX controls in Netscape Navigator, you'll find the results are far more reliable when you view ActiveX controls with Internet Explorer.

If you want to try out some controls—both free and licensed varieties—check out C|Net's ActiveX site at http://download.cnet.com/downloads/0-10081.html or Gamelan at www.gamelan.com. If you're so inclined, you can create ActiveX controls using popular Windows development packages, such as Visual Basic or Visual C++. You include ActiveX controls in a page just as you include multimedia elements: You use the object element—as discussed earlier in this chapter.

Where to Go from Here

This chapter showed you some of the more entertaining elements you can include in your HTML or XHTML documents. Although multimedia files don't always have practical uses, they do make your pages more interesting and give them the "up with technology" look and feel. You also learned, however, that multimedia effects have a big disadvantage: The files can be enormous, which slows download time considerably.

From here, you can reference several related chapters:

◆ See Chapter 9 to learn about developing Cascading Style Sheets, which let you add cool formatting to your documents.

◆ See Chapter 10 to learn how JavaScript can also make your pages shimmy and shake.

◆ See Chapter 13 to learn how to balance flashy elements (such as multimedia) with usability.

Part 4

Developing Web Sites

Chapter 12

Planning for a Coherent, Usable, Maintainable, and Accessible Web Site

THROUGHOUT THIS BOOK, WE'VE been looking at the document-level development process—that is, the steps for adding elements and attributes to pages so that you can include various features, capabilities, and functionality. But in most cases, you won't just be creating and publishing a single document, or even a handful of documents. Instead, you'll likely be creating documents that will be part of a bigger whole—for a Web site most likely, or possibly for a kiosk, help system, or personal digital assistant (PDA).

This chapter provides you with the tools, knowledge, and resources you'll need to develop sets of HTML or XHTML documents that are cohesive, maintainable, and accessible. The principles and steps offered in this chapter will work equally well if you're developing documents for nonprofit organizations, corporate intranets, or departmental sites, as well as for those other document uses.

We recommend that you start at the beginning and read through the sections in order. Along the way, you'll find advice that will help you make decisions that will improve your site. (Specific information about choosing and using software, coding documents, or applying effects is in other chapters throughout this book.)

This chapter covers the following topics:

◆ Planning for site development and maintenance

◆ Determining what information to provide

◆ Deciding how to organize the information

◆ Planning site navigation

◆ Ensuring accessibility

◆ Creating a master document

Planning for Site Development and Maintenance

You might be wondering why we're starting off with planning for site development and maintenance when we haven't even talked about content. Even before you get started typing those elements and attributes that comprise HTML and XHTML documents, you should think about the long-term goals for your Web site and realize that the site you create is likely going to start changing just as soon as you publish it. Therefore, a little planning is in order.

Planning for a Smooth Development (and Redesign) Process

You can take steps to help ensure that the site development—and "redesign" process—goes as smoothly as possible. Uh, why are we talking about redesigning the site, even before you develop the first site? Just as you have to update site content over time to meet users' changing needs, you also must take into account the fact that the initial site design will not meet user needs forever. Applying the following techniques will help ensure that designing the site goes as smoothly as it can and also help make sure your site is as "redesign-able" as possible:

Use XHTML and style sheets.   As we mentioned in Chapter 1, Web browsers handle HTML and XHTML equally well, and XHTML is not much more difficult to implement than HTML; XHTML is more flexible and more forward-looking than HTML, and using it can make moving toward XML much easier than if you are using HTML. Further, style sheets replace several elements and attributes in HTML that have been deprecated. If you use deprecated elements and attributes now, changing to style sheets later will require that you not only apply style sheets to the new site's documents, but also go through and remove all the deprecated elements and attributes. Even for a small site, removing deprecated elements is tedious and time-consuming—especially if you're doing so manually, but also if you develop a script or program to automate some of the process.

Use standard HTML or XHTML.   As tempting as it may be to include an element that's only supported by a specific browser or to use deprecated elements and attributes to achieve a particular effect, don't. By sticking to standard HTML or XHTML, you ensure that the features, functionality, and effects you include are available to the vast majority of your users. Perhaps more important in the context of planning for site updates, using standard HTML or XHTML helps ensure that your code is valid and that you won't have to manually weed out (or otherwise address) nonstandard code or features when you redesign your site.

Consider Your File Structure.   If you haven't worked with large Web sites, you may find it easy just to create a single site folder and save all of the site's files in that folder. And for smaller sites (that will remain small), this process *may* work fine. If, however, your site is more than just a few pages or you expect it to grow, strongly consider adding some structure to the files by grouping and saving them in different file folders. That is, rather than creating a single site folder, create a separate folder for each category of information you include on the site.

Doing so offers a few benefits. For example, users will be able to tell from the URL in their browser's location line where they are in the site: `www.wammi.com/troubleshooting/brakes/index.html` indicates that the page is the home page of the brakes section of the troubleshooting area on the site. Along those same lines, creating separate folders can allow you to easily use "breadcrumbing," which is another navigation aid (discussed in the section "Determining How to Organize the Information" later in this chapter). And, from a maintenance standpoint, having separate folders for separate areas of the site can help you more quickly locate files as you're maintaining them.

TIP   Develop your file structure as you're planning site contents, organization, and navigation, which we discuss next.

Plan for site styles and guidelines.   Before you start developing content and pages, take time to develop a site *style guide*—a reference document that includes rules and suggestions for writing style and presentation. By choosing or developing a style guide before creating the Web site, you can use the style guidelines to achieve consistency in the HTML and XHTML documents you create. And developing documents with consistent styles is much easier than editing and changing already-developed documents for consistency.

Often, the site style guide may be the same or similar to the corporate style guide for other documents your company creates, or it may be heavily based on a commercial style guide, such as *Chicago Manual of Style, Microsoft Manual of Style, Read Me First! A Style Guide for the Computer Industry*, or any number of style guides available. Remember, a style guide doesn't necessarily include the "right" styles or guidelines; it includes the styles that your company wants to apply consistently across a collection of documents. By choosing or developing a style guide before creating the Web site, you can use the style guidelines to achieve consistency in the HTML and XHTML documents you create.

TIP   For more information about style guides, see `www.raycomm.com/techwhirl/magazine/writing/styleguide.html`, *then search for "style guide" at your favorite online bookstore for ideas about the range of style guides available.*

TIP   At the end of this chapter, we discuss developing a master document, which is a template of sorts that includes some basic design elements that you'll use throughout your site. Although your site design—and therefore your master document— will depend a lot on issues discussed in this chapter, you might start thinking about the overall site themes as you're going through the rest of this chapter.

Planning for Development

Creating a development plan can significantly ease the overall process. If you're reading this chapter, you likely already have some idea of the development needs and expectations for your site; however, taking time to assess the resources you have available and the resources you need to develop the site can help smooth the process, minimize surprises, and ensure that you have the resources necessary to complete the project:

◆   What resources do you have available? What tools (for example, editors, browsers, validators, and conversion tools) do you have at your disposal? How about people resources—who can you call on? How about content resources (for example, existing documents that you can use as source material)? And what kind of Web server space do you have?

◆   What resources do you have yet to acquire? For example, will you be developing content from scratch? Do you need to gather existing documents and information? Will you be adding new team members who haven't been hired yet?

◆ Which team members will be working on the Web site? This list should include managers, worker-bees, technical folks, content folks, reviewers, testers, editors, and support people, as well as anyone else who might have a say in decisions, content, design, maintenance, administration, or production. Also, what is each team member responsible for? Be specific!

◆ What is the realistic schedule to complete phases of the project? Planning? Master document development? Content development? Document development? Testing? Revision? Additional testing? Publishing?

These questions are by no means exhaustive—issues can vary significantly depending on the company and site you're developing; however, these questions are a good starting point before you begin developing your site.

TIP   *Create the site development plan collaboratively with the input from others on the site development team, and then have the team review the plan before implementing it.*

Planning for Maintenance

Maintaining documents is the process of updating and revising existing pages, adding new pages, and deleting outdated pages. Regularly maintaining documents is essential if you want users to keep returning to your site; regular maintenance also helps make long-term maintenance less cumbersome.

DETERMINING MAINTENANCE NEEDS

Web site documents contain two types of information: static and dynamic. *Static* information remains constant. The company logo, most menus, and even product descriptions are examples of static information. Static information is usually what's included in your style sheet. *Dynamic* information, on the other hand, must be changed or updated regularly. Prices, schedules, specific or timely information, and product lists are examples of dynamic information. Figure 12.1 shows a Web page that includes both types.

With the exception of a few static elements, such as the logo, navigation links, contact information, and a few other page elements that likely won't change much, consider that other dynamic elements can—and should—be updated as needed to keep up with users' changing needs. In general, the more people involved in maintaining the site, the more time, effort, and coordination these process will take:

◆ Will more than one person be involved in developing the content?

◆ Will more than one person play an active role in maintaining the site?

◆ Will your site include more than about 20 documents?

◆ Will you frequently add or modify a significant numbers of pages—say, more than 20–25 percent of the total number of documents?

FIGURE 12.1

Static information remains constant (here, the logo and menus); dynamic information changes frequently (such as articles and ads)

DEVELOPING A MAINTENANCE PLAN

If you know that you'll be adding only tidbits of information every few weeks, you probably don't need a formal maintenance plan. However, if you're likely to receive pages and pages of information to add, or if you're likely to make significant changes, you should determine how you can make those additions and/or changes most effectively.

At a minimum, the maintenance plan should address the following areas:

- The site's purpose and goals

- The process for determining content

- Who provides content

- Who edits and prepares content

- When content providers should submit information, and how

- How content accuracy is tested, reviewed, or assessed

- When content is added to the site, and how

- What tools are required to maintain content

In addition, the maintenance plan should include a schedule for ensuring that the site in general is working as it should. For example, the following tasks are often included as regular site maintenance:

Checking for links that don't work or that point to outdated information (also known as _link rot_) As you add and remove information from your site, you'll find that some pages suddenly have no links to them, or that existing links don't go anywhere. Manually browse all your links, and take advantage of link-checking programs on the Web. (Look on sites such as www.tucows.com and www.zdnet.com and search for "link checkers".)

Ensuring that older pages still look good in new versions of browsers Often, changes in browser software affect how some elements—such as images, tables, and forms—are displayed.

Checking older pages for references to outdated information For example, you might want to update present-tense references to past presidential elections, sports records, or even products, prices, and schedules.

TIP   Develop the maintenance plan collaboratively with input from others on the site development team, and then have the team review the plan before implementing it, as with the site development plan.

Determining What Information to Provide

In using HTML or XHTML, you're mostly likely developing documents that provide information to those who need it. In this capacity, HTML and XHTML authoring is *user-centered*—in other words, it focuses on determining what users want and then providing that information.

However, Web sites have evolved into a marketing tool for millions of companies, organizations, and individuals worldwide. Rather than strictly providing information, the purpose of many Web sites is to tell users what a company wants them to know, to persuade them to purchase a product or service, and to keep them coming back for more. As a result, HTML and XHTML development is simultaneously user-centered and *author-centered*. Now, you need to consider not only what your users want to know, but also what information your organization wants to provide.

Therefore, before you start producing documents, you should do some content planning. In particular, you must determine what information your users want and what your organization wants to provide. Your goal is to reconcile these "wants" into a single list that accommodates both your users and your organization.

What Do Your Users Want?

When you visit a Web site, you usually have a reason for going there. Although you often stumble onto a site that interests you while browsing, you normally have something specific in mind when you start.

Therefore, as you begin the planning phase, you'll want to think about what users expect to see at your site. The process of figuring out what your users want to know is often called *audience analysis*, or *user analysis*. Just as the name implies, you analyze aspects of known and potential users to find out what information they want, need, or expect to find on your site.

How do you determine what your users want or need? The best way to find out is from the users themselves:

◆ Ask existing customers (or coworkers, if you're developing an intranet), because they can provide firsthand information about what they want and need. Often, asking about their wants and needs will result in minimal feedback; asking about what *problems* they have encountered related to the product, service, or other information resources will often result in more useful information.

◆ Check with your company's customer service center; it can provide information about what customers are calling and asking about.

◆ Read any communication, such as customer service e-mail messages, phone logs from customer calls, or notes or logs obtained from customer visits.

By starting with your customers, you can get an idea of what information they want and need. But what if you don't have direct access to customers or definitive information about their needs? Well, that's a bit trickier, although you may have more information available to you than you realize. For example, other departments in your company may have information about users, or they may have results of needs analyses, or documents that were developed based on audience analysis. For example, the product development team likely has design specifications that are based on user needs. The documentation department may have user documents that can provide valuable information about what people aim to *do* with a product. The marketing team may have information about existing customers that can help you determine what information potential users may want or need. Whatever the size or industry of your company, you likely have reliable customer information available to you.

If you don't have information available, then you can make some informed guesses about user needs. For example, suppose you have general information about your company and its general products and services, and you have specific product information, contact information, troubleshooting advice, safety information, prices, schedules, and order forms available. With those categories of information in mind, ask yourself:

◆ What skills, knowledge, or experience do users have in using the product or service?

◆ What existing information (product sheets, documentation, price lists, and so on) have already been given to users?

◆ What additional information will users need in order to use the product or service?

◆ What information would be especially helpful or convenient for users to access through your Web site?

TIP   Often, your competitors' Web sites can be a good resource for determining what information to include on your Web site. While you can't, of course, use their framework or information, you can look at the types of information they're providing to the same pool of users and potential users.

Finally, use yourself or your coworkers as guinea pigs for determining what information to provide on the Web site. What questions did you have when using (or learning to use) the product or service?

What obstacles did you encounter? What tidbits of information would have been useful to you? What information was tedious to look up (but would have been handy to have on the Web site)?

At WAMMI, our fictitious auto manufacturer, a survey revealed that users were interested in knowing what models were available, their cost, and their reliability and safety records. They also wanted to be able to request brochures and locate local dealerships. Their list of wants looked like this:

Available models

Cost

Safety record

Reliability record

Contact information

Request brochure

List of dealerships

What Do You Want to Provide?

Ideally, your Web site will provide all the information that your users want; however, what they want isn't necessarily what you can or want to provide. For example, you might not want to publicize a product's repair history—or at the very least, you might want to downplay it. Or, if you're developing pages for a corporate intranet—say, the R&D department—you don't want to publish *all* the information the department has available. You probably just want to include information about upcoming projects, recent successes and failures, and planned product improvements.

As mentioned in the context of assessing users' needs, you can start determining what information your company wants to provide by looking at materials your company already has on hand. For example, marketing materials often include information about the company, products, and services, information that is suitable for use on a Web site. Even if you're developing pages for an intranet, marketing materials often provide a jumping-off place.

If you don't have access to marketing materials (or the marketing guru), ask yourself a few questions:

♦ What do people want to know about my organization? What is my organization's mission statement? What are its goals?

♦ Why are we on the Web? What do we want out of it? Who are our users?

♦ What are our company's products or services? How do they help people? How do people use them?

♦ How do customers order our products?

♦ Is repair history or safety information so positive that we want to publicize it?

♦ Can we include product specifications?

◆ What product information can we send to people if they request it? Will customers download it? Or will we e-mail, or mail, the information to them?

◆ Can we provide answers to frequently asked questions? What are the frequently asked questions and their answers?

◆ Do we want to include information about employees? Do their skills and experience play a big part in how well our products are made or sold?

◆ Can we provide information that is more timely, useful, or effective than other marketing materials, such as brochures or pamphlets, provide?

After you answer these and any other questions that are helpful in your situation, you should be able to develop a list of what you want to provide. WAMMI decided to provide general information about the company, tell potential customers about the various models, show a few snazzy pictures, and brag about the cars' reliability records. WAMMI was unsure about discussing prices because they were higher than those of its competitors. Likewise, WAMMI was unsure whether to publicize safety records, which were only average. The final list looks like this:

Definite

Company information

Car models

Photos

Contact information

Maybe

Prices

Safety records

Reconciling the Want Lists

You may find that users want information that you simply can't provide. For example, they might want to know product release dates or be privy to product previews, which is probably information your company doesn't want to disclose. And, other times, you might want to provide your audience with information that they don't necessarily care about. For example, you might want to tell people that your company received a big award or just reached one million dollars in sales this year—certainly interesting information that's good for marketing, but it's not on your users' priority lists.

As you can see, what WAMMI wanted and what its users wanted didn't necessarily coincide:

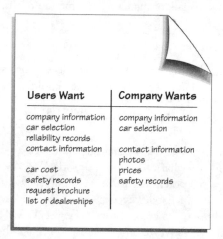

Users Want	Company Wants
company information	company information
car selection	car selection
reliability records	
contact information	contact information
	photos
car cost	prices
safety records	safety records
request brochure	
list of dealerships	

Although these two lists have items in common, each list also contains unique items. At the very least, we wanted to include all the items common to both lists. At WAMMI, the reconciled list includes the following:

Company information

Car selection

Safety records

Contact information

Now, what do you do about the items that are unique to each list? We suggest that you consult some of your colleagues, particularly those in marketing or public relations, and see what they think.

TIP   Getting a consensus before you start to build your Web site is always a good rule to follow. The last thing you want after your site goes public is a vice president announcing that you can't publish information that's already flaunted on your Web site. The information in this chapter will help you avoid encountering such problems.

At WAMMI, we decided to classify the items common to both lists as primary Web site information and to classify items unique to one list as secondary information.

Determining How to Organize the Information

After you decide what information to include in your site, you need to determine how you will arrange individual documents. Taking the time to organize the information carefully often makes the difference between having frequent users to your site and having none at all. How often do you return to a site that's not well organized? If you can't find what you need easily and quickly, you have no reason to go there, and the same will be true of visitors to your site.

You can use one or all of these types of organization, depending on your needs:

◆ Hierarchical

◆ Linear

◆ Webbed

Hierarchical Organization

When you organize information in a hierarchical structure, you present a group of equally important topics, followed by another group of equally important topics, and so on. If you've ever created or used an organizational chart, you're familiar with this technique. The hierarchy starts with top officials, then shows the managers who work for them, the employees who work for those managers, and so on. A document outline is another example of hierarchical organization. Multiple main points are followed by subpoints, which are followed by more subpoints. In both an organizational chart and a document outline, hierarchical organization allows you to provide multiple levels of structured information.

You can do the same with a Web site. You can provide several main points, and under each point, you can include subpoints. For example, the WAMMI Web site uses hierarchical organization to structure the main pages according to the major topics, as shown in Figure 12.2.

FIGURE 12.2

Hierarchical organization accommodates several main topics and subtopics

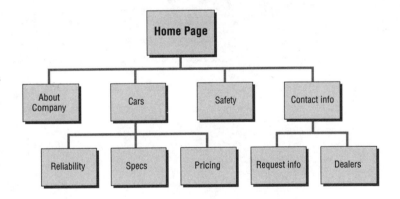

If you choose hierarchical organization, keep these guidelines in mind:

◆ Keep it simple. Visitors to your site will click through three or four levels of information, but after that, they're likely to give up.

◆ Provide an overview of the organization. You can do this by showing the categories and subcategories of information on the home page or by providing a site map.

TIP   Regardless of the type of site organization you choose, site maps and site indexes are excellent tools to help users determine the extent of information on your site, the topics your site covers, and the depth of information included. Check out HTML Indexer at `www.html-indexer.com` *for a starting point on an index; site maps tend to be best handled as a special HTML or XHTML page that you create along with the rest of your site.*

Linear Organization

When you organize information in a linear structure, you impose a particular order on it. Instructions and procedures are examples of this type of organization. If you've ever used a Microsoft Windows–type wizard, you've seen linear organization in action. You start the wizard and then you proceed in order from one screen to the next until you click Finish. You can back up a step or two if necessary, but if you don't complete all the steps, you terminate the procedure.

On a Web site that uses linear organization, a user can move forward and backward within a sequence of pages but cannot jump to other pages. Because this can frustrate users who want to get to other pages, you should use linear organization only when it's necessary. For example, at our WAMMI site, we used linear organization to walk a user through requesting a brochure, as shown in Figure 12.3.

FIGURE 12.3

Linear organization works well when you want users to perform actions in a specific order

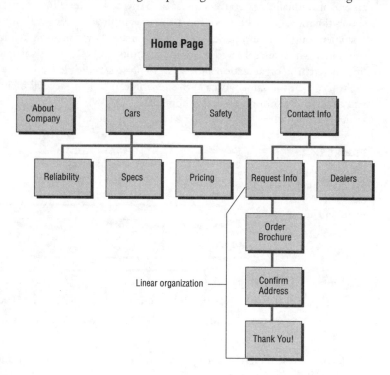

Here are some guidelines to keep in mind when you employ linear organization:

◆ When your site users are working through linear pages, they can't roam to other pages. Therefore, be sure the linear process is essential to the task at hand.

◆ Keep the linear sequence as short as possible so users focus on the process and complete it successfully.

◆ Provide prerequisites at the beginning of the process so that users know what information or other resources they should have on hand before starting. For example, if the process requires a product identification number or other information they may not have handy, suggest that they get this information before starting the procedure.

◆ Provide cues to users to let them know the extent of the linear process, as well as where they are in the process while completing it. For example, you might state that the upcoming process has 8 steps, or let them know "you are on step 3 of 8 in this process" (or whatever) so they know how far they've come and how far they have yet to go.

◆ Provide cues, as necessary, to let users know they've completed steps successfully. Many times, this will be obvious at the end of the process, but if interim steps have to be completed correctly in order for subsequent steps to work, then provide a screen capture or description during interim steps so that users know they've completed a step correctly and completely before moving on.

◆ Include a "success page," which acknowledges that a user has successfully completed the steps. This page might include just a short statement, a summary of what users just did, a summary of what they should do next, or information they should keep on hand.

Webbed Organization

Webbed organization provides users with multiple, unorganized paths to resources on a site. A user can link from one Web page to many other pages at the same Web site or at another Web site. You often hear stories about Web surfers becoming disoriented or lost—they don't know where they are or where they've been. Webbed organization is often the culprit.

An example of effective webbed organization, however, is an online index that's extensively cross-referenced. The WAMMI site provides an index of the available models, and cross-references each model to its specific features and to other models. Figure 12.4 shows how this works.

FIGURE 12.4

Webbed organization is a good technique to use when you want to cross-reference information

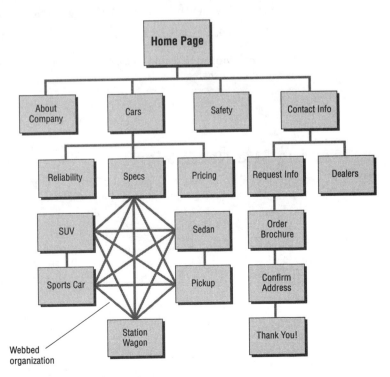

Here are some guidelines to keep in mind when you're using webbed organization:

◆ Provide navigation information consistently across the site so that readers can orient themselves even though content changes from page to page. For example, include a running footer or company logo (keep it small) on each page.

◆ Provide a link to your home page on all pages. If you do so, users can easily return to a familiar page.

◆ Provide "breadcrumbs" on the site, which are navigation links that indicate where a user is in the site, as in "Home ➤ Troubleshooting ➤ Brakes." Visit Chapter 18 for more information about including breadcrumbs.

STORYBOARDS: AN ESSENTIAL ORGANIZATIONAL TOOL

Storyboarding is the process of breaking information into discrete chunks and then grouping related chunks together. It's a technique that Web authors borrowed from the film industry, and it's a great way to help you determine the best organizational approach for your site.

Here's one way to do it (and the way the WAMMI site was storyboarded):

1. Write each topic or group of information on a separate note card.

2. Pin the note cards to a wall or spread them out on a table or the floor.

3. Group and rank related information.

4. Continue moving cards around until all the information is organized and ranked to your satisfaction.

5. When you've decided what should link to what, connect those note cards with string.

The resulting groups of information should follow one of the three organizational approaches we just discussed or some combination thereof.

Planning Site Navigation

Part of what makes a Web site usable (discussed in depth in Chapter 13) is how easily users can access it, browse through it, and find the information they want. Most users access your site through a home page, which is typically a single document that provides links to the other pages in the site. However, not all your users will drop in by using the home page. They can go directly to a page they've bookmarked, or they can access your site through a search engine and go straight to a specific page. In either case, you have little control over how users move through your site.

To ensure that your users can link to the information they're looking for and to encourage them to browse your site, you need to make your site easily navigable—that is, make accessing, browsing, and finding information intuitive and inviting. You can do this by using *navigation menus*, which are sets of links that appear from page to page.

Navigation menus come in two varieties:

◆ Textual, which is a set of text links

◆ Graphical, which is a set of images (or icons) used as links

Textual Navigation

Textual navigation is simply text that links users to other information in the Web site. As shown in Figure 12.5, a textual navigation menu doesn't offer glitz, but effectively conveys what information resides at the other end of the link.

Textual navigation, though somewhat unglamorous, offers several advantages over graphical navigation. Textual navigation is more descriptive than graphical navigation because, done right, the text clearly tells users about the information in the site. Textual navigation links can be as long as necessary to describe the information at the end of the link; the description is not limited by the size of a button. The smaller (thus faster to download) the button, the less text you can fit on it.

FIGURE 12.5

Textual navigation is often the most informative

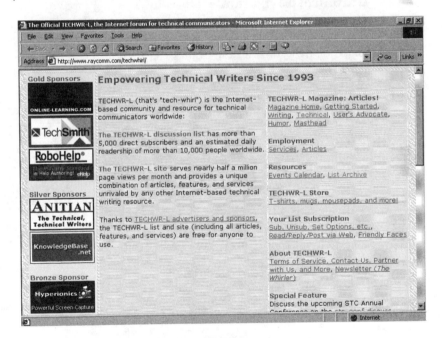

Textual navigation is also more reliable than graphical navigation because the link itself is part of the document, not a referenced element such as a navigation button.

Finally, text links download much faster than graphical navigation. The links download as part of the page, without the delays associated with images.

If you're considering using textual navigation, follow these guidelines:

◆ If your textual navigation menu appears as a vertical list, place the most important or most accessed links at the top.

◆ Make the text informative. Rather than calling links "More Information," "Contact Information," and "Related Information," add specific summaries. For example, call these links "Product Specs," "Contact Us!," and "Other Sportswear Vendors." Whatever you do, don't use instructions such as "Click Here," which is uninformative and wastes valuable space. Additionally, words such as *Information* rarely do anything but take up space. After all, what would be at the other end of the link besides information?

◆ Provide the same menu—or at least a very similar one—on each page. As your users link from page to page, they become familiar with the setup and location of the menu and actually (unconsciously) begin to expect that it contains certain information in a certain place.

◆ Customize the menu on each page so that the current page is listed, but not as a link. This approach helps users actually "see" where they are within the site, and it keeps menu locations consistent.

Graphical Navigation

Graphical navigation is a set of images that link to other information in the site. Most commonly, graphical navigation appears in the form of images with text on them, as shown in Figure 12.6. Graphical navigation can also be images that are pictures (called *icons*) representing what the buttons link to.

FIGURE 12.6

These navigation buttons include both text and images

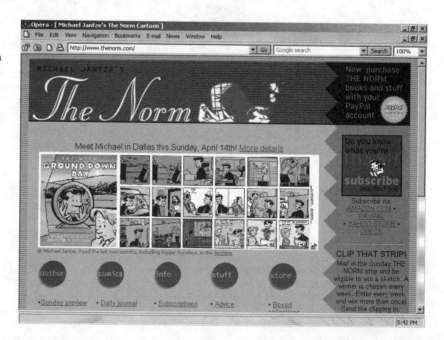

Graphical navigation has the distinct advantage of being visually more interesting than textual navigation. For example, because buttons and icons can include colors or patterns and can be almost any shape you can imagine, they are outstanding theme-bearing elements.

As colorful and interesting as graphical navigation might be, it has a few drawbacks. Primarily, it takes longer—sometimes much longer—to download than textual navigation. The download time depends on the file size and your user's connection speed, among other variables that aren't in your control.

TIP   Chapter 4 provides information about resizing images and making images quick to download.

Graphical navigation also tends to be less informative than textual navigation. For example, if you're using buttons with text on them, you might be limited by the size of the button. The text can be difficult to read, depending on the size of the button and the resolution of the user's computer.

If you want to use graphical navigation, consider these guidelines:

◆ Be sure that button text is easily readable. Sometimes, when images used to create buttons are made smaller to fit within a navigation menu, the text becomes too small to read or the letters get compacted. Your best bet is to try several button sizes to get a feel for which size is most effective.

◆ Be sure that the navigation menu integrates well with the other page elements. Images—including graphical navigation—are visually weighty page elements and often make other elements less apparent.

◆ Be sure that you include `alt` text for the graphics and provide a text-based alternative menu to accommodate users who cannot or will not use graphical menus.

◆ Plan the navigation menu before you actually create it. Graphical navigation takes longer to develop than textual navigation, and it's much more difficult to change once it's in place. Even if all the pages aren't in place (or fully planned yet), at least create a placeholder for the navigation menu so you don't have to revise the menu as you develop new content.

◆ Provide the same menu—or as close as possible—on every page. As with textual menus, users link from page to page and expect to see the same menu options in the same location on each page. Also, developing only one menu that you can use from page to page saves you time; you create it once and reuse it on each page.

TIP   Rather than creating several navigation buttons, you can create one image that includes several links. This single image with multiple links is called an image map. *See Chapter 4 for more information.*

Placing Navigation Menus

After you determine which kind of navigation menu to use, decide where to place the menu on your Web pages. Regardless of whether you use textual or graphical navigation, be sure to place menus where users are most likely to use them.

Because navigation menus, particularly graphical ones, often take up a lot of valuable page space, be sure to choose menu location(s) that don't interfere with other page elements. Here are some considerations when choosing a location for navigation menus:

Top of the page   Locating a navigation menu at the top of pages is particularly useful because it's easy to find and access. Users casually surfing your pages can easily link in and out, and those who link to a page in error can easily get out of the page. The big advantage to using the top of the page (from the user's perspective) is that he or she isn't forced to wade through information to access the menu.

Middle of the page   This location is effective in long pages because users can read through some of the information, but are not forced to return to the top or scroll to the bottom just to leave the page. Usually, with mid-page navigation menus, you'll want to use targeted links, as described in Chapter 3.

Bottom of the page   This location works well in a couple of situations. For example, you can put the navigation menu at the bottom when you want users to read the material that precedes it. Keep in mind that users don't want to be forced to read information they're not interested in, but they don't mind browsing through a short page to get to a navigation menu at the bottom. Bottom navigation also works well on pages that already include many elements at the top, such as logos or descriptions; in this case, adding a navigation menu would crowd other important information.

Right and left sides of the page   These locations are becoming increasingly common with the use of tables and frames. Although you can put the navigation on the right or left side, it's more commonly found on the left side of the page, with the content located in the larger area on the right. For example, you can use a framed layout to place the menu on the left side of the page and the information on the right. A menu at the left creates a two-column page appearance, which can make the page visually interesting and shorten the width of the right column to help readability. In addition, if the navigation menu appears in a separate frame, it can remain on screen at all times, regardless of which pages users link to or how far they scroll down a page. This is very useful for long documents. See Chapters 6 and 8 for more information on tables and frames, respectively.

Multiple locations   For most Web sites, you'll likely use a combination of these locations, which is fine, as long as you use at least one combination consistently. You could, for example, place a main menu at the top of all pages, place a menu of what's on the actual page on the left, and include a smaller text version of the main menu at the bottom of the page. Don't use this combination if you're space conscious.

Global navigation   For large Web sites, you might choose to have a high-level menu with links to the major sections of the site and submenus within each of the major sections. The global menu would be available on all pages, but the section-specific submenus would be available only within the sections. The menus on www.amazon.com are a good example of this technique.

Planning for Accessibility

As a Web site developer, you may assume that your potential users will interact with online information in the same way that you do. However, a significant number of these users—people with visual impairments—do not interact with online information in the same way others do. Instead, many visually impaired people rely on adaptive technologies, such as screen readers, enlargers, or a combination of these, to access and use the information you provide. Although adaptive technologies help make documents accessible and usable to this audience, they are not a panacea; they cannot read or interpret many of the visual communication techniques available to help make information more accessible and usable, such as tabular or column formats, frames, graphics, or colors. Because adaptive technologies cannot adequately accommodate these visual-communication techniques, you should take steps during the planning stages to help ensure that the information your site provides is accessible to everyone.

NOTE *The United States federal government now has Section 508 accessibility guidelines in place for companies selling anything to the government. See* `www.section508.gov` *for details.*

Understanding the Need to Address Accessibility Issues

According to the American Foundation for the Blind, an estimated 12 million people in the United States alone (5 percent of the population) have some degree of visual impairment. Other studies estimate that visual impairments affect up to 20 percent of the population. "Visual impairment," however, doesn't necessarily mean total blindness; it also refers to people with *low vision*, which includes any visual impairment that requires a person to use large type or a magnifying device, that requires a person to read at extremely close range, or that prevents a person from reading for long stretches of time.

But, what does this actually mean in terms of what visually impaired people might see when they try to access and use information? Consider the following examples of low vision and their effects. Figure 12.7 shows a screen as it's intended to be viewed, and Figures 12.8 through 12.12 illustrate how low vision might alter how the screen is perceived.

FIGURE 12.7

People with normal vision would see this screen

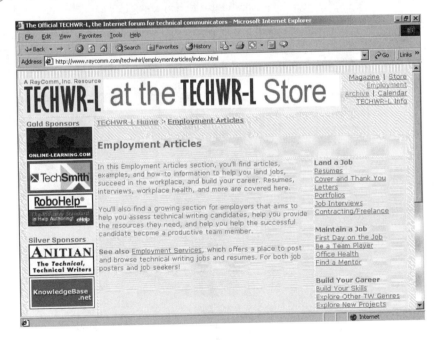

Tunnel vision   With tunnel vision, people can see only a portion of the normal field of vision. For example, rather than having the normal 150-to-180-degree field of vision, people with tunnel vision might be able to see only the width of a piece of paper or a small circle and have to rely on memory to cognitively assemble the pieces into a coherent whole.

FIGURE 12.8

People with tunnel vision might see as if looking through a paper towel tube

Colorblindness A person who is colorblind cannot distinguish between certain colors. Most common are problems distinguishing red from green, although some people cannot distinguish yellow from blue or cannot differentiate colors at all.

Age-related macular degeneration People with this visual impairment cannot see fine detail—they see only faded colors and shapes. This impairment occurs as part of the aging process and is, therefore, extremely common.

FIGURE 12.9

People with age-related vision impairments might not be able to see fine details

Diabetic retinopathy   This is a visual impairment that affects people's ability to focus; the severity can vary on a day-to-day basis. Additionally, blood vessels in the eye may leak, causing blood clots and scars that distort vision, turn it red, or possibly cause total blindness.

FIGURE 12.10

People with diabetic retinopathy might see distorted images, resulting from scarring within the eye

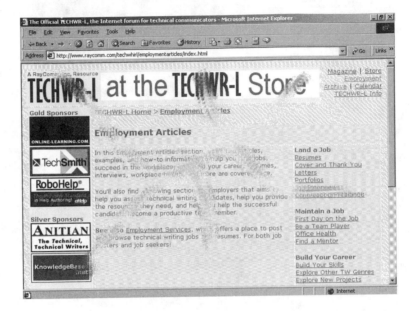

Cataracts   Cataracts cloud vision and affect the amount of light that enters the eye. This results in very hazy vision, as if you are looking through translucent glass.

FIGURE 12.11

People with cataracts experience cloudy vision that makes it very difficult to see anything

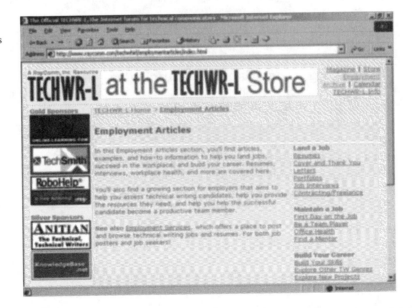

Vision field loss This visual impairment affects how messages are translated by the brain. For example, people might see only part of an image.

FIGURE 12.12

People with vision field loss perceive images incorrectly, often seeing only part of the image

TIP With this range of visual impairments in mind, you should take the time and effort to accommodate potential users who may have one or more of these impairments and ensure that they can access the information your site provides.

For much more information on accessibility, see the W3C's Web Accessibility Initiative (WAI) pages at www.w3.org/WAI/.

Understanding Adaptive Technologies

Despite technological advances in screen readers and enlargers, they have actually become *less* effective for visually impaired people because they do not provide complete access to increasingly complex graphical interfaces or complex document designs and layouts. In this sense, trends in Web design have been a step backward for accessibility and usability for this community. Although these trends often improve communication for sighted people, they hinder adaptive technologies' ability to make information accessible and usable. As you'll see in the next two sections, screen readers and enlargers do not offer visually impaired people complete access to the information they need.

SCREEN-READING TECHNOLOGY

Screen-reading technology allows people with little or no vision to navigate a graphical interface using keyboard tabs and arrows or using a "talking mouse cursor" to move through menus, buttons, icons, and other interface elements. Screen readers work by reading text associated with on-screen content—that is, text within a document, text descriptions of graphics, and text built into software programs (such as a name associated with a toolbar icon). For their users, screen readers identify interface elements, identify content, and then output the information through a synthesized voice or translate the information into Braille. For example, to oversimplify somewhat, if users navigate to a Save button, they might hear "button, save," which tells them specifically what they're pointing to (a button) and what the button is labeled (save).

Screen readers are not an ideal technology, however; many cannot interpret special formatting or graphics, so they cannot translate many visual cues that a sighted person might use to access information. For example, we commonly use multicolumn or tabular formats in documents to help group related information or to make information easier to access and read, as in this table:

PUBLICATION	CONTACT INFORMATION
TECHWR-L A RayComm, Inc. Resource for the Technical Writing Community	Visit www.raycomm.com/techwhirl to learn how to subscribe to the discussion list and to browse the variety of free resources.

This table breaks the information into clear and manageable pieces and communicates information one cell at a time. Rather than reading the contents of each cell, however, screen readers read from left to right and would likely read the table like this:

TECHWR-L visit A RayComm, Inc. www.Raycomm.com/techwhirl/ Resource for the Technical to learn how to subscribe to the Writing Community discussion list and to browse the variety of free resources.

In this case, screen readers can *technically* provide access to the information because it's rendered as text; however, the rendition is essentially unintelligible, making the content completely unusable. Perhaps a user could glean the URL from the mass of text, but the URL would have little value or context without the other pieces of information put in order.

Additionally, screen readers cannot make available information provided through graphics without the help of accompanying descriptive text. For example, if you use a chart to summarize data, screen readers would rely on the text—a caption or description within a paragraph—to convey the chart's contents. Without the descriptive text, the chart contents would be completely inaccessible to visually impaired people.

Likewise, screen readers also require descriptive text to interpret colors. For example, in an ordered list, we might use red text to show completed tasks and green text for the tasks yet to be done. Screen readers cannot convey the colors' implications without supplemental text to explain the context at each use. For example, we could add "You've just finished Lesson 1" at the end of a section of red text and add "You're about to begin Lesson 2" before the following section of green text. Only then could screen readers help visually impaired people discern the end of one lesson and the beginning of the next.

Essentially, screen readers can provide access to information, but only if the information is presented through simple text formats and descriptions.

SCREEN-ENLARGER TECHNOLOGY

Screen-enlarger technology, used by those with various degrees of low vision, helps people more easily access and use on-screen content. Screen enlargers magnify a small portion of the screen, enlarging the content by a factor users choose according to the software's capabilities. For example, they can enlarge an entire screen, specified screen portions (such as a single line), or just the area around the mouse (Figure 12.13).

on each aspect at a time, and you can incorporate changes on each issue separately, which is often easier than trying to incorporate changes to both issues at the same time.

◆ You can save time and effort by having to type only once any elements that will be included on every page.

◆ You can provide the master document to other people who will be contributing to the site.

TIP   After you create a master document, have it reviewed by others on the site development team and tested by potential users of your site to be sure that it appears the way you want, that it is usable and readable, and that it is error free. Finding and solving problems early on will save you lots of time in the overall process. See Chapter 13 for more information about testing.

TIP   You can easily use style sheets to create a template for your documents. See Chapter 9 for more on style sheets.

A master document should include elements that you want to appear on every page, such as the following:

◆ Background

◆ Navigational links

◆ Repeating images

◆ The corporate logo

◆ Icons

◆ Footer information

You might think of elements you include in the master document as being *theme-bearing elements*, which are Web page components that help unite multiple pages into a cohesive unit and convey the "brand" of the site. Your users might not notice that you've included theme-bearing elements, but they will certainly notice if you haven't or if you've used them inconsistently from page to page. In this sense, theme-bearing elements set up users' expectations. If your users browse several pages that contain a logo, they'll begin to expect to see the same logo in the same place on each page. They may not consciously notice that it's there, but they'll certainly notice if it's missing or in a different location—just as you never pay attention to that broken-down car at the house on the corner until it's gone.

Used correctly, theme-bearing elements make your site appear complete and professional, and they also help users know that they are in *your* site as they link from page to page. A user can view only one page at a time, so be sure that each page obviously belongs to the rest of the site and not to a page outside your site. The following sections describe the theme-bearing elements you can use in your master document to unify pages in your site.

Adding Backgrounds

Using consistent backgrounds—colors or images—is one of the easiest and most effective ways to unify Web pages, just as using the same color and style paper for multipage written correspondence identifies the material as a cohesive package. Using a different background for each Web page can lead to some unwanted results. Users might think they've somehow linked outside your site, or they might pay more attention to the differences in design than to your content.

TIP   Have you ever received business correspondence in which the first page is on heavy, cream-colored, linen-textured letterhead, and the second page is on cheap 20-pound copier paper? Using different backgrounds for Web pages produces a similar effect—users will notice.

Whether you use a solid color or an image depends on the effect you want to achieve. Background colors are less obtrusive and can effectively mark pages as belonging to a specific site. Imagine Figure 12.14 without the background color—just a plain white or gray background. You could use a solid color to adequately contrast the page elements and unify the other page elements without attracting attention to itself. The textured background in Figure 12.14, on the other hand, doesn't unify the page elements but instead becomes a visually interesting part of the page. Although the image background isn't overwhelming in itself, it does make reading a little more difficult.

FIGURE 12.14

Images create backgrounds that are more visually complex, yet they can complement—not overwhelm—page elements

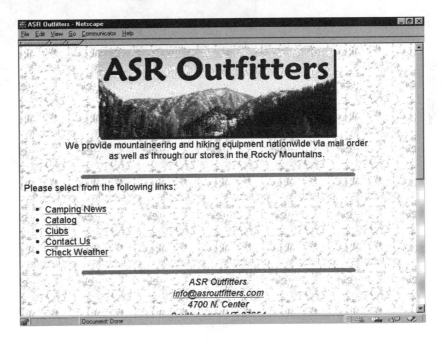

Some Web sites combine colors and images by using a mostly solid color but adding a small repeating graphic, such as the ASR logo shown in Figure 12.15.

By using a small logo—which, in Figure 12.15, appears more like a watermark than an image— you ensure that the image is less apparent and fades into the background. This is a great way to include a logo without significantly increasing download time or taking up valuable page space.

FIGURE 12.15

You can combine colors and images (or text) to create a subtle background

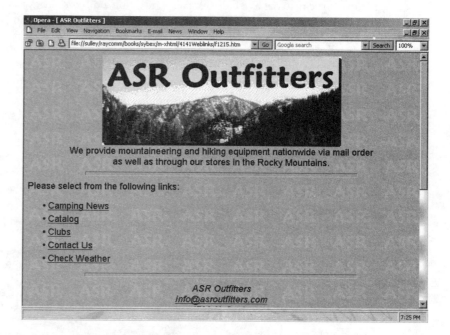

Regardless of whether you choose a color or an image background, follow these guidelines:

◆ Be sure that the background adequately contrasts with the text. Remember that online reading is inherently difficult because of monitor size and quality, resolution, lighting, and screen glare. If you use dark text, use a light background; if you use light text, use a dark background. If you have any doubt about whether the background contrasts adequately, it doesn't.

◆ Be sure that the background complements—not competes with—other elements such as images. For example, if you include images, be sure that the background doesn't overwhelm them. Often, placing a busy or colorful background under equally busy or colorful images makes online reading more difficult.

◆ Be sure that the background matches the style and tone of the Web site content. A solid black background makes an impression, but doesn't necessarily soothe and calm the user. It's not a good choice, for example, for the ASR Outfitters pages because it's quite obtrusive.

◆ Be sure that the foreground text is large and bold enough to be easily read against the background. Use the CSS font properties (or the deprecated font element) to increase the size and, optionally, set a font to help your users easily read text. A slightly increased font size can overcome the visual distractions of a textured or patterned background. (You'll find more information about changing fonts and font sizes in Chapter 2 and more about CSS in Chapter 9.)

◆ Be sure to choose a nondithering color (one that appears solid and nonsplotchy in Web browsers). Because backgrounds span the entire browser window, the colors you choose make a big difference in how the background integrates with the page elements. If, for example, you use a dithering color as a background, the resulting splotches may be more apparent than the page's content. Your best bet is to choose one of the 216 safe colors. To find out more, check out Master's Reference Part 6 or read the excellent, long article at

`http://hotwired.lycos.com/webmonkey/00/37/index2a.html`

◆ Be sure you view your Web pages in multiple browsers and with various color settings—particularly if you use an image background or don't choose from the 216 safe colors. A good background test includes changing your computer settings to 256 colors and then viewing all your pages again. Reducing the computer system's color depth may degrade the quality of the background.

TIP   You'll find information about how to include background colors in Chapter 2 and how to add background images in Chapter 4.

Choosing Colors

In most Web sites these days, colors abound—you see them in text, links, images, buttons, icons, and, of course, backgrounds. The key is to use color to enhance your Web pages and identify a theme from page to page.

When developing a color scheme, consider which elements you want to color—text (regular text as well as links, active links, visited links), logos, buttons, bullets, background, and so on. For smaller color areas—text or links—you can choose any color you can imagine. For larger color areas, such as panes or backgrounds, stick to one of the 216 safe colors. The goal is to choose the colors you'll use for each element and use them consistently.

Most Web-development software, from Netscape Composer to Microsoft FrontPage to Macromedia Dreamweaver, comes with prepared color schemes. If you're not good with colors, consider using these prematched colors. Because color is the primary visual element in your pages, problematic color choice will be woefully apparent to all users.

The colors you choose should match the site's content. For example, if you're developing a marketing site for a high-tech company, you'll likely choose small areas of bright, fast-paced colors (reds, bright greens, or yellows) that correspond to the site's purpose of catching and holding users' attention. If you're developing an intranet site, you'll likely choose mellow colors, such as beige and blue or dark green, or make the colors match the company colors, because the site's purpose is to inform users, not dazzle them.

If you choose particularly vivid colors, use them in small areas. As the old commercial goes, a little dab will do ya! A small area of red, for example, can attract attention and hold users to the page. A broad expanse of red—such as a background—will likely scare them off or at least discourage them from hanging around.

Including Logos

If you're developing a corporate Web site, consider using a logo on each page. In doing so, you not only help establish a theme, but you also explicitly provide readers with the name of your company or organization throughout the site. You can even make the logo a link to your home page, so regardless of which page users are on, they can jump to the home page via your logo. Logos often include multiple theme-bearing elements: the logo itself, its colors, and the fonts or emphasis of the letters. Take a look at Figure 12.16, which shows a sample logo used on the ASR Outfitters page.

The logo helps set up other page elements. For example, the font appears in other places on the page, the colors are consistent throughout the page, and the image used as the foundation for the logo conveys the appropriate impression.

You may have no control over the logo you use—sometimes you're required to use your company's logo, for example. If you can develop a logo or enhance an existing logo, do so. Logos used online, particularly in Web sites, must carry more information about the company or organization and its style than a logo designed primarily for hard copy. A traditional logo is established by determining paper choice, paper texture, and other elements. Often, an online logo stands nearly alone without the help of other images or background images.

FIGURE 12.16

ASR Outfitters' home page uses a nonscrolling logo as a theme-bearing element

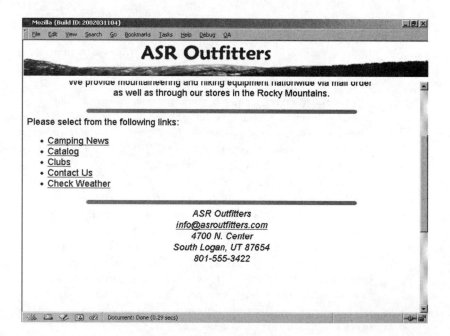

Where you place the logo depends on its emphasis. Many sites use a fairly large logo on the home page and a smaller version on subsequent pages. The logo thus appears on all pages, yet more space on subsequent pages is reserved for content.

An effective presentation is to combine small, classy logos with a clever arrangement of frames. For example, as shown in Figure 12.16, a logo can reside in a small frame at the top of a page that does not scroll, remaining visible while users are at the site. Because it does not have to be reloaded, other pages load more quickly.

Incorporating Other Graphical Elements

Other theme-bearing elements include buttons, graphical links, icons, and bullets. These elements, even more than colors and logos, add interest to your pages because they combine color and shape. What's more, these can be (and should be) small; you can include them throughout a page, adding a splash of color with each use.

You can also enhance a page with animated GIF images, which add visual attraction without increasing load time too much. See Chapter 11 for more information about animated GIF images.

Where to Go from Here

This chapter provided an overview of the HTML and XHTML document life cycle. In particular, it covered planning and organizing issues as well as issues about creating, publishing, publicizing, and maintaining HTML and XHTML documents. If you understand these topics, you'll be able to develop documents and use them for a variety of applications, including Web pages and sites, intranet sites, help files, and kiosks.

From here, you can refer to several chapters, depending on your proficiency and the specific application you're developing:

◆ Chapter 13 gives you general tips and advice for developing coherent Web sites.

◆ Chapter 14 gives you tips and advice for specifically developing public, personal, and intranet sites.

Chapter 13

Implementing a Good Web Site

IN THIS CHAPTER, WE'LL show you how to unite individual HTML or XHTML documents to develop a good Web site. What exactly makes up a *good* Web site? Well, if you ask five different people, you'll probably get five different answers. Furthermore, the specifics of a good Web site depend on a few factors, such as the purpose of the site and its users' needs. However, if you browse the Web, you'll find a handful of characteristics that effective sites often include. We'll discuss those characteristics in this chapter.

As you'll see, many of the characteristics relate to the concept of *usability*, which, among other things, measures how quickly users can find and access what they seek on a site, determines what obstacles users encounter, and observes how people actually use a site (regardless of the site developers' intentions).

This chapter covers the following topics:

◆ Understanding (and accommodating) your users' wants and needs

◆ Making your Web site cohesive

◆ Favoring content over flash

◆ Testing and maintaining your Web site

Understanding (and Accommodating) Your Users' Wants and Needs

Throughout this book, we've talked about developing your HTML or XHTML documents with your users in mind. While it's tempting to include information *you* happen to know, to develop a design that *you* like, or to incorporate flashy elements that *you* think are cool, that's not the idea. Instead, you should choose information, develop a design, and include extras that your *users* want or need.

In Chapter 12, we walked you through the process of performing a user analysis, in which you analyze aspects of known and potential users to discover the information they want, need, or expect to find on your site. Doing this analysis before even starting your first HTML or XHTML document for the site is an excellent step to take; however, user analysis shouldn't stop there. Instead, you should analyze your users on a continuous basis.

As described in Chapter 12, the best way to determine your users' needs and wants is to find out from the users themselves. You may not be able to meet with them in person and ask questions, but you can take advantage of other resources to find out. For example, your company's customer service center staff can describe the problems, questions, concerns, or obstacles your users have reported to them. They may even be able to tell you what pages, services, or features customers are finding most valuable. Similarly, any correspondence—phone discussions, e-mails, voice mail, and so on—can be useful. If a user picks up the phone or takes the time to e-mail your company, you can bet that there's a problem or issue to address at some level.

Site logs can be just as valuable in determining what your users want and what features they're using. Some of the things you can learn about users from site logs are:

What platforms, browsers, and versions people are using   Such information can help you determine how technically sophisticated your users are; what browsers, platforms, or versions you should test on; and how quickly your users are upgrading or changing their platform or browser.

What pages people are accessing (and not accessing)   Does a low-traffic page necessarily mean that users aren't interested in that information? Does a high-traffic page automatically indicate that users are particularly interested in that page's topic? Maybe, but maybe not. Although the topic, user-appropriateness, and quality of information do indeed play a part in whether users will access a page one or more times, another aspect plays a key role: how accessible that document is. For example, if links to the document are featured on the home page or on a topic-specific main page within a site, or if the links are cross-referenced on a featured document, chances are the page will get a lot of traffic. But if links to the document aren't as visible, or if they're buried in other links or content, the site logs may reveal lower traffic. So, while site logs can tell you about traffic to specific documents, you should consider that the visibility and availability of links to individual documents is a contributing factor.

Trends in what people are accessing over time   In addition to helping you gauge the timeliness or usefulness of a particular topic or document, trends revealed by site logs are useful for tracking how accessible different areas and pages of your site are. For example, on the TECHWR-L site, we used to feature new articles on the home page for a few weeks, and then feature the article within a specific content area on the site, and finally maintain a link to articles within the specific content area. (See Figure 13.1.) Surprisingly, we found that new articles drew relatively low traffic when featured on the site's home page, attracted the most traffic when featured within a specific content area, and drew little traffic once the article was available only by link. We've since revised the site organization and publishing process a bit: Articles are still featured on the home page when they're first published, but now the site includes more discrete topic areas, and each article within a topic area includes a summary that "features" articles within smaller topic areas, as illustrated in Figure 13.2. As a result, pages that received lower traffic before are now steadily receiving higher traffic.

TIP   *The bottom line: Take steps to find out what your users want and need, and then accommodate them.*

FIGURE 13.1

On the old TECHWR-L site, articles drew the most traffic when they were featured within a specific topic area, but the articles linked within the topic areas got much less traffic, buried in a long list of links

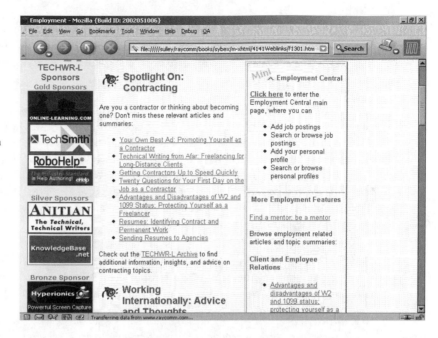

FIGURE 13.2

In the new TECHWR-L site, we have created smaller topic areas to minimize scrolling, and each article has an accompanying summary; consequently, articles that had once drew fairly low traffic are now steadily receiving more traffic

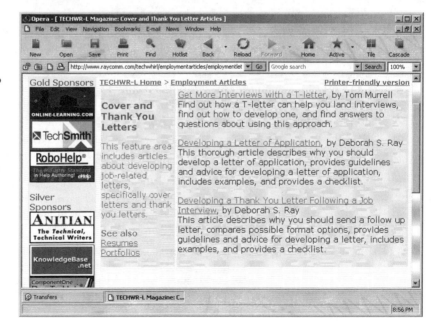

Favoring Content over Flash

In most cases, site developers should favor content over flashy elements. The exception to this guideline might be a marketing or corporate site whose product or service *is* the flashy design, gyrating thingie, or animated graphic.

For the rest of you, read on.

One of the most important principles of developing a Web site—particularly public and personal sites—is to balance flashy elements (ones that "dazzle" your users) with usability (which makes your site easy to use). If you've spent any time at all surfing the Web, you've probably noticed some really cool sites—in terms of using cutting-edge technology—ones that flash, make sounds, or have moving pictures, or ones that feature an unusual page layout or design elements. Even with faster Internet connections and reduced file size for some of these cool elements, flashy elements can still take a while to download. In this section, we'll take a look at the things you need to keep in mind if you're planning to use something that's a bit flashy.

Ensuring That the "Flash" Does Not Obscure Your Site's Content

How can you tell whether a particular effect overwhelms your site? Well, if you have to ask, then it probably does, and you should take steps to reduce or remove the flashy element.

WARNING *Just because you* can *provide an effect doesn't mean you should. If the effect doesn't help convey information, improve your user's overall experience, or help project your public image, don't include it.*

We can't tell you exactly how long each flashy element takes to download—too many variables exist, such as file size, the type and speed of the user's Internet connection, and the user's browser capability and computer resources. Table 13.1 summarizes the flashy effects you can add, the impact each can have on download time, and the availability in browsers.

TABLE 13.1: A SUMMARY OF WEB-PAGE ENHANCEMENTS

ENHANCEMENT	DESCRIPTION	AVAILABILITY
Images	These are the most common enhancements included in Web pages because they add color and flash, yet they're fairly easy to obtain or create. For this reason, they're probably the biggest culprits of waiting, because image files can grow to enormous sizes. However, you can modify images and image files so they take minimal time to download. Chapter 4 shows you how.	All graphical browsers.
Frames	These can slow things down slightly initially, but if used carefully they can speed overall performance considerably because only new information must be downloaded with every new page, leaving logos and other elements in place in adjacent frames. See Chapter 7 for more on frames.	Available on most versions of Netscape Navigator, Internet Explorer, and Opera.

Continued on next page

TABLE 13.1: A SUMMARY OF WEB-PAGE ENHANCEMENTS *(continued)*

ENHANCEMENT	DESCRIPTION	AVAILABILITY
Java applets	These can slow down pages considerably, particularly for users with older versions of Netscape Navigator. They can add power—both in terms of visual interest and through functional programs embedded in Web pages—but sometimes at a high cost. Java applets are sometimes avoided by the security conscious. Chapter 11 provides more information about Java applets.	Available on most versions of Internet Explorer, Netscape Navigator, and several other browsers.
JavaScript, also known as JScript or ECMAScript	This slows pages only slightly and can add attractive flash and glitz. However, many JavaScript effects are so overused as to be completely kitschy. Also avoided by the security conscious. See Chapter 10 for more details on JavaScript.	Available on most versions of Internet Explorer, Netscape Navigator, and Opera. Some effects are less widely available.
Multimedia	Sounds, video, Macromedia Flash animations, virtual reality worlds, and all the rest of the real flare formerly slowed pages nearly to a standstill. If you're adding important information or if you segregate the flare so only people who really want it will get it, it's okay, but use with consideration for those with older browser versions or slow Internet connections. See Chapter 11 for more information.	Available on newer browsers either already installed or with the proper plug-ins or controls.
Cascading Style Sheets (CSS)	These offer great formatting capabilities and lots of flexibility, but aren't quite universally available. However, browser support for CSS has increased to the point where CSS formatting is preferred for most purposes. Many HTML and XHTML formatting elements are deprecated in favor of CSS. See Chapter 9 for more information.	Netscape Navigator 4 and newer, Internet Explorer 3 and newer, and Opera 3 and newer. Specific capabilities vary greatly by browser.

TIP   *For a list of various browsers and the features they support, check out* `www.webreview.com/browsers/` `index.shtml`.

Be aware that some of these effects require users to have plug-ins installed on their computers, which can further impede users from accessing the information. A plug-in, discussed in detail in Chapter 11, is a program used to view an effect within a browser that doesn't typically support that effect. If you decide to include a Flash or Shockwave animation, for example, users need the appropriate plug-in to view it. If they don't already have the plug-in included in their browser's prepackaged software bundle and want to view the animation, they're forced to download the plug-in off the Internet and install it one time for every browser they use.

Is this a hassle? Yes, without a doubt. Most of your users won't take the time to download and install plug-ins just to view your site, unless the information provided through the plug-in is essential.

Being Aware of Other Obstacles That May Impede Your Users

Yes, flashy elements are often a big obstacle for your users; however, other factors can have a significant impact on your site visitors' experience (and affect how long they'll visit and whether they'll visit again):

Download time   Minimize it. Period. Even with Internet connection types and speeds improving all the time, remember that in the vast majority of cases, users go to your site because they want or need something. Don't make them wait to get it. How do you minimize download time?

- Use those flashy elements wisely.
- Minimize image file size, as described in Chapter 4.
- Specify image size in the img element, also described in Chapter 4.
- Specify table and cell size, as described in Chapter 5.
- Validate your HTML or XHTML document code, which eliminates any extraneous code that takes time to download and helps browsers parse your documents more quickly.

Glaring colors or color combinations, or colors that don't contrast enough   Again, if you have to ask whether two colors contrast enough (or whether the color scheme is garish), they probably don't (and it probably is). Opt for colors and combinations that aid readability, as discussed in Chapter 4.

Excessive scrolling   Don't require more than a single click to scroll down on topic and link pages (as opposed to article pages, for example, which are by nature often longer). If your pages are longer than a screen or two, consider breaking up the site contents into smaller chunks.

A complicated design   Back in Part II, we discussed using tables and frames to develop a more complex page layout. Rather than having left-aligned headings followed by left-aligned paragraphs, you can use tables and frames to *chunk*, or break up, content and place those chunks in different areas of the site. Although these elements can be useful in creating a less-boring page layout, remember to use your newly acquired powers in moderation. Even on a large monitor displaying a high resolution, screen space is still relatively limited, and table cells and frames can quickly become unusable and unreadable. What's more, while complex designs can be effective on larger monitors or at higher resolutions, they quickly become a total mess on smaller monitors or at lower resolutions. If you choose to develop a more complex (less boring!) page layout, keep these ideas in mind:

- Limit your frames to no more than two or three, regardless of your users' monitor size or resolution. Any more than that is just too many—the frames themselves consume a lot of screen space.
- Use JavaScript to force your page to adjust to the screen size. Otherwise, on smaller screens or at lower resolutions, your pages may be truncated on the right, forcing users to scroll

horizontally to access the width of your pages. Visit `www.hotscripts.com` for scripts that can accomplish this.

◆ Use the `cellspacing` and `cellpadding` attributes with the table data (`td`) element to increase the amount of space between cells and between the cell border and cell contents, respectively.

Excessive site or page-level changes   If you've done your job right, visitors to your site will quickly get a feel for the overall layout and design, as well as for where navigation menus are and how they work. If you change the overall design, remove sections, move or change navigation significantly, or make other similar changes, returning users will have to take time to relearn what's on your site and how to get to the information they are seeking. Certainly, site redesigns are a good idea from time to time—to correct problems or issues that users report, to give the site an updated look and feel, or to overhaul a site whose purpose or user base has changed. However, as much as possible, ensure that you plan these changes carefully, implement the changes during low-use times, and document the changes so that users can orient themselves quickly to the new site.

TIP   Remember that small-screen environments are becoming increasingly popular. Your Web site could very well be viewed on users' handheld devices or laptop computers.

Browser-specific elements   Throughout this book, we've focused on showing you how to use HTML and XHTML elements and attributes that are not browser-specific and are, instead, elements that the vast majority of your users can access. There are, however, a number of browser-specific elements available—ones that only Internet Explorer supports or that Netscape supports, for example. If you're tempted to use a browser-specific element, don't—or at least, realize that by doing so that information or effect may not be available to all of your users. Strongly consider choosing another element, or provide an alternative way for users to access the information, feature, or service.

Broken links   The Web is a living entity, in that sites and their contents are always changing. As a Web developer, you need to take steps to ensure that links on your site—whether to other pages on your site or to external sites—are kept current as much as possible. If you don't, you'll cause your users to waste time clicking through to content that's not available, and they may ultimately decide not to continue using your site. You'll find that the link-checking programs built into many editors are satisfactory. Or you can check out the resources at `http://directory.google.com/Top/Computers/Software/Internet/Site_Management/Link_Management/`. Also, be sure to publish a *Page Not Found (404 error)* page that loads whenever users try to access a page that no longer exists; if possible, go a step further and tell users where they can find the content they are looking for, or direct them to resources that do provide the needed information if your site no longer does. Figure 13.3 shows the TECHWR-L Page Not Found page.

FIGURE 13.3

By developing a detailed Page Not Found message, you can help redirect users to the information they are looking for

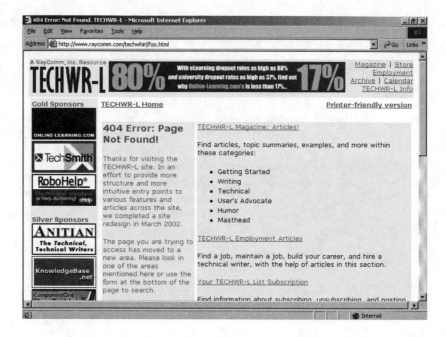

Testing Your Web Site

As we mentioned in Chapter 1, the appearance of your pages on your users' screens probably will differ from what you see on your screen because of browser and operating system differences. Therefore, you need to test your documents on as many computers and browsers as possible. By checking documents on various platforms and browsers, you can see how your documents will appear to various users, check readability and usability, and root out any layout or formatting problems. Remember that you want to test for these issues *before* you publish your pages on the Web or an intranet.

TIP *Web pages are similar to the marketing materials your company uses. Just as an editor checks corporate brochures closely for layout, design, organization, and accuracy, carefully check your Web pages or hire an editor to check them.*

Getting Ready to Test

Before you start testing, manually "expire" all the links. Most browsers are set by default to remember (for about 30 days) links that you've visited, and they color those links differently from unvisited links. You can easily see which sites you've visited, which is handy if you'd rather not browse in circles. By expiring links before you test your pages, you can see, for example, that the link colors (for links, active links, and visited links) appear as they should, and you can tell which links you haven't yet followed in your testing process.

Exactly how you expire links varies from browser to browser. The following steps give you the general procedure:

1. Look for a menu option that lets you change browser settings. For example, in Netscape 6, choose Edit ➤ Preferences. In Internet Explorer 5.5, choose Tools ➤ Internet Options.

2. In the resulting dialog box, look for an option that lets you change document history.

3. Expire the links by clicking the Clear History button.

4. Click OK when you're done.

Testing for Overall Appearance

With your links expired, open your Web pages in your browser(s), and ask yourself the following questions:

- Is the layout and design aesthetically appealing? Do page elements align as planned?
- Is all the content visible? All text? All images?
- Do all colors appear as they should? Are there any odd patterns or colors?
- Do all pages contain navigation tools?
- Do all frames, applets, and other objects appear as planned?

After you've answered these questions and are satisfied with the results, change the size of your display window and test the overall appearance again. For example, make your display window smaller. You'll find that some elements may not appear on the screen or align as intended. Make any necessary adjustments.

TIP   To quickly and easily evaluate different page sizes in Windows, create wallpaper with rectangles at 640 × 480, 800 × 600, and 1024 × 768 pixels. Then, assuming your display is set to at least 1024 × 768, you can simply resize the browser window to exactly overlap one of the rectangles.

TIP   Windows 95/98/ME/2000, Macintosh, and Unix users can all use built-in operating system functions to reset display characteristics. If you use Windows 95, go to **www.microsoft.com**, *download the Microsoft Power Toys, and use the Quick Res Power Toy to change display settings quickly and easily (without rebooting your machine). This utility is built into Windows 98 and higher.*

Now, change the color depth (that is, the number of colors being displayed) and see what happens to your pages. View your pages in millions of colors, in 256 colors, and in 16 colors in all your browsers. Check what happens to background and image color when you reduce the color depth. Yes, it's an incredible hassle—but, with some practice, you'll learn how HTML and XHTML effects appear at various resolutions, and you can improve your pages accordingly.

Testing for Usability

Usability refers to how easily a user can find and use information. The information may be there, but will users find it, wait for it to download, or go through layers of links to get to it? In testing for usability, consider the following:

- How long do the pages take to download? Remember, you're testing your pages on your local computer; therefore, you can expect the pages to download *much* more slowly when users access them over dial-up Internet connections. Of course, you should also test how the pages load using DSL and cable, if possible.

TIP   If your Web pages might be viewed on handheld devices, you'll also want to check your pages there. A better solution is to use XHTML and CSS to create separate, simpler versions of your Web pages for handheld devices.

- Do the benefits of the enhancements outweigh the extra download time? For example, do images or the JavaScript you've added merit the added time required to download?

- How easily can you find navigation tools? Are they readily available, or do you have to scroll to find them? Are they consistent from page to page?

- Do *all* links work—links to information within the site as well as to information outside the site? A variety of tools, both interactive, Web-based tools and downloadable programs, can help you check links automatically. Search on "link validation" at your favorite search service for specifics.

- Are the levels of links appropriate for the information provided? For example, is the information located in a third-level link clearly subordinate to information in the first- and second-level links? Do the main category links appropriately summarize links and content they contain? Also, if you've provided many link levels, is the information important enough that your users will take the time to wade through the other links?

*TIP   Jakob Nielsen's UseIt.com site (**www.useit.com**) provides excellent information about usability.*

TIP   See also Chapter 12, the section "Planning for Accessibility," for information about how screen readers and enlargers aid people with visual impairments, as well as how you can develop your pages with these users in mind.

PILOT-TESTING YOUR DOCUMENTS

Formal usability studies are conducted in carefully controlled environments, where the conditions are specified, tasks are identified, and participants' actions are closely monitored and recorded. If you don't have a formal usability lab or experts onsite to work with, you can still "pilot-test" your site by asking people to look at the site and identify problems and areas for improvement. The two main methods for pilot-testing are contextual inquiry and the talking-aloud protocol, which are often used in combination.

When you use *contextual inquiry*, you observe users in their own environments. One of the best ways to get started is to simply sit with a notebook and quietly watch your users. Pay attention to everything they do, including which information they refer to, which links they use most, and in what order they visit pages. Make notes about when they refer to your site for information, when they appear to get lost or frustrated, and when they head down the hall to ask someone else. Although this method is time consuming, it can be a real eye-opening experience, particularly if most of your information about your users' needs is based more on conjecture than on observation.

When you use the *talking-aloud protocol*, you listen to users describe what they're doing and why they're doing it as they navigate your site. Follow this process:

1. Make a list of five or fewer items that you want each user to find at your Web site.

2. Give the users the list and ask them to find each item.

3. Ask the users to talk out loud throughout the test, saying anything that pops into their heads about the search, the site, or overall tasks.

Continued on next page

If possible, record the session. In all likelihood, you'll end up with a transcript that is fairly disjointed but rich in information. For example: "Let's see, I'm supposed to find safety information about this particular car model. Hmmm. No menu items for safety. Maybe it'll be under the Reliability menu. Nope, don't see it. Let's see. Search. No search items. It must be under Reliability. Aha, there it is, hiding under Protection. I saw Protection the first time, but thought that had something to do with undercoating or paint."

Pilot-testing your site can identify how people *really* find information at your site and can indicate exactly where you need to make improvements.

Testing for Readability

Readability refers to how easily users can read information—text and images. Because several readability issues—fonts, font sizes, line spacing, kerning (amount of space between letters), emphases, and colors—contribute to a document's overall appearance, you may have addressed some of them already. However, you need to look at these same issues from a user's point of view.

To test readability, search for a specific piece of information on your site. Observe which information you are drawn to on the page—usually images and headings stand out. Be sure that important information stands out adequately and that you can easily read all text, headings, captions, addresses, and so on.

READING ONLINE

By nature, reading on a computer screen is more difficult than reading the printed page. Hindrances include the size of the monitor, screen glare, and difficulty in navigating windows. In addition, a computer screen has a much coarser resolution than the printed page (72 to 100 dots per linear inch, as compared with 600 to 2,650 dots for laser-printed or typeset ink on paper). Consequently, users get tired quickly, read more slowly, and frequently skip information when reading on a computer.

As an HTML or XHTML author, you can improve readability somewhat with a few design techniques:

◆ Use headings and subheadings to break up long sections of text and to announce to a reader what information is on the page.

◆ Use bulleted and numbered lists, which give readers at-a-glance information.

◆ Use short paragraphs to encourage reading.

◆ Use text and background colors that adequately contrast.

◆ Use images to illustrate difficult concepts, rather than describing concepts in words.

Always test readability after changing the size of your display window or decreasing the color depth settings. Often, decreasing the window size or color depth makes pages much more difficult to read. For example, a Web site with a nice menu down the left side, a banner on the top, and black text on the right looks great at 1024 × 768. At lower resolutions, however, the black text can end up over the dark background, as Figure 13.4 shows, and be impossible to read.

FIGURE 13.4

Reducing window size can hinder readability

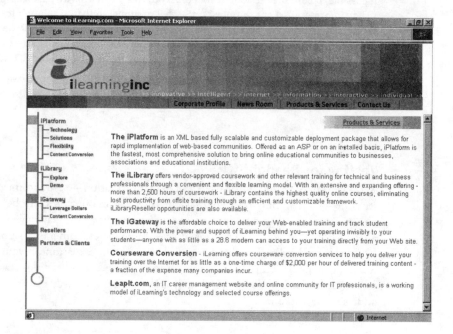

Testing for Accuracy

Be sure the information on your site is accurate. Pay attention to details. In particular, a site littered with typos and glaring grammatical errors has just about zero credibility. Your accuracy checklist also needs to ensure that:

- The content is correct and up-to-date.

- Headings summarize the content that follows.

- References to figures or illustrations are correct.

- The *date last modified* information is current. The date last modified, as the name indicates, tells your users how current the information is and helps them decide whether it's usable.

Maintaining Your Site

Finally, part of having a site that's well tested is also maintaining the usability, readability, and accuracy of information over time. Part of the difficulty in doing so is simply that content and the overall design do age, and any new information or features you add will need to be thoroughly tested beforehand as well. In addition, your users' needs, knowledge, and expectations change over time. In all, don't just think of "testing" as something you'll do before you launch your site, but as something you need to do regularly.

Where to Go from Here

Each of the topics introduced or further discussed in this chapter could all merit a chapter—or book—of its own! However, this chapter offers a good overview of issues and topics to explore as you're planning, designing, developing, and implementing your Web site. Keep these issues in mind and heed the advice as much as possible, and you'll be well on your way to developing a "good" Web site.

From here, you have several chapters at your fingertips that will add to the topics discussed in this chapter:

◆ Chapter 4 shows you how to include images in your Web pages and provides more information about choosing colors.

◆ Chapter 7 examines the advantages and disadvantages of using frames and shows you how to implement a framed site.

◆ Chapter 11 discusses including multimedia in your Web site.

◆ Chapter 12 provides a thorough discussion about planning your site (and includes many planning-related topics you may not have thought of).

◆ Chapter 14 provides tips and advice for developing specific types of sites—public, personal, or intranet.

Chapter 14

Tips for Web Sites:
Public, Personal, and Intranet

THROUGHOUT THIS BOOK, WE'VE talked about how to add elements and attributes to create various Web-page effects. In this chapter, we'll go a step further and discuss issues specific to the type of Web site you're developing. Broadly speaking, we can classify sites into three types:

Public

Personal

Intranet

A *public* site usually focuses on a company or an organization—for example, AltaVista or your local humane society. A *personal* site is a type of public site, but it focuses on an individual. Both types reside on the Web. However, an *intranet* is a different type of site altogether; it provides information about a company or organization, but it makes the information available only to people within that company or organization.

This chapter covers the following topics:

◆ Developing public sites

◆ Developing personal sites

◆ Developing intranet sites

Developing Public Sites

Public sites can address practically any topic and describe individuals as well as sell or describe products or services. They can also be published on any public Web server in the world. Public sites are those you find on the Internet. Presumably, if you've invested the time and resources to develop a Web site, you have a reason for wanting people to visit it. Although some users may happen upon it, you need to publicize your site to be sure that you reach the audience you intend to reach.

Publicizing Your Site

Your primary option is to publicize by submitting information about your site to directories and indexes. A *directory* is a categorized, hierarchical list. For example, Yahoo! (`www.yahoo.com`), one of the oldest and best-established directories, categorizes sites by subject.

Indexes (also called *search services*) use computer programs that roam the Internet and record every page they find. The site information, including titles, descriptions, and modification dates, is then fed into a huge database that anyone on the Internet can search. Google (`www.google.com`) is a well-known search service. As time goes by, the distinctions are disappearing—Google uses the Open Directory Project (`dmoz.org`) directory as a part of its search site, and Yahoo! licenses Google's search technology for its site. Other specialized sites, like Ask Jeeves at `http://ask.com`, use actual humans to identify and catalog information.

TIP   You can use the publicizing options discussed in the following few sections to publicize your personal site, too.

SUBMITTING DOCUMENTS YOURSELF

You can easily submit HTML and XHTML documents to directories and indexes by accessing their sites and completing online forms. For many years, this process was free; however, most commercial sites are now charging for business listings (or for all listings). Read the fine print before you click Submit.

For example, to submit your address to the Open Directory Project (currently free, and showing every indication of remaining so), follow these steps:

1. Go to the Open Directory Web site at `http://dmoz.org`.

2. Browse to the category that most closely fits your site.

3. Choose Add URL (currently found at the top of the page).

4. Enter the URL of your Web site and your e-mail address, and provide the title, description and other information requested.

5. Read the fine print, then click the Submit button to submit your site.

Other services may use slightly different procedures, but the basic process is the same and is typically just as easy. Look for a link at the bottom of the directory or index home page—the link is usually labeled "Add Your Site," "Submit Your Site," or "Add A URL." When your site is listed with these services, potential users have a much better chance of finding your site.

Your potential users determine which sites to visit based on these descriptions, so you need to make them informative. Unfortunately, not all services cull descriptions from the same place. For the most part, directories use information that you provide when you submit your site.

Providing Enticing Descriptions in Directories

Most directory services require—or at least request—a brief description about your site as part of the submission process. To draw people to your site, include the description and make it enticing and accurate. Even in the brief space provided by most directory services, you can summarize your site and lure potential users into clicking the link to your site. Here are a few suggestions:

Include key words.   Rather than saying, "Use this site to find tax information," include specific words and phrases, such as, "Find small business tax tips, tax forms, and tax-filing guidelines."

Start your description with active verbs that describe what users should do with the information. For example, begin your description with words such as *find, create,* or *develop.*

Include only major categories.   Don't ramble on about obscure or tangential topics.

Announce freebie files.   Many times, potential users are looking for images, sounds, or other information that they can download and use. If you have any freebies for them, let them know!

Announce that you've included updated, cutting-edge, or timely information.   Many potential users are looking for the latest information on a topic and will breeze past Web sites that seem to include only old news.

Helping Search Services Find Your Site

Some search services display the first several words of the document body as the site description, regardless of whether the words are headings, paragraphs, or even JavaScript code. For example, visit www .altavista.com and search for "xhtml". The results list the site addresses and a variety of descriptions.

TIP   Note that some nondirectory searches display the part of the page where the search term appears—usually the title, meta *tags (*keywords *or* description*), body, or some combination.*

You'll notice that descriptions vary considerably. Some sound like an introduction; others have nothing but jumbled information. Still others seem to summarize the document content, which is what potential users find most useful.

You can ensure that search services display an enticing description by including a meta element in the head of your HTML or XHTML document that specifies the description. Here's the process:

1. Open your document in a text editor.

2. In the document head (between the head elements), add a meta element, like this:

```
<head>
  <title>
      The Official TECHWR-L, the Internet forum for technical
      communicators
    </title><meta />
</head>
```

3. Add the name attribute to the element, and give it the value description:

```
<meta name="description" />
```

4. Add the content attribute to the element, and fill it with a concise, clear description of your page content. Stick to a few lines (200 characters or so), and be sure that the description accurately and effectively portrays your site.

```
<meta name="description"
      content="Welcome to TECHWR-L, which includes
the TECHWR-L discussion list, with over 5,000
subscribers and readership of over 10,000 and includes
the TECHWR-L site, with unrivaled content,
features, and services." />
```

WARNING *Remember that we have to break long lines, like this one, in print. You should type this all on one line, because including hard returns in attribute values can lead to unpredictable browser behavior.*

5. Save and close your document.

When search engines—such as Google, AltaVista, or Lycos—find your page, they display the description found within the `meta` element along with your site address.

In addition to using the text of your site, you can include keywords to help identify matches for user searches. *Keywords* provide synonyms for common words that might not appear in the actual text of the Web site. In addition, some search sites rank pages higher when the search term is in keywords than when it's just in the body. TECHWR-L uses keywords like these:

```
technical writing    technical communication    writing    editing
```

TECHWR-L

To include keywords, simply add another `meta` element. Follow these steps:

1. Open the document.

2. In the document head (between the `head` elements), add a `meta` element, as shown here. If you included a description in a `meta` element, you can place this one above or below it.

```
<head>
  <title>
      The Official TECHWR-L, the Internet forum for technical
      communicators
    </title><meta />
</head>
```

3. Add the `name` attribute to the element, with the value `keywords`:

```
<meta name="keywords" />
```

4. Add the `content` attribute to the tag, and fill it with a list of all the likely terms someone might use. Separate the terms with commas, but don't insert spaces after the commas.

```
<meta name="keywords"
    content="technical writing,
     technical communication,writing,editing,
     TECHWR-L" />
```

TIP *It's valuable to list variations of any important term—for example,* `biking,bikes,bicycles`*.*

5. Save and close your document.

TIP *For more information on search engines, including how they work, search engine placement tips, and a list of the top search engines and their URLs, go to* www.searchenginewatch.com*. This site also offers a free e-mail newsletter (as well as an expanded version by paid subscription) that details the latest updates in the frequently changing search engine field.*

HIDING PAGES AND FOLDERS FROM SEARCH ENGINES

If you've created a public site, you probably want robots or spiders to find your site and incorporate your pages into Internet-wide indexes such as Google and Lycos. You might also have specific pages or folders on your server that you want to exclude. For example, many sites have test folders that contain files that need to be on the server for testing purposes, but that are not designed to be accessed by users to the site or by search engines and indexes.

Fortunately, you can keep automated users from accessing specified pages and folders through an agreement called the *Robots Exclusion Standard*. Just put a plain-text document in the root (top) folder of your Web server and call the document robots.txt. In that file, use the following format to specify which robots to exclude and which folders to exclude them from. (All the lines that start with # are comments for you to read—they're disregarded by the robots.)

To keep robots out of your entire site, use a robots.txt file at your server root containing the following:

```
User-Agent: *
# The * specifies all agents or robots
Disallow: /
# The / indicates all documents under the server root.
```

To keep all robots out of the /test folder, for example, use a robots.txt file containing the following:

```
User-Agent: *
# The * specifies all agents or robots
Disallow: /test
# The / indicates that all folders immediately under the server root
# starting with /test should be excluded, including test and tests.
```

If you cannot access the robots.txt file at the server root, which could happen depending on your ISP and hosting arrangements, you can use a <meta name="robots" content="noindex" /> element and attributes in your document head. It is not as widely recognized as the robots.txt file, but is better than nothing.

USING SERVICES TO SUBMIT PAGES

Dozens of site submission services exist to relieve you of submitting your site manually. Some are free, and others charge a fee. Most free services submit your site to somewhere between 20 and 50 sites, including most of the popular ones. For a fee, they'll submit your site to many more sites—up to several hundred.

Is it worth your time to have your site submitted for free to several dozen sites? Perhaps, but remember that you often get what you pay for. It's worth the 15 minutes or so that it takes you to submit, but do not expect much in terms of results.

Is it worth the cost to have your site submitted for a fee to a few hundred directories and search engines? Possibly, but probably not. First, the 20 to 50 sites to which most services submit include those that your users are likely to use. Second, if your information is so precisely targeted that it wouldn't be adequately listed with the major directory and index services, you can probably market it more effectively through other channels or through specialty search engines and directories that target a specific content area—for example, book printing. You might also consider posting the information to e-mail list servers, newsgroups, or electronic magazines (*e-zines*), where you can target specific markets. Or, you might submit a press release about your site to a newsletter, magazine, or journal that targets specific markets.

TIP   Many search engines and directories now charge a fee for commercial sites. Some offer expedited review of your site for a fee, and others guarantee placement for a fee. If you're launching a new site (even a noncommercial one), it may be worth the fee to get an expedited review of your site by a directory such as Yahoo!. Otherwise, plan on at least six to eight weeks before your site appears in the search engines and directories.

OTHER PUBLICIZING METHODS

Because of the overwhelming number of new sites that appear on the Internet daily, simply adding your site to existing search engines and directories won't necessarily result in a flood of traffic.

Consider some of the following ways to publicize your new site:

◆ Include a brief announcement and URL in your e-mail signature.

◆ Add your URL and e-mail address to business cards and stationery.

◆ Add your URL to any advertising you do for your business, including yellow-page ads.

◆ Write an article about your site and submit it to newsletters or journals in your field.

◆ Send an e-mail message announcing your site to people in your field.

◆ Include links to other related sites, and ask those sites to provide a link back to your site.

Making Users Want to Browse Your Site

Think of your public Web site as being a retail store. The longer customers browse, the greater the chance that they'll buy something, even if they didn't go into the store intending to purchase anything. You want users to linger in your site for similar reasons. Longer visits likely mean that users will gather more information, notice more products and services, gain a better understanding of your organization, and purchase more merchandise (if you provide that option). Even if your public site serves more as a central clearinghouse for information—mostly providing links to information on the Web—you'll want users to spend time in your site and use the information you provide.

You can use several techniques to help keep visitors in your site longer. You'll find that you can easily combine these according to the site's purpose:

Minimize how long users have to wait to download pages, and be sure that your site loads quickly.   Pay extra attention to your home page, and make sure that it loads quickly enough that users will stay and visit the rest of the site. Check out Chapter 13 for information about balancing flashy elements with usability.

Use informative links.   Users won't spend much time at your site if you make them guess what information resides at the end of a link. Let them know if a link will take them to a different site. If you use links to graphics or other elements with large file sizes, let the user know in advance by putting the file size next to the link.

Provide links that go to real information.   Users tire easily of linking to pages that say, "This page under construction." At the very least, provide a date they can expect the information to be available—then do it.

Make the most useful and most-accessed information and links easily accessible.   You could force users to scroll through text to get to the information or links, but be careful. Users only tolerate a minimal amount of scrolling, and they're likely to move to another site if they can't reach information quickly.

Make the navigation obvious and easy for the user to figure out.   Never leave users at dead-end pages where they have no option except to leave the pages by using the browser's back button (or by leaving your site).

Provide services and information to make visiting worthwhile.   Offer free samples or added information about whatever you do.

Provide services that users can use while visiting your site.   For example, depending on your products or services, you could include an online mortgage amortization calculator, retirement planning advice, virtual coloring books, or a relocation calculator.

Making Users Yearn to Return

After users complete their business on your Web site, make them want to return to it. Here are some ideas to try:

Provide new information regularly and often.   Users won't return to a site that provides the same information time after time.

Provide accessible and complete contact information.   Many people use the Web as an enormous phone book; rather than looking up your company's phone number, they head to your Web site to find out how to contact you.

If you provide an e-mail link for contact, be sure to respond quickly to any e-mail you receive from the site.   If you're not able to answer right away, see if your ISP or Web hosting service offers auto-responders. These automatically send an e-mail response to let users know their e-mail was received and will be answered at a later time.

ISP AND WEB HOST: WHAT'S THE DIFFERENCE?

Internet service providers (ISPs) are usually the service you use to connect to the Internet. They provide dial-up access to the Internet via modems, and sometimes Digital Subscriber Line (DSL) and Integrated Services Digital Network (ISDN) access. Domain registration and domain hosting are usually available. Some ISPs offer Common Gateway Interface (CGI) directories (`cgi-bin`) for you to put your CGI scripts in, but usually do not offer any script templates or support for debugging scripts.

Web hosting services do not provide Internet connections for subscribers, but instead specialize in domain hosting and other services such as e-commerce, database connections, and Active Server Pages (ASP) services. Web hosts usually offer a variety of script templates for forms, guest books, and discussion forums. Most offer software or templates for e-commerce, and many provide chat services.

Update existing information.   Update product and service descriptions in particular, to reflect the current availability of your products and services, and make it clear that you've recently updated the information.

Include summaries of hot-off-the-press information that is related to your Web site.   Provide relevant, concise, and up-to-date news summaries for your readers. If readers get all the information they need in one place, they'll be more likely to come back.

Include links to related information.   Make your site a central information resource. For instance, we don't search for articles about the latest developments in browser technology; instead, we usually access reliable and current Web sites and link to articles from there.

Let your users register for e-mail notification of changes to the site.   You could collect addresses using a form on your site and send e-mail whenever you make substantive changes, or you could hire a service to automatically notify your registered users of changes.

Maintaining Public Sites

When you're running a public site, you'll probably have a steady stream of users. However, problems crop up when you're updating the site. Your goal is to develop a maintenance plan that eliminates downtime and provides users with uninterrupted service, as we discussed in Chapter 12. You want to eliminate even the shortest downtime stints—resulting from uploading files or encountering connectivity problems, for example. If your Web site is occasionally or unpredictably down for maintenance, users will not rely on it as an information resource.

You can avoid these problems if you follow these suggestions:

Keep backups of your site!   Be sure that your ISP, hosting service, and/or server administrator do the same.

Test the backups and confirm that you can restore the files in a reasonable amount of time.   If you house your site at your ISP or hosting service, be sure that you understand under which circumstances it's willing to restore the backup.

Provide redundant network connections (recommended for larger Web sites).   This ensures that users can access your site if a network connection goes down.

Find out what action your ISP or hosting service takes if it has technical difficulties.   Technical difficulties can include hard disk crashes, system problems, power outages, or network disruptions, or hackers may attack the system. While you—as a content provider—may not have to deal with these issues, you must take responsibility for ensuring that the Web site is adequately covered for all contingencies.

Use a *test environment* that duplicates your real server as nearly as possible, with the same software, the same physical platform, and the same configuration.   Viewing your site in a test environment gives you a good idea of what it will look like when you upload it to the server. See Chapter 13 for more information on test environments.

Consider using a tracking service as part of the maintenance of your site. Many free services are available, such as the tracker at www.extreme-dm.com/tracking, which features a counter and multiple site statistics, including when users visit your site, what browsers they're using, and what keywords they used in the search engines to find your site. The service is free for your home page, or you can purchase an expanded version that tracks every page.

For an expanded and very sophisticated tracking system, check out WebTrends at www.webtrends.com. This software provides a way for you to use your server access logs (these are generally available to you from your ISP or hosting service) to track the users to your site. WebTrends software can create reports about site users, including graphs and tables of information; among the extensive data it provides are these statistics:

- How long do users stay on a page?

- What pages are never accessed?

- What page do they leave the site from?

- What part of the country (or world) are they coming from?

Tracking information can be very useful to you for updating and maintaining your site to best meet the needs of your users.

Putting Ads on Your Site

If you're developing a public site, you may be considering selling ad space on your pages. For example, you might think about using some margins of your pages to promote related products or to advertise other, complementary sites. If your situation is typical, you probably won't make a fortune (or even a mini fortune). Even high-traffic sites such as Yahoo! don't yield high returns. However, selling ads directly or working with a reciprocal ad exchange service can have some benefits.

If you're sure you want to sell ads and do it all yourself, you'll need to use specialized, and possibly custom, software to track hits. For starters, check into eXtropia (www.extropia.com), Matt's Script Archive (www.worldwidemart.com/scripts), and HotScripts (www.hotscripts.com). All have custom applications to help manage ads and to track hits.

To begin placing ads on your site, you may consider doing ad exchanges with other companies. Perhaps the best option is to work with companies and organizations whose products or services would be of interest to your users, since doing so offers a few benefits. For example, if the ads are for products or services related to the topic of your site, users will more likely click through to find out more information than if the ads are not related to the reason they're visiting your site. Also, if users find ads on your site to be related to their needs (or related to the reason they're visiting your site), they'll be less likely to "tune out" ads on the site, an increasingly common fate for ads as they saturate the Internet. With these aspects in mind, providing targeted ads on your site can help improve the click-through rate for your advertisers, help you meet your users' needs, and help you develop a mutually beneficial relationship with your advertisers.

Another option is to use a link exchange service, such as those listed at http://directory.google .com/Top/Computers/Internet/Web_Design_and_Development/Promotion/Banner_Exchanges/. These link exchanges find homes for your ads while placing ads on your site. After you visit the link exchange site and register, you receive some code to put in your page—that code automatically displays the ad. You then also submit an image for your ad banner. The service counts the number of ads that you show, which is essentially the number of hits to your site. Typically, for every two hits to your site, your ad appears somewhere else once (some services provide a more favorable ratio). Participating in link exchange services is often less effective than working with companies whose products and services are of direct interest to your users simply because the ads placed on your site may or may not attract your users. And, sure, you may get your company's ad out there on other sites in exchange, but the ad may not hit people in your target audience.

TIP   *If you represent a company or an organization that's moving toward online sales of products, work with your ISP or Web hosting service to set up secure transactions so credit card transactions from your site are as secure as possible. Check what's available from your ISP or Web host, or go to your favorite search engine and search for "e-commerce" to get the latest services and software.*

Developing Personal Sites

A personal site is a special type of public Web site that focuses on an individual. Although you can use personal sites to publish general information about yourself, such as your hobbies and interests, you can also use personal sites to market your skills or publish information you've researched or developed—which is what the next few sections show you how to do.

Marketing Your Skills

You can use a personal Web site to market your skills through a Web-based resume, letter of introduction, or personal brochure. Most commonly, you'll market your skills to get a job (or a better job), although you could also use this vehicle to gain contract employment or to let companies know that you exist and are available. With one thoughtfully developed Web site, you can market yourself to millions of people around the world without the hassles or expense of traditional mailings.

A personal Web site represents your skills, experience, and creativity in much the same way that traditional tools do. When you're applying for a job, you generally develop a resume and a letter of application, and you probably pay particular attention to your personal appearance when you go to the interview. You create a package—one that informs a potential employer about your skills, shows your attention to detail and creativity, and projects some information about your personality. Your personal Web site should do the same.

Providing this information on the Web has several advantages over traditional job application materials. For example, your Web-page resume can't get buried on someone's desk, and multiple pages can't get separated or lost in the shuffle. Also, you can provide more details and examples on the Web than you could ever get away with in a traditional resume.

DEVELOPING A WEB RESUME

In developing a Web resume, you have the same options as you do in developing a paper resume—you can focus on experience or education, skills or training, or other aspects that might appeal to a future employer. The approaches break down into essentially two types: functional and skills-based, as shown in Figure 14.1.

FIGURE 14.1

Functional resumes focus on places of employment and educational institutions; skills-based resumes focus on your skills

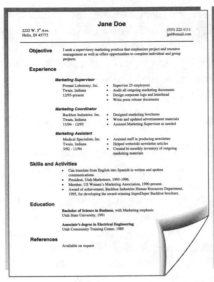

Functional Résumé

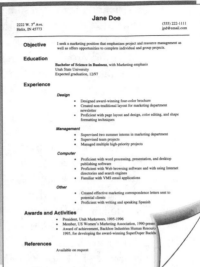

Skills-Based Résumé

Both types include basically the same sections—contact information, objective, education, employment, activities, and references. They differ only in emphasis, as shown by the summary in Table 14.1. When developing a Web resume, use either of these types or some combination of the two.

TABLE 14.1: FUNCTIONAL AND SKILLS-BASED RESUMES

	FUNCTIONAL RESUME	SKILLS-BASED RESUME
Purpose	Provides information about places you worked and/or educational institutions you attended	Provides information about skills you've developed or coursework you've completed
Advantages	Allows you to announce prestigious job titles, company names, university names, and degrees	Allows you to downplay multiple jobs, unfinished degrees, or positions in which you learned a lot without adequate compensation or title
Focus	Places you've worked or education	Skills
Categories	Objective, Education, Employment, Special Skills or Activities, and References	Objective, Skills, Education, Activities, and References

You'll probably combine features of both types of resumes. For example, you may have worked for companies with well-recognized names and held jobs with prestigious titles, but you also want to emphasize your specific skills. In this case, you primarily use a skills-based resume but add an employment history page that lists your previous employers. Or, perhaps you want to show your steady employment history and promotions through each job change. In this case, you want to primarily use a functional resume but include a separate skills page.

Organizing Web resumes is tricky because you must accommodate both a nonlinear read, in which users select topics that catch their attention, and a linear read, in which users start at the top and read sequentially (or print out the page). Many typical Web site users expect your pages to look flashy and provide information quickly. In this case, make available multiple, shorter documents with links between and among them. In doing so, you provide pages that download quickly and display information that's easy to find.

TIP   See Chapter 13 for more information about balancing flashy elements with quick loading time.

However, other users may want to print your documents, and you could spend a lot of time printing multiple pages from a site. For this reason, also provide a complete resume that users can read linearly and print easily.

Essentially, you develop two complete resume packages—one broken into chunks and the other in one document. This way, you accommodate virtually any user (think "potential employer"). These folks can easily view the information or print it, depending on their needs.

To meet both these structural needs, do two things. First, provide each of the resume categories in separate HTML or XHTML documents, as shown in Figure 14.2.

FIGURE 14.2

Put each resume category in a document of its own

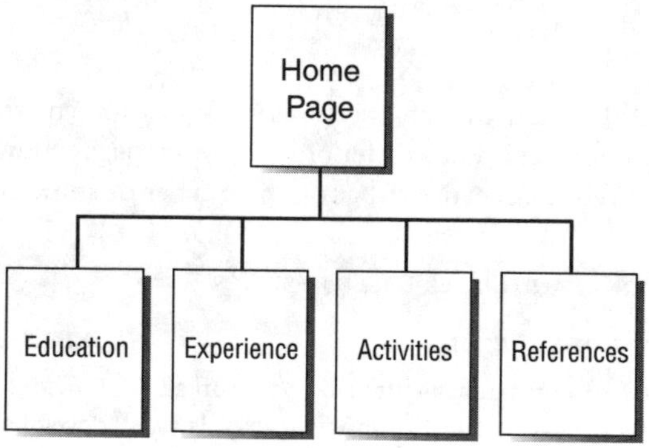

Why do this? You might recall from Chapter 1 that online reading produces some difficulties for users. For instance, users face obstacles such as computer resolution, small monitors, and screen glare, all of which make reading online difficult. The result is that users (or more specifically, their eyes) tire quickly, and they tend to gloss over information rather than read it thoroughly. By using multiple, shorter documents, as shown in Figure 14.2, you improve the chances that users take the time to browse. These shorter documents are more inviting because the pages don't appear so difficult to wade through, and very short documents virtually leap onto the screen, with little wait time. Also, users can choose which information they access and in what order. The result is that users spend more time browsing your site and—essentially—more time considering you as a possible applicant.

Next, provide a link pointing to a single document that includes the full resume package. You can easily include a link from the home page and let users view a longer single document (as opposed to multiple shorter documents).

WARNING *Resist the temptation to use the fanciest formatting options in your resume. Your resume should indeed look nice, but keep it quick to download and simply formatted (use standard fonts).*

Developing a Web Resume Home Page

Many Web resumes start on a home page, which is the most important page in the site because it's usually the first page that users access. Typically, it states your employment objective and includes links to each category of information, as shown in Figure 14.3.

FIGURE 14.3

Your resume home page should state your objectives and provide links to other information

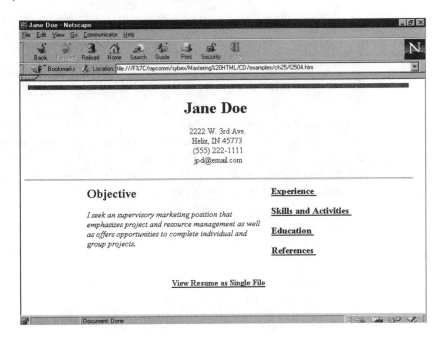

Don't overlook the *employment objective*, which can play a big role in luring users to link to other pages in the resume. Focus your objective on the skills you can offer a company. For example, rather than saying, "I seek a position in which I can use my existing skills and learn new ones," state the specific skills you want to use, like this: "I seek a position as Marketing Manager so that I can manage accounts, supervise people, and collaborate on marketing projects." Focus on what you offer the company, rather than on what you want from them.

When developing your resume home page, remember the following guidelines:

◆ Provide concise information about how, when, and where potential employers can contact you.

◆ Make browsing inviting—that is, minimize download time, provide links in a useful location, and provide informative link names.

◆ Be sure your home page portrays the image you want to present. Use colors and layout that express your professionalism and personality and align with those used by your target market.

For example, if your competitors use subdued blue and green tones, you probably do not want a sea of red for your site. See Chapters 2, 9, and 13 for information about applying formatting effectively.

◆ Be sure that users can easily link to other pages from the home page. If you provide a list of links, place the most important or most frequently accessed information at the top of it.

◆ Be sure the information at the end of links is complete. Never provide a link in a resume home page that goes to incomplete or unavailable information.

◆ Provide a link that goes to a full-length resume in addition to the Web resume that's divided into smaller pieces. That way, users can easily print your resume and have it on hand. (See "Publishing Your Resume in Other Formats" later in this chapter.)

◆ Include only original information, images, or files. Don't "borrow" materials from other sites and use them as your own. Doing so is illegal, not to mention unethical.

Developing Subsequent Resume Pages

Subsequent pages in the resume should reflect the topics that you announce in the home page. For example, if your home page announces categories such as work history, education, and references, develop a single HTML or XHTML document for each of those three categories.

When creating these subsequent pages, use the same background, fonts, and color scheme that appear on the home page. This unites pages into a cohesive unit and provides users with visual cues that the pages are part of your site.

TIP   See Chapter 12 for information about including theme-bearing elements throughout your Web site.

Here are a few tips to remember when developing subsequent pages:

◆ Include your contact information on *every* page.

◆ Provide navigation menus so users can access other main pages in the site easily and quickly.

◆ Be concise and clear. If you're tempted to go on to a second or third screen, move the less important information to a different page and provide a link to it.

Including a Letter of Introduction

Within your Web resume, you can include a link to a letter of introduction, which provides information that complements—not repeats—your resume. For example, your resume might indicate that you were a team leader on the AlphaDoowhichie project. The letter of introduction can supplement this information by telling users about your specific role in the project, discussing the project's success, or detailing how the company benefited from your performance. Letters of introduction give you the opportunity to highlight your successes and provide the details that aren't always appropriate in resumes.

Here are some guidelines about letters of introduction you might find useful:

◆ Make the application user-oriented—that is, not only give details about your successes, but also specify how these successes have prepared you to fill the position.

◆ Limit the letter to three or four paragraphs—long enough to highlight the main points, but not so long that you bore users.

◆ Provide your contact information.

Publishing Your Resume in Other Formats

Another option is to provide a link from your Web resume (probably from the home page) to your resume saved in other formats. Using Rich Text Format (RTF) and Adobe Acrobat PDF files, you overcome some difficulties inherent in Web pages—the biggest being that you have no control over how your resume appears in your users' browsers or in printed form.

These files are not actually part of your document—you link to them just as you link to any other files. Instead of automatically appearing in a user's Web browser as documents do, the RTF or PDF documents are downloaded to the user's computer and are saved to the hard drive or loaded in an appropriate viewing program (a word processor for RTF files, Acrobat Reader for PDF files). These formats also give you more control over how your document looks when it's printed.

Your easiest and cheapest option is to provide a link to your resume saved as an RTF file. RTF is a fairly standard word-processing format that, in this context, allows your users to view your resume in the word processor of their choice. Most formatting remains intact in RTF documents, and you can create them from the Save As command of most word-processing programs.

A few drawbacks are associated with using an RTF document, however:

◆ Users must take an extra step to download the file and open it in a word processor.

◆ Conversion problems can occur in the downloading process.

◆ Users can easily alter an RTF file.

A better, but more expensive, option is providing a link to a PDF version of your resume. PDF (which is short for *Portable Document Format* and uses the `.pdf` file extension) is a technology designed to facilitate document sharing and remote printing—keeping all fonts and formatting intact and making it impossible to change the document. Think of it as putting a fax copy of your resume on the Web—users view the document you created, complete with the layout and formatting you specified.

A few drawbacks are also associated with using PDF files. You, the resume provider, have to purchase Adobe Acrobat or have another program available that can create PDF files. PDF files are large, meaning that they take a while to download. Also, users must have Acrobat Reader or download and install it before they can view your resume. Granted, most readers do, but the last thing you want to do is to pose an extra obstacle for anyone interested in viewing your resume.

TIP   *Check out Adobe Acrobat at* `www.adobe.com` *for more information about Acrobat and purchasing information.*

INCORPORATING YOUR WEB RESUME INTO AN EXISTING PERSONAL SITE

If you're developing a Web resume as part of your personal site, consider that the personal site itself becomes part of the resume. In this case, a potential employer might visit your personal pages plus the resume-related pages.

Because of this, we recommend that you take some precautions:

♦ Make the personal pages as professional as possible.

♦ Store any potentially offensive documents in a subfolder without links to it. Send the complete URL to this subfolder only to the people you want to be able to see it.

♦ Use the robots.txt file to keep spiders and robots out of your personal stuff, as discussed in "Publicizing Your Site" earlier in this chapter.

♦ Consider password-protecting your personal pages. Anything from church activities, to hunting, to humor in arguably poor taste could offend some potential employers.

SUBMITTING YOUR RESUME ONLINE

In addition to posting your resume on your own Web site, strongly consider submitting your resume online. A multitude of employment Web sites is now available. These sites offer a variety of services, including job listings, career counseling, and often including online services such as tutorials and classes to increase your marketable skills. Most of these sites allow you to post your resume at no charge. Some allow you to post a text document version of your resume, but more often, they have their own forms for you to fill out online with details of your employment history, job skills, training, and education.

Check out several of these sites to see which one is best for the type of work you're looking for. A good place to start is www.monster.com, one of the largest online job sites. At this site, you can create up to five different online resumes with cover letters. In addition, an automatic job search service will e-mail you when a job listing matches your criteria. This site currently has over one million job postings and includes international listings.

Other well-known employment Web sites are www.guru.com, which includes job listings in media, marketing, management, information technology, and multiple types of Web-related employment, and www.dice.com, which specializes in job listings and online resumes for information technology jobs. Most employment sites cover both employee positions and contract or freelance work, but there are also sites that specialize in freelance jobs, such as www.elance.com. Do a search for "jobs" or "employment" using your favorite search engine to find additional Web sites with job listings and online resume services.

Self-Publishing Information

You might also develop a personal site to *self-publish* information you've researched or developed. For example, you might publish genealogical information, your in-progress soon-to-be-a-hit novel, short stories, class projects, research papers, recommendations, or advice. Whatever the topic, you can self-publish on the Web easily and inexpensively, which is the main reason self-publishing has become so popular.

However, before you self-publish, consider some of the downsides. First, most discerning readers are skeptical about the quality and reliability of self-published information, and your information may be perceived as unworthy. Assure users that the information you provide is reliable, researched, reviewed, or cross-referenced to other sources that support your claims. For example, include a bibliography, a works-cited list, or a list of experts with whom you consulted. Also, consider providing links to other information on the Web that supports your claims.

Second, Web surfers, whether they realize it or not, tend to take self-published information and use it as their own. Most folks don't realize that they're "stealing" your information; self-published information that lacks an official (and highly visible) copyright or statement of ownership appears available for public use. To ensure that your information stays yours, always provide a copyright statement or state that the information is available for reference, but not to be taken and subsumed into other people's work.

Finally, don't publish information that's been published elsewhere—in magazines, journals, newspapers, and so on—without obtaining prior permission. For example, if you're a Dilbert fan and you want to put your 10 favorite Dilbert cartoons on your Web page, remember that someone else holds the copyright to those cartoons. Contact the owners of the Web site and request their permission to use their material. Or, if you or someone else developed material for a company that's no longer in business, don't assume that the previously published material is available for you to use; on the contrary, the copyright to that defunct company's material is still likely held by someone. Although most people who publish on the Web (or post information to the Internet on newsgroups or in other forums) don't have lawyers watching for copyright infringements, it's still wrong to take other people's material.

WARNING   If you're publishing information about people, be sure that they want information published about them. When asking permission to publish information, provide the name and URL of your site, information about your intended use, and the length of time you'd like to publish the information on the site. Make sure you have all the permissions you need. The GigaLaw site (`www.gigalaw.com`*) provides extensive information about copyright and permissions-related topics, among many other topics.*

HAS INFORMATION BEEN TAKEN FROM YOUR SITE?

If you publish on the Web and you want to find out whether users have taken information and used it as their own, you can. Simply visit Google, AltaVista, HotBot, or another full-text search engine and do the following:

◆ Search for keywords that appear in your documents.

◆ Search for unique phrases.

◆ Search for typing or spelling errors that you find in your pages. For example, a search for "accomodates your needs" will get poor spellers as well as anyone who copied the misspelled text directly.

There's also a great Web site available that searches previously published works for you. It's called Digital Integrity and can be found at `www.d-integrity.com`.

When users access self-published research documents, their intent is usually to gather information so they can learn from it or apply it to their own projects. Users might actually read the information from start to finish, or they might print it.

For these reasons, consider presenting the information as one long page, rather than as sections in separate, shorter documents with links between and among them. One long document is easier to print for later reference.

Also, because these documents tend to be more than a screen or two, provide multiple navigation menus throughout the document, as shown in Figure 14.4. Place menus at the top and bottom of documents as well as throughout the body.

FIGURE 14.4

Placing navigation menus within long documents helps users wade through information

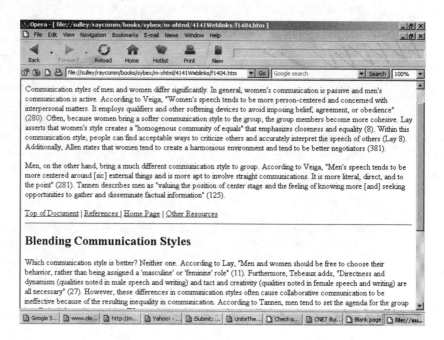

Developing Intranet Sites

Intranet sites are enterprise-wide Web sites accessible only by people within an organization. Intranets came about as a result of the need for improved corporate communications. As companies expand geographically, they face the challenges of providing company-wide information quickly and inexpensively—a feat not possible using traditional communication methods such as mailings, memorandums, faxes, or bulletin boards. Using an intranet, however, companies make information immediately accessible to all employees, regardless of their geographic location, and eliminate or significantly reduce the need for other forms of communication.

Although individuals or small groups generally develop and maintain public sites, employees often contribute content for intranets. For example, the information services department might actually run the intranet, but one or more employees in each department within an organization might assume responsibility for providing and updating pages pertaining to that department.

The result can be a hodgepodge of information that doesn't generally fit into a coherent information resource. Your goal as an information coordinator—whether you're the company owner, the head of information services, or the person who also develops and maintains the company's public site—is to ensure that the intranet is a valuable, uniform, usable information resource.

In the following sections, we'll look at how to coordinate content from contributors, suggest some ways that you can put out the word about what's new or updated on your intranet, and introduce intranet discussion groups. The "you" in these sections is the content coordinator for an intranet, and the "users" are employees or members of an organization that uses an intranet.

Determining Intranet Content

Intranets provide substantial, company-specific information that helps employees do their jobs, automates processes, and offers updates or news. If your intranet is part of a corporate environment, a good starting point for content is the human resources department, where you're likely to find company policy manuals, training schedules, safety guidelines, evacuation plans, and much more.

You can also use an intranet to publish product or service descriptions. For example, when you place boilerplate (standardized) information about your products and services on your intranet, users can easily access it and use it in marketing materials, documentation, or whatever.

You might also publish information that's not directly pertinent to employees' jobs, but that employees would find useful:

◆ The cafeteria menu

◆ The company newsletter

◆ New contract announcements

◆ Annual budgets

◆ Company and retirement-fund stock quotes

And, you can also include links to industry news or to sister-company Web sites.

Your next step is to talk with employees about the information that they provide, distribute, and update to other groups within the company and about the information that they need and might (or might not) get from other departments. Ask about the following:

◆ Forms

◆ Reports

◆ Budgets

◆ Schedules

◆ Guidelines

◆ Procedures

◆ Policies

◆ Legacy documents

You can probably obtain some of this information using existing materials such as human resources handbooks, marketing brochures, and company white papers.

Accommodating User Needs

Intranet site users generally have one thing in mind: They're looking for information necessary to do their jobs. They might, for example, use the information to write a report, develop marketing materials, plan their schedules, and so on. For this reason, make absolutely certain that the information you provide is accurate and timely.

Users also expect you to provide accessible information—information they can find consistently from day to day. As a starting point, develop the overall site organization, taking into account all categories of information you will provide. Be sure to leave room for growth—adding new categories and expanding existing categories. For example, in developing a navigation menu, include all the categories of information that you'll eventually need. If you end up including links that don't yet have content, provide a statement about the information coming soon, or better yet, specify a date when you'll provide the information (and of course make sure that you do provide the information by that date). You can also include contact information for people who can answer questions in the interim.

Finally, users don't usually expect an intranet site to be flashy. After all, they're accessing the site because they need information, not because they expect to be dazzled. Plan a site design that is visually appealing, but don't go overboard with sounds, colors, and other special effects. Consider including your company's logo and using its color scheme, but beyond that, think functional, not fancy.

TIP   *Visit Chapters 12 and 13 for information about Web site planning, accessibility, and usability.*

Helping Others Contribute

As you saw in the previous sections, intranets are not usually the work of one person. Although you may be in charge of developing the site, others will actually provide and update the content. And not all contributors will have the same HTML or XHTML proficiency; some will be novices, others will be experts. Striking a balance between consistency and creativity can be challenging. Here are some ideas that may help.

PROVIDE TEMPLATES AND EXAMPLES

If you maintain a consistent look and feel, your intranet will appear more established and polished than it actually is. Relying on information providers to care as much as you do about a consistent appearance is likely too much to hope for, so make it easy for them: Provide templates.

Templates include all the structure elements and other elements that set up the general document format. You can provide templates for departmental home pages, for contact information, for current projects, or for any other pages that are common to several departments. You might also provide references to company-specific graphics and symbols. Using a template complete with these items, contributors can copy and paste the code into their documents and fill in the specific content. Listing 14.1 and Figure 14.5 show a sample template and the resulting document format. Note that you don't see any text formatting in this template because it would be supplied in a separate CSS style sheet.

TIP   *Visit Chapter 12 for information about elements to include in a master document, which can be the basis for a template.*

LISTING 14.1: PROVIDING A TEMPLATE FOR INTRANET CONTENT

```
<!DOCTYPE html PUBLIC "-//W3C/DTD XHTML 1.0 Transitional//EN"
    "http://www.w3.org/TR/xhtml1/DTD/xhtml1-transitional.dtd">
<html xmlns="http://www.w3.org/1999/xhtml">
<head>
    <title>ASR Intranet</title>
    <link rel="stylesheet" href="style.css" type="text/css" />
</head>
<body>
    <div align="center">
    <img src="asrintra.jpg" border="0" alt="ASR intranet logo" />
    </div>
<!--Don't change anything above this line except the title.-->

    <h1 align="center">Put Your Department Name Here</h1>
    <p>Provide content here.</p>
    <p>And here.</p>
    <p>And here.</p>
    <ul>
        <li>List links here.</li>
        <li>And here.</li>
        <li>And here.</li>
    </ul>
<!--Replace department@intranet.asroutfitters.com in the
    following lines with your own e-mail address.-->
    <p>Send all questions to
    <a href="mailto:department@intranet.asroutfitters.com">
        department@intranet.asroutfitters.com</a>.</p>

<!--Please do not change anything below this line. The following
    command applies the document footer with the navigational
    toolbar and related information.-->
<!-- #include virtual="/boilerplate/footer.htm" -->
</body>
</html>
```

TIP   *If your company has standardized on Netscape Navigator or Internet Explorer 4 or later, you should provide style sheets to contributors. By supplying a style sheet, you help contributors concentrate on content and ensure a more consistent appearance throughout the site. (See Chapter 9 for more information about style sheets.)*

FIGURE 14.5

The same template viewed in a browser, before being customized for specific departmental use

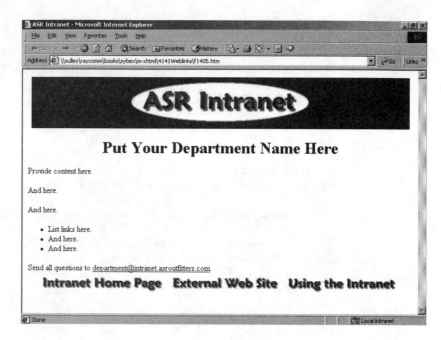

PROVIDING ACCESS TO IMAGES

An alternative to referencing image files is to store them in a folder that contributors can access. The easiest way is to put them all in a folder immediately off the server root, such as /graphics, and provide copy-and-paste text, like this:

```
<img src="/graphics/corplogo.gif" alt="ASR Corporate Logo"
    align="left" height="100" width="250" />
```

Moving further into the copy-and-paste realm, you can also include copy-and-paste snippets of code to automatically include document headers and footers by using *server-side includes*, such as:

```
<!--#include virtual="/includes/header.htm"-->
```

You provide the header, including anything that belongs at the top of the document, such as the corporate logo, copyright, confidentiality information, and anything else your company requires. The contributor includes the single line in the document, and, when it appears on the Web, all the header information appears in place of the include element. Check the Web server documentation for more information about using server-side includes.

PUBLISH INSTRUCTIONS AND GUIDELINES

Publish—on the intranet, of course—instructions and guidelines for providing information on the intranet:

- ◆ Documentation for publishing information
- ◆ Acceptable versions of HTML or XHTML (XHTML 1.0, tables, frames, or whatever)

- Formats for organizing and structuring the information

- Tools (and where to get them)

- Documentation for using tools

- HTML and XHTML resources (this book, right?)

- Acceptable enhancements—images, applets, JavaScript, and so on

Also, specify that contributors include their contact information on each page so that content questions will go to them, not you. Make it clear that the "contact the Webmaster" links are only for users having technical difficulties. Contributors need to give users a way to contact them—during and after hours.

PROVIDE CONVERSION SERVICES

Offer to convert existing documents to intranet pages. Most departments have pages of information that could easily be converted to HTML or XHTML.

If you offer this service, you could be overwhelmed with documents to convert. We strongly recommend providing one-time conversion services to help departments get material out on the intranet, but rather than assuming the responsibility for ongoing document conversion, take the time to train the contributors thoroughly so departments can support themselves.

TIP   See Chapter 8 for information about converting HTML to XHTML.

REMIND CONTRIBUTORS AS NECESSARY

Most content providers contribute information to the intranet in addition to their regular duties. You can help them manage their sections of the intranet by sending them e-mail reminders. Include information about how frequently users access their information, which information is not accessed, and so on—information that you (or the system administrator) can get from the access logs. If users aren't accessing certain pages, help find out why. Is the information outdated, hard to find, not needed? With this information, you can help weed out information that isn't being used and make room for more.

AUTOMATING PROCESSES

If you have programming resources available, consider automating some of the processes discussed in this chapter. For example, you can automatically:

- Generate "What's New" lists.

- Remind content providers of pages that haven't been updated in a specific amount of time.

- Consolidate and summarize access logs, changes to pages, and new sections for reports to management.

- Check incoming documents for compliance with corporate style, the correct version of HTML or XHTML, and functional links.

For more information, consult with your system administrator or internal programmers.

Announcing New or Updated Information

Users value new information, so be sure to notify them when the site is updated, and do so consistently. Even if users don't immediately need the information, making them aware that it's available might save them time later. Here are some ways to do so:

◆ Develop a What's New template that departments can use to feature new or updated information.

◆ Create New and Updated icons that contributors can include on their pages.

◆ E-mail employees regularly—say, weekly—and tell them what's new and updated.

◆ E-mail managers regularly about new and updated information, and request that they pass along the information to their employees.

Setting Up a Discussion Forum

In a real-time discussion forum, users can interact, regardless of time zones or schedules, using the intranet as the communication medium. For example, users can hold informal meetings, chat about projects, or even get live feedback about a document draft—all from their offices at their convenience.

You can choose from several forum options, based on the software you implement. For example, you can use one of the script archives mentioned earlier in this chapter and adapt discussion forums from the scripts. Your ISP or Web hosting service may also offer a discussion-forum package.

If you choose a more advanced software package, such as a Wiki (`c2.com/cgi/wiki`), users can post documents and request that other people edit and comment—right there online. The result is that users can open forums to large groups and get immediate feedback. Other users can monitor discussions for developments or news pertaining to their projects. By conducting meetings online through an intranet, companies move toward a newer, more open approach to communication.

TIP   When using scripts and server-side programs, you may need assistance from your system administrator to implement and debug them. Documentation, when available, is included with the scripts or embedded in the code.

Where to Go from Here

Armed with the information in this chapter, you have a running start on developing public, personal, or intranet sites. In fact, you'll likely be one step ahead of the Joneses if you follow the guidelines we provided.

From here, you can follow up with a visit to several chapters:

◆ See Chapter 12 for more information about planning for a coherent, usable, maintainable, and accessible web site, which applies to public, personal, and intranet sites.

◆ See Chapter 13 for tips and advice that apply to all Web sites.

◆ Check out Chapter 15 if you're interested in more information about servers and publishing your site.

◆ Visit Chapters 2 and 9 for information about applying formatting wisely.

Chapter 15

Publishing Your XHTML Documents

SO FAR IN THIS book, you've learned what HTML and XHTML documents are, what they look like, and why you'd use them, among many other topics. And, if you've been doing the examples, you've also created a few documents of your own. To this point, you've been developing and viewing the HTML and XHTML documents on your local computer. However, for other people to use and enjoy them, you must *publish* your documents.

In this chapter, we'll show you options for publishing your documents, and we'll walk you through the publishing process.

This chapter covers the following topics:

◆ Finding out where you can publish your HTML and XHTML documents

◆ Uploading HTML and XHTML documents to a Web server

Places to Publish

When you publish your HTML and XHTML documents, all you're doing is putting a copy of the documents on a *server* so the documents can be available on the Internet. You might think of a server as a waiter at a restaurant. You tell the server what, specifically, you want—"Yeah, I'll have the Big-Fuzz Cheeseburger, a Load-o-Fries, and a Choc-o-Yumm, please"—and the waiter gets the order and brings it to you. Likewise, when you visit a Web site, you ask the server to display a certain page—say, the page on the Web server (www), at the raycomm.com domain, and specifically the page called index.html (www.raycomm.com/index.html). You type that in the browser's location box and press Enter, the browser contacts the server, and then the server brings you the page you requested. So, to publish your HTML and XHTML documents, you need to make them available on a server so that the server can them make them available to the people (er, computers) that request them.

In general, you can publish your documents in three different ways:

◆ Your Internet service provider (ISP)

◆ Your corporate IS department

◆ Your own server

Publishing through Your ISP

One of the most common places to publish documents is on Web space provided by an Internet service provider (ISP). ISPs usually provide a slew of Internet-related services—including Web space—and help with your Web development needs. You can find out more about ISPs in your area by researching the following resources:

The Web For a comprehensive list of ISPs, along with contact information and services, visit your favorite search engine and search for "ISP" and your geographic area; for example, search for "ISP TX" if you live in Texas. Also, check out www.isps.com and www.webisplist.com.

Your local paper or yellow pages Often, you'll find ads for local ISPs in the Technology or Business section of your daily newspaper or in the Internet section of your local yellow pages.

Other people Ask friends, neighbors, business associates, or folks at your local computer store about the services they use and their experiences. The quality, reliability, and service of both ISPs and Web-hosting services vary, so get all the advice and input you can before you commit.

TIP Look for a guaranteed uptime figure, and always ask what you get if they fail to meet the guarantee. Then, after you find an ISP that appears to suit your needs, start by signing a short contract—say, no longer than six months—until you know that the service is satisfactory.

ISPs often provide a range of services, and you'll need to do some research to find out about them, as well as about start-up and monthly costs. In general, though, most ISPs offer either individual or business accounts.

FINDING A WEB-HOSTING SERVICE

Another option—one that's not quite an ISP, but similar—is a Web-hosting service. A Web-hosting service does not provide dial-up Internet access but simply provides a home from which you can serve your sites.

Generally, you use Web-hosting services in conjunction with an ISP, thus combining the best Web-hosting deal with reliable dial-up access. Although it's possible that a single company could meet all your needs, shopping for these services separately can be useful. For a fairly comprehensive list of Web-hosting services, check out this long but excellent URL:

```
http://dir.yahoo.com/Business_and_Economy/Business_to_Business/Communications_and_Net
working/Internet_and_World_Wide_Web/Network_Service_Providers/Hosting/Web_Site_Hosting/
Directories/
```

Alternatively, follow these steps in Yahoo! to find the Web-hosting information: Go to Home ➤ Business And Economy ➤ Business To Business ➤ Communications And Networking ➤ Internet And World Wide Web ➤ Web Site Hosting. (Note that the Web changes frequently, so these steps may not be identical by the time you read this book.)

Note that many free services (including Geocities, owned by Yahoo!) get you on the Web, but at the price of putting their ads in your pages (and in the pop-up pages that spring up when your page is accessed). For only a little money each month, you can avoid all that and keep your viewers happier.

ABOUT ISP INDIVIDUAL ACCOUNTS

Generally, ISPs provide individual subscribers—as opposed to business subscribers—with access to the Internet, to e-mail, and to a relatively small amount of space on a Web server. Many ISPs also provide other services, such as sending you the results of a form via e-mail. Exactly which services you'll need depends on what you want to do with your Web pages. For example, if you plan to create and publish a few documents, you may only need a little bit of Web space. On the other hand, if you plan to create a larger Web site loaded with multimedia and downloadable files, or an e-commerce site, you'll need more space. If you want to include forms or use server-specific capabilities, you may need some server access or specific programs. Therefore, when choosing an ISP account, determine how big of a site you'll be developing and what functionality it will include, and then find an ISP that can meet your needs.

In addition to finding out what general services an ISP provides, you may also want to ask these questions, depending on your needs:

What kind of server is it, and what platform does the server run on?   If you know the server and the platform, you can find the documentation on the Web, which should tell you which scripts you can easily add. For example, if an Apache server is running on a Sun workstation or Linux system (likely ISP scenarios), you can reasonably request that your server administrator install specific Perl scripts. However, if you're on an intranet with a Windows 2000–based IIS server and you hear of a cool enhancement to the WebStar server on a Macintosh, you can save yourself some embarrassment and just not ask for it.

Can I restrict access to my pages?   When testing pages on the server, you don't want the whole world to see them—setting password-restricted access to the whole site helps with this. Additionally, if you have some pages that you want to make available to only a few people (or to everyone except a few people), you need to be able to set passwords and ideally do that with little hassle and without wasting time.

WARNING   *Be careful about publishing pages on the Internet. Even if you don't provide links to a page or publish a page's URL, people may still come across it. Additionally, search engines can also index such pages, making them available.*

Can I install and run my own scripts?   If you can, you'll have a lot more flexibility and capabilities than you would otherwise. If you're limited to what your ISP has already installed for your use, you're likely to have access to certain limited special capabilities, such as chat rooms, but not the flexibility to go with what you really want.

Do you maintain access logs? How can I find out how many hits my site gets?   If you're selling services, promoting your company, or doing anything else that involves a significant number of people seeing your message, make sure that accesses are logged, and learn how to get to those logs.

TIP   *Ask your server administrator what kinds of tools are available to view and sort Web server access logs—the "raw" (unprocessed) logs are an ugly mess, but lots of neat programs exist to parse the logs into something useful. Although your server administrator might have some of these programs installed, the access instructions may not be publicized.*

TIP   Free or inexpensive services on the Web can provide logging and access counting for your pages. Look at www.hotscripts.com/Remotely_Hosted/ *and browse to the Counters (but check out the other cool stuff too).*

Who do I call if the server fails to respond at 2 PM? How about 2 AM?   Does the ISP make backups, or do you need to back up your own site? Under what circumstances will the ISP restore backup files—only if the server crashes or also if you make a mistake and delete your files?

TIP   You might also ask these questions if you're thinking about an ISP business account or publishing on a corporate server.

ABOUT ISP BUSINESS ACCOUNTS

If you're running a business and using the Internet (or if you're moving in that direction), consider getting a business account with an ISP. Business accounts, although somewhat more expensive than individual accounts, usually include more Web space, better access to server-side programs, and more comprehensive services, with guaranteed uptime, backups, and more attention to individual needs.

Many ISPs require a business account to have its own *domain name*, which replaces the ISP's name in the URL. For example, instead of our business's URL being:

www.example.com/~raycomm/index.html

(which includes the ISP name and a folder designated for us), it simply reads:

www.raycomm.com

Having your own domain name also offers a few practical advantages:

- It can enhance your professional appearance and can help make your business appear larger than it really is.

- It helps establish your identity. Each domain name is unique and can include the business name itself or other names. For example, our business name is RayComm, Inc., and our domain name is www.raycomm.com.

- You can keep a consistent address even if you move or change ISPs. Users (who may be your customers or potential customers) will always be able to find you because your address remains constant.

- You can easily expand your Web site as your needs grow. If you start by having your service provider host your domain (called a *virtual domain*), you can easily expand your capacity or add services, without changing your address or revising your advertising materials.

VIRTUAL DOMAINS

As an information provider, you're not limited to using the ISP's server name as the hostname portion of your URL. Instead, you can use a virtual domain, which gives you a hostname of your own, but your files still reside on a host computer. Virtual domains are a very popular way for small companies and organizations to look bigger than they really are.

For example, if you put your files on a server called `example.com`, your Web address might look something like the following:

```
http://www.example.com/~accountname/filename.html
```

In this example, the address includes the protocol indicator, a special folder on the server (indicated by the tilde [~]), an account name, and a filename.

A virtual domain changes the address to eliminate the special folder and account name and replaces these with a new host (domain) name. For example, a Web address using a virtual domain might look like this:

```
http://www.accountname.com/filename.html
```

This example includes the protocol indicator, the domain name (`www.accountname.com`), and the filename (`filename.html`).

The easiest way to get a virtual domain is to ask your ISP to set it up for you. You may pay in the neighborhood of $50 to $100 for setup, plus anywhere from $10 to $70 for registering your domain name for two years with one of the official Internet domain-name registrars. If you do a little homework with your ISP, however, you can set up a virtual domain yourself and save a few dollars. You can find a list of accredited registrars at

```
www.icann.org/registrars/accredited-list.html
```

TIP   If you're thinking about getting your own domain name, start your research and claim the name of your choice as soon as you can. If you don't claim the domain name you want, someone else likely will.

If you have a company name under which you operate, get a domain name immediately, even if you probably won't use it in the near future. Most of the most popular names are already taken. If you have a small business and aren't incorporated or are just thinking of incorporating, consider getting the domain name first and then incorporating under that name. It seems a little backward, but a domain name must be unique, and competition for good names is stiff. After you obtain your domain name, take care of registering to do business under that name.

Let's look at an example. Suppose your business's name is Laura's Toys and More. You look up `www.laurastoysandmore.com` and the domain name is already taken. You can try several variations, such as `www.laurastoysnmore.com` or `www.laurastoystore.com`, until you find one that is not taken.

At the time of writing, "registrar" companies such as Network Solutions or InterAccess handle most registrations for `.com`, `.org`, and `.net` names. However, you can also access a list of accredited domain registrars at the Internet Corporation for Assigned Names and Numbers (ICANN) site at

```
www.icann.org/registrars/accredited-list.html
```

TIP   Check with friends or acquaintances about registrars and recommendations. You can save quite a bit of money if you use an off-brand registrar (particularly if you are registering several names), and, in our experience, the customer service and support with the smaller registrars (one that we have used is www.gandi.net*) is actually better than with the big names.*

To register a domain name, follow this process:

1. Go to www.internic.net/whois.html. (InterNIC is the official body that supervises Internet naming; this is their "lookup" page.)

2. Enter your prospective domain name in the query field and press Enter. If you're lucky, you'll see a No Match message, which means that your domain name is available. If you're less fortunate, you'll see the InterNIC records for whoever owns the name you entered. If you want, you can contact them and see if they want to sell it or give it to you, but you're likely to have more success if you simply look for another name.

3. Either register the name or ask your ISP to do it for you. Most ISPs will register domain names for free if they'll be hosting them, or they charge a reasonable ($100 or less) fee for the service, plus hosting charges. If your ISP attempts to charge significantly more than $100, you might consider either doing it yourself or finding another ISP.

If you want to do it yourself, all the information and instructions you'll need are available at the sites owned by the various registrars, although you'll need to get a little information and cooperation from your ISP to complete the process.

Publishing through a Corporate Server

Another place you might publish your documents is on a corporate server—at your place of employment, most likely. If you work for a large company or an educational institution or if you work with an organization that handles system administration tasks, you'll probably have little to do when it comes to accessing a Web server. All the necessary pieces—access, administration, and security—are probably in place, and you'll simply step in and start using the server. This situation can be either the ideal or the worst possible case, depending on the group that actually runs the Web server.

The level of access and control you have on a corporate server varies from company to company. In the ideal situation, someone else takes care of running the server but lets you do anything you want, within reason. You get help setting up and running server-side programs and can essentially do anything you need to provide information. At the other extreme, you must adhere to a rigid process to submit information to the intranet. You'll submit documents and then have little control over where they're placed or how they're linked.

In all likelihood, your company will be somewhere in the middle, with an established procedure for accessing the corporate intranet but a substantial amount of freedom to do what you need to do. If not, or if the process of providing content is tightly controlled, you may want to see about running your own server. In any event, you'll need to find out how to contact the server administrators, get emergency contact numbers, find out about the corporate intranet policies, and go from there.

Publishing through Your Own Server

Finally, you might choose to publish your documents on your own server. If you have the technical savvy and existing infrastructure, running your own server affords you the most flexibility and best range of resources. One good reason to run your own server is that it's a more authentic environment for developing and testing pages. For example, if you have server-relative URLs in links, they'll work properly if you're loading the files from a server, but not if you're loading the same file locally. (See Chapter 3 for more about links and server-relative URLs.)

Particularly in a corporate or educational environment, where a network infrastructure exists, installing and running a server is straightforward. To run a public server, whether at home or at work, you'll need a dedicated network connection—anything from a full-time DSL line or cable modem (assuming you're allowed to run a Web server) to a T1 or similar commercial-grade connection will work. If you're just setting up a local server for your own testing purposes, you can even run the server on a stand-alone machine.

If you plan to host your own server, we suggest that you have a dedicated Web server with as few applications as possible on it. That will free up the computer for simply hosting the Web pages.

ASSESSING AND ADDRESSING SECURITY RISKS

As a small business owner or someone just interested in publishing documents on your own server, you may not think that you're at risk for being hacked—for computer hackers to break into your computer and read your documents, manipulate your computer, or even plant malicious software on your computer (which might lurk on your computer and relay information to the hacker or be used to attack other computer systems). With scripts and programs available on the Internet to let anyone—regardless of skill or expertise—become a hacker, you may be at risk. How do you assess your own security risks? Ask yourself these questions:

◆ Are you publishing information about your product or services that would be of interest to competitors or potential competitors?

◆ Are you storing source material or raw data about your products or services on your Internet-connected computer?

◆ Do you run instant messaging applications, file-sharing applications, or other software that you've downloaded from the Internet?

◆ Do you have a continuous Internet connection, or do you say online for extended periods of time?

◆ Do you have personal or private information anywhere on a computer connected to the Internet?

If you answered yes to one or more of these questions, you may be exposed to hackers, and your server could be used to stage attacks on others. You should take security measures. Consider these options:

◆ Change your passwords often—at least once per month.

◆ Use a firewall if you're running your own server. Check out the Firewall FAQ at www.interhack .net/pubs/fwfaq/ to find out more about firewalls.

Continued on next page

ASSESSING AND ADDRESSING SECURITY RISKS *(continued)*

◆ Use antivirus software regularly, and scan all incoming files you receive via e-mail before opening them, even if you know and trust the person who sent the file. Check out Google's Web Directory at `directory.google.com/Top/Computers/Security/Anti_Virus/` for more information and resources.

◆ Delay upgrades to software from all vendors as long as possible so that security holes are found and patched before you are vulnerable.

◆ Install patches and security upgrades as quickly as possible.

◆ Monitor antivirus sites, CIAC (Computer Incident Advisory Capability), and CERT (which, at one time, stood for Computer Emergency Response Team) for announcements of problems or security issues that affect your operating system or software.

◆ Monitor other sites for exploits that affect your operating system or software. Good starting points are `www.securityfocus.com` and `www.counterpane.com/alerts.html`.

◆ Find, download, and use network security products, including port scanners, intrusion-detection software, and published exploits against your own system. Start at `www.insecure.org` and go from there.

◆ Educate yourself about network security and how computers and the Internet work, starting with `www.insecure.org/reading.html`.

If you're considering running your own server, here are some issues to consider:

Security Web servers do present a security risk, although not a huge one. Letting other people access files on your computer, through any means, is inherently a little iffy. On an intranet, assuming you don't have highly confidential material on the server machine, you should be fine.

Uptime and access If you're going to set up and publicize a server, you must ensure that it stays up and available all the time. If you don't have a continuous Internet connection, you shouldn't host your own public Web server.

Time Running a Web server takes some time. If all you're doing is serving pages, it doesn't take much, but expect a certain investment. If you'll be generating pages from a database or installing and running other add-in programs, it'll take more time, both to keep the server going and to monitor security issues.

Capacity If your Web server provides only plain documents and a few graphics to others on an intranet or if it's just for testing purposes, almost any computer will do. If you expect heavy traffic or lots of access, however, be sure that the computer you use can handle the load or can easily be upgraded. If you choose a Windows operating system to host your pages, you'll need about 256 MB of RAM and 8 GB of hard disk space. For a Linux server, you could probably get away with 128 MB of RAM and 4 GB of hard disk space.

Backups If you're running your own server, you're responsible for backups. If the hard disk on your server suddenly stops working, will you be in a position to restore everything and get it all back up and running?

Installing, configuring, and running a server is beyond the scope of this book; however, if you'd like more information, you can visit the following Web sites:

www.microsoft.com   At this site, you can learn about the latest Microsoft Web server options. At the time of writing, Windows 2000 Server and Windows 2000 Professional ship with Internet Information Services (IIS) 5. Additionally, the Microsoft products also come with FrontPage, which is handy if you use that for Web development.

www.apache.org   At this site, you'll find Apache, the most popular Unix-based server software, although it's also available for other platforms, including Windows.

Finally, get the definitive server information at

http://serverwatch.internet.com/webservers.html

The Publishing Process

Before you get started, you'll need the following information:

The address of the HTTP server   For example, www.raycomm.com. Depending on your situation, you may need to know the folder name from which your files will be accessed.

The address of the FTP server, if required   For example, ftp://ftp.raycomm.com. Depending on how you get your files onto the server, you might have to use the File Transfer Protocol (FTP). Of course, it's also possible, particularly in a corporate or educational environment, that you would simply copy the files to a specific folder on a network drive, and that would be that.

Password and access restrictions   You need a user ID and password to upload files to the server. Table 15.1 summarizes this information and provides space for you to include your specific information.

TABLE 15.1: INFORMATION YOU'LL NEED BEFORE USING FTP

INFORMATION	EXAMPLE	YOUR INFORMATION
FTP server address	ftp.raycomm.com	
User ID	jsmith	
Password	JB14mN	Don't write it down or allow the FTP software to save it for you!
Folder on server to use	public_html	

TIP Passwords should always be something hard to guess, with a combination of lowercase and uppercase letters, and numbers. You shouldn't write down your entire password near your computer or save it on your computer. Another option is to break your password into two parts: something you know and something you write down.

Armed with this information, you're ready to *upload* your files to the server, which essentially just means to put a copy of your documents on the server. The process for uploading your documents to a server will be different for most servers and installations. It can be as easy as copying a file to a folder (on a corporate intranet) or as idiosyncratic as completing multiple page online forms and copying files to a folder (on intranets in Dilbert-esque companies—yes, we have examples). It can also be a straightforward process involving an FTP application (the common process on intranets and with ISPs).

The easiest way to upload files to a server is using the publishing tools included in many high-end HTML editing applications. These tools work well if all the files belong in one folder and if you're comfortable letting the programs "adjust" links as the files are uploaded.

However, you'll likely use either an FTP program or your browser to upload your documents, as described next.

Uploading with FTP

FTP is the Internet standard tool for transferring files. Regardless of which FTP program you choose, you'll probably be dealing with the commands outlined in Table 15.2. As you'll see in the following two sections, you can use these commands when uploading with a text-based FTP program or a graphical FTP program.

TABLE 15.2: FTP COMMANDS FOR TRANSFERRING FILES

COMMAND	DESCRIPTION
ftp	Starts an FTP application.
open "…"	Opens an FTP connection to the server name specified.
close	Closes an FTP connection without exiting the FTP application.
quit	Closes an FTP connection and the application.
put	Uploads files to the server computer.
get	Downloads files from the server computer.
ascii	Sets the file type to ASCII, to upload XHTML or other text documents.
binary	Sets the file type to binary, to upload image or class files and other binary documents.
cd	Changes directory on the server. Follow cd with a folder name to change into that folder; follow cd with .. to move up out of the current folder.
pwd	Tells you what folder you're in (stands for print working directory).

UPLOADING FILES WITH A TEXT-BASED FTP PROGRAM

Before you get started, you'll need the information specified in Table 15.1, and you'll need your documents and related files at hand. Follow these steps:

1. At a text prompt (a DOS prompt or a Linux/Unix shell), switch to the folder that contains the files you want to upload. For example, if you are at a `c:` prompt and your files are in the `TestWeb` subfolder, type **cd testweb**.

2. Type **ftp** to start the FTP application.

3. At the FTP> prompt, type **open** and the address of the FTP server—for example,

   `open ftp.raycomm.com`

4. When prompted, enter your user ID and then your password. Remember that these are case sensitive.

5. Change to the folder where you want to store the files. If you're uploading files to an ISP, your folder name will probably be `public_html` or `www` or something similar, such as `cd public_html`.

6. To upload HTML and XHTML documents, set the file type to ASCII. Type **ascii**.

7. Now, upload the documents with the `put` command. For example, type **put filename.htm**.

   If you have multiple files to upload, you can use the `mput` command and a wildcard. For example, to upload all files in the folder that have filenames ending with `.htm`, type **mput *.htm**.

8. To upload binary files (such as graphics), first set the file type to binary. Type **binary**.

9. Now, upload the documents with the `put` command. For example, type **put filename.htm**.

   If you have multiple files to upload, use the `mput` command and a wildcard. For example, to upload all files in the folder that have names ending with `.gif`, type **mput *.gif**.

10. When you've finished, type **quit** to leave the FTP application.

Now, open your Web browser and try to access the files you just uploaded. If you find broken image icons, odds are that you didn't specify binary before you uploaded the files (a common problem). Try again, being careful to specify binary.

TIP   If you used a WYSIWYG editor and your links do not work correctly, check out the raw HTML or XHTML code to verify that the links were not changed.

UPLOADING FILES WITH GRAPHICAL FTP PROGRAMS

An arguably easier procedure is available if you have a graphical FTP application (such as FTP Explorer for Windows, available from `www.ftpx.com`) or Fetch for Macintosh (available from `http://fetchsoftworks.com`). The specific procedure depends on the software, but generally resembles the following. Before you start, have at hand the same information you gathered for the text-based FTP application.

Use the following procedure to upload files with FTP Explorer, a Windows application:

1. Start the application, probably by double-clicking its icon.

2. Enter a name for the site and the hostname or IP address in the Connect dialog box that appears.

3. In the appropriate fields, fill in your login name, password, and any other information that your system administrator gave you.

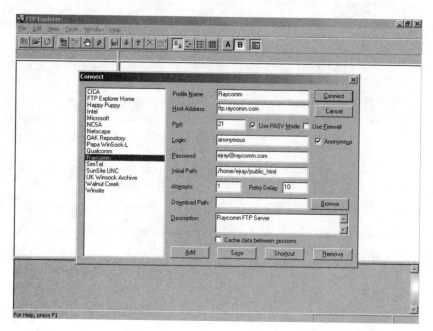

TIP *Both your user ID and password are case sensitive—if you substitute uppercase for lowercase or vice versa, access will be denied.*

4. Click Connect. You'll see a connecting message as your FTP client connects to the FTP server; then you'll see your folders and files on the server.

5. Drag files from your Windows Explorer window to the FTP Explorer window to upload; drag the other way to download.

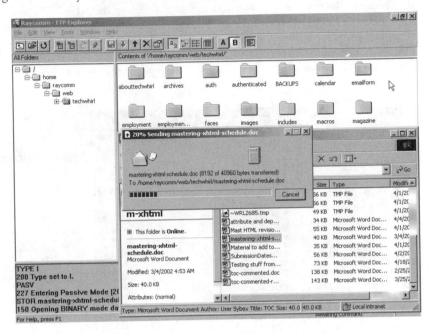

TIP   *If you can't open and read the file in Notepad, SimpleText, or vi, it's not a text file. You must transfer all word-processed documents, spreadsheets, and multimedia files as binary.*

That's all there is to it. Now, test all your uploaded files.

UPLOADING WITH HTTP

Some automatic publishing tools offer the option of uploading via HTTP instead of FTP. However, relatively few ISPs support HTTP uploads because of security considerations.

The primary difference is that with HTTP, you need provide only the Web address at which your files should end up, rather than the FTP server address.

For you, the Web developer, there's no real benefit to either approach as long as the files transfer correctly.

Uploading with Other Tools

In addition to using an FTP program to upload your documents, you can upload them through your browser or through specialized tools that come with various HTML software. Dreamweaver has an excellent site management tool, illustrated in Figure 15.1. The remote site appears on the left, and the local folders are on the right. This utility works much like an FTP utility and is very convenient. You can develop your pages and upload them to your server, all from the same interface.

You can often upload files by entering **ftp://yourid@yourftpserver.com/** in the location box of your favorite browser. You'll be prompted for your password. The only drawback to this approach is that you must be familiar with the structure of the files on the server. After you browse to the correct folder, choose File ➤ Upload File to select the file to upload (you can upload only one file at a time).

TIP　*If you upload through your browser, take a second to bookmark that long URL location of your files so you won't have to browse to it again.*

FIGURE 15.1

The Dreamweaver site management tool

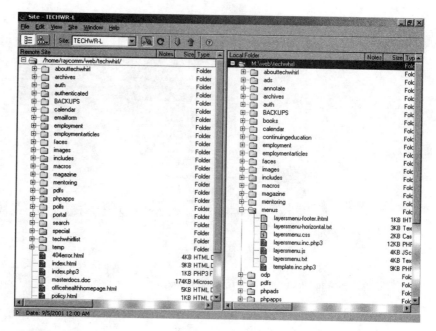

Where to Go from Here

So, there you have it! You can publish your documents using an ISP, on a corporate network, or on your own server just by transferring a copy of the documents from your computer to a server. By doing so, you make your documents accessible to other people, either at your company or on the Internet.

From here, you have lots of options. Here are a few suggestions:

- ◆ Visit Chapter 3 for a reminder about how URLs are constructed.

- ◆ Head to Chapter 4 to learn how to include images—and how to do so wisely.

- ◆ Visit Chapter 5 to learn how to develop and include tables.

- ◆ See Chapter 6 to learn how to include forms (remember, you'll need to get the server to process the form for you!).

- ◆ Check out Chapter 7 to learn how to use frames.

- ◆ Visit Chapter 14 for more information about public, personal, and intranet sites.

Chapter 16

Bringing Pages to Life with Dynamic HTML and XHTML

WHEN YOU DEVELOP A Web page using dynamic HTML or XHTML, your users can view new content without reloading the page, change screen colors with a mouse click, and view animations without installing a plug-in. Dynamic HTML or XHTML uses style sheets and scripting (such as JavaScript)—in tandem with standard HTML or XHTML—to produce dynamic effects. Only browsers that support style sheets and scripting can support dynamic HTML or XHTML.

In addition, you implement dynamic HTML or XHTML one way if you're developing for Microsoft Internet Explorer (IE) or current versions of Netscape Navigator and Opera (all of which support the Document Object Model, or DOM), but another way if you're developing for Netscape version 4. For example, IE users may encounter errors or see nothing at all if they open a page designed for Netscape Navigator. Therefore, taking advantage of the latest and greatest can be problematic if the new feature is not designed for your users' browsers. The introduction of fairly standard-compliant versions of browsers, such as Netscape Navigator 6 and IE 6, makes it easier to write dynamic cross-platform and cross-browser code, but you will still have to accommodate older browsers for a while.

If you're developing for newer browsers and you want to include dynamic effects on your pages, you'll want to know about and use dynamic HTML and XHTML. In this chapter, we introduce you to these technologies, look at some of the advantages and disadvantages associated with using them, and show you how to use them in your documents—for both Netscape Navigator and IE. We'll then use dynamic HTML and XHTML to develop a practical application: collapsing pages.

This chapter covers the following topics:

◆ Exploring dynamic HTML and XHTML

◆ Understanding the Document Object Model

◆ Developing standard-compliant dynamic HTML and XHTML

◆ Using dynamic HTML and XHTML to create collapsible pages

◆ Implementing browser detection

What Are Dynamic HTML and XHTML?

Dynamic HTML and XHTML expand on standard HTML or XHTML by giving you the formatting control of style sheets combined with the interactive capabilities of scripting languages such as JavaScript. When you develop pages with dynamic HTML or XHTML, users can spend far less time accessing information because it's available directly within the browser, rather than needing to be retrieved from the server.

TIP *You may see dynamic HTML or XHTML referred to as "DHTML" or "DXHTML." But because there's no defined DHTML or DXHTML language, we stick with calling it dynamic HTML or dynamic XHTML.*

WARNING *Dynamic HTML and XHTML are not languages; they're simply combinations of technologies.*

For example, suppose you have a table of contents page. If you develop it with standard HTML or XHTML, users click an item; the browser then requests the document from the server and displays it when it arrives. If you develop the table of contents page with dynamic HTML or XHTML, however, the trip to the server is eliminated. Figures 16.1 and 16.2 show this process.

FIGURE 16.1

Users can click items in the table of contents

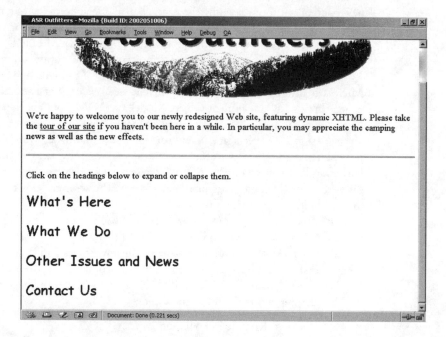

TIP *We show you how to create collapsible information in the section "Creating a Collapsible Document," later in this chapter.*

FIGURE 16.2

After selecting an item, the user can view the expanded content

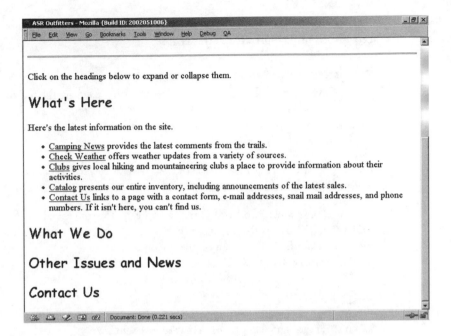

Before you go sprinting off to add dynamic HTML or XHTML capabilities to your documents, you need to be familiar with style sheets and JavaScript. Within dynamic HTML or XHTML, style sheets tell browsers what elements should look like, and JavaScript functions change the properties set by style sheets, which is how page elements know to do something—for example, move, change colors, and so on.

TIP   *We recommend that you have a firm understanding of style sheets and JavaScript before starting this chapter. For a quick review, flip back to Chapters 9 and 10, respectively.*

You might recall from Chapter 10 that you can use JavaScript's `onmouseover` event handler to change an image when a user moves the mouse over the image. For many browsers, dynamic HTML or XHTML and event handlers can do this with just about any page element. For example, you can change the color of text, increase the text size, or even make the text jump to a new location.

When you implement dynamic HTML or XHTML using the standard technologies, you use standard elements and attributes. As you'll see in the following section, this approach offers wider support along with better functionality, and it promises more in terms of long-range stability.

TIP   *For more information on scripting languages in general, including JavaScript, JScript, VBScript, and ECMAScript, see the section "What Is JavaScript?" in Chapter 10.*

The Document Object Model (DOM)

The W3C's *Document Object Model (DOM)* is a key (although behind-the-scenes) component of dynamic HTML or XHTML. It specifies how individual objects within Web pages (such as images, headings, or other tagged information) should be available to scripts. In browsers that support the DOM, dynamic documents will be more flexible, more powerful, and far easier to implement than in other browsers. This is illustrated in this chapter.

THE ORIGINAL DOM AND THE PROPRIETARY DOMs

The DOM is a model of how all the elements on a page are related to one another and to the document itself. Knowing these relationships allows scripts to access each of the elements (or groups of elements) and apply style or presentation changes to just that element (or group of elements) using JavaScript or other scripting languages.

NOTE   *The DOM Level 1 specification became a W3C recommendation in October 1998. You can view the full text of the recommendation at* `www.w3.org/TR/1998/REC-DOM-Level-1-19981001/`.

The easiest way to understand the DOM is by looking at a document as a tree structure. The highest level of the tree is the document itself, and all other elements on the page, including the **body** element, are classified as children of the document.

For example, let's look at a simple piece of code:

```
<html>
<body>
<h1>The document tree</h1>
<p>This is an example of a child element.</p>
<p>This is also a child element.</p>
```

This code can be illustrated as a tree:

In this simple form of a document tree, **html** is the parent element. It has one child, **body**, and the first child element of **html** (**body**) also has three children (**h1**, **p**, and **p**).

The original (Level 0) DOM was developed by Netscape for use in Netscape Navigator 2 with the newly developed scripting language JavaScript. It allowed access only to forms and links. In Netscape 3, access to images was added. IE 3 also added implementation of the Level 0 DOM; however, the implementation did not work quite like Netscape's implementation.

Netscape Navigator 4 and IE 4 continued to support the Level 0 DOM, but both also added their own proprietary DOMs to supplement the Level 0 DOM. The Netscape proprietary DOM is accessed using **document.layers** in the JavaScript code, and the IE proprietary DOM is accessed using **document.all** in the JavaScript code, so code that takes advantage of the fourth-generation browser DOM features cannot work on both Netscape and IE.

TIP   *Browser-detection scripts can determine which browser a visitor is using to access a site so that the browser is provided with the correct version. More details on browser detection, as well as a browser-detection script, are included at the end of this chapter.*

So, up through fourth-generation browsers, you've had two main choices for implementing dynamic documents:

◆ Using a browser-detection script and creating at least three versions of each page that includes dynamic features—a Netscape Navigator version, an IE version, and a version for browsers that don't support style sheets and JavaScript

◆ Writing a complex script that includes the options for all three but implements them all from a single document

Even with different versions of dynamic pages, the features supported by Netscape's DOM and IE's DOM are not the same, so similar effects are not always possible in both browsers. We explore some features of each proprietary DOM in more depth in the following section, and then return to the Level 1 DOM and the newest generation of Web browsers (version 6 for IE, Opera, and Netscape). According to statistics from www.thecounter.com, about 7 percent of the Web audience currently uses Netscape 4.*x* or IE 4.*x*, so it may be important to you to know how to use both of the proprietary DOMs—but, as always, it depends on what your users need.

LEVEL 1 DOM AND THE SIXTH-GENERATION BROWSERS

The W3C DOM Level 1 was designed to provide access to every part of an XML document. Because HTML and XHTML documents can also be *parsed* (broken down into component parts) like an XML document, this DOM is also accessible to JavaScript and other scripting and programming languages.

The Level 1 DOM treats each object of the document as a *node*, and the corresponding tree diagram is based on nodes.

If we look at the code sample from the previous section again, we can make a new tree diagram based on nodes:

```
<body>
<h1>Heading text</h1>
<p>This is a child element.</p>
<p>This is also a child element.</p>
```

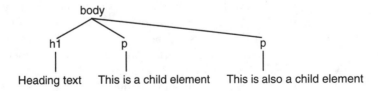

In this diagram, the parts break down as follows:

◆ body is an element node.

◆ h1 is an element node (and first child of html).

◆ Heading text is a text node, which is a child of h1.

- ◆ `p` is an element node (and child of `html`)

- ◆ `This is a child element` is a text node

- ◆ The second `p` is also an element node (and child of `html`)

- ◆ `This is also a child element` is a text node and child of the second `p`

You'll use three main node types for scripting: element nodes, text nodes, and attribute nodes. For example, if you add an `align` attribute to the second paragraph,

```
<p align="right">This is a child element.</p>
```

`align` is an attribute node, and `right` is a child of this attribute node.

This node structure allows you to access any node individually by giving it an `id` and by using two very useful access methods: `getElementsByTagName` and `getElementById`. Through these methods and `id`, you can apply a style and/or a script to a particular node.

The Level 1 DOM is supported by Netscape 6, IE 5, and Opera 4, 5, and 6 (although Opera 4 and 5 did not support all of the methods and properties of the Level 1 DOM).

ADDITIONAL DOM LEVEL 1 INFORMATION

Peter-Paul Koch's Web site offers several resources for more information on the Level 1 DOM:

- ◆ For more information on using the Level 1 DOM, see "Level 1 DOM - Introduction" at `www.xs4all.nl/ ~ppk/js/dom1.html`.

- ◆ For details on browser support and DOM, check out "Browsers" at `www.xs4all.nl/~ppk/ js/browsers.html`.

- ◆ For a detailed chart of support for DOM properties and methods, see `www.xs4all.nl/~ppk/js/version5.html`.

Although IE 5.*x* and 6 implement most of the Level 1 DOM, they also support IE's proprietary DOM. On the other hand, Netscape 6 supports the Level 1 DOM but does *not* offer support for Netscape's proprietary DOM. This means that scripts written for Netscape 4.*x* will not work in Netscape 6. Although you still need to use a browser-detection script for Level 4 browsers (if your audience includes users of these browsers) and separate scripts for Netscape 4.*x* and Netscape 6, the move toward standards compliance in the latest browsers offers the hope that eventually you'll have to create only one version of a Web page for all browsers and all platforms.

IE 6 takes a different approach to backward compatibility by making it dependent on the DTD used on your page. If you use an HTML 3.2 DTD, your pages will appear in IE 6 as they did in IE 4.*x* and 5.*x*. However, if you use the Strict form of the HTML 4.0 DTD or XHTML DTD, it will use the Level 1 DOM when executing your scripts.

For more details on creating dynamic pages in Netscape Navigator 6 and IE 6, check out the following resources:

- ◆ "Scripting for the 6.0 Browsers," by Scott Andrew LePera, at `www.scottandrew.com/index.php/articles/dom_1`

♦ "Mozilla Document Object Model Information," by Dave Eisenberg, at `www.alistapart.com/stories/dom/article.html`

♦ "IE 6 Switches to Standards," by Jeffrey Veen, at `http://hotwired.lycos.com/webmonkey/01/14/index0a.html?tw=authoring`

TIP   For an extensive script library to help support cross-browser scripting, see `www.cross-browser.com`.

Understanding the Standard Implementation

Dynamic HTML or XHTML in standard-compliant browsers exposes all page elements to scripting; that is, each page element can be manipulated—recolored, scrolled, jiggled, and so on. If you can specify what the element is, you can format it with style sheets and then change the style sheets using JavaScript. For example, you can identify a heading, specify in the style sheet that the heading is red, and then specify in the JavaScript that the red heading changes to green when a user passes the mouse pointer over the heading.

TIP   IE 6 offers implementation of most of the W3C DOM properties and includes backward compatibility for its proprietary DOM (`document.all`); therefore, scripts written for IE 4.x will also work in later versions. IE 5.x and 6 offer access to the DOM objects through scripting and also through Component Object Model (COM) interfaces.

TIP   If you haven't already done so, you might breeze through Chapters 9 and 10 before starting these examples. In particular, look closely at the `id` attribute description in Chapter 9 and check out the discussion of event handlers and functions in Chapter 10.

Let's take a look at the general process for adding dynamic capabilities to your documents using a standard-compliant implementation (good for current versions of IE, Opera, Mozilla, and Netscape):

1. Start with a functional document. The following code includes the XHTML structural elements and style sheet elements:

```
<!DOCTYPE html PUBLIC "-//W3C/DTD XHTML 1.0 Transitional//EN"
    "http://www.w3.org/TR/xhtml1/DTD/xhtml1-transitional.dtd">
<html xmlns="http://www.w3.org/1999/xhtml">
<head>
  <title>Fix Colors</title>
  <style type="text/css">
<!--
    h1 {color :red }
-->
</style>
<script type="text/javascript" language="javascript">
<!--
// -->
</script>
</head>
<body>
<h1>Changing Color</h1>
```

```
<p>
If you'd like to change the color of the heading above
from black to red for better contrast and easier reading,
just move your mouse over this paragraph.</p>
</body>
</html>
```

2. Add the `id` attribute for each instance that will be affected by a dynamic XHTML function. In this example, we'll change a text color, and apply the *changeme* id to a heading. Remember that `id` attributes must be unique in each instance.

```
<h1 id="changeme">Changing Color</h1>
```

3. Add the JavaScript event handlers. In this example, the event handlers each call a function—`swapit()` and `revert()`—to switch the color when a user clicks the text. Because standard-compliant dynamic document technology exposes all elements to scripting and style sheets, you can add the event handlers directly to the `p` elements. Because these functions are generic (so you could use the same function to change different elements at different times), you have to include in the function call the `id` of the element to change.

```
<h1 id="changeme">Changing Color</h1>
<p onmouseover="swapit('changeme')" onmouseout="revert('changeme')">
<p onmouseover="swapit('changeme')" onmouseout="revert('changeme')">
If you'd like to change the color of the heading above
from black to red for better contrast and easier reading,
just move your mouse over this paragraph.</p>
</body>
</html>
```

4. Add the JavaScript functions, which change the colors on command from the event handlers to the head section of the document (before the closing `head` element, for example). Each function sets the `myElement` variable to the element that should be changed (as specified in the event handlers added in the previous step). Next, each function specifies the color property of the element and sets it to a specific color.

```
<!--
function swapit(element) {
var myElement = document.getElementById(element);
myElement.style.color="red"
}
function revert(element) {
var myElement = document.getElementById(element);
myElement.style.color="black"
}
// -->
</script>
```

See the complete code in Listing 16.1.

LISTING 16.1: DYNAMIC COLOR CHANGES USING STANDARD-COMPLIANT DYNAMIC XHTML

```
<!DOCTYPE html PUBLIC "-//W3C/DTD XHTML 1.0 Transitional//EN"
    "http://www.w3.org/TR/xhtml1/DTD/xhtml1-transitional.dtd">
<html xmlns="http://www.w3.org/1999/xhtml">
<head>
  <title>Fix Colors</title>
 <script type="text/javascript" language="javascript">
<!--
function swapit(element) {
var myElement = document.getElementById(element);
myElement.style.color="red"
}
function revert(element) {
var myElement = document.getElementById(element);
myElement.style.color="black"
}
// -->
</script>
</head>
<body>
<h1 id="changeme">Changing Color</h1>
<p  onmouseover="swapit('changeme')" onmouseout="revert('changeme')">
If you'd like to change the color of the heading above
from black to red for better contrast and easier reading,
just move your mouse over this paragraph.</p>
</body>
</html>
```

When writing a function, you need to specify exactly which characteristics of which page element (technically, which *object*) the function applies to, and you do this most easily by setting a variable for the specific object name (think of it as an address), then modifying the properties. For example, in Step 4 the variable myElement is set to an element identified with a unique id by using document .getElementById(element), and then the properties of myElement are modified. As a result, the element with the id changeme changes color when a user moves the mouse over the paragraph. Table 16.1 shows you other sample addresses.

TABLE 16.1: DYNAMIC XHTML SAMPLE OBJECT AND PROPERTY IDENTIFIERS

THIS SAMPLE ADDRESS	DOES THIS
document.body.style.color	Specifies the color property of the style of the body of the document.
document.myElement.top	Specifies the top position property of the style for the myElement variable.
document.form(0).style.background	Specifies the background of the first form in the document.

TIP   *Elements in arrays are numbered starting with 0, as in* form(0) *in Table 16.1. If your document has three* form *elements, the* form *array would include* form(0), form(1), *and* form(2). *The numbering is based on when the* form *element is specified in the document code; the first form is* form(0), *etc. The length of the array is 3 because there are three* form *elements.*

Creating a Collapsible Document

A useful dynamic HTML or XHTML capability is providing collapsible information, such as the table of contents you saw earlier. The following section shows you how to develop such a feature for standard-compliant browsers, such as IE 5.5 or later, Netscape 6 and later, and Opera 6 and later.

TIP   *If your audience uses older browsers (which is possible, but fairly unlikely), you would need to provide additional scripts to accommodate those browsers and use a browser-detection script to switch. See* www.javascriptsource.com *for script samples.*

Collapsing a Document

To create a collapsible document, similar to the document shown in Figure 16.1 earlier in this chapter, follow these steps:

1. Start with a basic document.

    ```
    <!DOCTYPE html PUBLIC "-//W3C/DTD XHTML 1.0 Transitional//EN"
        "http://www.w3.org/TR/xhtml1/DTD/xhtml1-transitional.dtd">
    <html xmlns="http://www.w3.org/1999/xhtml">
    <head>
    <title>ASR Outfitters</title>
    <style type="text/css">
    <!--
    body {font-size : 110% }
    h1, h2, h3 {font-family : "Comic Sans MS"}
    h1 {font-size : 180% ; font-weight : bold}
    -->
    </style>
    </head>
    <body>
    <center>
    <img src="asrlogo.gif" alt="ASR logo" />
    </center>
    <p>We're happy to welcome you to our newly redesigned Web
        site, featuring dynamic XHTML. Please take the
        <a href="tour.html">tour of our site</a> if you haven't
        been here in a while. In particular, you may appreciate
        the camping news as well as the new effects. </p>
    <hr />
    <p>Click on the headings below to expand or collapse them.</p>
    <h2>What's Here</h2>
    ```

```
<p>Here's the latest information on the site.</p>
<ul>
<li><a href="camping.html">Camping News</a> provides the latest
    comments from the trails.</li>
<li><a href="weather.html">Check Weather</a> offers weather
    updates from a variety of sources. </li>
<li><a href="clubs.html">Clubs</a> gives local hiking and
    mountaineering clubs a place to provide information about
    their activities.</li>
<li><a href="catalog.html">Catalog</a> presents our entire
    inventory, including announcements of the latest sales.</li>
<li><a href="contact.html">Contact Us</a> links to a page with
    a contact form, e-mail addresses, snail mail addresses, and
    phone numbers. If it isn't here, you can't find us. </li>
</ul>
<h2>What We Do</h2>
<p>In addition to providing the latest camping and outdoor
    activities news, we do also provide mountaineering and
    hiking equipment nationwide via mail order as well as
    through our stores in the Rocky Mountains. Please take a
    few minutes to look through our <a href="catalog.html">
    online offerings</a>.</p>
<h2>Other Issues and News</h2>
<ul>
<li>As you may know, our URL was misprinted in the latest
    <i>Hiking News</i>. Please tell your hiking friends that
    the correct URL is
    <a href="http://www.asroutfitters.com/">
    http://www.asroutfitters.com/</a>.</li>
<li>To collect a $1000 reward, turn in the name of the person
    who set the fire in the Bear Lake area last weekend.
<ol>
<li>Call 888-555-1212. </li>
<li>Leave the name on the recording. </li>
<li>Provide contact information so we can send you the
    reward.</li>
</ol>
</li>
</ul>
<h2>Contact Us</h2>
<p>If you have suggestions or comments about the site or other
    information we could provide, we'd love to know about it.
    Drop us an e-mail at
<a href="mailto:asroutfitters@raycomm.com">
    asroutfitters@raycomm.com</a>.
    Of course, you could also contact us more traditionally at
    the following address: </p>
<address>ASR Outfitters<br />
4700 N. Center <br />
```

```
South Logan, UT 87654<br />
801-555-3422</address>
</body>
</html>
```

2. Add div elements around each of the elements that should individually expand or collapse. Add a unique id attribute to each. You'll use the id attribute to specify the name for later reference from scripts.

```
<h2>What's Here</h2>
<div id="whathere">
<p>Here's the latest information on the site.</p>
<ul>
<li><a href="camping.html">Camping News</a> provides the latest
    comments from the trails.</li>
<li><a href="weather.html">Check Weather</a> offers weather
    updates from a variety of sources. </li>
<li><a href="clubs.html">Clubs</a> gives local hiking and
    mountaineering clubs a place to provide information about
    their activities.</li>
<li><a href="catalog.html">Catalog</a> presents our entire
    inventory, including announcements of the latest sales.</li>
<li><a href="contact.html">Contact Us</a> links to a page with
    a contact form, e-mail addresses, snail mail addresses, and
    phone numbers. If it isn't here, you can't find us. </li>
</ul>
</div>
<h2>What We Do</h2>
<div id="whatwedo">
<p>In addition to providing the latest camping and outdoor
    activities news, we do also provide mountaineering and
    hiking equipment nationwide via mail order as well as
    through our stores in the Rocky Mountains. Please take a
    few minutes to look through our <a href="catalog.html">
    online offerings</a>.</p>
</div>
<h2>Other Issues and News</h2>
<div id="otherstuff" >
<ul>
<li>As you may know, our URL was misprinted in the latest
    <i>Hiking News</i>. Please tell your hiking friends that
    the correct URL is
    <a href="http://www.asroutfitters.com/">
    http://www.asroutfitters.com/</a>.</li>
<li>To collect a $1000 reward, turn in the name of the person
    who set the fire in the Bear Lake area last weekend.
<ol>
<li>Call 888-555-1212. </li>
<li>Leave the name on the recording. </li>
```

```
<li>Provide contact information so we can send you the
   reward.</li>
</ol>
</li>
</ul>
</div>
<h2>Contact Us</h2>
<div id="contactus">
<p>If you have suggestions or comments about the site or other
   information we could provide, we'd love to know about it.
   Drop us an e-mail at
<a href="mailto:asroutfitters@raycomm.com">
   asroutfitters@raycomm.com</a>.
   Of course, you could also contact us more traditionally at
   the following address: </p>
<address>ASR Outfitters<br />
4700 N. Center <br />
South Logan, UT 87654<br />
801-555-3422</address>
</div></body>
</html>
```

3. Add an event handler that invokes a script to make the display change. Note that each of the event handlers includes the unique id of the following div section, so the click that each event handler processes will control the display of the following section.

```
<h2 onclick="showOne('whathere')">What's Here</h2>
<div id="whathere">
<p>Here's the latest information on the site.</p>
<ul>
<li><a href="camping.html">Camping News</a> provides the latest
   comments from the trails.</li>
<li><a href="weather.html">Check Weather</a> offers weather
   updates from a variety of sources. </li>
<li><a href="clubs.html">Clubs</a> gives local hiking and
   mountaineering clubs a place to provide information about
   their activities.</li>
<li><a href="catalog.html">Catalog</a> presents our entire
   inventory, including announcements of the latest sales.</li>
<li><a href="contact.html">Contact Us</a> links to a page with
   a contact form, e-mail addresses, snail mail addresses, and
   phone numbers. If it isn't here, you can't find us. </li>
</ul>
</div>
<h2 onclick="showOne('whatwedo')">What We Do</h2>
<div id="whatwedo">
<p>In addition to providing the latest camping and outdoor
   activities news, we do also provide mountaineering and
   hiking equipment nationwide via mail order as well as
```

```
        through our stores in the Rocky Mountains. Please take a
        few minutes to look through our <a href="catalog.html">
        online offerings</a>.</p>
</div>
<h2 onclick="showOne('otherstuff')">Other Issues and News</h2>
<div id="otherstuff" >
<ul>
<li>As you may know, our URL was misprinted in the latest
    <i>Hiking News</i>. Please tell your hiking friends that
    the correct URL is
    <a href="http://www.asroutfitters.com/">
    http://www.asroutfitters.com/</a>.</li>
<li>To collect a $1000 reward, turn in the name of the person
    who set the fire in the Bear Lake area last weekend.
<ol>
<li>Call 888-555-1212. </li>
<li>Leave the name on the recording. </li>
<li>Provide contact information so we can send you the
    reward.</li>
</ol>
</li>
</ul>
</div>
<h2 onclick="showOne('contactus')">Contact Us</h2>
<div id="contactus" >
<p>If you have suggestions or comments about the site or other
    information we could provide, we'd love to know about it.
    Drop us an e-mail at
<a href="mailto:asroutfitters@raycomm.com">
    asroutfitters@raycomm.com</a>.
    Of course, you could also contact us more traditionally at
    the following address: </p>
<address>ASR Outfitters<br />
4700 N. Center <br />
South Logan, UT 87654<br />
801-555-3422</address>
</div>
</body>
</html>
```

4. Add the script at the top that controls all this. The first function hides all of the div sections within the document by looping through each and setting the display property to hidden. The second function (showOne()) first closes all the div elements, and then displays the element belonging to the id passed to it. This function allows users to toggle the headings to collapse and expand with each click.

```
<script type="text/javascript" language="javascript1.3">
<!--
function closeall() {
```

```
var divs = document.getElementsByTagName('div')
var elements = divs.length
for(var i = 0;i < elements;i++)
    {
    var divStyle = divs.item(i)
       divStyle.style.display = 'none';
           }
return;
}
function showOne(showme) {
closeall()
var element = document.getElementById(showme)
element.style.display = 'block'
return;
}
// -->
</script>
```

5. Finally, add an onload event handler to the body element to close all of the div elements as the page loads. This serves two purposes: First, it collapses all of the div elements. Second, it ensures that browsers (like Opera) that incorrectly claim to support display properties will still display everything to their users. (If we used a style sheet to hide those elements, then scripts to display them, the Opera users could not see them. By using the same script to hide and display, we ensure that, at the worst, the page will simply not be dynamic.)

```
<body onload="closeall()">
```

The complete code for a standard-compliant collapsible document is shown in Listing 16.2. This document works well in Netscape 6 and IE 6, but is not dynamic in Opera 6 because Opera does not properly support the CSS display property.

LISTING 16.2: COLLAPSIBLE DOCUMENT USING DYNAMIC XHTML

```
<!DOCTYPE html PUBLIC "-//W3C/DTD XHTML 1.0 Transitional//EN"
   "http://www.w3.org/TR/xhtml1/DTD/xhtml1-transitional.dtd">
<html xmlns="http://www.w3.org/1999/xhtml">
<head>
<title>ASR Outfitters</title>
<style type="text/css">
<!--
body {font-size : 110% }
h1, h2, h3 {font-family : "Comic Sans MS"}
h1 {font-size : 180% ; font-weight : bold}
-->
</style>
<script type="text/javascript" language="javascript1.3">
<!--
function closeall() {
var divs = document.getElementsByTagName('div')
```

```
var elements = divs.length
for(var i = 0;i < elements;i++)
    {
    var divStyle = divs.item(i)
       divStyle.style.display = 'none';
          }
return;
}
function showOne(showme) {
closeall()
var element = document.getElementById(showme)
element.style.display = 'block'
return;
}
// -->
</script>
</head>
<body>
<center>
<img src="asrlogo.gif" alt="ASR logo" />
</center>
<p>We're happy to welcome you to our newly redesigned Web
   site, featuring dynamic XHTML. Please take the
   <a href="tour.html">tour of our site</a> if you haven't
   been here in a while. In particular, you may appreciate
   the camping news as well as the new effects. </p>
<hr />
<!--<a onclick="closeall()" href="javascript:closeall();">Close All</a> -->

<p>Click on the headings below to expand or collapse them.</p>
<h2 onclick="showOne('whathere')">What's Here</h2>
<div id="whathere">
<p>Here's the latest information on the site.</p>
<ul>
<li><a href="camping.html">Camping News</a> provides the latest
   comments from the trails.</li>
<li><a href="weather.html">Check Weather</a> offers weather
   updates from a variety of sources. </li>
<li><a href="clubs.html">Clubs</a> gives local hiking and
   mountaineering clubs a place to provide information about
   their activities.</li>
<li><a href="catalog.html">Catalog</a> presents our entire
   inventory, including announcements of the latest sales.</li>
<li><a href="contact.html">Contact Us</a> links to a page with
   a contact form, e-mail addresses, snail mail addresses, and
   phone numbers. If it isn't here, you can't find us. </li>
</ul>
</div>
```

```
<h2 onclick="showOne('whatwedo')">What We Do</h2>
<div id="whatwedo">
<p>In addition to providing the latest camping and outdoor
   activities news, we do also provide mountaineering and
   hiking equipment nationwide via mail order as well as
   through our stores in the Rocky Mountains. Please take a
   few minutes to look through our <a href="catalog.html">
   online offerings</a>.</p>
</div>
<h2 onclick="showOne('otherstuff')">Other Issues and News</h2>
<div id="otherstuff" >
<ul>
<li>As you may know, our URL was misprinted in the latest
   <i>Hiking News</i>. Please tell your hiking friends that
   the correct URL is
   <a href="http://www.asroutfitters.com/">
   http://www.asroutfitters.com/</a>.</li>
<li>To collect a $1000 reward, turn in the name of the person
   who set the fire in the Bear Lake area last weekend.
<ol>
<li>Call 888-555-1212. </li>
<li>Leave the name on the recording. </li>
<li>Provide contact information so we can send you the
   reward.</li>
</ol>
</li>
</ul>
</div>
<h2 onclick="showOne('contactus')">Contact Us</h2>
<div id="contactus" >
<p>If you have suggestions or comments about the site or other
   information we could provide, we'd love to know about it.
   Drop us an e-mail at
<a href="mailto:asroutfitters@raycomm.com">
   asroutfitters@raycomm.com</a>.
   Of course, you could also contact us more traditionally at
   the following address: </p>
<address>ASR Outfitters<br />
4700 N. Center <br />
South Logan, UT 87654<br />
801-555-3422</address>
</div>
</body>
</html>
```

The resulting collapsible document should look similar to Figures 16.1 and 16.2.

Implementing Browser Detection

If you plan to include dynamic capabilities in your HTML or XHTML documents, strongly consider implementing a JavaScript that will detect which browser your users are using and then serve up different content for different browsers. Remember, if users are not using the browser for which the documents were developed, they'll get error messages or the page won't work as intended.

Browser detection in the past was generally a simple matter of determining whether users were using Netscape Navigator or IE using two simple JavaScript methods and properties:

◆ `navigator.appName` to determine the browser name

◆ `navigator.appVersion` to determine the browser version

This worked well for both Netscape Navigator and IE 4.*x* or lower (but not for Opera or other browsers), and enabled site developers to redirect users to an appropriate page with the appropriate JavaScript for the version of the browser that they were using and the DOM that the version implemented. With the introduction of newer versions of IE (5.5 and 6) and Netscape Navigator 6, other browsers (such as Opera, Mozilla, and Konqueror), and the multitude of possible operating systems, browser detection became much more complex.

Current browser detection requires use of the `userAgent` string. The HTTP 1.1 Specification uses a header called `userAgent`. This header identifies the client to the server and includes information about the operating system, the browser name, and the browser version. If you use the following simple script, you can find out the `userAgent` string returned by your current browser:

```
<script type="text/javascript" language="javascript">
    var agent = navigator.userAgent;
    document.write ("userAgent string: " + agent);
</script>
```

Here are a few examples of the `userAgent` string returned by this script:

```
userAgent string: Mozilla/4.75 [en] (Win98; U)
userAgent string: Mozilla/3.0 (compatible; Opera/3.0;
    Windows 95/NT4)
userAgent string: Mozilla/5.0 (Windows; U; Win98; en-US;
    CDonDemand) Gecko/20010131 Netscape6/6.01)
userAgent string:) Mozilla/4.0 (compatible; MSIE 5.5;
    Windows NT5.0)
userAgent string: Mozilla/4.78 (Windows 2000; U) Opera 6.01 [en]
```

The first string is returned from a computer running Netscape 4.75 on the Windows 98 platform, the second from Opera 3 on Windows 95, the third from Netscape 6 on Windows 98, and the fourth from IE 5.5 on Windows 2000 (note that the value returned for Windows 2000 is `Windows NT5.0`). The fifth string is returned from a computer running Opera (pretending to be Netscape 4.78) on Windows 2000. You can see how browser detection has become much more complex!

It's beyond the scope of this chapter to go into the details of pulling out the needed pieces of information from the `userAgent` string, but for more information on how browser detection works, see the Browser Detection tutorial by Richard Blaylock at `http://hotwired.lycos.com/webmonkey/99/02/index2a.html?tw=authoring`.

An excellent JavaScript called "The Ultimate JavaScript Client Sniffer: Version 3.02" is available from `www.mozilla.org/docs/web-developer/sniffer/browser_type.html`. We have provided this script in Listing 16.3, and we obtained copyright permission from Netscape for its reuse and distribution. This script covers every currently known combination of browser, operating system, and platform, and also includes WebTV and AOL. This script is updated as needed, so as future browser versions become available, check the previous URL for an updated script. It's a long script, but it offers the most comprehensive browser detection currently available, and you can modify it to suit your browser-detection needs.

This script goes in the head section of your document, but you must also use another JavaScript in the body section of your document so that the browser knows what action to take for the various combinations. Most commonly, you'll want to redirect your users to a particular version of your page for that browser and browser version. Therefore, an additional script using `location.replace` has been added to Listing 16.3 that redirects the user to a page specifically designed for Netscape 4.*x*, IE, Netscape 6.*x*, or a standard page for all other combinations. You can expand this script to include all the possibilities you want, such as an IE 4 page, an IE 5.5 page, and so on.

TIP You can link to an external JavaScript the same way you can link to an external style sheet. This browser-detection script is very comprehensive, but also quite long. You can save the script itself as a text file with a `.js` *extension to indicate that it's JavaScript; for example, save it as* **browserdetect.js**. *Then, in the head section of the document, use the* `link` *element to link to the script:* `<link rel="script" type="text/javascript" href="browserdetect.js"/>`. *For more information, see the section "Linking JavaScript" in Chapter 10.*

LISTING 16.3: THE ULTIMATE JAVASCRIPT CLIENT SNIFFER WITH PAGE REDIRECTS

```
//<!--
// Ultimate client-side JavaScript client sniff. Version 3.03
// (C) Netscape Communications 1999-2001.  Permission granted to reuse and
distribute.
// Revised 17 May 99 to add is_nav5up and is_ie5up (see below).
// Revised 20 Dec 00 to add is_gecko and change is_nav5up to is_nav6up
//                        also added support for IE5.5 Opera4&5 HotJava3 AOLTV
// Revised 22 Feb 01 to correct Javascript Detection for IE 5.x, Opera 4,
//                    correct Opera 5 detection
//                    add support for winME and win2k
//                    synch with browser-type-oo.js
// Revised 26 Mar 01 to correct Opera detection
// Revised 02 Oct 01 to add IE6 detection

// Everything you always wanted to know about your JavaScript client
// but were afraid to ask. Creates "is_" variables indicating:
// (1) browser vendor:
//     is_nav, is_ie, is_opera, is_hotjava, is_webtv, is_TVNavigator, is_AOLTV
// (2) browser version number:
//     is_major (integer indicating major version number: 2, 3, 4 ...)
//     is_minor (float   indicating full  version number: 2.02, 3.01, 4.04 ...)
```

```
// (3) browser vendor AND major version number
//      is_nav2, is_nav3, is_nav4, is_nav4up, is_nav6, is_nav6up, is_gecko, is_ie3,
//      is_ie4, is_ie4up, is_ie5, is_ie5up, is_ie5_5, is_ie5_5up, is_ie6, is_ie6up,
//      is_hotjava3, is_hotjava3up,
//      is_opera2, is_opera3, is_opera4, is_opera5, is_opera5up
// (4) JavaScript version number:
//      is_js (float indicating full JavaScript version number: 1, 1.1, 1.2 ...)
// (5) OS platform and version:
//      is_win, is_win16, is_win32, is_win31, is_win95, is_winnt, is_win98,
//      is_winme, is_win2k
//      is_os2
//      is_mac, is_mac68k, is_macppc
//      is_unix
//      is_sun, is_sun4, is_sun5, is_suni86
//      is_irix, is_irix5, is_irix6
//      is_hpux, is_hpux9, is_hpux10
//      is_aix, is_aix1, is_aix2, is_aix3, is_aix4
//      is_linux, is_sco, is_unixware, is_mpras, is_reliant
//      is_dec, is_sinix, is_freebsd, is_bsd
//      is_vms
//
// See http://www.it97.de/JavaScript/JS_tutorial/bstat/navobj.html and
// http://www.it97.de/JavaScript/JS_tutorial/bstat/Browseraol.html
// for detailed lists of userAgent strings.
//
// Note: You don't want your Nav4 or IE4 code to "turn off" or
// stop working when new versions of browsers are released, so
// in conditional code forks, use is_ie5up ("IE 5.0 or greater")
// is_opera5up ("Opera 5.0 or greater") instead of is_ie5 or is_opera5
// to check version in code which you want to work on future
// versions.

    // Convert all characters to lowercase to simplify testing
    var agt=navigator.userAgent.toLowerCase();

    // *** BROWSER VERSION ***
    // Note: On IE5, these return 4, so use is_ie5up to detect IE5.
    var is_major = parseInt(navigator.appVersion);
    var is_minor = parseFloat(navigator.appVersion);

    // Note: Opera and WebTV spoof Navigator.  We do strict client detection.
    // If you want to allow spoofing, take out the tests for Opera and WebTV.
    var is_nav  = ((agt.indexOf('mozilla')!=-1) && (agt.indexOf('spoofer')==-1)
                && (agt.indexOf('compatible') == -1) && (agt.indexOf('opera')==-1)
                && (agt.indexOf('webtv')==-1) && (agt.indexOf('hotjava')==-1));
    var is_nav2 = (is_nav && (is_major == 2));
    var is_nav3 = (is_nav && (is_major == 3));
    var is_nav4 = (is_nav && (is_major == 4));
```

```
var is_nav4up = (is_nav && (is_major >= 4));
var is_navonly     = (is_nav && ((agt.indexOf(";nav") != -1) ||
                      (agt.indexOf("; nav") != -1)) );
var is_nav6 = (is_nav && (is_major == 5));
var is_nav6up = (is_nav && (is_major >= 5));
var is_gecko = (agt.indexOf('gecko') != -1);


var is_ie     = ((agt.indexOf("msie") != -1) && (agt.indexOf("opera") == -1));
var is_ie3    = (is_ie && (is_major < 4));
var is_ie4    = (is_ie && (is_major == 4) && (agt.indexOf("msie 4")!=-1) );
var is_ie4up  = (is_ie && (is_major >= 4));
var is_ie5    = (is_ie && (is_major == 4) && (agt.indexOf("msie 5.0")!=-1) );
var is_ie5_5  = (is_ie && (is_major == 4) && (agt.indexOf("msie 5.5") !=-1));
var is_ie5up  = (is_ie && !is_ie3 && !is_ie4);
var is_ie5_5up =(is_ie && !is_ie3 && !is_ie4 && !is_ie5);
var is_ie6    = (is_ie && (is_major == 4) && (agt.indexOf("msie 6.")!=-1) );
var is_ie6up  = (is_ie && !is_ie3 && !is_ie4 && !is_ie5 && !is_ie5_5);

// KNOWN BUG: On AOL4, returns false if IE3 is embedded browser
// or if this is the first browser window opened.  Thus the
// variables is_aol, is_aol3, and is_aol4 aren't 100% reliable.
var is_aol   = (agt.indexOf("aol") != -1);
var is_aol3  = (is_aol && is_ie3);
var is_aol4  = (is_aol && is_ie4);
var is_aol5  = (agt.indexOf("aol 5") != -1);
var is_aol6  = (agt.indexOf("aol 6") != -1);

var is_opera = (agt.indexOf("opera") != -1);
var is_opera2 = (agt.indexOf("opera 2") != -1 || agt.indexOf("opera/2") != -1);
var is_opera3 = (agt.indexOf("opera 3") != -1 || agt.indexOf("opera/3") != -1);
var is_opera4 = (agt.indexOf("opera 4") != -1 || agt.indexOf("opera/4") != -1);
var is_opera5 = (agt.indexOf("opera 5") != -1 || agt.indexOf("opera/5") != -1);
var is_opera5up = (is_opera && !is_opera2 && !is_opera3 && !is_opera4);

var is_webtv = (agt.indexOf("webtv") != -1);

var is_TVNavigator = ((agt.indexOf("navio") != -1) ||
(agt.indexOf("navio_aoltv") != -1));
var is_AOLTV = is_TVNavigator;

var is_hotjava = (agt.indexOf("hotjava") != -1);
var is_hotjava3 = (is_hotjava && (is_major == 3));
var is_hotjava3up = (is_hotjava && (is_major >= 3));

// *** JAVASCRIPT VERSION CHECK ***
var is_js;
if (is_nav2 || is_ie3) is_js = 1.0;
```

```
else if (is_nav3) is_js = 1.1;
else if (is_opera5up) is_js = 1.3;
else if (is_opera) is_js = 1.1;
else if ((is_nav4 && (is_minor <= 4.05)) || is_ie4) is_js = 1.2;
else if ((is_nav4 && (is_minor > 4.05)) || is_ie5) is_js = 1.3;
else if (is_hotjava3up) is_js = 1.4;
else if (is_nav6 || is_gecko) is_js = 1.5;
// NOTE: In the future, update this code when newer versions of JS
// are released. For now, we try to provide some upward compatibility
// so that future versions of Nav and IE will show they are at
// *least* JS 1.x capable. Always check for JS version compatibility
// with > or >=.
else if (is_nav6up) is_js = 1.5;
// NOTE: ie5up on mac is 1.4
else if (is_ie5up) is_js = 1.3;

// HACK: no idea for other browsers; always check for JS version with > or >=
else is_js = 0.0;

// *** PLATFORM ***
var is_win    = ( (agt.indexOf("win")!=-1) || (agt.indexOf("16bit")!=-1) );
// NOTE: On Opera 3.0, the userAgent string includes "Windows 95/NT4" on all
//        Win32, so you can't distinguish between Win95 and WinNT.
var is_win95 = ((agt.indexOf("win95")!=-1) || (agt.indexOf("Windows 95")!=-1));

// is this a 16 bit compiled version?
var is_win16 = ((agt.indexOf("win16")!=-1) ||
            (agt.indexOf("16bit")!=-1) || (agt.indexOf("Windows 3.1")!=-1) ||
            (agt.indexOf("Windows 16-bit")!=-1) );

var is_win31 = ((agt.indexOf("Windows 3.1")!=-1) || (agt.indexOf("win16")!=-1)
||
                (agt.indexOf("Windows 16-bit")!=-1));

var is_winme = ((agt.indexOf("win 9x 4.90")!=-1));
var is_win2k = ((agt.indexOf("windows nt 5.0")!=-1));

// NOTE: Reliable detection of Win98 may not be possible. It appears that:
//        - On Nav 4.x and before you'll get plain "Windows" in userAgent.
//        - On Mercury client, the 32-bit version will return "Win98", but
//          the 16-bit version running on Win98 will still return "Win95".
 var is_win98 = ((agt.indexOf("win98")!=-1) || (agt.indexOf("Windows 98")!=-1));
 var is_winnt = ((agt.indexOf("winnt")!=-1) || (agt.indexOf("windows nt")!=-1));
 var is_win32 = (is_win95 || is_winnt || is_win98 ||
                ((is_major >= 4) && (navigator.platform == "Win32")) ||
                (agt.indexOf("win32")!=-1) || (agt.indexOf("32bit")!=-1));

var is_os2    = ((agt.indexOf("os/2")!=-1) ||
```

```
                      (navigator.appVersion.indexOf("OS/2")!=-1) ||
                      (agt.indexOf("ibm-webexplorer")!=-1));

    var is_mac    = (agt.indexOf("mac")!=-1);
    // hack ie5 js version for mac
    if (is_mac && is_ie5up) is_js = 1.4;
    var is_mac68k = (is_mac && ((agt.indexOf("68k")!=-1) ||
                                (agt.indexOf("68000")!=-1)));
    var is_macppc = (is_mac && ((agt.indexOf("ppc")!=-1) ||
                                (agt.indexOf("powerpc")!=-1)));

    var is_sun    = (agt.indexOf("sunos")!=-1);
    var is_sun4   = (agt.indexOf("sunos 4")!=-1);
    var is_sun5   = (agt.indexOf("sunos 5")!=-1);
    var is_suni86= (is_sun && (agt.indexOf("i86")!=-1));
    var is_irix   = (agt.indexOf("irix") !=-1);     // SGI
    var is_irix5  = (agt.indexOf("irix 5") !=-1);
    var is_irix6  = ((agt.indexOf("irix 6") !=-1) || (agt.indexOf("irix6") !=-1));
    var is_hpux   = (agt.indexOf("hp-ux")!=-1);
    var is_hpux9  = (is_hpux && (agt.indexOf("09.")!=-1));
    var is_hpux10= (is_hpux && (agt.indexOf("10.")!=-1));
    var is_aix    = (agt.indexOf("aix") !=-1);      // IBM
    var is_aix1   = (agt.indexOf("aix 1") !=-1);
    var is_aix2   = (agt.indexOf("aix 2") !=-1);
    var is_aix3   = (agt.indexOf("aix 3") !=-1);
    var is_aix4   = (agt.indexOf("aix 4") !=-1);
    var is_linux = (agt.indexOf("inux")!=-1);
    var is_sco    = (agt.indexOf("sco")!=-1) || (agt.indexOf("unix_sv")!=-1);
    var is_unixware = (agt.indexOf("unix_system_v")!=-1);
    var is_mpras    = (agt.indexOf("ncr")!=-1);
    var is_reliant  = (agt.indexOf("reliantunix")!=-1);
    var is_dec    = ((agt.indexOf("dec")!=-1) || (agt.indexOf("osf1")!=-1) ||
            (agt.indexOf("dec_alpha")!=-1) || (agt.indexOf("alphaserver")!=-1) ||
            (agt.indexOf("ultrix")!=-1) || (agt.indexOf("alphastation")!=-1));
    var is_sinix = (agt.indexOf("sinix")!=-1);
    var is_freebsd = (agt.indexOf("freebsd")!=-1);
    var is_bsd = (agt.indexOf("bsd")!=-1);
    var is_unix  = ((agt.indexOf("x11")!=-1) || is_sun || is_irix || is_hpux ||
                   is_sco ||is_unixware || is_mpras || is_reliant ||
                   is_dec || is_sinix || is_aix || is_linux || is_bsd || is_freebsd);

    var is_vms    = ((agt.indexOf("vax")!=-1) || (agt.indexOf("openvms")!=-1));

//--> end hide JavaScript // Following lines added for book example to serve
// up different pages for different browsers
if (is_gecko)
  {
  location.replace("Netscape6.htm");
```

```
        }
        else if (is_nav4)
        {
         location.replace("Netscape4.htm");
        }
        else if (is_ie5up)
        {
         location.replace("MSIEPage.htm");
        }
        else
        {
        location.replace("StandardPage.htm");
        }
//--> end hide JavaScript
</script>
</head>
<body>
<noscript>
   <h2>This website requires a browser supporting
   scripting</h2>
</noscript>

</body>
</html>
```

TIP *Take a look at* www.cross-browser.com *to see what you can do with browser detection and dynamic documents.*

Where to Go from Here

As you learned in this chapter, dynamic HTML and XHTML offers lots of potential for making your pages leap off the screen. Although this chapter covered only the basics, you can combine any style sheet characteristic with a JavaScript function to make your pages flash, change, and move.

If you feel confident using style sheets and JavaScript, we recommend that you experiment with combining these two aspects. You'll find a complete style sheet reference and JavaScript reference in the Master's Reference (Master's Reference 2 and 3, respectively). Or, if you're not quite up to speed with these two topics, we recommend visiting the following chapters:

- ◆ See Chapter 9 for information about developing and applying style sheets.

- ◆ See Chapter 10 to learn how to use JavaScript in your documents.

- ◆ Visit Chapter 17 to learn how to generate HTML and XHTML from a database.

- ◆ Visit Chapter 18 to learn how to make your Web site searchable.

Chapter 17

Generating HTML or XHTML from a Database

A *DATABASE* IS SIMPLY a collection of information arranged so you can easily access and use it. A phone directory, a catalog, and a mailing list are examples of databases you've probably used.

In a way, the Web is a database—the world's largest. It's a collection of information that anyone connected to the Internet can access and use. The Yahoo! site (at **www.yahoo.com**), which is a collection of information about Web sites, including descriptions and URLs, is another database within the larger World Wide Web database.

As an HTML or XHTML guru (you are one if you've made it to this chapter), you might need to move information from a database into a format that you can publish in an HTML or XHTML document. In this chapter, we'll show you how to convert database information into HTML or XHTML documents, look at a range of database tools, and step you through a general process for generating HTML or XHTML from a database.

This chapter covers the following topics:

◆ Enhancing your Web site with databases

◆ Determining your database needs

◆ Choosing database software

◆ Generating HTML or XHTML pages from databases

◆ Maintaining database documents

Why Generate HTML or XHTML from a Database?

Although it sounds complicated (it's not too bad, actually), generating HTML or XHTML from a database saves a tremendous amount of time. For example, suppose you work for a company that manufactures nuts and bolts. Management decides to make the enormous product catalog—which includes thousands of items—available on the corporate Web site. You could spend weeks doing the data entry, or you could spend almost as much time moving pages from the catalog into and out of your favorite Web development tools.

Your best bet is to develop the online catalog by pulling information directly from a database. Even developing a new database specifically for online information is a better choice than entering information into a document from scratch. Why? A computerized database is a dynamic entity, which means that you can constantly add, change, and remove information. If you use database software to create the online catalog, updating your documents is either almost or fully automatic—and a snap. The alternative is to find and manually edit each and every affected Web page every time some itty-bitty scrap of information changes.

When you generate Web pages from a database, you can also provide online information in any number of segments. For example, you can list products by size, weight, color, or whatever, and you can fairly easily change how you present information once you have a database in place.

Generating documents from a database is a good solution for the company that manufactures nuts and bolts; however, a database is not an ideal solution in all cases, particularly if the cost of setting up and maintaining the database outweighs the benefits. For example, if your company manufactures only one or two products, you might just as easily—perhaps more easily—develop an online catalog by simply creating a few HTML or XHTML documents.

Deciding to Use a Database

If you don't have a database in place yet—and, therefore, don't know whether generating information from a database will best meet your needs—here are some questions to ask yourself:

◆ Do you have a variety and/or large quantity of information?

◆ Does the data change frequently or require regular updates or maintenance?

◆ Does the data appear (in some form or another) in many pages throughout your Web site?

◆ Do you realistically have the technical and financial resources to create a database?

If you answered yes to the first, or second, or third questions, you probably have some need for a database. If you also answered no to the fourth, reassess your needs before you jump into it—this isn't a one-day project.

Our fictitious company, ASR Outfitters, decided to use a database for part of its site because of the variety of its products and ever-changing availability. Rather than editing every product page every time prices, products, or availability changes, ASR Outfitters developers want to update the master database and then quickly and easily make that information available through the Web.

As you consider a database, keep in mind that it could contain data in the traditional sense (as the examples in this chapter show) or it could contain text or other content. Most of the high-traffic sites on the Internet store articles in databases and serve HTML or XHTML pages directly from the databases to ease site maintenance. For example, sites like slashdot.org, cnn.com, weather.com, and many others rely on a database to manage content, user data, and the interactive features that attract visitors. Sites like docs.sun.com provide immense quantities of documentation through a Web server connected to an Oracle database backend. Our own site, TECHWR-L (www.raycomm.com/techwhirl), uses PHP and MySQL to manage a lot of the content. Figure 17.1 shows a page generated from a database.

FIGURE 17.1

TECHWR-L Employment Services draws content automatically from a MySQL database

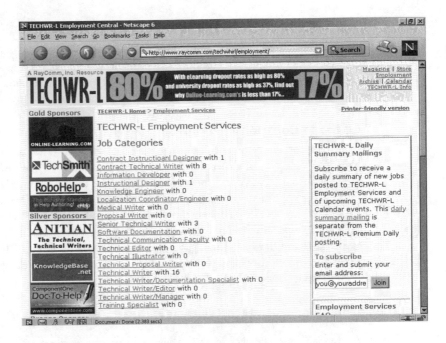

TIP   For more information about the value of database publishing, see `http://hotwired.lycos.com/webmonkey/01/21/index2a.html`.

DECIDING WHICH INFORMATION SHOULD GO ON THE WEB

At some point in this process, you'll need to decide which information within your database you should publish on the Web. (Obviously, this is a bigger issue if you're opening some of the content of an internal database to the Internet—using a database to manage Web-only content wouldn't necessarily require that you address these issues.) You may want to publish all the information, but if you don't, here are some other considerations:

◆ Which information will users find most useful? ASR Outfitters wants users to see all the available product information, so the company publishes it all.

◆ Which information won't users need? Aside from internal documentation, pricing, and marketing information (which is all kept in different databases), ASR decided that publishing nearly all product information was appropriate.

◆ Which information do you not want provided to the public? Because its product database is separate from confidential information, ASR did not have to contend with this problem. Management chose not to make cryptic acronyms and abbreviations available. This was not for security purposes, but was an effort to reduce users' confusion.

You don't have to answer these questions now, but keep them in mind as you're working through the remaining sections in this chapter.

Exploring Your Options

How you generate HTML or XHTML from a database depends on your specific needs and resources, which vary according to the size of your company and the size of the database. We're going to look briefly at the options for a very large company and for a small company. However, most situations fall somewhere in between—the basic principles apply in any situation.

The Large Company Scenario

If you work for a large organization that has company-wide database solutions in place, you're probably using Oracle, Sybase, Microsoft SQL Server, or Informix software. You probably also have programming resources at your disposal or have access to high-end (and fairly expensive) software, either built into the application or through additional software like ColdFusion that can automatically generate HTML or XHTML documents from your database.

If you have programming resources and can create a custom database solution, that's your most sophisticated and flexible option. Your goal, regardless of resources, is to develop a database that's suitable for Web publication, and you need an expedient solution to push the data onto the Web. Most of the solutions discussed in this chapter will work for you.

STRUCTURED QUERY LANGUAGE (SQL)

If you're a fairly motivated or savvy Web developer, or know someone who is, generating HTML or XHTML directly from a relational database management system (RDBMS), such as Oracle, Sybase, or Informix, using Structured Query Language (SQL) is a great technical solution for creating database-driven Web sites, and it can be a workable and flexible solution on most platforms and most servers at a reasonable cost. Even small companies with relatively few resources at their disposal can use products like PHP, MySQL, and Apache for a cost-effective database-driven solution. Check out any of these tutorials for more information on SQL:

◆ Simple SQL: Getting Started with SQL
  http://wdvl.internet.com/Authoring/DB/SQL/Start/

◆ Interactive/Online SQL Tutorial with SQL Interpreter and live practice database
  http://sqlcourse.com

◆ MySQL home page and links to examples
  www.mysql.org

The Small Company Scenario

In this situation, you generate HTML or XHTML from a database using moderately priced and easily accessible tools that also give you a broad range of capabilities. We assume that you have access to Windows (95/98/NT/ME/2000, or XP) or a Linux/Unix system, have access to the database, and need to get the information onto the Internet (or an intranet).

You can generate HTML or XHTML pages from a database using Microsoft Personal Web Server (included with Windows 95/98 or can be downloaded free from Microsoft's site at `http://msdn` `.microsoft.com/library/default.asp?URL=/library/officedev/office97/settinguppersonalweb-` `server.htm`), Microsoft Peer Web Services (included with Windows NT 4), or Internet Information Services 5.0 (included with Windows 2000 Professional) and Microsoft Access. This will be covered in more detail in the section "Generating HTML or XHTML Pages from Databases" later in this chapter. This is an easy and inexpensive solution for a small database and Web site, but will not work well for a busy site with a large database.

A more affordable solution (and one that is likely to scale to larger databases and higher-traffic sites more easily than the previous example) would be to use the Apache Web server and a MySQL database. This solution works on Linux/Unix, Macintosh, and Windows platforms. You need a little bit more technical savvy (or access to it) for this to be a good choice, but the flexibility and power of this solution makes it worth the investment in consultants or in building your own skills. Find more information at `www.apache.org`, `www.mysql.com`, and `www.php.net`.

Choosing Software

You need to select software that matches your budget, platform, and database size. Although we can't tell you exactly what you need (there are simply too many variables), we can tell you what your options are.

Tools for Database Publishing

You'll need two sets of tools to use a database to generate content for HTML or XHTML documents:

Database   A database is where the content for your pages is stored. Databases save content in tables, which are similar to spreadsheets. Each table has rows and columns, which create individual fields. A field has properties, such as what kind of data it can contain, how many characters the data can contain, and whether the field must contain data or can be empty.

Database management systems (DBMS) often use large and complex database programs, such as Oracle, Sybase, Informix, or Microsoft SQL Server. For smaller sites, a less complex and expensive system—such as MySQL, Microsoft Access, FileMaker Pro, or Paradox—may well be all that's needed.

Application Servers   These applications, often referred to as *middleware*, operate on the server side to link the Web server to the database content. These programs do not create databases, but they do help you create HTML or XHTML pages that can dynamically connect to a database and access its contents by using a server-side scripting language. The applications are designed to do two things with databases:

◆   They request data from the database using a server-side scripting language. The script contains the necessary information to make a connection to a database.

◆   They take the results of the database *query* (a request for information from a database) to a template so the results can be displayed on a Web page.

Scripting Languages for Database Publishing

There are several choices for the scripting language that makes up the largest part of the application. Your choices include Perl and Visual Basic Script (VBScript), as well as the following:

◆ ColdFusion Markup Language (CFML)

◆ Active Server Pages (ASP)/.NET

◆ JavaServlet Pages (JSP)

◆ PHP

TIP For a thorough review of server-side scripting languages, see "Server-Side Scripting Shootout" at `http://hotwired.lycos.com/webmonkey/99/46/index1a.html?tw=programming`.

ColdFusion Markup Language   ColdFusion Markup Language is a tag-based language, like HTML or XHTML; however, the tags are interpreted on the server (unlike HTML or XHTML, which are interpreted in the browser). ColdFusion also has a powerful server, which, among many other features, offers integration with databases and remote database administration, including database connections. The ColdFusion server can be used on many operating systems, including Windows, Solaris, HP-UX, and Linux.

For more information on ColdFusion, visit Macromedia's Web site at `www.macromedia.com`, or check out the ColdFusion tutorial at `http://hotwired.lycos.com/webmonkey/programming/coldfusion/tutorials/tutorial2.html`.

Active Server Pages (ASP)/.NET   ASP is a Microsoft technology that can be used to create dynamic pages that are a combination of HTML or XHTML, scripting, and ActiveX components. These pages can be used to access databases, among other things. ASP pages can be created using any text editor, and some software programs such as Microsoft FrontPage can create ASP pages. Any scripting language can be used in an ASP, but VBScript is the most common.

For more information on ASP, see the "Introduction to Active Server Pages" tutorial at `http://hotwired.lycos.com/webmonkey/98/39/index2a.html` or look at the content at `www.asp101.com`.

ASP now exists in forms that can be used on non-Windows platforms, such as Sun Chili!Soft ASP. For more details, visit the Web site at `www.chilisoft.com`.

JSP   JSP is similar to ASP, but it's a Sun technology based on the Java programming language. JSP can be used to create pages that include HTML or XHTML and scripting in Java, and can also be written in XML using Extensible Stylesheet Language Transformations (XSLT). JSP is available on all major Web platforms.

For more information on JSP, see the "Intro to JSP" tutorial at `http://hotwired.lycos.com/webmonkey/01/22/index3a.html?tw=programming`, or the Sun online JSP course at `http://developer.java.sun.com/developer/onlineTraining/JSPIntro/`.

PHP   PHP is another server-side scripting language that can be used to create dynamic database HTML or XHTML pages. It's usually used in combination with MySQL, a free, open-source database management system, but works with many database programs. PHP/MySQL is cross-platform and can be used on Windows, Macintosh, and Linux/Unix. PHP also supports XML.

For more information on PHP/MySQL, check out the introductory PHP tutorial at `www.php.net/tut.php`, the introduction to MySQL at `www.mysql.com/doc/W/h/What-is.html`, and the PHP/MySQL tutorial at `http://hotwired.lycos.com/webmonkey/programming/php/tutorials/tutorial4.html`.

Each of these applications can serve HTML or XHTML documents and exchange data through a server, thereby making them reasonable candidates for almost any database you'd want to create. You'll find that these software packages are flexible and easy to use to provide your database information as HTML or XHTML.

ASR Outfitters experimented with Microsoft Access as its desktop database program simply because the company uses Microsoft Office products; the consistent interface was a driving force. The company then tried ColdFusion as its database application software because it's easy to use and because developers could quickly get up to speed with it.

Generating HTML or XHTML Pages from Databases

If you decide to generate an HTML or XHTML page from a database, you'll find that the process is complicated, but certainly doable. You have to provide a way for the server (where your Web pages are published) to communicate with the database software.

The software that allows this communication (covered in the previous section) resides on the same computer system as the Web server, and it links the Web server to the data sources.

Exactly how you generate HTML or XHTML from a database depends on the software you choose; however, the general process is as follows:

1. Set up the data source. If you already have the data in a database—anything from Access to Oracle to MySQL—this part is done.

2. Set up the intermediary software (ColdFusion, in this case, but could easily have been PHP, JSPs, or other software) to communicate with the database and with the Web server. The intermediary software usually connects directly to the database (the information) itself and not to the data via the program used to create the data.

3. Set up query and change forms to get information out of and put information into HTML or XHTML documents.

4. Edit the documents to fit into the overall site appearance.

ASR used the ColdFusion Web Application Wizard to select information to display, to select fields to search on, and to select additional data to present on request. The result was a simple form in which users can enter search terms. Developing the form—linked to the data—is as simple as choosing options from menus, as shown here:

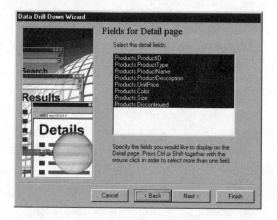

Furthermore, in addition to the plain-text boxes and the drop-down lists shown in Figure 17.2, users can add check boxes and radio buttons to their search form interface.

FIGURE 17.2

A simple and easily generated Cold-Fusion search form

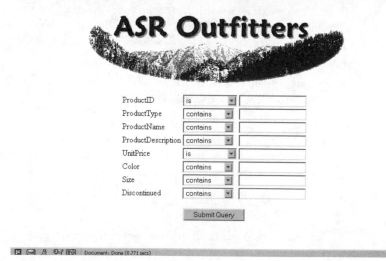

The files containing the HTML or XHTML markup for this search form has a `.cfm` extension. You'll find it easy to edit manually or with any HTML or XHTML editing application, but you will need to edit it to create well-formed and valid XHTML.

USING PREDEFINED SEARCHES

One technique that can save time for you and your users is a *predefined search*. Instead of users typing the search terms or even selecting terms from a list, they can simply click a link to automatically search in ways you define.

The easiest way to establish these searches is to go to the search form and run the query. Then, copy and paste the URL from the location line in the browser into the editing program. For example, at the hypothetical ASR site, a detailed view of information about skis is at www.example.com/ASROutfitters/ Detail.CFM?Products__ProductID=6.

Adding this URL to the a element (to create a link):

```
<a href="http://www.example.com/ASROutfitters/
    Detail.CFM?Products__ProductID=6" >Ski Information,
    Detailed</a>
```

makes it much easier for your users to find information.

Maintaining Pages Generated from a Database

After you are set up to generate HTML or XHTML from a database, you need to keep the pages current. Just because they're automatically generated does not mean that they require no maintenance. Unlike maintaining regular documents, though, maintaining database-generated documents involves both the data and the presentation.

First, you update the data or information in the database using the software in which you developed the database. When a browser requests the page from the Web server, the server-side script (which is part of the page) accesses the database for the information. Setting up a connection to the database to retrieve the database information is part of the server-side process. After the data has changed, this new information is then automatically displayed on the next Web page served, and the appearance continues to be based on the original HTML or XHTML documents that provide the structure.

You can change the HTML or XHTML in order to change the presentation as often as you feel is necessary just as you would maintain any of the pages on your Web site. When your changes are made, you can upload the new pages to the Web server so that the changes can take effect.

You can also change the code in the server-side script in your pages to access different information from the database.

Where to Go from Here

In this chapter, we showed you how generating HTML or XHTML from a database can be useful, which tools you have at your disposal, and which kinds of databases you can create, and we provided an overview of how to create pages from a database. Knowing how to integrate databases into your Web site can save hundreds if not thousands of hours of writing and maintaining HTML or XHTML pages and can add a whole new world of functionality to your site. Whether you're at a big company or organization, a small one, or somewhere in between, generating documents from a database offers you a powerful tool for giving users easy-to-use information.

Where to now?

◆ Chapter 6 covers HTML or XHTML forms.

◆ Chapter 15 gives you more information about Web servers.

◆ Chapter 18 shows you how to make your entire site searchable.

Chapter 18

Making Your Web Site Searchable

WHEN YOU MAKE YOUR Web site searchable, you give your site visitors flexibility in the way that they arrive at the information they're seeking. Rather than following the predefined links and path you set out on your site, users can jump to links to the information they've come to get. In this chapter, we're going to look at the techniques and tools you can use to add a search capability to your site.

First, we'll discuss the pros and cons of making your site searchable (doing so is not for every site), and then we'll talk about which search tools, known as *search engines*, are available and how to use them. Although some of this information gets into advanced concepts, your comfort level will be fine if you've read Chapter 15, which talks about understanding and using Web servers, and if you have a good grasp of the issues involved in HTML or XHTML coding.

This chapter covers the following topics:

◆ Exploring the benefits and drawbacks of a site search engine

◆ Using low-tech alternatives

◆ Preparing to implement a search service

◆ Choosing the right search service

Exploring the Benefits and Drawbacks of a Site Search Engine

One of the most important decisions that you, as a Web developer, must make is how to present navigation choices to your users. Some sites are carefully mapped to guide users through every step from point A to point B. Other sites use common navigation shortcuts, such as headers and footers or frames, to allow users to jump to specific points. Still other sites use database searches, and, of course, some sites combine any or all of these methods.

In addition to these methods, you have a more general tool for helping users find their way around your site: a search engine. A *search engine* is a tool that visitors can use to find words or phrases within your Web pages.

TIP   *If you've spent any time on the Internet, you've already used a search engine. For example, you may have tried AltaVista (`www.altavista.com`), Excite (`www.excite.com`), Google (`www.google.com`), or Yahoo! (`www.yahoo.com`), which all offer expedient ways to search the Internet. You simply enter a search query; the search engine plugs and churns for a second or two and then provides a list of results containing documents that should match your query.*

First, let's look at the benefits of providing a search engine on your site.

Benefits for Users

The primary benefit of including a search engine on your site is to provide users with the flexibility to access information in more than one way. That is, rather than forcing them to follow a predefined structure, you can include a search engine as an alternative route to information. In cases where the text and keywords you use are different from the ones your users have in mind when they arrive at your site, this alternative can be helpful.

In addition, a search engine can provide a list of pages on your site that include the keyword(s) users are looking for. Such a list can sometimes be a better starting point, depending on the text and links your site includes (and doesn't include).

Finally, search engines are often what users want to turn to when they can't find what they're looking for through the existing links.

Before you add a search engine to your Web site, though, be aware that while search engines do offer benefits, they have drawbacks as well—both for your users and for you, the site developer—as described in the following sections.

Potential Drawbacks for Users

As you're thinking about including a search engine on your site, carefully consider the following potential drawbacks it may pose to your users:

The results list can be overwhelming.   For example, if a user enters keywords that appear on a significant number of pages on your site, the results list may include more hits than users would want to wade through. Or, if `meta` elements included in the header of your documents aren't included or if the element's content isn't well developed, the search results may not be as specific or relevant as users would expect.

Users may have to spend time figuring out how your search feature works.   As we describe later in this chapter, search engines' capabilities and functionality can vary a bit, depending on the implementation you choose. To achieve useful results with your site's search engine, users may have to ask themselves certain questions: How much of the site's content (and what, specifically) is available through the search? Does the search feature use *Boolean language queries* (queries, for example, where keywords can be separated by AND or OR, and where keywords can be grouped with quote marks)? And, if the search results don't provide links to information, is that because the search query wasn't structured properly? Or does it indicate a problem with the search feature? Or is the problem simply user error, such as a typo or a keyword that was too general to be useful? When users don't find what they're looking for using a site's search engine, they are forced to wonder (and take further search steps to determine) whether the information is there but they've not yet found it, or if the information just isn't there at all.

Users may get a narrower view of your site through search results than by exploring through links. A recent Usability Interface Engineering (UIE) report indicates that "search equals failure of the links" in that users generally opt to use a site's search feature after they've determined that the site's links didn't meet their needs. The report further notes that, in getting users to explore your site, search results provide a narrow view of the site and minimize the potential for users to "discover additional content that interests them." As a Web developer, you may think that if users know what they're looking for, then typing keywords into a search feature is the most intuitive and direct way to access information. On the contrary, the UIE report states that "users who used the search engine took an average of 5.1 clicks to find their content," compared to the 4.4 clicks for users who followed category links.

TIP   We highly recommend you read the UIE report, "Getting Them to What They Want: Eight Best Practices to Get Users to the Content They Want (and to Content They Didn't Know They Wanted)," which is available for a relatively nominal fee from `www.uie.com`.

Potential Drawbacks for Developers

In addition to potential drawbacks for your users, search engines pose potential drawbacks for you, the Web site developer. For starters, adding a search engine can eat up significant resources in terms of both time and money (although some very easy and cost-effective solutions do exist). Before you make your site searchable, be absolutely sure that you have the resources to maintain it (both the search technology and the site itself). Once your site is searchable, you have to keep it current; a search engine that returns outdated information or dead links is a sure way to drive users from your site.

Privacy may also be a concern if your site contains sensitive documents. When dealing with search engines, there's no such thing as "security by obscurity." Be sure that you index only those pages that you want to be searchable, or don't add a search engine to your site. See the sidebar "A Word about Indexing" for information about how this works.

Another concern is site coherency. If your site has a clear, predefined path that you want users to traverse, adding a search engine may defeat the purpose of the predefined path. In your planning process, consider the type of site you're building and whether a search engine fits with the scheme.

A WORD ABOUT INDEXING

The terms *index, indexing,* and *indexer* appear often in this chapter, and their use in this electronic context is similar to their traditional use. In the index at the back of this book, important words appear in alphabetic order along with the number of the page(s) on which they're located. The purpose of an index is to help readers quickly locate a topic of interest.

The purpose of a computer index is very similar. All, or most, of the words in a group of files are listed along with their locations. If you want a specific word or concept, you can simply look it up in the index.

Once the index exists, special programs called *search front ends* allow users to search the index for relevant documents. The programs that create the index are called *indexers* and include applications such as Glimpse (`http://glimpse.cs.arizona.edu/`) or ht://Dig (`www.htdig.org`).

Using Low-Tech Alternatives

As described in the previous sections, including a search engine on your site does have some significant drawbacks, both for you and your users. If you think a search engine may not be the best solution for your Web site but you would still like to add some searching functionality, you might consider some of the following alternatives. These approaches don't involve the overhead or resource drain associated with adding and maintaining a search engine.

TIP   *Most of the best sites on the Internet use a combination of the approaches we describe in this chapter. As you can see, you can improve site navigation without a search engine.*

Developing Effective Navigation Menus

In Chapter 12, we discussed textual and graphical navigation menus—what they are and how to use them effectively. As a low-cost alternative to using a site search engine, navigation menus can be valuable. When planning your site's menus, keep the following tips in mind:

◆ Place navigation menus so that users can quickly and intuitively access them. Put the menus where users would most likely look to find them (given other page elements), and place them in the same location across all the pages of your site.

◆ Include in your navigation menus categories of information that use topics and keywords your users will be looking for.

◆ Ensure that your links use keywords that are familiar and helpful to your users.

TIP   *Ironically, a search engine's log is an excellent resource for finding out what keywords and terms your users are looking for.*

◆ Make sure that the keywords you choose for both categories and links do not overlap in meaning. Users should easily understand the difference in content behind links.

◆ Do not use catchy, ambiguous, or nondescriptive words or phrases in your category names or links. If the section contains content on employment topics, use the word "Employment" or "Jobs," not "The Job Store" or some such contrived name or jargon.

◆ Categories and links should be accompanied by descriptions of what they include.

◆ Provide alternative text (using the `alt` attribute, on the `img` element) if you're using graphical navigation.

Using "Breadcrumbs"

Breadcrumbs are those little navigation menus that you often see on larger Web sites that indicate where in the site a page is located. For example, in Figure 18.1, the breadcrumbs indicate that the page is in the User's Advocate feature of the Magazine area of the TECHWR-L site.

FIGURE 18.1

The TECHWR-L site breadcrumbs are located toward the top of every site page, helping users quickly locate where they are in the site

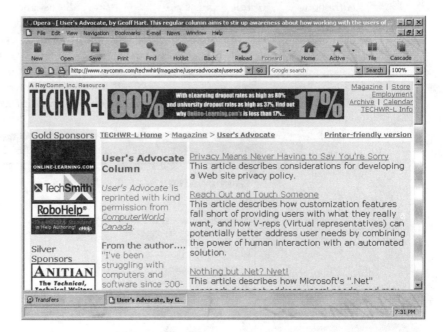

Although breadcrumbing is most often used along with a database backend, you can also use them in non-database sites, as long as you have a well-defined folder structure in place. If you have a small site, you can insert them manually. On larger sites, a variety of tools exist to automate the process. Visit `www.hotscripts.com` and search for "breadcrumb" to find more details and some sample scripts.

Taking the Guided Tour Approach

The guided tour approach is basically a series of HTML or XHTML pages with, at the extreme, only one link on each page: the link to the next page. This is probably the simplest and the least-flexible solution. Most sites that use this approach also provide links to the previous page and to the home page. However, it all amounts to the same thing—the user travels a set path and is not encouraged to deviate from that path.

Whether this approach will work for you depends on the type of site you're creating. This approach works well, for example, in the context of an online book, which might include links only to the next page, to the previous page, and to the table of contents.

Using Hierarchical Menus

Shortly before the advent of the Web, another method of information distribution became popular: gopher. *Gopher* is a predominantly text-based series of menus, similar to the one shown in Figure 18.2, that consists of links to either files or other menus, which may be on the same server or another.

Although the Web stole gopher's glory, gopher sites still exist and you can view them with any major Web browser. Many of the first Web sites looked just like gopher sites. Of course, the documents were more attractive because HTML could do what plain text never could, but the interface was still a series of hierarchical menus leading to a file.

If you want simplicity and ease of use, consider using hierarchical menus—built with HTML or XHTML, however—on your site. Users are familiar with menu structures and know how to use them. But let's face it: menus are boring when compared with the many visually appealing approaches.

FIGURE 18.2

A gopher site

Using a Back-of-the-Book Index

For many people seeking information in books, the traditional back-of-the-book index is an invaluable tool. You can create a similar tool for your Web site users by either manually (and somewhat laboriously) or automatically providing a site index. Although site indexes can require tedious maintenance, they do have the potential for helping your users find and use information on your site quickly and easily.

Figure 18.3 shows an index produced by HTML Indexer, a tool that helps you automatically generate a site index. You can find out more about this tool at `www.html-indexer.com`.

FIGURE 18.3

HTML Indexer is a handy tool for generating a site index

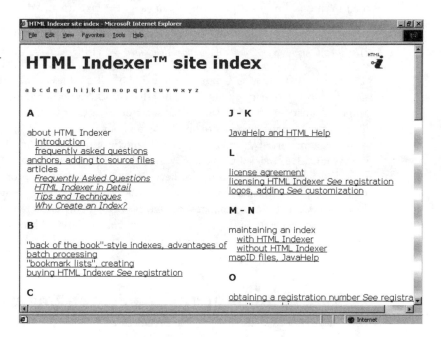

TIP   *A site index is an excellent tool for showing the breadth and depth of content on your site and for providing a resource users are familiar with.*

Using JavaScript

Perhaps one of the most useful JavaScript applications is one that allows users to search your site. It's fairly simple to run and does not require a full-blown search engine. Similar to the site index, a JavaScript search application can require a lot of maintenance and does not do very well with large sites, but it helps users find information quickly. You'll find JavaScript that you can copy, paste, and add to your site at `http://javascript.internet.com`.

Adding a Site Map

Even if you've lived in the same neighborhood your entire life, you probably need a map to get around the rest of the city. And when you visit a city for the first time, you most definitely need a map to find your way around. The same is true when you visit Web sites. After you've visited a site several times, you usually know where to find what you want, but on your first visit (especially if you arrive via a link), you may have no idea where you've landed or what else is on the site.

One solution to this problem is a *site map*, which is a page that includes a structural overview of the site. It could take the form of a traditional map, a tree structure, or simply a list of pages and their locations. From site maps, users can gauge the breadth and depth of the site, determine where they are within the site, and figure out how to go to another section.

TIP   A site map is an excellent solution for helping users get to the content they're looking for.

The simplest site map is a directory listing of all the files at the site. This solution is not necessarily ideal (or fascinating), but it can be effective. On the other hand, a site map can be completely graphical, giving users an instant, visual sense of what the site contains. You can create an animated, interactive site map using Java or similar technology.

Many commercial Web servers (such as SuiteSpot from Netscape, `http://home.netscape.com/suitespot/v3.5/index.html`) come with tools that allow you to easily generate graphical site maps. In addition, NetObjects Fusion (`www.netobjects.com`), Microsoft FrontPage (`www.microsoft.com/frontpage`), Macromedia Dreamweaver (`www.macromedia.com/software/dreamweaver/`), and Adobe GoLive (`www.adobe.com/products/golive/main.html`) include site-mapping programs. These programs do not generate site map pages for the public, but instead generate site maps for your use. With these, you can add and modify pages and move them around the hierarchy of your site, among many other things.

Preparing to Implement a Search Engine on Your Site

If you've examined all the options and have decided that adding a search engine to your site is worth the effort, the next step is to decide how to enable users to search within your site. Before you index your first page, answer the following questions (which are discussed in detail in the following sections):

◆ How much of your site will be indexed?

◆ Who can access your search engine?

◆ What can you do to improve the search engine's performance?

How Much of Your Site Will Be Indexed?

If you're absolutely confident that you want everyone to be able to hunt down every word on your site, the answer to this question is easy: Index the entire site. However, for most people, there are gray areas, and this question requires a great deal of thought. The following are some sections of your site that probably should not be indexed:

◆ Pages that exist only to help you maintain the site

◆ Any password-protected pages

TIP   You want password-protected information hidden from the public. Therefore, you can index those pages on a separate search engine that is accessible only from the password-protected area. Also, you don't want to annoy users by allowing them to link to a blocked area that they're then forbidden to access.

Before you put your search engine online, go through each page on your site (or each section if you have a large site) and decide whether you want to allow it on the search engine. If other people have a stake in the content of your site, be sure to have their consent before making their pages available via the search engine. Do not assume that a page should be on a search engine just because it's publicly available.

Who Can Access Your Search Engine?

As with the first question, if you want your site available to all users, this answer is easy: everybody. However, you may want to restrict access to the search engine to a selected group of people or keep a selected group of people out.

The easiest way to do this is to place a search program within a password-protected area of your site. With most search engines, you can create separate indexes for different parts of your site. This allows you to restrict access on a section-by-section basis.

TIP   Be sure that it's not possible to retrieve a reference to a password-protected page from a publicly available area of your Web site.

After you choose the parts of your site to index and decide who will have access to the index, make a list of all the directories that you will index. Almost all search engines index by directory. If you have a directory in which you want some files to be indexed but not other files, you'll probably have to split the directory into two directories—only one of which will be searchable. After you have a list of all the directories and files on your server, select the directories you want to index.

NOTE   If your Web server is on a Unix machine, run the command `ls -lR` from the root of your Web site to produce a list of all files within the site (not counting pages in user directories). From a Windows machine, use `dir /s` at a DOS prompt. On a Macintosh machine, use the system utilities to view a directory tree.

TIP   See Chapter 14 for information about a `robots.txt` file, which can keep spiders and indexers out of specific parts of your Web site.

What Can You Do to Improve the Search Engine's Performance?

Finally, before you begin researching specific search engine options, consider using these tips to help maximize the search engine's performance once it's in place on your site. Search technologies vary a bit in how they come up with the results lists; however, these tips will be generally useful:

◆   Use the `meta` element, and use it well. Plan to include the `meta` element and its `description` and `keyword` attributes, as discussed in Chapter 2. When choosing text and keywords to include, remember to think like the users of your site and not simply include text and keywords *you* happen to think of.

TIP   If you use a template, or use a basic HTML or XHTML document to copy and paste from, be careful to update the meta *information for each new document you create. It's easy to forget, and doing so helps ensure that search result links go to the content that users expect to find.*

◆   Use headings appropriately. Some search engine technologies use headings to help determine how closely a document matches the search query—figuring that if a word is used in a heading, it must be more important than words used only in paragraph text.

Choosing the Right Search Engine for Your Needs

Choosing the right search engine depends on your equipment and resources. The search engine choices for a Unix server are different from those for a Windows or Macintosh system. However, one commonality is the need for power. In general, search engines are resource intensive. Large amounts of hard disk space (often in the tens-of-gigabytes range) are needed to store the site index, and fast CPUs with lots of RAM are needed to run the front end for the searches. As in most cases, trade-offs are possible, and you can run a functional search engine with modest hardware. Still, if you want the performance of, for example, Google (in which a large portion of the entire Web is indexed but searches can still seem instantaneous), you have to pay for Google-level hardware, which is expensive.

Hosted Solutions

Some of the best solutions for the small to medium-sized Web site are the solutions hosted elsewhere on the Web by a service provider that takes care of indexing the site, serving up search results, and maintaining everything. These services are often quite inexpensive, at least for small sites, but can get pricey as your site grows. That said, they are certainly worth considering for most sites, because such a service relieves you of the need to manage the technology.

You may find that using an existing search engine will do the trick. Many of the big-name search engines, such as AltaVista or Google, allow you to use their search technology on your site.

NOTE   Use your favorite Web browser to view the source code of your favorite search service home pages to get some more ideas.

GOOGLE

For example, suppose you want to include the Google search engine on your site. Just go to the Google site (www.google.com), follow the link to Search Solutions, then fill out the forms to sign up for the free search service (it takes less than 5 minutes). They'll provide you with the code you need. After that, just find the place on the page where you want the search engine to go, and then include the code they provide (we were given the following):

```
<!-- Search Google -->
<center>
<FORM method=GET action=http://www.google.com/custom>
<TABLE bgcolor=#FFFFFF cellspacing=0 border=0>
<tr valign=top><td>
```

```
<A HREF=http://www.google.com/search>
<IMG SRC=http://www.google.com/logos/Logo_40wht.gif border=0
     ALT=Google align=middle></A>
</td>
<td>
<INPUT TYPE=text name=q size=31 maxlength=255 value="">
<INPUT type=submit name=sa VALUE="Google Search">
<INPUT type=hidden name=cof VALUE="AH:center;S:http://www.raycomm.
     com/techwhirl/;AWFID:f058688c78e10f4e;">
<font face=arial,sans-serif size=-1><input type=hidden name=domains
     value="raycomm.com"><br><input type=radio name=sitesearch value=""
     checked> Search WWW <input type=radio name=sitesearch
     value="raycomm.com"> Search raycomm.com </font><br>
</td></tr></TABLE>
</FORM>
</center>
<!-- Search Google -->
```

LETTING USERS SEARCH GOOGLE FROM YOUR SITE

In addition to using Google as a search engine for your own site, you can include a Google search on your site that searches Google itself for results. Google provides the text to use after you sign up; then all you have to do is paste it in.

ATOMZ SEARCH

Atomz Search is a hosted Web site search engine service. No special software is required to use Atomz Search because the application is hosted on the Atomz Search server. Three different types of services are currently available:

Atomz Express Search Free for sites with fewer than 500 pages, it indexes page title, keyword meta elements, description meta elements, and page content. Templates are provided, but the design layout can be changed to match the rest of your site. An Atomz Search logo appears on the search results page, but no additional banners or ads are required to use this free service.

Atomz Prime Search Atomz Prime offers advanced features, such as search reports showing what words or phrases users are using to search your site. You can set up daily site re-indexing if the content changes that frequently, or request re-indexing on demand when site content changes. Price is based on the number of pages in the site.

Atomz Enterprise Search More advanced features are available in Atomz Enterprise, including incremental indexing, parallel indexing, e-commerce support, and intranet support. Find out more information on Atomz Search at www.atomz.com.

For more information on similar search technologies, including comparative reviews, see www.searchtools.com/tools/tools-remote.html.

Unix Solutions

Perhaps the most common type of Web site found throughout the Internet is medium sized and powered by a Unix-based (usually a free Unix, such as Linux or FreeBSD) server running Apache Web Server. Because of the power and affordability of free Unix derivatives, as well as the decreasing costs of a permanent Internet connection, almost anyone can set up a Web server.

Creating a search engine for a site like this usually involves some programming, but the results can be effective. A free indexing system such as Glimpse is usually a good choice in this situation. You can then use either Webglimpse or SWISH as a search front end, but, in most cases, if you have the programming help available, the best bet is to create your own search front end that allows customized searches.

Unlike in the Windows world, few Unix solutions depend on a specific Web server. Some of these products are based on a scripting language such as PHP or Perl, in which case you need the language interpreter on your Web server machine (but it's probably already there). Still other products are distributed in source-code-only form. In such cases, you need a C compiler (and for some products, a C++ compiler) on your Web server machine (but again, it's probably already there).

TIP *If special software is needed, we've noted the requirement in the following descriptions.*

Here is a list of the most popular Unix search solutions:

Simple Search   Simple Search is a Perl script, offered by Matt's Script Archive, that implements a search according to your HTML or XHTML documents' `title` element. It's fairly straightforward to implement, and it's a great solution for small or low-traffic sites. Find Simple Search at `www.worldwidemart.com/scripts/`.

Glimpse   The University of Arizona created Glimpse as a kinder, gentler text-searching mechanism. Glimpse includes a text indexer and searching program with a myriad of simple, easy-to-use options for creating powerful searches. Additionally, an offshoot project called Webglimpse makes an entire site searchable. Find Glimpse at `http://glimpse.cs.arizona.edu/`.

ht://Dig   San Diego State University created ht://Dig to index its (then small) campus Web site. Designed for small sites and intranets, ht://Dig is fast and easy to use. It's not limited to a single server and can index pages from several related Web servers. It includes many features not found in larger search engines, such as *fuzzy searching* (searching for words using phonetic sounds or synonyms). You need a C compiler and a C++ compiler to implement this search engine on your site. You can find this search engine at `www.htdig.org`.

WAIS   In many ways, Wide Area Information Server (WAIS) is the grandfather of the current crop of search engines such as SWISH (see below), Glimpse, and the like. The official WAIS is a commercial product that has passed through several owners in the past few years, and is currently not available. However, there are a couple of freely available offshoots, such as freeWAIS and freeWAIS-sf. All versions of WAIS are robust and include many types of searches and even different ways of searching. Depending on the version you're using, creating a search interface can range from moderately tricky to downright impossible. You can find freeWAIS at `www.ensta.fr/internet/unix/wais/freewais.html`, and freeWAIS-sf is available at `http://ls6-www.informatik.uni-dortmund.de/ir/projects/freeWAIS-sf/`.

SWISH SWISH is a combination indexing/searching solution that you can also use as a searching-only front end to the WAIS indexer. SWISH was developed by Kevin Hughes of EIT as a WAIS-like indexing program and has many of the features of that system. SWISH has the advantage of small index files (generally about 1 to 5 percent of the total files you are indexing) and fast response time. You can find the latest version of SWISH, SWISH-E, at `http://swish-e.org/`. A C++ version, SWISH++, is available at `http://homepage.mac.com/pauljlucas/software/swish/` and can be run not only on Unix but also on Windows 95/98/NT.

mnoGoSearch mnoGoSearch is a combination indexing/searching solution that provides very flexible search capabilities. mnoGoSearch can use its own internal database for search indexes and tables, or it can use many of the commonly available database programs, including MySQL, PostgreSQL, and many more. mnoGoSearch provides a very flexible solution that easily scales to hundreds of thousands of documents, but configuring it can be a bit tricky. You can find the latest version at `www.mnogosearch.com`. The software is free on all platforms other than Windows, and a time- and feature-limited Windows version is available to try before you buy.

Windows Solutions

In the world of Microsoft Windows, the type of search engine you use for your Web site depends largely on the Web server you're running. Few third-party search engine front ends, and fewer still Web indexers, are available for Windows. Luckily, almost all the major commercial Web servers for Windows come with tools that allow you to index your site and make it searchable.

The second largest (and fastest-growing) segment of the Web server population consists of corporate sites that use Windows NT Server, and possibly even Windows 2000 Server. Most of these sites run Netscape SuiteSpot or the Microsoft Internet Information Server (called Internet Information Services in Windows 2000 and XP).

Creating a search engine for either of these servers is a simple matter of using the indexing tools that come with the server. Netscape Catalog Server and Microsoft Index Server are almost identical in form and function: Both allow you to easily select the areas of your site that you want to index and then automatically update the index. Both provide front ends and allow most common searches. Both allow you to create a custom front end, but neither makes it easy, and it's usually more trouble than it's worth.

TIP If you install Perl on the machine running your Web server, you can also use the Perl-based Unix solutions previously mentioned, such as Simple Search.

The most common utility for Microsoft is Index Server, which is a search application included as part of Internet Information Server (IIS). It can search and index ASCII text files, HTML files, and files created by the Microsoft Office and BackOffice suites of products. It can also search for document properties and HTML tags. It requires that IIS or Peer Web Server run continuously. However, once you've set it up, all index updates, optimization, and even crash recovery are automatic.

Where to Go from Here

In this chapter, we explored the world of interactive search engines. As you saw, although adding a search feature to your site does offer some benefits, you must keep in mind a few significant potential drawbacks. Fortunately, you can use some low-tech alternatives, as well as take advantage of existing search engines. If you do decide to use a search engine on your site, the advice and resources in this chapter should help you determine your needs and help you maximize the search engine's usefulness for your site visitors.

Where to now?

◆ See Chapter 6 for more information about forms.

◆ See Chapter 7 to find out how to use frames to provide navigation shortcuts to your users.

◆ See Chapter 12 for more information about planning navigation for your site.

◆ See Chapter 14 for information about publicizing your site.

◆ See Chapter 17 to find out how to use databases to provide other types of searches at your site.

Part 6

HTML and XHTML Development Tools

Chapter 19

Choosing Development Tools

CHOOSING THE DEVELOPMENT TOOLS that are right for you can be a daunting task. You'll find tons of software out there—both for developing documents and for developing and editing images.

In this chapter, we'll examine the options and take a look at some specific tools. Because XHTML is still relatively new as markup languages go, the only full-fledged development software choices you have are HTML- and XML-centric software packages. Obviously, if you're developing HTML documents, this will not pose a problem, but for XHTML, it could be more challenging. We'll discuss what each tool has to offer, point out any drawbacks, and recommend some tools. We can't tell you which tool to choose, but we can provide you with information that will help you determine which tools are best for your needs.

This chapter covers the following topics:

◆ Selecting development tools

◆ Comparing text editors and WYSIWYG editors

◆ Discovering XML development tools

◆ Getting to know some image-editing software

Choosing an Editing Tool

In general, there's no "right" kind of tool for developing HTML documents. It depends on you—your needs, preferences, and budget. In the following sections, we'll examine the three categories of development tools:

◆ Text editors, which give you a place to type and sometimes help with elements and attributes

◆ WYSIWYG editors, which give you a view of approximately how your document might look in a Web browser, and handle most of the coding for you

◆ High-end WYSIWYG editors, which provide the capabilities of WYSIWYG editors, plus Web site management tools

Text Editors

You use a text editor when you want to manually enter HTML or XHTML elements and attributes. If you've been following the sample markup in this book and entering elements and attributes, you've been using a text editor.

Although hand-coding HTML or XHTML is somewhat time-consuming and requires careful proofreading, doing so gives you much more flexibility and control over the documents you create. For example, when the XHTML specification became available, developers using text editors could immediately incorporate the latest XHTML rules and changes. However, developers using WYSI-WYG editors could not immediately make their documents XHTML-compliant; they're still waiting for the software to catch up with the latest specification.

Text editors come in two varieties:

◆ Plain text

◆ Enhanced

Plain-text editors, such as Notepad (Windows), Simple Text (Macintosh), and vi (Unix), offer nothing more than text-editing capabilities. Figure 19.1 shows a basic XHTML document in Notepad.

Enhanced editors, such as HomeSite and HTML-Kit (shown in Figure 19.2), give you editing capabilities and automated commands that let you add markup with a click of the mouse.

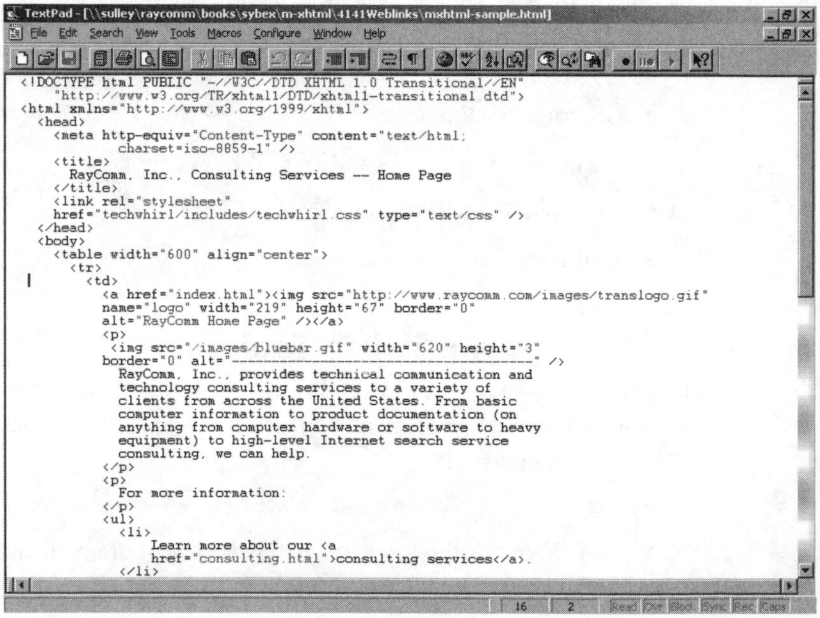

FIGURE 19.1

Plain-text editors, such as Notepad or TextPad, shown here, give you flexibility but no real help in creating HTML or XHTML documents

FIGURE 19.2

Some enhanced editors, such as HTML-Kit, provide space for you to enter code, as well as buttons and menu options that add code for you

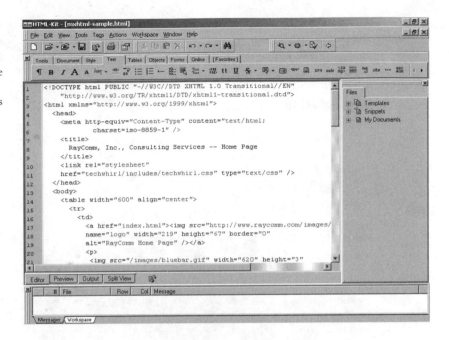

HTML-Kit, like most enhanced code-based editors, also offers a preview mode that mimics WYSIWYG (shown in Figure 19.3) as well as integration with HTML Tidy. The difference between these and true WYSIWYG editors is that you cannot make any editing changes in the preview mode.

FIGURE 19.3

Some enhanced text editors, such as HTML-Kit, display previews of the results

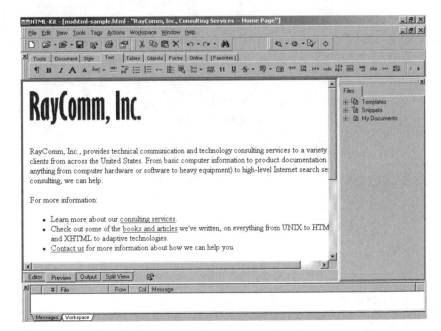

Whether you use a plain-text editor or an enhanced editor depends on your specific needs. If you want some help entering elements and attributes, use an enhanced editor. If you don't mind doing all the typing yourself or if you simply prefer a smaller, faster editor, you'll probably choose a plain-text editor.

WYSIWYG Editors

A WYSIWYG (What You See Is What You Get) editor lets you see roughly how the document will look in a browser as you're creating it. Rather than entering elements and attributes and then viewing the results in a browser, you can preview documents as you create them. Most WYSIWYG editors display only the actual text, not the markup (unless you choose to view the markup). Figure 19.4 shows how this works in Dreamweaver. For more information on Dreamweaver, visit `www.macromedia.com/software/dreamweaver/`.

FIGURE 19.4

Most WYSIWYG editors, such as Dreamweaver, don't display markup by default—only an approximation of what the page will look like in a browser

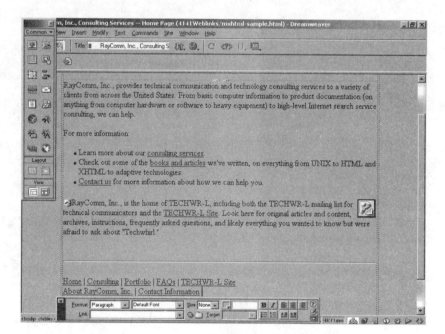

Other HTML WYSIWYG editors include:

◆ NetObjects Fusion MX `www.netobjects.com/products/html/nfmx.html`

◆ Adobe GoLive 6 `www.adobe.com/products/golive/main.html`

◆ Microsoft FrontPage `www.microsoft.com/frontpage/`

Although these editors can be rather expensive, they give you great control over formatting and can help you develop really spiffy Web pages.

High-end WYSIWYG editors treat page elements as objects, meaning that you can click and drag elements around on the page and place them where you want. In doing so, you can create interesting layouts that should look fairly consistent from browser to browser.

Most WYSIWYG editors also provide site-management services, which help you see how pages in the site connect and relate. For example, take a look at Figure 19.5, which shows Microsoft Front-Page. Each time you create a page, FrontPage automatically adds the page to the overall structure. All you have to do is name the page and add content to it.

Many WYSIWYG editors also include templates. For example, using the FrontPage Wizard, you can choose from several templates (called *themes* in FrontPage lingo), dozens of page options, and various color and background options. Similarly, in NetObjects Fusion, most templates include a banner, link buttons, bullets, and other formatting options. Templates come in a range of styles, from fun, as shown in Figure 19.6, to the more practical. And, if you want, you can pick and choose elements from the templates or start from scratch and create your own.

FIGURE 19.5

WYSIWYG editors, such as FrontPage, help you manage your site

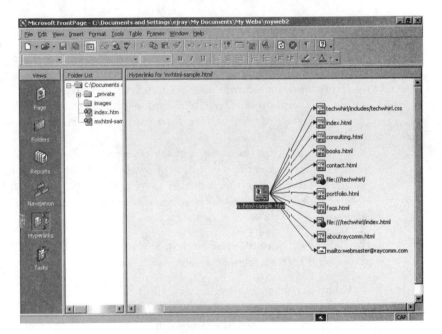

FIGURE 19.6

FrontPage templates provide formatting (themes) for all kinds of page elements

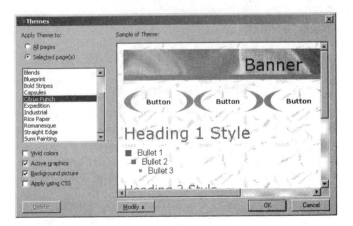

ADVANTAGES

WYSIWYG editors offer you a middle ground between ease of use and the ability to do exactly what you want with your Web pages. With a WYSIWYG editor, you can do the following:

◆ Quickly develop acceptable Web pages

◆ Create documents about as fast as you can type

◆ Add effects just by clicking a button or by choosing an option from a drop-down menu

◆ Concentrate more on the content because you see the text and formatting, and not the markup

DISADVANTAGES

Some drawbacks are associated with WYSIWYG editors, however. The biggest is that WYSIWYG editors commonly produce nonstandard markup to provide the effects most users expect. For example, using Netscape Composer you can indent page elements simply by clicking the Indent button. Although the ability to indent elements might be handy, the HTML and XHTML specifications don't provide any sort of element or attribute for indention (although you can indent using the CSS1 `text-indent` property). So, in this example, Composer produces nonstandard markup—and relies heavily on luck to work in most browsers.

Another drawback is that the WYSIWYG aspect is somewhat misleading. As we've mentioned throughout this book, the exact results of HTML and XHTML markup can vary significantly from browser to browser and from computer to computer. If you compare the WYSIWYG preview in any of these editors with the results in an actual browser, you might find that the display is somewhat different.

TIP   Check out Chapter 20 to find out how to validate your HTML and XHTML documents to fix the nonstandard markup that WYSIWYG editors sometimes produce.

A third drawback is that you can't use WYSIWYG editors to add the latest and greatest effects. For example, you couldn't use a WYSIWYG editor to add style sheets shortly after the release of the HTML 4 specification. The software companies have to develop the application after the latest specification or draft becomes available. For the time being, the best option is to use HTML Tidy (in one of its many forms) to clean up your documents, and to make sure your documents are valid and well formed. Chapter 8 of this book is devoted to converting HTML to XHTML and has an entire section on the various forms of HTML Tidy.

Discovering XML Development Tools

Some serious developers skip (X)HTML editors altogether and go straight for XML editors. Although XML editors do not recognize XHTML elements and attributes, they support DTDs, namespaces, and other XML-related features. If you choose to use an XML editor, we recommend that you create some basic XHTML templates to save you a little time.

You should be able to provide the editor with the appropriate DTD so you can use the XHTML elements and attributes. There's a chance, though, you may not be able to, so using these editors may be the equivalent of working with a text editor. However, if you use these tools, you can be sure that your XHTML documents comply with XML and the associated DTD, and therefore, XHTML rules, so your documents will definitely be well formed and valid.

XML Spy

XML Spy by Altova is more than just an XML editor. Using XML Spy, you can edit, create, and use existing DTDs; edit, view, and output XSL; edit XML Schemas, and more. If all of these terms seem too complicated, visit Part VI for more information about XML. XML Spy allows you to assign an existing DTD or schema to your documents. Therefore, using one of the XHTML DTDs with this tool is a definite possibility. Find out more about XML Spy at `www.xmlspy.com`.

XML Pro

XML Pro v2.0 by Vervet Logic isn't as versatile as XML Spy—it's simply an XML editor. You can't convert documents or create DTDs using XML Pro, but you can find out whether DTDs are valid. In addition, you need to have some in-depth knowledge of XML to be able to comfortably use XML Pro. You can find out more information about XML Pro at `www.vervet.com`.

epcEdit

If you want a flexible, powerful XML or XHTML (or HTML) editor, check out epcEdit (`www.epcedit.com`), shown in Figure 19.7. The interface is friendly and the tool is quite powerful—but probably not right for the XML or XHTML novice.

FIGURE 19.7

epcEdit shows the document structure, tags, and content

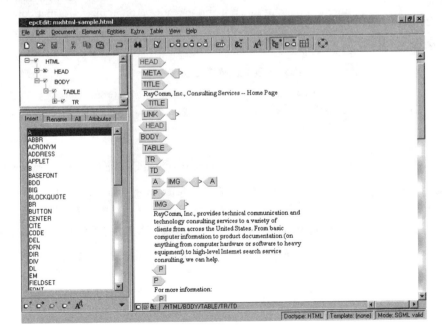

TIP   For information on a slew of XML tools, check out XMLSoftware at www.xmlsoftware.com. You'll find references to XML browsers, editors, parsers, conversion tools, and more on this site.

Choosing an Image-Editing Tool

Just as there's no "right" tool to generate HTML, there's also no one image-editing tool that will meet every need for every person. Which one you choose is up to you, your needs, and your budget. Here are some of the more popular image-editing tools:

Paint Shop Pro   Offers a wide range of capabilities, it's easy to use, and it's affordable. In fact, we used Paint Shop Pro to create the images used in the sample Web sites throughout this book. For more information, visit www.jasc.com.

Photoshop   Is a more expensive tool, but you can literally do anything with it. Take a look at any book or magazine cover—most were probably created with Photoshop. Unless you have very sophisticated image-editing needs or are already experienced with high-end image editing, this product might offer much more than you need. However, it's *the* tool if you're looking for power. For more information, check out www.adobe.com/products/photoshop/main.html.

GIMP   GIMP (GNU Image Manipulation Program) is a freely distributed program for Windows as well as Linux/Unix environments that is suitable for developing and editing images. Because GIMP is expandable with plug-ins and extensions, you can use it for a range of purposes, including as a simple paint program, an expert-quality photo-retouching program, an online batch-processing system, a mass production image renderer, or an image-format converter, among many other image-related uses. Find out more at www.gimp.org.

Where to Go from Here

So, those are your basic choices, folks! In this chapter, you saw the advantages and disadvantages of using text editors, WYSIWYG editors, and XML tools. You also got an idea of the image-editing tools you can use. Exactly which tools you choose depends on your specific needs.

From here:

◆   Visit Chapter 4 to learn how to include images in your documents.

◆   Take a look at Chapter 8 to learn more about converting your HTML documents to XHTML.

◆   See Part IV to learn how to use HTML or XHTML documents to develop Web sites.

◆   Go to Chapter 20 to learn about validation services.

Chapter 20

Validating HTML and XHTML Documents

BACK IN CHAPTER 1, we talked briefly about using a *validator*, which is a tool that examines your HTML or XHTML documents and verifies that they follow the rules for applying code and document structure. The DTD—the Document Type Definition, defined by the **doctype** element—defines what those document rules are; the validator checks your documents to see whether they followed the rules specified in the DTD. A document that complies with the DTD rules is said to be a *valid document*. A document that doesn't comply with the DTD rules is said to be...well, one that you need to work on some more.

In this chapter, we'll look at the following topics:

◆ Understanding validation

◆ Using the W3C validator

◆ Working with other available validators

Why Validate Your Documents?

Ultimately, only you can decide whether validation is a worthwhile exercise for your documents; however, we urge you to consider the pros and cons we present in this section. We want to candidly confess that we believe strongly in the virtues of validation and hope to sway you in that direction as you read through the pluses and minuses related to validation. Our hope is that we'll remain objective, but perhaps the best response to the question "Why validate?" is another question: "If you have to ask, why even bother with XHTML?"

First the validation pros:

◆ At a bare minimum, successful validation provides a guarantee that a document is syntactically correct and conforms to all of the rules set out by the DTD. Although browsers commonly accommodate and correctly display HTML code that isn't syntactically correct or that doesn't follow the rules precisely, remember that XHTML documents must be valid.

◆ With more and more markup being generated programmatically—such as from Active Server Pages (ASP), JavaServer Pages (JSP), PHP, database management systems, ColdFusion, and so forth—validation helps ensure that mechanically generated code is sound and error-free.

◆ Conformance to certain DTDs or XML Schemas (discussed in Chapter 29) is essential to ensure that specific modularizations for XHTML are used; therefore, when documents must work on personal digital assistants (PDAs), cell phones, or embedded systems, validation ensures that only legal markup is used.

◆ Next-generation software tools—including Web browsers—are expected to demand definitions for governing DTDs or XML Schemas to drive document parsing. As is already the case with some XML (and SGML) tools, such software may refuse to parse (and therefore display) documents that do not include DTD or XML Schema references and that do not validate against such references. Because this approach greatly simplifies (and therefore shrinks) the client software used to read and display XML and XHTML documents, it's expected to become an outright requirement for those same PDAs, cell phones, and embedded systems we mentioned earlier.

The bottom line is that valid HTML ideally works in virtually all Web browsers, whereas invalid HTML works in some but not in others. Because what works best for the broadest range of users is eminently desirable, what better argument for validation could we propose?

And now for the validation cons:

◆ Careful coding and development may be required to create documents that will validate, if you build them by hand. Alternatively, if you use a development tool that requires a DTD or an XML Schema from which to work, it's impossible to create invalid documents.

◆ Extra work and effort is required both to submit documents for validation and to keep working with them until they validate successfully.

◆ Validators don't always track new developments, specifications, or related DTDs and XML Schemas exactly. (As we write this chapter, in fact, to validate an XHTML 1.1 document certain workarounds are necessary—these include validating to the XHTML 1.0 Strict DTD instead of an XHTML 1.1 modularized DTD—and hand-checks are required to make sure no markup outside the restricted subset occurs in any XHTML document that uses only a subset of legal XHTML 1.0 markup.)

On the whole, we think the pros beat the cons hands down, but you can make your own decision on the subject. (Hint: If you decide against validation, you don't need to read any further in this chapter!)

TIP   If you're interested in validation, and in keeping up with the latest and greatest validation tools and techniques, we recommend that you sign up for the www-validator mailing list at `http://lists.w3.org/Archives/Public/www-validator/`*. You can also browse the list archives from this Web page. Past postings and current traffic are excellent sources of information about HTML, XHTML, related DTDs and schemas, and validation tools or techniques of all kinds.*

The Validation Process

Although the details vary, here's a step-by-step breakdown of what's involved in validating documents. Again, you'd use this same process for both HTML and XHTML documents; we're using XHTML as the example throughout the rest of this chapter:

1. Grab the document you want to validate or some other relevant document—we also cover a couple of Cascading Style Sheets (CSS) validators in this chapter—that you'd like to check for correctness and completeness.

2. Present that document to a validator (such as those we discuss throughout much of this chapter).

3. Read the validator's output, and respond to any error messages or warnings you might find by correcting the code.

4. Repeat the previous two steps until the validator produces no error messages—only warnings that you do not feel compelled to heed (usually, this requires changing your document to avoid certain markup elements, particularly deprecated elements).

If you recall from Chapter 1, some rules apply to both HTML and XHTML documents—for example, the rules for nesting elements correctly. Other rules, such as closing all elements (among several others), apply to XHTML documents. As you've been applying the rules outlined in Chapter 1 throughout this book, you're probably pretty good at using them by now; however, you'll often find that inadvertently breaking these rules is the cause of your documents being invalid:

◆ All XHTML elements must be closed.

◆ All attributes must have values.

◆ All attribute values must be enclosed in quotes ("").

◆ XHTML is case sensitive.

◆ Elements must be nested correctly.

TIP   *For detailed discussions and examples of these rules, revisit Chapter 1.*

Additionally, you'll often find that these common errors cause your documents to be invalid:

Ampersands in URLs   Many URLs contain ampersands; however, because the ampersand is a reserved character for XHTML, it's necessary to replace ampersands in URLs with the character entity (`&amp;`) so the validator does not flag this as an error. In fact, older browsers might also be unable to parse such URLs, so this is a good idea in any case. For example, you might change `http://www.example.com/test.pl?check&check` to `http://www.example.com/test.pl?check&amp;check`.

Invalid content model usage   When one markup element is nested within another, such nesting must be explicitly (or implicitly) part of the content model for the outermost element. The best way to be sure what's legal is to check the relevant DTD or to look in Master's Reference Part 1 of this book.

Invalid FPI   The name of the string that appears in quotes after the `PUBLIC` keyword in a `DOCTYPE` processing instruction is called a formal public identifier (FPI). The FPI is case sensitive; therefore, it's essential to match the formal declaration for any FPI exactly, or `"-//W3C/DTD XHTML 1.0 Strict//EN"` as an example. For precise FPI syntax, please visit "Choosing a DOCTYPE" at `www`
`.htmlhelp.com/tools/validator/doctype.html`, or refer to Chapter 1 of this book.

With a little practice, you'll become comfortable with your validator of choice. In the following sections, we present some of the better choices for such tools that are readily available online.

The W3C Validator

One of the easiest and best ways to validate an HTML or XHTML document is to use the W3C's free online validator. Provided by the W3C and easy to use, this validator is an excellent choice, and we'll discuss it in detail in the next few sections.

Validating a document using this tool is simple. You have two choices:

◆   You can point the validator to a public document on the Web. This option is handy for documents that you've already published or uploaded to a test site available on the Web.

◆   You can upload a local file. This option is handy for documents that you've not yet uploaded to the Web.

Validating Using the W3C's Web Interface

If the file you want to validate is on the Web, use this quick process:

   1.   Visit `http://validator.w3.org/`, as shown in Figure 20.1.

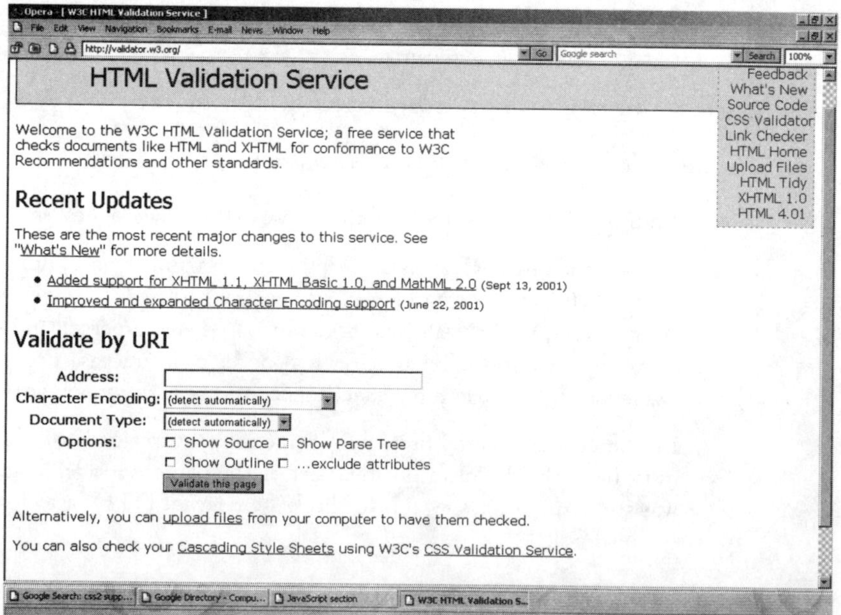

FIGURE 20.1

The primary interface for the W3C validator checks Internet-accessible documents

2. Enter the URL of the document in the Address field.

3. Select other options, if necessary:

   Character Encoding   Select the default value, Detect Automatically, to tell the validator to assume the character encoding that your Web server recommends when sending the page, or you can choose a particular encoding. Unless you know for sure that you must choose a different encoding, stick with the default value.

   Document Type   You can select the option Detect Automatically (which tells the validator to use the document's DOCTYPE declaration and other clues if necessary to determine the appropriate DTD), or you can select the version of XHTML or HTML you wish to use. You have eight options:

   XHTML 1.0 Strict

   XHTML 1.0 Transitional

   XHTML 1.0 Frameset

   HTML 4.01 Strict

   HTML 4.01 Transitional

   HTML 4.01 Frameset

   HTML 3.2

   HTML 2.0

WARNING   *If you specify a document type, be sure you specify the right one! Otherwise, you'll get a number of errors in the results, which may or may not reflect actual validation errors given the DTD you specified in the doctype element.*

   Show Source   Presents the user with a listing of the source document, including line numbers.

   Show Outline   Presents the user with a visual outline of the document based on heading markup.

   Show Parse Tree   Presents the user with a parsed tree of the document, using indentation for layout.

   Exclude Attributes   Tells the validator to exclude attributes from the parse tree. This function works only if you select to show the parse tree.

4. Click the Validate This Page button. The validator will do its work, and then return a report, which we discuss in the section "Translating Error Messages" later in this chapter.

Validating by Uploading a Document to the W3C Site

If the file you want to validate is on your local drive, you need to upload the file to the validator. To do this:

1. Visit http://validator.w3.org/.

2. Click Upload Files in the upper right of the window or under the Validate This Page button, then follow the Upload Files link to get to the page shown in Figure 20.2.

FIGURE 20.2

The file-upload interface for the W3C validator lets you select and upload single files

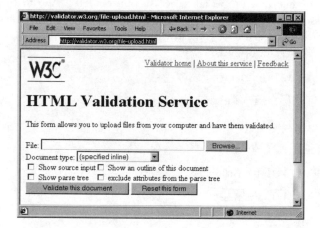

3. Click the Browse button.

4. Select the document to be validated from your hard drive.

5. Click the Validate This Document button. The validator will do its work, and then return a report, which we discuss next.

Translating Error Messages

If you make a mistake that violates any of the DTD's validity rules, or XML's well-formedness rules, the validator will present error messages. We used a sample document and ran it through the validator. The results are shown in Figure 20.3.

At first glance, the error messages seem a bit overwhelming. However, after you run a few documents through the validator, you'll get used to the cryptic messages. In Table 20.1, we've translated a few of the common error messages.

FIGURE 20.3

Some typical error messages

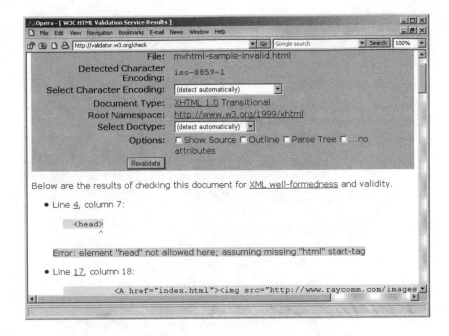

TABLE 20.1: COMMON W3C VALIDATOR ERROR MESSAGES

ERROR	TRANSLATION
Missing a required sub-element of "head"	You forgot to include a required child of the head element, such as the title element.
End tag for "p" omitted; end tags are required in XML for non-empty elements; empty elements require an end tag or the start tag must end with "/>"	You forgot to close the p element.
Required attribute "alt" not specified	You forgot to add the alt attribute to the img element, and it's required.
Element "p" not allowed here; possible cause is an inline element containing a block-level element	You accidentally nested a p element where it isn't allowed. Although the error message states "inline element containing a block-level element," the actual mistake made for this document involves the misuse of a block-level element.
End tag for "img" omitted; end tags are required in XML for non-empty elements; empty elements require an end tag or the start tag must end with "/>"	You forgot to terminate the empty element—for example, <img />.

Many other error messages can appear—and the possible causes of those errors are infinite. From experience, we can tell you that the easiest way to get your document to validate is to use the following process:

1. Submit your document.

2. Fix the first error reported. Don't get sidetracked into the actual error message if it's not immediately clear—the error is usually on the line mentioned or just above it, so just look for anything out of the ordinary.

3. Resubmit your document for validation. Even one little error at the top of a document can cause many other errors to appear (and go away as soon as the first error has been corrected), so fix the errors one at a time.

Adding the W3C Icon

If your HTML or XHTML document validates, and you receive a message like the following, you can add the appropriate icon to your Web page:

```
Congratulations, this document validates as XHTML 1.0
    Transitional!
```

The XHTML icon (shown in Figure 20.4) shows users that your page strictly conforms to the XHTML specification. Similarly, the HTML 4.01 icon shows that your page strictly conforms to the HTML 4.01 specification.

FIGURE 20.4

The XHTML icon appears when your document is validated against a DTD (in this case, the XHTML 1.0 Transitional DTD)

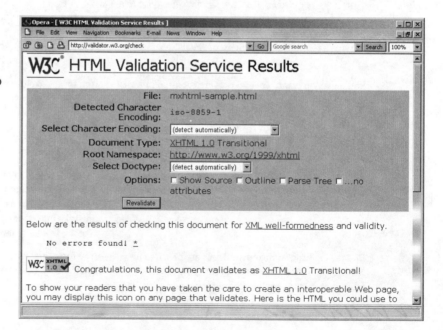

To add the icon to your page, just copy and paste the code suggested by the validator after your page has validated.

All in all, understanding the validator is not that difficult—just a bit tedious at times. Happy validating!

Working with Other Available Validators

Other validation services are available, and each has unique advantages and disadvantages over the others. If the W3C validator does not meet your needs exactly, feel free to check out some of the following validators.

The W3C Online CSS Validator

Because the W3C has deprecated much of the formatting-related markup in favor of style sheets (see Chapter 9), you'll likely be moving toward using style sheets, if you haven't already done so. Just as you use an HTML or XHTML validator to check your markup against specific DTDs, you can use a CSS validator to check inline or external style sheets against their governing specifications. The W3C CSS Validation Service page appears at `http://jigsaw.w3.org/css-validator/validator.html.en`, as shown in Figure 20.5.

In fact, the W3C CSS validator supports four ways to validate CSS instructions, whether they appear as inline text in HTML or XHTML documents, or in the form of stand-alone style sheets (ASCII text files that normally end with a `.css` extension):

- You can download the CSS validator to your local machine and perform validation there. Windows and a range of Unix systems are supported.

- You can validate a stand-alone CSS style sheet by URI—that is, by providing an Internet-accessible URL where the validator can access the document. An example of such access appears in Figure 20.6.

- You can validate an inline CSS style sheet by cutting the content of the `<style>...</style>` element and pasting it into a text area for analysis.

- You can validate a stand-alone CSS style sheet by uploading the file in which it resides for analysis, in much the same way you uploaded HTML or XHTML documents to the W3C validator in the preceding section.

Working with this tool will help you improve your understanding of style-sheet structures and syntax, because you'll learn as you interpret and act on its sometimes-arcane error and warning messages. As we became familiar with this tool, we found it extremely helpful to keep a good CSS reference handy to help us figure out exactly what the validator was trying to tell us. Start with the Master's Reference Part 2 from this book. If you need more depth, some good references include either of Eric A. Meyer's excellent CSS books from O'Reilly & Associates: *Cascading Style Sheets: The Definitive Guide*, ISBN 1565926226, or *CSS Pocket Reference*, ISBN 0596001207, as well as a couple of Web sites he's worked on, such as `www.meyerweb.com` and `http://style.webreview.com`.

FIGURE 20.5

The W3C CSS validator provides four ways to validate CSS instructions

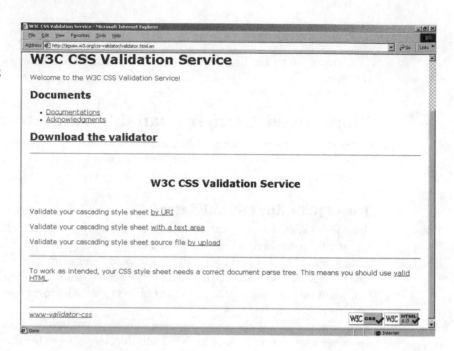

FIGURE 20.6

The W3C CSS Validation Service's URI-based interface lets you specify an Internet-accessible style sheet for analysis and reports your results

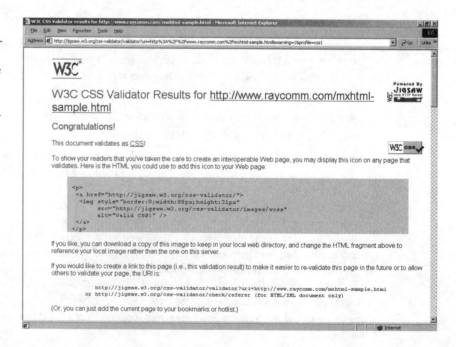

STG's Online XML Validator

Brown University in Providence, RI, is home to the Scholarly Technology Group (STG). This organization offers a general-purpose XML validation tool at `www.stg.brown.edu/service/xmlvalid/`. This tool is capable of handling XHTML documents, provided you edit such documents as needed to make sure they're also XML compliant.

The beauty of this tool is that it's useful for documents that include references to other XML namespaces, DTDs, or Schemas above and beyond those associated strictly with XHTML. If you're working with such hybrids, you'll find this tool an invaluable item in your validation toolbox, because it can handle just about anything you throw at it.

Although part of the interface to the STG XML Validation Form appears in Figure 20.7, the tool is capable of handling various kinds of input, including:

- ◆ File downloads, as shown in Figure 20.7, where a Choose button allows you to browse to the file to be uploaded and analyzed.

- ◆ URI access, where you can provide the address of an Internet-accessible document for analysis.

- ◆ Text box entry, where XML code can be pasted into a text area for analysis.

FIGURE 20.7

The STG XML Validation Form handles file uploads, URIs, and a paste buffer

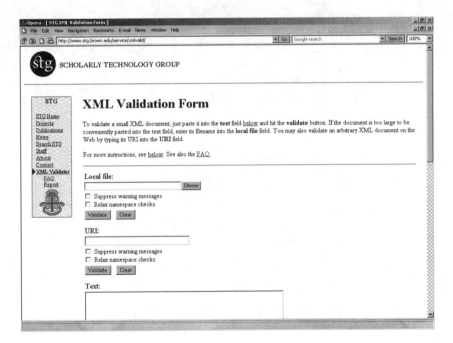

This tool is both easily accessible and quite convenient, particularly if you work in an environment where both XML and XHTML are broadly used (as many organizations are starting to do).

The WDG Validator

Under the oversight of Liam Quin, one of the developers of the W3C validator, the Web Design Group (WDG) has operated the HTML Help Web site for several years. An invaluable source for tools and information of all kinds, this site offers its own WDG validator at `www.htmlhelp.com/tools/validator/`. This tool appears to keep up with new and changed specifications much more quickly than its more official counterpart. In fact, the WDG validator supported the XHTML 1.1 Specification less than a month after its elevation to recommended status.

As with so many of the other tools of its ilk, the WDG validator supports URI-based validation of Internet-accessible files, upload and validation of local files from your current computer, and a text area into which you can paste markup for upload and subsequent analysis. Unlike many other such tools, however, this one also supports batch mode operation, where you can throw multiple URLs at it in a single file (one URL per line of text only) and it will happily chunk through as many of them as you'd care to line up in a row. The basic interface to the service, with its various options, appears in Figure 20.8.

FIGURE 20.8

The WDG Validator offers extra features, plus great documentation and support

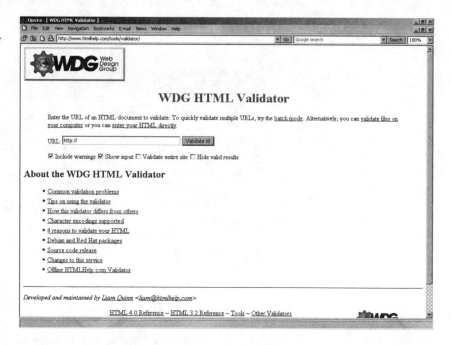

What we like best about the WDG validator is its infrastructure—that is, there's lots of documentation, additional information, and even access to source code for those alpha geeks interested in looking under the hood. Consequently, you'll find more information about common validation errors, tips on using the validator itself, rationales for validation, and so forth, than you'll find at other sites. Because it helps to soften the blow of learning to use a complex tool, this validator is recommended for those whose background in SGML, HTML, and markup terminology may not be as strong as they might like. This is particularly true for those who try the W3C validator and find themselves intimidated by its many and sometimes unintelligible error messages. In general, we find this validator's error messages a bit friendlier and therefore easier to understand.

TIP   Liam Quin also offers a Windows-compatible, downloadable tool called "A Real Validator," at `http://arealvalidator.com/`. *A 30-day evaluation copy is available for free; registration of this excellent tool costs a mere $30.00.*

WDG's CSSCheck

Simply as a friendlier alternative to the W3C's CSS validator, the WDG's CSSCheck is worth investigating. However, be warned that although this validator generally does a good job with CSS2 properties and selectors, it's not yet fully updated to support CSS2. For more information, or to try this tool, visit `www.htmlhelp.com/tools/csscheck/`. If you work with CSS and find the output from the W3C's tool intimidating, you might find that this one makes it a bit easier for you to understand what it's trying to tell you.

Page Valet

As we write this chapter, Page Valet is the only other XHTML validator (other than the validator from the W3C) equipped to handle XHTML 1.1. Page Valet is actually part of a suite of Web site–management tools called Site Valet (from a company named WebThing) that's available on a subscription basis. Although Page Valet is based on the W3C validator, it also does a good job of softening its error-reporting and warning messages, and it provides a generally friendlier validation tool than its official counterpart. You can access Page Valet at `http://valet.webthing.com/page/`. If properly invoked, Page Valet can also use an accessibility-enhanced DTD developed by the Web Design Group (mentioned previously in this chapter) to check XHTML and HTML documents for potential accessibility or backward compatibility problems with older Web browsers. For those interested in maximally accessible Web pages, this is a valuable added bonus. For more information about this DTD, visit `www.htmlhelp.org/design/dtd/`.

CAST's Bobby

In British English, a bobby is a (helpful and friendly) police officer; in the parlance of CAST (the Center for Applied Special Technology), Bobby is a friendly validation tool that looks for accessibility and usability violations that might keep those with disabilities from accessing or understanding content in a Web site. Section 508 of the U.S. Federal Rehabilitation Act requires that federal Web sites be accessible to people with disabilities, and Bobby is an important tool that can help organizations and agencies down the road meet this Act's requirements. In addition, because many federal contractors are also required to comply with this legislation, we see an "accessibility revolution" heading straight for the Web. Here again, Bobby can be a tremendous help. Visit `www.cast.org/bobby` for all kinds of information about accessibility and to access the Bobby service to check your HTML and XHTML documents for compliance with the Web accessibility initiative.

TIP   The National Cancer Institute has a great site on Section 508 information and initiatives at `www.niehs.nih.gov/websmith/508/home.htm`. *For the W3C's take on accessibility issues, please visit the Web Accessibility Initiative home page at* `www.w3.org/WAI/`. *Also, see Chapter 12 for information about planning for accessibility.*

Where to Go from Here

In this chapter, we explored the validation process for XML and XHTML documents. We covered the pros and cons regarding validation, and tried hard to make the case that validation is a good idea. Next, we examined the validation process in general, and took a look at a half-dozen available validation tools of several kinds. Now, not only should you be ready to make use of validation in working with XML and XHTML documents, but you should also be reasonably familiar with some interesting choices of tools and techniques to put the validation process to work.

Where to now?

◆ Chapter 1 provides a detailed discussion of the rules for applying HTML and XHTML elements and attributes.

◆ Chapter 19 discusses HTML and XHTML development tools, from FrontPage to Dreamweaver.

◆ Part VI introduces XML, covers extending XHTML with namespaces, and discusses creating a DTD.

◆ Master's Reference Part 2 provides a comprehensive listing of style sheet functions.

Part 7

A Bridge to XML

Chapter 21

An Overview of XML

WEB TECHNOLOGIES HAVE ALREADY provided much more useful and valuable tools than anyone could have envisioned only a few years ago. Along with the changes in Web site use and purpose have come many technological advances in Web-based information delivery. For example, as described in the Chapter 1 sidebar "Where Did HTML and XHTML Come From?", Microsoft and Netscape repeatedly extended HTML, adding features that provided flashy, useful effects that helped work around the limitations of basic, standard HTML 3.2. (Not all these features became part of the W3C recommendations, however.) The W3C has expanded the HTML standard on several occasions, each time adding a slew of features (some from the browser vendors) that let you more effectively control document appearance as well as make documents more accessible and usable.

However, these advances focus primarily on formatting Web sites. What's absent is an emphasis on technology that makes online information easy to present, maintain, and reuse. Even though you can create visually appealing Web sites with HTML or XHTML, you're limited to using simple document structures (*this is a heading; this is a paragraph*). You must employ complex and convoluted systems to automate information delivery, and maintaining documents is an exercise in tedium. A related technology changes this completely.

The *Extensible Markup Language (XML)* offers unique capabilities and flexibility. In particular, it bridges the gap between the two main markup languages, Standard Generalized Markup Language (SGML) and HTML, making the development of online information easier, more accessible, and more affordable. In this chapter, we'll introduce you to XML and show you how it handles specific needs that neither SGML nor HTML addresses directly.

This chapter covers the following topics:

◆ Understanding the purposes of markup languages

◆ Exploring the advantages and disadvantages of SGML

◆ Exploring the advantages and disadvantages of HTML and XHTML

◆ Understanding how XML bridges the gaps between SGML, XHTML, and HTML

Why Another Markup Language?

With HTML, SGML, and other markup languages available, you might be wondering why we need yet another such language. XML meets a specific need and compensates for certain limitations inherent in both SGML and HTML. We can most easily understand XML in the context of these other languages and their well-defined roles. So, before we dive into XML specifics in the "Understanding XML Markup" section, let's look at how these markup languages—SGML, HTML, XHTML, and XML—all relate to one another.

Understanding SGML Basics

SGML stands for Standard Generalized Markup Language and is based on work that Charles Goldfarb, Ed Mosher, and Ray Lorie undertook in the 1970s to create a platform-independent way of representing documents and their contents. This effort was so successful, in fact, that by 1986, SGML became enshrined as ISO standard 8879.

SGML is the original and the most powerful of the three markup languages we cover here. In fact, SGML lays a strong foundation for creating complex, large, or highly structured document sets. Using SGML, you can set up document rules that let you identify any structural part of a document, such as titles and subtitles, authors and editors, paragraphs and definitions, dates and times, and any other part you can imagine.

SGML is a *meta-language* used to describe and define other markup languages. The SGML rules that define these other markup languages are contained within a *Document Type Definition (DTD)*, which outlines what the language can and cannot do. Think of a DTD as defining a specific subset of SGML that contains only the SGML capabilities necessary to meet specific needs. For example, an SGML DTD originally defined HTML's capabilities; essentially, it included only those aspects of SGML needed for very simple Web information delivery. Therefore, HTML includes only the pieces necessary for its purpose and becomes markedly easier to use than SGML, but it also becomes more limited in its flexibility and effectiveness.

TIP   *A meta-language can define other, more specific markup languages.*

The key to understanding DTDs is realizing that they're completely customizable, meaning that you can specify which elements and attributes may be contained in documents and what rules they must follow. For example, the HTML (and XHTML) DTD specifies that you can include a maximum of six levels of headings (h1 through h6) and that you can include any heading at any point in a document—above or below paragraphs, images, other headings, addresses, or any other page element.

The result of this flexibility is that SGML DTDs can meet practically any need. In fact, many large and small organizations worldwide use SGML, including Lockheed-Martin, Boeing, the U.S. Department of Defense, the Association of American Publishers, Hewlett-Packard, Kodak, Sun Microsystems, the publications office of the European Community, Oxford University Press, the International Organization for Standardization (ISO), and even the publishers of this book, Sybex Inc., to name just a few. Although these organizations have very different document needs, their custom DTDs give them the specific capabilities needed to manage, use, and reuse hundreds of thousands of pages (or screens) of information.

SGML DTDs can require that you comply with the rules precisely as specified—that is, if the DTD says that a Chapter SubTitle follows a Chapter Title, you must include both the title and subtitle, in the order specified. If you don't follow the DTD exactly, you likely won't be able to view or use the documents because most SGML tools will refuse to display or use documents that don't validate successfully against a specific DTD. In this sense, the DTD ensures that documents always conform to an organization's standards; however, this strict compliance also makes developing documents potentially tedious and time-consuming—even when using custom software that helps tailor the information to the DTD.

The Advantages of SGML

First, because the SGML standard is accepted by the International Organization for Standardization (ISO 8879:1986), it lets you easily transfer and reuse information, with the confidence that the document format is mainstream and widely accepted. This helps both today—with the hodgepodge of available document formats—and in the future, for reusing documents, no matter how old those documents become. For example, you could create an SGML document set now and almost certainly be able to change, add to, or otherwise modify the documents 10 years from now.

Why is this significant? Well, imagine creating a document 10 years ago using a word processing program, and then consider the problems you might have trying to edit, add to, or modify that document using today's word processing software—that is, if you can even open the document file. SGML documents are not linked to specific software, companies, or versions; if you create an SGML document today, you should always be able to use or modify that document in the future.

Second, using SGML, you can custom-build SGML applications to meet your organization's needs. Rather than making do with an existing structure for a manual, you can tailor the SGML application to meet the specific needs of your organization. For example, if you create a series of manuals that must each have an introduction but have no need for glossaries, you can develop a DTD that requires introductions but makes no provision for glossaries.

Third, SGML's capabilities are limitless; therefore, SGML is ideal for extremely large or complex document sets, up to and including the documentation for a Boeing 777. If you developed that documentation using any other tool, you could easily suffer through many software versions, be limited by software restrictions, or be bound to the specific brand of software you choose. With SGML, you could create this documentation over a period of years, revise entire sections as information changed, and readily reuse information from other documentation sets, independent of tools or other limitations.

The Disadvantages of SGML

Although SGML offers limitless capabilities and flexibility, it does have a few drawbacks. First, with SGML, you must have a complete DTD *before* you can start creating documents or content. Planning first and creating later is usually a good idea, but you might not always have the time or resources to complete a DTD beforehand, or even to efficiently reuse an existing DTD, such as the DocBook DTD. Also, although you can (technically) change a DTD's organization and structure after you create it, you would also need to change all the existing documents to comply with the revised DTD.

Second, SGML is often very expensive to implement and use. The SGML specifications alone total 500 pages, and the software required to implement SGML can easily cost hundreds of thousands of dollars in equipment, software, and training. For this reason, your entire organization would have to commit to using SGML as its document-development tool to justify the investment.

Third, SGML's complexity makes constructing generalized parser software to support it quite costly. The SGML specification accommodates unlimited numbers and combinations of elements and attributes, plus different DTDs for different documents, which requires a more flexible and complex browser. Therefore, you're not likely to find many free or very inexpensive SGML browsers (such as Netscape Navigator or Microsoft Internet Explorer with SGML) on the Internet—at least not any time soon.

TIP   For more information about SGML, check out Robin Cover's comprehensive site at `www.oasis-open.org/cover/sgml-xml.html`. *Note the very strong emphasis on XML coverage. You'll have to search individual topic categories for SGML-specific entries.*

Why HTML and XHTML Were Built

HTML was developed as a specific SGML DTD that offered a relatively limited—but manageable—portion of SGML's most basic text-handling capabilities. HTML was developed at *CERN* (now the European Organization for Nuclear Research) as a simple and concise way for physicists to exchange information and publish papers over the fledgling Internet. SGML was just too big and complicated to address this relatively simple need, so the folks at CERN (mostly Tim Berners-Lee) developed a new markup language—HTML's first version—that included only a small subset of SGML capabilities.

Although intentionally limited in its capabilities, HTML has become the most widely used markup language because it's easy to use and straightforward. HTML includes basic formatting and document-structuring capabilities, such as the ability to identify headings, boldface, and italic, and to link to other documents, making it an ideal tool for publishing simple documents.

However, as the Web has grown, HTML changed to meet some of the increased demands on it. For example, people wanted better, more accurate page layout and design, and they wanted a less tedious way to maintain existing documents. As a result, today's HTML ventures way beyond its original capabilities and intent and includes much more functionality and capability in version 4.01 than was available in earlier versions. XHTML provides more structure and regularity, but the same functionality and capabilities as HTML 4.01 does.

The Advantages of HTML and XHTML

Both HTML and XHTML are easy to learn and use, making them ideal tools for not-so-techie people. As you've learned throughout this book, HTML and XHTML include a simple code structure, consisting of relatively few element and attribute names, angle brackets (<>), and a slash (/). Therefore, you can easily learn to apply elements and not be bogged down with complex code, overwhelming element choices, or hard-to-remember restrictions on where tags can be used.

Because these two markup languages are so simple, Web browsers—such as Netscape Navigator, Microsoft Internet Explorer, and Opera—can adequately present virtually any HTML or XHTML document you might create (with the exception of documents designed expressly to take advantage of browser-specific capabilities). This makes exchanging, presenting, and sharing information with HTML and XHTML easy and reliable for many purposes.

Finally, most Web browsers do not require strict compliance with a DTD—that is, you can use elements for things other than their intended purposes and still be able to view your documents in a browser. For example, whereas excluding a subtitle in an SGML document might cause a parser to completely reject a document, HTML browsers casually skip over unrecognized components, adapt to missing elements, and nonetheless present documents fairly accurately.

The Disadvantages of HTML and XHTML

Although the simplicity of HTML and XHTML lets you easily learn and use the markup, it also limits you in providing context for words on the page. For example, if we publish a chapter of this book on the Web, all the text and headings would look fine—and anyone reading the document online could certainly get as much out of the chapter as they would on paper. However, the chapter would lack several structural components, such as a chapter subtitle, notes, or sidebars, because HTML and XHTML DTDs do not provide elements that correspond to these document parts.

Because HTML and the XHTML DTDs don't provide elements for every possible document part, we could not accurately provide contexts for all page elements. Therefore, we have to use the elements that are available to represent the document parts that we need. For example, we would likely use a heading element (`h1`) for the subtitle, use an italic element (`i`) for notes, and use a table element (`table`) to insert sidebars, but neither users nor computers could automatically differentiate these parts from other headings, italicized words, or tables. Listing 21.1 shows how we might use heading 1, italic, and table elements to format subtitle, note, and sidebar elements using XHTML Transitional.

LISTING 21.1: USING ELEMENTS IN AN XHTML TRANSITIONAL DOCUMENT TO REPRESENT DOCUMENT PARTS

```
<!DOCTYPE html PUBLIC "-//W3C//DTD XHTML 1.0 Transitional//EN"
   "http://www.w3.org/TR/xhtml1/DTD/xhtml1-transitional.dtd">
<html xmlns="http://www.w3.org/1999/xhtml">
<head>
  <title>HTML Formatting Example</title>
</head>
<body bgcolor="#FFFFFF" text="#000000" link="#0000FF"
   vlink="#FF0000" alink="#80080">
<basefont face="Arial, Helvetica" size="4" />
<h1 align="center">Headings Foreshadow Information</h1>
<p><font size="-1">The first paragraph under a heading usually
   presents the key points about the topic and offers a brief
   sample of the information to follow.</font></p>
<table border="0">
<tr>
<td valign="top">
   <p>Following paragraphs further clarify the information
      and provide more detail. Some information is quoted from
      <cite>Romeo and Juliet</cite>, whereas other text might be
      <em>emphasized</em> for other reasons.</p>
   <p><strong>Warnings</strong> might be strongly emphasized,
      as well.</p>
</td>
</tr>
</table>
```

```
<table border="1" bgcolor="#E0E0E">
<tr>
<td>
    <h3>Sidebars Offer Extras</h3>
    Sidebars offer additional information on specific topics
    that aren't necessarily central to the issues discussed in
    the main flow.
</td>
</tr>
</table>

<p><font size="-1">
    The information above is in two different tables and
    includes a number of elements that describe the appearance
    but not the logical structure of the document.</font></p>
</body>
</html>
```

Figure 21.1 shows how this code appears in a browser; you'll notice that multiple document elements share similar formatting.

FIGURE 21.1

You can use HTML or XHTML elements to help format information, but the formatting does not describe the content

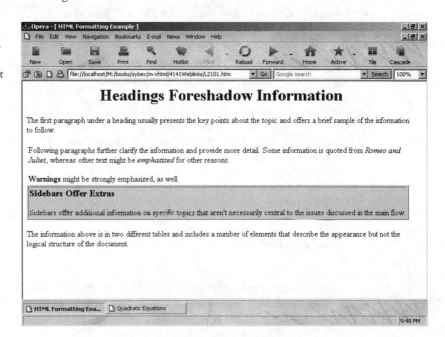

A related drawback is that the HTML and XHTML Transitional DTDs require no definite document structure because they are very flexible (reflecting the way most browsers interpret HTML

documents). For example, suppose you're developing a document featuring your company's Mongo-Mug product. You can choose to include a descriptive document title (using the `title` element), as in:

```
<title>MongoMug, the Choice of Serious Cocoa Drinkers</title>
```

Although the HTML DTDs require the `title` element and you cannot validate an HTML or XHTML document without including this element, you still don't have to include it! Browsers will still display the document even if you omit the title, or most other parts for that matter. Likewise, you might choose to use a heading level 6 (using the `h6` element) to provide your contact information, rather than using the heading element for its intended purpose—a heading.

```
<h6>All MongoMug pages are the property of BigGlug, Inc.
    Contact us at MongoMug@BigGlugInc.com.</h6>
```

TIP   *Revisit Chapter 2 for more information about the* `title` *element.*

Although misusing these elements may help you format a document the way you want it to appear, doing so also introduces all kinds of potential problems. For example, if you wanted to generate a table of contents from the headings, the table would include all elements you define as headings at any level, including the heading level 6 that is attached to your contact information. Also, rather than a document title appearing at the top of browser windows, the title area would be blank. Listing 21.2 shows an XHTML document that lacks a `title` element (which would normally follow the opening **head** element) and misuses the **h6** element. Figure 21.2 shows how it appears in a browser (and it does render despite its inability to be validated in its current form).

LISTING 21.2: XHTML DOCUMENT THAT LACKS A *title* ELEMENT

```
<!DOCTYPE html PUBLIC "-//W3C//DTD XHTML 1.0 Transitional//EN"
    "http://www.w3.org/TR/xhtml1/DTD/xhtml1-transitional.dtd">
<html xmlns="http://www.w3.org/1999/xhtml">
<head>
</head>

<body bgcolor="#FFFFFF" text="#000000" link="#0000FF"
vlink="#FF0000" alink="#80080">
<basefont face="Arial, Helvetica" size="4" />

<h1 align="center">MongoMug, the Choice of Serious
Cocoa Drinkers</h1>

<p><font size="-1">Once you've gulped from MongoMug, you'll
never sip again.</font></p>

<h6>All MongoMug pages are the property of BigGlug, Inc.
Contact us at MongoMug@BigGlugInc.com.</h6>

</body>
</html>
```

FIGURE 21.2

Even if you omit certain elements or use an element incorrectly, browsers will usually display the document as you intended

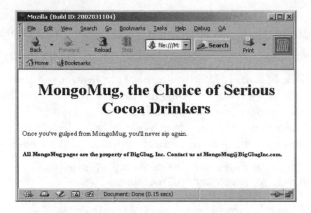

Understanding XML Markup

XML is a meta-language derived from SGML. It offers you virtually all the power of SGML and nearly all the simplicity of HTML. This is partially true for XHTML, which is nothing more than a reformulation of HTML according to XML's rules and syntax requirements. In other words, XHTML is XML that uses HTML 4.01 as its vocabulary. With XML, you can control virtually any document structure and meet any organizational need—and you can do so without necessarily dealing with an overwhelmingly complex language; without necessarily waiting for a committee to review, approve, and publish the new standards; and without necessarily dealing with expensive development and parsing tools.

Why are these features important? Let's look at an example: Suppose you must develop a Frequently Asked Questions (FAQ) document for maintaining houseplants. The FAQ would likely include those questions (and answers, obviously) that come up over and over again, as well as some basic information about the document, such as who maintains it and when it was last modified.

If you were to develop this FAQ page using HTML or XHTML, you'd be bound to the relevant DTD, which provides only limited predefined structure elements. For example, you'd likely end up using heading elements (such as h1 or h3) to list questions, use a paragraph element (p) or block-quote element (blockquote) to provide answers, and perhaps use an italic element (i) for the basic document information, such as the author and date. Take a look at Listing 21.3 and Figure 21.3 (which shows the resulting document viewed in a browser).

LISTING 21.3: A DOCUMENT THAT USES LIMITED STRUCTURE ELEMENTS

```
<!DOCTYPE html PUBLIC "-//W3C//DTD XHTML 1.0 Transitional//EN"
    "http://www.w3.org/TR/xhtml1/DTD/xhtml1-transitional.dtd">
<html xmlns="http://www.w3.org/1999/xhtml">
<head>
<title>House Plant FAQ</title>
</head>

<body bgcolor="#FFFFFF" text="#000000" link="#0000FF"
    vlink="#FF0000" alink="#80080">
```

```
<h1 align="center">Plant Care FAQ</h1>
<h3 align="center"><i><b>Motto:</b> All the plant questions
    you've lost sleep over, and then some.</i></h3>
<p align="center"><i>Maintained by Digit Brown</i><br />
<i>Last revised May 29, 2002</i></p>

<h2>Problems with Dying Plants</h2>
<ul>
    <li><h3>Why are my plants limp and yellow?</h3>
    <blockquote>Because you water them too much!</blockquote>
    </li>
    <li><h3>Why are my plants crispy and brown?</h3>
    <blockquote>Because you don't water them enough!
    </blockquote></li>
    <li><h3>Why don't my plants have a neat pattern like
    they should?</h3>
    <blockquote>Because we're not talking about tie-dying
    plants! </blockquote></li>
</ul>

</body>
</html>
```

FIGURE 21.3

Using HTML or XHTML, you're limited to the elements that the HTML or XHTML DTDs provide. Often, you end up using elements for purposes other than their intended uses

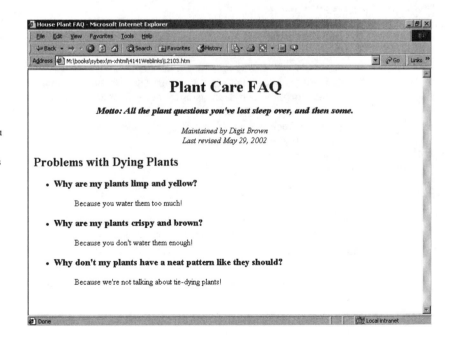

As Figure 21.3 shows, these elements only specify (to some extent) what each element will look like when viewed in a browser—that is, the questions will appear bigger and bolder than the answers, and the document information will appear in italics. They provide little context as to each element's purpose or the document structure.

If you used XML to create this FAQ, you could develop your own markup elements that not only specify what each element is, but also establish document structure. For example, your XML DTD could include a `question` element for questions, an `answer` element for answers, a `maintainer` element to list who maintains the page, and a `date` element to specify when the page was updated, as shown in Listing 21.4.

LISTING 21.4: THE FAQ WITH XML MARKUP

```
<?xml version="1.0"?>
<!DOCTYPE faq SYSTEM "faq1.dtd">
<faq>
<title>House Plant FAQ</title>
<motto>Motto: All the plant questions you've lost sleep over,
    and then some. </motto>
<maintainer>
    <who>Maintained by Digit Brown</who>
    <date>April 1, 2002</date>
</maintainer>

<category>
    <topic>Problems with Dying Plants</topic>
    <question>Why are my plants limp and yellow?</question>
    <answer>Because you water them too much!</answer>
    <question>Why are my plants crispy and brown?</question>
    <answer>Because you don't water them enough!</answer>
    <question>Why don't my plants have a neat pattern like
        they should?</question>
    <answer>Because we're not talking about tie-dying
        plants!</answer>
</category>
</faq>
```

These elements are much more logical for this purpose than the ones that HTML or XHTML provide, and they establish a specific document structure, as Figure 21.4 shows. XML documents can look like regular documents—this particular application formats the document as a "tree" so you can more easily see the structure.

In addition to creating custom elements, you could specify document rules to ensure that you or whoever uses the DTD to create future FAQ documents completes the FAQ documents correctly. For example, you could specify that all questions must have answers, that all FAQ documents must have at least one Q&A set, and so on. You do not have to specify such rules, but you certainly have the capability to do so.

FIGURE 21.4

Using XML, you can create custom elements that not only meet your specific document needs, but also help define document structure

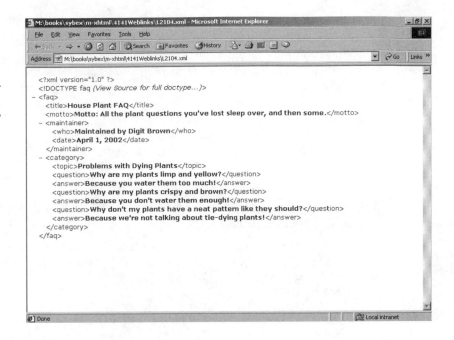

Or you could create interesting FAQ presentations. A user could view a list of FAQs, click a FAQ, and then see the answer pop up on screen —something you cannot do with HTML or unmodified XHTML. True, you could create the same general effect with dynamic XHTML (as described in Chapter 16), but to do so, you'd have to add scripts and specialized code to every FAQ and maintain them all. With XML, you could make this happen automatically in all your documents. See `www.nedit.org/faq` for an example of this kind of FAQ implementation, plus links to the FAQ's XML source and DTD.

TIP At this time, because few browsers can display XML directly (only IE supports XML), most Web sites that use XML for encoding information still automatically parse it into HTML or XHTML for display. For example, docs.sun.com uses XML behind the scenes, but converts documents to HTML so people with a variety of different browsers can access the content. Dynamic XHTML expands on standard XHTML by giving you precise formatting control combined with interactive capabilities. Take a look at Chapter 16 for more information.

If you're thinking that all this is a lot of work for a lonely FAQ page, you're right. But look at the bigger picture—that is, you might be developing a FAQ format that you will use for hundreds of documents or that other people could use to create compatible documents. In such cases, XML would be invaluable.

The Advantages of XML

The example in the previous section showed you a single comparison between HTML and XML, and in particular, it showed how XML can overcome HTML's limitations in a practical application. Let's take a broad look at XML's advantages, which apply to any XML application (but more to custom applications than XHTML).

XML PROVIDES CONTEXT FOR WORDS

XML gives you the capability to provide context for words on the page. For example, in traditional HTML or XHTML documents, the word *author* would have the same context (or lack thereof) no matter where it occurred in the document. That is, a casual mention in a paragraph of text (the author of the book was...), in a title (*Author, Author: The Story of Playwrights*), or in data about the publication itself (...author: Neil Simon) would simply be a word that appears in the document. Listing 21.5 shows how you might code the word *author* in a Web page as text, a title, or as the name of the person who wrote something. Notice that there's no specific context information in the markup itself that identifies Neil Simon as the author of the book under discussion. Figure 21.5 shows the resulting Web page.

LISTING 21.5: THE WORD *Author* IN A WEB PAGE AS TEXT, A TITLE, OR AS THE NAME OF THE PERSON WHO WROTE SOMETHING

```
<!DOCTYPE html PUBLIC "-//W3C//DTD XHTML 1.0 Transitional//EN"
   "http://www.w3.org/TR/xhtml1/DTD/xhtml1-transitional.dtd">
<html xmlns="http://www.w3.org/1999/xhtml">
<head>
<title>Author Section: Authoring a play can be hard
   work</title>
</head>

<body bgcolor="FFFFFF">
<h1 align="center">Author Section: Authoring a play can
   be hard work</h1>
<p>Many a would-be author (or playwright) has yearned for
the time that an audience will sing out "author, author" in
admiration for the hard work; however, as you might read in
the (actually not ever written) book by Neil Simon,
<i>Author, Author: The Story of Playwrights</i>,
this rarely comes to pass.
</p>
Title: <cite>Author, Author: The Story of
   Playwrights</cite><br />
Author: Neil Simon<br />
Published: Not really<br />
</body>
</html>
```

Again, notice that in the preceding code and in Figure 21.5 that the HTML or XHTML elements don't help identify the contexts for the different uses for the word *author*.

FIGURE 21.5

HTML or XHTML elements don't help identify context for document parts— that is, *author*, in any part of this example, is really just a word

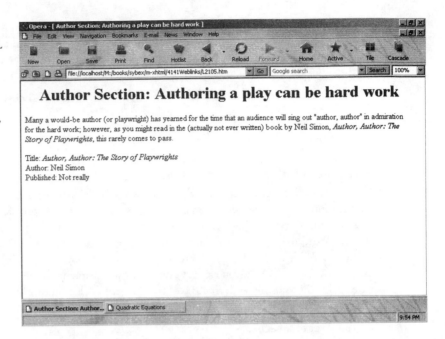

XML, on the other hand, lets you identify the context for each element by letting you specify how each is used. You could develop customized elements, such as the ones shown in bold in the following code, including the author element, which clearly identifies Neil Simon as the author of the hypothetical book under review. Thus, the markup itself provides lots of context information and clearly labels what's what.

```
<?xml version="1.0"?>
<!DOCTYPE review SYSTEM "review.dtd">
<review>

<heading>Author Section: Authoring a play can be hard work
   </heading>
<blurb>Many a would-be author (or playwright) has yearned
   for the time that an audience will sing out <quote>author,
   author</quote> in admiration for the hard work; however,
   as you might read in the (actually not ever written) book
   by Neil Simon, <booktitle>Author, Author: The Story of
   Playwrights</booktitle>, this rarely comes to pass.</blurb>

<citation>
   <title>Author, Author: The Story of Playwrights</title>
   <author>Neil Simon</author>
   <pub>Not really</pub>
</citation>

</review>
```

Using XML, you could also add attributes to provide additional information about any of the elements. For example, the following code shows how you might add `pubdate`, `publisher`, and `isbn` attributes to the `title` element and a `gender` attribute to the `author` element. Adding these attributes further adds context to words, as the following code shows:

```
<title pubdate="010199" publisher="Back Yard Press, Inc."
   isbn="1234123412">Author, Author: The Story of
   Playwrights</title>
   <author gender="Male">Neil Simon</author>
```

XML SPECIFIES DOCUMENT STRUCTURE

In addition to specifying context for words, XML lets you specify document structure—XML's second advantage. For example, a document might use italic for emphasis, for headings, and for the titles of publications. However, specifying that a word should be italicized does not indicate the role that the word plays in the document; it's simply a formatting tweak. If you indicate that a string of words is a publication title and the following string of words is the author, you add structure to the document. Using XML, you can develop your own elements that help identify the document structure, as in this example with a `publication` element enclosing title, author, and summary information about the publication:

```
<publicationrecord>
<title>Author, Author: The Story of Playwrights</title>
<author>Neil Simon</author>
<summary>Book provides a good range of readable
   information.</summary>
</publicationrecord>
```

XML ALLOWS EFFECTIVE SEARCH CAPABILITIES

Because XML provides context and structure, it lets users effectively search for information within your documents. Rather than simply searching for the word *author*, users could search for that word in a particular segment of the document, such as documents with *author* in a document title, or search only for that word in the body of a document. This control would clearly surpass the whole-text searches (available, for example, through Google) necessary to find information on the Internet today.

TIP   *For more information about Google, visit* **www.google.com**.

XML IS FLEXIBLE

XML documents do not absolutely require a DTD (you just can't validate the documents without one or something else equivalent to one), giving you more flexibility during the development process. For example, when you're developing a document, you can produce XML code and change it as necessary, without the hassles and process of changing a DTD every time you change your mind. After you've developed a structure and set of rules that suit your needs, you can then codify those rules by implementing a DTD that spells out the structure and organization you want. This flexibility makes XML ideal for trying out structured documents with minimal effort and time investment.

XML Is Accessible

Average people using average tools can use and access XML documents, so you can reach a wide audience. Already, a wide variety of software programs (Java applets, for example) let you provide XML data directly in conventional Web pages. Specifically, you could potentially provide information about your favorite books and authors (stored in XML format) directly in your (HTML- or XHTML-based) Web page, without recoding or converting your HTML documents. In doing so, you can keep structured XML information and still provide easy access to the information for all potential users.

XML Provides a Universal Format

Exchanging information and data between and among different systems has been challenging—at best—probably since the second computer system was developed. Different systems using different kinds of database software provide ample employment opportunities to do nothing but convert data (and clean up the messes when the conversion isn't so good). XML provides a standard and predictable format to encapsulate data, thus making data exchange and transfer (and as a direct result much of today's business-to-business commerce) possible.

The Disadvantages of XML

XML is a relatively new technology, and consequently, there's no plethora of tools available to develop and implement XML documents. A wide variety of XML applications exist—primarily but certainly not exclusively in the database world—but the acceptance of XML as a document-encoding format has been slower than many expected. The potential for widespread acceptance and popularity is certainly there—the number and quality of tools available improves daily—but you currently do not have nearly the breadth of options that you get with other technologies, such as HTML or XHTML.

For these reasons, you'll also need to take extra steps to ensure that people can view your XML documents. For example, when JavaScript became available, not all browsers supported it. HTML developers had to make decisions about disregarding the technology until it was more commonly available, developing an alternate non-JavaScript site so all possible users could access and view the pages, or living with the knowledge that some sites would be inaccessible to a portion of users.

The same idea applies to XML: You must take extra steps to ensure that users can view your pages because not all users will be able to directly access XML documents. Even when the newest generation of Web browsers adds XML capabilities, you still must take extra steps until a significant portion of your users begin using the newer browsers. These extra steps include providing CSS to add formatting information to XML documents, if users are permitted to access them directly, or providing XSLT style sheets to turn XML documents into HTML to make sure they'll work properly with the vast majority of Web browsers available today.

Where to Go from Here

In this chapter, we've explored XML in terms of how it differs from SGML, XHTML, and HTML and how it meets needs unmet by those languages. SGML sits at one end of the spectrum, with XHTML and HTML at the other end—SGML being a highly powerful tool, and HTML and XHTML being less capable, but more accessible tools—whereas XML combines the best features of the other markup languages.

Armed with this information, you're ready to get started with XML:

◆ Move on to Chapter 22 to learn about XML's special relationship with XHTML, and how that relationship can be expanded using namespaces.

◆ Visit Chapters 23 and 24 to find out how to create your own XML DTDs.

◆ Visit Chapter 25 to learn about XHTML modularization, a great technique that lets you pick only the parts of XHTML that your Web pages will actually use (designed for PDAs and Web-enabled cell phones, where memory and screen space are at an absolute premium).

Chapter 22

Extending XHTML Using Namespaces

As DISCUSSED IN CHAPTER 21, XHTML is an application of XML. Several benefits, such as simplicity and interoperability, can be gained by following XML's syntax requirements. In this chapter, we focus on the benefits of XML's extensibility.

Since XML was introduced, a number of optional features have been developed that provide element sets for specific tasks. For example, the Extensible Stylesheet Language (XSL) is a formatting vocabulary that defines presentation for XML documents. The XML Linking Language (XLink) defines a standard mechanism for adding hyperlinks to XML documents. The Mathematical Markup Language (MathML) provides document authors with a language for conveying mathematical expressions. If we wanted to stick with one language for the Web, we would have to extend the element set indefinitely. Instead, the XML community has separated specific tasks into manageable modules, each with a particular vocabulary.

To work with all of these different XML vocabularies, you must learn how to combine them within the same document. XML *namespaces* were created to resolve possible naming conflicts between combined vocabularies (such as the XHTML `title` element and the `title` element for a book-listing vocabulary). An XML namespace provides a formal mechanism for uniquely identifying a vocabulary. If you want to combine different XML vocabularies, you need to be familiar with XML namespaces.

This chapter covers the following topics:

◆ Identifying the benefits of extending XHTML markup

◆ Understanding namespaces

◆ Declaring the default namespace

◆ Declaring local namespaces

◆ Combining XML and XHTML vocabularies—extended examples

Benefits of Extending XHTML

The W3C promotes extensibility as the primary goal of the future of the Web. At the heart of extensibility is a collection of XML technologies. By separating functionality into discrete projects and approaches, Web developers will gain the advantages of flexibility. Combining XML vocabularies such as XLink and Scalable Vector Graphics (SVG) with XHTML will allow developers to take advantage of modularizing tasks—rather than the "everything in one big bucket" approach that characterized HTML up to and including the HTML 4.01 specification.

The *X* in XML means the vocabulary is extensible and that the author working with the markup can create his or her own elements and attributes. Therefore, as with XML, XHTML can be extended.

In a nutshell, the benefits to extending XHTML are:

◆ You can take advantage of emerging XML technologies, such as MathML, SVG, and XForms.

◆ You can embed your own XML vocabulary within an XHTML document.

◆ You can better organize the XML vocabularies you use.

◆ You have a more extensive toolset for problem solving.

In this chapter, we focus on XML namespaces because they are at the heart of extending XHTML.

COMMON NAMESPACES

Several namespaces have already been defined for common languages. As you begin to extend XHTML, you will possibly use some of these *common namespaces*. Here's a rather extensive list of namespaces:

◆ Chemical Markup Language (CML)
`www.xml-cml.org`

◆ Extensible Stylesheet Language (XSL) Working Draft 16-December-1998
`www.w3.org/TR/WD-xsl`

◆ Extensible Stylesheet Language (XSL) Version 1.0
`www.w3.org/1999/XSL/Format`

◆ Mathematical Markup Language (MathML)
`www.w3.org/1998/Math/MathML`

◆ Resource Description Framework (RDF) Model and Syntax Specification
`www.w3.org/1999/02/22-rdf-syntax-ns#`

◆ Description Framework (RDF) Schema Specification 1.0
`www.w3.org/2000/01/rdf-schema#`

◆ Scalable Vector Graphics (SVG) 1.0
`www.w3.org/2000/svg`

Continued on next page

COMMON NAMESPACES *(continued)*

◆ Simple Object Access Protocol (SOAP) 1.1 - Encoding
  `http://schemas.xmlsoap.org/soap/encoding/`

◆ Simple Object Access Protocol (SOAP) 1.1 - Envelope
  `http://schemas.xmlsoap.org/soap/envelope/`

◆ Synchronized Multimedia Integration Language (SMIL) 1.0 Specification
  `www.w3.org/TR/REC-smil`

◆ Synchronized Multimedia Integration Language (SMIL) 2.0 Specification
  `www.w3.org/TR/REC-smil/2000/SMIL20/LC/`

◆ The Schematron Assertion Language 1.5
  `www.ascc.net/xml/schematron`

◆ XHTML 1.0: The Extensible Hypertext Markup Language
  `www.w3.org/1999/xhtml`

◆ XInclude
  `www.w3.org/1999/XML/xinclude`

◆ XML Linking Language (XLink) Version 1.0
  `www.w3.org/1999/xlink`

◆ XML Schema Part 1: Structures
  `www.w3.org/1999/XMLSchema`

◆ XML Schema Part 2: Datatypes
  `www.w3.org/1999/XMLSchema-datatypes`

◆ XSL Transformations (XSLT) Version 1.0
  `www.w3.org/1999/XSL/Transform`

◆ XSL Transformations (XSLT) Specification Version 1.0 (Working Draft)
  `www.w3.org/TR/WD-xsl`

If you visit any of these namespace URIs, you would not find much because the namespace is only a symbolic identifier. With that said, some languages, but not all, use the namespace location to provide additional information about the standard. It also helps if you use an XML-capable browser to display some of these pages.

XML Namespaces

Although this book is dedicated to HTML and XHTML, it's important for you to understand how namespaces work from an XML perspective. Here's why: XML allows you to create your own elements and attributes. XML also enables developers to combine XML document types. For example, you could embed in an XHTML document elements from a document type that you created. The following would be an example of embedding your own elements into an XHTML document, but there's a possible problem; look at the bolded elements:

```
<!DOCTYPE html PUBLIC "-//W3C//DTD XHTML 1.0 Strict//EN"
    "http://www.w3.org/TR/xhtml1/DTD/xhtml1-strict.dtd">
<html xmlns="http://www.w3.org/1999/xhtml">
    <head>
        <title>Working with Namespaces</title>
    </head>
    <body>
        <h1>Online Class Offerings</h1>
        <class>
            <title>Introduction to XML</title>
            <instructor>William Ray</instructor>
        </class>
        <class>
            <title>TCP/IP for Webmasters</title>
            <instructor>Sarah Ray</instructor>
        </class>
    </body>
</html>
```

The bold lines illustrate the problem of element name conflicts. The first `title` element belongs to the XHTML document type; however, the next two `title` elements belong to our own document type. The problem arises when the processor has to decide what to do with them. How does the processor know which `title` element is which? The answer comes from XML namespaces.

XML namespaces allow you to use an element from one document type (such as an XML document) and embed it in another document type (such as an XHTML document). Because namespaces uniquely identify a set of elements that belongs to a given document type, they ensure that there are no element name conflicts.

The namespace in the XML recommendation document is seen as a complement to the XML specification and can be found at www.w3.org/TR/REC-xml-names. The recommendation document defines a special syntax to identify (declare) namespaces. The document defines how a collection of elements can be given unique identifiers; therefore, no matter where an element is used, you can be sure that it belongs to the namespace.

Declaring Namespaces

In each XHTML document you develop, you declare a namespace when you include the required `html` element:

```
<html xmlns="http://www.w3.org/1999/xhtml">
```

As you can see, `xmlns` is a required attribute of the `html` element, and the `xmlns` value is fixed as `http://www.w3.org/1999/xhtml`. The namespace declaration is a unique *Uniform Resource Identifier* (URI), which is the value of the `xmlns` namespace. A URI can be a Uniform Resource Locator (URL) or a Uniform Resource Name (URN). URLs are used most often. For example, `xmlns="http://www.raycomm.com/namespaces/onlinetraining/"` is a namespace that we created to uniquely identify our online-training vocabulary.

When you declare this namespace in the opening `html` element, you apply the namespace declaration to the entire XHTML document. In the next sections, we'll look more at this default namespace, as well as look at local namespaces, which are namespaces you can apply to specified elements within a document.

DEFAULT NAMESPACES

The preceding namespace example is also known as the *default namespace* because it's already part of the `html` element you include in your XHTML documents. The default namespace applies to the `html` element, as well as to all *child elements*—other elements within the document that are not specifically defined using other namespaces. You define the namespace as you would define an attribute: The attribute name is `xmlns`, and the value is the namespace name.

In the following snippet, the XHTML namespace is declared within the `html` opening element:

```
<html xmlns="http://www.w3.org/1999/xhtml">
  <head>
    <title>Example Transitional XHTML Document</title>
  </head>
  <body>
    <h1>My First XHTML Document</h1>
    <p><font color="#CCCC00" size="+1">After reading this book,
      we will become XHTML gods!</font></p>
  </body>
</html>
```

The namespace name is already defined for us when developing XHTML documents, because it belongs to a public document type that you're required to use. If you visit the URL in the preceding code, you'll find that no content resides there. This is because it's only meant to be a symbolic unique identifier used to resolve possible element name conflicts.

If you created your own XML document, you could create your own namespace name; for example:

```
<classListing
    xmlns="http://www.raycomm.com/namespace/onlinetraining/">
    <class>
        <title>Introduction to XML</title>
        <instructor>Sarah Ray</instructor>
    </class>
    <class>
        <title>TCP/IP for Webmasters</title>
        <instructor>William Ray</instructor>
    </class>
</classListing>
```

In this case, we've created our own unique namespace that uses our domain name. The `classListing` element and all of its children belong to the `http://www.raycomm.com/namespace/onlinetraining` namespace.

LOCAL NAMESPACES

You use *local namespaces* to define namespaces for child elements within an XHTML document. Local namespaces are similar to default namespaces; however, they include an additional identifier: a prefix. In this case, you define a namespace and associate a prefix that can later be used to reference the namespace.

Local namespaces are often used when embedding document types within another document. For example, in the previous section "XML Namespaces," we provided an example that uses both XHTML elements and our own class elements. The XHTML elements are uniquely identified by the XHTML default namespace, but what about our class elements? Because we already have a default namespace, we will have to define a local namespace for them. In the following example, we have bolded elements to illustrate this concept:

```
<!DOCTYPE html PUBLIC "-//W3C//DTD XHTML 1.0 Strict//EN"
    "http://www.w3.org/TR/xhtml1/DTD/xhtml1-strict.dtd">
<html xmlns="http://www.w3.org/1999/xhtml"
    xmlns:raycomm="http://www.raycomm.com/namespace/onlinetraining">
    <head>
        <title>Working with Namespaces</title>
    </head>
    <body>
        <h1>Online Class Offerings</h1>
        <raycomm:class>
            <raycomm:title>Introduction to XML</raycomm:title>
            <raycomm:instructor>Sarah Ray</raycomm:instructor>
        </raycomm:class>
        <raycomm:class>
            <raycomm:title>TCP/IP for Webmasters</raycomm:title>
            <raycomm:instructor>William Ray</raycomm:instructor>
        </raycomm:class>
    </body>
</html>
```

In the previous example, a local prefix is defined for the class elements:

```
xmlns:raycomm="http://www.raycomm.com/namespace/onlinetraining"
```

The xmlns attribute is used, but notice the colon and characters that follow (:raycomm). To define a local namespace, you must define a prefix that can be used as a reference later in the document. The colon separates the xmlns attribute name from the prefix. You can create your own prefix for your own document types; however, if you're using someone else's vocabulary, be sure to check and see if they have defined a prefix for you.

After you've defined the local namespace, you can reference it with the prefix. In our example, all elements identified with the prefix (raycomm) and a colon (:) belong to the http://www.raycomm .com/namespace/onlinetraining namespace. Most local namespaces are defined in the root element and then referenced when needed.

Combining Namespaces

In the section "Local Namespaces," our example combined two namespaces. This is becoming a common practice. The future of XHTML is as a document structure language. Gone are the days of using XHTML as a multipurpose language for structuring documents, presenting information, and describing metadata.

The W3C has turned its focus to creating XML applications that have dedicated tasks and that can work together. For example, the following XML applications could be combined:

- ◆ XHTML defines document markup.

- ◆ MathML (Mathematical Markup Language) defines mathematical expressions.

- ◆ SMIL (Synchronized Multimedia Integration Language) defines synchronized multimedia tasks.

- ◆ SVG defines a scalable vector graphic language.

For instance, you could add mathematical expressions to your XHTML document. The following example is defined by the XHTML specification (we've added the bold highlighting):

```
<html xmlns="http://www.w3.org/1999/xhtml"
   xml:lang="en" lang="en">
   <head>
      <title>A Math Example</title>
   </head>
   <body>
      <p>The following is MathML markup:</p>
      <math xmlns="http://www.w3.org/1998/Math/MathML">
         <apply>
            <log/>
            <logbase>
               <cn> 3 </cn>
            </logbase>
            <ci> x </ci>
         </apply>
      </math>
   </body>
</html>
```

There are a few ways to combine these document types. The first way, as demonstrated previously, is to define a default namespace for the root element and then redefine a default namespace for a child element. The nested default namespace is then applied to its current element and all its child elements. For example, all the elements in bold in the preceding code belong to the MathML namespace. The elements that are not in bold belong to the XHTML namespace.

The second way to combine namespaces is to define a default namespace and a local namespace in the root element. In this case, all elements that do not have a prefix belong to the default namespace, and all the elements that have a prefix belong to the associated local namespace. We used an example of this in the "Local Namespaces" section:

```
<!DOCTYPE html PUBLIC "-//W3C//DTD XHTML 1.0 Strict//EN"
    "http://www.w3.org/TR/xhtml1/DTD/xhtml1-strict.dtd">
<html xmlns="http://www.w3.org/1999/xhtml"
    xmlns:raycomm="http://www.raycomm.com/namespace/onlinetraining">
    <head>
        <title>Working with Namespaces</title>
    </head>
    <body>
        <h1>Online Class Offerings</h1>
        <raycomm:class>
            <raycomm:title>Introduction to XML</raycomm:title>
            <raycomm:instructor>Sarah Ray</raycomm:instructor>
        </raycomm:class>
        <raycomm:class>
            <raycomm:title>TCP/IP for Webmasters</raycomm:title>
            <raycomm:instructor>William Ray</raycomm:instructor>
        </raycomm:class>
    </body>
</html>
```

Finally, you can define only local namespaces and add prefixes to all the elements within the document. This is the least commonly used approach; however, there are conceivably times when you might want to use only local namespaces.

Combining XML Vocabularies with XHTML— Extended Examples

To demonstrate how you might combine XML vocabularies, we chose two of the most widely implemented XML vocabularies. In the following sections, we look at MathML and SVG, as well as an example using our own XML vocabulary.

MathML

Before we dive into how you might use MathML within an XHTML document, let's take a look at what MathML is. The MathML standard defines presentation elements *and* content elements. The presentation elements define how an expression should be displayed, whereas the content elements define the content of the expression.

MathML has been around for a while now—it's one of the oldest XML applications. For this reason, several browsers, plug-ins, and Java applets are already available that allow users to view MathML data (such as Amaya, at www.w3.org/Amaya/). MathML is almost always embedded into another document type, such as XHTML. This makes sense because, after all, who would want to view a page of strictly mathematical expressions?

The following are some common MathML elements from the W3C specification:

- `math` is the single top-level math element that contains all other MathML markup within the XHTML page.

- `mi` indicates that its content should be displayed as an identifier. Single-character identifiers (such as x or h) are commonly displayed in italics. Multicharacter identifiers (such as sin and log) are commonly displayed in an upright font.

- `mn` specifies that its content should be rendered as a number, which is commonly displayed in an upright font.

- `mo` specifies that its content should be displayed as an operator. There's no specific presentation format defined for operators. The presentation varies.

- `mrow` may contain any number of child elements. Its content is displayed aligned along the baseline in a horizontal row. In addition, `mrow` is commonly used to group terms into a single unit.

- `mfrac` may contain only two children. The first child is positioned as the numerator of a fraction, and the second is the denominator. It's commonly used for binomial coefficients; to do so, you must set the `linethickness` attribute to `0`, which removes the bar.

- `msqrt` may contain any number of children and displays them under a radical sign.

- `mroot` is similar to the `msqrt` element, except that it requires a second child, which is displayed above the radical in the location of the n in an nth root.

- `mfenced` is similar to the `mrow` element, except that it displays enclosed in parentheses. Using attributes, you can set the beginning and ending delimiter characters, as well as internal separator characters such as commas.

- `mstyle` is similar to the `mrow` element except that it handles attributes differently. The `mrow` element has almost no attributes of its own, and the `mstyle` elements can be used to set any MathML attribute.

The focus of this section is on how to embed MathML within an XHTML document, not necessarily on how to use MathML. Therefore, we focus on the MathML namespace and embedding MathML in an XHTML document.

TIP *Both languages are XML vocabularies and can therefore be combined using namespaces.*

MathML Namespace

Embedding MathML within other XML vocabularies, such as XHTML, requires that you keep track of namespaces. The MathML namespace is

```
http://www.w3.org/1998/Math/MathML
```

When you decide to embed MathML within another XML vocabulary, you have to identify all MathML markup as belonging to the scope of the MathML namespace. You do this by using a default namespace or using a namespace prefix, as described earlier.

The root MathML element is the `math` element; therefore, you use the `xmlns` attribute with the MathML namespace in it as shown here:

```
<math xmlns="http://www.w3.org/1998/Math/MathML">
<mrow>…</mrow>
</math>
```

When defined as a default namespace, the namespace is defined for the element to which it is attached, as well as any child elements.

If you choose to use a namespace prefix, the `xmlns` attribute is used with a prefix. The prefix can then be used to associate elements and attributes within the document with the defined namespace. For example:

```
<html xmlns:m="http://www.w3.org/1998/Math/MathML">
…
<m:math>
    <m:mrow>
    …
    </m:mrow>
</m:math>
…
</html>
```

You can use these two namespace declaration methods interchangeably. For example, you might declare a default XHTML namespace, while adding a document-wide namespace prefix for any MathML elements. You could accomplish the same thing by defining a default XHTML namespace and then adding a default MathML namespace to the outermost `math` element, thereby localizing the default MathML namespace.

WORKING WITH MathML NAMESPACES

It's common for MathML processors to use explicit namespace prefixes to attach rendering behaviors to an element. This practice is used for XSLT processors as well. On the other hand, several MathML authoring tools do not recognize namespaces and therefore lack the ability to use namespace prefixes.

If this is the case, it's likely that you'll want to use a combination of default and prefixed namespaces. For example:

```
<body xmlns:m="http://www.w3.org/1998/Math/MathML">
…
<m:math xmlns="http://www.w3.org/1998/Math/MathML">
<mrow>…<mrow>
</m:math>
…
</body>
```

EMBEDDING MATHML IN XHTML

Listing 22.1 is an example of an XHTML document containing MathML expressions.

LISTING 22.1: AN XHTML DOCUMENT WITH MATHML EXPRESSIONS

```
<!DOCTYPE html PUBLIC "-//W3C//DTD XHTML 1.0 Transitional//EN"
    "http://www.w3.org/TR/xhtml1/DTD/xhtml1-transitional.dtd">
<html xmlns="http://www.w3.org/1999/xhtml"
      xmlns:m="http://www.w3.org/1998/Math/MathML">
<head>
<title>Quadratic Equations</title>
</head>
<body>
<h1>Quadratic Equations</h1>
<p>The following is a quadratic equation:</p>
<p>
z = <math xmlns="http://www.w3.org/1998/Math/MathML">
    <mfrac>
     <mrow>
        <mo> - </mo>
        <mi> b </mi>
        <mo> &PlusMinus; </mo>
        <mi>   </mi>
        <msqrt>
          <msup>
            <mi> a </mi>
            <mn> 2 </mn>
          </msup>
          <mi>   </mi>
          <mo> - </mo>
          <mi>   </mi>
          <mn> 4 </mn>
          <mi> ac </mi>
        </msqrt>
      </mrow>
      <mrow>
        <mn> 3 </mn>
        <mi> c </mi>
        <mtext>   </mtext>
        <mtext>   </mtext>
        <mtext>   </mtext>
      </mrow>
    </mfrac>
  </math>
</p>

 <p>
 Sufficiently motivated readers might care to solve it. </p>
 </body>
</html>
```

FIGURE 22.1

In Amaya or other browsers that recognize MathML, all of the mathematical symbols end up looking just as they should

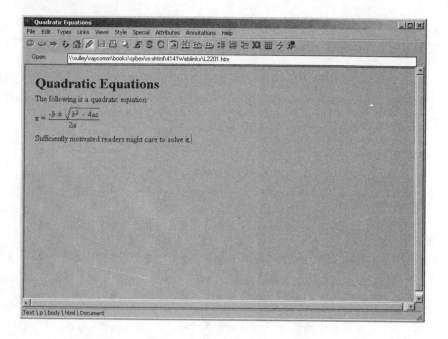

SVG

In case you're not familiar with SVG, let's take a moment to explain what it is. As defined by the W3C, SVG is a language for describing two-dimensional graphics in XML. Three types of graphical objects can be defined by SVG: vector graphic shapes, images, and text. SVG objects use the Document Object Model (DOM) to allow them to be both dynamic and interactive. Therefore, you can use event handlers such as `onmouseover` and `onclick` to attach behaviors to SVG objects. Many of the element and attribute names should be obvious. For example, the `circle` element is used to define a circle, and the `rect` element is used to define a rectangle. Attributes such as the familiar XHTML `style` attribute allow you to use Cascading Style Sheet (CSS) properties, such as `fill`, `stroke`, and `stroke-width`, to control appearance.

Working with SVG is not that different from working with MathML. Because this is a book on HTML and XHTML, we focus on embedding other XML vocabularies within an XHTML document. However, it's important for you to understand that you can use namespaces to embed other XML vocabularies within SVG or MathML documents too.

Many of the same rules that we defined in the MathML section apply when you're working with SVG. For example, you'll want to use a namespace prefix when declaring elements because it's best to use only one default namespace to help ensure uniqueness. Because XHTML is the parent vocabulary, it will be defined using a default namespace. For stylistic reasons, we declare the SVG prefixed namespace within the `html` root element. For our documents, we like to define all namespaces at the top of the document. With all namespaces defined at the same level, it's easier to maintain them.

The SVG namespace is

```
http://www.w3.org/2000/svg
```

You'll most likely define the SVG namespace using the svg prefix. Listing 22.2 is a sample XHTML document with embedded SVG elements.

LISTING 22.2: A SAMPLE XHTML DOCUMENT WITH EMBEDDED SVG ELEMENTS

```
<html xmlns="http://www.w3.org/1999/xhtml"
    xmlns:svg="http://www.w3.org/2000/svg">
    <head>
      <title>Shapes</title>
    </head>
    <body>
      <h1>Rectangle and Circle</h1>
    <svg:svg id="body" width="210px" height="23.5px"
      viewBox="0 0 210 135">
      <svg:rect x="15" y="25" width="150" height="70"
        style="fill:blue; stroke:red; stroke-width:2" />
    </svg:svg>
    <svg:svg width="20cm" height="10cm">
      <svg:circle style="stroke:#33CCCC; stroke-width:.2cm;
        stroke-opacity:1; fill:#000000; fill-opacity:0" cx="10cm"
        cy="5cm" r="3cm" />
    </svg:svg>
    <p>SVG makes it possible.</p>
    </body>
</html>
```

FIGURE 22.2

The Amaya browser, from the W3C, also supports SVG

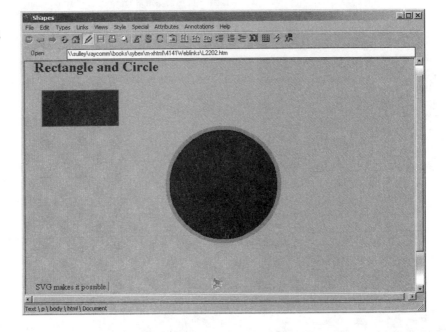

Listing 22.2 uses the XHTML namespace as its default namespace; therefore, we don't need to use element prefixes. It also declares an additional namespace for some SVG. These elements are prefixed using the XML namespaces notation. The `svg` prefix indicates the namespace in use by the `svg`, `rect`, and `circle` elements. If you add other elements and attributes that fall within the scope of other namespaces, you must prefix them to prevent any ambiguity.

TIP To learn more about SVG, visit the W3C's Web site dedicated to the topic at www.w3.org/Graphics/SVG/.

Your Own Vocabulary

More often than not, you'll want to mix XHTML elements with a grab bag of your own elements. When this is the case, you'll use a combination of default and prefix namespaces. For example:

```
<html xmlns="http://www.w3.org/1999/xhtml"
   xmlns:pdt="http://www.raycomm.com/namespaces/products">
  <head>
    <title>Products</title>
  </head>
  <body>
    <pdt:product name="fertilizer" price="5.00" />
    <pdt:product name="Aloe Vera" price="15.00" />
    <pdt:product name="Orchid" price="25.00" />
    <pdt:product name="Sand" price="3.00" />
    <pdt:product name="Cactus" price="15.00" />
  </body>
</html>
```

As with the SVG and MathML examples, the rules stay the same. XHTML uses the default namespace, and our vocabulary uses a prefixed namespace.

WARNING In the previous example, the product information would not be rendered in the browser window because the data is defined using attribute values. If you want to create a document that displays the data, you want to define the data using elements (or you could use XSLT to convert the document structure). If you choose to use elements, you'll need to use CSS style rules to define presentation information for the data. Remember that your own elements do not carry presentation information—all they do is describe the content.

Validation

One notable drawback to using DTDs is that they are not namespace aware—which means that they do not recognize namespace prefixes. To an XML validating processor, a namespace prefix (`m:math`) is just part of the element name. Therefore, the element type declaration for that element must define the qualified name as `m:math`. This is impractical if you're using multiple namespaces.

Namespace prefixes create problems for the DTD validation of documents that contain other XML vocabularies. DTD validation requires knowing the literal (possibly prefixed) element names used in the document. However, the namespaces in the XML recommendation allow the prefix to be changed at arbitrary points in the document, because namespace prefixes may be declared on any element.

There are a few ways around this problem; however, none of them is elegant. First, you can add the namespace prefix to the qualified name defined with the element type declaration; for example:

```
<!ELEMENT book:book (book:title, book:author)>
    <!ATTLIST book:book
            book:isbn CDATA #IMPLIED
            xmlns:book CDATA #FIXED "http://www.nspc.com/">
<!ELEMENT book:title (#PCDATA)>
<!ELEMENT book:author (#PCDATA)>
```

TIP *See Chapters 23 and 24 for more information about creating DTDs, like the snippets shown here.*

Although this syntax is legal, understand that the qualified names in the DTD have no special meaning. For example, `book:title` is just `book:title`. The processor does not recognize `title` as the element name to which the prefix `book` is mapped.

If you want to avoid namespace prefixes altogether, you can opt to use default namespaces. If you choose this method, remember that the `xmlns` attribute must be declared within the DTD. It's common practice to define the value as fixed; for example:

```
<!ELEMENT book (title, author)>
    <!ATTLIST book
            isbn CDATA #IMPLIED
            xmlns CDATA #FIXED "http://www.nspc.com/">
<!ELEMENT title (#PCDATA)>
<!ELEMENT author (#PCDATA)>
```

It's important to remember that whether or not you choose to use XML namespaces, the same rules apply for validity. You must include declarations for elements and attributes. Those declarations define qualified names. Although those qualified names may contain namespace prefixes, the process just views them as names with no special meaning. See the following section for validation tips and tricks.

Suggestions and Tips

In the ideal Web, you could follow our document examples, implement solutions, and walk away knowing all is well. Oftentimes, however, various processing agents are not in alignment with the W3C recommendations. XML-related technologies are evolving at a fast pace, and it's unrealistic to expect software products to keep up. In addition, many of the standards being defined by the W3C are still in flux. Even though we're in what you might call a transitional period, you should keep the following tips in mind:

◆ Do not create your own MathML namespace prefix. Use `m:` as a conventional prefix for the MathML namespace.

◆ When using namespace prefixes, pick one and use it consistently within a document.

◆ Declare the MathML namespace on all `math` elements.

- Avoid using DTDs and namespaces unless you're aware of the implications.
- Always declare all xmlns attributes in the DTD.
- Be sure to use the same qualified names in the DTD as used in the body of the document.
- Define only one prefix per XML namespace.
- Be careful to not use the same prefix for more than one XML namespace.
- Try not to use more than one default XML namespace. This will ensure uniqueness.

Where to Go from Here

In this chapter, we focused on extending XHTML using namespaces. If you want to extend XHTML, you need to read more about modularization techniques. Understanding namespace behavior is important, but the next step is to learn how to incorporate DTDs into the picture:

- See Chapters 23 and 24 to learn more about DTDs.
- See Chapter 25 to learn more about the modularization of XHTML.
- See Part 8 for many of the common XML vocabularies, such as XSL, XSLT, and SMIL.

Chapter 23

Getting Started with DTDs

As you learned in Chapter 21, creating a *DTD* (Document Type Definition) is often a big part of developing XML applications; therefore, you need to take the time to plan, organize, and develop DTDs thoroughly. If you can find an existing DTD that fits your needs (like the DocBook DTD for documentation at `www.docbook.org`), then by all means use it. However, if you cannot find an existing DTD that meets your needs, you'll have to create your own. In this chapter, we'll introduce you to DTD fundamentals, including the basic concept of validity (which determines whether a document adheres to all the rules set by the DTD) and the basic rules that govern how DTDs can be assembled and how they connect to XML documents.

DTDs will look a bit different from the HTML and XHTML documents you've developed throughout this book. Although you don't need to develop a DTD for your HTML or XHTML documents, we've included this chapter on DTDs so that you can see what they look like, what they include, and how to read and understand one, which can be helpful in furthering your HTML and XHTML knowledge. You can also apply this information to developing your own XML DTD.

This chapter covers the following topics:

- Understanding DTDs and validity
- Identifying the various types of declarations
- Understanding the basic rules and concepts of DTDs
- Connecting DTDs to XML documents

Understanding DTDs and Validity

You might think of DTDs as providing the grammar rules of markup languages. For example, the English language includes parts of speech—such as nouns, verbs, adjectives, and prepositions—and each of these parts appears in a particular order, depending on the kind of sentence and the amount of detail within the sentence. Likewise, a DTD specifies which elements you can include in markup language documents (such as HTML, XHTML, and XML), much the same way that the rules of English grammar specify all the possible parts of speech you can use. Also, a DTD identifies the order in which the elements should appear and specifies the details that each element can, may, or cannot include, similar to the way that the rules for English grammar specify how to build sentences.

So, a DTD serves two purposes:

◆ To specify which elements and attributes you can use to develop markup language documents

◆ To specify the document structure and rules you must adhere to while developing markup language documents

When you use XHTML, you're actually using one of three DTDs set forth by the W3C (remember the Strict, Transitional, and Frameset DTDs from Chapter 2), and the DTD is what you're checking your documents against when you run them through the W3C validator (which we mentioned in Chapter 1 and cover extensively in Chapter 20). For example, the XHTML DTD includes a declaration requiring that every document contain the `html` element and that the `html` element contain two child elements, `head` and `body`:

```
<html>
   <head>…</head>
   <body>…</body>
</html>
```

NOTE *The previous example is a simplified version of an XHTML document and we use it only to illustrate our point. For purposes of clarity, we intentionally left out some required components.*

The XHTML specification states that all XHTML documents must adhere to an XHTML DTD. If your documents adhere to the rules set forth and include only the elements and attributes specified in the DTD, then the documents are considered *valid*. Ahhh, right. That's why you've been running your XHTML documents through a validator—to determine whether they adhere to the XHTML DTD.

In XML, you can create your own DTD that specifies the rules you set forth for your documents and that specifies which elements and attributes your XML documents can contain. Unlike in XHTML, adhering to a DTD in XML is optional. In other words, an XML document is not required to be valid. Although XML seems to be more detailed and stringent compared to XHTML, it's also completely extensible, meaning that you make the rules—and you can even make a rule that you don't have to follow any rules set by a DTD.

Requirements aside, there are advantages to be gained by referencing a DTD. The most important of these is troubleshooting help. When creating a document by hand, you'll undoubtedly make mistakes. If you choose not to use a DTD, you'll have to comb the document with your eyes to find all your mistakes. However, if you use DTD, you can use a validator to locate errors. Additionally, by having (and validating to) a DTD, you ensure that your documents are regular and predictable, which makes it easier for programs to automatically extract or manipulate the content (for example, by selecting headings to create a table of contents automatically).

Declarations: The Heart of a DTD

The heart of a DTD is its *declarations*, which are statements of rules set out for a document. Four types of declarations exist:

TIP   For each declaration example, we've simplified actual XHTML element declarations to make it easier on the eyes. Our examples do not represent the complete declaration for a given element or attribute. Most XHTML DTD declarations use entities, and the syntax can become rather complex. If you're interested in seeing the real thing, visit `www.w3.org/TR/xhtml1/DTD/xhtml1-transitional.dtd`.

Element type declarations   Define element names and content models. Each content model defines the type of content an element can contain. For example, it could state that an element can contain only data, or that an element can contain only the `head` and `body` elements as children—for example,

```
<!ELEMENT html (head, body)>
```

Attribute list declarations   Define attribute names and the elements they can modify. Each attribute list declaration also defines default values and data types. For example, in XHTML, the `img` element requires both the `alt` and `src` attributes, and it allows the `height` and `width` attributes but makes them optional. Here's how an attribute list could look:

```
<!ELEMENT img EMPTY>
<!ATTLIST img src      CDATA   #REQUIRED
              alt      CDATA   #REQUIRED
              height   CDATA   #IMPLIED
              width    CDATA   #IMPLIED    >
```

Entity declarations   Define a data item and provide a way to reference that data item. Entities are used to define common data items that will be used throughout the XML document or the DTD itself. Once a data item is declared as an entity, you can reference it using an entity name, saving you time and effort. You can reference entities from within your document or from within a DTD subset. For example, if you want to create information that you reuse a lot in a DTD subset, such as the group of heading elements, you can create an entity for those values—for example,

```
<!ENTITY % heading "H1|H2|H3|H4|H5|H6">
```

Notation declarations   Identify elements or objects that are not to be *parsed*—or read—as XML. Because all text in an XML document is parsed by the XML parser (unless otherwise indicated), there must be some way to identify items that are not XML. For example, if you want to include a GIF image, you would need a way to tell the processor to not parse the GIF image as XML. A notation declaration does just that—for example,

```
<!NOTATION gif SYSTEM "image/gif">
```

These are the only four types of declarations that you will find in a DTD. Unfortunately, they are not as simple as they may appear. Each declaration type can take on many different forms—although these forms are not necessary for our discussion of DTDs. For more on these declarations, visit the XML specification at `www.w3.org/TR/1998/REC-xml-19980210` or just read on.

NOTE   A parser *is a program that reads and interprets the document markup and then translates it into the final Web page, screen, or file.*

Understanding DTD Rules and Concepts

Your first task in reading or developing DTDs is to understand a few rules and concepts. Taking the grammar analogy one step further, think of DTD rules as the spelling rules (such as, *i* before *e* except after *c*) and structure basics (such as, put a period, question mark, or exclamation point at the end of a sentence). These are the unexciting parts of developing DTDs, but they do provide the essential background you need. In the following few sections, we introduce you to these rules and concepts and show you how to apply them. Listing 23.1 illustrates a simple XML DTD. The following sections explain the concepts on which all DTDs are built.

TIP   In this chapter, we use the term processing application *generically to refer to a stand-alone parser or a specialized application or browser that includes the parser and other processing components. There are two types of parsers:* validating *and* non-validating *parsers. The validating parser parses a document according to the rules in the DTD and then passes the resulting information to the processor. A non-validating parser—the type found in most Web browsers—only checks the document (including any DTD subset) for well-formedness.*

LISTING 23.1: AN XML DTD

```
<!NOTATION gif SYSTEM "image/gif">
<!NOTATION jpeg SYSTEM "image/jpeg">
<!NOTATION png SYSTEM "image/png">
<!ENTITY mxhtml SYSTEM "graphics/mxhtml.gif" NDATA gif>
<!ENTITY jdgexj SYSTEM "graphics/jdgexj.gif" NDATA gif>
<!ENTITY jdgsj SYSTEM "graphics/jdgsj.gif" NDATA gif>
<!ELEMENT publications (book+)>
<!ATTLIST publications xmlns CDATA #FIXED
   "http://www.raycomm.com/namespaces/pubs">
<!ELEMENT book (title, authors, pubDate, publisher, size,
  cover?, topics, errata?, description, website?)>
<!ATTLIST book
        isbn CDATA #REQUIRED
        edition CDATA #REQUIRED
        cat NMTOKENS #REQUIRED
        id ID #IMPLIED
>
<!ELEMENT authors (author+)>
<!ATTLIST size pp CDATA #REQUIRED>
<!ELEMENT size EMPTY>
<!ELEMENT cover EMPTY>
<!ATTLIST cover img ENTITY #REQUIRED>
<!ELEMENT topics (topic+)>
<!ELEMENT errata EMPTY>
<!ATTLIST errata code CDATA #REQUIRED>
<!ELEMENT title (#PCDATA)>
<!ELEMENT pubDate EMPTY>
<!ATTLIST pubDate year CDATA #REQUIRED>
```

```
<!ELEMENT publisher (#PCDATA)>
<!ELEMENT description (#PCDATA)>
<!ELEMENT website (#PCDATA)>
<!ELEMENT author (#PCDATA)>
<!ELEMENT topic (#PCDATA)>
```

Characters and Names

When you're developing an XML document, you can use virtually any characters from any language in the world. You're limited only by what the processing application can interpret, and XML processing applications are very accommodating; by default, they support most characters available in most languages. So, for example, you can create XML documents with any combination of Western and Asian characters, rather than being restricted to the characters you can type on your computer keyboard.

TIP For more information about characters in DTDs, see Chapter 24.

When developing DTDs for XML documents, you must specify anything you want to include in the XML document by name. And you're required to use *legal names*, which are a grouping of characters that begin with a letter and include letters, numbers, hyphens, underscores, colons, or periods, as in `title`, `heading.2` or `doc-info`.

Names carry two restrictions:

◆ They can only contain four punctuation symbols—hyphens (-), underscores (_), colons (:), and periods (.). Any other punctuation characters are not acceptable in XML and will be rejected by the parser.

◆ They cannot begin with the character string "xml," "XML," or any other capitalization variation. All "xml" variations are reserved for future use by XML standards.

Valid sample names include `card`, `s2c`, or `card-shark`, which start with a letter and include only the allowed characters and symbols.

WARNING Although it's technically legal to use a colon within an attribute or element name, you should avoid doing so. Colons are reserved for use with namespaces, and any namespace-aware processor will mistake the element or attribute name as a namespace prefix.

Logic in a DTD

Logic refers to the characters and symbols you combine to construct a DTD. As you develop a DTD, you must have some way of connecting elements and of specifying the rules by which they can or must be applied.

Think of it this way. If you're making a sandwich, you have all sorts of pieces, such as bread, cheese, meat, lettuce, and perhaps mustard and/or mayonnaise. Also, you probably have a specific way of putting the pieces together, such as building it from the bottom up or putting goodies on both slices of bread and then putting the two slices together—goodies on the inside, of course. When describing how you build the sandwich, you need some way to specify what the pieces are, how they relate, and how they should be added. Without some sort of logical method in place (even if unstated), you could have all sorts of problems when building a sandwich, such as omitting the bottom piece of bread or adding the mustard to the outside of the bread.

Likewise, in developing an XML document DTD, you need some way to specify which elements can or must be included, how the elements relate, and how the elements should (or must) be put together in the XML document. DTDs use a system called *Extended Backus-Naur Format*, which gives you a method for specifying elements in XML documents, indicating how they relate and how they should be put together. Table 23.1 lists the Extended Backus-Naur operators and describes the function of each.

TABLE 23.1: Extended Backus-Naur Format Options

USE THIS...	TO DO THIS...	EXAMPLE
( )	Encloses a sequence or group of choices	(bread, meat, cheese)
,	Separates items in a list of required elements that must appear in order	(bread, filling, bread)
|	Separates items in a list of choices, only one of which must appear	(wheat | white | rye)
?	Shows that elements can occur zero or one time, but no more than once	(bread, filling, mustard?, bread)
*	Shows that elements can occur zero or more times	(bread, filling, mustard?, pickles*, bread)
+	Shows that elements occur one or more times	(bread, meat+, bread)

So, back to the sandwich example, you might specify

```
(bread, filling, bread)
```

indicating that bread, filling, and bread are each required, one time, and must occur in that order. You could also specify different bread choices, as in

```
((white | rye | wheat), filling, (white | rye | wheat))
```

which would give people the option to use white, rye, or wheat on either side of the sandwich. Additionally, you might specify that filling could occur multiple times, but at least once, like this:

```
((white | rye | wheat), filling+, (white | rye | wheat))
```

You might also specify that mustard can optionally be present, but no more than once, and it must go between the first bread and the filling:

```
((white | rye | wheat), mustard?, filling+,
   (white | rye | wheat))
```

Finally, you might add the option of having none, one, or many pickles:

```
((white | rye | wheat), mustard?, filling+, pickles*,
    (white | rye | wheat))
```

As you can see, using the Backus-Naur format involves nothing more than using a few symbols and putting the information in a specific order. You'll apply this system as you develop DTDs.

Data Types

When you write DTDs, you create elements for items such as headings, text, numbered lists, and links (among other elements) that will be parsed (processed) as part of the XML document. These parsed elements are called *parsed data* and will make up the vast majority of your XML documents.

In a DTD, you specify that you want elements to be parsed; you do so using the *parsed character data* (#PCDATA) content model, which will be processed by the XML parser as it looks for other elements or other variables that need to be changed or manipulated. For example, a section of an XML document that could contain other elements—such as a chapter that could contain paragraphs or notes—would be parsed to find the elements that indicate those embedded paragraphs or notes.

In some instances, however, you might not want all the data to be parsed and interpreted. Suppose you're creating an XML document that gives instructions for creating XML. How would you show XML markup within the instruction document? That is, if you say, `Step 1: Type in <coolness>Awesome idea</coolness>`, how do you indicate that you want the markup displayed as is and not parsed and interpreted by the processing application? In this case, you could not use parsed data to show the XML markup; it would be parsed and interpreted just like the rest of the document contents (and the parser would likely generate error messages because it didn't expect to see a `<coolness>` element). This is where *unparsed* data becomes handy. It lets you include XML markup (among other things) within a document that will appear exactly as you enter it—essential, in this case, for displaying the markup you want users to type.

TIP *You could also use character entities to display otherwise prohibited characters, such as <, >, or &. See Chapter 24 for more information.*

Whereas you specify parsed data in a DTD, you specify unparsed data in the XML document itself using *character data* (CDATA). Character data goes through a parser without being processed and, instead, gets passed directly to the processing application. In the XML document, then, you would include character data markup like this:

```
<![CDATA[Type in <coolness>Awesome idea</coolness>)]]>
```

Everything between <![CDATA[and]]> is not parsed and is passed directly to the processing application.

TIP *Character data also occurs in DTDs, not just in XML documents. We'll talk more about this in Chapter 24.*

Comments in a DTD

Comments are simply notes that you can include in a DTD that will not be processed along with the other DTD content. Think of a comment as a little yellow sticky note that you include in a DTD (or XML document). You can use comments to include reminders about the purpose of an element, make notes to other people developing or using a DTD, or include special instructions for revisions.

TIP   You can use comments in the XML documents as well—they are identical (`<!-- comment here -->`) in structure and purpose.

Your only restriction in using comments is that you must place them between elements (not inside them), and you must use only character data, not markup elements. The following markup shows how you might include a comment within a DTD:

```
<!ELEMENT faq (title, motto, maintainer, category)>
<!ELEMENT category (topic,(question, answer)+)>
<!-- Included date on maintainer element because of possibility
    of different maintainers at different times -->
<!ELEMENT maintainer (who, date)>
```

INCLUDE/IGNORE

When you're writing DTDs, you may want to either include or exclude parts of the DTD for processing. For example, after you've developed a fairly solid DTD, you might want to experiment with restructuring some of it to better meet your needs. You could create a set of new DTDs, copy and paste parts of the old DTD into them, and then change your XML documents to point to each different DTD to try them out. A better option, however, would be to use the INCLUDE and IGNORE options. By using these options, you can take an existing DTD and specify that only parts of it (such as experimental sections or working sections) should be read and used by the parser.

Let's look at an example. Suppose you've developed a FAQ (Frequently Asked Questions) DTD and want to begin adding new elements to it so the DTD supports extra information about questions, problem reporting, and resolutions. You can add to or tweak the DTD to include declarations for both purposes using the IGNORE and INCLUDE options. In the following example, a multipurpose DTD uses IGNORE and INCLUDE options to specify which parts the parser should parse or ignore:

```
<![IGNORE[
<!ELEMENT faq (title, motto, maintainer, category)>
<!ELEMENT category (topic,(question, answer)+)>
]]>
<![INCLUDE[
<!ELEMENT faq (title, motto, maintainer+, category)>
<!ELEMENT category (topic,(question, questioner, (answer,
    supporttech)+)+)>
]]>
```

Everything between the `<![IGNORE[` and `]]>` is ignored by the parser (the old part of the DTD that works and that you don't want to toss away until all the bugs are worked out), and everything between the `<![INCLUDE[` and `]]>` (the new stuff that should expand the DTD to address these new issues) is processed by the parser. Don't worry—we'll talk about the specific elements and how to define them in Chapter 24.

UNDERSTANDING THE DTD DECLARATION

The *DTD declaration* is the statement you'll include in the document markup that specifies—or declares—that your document uses a DTD, what the DTD is called, and where the DTD is. This declaration is essentially just a snippet of code. The DOCTYPE declaration syntax is not that complicated, but you should take a minute to see what components a declaration includes.

All XML declarations, including DOCTYPE declarations, begin with a less-than symbol and an exclamation point (<!). The declaration is closed with just a greater-than symbol (>). What we have so far is:

```
<!>
```

Note that this is not a comment tag.

All declarations use a keyword to identify their type. For DOCTYPE declarations, this keyword is DOCTYPE (all uppercase). The keyword must be added directly after the exclamation point. No white space is allowed. If you add the keyword, you have the following:

```
<!DOCTYPE>
```

You're not yet done, because after all, the DOCTYPE declaration must reference the file, and as of yet you've only identified the type of declaration. Four (or three, depending on the type of DOCTYPE declaration) other pieces of information must be added:

Type of document   This is essentially the root element—that is, the element that encloses all others in the document:

```
<!DOCTYPE rootelement>
```

In XHTML, this must be html, in all lowercase, as follows:

```
<!DOCTYPE html>
```

Type of DTD   Identifies whether the document is using a DTD that is not publicly defined (SYSTEM) or one that is and that has a public identifier available (PUBLIC). For example:

```
<!DOCTYPE html PUBLIC>
```

Public identifier of the DTD   A *Uniform Resource Name* (URN) that is recognized as a public identifier for the DTD. A public identifier is used only if the keyword PUBLIC is used; when you do include an identifier, the syntax looks like this:

```
<!DOCTYPE html PUBLIC "-//W3C//DTD XHTML 1.0 Strict//EN">
```

URL of the DTD   Defines the location of the external DTD subset (essentially, the DTD itself). When you've added this component, you get the following:

```
<!DOCTYPE html PUBLIC "-//W3C//DTD XHTML 1.0 Strict//EN"
    "http://www.w3.org/TR/xhtml1DTD/xhtml1-strict.dtd">
```

Connecting DTDs to XML Documents

Finally, before you start developing a DTD, you should be aware of how DTDs and XML documents are connected. Remember that each provides a parser with different information—the XML document provides content, and the DTD provides structure and rules for the XML document. For a processing application to read and display the XML document correctly, you need to tell it where to find the DTD so it knows which rules to apply.

You have three choices:

♦ You can embed the DTD within the XML document. In this case, the DTD is part of the XML document.

♦ You can reference a separate DTD. In this case, the DTD is a separate file.

♦ You can do both—embed declarations and reference an external file.

Embedding the DTD

When you embed DTD declarations in the XML document, you include the DTD information within the XML document itself. Specifically, you include the complete DTD, known as the *internal subset*, within the <!DOCTYPE> declaration, which you must include to create a valid XML document. The following markup shows a DTD embedded in the <!DOCTYPE> declaration:

```
<?xml version="1.0"?>
<!DOCTYPE faq [
<!ELEMENT faq ANY>
]>
<faq>
Some content might go here, as defined in the internal subset.
</faq>
```

The advantage to embedding the DTD is that you only have to deal with a single document, rather than separate ones. You might find an embedded DTD useful, particularly if you're debugging a new DTD and editing both an XML document and the DTD while you're experimenting. Additionally, if you're creating a relatively short DTD or one that you'll use for smaller documents, this would be a good option.

There are two drawbacks to embedding the DTD. In particular, your document could potentially become packed with markup, which makes the document more difficult to read. Rather than viewing only XML document content or DTD information, as you would with separate documents, you'll be forced to wade through the DTD information every time you want to view or modify the XML content. Also, the data in the XML document would be less readily reused and repurposed if it's physically tied to a DTD.

For these reasons, if you plan to create a complex DTD or one that you'll use repeatedly or for large documents (as you'll likely be doing), we recommend that you create a separate DTD and reference it in the <!DOCTYPE> declaration, as discussed in the following section.

Referencing the DTD

Your best choice for connecting the DTD to the XML document is to reference it within the XML document—that is, create a separate DTD document and point to it from the XML document. Referencing external DTD declarations, also known as the *external subset*, is similar to embedding it in that you use the <!DOCTYPE> declaration. The difference, as shown in the following markup, is that you include only the reference and provide no additional information about how your document should be structured:

```
<?xml version="1.0"?>
<!DOCTYPE faq SYSTEM "faq.dtd">
<faq>
```

The advantage to referencing a separate DTD is that it's ideal for long or complex DTDs. You can more easily access and modify DTD markup if it's in a separate file than you can if it's embedded in the XML document.

In addition, having a separate DTD makes reusing the DTD for other XML documents much easier. Rather than having to copy and paste DTD information, as you would if it's embedded, you can simply reference the DTD from multiple XML documents. You create the DTD one time and reference it as many times as you need.

The disadvantage to referencing a separate DTD is that you have to deal with two documents. For many uses, this may not be a problem; however, for small, simple DTDs, experimental DTDs, or ones under development, embedding the DTD might be a better option.

Combining External and Internal DTDs

External DTD subsets are good for defining a common vocabulary for a collection of XML documents. On the other hand, internal DTD subsets are beneficial for defining customized grammar rules for a specific document. More times than not, you'll find yourself wanting to take advantage of both of these approaches. The XML specification allows document authors to combine both internal and external subsets as a complete collection of declarations for a given document.

The syntax for combining internal and external subsets is as follows:

```
<?xml version="1.0"?>
<!DOCTYPE faq SYSTEM "faq.dtd" [
  <!ENTITY copy "Copyright 2002">
 ]>
<faq>
```

In the previous example, the XML document references the external DTD subset (`faq.dtd`), while including an internal `ENTITY` declaration. Although it's not recommended that you create conflicting declarations, if this does occur, the declaration that is read first by the processing application (the internal subset declarations) takes precedence.

Where to Go from Here

In this chapter, we introduced you to basic DTD rules and concepts and showed you how DTDs connect to XML documents. You may be thinking that these nitpicky rules, concepts, and markup are a lot to remember—and you're right. Keep in mind, though, that applying them (as you'll do starting in Chapter 24) is much easier than keeping them straight in your mind. With the information you learned in this chapter, you're ready to learn about the DTD development process and then move on to developing your first DTD.

Now, you're ready to move ahead:

◆ Go to Chapter 24 to create your own XML DTD.

◆ Check out Chapter 22 for more about XML's special relationship with XHTML, and how that relationship can be expanded using namespaces.

◆ See Chapter 21 for more about XML in general.

Chapter 24

Creating a DTD

In Chapter 23, we examined the basic rules and concepts you apply when developing DTDs. In this chapter, we'll discuss the basic DTD development process and DTD components that you'll need to become familiar with before you develop your first DTD.

As we'll show you, developing DTDs is basically a two-phase process:

1. You provide processing information, which tells parsers or specialized applications how to process the XML document. This step is the short and simple one—not many decisions to make here.

2. You fill in DTD content, which tells parsers or specialized applications the structure and rules it should apply.

In learning about these two phases, keep in mind that you'll complete the second one iteratively. Particularly when filling in DTD content, you'll undoubtedly add to, delete from, or otherwise modify the DTD so that it meets your specific needs. These two phases, however, are the basic aspects—one short and fixed, one longer and iterative—in building DTDs.

This chapter covers the following topics:

◆ Specifying processing instructions

◆ Filling in DTD content

◆ Putting it all together

Specifying Processing Instructions

Your first task in developing a DTD is to include some basics about how processing applications (parsers or other programs such as editors or browsers) should process DTD information. This information, called *processing instructions*, gives processing applications details about the XML document and helps ensure that they process the XML document correctly.

Although you don't have to include processing instructions (and whether you do depends completely on what your processing application requires), you should, at a minimum, include the *XML declaration*. In doing so, you state that the processing application adheres to the rules of a specific XML version, such as XML version 1.0 (currently) or version 3.4 (hypothetically) or whatever.

Just like the HTML specification, the XML specification might change a bit with new versions, so you need to tell processing applications with which version the XML document complies.

TIP   Although XML declarations use the same syntax as processing instructions, and even perform functions similar to those of other processing instructions, they're not technically processing instructions. The XML declaration is its very own unique piece of markup that defines version and encoding information about an XML document. This distinction may seem trivial, but it's important to understand.

As shown in the following brief excerpt from a DTD, the XML declaration is the first element in the DTD:

```
<?xml version="1.0"?>
<!ELEMENT faq (title, motto, maintainer, category)>
<!ELEMENT category (topic,(question, answer)+)>
<!ELEMENT maintainer (who, date)>
<!ELEMENT question (#PCDATA)>
<!ELEMENT answer (#PCDATA)>
<!ELEMENT motto (#PCDATA)>
<!ELEMENT title (#PCDATA)>
<!ELEMENT topic (#PCDATA)>
<!ELEMENT who (#PCDATA)>
<!ELEMENT date (#PCDATA)>
```

In this example, the XML declaration includes only information about the XML version—in this case, version 1.0—which is sufficient for telling processing applications to which XML version to adhere.

You can, however, also include two other bits of information in the XML declaration. First, you can specify that the DTD stands on its own and that it does not reference or link to other DTDs. To do this, simply add the standalone attribute, as shown in the following markup:

```
<?xml version="1.0" standalone="yes"?>
```

Or you can specify that the DTD does not stand on its own—that is, it references (includes) other DTDs. In this case, you add a no value to the standalone attribute, like this:

```
<?xml version="1.0" standalone="no"?>
```

TIP   You'll find more information about referencing other DTDs later in this chapter in the "Parameter Entities" section.

Second, you can specify an encoding for the DTD and XML document. *Encodings* specify character sets used, such as a Western character set, a Cyrillic character set, or various Asian character sets. By specifying that the processing application should expect a particular encoding, you help eliminate ambiguity in how it processes the information.

The default encoding is UTF-8, which includes all common ASCII characters in addition to most characters in common Western languages. The following markup adds the encoding attribute:

```
<?xml version="1.0" standalone="no" encoding="UTF-8"?>
```

TIP   You'll find more information about encodings in the "More about Encodings" sidebar at the end of this section.

In addition to including the XML declaration, you can add other processing declarations that meet your specific needs. Keep in mind that these instructions are just bits of information you provide so that the processing application knows how to parse and process your XML documents. To use other declarations, you'll either add them according to instructions provided with the processing application, or if you're writing a processing application, you can specify the instructions. Your only limitation in writing your own instructions is that you do *not* start them with <?xml, <?XML, or any variation in capitalization because this chunk of markup is reserved for future XML uses.

So, for example, if you want to create custom processing instructions for an application that counts the number of times a page is viewed, you might include markup that looks like

```
<?CustomProcessingApp increment PageViews?>
```

and CustomProcessingApp would presumably know what to do with the instructions. You begin the markup with an opening angle bracket (<) and question mark (?), and you end with a question mark (?) and a closing angle bracket (>). The information, or instructions, to be processed appears between these, but exactly what you fill in between the <? and the ?> depends on what your processing application requires. The documentation should tell you.

That's all there is to specifying processing instructions. At a minimum, you include the XML declaration, which specifies the XML version, whether the DTD stands alone, and encodings. Other declarations are optional.

MORE ABOUT ENCODINGS

XML supports *Unicode*, which is an international standard for character encodings. By requiring Unicode support for all XML applications, XML developers ensure that XML documents are internationally portable—unlike many other document formats. This means that you can include virtually any characters used in any language in the world in your XML documents by simply specifying the correct encoding.

All XML processors must be able to recognize and read UTF-8 encodings (which include ASCII characters and Western language characters) and UTF-16 encodings (which include UTF-8 encodings plus most other possible characters available internationally). If you're using either of these encodings, you don't have to include an encoding declaration—although it'd be a good idea to clearly specify which encoding you use anyway.

If you plan to use other encodings, you *must* specify them in the DTD.

Filling in DTD Content

After including processing instructions, your next step is to fill in DTD content, which consists of four general types of declarations:

- ◆ Element
- ◆ Attribute
- ◆ Entity
- ◆ Notation

As you're beginning to understand what each of these declarations does, keep in mind that you use these declarations to specify the rules and structure you must follow when developing an XML document. Each declaration directly corresponds to what you can or cannot include in an XML document. We'll show you markup samples throughout the following sections, but you might also refer to the "Putting It All Together" section to see how these declarations fit into a DTD.

Element Type Declarations

Element type declarations are perhaps the most common declarations you'll use because they let you identify specific and common parts of XML documents (called elements, logically). For example, using element type declarations, you can specify that an XML document contain items such as headings, citations, addresses, paragraphs, figure captions, and lists. Each of these refers to a different part of an XML document, and, therefore, each requires a separate element type declaration in the DTD. As a start, your element type declarations might look similar to the following bits of markup:

```
<!ELEMENT heading …>
<!ELEMENT citation …>
<!ELEMENT address …>
<!ELEMENT paragraph …>
<!ELEMENT caption …>
<!ELEMENT list …>
```

TIP   *Keep in mind that elements identify content, not presentation. In other words, a* list *element might indicate an enumeration of items; however, it does not necessarily mean that the items would appear aligned vertically with bullet characters in front of each item. You need to use style sheets to achieve that.*

In addition to specifying various elements that can occur within an XML document, you use element type declarations to identify what can be included within the element—that is, which elements will nest in the first element. In particular, you can specify that:

- Only specified elements can be included.

- Only data, such as words, numbers, or characters, can be included.

- Both specified elements and data can be included.

- Any element or data can be included.

- No elements or data can be included (the element is empty).

QUICK LOOKUP

In Chapter 23, we used the term *elements* generically to describe parts of an XML document—as in the elements that make up an XML document. In this chapter, we again use the term *element*, but in this more precise use, it refers to the *element* as used in an XML document, as in <!ELEMENT…>. An *element type declaration*, then, resides in the DTD.

SPECIFYING THAT ELEMENTS CAN BE INCLUDED

Within element type declarations, you'll commonly want to specify that other elements can be included. For example, the XHTML DTD specifies that an XHTML document must include an html element; it then further specifies that a head element *and* a body element be included with it. In doing so, it specifies that a particular element can be included within an existing element. The final code looks like this:

```
<!ELEMENT html (head, body)>
```

TIP   *For a reminder about the meanings and uses of parentheses and commas, refer to Chapter 23.*

Notice that each of these element type declarations begins with an opening angle bracket (<), includes !ELEMENT, identifies the name of the particular element being defined, and closes with a closing angle bracket (>). You'll use this format for all element type declarations.

This element type declaration, which declares an element and specifies what can be included in it, would allow you to create the following markup in an XHTML document:

```
<html>
  <head>...</head>
  <body>...</body>
</html>
```

As defined by the html element declaration, the html element includes the head element, followed by the body element.

SPECIFYING THAT DATA CAN BE INCLUDED

You can also specify that data can be included within an element. Data can include things such as words, numbers, or individual characters—practically any text that's not an element. All you have to do is include (#PCDATA) in the element type declaration, like this:

```
<!ELEMENT code (#PCDATA)>
```

TIP   *For a reminder about PCDATA, see Chapter 23.*

In this example, (#PCDATA) tells processing applications that any data can be included within the code element and that the data in the code element will be parsed. In using #PCDATA, you create what's called a *mixed content model*, which basically means that the element can contain mixed content, including normal characters and numbers, as well as entities, other elements (although the preceding example doesn't allow elements), numbers, or characters.

TIP   *Find out more about entities in the "Entity Declarations" section later in this chapter.*

In the following XML document markup, the data defined by (#PCDATA) appears as text included between opening and closing elements:

```
<code>info@example.com</code>
```

SPECIFYING THAT BOTH ELEMENTS AND DATA CAN BE INCLUDED

In other cases, you might want to specify that both elements and data can be included. For example, you might want to have a p element to mark a paragraph. Within a paragraph, you could reasonably have both text and other markup elements, like those for bold, emphasis, or italics. In this case, you'd structure the markup like this:

```
<!ELEMENT p (#PCDATA | b | em | i)*>
```

This is another example of a mixed content model, in which the element can be accompanied by data and a specific element. Notice the order in which the information appears. Like other element type declarations, it begins with <!ELEMENT, continues with the element name and an expression that closes with *, and concludes with >. Any time you mix data and elements, you must specify #PCDATA first, and then specify the element or elements and include the * to show that it can occur or recur any number of times.

TIP *An expression is a combination of logical operators and other objects that define what may or may not occur in parts of an XML document.*

The resulting XML document markup might look like the following sample:

```
<p>The paragraph element may contain text, <b>bold</b>,
    <em>emphasis</em>, and <i>italic</i> elements.</p>
```

SPECIFYING THAT ANYTHING CAN BE INCLUDED

Occasionally, you might want to specify that anything—data, elements, or characters—can be included. In doing so, you perhaps make it simpler to know what can and cannot be included with an element; however, you also make the resulting XML document less structured, which can make using and reusing the information more difficult. How? Well, if many elements can have any content, you could have as little structure or logic as you'd have in a merely well-formed, but not valid, document. You could not require that document developers adhere to any particular standard, which could lead to inconsistent document content and structure.

If, however, it's not important to guarantee consistency, use ANY in the element type declaration, as follows:

```
<!ELEMENT p ANY>
```

SPECIFYING THAT NOTHING CAN BE INCLUDED

Finally, you may want to specify that nothing can be included with an element—that the element is empty. If, for example, you provide specific information within attributes for an element but plan to have no information enclosed between the element's opening and closing tags, you would ensure that the element itself does not contain any information by defining it as empty.

To specify that nothing can be included with an element, use EMPTY in the element type declaration, like this:

```
<!ELEMENT meta EMPTY>
```

The resulting XML document markup might look like this:

```
<meta attributes="optional" />
```

or this:

```
<meta attributes="optional"></meta>
```

TIP   *Several empty elements are defined for XHTML, such as* `img`, `br`, `hr`, `meta`, `input`, `area`, `base`, `col`, `frame`, `link`, *and* `param`.

Attribute List Declarations

In XML documents, you often use elements in conjunction with attributes that provide additional information about the element. Logically, because you use an element type declaration to set the rules for the elements, you use an *attribute list declaration* to specify rules for using an attribute.

If you're thinking that you can already specify additional information about elements using elements nested within an element, you're right. In this sense, you're specifying additional information about elements, much the same way that attribute list declarations do. However, the difference is somewhat arbitrary—you could feasibly use nested elements to function as attributes or use attributes to function as nested elements. In deciding which declaration to use, consider the type of information you're specifying. Typically, you'll want to use element type declarations to include information that XML document users will view, and you'll want to use attribute list declarations for behind-the-scenes information that's only relevant to you, other developers, or perhaps processing applications.

For example, suppose you're developing a bibliography. Using element type declarations, you would likely declare a `book` element that requires a `title` element and specify that additional information be included as elements, such as authors and publication dates:

```
<!ELEMENT book (title | author | pubdate)>
```

The resulting markup in an XML document would look like this:

```
<book>
<title>Mastering HTML and XHTML</title>
<author>Ray and Ray</author>
<pubdate>2002</pubdate>
</book>
```

This additional information would be useful to potential XML document users; therefore, it makes sense to make it available as individual elements within the XML document.

In some XML applications, however, you'll want to specify information that's not necessarily useful to users. For example, you might want to provide information about the shelving category or potential audience. This information is useful for two reasons: It helps provide information that's valuable when developing and reusing XML documents, and it gives processing applications the context and targets that are necessary to sort or search for information. Because these reasons focus more on what's useful to you, as the developer, and a processing application—not a potential XML document user—you should consider including this information using attribute list declarations.

TIP *As a general rule, use* element type declarations *to provide additional information that's useful to XML document users. Use* attribute list declarations *to provide additional information that's useful to you or a processing application.*

You use attribute list declarations to do the following:

◆ Define the set of attributes for a given element type.

◆ Establish constraints for attributes.

◆ Provide default values for attributes.

◆ Provide information about whether the attribute is required and, if not, how the processing application should react if a declared attribute is absent.

Like element type declarations, attribute list declarations consist of specific information and are structured in a particular way. For example, the XHTML `img` element can accept a number of attributes. For simplicity sake, however, we pretend it can accept only one attribute, `src`:

```
<!ELEMENT img EMPTY>
```

To specify additional information about the `img` element, such as the kind of information that can go in it, you could develop an attribute list declaration:

```
<!ATTLIST img src CDATA #REQUIRED>
```

Notice that the attribute list declaration does the following:

◆ Begins with an opening angle bracket (<)

◆ Includes `!ATTLIST`, which specifies the declaration as an attribute list declaration

◆ Specifies the element name, `img`, that corresponds with the name of the element

◆ Specifies the attribute name, `src`

◆ Specifies the data type, `CDATA`

◆ Specifies an attribute setting, `#REQUIRED`

◆ Closes with an angle bracket (>)

No matter what information the attribute includes, you'll always follow this basic convention for forming attribute list declarations. Most of the information within the attribute list declaration will be fairly consistent from declaration to declaration; however, you'll always need to determine two essential components: name-value pairs and attribute settings.

SPECIFYING ATTRIBUTE NAME-VALUE PAIRS

Name-value pairs include the attribute name, which describes the attribute, and a value, which specifies parameters for the attribute. In developing a name-value pair, first determine the attribute name; you simply choose one that describes the attribute.

Determining the type of value, however, is a bit more complex because you can add three types of values. Your first option is to use *string values*, which include characters and/or numbers (such as 285, "One Fine Day," or "Pennsylvania6500"). These examples identify a specific attribute value—that is, the value associates with the attribute name. You could also develop a less specific string value that contains simply data, as follows:

```
<!ATTLIST img alt CDATA #REQUIRED>
```

In this example, the CDATA data type indicates that the attribute could contain any string for the value of the img attribute. So, for example, the corresponding attribute in the XML document might look like this:

```
<img alt="alternative text"/>
```

In most cases, however, you'll want to allow for any old string. As here, the value of the alt attribute is up to the document author. However, if there are only a few options for an attribute value, it might be more useful to precisely specify the acceptable values in the DTD.

Your second option is to use *enumerated values*, which specify the possible values (such as yes or no, or 1, 0, or unknown). You use enumerated values when you know the possible values for any given attribute. The following markup indicates that the border attribute for the img element could be either 1 or 0:

```
<!ATTLIST img border (1|0) "1">
```

This markup would require that either 1 or 0—and nothing else—be used as the value for the border attribute. (The final "1" sets the default value, as covered in the "Specifying Attribute Settings" section later in this chapter.)

Your third option is to use *tokenized values*, which refer to specific information within the DTD or XML document (such as the unique ID of an element in the document). These values are somewhat more complicated to develop—basically because you have even more options to choose from—but they can come in handy. In particular, you can use one of several tokenized attribute values, as listed in Table 24.1.

TIP   You'll recognize CDATA from discussions in Chapter 23.

TABLE 24.1: TOKENIZED ATTRIBUTE VALUES

TOKENIZED VALUE	FUNCTION	EXAMPLE
CDATA	Textual data—the broadest and most general possibility.	`<!ATTLIST img alt CDATA #IMPLIED)>`
ID	Provides a unique ID within a document. (Works similarly to ID in XHTML style sheets.)	`<!ATTLIST img id ID) #IMPLIED>`
IDREF, IDREFS	References an ID from the same document. It must be present and accurate for the parser to accept it.	`<!ATTLIST td headers IDREFS #IMPLIED>`
ENTITY, ENTITIES	References external, binary entity or entities, such as an image. Entity jpeg must be declared in the DTD for this example to work.	`<!ATTLIST img photo jpeg ENTITY #IMPLIED)>`

Continued on next page

TABLE 24.1: TOKENIZED ATTRIBUTE VALUES *(continued)*		
NMTOKEN, NMTOKENS	Provides for attribute values as a name or names that must be proper XML names, not simply unparsed data like the CDATA example. Provides more specific information than CDATA.	`<!ATTLIST contact photoformat NMTOKEN #IMPLIED >`
NOTATION	Refers to the name of a declared notation. In this example, the value provided in the XML document must correspond to a notation declared in the DTD. The NOTATION (enumerated) option would generally be better.	`<!ATTLIST contact photoformat NOTATION (viewer | editor) #IMPLIED >`
Enumerated	Provides a list of specific options; in this case, the value can only be ismap.	`<!ATTLIST img ismap (ismap) #IMPLIED >`
NOTATION (enumerated)	Itemizes the names of a declared notation. In this example, the value provided in the XML document must correspond to the viewer and editor notations declared in the DTD.	`<!ATTLIST contact photoformat NOTATION (viewer | editor) #IMPLIED >`

TIP   For the examples in Table 24.1, we used XHTML attribute list declarations. However, the XHTML DTD does not use each data type, and therefore, we had to create a few of our own.

SPECIFYING ATTRIBUTE SETTINGS

In addition to specifying name-value pairs, you need to specify *attribute settings*, which describe characteristics of the name-value pairs—whether the attribute and value must be present (`#REQUIRED`), whether they're implied when not explicitly included (`#IMPLIED`), whether they must always contain a certain value (`#FIXED`), or whether default values (rather than specific settings) are provided.

Your first setting choice is required (`#REQUIRED`), which means that the element requires the attribute. In this case, the attribute must be included with the element; otherwise, parsers will reject the document because the document doesn't follow the rules specified in the DTD. You add `#REQUIRED` to an attribute list declaration like this:

```
<!ATTLIST img src CDATA #REQUIRED>
```

Your next choice is implied (`#IMPLIED`), which means that the element does not require that an attribute be specified but that the default attribute value (null) be sent to the processing application if nothing else is specified. The following attribute list declaration specifies that the `width` attribute for the `img` element is optional:

```
<!ATTLIST img width CDATA #IMPLIED>
```

Another choice is fixed (#FIXED), followed by the value the attribute must take, which means that the attribute must contain the default attribute setting or it will be rejected by the parser. In the following example, the xmlns attribute must have the value http://www.w3.org/1999/xhtml:

```
<!ATTLIST html xmlns CDATA #FIXED
    "http://www.w3.org/1999/xhtml">
```

TIP   You might notice that the value of ATTLIST *has the XHTML namespace. Because the XHTML specification requires the XHTML namespace to be defined as a part of the* html *element, the XHTML DTD defines that value as fixed.*

Finally, rather than using these specific settings, you can simply provide a default value, if appropriate, by placing the value at the end of the attribute list declaration. Using a default value is handy for making sure information is provided to the processing application. The following markup shows that the attribute value can be either 1 or 0 and that the default value is 1:

```
<!ATTLIST img border (1|0) "1">
```

HANDLING WHITE SPACE

When writing DTDs, you can indicate how processing applications should handle white space. *White space* refers to spaces, carriage returns, line feeds, and tabs included in XML documents. In all cases, parsers must pass white space in XML documents to the processing application, but processing applications will likely ignore insignificant white space and present only the significant white space used. For example, in the following XML document fragment, the processing application would ignore the white space around elements because it's used only to make the XML markup easier to read:

```
<body>
<h1>House Plant FAQ</h1>
<p>Motto: All the plant questions you've lost sleep over,
    and then some. </p>
<div class="footer">
    <p>Maintained by Digit Brown</p>
    <p>April 1, 2002</p>
</div>
</body>
```

You include white space in XML documents primarily to make the (often-crowded) document easier to read.

In some instances, however, you might want to include white space in an XML document that should be retained and presented by a processing application. For example, if you're writing poetry or providing examples of computer programming languages, all spaces are likely significant. To indicate that the spaces matter, you simply add an extra instruction to the DTD—in particular, a special attribute, xml:space, for each element that you want the processing application to retain white space for in the processed document. In your DTD, you could include xml:space in the following attribute list declaration:

```
<!ATTLIST someelement xml:space 'preserve'>
```

In this example, the value default would signal that applications' default white-space processing modes are acceptable for this element. The value preserve would signal that applications preserve all the white space. The default value for the xml:space attribute is set to be preserve.

Entity Declarations

Entity declarations let you substitute information in a DTD, which is handy for easily reusing information in an XML document or even within the DTD itself. For example, if your company name is long and complex, you might want to use an entity declaration to allow people to use a shorter, substitute name in its place. By declaring an entity for a complex and hard-to-type name, you ensure that anyone developing a document can use the short entity and rely on the XML parser to put in the long name.

You can use three kinds of entity declarations—general entities, parameter entities, and character entities—each of which gives you specific capabilities.

GENERAL ENTITIES

General entities are substitutions that are made in the XML documents (as opposed to substitutions within the DTD). You define them in the DTD, but the changes and effects show up in the XML documents after processing.

Suppose your company is takeover-prone and you want a simpler way of replacing the old company name with a new company name. Rather than doing a search-and-replace through all your documents, you could more easily use general entities. All you have to do is use a general entity declaration in the DTD and then include the entity in the XML document. In doing so, every time the company name changes, you would only have to change the entity declaration in the DTD, and the parser would apply the new information in all the documents for you. No muss, no fuss.

For example, you might include an entity declaration in the DTD like this:

```
<!ENTITY companyname "John Smith and Sons">
```

WARNING *In an effort to keep our examples readable, throughout this section we do not use examples from the XHTML DTD. The XHTML DTD makes ample use of entities; however, they do not serve well as introductory examples. If you would like to see the XHTML entities in action, visit* www.w3.org/TR/xhtml1/DTD/xhtml1-transitional.dtd.

Then, your XML markup in a document associated with this DTD would look like this:

```
<P>Just remember, &companyname; has your best interests at
heart, and we'll always be here for you, whenever you need
us.</P>
```

The resulting parsed document would look like this:

```
Just remember, John Smith and Sons has your best interests
at heart, and we'll always be here for you, whenever you
need us.
```

What's particularly handy about general entities is that you can make changes to the DTD and easily apply them. For example, if your company name changes a week or so later, you could simply change the companyname entity in the DTD to specify the new name. Then all documents referencing the DTD would automatically be updated. The new parsed document might look like this:

```
Just remember, MegaCorporation has your best interests at
heart, and we'll always be here for you, whenever you need us.
```

In general, creating an entity is as easy as entering

```
<!ENTITY name "expansion">
```

In this example, *name* specifies the entity name (you make this up), and *expansion* specifies the replacement text that the parser should substitute whenever it encounters the entity. An entity name can include letters, numbers, dashes (-), underscores (_), periods (.), and colons (:), and it must begin with a letter or underscore.

Here, you're using a general entity in one DTD to substitute information in one or more XML documents—any documents that use that particular DTD. This is called an *internal entity* because it's completely contained within the DTD. You can also use what's called an *external entity* to reference an entity contained in a different file. For example, taking the company name change example one step further, suppose your company uses multiple DTDs, rather than just one. To change the company name throughout all XML documents, you'd need to replace the general entity in all the DTDs that include the company name. In this case, rather than making one quick change, you'd again be forced to change information in multiple documents. Instead, you could create a separate document—an external entity—that would contain the information to be changed and reference that document from every other document. Taking this approach, you could make the change one time in a single document and have that change affect many different XML documents. The following markup declares a `companyname` entity with the content of the `companyinfo.txt` file:

```
<!ENTITY companyname SYSTEM "companyinfo.txt">
```

External entities are either *system entities* or *public entities*; system entities are currently the most common and useful. Using system entities, you could reference information on the Internet or reference a graphics file, such as your company logo. To continue with the takeover-prone company example, in addition to substituting the company name, you may want to substitute a company logo in your document.

Therefore, if you wanted to include a reference to a `.jpg` format logo in the DTD, you could include something similar to the following:

```
<!ENTITY companylogo SYSTEM "johnsmithsonslogo.jpg" NDATA jpg>
```

In this example, the `SYSTEM` entity refers to a JPEG image, which is *non-text data* located outside the DTD. Non-text data can include such items as images or other binary files. You identify the non-text data using a *Uniform Resource Indicator (URI)*, which in this particular case is simply a graphic's filename, `johnsmithsonslogo.jpg`.

TIP   A URI is similar to a URL: It identifies a particular resource on the Internet. As a matter of fact, a URL is a type of URI.

If you're referencing non-text data, as we are here, you must also include a non-data reference (`NDATA`) and specify the type of data, in this case, `jpg`, so the processing applications know what kind of information to expect. If you're referencing text data, such as words or numbers or company names, you would not include the `NDATA` reference.

A WORD ABOUT PUBLIC ENTITIES AND IDENTIFIERS

In addition to using system entities and identifiers, as discussed here, you can use public entities and identifiers, which are commonly used by SGML applications. Confusingly, because anything on the Internet tends to be freely accessible and information in corporate networks tends to be restricted, "public entities" and "public identifiers" are the least public or accessible of anything you'll use in your XML journey.

You use public entities when you want to refer to standardized and publicly available data, such as a markup language standard. For example, an XHTML DOCTYPE declaration references a public identifier:

```
<!DOCTYPE HTML PUBLIC
    "-//W3C//DTD XHTML 1.0 Transitional//EN">
```

In this, the declaration (`"-//W3C//DTD XHTML 1.0 Transitional//EN"`) provides several bits of information: the organization that publishes the standard (W3C), what type of document it is (a DTD), what standard it references (XHTML 1.0), and which language it's written in (English).

You won't use public identifiers very often, unless you're coming from an SGML background and plan to continue to use your existing SGML tools for development.

PARAMETER ENTITIES

You use parameter entities to build and reuse DTDs more effectively. Parameter entities follow the same general principle outlined for general entities—they let you make automatic substitutions so you can more easily reuse information. Rather than making a substitution in the resulting XML document, however, the substitution occurs in the DTD.

Again, with parameter entities, you have both internal and external entities. You use an internal entity to expand information within a DTD. For example, you might use an internal parameter entity like this:

```
<!ENTITY % name definition>
```

Notice that this markup begins with a percent sign (%), followed by the entity name (`name`), and then the expansion text or definition of the entity (`definition`). The entity name must begin with a letter or an underscore (_), but you can use letters, numbers, dashes (-), underscores (_), periods (.), and/or colons (:) in the rest of the name.

If you have a set of elements in your current DTD that all have a common set of attributes (for example, `ModifiedDate` and `ModifiedBy`), you could define those attributes one time at the top of the DTD, as shown here:

```
<!ENTITY % commonAttributes
"ModifiedDate CDATA #REQUIRED
ModifiedBy CDATA #REQUIRED">
```

Then for each element that requires those two attributes, you can simply include the parameter entity `commonAttributes`, rather than the complete text. For instance, in this example:

```
<!ELEMENT report (#PCDATA | content )*>
```

```
<!ATTLIST report %commonAttributes;>
<!ELEMENT evaluation (#PCDATA | content )*>
<!ATTLIST evaluation %commonAttributes;>
```

a parser would expand the entity references to look like this:

```
<!ELEMENT report (#PCDATA | content )*>
<!ATTLIST report
ModifiedDate CDATA #REQUIRED
ModifiedBy CDATA #REQUIRED>
<!ELEMENT evaluation (#PCDATA | content )*>
<!ATTLIST evaluation
ModifiedDate CDATA #REQUIRED
ModifiedBy CDATA #REQUIRED>
```

You use an external parameter entity to reference standard parts of a DTD that are to be included in other DTDs. To return to the company name example, you could create a DTD that contains authoritative information about the company name and include an external parameter entity that specifies the company name. In doing so, you could change the company name one time in the master DTD and automatically make the change throughout the other DTDs.

So, in the master DTD, called `companyinfo.dtd`, you might have a `companyname` entity declaration, like this:

```
<!ENTITY companyname "John Smith and Sons">
```

and all other DTDs would reference the master DTD, like this:

```
<!ENTITY % companyinfo SYSTEM
   "http://www.company.com/companyinfo.dtd">
```

In this case, you could include the `companyinfo.dtd` file in all DTDs that referenced it and apply all entities (and everything else) defined in the DTD to all documents referencing it.

Finally, you can also use parameter entities to shorten DTDs and make them easier to use. For example, rather than creating a lengthy DTD that includes a set of commonly used character entities, elements to establish basic document structure for a memo, and additional elements to provide a structured status report within the memo, you might create three smaller, modular DTDs: one with common character entities, one with memo elements, and one with status report elements. Then, you can use parameter entities to include the three DTDs by reference. In doing so, you can reference the memo DTD for any or all memos you use, just as you can reference the character entities DTD for all documents that require those characters.

CHARACTER ENTITIES

You use character entities to add special characters and symbols to DTDs that you could not otherwise include. For example, suppose you need to include an opening angle bracket (<) in your DTD. In a non-markup language document, you could simply use the angle bracket key on your keyboard. However, because angle brackets are part of XML markup (for example, `<element>`), you cannot simply use the angle bracket key on your keyboard and have the symbol remain part of the document.

Processing applications would treat the angle bracket as part of the behind-the-scenes markup, which gets processed. So, to include an opening angle bracket and have it remain as part of the DTD, you must substitute the characters <, which translate to an opening angle bracket. XML comes with five built-in entities, as shown in Table 24.2.

You can include these five character entities in any XML document without having to specify that you've used them.

To include these entities, you simply include the markup directly in the XML document, like this:

```
<p>Few people have B&amp;W televisions any more.</p>
```

to yield

```
Few people have B&W televisions any more.
```

The & entity tells parsers to replace the entity with the ampersand symbol (&).

TABLE 24.2: BUILT-IN XML CHARACTER ENTITIES

CHARACTER ENTITY	RESULTING SYMBOL
&amp;	&
&lt;	<
&gt;	>
&apos;	'
&quote;	"

You're not limited to these five built-in character entities. You can use literally thousands of character entities derived from practically any language known internationally. You'll find a list of references to special characters in Master's Reference 5, which will meet most of your needs, or you can refer to specific resources for the language from which the characters are derived.

If you choose to use a character entity that's not built into XML, you must specify the entity in the DTD. For example, if you want to include a musical sharp symbol (#) in an XML document, you include markup like this in the DTD:

```
<!ENTITY sharp "&#x266F;">
```

The resulting XML document markup would look something like this:

```
<tip>Musicians must always remember the significance of
    the &sharp; symbol.</tip>
```

And, the parsed document would look something like this:

```
Musicians must always remember the significance of
    the # symbol.
```

TIP   *Character references that begin with &#x are a hexadecimal representation of the character number in the ISO/IEC 10646 standard. Character references that begin with &# are a decimal representation of the character number.*

Notation Declarations

You use notation declarations to help processing applications determine how to process non-XML references or information. For example, suppose you want to reference an object available in the Portable Network Graphics (PNG) image format. Because PNG is not an XML format, processing applications are not required to know what to do with the reference (although they might) and, therefore, may not be able to use the referenced image. In this case, you could use a notation entity to provide a suggestion about how the PNG file might be processed:

```
<!NOTATION png SYSTEM "graphview.exe">
```

Notice that this declaration includes !NOTATION, a name (png), and an external reference (graphview .exe). This markup suggests, but does not require, that processing applications use a graphics viewer (graphview.exe) to process the PNG file. Also, because the reference is platform specific, the suggestion does not provide useful information for Macintosh or Unix users—that's okay, though, because the external reference is only a suggestion for processing and does not require that the processing application actually use it.

Putting It All Together

In this chapter, we've given you lots of information—mostly bits and pieces of information you need to keep track of as you're developing DTDs. We expect that you'll probably refer to this chapter several times, at least until you get some practice developing DTDs. To see how all these tidbits fit together, take a look at the following:

- ◆ Listing 24.1 shows a sample DTD.
- ◆ Listing 24.2 shows the XML document.
- ◆ Listing 24.3 shows the style sheet.
- ◆ Figure 24.1 shows how all these pieces come together in the parsed document.

TIP   *Listings 24.1–24.3 can be found on this book's Web site.*

LISTING 24.1: A SAMPLE DTD

```
<!-- This is a comment in a DTD -->
<!ENTITY sponsor "John Smith and Associates, Inc.">
<!ENTITY % qa "(question, answer)+">

<!ELEMENT faq (title, motto, maintainer, category)>
<!ELEMENT category (topic,%qa;)>
<!ATTLIST category reviewed CDATA #FIXED "Jane Smith">
```

```
<!ELEMENT maintainer (who, date)>
<!ELEMENT question (#PCDATA)>
<!ELEMENT answer (#PCDATA)>
<!ELEMENT name (#PCDATA)>
<!ELEMENT motto (#PCDATA)>
<!ELEMENT title (#PCDATA)>
<!ELEMENT topic (#PCDATA)>
<!ATTLIST topic term (adv|elem) "adv">
<!ATTLIST topic revised (yes|no) "yes"
   import CDATA "low" >
<!ELEMENT who (#PCDATA)>
<!ELEMENT date (#PCDATA)>
```

LISTING 24.2: POSSIBLE RESULTING XML MARKUP THAT COMPLIES WITH THE DTD IN LISTING 24.1

```
<?xml version="1.0"?>
<?xml-stylesheet type="text/css" href="faq.css"?>
<!DOCTYPE faq SYSTEM "faq.dtd">
<faq>
<title>House Plant FAQ</title>
<motto>Motto: All the plant questions you've lost sleep over,
   and then some. </motto>
<maintainer>
   <who>Maintained by Digit Brown</who>
   <date>April 1, 2002</date>
</maintainer>

<category>
<topic revised="yes" term="adv">Problems with Dying Plants
   </topic>
   <question>Why are my plants limp and yellow?</question>
   <answer>Because you water them too much! </answer>
   <question>Why are my plants crispy and brown?</question>
   <answer>Because you don't water them enough! </answer>
   <question>Why don't my plants have a neat pattern like
   they should?</question>
   <answer>Because we're not talking about tie-dying
   plants! </answer>
</category>
</faq>
```

LISTING 24.3: ADD A STYLE SHEET TO ADD FORMATTING TO THE XML DOCUMENT

```
faq         {font-family : Arial}
motto       {display : block ;
             font-style : normal ;
             font-weight : normal ;
             font-size 14pt ;
             margin : 1em 1em 1em 1em ;
             font-family : "Comic Sans MS" ;
             float : right ;
             border : 1px black solid ;
             width : 50% ;
             padding : 8px
             }
maintainer  {display : block ;
             font-style : normal ;
             font-weight : normal ;
             margin : 1em 1em 1em 1em ;
             font-family : Technical
             }
email       {margin : 1em ; font-style : italic ;}
qacombo     {display : block ;
             margin-top : 1em}
topic       {display : block ;
             font-style : italic ;
             font-weight : bold ;
             font-size : 18pt ;
             margin-top : 2em}
question    {display : block ;
             font-style : italic ;
             font-weight : bold ;
             margin-top : 1em
             }
answer      {display : block ;
             font-style : normal ;
             font-weight : normal ;
             margin-left : 2em}
title       {display : block ;
             font-size : 24pt ;
             font-weight : bold ;
             border-top : solid 2px red ;
             font-family : "Comic Sans MS"}
```

FIGURE 24.1

The DTD, XML document, and style sheet all come together in this parsed document

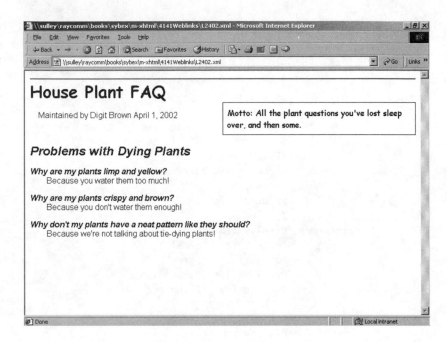

Where to Go from Here

In this chapter, we've examined the basic DTD development process, which gives you the foundation necessary to build DTDs. In particular, DTDs include two major components: processing information, which tells parsers or specialized applications how to process the XML document, and the rest of the DTD content, which specifies the elements and attributes that can be used in XML documents.

From here, you're ready to take these pieces and begin developing your own DTDs and XML documents. You'll likely refer to this chapter frequently as you're developing these.

- ◆ Refer to Chapter 23 for information about connecting documents to a DTD.

- ◆ Revisit Chapter 9 for a refresher on style sheets.

Chapter 25

XHTML 1.1 and XHTML Modularization

ON MAY 31, 2001, the W3C released a recommended specification titled "XHTML 1.1 - Module Based XHTML." (Note that when a W3C specification attains recommended status, it's become an official standard for all intents and purposes.) As the name for this specification indicates, this particular formulation for XHTML 1.1 follows "The Modularization of XHTML" specification closely, which itself attained recommended status on April 10, 2001 (www.w3.org/TR/2001/REC-xhtml-modularization-20010410).

To make a long story as straightforward as possible, we decided to use this chapter to not only cover the ins and outs of XHTML Modularization, but also to cover the XHTML 1.1 requirements. Because those requirements depend almost entirely on XHTML Modularization, this combination makes sense in the overall context of this book.

NOTE   *This chapter addresses a number of topics that are valuable for planning and design purposes, particularly if you will be using some variant of XHTML for cell phones or other nontraditional applications. At the time this was written, however, the information in this chapter is not supported by widely available tools or applications, and so is fairly abstract.*

This chapter covers the following topics:

◆ Understanding XHTML Modularization and XHTML 1.1

◆ Exploring the XHTML abstract modules

◆ Using DTDs for XHTML abstract modules

◆ Using schemas for XHTML abstract modules

◆ Mixing and matching XHTML abstract modules

Understanding XHTML Modularization

Basically, *modularization* breaks up the entire collection of markup defined in XHTML 1.0 (and, by direct extension, HTML 4.01) into a collection of independent markup subsets called abstract modules. Each abstract module is meant to address some specific set of data or functions—the specification states that each abstract module "...defines one kind of data that is semantically different from all others." The idea is to define individual sets of markup that may be mixed and matched to create tailored document types without requiring document designers to understand their underlying schemas or Document Type Definitions (DTDs) fully and completely. As needed, modules can be assembled into a whole that more closely matches the designers' needs.

The most important reason for modularizing XHTML is to support applications or platforms where displays may not support, or document data may not need, all the markup defined in the entire monolithic XHTML 1.0 DTDs (whether it be the Strict, Transitional, or Frameset version).

A popular example used to justify modularization is a Web-enabled personal digital assistant (PDA) or cell phone, where frames, tables, and graphics support may be overkill and may not display properly. Likewise, with all kinds of non-desktop devices adding Internet access (LG Electronics already offers an Internet-ready refrigerator and microwave oven, with other Internet-ready appliances under development) more uses for this technology are inevitable, if still not completely understood or familiar.

In a nutshell, XHTML Modularization lets document designers create document types that omit unwanted or unusable markup. It also creates flexible target document descriptions for documents created on the fly from XML data, for delivery to non-desktop devices. In turn, selecting a subset of XHTML abstract modules supports smaller, simpler parsers, smaller files, faster downloads, and so on—highly desirable for any kind of embedded or compact systems like the ones we've described. In fact, a cellular telephone manufacturers' consortium announced on March 21, 2001, that it will adopt XHTML for future wireless Internet applications for these very reasons.

Encapsulating XHTML Abstract Modules

In XHTML lingo, an *abstract XHTML module* is a subset of elements, attributes, and related content models, associated with a particular kind of markup or function within a typical XHTML document. In the abstract sense, an XHTML module is nothing more than a strict subset of some full-blown XHTML 1.0 DTD (or equivalent schema), taken as a stand-alone definition, ready for incorporation into some XHTML document or into some more general DTD or schema.

In practice, each module implementation consists of a set of element types, a set of attribute list declarations, and a set of content model declarations. This also explains how individual modules can be combined as needed to meet specific document requirements. Better yet, the modularization framework makes it possible to integrate multiple DTDs to create a new document type that can be validated using XML validation techniques. This makes the X in XHTML—which stands for *extensible*—more attainable using XHTML Modularization. (By extension, this applies to XHTML 1.1, as you'll learn in the following section.)

Table 25.1 provides a brief description of the abstract modules currently defined for XHTML; these will be more fully described later in this chapter.

TABLE 25.1: XHTML ABSTRACT MODULES

MODULE NAME	DESCRIPTION
Core Modules	All four core modules are required for minimal modular XHTML
Structure	XHTML structure elements (body, head, etc.)
Text	Basic text container elements (h1, p, etc.)
Hypertext	Basic hyperlinking (a element)
List	List-oriented elements (ol, ul, li, etc.)
Forms Modules	
Basic Forms	Minimal set of forms markup
Forms	Complete set of forms markup
Table Modules	
Basic Tables	Minimal set of table markup
Tables	Complete set of table markup
Text Extension Modules	
Presentation	Supports simple presentation markup
Edit	Supports del and ins elements
Bi-directional Text	Permits text to run right-to-left or left-to-right
Other Standard Modules	
Image	Provides basic image embedding
Client-Side Image Map	Handles client-side image maps
Server-Side Image Map	Handles server-side image map formats
Object	Supports general inclusion of external objects
Frames	Supports frames
Target	Supports destination targets for selections
Iframe	Supports use of inline frames
Intrinsic Events	Supports intrinsic XHTML events (onblur, onfocus, onload, onunload, and onchange)
Metainformation	Supports meta element
Scripting	Enables/disables support for executable scripts
Style Sheet	Enables declaration of internal style sheets
Style Attribute	Enables use of the style attribute

Continued on next page

TABLE 25.1: XHTML ABSTRACT MODULES *(continued)*

Link	For defining links to external resources
Base	Provides context for relative URLs
Deprecated Modules	
Applet	Supports the deprecated `applet` element
Name Identification	Supports the deprecated `name` attribute
Legacy	Supports other deprecated elements and attributes from HTML 4.0

Meet the XHTML 1.1 Specification

Here's some great news: XHTML 1.1 is nearly exactly equivalent to the version of XHTML 1.0 defined by the Strict XHTML DTD. This is the very same DTD invoked by the following DOCTYPE declaration:

```
<!DOCTYPE html PUBLIC "-//W3C//DTD XHTML 1.0 Strict//EN"
    "DTD/xhtml1-strict.dtd">
```

Because Appendix A of the XHTML 1.1 Specification describes the differences between XHTML 1.1 and XHTML 1.0 Strict, we quote the relevant sections document here, but add our own emphasis in bold:

> *XHTML 1.1 represents a departure from both HTML 4 and XHTML 1.0. Most significant is the **removal of features that were deprecated**. In general, the strategy is to define **a markup language that is rich in structural functionality, but that relies upon style sheets for presentation**.*
>
> *The differences can be summarized as follows:*
>
> ♦ *On every element, the **lang** attribute has been removed in favor of the **xml:lang** attribute (as defined in [XHTMLMOD]).*
>
> ♦ *On the **a** and **map** elements, the **name** attribute has been removed in favor of the **id** attribute (as defined in [XHTMLMOD]).*
>
> ♦ *The "ruby" collection of elements has been added (as defined in [RUBY]).*

For more information about the various items previously quoted or mentioned, please visit:

♦ XHTML 1.1 Appendix A: www.w3.org/TR/xhtml11/changes.html#a_changes

♦ XHTMLMOD: www.w3.org/TR/2001/REC-xhtml-modularization-20010410

♦ Ruby: www.w3.org/TR/2001/REC-ruby-20010531/

When approaching the contents of this book, if you want to stick strictly to XHTML 1.1, rather than the looser, more HTML-like XHTML 1.0 (using the Transitional or Frameset DTDs), please consider the following observations and provisos:

♦ The XHTML 1.0 Strict DTD omits numerous elements found in earlier implementations of HTML. Many of these omitted elements are used to control document appearance, including `basefont` for establishing a base document font, `font` for managing font selections explicitly, `center` for centering text, plus several text appearance and list style elements. Going forward, the W3C makes style sheets the only proper way to handle such things in XHTML 1.1. (Please note that deprecated modules can make this markup available if absolutely necessary, but it's highly unadvisable.)

♦ Deprecated elements and attributes disappear from XHTML 1.1 entirely. This means that many existing HTML or XHTML 1.0 documents must be "cleaned up" to validate to the XHTML 1.1 DTDs. Other elements in this category—some style-related ones are mentioned in the previous list element—include the `applet` element (replace with the `object` element) and the `isindex` element (replace with the `input` element). We provide a complete list of deprecated elements and attributes in Chapter 2, and also indicate which elements and attributes are deprecated in Master's Reference 1.

♦ XHTML 1.1 adheres to XHTML Modularization rules and naming conventions. Later in this chapter, we'll discuss what these rules are and how they work.

♦ Ruby annotations permit short snippets of text to appear beside the base text in an XHTML 1.1 document. Such annotations are used in many East Asian languages to supply pronunciation guides and notes. Ruby is defined in the form of an XHTML module for easy inclusion or omission. (Those creating documents in English or other European languages are less likely to use Ruby than those creating documents in East Asian languages, in any case.) For completeness, we also cover this module in this chapter, even though it's not part of the XHTML Modularization effort but rather belongs to the XHTML 1.1 Specification. For examples of this markup at work, see the examples section of the Ruby Annotation Specification at `www.w3.org/TR/2001/REC-ruby-20010531/`.

♦ Replacing the `lang` attribute with the `xml:lang` attribute, and the `name` attribute with the `id` attribute for a and map elements, makes XHTML syntax entirely consistent with XML going forward. Consider this a kind of practical simplification introduced in XHTML 1.1 to make XHTML more consistent with other forms of XML.

The removal of deprecated elements and attributes plus mandatory use of modularization are clearly the most significant changes here. Implementing these changes means that considerable effort, and in some cases, real redesign work, will be needed to convert XHTML 1.0 or HTML documents to XHTML 1.1. HTML-Tidy can help with this task, but until it's updated thoroughly (no word yet on when this might happen) manual effort will also be involved. Only you can decide if converting documents to XHTML 1.1 is something you should embrace, avoid, or postpone. That said, with no overriding need for the XHTML 1.1 capabilities and the unavailability of tools and browsers that take advantage of such features, you should prepare for, but not jump into, conversion.

Careful examination of Table 25.1 (and the related expanded sections on XHTML abstract modules that follow) shows that although the strict definition of XHTML 1.1 forbids the use of deprecated and presentation markup, abstract modules to support such markup have been defined and are available. In theory, this means you can start migrating to XHTML 1.1 and abstract XHTML modules without having to completely revise your code base. Nevertheless, we think planning for such a revision (and a possible redesign) is a good idea, because it's possible that the W3C may elect to make this deprecated markup obsolete in a future XHTML specification.

WARNING   *Remember, markup that is deprecated in XHTML 1.1 may no longer be legal or usable in subsequent revisions of XHTML.*

XHTML Modules: Abstract and Otherwise

In addition to the various specific abstract modules represented in Table 25.1, XHTML modules include various named attribute collections. To invoke an XHTML module within a document, however, you must include a definition of or a pointer to a real (not an abstract) module therein. Today, the W3C has defined DTDs that correspond to the XHTML abstract modules, and work is under way to build schema-based equivalents (more on that later in this chapter). For completeness, we include the complete URL for each XHTML module in the section that covers the elements and attributes that any module contains. Later on, as we present examples, we'll show how to use that information in a custom DTD to invoke the predefined module's DTD.

Because the Core XHTML modules must be included in any XHTML document definition to meet basic core markup requirements, it's not surprising that related core attribute sets are likewise required. These various attribute collections will be covered first in our detailed discussions of the various XHTML modules, and will be followed by the XHTML modules in their order of appearance in Table 25.1. Except for the Ruby module, which we cover last and which is defined in the XHTML 1.1 Specification at www.w3.org/TR/xhtml11/, all other predefined XHTML modules are documented at www.w3.org/TR/2001/REC-xhtml-modularization-20010410.

Modularization Rules and Naming Conventions

Because XHTML 1.1 essentially rests on the work done in the XHTML Modularization Specification, it should come as no surprise that XHTML 1.1 also follows basic XHTML Modularization rules and naming conventions. These may be briefly and succinctly stated as follows:

◆ All module names must be unique, so no conflicts are possible. A corollary to this rule is that you cannot define a module with the same name as an existing module, unless you intend to replace the existing module with the new one.

◆ Where any two modules contain definitions for the same markup elements or attributes, only one of those two modules may be referenced in a related DTD. (Note that this does not apply when one module extends another module's definition, as in adding a new attribute or default. Rather, it explains why we have basic and regular forms and table modules, and why you can use only the basic or regular module of each kind in a DTD.)

◆ Where attributes and elements have been renamed or replaced (for example, the `lang` attribute) to conform to XML syntax requirements and conventions, XHTML 1.1 conforms strictly to those requirements and conventions. (See Appendix A of the XHTML 1.1 Specification at `www.w3.org/TR/2001/REC-xhtml11-20010531/changes.html#a_changes` for more details.)

Attribute Collections

Although abstract modules require specialized attributes, they are normally defined within the context of the module's DTD. However, modular XHTML incorporates a collection of four named sets of attributes that are sometimes called common attributes. Two of these named sets—the *Core* and *I18N* (an abbreviation for "Internationalization") attributes—apply to many XHTML modules. The other two named sets—the *Events* and *Style* attributes—are defined only when related XHTML modules are invoked as part of an XHTML document's governing description. To be more specific, Events attributes are defined only when the Intrinsic Events module is invoked, and Style attributes are defined only when the Style Attribute module is invoked.

Table 25.2 describes all four of these attribute collections and their associated attribute names and data types. Note that this information is from the W3C site.

TABLE 25.2: XHTML ATTRIBUTE COLLECTIONS	
COLLECTION NAME	**ATTRIBUTES CONTAINED (DATA TYPE)**
Core	`class` (NMTOKENS), `id` (ID), `title` (CDATA)
I18N	`xml:lang` (NMTOKEN)
Events	`onclick`, `ondblclick`, `onmouseup`, `onmouseover`, `onmousemove`, `onmouseout`, `onkeypress`, `onkeydown`, `onkeyup` (all event attributes of type Script)
Style	`style` (CDATA)
Common	Core + Events + I18N + Style

Note that for convenience, a named collection of attributes—*Common*—represents the combination of all four of the previously named attribute collections.

Core XHTML Modules

All four of the core modules—*Structure, Text, Hypertext,* and *List*—must be present in any document that conforms to minimal requirements for valid XHTML markup. Each of these core modules is covered in more detail in the following sections.

XHTML STRUCTURE MODULE

The XHTML Structure module defines major document structure elements in XHTML. These elements thus define the basis for the content model instantiated in any XHTML document. Table 25.3 enumerates the relevant elements, attributes, and models.

TABLE 25.3: XHTML STRUCTURE MODULE

ELEMENT	ATTRIBUTES	MINIMAL CONTENT MODEL
body	Common	(Heading|Block|List)
head	I18N, profile (URI)	title
html	I18N, version (CDATA), xmlns (URI="http://www.w3.org/1999/xhtml")	head, body
title	I18N	PCDATA

For definitions of the Heading and Block content sets, see the text following Table 25.4; for the List content set, see Table 25.6. For further details on the Structure module, see

```
www.w3.org/TR/2001/REC-xhtml-modularization-20010410/
    dtd_module_defs.html#a_module_Structure
```

The module's DTD uses the following identifiers:

```
PUBLIC "-//W3C//ELEMENTS XHTML Document Structure 1.0//EN"
SYSTEM "http://www.w3.org/TR/xhtml-modularization/DTD/
    xhtml-struct-1.mod"
```

WARNING *Although we insert white space for readability here, each identifier should appear on one line with no spaces in the URL.*

XHTML TEXT MODULE

This module defines all basic XHTML text container elements, attributes, and related content models. This information appears in Table 25.4; be sure to read the explanation that follows to fully understand the named content sets used.

TABLE 25.4: XHTML TEXT MODULE

ELEMENT	ATTRIBUTES	MINIMAL CONTENT MODEL
abbr	Common	(PCDATA|Inline)*
acronym	Common	(PCDATA|Inline)*
address	Common	(PCDATA|Inline)*
blockquote	Common, cite (URI)	(PCDATA|Heading|Block|List)*
br	Core	EMPTY
cite	Common	(PCDATA|Inline)*
code	Common	(PCDATA|Inline)*
dfn	Common	(PCDATA|Inline)*

Continued on next page

TABLE 25.4: XHTML TEXT MODULE *(continued)*

ELEMENT	ATTRIBUTES	MINIMAL CONTENT MODEL
div	Common	(PCDATA|Flow)*
em	Common	(PCDATA|Inline)*
h1 – h6	Common	(PCDATA|Inline)*
kbd	Common	(PCDATA|Inline)*
p	Common	(PCDATA|Inline)*
pre	Commmon, xml:space="preserve"	(PCDATA|Inline)*
q	Common, cite (URI)	(PCDATA|Inline)*
samp	Common	(PCDATA|Inline)*
span	Common	(PCDATA|Inline)*
strong	Common	(PCDATA|Inline)*
var	Common	(PCDATA|Inline)*

The minimal content models for these elements introduce some content sets that must also be further defined:

- Heading: h1 | h2 | h3 | h4 | h5 | h6

- Block: address | blockquote | div | p | pre

- Inline: abbr | acronym | br | cite | code | dfn | em | kbd | q | samp | span | strong | var

- Flow: Heading | Block | Inline

TIP   *You can easily distinguish content set names from element names because elements are all lowercase and content set names start with an initial capital (Heading, Block, Inline, and Flow). Strings in ALL CAPS are standard DTD data types (PCDATA and EMPTY, in the preceding table; other entries elsewhere include NMTOKENS, CDATA, ID, URI, URL, and so on).*

For further details on the Text module, see

```
www.w3.org/TR/2001/REC-xhtml-modularization-20010410/
    dtd_module_defs.html#a_module_Text
```

The module's DTD uses the following identifiers:

```
PUBLIC "-//W3C//ELEMENTS XHTML Text 1.0//EN"
SYSTEM "http://www.w3.org/TR/xhtml-modularization/DTD/
    xhtml-text-1.mod"
```

XHTML HYPERTEXT MODULE

The Hypertext module provides the a element used to define standard hyperlinks to other resources in an XHTML document. Table 25.5 defines the related attributes and content model.

TABLE 25.5: XHTML HYPERTEXT MODULE

ELEMENT	ATTRIBUTES	MINIMAL CONTENT MODEL
a	Common, accesskey (Character), charset (Charset), href (URI), hreflang (LanguageCode), rel (LinkTypes), tabindex (Number), type (ContentType)	(PCDATA|Inline - a)*

For definitions of the data types mentioned in Table 24.5, please consult the XHTML Modularization Specification at

```
www.w3.org/TR/2001/REC-xhtml-modularization-20010410/
    abstract_modules.html#s_hypertextmodule
```

where each type name is a hyperlink to its definition. For further details on the Hypertext module itself, please see

```
www.w3.org/TR/2001/REC-xhtml-modularization-20010410/
    dtd_module_defs.html#a_module_Hypertext
```

The module's DTD uses the following identifiers:

```
PUBLIC "-//W3C//ELEMENTS XHTML Hypertext 1.0//EN"
SYSTEM "http://www.w3.org/TR/xhtml-modularization/DTD/
    xhtml-hypertext-1.mod"
```

XHTML LIST MODULE

The List module incorporates list-related XHTML elements to support basic list structures in even the most minimal XHTML documents. (Some designers disagree with this module's inclusion in the Core; however, because it adds only six elements, we don't view it as a major gaffe—if in fact it does represent an unnecessary inclusion, as some have argued.) Table 25.6 defines the elements, attributes, and content models associated with basic XHTML list structures.

TABLE 25.6: XHTML LIST MODULE

ELEMENT	ATTRIBUTES	MINIMAL CONTENT MODEL
dl	Common	(dt|dd)+
dt	Common	(PCDATA|Inline)*
dd	Common	(PCDATA|Flow)*
ol	Common	li+
ul	Common	li+
li	Common	(PCDATA|Flow)*

The module also defines a named content set, List, with an associated minimal content model of (dl | ol | ul)+. For further details on the List module, see

```
www.w3.org/TR/2001/REC-xhtml-modularization-20010410/
    dtd_module_defs.html#a_module_List
```

The module's DTD uses the following identifiers:

```
PUBLIC "-//W3C//ELEMENTS XHTML Lists 1.0//EN"
SYSTEM "http://www.w3.org/TR/xhtml-modularization/DTD/
    xhtml-list-1.mod"
```

XHTML Forms Modules

XHTML Modularization recognizes two forms modules: a *Basic Forms* module for bare-bones forms, and a *Forms* module for full-blown forms. These are described in the following sections.

XHTML BASIC FORMS MODULE

As its name is meant to suggest, the Basic Forms module supplies a minimal set of forms-related elements, attributes, and content models. These are described in Table 25.7.

TABLE 25.7: XHTML BASIC FORMS MODULE

ELEMENT	ATTRIBUTES	MINIMAL CONTENT MODEL
form	Common, action* (URI), method ("get"*|"post"), enctype (ContentType)	(Heading|List|Block-form)+
input	Common, accesskey (Character), checked ("checked"), maxlength (Number), name (CDATA), size (Number), src (URI), tabindex (Number), type ("text"*|"password"| "checkbox"|"radio"| "submit"|"reset"|"hidden"), value (CDATA)	EMPTY
label	Common, accesskey (Character), for (IDREF)	(PCDATA|Inline - label)*
select	Common, multiple ("multiple"), name (CDATA), size (Number), tabindex (Number)	option+
option	Common, selected ("selected"), value (CDATA)	PCDATA
textarea	Common, accesskey (Character), cols* (Number), name (CDATA), rows* (Number), tabindex (Number)	PCDATA

For further details on the Basic Forms module, see

```
www.w3.org/TR/2001/REC-xhtml-modularization-20010410/
    dtd_module_defs.html#a_module_Basic_Forms
```

The module's DTD uses the following identifiers:

```
PUBLIC "-//W3C//ELEMENTS XHTML Basic Forms 1.0//EN"
SYSTEM "http://www.w3.org/TR/xhtml-modularization/DTD/
    xhtml-basic-form-1.mod"
```

XHTML FORMS MODULE

The Forms module supports all the forms-related markup found in HTML 4, including the elements, attributes, and content models included in Table 25.8.

TABLE 25.8: XHTML FORMS MODULE

ELEMENT	ATTRIBUTES	MINIMAL CONTENT MODEL
form	Common, accept (ContentTypes), accept-charset (Charsets), action* (URI), method ("get"*| "post"), enctype (ContentType)	(Heading|List|Block-form | fieldset)+
input	Common, accept (ContentTypes), accesskey (Character), alt (Text), checked ("checked"), disabled ("disabled"), maxlength (Number), name (CDATA), readonly ("readonly"), size (Number), src (URI), tabindex (Number), type ("text"*|"password"|"checkbox"|"button"|"radio" | "submit"|"reset"|"file"|"hidden"|"image"), value (CDATA)	EMPTY
select	Common, disabled ("disabled"), multiple ("multiple"), name (CDATA), size (Number), tabindex (Number)	(optgroup|option)+
option	Common, disabled ("disabled"), label (Text), selected ("selected"), value (CDATA)	PCDATA
textarea	Common, accesskey (Character), cols* (Number), disabled ("disabled"), name (CDATA), readonly ("readonly"), rows* (Number), tabindex (Number)	PCDATA
button	Common, accesskey (Character), disabled ("disabled"), name (CDATA), tabindex (Number), type ("button"|"submit"*|"reset"), value (CDATA)	(PCDATA|Heading| List| Block-Form| Inline-Formctrl)*
fieldset	Common	(PCDATA|legend| Flow)*
label	Common, accesskey (Character), for (IDREF)	(PCDATA|Inline-label)*
legend	Common, accesskey (Character)	(PCDATA|Inline)+
optgroup	Common, disabled ("disabled"), label* (Text)	option+

The Forms module also mentions two named content sets—Form and Formctrl. These may be further described as follows:

◆ Form: form | fieldset

◆ Formctrl: input | select | textarea | label | button

When the Forms module is invoked, it adds the Form content set to the Block content set, and the Formctrl content set to the Inline content set as those are defined in the Text module.

TIP   *The Forms module is a superset of the Basic Forms module. Both modules may not appear together in any single document type; use only one or the other, as necessary.*

For further details on the Forms module, see

```
www.w3.org/TR/2001/REC-xhtml-modularization-20010410/
    dtd_module_defs.html#a_module_Forms
```

The module's DTD uses the following identifiers:

```
PUBLIC "-//W3C//ELEMENTS XHTML Forms 1.0//EN"
SYSTEM "http://www.w3.org/TR/xhtml-modularization/DTD/
    xhtml-form-1.mod"
```

XHTML Tables Modules

There are two XHTML Tables modules: Basic Tables and Tables. These two modules are explained in the following sections.

XHTML Basic Tables Module

The XHTML Basic Tables module provides access to a minimal set of table-related markup so that XHTML documents can accommodate simple tables when this module is invoked. The relevant markup, attributes, and content models appear in Table 25.9.

TABLE 25.9: XHTML Basic Tables Module

Element	Attributes	Minimal Content Model
caption	Common	(PCDATA|Inline)*
table	Common, summary (Text)	caption?,tr+
td	Common, abbr (Text), align ("left"|"center"|"right"), axis (CDATA), colspan (number), headers (IDREFS), rowspan (Number), scope ("row"|"col"), valign ("top"|"middle"|"bottom")	(PCDATA|Flow - table)*
th	Common, abbr (Text), align ("left"|"center"|"right"), axis (CDATA), colspan (number), headers (IDREFS), rowspan (Number), scope ("row"|"col"), valign ("top"|"middle"|"bottom")	(PCDATA|Flow - table)*
tr	Common, align ("left"|"center"|"right"), valign ("top"|"middle"|"bottom")	(td|th)+

When the Basic Tables module is invoked in an XHTML document, it adds the `table` element to the Block content set defined in the Text module.

For further details on the Basic Tables module, see

```
www.w3.org/TR/2001/REC-xhtml-modularization-20010410/
    dtd_module_defs.html#a_module_Basic_Tables
```

The module's DTD uses the following identifiers:

```
PUBLIC "-//W3C//ELEMENTS XHTML Basic Tables 1.0//EN"
SYSTEM "http://www.w3.org/TR/xhtml-modularization/DTD/
    xhtml-basic-table-1.mod"
```

XHTML TABLES MODULE

As the Basic Tables module provides minimal XHTML table markup, the XHTML Tables module provides complete XHTML table markup. The elements, attributes, and content models involved are documented in Table 25.10.

TABLE 25.10: XHTML TABLES MODULE

ELEMENT	ATTRIBUTES	MINIMAL CONTENT MODEL
caption	Common	(PCDATA|Inline)*
table	Common, border (Pixels), cellpadding (Length), cellspacing (Length), frame ("void"|"above"|"below"|"hsides"|"lhs"|"rhs"|"vsides"|"box"|"border"), rules ("none"|"groups"|"rows"|"cols"|"all"), summary (Text), width (Length)	caption?, (col*|colgroup*), ((thead?, tfoot?, tbody+)|(tr+))
td	Common, abbr (Text), align ("left"|"center"|"right"|"justify"| "char"), axis (CDATA), char (Character), charoff (Length), colspan (number), headers (IDREFS), rowspan (Number), scope ("row"|"col"|"rowgroup"|"colgroup"), valign ("top"|"middle"|"bottom")	(PCDATA|Flow - table)*
th	Common, abbr (Text), align ("left"|"center"|"right"), axis (CDATA), colspan (number), headers (IDREFS), rowspan (Number), scope ("row"|"col"), valign ("top"|"middle"|"bottom"|"baseline")	(PCDATA|Flow - table)*
tr	Common, align ("left"|"center"|"right""justify"|"char"), char (Character), charoff (Length), span (Number), valign ("top"|"middle"|"bottom"|"baseline")	(td|th)+

Continued on next page

TABLE 25.10: XHTML TABLES MODULE *(continued)*

ELEMENT	ATTRIBUTES	MINIMAL CONTENT MODEL
col	Common, align ("left"|"center"|"right""justify"| "char"), char (Character), charoff (Length), span (Number), valign ("top"|"middle"|"bottom"| "baseline"), width (MultiLength)	EMPTY
colgroup	Common, align ("left"|"center"|"right""justify"| "char"), char (Character), charoff (Length), span (Number), valign ("top"|"middle"|"bottom"| "baseline"), width (MultiLength)	col*
tbody	Common, align ("left"|"center"|"right""justify"| "char"), char (Character), charoff (Length), valign ("top"|"middle"| "bottom"|"baseline")	tr+
thead	Common, align ("left"|"center"|"right""justify"| "char"), char (Character), charoff (Length), valign ("top"|"middle"| "bottom"|"baseline")	tr+
tfoot	Common, align ("left"|"center"|"right""justify"| "char"), char (Character), charoff (Length), valign ("top"|"middle"| "bottom"|"baseline")	tr+

When this module is invoked, it adds the `table` element to the Block content set defined in the Text module. For further details on the Tables module, see

```
www.w3.org/TR/2001/REC-xhtml-modularization-20010410/
    dtd_module_defs.html#a_module_Tables
```

The module's DTD uses the following identifiers:

```
PUBLIC "-//W3C//ELEMENTS XHTML Tables 1.0//EN"
SYSTEM "http://www.w3.org/TR/xhtml-modularization/DTD/
    xhtml-table-1.mod"
```

TIP *The Tables module is a superset of the Basic Tables module. Both modules may not appear together in any single document type; use only one or the other, as necessary.*

XHTML Basic Defines Bare-bones XHTML

Let's assume that you wanted to declare the barest minimum collection of markup elements and related modules (where applicable) necessary to define a workable XHTML implementation. Perhaps it's because you want to send content to a cell phone, PDA, embedded system of some kind, or some other network-attached device with minimal display characteristics and a very small screen.

If you created a customized module declaration that included only the following markup:

◆ Basic text elements (including headings, paragraphs, and lists)—these are the h1 - h6 heading elements, the p element, and all the elements in the List module mentioned earlier in this chapter

◆ Hyperlinks and links to related documents (in other words, the Hypertext module)

◆ Basic forms (the module of the same name)

◆ Basic tables (the module of the same name)

◆ Images (the Image module, or img element, mentioned later in this chapter)

◆ Meta information (the meta element, covered in the Metainformation module later in this chapter)

and added the Common Attributes module to this mix, you'd define a minimalist collection of XHTML markup that even a cell phone could learn to live with. In fact, the W3C has done this for you: it's called XHTML Basic, and you can visit its equally short and minimal specification at www.w3.org/TR/xhtml-basic/.

Two closing remarks about this brief tour-de-force of XHTML Modularization:

◆ It does indeed define the bare usable markup minimum for XHTML and as such is eminently well suited to modest or minimal devices with small, character-only displays.

◆ It shows the power of the principles of modularization at work, which makes Appendix B of its specification—particularly the discussion and examples of the XHTML Basic Driver DTD—worth reading and using to inspire any XHTML module customization you might undertake.

Text Extension Modules

The Text Extension modules encompass a grab bag of text markup capabilities, including some limited presentation markup in the Presentation module, editing-related markup to mark insertions and deletions in the Edit module, and the Bi-directional Text module, which permits text to be displayed right-to-left instead of the more typical left-to-right. These modules are covered in the following sections.

XHTML PRESENTATION MODULE

The Presentation module provides some basic presentation elements, attributes, and content models for managing limited text presentation markup. Here again, markup purists find this questionable because style sheets can handle all the functions that this markup provides, but we believe the W3C's decision to include this very basic markup was sound, because handheld and embedded devices will have far less need of style sheets because of what this module contains. The various elements, attributes, and content models for the Presentation module appear in Table 25.11.

TABLE 25.11: XHTML PRESENTATION MODULE

ELEMENT	ATTRIBUTES	MINIMAL CONTENT MODEL
b	Common	(PCDATA|Inline)*
big	Common	(PCDATA|Inline)*
hr	Common	EMPTY
i	Common	(PCDATA|Inline)*
small	Common	(PDDATA|Inline)*
sub	Common	(PCDATA|Inline)*
sup	Common	(PCDATA|Inline)*
tt	Common	(PCDATA|Inline)*

When this module is invoked, it adds the hr element to the Block content set defined in the Text module; likewise, it adds the other elements—b, big, i, small, sub, sup, and tt—to the Inline content set defined in the Text module. For further details on the Presentation module, see

```
www.w3.org/TR/2001/REC-xhtml-modularization-20010410/
    dtd_module_defs.html#a_module_Presentation
```

The module's DTD uses the following identifiers:

```
PUBLIC "-//W3C//ELEMENTS XHTML Presentation 1.0//EN"
SYSTEM "http://www.w3.org/TR/xhtml-modularization/DTD/
    xhtml-pres-1.mod"
```

XHTML EDIT MODULE

The Edit module supports markup used to flag insertions and deletions in documents, which makes it easier to denote additions and removals therein. Table 25.12 describes the relevant elements, attributes, and content models.

TABLE 25.12: XHTML EDIT MODULE

ELEMENT	ATTRIBUTES	MINIMAL CONTENT MODEL
del	Common, cite (URL), datetime (Datetime)	(PCDATA|Flow)*
ins	Common, cite (URL), datetime (Datetime)	(PCDATA|Flow)*

When this module is invoked, it adds the del and ins elements to the Inline content set defined in the Text module. For further details on the Edit module, see

```
www.w3.org/TR/2001/REC-xhtml-modularization-20010410/
    dtd_module_defs.html#a_module_Edit
```

The module's DTD uses the following identifiers:

```
PUBLIC "-//W3C//ELEMENTS XHTML Editing Markup 1.0//EN"
SYSTEM "http://www.w3.org/TR/xhtml-modularization/DTD/
    xhtml-edit-1.mod"
```

XHTML BI-DIRECTIONAL TEXT MODULE

The Bi-directional Text module supports an element that governs the direction in which its content should be read. The relevant element, its attributes, and its content model are described in Table 25.13.

TABLE 25.13: XHTML BI-DIRECTIONAL TEXT MODULE

ELEMENT	ATTRIBUTES	MINIMAL CONTENT MODEL
bdo	Core, dir*("ltr"|"rtl")	(PCDATA|Inline)*

When this module is invoked, it adds the bdo element to the Inline content set defined in the Text module. For further details on the Bi-directional Text module, see

```
www.w3.org/TR/2001/REC-xhtml-modularization-20010410/
    dtd_module_defs.html#a_module_Bi-directional_Text
```

The module's DTD uses the following identifiers:

```
PUBLIC "-//W3C//ELEMENTS XHTML BDO Element 1.0//EN"
SYSTEM "http://www.w3.org/TR/xhtml-modularization/DTD/
    xhtml-bdo-1.mod"
```

Other Standard XHTML Modules

The remaining 14 standard XHTML modules aren't grouped in the specification (even though several, such as those related to frames markup, could have been). Thus, we simply present them here in their order of occurrence in Table 25.1.

XHTML IMAGE MODULE

The Image module supports an element that permits images to be embedded in XHTML documents. The relevant element, its attributes, and its content model are described in Table 25.14.

TABLE 25.14: XHTML IMAGE MODULE

ELEMENT	ATTRIBUTES	MINIMAL CONTENT MODEL
img	Common, alt* (Text), height (Length), longdesc (URI), src* (URI), width (Length)	EMPTY

When this module is invoked, it adds the img element to the Inline content set defined in the Text module. For further details on the Image module, see

```
www.w3.org/TR/2001/REC-xhtml-modularization-20010410/
    dtd_module_defs.html#a_module_Image
```

The module's DTD uses the following identifiers:

```
PUBLIC "-//W3C//ELEMENTS XHTML Images 1.0//EN"
SYSTEM "http://www.w3.org/TR/xhtml-modularization/DTD/
    xhtml-image-1.mod"
```

XHTML CLIENT-SIDE IMAGE MAP MODULE

The Client-Side Image Map module supports elements to enable use of client-side image maps. Because this requires an image to map to, the Image module must also be included in a document that uses this module, or some other reasonable alternative that supports the img element must be included. The relevant elements, their attributes, and their content models (where applicable) are described in Table 25.15.

When this module is invoked, it adds the map and area elements to the Inline content set defined in the Text module. For further details on the Client-Side Image Map module, see

```
www.w3.org/TR/2001/REC-xhtml-modularization-20010410/
    dtd_module_defs.html#a_module_Client-Side_Image_Map
```

The module's DTD uses the following identifiers:

```
PUBLIC "-//W3C//ELEMENTS XHTML Client-side Image Maps 1.0//EN"
SYSTEM "http://www.w3.org/TR/xhtml-modularization/DTD/
    xhtml-csismap-1.mod"
```

TABLE 25.15: XHTML CLIENT-SIDE IMAGE MAP MODULE

ELEMENT	ATTRIBUTES	MINIMAL CONTENT MODEL
a&	coords(CDATA), shape("rect"|"circle"|"poly"| "default")	No change
area	Common, accesskey (Character), alt* (Text), coords (CDATA), href (URI), nohref ("nohref"), shape("rect"* |"circle"|"poly"|"default"), tabindex (Number)	EMPTY
img&	usemap (IDREF)	No change
input&	usemap (IDREF)	No change; applies only when a Forms module is included
map	I18N, Events, class (NMTOKEN), id* (ID), title (CDATA)	((Heading|Block) |area)+
object& ·	usemap (IDREF)	Applies only when an Object module is included

TIP *The notation* `img&` *that appears in the Element column in Table 25.15 indicates that this module adds attributes to elements defined elsewhere. Thus, a corresponding "No change" entry in the content model means that the original content model is unchanged; when other modules must be included in a document for an element change to occur, it will be so noted, as with the* `object` *element in that table.*

XHTML SERVER-SIDE IMAGE MAP MODULE

The Server-Side Image Map module supports the use of server-side image maps, which means a mechanism to select coordinates on a client-side image, and to transmit those selections to the server's image map–handling facility. The relevant elements, their attributes, and content models are described in Table 25.16.

TABLE 25.16: XHTML SERVER-SIDE IMAGE MAP MODULE

ELEMENT	ATTRIBUTES	MINIMAL CONTENT MODEL
`img&`	`ismap ("ismap")`	No change
`input&`	`ismap ("ismap")`	No change; applies only when a Forms module is included

When this module is invoked, it adds no elements to the XHTML Core (it only defines additional attributes), but for this module to be used, the Image module (or some equivalent that defines the `img` element) must also be included. For further details on the Server-Side Image Map module, see

```
www.w3.org/TR/2001/REC-xhtml-modularization-20010410/
    dtd_module_defs.html#a_module_Server-side_Image_Map
```

The module's DTD uses the following identifiers:

```
PUBLIC "-//W3C//ELEMENTS XHTML Server-side Image Maps 1.0//EN"
SYSTEM "http://www.w3.org/TR/xhtml-modularization/DTD/
    xhtml-ssismap-1.mod"
```

XHTML OBJECT MODULE

The Object module supports an element that permits objects, such as applets, scripts, or other executables, to be embedded in XHTML documents. The relevant element, its attributes, and its content model are described in Table 25.17.

TABLE 25.17: XHTML OBJECT MODULE

ELEMENT	ATTRIBUTES	MINIMAL CONTENT MODEL
`object`	`Common, archive (URIs), classid (URI), codebase (URI), codetype (ContentType), data (URI), declare ("declare"), height (Length), name (CDATA), standby (Text), tabindex (Number), type (ContentType), width (Length)`	`(PCDATA|Flow|Param)*`
`param`	`id (ID), name* (CDATA), type (ContentType), value (CDATA), valuetype ("data"* | "ref" | "object")`	`EMPTY`

When this module is invoked, it adds the `object` element to the Inline content set defined in the Text module. For further details on the Object module, see

```
www.w3.org/TR/2001/REC-xhtml-modularization-20010410/
    dtd_module_defs.html#a_module_Object
```

The module's DTD uses the following identifiers:

```
PUBLIC "-//W3C//ELEMENTS XHTML Embedded Object 1.0//EN"
SYSTEM "http://www.w3.org/TR/xhtml-modularization/DTD/
    xhtml-object-1.mod"
```

XHTML FRAMES MODULE

The Frames module supports elements associated with framed document structures, and thereby permits frames to be used with XHTML documents. Table 25.18 describes the relevant elements, their attributes, and content models.

TABLE 25.18: XHTML FRAMES MODULE

ELEMENT	ATTRIBUTES	MINIMAL CONTENT MODEL
frameset	Core, cols (MultiLength), rows (MultiLength)	(frameset|frame)+, noframes?
frame	CCore, frameborder ("1"|"0"), longdesc (URI), marginheight (Pixels), marginwidth (Pixels), noresize ("noresize"), scrolling ("yes"|"no"| "auto"*), src (URI)	EMPTY
noframes	Common	body

When this module is invoked, it changes the minimal content model for the `html` element to (`head`, `frameset`). For further details on the Frames module, see

```
www.w3.org/TR/2001/REC-xhtml-modularization-20010410/
    dtd_module_defs.html#a_module_Frames
```

The module's DTD uses the following identifiers:

```
PUBLIC "-//W3C//ELEMENTS XHTML Frames 1.0//EN"
SYSTEM "http://www.w3.org/TR/xhtml-modularization/DTD/
    xhtml-frames-1.mod"
```

XHTML TARGET MODULE

The Target module supports the use of the `target` attribute in various XHTML elements so you can specify a frame target when you're defining a potential hypertext link or related context information. The relevant elements, the target attributes, and their content models are described in Table 25.19.

TABLE 25.19: XHTML TARGET

ELEMENT	ATTRIBUTES	MINIMAL CONTENT MODEL
a&	target (CDATA)	No change
area&	target (CDATA)	Applies when the Client-Side Image Map module is included
base&	target (CDATA)	Applies when the Legacy module is included
link&	target (CDATA)	Applies when the Link module is included
form&	target (CDATA)	Applies when a Forms module is included

When this module is invoked, it simply adds the `target` attribute to the various elements specified in the previous table. (When these go beyond the XHTML core, the applicable modules are mentioned in Table 25.19.) For further details on the Target module, see

```
www.w3.org/TR/2001/REC-xhtml-modularization-20010410/
    dtd_module_defs.html#a_module_Target
```

The module's DTD uses the following identifiers:

```
PUBLIC "-//W3C//ELEMENTS XHTML Target 1.0//EN"
SYSTEM "http://www.w3.org/TR/xhtml-modularization/DTD/
    xhtml-target-1.mod"
```

XHTML IFRAME MODULE

The Iframe module contains the `iframe` element, which is designed to support use of inline frames in XHTML documents. The relevant element, its attributes, and its content model are described in Table 25.20.

TABLE 25.20: XHTML IFRAME MODULE

ELEMENT	ATTRIBUTES	MINIMAL CONTENT MODEL
inframe	core, frameborder ("1"|"0"), height (Length), longdesc (URI), marginheight (Pixels), marginwidth (Pixels), scrolling ("yes"|"no"| "auto"*), src (URI), width (Length)	(PCDATA|Flow)*

When this module is invoked, it adds the `iframe` element to the Inline content set defined in the Text module. For further details on the Iframe module, see

```
www.w3.org/TR/2001/REC-xhtml-modularization-20010410/
    dtd_module_defs.html#a_module_Iframe
```

The module's DTD uses the following identifiers:

```
PUBLIC "-//W3C//ELEMENTS XHTML Inline Frame Element 1.0//EN"
SYSTEM "http://www.w3.org/TR/xhtml-modularization/DTD/
    xhtml-iframe-1.mod"
```

XHTML INTRINSIC EVENTS MODULE

The Intrinsic Events module defines attributes associated with handling events that occur when users perform specific actions. Note also that attributes covered in Table 25.21 are added to the indicated element only when the modules in which those elements are initially defined are also included in the XHTML document's DTD invocation. This set of attributes corresponds to the Events attribute set mentioned in the "Attribute Collections" section earlier in this chapter. The relevant elements and attributes are described in Table 25.21.

TABLE 25.21: XHTML INTRINSIC EVENTS MODULE

ELEMENT	ATTRIBUTES	NOTES
a&	onblur (Script), onfocus (script)	No change
area&	onblur (Script), onfocus (script)	Applies when the Client-Side Image Map module is included
frameset&	onload (Script), onunload (Script)	Applies when the Frames module is included
form&	onreset (Script), onsubmit (Script)	Applies when a Forms module is included
body&	onload(script), onunload (Script)	No change
label&	onblur (Script), onfocus (script)	Applies when a Forms module is included
input&	onblur (Script), onchange (Script), onfocus (Script), onselect (Script)	Applies when a Forms module is included
select&	onblur (Script), onchange (Script), onfocus (Script)	Applies when a Forms module is included
textarea&	Conblur (Script), onchange (Script), onfocus (Script), onselect (Script)	Applies when a Forms module is included
button&	onblur (Script), onfocus (Script)	Applies when a Forms module is included

For further details on the Intrinsic Events module, see

```
www.w3.org/TR/2001/REC-xhtml-modularization-20010410/
    dtd_module_defs.html#a_module_Intrinsic_Events
```

The module's DTD uses the following identifiers:

```
PUBLIC "-//W3C//ELEMENTS XHTML Intrinsic Events 1.0//EN"
SYSTEM "http://www.w3.org/TR/xhtml-modularization/DTD/
    xhtml-events-1.mod"
```

XHTML METAINFORMATION MODULE

The Metainformation module supports an element used to describe document contents, audience, and other attributes within the head element in an XHTML document. The relevant element, its attributes, and its content model are described in Table 25.22.

TABLE 25.22: XHTML METAINFORMATION MODULE

ELEMENT	ATTRIBUTES	MINIMAL CONTENT MODEL
meta	I18N, content* (CDATA), http-equiv (NMTOKEN), name (NMTOKEN), scheme (CDATA)	EMPTY

When this module is invoked, it adds the meta element to the content model for the head element defined in the Structure module. For further details on the Metainformation module, see

```
www.w3.org/TR/2001/REC-xhtml-modularization-20010410/
    dtd_module_defs.html#a_module_Metainformation
```

The module's DTD uses the following identifiers:

```
PUBLIC "-//W3C//ELEMENTS XHTML Metainformation 1.0//EN"
SYSTEM "http://www.w3.org/TR/xhtml-modularization/DTD/
    xhtml-meta-1.mod"
```

XHTML SCRIPTING MODULE

The Scripting module supports the invocation of executable scripts for user agents that can handle them, and provides information to user agents that cannot, in XHTML documents. The relevant elements, attributes, and content models are described in Table 25.23.

TABLE 25.23: XHTML SCRIPTING MODULE

ELEMENT	ATTRIBUTES	MINIMAL CONTENT MODEL
noscript	Common	(Heading|List|Block)+
script	charset (Charset), defer ("defer"), src (URI), type* (ContentType), xml:space="preserve"	PCDATA

When this module is invoked, it adds the script and noscript elements to the Block and Inline content sets defined in the Text module. The script element is also added to the head element's content model as defined in the Structure module. For further details on the Scripting module, see

```
www.w3.org/TR/2001/REC-xhtml-modularization-20010410/
    dtd_module_defs.html#a_module_Scripting
```

The module's DTD uses the following identifiers:

```
PUBLIC "-//W3C//ELEMENTS XHTML Scripting 1.0//EN"
SYSTEM "http://www.w3.org/TR/xhtml-modularization/DTD/
    xhtml-image-1.mod"
```

XHTML STYLE SHEET MODULE

The Style Sheet module supports an element that supports use of internal style sheets in XHTML documents. The relevant element, its attributes, and its content model are described in Table 25.24.

TABLE 25.24: XHTML STYLE SHEET MODULE

ELEMENT	ATTRIBUTES	MINIMAL CONTENT MODEL
style	CI18N, media (MediaDesc), title (Text), type* (ContentType), xml:space="preserve"	PCDATA

When this module is invoked, it adds the `style` element to the content model for the `head` element defined in the Structure module. For further details on the Style Sheet module, see

```
www.w3.org/TR/2001/REC-xhtml-modularization-20010410/
    dtd_module_defs.html#a_module_Style_Sheet
```

The module's DTD uses the following identifiers:

```
PUBLIC "-//W3C//ELEMENTS XHTML Style Sheets 1.0//EN"
SYSTEM "http://www.w3.org/TR/xhtml-modularization/DTD/
    xhtml-style-1.mod"
```

XHTML STYLE ATTRIBUTE MODULE

The Style Attribute module adds support for the `style` attribute to the Core attributes set, and must be defined before the Core attributes so as to be included when the Core attributes are invoked. Use this module if you want to add inline styles within an XHTML document body.

When this module is invoked, it adds the `style` attribute to the vast majority of XHTML core elements. For further details on the Style Attribute module, see

```
www.w3.org/TR/2001/REC-xhtml-modularization-20010410/
    dtd_module_defs.html#a_module_Style_Attribute
```

The module's DTD uses the following identifiers:

```
PUBLIC "-//W3C//ELEMENTS XHTML Inline Style 1.0//EN"
SYSTEM "http://www.w3.org/TR/xhtml-modularization/DTD/
    xhtml-inlstyle-1.mod"
```

XHTML LINK MODULE

The Link module supports an element that supports links to external resources. The relevant element and its attributes are described in Table 25.25.

TABLE 25.25: XHTML LINK MODULE

ELEMENT	ATTRIBUTES	MINIMAL CONTENT MODEL
link	Common, charset (Charset), href (URI), hreflang (LanguageCode), media (MediaDesc), rel (LinkTypes), rev (LinkTypes), type (ContentType)	EMPTY

When this module is invoked, it adds the `link` element to the content model for the `head` element defined in the Structure module. For further details on the Link module, see

```
www.w3.org/TR/2001/REC-xhtml-modularization-20010410/
    dtd_module_defs.html#a_module_Link
```

The module's DTD uses the following identifiers:

```
PUBLIC "-//W3C//ELEMENTS XHTML Link Element 1.0//EN"
SYSTEM "http://www.w3.org/TR/xhtml-modularization/DTD/
    xhtml-link-1.mod"
```

XHTML BASE MODULE

The Base module supports an element that supplies a base URI against which relative URIs in XHTML documents can be resolved. The relevant element and its attributes are described in Table 25.26.

TABLE 25.26: XHTML BASE MODULE

ELEMENT	ATTRIBUTES	MINIMAL CONTENT MODEL
base	href* (URI)	EMPTY

When this module is invoked, it adds the `base` element to the content model for the `head` element defined in the Structure module. For further details on the Base module, see

```
www.w3.org/TR/2001/REC-xhtml-modularization-20010410/
    dtd_module_defs.html#a_module_Base
```

The module's DTD uses the following identifiers:

```
PUBLIC "-//W3C//ELEMENTS XHTML Base Element 1.0//EN"
SYSTEM "http://www.w3.org/TR/xhtml-modularization/DTD/
    xhtml-base-1.mod"
```

This concludes our description of standard XHTML modules. Next, we present three additional modules that we categorize as deprecated (which is accurate, but is not a term used to characterize them in the XHTML Modularization Specification), after which we conclude the modules section of this chapter with a discussion of the Ruby module introduced in XHTML 1.1.

Deprecated XHTML Modules

Primarily for backward compatibility reasons, the XHTML Modularization Specification includes three additional modules that provide support for markup that would otherwise be unusable in the XHTML environment. This added support could be a significant boon to site designers, developers, and maintainers with Web sites that include older versions of HTML markup (HTML 4 or earlier) because it allows immediate migration to modularized XHTML—and, by extension, to XHTML 1.1—without requiring outright removal and replacement of all deprecated markup elements and attributes.

WARNING   *If an application requires XHTML Modularization and a restricted subset of XHTML, it's very likely that these modules would be inappropriate for use. Use these only with careful thought and consideration.*

XHTML APPLET MODULE

The Applet module supports the now-deprecated `applet` and `param` elements, which originally supported invocation of executable images embedded in HTML (particularly Java applets, hence the name for one of the elements involved). These elements have been superseded by the `object` element in HTML 4 and newer versions, but are supported for backward compatibility. The relevant elements, their attributes, and content models are described in Table 25.27.

When this module is invoked, it adds the `applet` and `param` elements to the Inline content set defined in the Text module. For further details on the Applet module, see

```
www.w3.org/TR/2001/REC-xhtml-modularization-20010410/
    dtd_module_defs.html#a_module_Applet
```

The module's DTD uses the following identifiers:

```
PUBLIC "-//W3C//ELEMENTS XHTML Java Applets 1.0//EN"
SYSTEM "http://www.w3.org/TR/xhtml-modularization/DTD/
    xhtml-applet-1.mod"
```

TABLE 25.27: XHTML APPLET MODULE

ELEMENT	ATTRIBUTES	MINIMAL CONTENT MODEL
applet	Core, alt* (Text), archive (CDATA), code (CDATA), codebase (URI), height* (Length), object (CDATA), width* (Length)	(PCDATA|Flow|param)*
param	id (ID), name* (CDATA), type (ContentType), value (CDATA), valuetype ("data"*|"ref"|"object")	EMPTY

XHTML NAME IDENTIFICATION MODULE

The Name Identification module adds the `name` attribute to numerous XHTML elements. The `name` attribute was used (historically) to identify specific elements in HTML documents. Modern usage, in keeping with the Document Object Model (DOM) and document parse trees, dictates that the `id` attribute (part of the XHTML Core) should be used instead. Here again, support is provided for backward compatibility, and the relevant elements, the `name` attribute, and relevant annotations appear in Table 25.28.

TABLE 25.28: XHTML NAME IDENTIFICATION MODULE

ELEMENT	ATTRIBUTES	NOTES
a&	name (CDATA)	Part of Core
applet&	name (CDATA)	Applies when the Applet module is included
form&	name (CDATA)	Applies when a Forms module is included
frame&	name (CDATA)	Applies when the Frames module is included

Continued on next page

When this module is invoked, it adds the various elements and attributes listed in Tables 25.29 and 25.30 to various modules. For further details on the Legacy module, see

```
www.w3.org/TR/2001/REC-xhtml-modularization-20010410/
    dtd_module_defs.html#a_module_Legacy
```

The module's DTD uses the following identifiers:

```
PUBLIC "-//W3C//ELEMENTS XHTML Legacy Markup 1.0//EN"
SYSTEM "http://www.w3.org/TR/xhtml-modularization/DTD/
    xhtml-legacy-1.mod"
```

This concludes our coverage of all modules covered in the XHTML Modularization Specification. In the following section, we provide similar coverage of the Ruby module added to the XHTML 1.1 Specification. (It, too, can be included in an XHTML 1.1 document using the same techniques we'll describe later in this chapter.)

The XHTML 1.1 Ruby Annotation Module

The Ruby Annotation module supports short bits ("runs") of text along with the base text in the document. Ruby is designed for use in East Asian documents to provide pronunciation details and other short annotations. The text involved is called "ruby text"—hence, the name of the module—and often provides a character-by-character or ideogram-by-ideogram translation from one Asian language to another. Thus, base text may be in Mandarin with ruby text in Hanggul, for instance, where for each Mandarin ideogram, a corresponding Hanggul ideogram is positioned immediately above it. The relevant Ruby markup elements, their attributes, and their content models are described in Table 25.31.

TABLE 25.31: XHTML 1.1 RUBY MODULE

ELEMENT	ATTRIBUTES	MINIMAL CONTENT MODEL
Ruby	Common	(rb, (rt|(rp,rt,rp)))
rbc	Common	rb+
rtc	Common	rt+
rb	Common	(PCDATA|Inline-ruby)*
rt	Common, rbspan (CDATA)	(PCDATA|Inline-ruby)*
rp	Common	PCDATA*

When this module is invoked, it adds the elements from Table 25.31 to the Inline content set defined in the Text module. For further details on the Ruby module, including some nicely formatted examples of what this baby can do, please visit:

```
www.w3.org/TR/2001/REC-ruby-20010531/#module
```

The module's DTD uses the following identifiers:

```
PUBLIC "-//W3C//ELEMENTS XHTML Ruby 1.0//EN"
SYSTEM "http://www.w3.org/TR/ruby/xhtml-ruby-1.mod"
```

Using XHTML Modules

When it comes to using modularized XHTML—be it to invoke and use the predefined modules covered earlier in this chapter or to invoke and use other publicly available or entirely custom-built modules—the technique is so simple that it's entirely anticlimactic. In a nutshell, you must create an internal DTD section in your XHTML documents, or make reference to an external DTD in your XHTML documents, that invokes the XHTML (or other) modules that you want to use.

It's important to observe, however, that the order of placement when invoking such modules is quite significant. Therefore, if you use modules that modify other modules (for example, the Style Attribute module or the Legacy module), you *must* invoke those modules before invoking the modules they modify. This is the only way that the parsing process that compiles the document definition can satisfy the references that those modifying modules make to the modules that they modify. In simpler terms, this means the extra modifications that modules outside the Core set make must occur before the Core modules—or other modified modules—can be invoked.

In practice, this means if the section on a module mentions that it alters or adds to a content set, you must invoke that module prior to invoking the module within which the altered content set is initially defined. For example, invoke the Core modules last, and other modules first, when custom-building a modularized XHTML DTD. We annotate the XHTML Basic DTD later in this section to provide a basic working example, with relevant explanations.

That said, the basic syntax for invoking an XHTML module is quite simple, and takes the following general form:

```
<!ENTITY % module-name.mod
    PUBLIC "-//W3C//ELEMENTS XHTML module-name 1.0//EN"
           "xhtml-mod-abbrev-1.mod" >
%module-name.mod;
```

Here, the `module-name` term is our notation for the string that appears in the `PUBLIC` string in our documentation of the various modules earlier in this chapter, and the `mod-abbrev` term is our notation for the related string that appears in the `SYSTEM` string in that same documentation. Thus, the equivalent code for the Text module (a member of the XHTML Core modules) is as follows (to demonstrate the substitutions involved):

```
<!ENTITY % xhtml-text.mod
    PUBLIC "-//W3C//ELEMENTS XHTML Text 1.0//EN"
           "xhtml-text-1.mod" >
%xhtml-text.mod;
```

Thus, the term text replaces both `module-name` and `mod-abbrev` in the real DTD invocation of that module. Because these terms sometimes differ for other XHTML modules, we used two terms in our description of the general form of this invocation. Do not assume you can always use the same string to replace both substitution terms.

Because using XHTML modules to create custom or special-purpose DTDs essentially limits your DTD writing efforts to nothing more than a carefully crafted series of invocations of other, publicly available XHTML module DTDs, it should come as no surprise that the W3C has come to call such DTDs *Driver DTDs*. We think this is because they simply invoke other necessary DTDs in the right order, and drastically limit the amount of original or custom SGML declarations and code otherwise. This makes them look a lot like Unix or Linux driver files, which often consist of nothing more than a bunch of invocations themselves. By looking for Driver DTDs in the XHTML 1.1 Specification, the XHTML Basic Specification, and so forth, you can find plenty of lengthy examples of this new abbreviated method of DTD composition to learn from. That's why we discuss the XHTML Basic DTD in this chapter as well.

WARNING *At this time, some of the currently available XHTML validation tools cannot yet validate documents based on modularized XHTML. See the sidebar "Validating Modularized XHTML" to help you cope with this problem, should it happen to you.*

VALIDATING MODULARIZED XHTML

Some of the currently available XHTML validation tools cannot yet validate documents based on modularized XHTML. We hope this will change by the time you read this book. If not, you can use a "trick" to get through validation by invoking the XHTML 1.0 DTD of your choice in documents as you validate them, then replacing your DTD invocation with a modularized equivalent for the production versions of your XHTML documents.

As long as you steer clear of Ruby Annotation and other external XHTML modules in your documents in the short term, this technique works fine. This is because the XHTML 1.0 Strict DTD is exactly equivalent to the non-deprecated XHTML modules (and the other XHTML 1.0 DTDs also work, as long as you invoke the necessary deprecated or additional standard modules to support legacy or frame-handling needs).

Looking at a more involved real-world example should help to cement your understanding of the process of constructing a modularized XHTML DTD. XHTML Basic is a subset of XHTML that became a W3C Recommendation in December 2000. It was designed to create the absolute minimum set of XHTML elements and attributes for use on handheld devices, cell phones, PDAs, and other systems with limited display capabilities. XHTML Basic defines a proper subset of the XHTML 1.0 DTD that includes the following modules:

- Text module
- Hypertext module
- List module
- Image module
- Tables module (basic only)
- Forms module (basic only)
- Link module
- Metainformation module
- Base Element module
- Param Element module
- Embedded Object module

Note that we reproduce the basic DTD from the W3C's Web site in Listing 25.1, except that where we remove tangential or extraneous information, or where we annotate the DTD, the SGML comments appear in italics below (and are not part of the original document itself). To see the document in its original form, please visit www.w3.org/TR/xhtml-basic/#a_dtd.

LISTING 25.1: THE BASIC DTD FROM THE W3C SITE

```
<!-- XHTML Basic 1.0 DTD -->
<!-- file: xhtml-basic10.dtd -->
<!-- XHTML Basic 1.0 DTD
     This is XHTML Basic, a proper subset of XHTML.

The Extensible HyperText Markup Language (XHTML)
Copyright 1998-2000 World Wide Web Consortium
(Massachusetts Institute of Technology, Institut National de
Recherche en Informatique et en Automatique, Keio University).
All Rights Reserved.

Permission to use, copy, modify and distribute the XHTML Basic
DTD and its accompanying documentation for any purpose and
without fee is hereby granted in perpetuity, provided that
the above copyright notice and this paragraph appear in all
copies. The copyright holders make no representation about the
suitability of the DTD for any purpose. It is provided "as is"
without expressed or implied warranty.
```

SNIP: Editorial attribution and revision history deleted here

```
-->
<!-- This is the driver file for version 1.0 of the XHTML
     Basic DTD.

This DTD is identified by the PUBLIC and SYSTEM identifiers:
     PUBLIC: "-//W3C//DTD XHTML Basic 1.0//EN"
     SYSTEM: "http://www.w3.org/TR/xhtml-basic/xhtml-basic10.dtd"
-->

<!ENTITY % XHTML.version  "-//W3C//DTD XHTML Basic 1.0//EN" >
<!-- Use this URI to identify the default namespace:
          "http://www.w3.org/1999/xhtml"
     See the Qualified Names module for information on the use of
     namespace prefixes in the DTD.
-->

<!ENTITY % NS.prefixed "IGNORE" >
<!ENTITY % XHTML.prefix  "" >
```

```
<!-- Reserved for use with the XLink namespace:
-->
<!ENTITY % XLINK.xmlns "" >
<!ENTITY % XLINK.xmlns.attrib "" >

<!-- For example, if you are using XHTML Basic 1.0 directly,
     use the FPI in the DOCTYPE declaration, with the xmlns
     attribute on the document element to identify the default
     namespace:
       <?xml version="1.0"?>
       <!DOCTYPE html PUBLIC "-//W3C//DTD XHTML Basic 1.0//EN"
         "http://www.w3.org/TR/xhtml-basic/xhtml-basic10.dtd">
     <html xmlns="http://www.w3.org/1999/xhtml" xml:lang="en" >
Unless you're invoking other modules outside the XHTML modules,
or modifying those modules, this is exactly what you must do!
     ...
     </html>
-->

<!-- SNIP: Extraneous content related to document profiles and
     the Bi-directional Text module removed here -->

<!-- :::::::::::::::::::::::::::::::::::::::::::::::::::::::::::: -->

<!ENTITY % xhtml-events.module   "IGNORE" >
<!ENTITY % xhtml-bdo.module      "%XHTML.bidi; " >

<!ENTITY % xhtml-model.mod
    PUBLIC "-//W3C//ENTITIES XHTML Basic 1.0
      Document Model 1.0//EN"
      "xhtml-basic10-model-1.mod" >
<!-- This invokes changes to the XHTML content model introduced
    in the XHTML Basic implementation. The related DTD is fully
    documented at
    http://www.w3.org/TR/xhtml-basic/#a_customization -->

<!ENTITY % xhtml-framework.mod
    PUBLIC "-//W3C//ENTITIES XHTML Modular Framework 1.0//EN"
      "xhtml-framework-1.mod" >
%xhtml-framework.mod;
<!-- This invokes the basic XHTML Modularization Framework that
    allows the monolithic XHTML 1.0 DTD to be broken into
    modules -->

<!ENTITY % pre.content
    "( #PCDATA
    | %InlStruct.class;
```

```
                    %InlPhras.class;
                    %Anchor.class;
                    %Inline.extra; )*"
>
<!-- This defines changes to preformatted content element in
    the Text module, which is why it must appear before the
    Text module is invoked in the next set of DTD definitions.
    -->

<!ENTITY % xhtml-text.mod
    PUBLIC "-//W3C//ELEMENTS XHTML Text 1.0//EN"
            "xhtml-text-1.mod" >
%xhtml-text.mod;

<!ENTITY % xhtml-hypertext.mod
    PUBLIC "-//W3C//ELEMENTS XHTML Hypertext 1.0//EN"
            "xhtml-hypertext-1.mod" >
%xhtml-hypertext.mod;

<!ENTITY % xhtml-list.mod
      PUBLIC "-//W3C//ELEMENTS XHTML Lists 1.0//EN"
              "xhtml-list-1.mod" >
%xhtml-list.mod;
<!-- This concludes the invocation of the XHTML Core modules
    that are unaltered by other invoked modules. Please note
    that the Structure module is invoked last herein because
    it's altered by some of the other modules that precede it.
    -->


<!-- :::::::::::::::::::::::::::::::::::::::::::::::::::::::: -->

<!-- Image Module ...................................... -->
<!ENTITY % xhtml-image.module "INCLUDE" >
<![%xhtml-image.module;[
<!ENTITY % xhtml-image.mod
    PUBLIC "-//W3C//ELEMENTS XHTML Images 1.0//EN"
            "xhtml-image-1.mod" >
%xhtml-image.mod;]]>
<!-- Notice that the syntax is more convoluted for the non-Core
    modules. Basically, it's necessary to create an internal
    image module entity, xhtml-image.module, to correspond to the
    external image module DTD before invoking that external
    module itself. The same approach applies to the Tables,
    Forms, Link, Metainformation, Base Element (Base), Param
    Element (Param), and Embedded Object (Object) modules that
    follow. -->
```

```
<!-- Tables Module ...................................... -->
<!ENTITY % xhtml-table.module "INCLUDE" >
<![%xhtml-table.module;[
<!ENTITY % xhtml-table.mod
    PUBLIC "-//W3C//ELEMENTS XHTML Basic Tables 1.0//EN"
           "xhtml-basic-table-1.mod" >
%xhtml-table.mod;]]>

<!-- Forms Module ...................................... -->
<!ENTITY % xhtml-form.module "INCLUDE" >
<![%xhtml-form.module;[
<!ENTITY % xhtml-form.mod
    PUBLIC "-//W3C//ELEMENTS XHTML Basic Forms 1.0//EN"
           "xhtml-basic-form-1.mod" >
%xhtml-form.mod;]]>

<!-- Link Element Module ............................... -->
<!ENTITY % xhtml-link.module "INCLUDE" >
<![%xhtml-link.module;[
<!ENTITY % xhtml-link.mod
    PUBLIC "-//W3C//ELEMENTS XHTML Link Element 1.0//EN"
           "xhtml-link-1.mod" >
%xhtml-link.mod;]]>

<!-- Document Metainformation Module ................... -->
<!ENTITY % xhtml-meta.module "INCLUDE" >
<![%xhtml-meta.module;[
<!ENTITY % xhtml-meta.mod
    PUBLIC "-//W3C//ELEMENTS XHTML Metainformation 1.0//EN"
           "xhtml-meta-1.mod" >
%xhtml-meta.mod;]]>

<!-- Base Element Module ............................... -->
<!ENTITY % xhtml-base.module "INCLUDE" >
<![%xhtml-base.module;[
<!ENTITY % xhtml-base.mod
    PUBLIC "-//W3C//ELEMENTS XHTML Base Element 1.0//EN"
           "xhtml-base-1.mod" >
%xhtml-base.mod;]]>

<!-- Param Element Module .............................. -->
<!ENTITY % xhtml-param.module "INCLUDE" >
<![%xhtml-param.module;[
<!ENTITY % xhtml-param.mod
    PUBLIC "-//W3C//ELEMENTS XHTML Param Element 1.0//EN"
           "xhtml-param-1.mod" >
%xhtml-param.mod;]]>
```

```
<!-- Embedded Object Module  ............................. -->
<!ENTITY % xhtml-object.module "INCLUDE" >
<![%xhtml-object.module;[
<!ENTITY % xhtml-object.mod
    PUBLIC "-//W3C//ELEMENTS XHTML Embedded Object 1.0//EN"
           "xhtml-object-1.mod" >
%xhtml-object.mod;]]>

<!ENTITY % xhtml-struct.mod
    PUBLIC "-//W3C//ELEMENTS XHTML Document Structure 1.0//EN"
           "xhtml-struct-1.mod" >
%xhtml-struct.mod;

<!-- end of XHTML Basic 1.0 DTD  ......................... -->
```

Modular XHTML and Schemas

Currently, the only way to build additional XHTML modules and to invoke such modules when constructing document definitions for related XHTML documents is to use DTDs. A *working draft*—or a formal statement of work in progress in a W3C working group that is still building a specification—titled "Modularization of XHTML in XML Schema" is available at www.w3.org/TR/2001/WD-xhtml-m12n-schema-20011219/. This document shows the state of the XML Schema equivalents to the existing DTDs that describe the various XHTML modules as of December 19, 2001. To find the latest version of this work, be sure to visit the HTML home page at www.w3.org/MarkUp/ and check the "News" and "Recommendations" sections to learn the latest status of this effort.

Many XML and XHTML experts believe that building and using XHTML modules will become easier when XML Schema–based descriptions of such modules become possible (when developing new modules or customizing existing ones) or available (when using predefined modules like the ones documented earlier in this chapter). Although this is a subject of some controversy that pits the "pro-SGML" or "pro-DTD" factions against the "pro-Schema" factions in the XML community, we believe most content developers will use whichever approach works best for them.

In the meantime, those interested in XML Schema–based implementations of XHTML modules will find section 3 of the working draft of "Modularization of XHTML in XML Schema" of great interest, because it documents proposed versions of XML Schemas for XHTML content models, infrastructure, and the individual modules themselves in detail. However, because the XML Schema definition only recently attained recommended status (May 5, 2001), we expect this draft to go through some minor changes and adjustments before it, too, attains recommended status. That's why we're unable to cover this information in depth in this book. Suffice it to say, in closing, that XML Schema–based modules should become available soon, perhaps even by the time you read this book. Please check www.w3.org/MarkUp to ascertain this important effort's current status as you read this material.

Where to Go from Here

In this chapter, we explored XHTML modules and modularization. We explored what motivates use of this technology for subsetting a monolithic definition of XHTML, and learned that XHTML Modularization produces more compact documents that are easier to parse and process, especially on handheld devices, cell phones, or embedded systems with Internet and Web access. We examined the contents and capabilities of the existing modules defined in the XHTML Modularization Specification and the Ruby module added to this collection in the XHTML 1.1 Specification. You should not only be ready to make use of this technology if your needs suggest or dictate its use, but should also be able to use the examples presented in this chapter to create and validate modular XHTML documents.

Where to now?

♦ Chapters 23 and 24 explore and explain the uses, syntax, and semantics of DTDs, should you wish to dig more deeply into the DTDs that describe XHTML modules, or the DTDs that pull them together (such as the XHTML Basic DTD presented earlier in this chapter).

♦ Chapter 29 explains XML Schemas, should you wish to investigate and learn more about XML Schema–based XHTML modules.

Part 8

The XML Family of Applications

Chapter 26

XSLT: Extensible Stylesheet Language Transformations

EXTENSIBLE STYLESHEET LANGUAGE TRANSFORMATIONS (XSLT) has become one of the most used XML vocabularies to date because it fulfills a significant need in adoption of XML. For those of us who are eager to use XML, XSLT is becoming a necessity to transform XML into XHTML or HTML. XSLT is a part of the Extensible Stylesheet Language (XSL). The T stands for *Transformations*, and that's just what this language does: It allows XML developers to *transform* their document model. In other words, it enables developers to convert an XML document into XHTML, or an XML document into a new XML document that uses a different vocabulary.

The benefits of transformation are already being experienced on the Web and in business-to-business transactions. Many developers use XSLT on the server side of their Web sites to transform their XML documents into HTML. This is a necessity if you want your Web site to be accessible to older browsers. Other uses include transforming XML data into the Wireless Markup Language (WML) for use on handheld devices. In this chapter, we'll outline the basics (although they're not very basic) of XSLT and provide some examples that you can build on if you implement XSLT.

This chapter covers the following topics:

◆ Understanding XSL and XSLT

◆ Working with XSLT

◆ Creating XSLT templates

◆ Working with XSLT elements

◆ Understanding XSLT elements and expressions

Understanding XSL and XSLT

The Extensible Stylesheet Language (XSL) is the parent of XSLT and is defined and maintained by the World Wide Web Consortium (W3C). Similar to Cascading Style Sheets (CSS), XSL is a formatting language. However, XSL extends CSS in two key ways:

◆ XSL is an application of XML and, therefore, follows XML's syntax rules.

◆ XSL allows you to format and transform XML documents.

TIP *For a tangible example of XSLT capabilities, look at the transformation in Listings 26.1, 26.2, and 26.3, as well as Figure 26.3, to see how an XML document can be automatically transformed into HTML.*

XSL ORIGINS

The origins of XSL can be found in a language called the Document Style Semantics and Specification Language (DSSSL). Introduced in the early 1990s, DSSSL was—and still is—used to format and transform Standard Generalized Markup Language (SGML) documents.

DSSSL allows you to describe the processing of documents using a standard syntax. DSSSL combines the two most common forms of document processing: formatting and transformation. XSL follows in DSSSL's footsteps and was introduced as XML's answer to formatting and transforming. This is not to say that CSS is on its way out. On the contrary, CSS works well with XML, in its context: CSS is a Web-specific formatting language. If all you need to do is display your XML document on the Web, CSS is the best candidate. However, XSL is a formatting language for multiple output formats, such as screen and print. In addition to defining formatting, XSL allows you to transform your document model.

Originally, XSL was defined by one specification document that covered both formatting and transforming XML documents. Later, the XSL working group at the W3C broke this document into two separate pieces: one, XSL, to cover formatting XML documents, and the other, XSL Transformations (XSLT), to cover transforming XML documents.

XSLT, the focus of this chapter, provides a set of rules to convert documents described by one set of elements to documents described by another set of elements. The two element sets don't even have to look similar.

For example, you may describe all of your data using an XML vocabulary that semantically makes sense. A company that sells books might use elements such as book, title, author, and price. However, these semantic elements don't define any formatting. Another problem is that the some of the desired user agents (browsers) don't support XML. Using XSLT, we can create a style sheet that transforms an XML document into two very different outputs: one that uses the WML needed to display data on cell phones and one that uses HTML to display data on desktop machines. Figure 26.1 illustrates this relationship.

FIGURE 26.1

Transforming XML documents for multiple outputs

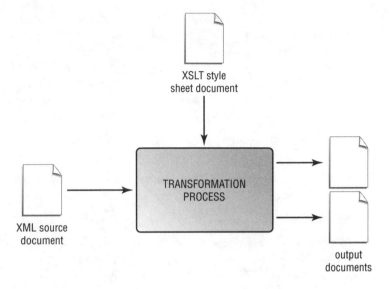

Working with XSLT

To work with XSLT, you must first understand the process. XSLT is designed to transform a document's vocabulary. It does so by applying an XSLT style sheet to an XML source document and producing a result document. In this section, we'll cover this process.

The Transformation Process

As the document author, you supply the XML source document and the XSLT style sheet document. The processor creates the output document by extracting data from the XML document and generating output based on the instructions in the XSLT style sheet. Figure 26.2 illustrates this concept.

FIGURE 26.2

The XSLT transformation process

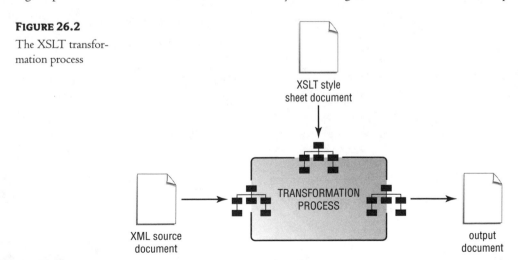

An XSLT processor is the tool that completes the process illustrated in Figure 26.2—represented by the box in the center of the figure. An XSLT processor can be used as a stand-alone processor, or can be part of a user agent (such as a browser). As the XSLT processor accepts the XML document and XSLT style sheet, it creates tree representations of them. Then it creates an output tree according to the instructions defined by the XSLT document and based on the data found in the XML input document. The last step is for the processor to generate an output document, if required by the receiving application. Three common XSLT processors are used:

◆ Saxon, a stand-alone processor used from the command prompt; it's available from the open source community at `sourceforge.net`.

◆ Xalan, another a stand-alone processor used from the command prompt; it's available from the Apache XML project (`http://xml.apache.org`).

◆ MSXML3, a processor that's a part of Microsoft's Internet Explorer (IE).

Processors are covered later in this chapter in the "XSLT Products" section.

As the document author, you supply the (well-formed) XML input document and the XSLT style sheet document. The processor creates the output document. An XSLT processor is allowed to produce three different types of output documents:

XML   The output document can be an XML vocabulary or XML fragment. Converting your XML vocabulary into another is often required when a specific vocabulary is necessary for exchanging data. For example, you might want to convert one XML vocabulary containing elements such as `book`, `title`, and `author` to another XML vocabulary that uses elements such as `publication`, `bookTitle`, and `bookAuthor`.

HTML   The output document adheres to the HTML 4 specification. If you want to produce an XHTML document, you should use the XML output method.

Text   The output document can be any text-based format. You might wish to transform your data into an EDI message or a PDF file. Because both of these documents are text based, you can transform your document with this output method.

XSLT allows you to process multiple documents. The processing model defines the following behavior:

◆ A style sheet can reference multiple-input XML documents. In this case, there must be one primary source file that will be associated with the style sheet; however, a style sheet could then reference additional input documents.

◆ The style sheet can reference additional style sheet documents, allowing you to modularize your style sheets. There must be one primary style sheet document. The style sheet could then use the XSLT `import` or `include` element to reference multiple style sheets.

TIP   *Another useful functionality present in most XSLT processors is the ability to produce multiple outputs with a single run of the processor. This is not currently supported by the XSLT standard; however, many products on the market provide this functionality.*

Understanding the Tree

XSLT processes trees, which are logical representations of the elements within the input document, rather than processing documents directly. Therefore, the first step in the transformation process is to create a tree representation of both the source and style sheet documents. Both the XML document and XSLT style sheet are processed using the same tree data model. The XSLT standard takes the XPath model (which is based on the concept of nodes) and tweaks it a bit for a perfect fit.

XPATH'S ROLE

XPath defines a regular syntax and semantics for addressing elements or objects within an XML document and is a key ingredient to using XSLT. XPath also provides syntax for manipulating strings, numbers, and Boolean variables. Much like the Document Object Model (DOM), XPath uses a tree model that defines various parts of an XML document as *nodes*. Specifically, XPath defines seven parts of an XML document that can be defined as a part of the node tree. For example, every element found in an XML document would have its own element node that identifies its name and string value. Once the data is defined as a part of a tree, it's easier to navigate that tree and locate the data needed for the output document. XSLT uses XPath expressions to identify nodes in the source tree, as well as select the nodes for data manipulation.

NODES

Nodes are objects defined using a data tree. Each of these nodes has a *string-value*, which you can generally think of as the content of the element (between the opening and closing elements) or the value of the attribute. The string-value is usually the information that XSLT extracts from the source documents and inserts into output documents. Some nodes also have extended names, which reflect additional XML namespaces used in the document. XPath defines seven types of nodes that make up the document's tree representation:

Root node   The root node is much like the document node in the DOM model in that it represents the entire document. Do not get this confused with the root element; the root node does not represent the root element. The root node is the root of the tree. The root element is defined as the first element node and is a child of the root node. The root node can also have comment and processing instruction nodes as children. The string-value of the root node is the total of all string-values of its descendants.

Element node   Element nodes represent an element. An element node can have an extended name that consists of the element name, plus a corresponding namespace prefix. If an element does not contain a namespace prefix, the expanded name is null. The string-value of an element node is the total of all string-values of its descendants.

Attribute node   An attribute node contains the name and value of a given attribute. An element node can be the parent of an attribute node. However, attribute nodes are not the children of element nodes. If an attribute is not present but has a default value defined in the Document Type Definition (DTD), the attribute is also represented as an attribute node (this is only required if the default value is found in the internal DTD subset). Although namespaces are typically defined as attributes, they're not included as attribute nodes (see the namespace node definition). The attribute node can have an extended name that consists of the attribute name, value, and a corresponding namespace prefix. If an attribute does not contain a namespace prefix, the expanded name is null. The string-value for an attribute node is the attribute value.

Comment node   A comment node exists for every comment written in the XML source document (`<!-- I am a comment -->`). The string-value of the comment node is the text of the comment.

Processing instruction node   A processing node exists for every processing instruction in the XML source document (`<?PITarget?>`). A processing instruction node's expanded name consists of the `PITarget`, and the namespace Uniform Resource Identifier (URI) is null. The string-value of the processing instruction node is everything that follows the `PITarget` (not including the `?>`).

WARNING   *Note that although the XML declaration (`<?xml version="1.0"?>`) looks like a processing instruction, it's not included as a node in the tree.*

Namespace node   A namespace node defines a namespace that's copied to each element node to which it applies. This means that every element node has one namespace node for every namespace declaration in the scope of an element.

Text node   The XPath tree model groups character data into text nodes. The string-value of a text node is the character data.

Each node type has a string-value. For some node types, the string-value is defined as a part of the node. For other node types, the string-value is determined by the string-values of descendant nodes.

When creating a document tree, a specific ordering must occur—a document order that defines the occurrence order of all nodes after expanding all entities defined in an internal DTD subset. The root node will be the first node. All element nodes must occur before their children, and they occur in order of the occurrence of their start element (after expansion of entities). Namespace nodes of an element occur first, then attribute nodes, and then children of the element.

Variables, Expressions, and Data Types

This section identifies and explains three of the key concepts needed to use XSLT effectively:

◆ Variables and parameters

◆ Expressions

◆ Data types

VARIABLES AND PARAMETERS

XSLT allows document authors to define global and local variables. You can use a global variable to define an expression that you intend to use repeatedly. The `xsl:variable` element defines a named string for use in the style sheet via an attribute value template. The primary difference between a variable and a parameter is that a parameter is designed to assign content from a source outside of the current template, while a variable is assigned internally.

EXPRESSIONS

As you begin to learn all the XSLT elements, you'll find that many of them use attributes that are set to expressions. So, just what is an expression? *Expressions*, which are defined as a part of the XPath specification document, are used to define a navigation path through a document tree. An expression begins at the current node or the root node, and then follows a sequence of steps in a defined direction.

Each step, or stage, of the path can branch, so for example, you can find all the attributes of all the children of a given node. The parts of an expression are defined as follows:

Axes Defines the direction of the path. For example, the child axis locates all the children of a given node, and the ancestor axis locates all the ancestors of a given node.

Node test Selects a set of nodes using the chosen axis.

Predicate Is an expression that filters a node set with respect to an axis to produce a new node set. The predicate is evaluated for each node in the node set. Each node for which the predicate evaluates to `true` is included in the new node set.

If you put them all together, you'll find a syntax that looks like this:

```
axis::nodetest[predicate]
```

Here, the double colon (`::`) separates the axis from the node test and the predicate is contained by square brackets (`[]`). You may include multiple predicates in an expression, as follows:

```
axis::nodetest[predicate][predicate][predicate]…
```

The combination of the three parts makes up a step. An expression can contain multiple steps. The syntax of an XPath expression uses the / as an operator to separate the successive steps; for example, `step/step/step`. If an expression begins with a /, the expression begins at the root node (this is said to be an absolute path—beginning at the very beginning). If the expression does not begin at the root node, it's a relative path.

The following is an example of an expression:

```
child::book[position()=5]
```

You'll find out more about expressions later in this chapter in the "XSLT Expressions" section.

DATA TYPES

Most expressions evaluate to node sets (a list of nodes) or a string-value (the string-value of a node); however, there are five different data types that expressions can evaluate to:

Boolean A Boolean type can have one of two values: `true` or `false`. Booleans are not defined with constants; rather, they can be called with functions: `true()` and `false()`. Boolean values may be obtained by comparing values of other data types using operators such as `=` and `!=`, and they may be combined using the two operators `and` and `or`.

Numbers The XPath specification states that a number is always a double-precision floating-point number.

Node set A node set is a list of nodes from the source document. A node set can contain a combination of different node types. For example, when a node set value is converted to a Boolean type, an empty node set is treated as `false` and a node set containing one or more nodes as `true`. For instance, the following test could be used: `<xsl:if test="@name">`. This example tests to find out whether the current element has a `name` attribute.

String-value A string-value is a series of characters. String-values can be included in XPath expressions using single or double quotes; for example, `"Paperback"` or `'Hardcover'`. String-values may be compared using operators such as `=` and `!=`. They are compared character by character.

Tree Also referred to as result tree fragments, this is a portion of an XML document that is not a complete node or set of nodes.

Style Sheet Structure

A XSLT style sheet usually begins with the `xsl:stylesheet` element. The `xsl:stylesheet` element is the document element (also referred to as the outermost element) for most XSLT style sheet documents.

Immediate children of the `xsl:stylesheet` element are considered top-level elements. The `xsl:stylesheet` element cannot contain any text nodes as immediate children, only top-level elements. These elements can occur in any order (with the exception of the `xsl:import` element).

Following top-level elements, you're likely to find a template rule that contains literal result elements to be copied—as is—to the result tree, coupled with instructions that locate and copy nodes from the XML source document.

Here's an example of the basic structure of an XSLT document:

```
<?xml version="1.0"?>
<xsl:stylesheet
   xmlns:xsl="http://www.w3.org/1999/XSL/Transform"
    version="1.0">
<!-- top-level elements go here -->

   <xsl:template match="/">

<!-- literal result elements and XSLT instructions go here -->

   </xsl:template>
</xsl:stylesheet>
```

Templates

On a very simple level, XSLT templates are similar to template documents used by Dreamweaver and other HTML editors. After a template is created, it can be applied to multiple documents (or multiple nodes). XSLT allows developers to define a template for the output document. For example, you can define a basic HTML template that will use list items. The template would consist of a few lines, such as:

```
<html>
   <head>
     <title>XML Message</title>
   </head>
   <body>
     <ul>
        <li>...</li>
     </ul>
   </body>
</html>
```

In this example, you can use XSLT to define how to populate the list item elements with content from a source XML file.

Most style sheets contain a template rule defined using the XSLT `xsl:template` element. Most template elements contain a `match` attribute that points to a pattern that defines the nodes to which the template rule applies. A style sheet can contain multiple template rules that match various node patterns. The following is an example of a template rule:

```
<xsl:template match="/">
   <html>
      <head>
        <title>XML Message</title>
      </head>

      <body>
       <ul>
         <xsl:for-each select="book">
           <li><xsl:value-of select="title" /></li>
         </xsl:for-each>
       </ul>
      </body>
   </html>
</xsl:template>
```

In this example, the `xsl:template` element defines a template rule to be applied to the root node (the pattern / in the first line matches the root node). The template uses an `xsl:for-each` element that states every time the processor comes across a `book` element node, it must use the contained XSLT instruction. In this case, the instruction is an `xsl:value-of` element that grabs the string-value of the `title` element node. Therefore, the result document would be a group of list item elements that contain all the book titles from the input document.

The template itself contains both XSLT elements (also known as *instructions* or *rules)* and literal result elements. The XSLT elements are instructions that contain patterns that match to the tree. For example, in the previous example, the `xsl:value-of` element contains a `select` attribute that matches an expression found in the XML source document tree. The `ul` and `li` elements are known as literal result elements. These types of elements make up the bulk of any template and are copied directly to the result tree.

Comments and processing instructions can be included within the template; however, they're ignored and treated as literal result elements and copied directly to the result tree. This is because the processor identifies literal result elements as any element that does not belong to the XSLT namespace—in other words, all elements that do not begin with `xsl:`

XSLT Products

To work with XSLT, you must use an XSLT processor. There are two common types of processors: stand-alone processors and processors that are part of an application, such as IE's MSXML3 processor. Here are some of the more common XSLT processors:

Saxon   Saxon is a stand-alone processor created by Michael Kay, a well-known XSLT expert. Saxon comes in two different versions: the full version, which includes source code and a Java library; and Instant Saxon, which includes only a Windows executable. Download it at `http://saxon.sourceforge.net/`.

Xalan   Xalan is a stand-alone processor from the Apache XML project at `http://xml.apache.org/`. Xalan can be used as a stand-alone executable or as a Java applet or servlet, or it can be incorporated into Java or C++ programs.

XT   Created by James Clark, XT is an easy-to-use stand-alone processor. Similar to Saxon, XT is a Java-based processor. Download it at `www.jclark.com/xml/xt.html`.

MSXML3   MSXML3 is Microsoft's XML processor, which is built into the latest versions of IE. If you do not use IE, simply search for "MSXML3" at the main Microsoft site.

Additionally, some Web servers include XSLT processors to transform documents from XML to HTML as they're served. Check with your Webmaster or in the Web server documentation for details.

A Working Example

In this section, we provide you with a working XSLT example. The following three code listings (Listing 26.1, Listing 26.2, and Listing 26.3) show three documents, which illustrate the original XML input document, the XSLT style sheet used to transform it, and the result document created by the transformation. We created the output document with the Saxon processor (although any processor should produce identical results). If you want to try this on your own, download and install the Saxon processor from `http://saxon.sourceforge.net/`, and download the sample files for this book from `www.sybex.com`.

Listing 26.1   An XML input document

Listing 26.2   An XSLT style sheet document

Listing 26.3   The result document that will be generated when you apply the XSLT style sheet to the XML document

LISTING 26.1: AN XML INPUT DOCUMENT

```xml
<?xml version="1.0" encoding="utf-8"?>
  <publications>
    <book>
      <title>Java Developer's Guide to E-Commerce with XML
        and JSP</title>
      <author>Bill Brogden</author>
      <publication_date>2001</publication_date>
    </book>
    <book>
      <title>Mastering HTML and XHTML</title>
      <author>Deborah S. Ray and Eric J. Ray</author>
      <publication_date>2002</publication_date>
    </book>
  </publications>
```

LISTING 26.2: AN XSLT STYLE SHEET DOCUMENT

```xml
<?xml version="1.0" encoding="utf-8"?>
  <xsl:stylesheet version="1.0"
    xmlns:xsl="http://www.w3.org/1999/XSL/Transform">
  <xsl:output indent="yes" />
  <xsl:template match="/">
    <html xmlns="http://www.w3.org/1999/xhtml">
      <head>
        <title>Books</title>
      </head>
      <body>
        <table>
          <tr>
            <th>Title</th>
            <th>Author</th>
          </tr>
          <xsl:for-each select="publications/book">
            <tr>
              <td><xsl:value-of select="title" /></td>
              <td><xsl:value-of select="author" /></td>
            </tr>
          </xsl:for-each>
        </table>
      </body>
    </html>
  </xsl:template>
</xsl:stylesheet>
```

LISTING 26.3: THE RESULT DOCUMENT

```
<html xmlns="http://www.w3.org/1999/xhtml">
  <head>
    <meta http-equiv="Content-Type"
      content="application/xml; charset=utf-8">
    <title>Books</title>
  </head>
  <body>
    <table>
      <tr>
        <th>Title</th>
        <th>Author</th>
      </tr>
      <tr>
        <td>Java Developer's Guide to E-Commerce with XML
          and JSP</td>
        <td>Bill Brogden</td>
      </tr>
      <tr>
        <td>Mastering HTML and XHTML</td>
        <td>Deborah S. Ray and Eric J. Ray</td>
      </tr>
    </table>
  </body>
</html>
```

Assuming all of the files are in the same directory and that you've installed Saxon correctly, you will be able to transform your XML into HTML by issuing the following command from within the folder your files are in:

```
java -jar saxon7.jar L2601.xml L2602.xsl
```

Alternatively, you can add to the XML file a processing instruction that specifies where the associated style sheet is (just as you would reference a CSS style sheet from an HTML or XHTML document). To do this, add to the code in Listing 26.1 a new line referencing the style sheet, as shown here. Then open the XML file from Internet Explorer (6 or later). Use whichever approach seems easier to you, because both produce the same results.

```
<?xml version="1.0" encoding="utf-8"?>
<?xml-stylesheet type="text/xsl" href="L2622.xsl" ?>
  <publications>
    <book>
```

You will see something similar to Figure 26.3.

FIGURE 26.3

The embedded XSLT processor in Internet Explorer converts XML to HTML on the fly

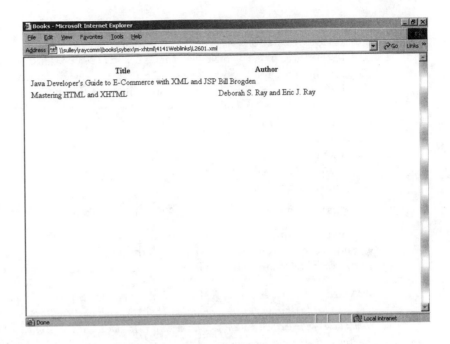

The remainder of this chapter is a reference to XSLT elements and expressions—the building blocks for your transformations. With these, and the working example above, you should be able to create your own transformations.

XSLT Elements Reference

The XSLT vocabulary defines a number of XSLT elements. And indeed, books are available that are dedicated to the subject. Because this is a book on HTML and XHTML, and not simply XSLT, we have only one chapter to dedicate to the subject matter, so cannot cover it comprehensively. However, in the following sections, we cover over half of the vocabulary, highlighting the most commonly used XSLT functions.

TIP *If you want to learn more about XSLT, we suggest you read Chuck White's excellent book,* Mastering XSLT *(Sybex, ISBN 0782140947). In addition, you can check out the W3C's XSLT Recommendation at* **www.w3.org/ TR/xslt**.

Defining Style Sheet Structure

The first thing you must know about creating XSLT documents is the basic structure for those documents. The following elements are used as a part of that basic structure:

◆ `xsl:stylesheet` (or `xsl:transform`)

◆ `xsl:include`

◆ `xsl:import`

XSL:STYLESHEET (XSL:TRANSFORM)

The `xsl:stylesheet` or `xsl:transform` element is normally used as the outermost element of an XSLT style sheet. These two elements are one and the same. They use the same attributes and have the same meaning. You'll most likely see the `xsl:stylesheet` element used; however, either is acceptable. Unless you're creating a simplified style sheet, you must always use one of these two elements.

The common attribute of the `xsl:stylesheet` element is `version="version-number"`. It defines the XSLT version used by the style sheet. Currently, the only valid version number is `"1.0"`. This attribute is required.

Although the XSLT namespace is not officially an attribute (remember in our tree representation, it's represented as a namespace node instead of an attribute node), you must not forget it. The official namespace is:

```
xmlns:xsl="http://www.w3.org/1999/XSL/Transform"
```

It must be written exactly as is. If you forget a / or misspell any piece of it, the XSLT processor will not recognize your elements. Although the XSLT namespace is a symbolic reference only, the processor is created to recognize it and, therefore, the XSLT elements associated with it.

WARNING *If you're creating an XML document that's going to be processed by an older version of IE's XML processor (MSXML) packaged as a part of IE 5.0 or IE 5.5, you must use a different namespace. The MSXML processor was created to recognize the XSLT namespace for an earlier Working Draft version of the XSLT standard. This not only means that you must use a different namespace, but also that there will be a few XSLT elements that won't be supported. The namespace for this processor is* `xmlns:xsl="http://www.w3.org/TR/WD-xsl"`. *To avoid this problem, you can download MSXML3, a newer version of the processor, from Microsoft's Web site.*

In the following example, the message node is the context node:

```
<?xml version="1.0"?>
<xsl:stylesheet
    xmlns:xsl="http://www.w3.org/1999/XSL/Transform"
    version="1.0">
<xsl:template match="message">
<html>
    <head>
      <title>Example Document</title>
    </head>
    <body>
      <xsl:value-of select="." />
    </body>
</html>
</xsl:template>
</xsl:stylesheet>
```

XSL:INCLUDE

The xsl:include element allows you to include external style sheets. The xsl:include element uses an href attribute to reference the additional style sheet you want to bring in; for example:

```
<xsl:include href="copyright.xsl">
```

Table 26.1 lists the common attributes of the xsl:include element.

TABLE 26.1: COMMON ATTRIBUTES OF THE xsl:include ELEMENT

ATTRIBUTE	DESCRIPTION
select="expression"	The value is an XPath expression that identifies the node set to be evaluated. If this attribute is not used, the node set identified by the context node is evaluated; optional.
mode="qname"	Defines the processing mode; optional.

The xsl:include element is a top-level element, so it should be an immediate child of the xsl:stylesheet element. You would use xsl:include in a primary XSLT style sheet like the following:

```
<xsl:stylesheet
    xmlns:xsl="http://www.w3.org/1999/XSL/Transform"
    version="1.0">
<xsl:include href="copyright.xsl" />
<xsl:template match="/">
    <p><xsl:value-of select="message" /></p>
</xsl:template>

<xsl:template match="copyright" />
    <copy><xsl:call-template name="copyright" /></copy>
</xsl:template>
</xsl:stylesheet>
```

The copyright.xsl style sheet would look like the following:

```
<xsl:stylesheet
    xmlns:xsl="http://www.w3.org/1999/XSL/Transform"
    version="1.0">
<xsl:variable name="raycomm">RayComm</xsl:variable>
<xsl:template name="copyright">
    Copyright 2001, <xsl:value-of select="$raycomm" />
</xsl:template>
</xsl:stylesheet>
```

In the primary style sheet, the xsl:include element brings in the copyright.xsl style sheet module. The template rule for the copy element calls a template named copyright. However, you should notice that there's no such named template in our primary style sheet. However, our copyright style sheet contains the named template copyright. Because we included the copyright style sheet, it's legal for the processor to grab the template from that document.

XSL:IMPORT

Similar to the xsl:include element, the xsl:import element allows you to import external style sheets. The xsl:import element is a top-level element that uses an href attribute to provide the URI of the style sheet to import. All xsl:import elements must appear before any other top-level elements. For example, the following would be a correct usage of the xsl:import element as a way to import a copyright.xsl style sheet:

```
<xsl:stylesheet
    xmlns:xsl="http://www.w3.org/1999/XSL/Transform"
    version="1.0">
<xsl:import href="copyright.xsl" />
...
</xsl:stylesheet>
```

If the rules in the copyright.xsl style sheet contradict rules defined by the primary style sheet, the primary style sheet wins. If you import multiple style sheets and the rules of the imported style sheets conflict, the last xsl:import element listed wins.

The common attribute of the xsl:import element is name="qname". It identifies the name of the template to be called and is required.

Applying and Invoking Template Rules

As explained in the section "Templates" earlier in this chapter, templates guide the transformation process. The following elements can be used to create, and then invoke, templates:

◆ xsl:template

◆ xsl:apply-templates

◆ xsl:call-template

XSL:TEMPLATE

A template rule is defined using the xsl:template element. This element contains both the literal result elements and XSLT instructions. The match attribute is used to define the node set to which the rule applies. By doing so, the match attribute defines the context node for the template.

The xsl:template (and xsl:apply-template) element enables you to use an optional mode attribute. Modes allow for the multiple processing of an element. Each time the element is processed, it could produce a different result. If the xsl:template element does not use the match attribute, it cannot use the mode attribute.

Table 26.2 lists the common attributes of the xsl:template element.

TABLE 26.2: COMMON ATTRIBUTES OF THE `xsl:template` ELEMENT

ATTRIBUTE	DESCRIPTION
match="pattern"	The value of the match attribute identifies the nodes that are eligible to be processed by the template rule. If this attribute is not used, the name attribute is required; optional.
name="qname"	The name attribute defines a name for the template that then can be used to reference the template; optional.
priority="number"	Defines a priority level for a template that can be used when multiple templates match the same node set; optional.
mode="qname"	The mode attribute is used in conjunction with the `xsl:apply-templates` element. When the `xsl:apply-templates` element is used to process the node set, the only templates considered are those with a matching mode; optional.

In Listing 26.4, the message node is the context node.

LISTING 26.4: XSLT STYLE SHEET USING AN *xsl:template* ELEMENT

```
<?xml version="1.0"?>
<xsl:stylesheet
    xmlns:xsl="http://www.w3.org/1999/XSL/Transform"
    version="1.0">
<xsl:template match="message">
<html>
    <head>
      <title>Example Document</title>
    </head>
    <body>
      <xsl:value-of select="." />
    </body>
</html>
</xsl:template>
</xsl:stylesheet>
```

XSL:APPLY-TEMPLATES

The `xsl:apply-templates` element selects a node set in the source tree and processes each child node (or child node set) individually by finding a matching template rule for that node. The node set is determined by the **select** attribute. Matching templates are processed according to the order the nodes occur within the source tree unless an `xsl:sort` element is present.

The **select** attribute can be used to define an expression that defines the node set to be processed. The **select** attribute can select nodes relative to the context node identified by the `xsl:template` element, or it can point to an absolute selection from the root node.

If the `select` attribute is not used, the template processes the children of the current node. This includes text nodes that consist of only white space, unless you use the `xsl:strip-space` element. Be sure to remember what can be defined as a child node.

Like the `xsl:template` element, the `xsl:apply-templates` element can accept a mode attribute. If it uses the mode attribute, it applies to any template rule that has the same mode.

Table 26.3 lists the common attributes of the `xsl:apply-templates` element.

TABLE 26.3: COMMON ATTRIBUTES OF THE `xsl:apply-templates` ELEMENT

ATTRIBUTE	DESCRIPTION
select="expression"	The value of the `select` attribute is an XPath expression that identifies the node set to be evaluated. If this attribute is not used, the node sets identified by the context node are evaluated; optional.
mode="qname"	Defines the processing mode; optional.

The `xsl:apply-templates` element can be defined as an empty element, or it can contain `xsl:sort` (to define sorting of the evaluated nodes) or `xsl:with-param` (to define a parameter). Listing 26.5 uses the `xsl:apply-templates` element.

LISTING 26.5: XSLT STYLE SHEET USING AN *xsl:apply-templates* ELEMENT

```
<?xml version="1.0"?>
<xsl:stylesheet
    xmlns:xsl="http://www.w3.org/TR/WD-xsl"
    version="1.0">
<xsl:template match="/">
<html>
   <head>
     <title>Example Document</title>
   </head>
   <body>
    <hr />
     <xsl:apply-templates />
    <hr />
   </body>
</html>
</xsl:template>

<xsl:template match="message">
<b>Message</b><br />
<xsl:apply-templates select="to" /><br />
<xsl:apply-templates select="from" /><br />
<xsl:apply-templates select="text" />
</xsl:template>
```

```
<xsl:template match="to">
<b>To:</b><xsl:value-of select="." />
</xsl:template>

<xsl:template match="from">
<b>From:</b><xsl:value-of select="." />
</xsl:template>

<xsl:template match="text">
<b>Text:</b><xsl:value-of select="." />
</xsl:template>

</xsl:stylesheet>
```

PUSH VERSUS PULL PROCESSING

As you begin to work with templates, you might come across the question, "Should I use the `xsl:apply-templates`, `xsl:value-of`, or `xsl:for-each` element?" There are two popular methods for working with templates.

Push processing with `xsl:apply-templates` This approach uses multiple template rules to define which nodes to process, rather than the template rule for the parent node that defines, in detail, how each of its children should be processed. If you're creating a rather lengthy style sheet and anticipate adding more rules, you might consider this approach. With each new element you add, all you have to do is add a new template rule.

Pull processing with `xsl:for-each` and `xsl:value-of` This approach uses the `xsl:value-of` instruction to grab data (string-values) from the XML source tree using complex XPath expressions. If you value structure and predictability, this approach might be for you. This approach tends to be useful with simpler style sheets and is the best choice when you know the location and order of data in the source tree. Two elements are used for this purpose: `xsl:value-of` for grabbing a string-value to add to the result tree, and `xsl:for-each` for allowing the process to loop until all nodes defined by the expression have been used.

XSL:CALL-TEMPLATE

The `xsl:call-template` element is an XSLT instruction used to invoke a named template. If this element is used, the name of the `xsl:template` element must match the name of the `xsl:call-template` element. If multiple templates exist with the same name, the author must define import precedence that will define which template is used.

The common attribute of the `xsl:call-template` element is `name="qname"`. It identifies the name of the template to be called and is required.

The `xsl:call-template` is either empty or may contain `xsl:with-param`. Listing 26.6 uses the `xsl:call-template` element to reference defined templates.

LISTING 26.6: XSLT STYLE SHEET USING THE *xsl:call-template* ELEMENT

```xml
<?xml version="1.0"?>
<xsl:stylesheet
    xmlns:xsl="http://www.w3.org/1999/XSL/Transform"
    version="1.0">
<xsl:template match="/">
<html>
  <head>
    <title>Example Document</title>
  </head>
  <body>
    <hr />
     <xsl:apply-templates select="message" />
    <hr />
  </body>
</html>
</xsl:template>

<xsl:template match="message">
<b>Message</b><br />
<xsl:call-template name="from" /><br />
<xsl:call-template name="to" /><br />
<xsl:call-template name="text" />
</xsl:template>

<xsl:template name="to">
<b>To:</b><xsl:value-of select="to" />
</xsl:template>

<xsl:template name="from">
<b>From:</b><xsl:value-of select="from" />
</xsl:template>

<xsl:template name="text">
<b>Text:</b><xsl:value-of select="text" />
</xsl:template>
</xsl:stylesheet>
```

Defining Variables and Parameters

The following elements are used to define variables and parameters:

◆ xsl:variable

◆ xsl:param

◆ xsl:with-param

The xsl:variable element defines a local or global variable. It can be used as a top-level element or as an instruction within a template. A variable allows you to create reusable information for your style sheet. To reference a defined variable, use the $ symbol in conjunction with the variable name ($name).

Table 26.4 lists the common attributes of the xsl:variable element.

TABLE 26.4: COMMON ATTRIBUTES OF THE xsl:variable ELEMENT

ATTRIBUTE	DESCRIPTION
name="qname"	Defines a name for the variable; required.
select="expression"	Defines the expression that is to be evaluated to provide the value for the variable. If used, the element can be defined as an empty element. If the attribute is not used, the contents of the xsl:variable element determine the value of the variable; optional.

The value for the variable can be expressed using the select attribute or defined as the content of the xsl:variable element. Listing 26.7 uses the xsl:variable element to define a variable that can be referenced throughout the style sheet.

LISTING 26.7: XSLT STYLE SHEET DEFINING A VARIABLE

```
<?xml version="1.0"?>
<xsl:stylesheet
    xmlns:xsl="http://www.w3.org/1999/XSL/Transform"
    version="1.0">

<xsl:variable name="font-color">blue</xsl:variable>

<xsl:template match="message">
    <div style="color:{$font-color}">
    <p>To: <xsl:value-of select="to" /></p>
    <p>From: <xsl:value-of select="from" /></p>
    <p>Message: <xsl:value-of select="text" /></p>
    </div>
</xsl:template>
</xsl:stylesheet>
```

XSL:PARAM

The xsl:param element defines a global parameter to a template when defined as a top-level element. However, when defined as a child of the xsl:template element, it's known as a local parameter.

Table 26.5 lists the common attributes of the xsl:param element.

TABLE 26.5: COMMON ATTRIBUTES OF THE xsl:param ELEMENT

ATTRIBUTE	DESCRIPTION
name="qname"	Defines a name for the parameter; required.
select="expression"	Defines the expression that is to be evaluated to provide the value for the parameter. If used, the element can be defined as an empty element. If the attribute is not used, the contents of the xsl:variable element determine the value of the parameter; optional.

Listing 26.8 provides an example of an XSLT parameter.

LISTING 26.8: XSLT STYLE SHEET THAT DEFINES A LOCAL PARAMETER

```
<?xml version="1.0"?>
<xsl:stylesheet
    xmlns:xsl="http://www.w3.org/1999/XSL/Transform"
    version="1.0">
<xsl:template match="/">
<html>
    <head>
      <title>Example Document</title>
    </head>
    <body>
      <hr />
       <xsl:apply-templates />
      <hr />
    </body>
</html>
</xsl:template>

<xsl:template match="message">
    <b>Message</b><br />
      <xsl:apply-templates select="to" /><br />
      <xsl:apply-templates select="from" /><br />
      <xsl:apply-templates select="text" />
</xsl:template>

<xsl:template match="to | from | text">
    <xsl:param name="pre">:</xsl:param>
    <b><xsl:value-of select="$pre" /></b>
      <xsl:value-of select="." />
</xsl:template>
</xsl:stylesheet>
```

XSL:WITH-PARAM

If used, xsl:with-param must be defined as a child of xsl:apply-templates or xsl:call-template. The xsl:with-param element is used to set the values of parameters when it's calling a template. Parameters are passed to templates using the xsl:with-param element. The required name attribute specifies the name of the parameter.

Table 26.6 lists the common attributes of the xsl:with-param element.

TABLE 26.6: COMMON ATTRIBUTES OF THE xsl:with-param ELEMENT

ATTRIBUTE	DESCRIPTION
name="qname"	Defines a name for the parameter; required.
select="expression"	Defines the expression that is to be evaluated to provide the value for the parameter; optional.

Listing 26.9 provides an example of an XSLT parameter.

LISTING 26.9: XSLT STYLE SHEET THAT USES THE *xsl:with-param* ELEMENT

```
<?xml version="1.0"?>
<xsl:stylesheet
   xmlns:xsl="http://www.w3.org/1999/XSL/Transform"
   version="1.0">
<xsl:template match="/">
<html>
   <head>
     <title>Example Document</title>
   </head>
   <body>
   <hr />
     <xsl:apply-templates />
   <hr />
   </body>
</html>
</xsl:template>

<xsl:template match="message">
<b>Message</b><br />

<xsl:apply-templates select="to">
<xsl:with-param name="pre">To:</xsl:with-param>
</xsl:apply-templates><br />

<xsl:apply-templates select="from">
<xsl:with-param name="pre">From:</xsl:with-param>
</xsl:apply-templates><br />
```

```
<xsl:apply-templates select="text" />

</xsl:template>

<xsl:template match="to | from | text">
<xsl:param name="pre">:</xsl:param>
<b><xsl:value-of select="$pre" /></b>
   <xsl:value-of select="." />
</xsl:template>
</xsl:stylesheet>
```

Copying Nodes

Although XSLT style sheets are used to transform a source document, XSLT also allows you to copy parts of the source document directly to the result document unchanged. The following two elements are used to copy nodes to the output tree:

◆ xsl:copy

◆ xsl:copy-of

The xsl:copy instruction copies the context node in the source document to the output tree. This element does not copy children, descendants, or attributes of the context node; it only copies the context node. For example, if the context node is an element, it will copy that element node to the result tree. This is known as performing a *shallow copy*.

The common attribute of the xsl:copy element is use-attribute-sets="qname". If the xsl:attribute-set element (see the section "Generating Output" for more information) is used to define a named set of attributes, the use-attribute-sets attribute can be used to call on the defined attribute set. The value of the use-attribute-sets attribute can be a white space–separated list of named attribute sets. This attribute is optional.

Listing 26.10 illustrates how you might copy a node to the output tree using the xsl:copy element.

LISTING 26.10: XSLT STYLE SHEET THAT USES THE *xsl:copy* ELEMENT

```
<?xml version="1.0"?>
<xsl:stylesheet
   xmlns:xsl="http://www.w3.org/1999/XSL/Transform"
   version="1.0">
<xsl:template match="/">
<html>
   <head>
     <title>Example Document</title>
   </head>
   <body>
     <hr />
       <xsl:apply-templates />
     <hr />
   </body>
```

```
</html>
</xsl:template>

<xsl:template match="message">
  <div id="message">
   To: <xsl:value-of select="to" />
   From: <xsl:value-of select="from" />
  <xsl:copy>
     <xsl:value-of select="text" />
  </xsl:copy>
   </div>

</xsl:template>
</xsl:stylesheet>
xsl:copy-of
```

The xsl:copy-of element can be used to copy a node set to the result tree. In addition to copying the context node, it copies descendant nodes. This is known as performing a *deep copy*.

The common attribute of the xsl:copy-of element is select="qname". It defines the node set or result tree fragment to be copied to the output tree and is required.

Listing 26.11 illustrates how you might copy a node set to the output tree using the xsl:copy-of element.

LISTING 26.11: XSLT STYLE SHEET THAT USES THE *xsl:copy-of* ELEMENT

```
<?xml version="1.0"?>
<xsl:stylesheet
   xmlns:xsl="http://www.w3.org/1999/XSL/Transform"
   version="1.0">
<xsl:template match="/">
<html>
   <head>
   <title>Example Document</title>
   </head>
   <body>
     <hr />
       <xsl:apply-templates />
     <hr />
   </body>
</html>
</xsl:template>

<xsl:template match="message">
<h1>Message</h1>
<xsl:copy-of select="." />
</xsl:template>

</xsl:stylesheet>
```

Conditional Processing

Conditional processing allows the developer to identify a choice of two or more alternative instructions. XSLT allows for two types of conditional processing. The `xsl:if` instruction provides simple if-then conditionality, and the `xsl:choose` instruction supports selection of one choice when there are several possibilities. The following elements can be used for conditional processing:

- ◆ `xsl:if`
- ◆ `xsl:choose`
- ◆ `xsl:when`
- ◆ `xsl:otherwise`
- ◆ `xsl:for-each`

XSL:IF

The `xsl:if` element encloses a template body that will be instantiated only if a specified condition tests `true`. This means that you can change the output based on a pattern. The `test` attribute contains an expression that evaluates to a Boolean condition. If the expression tests `true`, the contents of the `xsl:if` attribute are passed to the result tree. If the expression tests `false`, the contents are not passed to the result tree.

The required attribute of the `xsl:if` element is `test="expression"`. It defines the Boolean condition to be tested.

Listing 26.12 illustrates how you use the `xsl:if` element.

LISTING 26.12: XSLT STYLE SHEET THAT USES THE *xsl:if* ELEMENT

```
<?xml version="1.0"?>
<xsl:stylesheet
   xmlns:xsl="http://www.w3.org/1999/XSL/Transform"
   version="1.0">
<xsl:template match="/">
<html>
   <head>
     <title>Example Document</title>
   </head>
   <body>
     <hr />
      <xsl:apply-templates />
     <hr />
   </body>
</html>
</xsl:template>

<xsl:template match="message">
    <xsl:if test="to='Sam'">
     <h1>Sam's Message</h1>
```

```
        <xsl:value-of select="to" /><br />
        <xsl:value-of select="from" /><br />
        <xsl:value-of select="text" />
      </xsl:if>
  </xsl:template>
</xsl:stylesheet>
```

XSL:CHOOSE

The xsl:choose element defines a choice between a number of alternatives. The xsl:choose element must contain at least one xsl:when element that provides a condition to be tested. An xsl:otherwise element can be included and is selected if the test defined by the xsl:when element(s) is found to be false. The xsl:choose element does not accept any attributes.

Listing 26.13 illustrates how you use the xsl:choose element.

LISTING 26.13: XSLT STYLE SHEET THAT USES THE *xsl:choose* ELEMENT

```
<?xml version="1.0"?>
<xsl:stylesheet
   xmlns:xsl="http://www.w3.org/1999/XSL/Transform"
   version="1.0">
<xsl:template match="/">
<html>
   <head>
   <title>HTML Output; choose, when, otherwise example</title>
   </head>
   <body>
     <hr />
       <xsl:apply-templates />
     <hr />
   </body>
</html>
</xsl:template>

<xsl:template match="message">
   <b>Message</b><br />
     <xsl:apply-templates select="to">
       <xsl:with-param name="pre">T</xsl:with-param>
     </xsl:apply-templates><br />
     <xsl:apply-templates select="from">
       <xsl:with-param name="pre">F</xsl:with-param>
     </xsl:apply-templates><br />
     <xsl:apply-templates select="text" />
     </xsl:template>
<xsl:template match="to | from | text">
     <xsl:param name="pre">:</xsl:param>
       <xsl:choose>
```

```
        <xsl:when test="$pre='T'">To:</xsl:when>
        <xsl:when test="$pre='F'">From:</xsl:when>
        <xsl:when test="$pre='Text'">Text:</xsl:when>
        <xsl:otherwise>
          <xsl:value-of select="$pre" />
        </xsl:otherwise>
        </xsl:choose>
        <xsl:value-of select="." />
    </xsl:template>

    </xsl:stylesheet>
```

XSL:WHEN

The xsl:when element defines a condition to be tested and the action to be performed if the condition is true. This element is a required child of the xsl:choose element. This element defines a condition to be tested.

The required attribute of the xsl:when element is test="expression". It defines the Boolean condition to be tested.

For an example, see Listing 26.13.

XSL:OTHERWISE

This element is an optional child of the xsl:choose instruction and indicates the action that should be taken when none of the xsl:when conditions are satisfied. The xsl:otherwise element does not accept any attributes.

For an example, see Listing 26.13.

XSL:FOR-EACH

This instruction uses an XPath expression to select a node set and performs the same processing for each node in the set. The result is a looping effect. It has a required select="expression" attribute that specifies the node set to be evaluated.

Listing 26.14 illustrates how to use the xsl:for-each element.

LISTING 26.14: XSLT STYLE SHEET THAT USES THE *xsl:for-each* ELEMENT

```
<?xml version="1.0"?>
<xsl:stylesheet
   xmlns:xsl="http://www.w3.org/1999/XSL/Transform"
   version="1.0">
<xsl:template match="/">
   <html>
   <head><title>HTML Output; choose, when, otherwise
     example</title></head>
   <body>
   <xsl:for-each select="message">
```

```
      <hr />
        <b>To:</b><xsl:value-of select="." />
        <b>From:</b><xsl:value-of select="." />
        <b>Text:</b><xsl:value-of select="." />
      <hr />
      </xsl:for-each>
      </body>
      </html>
  </xsl:template>
  </xsl:stylesheet>
```

Sorting and Numbering

The title of this section gives it away. If you need to sort or number using nodes, you have to use one of these two elements:

◆ xsl:sort

◆ xsl:number

XSL:SORT

This element is always defined as a child of the xsl:apply-templates or xsl:for-each element. The xsl:sort element is used to define a sort key and defines the order in which nodes selected by xsl:apply-templates or xsl:for-each are processed. This element is useful for all types of sorting; for example, you may want to sort using an attribute value or maybe even alphabetically. Both of these sorts can be accomplished using the xsl:sort element.

Table 26.7 lists the common attributes of the xsl:sort element.

TABLE 26.7: COMMON ATTRIBUTES OF THE xsl:sort ELEMENT

ATTRIBUTE	DESCRIPTION
select="expression"	Defines the sort key; optional.
lang="lang-type"	Defines the language being used; optional.
data-type="text|number|qname"	Defines how the values are to be sorted; optional.
order="ascending|descending"	Defines how the nodes should be sorted, in either ascending or descending order; optional.
case-order="upper-first|lower-first"	Applies when the data-type attribute is set equal to text. If set to upper-first, it specifies that uppercase letters should sort before lowercase letters; optional.

Listing 26.15 illustrates how to use the xsl:sort and xsl:number elements.

LISTING 26.15: XSLT STYLE SHEET THAT USES THE *xsl:sort* AND *xsl:number* ELEMENTS

```xml
<?xml version="1.0"?>
<xsl:stylesheet
   xmlns:xsl="http://www.w3.org/1999/XSL/Transform"
   version="1.0">
<xsl:template match="/">
   <html>
   <head>
     <title>Example Document</title>
   </head>
   <body>
     <hr />
      <xsl:apply-templates />
     <hr />
   </body>
   </html>
</xsl:template>

<xsl:template match="messages">
   <xsl:for-each select="message">
     <xsl:sort select="position()" order="descending" />
     Number=<xsl:number format="01" />
     Position=<xsl:value-of select="position()" /><br />
     <xsl:apply-templates select="." /><br />
   </xsl:for-each>
</xsl:template>

<xsl:template match="message">
   <b>Message</b><br />

   <xsl:apply-templates select="to">
     <xsl:with-param name="pre">1</xsl:with-param>
   </xsl:apply-templates><br />

   <xsl:apply-templates select="from">
     <xsl:with-param name="pre">2</xsl:with-param>
   </xsl:apply-templates><br />

   <xsl:apply-templates select="text" />
   </xsl:template>

<xsl:template match="to | from | text">
   <xsl:param name="pre">:</xsl:param>
   <b>
   <xsl:choose>
     <xsl:when test="$pre=1">To:</xsl:when>
     <xsl:when test="$pre=2">From:</xsl:when>
```

```
        <xsl:when test="$pre=3">Text:</xsl:when>
        <xsl:otherwise><xsl:value-of select="$pre" /></xsl:otherwise>
      </xsl:choose>
      </b>
      <xsl:value-of select="." />
    </xsl:template>
    </xsl:stylesheet>
```

XSL:NUMBER

This instruction is used to insert a formatted integer into the current node and/or to format a number for output.

Table 26.8 lists the common attributes of the xsl:number element.

TABLE 26.8: COMMON ATTRIBUTES OF THE xsl:number ELEMENT

ATTRIBUTE	DESCRIPTION
level="single|multiple|any"	Defines what level of the source tree that is to be considered. The default value is single; optional.
count="pattern"	Defines what nodes should be counted at the defined level; optional.
from="pattern"	Defines where the counting is to begin; optional.
value="number-expression"	A user-supplied number to be formatted; optional.
format="string"	Defines the formatting for the output; optional.
lang="lang-type"	Defines the language to be used; optional.
letter-value="alphabetic|transitional"	Specifies either alphabetical or traditional numbering; optional.
grouping-separator="character"	Defines the character to be used between groups of digits; optional.
grouping-size="number"	Defines the number of digits for grouping, therefore defining where the group separator should be added; optional.

For an example, see Listing 26.15.

Generating Output

The main goal of XSLT is to generate a specific output. This section is dedicated to this goal. Several elements are essential to specifying how to generate output. They are as follows:

◆ xsl:value-of

◆ xsl:element

- ◆ `xsl:attribute`
- ◆ `xsl:attribute-set`
- ◆ `xsl:comment`
- ◆ `xsl:processing-instruction`

XSL:VALUE-OF

The `xsl:value-of` element copies the string-value of a single source node to the output tree. The `select` attribute defines the source node to be evaluated. The instruction is always empty.

Table 26.9 lists the common attributes of the `xsl:value-of` element.

TABLE 26.9: COMMON ATTRIBUTES OF THE `xsl:value-of` ELEMENT

ATTRIBUTE	DESCRIPTION
`select="string-expression"`	Identifies the node to be evaluated. The processor will grab the string-value of the evaluated node and output it to the result tree; required.
`disable-output-escaping="yes|no"`	The XML output method escapes & and < when outputting text nodes. As a way around this rule, you can set the value equal to `yes`, which defines that special characters in the string-value, such as <, are passed to the result tree as is, rather than using `&lt;`; optional.

XSL:ELEMENT

The `xsl:element` element can be used in XSLT templates to compute new elements in result trees. This instruction is particularly useful when the name or namespace of the element to be created in the result node needs to be calculated.

Table 26.10 lists the common attributes of the `xsl:element` element.

TABLE 26.10: COMMON ATTRIBUTES OF THE `xsl:element` ELEMENT

ATTRIBUTE	DESCRIPTION
`name="qname"`	The name attribute defines a name for the element; required.
`namespace="URI"`	Defines a namespace for the result element node; optional.
`use-attribute-sets="qname"`	Specifies a list of attributes (defined using `xsl:attribute-set` elements) that will be added to the new element node; optional.

The contents of the `xsl:element` element are the contents of the new element in our result tree. For example, in Listing 26.16 we create a `div` element for our result tree that contains the text of the text element node. If no content is defined, the new element is empty.

LISTING 26.16: XSLT STYLE SHEET USING AN *xsl:element* ELEMENT

```
<?xml version="1.0"?>
<xsl:stylesheet
   xmlns:xsl="http://www.w3.org/1999/XSL/Transform"
   version="1.0">

<xsl:template match="/">
   <xsl:for-each select="message">
     <xsl:element name="div">
     The message states <xsl:value-of select="text" />.
     </xsl:element>
   </xsl:for-each>
</xsl:template>

</xsl:stylesheet>
```

XSL:ATTRIBUTE

The `xsl:attribute` element can be used to add attributes to result elements. The element outputs an attribute name and value to the current node.

Table 26.11 lists the common attributes of the `xsl:attribute` element.

TABLE 26.11: COMMON ATTRIBUTES OF THE `xsl:attribute` ELEMENT

ATTRIBUTE	DESCRIPTION
name="qname"	The name attribute defines the name for the attribute; required.
namespace="URI"	Names the namespace to be added to the attribute node; optional.

The `xsl:attribute` element works much like `xsl:element`. The contents of the `xsl:attribute` element will be the value of the newly created attribute. For example, in Listing 26.17 we create an attribute, `align`, to be used with the `div` element we created in Listing 26.16.

LISTING 26.17: XSLT STYLE SHEET USING AN *xsl:attribute* ELEMENT

```
<?xml version="1.0"?>
<xsl:stylesheet
   xmlns:xsl="http://www.w3.org/1999/XSL/Transform"
   version="1.0">

<xsl:template match="/">
   <xsl:for-each select="message">
     <xsl:element name="div">
       <xsl:attribute name="align">center</xsl:attribute>
```

```
            The message states <xsl:value-of select="text" />.
        </xsl:element>
      </xsl:for-each>
  </xsl:template>

</xsl:stylesheet>
```

XSL:ATTRIBUTE-SET

A named attribute set is a set of attributes that can be referenced in an XSLT template using just one name. The top-level element used for declaring named attribute sets is `xsl:attribute-set`.

Defined attribute sets can be referenced with the `use-attribute-sets` attribute of the `xsl:element`, `xsl:copy`, and `xsl:attribute-set` elements. You can also use attribute sets by adding a `use-attribute-sets` attribute to a literal result element.

Specifying an attribute set in the `use-attribute-sets` attribute of one of these elements is the same as using an `xsl:attribute` instruction for each of the attributes declared in the attribute set.

Table 26.12 lists the common attributes of the `xsl:attribute-set` element.

TABLE 26.12: COMMON ATTRIBUTES OF THE `xsl:attribute-set` ELEMENT

ATTRIBUTE	DESCRIPTION
`name="qname"`	The name attribute defines a name for the attribute set; required.
`use-attribute-sets="qname"`	References names of other attribute sets to be added to the current attribute set; optional.

In Listing 26.18, we create attribute sets named `bodySet` and `centerSet`, and then reference those attribute sets within our template.

LISTING 26.18: XSLT STYLE SHEET USING AN *xsl:attribute-set* **ELEMENT**

```
<?xml version="1.0"?>
<xsl:stylesheet
   xmlns:xsl="http://www.w3.org/1999/XSL/Transform"
   version="1.0">

<xsl:attribute-set name="bodySet">
   <xsl:attribute name="bgcolor">#f7f7f7</xsl:attribute>
   <xsl:attribute name="text">#000000</xsl:attribute>
</xsl:attribute-set>

<xsl:attribute-set name="centerSet">
   <xsl:attribute name="align">center</xsl:attribute>
</xsl:attribute-set>
```

```
<xsl:template match="/">
<html>
  <head>
     <title>Example Document</title>
  </head>
  <xsl:element name="body" use-attribute-sets="bodySet">
     <xsl:apply-templates />
  </xsl:element>
</html>
</xsl:template>

<xsl:template match="message">
  <xsl:element name="div" use-attribute-sets="centerSet">
    Message:
     <xsl:value-of select="text" /><br />
    To:
     <xsl:value-of select="to" /><br />
    From:
     <xsl:value-of select="from" />
  </xsl:element>
</xsl:template>

</xsl:stylesheet>
```

XSL:COMMENT

The `xsl:comment` instruction is used to create comments in the output of a style sheet. The `xsl:comment` instruction has very few rules, one of which is that it cannot contain any attributes. The text generated by the content of this element is written into an XML comment.

In Listing 26.19 we create a comment with the following text: "A work-related message." The output would be the following comment:

```
<!-- A work-related message -->
```

LISTING 26.19: XSLT STYLE SHEET USING AN *xsl:comment* ELEMENT

```
<?xml version="1.0"?>
<xsl:stylesheet
   xmlns:xsl="http://www.w3.org/1999/XSL/Transform"
   version="1.0">

<xsl:template match="/">
<html>
  <head>
     <title>Example Document</title>
```

```
    </head>
    <body>
        <xsl:apply-templates />
    </body>
</html>
</xsl:template>

<xsl:template match="message">
    <xsl:comment>A work-related message</xsl:comment>
    <div>
    Message:
    <xsl:value-of select="text" /><br />
    To:
    <xsl:value-of select="to" /><br />
    From:
    <xsl:value-of select="from" />
    </div>
</xsl:template>

</xsl:stylesheet>
```

XSL:PROCESSING-INSTRUCTION

To create a processing instruction in the result tree, you can use the `xsl:processing-instruction` element. The name given to a processing instruction created using the `xsl:processing-instruction` element must conform to the definition of an *NCName*, as defined in the XML Namespace recommendation. An NCName is a valid XML name that doesn't contain any colons. Also, the `name` attribute cannot be `xml`, in any combination of uppercase or lowercase letters.

The required attribute for `xsl:processing-instruction` is `name="qname"`, which defines the PITarget name of the processing instruction node to be passed to the result tree.

In Listing 26.20, we create an XML style sheet processing instruction.

LISTING 26.20: XSLT STYLE SHEET USING AN *xsl:processing-instruction* ELEMENT

```
<?xml version="1.0"?>
<xsl:stylesheet
    xmlns:xsl="http://www.w3.org/1999/XSL/Transform"
    version="1.0">

<xsl:template match="/">
<xsl:processing-instruction name="xsl-stylesheet">
    href="housestyle.css" type="text/css"
</xsl:processing-instruction>
```

```
<messages>
   <xsl:apply-templates />
</messages>
</xsl:template>
<xsl:template match="message">
   <message>
    <xsl:attribute name="number"><xsl:number /></xsl:attribute>
    <xsl:for-each select="@*">
     <xsl:element name="{name()}">
        <xsl:value-of select="." />
     </xsl:element>
    </xsl:for-each>
    <xsl:value-of select="." />
   </message>
</xsl:template>

</xsl:stylesheet>
```

Manipulating White Space in the Output

White space can be a tricky issue. Because XML and XSLT treat white space differently, it's important to understand how the following elements work:

◆ xsl:text

◆ xsl:preserve-space

◆ xsl:strip-space

XSL:TEXT

Text nodes can be computed in XSLT result trees using the xsl:text element. The contents of an xsl:text element must be text only; therefore, instructions cannot be nested inside xsl:text elements. An XSLT processor will copy text appearing in an XSLT template to the result tree whether it's enclosed in an xsl:text element or not. Therefore, the xsl:text instruction is only necessary in the following two circumstances:

◆ When you need to control the output of white space

◆ When you need to control how special characters are output

The common attribute of the xsl:text element is disable-output-escaping="yes|no". The XML output method escapes & and < when outputting text nodes. As a way around this rule, you can set the value equal to yes, which defines that special characters in the string-value, such as <, will be passed to the result tree as is, rather than using <. This element is optional.

Listing 26.21 uses the xsl:text element.

LISTING 26.21: XSLT STYLESHEET USING AN *xsl:text* ELEMENT

```xml
<?xml version="1.0"?>
<xsl:stylesheet
    xmlns:xsl="http://www.w3.org/1999/XSL/Transform"
    version="1.0">
<xsl:template match="/">
    <html>
      <head>
      <title>Example Document</title>
      </head>
      <body>
      <hr /><xsl:apply-templates /><hr />
      </body>
      </html>
</xsl:template>

<xsl:template match="message">
<b>
    <xsl:text>Mess</xsl:text>
    <xsl:text>age</xsl:text>
</b>
<br />

<xsl:apply-templates select="to">
    <xsl:with-param name="pre">To:</xsl:with-param>
</xsl:apply-templates><br />

<xsl:apply-templates select="from">
    <xsl:with-param name="pre">From:</xsl:with-param>
</xsl:apply-templates><br />

<xsl:apply-templates select="text" />
</xsl:template>

<xsl:template match="to | from | text">
    <xsl:param name="pre">:</xsl:param>
      <b><xsl:value-of select="$pre" /></b>
    <xsl:value-of select="." />
</xsl:template>

</xsl:stylesheet>
```

XSL:PRESERVE-SPACE

This element defines the way white space—only text nodes (in the source document) are handled. All character data is lumped into a text node.

The `xsl:preserve-space` element has a required attribute: `elements="name"`. It defines the element node found in the source document whose white space is to be preserved (it preserves white space text nodes).

Listing 26.22 uses the `xsl:preserve-space` element.

LISTING 26.22: XSLT STYLESHEET USING AN *xsl:preserve-space* ELEMENT

```
<?xml version="1.0"?>
<xsl:stylesheet
    xmlns:xsl="http://www.w3.org/1999/XSL/Transform"
    version="1.0">
    <xsl:output method="xml" indent="yes" />
      <xsl:preserve-space elements="message" />
    <xsl:template match="/message">
      <p>
      <xsl:value-of select="." />
      </p>
    </xsl:template>
</xsl:stylesheet>
```

XSL:STRIP-SPACE

The `xsl:strip-space` element strips white space nodes from elements as they're sent to the output tree. Its required attribute is `elements="name"`, which defines the element node found in the source document that is to be trimmed of white space (it removes white space text nodes).

Listing 26.23 uses the `xsl:strip-space` element.

LISTING 26.23: XSLT STYLESHEET USING AN *xsl:strip-space* ELEMENT

```
<?xml version="1.0"?>
<xsl:stylesheet
    xmlns:xsl="http://www.w3.org/1999/XSL/Transform"
    version="1.0">
    <xsl:output method="xml" indent="yes" />
    <xsl:strip-space elements="message" />
      <xsl:template match="/message">
    <p>
      <xsl:value-of select="." />
    </p>
      </xsl:template>
</xsl:stylesheet>
```

XSLT Expressions Reference

As previously discussed, XSLT expressions use XPath expressions to navigate the source tree. XSLT expressions are made up of XPath location paths. Location paths consist of steps that help the processor navigate a document tree.

LOCATION PATHS

The basic syntax of a location path is as follows:

```
/step/step/step
```

The forward slash (/) separates each step. Location paths can be defined as absolute or relative:

Absolute   The location path selects a set of nodes relative to the root node; for example, /person/name/first. In this case, the initial / represents the root node. The person element is a child of the root node; name is a child of person; and first is a child of name. The XSLT processor will look for this pattern in the source tree.

Relative   The location path selects a set of nodes relative to the context node; for example, name/first. In this case, it selects all the first elements that are children of the name element. A location path consists of three basic parts:

- Axis, which defines the direction of the path
- Node test, which selects a given node set
- Predicate, which provides testing conditions for the node set

AXIS

An *axis* is used as part of a step to define the path for the expression. The axis provides directional information. There are 13 axes defined for XPath expressions, as shown in Table 26.13.

TABLE 26.13: THE XPATH AXES

AXIS	DESCRIPTION
child	Selects all direct children of the context node (in document order). Does not include attribute or namespace nodes.
descendant	Selects all descendants (children, children's children, etc.) of the context node. Does not include attribute or namespace nodes.
parent	Selects the direct parent of the context node. If the context node is the root node, this axis is empty.
ancestor	Selects all the ancestor nodes of the context node, in reverse document order. This axis always includes the root node (unless the root node is the context node).
following-sibling	Selects all sibling nodes of the context node that appear later in the document (in document order), if they exist.

Continued on next page

TABLE 26.13: THE XPATH AXES *(continued)*

AXIS	DESCRIPTION
preceding-sibling	Selects all sibling nodes of the context node that appear earlier in the document in reverse document order.
following	Selects all nodes in the document that come after the context node (in document order), excluding all descendants of the context node. Does not include attribute or namespace nodes.
preceding	Selects all nodes in the document that come before the context node (in reverse document order).
attribute	Selects all the attribute nodes for a given context node. Because attributes can occur in any order, the node order is arbitrary.
namespace	Selects the namespace nodes of the context node. If none exists, this axis is empty. This includes an entry for the default namespace and the implicitly declared XML namespace.
self	Selects only the context node itself.
descendant-or-self	Selects all descendant nodes and the context node itself (in document order). Does not include attribute or namespace nodes.
ancestor-or-self	Selects all ancestor nodes and the context node itself (in document order).

NODE TEST

Node tests allow specific elements or node types to be selected from the specified axis. One of the most common node tests is to use the name of element nodes. For example, `child::book` selects the book element node that is a child of the context node. Table 26.14 defines a few other node tests you can use.

TABLE 26.14: NODE TESTS

NODE TEST	DESCRIPTION
*	A wildcard that selects all nodes defined by the axis. For example, `attribute::*` selects all attributes of the context node.
name	Selects all elements (or attributes if the attribute is used) with the given name. For example, book selects all book elements nodes.
node()	Selects all nodes on the axis.
text()	Selects all text nodes on the axis.
processing-instruction()	Selects all processing instruction nodes on the axis.
comment()	Selects all comment nodes on the axis.

PREDICATE

A *predicate* defines further filtering of the node set identified by the axis and node test. A predicate is a Boolean expression that is evaluated for each node in the resultant node set. Each node that is evaluated to true is added to the new node set.

Each predicate expression can include location steps, function calls, union operations on node sets, relational expressions, and expressions grouped with or and and operators.

The idea is that you can use a function that can test for the nodes you want. Each test will return values in various forms, such as strings, numbers, node sets, and Booleans. These return values can be compared using comparative operators, such as =, !=, <+, <, >=, and >. You can also separate larger expressions with the Boolean operators and and or.

While predicates can return values of various data types, they can only be written as a Boolean or numeric expression. The basic syntax is as follows:

```
axis::nodetest[predicate]
```

The predicate is always defined within an opening bracket ([) and a closing bracket (]). Table 26.15 provides a few examples.

TABLE 26.15: XPATH EXAMPLES

LOCATION PATH	DESCRIPTION
`child::book`	Selects the book element node that is a child of the context node.
`child::*`	Selects all child element nodes of the context node to the result tree.
`attribute::isbn`	Selects the isbn attribute node that is a child of the context node.
`self::book`	Selects the context node if it's a book element node.
`child::book[position()=2]`	Selects the second book element node that is a child of the context node.
`child::book[title="Mastering HTML and XHTML"]`	Selects the book element node that is a child of the context node if a title child node has the string value Mastering HTML and XHTML.
`child::book[@isbn="0782128203"]`	Selects the book node that is a child of the context node if that child has an isbn attribute with the value 0782128203.

XSLT Patterns

XSLT patterns are a subset of expressions. The pattern defines a set of conditions. Any node that tests true according to those conditions matches the pattern. Because patterns use the same syntax as expressions, location paths can be used as patterns.

A pattern can define alternatives by separating location paths with pipe bars (|). When used, the pattern matches if any one or more of the alternatives is found to be true. Patterns are restricted to using only the child or attribute axis. In addition to using those two axes, a pattern can use the // (descendant nodes) and / (root node) operators.

The most common usage for this feature is as the value of the xsl:template match attribute:

```
<xsl:template match="pattern">
```

Where to Go from Here

In this chapter, we covered basic XSLT transformations. There's so much more to learn about XSLT than what is covered in this chapter. We recommend some outside reading. Whether you visit online resource sites, or a book, you'll want to learn more.

From here, you can follow up with a visit to several chapters:

◆ See Chapter 28 to learn more about XPath.

◆ See Chapter 9 for more on style sheets.

Chapter 27

SMIL

THE SYNCHRONIZED MULTIMEDIA INTEGRATION Language (SMIL, pronounced *smile*) is an XML language specifically designed for multimedia. SMIL synchronizes multimedia files (such as audio, video, and animation files) to play in the order and time sequence you specify, and to act as a single stream during download and playback. *Streaming* media is media that plays as it downloads—in other words, you don't have to wait for the whole file to download before playback begins. SMIL is easy to learn and easy to use.

This chapter covers the following topics:

◆ Understanding what SMIL can do

◆ Reviewing the history of SMIL

◆ Creating SMIL files

◆ Working with SMIL

◆ Examining SMIL tools and resources

What Can SMIL Do?

SMIL offers many advantages for interactive multimedia presentations. It also includes accessibility features and search features not available with other multimedia files in Web pages, such as:

◆ SMIL provides a structural framework for synchronizing multimedia files into a unified interactive presentation. For example, if you want an audio file to start playing a few seconds after a video clip begins, or if you want a series of images to be presented as a slide show while an audio track plays, you can specify this in a SMIL file.

◆ SMIL is much easier to use than JavaScript and dynamic HTML (DHTML) for interactive presentations. SMIL uses all the standard events of JavaScript (see Chapter 10 for more on JavaScript) as part of the SMIL language, but does not require any script coding.

- SMIL includes features to set the start and end times for multimedia file playback, to play multimedia files in parallel or sequential order, and to map paths for objects to move along (for example, you can specify an oval path for a graphics file to follow across the screen).

- SML allows you to include different versions of files, such as different file sizes depending on the user's bandwidth, or versions in several different languages. SMIL incorporates elements that can determine which version of a file should be accessed for a particular group of viewers.

- SMIL incorporates accessibility features in its basic design and can be used to present alternative content, such as a synchronized text display for a slide show that incorporates all the content of an audio track for users with auditory or visual disabilities.

- SMIL supports alternative text content, which makes it possible for search engines to index SMIL files (unlike other multimedia files, such as Flash animations, which are not indexed and can't be searched directly by content).

SMIL is supported in Internet Explorer 5 and higher, RealPlayer, Apple's QuickTime player, and Windows Media Player.

STREAMING MEDIA

Streaming media are digital media files that can be listened to and/or viewed in real time. In other words, the media is broadcast to your computer and played back as the information is received from the server.

To create streaming media, you start with content files such as images, text, animation, audio, or video. You convert these files (if necessary) to a digital format using hardware called a capture card. The files are then compressed with encoding software or hardware, which compresses the files into small packets of information that can then be streamed from a server to a player or a browser. The server software determines the types of digital media that can be streamed. It's preferable, but not mandatory, to use a streaming server to deliver these files to a user. See "Server Issues" later in this chapter for more information on servers for streaming media.

Bandwidth is an important issue in delivering streaming content to viewers. Your site users will likely include users with both broadband connections and narrowband connections. Broadband connections are high-speed, 200 kilobits per second (Kbps) or higher, and include most Digital Subscriber Lines (DSL), cable modems, T1, and T3 connections. Narrowband connections are less than 200 Kbps, and include dial-up modems. SMIL allows you to adjust media content depending on the user's bandwidth.

A Brief History of SMIL

After many workshops and conferences on the use of real-time multimedia on the Web, SMIL 1.0 was presented as a Proposed Recommendation by the W3C in April 1998. Beginning in August 1999, several working drafts were formulated to present SMIL in modular form. These versions of SMIL, referred to as SMIL Boston, consisted of nine modules. In August 2001, the SMIL 2.0 specification became a full-fledged Recommendation.

SMIL 2.0 consists of the following 10 modules:

Animation   Incorporates animation on a time line. It includes a BasicAnimation module and a SplineAnimation module (for animation on a motion path and uneven spacing of points in time).

Content Control   Provides runtime content choices and optimized content delivery. It enables content to be adjusted depending on attributes on the user's system; for example, different versions can be played depending on the user's bandwidth.

Layout   Positions media elements visually and controls audio volume.

Linking   Navigation through the presentation can be triggered by user interaction or by setting times for certain events to occur.

Media Objects   Defines the seven types of media objects recognized by SMIL: `ref`, `animation`, `audio`, `img`, `text`, `textstream`, and `video`.

Metainformation   Describes SMIL documents with a `meta` element and a `metadata` element (for the Resource Description Framework, or RDF).

Structure   Describes the basic elements of the SMIL structure (`smil`, `head`, and `body`).

Timing and Synchronization   Coordinates and synchronizes playback of media objects. It allows media objects to be played in parallel (at the same time), sequentially, or (new to SMIL 2.0) exclusively, which is similar to parallel but allows only one object to play at a time and adds the ability to pause and resume playback.

Time Manipulations (added in SMIL 2.0)   Manipulates the timing of a media object through controlling its rate, and adds support for reverse playback and for acceleration and deceleration of an element. This module is especially suited for animation.

Transition Effects   Coordinates transitions among multiple visual media in playback, including fades and multiple types of wipes.

More information on the history of the SMIL language can be found at the W3C site at `www.w3.org/AudioVideo/`, and you can find full details of the SMIL 2.0 specification at the W3C site at `www.w3.org/TR/2001/PR-smil20-20010605/`.

SMIL Support

RealNetwork supports SMIL through the RealPlayer multimedia player. The current version is RealPlayerONE, and you can download a free version from `www.real.com/player/index.html?src=downloadr`. RealPlayer can be used to display SMIL files in any browser.

QuickTime has also incorporated SMIL support within the QuickTime player, which includes several QuickTime extensions to SMIL. For more information, see "QuickTime and SMIL" at `www.apple.com/quicktime/authoring/qtsmil.html`.

Direct browser support would eliminate the need for multimedia players and plug-ins, and give you more options for the presentation of your multimedia files on a Web page without the window and other limitations of a multimedia player.

The first browser support for SMIL appeared in Internet Explorer 5. Microsoft used what it calls *HTML + Time*. HTML + Time adds time-based attributes to HTML elements and uses Cascading Style Sheets (CSS) for adding styles as well as positioning. In Internet Explorer 5.5, HTML + Time was updated to version 2.0, and it incorporated SMIL Boston's HTML + SMIL Language Profile. Internet Explorer 5.5 supports three of the SMIL modules (Animation, Media Objects, and Timing and Synchronization), and Internet Explorer 6 also supports the new SMIL 2.0 module Transition Effects. Neither Netscape nor Opera currently directly supports SMIL (although they support it through the RealPlayer plug-in), but support is expected in future versions of both browsers.

For more information, see the Streaming Media World site at

```
http://smw.internet.com/smil/tutor/htmltime1/index.html
```
Information on the HTML + SMIL Language Profile is available at

```
www.w3.org/TR/2000/WD-smil-boston-20000622/html-smil-profile.html
```

TIP   *To learn more about multimedia players and multimedia files, see Chapter 11.*

Creating SMIL Files

SMIL files can be created with any text editor. In addition, many tools are available for creating SMIL files, and we will cover these tools later in this chapter in the "SMIL Tools" section.

The first step in creating a SMIL file is to create the multimedia files that you want to utilize for a multimedia presentation on the Web. A SMIL file references the multimedia files but does not include them as part of the SMIL file. The available file types include audio, video, animation, image, and text files. RealNetworks offers many different software packages for creating multimedia files, including RealProducer (RealAudio and RealVideo files), RealPix (image files), RealText (streaming text files), and RealSlideShow. Multimedia files can also be created in other graphic and media software, including Adobe Photoshop, Adobe Illustrator, Adobe Premiere, Macromedia Fireworks, Macromedia Flash, and Apple QuickTime.

SMIL files use the file extension `.smil` or `.smi`. All SMIL files start and end with the SMIL opening and closing elements, `<smil>` and `</smil>`, respectively.

The SMIL syntax rules are very similar to XHTML's rules because SMIL is an XML application:

- Tags and attributes in SMIL must be lowercase.
- All attribute values must be in quotation marks.
- All tags must be closed, either with a matching closing tag or with `/>`.

A SMIL file includes a head section and a body section. The head section can include the following elements:

- `meta` elements
- The `layout` element, which is used to position elements on the page

The `layout` element can also contain the following child elements:

◆ The `root-layout` element, which sets the total size of the playback area—the multimedia clips play in specified regions of the root layout.

◆ The `region` element, which includes a size and a position relative to the root layout. The `region` element should also have the following attributes:

    ◆ `id` identifies the region element.

    ◆ `fit` specifies how you want the display to occur if the size of the media display does not exactly match the size of the region. Table 27.1 shows the values for the `fit` attribute.

    ◆ `z-index` specifies the order of the region layout.

TABLE 27.1: VALUES FOR THE `fit` ATTRIBUTE

VALUE	HEIGHT/WIDTH RATIO	DESCRIPTION
`fill`	May be distorted	Scales the clip to fit the region exactly.
`hidden` (default)	Preserved	Keeps the clip at a specified size, placed in the upper-left corner of the region. The clip is cropped if it's bigger than the region; if it's smaller, the background color displays in the rest of the region.
`meet`	Preserved	Places the clip at the upper-left corner of the region and scales the clip until its height and width are within the region boundaries.
`slice`	Preserved	Places the clip at the upper-left corner of the region, scales the clip until its height and width are within the region boundaries, and crops any overflow area.

The body section is where you specify the source of the media files using clip types. There are seven clip types (called Media Object Elements in the specification), and each clip type is an empty element, as listed in Table 27.2.

TABLE 27.2: SMIL CLIP TYPES

VALUE	DESCRIPTION
`animation`	Animation files, such as Flash files (`.swf`)
`audio`	Audio clips
`img`	JPEG (`.jpg`), GIF (`.gif`), or PNG (`.png`)
`ref`	Any clip type not covered by another attribute
`text`	Static text (`.txt`)
`textstream`	Streaming RealText clips (`.rt`)
`video`	Video clips

If you are unsure of which clip type to use, remember that ref can be used as a generic clip type.

Table 27.3 shows just some of the attributes you can use for the various clip types. You can use these attributes with any of the clip types. For a full list of attributes for clip types, see the SMIL Quick Reference at `http://service.real.com/help/library/guides/production/htmfiles/smilref.htm#997503`.

TABLE 27.3: ATTRIBUTES OF CLIP TYPES

NAME	VALUE	DESCRIPTION
begin	h, min, s, or ms	Sets timing for the start of playback
dur	h, min, s, or ms	Sets total playback time (do not use with end)
end	h, min, s, or ms	Sets the end time relative to the begin time (do not use with dur)
fill	freeze or remove	Freezes or removes the clip from the screen when playback is complete
repeat	number	Repeats the playback the specified number of times

ASR Outfitters (our fictional company) decided to put an audiovisual presentation on its Web site to feature hiking trails in the southern Rocky Mountains. This presentation included images of maps and an audio file narrative highlighting key features. ASR used SMIL to coordinate its multimedia files into a synchronized Web presentation. Here are the steps:

1. Open a SMIL file with the smil element:

```
<smil>
…</smil>
```

2. Add a head element with meta elements:

```
<smil>
   <head>
   <meta name="copyright"
     content="(c)2001 ASR Outfitters" />
   <meta name="author" content="ASR Outfitters" />
   <meta name="title"
     content="Hiking the Southern Rockies" />
   </head>
…<smil>
```

3. Add the layout element with the child elements root-layout and the region element between the head elements:

```
<smil>
   <head>
   <meta name="copyright"
     content="(c)2001 ASR Outfitters" />
   <meta name="author" content="ASR Outfitters" />
   <meta name="title"
```

```
        content="Hiking the Southern Rockies" />
    <layout>
    <root-layout width="800" height="600"
      background-color="black" />
    <region id="map" left="0" top="25" width="450"
      height="450" fit="meet" />
    <region id="image" left="450" top="25" width="350"
      height="450" fit="slice" />
    <region id="text" left="0" top="475" width="800"
      height="125" fit="meet" />
    </layout>
    </head>…
</smil>
```

4. Next add a body section, and specify the source of the media files using the clip types, as listed back in Table 27.2.

```
<body>
    <img src="map.gif" alt="map" region="map" />
    <img src="image1.jpg" alt="marmot" region="image" />
    <textstream src="hiking.rt" alt="a narrative of the
      hiking trail" region="text" />
    <audio src="hiking.rm" alt="trail sounds" />
</body>
```

5. All the media files are specified for the presentation, but now we need to specify their timing and sequence. Add attributes to the clip types to specify timing. First, we specify all six of the images for the map region and their timing attributes:

```
<body>
<img src="map.gif" alt="map" region="map" begin="2s"
   dur="10s" />
<img src="map2.gif" alt="map" region="map" begin="12s"
   dur="10s" />
<img src="map3.gif" alt="map" region="map" begin="22s"
   dur="10s" />
<img src="map4.gif" alt="map" region="map" begin="32s"
   dur="10s" />
<img src="map5.gif" alt="map" region="map" begin="42s"
   dur="10s" />
<img src="map6.gif" alt="map" region="map" begin="52s"
   dur="8s" />
```

6. Then we specify all five of the images for the image region and their timing attributes:

```
<img src="image1.jpg" alt="marmot" region="image" begin="0s"
   dur="10s" />
<img src="image2.jpg" alt="ground_squirrel" region="image"
   begin="10s" dur="10s" />
<img src="image3.jpg" alt="bluejay" region="image"
```

```
          begin="20s" dur="10s" />
<img src="image4.jpg" alt="snake" region="image" begin="30s" dur="10s" />
<img src="image5.jpg" alt="blackbear" region="image"
     begin="40s" dur="20s" fill="freeze" />
```

7. Next, we specify the timing for the streaming text file and for the audio file:

```
<textstream src="hiking.rt" alt="a narrative of the hiking
     trail" region="text" begin="2s" dur="58s" />
<audio src="hiking.rm" alt="trail sounds" begin="0s"
     repeat="2" />
```

8. Our next step is to synchronize our multimedia presentation. SMIL has two elements for synchronizing playback: the par element and the seq element. The par element specifies that clips play in parallel, i.e., at the same time. The seq element specifies that clips play sequentially.

ASR Outfitters wants the audio track and the text stream to play at the same time. The image clips play sequentially, but one sequence plays in the map region while the other plays in the image region.

```
<body>
<par>
    <textstream src="hiking.rt" alt="a narrative of the
     hiking trail" region="text" begin="2s" dur="58s" />
    <audio src="hiking.rm" alt="trail sounds" begin="0s"
     repeat="2" />
    <seq>
      <img src="map.gif" alt="map" region="map" begin="2s"
         dur="10s" />
      <img src="map2.gif" alt="map" region="map" begin="12s"
         dur="10s" />
      <img src="map3.gif" alt="map" region="map" begin="22s"
         dur="10s" />
      <img src="map4.gif" alt="map" region="map" begin="32s"
         dur="10s" />
      <img src="map5.gif" alt="map" region="map" begin="42s"
         dur="10s" />
      <img src="map6.gif" alt="map" region="map" begin="52s"
         dur="8s" />
    </seq>
    <seq>
      <img src="image1.jpg" alt="marmot" region="image"
         begin="0s" dur="10s" />
      <img src="image2.jpg" alt="ground_squirrel"
         region="image" begin="10s" dur="10s" />
      <img src="image3.jpg" alt="bluejay" region="image"
         begin="20s" dur="10s" />
      <img src="image4.jpg" alt="snake" region="image"
         begin="30s" dur="10s" />
      <img src="image5.jpg" alt="blackbear" region="image"
```

```
      begin="40s" dur="20s" fill="freeze" />
    </seq>
  </par>
  </body>
```

We've nested two sequences of images to play in parallel with the audio track and the text stream.

9. Finally, add the `switch` element to specify different audio files depending on the bandwidth available to the user:

```
<body>
  <par>
  <textstream src="hiking.rt" alt="a narrative of the
    hiking trail" region="text" begin="2s" dur="58s" />
  <switch>
    <audio src="hiking.rm" alt="trail sounds" begin="0s"
      repeat="2" system-bit-rate="47000" />
      <!-- for 56K modems -->
    <audio src="hiking2.rm" alt="trail sounds" begin="0s"
      repeat="2" system-bit-rate="20000" />
      <!-- for 28.8 modems -->
  </switch>
  <seq>
    ...
```

The system will check the user's bandwidth and play the appropriate clip. The switch options are evaluated in the order the code is read, so it's important to put the highest bit rate at the top. If the first statement after the switch evaluates to `true` (i.e., if the user's bit rate is 47,000 or greater), the first clip will be played and the second statement is not evaluated. You can include several different choices in a switch statement, but be sure that the last choice you specify is a viable option—if no choice evaluates to `true`, that part of your presentation will not play.

The `switch` element can also be used to specify different language versions of a presentation. The language preference in the user's browser is used to choose the version that plays. Other attributes of `switch` are captions (on or off), screen depth (bits per pixel), and screen dimension (640 × 480, 800 × 600, and so on).

The complete code is shown in Listing 27.1.

LISTING 27.1: A MULTIMEDIA PRESENTATION USING SMIL

```
<smil>
<head>
  <meta name="copyright" content=" (c)2001 ASR Outfitters" />
  <meta name="author" content="ASR Outfitters" />
  <meta name="title" content="Hiking the Southern Rockies" />
  <layout>
    <root-layout width="800" height="600"
      background-color="black" />
    <region id="map" left="0" top="25" width="450"
```

```
                      height="450" fit="meet" />
              <region id="image" left="450" top="25" width="350"
                      height="450" fit="slice" />
              <region id="text" left="0" top="475" width="800"
                      height="125" fit="meet" />
          </layout>
      </head>
      <body>
          <par>
          <textstream src="hiking.rt" alt="a narrative of the
             hiking trail" region="text" begin="2s" dur="58s" />
          <switch>
             <audio src="hiking.rm" alt="trail sounds" begin="0s"
                 repeat="2" system-bit-rate="47000" />
                 <!-- for 56K modems -->
             <audio src="hiking2.rm" alt="trail sounds" begin="0s"
                 repeat="2" system-bit-rate="20000" />
                 <!-- for 28.8 modems -->
          </switch>
          <seq>
             <img src="map.gif" alt="map" region="map" begin="2s"
                 dur="10s" />
             <img src="map2.gif" alt="map" region="map" begin="12s"
                 dur="10s" />
             <img src="map3.gif" alt="map" region="map" begin="22s"
                 dur="10s" />
             <img src="map4.gif" alt="map" region="map" begin="32s"
                 dur="10s" />
             <img src="map5.gif" alt="map" region="map" begin="42s"
                 dur="10s" />
             <img src="map6.gif" alt="map" region="map" begin="52s"
                 dur="8s" />
          </seq>
          <seq>
             <img src="image1.jpg" alt="marmot" region="image"
                 begin="0s" dur="10s" />
             <img src="image2.jpg" alt="ground_squirrel"
                 region="image" begin="10s" dur="10s" />
             <img src="image3.jpg" alt="bluejay" region="image"
                 begin="20s" dur="10s" />
             <img src="image4.jpg" alt="snake" region="image"
                 begin="30s"dur="10s" />
             <img src="image5.jpg" alt="blackbear" region="image"
                 begin="40s" dur="20s" fill="freeze" />
          </seq>
          </par>
      </body>
      </smil>
```

Creating SMIL Files Using HTML + Time

It's also easy to create a SMIL file using Microsoft's current implementation of SMIL, HTML + Time. See the section "SMIL Support" earlier in this chapter for more information on HTML + Time.

In this example, you'll create three mouseovers without using JavaScript. Each of the three elements you create will change in color after a mouseover event:

1. Start by declaring an XML namespace (smil) in the opening html element:

```
<html xmlns:smil="urn:schemas-microsoft-com:time">...
</html>
```

2. Associate smil and time with Microsoft's HTML + Time time2 behavior. You can do this by using an embedded style in the document head section:

```
<head>
    <style>
      smil\:* {behavior:url(#default#time2)}
      time:* {behavior:url(#default#time2)}
    </style>
...</head>
```

3. Add style declarations for the body of the page and for the three elements for the mouseover behavior. Create three blocks that are each 75 pixels wide, 35 pixels high, and have a blue background color.

```
<style>
    smil\:* {behavior:url(#default#time2)}
    time:* {behavior:url(#default#time2)}
    body   {background-color:#000000}
    #home {width:75;
           height:35;
           background-color:blue;
           color:#ffffff;font-size:16pt
           }
    #part1 {width:75;
            height:35;
            background-color:blue;
            color:#ffffff;
            font-size:16pt
            }
    #part2 {width:75;
            height:35;
            background-color:blue;
            color:#ffffff;font-size:16pt
            }
</style>
```

4. Using the `div` element, add text to the three blocks, which will be 16-point white text, as declared in the style section.

```
</head>
<body>
   <div id="home"> Home</div><br />
   <div id="part1"> Part I</div><br />
   <div id="part2">Part II</div>
</body>
```

5. Now that you've created the blocks of color and added text to them, add a behavior using SMIL. First, open a `smil` element and a `par` element (`smil:par`). As you can see, Microsoft's use of `smil` and `par` have a different structure than the previous example. Then, add `begin` to define when the behavior starts. This behavior will begin when the viewer mouses over the element with the `id` value of `home`.

```
<smil:par begin="home.onmouseover">
```

6. Add the specific behavior that occurs with a mouseover event. Start with the `animateColor` element—`animateColor` is part of the Animation module in SMIL 2 and specifies the animation of a color attribute.

```
<smil:animateColor />
```

7. Specify a value for `targetElement`. `targetElement` is an attribute that specifies the element to be animated; in this case, the element with the `id` value of `home`.

```
<smil:animateColor targetElement="home" />
```

8. Add a value for `attributeName`, which is used to define which style you want to affect with this behavior; in this case, `background-color`. You could have chosen any style that can have a color value; for example, if you used `color` instead of `background-color`, the text color would change with the mouseover event rather than the background color.

```
<smil:animateColor targetElement="home"
   attributeName="color" />
```

9. The next attribute is `values`, which tells Internet Explorer 5.5 and higher to animate from `blue` to `green` to `red` over a duration of three seconds. You can also use hex for the color values—just precede the hex code with a #; for example, `values="#ffff00;#008000;#ff0000"`.

```
<smil:animateColor targetElement="home"
   attributeName="color" values="yellow;green;red" />
```

10. Add a `begin` attribute. The `begin` attribute specifies when the animation should start; in this case, as soon as the mouseover occurs. Also add a `dur` attribute, which specifies the total duration in seconds of the color animation.

```
<smil:animateColor targetElement="home"
   attributeName="color" values="blue;green;red"
   begin="0s" dur="3s" />
```

11. The last attribute, `autoreverse`, tells the browser whether to play back the animation in reverse once it has completed playing forward. In this case, use a value of `false` so the animation does not play in reverse.

```
<smil:animateColor targetElement="home"
    attributeName="color" values="blue;green;red"
    begin="0s" dur="3s" autoreverse="false" />
</smil:par>
```

12. Add the behaviors for the other two elements: `part1` and `part2`. Note that each one requires a `smil:par` statement to define when the behavior occurs, and a `smil:animateColor` statement to define what the behavior is. The second element, `part1`, has an `attributeName` of `color`, so the color animation will affect the text color. Also note that the last two elements have an `autoreverse` value of `true`, which means the animations will play forward and then backwards, with a total time duration of six seconds each.

```
<smil:par begin="part1.onmouseover">
   <smil:animateColor targetElement="part1"
     attributeName="color" values="purple;yellow;red"
     begin="0s" dur="3s" autoreverse="true" />
</smil:par>
<smil:par begin="part2.onmouseover">
   <smil:animateColor targetElement="part2"
     attributeName=" background-color"
     values="red;magenta;purple" begin="0s"
     dur="3s" autoreverse="true" />
</smil:par>
</body>
</html>
```

The complete code for this example is shown in Listing 27.2. This example will work only in Internet Explorer 5.5 or later.

LISTING 27.2: COLOR ANIMATION USING HTML + TIME IN INTERNET EXPLORER

```
<html xmlns:smil="urn:schemas-microsoft-com:time">
<head>
   <title>SMIL example</title>
 <style>
   smil\:* {behavior:url(#default#time2)}
   time:* {behavior:url(#default#time2)}
   body    {background-color:#000000}
   #home {width:75;
          height:35;
          background-color:blue;
          color:#ffffff;font-size:16pt
          }
   #part1 {width:75;
```

```
                height:35;
                background-color:blue;
                color:#ffffff;
                font-size:16pt
                }
      #part2  {width:75;
                height:35;
                background-color:blue;
                color:#ffffff;font-size:16pt
                }
   </style>
 </head>
<body>
   <div id="home"> Home</div><br />
   <div id="part1"> Part I</div><br />
   <div id="part2">Part II</div>
   <smil:par begin="home.onmouseover">
     <smil:animateColor targetElement="home"
     attributeName="background-color" values="yellow;green;red"
     begin="0s" dur="3s" autoreverse="false" />
   </smil:par>
   <smil:par begin="part1.onmouseover">
     <smil:animateColor targetElement="part1"
      attributeName="color" values="purple;yellow;red"
       begin="0s" dur="3s" autoreverse="true" />
   </smil:par>
   <smil:par begin="part2.onmouseover">
     <smil:animateColor targetElement="part2"
      attributeName="background-color"
      values="red;purple;magenta" begin="0s"
      dur="3s" autoreverse="true" />
   </smil:par>
 </body>
 </html>
```

Working with SMIL

SMIL files can be included within HTML or XHTML documents using the object elements, as discussed in Chapter 11. Because SMIL files stream (meaning that they start playing as soon as the beginning material reaches the browser, rather than waiting for everything to be downloaded), the user can start seeing your multimedia presentation much more quickly in a SMIL file than if you use a multimedia file directly on your page. The SMIL file will be shown in a separate media player window unless you're using Internet Explorer and HTML + Time to view the files directly in the browser window.

Server Issues

RealServer is a streaming media server designed to deliver streaming files. RealServer, created by Real-Networks, is available from a multitude of Web-hosting services. Web-hosting accounts that include access to a streaming server are generally available, although at a higher cost than standard Web hosting. The main advantage to using RealServer or any streaming media server is its ability to serve your multimedia content smoothly despite varying network conditions—it can adapt playback to network conditions and keep the multimedia files synchronized despite changing conditions. A list of hosting services that offer RealServer is available at `www.realnetworks.com/solutions/infrastructure/isp/index.html`.

Microsoft also offers a streaming media server called Microsoft Media Server (short for Windows NT Server Windows Media Services). For more details on this server option, and further discussion on HTTP servers versus streaming servers, see "Streaming Methods: Web Server vs. Streaming Media Server" at `www.microsoft.com/windows/windowsmedia/en/compare/webservvstreamserv.asp`. Windows Media Technologies 4, however, supports HTML + Time but does not support SMIL.

You don't have to use a streaming server. You can also serve SMIL presentations from an HTTP server, although the disadvantage is that the HTTP protocol does not pay attention to timelines when it downloads files; therefore, clips that have timelines are more likely to stall when served from an HTTP server.

SMIL Tools

Many tools are currently available to create and play SMIL documents.

RealNetworks   RealNetworks was one of SMIL's earliest supporters. It offers several products for creating and using streaming multimedia files, including:

- RealPlayer; both a free version and an expanded commercial version
- RealProducer for creating streaming RealAudio and RealVideo files
- RealPix for streaming graphics
- RealText for streaming text files
- RealSlideShow for graphics plus voice-over and text annotations

RealNetworks is also the developer of RealServer, a streaming media server, and it also offers many SMIL resources on its site.

GRiNS (Graphical iNterface to SMIL)   GRiNS/G2 Pro is available for both Windows and Macintosh, and offers a structured interface for creating multimedia presentations. GRiNS also offers the GRiNS/SMIL 2.0 Player, which supports the features of the SMIL 2.0 specification as well as Scalable Vector Graphics (SVG) and Microsoft's HTML + Time implementation of SMIL.

These products are available at `www2.oratrix.nl/`.

Fluition   Confluent Technologies offers Fluition 1.51 for Windows and Fluition 1.31 for Macintosh. Fluition features a wizard interface to walk you through the steps of creating a SMIL presentation.

More information on Fluition is available at `www.confluenttechnologies.com/products.html`.

MAGpie   Media Access Generator (MAGpie) is software designed to make multimedia files accessible to users with disabilities. MAGpie creates captions for use with SMIL files, and also can integrate audio descriptions into SMIL files.

MAGpie is available at `http://ncam.wgbh.org/webaccess/magpie/`.

SMIL Resources

There are many SMIL resources online, including tutorials, articles, and SMIL examples. The following are particularly helpful for learning SMIL:

JustSMIL   JustSMIL is hosted on the Streaming Media Network site. It includes links to many different SMIL tutorials and streaming multimedia guides, and is also a great resource for the latest news on SMIL and browser implementations. Visit JustSMIL at `http://smw.internet.com/smil/smilhome.html`.

Helio   Helio offers an extensive SMIL tutorial on its site. Although the tutorial is for SMIL 1.0, the information is still useful for getting started with SMIL, because most of SMIL 2.0 is added on to SMIL 1.0. The tutorial is located at `www.helio.org/products/smil/tutorial/toc.html`.

RealNetworks   RealNetworks offers a SMIL tutorial on its site at `www.realnetworks.com/resources/tutorials/index.html`. It also offers a free RealSystem Authoring Kit, which includes detailed guides on SMIL and on RealSystem software for creating multimedia content: RealAudio, RealVideo, RealPix, and RealText. It can be downloaded at `www.realnetworks.com/products/authkit/index.html`.

Larry Bouthillier's SMIL Authoring Page   Larry Bouthillier's SMIL Authoring Page (`www.people.hbs.edu/lbouthillier/smil/`) includes links to articles he has written on SMIL and on streaming media. His article from *Web Techniques*, September 1998, can be accessed from this page, and is a very comprehensive introduction to the basics of the SMIL language. The article includes several SMIL sample files.

Where to Go from Here

This chapter introduced SMIL and streaming multimedia. SMIL is easy to use, and offers a means to include very simple to extremely complex multimedia presentations on your Web site. SMIL is a great way to provide multimedia educational presentations as well as just add some fun and excitement to your pages.

From here you can reference several related chapters:

◆ See Chapter 9 to learn about developing Cascading Style Sheets, which let you add formatting to your page presentation.

◆ See Chapter 10 to learn more about JavaScript and using scripts and event handlers.

◆ See Chapter 11 for the basics of including multimedia elements in your HTML or XHTML pages.

◆ See Chapter 16 to learn more about dynamic HTML and XHTML.

Chapter 28

XML Tree Model Reference

THIS CHAPTER PROVIDES ADVANCED material that augments the information presented in the Mastering HTML and XHTML book. This content is intended for advanced users who have experience using XHTML or XML. To get a sample of the book's core material, you can download the sample chapter, available at www.sybex.com/SybexBooks.nsf/booklist/4141.

As you begin to tackle XML, you'll quickly discover that there's a lot of information to digest—especially when it comes to handling XML data. This is because several different standards exist that define just how an XML parser handles an XML document fragment. In some cases, XPath is used to create a tree representation of the document, which can then be used by Extensible Stylesheet Language Transformations (XSLT) or XPointer. On the other hand, some applications require the processor to use the Document Object Model (DOM) to create a tree representation of the XML document fragment.

Either way, you need to know how a processor will handle an XML document. In this chapter, we've created a handy reference that identifies three of the most common data models used for XML. All of this information is derived from the corresponding W3C XML specifications. We also provide pointers to each specification so you can learn more.

This chapter covers the following topics:

◆ Uncovering the XML Information Set

◆ Working with XML DOM objects

◆ Understanding XPath nodes

XML Information Set

The XML Information Set (Infoset) identifies an abstract data set of information items (objects) within an XML document. For each information item, properties are defined. It's a basic model that identifies important items in an XML document. It's not meant to be an exhaustive list, just a point of departure for other specifications that need to define data models for XML documents (for example, XPath). Each information item was chosen based on expected usefulness.

Another distinction between the Infoset and other data models is that the Infoset does not define an interface model. Unlike XPath, which uses a tree structure, the Infoset does not require information items to be defined in a tree. Keep in mind that the primary function of the Infoset is to define a point of departure for other data models. As a common reference point, the Infoset is meant to provide interoperability between XML-related specifications.

As defined by the XML Information Set Requirements document, the following are the goals of the Infoset standard:

◆ It should provide an abstract model for describing the logical structure of a well-formed XML 1.0 document. (Note that all valid XML 1.0 documents are also, by definition, well formed.)

◆ It should be suitable for use as a common reference model for specifications, such as parsing application programming interfaces (APIs) and query languages, and applications, such as editors and browsers, that deal with the structure of XML 1.0 documents.

◆ The normative portion of the XML Information Set specification should be human readable.

◆ It should include a non-normative formal model that allows for machine testing and verification of the information set.

◆ It should be designed to be interoperable with the W3C's DOM Level 1 Recommendation and, as far as possible, with the XPointer Working Draft and the XSL Working Draft.

◆ The working group will consider the issue of document validation while designing the XML Information Set.

Where to Use it

As stated previously, the Infoset is not itself used directly in an XML application. However, several data models and specifications benefit from the definitions defined by the Infoset. The Infoset can be a common reference for specifications, such as:

◆ The DOM (www.w3.org/DOM/)

◆ XPath (www.w3.org/TR/xpath)

◆ XML Canonicalization (www.w3.org/Signature/)

◆ XML Inclusions (XInclude—www.w3.org/TR/xinclude/)

◆ XML Schema (www.w3.org/XML/Schema)

◆ XML Query (www.w3.org/XML/Query)

Information Items

The Infoset is a descriptive standard that defines primary information items for an XML document. The 11 information items are defined in the following sections. For each information item, we list the allowed properties. These lists are derived from the XML Information Set Candidate Recommendation at www.w3.org/TR/xml-infoset/.

THE DOCUMENT INFORMATION ITEM

The document information items define the entire document. Nine properties are allowed:

all declarations processed   This property is not, strictly speaking, part of the Infoset of the document. Rather, it's an indication of whether the processor has read the complete DTD. Its value is a Boolean. If it's `false`, certain properties may be unknown. If it's `true`, those properties are never unknown.

base URI   The base URI of the document entity.

character encoding scheme   The name of the character-encoding scheme in which the document entity is expressed.

children   A list of child information items defined in document order.

document element   The element information item for the root element.

notations   An unordered list of notation information items—one for each notation declared in the DTD.

standalone   An indication of the stand-alone status of the document: either `yes` or `no`.

unparsed entities   An unordered list of unparsed entity information items, one for each unparsed entity declared in the DTD.

version   Defines the XML version of the document. This property, derived from the XML declaration optionally present at the beginning of the document entity, has no value if there's no XML declaration.

ELEMENT INFORMATION ITEMS

For every element in an XML document, there's a corresponding element information item. An element information item has the following properties:

attributes   An unordered list of attribute information items, one for each of the attributes defined for the element. Namespace declarations do not appear in this set.

base URI   The base URI of the element.

children   A list of child information items defined in document order. This list contains element, processing instruction, unexpanded entity reference, character, and comment information items, one for each element, processing instruction, reference to an unprocessed external entity, data character, and comment appearing immediately within the current element.

in-scope namespaces   An unordered list of namespace information items, one for each of the namespaces defined for the element. There's always an item in this list with the prefix `xml`, which is always bound to the namespace name `http://www.w3.org/XML/1998/namespace`. This list doesn't contain any items with the prefix `xmlns` (which is used for declaring namespaces), because an application can never encounter an element or attribute with that prefix. The set will include namespace items corresponding to all of the members of namespace attributes, except for any representing a declaration of the form xmlns="...", which does not declare a namespace but rather "undeclares" the default namespace.

local name   The local part of the element-type name. This does not include any namespace prefix or following colon.

namespace attributes   An unordered list of attribute information items, one for each of the namespace declarations defined for the element.

namespace name   Defines a name for any namespace present. If the element does not belong to a namespace, this property has no value.

parent   The document or element information item.

prefix   The namespace prefix part of the element-type name. If the name is "unprefixed," this property has no value.

ATTRIBUTE INFORMATION ITEMS

For every attribute used in an XML document, there's a corresponding attribute information item for each attribute (specified or defaulted). The following properties are allowed for attribute information items:

attribute type   Defines the data type declared for this attribute in the DTD. Values can include: ID, IDREF, IDREFS, ENTITY, ENTITIES, NMTOKEN, NMTOKENS, NOTATION, CDATA, and ENUMERATION. If there's no declaration for the attribute, this property has no value.

local name   The local part of the attribute name. This does not include any namespace prefix or following colon.

namespace name   The namespace name, if any, of the attribute. Otherwise, this property has no value.

normalized value   The normalized attribute value.

owner element   The element information item associated with the attribute in question.

prefix   The namespace prefix part of the attribute name. If the name is unprefixed, this property has no value.

references   If the attribute type is ID, NMTOKEN, NMTOKENS, CDATA, or ENUMERATION, the property has no value. If the attribute type is unknown, the value of this property is unknown. If the attribute type is IDREF, IDREFS, ENTITY, ENTITIES, or NOTATION, the value of this property is an ordered list of the element, unparsed entity, or notation information items referred to in the attribute value, in the order that they appear there.

specified   Indicates whether this attribute was actually specified in the start tag of its element or was defaulted from the DTD.

PROCESSING INSTRUCTION INFORMATION ITEMS

For every processing instruction present in an XML document, there's a corresponding processing instruction information item. The XML declaration and text declarations for external parsed entities are not considered processing instructions. The following properties are allowed for the processing instruction information item:

content   A string representing the content of the processing instruction. This does not include the processing instruction target (`PITarget`). If there's no such content, the value of this property will be an empty string.

base URI   The base URI of the processing instruction.

notation   Defines any notation information items named by the `PITarget`. If there's no declaration for a notation with that name, this property has no value.

parent   The document, element, or DTD information item that contains the processing instruction.

target   A string representing the `PITarget`.

UNEXPANDED ENTITY REFERENCE INFORMATION ITEMS

An unexpanded entity reference information item serves as a placeholder by which an XML processor can indicate that it has not expanded an external parsed entity. For each unexpanded reference, there's an unexpanded entity reference information item. If the processor reads all external general entities, the unexpanded entity reference information items will not be generated.

The following properties are allowed for the unexpanded entity reference information items:

declaration base URI   The base URI relative to which the system identifier should be resolved.

name   The name of the entity referenced.

parent   The element information item that contains an unexpanded reference.

public identifier   The public identifier of the entity. If there's no declaration for the entity, or the declaration does not include a public identifier, this property has no value.

system identifier   The system identifier of the entity. If there's no declaration for the entity, this property has no value.

CHARACTER INFORMATION ITEMS

For character data in an XML document, there's a character information item. This includes character data contained by CDATA sections. According the Infoset specification, each character is a logically separate information item. However, XML applications are allowed to group characters together. The following properties are allowed for the character information item:

character code   The ISO 10646 character code of the character.

element content whitespace   A Boolean defining if the character is white space appearing within element content. It's always `false` for characters that are not white space.

parent   The element information item that contains the character information item.

COMMENT INFORMATION ITEMS

There's a comment information item for each XML comment in the XML document. This does not include comments defined with the DTD. The following properties are allowed for the comment information item:

content   A string representing the content of the comment.

parent   The document or element information item that contains the comment.

THE DOCUMENT TYPE DECLARATION INFORMATION ITEM

If the XML document has a document type (`DOCTYPE`) declaration, a document type declaration information item is defined. The following properties are allowed for the document type declaration information item:

children   An ordered list of processing instruction information items representing processing instructions appearing in the DTD, in the original document order.

parent   The document information item.

public identifier   The public identifier of the external subset. If there's no external subset or if it has no public identifier, this property has no value.

system identifier   The system identifier of the external subset, if it exists. If none exists, then the property has no value.

UNPARSED ENTITY INFORMATION ITEMS

There's an unparsed entity information item for each unparsed general entity declared in the DTD. The following properties are allowed for the unparsed entity information item:

name   The name of the entity.

declaration base URI   The base URI relative to the system identifier.

notation   The notation information item named by the notation name.

notation name   The notation name associated with the entity.

public identifier   The public identifier of the entity. If the entity has no public identifier, this property has no value.

system identifier   The system identifier of the entity.

NOTATION INFORMATION ITEMS

If a notation is declared in the DTD, then there's a notation information item defined. The following properties are allowed for the notation information item:

declaration base URI   The base URI relative to the system identifier.

name   The name of the notation.

public identifier   The public identifier of the notation. If the notation has no public identifier, this property has no value.

system identifier   The system identifier of the notation.

NAMESPACE INFORMATION ITEMS

For each element defined within the scope of a namespace, a namespace information item is defined. The following properties are allowed for the namespace information item:

namespace name   The namespace name to which the prefix is defined.

prefix   The prefix defined with the namespace. If the item in question is a default namespace, the property has no value.

XML DOM

The Document Object Model (DOM) uses a tree model to define XML objects. Specifically, the DOM creates a tree of nodes for all important objects. Many applications use the DOM as a programming interface. For example, if you want to use JavaScript with HTML or XHTML, you're using the DOM (whether you knew it or not). The DOM is not the only answer for parsing an XML document. However, it's a common method for working with both Java and JavaScript. If you're familiar with XPath, the DOM will make sense. Both use a tree model to define accessible objects in the XML document.

SAX VERSUS DOM

An API is a well-defined and well-documented set of interfaces or objects designed to permit application programmers to invoke external services outside the normal execution boundaries of their programs. APIs are essential to modern programming, for everything from file system access, to communications between programs, to access to databases, and so forth.

Currently, two popular API specifications are used to define how to parse XML documents: SAX and DOM. The W3C's DOM specification defines a tree-based approach to navigating an XML document. The DOM parser processes the XML input document and creates an object-oriented hierarchical representation of the document that you can navigate at runtime.

Continued on next page

SAX VERSUS DOM *(continued)*

SAX stands for the Simple API for XML. Whereas the DOM creates a tree representation of the XML input document, SAX defines an object model and an event-based approach. The SAX parser processes the XML input document. As the parser encounters a part of the document, such as an element or attribute, the parser treats it as an event and calls handler functions that you define to handle that event. For example, if the SAX parser comes across an element, it will call on the code you specified to handle elements. The same can be said for such items as attributes, text, and processing instructions.

Both approaches, SAX and DOM, use different methods for parsing the XML document. For those of you just starting out designing XML applications, you might wonder why two different ways to parse XML documents are needed, and whether defining two different methods ever becomes a problem for developers. Because the DOM and SAX approaches both use different methods, there are varying strengths and weaknesses to both. For example, the DOM provides for an intuitive structure for defining and housing your XML data, but there's a drain on processing because the DOM requires the parser to store the tree in its memory. Once the tree is in memory, you can manipulate it at runtime and stream the updated data as XML, or transform it to your own format if you require.

On the other hand, the SAX specification is able to parse XML documents faster without reaching resource limits, because it doesn't store an object model in its memory. Because of this design, the SAX implementation is generally faster and requires fewer resources.

Core Objects

The DOM represents a tree view of the XML document. The `documentElement` element is the top level of the tree. This element has one or many `childNodes` attributes that represent the branches of the tree. In this section, we define each node type defined by the Core DOM. The object is defined first, followed by a brief description.

Attr   Defines a node for every attribute.

CDATASection   Defines a node for every occurrence of a CDATA section.

Comment   Defines a node for every comment.

Document   Defines a node for the document object (the node represents the entire document).

DocumentFragment   Defines a node that is a reference to a document fragment.

DocumentType   Defines a node for the `DOCTYPE` declaration.

Element   Defines a node for every element.

Entity   Defines a node for parsed and unparsed entities.

EntityReference   Defines a node for each occurrence of an entity reference.

Notation   Defines a node for each notation present in the XML document.

ProcessingInstruction   Defines a node for each processing instruction.

Text   Defines a node for data contained by an element or attribute.

TIP *Microsoft has a slightly different implementation of the DOM. For more information on Microsoft's implementation, see the company's Web site at* `http://msdn.microsoft.com/library/default.asp?url=/library/en-us/xmlsdk/htm/dom_concepts_21kd.asp`.

To read more about the DOM, see Chapter 16.

XPath

XPath defines a regular syntax and semantics for addressing into an XML document. Using a tree model, XPath is a key ingredient to using XSLT and XPointer. XPath also provides syntax for manipulating strings, numbers, and Booleans. Much like the DOM, XPath uses a tree model that defines various parts of an XML document as nodes. Specifically, XPath defines seven parts of an XML document that can be defined as a part of the node tree. For example, every element found in an XML document would have its own element node that identified its name and string value. Once the data is defined as a part of a tree, it's easier to navigate that tree and locate the data needed for the output document. XSLT and XPointer use XPath expressions to identify nodes in the source tree, as well as select the nodes for data manipulation.

XPath has two very specific uses: XSLT and XPointer. Originally, the data models used for both of these specifications were defined as a part of each specification. However, the data models were so similar, one separate data model document was created instead: XPath.

XPath is used in the following ways:

◆ XSLT uses XPath to access objects within an XML document for use in its transformation process.

◆ XPointer uses XPath to address the internal structures of XML documents. XPath allows for navigation of a document tree (the XPath tree).

Nodes

An XPath tree is made up of nodes (similar to DOM objects). XPath defines seven types of nodes that make up the document's tree representation. The allowable node types are:

◆ Root node

◆ Element node

◆ Attribute node

◆ Comment node

◆ Processing instruction node

◆ Namespace node

◆ Text node

These nodes are discussed in detail in Bonus Chapter 26 (on the Web at `www.sybex.com`).

Unlike the DOM, XPath also defines a regular syntax for navigating the tree. Both XPointer and XSLT use this syntax to access, select, or refer to nodes within the tree. An XPath expression is used to navigate to a particular node or node set in the tree. Expressions are defined by a location path that is in turn made up of steps:

```
step/step/step
```

Each step is made up of three possible items: axis, node test, and predicate. The axis defines the direction that you're navigating. The node test selects a node set. The predicate filters the node set. The syntax used for each step is:

```
axis::nodetest[predicate]
```

The following are the allowable axes and are discussed in detail in Bonus Chapter 26 (on the Web at www.sybex.com):

- `child`
- `descendant`
- `parent`
- `ancestor`
- `following-sibling`
- `preceding-sibling`
- `following`
- `preceding`
- `attribute`
- `namespace`
- `self`
- `descendant-or-self`
- `ancestor-or-self`

Where to Go from Here

In this chapter, we provided you with an overview of three common data models used with XML. XPath is used for XPointer and XSLT, and the DOM is used as a common API for programming languages such as Java. The XML Information Set is a behind-the-scenes standard that helps drive many other specifications, such as XPath and the DOM. If you're interested in learning more about either XPath or the DOM, visit the following chapters:

- See Chapter 16 to learn more about the DOM.
- See Chapter 26 to learn more about XPath.

Chapter 29

XML Schemas

SCHEMAS, MUCH LIKE DTDs, are used to validate XML documents. Schemas were designed as a more complex alternative to DTDs. The need for an alternative arose for several reasons, but one of the most important reasons is data typing. XML Schemas allow document authors to define strict data types for element and attribute values. For example, an e-commerce or business-to-business (B2B) application requires your data to follow specific patterns; a given attribute value must have two decimal places; or the contents of an element used for a password must be eight characters long. Although DTDs don't allow for much data typing, schemas offer 45 built-in data types and the ability to create your own.

It's thought by many in the industry that various data-centric applications will make the move to XML Schemas for validation in the near future—if they haven't already. If you plan to work with XML, you'll want to take a look at XML Schemas.

Although XHTML uses DTDs for validation, there's been an initiative to create schema modules for XHTML. These modules are based on the modularization of XHTML and will be a big part of XHTML's future.

This chapter covers the following topics:

◆ Deciding between DTDs and XML Schemas

◆ Creating element and attribute declarations

◆ Working with schema data types

◆ Discovering alternative schema languages

Schema Overview

The XML community has waited a long time for XML Schemas. As a matter of fact, while everyone was waiting for the W3C version, several alternative schema languages began to pop up. Unlike many XML vocabularies based on well-implemented SGML-related languages, XML Schemas are brand-new. They were created as an alternative to DTDs. On the one hand, DTDs seem to make sense in a document-centric environment, where element data types are primarily character data. However, in a data-centric environment, where every decimal place counts, better alternatives were called for that could help you enforce data types. One of the original goals of DTDs was simplicity. Simplicity is important; however, so is the ability for a programmer to insist that the data is defined stringently. XML Schemas are here to address that issue.

TIP If you're interested in learning more about XML Schemas, check out XML Schemas, *by Chelsea Valentine and Lucinda Dykes (Sybex, 2002).*

XML Schemas versus DTDs

As XML evolves, so do the related technologies. In the beginning, the DTD was the best mechanism for defining the logical structure or content model of an SGML document. Implementation and experience with this environment helped foster the development of XML Schemas. The focus was on developing a more descriptive way to specify element content models, in addition to specifying data types used in the document.

DTDs, stemming from the days of SGML, are prevalent in the marketplace today. This cannot yet be said about schemas. However, they're gaining support because of the increased functionality and extensibility they provide over the DTD.

This is not to say that DTDs are on their way out. On the contrary, both methods of validation are likely to be around for some time. What you need to be able to do is to identify the strengths and weaknesses of both methods and choose the appropriate method for your application.

First, let's take a look at the advantages and disadvantages of using XML Schemas.

Some advantages are:

◆ Schemas use XML syntax and can therefore be parsed to check for well-formedness.

◆ Schemas support namespaces.

◆ Schemas support 45 built-in data types.

◆ Schemas allow authors to create their own data types (in case the data has special formatting needs).

◆ Schemas allow for more rigorous validation.

◆ Schemas allow for extensibility.

Some disadvantages are:

◆ Schemas have not seen widespread implementation yet.

◆ Microsoft Internet Explorer supports its own schema vocabulary (this is changing with newest version of IE's XML processor, MSXML4).

◆ The schema language is more complex than DTDs.

With XML Schemas, not only can you use one of the 45 built-in data types, but you can also create your own. For example, if you sell books on the Web, you could keep track of the books using catalog numbers (for example, n4887). A DTD would only allow you to define the value to be CDATA (character data). However, with schemas, for example, you could define the value to begin with a character such as s or n (for science fiction or nonfiction). Then, you could define that the value contains exactly four digits.

This is not to say that you should drop DTDs and run to purchase a schema editor. DTDs are not without their advantages:

◆ Plenty of tools are available for DTDs. (Some even auto-generate DTDs.)

◆ DTDs are simple to read and write.

◆ There's plenty of documentation on DTDs.

The main advantage to using DTDs is that they are easy. There's a time and place to use XML Schemas. The general rule is that if you're dealing with document-centric data and don't need to use namespaces, DTDs will serve you well. However, if you're concerned about data typing, namespaces, or complex content models, you'll want to use a schema vocabulary.

TIP   XML Schemas do not define a mechanism for creating entities similar to the ones used for data abstraction in DTDs. According to the W3C, the reasoning is that in most cases, the functionality of entities can be replaced through other XML-based mechanisms.

XML Schema Specification Documents

If you want to visit the official XML Schema language specification, you can do so at the W3C's Web site. The standard is defined by two separate recommendation documents because the XML Schema language was broken up into two parts: structures and data types. The structures portion defines the XML Schema vocabulary, and the data types portion defines how to use XML Schema data types. The two XML Schema recommendation documents are:

XML Schema Part 1: Structures (Recommendation)   The first specification document defines the schema vocabulary. By defining the vocabulary, the document defines the rules governing schema validation of documents. The most recent version was defined on May 2, 2001. You can find this document at www.w3.org/TR/xmlschema-1/.

XML Schema Part 2: Datatypes (Recommendation)   The second specification document defines all possible data types, in addition to describing how to create your own data types. The most recent version was also defined on May 2, 2001. You can find this document at www.w3.org/TR/xmlschema-2/.

TIP   The W3C also offers a third recommendation document, "XML Schema Part 0: Primer," which provides examples and illustrations for using XML Schemas. This document can be found at www.w3.org/TR/xmlschema-0/.

XML Schema Namespaces

One of the weaknesses of DTDs is that they are not namespace aware. XML Schemas were created with namespaces in mind and therefore take full advantage of them. You need to be familiar with namespaces if you want to work with XML Schemas. There are two schema-dedicated namespaces:

`http://www.w3.org/2000/10/XMLSchema` This namespace defines the scope for W3C XML Schema elements. You must use this namespace; however, you can define it as a default namespace or with an `xsd` prefix. If you use the `xsd` prefix, every schema element must use the prefix (for example, `<xsd:attribute>...</xsd:attribute>`).

`http://www.w3.org/2000/10/XMLSchema-instance` This namespace is used to define the scope for any W3C XML Schema extensions that are used in instance documents. If you use this namespace, you want to define it using its `xsi` prefix. You should use this namespace only if you'll be using XML Schema extensions.

XML Schemas are namespace aware and, therefore, allow you to define your own namespace to be used in the corresponding XML document. If you plan to use a namespace in your XML document, you need to define a target namespace in the XML Schema document. For example, this XML document adheres to the defined namespace `http://www.raycomm.com/namespace/books`. Here's what the markup might look like (remember, this is just an example):

```
<?xml version="1.0"?>
<book-tracking xmlns="http://www.raycomm.com/namespace/books">
   <book>
      <title>Mastering HTML and XHTML</title>
      <author type="staff" email="debray@raycomm.com">Deborah S. Ray
         </author>
      <author type="staff" email="ejray@raycomm.com">Eric J.
         Ray</author>

      <editor email="willem@example.com">Willem Knibbe</editor>
   </book>
   <book>
      <title>XML Schemas</title>
      <author type="staff" email="etittel@lanw.com">Ed Tittel
         </author>
      <author type="staff" email="chelsea@lanw.com">Chelsea
         Valentine</author>
      <author type="contractor" email="lucinda@thuntek.net">
         Lucinda Dykes</author>
      <editor email="mary@lanw.com">Mary Burmeister</editor>
   </book>
</book-tracking>
```

TIP *Because DTDs don't support namespaces, you'd be forced to define the namespace using an attribute list declaration, where* `xmlns` *is the attribute name and* `http://www.raycomm.com/namespace/books` *is the fixed value (for example,* `<!ATTLIST enrollment xmlns CDATA FIXED "http://www.raycomm.com/namespace/books">`*). Note that this method doesn't truly represent a namespace.*

In the XML Schema document, you'd use the `targetNamespace` attribute with the corresponding namespace URI as the value; for example:

```
<schema targetNamespace="http://www.raycomm.com/namespace/books">
...
</schema>
```

If we pulled all the necessary namespaces together, our root schema element might look like this:

```
<xsd:schema
    xmlns:xsd="http://www.w3.org/2000/10/XMLSchema"
    targetNamespace="http://www.raycomm.com/namespaces/books">
```

Please note that we added the `xsd` namespace prefix to the `schema` element in accordance with the prefix namespace declaration.

XML Schema Syntax

As you might have already guessed, XML Schemas follow XML syntax. This happens to be one of the advantages to using XML Schemas. Not only is it easier for you to learn the language, but it also means that XML Schema documents can be parsed using an XML parser. In case you need a quick refresher, the syntax rules are:

- ◆ All non-empty elements must be closed with a closing tag.
- ◆ All empty elements must be terminated: `<empty />`.
- ◆ All attributes must have values in quotation marks.
- ◆ All elements must nest correctly.
- ◆ Elements and attributes are case sensitive.

XML Schema Vocabulary

Much of the XML Schema vocabulary is intuitive. To declare an element, you use the `element` element. To declare an attribute, you use the `attribute` element. It would take an entire book to cover everything in the schema vocabulary, but we touch on many of the basics in this chapter:

- ◆ Declaring elements
- ◆ Declaring attributes
- ◆ Declaring reusable chunks of information (similar to DTD parameter entities)

There are several similarities between DTD and schema functionality. This is not by mistake. Table 29.1 compares and contrasts some of the features found in both DTDs and XML Schemas.

TABLE 29.1: DTD AND XML SCHEMA FEATURES

DTD CONCEPT	DTD SYNTAX	XML SCHEMA EQUIVALENT

Element type declaration	`<!ELEMENT book (content model)>`	`<xsd:element name="book">`
		`...content model...`
		`</xsd:element>`

Mixed content models (#PCDATA only)	`<!ELEMENT title (#PCDATA)>`	`<xsd:element name="title"` `type="xsd:string"/>`

Mixed content models	`<!ELEMENT para (#PCDATA | bold)*>`	`<xsd:element name="para">`
		`<xsd:complexType mixed="true">`
		`<xsd:sequence>`
		`<xsd:element name="bold"`
		`type="xsd:string"/>`
		`</xsd:sequence>`
		`</xsd:complexType>`
		`</xsd:element>`

ANY content model	`<!ELEMENT book ANY>`	`<element name="book">`
		`<complexType>`
		`<sequence>`
		`<any minOccurs="1" maxOccurs="unbounded"`
		`processContents="skip"/>`
		`</sequence>`
		`</complexType>`
		`</element>`

EMPTY content model	`<!ELEMENT img EMPTY>`	`<xsd:element name="img">`
		`<xsd:complexType>`
		`<xsd:attribute name="alt"`
		`type="xsd:string"/>`
		`<xsd:attribute name="src"`
		`type="xsd:uriReference"/>`
		`</xsd:complexType>`
		`</xsd:element>`

, (sequence connector)	`<!ELEMENT html (head, body)>`	`<xsd:element name="html">`
		`<xsd:complexType>`
		`<xsd:sequence>`
		`<xsd:element name="head"`
		`type="head.content"/>`
		`<xsd:element name="body"`
		`type="body.content"/>`
		`</xsd:sequence>`
		`</xsd:complexType>`
		`</xsd:element>`

Continued on next page

TABLE 29.1: DTD AND XML SCHEMA FEATURES *(continued)*

DTD CONCEPT	DTD SYNTAX	XML SCHEMA EQUIVALENT

| (choice connector)	`<!ELEMENT contact (email | address)>`	`<xsd:element name="contact">`
		`<xsd:complexType>`
		`<xsd:choice>`
		`<xsd:element name="email"`
		`type="xsd:string"/>`
		`<xsd:element name="address"`
		`type="xsd:string"/>`
		`</xsd:choice>`
		`</xsd:complexType>`
		`</xsd:element>`

? (optional occurrence indicator)	`<!ELEMENT table (caption?, tr)>`	`<xsd:element name="table">`
		`<xsd:complexType>`
		`<xsd:sequence>`
		`<xsd:element name="caption"`
		`type="xsd:string" minOccurs="0"`
		`maxOccurs="1"/>`
		`<xsd:element name="tr" type="tr.content"/>`
		`</xsd:sequence>`
		`</xsd:complexType>`
		`</xsd:element>`

+ (required and repeatable occurrence indicator)	`<!ELEMENT head (title, meta+)>`	`<xsd:element name="head">`
		`<xsd:complexType>`
		`<xsd:sequence>`
		`<xsd:element name="title"`
		`type="xsd:string"/>`
		`<xsd:element name="meta" type="meta`
		`.content" minOccurs="1"`
		`maxOccurs="unbounded"/>`
		`</xsd:sequence>`
		`</xsd:complexType>`
		`</xsd:element>`

* (optional and repeatable occurrence indicator)	`<!ELEMENT head (title, meta*)>`	`<xsd:element name="head">`
		`<xsd:complexType>`
		`<xsd:sequence>`
		`<xsd:element name="title"`
		`type="xsd:string"/>`
		`<xsd:element name="meta" type=`
		`"meta.content" minOccurs="0"`
		`maxOccurs="unbounded"/>`
		`</xsd:sequence>`
		`</xsd:complexType>`
		`</xsd:element>`

Continued on next page

TABLE 29.1: DTD AND XML SCHEMA FEATURES *(continued)*

DTD CONCEPT	DTD SYNTAX	XML SCHEMA EQUIVALENT

( ) (grouping)	`<!ELEMENT customer (name, (email | address))>`	`<xsd:element name="customer">`
		`<xsd:complexType>`
		` <xsd:sequence>`
		`  <xsd:element name="name"`
		`type="xsd:string"/>`
		`  <xsd:group   ref="contact"/>`
		` </xsd:sequence>`
		` <xsd:attribute name="orderDate"`
		` type="xsd:date"/>`
		`</xsd:complexType>`
		`</xsd:element>`
		
		`<xsd:group name="contact">`
		`  <xsd:choice>`
		`   <xsd:element name="email" type=`
		`   "xsd:string"/>`
		`   <xsd:element name="address" type=`
		`   "xsd:string"/>`
		`  </xsd:choice>`
		`</xsd:group>`

attribute list declarations	`<!ATTLIST img src CDATA #REQUIRED>`	`<xsd:element name="img">`
		` <xsd:complexType>`
		`  <xsd:attribute name=`
		`  "src" type="xsd:uriReference"`
		`use="required"/>`
		` </xsd:complexType>`
		`</xsd:element>`

Multiple attribute list declarations	`<!ATTLIST img src CDATA #REQUIRED alt CDATA #REQUIRED>`	Not supported in the strict sense, however, you can define a group of attributes that can then be references from within content models:
		`<xsd:element name"img">`
		`<xsd:complexType>`
		`<xsd:attributeGroup ref="img.att"/>`
		`</xsd:complexType>`
		`<xsd:element>`
		`<xsd:attributeGroup name="img.att">`
		`<xsd:attribute name="src" type=`
		`   "xsd:uriReference" use="required"/>`
		`<xsd:attribute name="alt" type="xsd:string"`
		`   use="required"/>`
		`</xsd:attributeGroup>`

Continued on next page

TABLE 29.1: DTD AND XML SCHEMA FEATURES *(continued)*

DTD CONCEPT	DTD SYNTAX	XML SCHEMA EQUIVALENT
Attribute default value	`<!ATTLIST book author CDATA "unknown">`	`<xsd:attlist name="author" default="unknown"/>`
Required attribute (#REQUIRED)	`<!ATTLIST img src CDATA #REQUIRED>`	`<xsd:attribute name="src" type="xsd:uriReference" use="required"/>`
Optional attribute (#IMPLIED)	`<!ATTLIST img src CDATA #OPTIONAL>`	`<xsd:attribute name="width" type="xsd:number" use="optional"/>`
Fixed attribute (#FIXED)	`<!ATTLIST book-list version CDATA #FIXED "1.0">`	`<xsd:attribute name="version" type="xsd:number" fixed="1.0"/>`
Comments	`<!-- comment text -->`	You can still use XML comments; however, you can also use the Schema annotation element: `<xsd:annotation>` `<xsd:documentation>` `Text of comment` `</xsd:documentation>` `</xsd:annotation>`

Declarations

The first step to understanding how an XML Schema works is to understand the concept of declarations. When you create a DTD or schema document, you must declare all elements and attributes for the XML document. Each element and attribute will have its own declaration that defines its name, content model, and behavior. For example, for the following markup, we'd declare that the book-tracking element can only contain book elements:

```
<book-tracking>
    <book>…</book>
    <book>…</book>
    <book>…</book>
</book-tracking>
```

Not only do we want to declare that the book-tracking element can contain only other book elements, but we also want to require at least one occurrence of a book element. The following markup uses DTD syntax to define the declaration:

```
<!ELEMENT book-tracking (book)+>
```

However, if we used XML Schema syntax, the declaration would be:

```
<xsd:element name="book-tracking">
    <xsd:complexType>
```

```
      <xsd:sequence minOccurs="1" maxOccurs="unbounded">
       <xsd:element name="book">
          ...
       </xsd:element>
      </xsd:sequence>
    </xsd:complexType>
  </xsd:element>
```

We know this looks foreboding because there are many more lines of markup, but remember the advantages of schemas discussed back in the "XML Schemas versus DTDs" section.

When declaring elements and attributes, you have two options:

Global declarations   You can define an element or attribute as the child of the schema element. This is known as a *global declaration*. Once you've created a global declaration, you can reference that declaration throughout the schema document by using a `ref` attribute. We use this method for most of our examples in this chapter. In the following example, both elements are declared globally:

```
  <xsd:element name="book-tracking">
    <xsd:complexType>
      <xsd:element ref="book:book"/>
    </xsd:complexType>
  </xsd:element>
  <xsd:element name="book" type="xsd:string"/>
```

Local declarations   You can declare an element or attribute as a child of another element declaration. The term *local* is not used often, but it helps define the distinction between the two. In the following example, the book element is defined locally:

```
  <xsd:element name="book-tracking">
    <xsd:complexType>
      <xsd:element name="book" type="xsd:string"/>
    </xsd:complexType>
  </xsd:element>
```

You've already seen a preview to element declarations, but let's take a more detailed look.

Declaring Elements

In the previous section, we discussed the difference between global and local declarations. When it comes to element declarations, there's another distinction that needs to be made: complex versus simple.

COMPLEX TYPES

If an element contains attributes or other child elements, it must be defined as a complex type. Complex types can get interesting because there are two different ways you can define them. One way to work with complex types is to define them on a global level, and then reference them from within a declaration. This works much like a DTD parameter entity. (See Chapter 23 for more on parameter entities.) The advantage of using complex types is that you can create the complex type and then reuse it when needed. For example, the following is a complex-type definition:

```
<xsd:complexType name="bookcontentType">
  <xsd:sequence>
    <xsd:element name="title" type="xsd:string" />
    <xsd:element name="author" type="xsd:string" />
  </xsd:sequence>
</xsd:complexType>
```

In this example, the complex type is defined as a child of the schema element (similar to that of a global declaration). When you want to use the complex type, you do so by calling it with a type attribute:

```
<xsd:element name="book" type="bookcontentType" />
```

However, if you want to create a complex type that's used only once, there's no need to declare it globally. In this case, the complex type can be defined as a part of the declaration itself. In this case, you do not define a complex type that you reference later; for example:

```
<xsd:element name="book">
  <xsd:complexType>
    <xsd:sequence>
      <xsd:element name="title" type="xsd:string" />
      <xsd:element name="author" type="xsd:string" />
    </xsd:sequence>
  </xsd:complexType>
</xsd:element>
```

SIMPLE TYPES

If an element doesn't contain any attributes or child elements, it's called a simple type. For simple type declarations, there's nothing needed except the element element, which is empty. In the following markup, the declarations for both the title and author elements are simple types:

```
<xsd:element name="book">
  <xsd:complexType>
    <xsd:sequence>
      <xsd:element name="title" type="xsd:string" />
      <xsd:element name="author" type="xsd:string" />
    </xsd:sequence>
  </xsd:complexType>
</xsd:element>
```

TIP   *Because an attribute can contain only a value, its declaration is, by default, a simple type.*

ELEMENT DECLARATION EXAMPLE

The odds are you'll use a combination of both simple and complex type declarations. Listing 29.1 illustrates element declarations.

LISTING 29.1: *book-tracking.xml*

```
<?xml version="1.0"?>
<book-tracking>
  <book>
    <title>Mastering HTML and XHTML</title>
    <author>Deborah S. Ray</author>
    <author>Eric J. Ray</author>
    <editor>Willem Knibbe</editor>
  </book>
  <book>
    <title>XML Schemas</title>
    <author>Ed Tittel</author>
    <author>Chelsea Valentine</author>
    <author>Lucinda Dykes</author>
    <editor>Mary Burmeister</editor>
  </book>
</book-tracking>
```

The DTD declarations for `book-tracking.xml` are shown in the following DTD subset:

```
<!ELEMENT book-tracking (book)+>
<!ELEMENT book (title, author+, editor)>
<!ELEMENT title (#PCDATA)>
<!ELEMENT author (#PCDATA)>
<!ELEMENT editor (#PCDATA)>
```

In the XML document, we use five elements, and indeed, our DTD example contains five element type declarations. The XML Schema equivalent is shown in Listing 29.2:

LISTING 29.2: THE XML SCHEMA EQUIVALENT OF THE DTD FOR LISTING 29.1

```
<xsd:element name="book-tracking">
  <xsd:complexType>
    <xsd:sequence minOccurs="1" maxOccurs="unbounded">
     <xsd:element ref="book:book"/>
    </xsd:sequence>
  </xsd:complexType>
</xsd:element>
<xsd:element name="book">
  <xsd:complexType>
    <xsd:sequence>
     <xsd:element ref="book:title"/>
```

```
      <xsd:element ref="book:author" minOccurs="1"
        maxOccurs="unbounded"/>
      <xsd:element ref="book:editor"/>
    </xsd:sequence>
  </xsd:complexType>
</xsd:element>
<xsd:element name="title" type="xsd:string"/>
<xsd:element name="author" type="xsd:string"/>
<xsd:element name="editor" type="xsd:string"/>
```

In this example, there are five globally declared elements. But, remember, you can declare your elements in one of two ways (globally or locally). In the following example, the XML Schema document uses local declarations:

```
<xsd:element name="book-tracking">
  <xsd:complexType>
    <xsd:sequence minOccurs="1" maxOccurs="unbounded">
      <xsd:element name="book">
        <xsd:complexType>
          <xsd:sequence>
            <xsd:element name="title" type="xsd:string"/>
            <xsd:element name="author" minOccurs="1"
              maxOccurs="unbounded" type="xsd:string"/>
            <xsd:element name="editor" type="xsd:string"/>
          </xsd:sequence>
        </xsd:complexType>
      </xsd:element>
    </xsd:sequence>
  </xsd:complexType>
</xsd:element>
```

When you're declaring elements, there are several attributes that you can use with the `element` element. The most common attributes are:

- `name="name"` names the element.

- `type="name"` defines schema data type or references a globally defined complex type definition.

- `ref="name"` references global element declarations.

- `minOccurs="nonNegativeInteger"` defines the minimum number of occurrences. The default value is 1, so if you leave out the attribute, it's assumed that the choice is required.

- `maxOccurs="nonnegativeInteger | unbounded"` defines the maximum number of occurrences. The default value is 1, so if you leave out the attribute, it's assumed that the choice cannot repeat.

If we pull it all together, you'd have a schema document (Listing 29.2) that would validate Listing 29.1 (`book-tracking.xml`), as shown in Listing 29.3.

LISTING 29.3: *book-tracking.xsd*

```xml
<?xml version="1.0" encoding="UTF-8"?>
<xsd:schema
    xmlns:xsd="http://www.w3.org/2000/10/XMLSchema"
    xmlns:book="http://www.raycomm.com/namespaces/books"
    targetNamespace="http://www.raycomm.com/namespaces/books"
    elementFormDefault="qualified">
<xsd:element name="book-tracking">
  <xsd:complexType>
    <xsd:sequence minOccurs="1" maxOccurs="unbounded">
     <xsd:element ref="book:book"/>
    </xsd:sequence>
  </xsd:complexType>
</xsd:element>
<xsd:element name="book">
  <xsd:complexType>
    <xsd:sequence>
     <xsd:element ref="book:title"/>
     <xsd:element ref="book:author" minOccurs="1"
       maxOccurs="unbounded"/>
     <xsd:element ref="book:editor"/>
    </xsd:sequence>
  </xsd:complexType>
</xsd:element>
<xsd:element name="title" type="xsd:string"/>
<xsd:element name="author" type="xsd:string"/>
<xsd:element name="editor" type="xsd:string"/>
</xsd:schema>
```

Let's break this example down, piece by piece:

Schema root element In the previous example, the schema element is defined as the root element. You must define the schema namespace in any schema document.

We also include a namespace for our book-tracking elements that are prefixed with book. By doing this, we can then refer to elements declared within the document (more on that shortly).

The last namespace defined is known as the target namespace. As you know, a target namespace defines the namespace for the corresponding XML document.

The element element The element element declares an element. The name attribute names the element. There are five element declarations for the following elements: book-tracking, book, title, author, and editor.

If an element contains child elements, it must be declared using a complex type. In Listing 29.3, there are two elements that contain other child elements: book-tracking and book. Each of these elements is defined using a complex type. Each complex type contains a content model—remember

DTDs: (`title`, `author+`, `editor`). Schemas allow for several different types of content models to be defined, all using different schema elements and attributes. For example, Table 29.2 identifies the XML Schema equivalent for common DTD content models.

TABLE 29.2 SCHEMA CONTENT MODELS

SCHEMA ELEMENT	DTD EQUIVALENT
`<all>`	No DTD equivalent
`<any>`	Similar to the ANY keyword
`<choice>`	Similar to the pipe bar (|) connector
`<group>`	No DTD equivalent
`<sequence>`	Similar to the comma (,) connector

As with the `element` element, you can use the `minOccurs` and `maxOccurs` attributes with any of the elements defined in Table 29.2:

◆ `minOccurs` is similar to the DTD occurrence indicators (?, +, and *).

◆ `maxOccurs` is similar to the DTD occurrence indicators (?, +, and *).

In the following sections, we'll look at using some of the elements defined in Table 29.2.

In Listing 29.3, we used the `sequence` element to require that the child elements for `book` occur in the following order: `title`, `author`, and `editor`.

```
<xsd:sequence>
    <xsd:element ref="book:title"/>
      <xsd:element ref="book:author" minOccurs="1"
        maxOccurs="unbounded"/>
    <xsd:element ref="book:editor"/>
</xsd:sequence>
```

Finally, we create element references. In the previous markup, each element declaration references a global declaration. To reference a global declaration, you have to use the `ref` attribute. The value of the `ref` attribute is the name of the element. Because we declared the `title`, `author`, and `editor` elements within the scope of a target namespace, we must reference it as part of that namespace, no matter where we use it. In this case, we reference the element as part of the `ref` attribute, so we must use the namespace prefix.

Take a second to look back at the namespace definitions:

```
<xsd:schema xmlnsxsd:="http://www.w3.org/2000/10/XMLSchema"
    xmlns:book="http://www.raycomm.com/namespaces/books"
    targetNamespace="http://www.raycomm.com/namespaces/song">
```

Remember that the first namespace is the default namespace for schema elements. This means that if we use (or reference) any non-schema elements, they must be defined with an alternative prefix.

The last two namespaces work together. The last one (`targetNamespace`) defines a namespace to be associated with all declared elements. The target namespace is not technically an `xmlns` namespace definition; this simply states that if these elements are used in a document, they must belong to the defined namespace.

THE *choice* ELEMENT

In the examples we've used so far, we used the `sequence` element. However, in many cases you might want to allow for a choice within your content model. For example, using DTD syntax we can require the document author to choose among one of three possible child elements:

```
<!ELEMENT book (title | author | editor)>
```

The DTD element type declaration uses the pipe bar to signify a choice. The schema equivalent is shown in Listing 29.4.

LISTING 29.4: THE *choice* ELEMENT

```
<?xml version="1.0" encoding="UTF-8"?>
<xsd:schema
    xmlns:xsd="http://www.w3.org/2000/10/XMLSchema"
    xmlns:book="http://www.raycomm.com/namespaces/books"
    targetNamespace="http://www.raycomm.com/namespaces/books"
    elementFormDefault="qualified">
<xsd:element name="book-tracking">
  <xsd:complexType>
    <xsd:sequence minOccurs="1" maxOccurs="unbounded">
     <xsd:element ref="book:book"/>
    </xsd:sequence>
  </xsd:complexType>
</xsd:element>
<xsd:element name="book">
  <xsd:complexType>
    <xsd:choice>
     <xsd:element ref="book:title"/>
     <xsd:element ref="book:author" minOccurs="1"
        maxOccurs="unbounded"/>
     <xsd:element ref="book:editor"/>
    </xsd:choice>
  </xsd:complexType>
</xsd:element>
<xsd:element name="title" type="xsd:string"/>
<xsd:element name="author" type="xsd:string"/>
<xsd:element name="editor" type="xsd:string"/>
</xsd:schema>
```

In this case, we added a `choice` element. Because we did not use the `minOccurs` or `maxOccurs` attribute, the choice can be made only once. If you want to require the choice to occur at least once, but want to limit the number of times the choice can be made (for example, you could limit the maximum number of occurrences to 10), you add the `minOccurs` and `maxOccurs` attributes as shown here:

```
<xsd:element name="book">
  <xsd:complexType>
    <xsd:choice minOccurs="1" maxOccurs="10">
      <xsd:element ref="book:title"/>
      <xsd:element ref="book:author" minOccurs="1"
        maxOccurs="unbounded"/>
      <xsd:element ref="book:editor"/>
    </xsd:choice>
  </xsd:complexType>
</xsd:element>
```

THE *minOccurs* AND *maxOccurs* ATTRIBUTES

When using DTDs, you can use one of three occurrence indicators (*, +, or ?) to define the number of times a content model can be used. XML Schemas offer a higher level of occurrence manipulation. To define occurrences for content models, you use the `minOccurs` and `maxOccurs` attributes.

For example, you could use the following DTD element type declaration to allow the content model to repeat an unlimited number of times:

```
<!ELEMENT book (title | author | editor)*>
```

The schema equivalent is:

```
  <xsd:choice minOccurs="0" maxOccurs="unbounded">
   <xsd:element ref="book:title"/>
     <xsd:element ref="book:author" minOccurs="0"
       maxOccurs="unbounded"/>
     <xsd:element ref="book:editor"/>
   </xsd:choice>
  </xsd:complexType>
</xsd:element>
```

You can apply these attributes to the `element` element as well. In this case, they define the number of times an element may occur, as shown in Listing 29.5.

LISTING 29.5: APPLYING *minOccurs* AND *maxOccurs* TO THE *element* ELEMENT

```
<?xml version="1.0" encoding="UTF-8"?>
<xsd:schema
    xmlns:xsd="http://www.w3.org/2000/10/XMLSchema"
    xmlns:book="http://www.raycomm.com/namespaces/books"
    targetNamespace="http://www.raycomm.com/namespaces/books"
    elementFormDefault="qualified">
<xsd:element name="book-tracking">
```

```
    <xsd:complexType>
      <xsd:sequence minOccurs="1" maxOccurs="unbounded">
       <xsd:element ref="book:book"/>
      </xsd:sequence>
    </xsd:complexType>
  </xsd:element>
  <xsd:element name="book">
    <xsd:complexType>
      <xsd:choice>
       <xsd:element ref="book:title"/>
       <xsd:element ref="book:author" minOccurs="1"
           maxOccurs="10"/>
       <xsd:element ref="book:editor"/>
      </xsd:choice>
    </xsd:complexType>
  </xsd:element>
  <xsd:element name="title" type="xsd:string"/>
  <xsd:element name="author" type="xsd:string"/>
  <xsd:element name="editor" type="xsd:string"/>
</xsd:schema>
```

In this example, the author element is required to occur once but can repeat up to 10 times.

THE *any* ELEMENT

The last content model—related element we look at is the any element. The any element can be used to allow child elements to occur in any order, as shown in Listing 29.6. For example, in the corresponding XML document, the title, author, and editor elements may occur in any order.

LISTING 29.6: THE *any* ELEMENT

```
<?xml version="1.0" encoding="UTF-8"?>
<xsd:schema
xmlns:xsd="http://www.w3.org/2000/10/XMLSchema"
xmlns:book="http://www.raycomm.com/namespaces/books"
targetNamespace="http://www.raycomm.com/namespaces/books"
elementFormDefault="qualified">
<xsd:element name="book-tracking">
  <xsd:complexType>
    <xsd:sequence minOccurs="1" maxOccurs="unbounded">
     <xsd:element ref="book:book"/>
   </xsd:sequence>
  </xsd:complexType>
</xsd:element>
<xsd:element name="book">
  <xsd:complexType>
    <xsd:any>
```

```
        <xsd:element ref="book:title"/>
        <xsd:element ref="book:author" minOccurs="1"
           maxOccurs="unbounded"/>
        <xsd:element ref="book:editor"/>
      </xsd:any>
    </xsd:complexType>
</xsd:element>
<xsd:element name="title" type="xsd:string"/>
<xsd:element name="author" type="xsd:string"/>
<xsd:element name="editor" type="xsd:string"/>
</xsd:schema>
```

THE *group* ELEMENT

The group element allows you to create reusable chunks of declarations. When you're dealing with content models that you want to reuse, the group element is your best bet. In the following example, we have created a group element and given it the name bookContent. The name is used to reference the group throughout the schema document. In this case, the bookContent group defines the content model we want to use within the book element. To call on a defined group, you use the group element again. This time, you use the ref attribute to call on the defined group, as shown in Listing 29.7.

LISTING 29.7: THE *group* ELEMENT

```
<?xml version="1.0" encoding="UTF-8"?>
<xsd:schema xmlns:xsd="http://www.w3.org/2000/10/XMLSchema"
    xmlns:book="http://www.raycomm.com/namespaces/books"
    targetNamespace="http://www.raycomm.com/namespaces/books"
    elementFormDefault="qualified">
<xsd:group name="bookContent">
    <xsd:sequence>
      <xsd:element ref="book:title"/>
      <xsd:element ref="book:author" minOccurs="1"
        maxOccurs="unbounded"/>
      <xsd:element ref="book:editor"/>
    </xsd:sequence>
</xsd:group>

<xsd:element name="author">
    <xsd:complexType>
      <xsd:simpleContent>
        <xsd:restriction base="xsd:string">
          <xsd:attribute name="type" type="xsd:string"
              use="required"/>
          <xsd:attribute name="email" type="xsd:string"
              use="required"/>
```

```
          </xsd:restriction>
        </xsd:simpleContent>
      </xsd:complexType>
  </xsd:element>
  <xsd:element name="book">
    <xsd:complexType>
      <xsd:group ref="bookContent"/>
    </xsd:complexType>
  </xsd:element>
  <xsd:element name="book-tracking">
    <xsd:complexType>
      <xsd:sequence minOccurs="1" maxOccurs="unbounded">
       <xsd:element ref="book:book"/>
      </xsd:sequence>
    </xsd:complexType>
  </xsd:element>
  <xsd:element name="editor">
    <xsd:complexType>
      <xsd:simpleContent>
        <xsd:restriction base="xsd:string">
          <xsd:attribute name="email" type="xsd:string"
             use="required"/>
        </xsd:restriction>
      </xsd:simpleContent>
    </xsd:complexType>
  </xsd:element>
  <xsd:element name="title" type="xsd:string"/>
</xsd:schema>
```

Declaring Attributes

If you understand how to declare an element, then working with attribute declarations will be a breeze. Attributes are simple types, and therefore aren't defined using content models. Just like element declarations, attributes can be declared locally or globally. For attribute declarations, we use the **attribute** element. In the following examples, we use the same book-tracking.xsd document; however, this time, we add an email attribute to the author and editor elements. To allow for these new attributes, we could use DTD syntax like so:

```
<!ELEMENT author (#PCDATA)>
<!ATTLIST  author email CDATA #REQUIRED>
<!ELEMENT editor (#PCDATA)>
<!ATTLIST  editor email CDATA #REQUIRED>
```

Listing 29.8 illustrates how we might add equivalent attribute declarations to our schema document.

LISTING 29.8: DECLARING ATTRIBUTES WITH XML SCHEMA

```
<?xml version="1.0" encoding="UTF-8"?>
<xsd:schema xmlns:xsd="http://www.w3.org/2000/10/XMLSchema"
    xmlns:book="http://www.raycomm.com/namespaces/books"
    targetNamespace="http://www.raycomm.com/namespaces/books"
    elementFormDefault="qualified">
<xsd:element name="author">
  <xsd:complexType>
     <xsd:simpleContent>
        <xsd:restriction base="xsd:string">
           <xsd:attribute name="email" type="xsd:string"
              use="required"/>
        </xsd:restriction>
     </xsd:simpleContent>
  </xsd:complexType>
</xsd:element>
<xsd:element name="book">
  <xsd:complexType>
     <xsd:sequence>
        <xsd:element ref="book:title"/>
        <xsd:element ref="book:author" minOccurs="1"
          maxOccurs="unbounded"/>
        <xsd:element ref="book:editor"/>
     </xsd:sequence>
  </xsd:complexType>
</xsd:element>
<xsd:element name="book-tracking">
  <xsd:complexType>
     <xsd:sequence minOccurs="1" maxOccurs="unbounded">
        <xsd:element ref="book:book"/>
     </xsd:sequence>
  </xsd:complexType>
</xsd:element>
<xsd:element name="editor">
  <xsd:complexType>
     <xsd:simpleContent>
        <xsd:restriction base="xsd:string">
           <xsd:attribute name="email" type="xsd:string"
              use="required"/>
        </xsd:restriction>
     </xsd:simpleContent>
  </xsd:complexType>
</xsd:element>
<xsd:element name="title" type="xsd:string"/>
</xsd:schema>
```

To declare attributes, all you have to do is add an `attribute` element. When you use the `attribute` element, there are a few attributes you need to be aware of:

◆ `name="name"` defines the name for the attribute.

◆ `ref="name"`, like the `ref` attribute used with the `element` element, allows you to reference a global attribute declarations

◆ `type="name"` defines the data type for the attribute.

◆ `use="prohibited | optional | required"` is used to indicate whether the attribute is required or optional.

◆ `default="value"` defines a default value.

◆ `fixed="value"` defines a fixed value.

In this example, we add a default value for our `email` attribute:

```
<xsd:attribute name="email" type="xsd:string"
   use="optional" default="unknown"/>
```

You'll also want to use the `type` attribute to define the data type for your new attribute. For example, if we add an attribute to the root element that identifies the URL location of the `book-tracking` document, you could define the attribute like so:

```
<xsd:attribute name="location" type="xsd:uriReference"
   use="required"/>
```

One of the benefits to using XML Schemas over DTDs is that you have an endless number of data types to choose from. Whereas DTDs allow for only 7 data types, XML Schemas offers 45 predefined data types, as well as the ability to create your own data type patterns. The following section is dedicated to this topic.

Schema Data Types

As we mentioned, data typing is not a strong suit of DTDs. As a matter of fact, you have only seven different data types to choose from for your attributes—`ID`, `IDREF(S)`, `CDATA`, `NOTATION`, `ENTITY`, `ENTITIES`, `NMTOKEN(S)`, and enumerated values—and for elements you only have two. One of the benefits to working with XML Schemas is the ability to use predefined data types. For example, you might want to add an `isbn` attribute to a `book` element. If this were the case, the DTD data type used might be `CDATA`. However, if you choose to use XML Schemas, you would build a data type pattern that would require the attribute value to consist of exactly 10 digits. The technique of data typing is defined by the XML Schema Part 2: Datatypes document.

To illustrate our point, let's look at a simple example:

```
<!ATTLIST book price CDATA #IMPLIED>
```

For this example, the document author can use any character string as the value of the price attribute. For example, the following values could be used: `"don't know"`, `"how about it"`, or `"*"`. These are not very helpful.

However, if you wanted to use XML Schema data types, you could define the data types as a decimal:

```
<attribute name="price" type="decimal" />
```

Learning data types is not a quick and easy task. The specification document is long, and there are several different types of data types to learn.

The advantages to using data types are many, but learning them can take some time. We wish we could dedicate an entire chapter to this topic, but we can't. For this reason, we focus on only one type of data type: built-in data types. However, before we get there, let's take a look at the different categories of data types:

Built-in or user-derived Built-in data types are those that are defined by the specification. User-derived data types are derived data types that are defined by schema authors.

Primitive or derived Primitive data types are the core data types defined and are not defined in terms of other data types; derived data types are defined in terms of primitive data types.

Atomic, list, or union Atomic data types are those with indivisible values. List data type values consist of a finite-length sequence of values of an atomic data type. Union data types occur when there is a union of two or more data types.

Built-in data types are defined by the XML Schema specification. Built-in data types can be divided into two different categories: *primitive data types*, which are the basis for all other data types, and *derived data types*, which are derived from the primitive data types. As the schema author, you can select any one of these predefined (or built-in) data types.

We look at primitive data types first. Table 29.3 defines each primitive data type defined by the XML Schema specification.

TABLE 29.3 XML SCHEMA PRIMITIVE DATA TYPES

PRIMITIVE DATA TYPE	EXAMPLE VALUE
string	Hello World
boolean	{true, false}
float	12.56E3, 12, 12560, 0, -0, INF, -INF, NAN
double	12.56E3, 12, 12560, 0, -0, INF, -INF, NAN
decimal	12.68
duration	P0Y1347M
dateTime	2001-07-31T17:20:00-03:00
time	17:20:00-03:00
date	2001-08-13
gYearMonth	2001-08

Continued on next page

TABLE 29.3 XML SCHEMA PRIMITIVE DATA TYPES *(continued)*

PRIMITIVE DATA TYPE	EXAMPLE VALUE
gYear	2001
gMonthDay	08-13
gDay	13
gMonth	08
hexBinary 0FB7	
base64Binary	
anyURI	http://www.raycomm.com
Qname	book:title
Notation	Notation

Most of the primitive data types should look familiar. The most common of the primitive data types is string. From those core data types, additional data types have been derived. The following list identifies all derived data types defined by the Datatypes document:

normalizedString

token

language

ID

IDREF

IDREFS

ENTITY

ENTITIES

NMTOKEN

NMTOKENS

Name

NCName

integer

nonPositiveInteger

negativeInteger

long

int

short

byte

```
nonNegativeInteger

unsignedLong

unsignedInt

unsignedShort

unsignedByte

positiveInteger
```

To use any of these data types, all you have to do is use them as the value of the **type** attribute; for example:

```
<xsd:attribute name="id" type="xsd:ID"/>
```

It's really that simple.

WARNING   For this chapter, we highlight built-in data types. However, there's much more to data types than what we defined in this section. For more information on data types, see the XML Schema Datatypes specification at **www.w3** **.org/TR/xmlschema-2/.**

Other Schema Vocabularies

It's taken the W3C a long time to complete the XML Schema specification. Even with the first official version complete, there's plenty of discussion within the XML community. The advantages to using schemas are many, and most XML developers didn't want to wait for the W3C version to come out to begin taking advantage of them. In the meantime, several alternative schema languages were developed, most notably, TREX, RELAX, and Schematron. More recently, TREX and RELAX have been combined to bring us RELAX NG.

RELAX NG

RELAX NG is a schema language based on Tree Regular Expressions for XML (TREX) and the Regular Language description for XML (RELAX). As a schema language, RELAX NG is an XML vocabulary that specifies a pattern for defining the structure and content of an XML document.

The language itself is very similar to the schema vocabulary. For example, RELAX NG uses elements such as **element**, **attribute**, **choice**, and **text**. Consider the following XML document:

```
<?xml version="1.0"?>
<book-tracking>
   <book>
      <title>Mastering HTML or XHTML</title>
      <author>Deborah S. Ray</author>
   </book>
   <book>
      <title>XML Schemas</title>
      <author>Ed Tittel</author>
   </book>
</book-tracking>
```

The corresponding RELAX NG schema document would be:

```
<element name="book-tracking"
   xmlns="http://relaxng.org/ns/structure/0.9">
   <zeroOrMore>
     <element name="book">
      <element name="title">
         <text/>
      </element>
      <element name="author">
         <text/>
      </element>
     </element>
   </zeroOrMore>
</element>
```

RELAX NG is a simple alternative to working with XML Schemas. To read more about it, visit www.oasis-open.org/committees/relax-ng/spec.html. The standard is currently in progress, so expect some changes over time.

Schematron

Brought to us by Rick Jelliffee, Schematron is an alternative schema language that takes a different approach to validation. Instead of using a grammar-based approach, Schematron locates tree patterns in the parsed document. If you're familiar with using XPath or XSLT, you'll find Schematron easy to understand.

Schematron works off trees by initially using XPath to find content nodes in the parsed document and then to verify if XPath expressions are true for each node.

Schematron is especially easy to learn because it has only six primary elements. Although you can use other elements, these six define the basic validation functionality. A large part of understanding Schematron is understanding XPath. If you're not familiar with XPath, you will want to read Chapter 28 before learning Schematron.

The six primary elements are `schema`, `title`, `ns`, `pattern`, `rule`, `assert`, and `report`. The `assert` and `report` elements both use XPath expressions to test and report possible errors.

The following is a sample Schematron document that uses these six elements and is taken from the Schematron specification:

```
<schema xmlns="http://www.ascc.net/xml/schematron">
   <title>A Schematron Mini-Schema for Schematron</title>
   <ns prefix="sch" uri="http://www.ascc.net/xml/schematron">
   <pattern>
     <rule context="sch:schema">
      <assert test="sch:pattern">
      A schema contains patterns.</assert>
      <assert test="sch:pattern/sch:rule[@context] ">
      A pattern is composed of rules.
      These rules should have context attributes.</assert>
```

```
      <assert test="sch:pattern/sch:rule/sch:assert[@test] or
       sch:pattern/sch:rule/sch:report[@test] ">
      A rule is composed of assert and report statements.
      These rules should have a test attribute.</assert>
    </rule>
  </pattern>
</schema>
```

To learn more about Schematron, visit `www.ascc.net/xml/schematron/`.

Where to Go from Here

In this chapter, we covered the basics of schema validation. If you want to learn more about using XHTML and XML Schemas, see the following chapters:

◆ See Chapter 25, which covers the future of XHTML.

◆ See Chapter 28 if you're interested in learning more about XPath to prepare you for Schematron.

Part 9

Master's Reference

In This Section:

HTML and XHTML Elements and Attributes

THIS SECTION IS A comprehensive reference guide to all HTML and XHTML elements (often referred to as *tags*), including all standard elements and some other elements introduced by Netscape Navigator and Microsoft Internet Explorer. For each element, we provide sample code and indicate:

Standard/Usage: The version of HTML in which the element was introduced

Widely Supported: Whether browsers widely support the element

Empty: Whether the element is an empty element

For each element, we also list the available attributes; then, for each attribute, we again describe its use with values, provide HTML version and browser-support information, and show some sample HTML or XHTML code.

TIP *If an element or attribute says it was introduced in HTML 2, 3.2, or 4, you can use that item in XHTML as well.*

If elements and attributes were introduced in the HTML 4, HTML 3.2, or HTML 2 specifications, that version number appears next to Standard/Usage. For browser-specific elements and attributes, Standard/Usage tells you which browsers or browser versions support them.

TIP *You might bookmark and reference the following chapters as you're using this Reference section:*

Chapters 2 through 8 for instructions on using various kinds of elements for developing HTML or XHTML documents.

Chapters 9 through 11 if you're combining HTML or XHTML with style sheets, JavaScript, or multimedia.

Chapters 16 and 17 if you're using dynamic HTML or XHTML, or if you're generating HTML or XHTML from a database.

You can safely use all HTML 2 elements and attributes—they provide basic functionality, but few layout or design-oriented features.

HTML 3.2 remained backward compatible with HTML 2 but provided many new elements. Included in HTML 3.2 was support for tables, client-side image maps, embedded applets, and many new attributes that help control alignment of objects within documents. You can assume that all common browsers support all HTML 3.2 elements and attributes.

HTML 4 remained backward compatible with other versions of HTML and expanded the capabilities to better address multiple languages and browser technologies, such as speech or Braille. Additionally, most formatting elements and attributes were deprecated in HTML 4 in favor of style sheets, which provide better formatting capabilities.

NOTE *Deprecated means the element is no longer recommended for use and is likely to be removed in a future version of the specification. You should use alternatives if at all possible.*

Because XHTML is a reformulation of HTML 4 as XML, the elements and attributes used are the same. Therefore, if an element or attribute can be used with HTML 4 or earlier, it can be used with XHTML. However, you should consider using style sheets instead of the deprecated elements or attributes.

The current HTML 4 and XHTML specifications provide three subtypes: Transitional, Frameset, and Strict. The Transitional DTD accepts the elements and attributes that are deprecated for use in HTML 4 and XHTML 1. For general-purpose Web authoring, this continues to be the best choice. The XHTML Frameset DTD supports frames.

The XHTML Strict DTD focuses on document structure elements, and leaves out all deprecated elements (shown in Table MR1.1) and attributes. This DTD is good if you're authoring for:

◆ Netscape Navigator 4 or later versions

◆ Internet Explorer 4 or later versions

◆ Opera 5 or later versions

We strongly emphasize using clean XHTML markup and style sheets. See Chapter 2 for details on the different specifications and when to use them.

If you want to comply with the XHTML 1.1 specification (released May 31, 2001), you need to stay away from the deprecated elements shown in Table MR1.1. See Master's Reference Part 7 for more on official specifications.

TABLE MR1.1: DEPRECATED ELEMENTS IN XHTML 1.0

DEPRECATED ELEMENT	DESCRIPTION	NOTES
applet	Java applet	Deprecated in favor of the object element
basefont	Base font size	Deprecated in favor of CSS
center	Shorthand for div align="center"	Deprecated in favor of CSS
dir	Directory list	Deprecated in favor of unordered lists
font	Local change to font	Deprecated in favor of CSS
isindex	Single-line prompt	Deprecated in favor of using input elements to create text-input controls
menu	Menu list	Deprecated in favor of unordered lists

Continued on next page

TABLE MR1.1: DEPRECATED ELEMENTS IN XHTML 1.0 *(continued)*		
s	Strikethrough text	Deprecated in favor of CSS
strike	Strikethrough text	Deprecated in favor of CSS
u	Underlined text	Deprecated in favor of CSS

TIP   *To see a table that shows which attributes are deprecated in which elements in HTML 4.01, visit* **www.w3.org/ TR/html401/index/attributes.html** *and check out the Depr column.*

Elements labeled as deprecated throughout this section are acceptable to the Transitional and Frameset DTDs, but not to the Strict DTD. Elements labeled with earlier versions of HTML but not as deprecated are acceptable for all HTML DTDs, including Strict. Elements in the Frameset DTD are labeled as HTML 4 (Frames).

Specifying that an element or attribute is Widely Supported means that approximately 85 to 90 percent of browsers in common use accommodate the element. All commonly used versions of Internet Explorer (5.5 and later) and Netscape Navigator (6 and later), as well as alternative browsers like Opera (5 and later) and Mozilla (.9 and later), recognize all Widely Supported elements and attributes.

We indicate common variables as follows:

Variable	What You Substitute
n	A number (such as a size)
url	Some form of address (as in a hyperlink)
#rrggbb	A color value (in hex format) *or* a standard color name
...	Some other value, such as a title or a name

TIP   *Where values are given as a comma-separated list, the values are variable. Where values are given as a pipe-separated list, they're fixed values and you should choose one.*

Common Attributes

Some attributes apply to almost all elements. These are called *common attributes*, and they are as follows.

lang="..."

Specifies the language used within the section. This attribute is used most often within documents to override site-wide language specifications. Use standard codes for languages, such as DE for German, FR for French, IT for Italian, and HE for Hebrew. See ISO International Standard 639 at

    http://www.oasis-open.org/cover/iso639a.html

for more information about language codes.

Although these codes aren't case sensitive as HTML or XHTML attribute values, the ISO requires them to be uppercase in other contexts, such as SGML, so it's better to use capital letters.

Standard/Usage: HTML 4   **Widely Supported:** No

Sample:
```
<p>The following quote is in German. <q lang="DE">Guten tag!</q></p>
```

dir="ltr|rtl"

Specifies the direction (left to right or right to left) for the text used within the section. This attribute is used most often within documents to override site-wide language direction specifications.

Standard/Usage: HTML 4   **Widely Supported:** No

Sample:
```
<p>The following quote is in Hebrew; therefore, it's written right to left, not
left to right. <q lang="HE" dir="rtl">Hebrew text goes here and is presented right
to left, not left to right.</q></p>
```

Event Handlers

Each of the following event handlers helps link user actions to scripts. See Master's Reference Part 3, "Scripting Reference," for a fuller explanation of their uses, and see Chapter 10 for JavaScript instructions.

onload="..."

Occurs when the browser finishes loading a window or all frames within a `frameset`. This handler works with `body` and `frameset` elements.

onunload="..."

Occurs when the browser removes a document from a window or frame. This handler works with `body` and `frameset` elements.

onclick="..."

Occurs when a user clicks the mouse over an element. This handler works with most elements.

ondblclick="..."

Occurs when a user double-clicks the mouse over an element. This handler works with most elements.

onmousedown="..."

Occurs when a user presses the mouse button over an element. This handler works with most elements.

onmouseup="..."

Occurs when a user releases the mouse button over an element. This handler works with most elements.

onmouseover="..."

Occurs when a user moves the mouse over an element. This handler works with most elements.

onmousemove="..."

Occurs when a user moves the mouse while still over an element. This handler works with most elements.

onmouseout="..."

Occurs when a user moves the mouse away from an element. This handler works with most elements.

onfocus="..."

Occurs when a user moves the focus to an element, either with the mouse or the Tab key. This handler works with `label`, `input`, `select`, `textarea`, and `button`.

onblur="..."

Occurs when a user moves focus away from an element, either with the mouse or the Tab key. This handler works with `label`, `input`, `select`, `textarea`, and `button`.

onkeypress="..."

Occurs when a user presses and releases a key over an element. This handler works with most elements.

onkeydown="..."

Occurs when a user presses a key over an element. This handler works with most elements.

onkeyup="..."

Occurs when a user releases a key over an element. This handler works with most elements.

onsubmit="..."

Occurs when a user submits a form. This handler works only with the `form` element.

onreset="..."

Occurs when a user resets a form. This handler works only with the `form` element.

onselect="..."

Occurs when a user selects text in a text field. This handler works with the `input` and `textarea` elements.

onchange="..."

Occurs when a user modifies a field and moves the input focus to a different control. This handler works with the `input`, `select`, and `textarea` elements.

!

<!-- -->

Inserts comments into a document. Browsers do not display comments, although comments are visible in the document source.

Standard/Usage: HTML 2   **Widely Supported:** Yes   **Empty:** No

Sample:
```
<!-- This paragraph was modified on 4-15-02 -->
<p>XML is the latest and greatest in markup languages.</p>
```

<!DOCTYPE>

Appears at the beginning of the document and indicates the version of the document.

Standard/Usage: HTML 2   **Widely Supported:** Yes

Samples:
The HTML Strict standard:
```
<!DOCTYPE HTML PUBLIC "-//W3C//DTD HTML 4.01//EN"
          "http://www.w3.org/TR/html401/strict.dtd">
```

The HTML Transitional standard:
```
<!DOCTYPE html PUBLIC "-//W3C//DTD HTML 4.01 Transitional//EN"
     "http://www.w3.org/TR/html401/loose.dtd">
```

The HTML Frameset standard:
```
<!DOCTYPE html PUBLIC "-//W3C//DTD HTML 4.01 Frameset//EN"
     "http://www.w3.org/TR/html401/frameset.dtd">
```

The XHTML Strict standard:
```
<!DOCTYPE html PUBLIC "-//W3C//DTD XHTML 1.0 Strict//EN"
     "http://www.w3.org/TR/xhtml1/DTD/xhtml1-strict.dtd">
```

The XHTML Transitional standard:
```
<!DOCTYPE html PUBLIC "-//W3C//DTD XHTML 1.0 Transitional//EN"
     "http://www.w3.org/TR/xhtml1/DTD/xhtml1-transitional.dtd">
```

The XHTML Frameset standard:
```
<!DOCTYPE html PUBLIC "-//W3C//DTD XHTML 1.0 Frameset//EN"
     "http://www.w3.org/TR/xhtml1/DTD/xhtml1-frameset.dtd">
```

WARNING   DOCTYPE *is not an element; therefore, it's not written with a closing tag or a trailing /. It's a document type definition and should be written as shown in this section.*

A

a

Also called the *anchor* element; identifies a link to another document or a link to a location within a document. You commonly use this element to create a hyperlink, using the `href` attribute. You can also use the a element to identify sections within a document, using the `name` attribute.

Standard/Usage: HTML 2   **Widely Supported:** Yes   **Empty:** No

Sample:
```
<a href="http://www.raycomm.com/">Visit RayComm, Inc.</a>
```

accesskey="..."
Assigns a single keyboard key to the element.

Standard/Usage: HTML 4   **Widely Supported:** No

Sample:
```
<a href="help.html" accesskey="h">Help</a>
```

charset="..."
Specifies character encoding of the data designated by the link. Use the name of a character set defined in RFC2045. The default value for this attribute, appropriate for all Western languages, is ISO-8859-1.

Standard/Usage: HTML 4   **Widely Supported:** No

Sample:
```
<a href="help.html" charset="ISO-8859-1">Help</a>
```

class="..."
Indicates the style class to apply to the a element. Note that you must define the class in a style sheet.

Standard/Usage: HTML 4   **Widely Supported:** Yes

Sample:
```
<a href="next.html" class="casual">Next</a>
```

coords="x1,y1,x2,y2,... "
Identifies the coordinates that define a clickable area in a client-side image map. Measures coordinates, in pixels, from the top-left corner of the image.

Standard/Usage: HTML 4   **Widely Supported:** No

Sample:
```
<a shape="rect" coords="20,8,46,30" href="food.html">Food</a>
```

href="url"

Specifies the relative or absolute location of a file to which you want to provide a hyperlink.

> **Standard/Usage:** HTML 2   **Widely Supported:** Yes
>
> **Sample:**
> ```
> <a href="details.html">More Info</a>
> ```

hreflang="..."

Specifies the language used in the document linked to, which can be useful for aural browsers. Use standard codes for languages, such as DE for German, FR for French, IT for Italian, and HE for Hebrew. See ISO International Standard 639 at

> www.oasis-open.org/cover/iso639a.html

for more information about language codes.

> **Standard/Usage:** HTML 4   **Widely Supported:** No
>
> **Sample:**
> ```
> <a href="german.html" hreflang="DE">Read this in German!</a>
> ```

id="..."

Assigns a unique ID selector to an instance of the a element. When you then assign a style to that ID selector, it affects only that one instance of the a element.

> **Standard/Usage:** HTML 4   **Widely Supported:** Yes
>
> **Sample:**
> ```
> <a href="next.html" id="123">Next</a>
> ```

name="..."

Marks a location within the current document with a name. The browser can then quickly move to specific information within a document. You can link to existing named locations in a document by using a partial URL, consisting of just a pound sign (#) and the name (from within that document), or by using a more complete URL with a pound sign and a name at the end (from other documents or sites). This attribute is deprecated; use the id attribute instead of or together with name.

> **Standard/Usage:** HTML 2; deprecated   **Widely Supported:** Yes
>
> **Sample:**
> ```
> <a href="#ingredients">Ingredients</a>
> ...
> <a name="ingredients" id="ingredients"><h1>Ingredients</h1></a>
> ```

rel="..."

Specifies forward relationship hyperlinks.

> **Standard/Usage:** HTML 3.2   **Widely Supported:** No

Sample:
```
<a rel="Next" href="otherdoc.html">Other Doc</a>
```

rev="..."

Specifies reverse relationship hyperlinks.

Standard/Usage: HTML 3.2   **Widely Supported:** No

Sample:
```
<a rev="Prev" href="http://www.raycomm.com/">Link</a>
```

shape="rect|circle|poly"

Specifies the type of shape used to represent the clickable area in a client-side image map.

Value	Shape Indicated
Rect	Rectangle
Circle	Circle
Poly	Polygon bounded by three or more sides

Standard/Usage: HTML 4   **Widely Supported:** No

Sample:
```
<a shape="rect" coords="20,8,46,30" href="food.html">...</a>
```

style="..."

Specifies style sheet commands that apply to the contents of the a element.

Standard/Usage: HTML 4   **Widely Supported:** Yes

Sample:
```
<a style="background: red" href="page2.html">Page 2</a>
```

tabindex="n"

Indicates where the element appears in the tabbing order of the document.

Standard/Usage: HTML 4   **Widely Supported:** No

Sample:
```
<a href="food.html" tabindex="4">Food</a>
```

target="..."

Indicates the name of a specific frame into which you load the linked document. You establish frame names within the frame element. The value of this attribute can be any word you specify.

Standard/Usage: HTML 4 (Frames)   **Widely Supported:** Yes

Sample:
```
<a href="/frames/frame2.html" target="pages">Go to Page 2</a>
```

title="..."

Specifies text assigned to the element that you can use for context-sensitive help within the document. Browsers may use this to show tooltips over the hyperlink.

> **Standard/Usage:** HTML 4 **Widely Supported:** Yes
>
> **Sample:**
> ```
> <a href="page2.html" title="Go to the next page">Next page</a>
> ```

type="..."

Indicates the MIME type of the linked file or object. For example, specify `text/html`, `image/jpeg`, `application/java`, `text/css`, or `text/javascript`. For the full list of types, see

```
ftp://ftp.isi.edu/in-notes/iana/assignments/media-types/media-types
```

> **Standard/Usage:** HTML 4 **Widely Supported:** No
>
> **Sample:**
> ```
> <a href="shocknew.dcr" type="application/x-director">Choose Shockwave</a>
> ```

NOTE *The* `a` *element also accepts the* `lang`, `dir`, `onclick`, `ondblclick`, `onmousedown`, `onmouseup`, `onmouseover`, `onmousemove`, `onmouseout`, `onkeypress`, `onkeydown`, *and* `onkeyup` *attributes.*

abbr

Indicates an abbreviation in a document.

> **Standard/Usage:** HTML 4 **Widely Supported:** No **Empty:** No
>
> **Sample:**
> ```
> <p><abbr>ABBR</abbr> is an abbreviation for abbreviation.</p>
> ```

class="..."

Indicates which style class applies to the `abbr` element.

> **Standard/Usage:** HTML 4 **Widely Supported:** Yes
>
> **Sample:**
> ```
> <p><abbr class="casual">ABBR</abbr> is short for abbreviation.</p>
> ```

id="..."

Assigns a unique (within the document) ID selector to an instance of the `abbr` element. When you then assign a style to that ID selector, it affects only that one instance of the `abbr` element.

> **Standard/Usage:** HTML 4 **Widely Supported:** Yes
>
> **Sample:**
> ```
> <p><abbr id="123">ABBR</abbr> is short for abbreviation.</p>
> ```

style="..."

Specifies style sheet commands that apply to the abbreviation.

> **Standard/Usage:** HTML 4   **Widely Supported:** Yes
>
> **Sample:**
> ```
> <p><abbr style="background: blue; color: white">abbr</abbr> is short for
> abbreviation.</p>
> ```

title="..."

Specifies text assigned to the element. For the abbr element, use this to provide the expansion of the term. You can also use this attribute for context-sensitive help within the document. Browsers may use this to show tooltips over the text.

> **Standard/Usage:** HTML 4   **Widely Supported:** No
>
> **Sample:**
> ```
> <p><abbr title="Abbreviation">ABBR</abbr> is short for abbreviation.</p>
> ```

NOTE   *The* abbr *element also accepts the* lang, dir, onclick, ondblclick, onmousedown, onmouseup, onmouseover, onmousemove, onmouseout, onkeypress, onkeydown, *and* onkeyup *attributes.*

acronym

Indicates an acronym in a document.

> **Standard/Usage:** HTML 4   **Widely Supported:** No   **Empty:** No
>
> **Sample:**
> ```
> <p><acronym>HTTP</acronym> stands for Hypertext Transfer Protocol.</p>
> ```

class="..."

Indicates which style class applies to the acronym element.

> **Standard/Usage:** HTML 4   **Widely Supported:** Yes
>
> **Sample:**
> ```
> <p><acronym class="casual">HTTP</acronym> stands for Hypertext Transfer
> Protocol.</p>
> ```

id="..."

Assigns a unique ID selector to an instance of the acronym element. When you then assign a style to that ID selector, it affects only that one instance of the acronym element.

> **Standard/Usage:** HTML 4   **Widely Supported:** Yes
>
> **Sample:**
> ```
> <p><acronym id="123">HTTP</acronym> stands for Hypertext Transfer Protocol.</p>
> ```

style="..."

Specifies style sheet commands that apply to the acronym.

> **Standard/Usage:** HTML 4   **Widely Supported:** Yes

> **Sample:**

```
<p><acronym style="background: blue; color: white">ESP</acronym> stands for extra-
sensory perception.</p>
```

title="..."

Specifies text assigned to the element. For the acronym element, use this to provide the expansion of the term. You can also use this attribute for context-sensitive help within the document. Browsers may use this to show tooltips over the text.

> **Standard/Usage:** HTML 4   **Widely Supported:** No

> **Sample:**

```
<p><acronym title="Hypertext Transfer Protocol">HTTP</acronym> stands for Hypertext
Transfer Protocol.</p>
```

NOTE   The acronym *element also accepts the* lang, dir, onclick, ondblclick, onmousedown, onmouseup, onmouseover, onmousemove, onmouseout, onkeypress, onkeydown, *and* onkeyup *attributes.*

address

Used to provide contact information in a document. This element is sometimes used to contain footer information. The enclosed text is usually rendered in italics.

> **Standard/Usage:** HTML 2   **Widely Supported:** Yes   **Empty:** No

> **Sample:**

```
<address>RayComm, Inc.<br />
    <a href="mailto:webmaster@raycomm.com">Webmaster</a><br />
</address>
```

class="..."

Indicates the style class to apply to the address element.

> **Standard/Usage:** HTML 4   **Widely Supported:** Yes

> **Sample:**

```
<address class="casual">Author info</address>
```

id="..."

Assigns a unique ID selector to an instance of the address element. When you then assign a style to that ID selector, it affects only that one instance of the address element.

> **Standard/Usage:** HTML 4   **Widely Supported:** Yes

Sample:
```
<address id="123">Author info</address>
```

style="..."

Specifies style sheet commands that apply to the contents of the `address` element.

Standard/Usage: HTML 4   **Widely Supported:** Yes

Sample:
```
<address style="background: red">Author info</address>
```

title="..."

Specifies text assigned to the element. You can use this attribute for context-sensitive help within the document. Browsers may use this to show tooltips over the address text.

Standard/Usage: HTML 4   **Widely Supported:** No

Sample:
```
<address title="My Address">Author info</address>
```

NOTE   *The* `address` *element also accepts the* `lang`, `dir`, `onclick`, `ondblclick`, `onmousedown`, `onmouseup`, `onmouseover`, `onmousemove`, `onmouseout`, `onkeypress`, `onkeydown`, *and* `onkeyup` *attributes.*

applet

Embeds a Java applet object into an XHTML document. Typically, items that appear inside the `applet` element allow browsers that do not support Java applets to view alternative text. Browsers that do support Java ignore all information between the `applet` elements. This element is deprecated in HTML 4 in favor of the `object` element.

Standard/Usage: HTML 3.2; deprecated   **Widely Supported:** Yes   **Empty:** No

Sample:
```
<applet code="game.class">It appears your browser does not support Java. You're
missing out on a whole world of neat things!</applet>
```

align="left | center | right"

Specifies the relative horizontal alignment of the Java applet displayed. For example, a value of `center` tells the browser to place the applet evenly spaced between the left and right edges of the browser window. This attribute is deprecated in HTML 4 in favor of style sheets.

Standard/Usage: HTML 3.2; deprecated   **Widely Supported:** No

Sample:
```
<applet align="center" code="hangman.class">You lose. Would you like to play again?
Hit the RELOAD button.</applet>
```

alt="..."

Displays a textual description of a Java applet, if necessary.

Standard/Usage: HTML 3.2   **Widely Supported:** No

Sample:
```
<applet code="hangman.class" alt="A Game of Hangman">We could have had a relaxing
game of Hangman if your browser supported Java applets.</applet>
```

archive="url, url"

Used to provide a comma-separated list of URLs of classes and other resources to be preloaded to improve applet performance.

Standard/Usage: HTML 4   **Widely Supported:** Yes

Sample:
```
<applet code="hangman.class" archive="hgman.htm, hgman2.htm">Hangman</applet>
```

code="url"

Specifies the relative or absolute location of the Java bytecode file on the server.

Standard/Usage: HTML 3.2   **Widely Supported:** No

Sample:
```
<applet code="hangman.class">Hangman</applet>
```

codebase="url"

Specifies the directory where you can find all necessary Java class files on a Web server. If you set this attribute, you don't need to use explicit URLs in other references to the class files. For example, you would not need an absolute reference in the code attribute.

Standard/Usage: HTML 3.2   **Widely Supported:** No

Sample:
```
<applet codebase="http://www.raycomm.com/" code="hangman.class">If your browser
supported inline Java applets, you'd be looking at a Hangman game right
now.</applet>
```

height="n"

Specifies the height (in pixels or percentage of available space) of the Java applet object within the document.

Standard/Usage: HTML 3.2   **Widely Supported:** No

Sample:
```
<applet height="200" code="hangman.class">Because your browser does not support inline
Java applets, we won't be playing Hangman today.</applet>
```

hspace="n"

Specifies an amount of blank space (in pixels) to the left and right of the Java applet within the document.

Standard/Usage: HTML 3.2   **Widely Supported:** No

Sample:
```
<applet hspace="10" code="hangman.class">Sorry. Because your browser does not
support embedded Java applets, you'll have to play Hangman the old way.</applet>
```

name="..."

Assigns the applet instance a name so other elements can identify it within the document. This attribute is deprecated; use the id attribute instead of or together with name.

Standard/Usage: HTML 3.2; deprecated   **Widely Supported:** No

Sample:
```
<applet code="hangman.class" name="Hangman" id="Hangman"></applet>
```

object="url"

Specifies the relative or absolute location of the locally saved Java program.

Standard/Usage: HTML 4   **Widely Supported:** No

Sample:
```
<applet object="http://www.raycomm.com/hangman.class">Whoops! Your browser does not
support serialized Java applets. You may want to install a newer Web
browser.</applet>
```

title="..."

Specifies text assigned to the element. You can use this attribute for context-sensitive help within the document. Browsers may use this to show tooltips over the embedded applet, while aural browsers or accessibility aids might read it aloud.

Standard/Usage: HTML 4   **Widely Supported:** No

Sample:
```
<applet code="/java/thing.class" title="Thing">Thing</applet>
```

vspace="n"

Specifies the amount of vertical space (in pixels) above and below the Java applet.

Standard/Usage: HTML 3.2   **Widely Supported:** No

Sample:
```
<applet vspace="10" code="/hangman.class">If you had a Java-capable browser, you could
be playing Hangman!</applet>
```

width="n"

Specifies the width (in pixels) of a Java applet within a document.

>   **Standard/Usage:** HTML 3.2   **Widely Supported:** No

>   **Sample:**
>    ```
>    <applet width="350" code="hangman.class">Hangman can be a lot of fun, but it's more fun
>    if your browser supports Java. Sorry.</applet>
>    ```

NOTE   *The* `applet` *element also accepts the* `lang`, `dir`, `onclick`, `ondblclick`, `onmousedown`, `onmouseup`, `onmouseover`, `onmousemove`, `onmouseout`, `onkeypress`, `onkeydown`, *and* `onkeyup` *attributes.*

area

Defines an active area within a client-side image map definition (see the `map` element). It indicates an area where audiences can choose to link to another document.

>   **Standard/Usage:** HTML 3.2   **Widely Supported:** Yes   **Empty:** Yes

>   **Sample:**
>    ```
>    <area shape="rect" coords="20,8,46,30" href="food.html" />
>    ```

alt="..."

Provides a textual description for users who have text-only browsers, and should be used (and is required by the specifications to be included) for all images.

>   **Standard/Usage:** HTML 4; required   **Widely Supported:** Yes

>   **Sample:**
>    ```
>    <area alt="This blue rectangle links to blue.html" href="blue.html" />
>    ```

accesskey="..."

Associates a single keyboard key with the area.

>   **Standard/Usage:** HTML 4   **Widely Supported:** No

>   **Sample:**
>    ```
>    <area accesskey="b" />
>    ```

class="..."

Indicates the style class you want to apply to the `area` element.

>   **Standard/Usage:** HTML 4   **Widely Supported:** Yes

>   **Sample:**
>    ```
>    <area class="casual" shape="rect" coords="20,8,46,30" href="food.html" />
>    ```

coords="x1,y1,x2,y2..."

Identifies the coordinates within an image map that define the image map area. Measure coordinates, in pixels, from the top-left corner of the image.

Standard/Usage: HTML 3.2   Widely Supported: Yes

Sample:
```
<area shape="rect" coords="20,8,46,30" href="food.html" />
```

href="url"

Identifies the location of the document you want to load when the indicated image map area is selected.

Standard/Usage: HTML 3.2   Widely Supported: Yes

Sample:
```
<area shape="rect" coords="20,8,46,30" href="food.html" />
```

id="..."

Assigns a unique ID selector to an instance of the area element. When you then assign a style to that ID selector, it affects this instance of the area element.

Standard/Usage: HTML 4   Widely Supported: Yes

Sample:
```
<area id="123" />
```

nohref="nohref"

Defines an image map area that does not link to another document.

Standard/Usage: HTML 3.2   Widely Supported: Yes

Sample:
```
<area shape="rect" coords="20,8,46,30" nohref="nohref" />
```

shape="default | rect | circle | poly"

Specifies the type of shape used to represent the image map area.

Value	Shape Indicated
rect	Rectangle
circle	Circle
poly	Polygon bounded by three or more sides
default	Any area not otherwise defined

Standard/Usage: HTML 3.2   **Widely Supported:** Yes

Sample:
```
<area shape="rect" coords="20,8,46,30" href="food.html" />
```

style="..."

Specifies style sheet commands that apply to the image map area.

Standard/Usage: HTML 4   **Widely Supported:** No

Sample:
```
<area shape="rect" coords="20,8,46,30" href="food.html" style="background: red" />
```

tabindex="n"

Indicates where the image map area appears in the tabbing order of the document.

Standard/Usage: HTML 4   **Widely Supported:** Yes

Sample:
```
<area shape="rect" coords="20,8,46,30" href="food.html" tabindex="4" />
```

target="..."

Identifies the named frame in which the linked document should load. For example, when users select an area within an image map, the linked document may load in the same frame (the default if target is omitted) or in a different frame, specified by the value of target.

Standard/Usage: HTML 4 (Frames)   **Widely Supported:** Yes

Sample:
```
<area shape="rect" coords="20,8,46,30" href="food.html" target="leftframe" />
```

title="..."

Specifies text assigned to the element. You can use this attribute for context-sensitive help within the document. Browsers may use this to show tooltips over the image map area.

Standard/Usage: HTML 4   **Widely Supported:** No

Sample:
```
<area shape="rect" coords="20,8,46,30" href="food.html" title="food" id="food"/>
```

NOTE   The area *element also accepts the* lang, dir, onclick, ondblclick, onmousedown, onmouseup, onmouseover, onmousemove, onmouseout, onkeypress, onkeydown, *and* onkeyup *attributes.*

B

b

Indicates text that should appear in boldface.

Standard/Usage: HTML 2   **Widely Supported:** Yes   **Empty:** No

Sample:
```
The afternoon was <b>so</b> hot!
```

class="..."

Indicates which style class applies to the b element.

Standard/Usage: HTML 4   **Widely Supported:** Yes

Sample:
```
<b class="casual">Boom!</b>
```

id="..."

Assigns a unique ID selector to an instance of the b element. When you assign a style to that ID selector, it affects only that one instance of the b element.

Standard/Usage: HTML 4   **Widely Supported:** Yes

Sample:
```
I work for <b id="123">Widgets, Inc.</b>
```

style="..."

Specifies style sheet commands that apply to the contents of the b element.

Standard/Usage: HTML 4   **Widely Supported:** Yes

Sample:
```
<b style="background: red">text with red background</b>
```

title="..."

Specifies text assigned to the element. You can use this attribute for context-sensitive help within the document. Browsers may use this to show tooltips over the boldface text.

Standard/Usage: HTML 4   **Widely Supported:** No

Sample:
```
<b title="Species">Dog Species</b>
```

NOTE   *The* b *element also accepts the* lang, dir, onclick, ondblclick, onmousedown, onmouseup, onmouseover, onmousemove, onmouseout, onkeypress, onkeydown, *and* onkeyup *attributes.*

base

Identifies the location where all relative URLs in your document originate.

Standard/Usage: HTML 2   **Widely Supported:** Yes   **Empty:** Yes

Sample:
```
<base href="http://www.raycomm.com/techwhirl/" />
```

href="url"

Indicates the relative or absolute location of the base document.

Standard/Usage: HTML 2; required   **Widely Supported:** Yes

Sample:
```
<base href="http://www.raycomm.com/" />
```

target="..."

Identifies the named frame in which you load a document (see the href attribute).

Standard/Usage: HTML 4 (Frames)   **Widely Supported:** Yes

Sample:
```
<base href="http://www.raycomm.com/frames/" target="main" />
```

basefont

Provides a font setting for normal text within a document. Font settings (see the font element) within the document are relative to settings specified with this element. Use this element in the document header (between the head elements). The basefont element is deprecated in HTML 4 in favor of style sheets.

Standard/Usage: HTML 3.2; deprecated   **Widely Supported:** Yes   **Empty:** Yes

Sample:
```
<basefont size="5" />
```

color="#rrggbb" or "..."

Sets the font color of normal text within a document. Color names may substitute for the explicit RGB hexadecimal values. This attribute is deprecated in HTML 4 in favor of style sheets.

Standard/Usage: HTML 3.2; deprecated   **Widely Supported:** Yes

Sample:
```
<basefont size="2" color="#ff00cc" />
```

face="...", ..."

Specifies the font face of normal text within a document. You can set this attribute to a comma-separated list of font names. The browser will select the first font from the list provided that the font is installed on the user's computer. This attribute is deprecated in HTML 4 in favor of style sheets.

Standard/Usage: HTML 3.2; deprecated   **Widely Supported:** Yes

Sample:
```
<basefont face="Verdana, Helvetica, Arial" />
```

id="..."

Assigns a unique ID selector to an instance of the basefont element. When you then assign a style to that ID selector, it affects only that one instance of the basefont element.

Standard/Usage: HTML 4   **Widely Supported:** Yes

Sample:
```
<basefont size="+2" id="d3e" />
```

size="n"

Specifies the default font size of normal text within a document. Valid values are integer numbers in the range 1 and 7, with 3 being the default setting. This attribute is deprecated in HTML 4 in favor of style sheets.

Standard/Usage: HTML 3.2; deprecated   **Widely Supported:** Yes

Sample:
```
<basefont size="5" />
```

NOTE   The basefont *element also accepts the* lang *and* dir *attributes.*

bdo

Indicates text that should appear with the direction (left to right or right to left) specified, overriding other language-specific settings. The bdo element accepts the lang and dir attributes.

Standard/Usage: HTML 4   **Widely Supported:** No   **Empty:** No

Sample:
```
<p lang="HE" dir="rtl">This Hebrew text contains a number, <bdo="ltr">29381</bdo>,
that must appear left to right.</p>
```

bgsound

Embeds a background sound file within documents. Use in the document head of documents intended for users who use Internet Explorer.

Standard/Usage: Internet Explorer 2   **Widely Supported:** No   **Empty:** Yes

Sample:
```
<bgsound src="scream.wav" />
```

loop="n | infinite"

Specifies the number of times a background sound file repeats. The value infinite is the default.

> **Standard/Usage:** Internet Explorer 2   **Widely Supported:** No
>
> **Sample:**
> ```
> <bgsound src="bugle.wav" loop="2" />
> ```

src="url"

Indicates the absolute or relative location of the sound file.

> **Standard/Usage:** Internet Explorer 2   **Widely Supported:** No
>
> **Sample:**
> ```
> <bgsound src="wah.wav" />
> ```

big

Indicates that text displays in a larger font. Although this element is not deprecated, big is a presentational element and its use is discouraged in favor of style sheets.

> **Standard/Usage:** HTML 3.2   **Widely Supported:** Yes   **Empty:** No
>
> **Sample:**
> ```
> <big>Lunch</big>
> <p>Lunch will be served at 2 P.M.</p>
> ```

class="..."

Indicates which style class applies to the big element.

> **Standard/Usage:** HTML 4   **Widely Supported:** Yes
>
> **Sample:**
> ```
> <big class="casual">Instructions</big>
> ```

id="..."

Assigns a unique ID selector to an instance of the big element. When you then assign a style to that ID selector, it affects only that one instance of the big element.

> **Standard/Usage:** HTML 4   **Widely Supported:** Yes
>
> **Sample:**
> ```
> <big id="123">REMINDER:</big>
> Eat five servings of fruits and vegetables every day!
> ```

style="..."

Specifies style sheet commands that apply to the contents of the big element.

Standard/Usage: HTML 4   Widely Supported: Yes

Sample:
```
<big style="background: red">This text is red and big.</big>
```

title="..."

Specifies text assigned to the element. You can use this attribute for context-sensitive help within the document. Browsers may use this to show tooltips over the text inside the big element.

Standard/Usage: HTML 4   Widely Supported: No

Sample:
```
<big title="Bigger">This text is bigger.</big>
```

NOTE   *The* big *element also accepts the* lang, dir, onclick, ondblclick, onmousedown, onmouseup, onmouseover, onmousemove, onmouseout, onkeypress, onkeydown, *and* onkeyup *attributes.*

blink

A Netscape-specific element that makes text blink on and off. Style sheets offer the same functionality in a more widely recognized syntax (the **text-decoration** property with a value of blink).

Standard/Usage: Netscape Navigator   Widely Supported: No   Empty: No

Sample:
```
<p><blink>NEW INFO</blink>: We moved!</p>
```

class="..."

Indicates which style class applies to the blink element.

Standard/Usage: HTML 4   Widely Supported: Yes

Sample:
```
<blink class="casual">NEW INFORMATION</blink>
```

id="..."

Assigns a unique ID selector to an instance of the blink element. When you then assign a style to that ID selector, it affects only that one instance of the blink element.

Standard/Usage: HTML 4   Widely Supported: Yes

Sample:
```
<blink id="123">12-Hour Sale!</blink>
```

style="..."

Specifies style sheet commands that apply to the contents of the blink elements.

Standard/Usage: HTML 4   **Widely Supported:** No

Sample:
```
<blink style="background: red">This text is blinking and has a red background if
you're using Netscape Navigator.</blink>
```

blockquote

Useful for quoting a direct source within a document (a block quotation).

Standard/Usage: HTML 2   **Widely Supported:** Yes   **Empty:** No

Sample:
```
In So Long and Thanks for All the Fish, Douglas Adams wrote:
<blockquote>Man had always assumed that he was more intelligent than dolphins
because he had achieved so much... the wheel, New York, wars, and so on, whilst all
the dolphins had ever done was muck about in the water having a good time. But
conversely the dolphins believed themselves to be more intelligent than man for
precisely the same reasons.</blockquote>
```

cite="..."

Specifies a reference URL for the quotation.

Standard/Usage: HTML 4   **Widely Supported:** No

Sample:
```
<blockquote cite="http://www.clementmoore.com/">Twas the night...</blockquote>
```

class="..."

Indicates which style class applies to the blockquote element.

Standard/Usage: HTML 4   **Widely Supported:** Yes

Sample:
```
<blockquote class="holiday">Twas the night before Christmas... </blockquote>
```

id="..."

Assigns a unique ID selector to an instance of the blockquote element. When you then assign a style to that ID selector, it affects only that one instance of the blockquote element.

Standard/Usage: HTML 4   **Widely Supported:** Yes

Sample:
```
In So Long and Thanks for All the Fish, Douglas Adams wrote:
<blockquote id="DAq1">Man had always assumed that he was more intelligent than dolphins
because he had achieved so much...</blockquote>
```

style="..."
Specifies style sheet commands that apply to the contents of the blockquote element.

Standard/Usage: HTML 4   Widely Supported: Yes

Sample:
`<blockquote style="background: red">This quote is red.</blockquote>`

title="..."
Specifies text assigned to the element. You can use this attribute for context-sensitive help within the document. Browsers may use this to show tooltips over the quoted text.

Standard/Usage: HTML 4   Widely Supported: No

Sample:
`<blockquote title="Quotation">Quoted text goes here.</blockquote>`

NOTE   *The* blockquote *element also accepts the* lang, dir, onclick, ondblclick, onmousedown, onmouseup, onmouseover, onmousemove, onmouseout, onkeypress, onkeydown, *and* onkeyup *attributes.*

body

Acts as a container for the body of the document. It is a child of the html element and appears after the head element. In previous versions of HTML, the body element was used to set various color settings and background characteristics of the document; however, in HTML 4 and XHTML, those formatting attributes are deprecated in favor of style sheets.

Standard/Usage: HTML 2; required   Widely Supported: Yes   Empty: No

Sample:
```
<html xmlns="http://www.w3.org/1999/xhtml">
   <head>...</head>
   <body>
      <h1>hello!</h1>
   </body>
</html>
```

alink="#rrggbb" or "..."
Indicates the color of hyperlink text while the text is selected. Color names can substitute for the RGB hexadecimal values. This attribute is deprecated in HTML 4 in favor of style sheets.

Standard/Usage: HTML 3.2; deprecated   Widely Supported: Yes

Sample:
```
<body bgcolor="#000abc" text="#000000" link="#ffffff" vlink="#999999" alink="#ff0000">
   The rest of your document
</body>
```

background="url"

Specifies the relative or absolute location of an image file that tiles across the document's background. This attribute is deprecated in HTML 4 in favor of style sheets.

Standard/Usage: HTML 3.2; deprecated   **Widely Supported:** Yes

Sample:
```
<body background="images/slimey.gif">The rest of your document</body>
```

bgcolor="#rrggbb" or "..."

Indicates the color of a document's background. Color names can substitute for the RGB hexadecimal values. This attribute is deprecated in HTML 4 in favor of style sheets.

Standard/Usage: HTML 3.2; deprecated   **Widely Supported:** Yes

Sample:
```
<body bgcolor="#000abc" text="#000000" link="#ffffff" vlink="#999999" alink="#ff0000">
    The rest of your document
</body>
```

bgproperties="fixed"

Specifies the behavior of the background image (see the background attribute). The only current value for this attribute is fixed, which indicates that the background image remains in place as you scroll the document, creating a watermark effect.

Standard/Usage: Internet Explorer 2   **Widely Supported:** No

Sample:
```
<body background="waves.jpg" bgproperties="fixed">The rest of your document</body>
```

class="..."

Indicates which style class applies to the body element.

Standard/Usage: HTML 4   **Widely Supported:** Yes

Sample:
```
<body class="casual">The rest of your document</body>
```

id="..."

Assigns a unique ID selector to an instance of the body element. When you then assign a style to that ID selector, it affects only that one instance of the body element.

Standard/Usage: HTML 4   **Widely Supported:** Yes

Sample:
```
<body id="123">The rest of your document</body>
```

leftmargin="n"

Specifies the width (in pixels) of a margin of white space along the left edge of the entire document.

Standard/Usage: Internet Explorer 2   **Widely Supported:** No

Sample:
```
<body leftmargin="30">The rest of your document</body>
```

link="#rrggbb" or "..."

Indicates the color of hyperlink text within the document for documents not already visited by the browser. Color names can substitute for the RGB hexadecimal values. This attribute is deprecated in HTML 4 in favor of style sheets.

Standard/Usage: HTML 3.2; deprecated   **Widely Supported:** Yes

Sample:
```
<body bgcolor="#000abc" text="#000000" link="#ffffff" vlink="#999999" alink="#ff0000">
   The rest of your document
</body>
```

scroll="yes | no"

Indicates whether scrolling is possible within the document body.

Standard/Usage: Internet Explorer 4   **Widely Supported:** No

Sample:
```
<body bgcolor="silver" scroll="no">The rest of your document</body>
```

style="..."

Specifies style sheet commands that apply to the document body.

Standard/Usage: HTML 4   **Widely Supported:** Yes

Sample:
```
<body style="background: red">The rest of your document</body>
```

text="#rrggbb" or "..."

Indicates the color of normal text within the document. Color names can substitute for the RGB hexadecimal values. This attribute is deprecated in HTML 4 in favor of style sheets.

Standard/Usage: HTML 3.2; deprecated   **Widely Supported:** Yes

Sample:
```
<body bgcolor="#000abc" text="#000000" link="#ffffff" vlink="#999999"
alink="#ff0000"> The rest of your document
</body>
```

title="..."

Specifies text assigned to the element. You can use this attribute for context-sensitive help within the document. Browsers may use this to show tooltips.

Standard/Usage: HTML 4   **Widely Supported:** No

Sample:
```
<body title="Document body">The rest of your document</body>
```

topmargin="n"

Specifies the size (in pixels) of a margin of white space along the top edge of the entire document.

Standard/Usage: Internet Explorer 2   **Widely Supported:** No

Sample:
```
<body topmargin="10">The rest of your document</body>
```

vlink="#rrggbb" or "..."

Indicates the color of hyperlink text within the document for documents already visited by the browser. Color names can substitute for the RGB hexadecimal values. This attribute is deprecated in HTML 4 in favor of style sheets.

Standard/Usage: HTML 3.2; deprecated   **Widely Supported:** Yes

Sample:
```
<body bgcolor="#000abc" text="#000000" link="#ffffff" vlink="#999999" alink="#ff0000">
    The rest of your document</body>
```

NOTE *The* body *element also accepts the* lang, dir, onload, onunload, onclick, ondblclick, onmouse-down, onmouseup, onmouseover, onmousemove, onmouseout, onkeypress, onkeydown, *and* onkeyup *attributes.*

br

Breaks a line of continuous text and prevents text alignment around images.

Standard/Usage: HTML 2   **Widely Supported:** Yes   **Empty:** Yes

Sample:
```
I live at: <p>123 Nowhere Ave.<br />New York, NY 12345</p>
```

class="..."

Indicates which style class applies to the element.

Standard/Usage: HTML 4   **Widely Supported:** Yes

Sample:
```
<br class="casual" />
```

clear="all | left | right | none"

Discontinues alignment of text to inline graphic images. The sample demonstrates how you can force the text to appear after the image and not alongside it.

> **Standard/Usage:** HTML 3.2; deprecated   **Widely Supported:** Yes
>
> **Sample:**
> ```
> <img src="portrait.jpg" align="right" /><br clear="all" />
> <p>The above photo was taken when I was in Florida.</p>
> ```

id="..."

Assigns a unique ID selector to an instance of the br element. When you then assign a style to that ID selector, it affects only that one instance of the br element.

> **Standard/Usage:** HTML 4   **Widely Supported:** Yes
>
> **Sample:**
> ```
> <br id="123" />
> ```

style="..."

Specifies style sheet commands that apply to the br element, although applying a style to an element, like br, that is not visible is not likely to be effective most of the time.

> **Standard/Usage:** HTML 4   **Widely Supported:** Yes
>
> **Sample:**
> ```
> <br style="background: red" />
> ```

title="..."

Specifies text assigned to the element. You can use this attribute for context-sensitive help within the document. Browsers may use this to show tooltips.

> **Standard/Usage:** HTML 4   **Widely Supported:** No
>
> **Sample:**
> ```
> <br clear="all" title="stop image wrap" />
> ```

button

Sets up a button to submit or reset a form as well as to activate a script. Use the img element between the opening and closing button elements to specify a graphical button.

> **Standard/Usage:** HTML 4   **Widely Supported:** No   **Empty:** No
>
> **Sample:**
> ```
> <button type="button" value="Run Program" onClick(doit)>
>    <img src="button.gif" alt="Button" /></button>
> ```

accesskey="..."

Associates a single keyboard key with the button.

Standard/Usage: HTML 4   **Widely Supported:** Yes

Sample:
```
<button accesskey="B">Click Me! </button>
```

class="..."

Indicates which style class applies to the button element.

Standard/Usage: HTML 4   **Widely Supported:** Yes

Sample:
```
<button class="casual" type="submit" value="Submit">
   <img src="submit.gif" alt="submit" /></button>
```

disabled="disabled"

Denies access to the input method.

Standard/Usage: HTML 4   **Widely Supported:** No

Sample:
```
<button type="submit" disabled="disabled"><img src="button.gif" alt="button" />
</button>
```

id="..."

Assigns a unique ID selector to an instance of the input element. When you then assign a style to that ID selector, it affects only that one instance of the input element.

Standard/Usage: HTML 4   **Widely Supported:** Yes

Sample:
```
<button id="123" type="submit" value="Submit">
   <img src="button.gif" alt="Button" /></button>
```

name="..."

Gives a name for the value you pass to the form processor.

Standard/Usage: HTML 4   **Widely Supported:** Yes

Sample:
```
<button type="button" name="runprog" value="Click to run">
   <img src="button.gif" alt="Button" /></button>
```

style="..."

Specifies style sheet commands that apply to the element.

Standard/Usage: HTML 4   **Widely Supported:** Yes

Sample:
```
<button style="background: red" type="button" name="runprog" value="Click to Run">
   <img src="button.gif" alt="Button" /></button>
```

tabindex="n"

Specifies where the input method appears in the tab order. For example, `tabindex="3"` places the cursor at the button element after the user presses the Tab key three times.

Standard/Usage: HTML 4   **Widely Supported:** No

Sample:
```
<button type="button" name="runprog" value="Click to run" tabindex="5">
   <img src="button.gif" alt="Button" /></button>
```

title="..."

Specifies text assigned to the element. You can use this attribute for context-sensitive help within the document. Browsers may use this to show tooltips over the input method.

Standard/Usage: HTML 4   **Widely Supported:** No

Sample:
```
<button type="submit" name="cc" value="visa" title="VisaCard">
   <img src="visacard.gif" alt="VisaCard button" /></button>
```

type="submit | button | reset"

Indicates the kind of button to create. `submit` produces a button that, when selected, submits all the name-value pairs to the form processor. `reset` sets all the input methods to empty or default settings (as specified when the page was loaded). `button` creates a button with no specific behavior that can interact with scripts.

Standard/Usage: HTML 4   **Widely Supported:** Yes

Sample:
```
<button type="button" value="Send Data" onClick(verify())>Send Data
   <img src="button.gif" alt="Button" /></button>
```

value="..."

Sets the default value for the button face.

Standard/Usage: HTML 4   **Widely Supported:** No

Sample:
```
<button type="button" name="id" value="Press Me">
   <img src="button.gif" alt="Button" /></button>
```

NOTE The button *element also accepts the* lang, dir, onfocus, onblur, onclick, ondblclick, onmousedown, onmouseup, onmouseover, onmousemove, onmouseout, onkeypress, onkeydown, *and* onkeyup *attributes.*

C

caption

Used inside a table element to specify a description for the table.

Standard/Usage: HTML 3.2   **Widely Supported:** Yes   **Empty:** No

Sample:
```
<table>
    <caption valign="top" align="center">Test Grades for Cooking 101</caption>
    <tr><th>Student</th>  <th>Grade</th> </tr>
    <tr><td>B. Smith</td>  <td>88</td>     </tr>
    <tr><td>J. Doe</td>    <td>45</td>     </tr>
</table>
```

align="top | bottom | left | right"

Indicates whether the caption appears at the top (default) or the bottom, left, or right of the table. The values left and right were added in HTML 4, but this attribute is deprecated in HTML 4 in favor of style sheets.

Standard/Usage: HTML 3.2; deprecated   **Widely Supported:** Yes

Sample:
```
<caption align="top">Seattle Staff Directory</caption>
```

class="..."

Indicates which style class applies to the caption element.

Standard/Usage: HTML 4   **Widely Supported:** Yes

Sample:
```
<caption class="chemical">Hydrogen vs. Oxygen</caption>
```

id="..."

Assigns a unique ID selector to an instance of the caption element. When you then assign a style to that ID selector, it affects only that one instance of the caption element.

Standard/Usage: HTML 4   **Widely Supported:** Yes

Sample:
```
<table>
    <caption id="123">Great Painters</caption>…
</table>
```

style="..."

Specifies style sheet commands that apply to the contents of the caption element.

Standard/Usage: HTML 4   Widely Supported: Yes

Sample:
```
<caption style="background: red">This title caption will have a red
background.</caption>
```

title="..."
Specifies text assigned to the element. You can use this attribute for context-sensitive help within the document. Browsers may use this to show tooltips over the caption.

Standard/Usage: HTML 4   Widely Supported: Yes

Sample:
```
<caption title="Table caption">Great Painters</caption>
```

NOTE *The* caption *element also accepts the* lang, dir, onclick, ondblclick, onmousedown, onmouseup, onmouseover, onmousemove, onmouseout, onkeypress, onkeydown, *and* onkeyup *attributes.*

center

Positions text an equal distance between the left and right edges of the document. This element, now officially replaced by the <div align="center">, was included in HTML 3.2 only because of its widespread use.

Standard/Usage: HTML 3.2; deprecated   Widely Supported: Yes   Empty: No

Sample:
```
<center><h1>ONE-DAY SALE!</h1></center>
```

cite

Provides an in-text citation of a proper title such as the title of a book. Most browsers display the text inside the cite elements in italics.

Standard/Usage: HTML 2   Widely Supported: Yes   Empty: No

Sample:
```
<p>I've read <cite>The Hitchhiker's Guide to the Galaxy</cite> by Douglas Adams.</p>
```

class="..."
Indicates which style class applies to the cite element.

Standard/Usage: HTML 4   Widely Supported: Yes

Sample:
```
This came from Homer's <cite class="classic">Odyssey</cite>.
```

id="..."

Assigns a unique ID selector to an instance of the `cite` element. When you then assign a style to that ID selector, it affects only that one instance of the `cite` element.

Standard/Usage: HTML 4   **Widely Supported:** Yes

Sample:
```
I read about this in <cite id="123">World Weekly News</cite>.
```

style="..."

Specifies style sheet commands that apply to the contents of the `cite` element.

Standard/Usage: HTML 4   **Widely Supported:** Yes

Sample:
```
<cite style="background: red">...</cite>
```

title="..."

Specifies text assigned to the element. You can use this attribute for context-sensitive help within the document. Browsers may use this to show tooltips over the cited text.

Standard/Usage: HTML 4   **Widely Supported:** No

Sample:
```
<cite title="citation">FDA Vegetable Pamphlet</cite>
```

NOTE   The cite *element also accepts the* `lang`, `dir`, `onclick`, `ondblclick`, `onmousedown`, `onmouseup`, `onmouseover`, `onmousemove`, `onmouseout`, `onkeypress`, `onkeydown`, *and* `onkeyup` *attributes.*

code

Embeds excerpts of program source code into your document text. This is useful if you want to show program source code within a paragraph of normal text. For showing formatted segments of source code longer than one line, use the `pre` element.

Standard/Usage: HTML 2   **Widely Supported:** Yes   **Empty:** No

Sample:
```
To see the variable's value, use the <code>printf("%0.2f\n", cost);</code> function
call.
```

class="..."

Indicates which style class applies to the `code` element.

Standard/Usage: HTML 4   **Widely Supported:** Yes

Sample:
```
The <code class="casual">html</code> element is required.
```

id="..."

Assigns a unique ID selector to an instance of the code element. When you then assign a style to that ID selector, it affects only that one instance of the code element.

Standard/Usage: HTML 4   **Widely Supported:** Yes

Sample:
```
<code id="123">while(x) x--;</code>
```

style="..."

Specifies style sheet commands that apply to the contents of the code element.

Standard/Usage: HTML 4   **Widely Supported:** Yes

Sample:
```
<code style="background: red">while(x) x--;</code>
```

title="..."

Specifies text assigned to the element. You can use this attribute for context-sensitive help within the document. Browsers may use this to show tooltips over the code text.

Standard/Usage: HTML 4   **Widely Supported:** No

Sample:
```
<code title="c code">exit(1);</code>
```

NOTE   The code *element also accepts the* lang, dir, onclick, ondblclick, onmousedown, onmouseup, onmouseover, onmousemove, onmouseout, onkeypress, onkeydown, *and* onkeyup *attributes.*

col

Specifies properties for table columns.

Standard/Usage: HTML 4   **Widely Supported:** No   **Empty:** Yes

Sample:
```
<table>
   <colgroup>
      <col align="right" />
      <col align="center" />
   </colgroup>
   <tr>
      <td>This cell is aligned right.</td>
      <td>This cell is centered.</td>
   </tr>
</table>
```

align="left | right | center | justify | char"

Specifies how text within the table columns will line up with the edges of the table cells, or if the value is char, on a specific character (the decimal point by default).

Standard/Usage: HTML 4   **Widely Supported:** No

Sample:
```
<col align="center" />
```

char="..."

Specifies the character on which cell contents will align, if align="char". If you omit the char attribute, the default value is the decimal point in the specified language.

Standard/Usage: HTML 4   **Widely Supported:** No

Sample:
```
<col align="char" char="," />
```

charoff="n"

Specifies the number of characters from the left at which the alignment character appears.

Standard/Usage: HTML 4   **Widely Supported:** No

Sample:
```
<col align="char" char="," charoff="7" />
```

id="..."

Assigns a unique ID selector to an instance of the col element. When you assign a style to that ID selector, it affects only that one instance of the col element.

Standard/Usage: HTML 4   **Widely Supported:** Yes

Sample:
```
<col id="123" />
```

span="n"

Indicates the number of columns in the group.

Standard/Usage: HTML 4   **Widely Supported:** No

Sample:
```
<colgroup><col align="right" span="2" /></colgroup>
```

style="..."

Specifies style sheet commands that apply to the columns.

Standard/Usage: HTML 4   **Widely Supported:** Yes

Sample:
```
<col style="background: black" />
```

title="..."

Specifies text assigned to the element. You can use this attribute for context-sensitive help within the document. Browsers may use this to show tooltips over the table column.

Standard/Usage: HTML 4   **Widely Supported:** No

Sample:
```
<col title="Table column" />
```

width="n"

Specifies the horizontal dimension of a column (in pixels or as a percentage). Special values of `"0*"` force the column to the minimum required width, and `"2*"` requires that the column receive proportionately twice as much space as it otherwise would.

Standard/Usage: HTML 4   **Widely Supported:** No

Sample:
```
<col width="100" />
```

valign="top | bottom | middle | baseline"

Vertically position the contents of the table column.

Value	Effect
top	Positions the contents flush with the top of the column
bottom	Positions the contents flush with the bottom of the column
middle	Centers the contents between the top and bottom of the column
baseline	Aligns the contents with the baseline of the current text font

Standard/Usage: HTML 4   **Widely Supported:** No

Sample:
```
<col valign="top" />
```

NOTE   *The* col *element also accepts the* lang, dir, onclick, ondblclick, onmousedown, onmouseup, onmouseover, onmousemove, onmouseout, onkeypress, onkeydown, *and* onkeyup *attributes.*

colgroup

Specifies characteristics for a group of table columns.

Standard/Usage: HTML 4   **Widely Supported:** No   **Empty:** No

Sample:
```
<table>
   <colgroup valign="top">
      <col align="right" />
```

```
      <col align="center" />
   </colgroup>
   <tr>
      <td>This cell is aligned top and right.</td>
      <td>This cell is aligned top and centered.</td>
   </tr>
</table>
```

align="left | right | center | justify | char"

Specifies how text within the table columns lines up with the edges of the table cells, or if the value is char, on a specific character (the decimal point by default).

Standard/Usage: HTML 4   **Widely Supported:** No

Sample:
```
<colgroup align="center">...</colgroup>
```

char="..."

Specifies the character on which cell contents align, if align="char". If you omit the char attribute, the default value is the decimal point in the specified language.

Standard/Usage: HTML 4   **Widely Supported:** No

Sample:
```
<colgroup align="char" char=",">...</colgroup>
```

charoff="n"

Specifies the number of characters from the left at which the alignment character appears.

Standard/Usage: HTML 4   **Widely Supported:** No

Sample:
```
<colgroup align="char" char="," charoff="7">...</colgroup>
```

id="..."

Assigns a unique ID selector to an instance of the element. When you then assign a style to that ID selector, it affects only that one instance of the element.

Standard/Usage: HTML 4   **Widely Supported:** Yes

Sample:
```
<colgroup id="123">...</colgroup>
```

span="n"

Indicates how many consecutive columns exist in the column group and to which columns the specified attributes apply.

Standard/Usage: HTML 4   **Widely Supported:** No

Sample:
```
<colgroup span="2" align="left">…</colgroup>
```

style="..."

Specifies style sheet commands that apply to the contents of the `colgroup` element.

Standard/Usage: HTML 4   **Widely Supported:** Yes

Sample:
```
<colgroup style="color: red">…</colgroup>
```

title="..."

Specifies text assigned to the element. You can use this attribute for context-sensitive help within the document. Browsers may use this to show tooltips over the column group.

Standard/Usage: HTML 4   **Widely Supported:** No

Sample:
```
<colgroup title="column group">…</colgroup>
```

width="n"

Specifies the horizontal dimension of columns within the column group (in pixels or as a percentage).

Standard/Usage: HTML 4   **Widely Supported:** No

Sample:
```
<colgroup width="100"><col align="right" />…</colgroup>
```

valign="top | bottom | middle | baseline"

Vertically positions the contents of the table column.

Value	Effect
top	Positions the contents flush with the top of the column group
bottom	Positions the contents flush with the bottom of the column group
middle	Centers the contents between the top and bottom of the column group
baseline	Aligns the contents with the baseline of the current text font

Standard/Usage: HTML 4   **Widely Supported:** No

Sample:
```
<colgroup valign="top">…</colgroup>
```

NOTE *The* `colgroup` *element also accepts the* `lang`, `dir`, `onclick`, `ondblclick`, `onmousedown`, `onmouseup`, `onmouseover`, `onmousemove`, `onmouseout`, `onkeypress`, `onkeydown`, *and* `onkeyup` *attributes.*

D

dd

Contains a definition in a definition list (dl). Use this element inside the dl element. The dd element can contain block-level elements.

Standard/Usage: HTML 2   **Widely Supported:** Yes   **Empty:** No

Sample:
```
<dl>
    <dt>Butter</dt>
    <dd>Butter is a dairy product.</dd>
</dl>
```

class="..."

Indicates which style class applies to the dd element.

Standard/Usage: HTML 4   **Widely Supported:** Yes

Sample:
```
<dl>
    <dt>HTML</dt>
    <dd class="casual">Hypertext Markup Language</dd>
</dl>
```

id="..."

Assigns a unique ID selector to an instance of the dd element. When you then assign a style to that ID selector, it affects only that one instance of the dd element.

Standard/Usage: HTML 4   **Widely Supported:** Yes

Sample:
```
<dl>
    <dt>RS-232C</dt>
    <dd id="123">A standard for serial communication between computers.</dd>
</dl>
```

style="..."

Specifies style sheet commands that apply to the definition.

Standard/Usage: HTML 4   **Widely Supported:** Yes

Sample:
```
<dd style="background: blue; color: white">…</dd>
```

title="..."

Specifies text assigned to the element. You can use this attribute for context-sensitive help within the document. Browsers may use this to show tooltips over the definition.

Standard/Usage: HTML 4   **Widely Supported:** No

Sample:
```
<dd title="Definition">…</dd>
```

NOTE   *The* dd *element also accepts the* lang, dir, onclick, ondblclick, onmousedown, onmouseup, onmouseover, onmousemove, onmouseout, onkeypress, onkeydown, *and* onkeyup *attributes.*

del

Indicates text marked for deletion in the document. May be either block-level or inline, as necessary.

Standard/Usage: HTML 4   **Widely Supported:** No   **Empty:** No

Sample:
```
<p>HTTP stands for Hypertext Transfer <del>Transport</del>Protocol.</p>
```

cite="url"

Indicates the address of the reference (a definitive source, for example) for the deletion.

Standard/Usage: HTML 4   **Widely Supported:** No

Sample:
```
<del cite="http://www.w3.org/">HTML 3.0 was used for 10 years.</del>
```

class="…"

Indicates which style class applies to the del element.

Standard/Usage: HTML 4   **Widely Supported:** Yes

Sample:
```
<del class="casual">POP stands for Post Office Protocol.</del>
```

datetime="…"

Indicates the date and time in precisely this format: YYYY-MM-DDThh:mm:ssTZD. For example, 2001-07-14T08:30:00-07:00 indicates July 14, 2001, at 8:30 AM, in U.S. Mountain Time (7 hours from Greenwich time). This time could also be presented as 2001-07-14T08:30:00Z.

Standard/Usage: HTML 4   **Widely Supported:** No

Sample:
```
<del datetime="2001-07-14T08:30:00Z">POP stands for Post Office Protocol.</del>
```

id="…"

Assigns a unique ID selector to an instance of the element. When you then assign a style to that ID selector, it affects only that one instance of the del element.

Standard/Usage: HTML 4   **Widely Supported:** Yes

Sample:
```
<del id="123">WWW stands for World Wide Web.</del>
```

style="..."

Specifies style sheet commands that apply to the deleted text.

Standard/Usage: HTML 4   **Widely Supported:** Yes

Sample:
```
<del style="background: blue; color: white">ESP stands for extra-sensory
perception.</del>
```

title="..."

Specifies text assigned to the element. You can use this attribute for context-sensitive help within the document. Browsers may use this to show tooltips over the text.

Standard/Usage: HTML 4   **Widely Supported:** No

Sample:
```
<del title="Definition">More deleted text.</del>
```

NOTE   The del *element also accepts the* lang, dir, onclick, ondblclick, onmousedown, onmouseup, onmouseover, onmousemove, onmouseout, onkeypress, onkeydown, *and* onkeyup *attributes.*

dfn

Indicates the definition of a term in the document.

Standard/Usage: HTML 3.2   **Widely Supported:** No   **Empty:** No

Sample:
```
<dfn>HTTP stands for Hypertext Transfer Protocol.</dfn>
```

class="..."

Indicates which style class applies to the dfn element.

Standard/Usage: HTML 4   **Widely Supported:** Yes

Sample:
```
<dfn class="computer">POP stands for Post Office Protocol.</dfn>
```

id="..."

Assigns a unique ID selector to an instance of the dfn element. When you then assign a style to that ID selector, it affects only that one instance of the dfn element.

Standard/Usage: HTML 4   **Widely Supported:** Yes

Sample:
```
<dfn id="123">WWW stands for World Wide Web.</dfn>
```

style="..."

Specifies style sheet commands that apply to the definition.

Standard/Usage: HTML 4   Widely Supported: Yes

Sample:
```
<dfn style="background: blue; color: white">ESP stands for extra-sensory
perception.</dfn>
```

title="..."

Specifies text assigned to the element. You can use this attribute for context-sensitive help within the document. Browsers may use this to show tooltips over the definition text.

Standard/Usage: HTML 4   Widely Supported: No

Sample:
```
<dfn title="Definition">...</dfn>
```

NOTE   *The* dfn *element also accepts the* lang, dir, onclick, ondblclick, onmousedown, onmouseup, onmouseover, onmousemove, onmouseout, onkeypress, onkeydown, *and* onkeyup *attributes.*

dir

Contains a directory list. Use the li element to indicate list items within the list. Use ul rather than this deprecated element.

Standard/Usage: HTML 2; deprecated   Widely Supported: Yes   Empty: No

Sample:
```
Choose a music genre:
<dir>
   <li><a href="rock/">Rock</a></li>
   <li><a href="country/">Country</a></li>
   <li><a href="newage/">New Age</a></li>
</dir>
```

class="..."

Indicates which style class applies to the dir element.

Standard/Usage: HTML 4   Widely Supported: Yes

Sample:
```
<dir class="food">
   <li>Apples</li>
   <li>Kiwis</li>
   <li>Mangos</li>
   <li>Oranges</li>
</dir>
```

compact="compact"

Causes the list to appear in a compact format. This attribute probably will not affect the appearance of the list because most browsers do not present lists in more than one format. It's deprecated in HTML 4.

Standard/Usage: HTML 2; deprecated   **Widely Supported:** No

Sample:
```
<dir compact="compact">...</dir>
```

id="..."

Assigns a unique ID selector to an instance of the dir element. When you then assign a style to that ID selector, it affects only that one instance of the dir element.

Standard/Usage: HTML 4   **Widely Supported:** Yes

Sample:
```
<dir id="123">
   <li>Thingie 1</li>
   <li>Thingie 2</li>
</dir>
```

style="..."

Specifies style sheet commands that apply to the dir element.

Standard/Usage: HTML 4   **Widely Supported:** Yes

Sample:
```
<dir style="background: blue; color: white">
   <li>Thingie 1</li>
   <li>Thingie 2</li>
</dir>
```

title="..."

Specifies text assigned to the element. You can use this attribute for context-sensitive help within the document. Browsers may use this to show tooltips over the directory list.

Standard/Usage: HTML 4   **Widely Supported:** No

Sample:
```
<dir title="Directory List">...</dir>
```

NOTE   *The* dir *element also accepts the* lang, dir, onclick, ondblclick, onmousedown, onmouseup, onmouseover, onmousemove, onmouseout, onkeypress, onkeydown, *and* onkeyup *attributes.*

div

Indicates logical divisions within a document. You can use this element to apply alignment, line-wrapping, and particularly style sheet attributes to a section of your document. `<div align="center">` is the official replacement for the `center` element—although it's also deprecated in favor of using style sheets.

> **Standard/Usage:** HTML 3.2; deprecated   **Widely Supported:** No   **Empty:** No
>
> **Sample:**
> ```
> <div align="center" style="background: blue">All About Formic Acid</div>
> ```

align="left | center | right | justify"

Specifies whether the content of the section aligns with the left or right margins (`left`, `right`), if it's evenly spaced between them (`center`), or if it stretches between the left and right margins (`justify`). This attribute is deprecated in HTML 4 in favor of style sheets.

> **Standard/Usage:** HTML 3.2; deprecated   **Widely Supported:** No
>
> **Sample:**
> ```
> <div align="right">Look over here!</div>
> <div align="left">Now, look over here!</div>
> ```

class="..."

Indicates which style class applies to the `div` element.

> **Standard/Usage:** HTML 4   **Widely Supported:** Yes
>
> **Sample:**
> ```
> <div class="casual">...</div>
> ```

id="..."

Assigns a unique ID selector to an instance of the `div` element. When you then assign a style to that ID selector, it affects only that one instance of the `div` element.

> **Standard/Usage:** HTML 4   **Widely Supported:** Yes
>
> **Sample:**
> ```
> <div id="123">...</div>
> ```

nowrap="nowrap"

Disables line-wrapping for the section.

> **Standard/Usage:** Internet Explorer 4   **Widely Supported:** No
>
> **Sample:**
> ```
> <div align="left" nowrap="nowrap">The contents of this section will not automatically
> wrap as you size the window.</div>
> ```

style="..."

Specifies style sheet commands that apply to the contents of the div element.

> **Standard/Usage:** HTML 4   **Widely Supported:** Yes

> **Sample:**
> ```
> <div style="background: red">...</div>
> ```

title="..."

Specifies text assigned to the element. You can use this attribute for context-sensitive help within the document. Browsers may use this to show tooltips over the contents of the div element.

> **Standard/Usage:** HTML 4   **Widely Supported:** No

> **Sample:**
> ```
> <div title="Title" class="casual">...</div>
> ```

NOTE   The div element also accepts the lang, dir, onclick, ondblclick, onmousedown, onmouseup, onmouseover, onmousemove, onmouseout, onkeypress, onkeydown, *and* onkeyup *attributes.*

dl

Contains the dt and dd elements that form the term and definition portions of a definition list.

> **Standard/Usage:** HTML 2   **Widely Supported:** Yes   **Empty:** No

> **Sample:**
> ```
> <dl>
>    <dt>Hygeine</dt>
>    <dd>Being clean.</dd>
> </dl>
> ```

class="..."

Indicates which style class applies to the dl element.

> **Standard/Usage:** HTML 4   **Widely Supported:** Yes

> **Sample:**
> ```
> <dl class="computer">
>    <dt>RAM</dt>
>    <dd>Random Access Memory</dd>
> </dl>
> ```

compact="compact"

Causes the definition list to appear in a compact format. This attribute probably will not affect the appearance of the list because most browsers do not present lists in more than one format. It's deprecated in HTML 4.

Standard/Usage: HTML 2; deprecated   **Widely Supported:** No

Sample:
```
<dl compact="compact">...</dl>
```

id="..."
Assigns a unique ID selector to an instance of the dd element. When you then assign a style to that ID selector, it affects only that one instance of the dd element.

Standard/Usage: HTML 4   **Widely Supported:** Yes

Sample:
```
<dl id="123">
   <dt>food</dt>
   <dd>We will be eating three meals/day.</dd>
</dl>
```

style="..."
Specifies style sheet commands that apply to contents of the dl element.

Standard/Usage: HTML 4   **Widely Supported:** Yes

Sample:
```
<dl style="background: red">...</dl>
```

title="..."
Specifies text assigned to the element. You can use this attribute for context-sensitive help within the document. Browsers may use this to show tooltips over the definition list.

Standard/Usage: HTML 4   **Widely Supported:** No

Sample:
```
<dl title="Definition List">...</dl>
```

NOTE   *The* dl *element also accepts the* lang, dir, onclick, ondblclick, onmousedown, onmouseup, onmouseover, onmousemove, onmouseout, onkeypress, onkeydown, *and* onkeyup *attributes.*

dt
Contains the terms inside a definition list. Place the dt element inside dl elements.

Standard/Usage: HTML 2   **Widely Supported:** Yes   **Empty:** No

Sample:
```
<dl>
   <dt>Hygeine</dt>
   <dd>Being clean.</dd>
</dl>
```

class="..."

Indicates which style class applies to the dt element.

Standard/Usage: HTML 4   Widely Supported: Yes

Sample:
```
<dl>
    <dt class="casual">CUL8R</dt>
    <dd>See You Later</dd>
</dl>
```

id="..."

Assigns a unique ID selector to an instance of the dt element. When you then assign a style to that ID selector, it affects only that one instance of the dt element.

Standard/Usage: HTML 4   Widely Supported: Yes

Sample:
```
<dl>
    <dt id="123">Caffeine</dt>
    <dd>What most people need to start their days.</dd>
</dl>
```

style="..."

Specifies style sheet commands that apply to the contents of the dt element.

Standard/Usage: HTML 4   Widely Supported: Yes

Sample:
```
<dt style="background: red">...</dt>
```

title="..."

Specifies text assigned to the element. You can use this attribute for context-sensitive help within the document. Browsers may use this to show tooltips over the definition term.

Standard/Usage: HTML 4   Widely Supported: No

Sample:
```
<dt title="Term">XHTML</dt>
<dd>HTML reformulated as an XML application</dd>
```

NOTE   *The* dt *element also accepts the* lang, dir, onclick, ondblclick, onmousedown, onmouseup, onmouseover, onmousemove, onmouseout, onkeypress, onkeydown, *and* onkeyup *attributes.*

E

em

Makes the text stand out. Browsers usually render the enclosed text in italics or boldface.

Standard/Usage: HTML 2   **Widely Supported:** Yes   **Empty:** No

Sample:
```
It's <em>very</em> important to read the instructions before beginning.
```

class="..."

Indicates which style class applies to the em element.

Standard/Usage: HTML 4   **Widely Supported:** Yes

Sample:
```
Did you say my house was on <em class="urgent">FIRE?!</em>
```

id="..."

Assigns a unique ID selector to an instance of the em element. When you then assign a style to that ID selector, it affects only that one instance of the em element.

Standard/Usage: HTML 4   **Widely Supported:** Yes

Sample:
```
I have complained <em id="123">ten</em> times about the leaking faucet.
```

style="..."

Specifies style sheet commands that apply to the contents of the em element.

Standard/Usage: HTML 4   **Widely Supported:** Yes

Sample:
```
You want this <em style="background: red">when</em>?
```

title="..."

Specifies text assigned to the element. You can use this attribute for context-sensitive help within the document. Browsers may use this to show tooltips over the emphasized text.

Standard/Usage: HTML 4   **Widely Supported:** No

Sample:
```
<em title="Emphasis">…</em>
```

NOTE   The em *element also accepts the* lang, dir, onclick, ondblclick, onmousedown, onmouseup, onmouseover, onmousemove, onmouseout, onkeypress, onkeydown, *and* onkeyup *attributes.*

embed

Places an embedded object into a document. Examples of embedded objects include MIDI files and digital video files. Because the embed element is not part of the HTML standard, you should use the object element instead. If the browser does not have built-in support for an object, users will need a plug-in to use the object within the document. This element was introduced in Netscape Navigator, but it's also supported by Internet Explorer.

Standard/Usage: Netscape Navigator, Internet Explorer 3   **Widely Supported:** No
Empty: Yes

Sample:
```
<embed src="fur_elise.midi" />
```

accesskey="..."

Specifies a single keyboard key that binds to the embedded object.

Standard/Usage: Internet Explorer 4   **Widely Supported:** No

Sample:
```
<embed src="st.ocx" accesskey="e" />
```

align="left│right│center│texttop│top│absbottom│absmiddle│baseline│bottom"

Indicates how an embedded object is positioned relative to the document borders and surrounding contents.

Value	Effect
left	Floats the embedded object between the edges of the window, on the left side
right	Floats the embedded object between the edges of the window, on the right side
center	Floats the embedded object between the edges of the window, evenly between left and right
texttop	Aligns the top of the embedded object with the top of the current text
top	Aligns the top of the embedded object with the top of the current text
absmiddle	Aligns the middle of the embedded object with the middle of the current text
absbottom	Aligns the bottom of the embedded object with the bottom of the current text
baseline	Aligns the bottom of the embedded object with the baseline of the surrounding text
bottom	Aligns the bottom of the embedded object with the baseline of the surrounding text

Standard/Usage: Internet Explorer 4   **Widely Supported:** No

Sample:
```
<embed src="song.mid" align="center" />
```

height="n"

Specifies the vertical dimension of the embedded object.

> **Standard/Usage:** Netscape Navigator, Internet Explorer 3; required   **Widely Supported:** No

> **Sample:**
> ```
> <embed src="rocket.avi" width="50" height="40" />
> ```

src="url"

Indicates the relative or absolute location of the file containing the object you want to embed.

> **Standard/Usage:** Netscape Navigator, Internet Explorer 3; required   **Widely Supported:** No

> **Sample:**
> ```
> <embed src="beethoven_9.midi" />
> ```

title="..."

Specifies text assigned to the element. You can use this attribute for context-sensitive help within the document. Browsers may use this to show tooltips over the embedded object.

> **Standard/Usage:** Internet Explorer 4   **Widely Supported:** No

> **Sample:**
> ```
> <embed src="explode.avi" title="movie" />
> ```

width="n"

Indicates the horizontal dimension of the embedded object.

> **Standard/Usage:** Netscape Navigator, Internet Explorer 3; required   **Widely Supported:** No

> **Sample:**
> ```
> <embed src="cartoon.avi" width="50" />
> ```

NOTE   *The* embed *element also accepts the* lang, dir, onclick, ondblclick, onmousedown, onmouseup, onmouseover, onmousemove, onmouseout, onkeypress, onkeydown, *and* onkeyup *attributes.*

F

fieldset

Groups related form elements.

> **Standard/Usage:** HTML 4   **Widely Supported:** No   **Empty:** No

> **Sample:**
> ```
> <form>
>    <fieldset>
>       ...Logically related field elements...
>    </fieldset>...
> </form>
> ```

class="..."

Indicates which style class applies to the `fieldset` element.

Standard/Usage: HTML 4   **Widely Supported:** Yes

Sample:
```
<fieldset class="casual">…</fieldset>
```

id="..."

Assigns a unique ID selector to an instance of the `fieldset` element. When you then assign a style to that ID selector, it affects only that one instance of the `fieldset` element.

Standard/Usage: HTML 4   **Widely Supported:** Yes

Sample:
```
<fieldset id="123">…</fieldset>
```

style="..."

Specifies style sheet commands that apply to the contents of the `fieldset` element.

Standard/Usage: HTML 4   **Widely Supported:** Yes

Sample:
```
<fieldset style="background: red">…</fieldset>
```

title="..."

Specifies text assigned to the element. You can use this attribute for context-sensitive help within the document. Browsers may use this to show tooltips over the text.

Standard/Usage: HTML 4   **Widely Supported:** No

Sample:
```
<fieldset title="Personal data fields">…</fieldset>
```

NOTE   *The* `fieldset` *element also accepts the* `lang`, `dir`, `onclick`, `ondblclick`, `onmousedown`, `onmouseup`, `onmouseover`, `onmousemove`, `onmouseout`, `onkeypress`, `onkeydown`, *and* `onkeyup` *attributes.*

font

Alters or sets font characteristics of the font the browser uses to display text. This element is deprecated in HTML 4 in favor of style sheets.

Standard/Usage: HTML 3.2; deprecated   **Widely Supported:** Yes   **Empty:** No

Sample:
```
That cat was really <font size="+3">BIG</font>!
```

color="#rrggbb" or "..."
Indicates the color the browser uses to display text. Color names can substitute for the RGB hexadecimal values. This attribute is deprecated in HTML 4 in favor of style sheets.

Standard/Usage: HTML 3.2; deprecated   **Widely Supported:** Yes

Sample:
```
<font color="#ff0000"><h2>Win A Trip!</h2></font>
<font color="lightblue"><p>That's right! A trip to Hawaii can be yours if you
scratch off the right number!</font>
```

face="..., ..."
Specifies a comma-separated list of font names the browser uses to render text. If the browser does not have access to the first named font, it tries the second, then the third, and so forth. This attribute is deprecated in favor of style sheets.

Standard/Usage: HTML 4; deprecated   **Widely Supported:** Yes

Sample:
```
<font size="+1" face="AvantGarde, Helvetica, Lucida Sans, Arial">This text will appear
in AvantGarde if it's available.</font>
```

size="n"
Specifies the size of the text affected by the font element. You can specify the size relative to the base font size (see the basefont element), which is normally 3. You can also specify the size as a digit in the range 1 through 7. This attribute is deprecated in HTML 4 in favor of style sheets.

Standard/Usage: HTML 3.2; deprecated   **Widely Supported:** Yes

Sample:
```
<basefont size="4" />
<font size="+2">This is a font of size 6.</font>
<font size="1">This is a font of size 1.</font>
```

form

Sets up a container for a form element. Within the form element, you can place form input elements such as fieldset, input, select, and textarea.

Standard/Usage: HTML 2   **Widely Supported:** Yes

Empty: No

Sample:
```
<form method="post" action="/cgi-bin/search.pl">
   Search: <input type=text name="name" size="20" /><br />
   <input type="submit" value="Start Search" />
   <input type="reset" />
</form>
```

accept-charset="..."

Specifies the character encodings for input data that the server processing the form must accept. The value is a list of character sets as defined in RFC2045, separated by commas or spaces.

Standard/Usage: HTML 4   **Widely Supported:** No

Sample:
```
<form method="post" accept-charset="ISO-8859-1" action="/stat-collector.cgi">…</form>
```

accept="..."

Specifies a list of MIME types, separated by commas, that the server processing the form will handle correctly.

Standard/Usage: HTML 4   **Widely Supported:** No

Sample:
```
<form method="post" accept="image/gif, image/jpeg" action="/image-
collector.cgi">…</form>
```

action="url"

Specifies the absolute or relative location of the form-processing CGI application.

Standard/Usage: HTML 2; required   **Widely Supported:** Yes

Sample:
```
<form method="post" action="/stat-collector.cgi">…</form>
```

class="..."

Indicates which style class applies to the `form`.

Standard/Usage: HTML 4   **Widely Supported:** Yes

Sample:
```
<form method="post" class="casual" action="/stat-collector.cgi">…</form>
```

enctype="..."

Specifies the MIME type used to submit (post) the form to the server. The default value is `"appli-cation/x-www-form-urlencoded"`. Use the value `"multipart/form-data"` when the returned document includes files.

Standard/Usage: HTML 4   **Widely Supported:** No

Sample:
```
<form method="post" enctype="application/x-www-form-urlencoded"
    action="/stat-collector.cgi">…</form>
```

id="..."

Assigns a unique ID selector to an instance of the `form` element. When you then assign a style to that ID selector, it affects only that one instance of the `form` element.

Standard/Usage: HTML 4   **Widely Supported:** Yes

Sample:
```
<form action="/cgi-bin/ttt.pl" method="get" id="123">...</form>
```

method="post | get"

Changes how form data is transmitted to the form processor. When you use `get`, the form data is given to the form processor in the form of an environment variable (`query_string`). When you use `post`, the form data is given to the form processor as the standard input to the program.

Standard/Usage: HTML 2   **Widely Supported:** Yes

Sample:
```
<form method="post" action="/cgi-bin/www-search">
    Enter search keywords: <input type="text" name="query" size="20" />
    <input type="submit" value="search" />
</form>
```

name="..."

Assigns the form a name accessible by bookmark, script, and applet resources. This attribute is deprecated; use the `id` attribute instead of or together with `name`.

Standard/Usage: HTML 4; deprecated   **Widely Supported:** No

Sample:
```
<form method="post" action="/cgi-bin/ff.pl" name="ff" id="ff">...</form>
```

style="..."

Specifies style sheet commands that apply to the contents of the `form` element.

Standard/Usage: HTML 4   **Widely Supported:** Yes

Sample:
```
<form style="background: red">...</form>
```

target="..."

Identifies in which previously named frame the output from the form processor should appear.

Standard/Usage: HTML 4 (Frames)   **Widely Supported:** Yes

Sample:
```
<form target="output" method="get" action="/cgi-bin/thingie.sh">...</form>
```

title="..."

Specifies text assigned to the element. You can use this attribute for context-sensitive help within the document. Browsers may use this to show tooltips over the fill-out form.

Standard/Usage: HTML 4   **Widely Supported:** No

Sample:
```
<form method="post" action="/cgi-bin/ff.pl" title="Fill-out form">…</form>
```

NOTE   *The* form *element also accepts the* lang, dir, onsubmit, onreset, onclick, ondblclick, onmousedown, onmouseup, onmouseover, onmousemove, onmouseout, onkeypress, onkeydown, *and* onkeyup *attributes.*

frame

Defines a frame within a frame set (see the frameset element). The frame element specifies the source file and visual characteristics of a frame.

Standard/Usage: HTML 4 (Frames)   **Widely Supported:** Yes   **Empty:** Yes

Sample:
```
<frameset rows="*,70">
  <frame src="frames/body.html" name="body" />
  <frame src="frames/buttons.html" name="buttons" scrolling="no"
      noresize="noresize" />
</frameset>
```

bordercolor="#rrggbb" or "..."

Specifies the color of the border around the frame. Use the color's hexadecimal RGB values or the color name.

Standard/Usage: Internet Explorer 4, Netscape Navigator 3   **Widely Supported:** Yes

Sample:
```
<frame src="hits.html" bordercolor="red" />
```

class="..."

Indicates which style class applies to the frame element.

Standard/Usage: HTML 4   **Widely Supported:** Yes

Sample:
```
<frame src="hits.html" class="casual" />
```

frameborder="1|0"

Indicates whether the frame's border is visible. A value of 1 (default) indicates that the border is visible; 0 indicates that it's invisible.

Standard/Usage: HTML 4 (Frames)   **Widely Supported:** Yes

Sample:
```
<frame src="weather.html" frameborder="0" />
```

id="..."
Assigns a unique ID selector to an instance of the frame element. When you then assign a style to that ID selector, it affects only that one instance of the frame element.

Standard/Usage: HTML 4   **Widely Supported:** Yes

Sample:
```
<frame src="weather.html" id="123" />
```

longdesc="url"
Specifies the URL of a long description of the frame.

Standard/Usage: HTML 4 (Frames)   **Widely Supported:** Yes

Sample:
```
<frame src="cats.html" longdesc="whycatsrcool.htm" />
```

marginheight="n"
Specifies the vertical dimension (in pixels) of the top and bottom margins in a frame.

Standard/Usage: HTML 4 (Frames)   **Widely Supported:** Yes

Sample:
```
<frame src="cats.html" marginheight="10" />
```

marginwidth="n"
Specifies the horizontal dimension (in pixels) of the left and right margins in a frame.

Standard/Usage: HTML 4 (Frames)   **Widely Supported:** Yes

Sample:
```
<frame src="dogs.html" marginwidth="10" />
```

name="..."
Gives the frame you're defining a name. You can use this name later to load new documents into the frame (see the target attribute) and within scripts to control attributes of the frame. Reserved names with special meaning include _blank, _parent, _self, and _top.

Standard/Usage: HTML 4 (Frames)   **Widely Supported:** Yes

Sample:
```
<frame src="/cgi-bin/weather.cgi" name="weather" id="weather" />
```

noresize="noresize"

Makes a frame's dimensions unchangeable. Otherwise, if a frame's borders are visible, users can resize the frame by selecting a border and moving it with the mouse.

Standard/Usage: HTML 4 (Frames)   **Widely Supported:** Yes

Sample:
```
<frame src="bottom.html" name="bottom" id="bottom" noresize="noresize"
scrolling="no" />
```

scrolling="yes|no|auto"

Indicates whether a scroll bar is present within a frame when text dimensions exceed the dimensions of the frame. Set `scrolling="no"` when using a frame to display only an image.

Standard/Usage: HTML 4 (Frames)   **Widely Supported:** Yes

Sample:
```
<frame name="titleimg" id="titleimg" src="title.gif" scrolling="no" />
```

src="url"

Specifies the relative or absolute location of a document that you want to load within the defined frame.

Standard/Usage: HTML 4 (Frames)   **Widely Supported:** Yes

Sample:
```
<frame name="main" id="main" src="intro.html" />
```

style="..."

Specifies style sheet commands that apply to the frame.

Standard/Usage: HTML 4   **Widely Supported:** Yes

Sample:
```
<frame name="main" id="main" src="intro.html" style="background: red" />
```

title="..."

Specifies text assigned to the element. You can use this attribute for context-sensitive help within the document. Browsers may use this to show tooltips over the fill-out form.

Standard/Usage: HTML 4   **Widely Supported:** No

Sample:
```
<frame name="main" id="main" src="intro.html" title="Main Frame" />
```

frameset

Contains frame definitions and specifies frame spacing, dimensions, and attributes. Place `frame` and `noframes` elements inside `frameset` elements.

Standard/Usage: HTML 4 (Frames)   **Widely Supported:** Yes   **Empty:** No

Sample:
```
<frameset cols="*,70">
   <frame src="frames/body.html" name="body" id="body" />
   <frame src="frames/side.html" name="side" id="side" />
</frameset>
```

border="n"

Specifies the thickness of borders (in pixels) around frames defined within the frameset. You can also control border thickness with the frame element.

Standard/Usage: Netscape Navigator 3, Internet Explorer 4   **Widely Supported:** No

Sample:
```
<frameset cols="*,150" border="5">
   <frame src="left.html" name="main" id="main" />
   <frame src="side.html" name="side" id="side" />
</frameset>
```

bordercolor="#rrggbb" or "…"

Sets the color of the frame borders. Color names can substitute for the hexadecimal RGB color values.

Standard/Usage: Netscape Navigator 3, Internet Explorer 4   **Widely Supported:** Yes

Sample:
```
<frameset bordercolor="red" rows="100,* ">
   <frame src="top.html" name="title" id="title" />
   <frame src="story.html" name="story" id="story" />
</frameset>
```

class="…"

Indicates which style class applies to the frameset.

Standard/Usage: HTML 4   **Widely Supported:** Yes

Sample:
```
<frameset bordercolor="red" class="casual">
   <frame src="top.html" name="title" id="title" />
   <frame src="story.html" name="story" id="story" />
</frameset>
```

cols="…"

Specifies the number and dimensions of the vertical frames within the current frameset.

Set cols to a comma-separated list of numbers or percentages to indicate the width of each frame. Use the asterisk (*) to represent a variable width. A frame of variable width fills the space left over after the browser formats space for the other frames (<frameset cols="100,400,* ">).

Setting cols with percentage values controls the ratio of frame horizontal space relative to the amount of space available within the browser (<frameset cols="10%,*">).

You cannot use cols and rows in the same element.

Standard/Usage: HTML 4 (Frames)   **Widely Supported:** Yes

Sample:
```
<frameset cols="*,100,* ">
   <frame src="left.html" name="left" id="left" />
   <frame src="middle.html" name="middle" id="middle" />
   <frameset rows="2">
      <frame src="top.html" name="top" id="top" />
      <frame src="bottom.html" name="bottom" id="bottom" />
   </frameset>
</frameset>
```

framespacing="n"

Specifies the space (in pixels) between frames within the browser window.

Standard/Usage: Internet Explorer 3   **Widely Supported:** No

Sample:
```
<frameset rows="*,100" framespacing="10">
   <frame src="top.html" name="top" id="top" />
   <frame src="middle.html" name="middle" id="middle" />
</frameset>
```

id="..."

Assigns a unique ID selector to an instance of the frameset element. When you then assign a style to that ID selector, it affects only that one instance of the frameset element.

Standard/Usage: HTML 4   **Widely Supported:** Yes

Sample:
```
<frameset rows="*,100" framespacing="10" id="123" >
   <frame src="top.html" name="top" id="top" />
   <frame src="middle.html" name="middle" id="middle" />
</frameset>
```

rows="..."

Specifies the number and dimensions of the horizontal frames within the current frameset.

Set rows to a comma-separated list of numbers or percentages to indicate the height of each frame. Use the asterisk (*) to represent a variable height. A frame of variable height fills the space remaining after the browser formats space for the other frames (<frameset rows="100,400,* ">).

Setting rows to a comma-separated list of percentages allows you to control the ratio of frame vertical space relative to the space available within the browser (<frameset rows="10%,*">).

You cannot use rows and cols in the same element.

Standard/Usage: HTML 4 (Frames)   **Widely Supported:** Yes

Sample:
```
<frameset rows="*,100,* ">
   <frame src="top.html" name="top" id="top" />
```

```
    <frame src="middle.html" name="middle" id="middle" />
    <frameset cols="2">
        <frame src="bottom1.html" name="left" id="left" />
        <frame src="bottom2.html" name="right" id="right" />
    </frameset>
</frameset>
```

style="..."

Specifies style sheet commands that apply to the contents of the `frameset` element.

Standard/Usage: HTML 4   **Widely Supported:** No

Sample:
```
<frameset rows="100,* " style="background: red">
    <frame src="top.html" name="title" id="title" />
    <frame src="story.html" name="story" id="story" />
</frameset>
```

title="..."

Specifies text assigned to the element. You can use this attribute for context-sensitive help within the document. Browsers may use this to show tooltips over the frame.

Standard/Usage: HTML 4   **Widely Supported:** No

Sample:
```
<frameset rows="100,* " title="Stories">
    <frame src="top.html" name="title" id="title" />
    <frame src="story.html" name="story" id="story" />
</frameset>
```

NOTE   The `frameset` *element also accepts the* `onload` *and* `onunload` *attributes.*

H

h*n*

Specifies headings in a document. Headings are numbered 1–6, with `h1` representing the heading for the main heading in the document and `h3` representing a nested subtopic. Generally, text inside heading elements appears in boldface and may be larger than normal document text.

Standard/Usage: HTML 2   **Widely Supported:** Yes   **Empty:** No

Sample:
```
<h1>Caring for Your Canary</h1>
<p>This document explains how you should take care of a canary.</p>
<h2>Feeding</h2>
<h2>Caging</h2>
```

align="left | center | right"

Positions the heading in the left, right, or center of a document. This attribute is deprecated in HTML 4 in favor of style sheets.

Standard/Usage: HTML 3.2; deprecated   **Widely Supported:** Yes

Sample:
```
<h3 align="center">History of the Platypus</h3>
```

class="..."

Indicates which style class applies to the hn element.

Standard/Usage: HTML 4   **Widely Supported:** Yes

Sample:
```
<h1 class="casual" align="left">River Tours</h1>
```

id="..."

Assigns a unique ID selector to an instance of the hn element. When you then assign a style to that ID selector, it affects only that one instance of the hn element.

Standard/Usage: HTML 4   **Widely Supported:** Yes

Sample:
```
<h2 id="123">Paper Products</h2>
```

style="..."

Specifies style sheet commands that apply to the heading.

Standard/Usage: HTML 4   **Widely Supported:** Yes

Sample:
```
<h1 style="background: red">Heading 1</h1>
```

title="..."

Specifies text assigned to the element. You can use this attribute for context-sensitive help within the document. Browsers may use this to show tooltips over the heading.

Standard/Usage: HTML 4   **Widely Supported:** No

Sample:
```
<h1 title="Headline">Meals On Wheels Gets New Truck</h1>
```

NOTE   *The* hn *elements also accept the* lang, dir, onclick, ondblclick, onmousedown, onmouseup, onmouseover, onmousemove, onmouseout, onkeypress, onkeydown, *and* onkeyup *attributes.*

head

Contains document head information. The following elements can be used within the document head: `link`, `meta`, `title`, `script`, `base`, and `style`.

> **Standard/Usage:** HTML 2; required   **Widely Supported:** Yes   **Empty:** No
>
> **Sample:**
> ```
> <html>
>    <head>
>       <title>Making a Peanut Butter and Jelly Sandwich</title>
>       <link rel="parent" href="sandwiches.html" />
>    </head>
> ...</html>
> ```

profile="url"

Specifies the address of meta-data profiles. You can use this attribute to specify the location of, for example, `meta` element information.

> **Standard/Usage:** HTML 4   **Widely Supported:** No
>
> **Sample:**
> ```
> <head profile="http://www.raycomm.com/books.html">...</head>
> ```

NOTE   The head *element also accepts the* lang *and* dir *attributes.*

hr

Draws horizontal lines (rules) in your document. This is useful for visually separating document sections.

> **Standard/Usage:** HTML 2   **Widely Supported:** Yes   **Empty:** Yes
>
> **Sample:**
> ```
> <h2>Birthday Colors</h2>
> <hr align="left" width="60%" />
> <p>Birthdays are usually joyous celebrations so we recommend bright colors.</p>
> ```

align="left | center | right"

Positions the line flush left, flush right, or in the center of the document. These settings are irrelevant unless you use the `width` attribute to make the line shorter than the width of the document. This attribute is deprecated in HTML 4 in favor of style sheets.

> **Standard/Usage:** HTML 3.2; deprecated   **Widely Supported:** Yes
>
> **Sample:**
> ```
> <h2 align="left">Shopping List</h2>
> <hr width="40%" align="left" />
> <ul type="square">
>    <li>eggs</li> <li>butter</li> <li>bread</li> <li>milk</li>
> </ul>
> ```

class="..."
Indicates which style class applies to the hr element.

Standard/Usage: HTML 4   **Widely Supported:** Yes

Sample:
```
<hr class="casual" width="50%" />
```

color="#rrggbb" or "..."
Specifies the color of the line. A color name can be substituted for the hexadecimal RGB values. This attribute on the hr element is only supported by Internet Explorer; style sheets provide more functionality for a wider variety of browsers.

Standard/Usage: Internet Explorer 3   **Widely Supported:** No

Sample:
```
<hr color="#09334c" />
```

id="..."
Assigns a unique ID selector to an instance of the hr element. When you then assign a style to that ID selector, it affects only that one instance of the hr element.

Standard/Usage: HTML 4   **Widely Supported:** Yes

Sample:
```
<hr id="123" />
```

noshade="noshade"
Specifies that the browser should not shade the line.

Standard/Usage: HTML 3.2; deprecated   **Widely Supported:** Yes

Sample:
```
<hr noshade="noshade" align="center" width="50%" />
<img src="bobby.jpg" align="center" border="0" alt="bobby" />
<br clear="all" />
<hr noshade="noshade" align="center" width="50%" />
```

size="n"
Specifies the thickness of the line (in pixels). This attribute is deprecated in HTML 4 in favor of style sheets.

Standard/Usage: HTML 3.2; deprecated   **Widely Supported:** Yes

Sample:
```
<hr size="10" />
```

style="..."

Specifies style sheet commands that apply to the horizontal rule.

    Standard/Usage: HTML 4   **Widely Supported:** Yes

    Sample:
```
<hr width="50%" style="color: red" />
```

width="n"

Specifies the length of the line. You can specify the value with an absolute number of pixels or as a percentage to indicate how much of the total width available is used. This attribute is deprecated in HTML 4 in favor of style sheets.

    Standard/Usage: HTML 3.2; deprecated   **Widely Supported:** Yes

    Sample:
```
<h2 align="center">The End!</h2>
<hr width="85%" />
```

title="..."

Specifies text assigned to the element. You can use this attribute for context-sensitive help within the document. Browsers may use this to show tooltips over the horizontal rule.

    Standard/Usage: HTML 4   **Widely Supported:** No

    Sample:
```
<hr title="A line" />
```

NOTE *The* hr *element also accepts the* onclick, ondblclick, onmousedown, onmouseup, onmouseover, onmousemove, onmouseout, onkeypress, onkeydown, *and* onkeyup *attributes.*

html

Contains the entire document. Place the opening html tag at the top and the closing html tag at the bottom of all your HTML files. (The only code outside of the html tag should be the required DOC-TYPE declaration and the optional XML declaration.) The html element is required. Remember the XHTML namespace for XHTML documents.

    Standard/Usage: HTML 2; required   **Widely Supported:** Yes   **Empty:** No

    Sample:
```
<?xml version="1.0" encoding="UTF-8" standalone="no"?>
<!DOCTYPE html PUBLIC "-//W3C//DTD XHTML 1.0 Transitional//EN"
    "http://www.w3.org/TR/xhtml1/DTD/xhtml1-transitional.dtd">
<html xmlns="http://www.w3.org/1999/xhtml">
    <head><title>Test Page</title></head>
    <body><h1>Is this working?</h1></body>
</html>
```

version="..."
Specifies the version of HTML used. This attribute is deprecated in XHTML because it contains the same information as the DOCTYPE declaration.

Standard/Usage: HTML 4; deprecated   **Widely Supported:** No

Sample:
```
<html version="-//W3C//DTD HTML 4.0 Transitional//EN">This is an HTML 4.0 document.
Not valid XHTML…</html>
```

xmlns="..."
Specifies the XHTML namespace. There's only one possible value for XHTML at this time: xmlns="http://www.w3.org/1999/xhtml".

Standard/Usage: XHTML 1; required   **Widely Supported:** No

Sample:
```
<html xmlns="http://www.w3.org/1999/xhtml">…</html>
```

NOTE *The* html *element also accepts the* lang *and* dir *attributes.*

I

i
Italicizes text.

Standard/Usage: HTML 2   **Widely Supported:** Yes   **Empty:** No

Sample:
```
Mary told me to read <i>Mostly Harmless</i>.
```

class="..."
Indicates which style class applies to the i element.

Standard/Usage: HTML 4   **Widely Supported:** Yes

Sample:
```
This mouse is <i class="casual">enhanced</i>.
```

id="..."
Assigns a unique ID selector to an instance of the i element. When you then assign a style to that ID selector, it affects only that one instance of the i element.

Standard/Usage: HTML 4   **Widely Supported:** Yes

Sample:
```
He called it a <i id="123">doohickie</i>!
```

style="..."

Specifies style sheet commands that apply to the italicized text.

> Standard/Usage: HTML 4   Widely Supported: Yes

> Sample:
> ```
> <i style="color: green">green, italicized text</i>
> ```

title="..."

Specifies text assigned to the element. You can use this attribute for context-sensitive help within the document. Browsers may use this to show tooltips over the italicized text.

> Standard/Usage: HTML 4   Widely Supported: No

> Sample:
> ```
> <i title="italicized">italicized text</i>
> ```

NOTE   *The* i *element also accepts the* lang, dir, onclick, ondblclick, onmousedown, onmouseup, onmouseover, onmousemove, onmouseout, onkeypress, onkeydown, *and* onkeyup *attributes.*

iframe

Creates floating frames within a document. Floating frames differ from normal frames because they can be manipulated independently within another HTML document.

> Standard/Usage: HTML 4 (Frames)   Widely Supported: No   Empty: No

> Sample:
> ```
> <iframe name="new_win" id="new_win" src="http://www.raycomm.com ">iframe>
> ```

align="left | center | right"

Specifies how the floating frame lines up with respect to the left and right sides of the browser window. This attribute is deprecated in favor of style sheets.

> Standard/Usage: HTML 4; deprecated   Widely Supported: No

> Sample:
> ```
> <iframe align="left" src="goats.html" name="g1" id="g1">...</iframe>
> ```

frameborder="1 | 0"

Indicates whether the floating frame has visible borders. A value of 1 (default) indicates that the border is visible, and a value of 0 indicates that it is not visible.

> Standard/Usage: HTML 4 (Frames)   Widely Supported: No

> Sample:
> ```
> <iframe src="main.html" name="main" id="main" frameborder="0">...</iframe>
> ```

height="n"

Specifies the vertical dimension (in pixels) of the floating frame.

Standard/Usage: HTML 4 (Frames)   **Widely Supported:** No

Sample:
```
<iframe src="joe.html" name="Joe" id="Joe" width="500" height="200">…</iframe>
```

hspace="n"

Indicates the size (in pixels) of left and right margins within the floating frame.

Standard/Usage: Internet Explorer 4   **Widely Supported:** No

Sample:
```
<iframe src="joe.html" name="Joe" id="Joe" hspace="10" vspace="10">…</iframe>
```

id="..."

Assigns a unique ID selector to an instance of the iframe element. When you then assign a style to that ID selector, it affects only that one instance of the iframe element.

Standard/Usage: HTML 4 (Frames)   **Widely Supported:** Yes

Sample:
```
<iframe src="joe.html" name="Joe" id="Joe">…</iframe>
```

marginheight="n"

Specifies the size of the top and bottom margins (in pixels) within the floating frame.

Standard/Usage: HTML 4 (Frames)   **Widely Supported:** No

Sample:
```
<iframe src="top.html" name="topbar" id="topbar" marginheight="50">…</iframe>
```

marginwidth="n"

Specifies the size of the left and right margins (in pixels) within the floating frame.

Standard/Usage: HTML 4 (Frames)   **Widely Supported:** No

Sample:
```
<iframe src="body.html" name="body" id="body" marginwidth="50">…</iframe>
```

name="..."

Assigns the frame a unique name. You can use this name within other frames to load new documents in the frame and to manipulate the attributes of the frame.

Standard/Usage: HTML 4 (Frames)   **Widely Supported:** No

Sample:
```
<iframe src="jane.html" name="Jane" id="Jane" width="500" height="200">…</iframe>
```

scrolling="yes | no | auto"

Indicates whether the floating frame has scroll bars. The default is auto.

Standard/Usage: HTML 4 (Frames)   **Widely Supported:** No

Sample:
```
<iframe src="top.html" scrolling="auto">...</iframe>
```

src="url"

Specifies the relative or absolute location of the document file to load in the floating frame.

Standard/Usage: HTML 4 (Frames)   **Widely Supported:** No

Sample:
```
<iframe name="pics" id="pics" src="pics.htm">...</iframe>
```

style="..."

Specifies style sheet commands that apply to the floating frame.

Standard/Usage: HTML 4 (Frames)   **Widely Supported:** No

Sample:
```
<iframe src="dots.html" name="dots" id="dots" style="background: red">...</iframe>
```

width="n"

Specifies the horizontal dimension (in pixels) of the floating frame.

Standard/Usage: HTML 4 (Frames)   **Widely Supported:** No

Sample:
```
<iframe src="joe.html" name="Joe" id="Joe" width="500" height="200">...</iframe>
```

vspace="n"

Indicates the size (in pixels) of top and bottom margins within the floating frame.

Standard/Usage: Internet Explorer 4   **Widely Supported:** No

Sample:
```
<iframe src="joe.html" name="Joe" id="Joe" hspace="10" vspace="10">...</iframe>
```

NOTE *The* iframe *element also accepts the* lang, dir, onclick, ondblclick, onmousedown, onmouseup, onmouseover, onmousemove, onmouseout, onkeypress, onkeydown, *and* onkeyup *attributes.*

img

Places an inline image in a document. You can use the attributes ismap and usemap with the img element to implement image maps.

Standard/Usage: HTML 2   **Widely Supported:** Yes   **Empty:** Yes

Sample:
```
<img src="images/left_arrow.gif" alt="&lt;- " />
```

align="left|right|top|middle|bottom"

Specifies the appearance of text that is near an inline graphic image. For example, if you use right, the image appears flush to the right edge of the document, and the text appears to its left. Using left produces the opposite effect.

HTML 2 mentions only attribute values of top, middle, and bottom. top aligns the top of the first line of text after the img element to the top of the image. bottom (the default) aligns the bottom of the image to the baseline of the text. middle aligns the baseline of the first line of text with the middle of the image.

HTML 3.2 added left and right to the list of attribute values.

You can use the br element to control specific points where text stops wrapping around an image and continues below the instance of the image.

The align attribute is deprecated in HTML 4 in favor of style sheets.

Standard/Usage: HTML 2; deprecated   **Widely Supported:** Yes

Sample:
```
<img src="red_icon.gif" align="left" />
It's about time for volunteers to pitch in.<br clear="all" />
```

alt="..."

Provides a textual description of images, which is both useful for users who have text-only browsers and required by the specifications. Some browsers may also display the alt text as a tooltip when the user places the mouse pointer over the image.

Standard/Usage: HTML 2; required   **Widely Supported:** Yes

Sample:
```
<img src="smiley.gif" alt=":-)" />
```

border="n"

Specifies the width (in pixels) of a border around an image. The default value is usually 0 (no border). The border color is the color of normal text within your document. This attribute is deprecated in favor of style sheets.

Standard/Usage: HTML 3.2; deprecated   **Widely Supported:** Yes

Sample:
```
<img src="portrait.jpg" border="2" />
```

class="..."

Indicates which style class applies to the image.

Standard/Usage: HTML 4 **Widely Supported:** Yes

Sample:
```
<img class="casual" src="dots.gif" />
```

controls="control"

If the image is a video file, indicates the playback controls that appear below the image.

Standard/Usage: Internet Explorer 2 **Widely Supported:** No

Sample:
```
<img dynsrc="foo.avi" controls="controls" />
```

dynsrc="url"

Specifies the relative or absolute location of a dynamic image (VRML, video file, and so on).

Standard/Usage: Internet Explorer 2 **Widely Supported:** No

Sample:
```
<img dynsrc="foo.avi" />
```

height="n"

Specifies the vertical dimension of the image (in pixels). If you don't use this attribute, the image appears in its default height. Use this attribute, along with the width attribute, to fit an image within a space. You can fit a large image into a smaller space, and you can spread a smaller image. Some Web designers use the width and height attributes to spread a single pixel image over a large space to produce the effect of a larger solid-color image.

Standard/Usage: HTML 3.2 **Widely Supported:** Yes

Sample:
```
<img src="images/smiley.jpg" width="50" height="50" />
```

hspace="n"

Establishes a margin of white space (in pixels) to the left and right of a graphic image. (See the vspace attribute for how to control the top and bottom margins around an image.) This attribute is deprecated in favor of style sheets.

Standard/Usage: HTML 3.2; deprecated **Widely Supported:** Yes

Sample:
```
<img src="pics/pinetree.jpg" hspace="20" vspace="15" />
```

id="..."

Assigns a unique ID selector to an instance of the img element. When you then assign a style to that ID selector, it affects only that one instance of the img element.

Standard/Usage: HTML 4   **Widely Supported:** Yes

Sample:
```
<img src="grapes.jpg" id="123" />
```

ismap="ismap"

Indicates that the graphic image functions as a clickable image map. The ismap attribute instructs the browser to send the pixel coordinates to the server image map CGI application when a user selects the image with the mouse pointer. When HTML 2 established the ismap attribute, image maps were implemented in a server-side fashion only. Now, client-side image maps are more popular (see the usemap attribute).

Standard/Usage: HTML 2   **Widely Supported:** Yes

Sample:
```
<a href="/cgi-bin/imagemap/mymap">
<img ismap="ismap" src="images/main.gif" /></a>
```

longdesc="..."

Provides a long textual description of images, which is useful for users who have text-only browsers or who cannot view images for other reasons.

Standard/Usage: HTML 4   **Widely Supported:** No

Sample:
```
<img src="smiley.gif" alt=":-)"
    longdesc="This is a smiley face, placed here for decoration. " />
```

loop="n|infinite"

Indicates the number of times a video file plays back.

Standard/Usage: Internet Explorer 2   **Widely Supported:** No

Sample:
```
<img dynsrc="bar.avi" loop="infinite" />
```

name="..."

Specifies a name by which bookmarks, scripts, and applets can reference the image. This attribute is deprecated; use the id attribute instead of or together with name.

Standard/Usage: HTML 2; deprecated   **Widely Supported:** No

Sample:
```
<img src="tweakie.jpg" name="img_1" id="img_1" />
```

src="url"

Specifies the relative or absolute location of a file that contains the graphic image you want to embed in a document.

Standard/Usage: HTML 2; required   **Widely Supported:** Yes

Sample:
```
<img src="images/left_arrow.gif" alt="&lt;- " />
```

style="..."

Specifies style sheet commands that apply to the inline image.

Standard/Usage: HTML 4   **Widely Supported:** Yes

Sample:
```
<img src="dots.gif" style="background: red" />
```

title="..."

Specifies text assigned to the element. You can use this attribute for context-sensitive help within the document. Browsers may use this to show tooltips over the image.

Standard/Usage: HTML 4   **Widely Supported:** No

Sample:
```
<img src="pics/jill.jpg" title="Image" />
```

usemap="url"

Specifies the location of the client-side image map data (see the map element). Because the map element gives the map data an anchor name, be sure to include the name with the URL of the document that contains the map data.

Standard/Usage: HTML 3.2   **Widely Supported:** Yes

Sample:
```
<img ismap="ismap" src="map1.gif" usemap="maps.html#map1" />
```

vrml="..."

Specifies the absolute or relative location of a VRML (Virtual Reality Markup Language) world to embed in a document.

Standard/Usage: Internet Explorer 2   **Widely Supported:** No

Sample:
```
<img vrml="vr/myroom.vrml" />
```

vspace="n"

Establishes a margin of white space (in pixels) above and below a graphic image. (See the hspace attribute for how to control the left and right margins of an image.) This attribute is deprecated in favor of style sheets.

Standard/Usage: HTML 3.2; deprecated   **Widely Supported:** Yes

Sample:
```
<img src="pics/pinetree.jpg" hspace="20" vspace="15" />
```

width="n"

Specifies the horizontal dimension of the image (in pixels). If you don't use this attribute, the image appears in the default width. Use this attribute, along with the `height` attribute, to fit an image within a space. You can fit a large image into a smaller space, and you can spread a smaller image. Some Web designers use `width` and `height` to spread a single pixel image over a large space to produce the effect of a larger solid-color image.

Standard/Usage: HTML 3.2   **Widely Supported:** Yes

Sample:
```
<img src="images/smiley.jpg" width="50" height="50" />
```

NOTE   *The* `img` *element also accepts the* `lang`, `dir`, `onclick`, `ondblclick`, `onmousedown`, `onmouseup`, `onmouseover`, `onmousemove`, `onmouseout`, `onkeypress`, `onkeydown`, *and* `onkeyup` *attributes.*

input

Identifies several input methods for forms. This element must appear between the opening and closing `form` elements.

Standard/Usage: HTML 2   **Widely Supported:** Yes   **Empty:** Yes

Sample:
```
<form action="/cgi-bin/order/" method="post">
   <input name="qty" type="text" size="5" />
   <input type="submit" value="order" />
</form>
```

align="left | center | right"

Lines up a graphical submit button (`type="image"`). The behavior of this element is identical to that of the `align` attribute of the `img` element. This attribute is deprecated in HTML 4 in favor of style sheets.

Standard/Usage: HTML 3.2; deprecated   **Widely Supported:** Yes

Sample:
```
<input type="image" src="picture.gif" align="right" />
```

accept="..."

Specifies a comma-separated list of acceptable MIME types for submitted files.

Standard/Usage: HTML 4   **Widely Supported:** No

Sample:
```
<input type="file" accept="image/gif, image/jpg" />Please submit an image.
```

accesskey="..."

Specifies a single keyboard key that users can use to navigate to the input field.

Standard/Usage: HTML 4   **Widely Supported:** No

Sample:
```
<input type="checkbox" name="test" value="unproven" accesskey="t" />
```

alt="..."

Provides a textual description of the input element, which is useful for users who have text-only browsers. Some browsers may also display the alt text as a floating message when the user places the mouse pointer over the image.

Standard/Usage: HTML 2   **Widely Supported:** Yes

Sample:
```
Age: <input type="text" name="age" alt="age" id="123" />
```

checked="checked"

Use with the type="radio" or type="checkbox" to set the default state of those input methods to true.

Standard/Usage: HTML 2   **Widely Supported:** Yes

Sample:
```
One <input type="checkbox" checked="checked" name="foo" value="1" /><br />
Two <input type="checkbox" name="foo" value="2" /><br />
```

class="..."

Indicates which style class applies to the input element.

Standard/Usage: HTML 4   **Widely Supported:** Yes

Sample:
```
<input class="casual" type="text" name="age" />
```

disabled="disabled"

Disables an instance of the input method so data cannot be accepted or submitted. Also removes this element from the tab sequence.

Standard/Usage: HTML 4   **Widely Supported:** No

Sample:
```
<input type="password" name="pass" disabled="disabled" />
```

id="..."

Assigns a unique ID selector to an instance of the input element. When you then assign a style to that ID selector, it affects only that one instance of the input element.

Standard/Usage: HTML 4   Widely Supported: Yes

Sample:
```
Age: <input type="text" name="age" id="123" />
```

ismap="ismap"

Indicates that the input element functions as a clickable image map. type must be equal to image.

Standard/Usage: HTML 2   Widely Supported: Yes

Sample:
```
<input src="mapimage.gif" type="image" ismap="ismap" />
```

maxlength="n"

Indicates the number of characters you can enter into a text input field; only useful to input methods of type text or password. Unlike the size attribute, maxlength does not affect the size of the input field shown on the screen.

Standard/Usage: HTML 2   Widely Supported: Yes

Sample:
```
Phone: <input type="text" name="phone" maxlength="11" />
```

name="..."

Gives a name to the value you pass to the form processor. For example, if you collect a person's last name with an input method of type text, you assign a value to the name attribute similar to lastname. This establishes a *name-value pair* for the form processor.

Standard/Usage: HTML 2   Widely Supported: Yes

Sample:
```
Enter your last name: <input type="text" name="lastname" size="25" />
```

readonly="readonly"

Indicates that changes to the input method data cannot occur.

Standard/Usage: HTML 4   Widely Supported: No

Sample:
```
<input type="text" name="desc" value="1/4 inch flange assembly" readonly="readonly" />
```

size="n"

Specifies the width of the input field, in characters for input fields of type text or password and in pixels for all other input methods.

Standard/Usage: HTML 2   Widely Supported: Yes

Sample:
```
Your Age: <input type="text" name="age" size="5" />
```

src="url"

Implements a graphic image for a submit button. For this to work, indicate `type="image"`.

> **Standard/Usage:** HTML 3.2   **Widely Supported:** Yes
>
> **Sample:**
> ```
> <input type="image" src="/images/push-button.gif" />
> ```

style="..."

Specifies style sheet commands that apply to this `input` element.

> **Standard/Usage:** HTML 4   **Widely Supported:** Yes
>
> **Sample:**
> ```
> <input type="radio" name="food" value="1" style="background: red" />
> ```

tabindex="n"

Specifies where the input method appears in the tab order.

> **Standard/Usage:** HTML 4   **Widely Supported:** No
>
> **Sample:**
> ```
> Information:
> <input type="text" name="first name" tabindex="1" />
> <input type="text" name="middle name" tabindex="2" />
> <input type="text" name="last name" tabindex="3" />
> ```

title="..."

Specifies text assigned to the element. You can use this attribute for context-sensitive help within the document. Browsers may use this to show tooltips over the input method.

> **Standard/Usage:** HTML 4   **Widely Supported:** No
>
> **Sample:**
> ```
> <input type="radio" name="cc" value="visa" title="visacard" />
> ```

type="button | checkbox | file | hidden | image | password | radio | reset | submit | text"

Indicates the kind of input method to use:

Value	Effect
button	Creates a generic button that can interact with scripts.
checkbox	Produces a small check box that the user can check or uncheck, depending on the settings.
file	Allows the user to submit a file with the form.
hidden	Creates a hidden field that the user cannot interact with. This field is typically used to transmit data to between the client and server.

image	Replaces the Submit button with an image. The behavior of this value is identical to that of the Submit button, except that the x,y coordinates of the mouse position over the image when selected are also sent to the form processor.
password	Gives the user a simple one-line text input field similar to the text type. However, when users enter data into the field, they do not see individual characters; rather, they see asterisks.
radio	Produces a small radio button that can be turned on and off (in groups of two or more). Use radio buttons when you want a user to select only one of several items. For multiple-value selections, see the checkbox type or the select element.
reset	Sets all the input methods to their empty or default settings.
submit	Produces a button that, when selected, submits all the name-value pairs to the form processor.
text	Produces a simple one-line text input field that is useful for obtaining simple data such as a person's name, a person's age, a dollar amount, and so on. To collect multiple lines of text, use the textarea element.

Standard/Usage: HTML 2 **Widely Supported:** Yes

Sample:
```
<form method="post" action="/cgi-bin/thingie">
   Name:        <input type="text" name="name" /><br />
   Password:  <input type="password" name="pass" /><br />
   Ice Cream: Vanilla<input type="radio" value="1" checked="checked"
                name="ice_cream" />
                Chocolate<input type="radio" value="2" name="ice_cream" /><br />
                <input type="submit" value="Send Data…" />
</form>
```

usemap="url"
Indicates the relative or absolute location of a client-side image map to use with the form.

Standard/Usage: HTML 4 **Widely Supported:** No

Sample:
```
<input src="mapimage.gif" usemap="maps.html#map1" />
```

value="…"
Sets the default value input method. Required when input is set to type="radio" or type="checkbox".

Standard/Usage: HTML 2 **Widely Supported:** Yes

Sample:
```
<input type="hidden" name="id" value="123" />
```

NOTE *The* input *element also accepts the* lang, dir, onfocus, onblur, onselect, onchange, onclick, ondblclick, onmousedown, onmouseup, onmouseover, onmousemove, onmouseout, onkeypress, onkeydown, *and* onkeyup *attributes.*

ins

Indicates text to be inserted in the document. May be either block-level or inline, as necessary.

Standard/Usage: HTML 4   **Widely Supported:** No   **Empty:** No

Sample:
```
<p>HTTP stands for Hypertext <ins>Transfer</ins> Protocol.</p>
```

cite="url"

Indicates the address of the reference (a definitive source, for example) for the insertion.

Standard/Usage: HTML 4   **Widely Supported:** No

Sample:
```
<ins cite="http://www.w3.org/">HTML 2 was used for two years.</ins>
```

class="..."

Indicates which style class applies to the ins element.

Standard/Usage: HTML 4   **Widely Supported:** Yes

Sample:
```
<ins class="joeadd">POP stands for Post Office Protocol.</ins>
```

datetime="..."

Indicates the date and time in precisely this format: YYYY-MM-DDThh:mm:ssTZD. For example, 2001-07-14T08:30:00-07:00 indicates July 14, 2001, at 8:30 AM, in U.S. Mountain Time (7 hours from Greenwich time). This time could also be presented as 2001-07-14T08:30:00Z.

Standard/Usage: HTML 4   **Widely Supported:** No

Sample:
```
<ins datetime="2001-07-14T08:30:00Z">POP stands for Post Office Protocol.</ins>
```

id="..."

Assigns a unique ID selector to an instance of the ins element. When you then assign a style to that ID selector, it affects only that one instance of the ins element.

Standard/Usage: HTML 4   **Widely Supported:** Yes

Sample:
```
<ins id="123">WWW stands for World Wide Web.</ins>
```

style="..."

Specifies style sheet commands that apply to the inserted text.

Standard/Usage: HTML 4   **Widely Supported:** Yes

Sample:
```
<ins style="background: blue; color: white">ESP stands for extra-sensory
perception.</ins>
```

title="..."

Specifies text assigned to the element. You can use this attribute for context-sensitive help within the document. Browsers may use this to show tooltips over the inserted text.

Standard/Usage: HTML 4   **Widely Supported:** No

Sample:
```
<ins title="Definition">More inserted text.</ins>
```

NOTE   The ins *element also accepts the* lang, dir, onclick, ondblclick, onmousedown, onmouseup, onmouseover, onmousemove, onmouseout, onkeypress, onkeydown, *and* onkeyup *attributes.*

isindex

Inserts an input field into the document so users can enter search queries. The queries then go to a CGI application indicated by the action attribute. This element is deprecated in HTML 4 in favor of the input element.

Standard/Usage: HTML 2; deprecated   **Widely Supported:** Yes   **Empty:** Yes

Sample:
```
<isindex prompt="keyword search" action="/cgi-bin/search.cgi" />
```

prompt="..."

Changes the input prompt for keyword index searches. If you don't specify prompt, the browser displays a default prompt.

Standard/Usage: HTML 3.2   **Widely Supported:** Yes

Sample:
```
<isindex prompt="Search for something" />
```

NOTE   The isindex *element also accepts the* lang, dir, id, class, style, *and* title *attributes.*

K

kbd

Specifies text to be entered at the keyboard or keystrokes to be done by the user within a document.

Standard/Usage: HTML 2   **Widely Supported:** Yes   **Empty:** No

Sample:
```
Press <kbd>Ctrl+S</kbd> to save your document.
```

class="..."

Indicates which style class applies to the kbd element.

Standard/Usage: HTML 4   **Widely Supported:** Yes

Sample:
```
Now press the <kbd class="casual">F4</kbd> key!
```

id="..."

Assigns a unique ID selector to an instance of the kbd element. When you then assign a style to that ID selector, it affects only that one instance of the kbd element.

Standard/Usage: HTML 4   **Widely Supported:** Yes

Sample:
```
Press <kbd id="123">F1</kbd> for help.
```

style="..."

Specifies style sheet commands that apply to the text within the kbd element.

Standard/Usage: HTML 4   **Widely Supported:** Yes

Sample:
```
<kbd style="background: red">Type me</kbd>
```

title="..."

Specifies text assigned to the element. You can use this attribute for context-sensitive help within the document. Browsers may use this to show tooltips over the keyboard text.

Standard/Usage: HTML 4   **Widely Supported:** No

Sample:
```
Now press the <kbd title="Keyboard stuff">F4</kbd> key.
```

NOTE *The* kbd *element also accepts the* lang, dir, onclick, ondblclick, onmousedown, onmouseup, onmouseover, onmousemove, onmouseout, onkeypress, onkeydown, *and* onkeyup *attributes.*

L

label

Provides identifying text for a form widget.

Standard/Usage: HTML 4   **Widely Supported:** No   **Empty:** No

Sample:
```
<label for="idname">First Name</label><input type="text" id="idname" />
```

accesskey="..."

Assigns a keystroke to the element.

Standard/Usage: HTML 4   **Widely Supported:** No

Sample:
```
<label for="idname" accesskey="h">...</label>
```

class="..."

Indicates which style class applies to the label element.

Standard/Usage: HTML 4   **Widely Supported:** Yes

Sample:
```
<label for="idname" class="short">First Name</label><input type="text" id="idname" />
```

disabled="disabled"

Denies access to the label input method.

Standard/Usage: HTML 4   **Widely Supported:** No

Sample:
```
<label for="idname" accesskey="h" disabled="disabled">...</label>
```

for="..."

Specifies the ID of the widget associated with the label.

Standard/Usage: HTML 4   **Widely Supported:** No

Sample:
```
<label for="idname">First Name</label><input type="text" id="idname" />
```

id="..."

Assigns a unique ID selector to an instance of the label element. When you then assign a style to that ID selector, it affects only that one instance of the label element.

Standard/Usage: HTML 4   **Widely Supported:** Yes

Sample:
```
<label for="idname" id="234">First Name</label><input type="text" id="idname" />
```

style="..."

Specifies style sheet commands that apply to this `label` element.

Standard/Usage: HTML 4   **Widely Supported:** Yes

Sample:
```
<label for="idname" style="background: red">First Name</label>
<input type="text" id="idname" />
```

tabindex="n"

Specifies where the label input method appears in the tab order. For example, `tabindex="3"` places the cursor at the `label` element after the user presses the Tab key three times.

Standard/Usage: HTML 4   **Widely Supported:** No

Sample:
```
Credit card number: <label for="ccard" tabindex="5">Credit Card</label>
<input type="text" name="ccard" />
```

title="..."

Specifies text assigned to the element. You can use this attribute for context-sensitive help within the document. Browsers may use this to show tooltips over the label.

Standard/Usage: HTML 4   **Widely Supported:** No

Sample:
```
<label for="ccard" title="credit card">Credit Card</label>
```

NOTE *The* `label` *element also accepts the* `lang`, `dir`, `onfocus`, `onblur`, `onselect`, `onchange`, `onclick`, `ondblclick`, `onmousedown`, `onmouseup`, `onmouseover`, `onmousemove`, `onmouseout`, `onkeypress`, `onkeydown`, *and* `onkeyup` *attributes.*

layer

Defines a layer within a document, which you can then manipulate with JavaScript. You specify the layer's contents by placing markup between the `layer` elements or by using the `src` attribute. Netscape Navigator 6 or later, Internet Explorer 4 or later, and Opera 5 or later support the DOM, which allows comparable functionality in a more generally accessible form. See Chapter 16, "Bringing Pages to Life with Dynamic HTML and XHTML," for details.

Standard/Usage: Netscape Navigator 4   **Widely Supported:** No   **Empty:** No

Sample:
```
<layer src="top.html" height="100" width="100" z-index="4" name="top"
visibility="show">...</layer>
```

above="..."

Specifies the name of a layer above which the current layer should appear.

Standard/Usage: Netscape Navigator 4   **Widely Supported:** No

Sample:
```
<layer src="grass.gif" z-index="1" name="grass" visibility="show">
   <layer src="dog.gif" above="grass" name="dog">…</layer>
</layer>
```

background="url"

Specifies the relative or absolute location of an image file that the browser tiles as the background of the layer.

Standard/Usage: Netscape Navigator 4   **Widely Supported:** No

Sample:
```
<layer z-index="5" name="info" background="goo.gif"><h1>Hi there</h1></layer>
```

below="..."

Specifies the name of a layer below which the current layer should appear.

Standard/Usage: Netscape Navigator 4   **Widely Supported:** No

Sample:
```
<layer background="road.jpg" name="Road" below="Car">…</layer>
```

bgcolor="#rrggbb" or "..."

Specifies the background color of the layer. Use either the hexadecimal RGB values or the color name.

Standard/Usage: Netscape Navigator 4   **Widely Supported:** No

Sample:
```
<layer bgcolor="#ff0011">
<div align="center"><h1><blink>EAT AT JOE'S!</blink></h1></div></layer>
```

clip="x1,y1,x2,y2"

Indicates the dimensions of a clipping rectangle that specifies which areas of the layer are visible. Areas outside this rectangle become transparent.

You can give the x and y coordinates in pixels or as percentages to indicate relative portions of the layer. You can omit x1 and y1 if you want to clip from the top-left corner of the layer.

Standard/Usage: Netscape Navigator 4   **Widely Supported:** No

Sample:
```
<layer src="hawk.jpg" clip="20%,20%">…</layer>
```

height="n"

Specifies the vertical dimension of the layer (in pixels or as a percentage of the browser window height).

Standard/Usage: Netscape Navigator 4   **Widely Supported:** No

Sample:
```
<layer src="frame.gif" above="bg" name="frame" width="200" height="200">…</layer>
```

left="n"

Specifies the layer's horizontal position (in pixels) relative to the left edge of the parent layer. Use the top attribute for vertical positioning.

Standard/Usage: Netscape Navigator 4   **Widely Supported:** No

Sample:
```
<layer left="100" top="150">This layer is at {100,150}.</layer>
```

name="..."

Gives the layer a name by which other layer definitions and JavaScript code can reference it.

Standard/Usage: Netscape Navigator 4   **Widely Supported:** No

Sample:
```
<layer src="car.gif" name="carpic" above="road">…</layer>
```

src="url"

Specifies the relative or absolute location of the file containing the contents of the layer.

Standard/Usage: Netscape Navigator 4   **Widely Supported:** No

Sample:
```
<layer src="ocean.jpg">…</layer>
```

top="n"

Specifies the layer's vertical position (in pixels) relative to the top edge of the parent layer. Use the left attribute for horizontal positioning.

Standard/Usage: Netscape Navigator 4   **Widely Supported:** No

Sample:
```
<layer left="100" top="150">This layer is at {100,150}.</layer>
```

visibility="show | hide | inherit"

Indicates whether the layer is initially visible. A value of show indicates the layer is initially visible; hide indicates the layer is not initially visible; and inherit indicates the layer has the same initial visibility attributes as its parent layer.

Standard/Usage: Netscape Navigator 4   **Widely Supported:** No

Sample:
```
<layer src="grass.gif" z-index="1" name="grass" visibility="show">…</layer>
```

width="n"

Specifies the horizontal dimension of the layer (in pixels or as a percentage of the browser window width).

Standard/Usage: Netscape Navigator 4   **Widely Supported:** No

Sample:
```
<layer src="frame.gif" above="bg" name="frame" width="200" height="200">…</layer>
```

z-index="n"

Specifies where the layer appears in the stack of layers. Higher values indicate a position closer to the top of the stack.

Standard/Usage: Netscape Navigator 4   **Widely Supported:** No

Sample:
```
<layer z-index="0" name="bottom">
You may never see this text if other layers are above it.</layer>
```

NOTE *The* layer *element also accepts the* onfocus, onblur, onselect, onchange, onclick, ondblclick, onmousedown, onmouseup, onmouseover, onmousemove, onmouseout, onkeypress, onkeydown, *and* onkeyup *attributes.*

legend

Specifies a description for a fieldset. Use inside the fieldset element.

Standard/Usage: HTML 4   **Widely Supported:** No   **Empty:** No

Sample:
```
<fieldset><legend valign="top" align="center">Grades for Cooking
101</legend>…</fieldset>
```

align="top | bottom | left | right"

Indicates whether the legend appears at the top or bottom, left or right of the fieldset element. This attribute is deprecated in favor of style sheets.

Standard/Usage: HTML 4; deprecated   **Widely Supported:** No

Sample:
```
<legend align="top">Seattle Staff Directory</legend>
```

accesskey="..."

Specifies a single keyboard key that users can use to navigate to the legend.

Standard/Usage: HTML 4   **Widely Supported:** No

Sample:
```
<legend accesskey="c">Criteria for Judging</legend>
```

class="..."

Indicates which style class applies to the legend element.

Standard/Usage: HTML 4   **Widely Supported:** Yes

Sample:
```
<legend class="chemical">Hydrogen vs. Oxygen</legend>
```

id="..."

Assigns a unique ID selector to an instance of the legend element. When you then assign a style to that ID selector, it affects only that one instance of the legend element.

Standard/Usage: HTML 4   **Widely Supported:** Yes

Sample:
```
<legend id="123">Great Painters</legend>
```

style="..."

Specifies style sheet commands that apply to the contents of the legend element.

Standard/Usage: HTML 4   **Widely Supported:** Yes

Sample:
```
<legend style="background: red">…</legend>
```

title="..."

Specifies text assigned to the element. You can use this attribute for context-sensitive help within the document. Browsers may use this to show tooltips over the legend.

Standard/Usage: HTML 4   **Widely Supported:** Yes

Sample:
```
<legend title="sleepy hollow">…</legend>
```

NOTE The legend *element also accepts the* lang, dir, onclick, ondblclick, onmousedown, onmouseup, onmouseover, onmousemove, onmouseout, onkeypress, onkeydown, *and* onkeyup *attributes.*

li

Identifies items in ordered (see the ol element), menu (see the menu element), directory (see the dir element), and unordered (see the ul element) lists.

Standard/Usage: HTML 2   **Widely Supported:** Yes   **Empty:** No

Sample:
```
<p>My favorite foods are:
<ul>
    <li>Pepperoni pizza</li>
    <li>Lasagna</li>
    <li>Taco salad</li>
    <li>Bananas</li>
</ul></p>
```

class="..."

Indicates which style class applies to the li element.

Standard/Usage: HTML 4   **Widely Supported:** Yes

Sample:
```
<li class="casual">Dogs</li>
```

compact="compact"

Specifies that the list item appears in a space-saving form. This attribute may not affect the appearance of the list because most browsers do not present lists in more than one format. The attribute is deprecated in HTML 4.

Standard/Usage: HTML 2; deprecated   **Widely Supported:** Yes

Sample:
```
<ul>
    <li>Cola</li>
    <li>Fruit drink</li>
    <li compact="compact">Orange juice</li>
    <li>Water</li>
</ul>
```

id="..."

Assigns a unique ID selector to an instance of the li element. When you then assign a style to that ID selector, it affects only that one instance of the li element.

Standard/Usage: HTML 4   **Widely Supported:** Yes

Sample:
```
<li id="123">Bees</li>
```

style="..."

Specifies style sheet commands that apply to the list item.

Standard/Usage: HTML 4   **Widely Supported:** Yes

Sample:
```
<li style="background: red">Fruit drink</li>
```

title="..."

Specifies text assigned to the element. You can use this attribute for context-sensitive help within the document. Browsers may use this to show tooltips over the list item.

Standard/Usage: HTML 4   **Widely Supported:** No

Sample:
```
<li title="List Item">Thingie</li>
```

type="..."

Specifies the bullets for each unordered list item (see the ul element) or the numbering for each ordered list item (see the ol element). If you omit the type attribute, the browser chooses a default type.

Valid type values for unordered lists are disc, square, and circle.

Valid type values for ordered lists are 1 for Arabic numbers, a for lowercase letters, A for uppercase letters, i for lowercase Roman numerals, and I for uppercase Roman numerals.

The type attribute is deprecated in favor of style sheets.

Standard/Usage: HTML 3.2; deprecated   **Widely Supported:** Yes

Sample:
```
<ul>
    <li type="square">Food</li>
    <ol>
        <li type="1">Spaghetti</li>
        <li type="1">Tossed salad</li>
    </ol>
</ul>
```

value="..."

Sets a number in an ordered list. Use this attribute to continue a list after interrupting it with something else in your document. You can also set a number in an ordered list with the start attribute of the ol element.

Because unordered lists do not increment, the value attribute is meaningless when used with them. This attribute is deprecated in favor of style sheets.

Standard/Usage: HTML 3.2; deprecated   **Widely Supported:** Yes

Sample:
```
<ol type="1">
    <li value="5">Watch</li>
    <li>Compass</li>
</ol>
```

NOTE   The li element also accepts the lang, dir, onclick, ondblclick, onmousedown, onmouseup, onmouseover, onmousemove, onmouseout, onkeypress, onkeydown, *and* onkeyup *attributes.*

link

An empty element that establishes relationships between the current document and other documents. Use this element within the head section. For example, if you access the current document by choosing a hyperlink from the site's home page, you can establish a relationship between the current document and the site's home page (see the rel attribute). At this time, however, most browsers don't use most of these relationships; only rel="stylesheet" is widely supported. You can place several link elements within the head section of your document to define multiple relationships.

With newer implementations of HTML, you use the link element to establish information about Cascading Style Sheets (CSS). Some other relationships (link types) that the link element defines with either the rel or rev attribute include the following:

Value of rel or rev	References
alternate	A different version of the same document. When used with lang, alternate implies a translated document; when used with media, it implies a version for a different medium.
appendix	An appendix
bookmark	A bookmark, which links to an important entry point within a longer document
chapter	A chapter
contents	A table of contents
copyright	A copyright notice
glossary	A glossary of terms
help	A document offering help or more information
index	An index
next	The next document in a series (use with rel)
prev	The previous document in a series (use with rev)
section	A section
start	The first document in a series
stylesheet	An external style sheet
subsection	A subsection

Standard/Usage: HTML 2   **Widely Supported:** Yes   **Empty:** Yes

Sample:
```
<head>
   <title>Prices</title>
   <link rel="top" href="http://www.raycomm.com/" />
   <link rel="stylesheet" href="http://www.raycomm.com/styles.css" />
</head>
```

charset="..."

Specifies character encoding of the data designated by the link. Use the name of a character set defined in RFC2045. The default value for this attribute, appropriate for all Western languages, is ISO-8859-1.

Standard/Usage: HTML 4   **Widely Supported:** No

Sample:
```
<link rel="top" href="http://www.raycomm.com/" charset="ISO-8859-1" />
```

href="url"

Indicates the relative or absolute location of the resource you're establishing a relationship to/from.

Standard/Usage: HTML 2   **Widely Supported:** Yes

Sample:
```
<link rel="prev" href="page1.html" />
```

hreflang="..."

Specifies the language used in the document linked to. Use standard codes for languages, such as DE for German, FR for French, IT for Italian, and HE for Hebrew. See ISO International Standard 639 at

```
www.oasis-open.org/cover/iso639a.html
```
for more information about language codes.

Standard/Usage: HTML 4   **Widely Supported:** No

Sample:
```
<link href="german.html" hreflang="DE" />
```

media="..."

Specifies the destination medium for style information. It may be a single type or a comma-separated list. Media types include the following:

Value	Description
all	Applies to all devices
braille	For Braille tactile feedback devices
print	For traditional printed material and for documents on screen viewed in print pre-view mode
projection	For projectors
screen	For online viewing (default setting)
speech	For a speech synthesizer

Standard/Usage: HTML 4   **Widely Supported:** No

Sample:
```
<link media="screen" rel="stylesheet" href="/global.css" />
```

rel="..."

Defines the relationship you're establishing between the current document and another resource. The values for this attribute are the link types provided in the element definition section.

Standard/Usage: HTML 2   **Widely Supported:** Yes

Sample:
```
<head>
    <link rel="help" href="/help/index.html" />
    <link rel="stylesheet" href="sitehead.css" />
</head>
```

rev="..."

Establishes reverse relationships between the current document and other resources. The values for this attribute are the link types provided in the element definition section.

Standard/Usage: HTML 2   **Widely Supported:** Yes

Sample:
```
<link rev="stylesheet" href="/global.css" />
```

target="..."

Specifies the name of a frame in which the referenced link appears.

Standard/Usage: HTML 4   **Widely Supported:** No

Sample:
```
<link target="_blank" rel="home" href="http://www.raycomm.com/" />
```

title="..."

Specifies text assigned to the element that can be used for context-sensitive help within the document. Browsers may use this to show tooltips.

Standard/Usage: HTML 4   **Widely Supported:** Yes

Sample:
```
<link rel="top" href="/index.html" title="Home Page" />
```

type="..."

Specifies the MIME type of a style sheet to import with the link element.

Standard/Usage: HTML 4   **Widely Supported:** No

Sample:
```
<link rel="stylesheet" type="text/css" href="/style/main.css" />
```

NOTE *The* link *element also accepts the* lang, dir, onfocus, onblur, onchange, onselect, onclick, ondblclick, onmousedown, onmouseup, onmouseover, onmousemove, onmouseout, onkeypress, onkeydown, *and* onkeyup *attributes.*

MAP | 779

M

map

Specifies a container for client-side image map data. You use the area element inside the map element.

Standard/Usage: HTML 3.2   **Widely Supported:** Yes   **Empty:** No

Sample:
```
<map name="mainmap" id="mainmap">
    <area nohref="nohref"    alt="home"   shape="rect"  coords="0,0,100,100" />
    <area href="yellow.html" alt="yellow" shape="rect"  coords="100,0,200,100" />
    <area href="blue.html"   alt="blue"   shape="rect"  coords="0,100,100,200" />
    <area href="red.html"    alt="red"    shape="rect"  coords="100,100,200,200" />
</map>
```

class="..."
Indicates which style class applies to the element.

Standard/Usage: HTML 4   **Widely Supported:** Yes

Sample:
```
<map class="casual" name="simba" id="simba">...</map>
```

id="..."
Indicates an identifier to associate with the map. You can also use this to apply styles to the object.

Standard/Usage: HTML 4   **Widely Supported:** Yes

Sample:
```
<map id="123" name="simba" id="simba">...</map>
```

name="..."
Establishes a name for the map information you can later reference using the usemap attribute of the img element.

Standard/Usage: HTML 3.2   **Widely Supported:** Yes

Sample:
```
<map name="housemap" id="housemap">
    <img src="house.gif" usemap="#housemap" alt="map of house" />...</map>
```

style="..."
Specifies style sheet commands that apply to the contents of the map element.

Standard/Usage: HTML 4   **Widely Supported:** Yes

Sample:
```
<map style="background: black">...</map>
```

title="…"

Specifies text assigned to the element. You can use this attribute for context-sensitive help within the document. Browsers may use this to show tooltips.

Standard/Usage: HTML 4 **Widely Supported:** No

Sample:
```
<map title="image map spec">…</map>
```

marquee

Displays a scrolling text message within a document. Only Internet Explorer recognizes this element. Use the more widely supported Java, JavaScript, or Flash to achieve the same effect for a broader audience.

Standard/Usage: Internet Explorer 2 **Widely Supported:** No **Empty:** No

Sample:
```
<marquee direction="left" behavior="scroll" scrolldelay="250" scrollamount="10">
    Big sale today on fuzzy-wuzzy widgets!</marquee>
```

behavior="scroll | slide | alternate"

Indicates the type of scrolling. A value of `scroll` scrolls text from one side of the marquee, across, and off the opposite side; `slide` scrolls text from one side of the marquee, across, and stops when the text reaches the opposite side; and `alternate` bounces the marquee text from one side to the other.

Standard/Usage: Internet Explorer 2 **Widely Supported:** No

Sample:
```
<marquee direction="left" behavior="alternate">Go Bears! Win Win Win!</marquee>
```

bgcolor="#rrggbb" or "…"

Specifies the background color of the marquee. You use a hexadecimal RGB color value or a color name.

Standard/Usage: Internet Explorer 2 **Widely Supported:** No

Sample:
```
<marquee bgcolor="red" direction="left">Order opera tickets here!</marquee>
```

direction="left | right"

Indicates the direction in which the marquee text scrolls.

Standard/Usage: Internet Explorer 2 **Widely Supported:** No

Sample:
```
<marquee direction="left">Order opera tickets here!</marquee>
```

height="n"

Specifies the vertical dimension of the marquee (in pixels).

> **Standard/Usage:** Internet Explorer 2   **Widely Supported:** No
>
> **Sample:**
> ```
> <marquee width="300" height="50">Go Bears!</marquee>
> ```

hspace="n"

Specifies the size of the margins (in pixels) to the left and right of the marquee.

> **Standard/Usage:** Internet Explorer 2   **Widely Supported:** No
>
> **Sample:**
> ```
> <marquee direction="left" hspace="25">Check out our detailed product specs!</marquee>
> ```

id="..."

Assigns a unique ID selector to an instance of the marquee element. When you then assign a style to that ID selector, it affects only that one instance of the marquee element.

> **Standard/Usage:** Internet Explorer 4   **Widely Supported:** No
>
> **Sample:**
> ```
> <marquee id="3d4">…</marquee>
> ```

loop="n | infinite"

Controls the appearance of the marquee text.

> **Standard/Usage:** Internet Explorer 2   **Widely Supported:** No
>
> **Sample:**
> ```
> <marquee loop="5">December 12 is our big, all-day sale!</marquee>
> ```

scrollamount="n"

Indicates how far (in pixels) the marquee text shifts between redraws. Decrease this value for a smoother (but slower) scroll; increase it for a faster (but bumpier) scroll.

> **Standard/Usage:** Internet Explorer 2   **Widely Supported:** No
>
> **Sample:**
> ```
> <marquee scrollamount="10" scrolldelay="40">Plant a tree for Arbor Day!</marquee>
> ```

scrolldelay="n"

Indicates how often (in milliseconds) the marquee text redraws. Increase this value to slow the scrolling action; decrease it to speed the scrolling action.

Standard/Usage: Internet Explorer 2   **Widely Supported:** No

Sample:
```
<marquee direction="right" scrolldelay="30">Eat at Joe's!</marquee>
```

style="..."

Specifies style sheet commands that apply to the text within the marquee element.

Standard/Usage: Internet Explorer 4   **Widely Supported:** No

Sample:
```
<marquee style="background: red">...</marquee>
```

title="..."

Specifies text assigned to the element. You can use this attribute for context-sensitive help within the document. Browsers may use this to show tooltips over the marquee.

Standard/Usage: Internet Explorer 4   **Widely Supported:** No

Sample:
```
<marquee title="scrolling marquee">...</marquee>
```

truespeed="truespeed"

A stand-alone attribute that specifies that the scrolldelay values should be maintained. If this attribute is not used, scrolldelay values under 59 are rounded up to 60 milliseconds.

Standard/Usage: Internet Explorer 2   **Widely Supported:** No

Sample:
```
<marquee direction="right" scrolldelay="30" truespeed="truespeed">Eat at
Joe's!</marquee>
```

vspace="n"

Specifies the size of the margins (in pixels) at the top and bottom of the marquee.

Standard/Usage: Internet Explorer 2   **Widely Supported:** No

Sample:
```
<marquee direction="left" vspace="25">Check out our detailed product specs!</marquee>
```

width="n"

Specifies the horizontal dimension (in pixels) of the marquee.

Standard/Usage: Internet Explorer 2   **Widely Supported:** No

Sample:
```
<marquee width="300">Go Bears!</marquee>
```

menu

Defines a menu list. Use the li element to indicate list items. However, use ul instead of this deprecated element.

> **Standard/Usage:** HTML 2; deprecated   **Widely Supported:** No   **Empty:** No
>
> **Sample:**
> ```
> Now you can:<menu>
>    <li>Eat the sandwich.</li>
>    <li>Place the sandwich in the fridge.</li>
>    <li>Feed the sandwich to the dog.</li>
> </menu>
> ```

class="..."

Indicates which style class applies to the menu element.

> **Standard/Usage:** HTML 4   **Widely Supported:** Yes
>
> **Sample:**
> ```
> <menu class="casual">
>    <li>Information</li>
>    <li>Members</li>
>    <li>Guests</li>
> </menu>
> ```

compact="compact"

Specifies that the menu list appears in a space-saving form. This attribute may not affect the appearance of the list because most browsers do not present lists in more than one format. This attribute is deprecated in HTML 4.

> **Standard/Usage:** HTML 2; deprecated   **Widely Supported:** Yes
>
> **Sample:**
> ```
> <h2>Drinks Available</h2>
> <menu compact="compact">
>    <li>Cola</li>
>    <li>Fruit drink</li>
>    <li>Orange juice</li>
>    <li>Water</li>
> </menu>
> ```

id="..."

Assigns a unique ID selector to an instance of the menu element. When you then assign a style to that ID selector, it affects only that one instance of the menu element.

> **Standard/Usage:** HTML 4   **Widely Supported:** Yes

Sample:
```
You'll need the following:<menu id="123">
    <li>Extra socks</li>
    <li>Snack crackers</li>
    <li>Towel</li>
</menu>
```

style="..."

Specifies style sheet commands that apply to the menu list.

Standard/Usage: HTML 4   **Widely Supported:** Yes

Sample:
```
<menu style="background: black; color: white">...</menu>
```

title="..."

Specifies text assigned to the element. You can use this attribute for context-sensitive help within the document. Browsers may use this to show tooltips over the menu list.

Standard/Usage: HTML 4   **Widely Supported:** No

Sample:
```
<menu title="menu list">...</menu>
```

NOTE   *The* menu *element also accepts the* lang, dir, onclick, ondblclick, onmousedown, onmouseup, onmouseover, onmousemove, onmouseout, onkeypress, onkeydown, *and* onkeyup *attributes.*

meta

This empty element specifies information about the document to browsers, applications, and search engines. Place the meta element within the document head. For example, you can use the meta element to instruct the browser to load a new document after 10 seconds (client-pull), or you can specify keywords for search engines to associate with your document.

Standard/Usage: HTML 2   **Widely Supported:** Yes   **Empty:** Yes

Sample:
```
<head>
    <title>Igneous Rocks in North America</title>
    <meta http-equiv="keywords" content="geology, igneous, volcanoes" />
</head>
```

content="..."

Assigns values to the HTTP header field. For example, when using the refresh HTTP header, assign a number along with a URL to the content attribute; the browser then loads the specified URL after the specified number of seconds.

Standard/Usage: HTML 2; required   **Widely Supported:** Yes

Sample:
```
<meta http-equiv="refresh" content="2;url=nextpage.html" />
```

http-equiv="..."

Indicates the HTTP header value you want to define, such as refresh, expires, or content-language. Other header values are listed in RFC2068.

Standard/Usage: HTML 2   **Widely Supported:** Yes

Sample:
```
<meta http-equiv="expires" content="Tue, 04 Aug 2002 22:39:22 GMT" />
```

name="..."

Specifies the name of the association you are defining, such as keywords or description.

Standard/Usage: HTML 2   **Widely Supported:** Yes

Sample:
```
<meta name="keywords" content="travel,automobile" />
<meta name="description" content="The Nash Metro moves fast and goes beep beep. " />
```

scheme="..."

Specifies additional information about the association you're defining.

Standard/Usage: HTML 4   **Widely Supported:** No

Sample:
```
<meta name="number" scheme="priority" content="1" />
```

NOTE   *The* meta *element also accepts the* lang *and* dir *attributes.*

multicol

Formats text into newspaper-style columns.

Standard/Usage: Netscape Navigator 4   **Widely Supported:** No   **Empty:** No

Sample:
```
<multicol cols="2" gutter="10">...</multicol>
```

cols="n"

Indicates the number of columns.

Standard/Usage: Netscape Navigator 4   **Widely Supported:** No

Sample:
```
<multicol cols="4">...</multicol>
```

gutter="n"

Indicates the width of the space (in pixels) between multiple columns.

>   **Standard/Usage:** Netscape Navigator 4   **Widely Supported:** No
>
>   **Sample:**
>   ```
>   <multicol cols="3" gutter="15">…</multicol>
>   ```

width="n"

Indicates the horizontal dimension (in pixels or as a percentage of the total width available) of each column.

>   **Standard/Usage:** Netscape Navigator 4   **Widely Supported:** No
>
>   **Sample:**
>   ```
>   <multicol cols="2" width="30%">…</multicol>
>   ```

N

nobr

Disables line-wrapping for a section of text. To force a word break within a nobr clause, use the wbr empty element. The nobr element is a proprietary Internet Explorer element, which is also supported by Netscape but not the XHTML or HTML specification.

>   **Standard/Usage:** Internet Explorer, Netscape Navigator   **Widely Supported:** Yes   **Empty:** No
>
>   **Sample:**
>   ```
>   <nobr>All this text will
>   remain on one single line in the
>   browser window, no matter how wide the
>   window is, until the closing
>   tag appears. That doesn't happen
>   until right now.</nobr>
>   ```

class="..."

Indicates which style class applies to the element.

>   **Standard/Usage:** Internet Explorer 3, Netscape Navigator 4   **Widely Supported:** Yes
>
>   **Sample:**
>   ```
>   <nobr class="casual">…</nobr>
>   ```

id="..."

Assigns a unique ID selector to an instance of the nobr element. When you then assign a style to that ID selector, it affects only that one instance of the nobr element.

Standard/Usage: Internet Explorer 3, Netscape Navigator 4   **Widely Supported:** No

Sample:
```
You'll need the following:<nobr id="123">...</nobr>
```

style="..."
Specifies style sheet commands that apply to the nonbreaking text.

Standard/Usage: Internet Explorer 4, Netscape Navigator 3   **Widely Supported:** Yes

Sample:
```
<nobr style="background: black">...</nobr>
```

noframes

Provides content for browsers that do not support frames or are configured not to present frames. The body element is required within the noframes section. It provides additional formatting and style sheet features.

Standard/Usage: HTML 4 (Frames)   **Widely Supported:** Yes   **Empty:** No

Sample:
```
<frameset cols="*,70">...
   <noframes>
      <body>
         <p>Your browser doesn't support frames. Please follow the links below for
            the rest of the story.</p>
         <p><a href="prices.html">Prices</a> |
            <a href="about.html">About Us</a> |
            <a href="contact.html">Contact Us</a></p>
      </body>
   </noframes>
</frameset>
```

class="..."
Indicates which style class applies to the noframes element.

Standard/Usage: HTML 4   **Widely Supported:** Yes

Sample:
```
<noframes class="short"><body>...</body></noframes>
```

id="..."
Assigns a unique ID selector to an instance of the noframes element. When you then assign a style to that ID selector, it affects only that one instance of the noframes element.

Standard/Usage: HTML 4   **Widely Supported:** Yes

Sample:
```
<noframes id="234"><body>...</body></noframes>
```

style="..."

Specifies style sheet commands that apply to the noframes element.

Standard/Usage: HTML 4   **Widely Supported:** No

Sample:
```
<noframes style="background: red"><body>…</body></noframes>
```

title="..."

Specifies text assigned to the element. You can use this attribute for context-sensitive help within the document. Browsers may use this to show tooltips.

Standard/Usage: HTML 4   **Widely Supported:** No

Sample:
```
<noframes title="XHTML for nonframed browsers"><body>…</body></noframes>
```

NOTE   The noframes *element also accepts the* lang, dir, onclick, ondblclick, onmousedown, onmouseup, onmouseover, onmousemove, onmouseout, onkeypress, onkeydown, *and* onkeyup *attributes.*

noscript

Provides alternative content for browsers that do not support scripts. Use the noscript element inside a script definition.

Standard/Usage: HTML 4   **Widely Supported:** No   **Empty:** No

Sample:
```
<noscript>Because you can see this, you can tell that your browser will not run (or
is set not to run) scripts.</noscript>
```

class="..."

Indicates which style class applies to the noscript element.

Standard/Usage: HTML 4   **Widely Supported:** Yes

Sample:
```
<noscript class="short">…</noscript>
```

id="..."

Assigns a unique ID selector to an instance of the noscript element. When you then assign a style to that ID selector, it affects only that one instance of the noscript element.

Standard/Usage: HTML 4   **Widely Supported:** Yes

Sample:
```
<noscript id="234">…</noscript>
```

style="..."
Specifies style sheet commands that apply to the noscript element.

> **Standard/Usage:** HTML 4   **Widely Supported:** Yes
>
> **Sample:**
> ```
> <noscript style="background: red">...</noscript>
> ```

title="..."
Specifies text assigned to the element. You can use this attribute for context-sensitive help within the document. Browsers may use this to show tooltips.

> **Standard/Usage:** HTML 4   **Widely Supported:** No
>
> **Sample:**
> ```
> <noscript title="XHTML for nonscript browsers">...</noscript>
> ```

NOTE   *The* noscript *element also accepts the* lang, dir, onclick, ondblclick, onmousedown, onmouseup, onmouseover, onmousemove, onmouseout, onkeypress, onkeydown, *and* onkeyup *attributes.*

object

Embeds a software object into a document. The object can be an ActiveX object, a QuickTime movie, a Flash animation, or any other object or data that a browser supports.

Use the param element to supply parameters to the embedded object. You can place messages and other elements between the object elements for browsers that do not support embedded objects.

> **Standard/Usage:** HTML 4   **Widely Supported:** No   **Empty:** No
>
> **Sample:**
> ```
> <object classid="/thingie.py">
>    <param name="thing" value="1" />
>    <param name="autostart" value="true" />
>    Sorry. Your browser does not support embedded objects.
>    If it supported these objects, you would not see this message.
> </object>
> ```

align="left | center | right | texttop | middle | textmiddle | baseline | textbottom"
Indicates how the embedded object lines up relative to the edges of the browser windows and/or other elements within the browser window. This attribute is deprecated in favor of style sheets.

Value	Effect
left	Floats the embedded object between the edges of the window, on the left side
right	Floats the embedded object between the edges of the window, on the right side
center	Floats the embedded object between the edges of the window, evenly between left and right

texttop	Aligns the top of the embedded object with the top of the surrounding text
textmiddle	Aligns the middle of the embedded object with the middle of the surrounding text
textbottom	Aligns the bottom of the embedded object with the bottom of the surrounding text
baseline	Aligns the bottom of the embedded object with the baseline of the surrounding text
middle	Aligns the middle of the embedded object with the baseline of the surrounding text

Standard/Usage: HTML 4; deprecated   **Widely Supported:** No

Sample:
```
<object data="shocknew.dcr" type="application/director" width="288" height="200"
align="right">...</object>
```

archive="url url url"

Specifies a *space-separated* list of URIs for archives containing resources relevant to the object, which may include the resources specified by the `classid` and `data` attributes. Preloading archives generally results in reduced load times for objects.

Standard/Usage: HTML 4   **Widely Supported:** No

Sample:
```
<object archive="bear.htm lion.htm">...</object>
```

border="n"

Indicates the width (in pixels) of a border around the embedded object. `border="0"` indicates no border. This attribute is deprecated in favor of style sheets.

Standard/Usage: HTML 4; deprecated   **Widely Supported:** No

Sample:
```
<object data="shocknew.dcr" type="application/director" width="288" height="200"
border="10">...</object>
```

classid="url"

Specifies the location of an object resource, such as a Java applet. Use `classid="java:appletname.class"` for Java applets.

Standard/Usage: HTML 4   **Widely Supported:** No

Sample:
```
<object classid="java:appletname.class">...</object>
```

codebase="url"

Specifies the absolute or relative location of the base directory in which the browser will look for data and other implementation files.

Standard/Usage: HTML 4   Widely Supported: No

Sample:
```
<object codebase="/fgm/code/">...</object>
```

codetype="..."
Specifies the MIME type for the embedded object's code.

Standard/Usage: HTML 4   Widely Supported: No

Sample:
```
<object codetype="application/x-msword">...</object>
```

class="..."
Indicates which style class applies to the element.

Standard/Usage: HTML 4   Widely Supported: Yes

Sample:
```
<object class="casual" codetype="application/x-msword">...</object>
```

classid="url"
Specifies the URL of an object resource.

Standard/Usage: HTML 4   Widely Supported: No

Sample:
```
<object classid="http://www.raycomm.com/bogus.class">...</object>
```

data="url"
Specifies the absolute or relative location of the embedded object's data.

Standard/Usage: HTML 4   Widely Supported: No

Sample:
```
<object data="/fgm/goo.avi">...</object>
```

declare="declare"
Defines the embedded object without actually loading it into the document.

Standard/Usage: HTML 4   Widely Supported: No

Sample:
```
<object classid="clsid:99B42120-6EC7-11CF-A6C7-00AA00A47DD3"
declare="declare">...</object>
```

height="n"

Specifies the vertical dimension (in pixels) of the embedded object.

Standard/Usage: HTML 4   Widely Supported: No

Sample:
```
<object data="shocknew.dcr" type="application/director" width="288"
height="200">...</object>
```

hspace="n"

Specifies the size of the margins (in pixels) to the left and right of the embedded object.

Standard/Usage: HTML 4   Widely Supported: No

Sample:
```
<object data="shocknew.dcr" width="288" height="200" hspace="10">...</object>
```

id="..."

Indicates an identifier to associate with the embedded object. You can also use this to apply styles to the object.

Standard/Usage: HTML 4   Widely Supported: Yes

Sample:
```
<object data="shocknew.dcr" width="288" height="200" id="swave2">...</object>
```

name="..."

Specifies the name of the embedded object.

Standard/Usage: HTML 4   Widely Supported: No

Sample:
```
<object data="shocknew.dcr" name="Very Cool Thingie">...</object>
```

standby="..."

Specifies a message that the browser displays while the object is loading.

Standard/Usage: HTML 4   Widely Supported: No

Sample:
```
<object standby="Please wait. Movie loading. " width="100" height="250">...</object>
```

tabindex="n"

Indicates the place of the embedded object in the tabbing order.

Standard/Usage: HTML 4   Widely Supported: No

Sample:
```
<object classid="clsid:99b42120-6ec7-11cf-a6c7-00aa00a47dd3" tabindex="3">...</object>
```

title="..."

Specifies text assigned to the element. You can use this attribute for context-sensitive help within the document. Browsers may use this to show tooltips over the embedded object.

Standard/Usage: HTML 4   **Widely Supported:** No

Sample:
```
<object title="Earth Movie" width="100" height="250">…</object>
```

type="..."

Indicates the MIME type of the embedded object.

Standard/Usage: HTML 4   **Widely Supported:** No

Sample:
```
<object data="shock.dcr" type="application/x-director" width="288"
height="200">…</object>
```

usemap="url"

Indicates the relative or absolute location of a client-side image map to use with the embedded object.

Standard/Usage: HTML 4   **Widely Supported:** No

Sample:
```
<object usemap="maps.html#map1">…</object>
```

vspace="n"

Specifies the size of the margin (in pixels) at the top and bottom of the embedded object.

Standard/Usage: HTML 4   **Widely Supported:** No

Sample:
```
<object data="shocknew.dcr" width="288" height="200" vspace="10">…</object>
```

width="n"

Indicates the horizontal dimension (in pixels) of the embedded object.

Standard/Usage: HTML 4   **Widely Supported:** No

Sample:
```
<object data="shock.dcr" type="application/director" width="288"
height="200">…</object>
```

NOTE *The* object *element also accepts the* lang, dir, onclick, ondblclick, onmousedown, onmouseup, onmouseover, onmousemove, onmouseout, onkeypress, onkeydown, *and* onkeyup *attributes.*

ol

Contains a numbered (ordered) list.

> **Standard/Usage:** HTML 2   **Widely Supported:** Yes   **Empty:** No
>
> **Sample:**
> ```
> <ol>
>    <li>Introduction</li>
>    <li>Part One</li>
>    <ol type="A">
>       <li>Chapter 1</li>
>       <li>Chapter 2</li>
>    </ol>
> </ol>
> ```

class="..."

Indicates which style class applies to the ol element.

> **Standard/Usage:** HTML 4   **Widely Supported:** Yes
>
> **Sample:**
> ```
> <ol class="car">
>    <li>Check engine oil</li>
>    <li>Check tire pressures</li>
>    <li>Fill with gasoline</li>
> </ol>
> ```

compact="compact"

Indicates that the ordered list appears in a compact format. This attribute may not affect the appearance of the list because most browsers do not present lists in more than one format. This attribute is deprecated in HTML 4.

> **Standard/Usage:** HTML 2; deprecated   **Widely Supported:** No
>
> **Sample:**
> ```
> <ol compact="compact">...</ol>
> ```

id="..."

Assigns a unique ID selector to an instance of the ol element. When you then assign a style to that ID selector, it affects only that one instance of the ol element.

> **Standard/Usage:** HTML 4   **Widely Supported:** Yes
>
> **Sample:**
> ```
> <ol id="123">...</ol>
> ```

start="..."

Specifies the value at which the ordered list should start. This attribute is deprecated in HTML 4.

Standard/Usage: HTML 2; deprecated   Widely Supported: Yes

Sample:
```
<ol type="a" start="f">...</ol>
```

style="..."

Specifies style sheet commands that apply to the ordered list.

Standard/Usage: HTML 4   Widely Supported: Yes

Sample:
```
<ol style="background: black; color: white">...</ol>
```

title="..."

Specifies text assigned to the element. You can use this attribute for context-sensitive help within the document. Browsers may use this to show tooltips over the ordered list.

Standard/Usage: HTML 4   Widely Supported: No

Sample:
```
<ol title="ordered list">...</ol>
```

type="..."

Specifies the numbering style of the ordered list. Possible values are 1 for Arabic numbers, i for lowercase Roman numerals, I for uppercase Roman numerals, a for lowercase letters, and A for uppercase letters. This attribute is deprecated in HTML 4 in favor of style sheets.

Standard/Usage: HTML 2; deprecated   Widely Supported: Yes

Sample:
```
<ol type="a">
    <li>is for apple.</li>
    <li>is for bird.</li>
    <li>is for cat.</li>
    <li>is for dog.</li>
</ol>
```

NOTE   *The* ol *element also accepts the* lang, dir, onclick, ondblclick, onmousedown, onmouseup, onmouseover, onmousemove, onmouseout, onkeypress, onkeydown, *and* onkeyup *attributes.*

optgroup

Specifies a description for a group of options. Use inside select elements, and use the option element within the optgroup element.

Standard/Usage: HTML 4   Widely Supported: No   Empty: No

Sample:
```
<select name="dinner">
   <optgroup label="choices">
      <option>Vegan</option>
      <option>Vegetarian</option>
      <option>Traditional</option>
   </optgroup>
</select>
```

class="..."

Indicates which style class applies to the optgroup element.

Standard/Usage: HTML 4   **Widely Supported:** Yes

Sample:
```
<optgroup label="Fake or False" class="casual">
   <option>Fake</option>
   <option>False</option>
</optgroup>
```

disabled="disabled"

Denies access to the group of options.

Standard/Usage: HTML 4   **Widely Supported:** No

Sample:
```
<optgroup label="food" disabled="disabled">
   <option>Prime Rib</option>
   <option>Lobster</option>
</optgroup>
```

id="..."

Assigns a unique ID selector to an instance of the optgroup element. When you then assign a style to that ID selector, it affects only that one instance of the optgroup element.

Standard/Usage: HTML 4   **Widely Supported:** Yes

Sample:
```
<optgroup label="Fake or False" id="123">
   <option>Fake</option>
   <option>False</option>
</optgroup>
```

label="..."

Specifies alternative text assigned to the element. You can use this attribute for context-sensitive help within the document.

Standard/Usage: HTML 4; required   **Widely Supported:** Yes

Sample:
```
<optgroup label="Dinner selections">
   <option>Prime Rib</option>
   <option>Lobster</option>
</optgroup>
```

style="..."

Specifies style sheet commands that apply to the contents of the optgroup element.

Standard/Usage: HTML 4   **Widely Supported:** No

Sample:
```
<optgroup label="dinner" style="background: red">...</optgroup>
```

title="..."

Specifies text assigned to the element. You can use this attribute for context-sensitive help within the document.

Standard/Usage: HTML 4   **Widely Supported:** No

Sample:
```
<optgroup label="party" title="Select a political party">...</optgroup>
```

NOTE   *The* optgroup *element also accepts the* lang, dir, onfocus, onblur, onchange, onselect, onclick, ondblclick, onmousedown, onmouseup, onmouseover, onmousemove, onmouseout, onkeypress, onkey-down, *and* onkeyup *attributes.*

option

Indicates items in a fill-out form selection list (see the select element).

Standard/Usage: HTML 2   **Widely Supported:** Yes   **Empty:** No

Sample:
```
Select an artist from the 1970s:<select name="artists">
   <option>Simon and Garfunkel</option>
   <option selected="selected">Pink Floyd</option>
   <option>Boston</option>
</select>
```

class="..."

Indicate which style class applies to the element.

Standard/Usage: HTML 4   **Widely Supported:** Yes

Sample:
```
<option name="color" class="casual">...</option>
```

disabled="disabled"

Denies access to the input method.

    Standard/Usage: HTML 4   **Widely Supported:** No

    Sample:
```
<option value="Bogus" disabled="disabled">Nothing here.</option>
```

id="..."

Assigns a unique ID selector to an instance of the option element. When you then assign a style to that ID selector, it affects only that one instance of the option element.

    Standard/Usage: HTML 4   **Widely Supported:** Yes

    Sample:
```
<option id="123">Mastercard</option>
```

label="..."

Specifies shorter, alternative text assigned to the option element. You can use this attribute for context-sensitive help within the document. Browsers may use this to show tooltips over the group.

    Standard/Usage: HTML 4   **Widely Supported:** Yes

    Sample:
```
<option label="Trad">Traditional Dinner Menu</option>
```

selected="selected"

Marks a selection list item as preselected.

    Standard/Usage: HTML 2   **Widely Supported:** Yes

    Sample:
```
<option selected="selected" value="1">Ice Cream</option>
```

title="..."

Specifies text assigned to the element. You can use this attribute for context-sensitive help within the document. Browsers may use this to show tooltips over the selection list option.

    Standard/Usage: HTML 4   **Widely Supported:** No

    Sample:
```
<option title="Option">Thingie</option>
```

value="..."

Indicates which data is sent to the form processor if you choose the selection list item. If the value attribute is not present within the option element, the text between the option elements is sent instead.

Standard/Usage: HTML 2   **Widely Supported:** Yes

Sample:
```
<option value="2">Sandwiches</option>
```

NOTE *The* option *element also accepts the* lang, dir, onfocus, onblur, onchange, onselect, onclick, ondblclick, onmousedown, onmouseup, onmouseover, onmousemove, onmouseout, onkeypress, onkeydown, *and* onkeyup *attributes.*

P

p

Indicates a paragraph in a document.

Standard/Usage: HTML 2   **Widely Supported:** Yes   **Empty:** No

Sample:
```
<p>I'm a paragraph.</p>
<p>I'm another paragraph.</p>
```

align="left | center | right"

Aligns paragraph text flush left, flush right, or in the center of the document. This attribute is deprecated in HTML 4 in favor of style sheets.

Standard/Usage: HTML 3.2; deprecated   **Widely Supported:** Yes

Sample:
```
<p align="center">There will be fun and games for everyone!</p>
```

class="..."

Indicates which style class applies to the p element.

Standard/Usage: HTML 4   **Widely Supported:** Yes

Sample:
```
<p class="casual">Tom turned at the next street and stopped.</p>
```

id="..."

Assigns a unique ID selector to an instance of the p element. When you then assign a style to that ID selector, it affects only that one instance of the p element.

Standard/Usage: HTML 4   **Widely Supported:** Yes

Sample:
```
<p id="123">This paragraph is yellow on black!</p>
```

style="..."

Specifies style sheet commands that apply to the contents of the paragraph.

Standard/Usage: HTML 4   **Widely Supported:** Yes

Sample:
```
<p style="background: red; color: white">...</p>
```

title="..."

Specifies text assigned to the element. You can use this attribute for context-sensitive help within the document. Browsers may use this to show tooltips over the paragraph.

Standard/Usage: HTML 4   **Widely Supported:** No

Sample:
```
<p title="paragraph">...</p>
```

NOTE   The p element also accepts the lang, dir, onclick, ondblclick, onmousedown, onmouseup, onmouseover, onmousemove, onmouseout, onkeypress, onkeydown, *and* onkeyup *attributes.*

param

Specifies parameters passed to an embedded object. Use the param element within the object or applet elements.

Standard/Usage: HTML 3.2   **Widely Supported:** No   **Empty:** Yes

Sample:
```
<object classid="/thingie.py">
    <param name="thing" value="1" />
    Sorry. Your browser does not support embedded objects.
</object>
```

name="..."

Indicates the name of the parameter passed to the embedded object.

Standard/Usage: HTML 3.2; required   **Widely Supported:** No

Sample:
```
<param name="startyear" value="1920" />
```

type="..."

Specifies the MIME type of the data found at the specified URL. Use this attribute with the value-type="ref" attribute.

Standard/Usage: HTML 4   **Widely Supported:** No

Sample:
```
<param name="data" value="/data/sim1.zip" valuetype="ref"
    type="application/x-zip-compressed" />
```

value="..."

Specifies the value associated with the parameter passed to the embedded object.

> **Standard/Usage:** HTML 3.2   **Widely Supported:** No

> **Sample:**
> ```
> <param name="startyear" value="1920" />
> ```

valuetype="ref | object | data"

Indicates the kind of value passed to the embedded object. A value of `ref` indicates that the value of `value` is a URL passed to the embedded object; `object` indicates that the `value` attribute specifies the location of object data; and `data` indicates that the `value` attribute is set to a plain-text string. Use this for passing alphanumeric data to the embedded object.

> **Standard/Usage:** Internet Explorer 3, HTML 4   **Widely Supported:** No

> **Sample:**
> ```
> <param name="length" value="9" valuetype="data" />
> ```

pre

Contains preformatted (including line breaks and spaces) plain text. This is useful for including computer program output or source code within your document.

> **Standard/Usage:** HTML 2   **Widely Supported:** Yes   **Empty:** No

> **Sample:**
> ```
> Here's the source code:
> <pre>
> #include <stdio.h>
> void main()
> {
>  printf("Hello World!\n");
> }
> </pre>
> ```

class="..."

Indicates which style class applies to the `pre` element.

> **Standard/Usage:** HTML 4   **Widely Supported:** Yes

> **Sample:**
> ```
> <pre class="food">BBQ Info</pre>
> ```

id="..."

Assigns a unique ID selector to an instance of the `pre` element. When you then assign a style to that ID selector, it affects only that one instance of the `pre` element.

Standard/Usage: HTML 4   **Widely Supported:** Yes

Sample:
```
An example of an emoticon:<pre id="123"> :-) </pre>
```

style="..."
Specifies style sheet commands that apply to the contents of the pre element.

Standard/Usage: HTML 4   **Widely Supported:** Yes

Sample:
```
<pre style="background: red">…</pre>
```

title="..."
Specifies text assigned to the element. You can use this attribute for context-sensitive help within the document. Browsers may use this to show tooltips over the preformatted text.

Standard/Usage: HTML 4   **Widely Supported:** No

Sample:
```
<pre title="preformatted text">…</pre>
```

width="n"
Specifies the horizontal dimension of the preformatted text (in pixels). This attribute is deprecated in favor of style sheets.

Standard/Usage: HTML 4; deprecated   **Widely Supported:** No

Sample:
```
<pre width="80">…</pre>
```

NOTE   The pre *element also accepts the* lang, dir, onclick, ondblclick, onmousedown, onmouseup, onmouseover, onmousemove, onmouseout, onkeypress, onkeydown, *and* onkeyup *attributes.*

Q

q
Quotes a direct source within a paragraph. Use blockquote to signify a longer or block quotation.

Standard/Usage: HTML 4   **Widely Supported:** No   **Empty:** No

Sample:
```
Dr. Bob said <q>I really like the procedure.</q>
```

cite="url"

Specifies a reference URL for a quotation.

Standard/Usage: HTML 4   **Widely Supported:** No

Sample:
```
<q cite="http://www.example.com/url.html">The book was good.</q>
```

class="..."

Indicates which style class applies to the q element.

Standard/Usage: HTML 4   **Widely Supported:** Yes

Sample:
```
<q class="holiday">Twas the night before Christmas</q>
```

id="..."

Assigns a unique ID selector to an instance of the q element. When you then assign a style to that ID selector, it affects only that one instance of the q element.

Standard/Usage: HTML 4   **Widely Supported:** Yes

Sample:
```
On July 12, John wrote a profound sentence in his diary:
<q id="123">I woke up this morning, and it was raining.</q>
```

style="..."

Specifies style sheet commands that apply to the contents of the q element.

Standard/Usage: HTML 4   **Widely Supported:** Yes

Sample:
```
<q style="background: red">...</q>
```

title="..."

Specifies text assigned to the element. You can use this attribute for context-sensitive help within the document. Browsers may use this to show tooltips over the quoted text.

Standard/Usage: HTML 4   **Widely Supported:** No

Sample:
```
<q title="quotation">Quoted text goes here.</q>
```

NOTE *The* q *element also accepts the* lang, dir, onclick, ondblclick, onmousedown, onmouseup, onmouseover, onmousemove, onmouseout, onkeypress, onkeydown, *and* onkeyup *attributes.*

S

s

Deprecated. See `strike`.

samp

Indicates a sequence of literal characters.

Standard/Usage: HTML 2   **Widely Supported:** Yes   **Empty:** No

Sample:
```
An example of a palindrome is the word <samp>MOM</samp>.
```

class="..."
Indicates which style class applies to the `samp` element.

Standard/Usage: HTML 4   **Widely Supported:** Yes

Sample:
```
The PC screen read: <samp class="casual">Command Not Found</samp>.
```

id="..."
Assigns a unique ID selector to an instance of the `samp` element. When you then assign a style to that ID selector, it affects only that one instance of the `samp` element.

Standard/Usage: HTML 4   **Widely Supported:** Yes

Sample:
```
Just for fun, think of how many words end with the letters <samp id="123">ing</samp>.
```

style="..."
Specifies style sheet commands that apply to the contents of the `samp` element.

Standard/Usage: HTML 4   **Widely Supported:** Yes

Sample:
```
<samp style="background: red">...</samp>
```

title="..."
Specifies text assigned to the element. You can use this attribute for context-sensitive help within the document. Browsers may use this to show tooltips.

Standard/Usage: HTML 4   **Widely Supported:** No

Sample:
```
<samp title="Sample">...</samp>
```

NOTE   *The* samp *element also accepts the* lang, dir, onclick, ondblclick, onmousedown, onmouseup, onmouseover, onmousemove, onmouseout, onkeypress, onkeydown, *and* onkeyup *attributes.*

script

Places a script within a document. Examples include JavaScript and VBScript.

> **Standard/Usage:** HTML 3.2   **Widely Supported:** Yes   **Empty:** No
>
> **Sample:**
> `<script type="text/javascript">...</script>`

charset="..."

Specifies character encoding of the data designated by the script. Use the name of a character set defined in RFC2045. The default value for this attribute, appropriate for all Western languages, is ISO-8859-1.

> **Standard/Usage:** HTML 4   **Widely Supported:** No
>
> **Sample:**
> `<script type="text/javascript" charset="ISO-8859-1">...</script>`

defer="defer"

Indicates to the browser that the script does not affect the initial document display, so the script can be processed after the page loads.

> **Standard/Usage:** HTML 4   **Widely Supported:** No
>
> **Sample:**
> `<script type="text/javascript" defer="defer">...</script>`

language="..."

Indicates the type of script; deprecated in favor of type="...".

> **Standard/Usage:** HTML 4; deprecated   **Widely Supported:** Yes
>
> **Sample:**
> `<script language="JavaScript">...</script>`

src="url"

Specifies the relative or absolute location of a script to include in the document.

> **Standard/Usage:** HTML 4   **Widely Supported:** Yes
>
> **Sample:**
> `<script type="text/javascript" src="http://www.example.com/sc/script.js">...</script>`

type="..."

Indicates the MIME type of the script. This is a preferred alternative to the language element for declaring the type of scripting.

Standard/Usage: HTML 3.2; required   **Widely Supported:** Yes

Sample:
```
<script type="text/javascript">document.write ("<em>Great!</em>")</script>
```

select

Specifies a selection list within a form. Use the option element to specify items in the selection list.

Standard/Usage: HTML 2   **Widely Supported:** Yes   **Empty:** No

Sample:
```
What do you use our product for?<br />
<select multiple="multiple" name="use">
   <option value="1">Pest control</option>
   <option selected="selected" value="2">Automotive lubricant</option>
   <option value="3">Preparing pastries</option>
   <option value="4">Other</option>
</select>
```

accesskey="..."

Indicates a keystroke sequence associated with the selection list.

Standard/Usage: Internet Explorer 4   **Widely Supported:** No

Sample:
```
<select name="size" accesskey="s">...</select>
```

class="..."

Indicates which style class applies to the element.

Standard/Usage: HTML 4   **Widely Supported:** Yes

Sample:
```
<select name="color" class="casual">...</select>
```

disabled="disabled"

Denies access to the selection list.

Standard/Usage: HTML 4   **Widely Supported:** No

Sample:
```
<select name="color" disabled="disabled">...</select>
```

id="..."

Assigns a unique ID selector to an instance of the `select` element. When you then assign a style to that ID selector, it affects only that one instance of the `select` element.

Standard/Usage: HTML 3   **Widely Supported:** Yes

Sample:
```
<select id="123" name="salary">...</select>
```

multiple="multiple"

Indicates that a user can select more than one selection list item at the same time.

Standard/Usage: HTML 2   **Widely Supported:** Yes

Sample:
```
<select multiple="multiple">...</select>
```

name="..."

Gives a name to the value you are passing to the form processor. This establishes a name–value pair with which the form processor application can work.

Standard/Usage: HTML 2   **Widely Supported:** Yes

Sample:
```
What is your shoe size?
<select size="4" name="size">
   <option>5</option>
   <option>6</option>
   <option>7</option>
   <option>8</option>
   <option>9</option>
   <option>10</option>
</select>
```

size="n"

Specifies the number of visible items in the selection list. If there are more items in the selection list than are visible, a scroll bar provides access to the other items.

Standard/Usage: HTML 2   **Widely Supported:** Yes

Sample:
```
<select size="3">...</select>
```

style="..."

Specifies style sheet commands that apply to the contents of the `select` element.

Standard/Usage: HTML 4   **Widely Supported:** Yes

Sample:
```
<select style="background: red" name="color">...</select>
```

tabindex="n"

Indicates where in the tabbing order the selection list is placed.

>   Standard/Usage: HTML 4   Widely Supported: No

>   Sample:
>   ```
>   <select name="salary" tabindex="3">…</select>
>   ```

title="..."

Specifies text assigned to the element. You can use this attribute for context-sensitive help within the document. Browsers may use this to show tooltips over the selection list.

>   Standard/Usage: HTML 4   Widely Supported: No

>   Sample:
>   ```
>   <select title="select list" name="car">…</select>
>   ```

NOTE   *The* select *element also accepts the* lang, dir, onfocus, onblur, onchange, onselect, onclick, ondblclick, onmousedown, onmouseup, onmouseover, onmousemove, onmouseout, onkeypress, onkey-down, *and* onkeyup *attributes.*

small

Specifies text that should appear in a small font.

>   Standard/Usage: HTML 3.2   Widely Supported: Yes   Empty: No

>   Sample:
>   ```
>   <p>Our lawyers said we need to include some fine print:</p>
>   <p><small>By reading this document, you're breaking the rules and will be assessed
>   a $2000 fine.</small></p>
>   ```

class="..."

Indicates which style class applies to the small element.

>   Standard/Usage: HTML 4   Widely Supported: Yes

>   Sample:
>   ```
>   <small class="casual">Void where prohibited.</small>
>   ```

id="..."

Assigns a unique ID selector to an instance of the small element. When you then assign a style to that ID selector, it affects only that one instance of the small element.

>   Standard/Usage: HTML 4   Widely Supported: Yes

>   Sample:
>   ```
>   <p>Most insects are <small id="123">small</small>.</p>
>   ```

style="..."
Specifies style sheet commands that apply to the contents of the small element.

> **Standard/Usage:** HTML 4   **Widely Supported:** Yes

> **Sample:**
> ```
> <small style="background: red">...</small>
> ```

title="..."
Specifies text assigned to the element. You can use this attribute for context-sensitive help within the document. Browsers may use this to show tooltips over the text inside the small element.

> **Standard/Usage:** HTML 4   **Widely Supported:** No

> **Sample:**
> ```
> <small title="Legalese">This will subject you to risk of criminal prosecution.</small>
> ```

NOTE   The small *element also accepts the* lang, dir, onclick, ondblclick, onmousedown, onmouseup, onmouseover, onmousemove, onmouseout, onkeypress, onkeydown, *and* onkeyup *attributes.*

spacer

A Netscape-specific element that specifies a blank space within the document. We strongly recommend using style sheets or other formatting techniques.

> **Standard/Usage:** Netscape Navigator 3   **Widely Supported:** No   **Empty:** Yes

> **Sample:**
> ```
> <spacer type="horizontal" size="150" />
> Doctors Prefer MediWidget 4 to 1
> ```

align="left | right | top | texttop | middle | abbsmib | baseline | bottom | absbottom"
Specifies the alignment of text around the spacer. Only used when type="block".

> **Standard/Usage:** Netscape Navigator 3   **Widely Supported:** No

> **Sample:**
> ```
> <spacer type="block" align="left" />
> ```

height="n"
Specifies the height of the spacer (in pixels). Only used when type="block".

> **Standard/Usage:** Netscape Navigator 3   **Widely Supported:** No

> **Sample:**
> ```
> <spacer type="block" height="50" />
> <img src="rosebush.jpg" />
> ```

size="n"

Specifies the dimension of the spacer (in pixels).

> **Standard/Usage:** Netscape Navigator 3   **Widely Supported:** No
>
> **Sample:**
> ```
> <spacer type="horizontal" size="50" />
> <img src="rosebush.jpg" />
> ```

type="horizontal | vertical | block"

Indicates whether the spacer measures from left to right, from top to bottom, or a block (acts like a transparent image).

> **Standard/Usage:** Netscape Navigator 3   **Widely Supported:** No
>
> **Sample:**
> ```
> <p>After you've done this, take a moment to review your work.
> <spacer type="vertical" size="400" /></p>
> <p>Now, isn't that better?</p>
> ```

span

Defines an inline section of a document affected by style sheet attributes. Use `div` to apply styles at the block element level.

> **Standard/Usage:** HTML 4   **Widely Supported:** Yes   **Empty:** No
>
> **Sample:**
> ```
> <span style="background: red">...</span>
> ```

class="..."

Indicates which style class applies to the `span` element.

> **Standard/Usage:** HTML 4   **Widely Supported:** Yes
>
> **Sample:**
> ```
> <span class="casual">...</span>
> ```

id="..."

Assigns a unique ID selector to an instance of the `span` element. When you then assign a style to that ID selector, it affects only that one instance of the `span` element.

> **Standard/Usage:** HTML 4   **Widely Supported:** Yes
>
> **Sample:**
> ```
> <span id="123">...</span>
> ```

style="..."

Specifies style sheet commands that apply to the contents of the `span` element.

Standard/Usage: HTML 4   Widely Supported: Yes

Sample:
```
<span style="background: red">...</span>
```

title="..."

Specifies text assigned to the element. You can use this attribute for context-sensitive help within the document. Browsers may use this to show tooltips.

Standard/Usage: HTML 4   Widely Supported: No

Sample:
```
<span title="section" style="background: red">...</span>
```

NOTE   The span *element also accepts the* lang, dir, onclick, ondblclick, onmousedown, onmouseup, onmouseover, onmousemove, onmouseout, onkeypress, onkeydown, *and* onkeyup *attributes.*

strike

Indicates strikethrough text. This element is deprecated in HTML 4 in favor of style sheets.

Standard/Usage: HTML 3.2; deprecated   Widely Supported: Yes   Empty: No

Sample:
```
My junior high biology teacher was <strike>sort of</strike> really smart.
```

class="..."

Indicates which style class applies to the strike element.

Standard/Usage: HTML 4   Widely Supported: Yes

Sample:
```
<strike class="casual">Truman</strike> lost.
```

id="..."

Assigns a unique ID selector to an instance of the strike element. When you then assign a style to that ID selector, it affects only that one instance of the strike element.

Standard/Usage: HTML 4   Widely Supported: Yes

Sample:
```
Don <strike id="123">ain't</strike> isn't coming tonight.
```

style="..."

Specifies style sheet commands that apply to the contents of the strike element.

Standard/Usage: HTML 4   Widely Supported: Yes

Sample:
```
<strike style="background: red">...</strike>
```

title="..."

Specifies text assigned to the element. You can use this attribute for context-sensitive help within the document. Browsers may use this to show tooltips over the text.

Standard/Usage: HTML 4   **Widely Supported:** No

Sample:
```
<p>He was <strike title="omit">ambitious</strike>enthusiastic.</p>
```

NOTE *The* strike *element also accepts the* lang, dir, onclick, ondblclick, onmousedown, onmouseup, onmouseover, onmousemove, onmouseout, onkeypress, onkeydown, *and* onkeyup *attributes.*

strong

Indicates strong emphasis. The browser will probably display the text in a boldface font.

Standard/Usage: HTML 2   **Widely Supported:** Yes   **Empty:** No

Sample:
```
If you see a poisonous spider in the room then <strong>get out of there!</strong>
```

class="..."

Indicates which style class applies to the strong element.

Standard/Usage: HTML 4   **Widely Supported:** Yes

Sample:
```
Did you say my dog is <strong class="urgent">missing?!</strong>
```

id="..."

Assigns a unique ID selector to an instance of the strong element. When you then assign a style to that ID selector, it affects only that one instance of the strong element.

Standard/Usage: HTML 4   **Widely Supported:** Yes

Sample:
```
Sure, you can win at gambling. But you'll probably <strong id="123">lose</strong>.
```

style="..."

Specifies style sheet commands that apply to the contents of the strong element.

Standard/Usage: HTML 4   **Widely Supported:** Yes

Sample:
```
<strong style="background: red">...</strong>
```

title="..."

Specifies text assigned to the element. You can use this attribute for context-sensitive help within the document. Browsers may use this to show tooltips over the emphasized text.

Standard/Usage: HTML 4   **Widely Supported:** No

Sample:
```
I mean it was <strong title="emphasis">HOT!</strong>
```

NOTE   *The* strong *element also accepts the* lang, dir, onclick, ondblclick, onmousedown, onmouseup, onmouseover, onmousemove, onmouseout, onkeypress, onkeydown, *and* onkeyup *attributes.*

style

Contains style sheet definitions and appears in the document head (see the **head** element). Place style sheet data within comment markup (<!--...-->) to accommodate browsers that do not support the style element.

Standard/Usage: HTML 3.2   **Widely Supported:** Yes   **Empty:** No

Sample:
```
<html xmlns="http://www.w3.org/1999/xhtml">
   <head>
      <title>Edible Socks: Good or Bad?</title>
      <style type="text/css">
         <!--
            h1    { background: black; color: yellow }
            li dd { background: silver; color: black }
         -->
      </style>
   </head>
```

media="..."
Specifies the destination medium for style information. It may be a single type or a comma-separated list. Media types include the following:

Value	Media Type
all	Applies to all devices
aural	Speech synthesizer
braille	Braille tactile feedback devices
handheld	Handheld devices
print	Traditional printed material and documents on screen viewed in print preview mode
projection	Projectors
screen	Online viewing (default setting)
tty	Teletypes, terminals, or portable devices with limited display capabilities
tv	Television-type devices

Standard/Usage: HTML 4   **Widely Supported:** No

Sample:

```
<style type="text/css" media="all">
   <!--
      h1    { background: black; color: white }
      li dd { background: silver; color: darkgreen }
   -->
</style>
```

title="..."

Specifies text assigned to the element. You can use this attribute for context-sensitive help within the document. Browsers may use this to show tooltips, although there's really nothing for them to show the tooltips over.

Standard/Usage: HTML 4   **Widely Supported:** No

Sample:

```
<style title="Stylesheet 1" type="text/css">
   <!--
      h1 { background: black; color: yellow }
      li dd { background: silver; color: black }
   -->
</style>
```

type="..."

Specifies the MIME type of the style sheet specification standard used.

Standard/Usage: HTML 4; required   **Widely Supported:** No

Sample:

```
<style type="text/css">
   <!--
      h1 { background: black; color: white }
      li dd { background: silver; color: darkgreen }
   -->
</style>
```

NOTE   *The* style *element also accepts the* lang *and* dir *attributes.*

sub

Indicates subscripted text.

Standard/Usage: HTML 3.2   **Widely Supported:** Yes   **Empty:** No

Sample:

```
<p>Chemists refer to water as H<sub>2</sub>0.</p>
```

class="..."
Indicates which style class applies to the sub element.

> **Standard/Usage:** HTML 4   **Widely Supported:** Yes
>
> **Sample:**
> `H<sub class="chemical">2</sub>0`

id="..."
Assigns a unique ID selector to an instance of the sub element. When you then assign a style to that ID selector, it affects only that one instance of the sub element.

> **Standard/Usage:** HTML 4   **Widely Supported:** Yes
>
> **Sample:**
> `At the dentist I ask for lots of NO<sub id="123">2</sub>.`

style="..."
Specifies style sheet commands that apply to the contents of the sub element.

> **Standard/Usage:** HTML 4   **Widely Supported:** Yes
>
> **Sample:**
> `<sub style="background: red">...</sub>`

title="..."
Specifies text assigned to the element. You can use this attribute for context-sensitive help within the document. Browsers may use this to show tooltips over the subscripted text.

> **Standard/Usage:** HTML 4   **Widely Supported:** No
>
> **Sample:**
> `Before he fell asleep, he uttered, "Groovy. "<sub title="Footnote">2</sub>`

NOTE *The* sub *element also accepts the* lang, dir, onclick, ondblclick, onmousedown, onmouseup, onmouseover, onmousemove, onmouseout, onkeypress, onkeydown, *and* onkeyup *attributes.*

sup

Indicates superscripted text.

> **Standard/Usage:** HTML 3.2   **Widely Supported:** Yes   **Empty:** No
>
> **Sample:**
> `<p>Einstein's most famous equation is E=mc<sup>2</sup>.</p>`

class="..."
Indicates which style class applies to the sup element.

Standard/Usage: HTML 4   **Widely Supported:** Yes

Sample:
```
z<sup class="exp">2</sup> = x<sup class="exp">2</sup> + y<sup class="exp">2</sup>
```

id="..."

Assigns a unique ID selector to an instance of the sup element. When you then assign a style to that ID selector, it affects only that one instance of the sup element.

Standard/Usage: HTML 4   **Widely Supported:** Yes

Sample:
```
The Pythagorean theorem says z<sup id="123">2</sup> = 4 + 16.
```

style="..."

Specifies style sheet commands that apply to the contents of the sup element.

Standard/Usage: HTML 4   **Widely Supported:** Yes

Sample:
```
<sup style="background: red">...</sup>
```

title="..."

Specifies text assigned to the element. You can use this attribute for context-sensitive help within the document. Browsers may use this to show tooltips over the superscripted text.

Standard/Usage: HTML 4   **Widely Supported:** No

Sample:
```
x<sup title="Exponent">2</sup>
```

NOTE *The* sup *element also accepts the* lang, dir, onclick, ondblclick, onmousedown, onmouseup, onmouseover, onmousemove, onmouseout, onkeypress, onkeydown, *and* onkeyup *attributes.*

T

table

Specifies a container for a table within your document. Inside these elements you can place tr, td, th, caption, and other table elements.

Standard/Usage: HTML 3.2   **Widely Supported:** Yes   **Empty:** No

Sample:
```
<table border="0">
  <tr>
    <td><img src="pine.jpg" border="0" alt="pine" /></td>
    <td valign="middle">Pine trees naturally grow at higher elevations. They require
```

TABLE | **817**

```
                less water and do not shed leaves in the fall.</td>
        </tr>
    </table>
```

align="left | right | center"

Positions the table flush left, flush right, or in the center of the window. This attribute is deprecated in favor of style sheets.

Standard/Usage: HTML 3.2; deprecated   **Widely Supported:** Yes

Sample:
```
<table align="center">...</table>
```

background="url"

Specifies the relative or absolute location of an image file loaded as a background image for the entire table.

Standard/Usage: Internet Explorer 3, Netscape Navigator 4; deprecated   **Widely Supported:** No

Sample:
```
<table background="paper.jpg">...</table>
```

bgcolor="#rrggbb" or "..."

Specifies the background color within all table cells in the table. You can substitute color names for the hexadecimal RGB values. This attribute is deprecated in favor of style sheets.

Standard/Usage: HTML 4; deprecated   **Widely Supported:** No

Sample:
```
<table bgcolor="peach">...</table>
```

border="n"

Specifies the thickness (in pixels) of borders around each table cell. Use a value of 0 to produce a table with no visible borders.

Standard/Usage: HTML 3.2   **Widely Supported:** Yes

Sample:
```
<table border="0">...</table>
```

bordercolor="#rrggbb" or "..."

Specifies the color of the borders of all the table cells in the table. You can substitute color names for the hexadecimal RGB values.

Standard/Usage: Internet Explorer 2, Netscape Navigator 4   **Widely Supported:** No

Sample:
```
<table bordercolor="#3f9a11">...</table>
```

bordercolordark="#rrggbb" or "..."

Specifies the darker color used to draw 3D borders around the table cells. You can substitute color names for the hexadecimal RGB values.

> **Standard/Usage:** Internet Explorer 2   **Widely Supported:** No
>
> **Sample:**
> ```
> <table bordercolordark="silver">…</table>
> ```

bordercolorlight="#rrggbb" or "..."

Specifies the lighter color used to draw 3D borders around the table cells. You can substitute color names for the hexadecimal RGB values.

> **Standard/Usage:** Internet Explorer 2   **Widely Supported:** No
>
> **Sample:**
> ```
> <table bordercolorlight="white">…</table>
> ```

cellpadding="n"

Specifies the space (in pixels) between the edges of table cells and their contents.

> **Standard/Usage:** HTML 3.2   **Widely Supported:** Yes
>
> **Sample:**
> ```
> <table cellpadding="5">…</table>
> ```

cellspacing="n"

Specifies the space (in pixels) between the borders of table cells and the borders of adjacent cells.

> **Standard/Usage:** HTML 3.2   **Widely Supported:** Yes
>
> **Sample:**
> ```
> <table border="2" cellspacing="5">…</table>
> ```

class="..."

Indicates which style class applies to the `table` element.

> **Standard/Usage:** HTML 4   **Widely Supported:** Yes
>
> **Sample:**
> ```
> <table class="table" border="2">…</table>
> ```

cols="n"

Specifies the number of columns in the table.

> **Standard/Usage:** Internet Explorer 3, Netscape Navigator 4   **Widely Supported:** No
>
> **Sample:**
> ```
> <table border="2" cols="5">…</table>
> ```

TABLE | 819

frame="void | border | above | below | hsides | lhs | rhs | vsides | box"

Specifies the external borderlines *around* the table. For the frame attribute to work, set the border attribute to a nonzero value.

Value	Specifies
void	No borderlines
box or border	Borderlines around the entire table (the default)
above	A borderline along the top edge
below	A borderline along the bottom edge
hsides	Borderlines along the top and bottom edges
lhs	A borderline along the left edge
rhs	A borderline along the right edge
vsides	Borderlines along the left and right edges

Standard/Usage: HTML 4   **Widely Supported:** No

Sample:
```
<table border="2" rules="all" frame="vsides">…</table>
```

id="…"

Assigns a unique ID selector to an instance of the table element. When you then assign a style to that ID selector, it affects only that one instance of the table element.

Standard/Usage: HTML 4   **Widely Supported:** Yes

Sample:
```
<table id="123">…</table>
```

rules="none | rows | cols | all | groups"

Specifies where rule lines appear *inside* the table. For the rules attribute to work, set the border attribute to a nonzero value.

Value	Specifies
none	No rule lines
rows	Rule lines between rows
cols	Rule lines between columns
all	All possible rule lines
groups	Rule lines between the groups defined by the tfoot, thead, tbody, and colgroup elements

Standard/Usage: HTML 4   **Widely Supported:** No

Sample:
```
<table border="2" rules="all">…</table>
```

style="..."

Specifies style sheet commands that apply to the contents of cells in the table.

Standard/Usage: HTML 4   **Widely Supported:** Yes

Sample:
```
<table style="background: red">…</table>
```

summary="..."

Specifies descriptive text for the table. It's recommended that you use this attribute to summarize or describe the table for use by browsers that do not visually display tables (for example, Braille or text-only browsers).

Standard/Usage: HTML 4   **Widely Supported:** No

Sample:
```
<table summary="This table shows that 50% of sick days are taken on Mondays. ">
…</table>
```

title="..."

Specifies text assigned to the element. You can use this attribute for context-sensitive help within the document. Browsers may use this to show tooltips over the table.

Standard/Usage: HTML 4   **Widely Supported:** No

Sample:
```
<table title="table">…</table>
```

width="n"

Specifies the width of the table. You can set this value to an absolute number of pixels or to a percentage amount so the table is proportionally as wide as the available space.

Standard/Usage: HTML 3.2   **Widely Supported:** Yes

Sample:
```
<table align="center" width="60%">…</table>
```

NOTE *The* `table` *element also accepts the* `lang`, `dir`, `onclick`, `ondblclick`, `onmousedown`, `onmouseup`, `onmouseover`, `onmousemove`, `onmouseout`, `onkeypress`, `onkeydown`, *and* `onkeyup` *attributes.*

tbody

Defines the table body within a table. This element must *follow* the tfoot element.

> **Standard/Usage:** HTML 4   **Widely Supported:** No   **Empty:** No
>
> **Sample:**
> ```
> <table>
>    <thead>...</thead>
>    <tfoot>...</tfoot>
>    <tbody>...</tbody>
> </table>
> ```

align="left | right | center | justify | char"

Specifies how text within the table footer will line up with the edges of the table cells, or if align="char", on a specific character (the decimal point by default).

> **Standard/Usage:** HTML 4   **Widely Supported:** Yes
>
> **Sample:**
> ```
> <tbody align="left">...</tbody>
> ```

char="..."

Specifies the character on which cell contents will align, if align="char". If you omit the char attribute, the default value is the decimal point in the specified language.

> **Standard/Usage:** HTML 4   **Widely Supported:** No
>
> **Sample:**
> ```
> <tbody align="left" char="a">...</tbody>
> ```

charoff="n"

Specifies the number of characters from the left at which the alignment character appears.

> **Standard/Usage:** HTML 4   **Widely Supported:** No
>
> **Sample:**
> ```
> <tbody align="char" char="," charoff="7">...</tbody>
> ```

class="..."

Indicates which style class applies to the tbody element.

> **Standard/Usage:** HTML 4   **Widely Supported:** Yes
>
> **Sample:**
> ```
> <tbody class="casual">...</tbody>
> ```

id="..."

Assigns a unique ID selector to an instance of the tbody element. When you then assign a style to that ID selector, it affects only that one instance of the tbody element.

Standard/Usage: HTML 4   **Widely Supported:** Yes

Sample:
```
<tbody id="123"></tbody>
```

style="..."

Specifies style sheet commands that apply to the contents of the tbody element.

Standard/Usage: HTML 4   **Widely Supported:** Yes

Sample:
```
<tbody style="background: red">...</tbody>
```

title="..."

Specifies text assigned to the element. You can use this attribute for context-sensitive help within the document. Browsers may use this to show tooltips over the table body.

Standard/Usage: HTML 4   **Widely Supported:** No

Sample:
```
<tbody title="Table Body">...</tbody>
```

valign="top | bottom | middle | baseline"

Specifies the vertical alignment of the contents of the table body.

Standard/Usage: Internet Explorer 4   **Widely Supported:** No

Sample:
```
<tbody valign="middle">...</tbody>
```

NOTE   The tbody *element also accepts the* lang, dir, onclick, ondblclick, onmousedown, onmouseup, onmouseover, onmousemove, onmouseout, onkeypress, onkeydown, *and* onkeyup *attributes.*

td

Contains a table cell. These elements go inside tr elements.

Standard/Usage: HTML 3.2   **Widely Supported:** Yes   **Empty:** No

Sample:
```
<tr>
   <td>Bob Jones</td>
   <td>555-1212</td> <td>Democrat</td>
</tr>
```

abbr="..."

Specifies short replacement text associated with the element contents. When appropriate, browsers may use this text in place of the actual contents.

Standard/Usage: HTML 4   **Widely Supported:** No

Sample:
```
<td title="Year to Date Summary" abbr="ytd">Year to Date</td>
```

axis="..."

Specifies cell categories. The values can be a comma-separated list of category names.

Standard/Usage: HTML 4   **Widely Supported:** No

Sample:
```
<td axis="TV">Television</td>
```

align="left | right | center | justify | char"

Specifies how text within the table header will line up with the edges of the table cells, or if `align="char"`, on a specific character (the decimal point by default).

Standard/Usage: HTML 4   **Widely Supported:** Yes

Sample:
```
<tr>
   <td align="center">Television</td>
   <td><img src="tv.gif" alt="TV" border="0" /></td>
</tr>
```

background="url"

Specifies the relative or absolute location of an image file for the browser to load as a background graphic for the table cell.

Standard/Usage: Internet Explorer 4, Netscape Navigator 3   **Widely Supported:** No

Sample:
```
<td background="waves.gif">Oceanography</td>
```

bgcolor="#rrggbb" or "..."

Specifies the background color inside a table cell. You can substitute the hexadecimal RGB values for the appropriate color names. This attribute is deprecated in favor of style sheets.

Standard/Usage: HTML 4; deprecated   **Widely Supported:** No

Sample:
```
<td bgcolor="pink">Course Number</td>
```

bordercolor="#rrggbb" or "..."

Indicates the color of the border of the table cell. You can specify the color with hexadecimal RGB values or by the color name.

> **Standard/Usage:** Internet Explorer 2   **Widely Supported:** No
>
> **Sample:**
> ```
> <td bordercolor="blue">Time Taught</td>
> ```

bordercolordark="#rrggbb" or "..."

Indicates the darker color used to form 3D borders around the table cell. You can specify the color with its hexadecimal RGB values or with its color name.

> **Standard/Usage:** Internet Explorer 2   **Widely Supported:** No
>
> **Sample:**
> ```
> <td bordercolorlight="#ffffff" bordercolordark="#88aa2c">…</td>
> ```

bordercolorlight="#rrggbb" or "..."

Indicates the lighter color used to form 3D borders around the table cell. You can specify the color with its hexadecimal RGB values or with its color name.

> **Standard/Usage:** Internet Explorer 2   **Widely Supported:** No
>
> **Sample:**
> ```
> <td bordercolorlight="#ffffff" bordercolordark="#88aa2c">…</td>
> ```

char="..."

Specifies the character on which cell contents will align, if `align="char"`. If you omit the `char` attribute, the default value is the decimal point in the specified language.

> **Standard/Usage:** HTML 4   **Widely Supported:** No
>
> **Sample:**
> ```
> <td align="char" char=",">…</td>
> ```

charoff="n"

Specifies the number of characters from the left at which the alignment character appears.

> **Standard/Usage:** HTML 4   **Widely Supported:** No
>
> **Sample:**
> ```
> <td align="char" char="," charoff="7">…</td>
> ```

class="..."

Indicates which style class applies to the `td` element.

> **Standard/Usage:** HTML 4   **Widely Supported:** Yes

Sample:
```
<td class="casual">Jobs Produced</td>
```

colspan="n"

Specifies that a table cell occupies more columns than the default of 1. This is useful when you have a category name that applies to multiple columns of data.

Standard/Usage: HTML 3.2   **Widely Supported:** Yes

Sample:
```
<tr>
    <td colspan="2">Students</td>
</tr>
<tr>
    <td>Bob Smith</td>
    <td>Jane Doe</td>
</tr>
```

id="..."

Assigns a unique ID selector to an instance of the td element. When you then assign a style to that ID selector, it affects only that one instance of the td element.

Standard/Usage: HTML 4   **Widely Supported:** Yes

Sample:
```
<td id="123">...</td>
```

headers="..."

Specifies the ID names of table header cells associated with the current cell for use by browsers in presenting the table contents.

Standard/Usage: HTML 4   **Widely Supported:** No

Sample:
```
<td title="Year to Date Summary" headers="th1,th4">Year to Date</td>
```

height="n"

Specifies the vertical dimension (in pixels) of the cell. This attribute is deprecated in favor of style sheets.

Standard/Usage: HTML 3.2; deprecated   **Widely Supported:** No

Sample:
```
<td title="Year to Date Summary" height="200">Year to Date</td>
```

nowrap="nowrap"

Disables the default word-wrapping within a table cell, thus maximizing the amount of the cell's horizontal space. This attribute is deprecated in favor of style sheets.

Standard/Usage: HTML 3; deprecated   **Widely Supported:** No

Sample:
```
<td nowrap="nowrap">The contents of this cell will not wrap at all.</td>
```

rowspan="n"

Specifies that a table cell occupies more rows than the default of 1. This is useful when several rows of information are related to one category.

Standard/Usage: HTML 3.2   **Widely Supported:** Yes

Sample:
```
<tr>
   <td valign="middle" align="right" rowspan="3">Pie Entries</td>
   <td>Banana Cream</td>
   <td>Mrs. Robinson</td></tr>
<tr>
   <td>Strawberry Cheesecake</td>
   <td>Mr. Barton</td></tr>
<tr>
   <td>German Chocolate</td>
   <td>Ms. Larson</td></tr>
```

scope="row | col | rowgroup | colgroup"

Specifies the row, row group, column, or column group to which the specific header information contained in the current cell applies. When appropriate, browsers may use this information to help present the table.

Standard/Usage: HTML 4   **Widely Supported:** No

Sample:
```
<td title="Year to Date Summary" scope="rowgroup">Year to Date</td>
```

style="..."

Specifies style sheet commands that apply to the contents of the table cell.

Standard/Usage: HTML 4   **Widely Supported:** Yes

Sample:
```
<td style="background: red">...</td>
```

title="..."

Specifies text assigned to the element. You can use this attribute for context-sensitive help within the document. Browsers may use this to show tooltips over the table header.

Standard/Usage: HTML 4   **Widely Supported:** No

Sample:
```
<td title="table cell heading">...</td>
```

valign="top | middle | bottom | baseline"

Aligns the contents of a cell within the cell.

>   **Standard/Usage:** HTML 3.2   **Widely Supported:** Yes

>   **Sample:**
>   `<td valign="top"><img src="images/bud.gif" alt="bud.gif" border="0" /></td>`

width="n"

Specifies the horizontal dimension of the cell in pixels or as a percentage of the table width. This attribute is deprecated in favor of style sheets.

>   **Standard/Usage:** HTML 3.2; deprecated   **Widely Supported:** Yes

>   **Sample:**
>   `<td width="200" align="left">African Species</td>`

NOTE   The `td` *element also accepts the* `lang, dir, onclick, ondblclick, onmousedown, onmouseup,` `onmouseover, onmousemove, onmouseout, onkeypress, onkeydown,` *and* `onkeyup` *attributes.*

textarea

Defines a multiple-line text input field within a form. Place the `textarea` elements inside the `form` elements. To specify a default value in a `textarea` field, place the text between the `textarea` elements.

>   **Standard/Usage:** HTML 2   **Widely Supported:** Yes   **Empty:** No

>   **Sample:**
>   `Enter any comments here:`
>   `<textarea name="comments" cols="40" rows="5">No Comments.</textarea>`

accesskey="..."

Assigns a keystroke sequence to the `textarea` element.

>   **Standard/Usage:** HTML 4   **Widely Supported:** No

>   **Sample:**
>   `<textarea cols="40" rows="10" name="story" accesskey="s">...</textarea>`

class="..."

Indicates which style class applies to the `textarea` element.

>   **Standard/Usage:** HTML 4   **Widely Supported:** Yes

>   **Sample:**
>   `<textarea cols="50" rows="3" class="casual">...</textarea>`

cols="n"

Indicates the width (in characters) of the text input field.

Standard/Usage: HTML 2; required   **Widely Supported:** Yes

Sample:
```
<textarea name="desc" cols="50" rows="3">…</textarea>
```

disabled="disabled"

Denies access to the text input field.

Standard/Usage: HTML 4   **Widely Supported:** No

Sample:
```
<textarea rows="10" cols="10" name="comments" disabled="disabled">…</textarea>
```

id="…"

Assigns a unique ID selector to an instance of the textarea element. When you then assign a style to that ID selector, it affects only that one instance of the textarea element.

Standard/Usage: HTML 4   **Widely Supported:** Yes

Sample:
```
<textarea rows="10" cols="10" id="123">…</textarea>
```

name="…"

Names the value you pass to the form processor. For example, if you collect personal feedback, assign the name attribute something like comments. This establishes a name-value pair with which the form processor can work.

Standard/Usage: HTML 2   **Widely Supported:** Yes

Sample:
```
<textarea cols="30" rows="10" name="comments">…</textarea>
```

readonly="readonly"

Specifies that the user cannot change the contents of the text input field.

Standard/Usage: HTML 4   **Widely Supported:** No

Sample:
```
<textarea rows="10" cols="10" name="notes" readonly="readonly">…</textarea>
```

rows="n"

Indicates the height (in lines of text) of the text input field.

Standard/Usage: HTML 2; required   **Widely Supported:** Yes

Sample:
```
<textarea name="desc" cols="50" rows="3">…</textarea>
```

style="..."

Specifies style sheet commands that apply to the textarea element.

> **Standard/Usage:** HTML 4   **Widely Supported:** Yes

> **Sample:**
> ```
> <textarea rows="5" cols="40" style="background: red">...</textarea>
> ```

tabindex="n"

Indicates where textarea appears in the tabbing order.

> **Standard/Usage:** HTML 4   **Widely Supported:** No

> **Sample:**
> ```
> <textarea rows="5" cols="40" name="story" tabindex="2">...</textarea>
> ```

title="..."

Specifies text assigned to the element. You can use this attribute for context-sensitive help within the document. Browsers may use this to show tooltips over the text entry input method.

> **Standard/Usage:** HTML 4   **Widely Supported:** No

> **Sample:**
> ```
> <textarea cols="10" rows="2" name="tt" title="text entry box">...</textarea>
> ```

NOTE   *The* textarea *element also accepts the* lang, dir, onfocus, onblur, onchange, onselect, onclick, ondblclick, onmousedown, onmouseup, onmouseover, onmousemove, onmouseout, onkeypress, onkey-down, *and* onkeyup *attributes.*

tfoot

Defines a table footer within a table. It must *precede* the tbody element.

> **Standard/Usage:** HTML 4   **Widely Supported:** No   **Empty:** No

> **Sample:**
> ```
> <table>
>    <thead>...</thead>
>    <tfoot>
>       <tr><td>Totals</td><td>$100.25</td></tr>
>    </tfoot>
>    <tbody>...</tbody>
> </table>
> ```

align="left | right | center | justify | char"

Specifies how text within the table footer will line up with the edges of the table cells, or if align="char", on a specific character.

> **Standard/Usage:** HTML 4   **Widely Supported:** Yes
>
> **Sample:**
> ```
> <tfoot align="center">...</tfoot>
> ```

char="..."

Specifies the character on which cell contents will align, if `align="char"`. If you omit the `char` attribute, the default value is the decimal point in the specified language.

> **Standard/Usage:** HTML 4   **Widely Supported:** No
>
> **Sample:**
> ```
> <tfoot align="char" char=",">...</tfoot>
> ```

charoff="n"

Specifies the number of characters from the left at which the alignment character appears.

> **Standard/Usage:** HTML 4   **Widely Supported:** No
>
> **Sample:**
> ```
> <tfoot align="char" char="," charoff="7">...</tfoot>
> ```

class="..."

Indicates which style class applies to the **tfoot** element.

> **Standard/Usage:** HTML 4   **Widely Supported:** Yes
>
> **Sample:**
> ```
> <tfoot class="casual">...</tfoot>
> ```

id="..."

Assigns a unique ID selector to an instance of the **tfoot** element. When you then assign a style to that ID selector, it affects only that one instance of the **tfoot** element.

> **Standard/Usage:** HTML 4   **Widely Supported:** Yes
>
> **Sample:**
> ```
> <tfoot id="123">...</tfoot>
> ```

style="..."

Specifies style sheet commands that apply to the contents of the **tfoot** element.

> **Standard/Usage:** HTML 4   **Widely Supported:** Yes
>
> **Sample:**
> ```
> <tfoot style="background: red">...</tfoot>
> ```

title="..."

Specifies text assigned to the element. You can use this attribute for context-sensitive help within the document. Browsers may use this to show tooltips over the table footer.

Standard/Usage: HTML 4   **Widely Supported:** No

Sample:
```
<tfoot title="Table Footer">...</tfoot>
```

valign="top | bottom | middle | baseline"

Aligns the contents of the table footer with the top, bottom, or middle of the footer container.

Standard/Usage: HTML 4   **Widely Supported:** No

Sample:
```
<tfoot align="center" valign="top">...</tfoot>
```

NOTE   The `tfoot` *element also accepts the* `lang`, `dir`, `onclick`, `ondblclick`, `onmousedown`, `onmouseup`, `onmouseover`, `onmousemove`, `onmouseout`, `onkeypress`, `onkeydown`, *and* `onkeyup` *attributes.*

th

Contains table cell headings. The `th` element is identical to the `td` element except that text inside `th` is usually emphasized with boldface font, centered within the cell, and represents a table heading instead of table data.

Standard/Usage: HTML 3.2   **Widely Supported:** Yes   **Empty:** No

Sample:
```
<table>
   <tr>
      <th>Name</th>
      <th>Phone No.</th>
   </tr>
   <tr>
      <td>Jane Doe</td>
      <td>555-1212</td>
   </tr>
   <tr>
      <td>Bob Smith</td>
      <td>555-2121</td>
   </tr>
</table>
```

abbr="..."

Specifies short replacement text associated with the element contents. When appropriate, browsers may use this text in place of the actual contents.

Standard/Usage: HTML 4   **Widely Supported:** No

Sample:
```
<th title="Year to Date Summary" abbr="ytd">Year to Date</th>
```

align="left | right | center | justify | char"

Specifies how text within the table header will line up with the edges of the table cells or, if align="char", on a specific character (by default, the decimal point).

Standard/Usage: HTML 4   **Widely Supported:** Yes

Sample:
```
<th align="right">Television</th>
<th align="left"><img src="tv.gif" alt="tv" border="0" /></th>
```

axis="..."

Specifies cell categories. The value can be a comma-separated list of category names.

Standard/Usage: HTML 4   **Widely Supported:** No

Sample:
```
<th axis="TV">Television</th>
```

background="url"

Specifies the relative or absolute location of an image file for the browser to load as a background graphic for the table cell.

Standard/Usage: Internet Explorer 4, Netscape Navigator 3   **Widely Supported:** Yes

Sample:
```
<th background="waves.gif">Oceanography</th>
```

bgcolor="#rrggbb" or "..."

Specifies the background color inside a table cell. You can substitute the hexadecimal RGB values for the appropriate color names. This attribute is deprecated in favor of style sheets.

Standard/Usage: HTML 4; deprecated   **Widely Supported:** Yes

Sample:
```
<th bgcolor="pink">Course Number</th>
```

bordercolor="#rrggbb" or "..."

Indicates the color of the border of the table cell. You can specify the color with hexadecimal RGB values or by the color name.

Standard/Usage: Internet Explorer 2   **Widely Supported:** Yes

Sample:
```
<th bordercolor="blue">Time Taught</th>
```

bordercolordark="#rrggbb" or "…"

Indicates the darker color used to form 3D borders around the table cell. You can specify the color with its hexadecimal RGB values or with its color name.

Standard/Usage: Internet Explorer 2   **Widely Supported:** No

Sample:
```
<th bordercolorlight="#ffffff" bordercolordark="#88aa2c">…</th>
```

bordercolorlight="#rrggbb" or "…"

Indicates the lighter color used to form 3D borders around the table cell. You can specify the color with its hexadecimal RGB values or with its color name.

Standard/Usage: Internet Explorer 2   **Widely Supported:** No

Sample:
```
<th bordercolorlight="#ffffff" bordercolordark="#88aa2c">…</th>
```

char="…"

Specifies the character on which cell contents align, if `align="char"`. If you omit the `char` attribute, the default value is the decimal point in the specified language.

Standard/Usage: HTML 4   **Widely Supported:** No

Sample:
```
<th align="char" char=",">…</th>
```

charoff="n"

Specifies the number of characters from the left at which the alignment character appears.

Standard/Usage: HTML 4   **Widely Supported:** No

Sample:
```
<th align="char" char="," charoff="7">…</th>
```

class="…"

Indicates which style class applies to the th element.

Standard/Usage: HTML 4   **Widely Supported:** Yes

Sample:
```
<th class="casual">Jobs Produced</th>
```

colspan="n"

Specifies that a table header cell occupies more columns than the default of 1. Use this, for example, if a category name applies to more than one column of data.

Standard/Usage: HTML 3.2   **Widely Supported:** Yes

Sample:
```
<tr>
    <th colspan="2">Students</th>
</tr>
<tr>
    <td>Bob Smith</td>
    <td>Jane Doe</td>
</tr>
```

height="n"

Specifies the vertical dimension (in pixels) of the cell. This attribute is deprecated in favor of style sheets.

Standard/Usage: HTML 3.2; deprecated   **Widely Supported:** No

Sample:
```
<th title="Year to Date Summary" height="200">Year to Date</th>
```

id="..."

Assigns a unique ID selector to an instance of the th element. When you then assign a style to that ID selector, it affects only that one instance of the th element.

Standard/Usage: HTML 4   **Widely Supported:** Yes

Sample:
```
<th id="123">...</th>
```

headers="..."

Specifies the ID names of table header cells associated with the current cell for use by browsers in presenting the table contents.

Standard/Usage: HTML 4   **Widely Supported:** No

Sample:
```
<th title="Year to Date Summary" headers="th1,th4">Year to Date</th>
```

nowrap="nowrap"

Disables default word wrapping within a table cell, maximizing the cell's horizontal space. This attribute is deprecated in favor of style sheets.

Standard/Usage: HTML 4; deprecated   **Widely Supported:** No

Sample:
```
<th nowrap="nowrap">The contents of this cell will not wrap at all.</th>
```

rowspan="n"

Specifies that a table header cell occupies more rows than the default of 1. This is useful if several rows of information relate to one category.

Standard/Usage: HTML 3.2   **Widely Supported:** Yes

Sample:
```
<tr>
   <th valign="middle" align="right" rowspan="3">Pie Entries</th>
   <td>Banana Cream</td>
   <td>Mrs. Robinson</td></tr>
<tr>
   <td>Strawberry Cheesecake</td>
   <td>Mr. Barton</td></tr>
<tr>
   <td>German Chocolate</td>
   <td>Ms. Larson</td></tr>
```

scope="row | col | rowgroup | colgroup"

Specifies the row, row group, column, or column group to which the specific header information contained in the current cell applies. When appropriate, browsers may use this information to help present the table.

Standard/Usage: HTML 4   **Widely Supported:** No

Sample:
```
<th title="Year to Date Summary" scope="rowgroup">Year to Date</th>
```

style="..."

Specifies style sheet commands that apply to the contents of the table header.

Standard/Usage: HTML 4   **Widely Supported:** Yes

Sample:
```
<th style="background: red">...</th>
```

title="..."

Specifies text assigned to the element. You can use this attribute for context-sensitive help within the document. Browsers may use this to show tooltips over the table header.

Standard/Usage: HTML 4   **Widely Supported:** No

Sample:
```
<th title="Table Cell Heading">...</th>
```

valign="top | middle | bottom | baseline"

Aligns the contents of a cell within the cell.

Standard/Usage: HTML 3.2   **Widely Supported:** Yes

Sample:
```
<th valign="top"><img src="images/bud.gif" alt="bud.gif" border="0" /></th>
```

width="n"

Specifies the horizontal dimension of the cell in pixels or as a percentage of the table width. This attribute is deprecated in favor of style sheets.

Standard/Usage: HTML 3.2; deprecated **Widely Supported:** Yes

Sample:
```
<th width="200" align="left">African Species</th>
```

NOTE *The* th *element also accepts the* lang, dir, onclick, ondblclick, onmousedown, onmouseup, onmouseover, onmousemove, onmouseout, onkeypress, onkeydown, *and* onkeyup *attributes.*

thead

Defines a table header section. At least one table row must go within thead.

Standard/Usage: HTML 4 **Widely Supported:** No **Empty:** No

Sample:
```
<table rules="rows">
   <thead>
      <tr><td>Column 1</td><td>Column 2</td></tr>
   </thead>
</table>
```

align="left|right|center|justify|char"

Specifies how text within the table header will line up with the edges of the table cells, or if align="char", on a specific character (by default, the decimal point).

Standard/Usage: HTML 4 **Widely Supported:** Yes

Sample:
```
<thead align="center">
   <tr>
      <th>Television</th>
      <th>Radio</th>
   </tr>
</thead>
```

char="..."

Specifies the character on which cell contents align, if align="char". If you omit the char attribute, the default value is the decimal point in the specified language.

Standard/Usage: HTML 4 **Widely Supported:** No

Sample:
```
<thead align="char" char=",">...</thead>
```

charoff="n"

Specifies the number of characters from the left at which the alignment character appears.

Standard/Usage: HTML 4   **Widely Supported:** No

Sample:
```
<thead align="char" char="," charoff="7">…</thead>
```

class="..."

Indicates which style class applies to the thead element.

Standard/Usage: HTML 4   **Widely Supported:** Yes

Sample:
```
<thead class="casual">…</thead>
```

id="..."

Assigns a unique ID selector to an instance of the thead element. When you then assign a style to that ID selector, it affects only that one instance of the thead element.

Standard/Usage: HTML 4   **Widely Supported:** No

Sample:
```
<thead id="123">…</thead>
```

style="..."

Specifies style sheet commands that apply to the contents of the thead element.

Standard/Usage: HTML 4   **Widely Supported:** Yes

Sample:
```
<thead style="background: red">…</thead>
```

title="..."

Specifies text assigned to the element. You can use this attribute for context-sensitive help within the document. Browsers may use this to show tooltips over the table head.

Standard/Usage: HTML 4   **Widely Supported:** No

Sample:
```
<thead title="table heading">…</thead>
```

valign="top|middle|bottom|baseline"

Aligns the contents of the table header with respect to the top and bottom edges of the header container.

Standard/Usage: HTML 4   **Widely Supported:** No

Sample:
```
<thead align="left" valign="top">…</thead>
```

NOTE *The* thead *element also accepts the* lang, dir, onclick, ondblclick, onmousedown, onmouseup, onmouseover, onmousemove, onmouseout, onkeypress, onkeydown, *and* onkeyup *attributes.*

title

Gives the document an official title. The title element appears in the document header inside the head elements and is required for valid XHTML.

Standard/Usage: HTML 2; required   **Widely Supported:** Yes   **Empty:** No

Sample:
```
<head><title>How To Build a Go-Cart</title>…</head>
```

This element accepts the lang and dir attributes.

tr

Contains a row of cells in a table. You must place the tr elements inside the table container, which can contain th and td elements.

Standard/Usage: HTML 3.2   **Widely Supported:** Yes   **Empty:** No

Sample:
```
<table>
   <tr>
      <th colspan="3">Test Scores</th></tr>
   <tr>
      <td>Bob Smith</td>
      <td>78</td>
      <td>85</td></tr>
   <tr>
      <td>Jane Doe</td>
      <td>87</td>
      <td>75</td></tr>
</table>
```

align="left | right | center | justify | char"
Specifies how text within the table row will line up with the edges of the table cells or, if align="char", on a specific character (by default, the decimal point).

Standard/Usage: HTML 4   **Widely Supported:** Yes

Sample:
```
<tr align="center">
   <td>Television</td>
   <td>Internet</td>
</tr>
```

bgcolor="#rrggbb" or "..."
Specifies the background color of table cells in the row. You can substitute the color names for the hexadecimal RGB values. This attribute is deprecated in favor of style sheets.

Standard/Usage: HTML 4; deprecated   **Widely Supported:** No

Sample:
```
<tr bgcolor="yellow">
   <td><img src="bette.jpg" alt="bette" border="0" /></td>
   <td align="left" valign="middle">Bette Smith sitting at her desk.</td>
</tr>
```

bordercolor="#rrggbb" or "..."
Specifies the color of cell borders within the row. Only Internet Explorer supports this attribute. You can substitute color names for the hexadecimal RGB values.

Standard/Usage: Internet Explorer 2   **Widely Supported:** No

Sample:
```
<tr bordercolor="#3F2A55">
   <td align="right" valign="middle">Computers</td>
   <td><img src="computers.jpg" /></td>
</tr>
```

bordercolordark="#rrggbb" or "..."
Indicates the darker color for the 3D borders around the table row. You can specify the color with its hexadecimal RGB values or with its color name.

Standard/Usage: Internet Explorer 2   **Widely Supported:** No

Sample:
```
<tr bordercolorlight="silver" bordercolordark="black">...</tr>
```

bordercolorlight="#rrggbb" or "..."
Indicates the lighter color for 3D borders around the table row. You can specify the color with its hexadecimal RGB values or with its color name.

Standard/Usage: Internet Explorer 2   **Widely Supported:** No

Sample:
```
<tr bordercolorlight="silver" bordercolordark="black">...</tr>
```

char="..."
Specifies the character on which cell contents align, if align="char". If you omit the char attribute, the default value is the decimal point in the specified language.

Standard/Usage: HTML 4   **Widely Supported:** No

Sample:
```
<tr align="char" char=",">...</tr>
```

charoff="n"

Specifies the number of characters from the left at which the alignment character appears.

Standard/Usage: HTML 4 **Widely Supported:** No

Sample:
```
<tr align="char" char="," charoff="7">…</tr>
```

class="..."

Indicates which style class applies to the tr element.

Standard/Usage: HTML 4 **Widely Supported:** Yes

Sample:
```
<tr class="elementary">
   <td>Uranium</td>
   <td>Plutonium</td>
   <td>Radon</td>
</tr>
```

id="..."

Assigns a unique ID selector to an instance of the tr element. When you then assign a style to that ID selector, it affects only that one instance of the tr element.

Standard/Usage: HTML 4 **Widely Supported:** Yes

Sample:
```
<tr id="123">…</tr>
```

style="..."

Specifies style sheet commands that apply to all cells in the table row.

Standard/Usage: HTML 4 **Widely Supported:** Yes

Sample:
```
<tr style="background: red">…</tr>
```

title="..."

Specifies text assigned to the element. You can use this attribute for context-sensitive help within the document. Browsers may use this to show tooltips.

Standard/Usage: HTML 4 **Widely Supported:** No

Sample:
```
<tr title="table row">…</tr>
```

valign="top | middle | bottom | baseline"

Specifies the vertical alignment of the contents of all cells within the row.

Standard/Usage: HTML 3.2 **Widely Supported:** Yes

Sample:
```
<tr valign="top">
    <td align="center">Jane Smith</td>
    <td align="center">Bob Doe</td>
</tr>
```

NOTE   *The* tr *element also accepts the* lang, dir, onclick, ondblclick, onmousedown, onmouseup, onmouseover, onmousemove, onmouseout, onkeypress, onkeydown, *and* onkeyup *attributes.*

tt

Displays text in a monospace font.

Standard/Usage: HTML 2   **Widely Supported:** Yes   **Empty:** No

Sample:
```
After I typed help, the words <tt>help: not found</tt> appeared on my screen.
```

class="..."

Indicates which style class applies to the tt element.

Standard/Usage: HTML 4   **Widely Supported:** Yes

Sample:
```
<p>I began to type. <tt class="casual">It was a dark and stormy night.</tt></p>
```

id="..."

Assigns a unique ID selector to an instance of the tt element. When you then assign a style to that ID selector, it affects only that one instance of the tt element.

Standard/Usage: HTML 4   **Widely Supported:** Yes

Sample:
```
<tt id="123">...</tt>
```

style="..."

Specifies style sheet commands that apply to the contents of the tt elements.

Standard/Usage: HTML 4   **Widely Supported:** Yes

Sample:
```
<tt style="background: red">...</tt>
```

title="..."

Specifies text assigned to the element. You can use this attribute for context-sensitive help within the document. Browsers may use this to show tooltips over the text within the tt elements.

Standard/Usage: HTML 4   **Widely Supported:** No

Sample:
```
<p>Now, type <tt title="user typing">mail</tt> and hit the <kbd>Enter</kbd> key.</p>
```

NOTE   The tt *element also accepts the* lang, dir, onclick, ondblclick, onmousedown, onmouseup, onmouseover, onmousemove, onmouseout, onkeypress, onkeydown, *and* onkeyup *attributes.*

U

u

Underlines text in a document. Use this element in moderation; underlined text can confuse users, because they're accustomed to seeing hyperlinks underlined. This element is deprecated in HTML 4 in favor of style sheets.

Standard/Usage: HTML 2; deprecated   **Widely Supported:** Yes   **Empty:** No

Sample:
```
After waterskiing, I was <u>really</u> tired.
```

class="..."
Indicates which style class applies to the u element.

Standard/Usage: HTML 4   **Widely Supported:** Yes

Sample:
```
Have you seen <u class="casual">Tomb Raider</u> yet?
```

id="..."
Assigns a unique ID selector to an instance of the u element. When you then assign a style to that ID selector, it affects only that one instance of the u element.

Standard/Usage: HTML 4   **Widely Supported:** Yes

Sample:
```
<u id="123">…</u>
```

style="..."
Specifies style sheet commands that apply to the contents of the u element.

Standard/Usage: HTML 4   **Widely Supported:** Yes

Sample:
```
<u style="background: red">…</u>
```

title="..."

Specifies text assigned to the element. You can use this attribute for context-sensitive help within the document. Browsers may use this to show tooltips over the underlined text.

Standard/Usage: HTML 4   **Widely Supported:** No

Sample:
```
<p>Read the book <u title="BookTitle">Walden</u> and you'll be enlightened.</p>
```

NOTE *The* u *element also accepts the* lang, dir, onclick, ondblclick, onmousedown, onmouseup, onmouseover, onmousemove, onmouseout, onkeypress, onkeydown, *and* onkeyup *attributes.*

ul

Contains a bulleted (unordered) list. You then use the li (list item) element to add bulleted items to the list.

Standard/Usage: HTML 2   **Widely Supported:** Yes   **Empty:** No

Sample:
```
Before you can begin, you need:
<ul>
    <li>Circular saw</li>
    <li>Drill with Phillips bit</li>
    <li>Wood screws</li>
</ul>
```

class="..."

Indicates which style class applies to the ul element. Use li elements within the ul element.

Standard/Usage: HTML 4   **Widely Supported:** Yes

Sample:
```
<ul class="casual">...</ul>
```

compact="compact"

Indicates that the unordered list appears in a compact format. This attribute may not affect the appearance of the list because most browsers do not present lists in more than one format. This attribute is deprecated in HTML 4.

Standard/Usage: HTML 2; deprecated   **Widely Supported:** No

Sample:
```
<ul compact="compact">...</ul>
```

id="..."

Assigns a unique ID selector to an instance of the ul element. When you then assign a style to that ID selector, it affects only that one instance of the ul element.

> **Standard/Usage:** HTML 4   **Widely Supported:** Yes
>
> **Sample:**
> `<ul id="123">...</ul>`

style="..."

Specifies style sheet commands that apply to the contents of the unordered list.

> **Standard/Usage:** HTML 4   **Widely Supported:** Yes
>
> **Sample:**
> `<ul style="background: red">...</ul>`

title="..."

Specifies text assigned to the element. You can use this attribute for context-sensitive help within the document. Browsers may use this to show tooltips over the unordered list.

> **Standard/Usage:** HTML 4   **Widely Supported:** No
>
> **Sample:**
> ```
> <ul title="Food List">
>    <li>Spaghetti</li>
>    <li>Pizza</li>
>    <li>Fettuccini Alfredo</li>
> </ul>
> ```

type="square | circle | disc"

Specifies the bullet type for each unordered list item. If you omit the type attribute, the browser chooses a default type.

> **Standard/Usage:** HTML 2; deprecated   **Widely Supported:** Yes
>
> **Sample:**
> ```
> <ul type="disc">
>    <li>Spaghetti</li>
>    <ul type="square">
>       <li>Noodles</li>
>       <li>Sauce</li>
>       <li>Cheese</li>
>    </ul>
> </ul>
> ```

NOTE   *The* ul *element also accepts the* lang, dir, onclick, ondblclick, onmousedown, onmouseup, onmouseover, onmousemove, onmouseout, onkeypress, onkeydown, *and* onkeyup *attributes.*

V

var

Indicates a placeholder variable in document text. This is useful when describing commands for which the user must supply a parameter.

Standard/Usage: HTML 2   **Widely Supported:** Yes   **Empty:** No

Sample:
```
To copy a file in DOS, type <samp>COPY <var>file1</var> <var>file2</var></samp>
    and press the Enter key.
```

class="..."
Indicates which style class applies to the var element.

Standard/Usage: HTML 4   **Widely Supported:** Yes

Sample:
```
<p>I, <var class="casual">your name</var>, solemnly swear to tell the truth.</p>
```

id="..."
Assigns a unique ID selector to an instance of the var element. When you then assign a style to that ID selector, it affects only that one instance of the var element.

Standard/Usage: HTML 4   **Widely Supported:** Yes

Sample:
```
<var id="123">…</var>
```

style="..."
Specifies style sheet commands that apply to the contents of the var element.

Standard/Usage: HTML 4   **Widely Supported:** Yes

Sample:
```
<var style="background: red">…</var>
```

title="..."
Specifies text assigned to the element. You can use this attribute for context-sensitive help within the document. Browsers may use this to show tooltips over the text within the var elements.

Standard/Usage: HTML 4   **Widely Supported:** No

Sample:
```
Use an <code>h</code><var title="Heading level number">n</var> element.
```

NOTE   *The* var *element also accepts the* lang, dir, onclick, ondblclick, onmousedown, onmouseup, onmouseover, onmousemove, onmouseout, onkeypress, onkeydown, *and* onkeyup *attributes.*

W

wbr

Forces a word break. This is useful in combination with the nobr element to permit line breaks where they would otherwise not occur. This element has no attributes.

Standard/Usage: Netscape Navigator   **Widely Supported:** No   **Empty:** Yes

Sample:
```
<nobr>This line would go on
forever, except that I have
this neat tag called wbr
that does <wbr />this!</nobr>
```

Master's Reference Part 2

Cascading Style Sheets Reference

THIS REFERENCE LISTS PROPERTIES that you can use to set up style sheets or to introduce styles into a document. For a thorough introduction to style sheets and their capabilities, including an introduction to some of the specialized terminology used in this reference section, see Chapter 9.

This section includes a complete discussion of Cascading Style Sheets level 1 (traditionally noted as CSS1) as well as introductions to some of the Cascading Style Sheets level 2 (noted as CSS2) features that might be of value to you as you're developing your HTML or XHTML documents. At the time of this writing, most commonly available browsers support CSS1 completely, but only a few browsers support any CSS2 features (and then do not support all of them). So, as always, test your documents thoroughly on as many browsers and computers as possible before you use new features.

NOTE   *As described in Chapter 9, CSS3 is currently being developed, but as of the time of this writing, does not yet have any browser support. You can keep up with the latest CSS3 developments at the W3C site:* www.w3.org/TR/css3-roadmap/.

TIP   *You might refer to the following chapters as you're reading this section:*

Chapter 4, specifically the section called "Choosing Suitable Colors"

Chapter 9, if you're getting started with style sheets

Chapter 13, for information on implementing a coherent Web site

Chapter 20, to learn how you can validate style sheets

General Information

The CSS properties are organized into the following categories:

♦ Selectors, which summarize the combinations of selectors you can use

♦ Colors, which describe the many ways to specify colors in style sheets

♦ Universal properties and values, which apply in many or most cases through style sheets

♦ Font properties, which affect the style of the typeface

♦ Text properties, which control paragraph and line values

♦ Box padding, border, margin, and position properties, which place the box contents within its boundaries on a page

♦ Color and background properties, which specify background colors and images, not just for the whole page, but for each element

♦ Classification properties, which control the presentation of standard elements, such as display and lists

♦ Aural style sheet properties, which control the aural presentation of HTML and XHTML documents

♦ Printed style sheet properties, which add features specifically to control printed output of HTML and XHTML documents

♦ Auto-generated content properties, which add features that help automatically insert content or automatically number parts of HTML and XHTML documents

WARNING   We don't cover the CSS2 table properties in this Master's Reference because they're currently not widely supported and the traditional HTML and XHTML table elements are still widely supported. If you're feeling brave and lucky (or if you know you're writing for browsers that do implement CSS2) and want to check out CSS2 tables for yourself, visit the CSS2 tables section at `www.w3.org/TR/REC-CSS2/tables.html`*. If not, use the HTML and XHTML table elements discussed in Chapter 5 to develop your tables.*

In this reference, you'll generally find a description of the property, a list of the property's values, notes about the use of the property, and examples of the property used in statements. Note that in the "Values" sections, if the value is a keyword, it's in program font (`like this`) and you use it as written; if it's a category of value, such as "Length" or "Percentage," it just appears in the normal font and you use the appropriate values as discussed in the description.

WARNING   At the time of this writing, the newest versions of Internet Explorer 6 and Netscape 6 support CSS1 almost completely (but not always consistently), and support for the CSS2 features is buggy and sketchy. Be sure to test extensively on a variety of browsers before relying on any of the properties listed in this reference. See Chapter 9 for additional information about tailoring your style sheets to specific browser capabilities. See `www.webreview.com/style/css1/charts/mastergrid.shtml` *for a good reference of browser support for various features.*

Throughout this reference, you'll also see references to various element types. The common element types are defined as follows:

Inline element   Does not start and stop on its own line, but is included in the flow of another element. A standard inline element is em, for emphasis; you can also include images in the stream of text as an inline element.

Block element   Starts on its own line and ends with another line break.

List item   Is a subset of block elements, but is contained within a larger block element.

Comments

Comments in CSS begin with the characters /* and end with the characters */. Don't use the traditional HTML and XHTML comment markup <!-- --> within your CSS markup. Additionally, don't nest comments inside each other.

```
/* this is a comment in a CSS file */
```

Selectors

You use selectors to indicate to which HTML or XHTML elements a style statement applies. You can assemble selectors in several combinations, which will each have different meanings.
Table MR2.1 shows selectors, examples, and descriptions. The first five selectors come from CSS1 and work for all CSS implementations; the remaining selectors come from CSS2 and work only in CSS2-compliant browsers. You can use these selectors individually or together.

TABLE MR2.1: SELECTORS

SELECTOR PATTERN	EXAMPLE	DESCRIPTION
element	p {color: black}	Sets all p elements to black. (CSS1)
element element	p em {color: black}	Sets all em elements contained in p elements to black. This contextual selector does not affect em elements contained in other elements (such as h1, for example). (CSS1)
element.classname	p.newclass {color: black}	Sets all p elements that have class="newclass" to black. (CSS1)
.classname	.newclass {color: black}	Sets all elements that have class="newclass" to black. (CSS1)
#idvalue	#uniqueid {color: black}	Sets the element with id="uniqueid" to black. (CSS1)
*	* {color: black}	Sets all elements to black. (CSS2)
element > element	p > em {color: black}	Sets any em element that is contained in a p element to black. (CSS2)

Continued on next page

TABLE MR2.1: SELECTORS *(continued)*

SELECTOR PATTERN	EXAMPLE	DESCRIPTION
element + element	p + blockquote {color: black}	Sets any blockquote element that immediately follows a p element to black. (CSS2)
element[attribute]	a[href] {color: black}	Sets any a element that includes an href attribute to black. (CSS2)
element[attribute ="value"]	a[href="http://www.example .com/"] {color: black}	Sets any a element that includes an href attribute with the value "http://www.example .com/" to black (the value must be exact). (CSS2)
element[attribute~ ="value"]	a[href~="index"] {color: black}	Sets any a element that includes an href attribute with a value of a space-separated list of words containing "index" to black. (CSS2)
element[attribute| ="value"]	a[lang|="en"] {color: black}	Sets any a element that includes a language attribute beginning with the value "en" in a hyphen-separated list of words to black (CSS2)

Pseudoclasses

Pseudoclasses, which are closely related to selectors, refer to elements that do not explicitly exist in HTML and XHTML documents but that can be inferred from location. For example, CSS1 offers the pseudoclasses :first-letter and :first-line (although browsers have not yet done anything with these features). Table MR2.2 summarizes CSS1 and CSS2 pseudoclasses.

TABLE MR2.2: PSEUDOCLASSES

PSEUDOCLASS	EXAMPLE	DESCRIPTION
:first-line	p:first-line {color: red} p {color: black}	Sets the first line of all p elements to red, with the remaining lines black. (CSS1)
:first-letter	p:first-letter {color: red} p {color: black}	Sets the first letter of all p elements to red, with the remaining letters and lines black. (CSS1)
:first-child	h1:first-child {color: red}	Sets the first child element under a h1 element to red. (CSS2)
:hover	p:hover {color: red}	Sets all p elements to red when the mouse cursor hovers over them. (CSS2)
:lang	p:lang(en) {color: red}	Sets all p elements set to language "en" (English) to red. (CSS2)

Continued on next page

TABLE MR2.2: PSEUDOCLASSES *(continued)*

PSEUDOCLASS	EXAMPLE	DESCRIPTION
:first	@page:first {page-break-before: left}	Specifies that the first printed page start on the left. (CSS2)
:left	@page:left {margin: 2in}	Specifies 2-inch margins on all left printed pages. (CSS2)
:right	@page:right {margin: 2in}	Specifies 2-inch margins on all right printed pages. (CSS2)
:before	p:before {content: "para: "}	Specifies content to insert before an element.
:hover:after	p:after {content: "\""}	Places " after all paragraph elements (the \ escapes the " in the statement). (CSS2)
:focus	button:focus {color: red}	Sets properties for a form element when the element has the focus. This example sets button elements to red when they have the cursor focus. (CSS2)
:active	button:active {color: red}	Sets properties for a form element when the element is active. This example sets button elements to red when they are active. (CSS2)

See also the outline-color, outline-style, outline-width, and outline properties, which can be used with the :focus pseudoclass above.

Inherit Values

The inherit value can apply for any property in a style sheet. It explicitly indicates that the value of that property must be inherited from the parent element's value. This value is new (and only available) in CSS2. For example,

```
p {font-family: inherit}
```

means that every p element should inherit its font-family from its immediate parent.

Colors

You can set color values for many CSS properties. In all CSS properties that accommodate color specifications, you can use either color keywords or RGB values to specify border colors. If you name a color, the browser must be able to recognize the keyword. Because all browsers recognize the RGB colors, they're generally a safer choice.

Table MR2.3 lists the keyword, hexadecimal, integer, and percentage values for all colors that have generally recognized keywords (these colors are taken from the Windows VGA palette). You can actually include many more colors in style sheets.

WARNING   Even though browsers recognize the RGB colors and you can use more than the ones listed here, they may not render some of the more obscure colors the way you expect. Therefore, always test your pages on as many browsers as you can.

TABLE MR2.3: EQUIVALENT COLOR SPECIFICATIONS IN VARIOUS SYSTEMS

COLOR KEYWORD	RGB HEX	RGB INTEGER	RGB PERCENTAGE
aqua	#00ffff	rgb(0,255,255)	rgb(0%,100%,100%)
black	#000000	rgb(0,0,0)	rgb(0%,0%,0%)
blue	#0000ff	rgb(0,0,255)	rgb(0%,0%,100%)
fuchsia	#ff00ff	rgb(255,0,255)	rgb(100%,0%,100%)
gray	#808080	rgb(128,128,128)	rgb(50%,50%,50%)
green	#008000	rgb(0,128,0)	rgb(0%,50%,0%)
lime	#00ff00	rgb(0,255,0)	rgb(0%,100%,0%)
maroon	#800000	rgb(128,0,0)	rgb(50%,0%,0%)
navy	#000080	rgb(0,0,128)	rgb(0%,0%,50%)
olive	#808000	rgb(128,128,0)	rgb(50%,50%,0%)
purple	#800080	rgb(128,0,128)	rgb(50%,0%,50%)
red	#ff0000	rgb(255,0,0)	rgb(100%,0%,0%)
silver	#c0c0c0	rgb(192,192,192)	rgb(75%,75%,75%)
teal	#008080	rgb(0,128,128)	rgb(0%,50%,50%)
white	#ffffff	rgb(255,255,255)	rgb(100%,100%,100%)
yellow	#ffff00	rgb(255,255,0)	rgb(100%,100%,0%)

When specifying colors with RGB numbers, in any system, it's helpful (and good code form) to include a comment that indicates what color you expect. For example, reading this line,

```
p {border-color: #000080 #00008b blue #0000cd}
```

it's a little difficult to tell what the outcome should look like. But this code

```
p {border-color: #000080 #00008b blue #0000cd}
    /* TOP navy blue, R dark blue, BOT blue, L med. blue */
```

is much easier to picture.

TIP *For more information about choosing colors, visit Chapters 4 and 13. Or, for additional resources regarding browser-safe colors and values, visit Part 5 of this Master's Reference.*

CSS2 COLOR FEATURES

The following additional CSS2 color values let your HTML and XHTML documents use the user's operating system colors:

ActiveBorder	InfoBackground
ActiveCaption	InfoText
AppWorkspace	Menu
Background	MenuText
ButtonFace	Scrollbar
ButtonHighlight	ThreeDDarkShadow
ButtonText	ThreeDFace
CaptionText	ThreeDHighlight
GrayText	ThreeDLightshadow
Highlight	ThreeDShadow
HighlightText	Window
InactiveBorder	WindowFrame
InactiveCaption	WindowText

For example, the code

```
p {color: MenuText}
```

makes paragraph text the same color as the menu text on the user's computer.

Lengths

Many properties can be defined as a length. Length values set a property as a number plus a unit abbreviation. Some standard units of measurement are described in Table MR2.4.

TABLE MR2.4: STANDARD UNITS OF MEASUREMENT

ABBREVIATION	UNIT	EXAMPLE	NOTES
cm	Centimeters	2.5cm	
em	Ems	3em	1 em equals the font's point size.
in	Inches	1in	
mm	Millimeters	25mm	
pc	Picas	6pc	1 inch = 6 picas
px	Pixels	96px	
pt	Points	72pt	1 inch = 72 points
ex	X-heights	2ex	1 x-height usually equals the height of the lowercase letter *x*.

When you specify a length, relative units set up the property in relation to other font and size properties. Use relative units wherever you can, because they scale more easily from situation to situation (for example, in different browsers and displays, or in the transition from display to printer). Relative units include em (in CSS, 1 em is equal to the font's point size), ex (usually the height of the lowercase letters that have no ascenders or descenders: x or e), and px (screen pixels). The em and ex settings usually generate a font size relative to the parent font.

Absolute lengths are useful when the properties of the browser are well known or when you want to set a particular value to conform to a specification. Absolute units include inches, millimeters, centimeters, points (1 point = 1/72 inch), and picas (1 pica = 12 points = 1/6 inch).

Percentages

You can set many properties as a percentage of something else—a percentage of the parent element's value for the property, or a percentage of another property of the current element. Specify this type of value simply by including a % symbol after the number, as in font-size: 90%.

Font Properties

The font properties control the display of text elements, such as headings and paragraphs. This is the most common type of formatting you'll use in style sheets. These properties—particularly the font-family property—are also the most problematic, because no standard exists for fonts. Therefore, what works on one system or one platform may not work on another. Fortunately, you can specify alternative font families, as well as a generic font family.

The six font properties cover the font family (typeface), weight, and effects such as small caps or italics. The first property, font, is a *shorthand* property, as explained next.

font

Use this property as a shortcut to incorporate any or all of the other font properties. If you use the font shorthand property, you can also set the line spacing, using the line-height property (listed later in the "Text Properties" section of this reference). You can include one, many, or all of the font properties in this one property.

If you do not set the font-style, font-variant, font-weight, or font-family in this statement, you're essentially accepting the document default values for these properties. Shorthand properties do not have default settings; refer to entries for the individual properties for their default values.

If you set the font properties for an element, these settings are used by inline elements (such as em) that are nested within such an element and by all elements of that type unless a class definition overwrites the settings.

VALUES

The possible values for the font property are the set of all possible values listed in the individual property entries, which must be set in this order (though optional properties can be omitted altogether):

Property	Effect
`font-style`	Sets the font to an oblique or italic face (optional), or back to normal face.
`font-weight`	Sets the font to lighter or bolder (optional).
`font-variant`	Sets the font to small caps (optional).
`font-size`	Sets the size of the font (required).
`line-height`	Sets the line spacing for the font (optional).
`font-family`	Sets the font face or type used (required).

See the entries for the individual properties for more details about these values. (Note that the sections for the individual properties are arranged alphabetically, whereas this table is arranged in the order in which the properties should occur.)

NOTES

If you do not include a setting for a particular property (such as `font-variant`), the browser uses the parent value of that property.

EXAMPLES

```
h1 {font: bold 14pt/18pt Arial, Helvetica, sans-serif}
```

This statement uses values for the `font-style`, `font-size`, `line-height`, and `font-family` (in that order). The `font-style` is bold. The `font-size` is 14 points, and the `line-height` is 18 points. For the `font-family`, three values are listed, telling the browser to use Arial, and if Arial is not available use Helvetica, and if Helvetica is not available use a generic sans-serif font.

```
h3 {font: 12pt/120% serif}
```

This statement sets the `font-size`, `line-height`, and `font-family` using a 12-point font, a line height of 120% (14.4 points), and a generic serif font family.

```
body {font: italic 100%/130% Helvetica}
```

This statement sets the base class for the document; all other elements will default to these values. It sets the `font-style` to italic, the `font-size` to normal (100% of the browser default), the `line-height` to 130%, and the `font-family` to Helvetica.

CSS2 FONT FEATURES

CSS2 adds values for `caption`, `icon`, `menu`, `messagebox`, `smallcaption`, and `statusbar`. Each of these should set the font characteristics to the same values used in the user's system. For example, if you want text in your HTML and XHTML document to look like the text displayed in your user's status bar, use a statement such as the following:

```
p {font: statusbar}
```

font-family

Use this property when you want to change just the font family for an HTML or XHTML element. This sets the font to a particular or generic font family. You can set a comma-separated list of font families and include a generic family at the end of the list. The browser works through the list until it finds a matching font family on the user's system.

The `font-family` property defaults to the browser settings, which may be the browser preferences, the browser default style sheet, or the user's default style sheet. If the setting is the browser preferences or style sheet, your settings take precedence, but if it's the user's style sheet, your settings are overridden by the user's style sheet.

Inline elements (such as `em`) use this property, as do child elements and all elements of that type unless the settings are overwritten by a class definition.

*TIP   A paragraph (`p`) or heading (`h1`, `h2`, and so on) element is the child of the **body** element; list items (`li`) are the children of a list element (`ol` and `ul`). Class definitions allow you to have more than one type or version of an element for formatting. For example, a warning note could have its own class of paragraph element, as discussed in Chapter 9.*

VALUES

Family name   Use any specific font family name. For font names, check the list of fonts on your system.

Generic family   Use one of the following generic family names: `serif` for fonts such as Times or Palatino, `sans-serif` for fonts such as Helvetica, `cursive` for fonts such as Zapf Chancery, `fantasy` for fonts such as Western or Circus, or `monospace` for fonts such as System or Courier.

You can list several choices for the font family, specific or generic; it's best to at least conclude your list with one choice for a generic family. Separate the list members with a comma, and put single quotes around font names with white space, like the `'Times New Roman'` face.

NOTES

With this property, you have the option of listing a series of alternatives separated by commas. You should *end* each list with a generic family name; the browser can then substitute an available font of the correct generic type when none of your specific family types are available. The browser works through the list from left to right until it finds a match on the user's system.

If a font family name contains spaces, place that name in quotation marks.

EXAMPLES

```
h1 {font-family: "Comic Sans MS", Architecture, sans-serif}
```

In this statement, the font choices for heading 1 elements are Comic Sans MS, Architecture, and a generic sans-serif. If the user's system has Comic Sans MS, it will use that font. Notice that Comic Sans MS is enclosed in quotation marks, because it includes spaces. If Comic Sans MS is not available, the browser looks for Architecture. If neither font family is available, the browser uses a generic sans-serif font.

```
body {font-family: Arial, Helvetica, sans-serif}
```

This statement sets body, the base class for all text elements in your page, to Arial or Helvetica (in order of preference). If neither of these families is available, the browser uses a generic sans-serif font. Because this is a base class, all the elements in your page inherit this property. Apply the properties you want as defaults for the page to the body element.

font-size

Use this property when you want to control the size of text. This property lets you set the size using a variety of measurements. It's more flexible than the font element in the HTML and XHTML specifications, which scales text only by reference to the default size.

VALUES

Absolute size   Defines the font-size using a table of computed font sizes. These values can be one of the following: xx-small, x-small, small, medium (the default), large, x-large, or xx-large. Different font families may have different table values; thus, a small in one family might not be exactly the same size as a small in another family.

Relative size   Defines the font-size by increasing it (larger) or decreasing it (smaller) relative to the parent container font size rather than to the base browser font size.

Length   Sets the font-size as a number plus a unit abbreviation as a measurement. See the "Lengths" section earlier in this reference.

Percentage   Sets the font-size as a percentage of the parent element's font-size.

NOTES

You can assign a single value for this property. If you use a keyword, such as x-large or larger, the browser recognizes the keyword and acts accordingly. If you use a numeric value, be sure to follow it with the appropriate measurement indicator, such as pt to indicate a point size or % to indicate a percentage.

When you use the absolute size value, the browser adjusts the font size according to the user's preferences. For example, if the default font size for the browser is 10 points, this corresponds to the medium value. The adjustment from medium is a multiplier of 1.5 for each increment in the list. So, if medium is 10 points, small is 6.7 points, and large is 15 points. Relative size is the best choice for sizing fonts, because if the user changes the base font from 10 points to 14 points, your document scales with the change.

In terms of absolute size and relative size, the default is expressed as medium.

Length and percentage values do not use the absolute or relative tables of values. The font sizes are interpreted, so they may appear different in different situations.

For length values, the default is taken from the browser or user's settings. The em and ex values are interpreted as references to the parent font size. For example, 1.5em is equivalent to large, larger, and 150% for absolute, relative, and percentage font sizes.

If the size is expressed as a percentage, the default is 100%. Any value less than 100% is smaller than the parent, and any value more than 100% is larger than the parent. For example, if the parent font is 12 points, and this property is set to 110%, the font size for this element is 13.2 points. If the font size is set to 80% of the 12-point parent, the element appears as 9.6 points.

EXAMPLES

```
body {font-size: 14pt}
```

This statement sets the base class `font-size` to 14 points. This is useful for sites where you want the presentation of text to be large, such as a site for the visually impaired or for children.

```
p {font-size: 90%}
```

This statement uses a percentage value to make the `font-size` depend on the settings in the body element. So, if this statement and the preceding one appear in the same style sheet, the font in the paragraph (p) will be 12.6 points.

```
address {font-size: x-small}
```

This statement sets the `font-size` for the `address` element using an absolute value. If this statement appears in the same style sheet as the first example, the `font-size` for the `address` element will be 4 points.

font-style

Use this property to add emphasis with an oblique or italic version of the font. If the default setting inherited for a particular element is an italic style font, you can use the `font-style` property to set the current element to `normal`, sometimes called roman (or upright).

When you set the `font-style` for an element, inline elements (such as em) and included block elements use this style. Also, if you set the `font-style` for a body or list container, all the elements within it use the setting.

VALUES

Value	Effect
normal	Chooses the roman or upright style in a font family.
italic	Chooses the italic style in a font family. Fonts with *italic, cursive,* or *kursiv* in their names are usually listed as "italic" in the browser's database.
oblique	Chooses the oblique style in a font family. Fonts with *oblique, slanted,* or *incline* in their names are usually listed in the browser's database as "oblique" fonts. The browser may also generate an oblique font from a family that does not have an oblique or italic style.

NOTES

The browser maintains a list of the fonts available on the system, with the font name, font family, and values of the font, such as oblique or italic.

EXAMPLES

```
body {font-style: oblique}
h1, h2, h3 {font-style: normal}
```

The first statement sets the base body (body) to an oblique version of the font. Because the heading levels 1, 2, and 3 (h1, h2, h3) inherit this from the body class, the second statement sets them to normal. If the base font is not oblique or italic, you do not need to set the font-style to normal.

```
body em {font-style: italic}
```

This statement sets up the emphasis element to be an italic font-style. This means that when you emphasize some inline text, it will be italicized automatically.

font-variant

Use this property to switch between normal and small-caps fonts. Similar to the font-style property, font-variant handles one piece of font information. If you assign this property to an element, all included blocks and inline elements use the setting.

VALUES

A value of small-caps sets the lowercase letters to display as uppercase letters in a smaller font size. If the element has inherited a small-caps setting from its parent, a value of normal sets the font-variant to the usual uppercase and lowercase; this is the default value.

NOTES

In some cases, when a small-caps version of the font is not available to the browser, the browser creates small-caps by using scaled uppercase letters.

EXAMPLES

```
h1 {font-variant: small-caps}
```

This statement sets the level 1 headings to a small-cap version of the default font.

```
address {font-variant: small-caps}
```

This statement sets the contents of any address element to appear in small caps, using the default body font.

```
body em {font-variant: small-caps}
```

This statement sets text in the inline element em to use the small-caps version of the default font.

font-weight

Use this property to set the weight of a font, creating darker or lighter versions of the normal font. You can set the font-weight property as a relative weight or as a specific numeric value that represents a degree of darkness (or heaviness) or lightness for the font.

VALUES

Use only one value from the following lists:

Relative weight   Sets the font-weight relative to the weight inherited by the element. In this method, the value can be either bolder or lighter; these increase (bolder) or decrease (lighter) the font-weight by one setting from its current weight (but not beyond the limits of 100 and 900).

Absolute weight   Sets the font-weight as a degree of heaviness on a nine-point scale. The value can be one of the following: 100, 200, 300, 400 or normal (these two values are equivalent), 500, 600, 700 or bold (these two values are equivalent), 800, or 900. The default is normal.

NOTES

When you set a font-weight value for an element, its child elements inherit the weight of the font. This weight becomes their default weight, and you can increase or decrease the weight based on the inherited weight. When you then set a child element's weight using a relative weight (for example, bolder or lighter), it's relative to the weight of the parent element's font. (However, the weight will never exceed 900 or go below 100; if you set bolder on an element that is already inheriting 900, it stays at 900.)

The numeric, gradient weight values give you greater control over the weight of the font. These values must be stated exactly; intermediate values such as 250 are not acceptable.

There are no guarantees that the font family will include the full range of weight values. The browser will map the values you assign to those available for the font it uses. Fonts that have a weight lighter than normal are usually listed in the browser's database as *thinner, light,* or *extra-light.*

EXAMPLES

```
p {font-weight: bold}
```

This statement makes the weight of the paragraph (p) font bold. Use this when your layout requires a heavier text presentation.

```
body {font-weight: 500}
```

This statement uses the numerical representation to set the base font weight to slightly heavier than normal. This will make the text for all the elements appear darker. All included and inline elements use this as their normal weight. If you then use the relative keywords, as in the next statement, the text is bolder or lighter (we specify bolder here) than the 500 weight set in body.

```
h1 {font-weight: bolder}
```

This statement makes the h1 elements darker than the base font, regardless of what setting the base font has for its weight. However, if your body element base font is 900, there's no value that is bolder; therefore, the browser cannot make the h1 text bolder.

```
body em {font-weight: 400}
```

This statement controls the weight of emphasized text in the document. If the body weight is 500, the emphasized text will be lighter. If you include emphasized text in a paragraph set to bold, as in the first statement in this section, the emphasized text would appear lighter.

Text Properties

Text properties control the layout or display of lines and words on a page and within a text element. These properties include the familiar values for spacing and aligning text within an area, as well as values for controlling text capitalization and effects (such as underlining and blinking). Combined with the font properties, the text properties give you almost complete control over the appearance of the text on your page. The font properties control the typeface; the text properties control the paragraph settings.

letter-spacing

Use this property to control the spacing between characters in words in a text element. The distance you set applies across the elements; you cannot insert larger or smaller spaces between characters. This property is useful if you want to add space between characters for an open-looking presentation.

This property defaults to the spacing set in the parent element, or in the browser if no style is set. Inline and included block elements use the value set with the `letter-spacing` property.

VALUES

Sets standard spacing length between characters with a number plus a unit abbreviation. (See the "Lengths" section earlier in this reference.) The value adds to the normal length inherited by the element from its parent, or reduces the normal length if you use a negative value.

To reset the distance between characters to whatever is common for the font and font size in use, use a value of `normal`. This is the default.

NOTES

When you use a length unit, you can use a positive or negative number, or a decimal number (for example, `0.4em` or `1.2em`). If you use a negative value, be sure that you don't make your text illegible with spacing too small between characters.

EXAMPLES

    h1 {letter-spacing: 2em}

This statement increases the character spacing in words found in the level 1 headings to twice the font size.

    p {letter-spacing: -0.5em}

This statement decreases the character spacing for paragraphs in the document to half the font size.

line-height

Use this property to set the distance (leading or spacing) between lines of text within an element. Elements inherit the settings for this property; if you change the settings in the child element, you change the inherited results. For example, if you set unordered lists (`ul`) to 2 (for double-spaced) and then set list items (`li`) to `1.5`, you've effectively triple-spaced list items (2×1.5). In other words, the inheritance is cumulative, rather than a setting for a child element replacing the parent's setting.

VALUES

To set the spacing value to default to the browser-specific setting, which is usually 1 to 1.2 times the font size, use the default value of `normal`. To change the spacing, use one of the following techniques:

Number   Sets the distance between the baselines of each line of text in the element to the font size multiplied by the specified number. For example, if the font size is 10 points and you set `line-height` to 2, the spacing will be 20 points.

Length   Sets the spacing using one of the standard relative or absolute measurements. See the "Lengths" section earlier in this reference.

Percentage   Sets the spacing to a percentage of the line's font size.

NOTES

When you use a length unit, you can use a positive or negative number. If you use a negative number, you'll create overlapping text, which may make it illegible.

Using a percentage for the `line-height` property is a flexible way to set line spacing, because it adapts to the font and display of the browser. Child elements will inherit the result of this setting.

EXAMPLES

```
p {line-height: 1.2;    font-size: 10pt}
p {line-height: 1.2em; font-size: 10pt}
p {line-height: 120%;  font-size: 10pt}
```

These three statements produce the same result: The text will have 12 points between each line.

outline

Using this CSS2 shorthand property, you can outline individual elements, such as buttons, fields, or emphasized text. Outlines do not take space—they fit just outside the border (if any) and do not affect the layout of any elements. Additionally, they precisely enclose the text, even if the lines result in irregular shapes, rather than forming a rectangle.

The `outline` property is a shorthand property and sets any of `outline-color`, `outline-style`, and `outline-width`.

VALUES

The possible values for the `outline` property are the set of all possible values listed in the individual property entries:

Property	Effect
`outline-color`	Sets the color for all sides of the outline.
`outline-style`	Sets the pattern used for the outline.
`outline-width`	Sets the outline width.

See the `border-color` for `outline-color` values, `border-style` for `outline-style` values, and `border-width` for `outline-width` values. Possible values for `outline-style` are the same as for the `border-style` property, except that `hidden` is not permitted for `outline-style`.

The `outline-color` property accepts all colors, as well as the keyword `invert`, which is expected to perform a color inversion on the pixels on the screen. This is a trick you can use to ensure that the focus border is visible, regardless of color background.

NOTES

This property is a CSS2 property and, therefore, won't work in browsers that don't support CSS2.

See the "Notes" sections for the `border-width`, `border-style`, and `border-color` properties, under "Box Border Properties" later in this reference.

EXAMPLE

```
input:focus {outline: 2px inset red}
```

This statement generates an outline around the `input` element that has the focus. The outline is a red, inset line that is 2 pixels wide.

text-align

Use this property to arrange the text horizontally within the element box. This is useful for centering headings or creating effects with justification. You can set the alignment on any block-level element, such as `p`, `h1`, `ul`, and so on. The browser sets the property default (either from the browser properties, browser style sheet, or user's style sheet). Inline and included block elements use the settings. For example, if you justify an unordered list (`ul`), the list items (which are included block elements) are justified.

VALUES

Value	Effect
left	Aligns text along the left margin, for a "ragged-right" layout.
right	Aligns text along the right margin, for a "ragged-left" layout.
center	Places the text a uniform distance from the left and right margins.
justify	Creates uniform line lengths. The browser will use word and letter spacing to create lines of text that touch both the left and right margins of the element box.

EXAMPLES

```
h1, h2 {text-align: center}
```

This statement centers both level 1 and level 2 headings across the width of the page (however wide or narrow the display is).

```
p.emerg {text-align: right;
         background: url(exclaim.gif) no-repeat}
```

This statement aligns paragraphs of class emerg (that is, `<p class="emerg">...</p>`) with the right margin of the element box. `p.emerg` also has an icon that appears once in the top-left corner of the element box as a background.

text-decoration

Use this property to control the effects used on text elements. This property is particularly useful for drawing attention to text elements, such as notes and warnings.

The default is not to use any text decoration, and the property is not inherited, although some properties do continue throughout sections. For example, a `p` with underlining will be underlined throughout, even through sections with other formatting, such as boldface. The decoration uses the settings from the `color` property (listed in the "Background and Color Properties" section).

VALUES

Value	Effect
none	Leaves the text plain (unadorned). This is the default.
underline	Draws a single, thin line under the text.
overline	Draws a single, thin line above the text.
line-through	Draws a single, thin line through the text, similar to strikethrough text.
blink	Makes the text blink.

You can combine `underline`, `overline`, `line-through`, and `blink` in a single statement—though that would be pretty ugly.

NOTES

If you apply the `text-decoration` to an empty element (such as `br`) or an element that has no text, the property has no effect.

Be careful using underlined text in your Web pages. Users are accustomed to underlined text representing hyperlinks and may get confused if you use it for other reasons.

The `blink` element will get readers' attention, but will also make pages look amateurish. Think carefully before you use it.

EXAMPLES

```
h1 {color: purple; text-decoration: underline}
```

This statement sets level 1 headings as purple underlined text.

```
p em {text-decoration: blink}
```

This statement sets the emphasis in paragraphs (`p em`) to `blink`. Because nothing else is set, the emphasis will use all the other paragraph (`p`) properties that you have set.

```
h1 em {text-decoration: overline}
```

This statement sets the emphasized text in level 1 headings to have a line above it. If this statement appears in the same style sheet as the first statement in this section, this emphasized text will have a line above and a line below.

text-indent

Use this property to create paragraphs with the first line indented. Traditionally, indented first lines compensate for a lack of space between paragraphs and act as a visual cue for the reader. You can set the indent as an absolute or relative measurement.

Elements use whatever setting the parent has, so if you set `text-indent` for `body`, all block elements, such as `h1` and `p`, default to first-line indentation. The default value is 0, for no indentation. Negative values can be used to "outdent" the element to the left from the rest of the block.

VALUES

Length   Sets the size of the first-line indent to the specified measurement. Some measurements are relative, and some are absolute. See the "Lengths" section earlier in this reference.

Percentage   Sets the first-line indent to a percentage of the line length.

NOTES

For most browsers, you can use negative values to create a hanging-indent format.

An indent is not added to the first line of the second text stream if the text within the element is separated by an inline element that breaks the line (such as `br`).

EXAMPLES

```
body {text-indent: 1%}
```

This statement creates a base class `body` with a first-line indent of 1 percent of the line length. Because a percentage is used, the ratio of indent to line length stays the same whether the browser window or font is sized larger or smaller.

```
h1 {text-indent: 3em}
```

In this statement, the indentation for level 1 headings is also relative to the font size (`em` measurements are based on the font size). If this line appears in the same style sheet as the first statement, the indentation is the base 1% *plus* an additional 3 ems.

```
p.warn {text-indent: 2cm}
```

This statement specifies a 2-centimeter first-line indent. Because this is an absolute measurement, this setting can produce unexpected results on different systems.

text-shadow

Use this CSS2 property to control shadow effects on text elements. We recommend using this effect sparingly, because too much text shadow can make text difficult to read.

VALUES

To restore an element to no text shadow, use the default value `none`.

To set a text shadow, you *must* provide the horizontal and vertical shadow offsets, but the blur radius and color are optional. You can also specify separate groups of settings for multiple shadows under the same text.

Horizontal shadow offset   Specifies the horizontal distance to the right that the shadow appears. Use negative numbers to move the shadow to the left from the text. Specify measurements in any units.

Vertical shadow offset   Specifies the vertical distance down that the shadow appears. Use negative numbers to move the shadow above the text. Specify measurements in any units.

Blur radius   Specifies the fuzziness of the shadow. Specify measurements in any units.

Color   Specifies the shadow color. See the "Colors" section earlier in this reference for more about colors.

NOTES

This property is new in CSS2 and is supported only by CSS2-compliant browsers.

If you apply the text shadow to an empty element (such as `br`) or an element that has no text, the property has no effect.

EXAMPLES

```
h1 {text-shadow: 1px 1px}
```

This statement sets a shadow offset by 1 pixel horizontally and vertically for level 1 headings.

```
h1 {text-shadow: 2px 2px 1px blue}
```

This statement sets the level 1 headings to have a blue shadow offset by 2 pixels horizontally and vertically, with a 1-pixel blur radius for level 1 headings.

```
h1 {text-shadow: 2px 2px 1px blue, 1px 1px red}
```

This statement sets a blue shadow offset by two pixels horizontally and vertically, with a 1-pixel blur radius, and a red shadow offset by 2 pixel in both directions for level 1 headings.

text-transform

Use this property to set the capitalization standard for one or more elements. For example, if you want all uppercase letters for a warning or title case for all headings, you can set this property in one place and allow the browser to adjust the text. Child elements, including both block and inline elements, use the parent's setting for this property.

VALUES

Value	Effect
none	Does not change the case for any of the text. This is the default.
capitalize	Creates a title-cased element, capitalizing the first letter of each word in the element.
lowercase	Sets all the text to lowercase, eliminating any uppercase letters from the element text.
uppercase	Sets all the text to uppercase.

EXAMPLES

```
h1 {text-transform: capitalize}
```

This statement forces all the text in level 1 headings to use uppercase for the first letter of each word. This is a form of the title case.

```
p.headline {text-transform: uppercase}
```

In this statement, paragraphs with the class `headline` are rendered in uppercase (all capital letters). This is not the same as setting a small-caps font (`font-variant: small-caps`), because no adjustment is made to the size of the lowercase letters.

vertical-align

Use this property to set inline text elements within a parent element to have different vertical alignment from the parent. The `vertical-align` property is an important layout tool for document designers. You could, for example, define a class for superscripted or subscripted text and apply it where required. This property is typically used to set the alignment between inline graphics (such as keycaps or toolbar icons) and the surrounding text. The default value is for alignment along the baselines of the elements. These settings are not used by any other elements.

VALUES

Value	Effect
baseline	Aligns the bottom of lowercase letters in the two elements (the default setting).
bottom	Aligns the inline element with the lowest part of the parent element on the same line. Use with caution—may produce unexpected results.
middle	Centers the inline text and the parent element text, aligning the midpoints of the two elements. May be required when the two elements have different sizes or when the inline element is an image.
sub	Moves the inline element down below the baseline of the parent element.
super	Moves the inline element up from the baseline of the parent element.
text-bottom	Aligns the bottom of the inline element with the bottom of the parent font's descender. Preferred method for aligning inline elements with the bottom of a textual parent element.
text-top	Aligns the inline element with the top of the ascender in the parent element.
top	Aligns the inline element with the highest part of the parent element, similar to superscript. Works line by line—for example, if the line has no ascenders, `top` moves the inline text to the top of the x-height for the parent element.

The `vertical-align` property can also be set as a percentage, raising or lowering (with negative values) the baseline of the inline element the given percentage above or below the baseline of the parent element. Use this in combination with the `line-height` property of the element.

NOTES

If you use subscript (`sub`) or superscript (`super`) alignment, decrease the font size in relation to the parent element.

If you want to include inline images that replace words or letters in your text (such as toolbar buttons or keycaps), use a percentage value with the `vertical-align` property. This allows you to obtain precision in the placement of inline elements, such as images, that do not have true baselines.

EXAMPLES

```
img.keycap {vertical-align: -20%}
```

This statement creates an image class (`img`) called `keycap`. Elements that you apply this class to will drop below the baseline of the parent text element; 20% of the image will be below the baseline of the parent element's text.

```
code.expo {vertical-align: super}
```

This statement creates a code class called `expo` for superscripting. You could, for example, use this for the exponents in equations.

```
.regmark {vertical-align: text-top}
```

In this statement, a generic class, called `regmark`, aligns the inline element to the top of the parent font.

word-spacing

Use this property to control the spacing between words in a text element. As with the `letter-spacing` property, the distance you set applies across the elements; you cannot insert larger and smaller spaces between words, as in typesetting. This property is useful if you want to add space between words for an open-looking presentation.

This property assumes the settings for its parent element or the browser, and inline or included block elements use any changes you make in the `word-spacing` property.

VALUES

Sets a standard spacing between words with a length value. (See the "Lengths" section earlier in this reference.) The value adds to the length inherited by the element from its parent, or reduces the length if you use a negative value. For example, if `body` sets the font size to `10pt` and the word spacing to `1em`, the child elements will use a 10-point word spacing (1 em = the point size). If you then add `0.4em` to the word spacing, the child element has a wider word spacing than the parent.

To reset the distance between words to whatever is usual for the font and font size in use, use a value of `normal` (which is the default).

NOTES

When you use a length unit, you can use a positive or negative number, as well as a decimal number (such as `0.4em`). If you use a negative value, be careful that you do not eliminate the spaces between words, making your text unreadable.

EXAMPLES

```
h1 {word-spacing: 1em}
p {word-spacing: 0.4em}
```

In both these statements, the space between words in the elements will increase; the spacing in heading level 1 elements increases by 1 em, and the spacing in paragraph elements increases by 0.4 (4/10 of the font size).

Box Padding Properties

In the element box, the padding provides the distance between the element contents and the border. You can use the `padding` shorthand property to set the padding on all sides of the element or use the individual properties to set the padding on each side separately.

TIP   With box properties, you can manipulate the layers around the element. These layers, from the element out, are padding, border, margin, and position. Each of these layers has its own set of properties, which are included in this reference in the order listed, beginning with box padding.

padding

Use this shorthand property to set the distance for all four padding directions (top, right, bottom, and left). This area uses the element's settings for background (such as color and image).

Padding is not inherited, so included and inline elements use the default of zero rather than the settings from the parent element.

VALUES

Length   Sets an absolute or relative distance between the element contents and the inside of the box border. See the "Lengths" section earlier in this reference.

Percentage   Sets the distance between the element contents and the inside of the box border as a percentage of the parent element.

Use a single value to make the padding on each side equidistant. If you use two values, the browser uses the first one for the top and bottom padding, and the second one for the left and right padding. If you provide three values, the browser assigns them to the top padding, the left and right padding, and the bottom padding. If you provide all four values, the browser assigns them, in order, to the top, right, bottom, and left padding. You can mix value types—specifying padding in percentage for some and absolute measurements for other values.

NOTES

You cannot have negative padding values; however, you can use decimal numbers, such as `0.4` or `1.2`.

EXAMPLES

```
h1 {font-size:. 20pt; padding: 1em 0.5em; color: red;}
h2 {font-size: 15pt; font-weight: normal; padding: 1em 0.5em;
    color: blue;}
```

If you include these two statements in a style sheet, the headings at levels 1 and 2 will have 20 and 15 points, respectively, between the content and the top and bottom borders. Heading 1s will have a left and right padding of 10 points and be red; heading 2s will have a left and right padding of 7.5 points and be blue with a normal font weight.

padding-bottom

Use this property to add space between the bottom of the contents and the border below. Padding is not inherited, so included and inline elements use the default of zero rather than the settings from the parent element.

VALUES

Length   Sets an absolute or relative distance between the bottom of the contents and the border below. See the "Lengths" section earlier in this reference.

Percentage   Sets the bottom padding size to a percentage of the parent element.

NOTES

You cannot have negative padding values; however, you can use decimal numbers, such as 0.4 or 1.2.

EXAMPLES

```
body {padding-bottom: 3em}
```

This statement sets the padding distance between the bottom of the page to 3 ems, which allows it to vary with the font size.

```
h1 {padding-bottom: 2pt}
```

This statement sets the distance for the bottom padding to 2 points for level 1 headings. It will add a distance of 2 points to the space between the text of the heading and the location of the border, regardless of the font size of the heading.

```
p.cap {padding-bottom: 0.5cm}
```

This statement sets up a paragraph class called cap (that is, `<p class="cap">...</p>`) in which the distance between the bottom of the element contents and the border location is an absolute value of 0.5 centimeters.

padding-left

Use this property to add space between the left edge of the contents and the border location. Padding is not inherited, so included and inline elements use the default of zero rather than the settings from the parent element.

VALUES

Length   Sets an absolute or relative distance between the left edge of the contents and the border. See the "Lengths" section earlier in this reference.

Percentage   Sets the left padding size to a percentage of the parent element.

NOTES

You cannot have negative padding values; however, you can use decimal numbers, such as `0.4` or `1.2`.

EXAMPLE

```
address {padding-left: 10%}
```

This statement adds space to the left of the `address` elements. Unlike the left margin space, this padding space shows the element background. This space is a relative space; the amount of the space depends on the size of the element.

padding-right

Use this property to add space between the right edge of the contents and the border location. Padding is not inherited, so included and inline elements use the default of zero rather than the settings from the parent element.

VALUES

Length   Sets an absolute or relative distance between the right edge of the contents and the border. See the "Lengths" section earlier in this reference.

Percentage   Sets the right padding size to a percentage of the parent element.

NOTES

You cannot have negative padding values; however, you can use decimal numbers, such as `0.4` or `1.2`.

EXAMPLES

```
p {padding-left: 8px; padding-right: 8px}
p {padding: 0 8px}
```

These two statements produce the same result. The first one uses the individual properties to set the left and right padding to 8 pixels. The second one uses the shorthand `padding` property to set the top and bottom padding to zero and the left and right padding to 8 pixels.

padding-top

Use this property to add space between the top of the contents and the border location. Padding is not inherited, so included and inline elements use the default of zero rather than the settings from the parent element.

VALUES

Length Sets an absolute or relative distance between the top of the contents and the border. See the "Lengths" section earlier in this reference.

Percentage Sets the top padding size to a percentage of the parent element.

NOTES

You cannot have negative padding values; however, you can use decimal numbers, such as 0.4 or 1.2.

EXAMPLE

```
address {padding-top: 1cm}
```

This statement adds a centimeter above the element contents before placing the border. Using an absolute measurement such as this is less browser-sensitive than the relative values.

Box Border Properties

Every container has a border. Element borders reside between the padding and margin in the element container. By default, borders have no style set (are not visible), regardless of color or width.

The default for the border is a medium-width line with no pattern that inherits the color (foreground) setting for the parent element.

You can use the border shorthand property to set any of the border properties, or use the individual properties.

border

Use this shorthand property to set some or all of the border properties. You can set a single value for all four sides of the border.

See the sections on the border-color, border-style, and border-width properties for values and notes on each.

VALUES

The possible values for the border property are the set of all possible values listed in the individual property entries:

Property	Effect
border-color	Sets the color for all sides of the border.
border-style	Sets the pattern used to fill the border.
border-width	Sets the border width for the border.

NOTES

Unlike other shorthand properties, you can use only one setting for each value you include (as opposed to separate settings for top, bottom, etc.). The property is applied evenly to all sides of the box border. To set borders differently on various sides, use the more specific shorthand properties such as border-bottom.

```
p.warn {border: 2em double red}
```

This statement generates a border around the paragraph class element warn (that is, <p class="warn<">...</p>). The border is a red, double-line border that is 2 ems wide.

```
p.note {border: 2px ridge blue}
```

This statement generates borders around the paragraph elements of the class note. The border is a ridged, blue border that is 2 pixels wide.

border-bottom

Use this shorthand property to set some or all of the border properties for the bottom border of the element container.

See the sections on the border-color, border-style, and border-width properties for values and notes on each.

VALUES

The possible values for the border-bottom property are the set of all possible values listed in the individual property entries:

Property	Effect
border-color	Sets the color for the bottom border.
border-style	Sets the pattern used to fill the bottom border.
border-width	Sets the width for the bottom border.

EXAMPLES

```
p.sectend {color: blue; border-bottom: 0.5em dashed #ff0000}
```

This statement overrides the foreground color for the sectend class of paragraphs (that is, <p class="sectend">...</p>) and replaces it with an RGB value (#ff0000). See the entry for the border-color property for more information about specifying border colors. sectend paragraph text will appear blue and conclude with a dashed, red line that is 0.5 em thick. The em thickness associates the width of the border with the font size for the paragraph.

```
p.note {color: green; border-bottom: 5em groove}
```

This statement specifies that note-class paragraphs (that is, <p class="note">...</p>) will use the color green for foreground objects (such as text and the border) and have a grooved, 5 em terminating line.

border-bottom-width

Use this property to set the thickness of the bottom border for an element. The border width is, by default, a medium thickness, and is unaffected by any border settings for the parent element.

VALUES

Sets the bottom border width, using an absolute or a relative measurement. For valid absolute-value measurements, see the "Lengths" section earlier in this reference. Possible relative values are thin, medium (the default), and thick; the specific interpretation of these thicknesses is up to the browser.

NOTES

See the "Notes" section for the border-width property.

EXAMPLES

```
p.under {border-style: solid; border-bottom-width: 0.5cm;
        border-color: gray}
```

This creates a class of paragraph called under (that is, `<p class="under">...</p>`) in which the bottom border is 0.5 centimeter. This is an absolute setting, unaffected by the browser, page size, or element properties such as font.

```
h1 {border-style: solid; border-bottom-width: thin;
    border-color: #f0f8ff}
```

This statement specifies the bottom border as a standard, thin line.

border-color

Use this property to create a border using different colors than the foreground color for the element. The border color uses the foreground color of the element as a default setting. This shorthand property sets the visible border to the selected color(s).

VALUES

The values for border-color can be predefined color names or RGB values. See the "Colors" section earlier in this reference.

NOTES

If you specify a single color, all four borders will appear as that color. If you include two colors, the top and bottom borders use the first color, and the left and right borders use the second color. If you include three colors, the top border uses the first color, the left and right borders use the second color, and the bottom border uses the third color. To give each border a unique color, list four colors; the browser will use them in the following order: top, right, bottom, left.

EXAMPLES

```
p.warn {border-color: #8b0000}
```

This statement specifies that the paragraphs of class warn (that is, `<p class="warn">...</p>`) are outlined with a dark red border.

```
p.dancing {border-color: #000080 #00008b blue #0000cd}
```

This statement sets the border on each side of the element to a different color. This creates a multi-hued line around paragraphs of class dancing. The top is navy blue, the right is dark blue, the bottom is blue, and the left is medium blue.

border-left

Use this shorthand property to set some or all of the border properties for the border on the left side of the element container.

See the sections on the border-color, border-style, and border-width properties for values and notes on each.

VALUES

The possible values for the border-left property are the set of all possible values listed in the individual property entries:

Property	Effect
border-color	Sets the color for the left border.
border-style	Sets the pattern used to fill the left border.
border-width	Sets the width for the left border.

EXAMPLE

```
p.insert {border-left: thin solid red}
```

This statement places a thin, solid, red line next to the insert class paragraphs (that is, `<p class="insert">…</p>`). This is a useful way to create a class for all your elements that inserts "change bars" (a line that shows that changes have been made in the text) in the left border.

border-left-width

Use this property to set the thickness of the border on the left side of an element. The border width is, by default, a medium thickness, and is unaffected by any border settings for the parent element.

VALUES

Sets the left border width, using an absolute or a relative measurement. Possible relative values are thin, medium (the default), and thick; the specific interpretation of these thicknesses is up to the browser. For absolute values and other valid relative measurements, see the "Lengths" section earlier in this reference.

NOTES

See the "Notes" section for the border-width property.

EXAMPLE

```
p.insert {border-style: dashed;
          border-left-width: 5em;
          border-color: red}
```

This statement creates a paragraph class called `insert` (that is, `<p class="insert">…</p>`) that uses a dashed, red line on the left border. The thickness of the line depends on the size of the paragraph font.

border-right

Use this shorthand property to set some or all of the border properties for the border to the right of the element contents.

See the sections on the `border-color`, `border-style`, and `border-width` properties for values and notes on each.

VALUES

The possible values for the `border-right` property are the set of all possible values listed in the individual property entries:

Property	Effect
border-color	Sets the color for the right border.
border-style	Sets the pattern used to fill the right border.
border-width	Sets the width for the right border.

EXAMPLES

```
p.news {padding-right: 15em;
        border-right: thick dotted navy}
```

This creates a thick, dotted line that appears to the right of paragraphs of the class `news` (that is, `<p class="news">…</p>`). The line is navy blue and is 15 ems from the element contents.

```
h3.strike {border-right: thick groove black}
```

This adds a thick, grooved, black line to the right of level 3 headings of the class `strike` (that is, `<h3 class="strike">…</h3>`). This is a useful way to create a class that inserts an indicator that the information is out-of-date and about to be removed.

border-right-width

Use this property to set the thickness of the border on the right side of an element. The border width is, by default, a medium thickness, and is unaffected by any border settings for the parent element.

VALUES

Sets the right border width, using an absolute or a relative measurement. Possible relative values are
`thin`, `medium` (the default), and `thick`; the specific interpretation of these thicknesses is up to the
browser. For absolute values and other valid relative measurements, see the "Lengths" section earlier
in this reference.

NOTES

See the "Notes" section for the `border-width` property.

EXAMPLE

```
p.strike {border-style: dashed;
          border-right-width: 5px;
          border-color: blue}
```

This statement creates a paragraph class called `strike` (that is, `<p class="strike">...</p>`) that
uses a dashed, blue, 5-pixel-wide line on the right border of the element.

border-style

Use this property to display a border and specify a border style. You can create different effects by
combining line styles with color and width. This property uses `none` as the default, which doesn't display the border at all, regardless of the color or width settings.

VALUES

Value	Effect
none	Prevents the display of one or more borders. This is the default.
dashed	Sets the border as a series of dashes, alternating the element background and the border color.
dotted	Sets the border as a dotted line, with spaces where the element background shows through.
double	Sets the border as two solid lines in the border color or element foreground color.
groove	Sets the border as a 3D rendering of a grooved line drawn in the border color.
hidden	Identical to none except in reference to table element border conflict resolution.
inset	Sets the border as a 3D rendering, creating the illusion that the inside of the element is sunken into the page.
outset	Sets the border as a 3D rendering, creating the illusion that the inside of the element is raised above the page.
ridge	Sets the border as a raised 3D rendering, peaking in the middle of the line, drawn in the border color.
solid	Sets the border as a single, solid line in the border color or element foreground color.

Use up to four values from the preceding list to stylize the borders around an element. Because the initial setting for the `border-style` property is `none`, no borders are visible unless you set them up with a style and width.

NOTES

Not all browsers are capable of displaying the more esoteric styles, such as `ridge`, `inset`, and `outset`. If the browser cannot interpret the style, it substitutes a solid line. Some browsers may simply render all borders as solid lines.

EXAMPLES

```
p.looknew {border-style: outset; border-width: 0.5cm;
          border-color: gray}
```

This statement creates the illusion that the `looknew` class paragraph elements (that is, `<p class="looknew">...</p>`) are set above the page in a raised box.

```
p.dancing {border-style: groove ridge inset outset;
          border-color: #f0f8ff #f0ffff blue #5f9ea0}
```

With these properties, each side of the paragraphs in the class `dancing` is a different shade of blue and a different style.

border-top

Use this shorthand property to set some or all of the border properties for the top border of the element container.

See the sections on the `border-color`, `border-style`, and `border-width` properties for values and notes on each.

VALUES

The possible values for the `border-top` property are the set of all possible values listed in the individual property entries:

Property	Effect
border-color	Sets the color for the top border.
border-style	Sets the pattern used to fill the top border.
border-width	Sets the width for the top border.

EXAMPLE

```
h1 {margin-top: 0.5in; color: red; background: white;
    padding: 9em; border-top: thin solid blue}
```

This statement creates level 1 headings that have red text on a white background and a thin, solid, blue line positioned 9 ems above the text. There is another line 0.5 inch above the heading. The 9-em padding is a relative value that depends on the font size and is equivalent to nine blank lines above the heading.

border-top-width

Use this property to set the thickness of the border along the top of an element. The border width is, by default, a medium thickness, and is unaffected by any border settings for the parent element.

VALUES

Sets the top border width, using an absolute or a relative measurement. Possible relative values are thin, medium (the default), and thick; the specific interpretation of these thicknesses is up to the browser. For absolute values and other valid relative measurements, see the "Lengths" section earlier in this reference.

NOTES

See the "Notes" section for the border-width property.

EXAMPLE

```
h1, h2, h3 {font-style: Futura, sans-serif;
            font-size: 15pt;
            border-style: solid;
            border-top-width: 1.5em}
```

This statement applies to the three levels of headings, giving each heading a solid line that is 1.5 ems wide. Because this is relative to the font, the line will be about 22.5 points wide. The border color is not set, so the border uses the foreground color of the element.

border-width

Use this shorthand property to set the thickness of all the borders for an element. You can give the borders unique widths, or you can use a single width for all the borders.

VALUES

Sets the width of the border on all sides, using an absolute or a relative measurement. Possible relative values are thin, medium (the default), and thick; the specific interpretation of these thicknesses is up to the browser. For absolute values and other valid relative measurements, see the "Lengths" section earlier in this reference.

If you use one value, it applies evenly to the borders on the four sides of the element. If you use two values, the browser applies the first to the top and bottom borders of the element, and the second to the left and right borders. If you include three values, the browser uses the first for the top border, the second for the left and right borders, and the last for the bottom border. If you use four values, the browser applies them in the following order: top, right, bottom, left.

NOTES

The thin setting will always be less than or equal to the medium setting, which will always be less than or equal to the thick setting. The border widths do not depend on the element font or other settings. The thick setting, for example, is rendered in the same size wherever it occurs in a document. You can use the relative length values to produce variable (font-dependent) widths.

With a length setting, you cannot have a border with a negative width. However, you can use a decimal number, for example, 0.4 or 1.2.

EXAMPLES

```
p.looknew {border-style: outset; border-width: 0.5cm;
          border-color: gray}
```

This statement sets all the borders for the paragraphs of class looknew (that is, <p class="looknew">...</p>) at 0.5 centimeter, outset, and gray.

```
p.dancing {border-style: groove ridge inset outset;
           border-width: thin thick medium 1cm;
           border-color: #f0f8ff #f0ffff blue #5f9ea0}
```

This statement sets each border in the paragraphs of class dancing at different widths. The top border is thin and grooved, the right border is thick and ridged, the bottom is medium and inset, and the left border is 1 centimeter and outset. Each border is also a different shade of blue.

CSS2 Border Properties

CSS2 also provides border properties that offer you even more control over border appearance. Choose from:

border-bottom-color

border-bottom-style

border-left-color

border-left-style

border-right-color

border-right-style

border-top-color

border-top-style

For example,

```
h1, h2, h3 {font-size: 15pt; font-style: Futura, sans-serif;
            border-left-style: solid; border-left-color: blue}
```

applies to the three levels of headings, giving each heading a solid blue line on the left. See the corresponding CSS1 properties for valid values and notes.

Box Margin Properties

Margins set the size of the box around an element. You measure margins from the border area to the edge of the box.

margin

This property is shorthand to set up all the margins for an element's box. This measurement gives the browser the distance between the element border and the edge of the box. This area is always transparent, so you can view the underlying page background.

VALUES

The value `auto` sets the margin to the browser's default.

Length   Sets an absolute or relative distance between the border and the box edge. See the "Lengths" section earlier in this reference.

Percentage   Sets the margin size as a percentage of the parent element's width.

Use one of the preceding values. For length and percentage, you can use one, two, three, or four numbers. If you use one number, the browser applies it to all four margins (top, right, bottom, and left). If you use two numbers, the first number sets the top and bottom margin, and the second number sets the left and right margin. If you use three numbers, you set the top margin with the first, the right and left margins with the second, and the bottom margin with the third. You can mix length and percentage values.

NOTES

You can use negative values for margins, but not all browsers will handle the settings correctly, and some may ignore the setting and substitute the default of zero or use their own algorithm.

EXAMPLES

    p.1 {margin: 5%}

This statement establishes paragraph margins, for paragraphs of class 1 (that is, `<p class="1">`...`</p>`), to 5% each of the total width of the box.

    p {margin: 2em 3pt}

This statement sets all paragraph elements' top and bottom margins to 2 ems (relative to the size of the font) and the left and right margins to 3 points.

    p.note {margin: 1em 3em 4em}

This statement sets the margins for paragraphs of class note (that is, `<p class= "note">`...`</p>`). The top margin is 1 em (relative to the font size), the left and right margins are 3 ems, and the bottom margin is 4 ems. If the font size is 10 points, the top margin will be 10 points, the left and right margins will be 30 points, and the bottom margin will be 40 points.

margin-bottom

Use this property to set just the bottom margin of an element's box. The bottom margin is the distance between the bottom border and the bottom edge of the box. This generally defaults to zero and is not used by included block or inline elements.

VALUES

The value `auto` sets the bottom margin to the browser's default.

Length Sets an absolute or relative distance between the border and the box's bottom edge. See the "Lengths" section earlier in this reference.

Percentage Sets the bottom margin size as a percentage of the parent element's width.

NOTES

You can use negative values for margins, but not all browsers will handle the settings correctly, and some may ignore the setting and substitute the default of zero or use their own algorithm.

EXAMPLES

```
p {margin-bottom: 4em}
```

This statement sets all paragraphs to have a bottom margin that is 4 ems. This is a relative measurement, so the actual distance depends on the font. For example, if the font size is 10 points, the bottom margin will be the equivalent of 4 blank lines, or 40 points. This establishes a distance of 4 ems between the border and the box bottom.

```
h1 {margin-top:5em; margin-bottom: 1em}
```

This statement positions level 1 headings with the equivalent of five lines above and one line below. This creates a separation between the preceding topic and the heading and strengthens the association between the heading and its topic contents below.

margin-left

Use this property to set just the left margin of an element's box. The left margin is the distance between the border and the left edge of the box. You can use this to create indented text or other element placements. The default for the left margin is zero, or no space. The settings in one element are not used by its included or inline elements.

VALUES

The value `auto` sets the left margin to the browser's default.

Length Sets an absolute or relative distance between the border and the box's left edge. See the "Lengths" section earlier in this reference.

Percentage Sets the left margin size as a percentage of the parent element's width.

NOTES

You can use negative values for margins, but not all browsers will handle the settings correctly, and some may ignore the setting and substitute the default of zero or use their own algorithm.

EXAMPLES

```
body {margin-left: 3%}
```

This statement sets up a basic left margin for the page using the **body** element. The browser should display this margin as 3% of the width of the page. No element within the page will appear outside this margin. If the browser shows 600 × 480 pixels, the body's left margin uses 18 pixels.

```
p {margin-left: 1cm; margin-top: 0.5cm}
```

This statement sets a left margin for paragraphs at the absolute value of 1 centimeter. With this, you can add a left gutter to your page. It also sets the top margin to 0.5 centimeters.

```
p {margin-left: 4em}
```

This statement creates a variable gutter for the paragraphs on a page. The actual size of the 4-em margin depends on the font size used for the paragraphs.

margin-right

Use this property to set just the right margin of an element's box. The right margin is the distance between the border and the right edge of the box. You can use this to force the element away from the right edge of the page. This generally defaults to zero and is not used by included block or inline elements.

VALUES

The value auto sets the right margin to the browser's default.

Length   Sets an absolute or relative distance between the border and the box's right edge. See the "Lengths" section earlier in this reference.

Percentage   Sets the right margin size as a percentage of the parent element's width.

NOTES

You can use negative values for margins, but not all browsers will handle the settings correctly, and some may ignore the setting and substitute the default of zero or use their own algorithm.

EXAMPLES

```
body {margin-right: 0.5in}
```

This statement creates a margin on your page that is a 0.5 inches wide. Nothing will appear in this margin area.

```
p {margin-right: 10%}
```

This statement establishes an outside gutter that is 10% of the paragraph width. The actual distance depends on the paragraph width.

```
h1 {margin-right: 15em}
```

This statement creates an outside gutter whose size depends on the heading font size. It inserts a distance equal to 1.5 times the heading font size. This means that if the level 1 heading uses a 15-point font, for example, the distance between the border and box edge would be less than it would be with a 20-point font. If you want all headings to wrap before the edge of the box, but at the same place in the page, use percentage or absolute measurements.

margin-top

Use this property to set just the top margin of an element's box. The top margin is the distance between the border and the top of the box. You can use this to insert space above an element, perhaps to visually reinforce its relationship with the elements around it. This generally defaults to zero and is not used by included block or inline elements.

VALUES

The value auto sets the top margin to the browser's default.

Length   Sets an absolute or relative distance between the border and the box's top edge. See the "Lengths" section earlier in this reference.

Percentage   Sets the top margin size as a percentage of the parent element's width.

NOTES

You can use negative values for margins, but not all browsers will handle the settings correctly, and some may ignore the setting and substitute the default of zero or use their own algorithm.

EXAMPLES

```
h1 {margin-top:5em; margin-bottom: 1em}
```

This statement positions level 1 headings with the equivalent of five lines above and one line below. This creates a separation between the preceding topic and the heading and strengthens the association between the heading and its topic contents below.

```
body {margin-top: 1em}
```

This statement adds the equivalent of one line to the margin of any element inside the body of the document. The actual distance depends on the font size for the element.

```
p {margin-top: 5%}
```

This statement adds a variable distance (5% of the height) to paragraph elements.

```
h1 {margin-top: 1cm}
```

This statement adds an absolute distance of 1 centimeter to the space between the box edge and the border of level 1 headings. Whatever the environment, the browser tacks on a centimeter of transparent margin to the element's box.

Box Position Properties

The box position properties control the arrangement of elements in relation to each other and the page, rather than within themselves. The `float` and `clear` properties control which elements can sit next to each other. The `width` and `height` properties set dimensions for elements, giving you more control of the page layout.

clear

Use this property to allow or disallow other elements, usually inline images, to float beside the element specified. You can allow floating elements on either side, both sides, or neither side. The default is to allow floating elements on both sides of the element (the `none` setting). This property is not used by inline and included elements.

VALUES

Value	Effect
none	Allows floating elements on either side of this element. This is the default.
both	Does not allow floating elements on either side of this element.
left	Not on the left; moves the element below any floating elements on the left.
right	Not on the right; moves the element below any floating elements on the right.

Use one of these values to designate the position for floating elements in relation to a particular element.

NOTES

This property indicates where floating elements are not allowed.

EXAMPLES

```
p.prodname {clear: none}
```

This statement creates a paragraph class called `prodname` (that is, `<p class="prodname">...</p>`) that allows floating elements to appear on either side of it.

```
p {clear: right}
```

In this statement, the paragraph element allows floating elements on its left side, but not the right.

```
h1, h2, h3 {clear: both}
```

This statement prevents elements from appearing next to the headings in the document. All floating elements, usually images, are pushed up or down and appear above or below the headings.

float

Use this property to set an element in a position outside the rules of placement for the normal flow of elements. For example, the `float` property can raise an element from an inline element to a block element. This is usually used to place an image. The default, which is not an inherited value, is to display the element where it appears in the flow of the document (`none`).

VALUES

Value	Effect
none	Displays the element where it appears in the flow of the parent element. This is the default.
left	Wraps other element contents to the right of the floating element.
right	Wraps other element contents to the left of the floating element.

NOTES

A floating element cannot overlap the margin in the parent element used for positioning. For example, an illustration that is a left-floating element (pushes other contents to the right of itself) cannot overlap the left margin of its parent container.

EXAMPLES

```
p {clear: none}
img.keycap {float: none}
img.prodlogo {float: left}
```

These statements specify that if an image of class `keycap` (that is, `<img class="keycap" />`) is inserted in the course of a paragraph, it appears within the flow of the text. If an image of class `prodlogo` is inserted, it appears against the left margin of the parent element and the text wraps on its right.

height

Use this property to set the height of an element on a page. Browsers will enforce the height, scaling the image to fit. This property will be familiar to anyone who has used the `height` and `width` attributes of an image (`img`) element in HTML or XHTML.

VALUES

The value `auto` allows the browser to either set the `height` to the actual image height or, if the `width` is set, preserve the aspect ratio of images. You can instead use absolute or relative length measurements, as described in the "Lengths" section earlier in this reference. Use a percentage to set the image size as a percentage of the parent element's height.

NOTES

Some browsers may not handle the `height` (or `width`) property if the element is not a replaced element (one that uses a pointer in the HTML or XHTML source to indicate the file with the actual content, like an `img` element).

Generally, replaced elements have their own, intrinsic, measurements. If you want to replace these dimensions with a `height` (and/or `width`) property setting, the browser tries to resize the replaced element to fit. To maintain the aspect ratio, you need to set one of the properties, `height` or `width`, to `auto`. To preserve the aspect ratio of images positioned with `height`, include the `width` property in the statement and set the `width` to `auto`. If you position an image with the `width` property, include the `height` property in the statement and set `height` to `auto`.

If you need to set the size of an image, it's usually best to set it in proportion to the container element (using a relative setting); otherwise, leave these settings at `auto`, which allows the browser to use the image's original size.

You cannot use a negative value for the `height` or `width` property of an element.

EXAMPLES

```
img.keycap {float: none; width: auto; height: 1.2em;
            vertical-align: middle}
```

This statement creates an img class (that is, `<img class="keycap" />`) where the images appear in the text stream. These images have a controlled width, and a height that is 1.2 ems. For example, in a stream of text with a font size of 12 points, the image will be 14.4 points. The statement also adjusts the vertical position of the image in relation to the line.

```
img.prodlogo {float: left; width: 2cm; height: auto}
```

In this statement, images of class `prodlogo`, which have the text wrap on the right around them, have a controlled width of 2 centimeters. However, it's better to avoid absolute measurements and use relative values or the image's values (by setting `width` and `height` to `auto`).

width

Use this property to set the width of an element on a page. Browsers will enforce the width, scaling the image to fit. This property will be familiar to anyone who has used the `height` and `width` attributes of an image (`img`) element in HTML or XHTML.

VALUES

The value `auto` allows the browser to either set the `width` to the actual image height or, if the `height` is set, preserve the aspect ratio of images.

Length   Sets an absolute or relative width for images in a particular element or class. See the "Lengths" section earlier in this reference.

Percentage   Sets the image size as a percentage of the parent element's width.

NOTES

See the "Notes" section for the `height` property.

EXAMPLES

```
img.keycap {float: none; width: auto; vertical-align: middle;
            height: 1.2em}
```

In this statement, images of class `keycap` (that is, `<img class="keycap" />`) will appear in the text stream aligned to the middle of the line of text where it appears. Its height is set to 1.2 ems and the width to `auto`, which allows the browser to position it properly (the height does not disturb the paragraph formatting around it, and the width is adjusted to fit).

```
img.prodlogo {float: left; height: auto; width: 2cm}
```

This statement creates an image class `prodlogo` that forces the text to wrap on the right of it, is 2 centimeters wide, and has whatever height is proportionate to the 2-centimeter width.

Background and Color Properties

Color affects the foreground elements, such as text and borders, and background properties affect the surface on which the document elements appear. You can set these globally and locally for individual elements. When you paint the background for an element, you're layering on top of the document's background. If you do not set a background for an element, it defaults to transparent, allowing the document background to show. The `color` property inherits from the document body.

You can control a wide variety of properties for backgrounds, including the position, repetition, and scrolling. You can use the `background` shorthand property to set all the background properties, or use the individual properties. The background is set relative to the element's box properties.

background

This is a shorthand property used to include the full collection of background values. The `background` property will be familiar to anyone who has changed the page color of a Web page or added a graphic as wallpaper. This property now extends to individual elements, allowing you to have a variety of backgrounds. It also allows more functionality in the background, including scrolling and repetitions.

VALUES

The possible values for background are the set of all possible values listed in the individual property entries:

Property	Effect
background-attachment	Sets up a background that scrolls with the element.
background-color	Sets a background color for the page or elements on the page.
background-image	Sets an image behind the element.
background-position	Positions the background within the element's box.
background-repeat	Sets the number of times and direction that a background repeats.

See the sections for the individual properties for details about these values.

NOTES

If you do not include a property (such as `background-repeat`), the browser uses the default.

The order of the properties in a statement is not important.

EXAMPLES

```
body {background: url(sunshine.gif) blue repeat-y}
```

This statement sets up a background for the page using the `body` element. If the browser cannot find the image, it uses a blue background. If needed, the background image repeats down the page (but not across the page).

```
h1 {background: white}
```

This statement changes the background for level 1 headings to white using a color keyword. If this statement appears in the same style sheet as the first statement, the sunshine background is over-laid with a white box where the level 1 headings appear.

```
p em {background: url(swirl.gif) yellow top left}
```

In this statement, any emphasis (`em`) within a paragraph (`p`) is changed to use as a background a `swirl.gif` file that starts at the top-left corner of the element's box. If the `swirl.gif` file cannot be found, the browser uses a yellow background.

background-attachment

Use this property to specify whether an image used for the background of an element will scroll with the element or remain at a fixed location on the page. If the image is larger than the element box, when users scroll down the screen, they either see different parts of the background image (a fixed attachment) or a single part of the image (a scrolling attachment) that moves with the display of the element down the page.

Inline and included block elements do not inherit this property.

VALUES

A value of `scroll` moves the image with the element on the page, so the same part is visible when users scroll down the screen. This is the default and it applies only to the element in the statement. A value of `fixed` keeps the image fixed in relation to the page so different parts are visible when users scroll down the screen.

NOTES

Use this property in conjunction with the `background-image` property.

EXAMPLE

```
p {background-image: url(logo.gif);
   background-attachment: fixed}
```

This statement uses the image `logo.gif` as the background for the paragraphs in the document. The image is fixed to the page, not the contents of the paragraph.

background-color

Use this property to set the background color for the page or elements on the page. If you set the background for the base class body, your other elements will appear to inherit that color unless you change their background colors from transparent.

VALUES

Sets the color for the background. This value can be one of the color names or RGB values. See the "Colors" section earlier in this reference. The keyword value transparent makes the page background the default for viewing.

NOTES

This value sets the background color only. To set the background as an image, you need to use either the background property or the background-image property.

This property affects the box area owned by the element. This is set using the margin and padding properties, listed in the "Box Margin Properties" and "Box Padding Properties" sections.

When you set an element's background to transparent, or don't set it at all, the page's background color or image appears in its place.

EXAMPLES

```
h1 {background-color: blue}
```

In this statement, the background color for level 1 headings is set to blue using the color keyword.

```
p.note {background-color: #800000}
```

This statement creates a paragraph class called note (that is, <p class="note"> ...</p>) that has a background color of maroon using the RGB hexadecimal value for the color.

background-image

Use this property to define an image for the background. The browser will look for additional information about the image's position, repetition, and attachment (or association). If you accept the defaults for these properties, your background image will not repeat, will be attached to the page (not the element), and will have a starting position at the upper-left corner of the element's box.

VALUES

The default value, none, does not use an image for the background. A value of url(...) cues the browser that you're going to provide a filename. You must include the file with the page.

NOTES

The images you use should be gif or jpg image files to ensure that all graphical browsers can read them.

You should also include a background-color property in case the image you have selected is not available.

EXAMPLE

```
p {background-image: url(litelogo.jpg);
   background-repeat: no-repeat;
   background-attachment: fixed;}
```

This statement sets up the document paragraphs to have a background image (called `litelogo.jpg`) that does not repeat and is fixed to the document canvas rather than to the element.

background-position

Use this property to position the element background within its space, using the initial position as a mark. Every element has a box that describes the area it controls. The `background-position` property is useful when your image is not the same size as the element it provides a background for. With this property, you can indicate the position of the image relative to the element box.

VALUES

Length   Sets the starting point on the element's box edge, in an absolute or a relative measurement, and also gives the coordinates as measurements. See the "Lengths" section earlier in this reference.

Percentage   Indicates, as a percentage, where on the box edge the browser begins placing the image. You can repeat this value to give a vertical and horizontal starting point.

Vertical position   Sets the vertical starting position. Use the keyword `top`, `center`, or `bottom`. The browser determines the size of the element box and works from there.

Horizontal position   Sets the horizontal starting position. Use the keyword `left`, `center`, or `right`. The browser determines the width of the element box and works from there.

With the length and percentage settings, you can use two numbers to indicate the vertical and horizontal starting point. Unlike percentage, however, the length measurement does not apply to both the image and the element box in the same way. The length measurement indicates the coordinates inside the element box where the top-left corner of the image appears.

NOTES

Using `0% 0%` is synonymous with using `top left`. In the first case, the initial position of the image is determined this way; the upper-left corner of the image is considered to be 0% horizontal and 0% vertical, and the same is done with the element box. You could position an image using `50% 50%`, and the browser would then begin at the middle of the element and the image. If the image is larger than the element box, you lose the edges that extend beyond the element box. Similarly, if your image is smaller than the element box, you will have an edge, inside your element box, with no image.

You can combine the percentage and length measurements. It's legal to set the property using `25% 2cm`. This would start rendering the image at one-fourth the way into the image and at one-fourth the distance across the element box. The image would begin to appear 2 centimeters below the top of the element box.

The length measurements indicate the distance from the box border where the browser starts to render the image.

When you use a length unit, you can use a positive or negative number. You can, in some cases, use a decimal number. Whichever system of measurement you choose to use must be communicated with the short form for the system (for example, cm or in).

You can also use keywords to position the image within the element's box. Table MR2.5 gives you some corresponding values to work with.

TABLE MR2.5: BACKGROUND POSITION KEYWORDS

KEYWORD	PERCENTAGE	DESCRIPTION
top left, left top	0% 0%	The top-left corner of the image starts at the top-left corner of the element box.
top, top center, center top	50% 0%	The horizontal middle of the image appears in the horizontal middle of the element box. The top of the image begins at the top of the element box.
right top, top right	100% 0%	The top-right corner of the image starts at the top-right corner of the element box.
left, left center, center left	0% 50%	The vertical middle of the image appears in the vertical middle of the element box. The left side of the image is flush against the left side of the element box.
center, center center	50% 50%	The absolute middle of the image is positioned over the absolute middle of the element box.
right, right center, center right	100% 50%	The vertical middle of the image positions over the vertical middle of the element box. The right edge of the image is flush against the right side of the element box.
bottom left, left bottom	0% 100%	The bottom-left corner of the image is positioned at the bottom-left corner of the element box.
bottom center, center bottom	50% 100%	The horizontal centers of the image and element box appear together, and the bottom edges of each remain together.
bottom right, right bottom	100% 100%	The lower-right corner of the image positions in the lower-right corner of the element box.

EXAMPLES

```
body {background-image: url(litelogo.gif);
      background-position: 50% 50%}
```

This sets the class, body, to position a background image centered on the page.

```
h1 {background-image: url(exclaim.gif);
    background-position: top left}
```

In this statement, an image has been assigned to the background of heading level 1 elements that starts rendering at the upper-left corner of the element box.

background-repeat

Use this property to control whether an image repeats horizontally, vertically, both, or neither. Images normally repeat both horizontally and vertically, filling in the area within the element's margins. By default, backgrounds repeat both horizontally and vertically.

VALUES

Value	Effect
repeat	Sets horizontal and vertical repetitions of the image. This is the default.
repeat-x	Sets horizontal repetitions only.
repeat-y	Sets vertical repetitions only.
no-repeat	Prevents repeated copies of the image from displaying.

NOTES

This property works in conjunction with the `background-image` and `background-position` properties. Combining these properties into a single statement enables you to create a pattern of background images that enhances the presentation of information.

EXAMPLE

```
p {background-image: url(logo1.gif); background-color: blue;
   background-position: top left; background-repeat: repeat-y}
```

This statement adds a background to your document paragraphs. The first copy of the image, `logo1.gif`, appears in the top-left corner of the page and repeats down the page. If the image is not found, the browser uses a blue background.

color

Use this property to set the foreground, or element, color. If the element is text, you can set the color of the text with this property. Both inline (such as a) and included block elements (such as p) use this property.

VALUES

Sets the color using color names or RGB values. See the "Colors" section earlier in this reference.

NOTES

You can set this property using one of the three RGB systems or by using a color keyword. Although most browsers should recognize the color keyword, individual browser/system configurations may display the same color differently.

EXAMPLES

```
body {color: black}
```

This statement uses the keyword `black` to set the default foreground color in the document to black.

```
p {color: #0000ff}
```

This statement changes the paragraph (p) foreground color to blue using the RGB hexadecimal value.

```
em {color: rgb(75%,0%,0%)}
```

In this statement, emphasis elements are set to maroon using the RGB percentage value.

Classification Properties

This group of properties controls the presentation of some standard elements, such as the display and lists. The properties can change the type of an element from an inline to a block, from a list item to an inline element, and so on. These properties also include controls for lists and list items, giving you more control over the presentation of the bulleted lists on your page.

display

Use this property to change the display values of an element. Every element has its own default value for display.

VALUES

Value	Effect
block	Sets the element with a line break before and after.
compact	Sets the display to compact, running the element into the margin of the next element if possible. This value is new in CSS2.
inline	Removes the line breaks from an element and forces it into the flow of another element.
list-item	Sets the element as an item in a list.
marker	Sets the display of an element to be a marker (for example, a bullet in a list). This value is new in CSS2.
none	Prevents the display of the element.
run-in	Sets the display to "run in," making the element an inline element at the beginning of the following block element. This value is new in CSS2.
table, inline-table, table-row-group, table-column, table-column-group, table-header-group, table-footer-group, table-row, table-cell, and table-caption	Makes the element act like a table element.

You can use the `display` property values to create special elements such as run-in headings and running lists, as well as to force images into inline presentations.

EXAMPLES

```
h1 {display: inline}
```

This statement sets the browser not to force the level 1 headings onto a separate line. You could combine this with a line break (`br`) before the heading, to start a new line, but let the contents of the section start right after the heading. You may want to extend the right margin of the heading to add some space between the heading and the content.

```
li.intext {display: inline}
```

Use this if you want to reformat your lists of the class `intext` (that is, `<li class="intext">...</li>`) as an integral part of a paragraph. For example, you could list:

```
block
inline
list-item
none
```

Or you could list them inline as `block`, `inline`, `list-item`, `none`.

list-style

Use this shorthand property to set all the list properties in a single statement. If you set this property for a list element (as opposed to the list-item elements), the list items use the settings you establish. You can override the list settings with individual list-item settings.

VALUES

The possible settings values for `list-style` are the set of all possible values listed in the individual property entries:

Property	Effect
list-style-image	Sets an image to use for a bullet.
list-style-position	Sets a traditional hanging bullet, which is not flush with the text of the list item, or an indented one that is flush with the text.
list-style-type	Sets the type of bullet used in the list.

See the entries for the individual properties for details about these values.

NOTES

These values apply only to elements with a display characteristic of `list-item`.

If you use a URL to specify an image, you don't need to set the type, because the bullet position will be occupied by the image.

EXAMPLES

```
ol.outline {list-style: lower-roman inside}
```

This creates a list class called outline (that is, <ol class="outline">...</ol>) that numbers the list items.

```
li.comment {list-style: none}
```

If you use this statement in the same style sheet as the first statement, you can insert list items that have no numbering.

list-style-image

Use this property to replace the standard bullet characters with an image of your choice. If you set this property for a list element (as opposed to the list-item elements), the list items use the settings you establish. You can override the list settings with individual list-item settings.

VALUES

The keyword none (the default) suppresses the image bullets that the element may have inherited. A URL, in the format url(...), identifies the URL of an image you want to use for a bullet.

NOTES

If you use an image, be sure to resize it so it's a small image before using it as a bullet.

If the browser cannot find the image identified in the URL, it will default to the list-style-type setting.

List items use the settings from the lists. You can insert list items with different settings, creating a series of effects (such as comments or highlights by using a different bullet or position).

EXAMPLE

```
li.prodicon {list-style-image: url(logo.gif)}
```

This replaces the bullet character for list items of type prodicon (that is, <li class="prodicon">... </li>) with an image called logo.gif.

list-style-position

Use this property to set an indent or "outdent" for the bullet. This property allows the bullet to stand out from the list contents (outside) or lays it flush with the list items (inside). If you set this property for a list element (as opposed to the list-item elements), the list items use the settings you establish. You can override the list settings with individual list-item settings.

VALUES

A value of inside indents the bullet character with the left margin of the list-item contents. A value of outside creates a hanging-indent (or "outdent") effect, with the bullet standing out from the left margin of the list-item contents.

NOTES

List items use the settings from the lists. You can insert list items with different settings, creating a series of effects (such as comments or highlights by using a different bullet or position).

EXAMPLES

```
ul {list-style-position: outside; list-style-type: circle}
li.level2 {list-style-position: inside}
li.prodstart {list-style-image: url(logolitl.gif)}
```

If you combine these three statements in a style sheet, your basic list items in an unordered list will have a hollow circle that hangs outside the left margin of the list contents. You can add "second-level" list items (that is, `<li class="level2">......</li>`) that use the circle bullet but lay it flush to the list-item contents. This creates a visual effect where these list items appear to be secondary. The third statement creates the effect of list headings by replacing the circle with a logo, and these list items use the parent's `list-style-position` setting.

list-style-type

Use this property to indicate a style of bullet or numbering you want for your lists. You can create several list classes and list-item classes, and then combine them to give your information navigational structure. If you set this property for a list element (as opposed to the list-item elements), the list items use the settings you establish. You can override the list settings with individual list-item settings.

VALUES

Value	Effect
none	Suppresses the display of bullet characters.
circle	Places a hollow circle as the bullet.
disc	Places a filled circle as the bullet.
square	Places a filled square as the bullet.
decimal	Numbers the list items using Arabic numerals (1, 2, 3, ...).
decimal-leading-zero	Numbers the list items using Arabic numerals with initial zeros (01, 02, 03, ... , 10, 11, ...).
lower-roman	Numbers the list items using lowercase Roman numerals (i, ii, iii, ...).
upper-roman	Numbers the list items using uppercase Roman numerals (I, II, III, ...).
lower-alpha	Letters the list items using lowercase letters (a, b, c, ...).
upper-alpha	Letters the list items using uppercase letters (A, B, C, ...).
armenian	Armenian numbering (CSS2).

Continued on next page

Value	Effect
cjk-ideographic	Ideographic numbering (CSS2).
georgian	Georgian numbering (an, ban, gan, ..., he, tan, in, in-an, ...) (CSS2).
hebrew	Hebrew numbering (CSS2).
hiragana	A, i, u, e, o, ka, ki, ... (CSS2).
hiragana-iroha	i, ro, ha, ni, ho, he, to, ... (CSS2).
katakana	A, I, U, E, O, KA, KI, ... (CSS2).
katakana-iroha	I, RO, HA, NI, HO, HE, TO, ... (CSS2).

NOTES

If you use numbering or lettering, and you insert list items with an alternate type, the numbering includes the unnumbered list items in its counts. For example:

```
a    full-featured
     WYSIWIG
     compliant
D    backward compatible
```

EXAMPLES

```
ol {list-style-type: lower-roman}
```

This statement sets up a numbering system for the ordered lists in the document. These lists will use i, ii, iii, and so on, as a "bullet" for each list item.

```
li.comment {list-style-type: none}
```

You can override the list settings with a list-item setting. If you apply the list-item class comment (that is, `<li class="comment">...</li>`) to an item in a numbered list, the browser includes it in the numbering, but does not display the number for the list item.

CSS2 NOTES

CSS2 supports additional keywords for other numbering systems. Use the keywords hebrew, armenian, georgian, cjk-ideographic, hiragana, hiragana-iroha, katakana, and katakana-iroha. For example, if you want to use a Hebrew numbering system, your code might look like this:

```
ol {list-style-type: hebrew}
```

white-space

Use this property to control the white space within an element. This setting controls the wrapping of text within the element.

VALUES

Value	Effect
normal	Keeps the default of wrapping lines at the browser page size. This is the default and produces results similar to what you see in Web pages already.
nowrap	Prevents the user from wrapping lines within an element.
pre	Assigns the formatting in the document source to the document display.

When you want to control the line wrap in paragraphs or headings, you can do it with this property. If you select normal, it overrides the settings of a parent element because browsers default to this setting. If your element is a preformatted entity (such as sample code), you may want to use the pre keyword to force the browser to display it exactly as it occurs in the source text. Use the nowrap keyword to prevent the browser from ending the line without an explicit instruction, such as br, in the source.

NOTES

Some browsers may ignore this setting and retain their own defaults. Even though the default value for white-space is listed as normal, some browsers will have a default setting for all HTML or XHTML elements as proposed in a specification.

EXAMPLES

```
pre {white-space: pre}
```

This statement indicates that the text in the element is preformatted. The spacing between characters, words, and lines is set in the source, as are the line breaks.

```
p {white-space: normal}
```

This statement sets the spacing in the paragraph elements (p) to normal, which is how text is currently displayed.

```
h1 {white-space: nowrap}
```

This statement prevents the browser from wrapping the level 1 headings. For these headings to break across more than one line, you explicitly add br elements at the break spots.

Positioning

Using positioning, one of the first CSS2 features to be supported by browsers, you can add properties to style rules to control the positioning of the element. For example, you can identify specific locations for elements, as well as specify locations that are relative to other elements. You can use other box properties to control the layout as well, in conjunction with the positioning features. Furthermore, these features, used with scripting features, allow you to create dynamic HTML or XHTML documents.

bottom

Use this property to specify how far a box's bottom content edge is offset above the bottom of the box's containing block.

VALUES

The value `auto` specifies automatic offset, based on related settings.

Length   Specifies offset as a distance from the edge of the containing element. See the "Lengths" section earlier in this reference.

Percentage   Specifies offset as a percentage of the containing element's size (vertical or horizontal, as appropriate).

EXAMPLE

```
img.logo {position: fixed; bottom: 0px; right: 0px}
```

This sets the image with class `logo` to stay at the bottom right of the display at all times.

clear

Use this property to indicate which sides of an element's box(es) may not be adjacent to an earlier floating box.

VALUES

Value	Effect
left	Specifies that the element start below any left-floating elements above the current element.
right	Specifies that the element start below any right-floating elements above the current element.
both	Specifies that the element start below all floating boxes of earlier elements.
none	Specifies no constraints on element placement.

EXAMPLE

```
img.picture {clear: all; float: left}
```

This sets the image with class `picture` to float to the left side with the text flowing around to the right. It also sets the `clear` property to ensure that no other floating elements appear on the same line.

clip

A clipping region defines which portion of an element's rendered content is visible. By default, the clipping region has the same size and shape as the element's box(es). However, the clipping region may be modified by the `clip` property.

VALUES

Specifies `rect` (for rectangle, which is the only valid shape in CSS2). Use code `rect (top, right, bottom, left)` with each value specifying the length offset from the respective sides of the box. Substitute an absolute or relative length or `auto` for each of top, right, bottom, and left. The keyword `auto` specifies that the clipping region has the same size and location as the element's box(es).

```
p {clip: 15px 15px 15px 15px; overflow: hidden}
```

This example defines a clipping area 15 pixels in from the edges of the box and hides the extra content.

float

Use this property to specify that a box may shift to the left or right on the current line. The HTML and XHTML `img` elements with `clear` and `align` attributes are similar to `float`.

VALUES

Value	Effect
left	Specifies a box that is floated to the left with other content flowing around the right.
right	Specifies a box that is floated to the right with other content flowing around the left.
none	Specifies that the box does not float.

EXAMPLE

```
img.picture {float: left}
```

This sets the image with class `picture` to float to the left side with the text flowing around to the right.

left

Use this property to specify how far a box's left content edge is offset to the right of the left edge of the box's containing block.

VALUES

The value `auto` specifies automatic offset, based on related settings.

Length   Specifies offset as a distance from the edge of the containing element. See the "Lengths" section earlier in this reference.

Percentage   Specifies offset as a percentage of the containing element's size (vertical or horizontal, as appropriate).

EXAMPLE

```
img.logo {position: fixed; top: 0px; left: 0px}
```

This sets the image with class `logo` to stay at the top left of the display at all times.

overflow

Use this property to specify what happens to the extra content when a box is too small for the content it includes. In this case, the box is often called "clipped."

VALUES

Value	Effect
auto	Specifies that a scrolling mechanism is to be provided when necessary, but not always.
hidden	Specifies that content is clipped and that users should be unable to access the hidden region.
scroll	Specifies that the content is clipped and that scroll bars (if applicable) should always be shown to allow access to the content.
visible	Specifies that content not be clipped to box boundaries.

EXAMPLE

```
p {clip: 15px 15px 15px 15px; overflow: hidden}
```

This example defines a clipping area 15 pixels in from the edges of the box and hides the extra content.

position

Use this property to control the positioning of elements.

VALUES

Value	Effect
absolute	Specifies the element position and, optionally, size with respect to the containing element.
fixed	Specifies the element position and, optionally, size as with the absolute value, but with respect to a specific reference point (in the browser window or on a printed sheet, for example).
relative	Specifies that the position be calculated relative to the position in the normal flow, with no effect on other elements. Relatively positioned elements can overlap.
static	Specifies that the element belongs to the normal document flow with no specific positioning requirements.

EXAMPLE

```
img.logo {position: fixed; top: 0px; right: 0px}
```

This sets the image with the class logo (that is, <img class="logo" />) to stay at the top right of the display at all times.

right

Use this property to specify how far a box's right content edge is offset to the left of the right edge of the box's containing block.

VALUES

The value auto specifies automatic offset, based on related settings.

Length Specifies offset as a distance from the edge of the containing element. See the "Lengths" section earlier in this reference.

Percentage Specifies offset as a percentage of the containing element's size (vertical or horizontal, as appropriate).

EXAMPLE

```
img.logo {position: fixed; top: 0px; right: 0px}
```

This sets the image with class logo to stay at the top right of the display at all times.

top

Use this property to specify the vertical offset for an element in relation to the containing block.

VALUES

The value auto specifies automatic offset, based on related settings.

Length Specifies offset as a distance from the edge of the containing element. See the "Lengths" section earlier in this reference.

Percentage Specifies offset as a percentage of the containing element's size (vertical or horizontal, as appropriate).

EXAMPLE

```
img.logo {position: fixed; top: 0px; right: 0px}
```

This sets the image with class logo to stay at the top right of the display at all times.

visibility

Use the visibility property to specify whether the boxes generated by an element are rendered. Invisible boxes still affect layout; set the display property to none to suppress box generation altogether.

VALUES

Value	Effect
collapse	Specifies a collapsed (hidden) display for table rows and columns, or same as hidden for other elements.
hidden	Specifies that the box is invisible, but present for layout purposes.
visible	Specifies that the box is visible.

EXAMPLES

```
p.chosen {visibility: visible}
p.unchosen {visibility: hidden}
```

This example shows two paragraphs, each of which takes the same space, that can be either revealed or hidden (likely through scripts).

z-index

Using CSS2, you can *layer* box elements. Each box element has a position in three dimensions, including the normal horizontal and vertical positions and a vertical dimension, which is described on a *z*-axis. Each box belongs to one *stacking context* and has a number that indicates its position relative to other elements in the stack—the higher the number, the closer to the top (revealed) portion of the stack.

Use this property to specify the stack level of the box in the current stacking context. This property also implicitly specifies that new context is started.

VALUES

A numeric value specifies the stack level of the current element using an integer. The keyword `auto` specifies that the stack level is the same as the parent.

EXAMPLES

```
p.foreground {z-index: 10}
p.background {z-index: 3}
```

This sets the paragraphs with class `foreground` to have a `z-index` of 10, while the paragraphs with class `background` have a `z-index` of 3, so the background is behind the foreground.

Aural Style Sheets

Aural style sheets were introduced in CSS2; they specify how a document should be read aloud—for example, to a visually impaired person, in situations where reading is not possible, or as a supplement to the visual presentation.

With aural style sheets, you can specify where sound should come from, the characteristics of the sound, and other sounds to precede or follow the sound. These properties are important for accessibility reasons.

azimuth

You use the `azimuth` property to specify which direction the sound comes from on the horizontal plane—either from the left or right, from in front of or from behind, or from any point in between.

VALUES

Describes the sound source as an angle with 0 degrees directly in front of the listener, 90 degrees to the listener's right, 180 degrees behind the listener, and 270 degrees to the listener's left. All points in between are possible. Use a number to express the angle, or use one of the following keyword equivalents:

Value	Equivalent to
left-side	270 degrees
far-left	300 degrees (used with behind, specifies 240 degrees)
left	320 degrees (used with behind, specifies 220 degrees)
center-left	340 degrees (used with behind, specifies 200 degrees)
center	0 degrees (used with behind, specifies 180 degrees)
center-right	20 degrees (used with behind, specifies 160 degrees)
far-right	60 degrees (used with behind, specifies 120 degrees)
right-side	90 degrees
behind	180 degrees
leftwards	Moving the sound source counterclockwise by 20 degrees (subtracting 20 degrees)
rightwards	Moving the sound source clockwise by 20 degrees (adding 20 degrees)

EXAMPLE

```
p.trick {azimuth: right-side; volume: 100}
```

This example sets the sound for all paragraphs with the trick attribute to come from the right at a volume of 100.

cue

You use this property to specify a sound to play before and after the specified element. The W3C suggests cues as "auditory icons." If you specify one value, it applies to both before and after; if you specify two values, one applies to before, and one applies to after.

VALUES

Specify the address of a sound file to play with the format url(...). The value none specifies no cueing.

EXAMPLE

```
.example, .code {cue: url(codewarning.au);
                 pause-before: 20ms; pause-after: 50ms}
```

This example specifies that the codewarning.au sound should precede and follow anything in example or code classes. It also specifies that codewarning.au has a 50-millisecond pause before it plays and a 20-millisecond pause after it's played.

cue-after

Use this property to specify a sound to play after the specified element.

VALUES

Specify the address of a sound file to play with the format url(...). The value none specifies no cueing.

EXAMPLE

```
.example, .code {cue-after: url(donenow.au);
                 pause-after: 5%}
```

This example specifies that the donenow.au sound follow anything in example or code classes and have a 5% pause after it's played.

cue-before

Use this property to specify a sound to play before the specified element.

VALUES

Specify the address of a sound file to play with the format url(...). The value none specifies no cueing.

EXAMPLE

```
.example, .code {cue-before: url(codewarning.au);
                 pause-after: 5%}
```

This example specifies that the codewarning.au sound precede anything in example or code classes and have a 5% pause after it's played.

elevation

You use this property to specify the sound source in the vertical plane—points above or below the listener.

VALUES

Specifies the sound source as an angle between −90 degrees (directly below the listener) and +90 degrees (directly above the listener). Use a number to express the angle, or use one of the following keyword equivalents:

Value	Equivalent to
below	−90 degrees
level	0 degrees
above	+90 degrees
higher	Increasing elevation by 10 degrees
lower	Decreasing elevation by 10 degrees

EXAMPLE

```
p.downhere {elevation: below; volume: 100}
```

This example sets the sound for all paragraphs with the class `downhere` to come from below.

pause

Use this property to specify the duration of a pause before or after an element is read. The pause occurs between element content and cues. If you specify one value, it applies before and after the element is read. If you specify two values, the first applies before and the second applies after an element is read.

VALUES

Time   Specifies the duration of the pause as a number of milliseconds.

Percentage   Specifies the duration of the pause as a percentage of the overall element length.

EXAMPLES

```
.example, .code {volume: 50; speak: spell-out; pause: 10 20}
```

This example specifies that anything in `example` or `code` classes should be spelled out at a volume of 50, preceded by a 10-millisecond pause and followed by a 20-millisecond pause.

```
.example, .code {volume: 50; speak: spell-out; pause: 10}
```

This example is the same as the first one, but the element will be preceded *and* followed by a 10-millisecond pause.

pause-after

Use this property to specify the length of a pause after an element is read. The pause occurs between element content and cues.

VALUES

Time   Specifies the duration of the pause as a number of milliseconds.

Percentage   Specifies the duration of the pause as a percentage of the overall element length.

EXAMPLE

```
.example, .code {volume: 50; speak: spell-out;
                 pause-before: 10; pause-after: 5%}
```

This example specifies that anything in `example` or `code` classes be spelled out at a volume of 50, be preceded by a 10-millisecond pause, and be followed by a pause lasting 5% of the length of the element.

pause-before

Use this property to specify the length of a pause before an element is read.

VALUES

Time   Specifies the duration of the pause as a number of milliseconds.

Percentage   Specifies the duration of the pause as a percentage of the overall element length.

EXAMPLE

```
.example, .code {volume: 50; speak: spell-out; pause-before: 10}
```

This example specifies that anything in example or code classes be spelled out and preceded by a 10-millisecond pause at a volume of 50.

pitch

Use this property to specify the pitch (frequency) of the voice.

VALUES

Specifies the pitch of the voice in hertz (Hz). Use a number for the value, or use x-low, low, medium, high, and x-high to specify relative pitches.

EXAMPLE

```
.example, .code {pitch: medium}
```

This example specifies that anything in example or code classes be of medium pitch.

pitch-range

You use this property to specify variation in the pitch, which can range from a monotone to a highly inflected voice.

VALUES

Specifies a number in the range from 0 (monotone) to 100 (very energetic, highly inflected).

EXAMPLE

```
.example, .code {volume: 50; pitch: medium; pitch-range: 10}
```

This example specifies that anything in example or code classes be inflected very little in a medium pitch at a volume of 50.

play-during

Use this property to specify a sound to play while the element's content is read.

Value	Effect
url(...)	Specifies the address of a sound file.
Mix	Specifies that any sound from the parent element should continue to play in addition to the sound named in the url(...) value.
Repeat	Specifies that the sound should repeat if necessary to fill the time that the element occupies. Otherwise, the sound plays once and then stops.
Auto	Specifies that the sound of the parent element continues but no other sound plays. This is the default.
None	Specifies no cueing.

```
.example, .code {volume: 50;
                 speak: spell-out;
                 cue-before: url(codewarning.au)
                 play-during: url(special.mid) repeat;
                 pause-after: 5%}
```

This example specifies that the special.mid sound should accompany anything in example or code classes.

richness

Use this property to specify the brightness or richness of the sound.

Specifies a number in the range from 0 (a "smooth" voice that carries little) to 100 (a "rich" voice that carries well).

```
.example, .code {volume: 50; richness: 90}
```

This example specifies that anything in example or code classes be very rich and played at a volume of 50.

speak

Use this property to specify whether text should be spoken, not spoken, or spelled out.

VALUES

Value	Effect
none	Specifies that the element not be spoken.
normal	Specifies that the element should be spoken.
spell-out	Specifies that the element should be spelled one letter at a time.

EXAMPLE

```
.example, .code {volume: 50; stress: 50;
                 richness: 90; speak: spell-out;}
```

This example specifies that anything in example or code classes be spelled out at a volume and stress of 50 and a richness of 90.

speak-numeral

Use this property to control how numbers are read.

VALUES

The value digits specifies that numbers be read as individual digits. The (default) value continuous specifies that numbers be read as a complete number.

EXAMPLE

```
.example, .code {pitch: medium;
                 speak: spell-out;
                 speak-numeral: digits}
```

This example specifies that all numerals in example or code classes be spelled out and read digit by digit in a medium pitch.

speak-punctuation

Use this property to specify if or how punctuation should be spoken.

VALUES

The value code specifies that punctuation should be spoken explicitly. The (default) value none specifies that punctuation should be interpreted as pauses or inflection, but not spoken.

```
.example, .code {volume: 50;
                 speak: spell-out;
                 speak-punctuation: code}
```

This example specifies that all punctuation in `example` or `code` classes be spelled out and spoken explicitly at a volume of 50.

speech-rate

Use this property to specify the rate of speech output for aural browsers.

VALUES

Specifies the rate in words per minute. Use a number to express the rate, or use one of the following keyword equivalents:

Value	Equivalent to
x-slow	80 words per minute
slow	120 words per minute
medium	180–200 words per minute (the default)
fast	300 words per minute
x-fast	500 words per minute
faster	Increasing rate by 40 words per minute
slower	Decreasing rate by 40 words per minute

EXAMPLE

```
.example, .code {speech-rate: slow}
```

This example specifies that anything in `example` or `code` class be read slowly.

stress

This property is similar to `pitch-range`; however, it allows you to specify the amount of stress (inflection) of words and syllables.

VALUES

Specifies a number in the range from 0 (monotone) to 100 (highly inflected).

EXAMPLE

```
.example, .code {volume: 50; pitch: medium; stress: 90}
```

This example specifies that anything in `example` or `code` classes be highly inflected at a volume of 50 and a medium pitch.

voice-family

Use this property to specify voice family names. You can specify multiple voice families, just as you can specify multiple font families.

VALUES

Specify either a generic voice, using the keywords `male`, `female`, or `child`, or a specific voice, assuming availability to the listener.

EXAMPLE

```
h1 {voice-family: narrator, female}
```

This example specifies all level 1 headings be read in the `narrator` voice, or in a female voice if `narrator` is not available.

volume

Use this property to specify the relative volume of the text, where 1 is the minimum and 100 is the maximum. Users will likely be able to adjust or override volume settings.

VALUES

Value	Effect
nn	Sets a specific number between 1 and 100.
nn%	Sets a volume percentage.
x-soft	Identical to a value of 0.
soft	Identical to a value of 25.
medium	Identical to a value of 50.
loud	Identical to a value of 75.
x-loud	Identical to a value of 100.

EXAMPLE

```
h1 {volume: 70}
```

This example sets a relatively high volume for level 1 headings.

Printed Media Style Sheets

Your users will view many of your documents online and scroll up or down to access page content. In some cases, however, your users might print your documents, rather than reading them online. You can use printed (or paged) media style sheets to set up documents to accommodate printing needs. These CSS2 properties let you set values for the page box, which you can think of as the area of your printout. For example, in hard copy, your page box might be the 8.5 × 11 piece of paper; the page box is the content, margins, and edges. Remember that these are only available to users using CSS2-compliant browsers.

@page

Use this special element to specify the dimensions, orientation, and margins of a page box. Use @page, which selects a page. For example,

```
@page {size: 8.5in 11in}
```

sets a standard North American paper size.

You can also use optional pseudoclasses, which are :first, :left, and/or :right to specify styles for the first, left, or right page of a document, respectively. For example,

```
@page :first {margin-top: 2em}
```

You can also use the names of specific pages, and any properties and declarations you want. For example,

```
@page squirrel {margin-bottom: 1in}
```

margin

Use this property to set up all the margins for a page. This shorthand measurement specifies the distance between the page box and the edge of the media.

VALUES

Length   Sets the border width using an absolute or a relative measurement. See the "Lengths" section earlier in this reference.

Percentage   Sets the margin size as a percentage of the page width.

Browser default   The value auto sets the margin to the browser's default on all four sides.

For length and percentage, you can use one, two, three, or four numbers. If you use one number, the browser applies it to all four margins (top, right, bottom, and left). If you use two numbers, the first number sets the top and bottom margins, and the second number sets the left and right margins. If you use three numbers, you're setting the top margin with the first, the right and left margins with the second, and the bottom margin with the third. You can mix length and percentage values.

EXAMPLE

```
@page {margin: 1in}
```

This example sets a 1-inch margin around all sides of the pages.

margin-bottom

Use this property to set only the bottom margin of a page box. The bottom margin is the distance between the bottom border and the bottom edge of the box. This generally defaults to zero and is not used by included block or inline elements.

VALUES

Length   Sets an absolute or relative distance between the border and the box's bottom edge. See the "Lengths" section earlier in this reference.

Percentage   Sets the bottom margin size as a percentage of the parent element's width.

Browser default   The value `auto` sets the bottom margin to the browser's default.

EXAMPLE

```
@page {margin: 1in; margin-bottom: 0.5in}
```

This example sets a 1-inch margin around all sides of the pages with a 0.5-inch margin at the bottom.

margin-left

Use this property to set only the left margin of a page box. The left margin is the distance between the border and the left edge of the box.

VALUES

Length   Sets an absolute or relative distance between the border and the box's left edge. See the "Lengths" section earlier in this reference.

Percentage   Sets the left margin size as a percentage of the parent element's width.

Browser default   The value `auto` sets the left margin to the browser's default.

EXAMPLE

```
@page {margin: 1in; margin-left: 0.5in}
```

This example sets a 1-inch margin around all sides of the pages with a 0.5-inch margin at the left.

margin-right

Use this property to set only the right margin of a page. The right margin is the distance between the border and the right edge of the page. You can use this to force the element away from the right edge of the page.

VALUES

Length   Sets an absolute or relative distance between the border and the box's right edge. See the "Lengths" section earlier in this reference.

Percentage   Sets the right margin size as a percentage of the parent element's width.

Browser default   The value `auto` sets the right margin to the browser's default.

EXAMPLE

```
@page:left {margin-left: 5cm; margin-right: 6cm}
```

This example sets the left margin at 5 cm and the right margin at 6 cm.

margin-top

Use this property to set only the top margin of a page box. The top margin is the distance between the page and the top of the physical page.

VALUES

Length   Sets an absolute or relative distance between the border and the box's top edge. See the "Lengths" section earlier in this reference.

Percentage   Sets the top margin size as a percentage of the parent element's width.

Browser default   The value `auto` sets the top margin to the browser's default.

EXAMPLE

```
@page:first {margin-top: 8cm}
```

Here, we set the top margin to 8 cm.

marks

You use this property to specify whether crop or cross marks should be printed outside the page box (if the output device can do so) to help with alignment of physical media for binding.

VALUES

The value `crop` specifies to print crop marks. The value `cross` specifies to print cross marks. The default value is `none`.

EXAMPLE

```
@page {marks: crop}
```

This example specifies to print crop marks.

orphans

Use this property to specify the minimum number of lines of a paragraph that must be left at the bottom of a page. By using the `orphans` property, you can avoid a single line dangling at the bottom of a page.

VALUES

An integer that sets the minimum number of lines of a paragraph that must appear at the bottom of a page.

EXAMPLE

```
p {orphans: 3}
```

This example requires at least three lines of a new paragraph to appear at the bottom of a page.

page

Using the `page` property, you can specify the specific page on which an element should appear.

VALUES

The value specifies the name or identification of a page.

EXAMPLE

```
@page summary
h1 {page: summary}
```

This example specifies that the `h1` element appear on the `summary` page.

page-break-after

Use this property to control page breaks after elements.

VALUES

Value	Effect
always	Specifies a page break after the element.
auto	Specifies default action for page breaks (this is the default value).
avoid	Specifies no page break after the element.
left	Specifies a page break after the element to make sure the element starts on a left-side page.
right	Specifies a page break after the element to make sure the element starts on a right-side page.

EXAMPLE

```
table {page-break-after: auto}
```

This example specifies automatic page breaks after `table` elements.

page-break-before

Use this property to control page breaks before elements.

VALUES

Value	Effect
always	Specifies a page break before the element.
auto	Specifies default action for page breaks (this is the default value).
avoid	Specifies no page break before the element.
left	Specifies a page break before the element to make sure the element starts on a left-side page.
right	Specifies a page break before the element to make sure the element starts on a right-side page.

EXAMPLE

```
h1 {page-break-before: right}
```

This example specifies a page break before h1 elements and forces them to start on a right-hand page.

page-break-inside

Use this property to control page breaks within elements.

VALUES

The (default) value auto specifies a default action for page breaks. The value avoid specifies no page break within the element.

EXAMPLE

```
table {page-break-inside: avoid}
```

Using the page-break-inside property, we can avoid all page breaks within table elements.

size

Use this property to specify the size of the page box.

VALUES

Use a keyword value or a number. Numeric values specify the dimensions (horizontal and vertical) of the box, using an absolute or (in the case of pixels) a relative measurement. This type of sizing forces a particular measurement to be used for the element, ignoring any browser's settings. Specify the measurement after the number as follows: in for inches, mm for millimeters, cm for centimeters, pt for points, px for pixels, or pc for picas. If you provide one measurement, the box will be square. If you provide two, you specify the width and length of the box.

Possible keyword values are as follows:

Value	Effect
auto	Specifies that the page box be set to the size and orientation of the target sheet. This is the default.
landscape	Specifies that the long sides of the page box are horizontal.
portrait	Specifies that the long sides of the page box are vertical.

If you use auto, you can follow it with landscape or portrait to override the default orientation while maintain the auto setting for size.

EXAMPLES

```
@page {size: 8.5in 11in}
```

This example sets a standard North American paper size.

```
@page {size: auto landscape}
```

This example sets a horizontally oriented page of the default size for the output device.

widows

Use this property to set the minimum number of lines of a paragraph that must appear at the top of a page. Similar to the orphans property, widows will prevent a single line dangling at the top of a new page.

VALUES

An integer that sets the minimum number of lines of a paragraph that must appear at the top of a page.

EXAMPLE

```
p {widows: 3}
```

This example requires at least three lines of a new paragraph to appear at the top of a page.

Auto-Generated Content

The properties in this section allow you to use CSS2 to automatically generate content for your pages. These properties are handy for generating content that you'd otherwise have to retype from document to document or line to line, such as boilerplate text, dates, or even counters.

content

With the content property, you can automatically include whatever text you want. You'll use this property with the :before and :after pseudoclasses.

Value	Effect
text	Specifies text content.
url(…)	Specifies the URL from which the content should come.
open-quote	Specifies opening quotation marks based on the `quote` property.
close-quote	Specifies closing quotation marks based on the `quote` property.
no-close-quote	Specifies not to display closing quotation marks, but to consider the quote closed.
no-open-quote	Specifies not to display opening quotation marks, but to consider a quote open.

EXAMPLES

```
q:before {content: open-quote}
q:after {content: close-quote}
```

This example places an opening quote before q elements and a closing quote after q elements.

counter

Use this property to set and display counters.

VALUES

This property takes two values: the name of the counter, and an optional style. `counter(name, style)` specifies to display the current count for *name*, with the count displayed in *style* format. All the styles shown as possible values for `list-style-type` are allowed here, including `disc`, `circle`, `square`, and `none`; see the section on `list-style-type` earlier in this reference.

NOTES

If an element increments or resets a counter and also uses it (in the `content` property of its `:before` or `:after` pseudoclass), the counter is used *after* being incremented or reset.

EXAMPLES

```
ol {counter-reset: list}
li:before {content: counter(list) ". ";
           counter-increment: list}
```

This example resets the `list` counter and then displays the `list` counter before each item in the list.

```
ol {counter-reset: list}
li:before {content: counter(name, roman) ". ";
           counter-increment: list}
```

This example is the same as the previous, but sets the counter to display as Roman numerals.

counter-increment

The `counter-increment` property adjusts the value of one or more counters as a particular selector occurs in your document.

VALUES

This property takes a counter name or names as a value (the name of the counter[s] to increment) and an optional integer by which to increment. The default increment is 1. Zero and negative integers are allowed.

EXAMPLE

```
h2:before {content: counter(chapter) "." counter(section) " ";
           counter-increment: section}
```

This example displays a heading format like *1.2* and increments the counter on the section (h2) part by 1.

counter-reset

Use this property to reset counters to zero or another value when a particular selector occurs in your document.

VALUES

This property takes the name(s) of a counter to reset, and an optional integer that the counter is reset to (the default is to reset to zero).

EXAMPLE

```
h1:before {counter-reset: section 1 headlevel 1}
```

This example resets the counter named section to 1 and also resets the counter named headlevel to 1.

quotes

Use this property to specify quotation marks for any number of embedded quotations.

VALUES

The value none specifies that open-quote and close-quote values of the content property produce no quotations marks.

To specify quotation marks for the open-quote and close-quote values of the content property, provide paired strings of quotation characters. The first pair represents the opening and closing characters for the first (or outer) level of quotation, the second pair defines the next included level of quotation, and so forth.

EXAMPLES

```
q:lang(en) {quotes: '"''"''''''''''"'}
q:lang(fr) {quotes: "«" "»" "<" ">"}
```

This example sets double and single quotes for English-language quotations and double and single chevrons for French-language quotations.

Master's Reference Part 3

Scripting Reference

THIS REFERENCE COVERS SCRIPTING statement keywords, objects, methods and functions, event handlers, and properties. These are all the pieces that you need to build a script for your page. The information in this section is based on Netscape's JavaScript 1.3, which is compatible with the international standard ECMA-262 (ECMAScript) and to a large extent with Microsoft's JScript (which is itself ECMA-262-compatible).

TIP *You might refer to the following chapters as you're reading this section:*
Chapter 10 (if you're adding JavaScript to your documents)
Chapter 16 (if you're using Dynamic HTML or XHTML)

We've included some examples here, but look in Chapter 10 to find the details of how to write scripts for your Web pages. Keep in mind that you should test your scripts in as many different browsers on as many different platforms as you can. Additionally, we have chosen not to include most scripting features that are in only a particular version of JavaScript or JScript. Although extra or additional features in HTML or XHTML cause no problems for browsers lacking support for those features, extra or additional script commands do not work and simply generate error messages in noncompliant browsers. For a complete JavaScript reference, see *Mastering JavaScript: Premium Edition* by James Jaworski (also published by Sybex).

Throughout this reference, in explanations of the examples, we've used the term *entry* (rather than parameter or operator) to refer to the various parts of the syntax.

NOTE *The HTML and XHTML code samples throughout this section are all technically XHTML, because XHTML requires the most careful use of elements and attributes. If you're using XHTML, you can use the examples as shown. As you remember from Chapter 2, HTML is more forgiving and flexible than XHTML, so the samples here all work equally well and can be used "as is" if you're using plain HTML.*

This reference sorts entries by general purpose; the sections cover the constructs, operators, escape character, reserved words, objects, methods and functions, event handlers, and properties.

Category	Description
Constructs	Statement types that you can use to control the flow of a script
Operators	Algebraic, logical, and bitwise symbols for working with values in your statements
The escape character	Allows you to insert a special character into your text
Reserved words	Terms that JavaScript either currently uses or plans to use in the future
Objects	Containers in which properties reside and that are affected by methods and functions
Event handlers	Wait for the user or browser to do something and then tell the script to act, based on that event
Properties	Describe browser or scripting characteristics

WARNING   *Although we often use extra spaces, indents, and line breaks for readability in our printed code, do not insert any additional spaces or line returns in your JavaScript code. Make sure that each JavaScript statement is on a single line, and allow the text to wrap without a line return. JavaScript sees line returns as JavaScript characters and adds them to your code (which will make the code nonfunctional). It's fine to use line returns at the actual end of a line of code, before you start the next line, but not in the middle of a line of code.*

Constructs

Constructs are the structures that you can use in JavaScript to control the flow of the script. If the course of the script depends on input or circumstance, you use a construct to direct the processing of the script. For example, to display the answer to a test question after a user has tried unsuccessfully to respond correctly, you can use a construct called an `if` statement.

This section contains an alphabetical list of JavaScript constructs. Each entry describes a single construct and provides its syntax and an example.

break

A `break` statement ends a repetitive series of `while` or `for` statements. Sometimes you want a condition that ignores everything else and jumps out of the loop to carry on with the rest of the script. You do this with a `break` statement. The syntax for the `break` statement is:

```
break;
```

EXAMPLE

```
function alphacount (x) {
    var count = 0
    while (count < 1000) {
        if (990 == count)
            break;
        count += (getUserNumber())  }  }
```

This example is a function, `alphacount`, that adds user input until at least 990, but it could conceivably go as high as 1000. If the value is exactly 990, the `break` statement is triggered and the `while` statement ends.

comment

You place comments within your scripts to help you recall what variables represent or which conditions that change over time may affect loops or other calls. A comment does not perform a function; it's simply a note to yourself or to future users of the script. The syntax of the `comment` statement is:

```
// comment text
```

EXAMPLE

```
readMe = "" // set the readMe variable to null
bigNews = 1 // set the bigNews variable to 1
if (readMe < bigNews) {
    bigNews += song
    // Add song to bigNews, increments bigNews by a user.
    variable getStory(readMe)
    // This function retrieves the user's guess.
}
```

In this example, the variable declarations and the `if` statement are documented with comments.

continue

Like the `break` statement, `continue` breaks out of a `for` or `while` loop. Instead of going to the next set of instructions past the loop, the `continue` statement sends the script back to the condition in the `while` statement or to the `update` expression in a `for` loop. The syntax of the `continue` statement is:

```
continue;
```

or

```
continue label;
```

where the optional `label` is the name of the label in the script where the execution should continue.

EXAMPLE

```
while (cows != "home") {
    if (barnDoor = "open") {
        cows = "home"
        continue;   }
    callCows()
}
```

In this `while` loop, the condition checks the value of the variable `cows`. As long as the value is not equal to "home", the loop continues. Within the loop is an `if` statement that checks the state of the `barnDoor` variable; when `barnDoor` is "open", the statement sets the value of `cows` to "home" and sends the script back up to the condition statement. Otherwise, the loop continues to run the function `callCows`.

for

The for statement repeats an action for a specified number of times. You give the script the starting conditions, ending conditions, and iteration information. A starting condition could be month=1, indicating the repetitions begin at January. The ending condition, in this case, could be month=12, indicating the repetitions continue through the months of the year. Inside this repetition, you include a series of statements that perform a function (such as displaying a result: "in January our sales were $1,500,000"). The increment would likely be month++, indicating that the value of month is increased by 1 as each repetition is completed. The syntax of the for statement is:

```
for ([initial expression]; [condition]; [update expression]) {
    statements; }
```

The initial expression entry is the statement or variable declaration, condition is the Boolean or comparison statement, and update expression is the scheme for incrementing, tied in with a variable in the condition.

EXAMPLE

```
horse = 100;
for (cows = 0; cows <= horse; cows++) {
    getCowCount(cows); }
```

This example simply repeats the function getCowCount until the number of cows is more than the number of horses. Each time the result of getCowCount is less than or equal to the number of horses (in the variable horse), the number of cows is incremented by 1. This loop could go on for a long time.

for in

The for in statement doesn't need counters to complete its repetitions. If, for example, you have a list of commands in objects that use the menu name (the File object contains all the menu items found under the File menu), you can iterate through the list, presenting them as part of a list of options. The benefit is that you can store the information in an object and update it once to use many times. When the list of menu items is complete, the script moves on to the next set of instructions. The syntax of the for in statement is:

```
for (variable in object) { statements; }
```

The variable entry represents a value, and object is an array of object properties.

EXAMPLE

```
function house (rooms, location, floors, residents) {
    this.rooms = rooms;
    this.location = location;
    this.floors = floors;
    this.residents = residents;  }
while (newHome != "no") {
    description = "";
    var info;
    for (info in house) { description += house + "." + info +
```

```
        " = " + house[info] + "<br />" }
    description += "<hr />";
    return description;
    getNewHouse (newHome);   }
```

In this example, the function house fills the information about the object house. The object house contains the properties rooms, location, floors, and residents. The statement inside the for in loop generates a series of statements that fill the object. For example, if the user provided the following information—**10**, **London**, **5**, and **9**—the variable description would end up being this series:

```
house.rooms = 10;
house.location = London;
house.floors = 5;
house.residents = 9;
```

function

This construct sets up a JavaScript function. The function makes some kind of calculation or performs a specific task using information provided—words, numbers, or objects. With a function command, you can fill an object with the selected information. For example, if you collect information from a user in several boxes, you can put this together into a single variable that you then use to address the user throughout the session. It's best to define functions in the head section of the Web page, because functions must be declared before they can be used. The syntax of the function statement is:

```
function name ([parameter], [parameter], [parameter]) {
    statements; }
```

EXAMPLE

```
// This function works out the grade for the test.
// The variables ans_right, ans_wrong, and ans_blank are used
// in other functions to determine the user's improvement over
// a series of tests.
function calc_pass_fail (ans_right, ans_wrong, ans_blank) {
    return ans_right / (ans_right + ans_wrong + ans_blank);   }
```

In this example, the function calc_pass_fail reads in the variables ans_right, ans_wrong, and ans_blank to produce the person's percentage grade for the most recent test. Subsequent scripts can control which page users see, depending on their grade.

if

The if statement works just like the spoken equivalent: *If this is true, do this; if it is not true, do something else.* Use this construct when you want the script to perform a task when the right conditions arise. For example, to include some information in a result page, use the if construct—if the user selects examples, include examples in the results page. The syntax of the if statement is:

```
if (condition) {
    statements; }
```

EXAMPLE

```
if (tests == 0) {
    window.location.href = "test.html"; }
```

In this example, the if statement determines whether the user has taken any tests. If the user has not taken any tests (tests = 0), the user is taken to the test pages.

if else

Like the if statement, this construct allows you to apply decision-making to the script: *If this is true, do this; otherwise, do this*. Use this construct when you have two alternatives that depend on the conditions. For example, suppose you want to display correct or incorrect notes next to the user's response in a test. If the user answers correctly, you want to include a congratulations message; otherwise, you want to show the correct answer. The syntax of the if else statement is:

```
if (condition) {
    statements; }
else {
    statements; }
```

EXAMPLE

```
if (tests != 0) {
    if (tests == 1) {
        document.write("lesson 2"); }
    else {
        if (tests == 2) {
            document.write("lesson 3"); }
            else {
            if (tests == 3) {
                document.write("lesson 4"); }
            } } }
else {
    document.write("lesson 1"); }
```

In this example, the if statements check which test the user has completed and print the name of the next lesson. The first if statement simply tests whether the user has taken any tests; the test counter is incremented at the end of each test (not in this function or loop).

new

Use this construct to create a user-defined object. Creating an object is a two-step process:

1. Define the object with a function.

2. Create an instance of the object with the new statement.

The syntax of the new statement is:

```
objectName = new objectType (
    [parameter1], [parameter2], [parameterN] );
```

The objectName entry is the name of the new object; this is how you refer to it in later code. The objectType entry is the object type, a function that defines the object. The parameter1 … parameterN entries are the properties for the object.

EXAMPLE

```
function house (rooms, location, floors, residents) {
   this.rooms = rooms;
   this.location = location;
   this.floors = floors;
   this.residents = residents;  }
newHouse = new house (8, Prairieville, 3, 4);
```

This example creates an object type called house and populates newHouse, which is of type house, with 8 rooms, a Prairieville location, 3 floors, and 4 residents.

return

The return statement works in conjunction with the function statement to specify that a value be returned by the function. To display a calculated value, you include a return statement to bring the value back to the script. The syntax of the return statement is:

```
return;
```

or

```
return expression;
```

where the optional expression can specify what is to be returned.

EXAMPLE

```
function square (x) {
   return (x * x); }
```

This simple example uses the return statement with the expression that generates the value that should be returned (the square of the number x passed to the function).

switch

The switch statement is similar to the if else statement in that it presents the script with a series of alternate routes that depend on conditions found. If a given condition is true, then the associated case is executed. If no conditions match, then the default case is executed. The switch statement is cleaner than nesting a series of if else statements. The syntax of the switch statement is:

```
switch (expression) {
   case1: statements;
      break;
   case2: statements;
      break;
   default: statements;
}
```

EXAMPLE

```
switch (infoType) {
   case ("reference") : destination = "jref.html";
      break;
   case ("how-to") : destination = "instruct.html";
      break;
   case ("overview") : destination = "intro.html";
      break;
   default : destination = "toc.html";
}
```

This example takes the value in the variable infoType and compares it to a list of known values. If the value in infoType matches any of the stated cases (reference, how-to, or overview), the script stores a page name in the destination variable. If no match is found, the script sets the destination to the table of contents (toc.html).

this

The construct this refers to the object in focus. For example, when filling an object's array (list of properties), you would have a series of this statements, one for each property. The syntax of the this statement is:

```
this[.propertyName]
```

EXAMPLE

```
function house (rooms, location, floors, residents) {
   this.rooms = rooms;
   this.location = location;
   this.floors = floors;
   this.residents = residents;  }
newHouse = new house (8, Prairieville, 3, 4);
```

This example creates an object type called house and populates newHouse, which is of type house, with 8 rooms, a Prairieville location, 3 floors, and 4 residents.

var

This keyword indicates that the statement is performing an assignment to a variable. You can use it to set the initial value of the variables (always a good idea!) outside the function (particularly if it has repetitions) or inside the function. The syntax of the var keyword is either one of the following lines:

```
var varName;
var varName = value;
```

The varName entry is the name of the variable, and value becomes the original contents of the variable.

EXAMPLE

```
var cust_id = 0, reading = 0;
```

In this simple statement, customer ID (`cust_id`) and usage (`reading`) variables are set to zero. This is in preparation for a function in which a customer number is assigned and a variable that tracks session activities is launched.

while

The `while` statement is similar to the `for` statement; it creates a loop that repeats a set of statements as long as a condition is true. The syntax of the `while` statement is:

```
while (condition) { statements }
```

EXAMPLE

```
copies = 0;
original = 0;
while (copies < 5) {
    copies++;
    while (original < 10) {
        original++; }
    original = 0;
    //reset original to 0 before reentering the first while loop
}
```

In this example, the two variables, `copies` and `original`, are set to zero before entering the `while` loop. The outside loop checks that the number of copies made is less than 5. If that condition is true, the number of copies is incremented by 1, and then a second `while` loop iterates through the pages in the original.

with

To use a series of statements from the same object, such as the `Math` object, place them inside a `with` statement. You then need not identify each function, method, or property as belonging to the `Math` object. Usually when you write a statement that uses a function from an object, you have to include the object in the statement. The `with` construct lets you group a series of statements and identifies the parent object for the functions, methods, and properties. The syntax of the `with` statement is:

```
with (object) { statements; }
```

EXAMPLE

```
with (Math) {
    a = PI * r * r;
    x = r * cos(theta);
    y = r * sin(theta);
}
```

In this example, values are assigned to the properties `Math.a`, `Math.x`, and `Math.y`.

Operators

An operator is a symbol that represents an action; the most familiar operators are the mathematical symbols for addition, subtraction, multiplication, and division. JavaScript includes these basic actions and some more complex operations, each with a special symbol. As is the case with those familiar mathematical symbols, an order of operation defines the precedence (that is, which operator is dealt with first) of each operator in an expression.

Table MR3.1 defines the operators and presents them in their order of operation. You can use parentheses to control the order or precedence in a statement. In the table, operators of equal precedence are grouped together, and the groups are divided by a single line. For example, ( ), [ ], and . (period) have the same precedence in the order of operation.

Some of these operators work on the bits in your values. To work on the bits, JavaScript converts your values to bits, performs the operation, and converts the value back to its original type. This can lead to some interesting results, particularly if you're unfamiliar with the bit values or if you miscalculate.

Because the category of "assignment" is so extensive, we've listed the assignment operators separately, in Table MR3.2.

TABLE MR3.1: JavaScript Operators

OPERATOR	DESCRIPTION	WHAT IT DOES
( )	Function call or statement organizer	Organizes functions and forces a different order on the equations: x+2*y is the same as x+(2*y) because multiplication takes precedence over addition.
[ ]	Subscript	Use when you have a pointer and an element. For example, if you have an associative list (a variable that contains a set of values), you can use this to identify individual members in the list. These lists are called arrays.
.	Members	Use when you're using the methods and properties for an object. For example, Math.abs() calls the absolute function from the Math object.
!	NOT	The Boolean negation symbol. Use it when your expression is designed to include everything except the item marked with this NOT symbol. For example, if name !Bob, call calls everyone except people named Bob.
~	One's complement	The bitwise equivalent of the NOT operator. Using this changes a 0 (zero) to a 1 (one) and vice versa.
++	Increment	Use in front of or behind a variable to add one to its value. For example, right++ is the same as right+1.
--	Decrement	Use in front of or behind a variable to subtract one from its value. For example, submits-- is the same as submits-1.

Continued on next page

TABLE MR3.1: JAVASCRIPT OPERATORS *(continued)*

OPERATOR	DESCRIPTION	WHAT IT DOES
*	Multiply	Use to multiply two numeric values. These must be numbers.
/	Divide	Use to divide two numeric values. These must be numbers. If you use integers on both sides of the division expression, you won't get any decimal values. For example, if in and out are declared as integers, and in is 12 and out is 7, in/out = 1.
%	Modulo	Integer division does not use the remainder; it does not give you a decimal place in the result. If the division is not a clean division, you lose the remainder. Use this when you want the remainder from a division operation. For example, 7/2 as an integer division gives you a result of 3; 7%2 gives you 1.
+	Addition	Combines two values (numbers or words).
–	Subtraction	Takes one value (number or word) out of another.
<<	Bitwise left shift	Moves the contents of an object or element left. This works on the bits in the object, moving them left and filling in the right with zeros. For example, 7<<2 takes 111 (the binary representation of 7) and shifts it left 2 places (11100), which, when converted back to integer values, is 28.
>>	Bitwise right shift	Similar to the left shift in the preceding row, this moves the bits to the right; unlike the left shift, the bits shifted right drop out of the value. So, using the same example, 7>>2 becomes 1.
>>>	Zero-fill right shift	This bitwise shift operator moves bits to the right and pads the left with zeros.
<	Less than	Compares two values. If the value on the right is larger than the value on the left, this operation returns True.
>	Greater than	Compares two values. If the value on the left is larger than the value on the right, this operation returns True.
<=	Less than or equal to	Compares two values. If the value on the right is equal to or larger than the value on the left, this operation returns True.
>=	Greater than or equal to	Compares two values. If the value on the left is equal to or larger than the value on the right, this operation returns True.
==	Equality	Compares two values. If they're equal, the operation returns True.
===	Strict equality	Compares two values. If they're equal and the same type, the operation returns True.

Continued on next page

TABLE MR3.1: JAVASCRIPT OPERATORS *(continued)*

OPERATOR	DESCRIPTION	WHAT IT DOES
!=	Inequality	Compares two values. If they're not equal, the operation returns True.
!==	Strict inequality	Compares two values. If they're the same type and not equal, the operation returns True.
&	Bitwise AND	Checks the bits of two values and determines where they're both the same. If the value is a multibit value, the operation checks each position. If the two values do not have a matching number of bits, the smaller value is left-padded until the number of positions match. If they match, a 1 is returned. For example, 10&7 returns 2 because 1010 & 0111 only match in the second-to-last position, giving you 0010, which is 2.
^	Bitwise EOR (exclusive OR)	Returns True if one or the other of the values is 1. When the values match, it returns a 0. So, using the previous example, 10^7 returns 1101, which is 13.
|	Bitwise OR (inclusive OR)	Returns True (1) if one value is 1. Unlike EOR, this operator returns True if both values are 1. So, the 10|7 expression returns 1111, which is 15.
&&	Logical AND	Unlike bitwise operators, logical operators compare expression results. Use the logical operators to link Boolean comparisons into a test for a branching statement. For example, if Bob is older than Ray, AND Ray is not working today, send the package to Ray. The package is sent to Ray only if the two conditions are met.
||	Logical OR	Results in True if either expression is true. So, using the same example as the previous cell, Ray would receive the package if either he was younger than Bob or was not working that day.
?:	If-else	This is the symbol for the if else construct, which is described in the "Constructs" section.
operator=	Assignment	Creates assignments. Table MR3.2 shows the range of possibilities.
,	Comma	Separates values in a sequence, such as assignments to an object that contains an array.

TABLE MR3.2: THE ASSIGNMENT OPERATORS

OPERATOR	WHAT IT DOES
=	Puts the value on the right into the variable on the left; any contents of the variable on the left are replaced.
+=	Adds the value on the right to the variable on the left; the contents of the variable on the left are augmented.
-=	Subtracts the value on the right from the variable on the left; the contents of the variable on the left are decremented.
*=	Multiplies the variable on the left by the value on the right and places the result in the variable on the left.
/=	Divides the variable on the left by the value on the right and places the result in the variable on the left.
%=	Divides the variable on the left by the value on the right and places the difference in the variable on the left.
<<=	Performs a bitwise shift on the variable on the left equal to the value on the right; the result is placed in the variable on the left.
>>=	Performs a bitwise shift on the variable on the left equal to the value on the right; the result is placed in the variable on the left.
>>>=	Performs a bitwise shift on the variable on the left equal to the value on the right; the result is placed in the variable on the left.
&=	Performs a bitwise AND on the variable on the left and value on the right; the result is placed in the variable on the left.
^=	Performs a bitwise EOR on the variable on the left and the value on the right; the result is placed in the variable on the left.
|=	Performs a bitwise OR on the variable on the left and the value on the right; the result is placed in the variable on the left.

Escape Character

The backslash (\) is the escape character in JavaScript. An escape character tells the system that the next character in the sequence is either a special instruction or a reserved character being used in quoted text. Table MR3.3 lists the escape sequences that JavaScript uses.

TABLE MR3.3: THE JAVASCRIPT ESCAPE SEQUENCES

CHARACTER	FUNCTION
\b	Backspace
\n	New line
\t	Tab
\r	Carriage return
\f	Form feed
\uhhhh	Unicode character (u + four-digit hexadecimal number)
\\	Backslash (in text)
\'	Single quote (in text)
\"	Double quote (in text)
\ooo	Octal number
\xhh	Latin-1 character (x + two-digit hexadecimal number)

Reserved Words

JavaScript has many reserved words—words that you cannot use for variables in your script. These words, listed in Table MR3.4, are either in use—as functions, for example—or reserved for future use.

TABLE MR3.4: JAVASCRIPT RESERVED WORDS

abstract	final	protected
boolean	finally	public
break	float	return
byte	For	short
case	function	static
catch	goto	super
char	if	switch
class	implements	synchronized
comment	import	this
const	in	throw
continue	instanceof	throws
debugger	int	transient

Continued on next page

TABLE MR3.4: JavaScript Reserved Words *(continued)*		
default	interface	true
delete	label	try
do	long	typeof
double	native	var
else	new	void
enum	null	volatile
export	package	while
extends	private	with
false		

Also, operators (the following characters) may not be used in variable names:

```
-   !   ~   %   /   *   >   <   =   &   |   +   ?
```

Objects

An object is a simple way of referring to parts of a Web page. Using objects gives structure to your Web pages and JavaScript scripts. In general, you apply methods, functions, and properties to objects to achieve a result.

This section contains an alphabetical listing of the available JavaScript objects. Each entry describes the object, gives its format, and (in most cases) shows an example. Each entry also contains a list of the associated properties, methods, and event handlers.

anchor

The anchor object is text on a page that represents a destination for a link. The anchor object can also be a link object if it includes an href attribute. The browser creates an anchors array when it opens a page containing anchors. This array contains information about each anchor object. You can access the anchors or their length from this array.

The anchor object has the following format:

```
<a name="anchorname" id="anchorname">anchorText</a>
```

To access the anchor object:

```
document.anchor.name
```

To access the anchors array:

```
document.anchors.length
document.anchors.[index]
```

The index entry is an integer representing an anchor in the document.

The anchor object had no properties or methods prior to the version 4 browsers, in which the property name was introduced. The anchors array has the property length, which you can use to get the number of anchors on the page from the number of elements in the anchors array.

There are no event handlers for the anchor object, which is a property of document.

button

The button object represents an HTML or XHTML button element and creates a pushbutton on a form. The browser sets the appearance of the button, but you can control the text prompt on the button and the action it performs. You create a button object by using the input element with a type attribute set to the value button. The button object has the following format:

```
<input type="button" name="buttonName" value="buttonText"
   [onclick="handlerText"] />
```

The buttonName entry is the name for the button, which is how you identify the button. Each button on the page needs a unique name. The buttonText entry is the label that appears on the button.

The name property corresponds to the value of the name attribute, and the value property corresponds to the value specified in the value attribute. The button uses the click, blur, and focus methods and the onblur, onclick, onfocus, onmousedown, and onmouseup event handlers. The button object is a property of the form object.

EXAMPLE

```
<input type="button" name="goNow" value="Let's Go"
   onclick="buttonClick(this.form)" />
```

In this example, a Let's Go button appears on the form. When the user clicks the button, the event handler onclick runs the buttonClick function that processes the form.

```
var button1 = document.forms['form1'].elements['goNow'];
```

In this example, a variable named button1 has been created to represent the button named goNow in the form named form1.

checkbox

The checkbox object represents an HTML or XHTML checkbox element. A check box appears on a form to let users make selections (none, one, or more) from a list. You create a checkbox object by using the input element with a type attribute set to the value checkbox. The checkbox object has the following format:

```
<input type="checkbox" name="checkboxName"
   value="checkboxValue" [checked="checked"]
   [onclick="handlerText"] /> textToDisplay
```

The checkboxName entry is the name for the checkbox object; you identify the check box with this name if you reference it in your script. The checkboxValue entry is the return value when the check box is selected; the default is On. The checked entry specifies that the check box appear as checked when the browser first displays it. The `textToDisplay` entry is the label, the text next to the check box on the page.

You can set the check box's `checked` property, changing the state (On or Off) of the check box. The `checked` property indicates whether the check box is currently checked. The `defaultChecked` property indicates if the check box is checked by default (`checked="checked"`). The `name` property corresponds to the value of the `name` attribute, and the `value` property corresponds to the value specified in the `value` attribute. The `checkbox` object uses the `blur`, `click`, and `focus` methods and the `onblur`, `onclick`, and `onfocus` event handlers; `checkbox` is a property of the `form` object.

EXAMPLE

```
<h3>Pick the modules that you want to study:</h3>
<input type="checkbox" name="studymodul_newdocs"
    checked="checked" />Creating a new document<br />
<input type="checkbox" name="studymodul_trackdocs" />
    Tracking documents in the system<br />
<input type="checkbox" name="studymodul_routedocs" />
    Routing documents on the system<br />
…
```

In this example, you have a list of options; the first option appears with its check box selected.

```
var check1 = document.forms["modules"].
    elements["studymodul_newdocs"];
```

In this example, a variable named `check1` has been created to represent the check box named `studymodul_newdocs` in the form named `modules`.

date

The `date` object, which is built in, lets you work with dates. It includes a large number of methods for getting date information, such as the calendar date or the time of day. Dates prior to 1970 are not allowed. The `date` object has the following format:

```
dateObjectName = new Date();
dateObjectName = new Date(
    "month day, year hours: minutes:seconds");
dateObjectName = new Date(year, month, day);
dateObjectName = new Date(
    year, month, day, hours, minutes, seconds, milliseconds);
```

The `new` keyword generates a new object using the `date` object. In the second statement, the properties `month day, year hours: minutes:seconds` are string values. In the third and fourth statements, they are integers.

The `date` method has the following format:

```
dateObjectName.methodName(parameters);
```

The date object has no properties and uses the following methods:

getDate	getUTCMilliseconds	setUTCDate
getDay	getUTCMinutes	setUTCFullYear
getFullYear	getUTCMonth	setUTCHours
getHours	getUTCSeconds	setUTCMilliseconds
getMilliseconds	getYear	setUTCMinutes
getMinutes	parse	setUTCMonth
getMonth	setDate	setUTCSeconds
getSeconds	setFullYear	setYear
getTime	setHours	toLocaleString
getTimeZoneOffset	setMilliseconds	toUTCString
getUTCDate	setMinutes	UTC
getUTCDay	setMonth	valueOf
getUTCFullYear	setSeconds	
getUTCHours	setTime	

The date object has no event handlers because built-in objects have no event handlers. The date object is the property of no other object.

EXAMPLE

```
var logofftime= new Date();
logofftime = logofftime.getHours() + ":" +
    logofftime.getMinutes() + ":" + logofftime.getSeconds();
```

In this example, the script creates a new date variable called logofftime and then populates that variable with the current time.

document

The document object is the container for the information on the current page. This object controls the display of HTML or XHTML information for the user. The document object has the following format:

```
function setMeUp() {
    document.alinkColor="darkcyan";
    document.linkColor="yellow";
    document.vlinkColor="white";   }
...
<body onload="setMeUp()">...</body>
```

In this example, the settings for the link colors use the document properties alinkColor, linkColor, and vlinkColor. This is equivalent to the following body declaration:

```
<body alink="darkcyan" link="yellow" vlink="white">...</body>
```

The document object has the properties shown in Table MR3.5.

TABLE MR3.5: PROPERTIES OF THE **document** OBJECT

PROPERTY	WHAT IT IS
alinkColor	Active link color
anchors	Array containing a list of the anchors in the document
applets	Array containing a list of the applets in the document
bgColor	Background color
cookie	Cookie (information about the user/session)
domain	Domain name of the server from which the document was served
embeds	Array containing a list of the embedded objects in the document
fgColor	Foreground color for text and other foreground elements, such as borders or lines
formname	Name of a form in the document
forms	Array containing a list of the forms in the document
images	Array containing a list of the images in the document
lastModified	Date the document was last changed
layers	Array containing a list of the layers in the document
linkColor	Basic link color
links	Link attributes
location	Location (URL) of the document
plugins	Array containing a list of the plug-ins used in the document
referrer	Location (URL) of the parent or calling document
title	Contents of the title element
vlinkColor	Color of past links activity

The document object also uses 10 methods—captureEvents, close, getSelection, handleEvent, open, releaseEvents, routeEvent, write, and writeln—but uses no event handlers. Although the onload and onunload event handlers are included in the body element, they are window events. The document object is a property of the window object.

```
function hello() {
    document.write("Hello, welcome to my site");  }
```

In this example, the message "Hello, welcome to my site" is written to the page when the `hello` function is called, using the `write` method of the `document` object.

elements

The `elements` object is an array of the `form` objects in the order in which they occur in the source code. This gives you an alternate access path to the individual `form` objects. You can also determine the number of `form` objects by using the `length` property. This is similar to the `anchors` array in that you can read from it but not write to it. The `elements` object has the following format:

```
formName.elements[index]
formName.elements.length
```

The `formName` entry is either the name of the form or an element in the `forms` array. The `index` entry is an integer representing an object on a form.

The `elements` object uses the `length` property, which reflects the number of elements in a form. There are no methods and no event handlers for the `elements` object, which is a property of the `form` object.

```
userInfo.username.value
userInfo.elements[0].value
```

Both statements return the same value if the element `username` is the first item in the `elements` array.

form

This object defines the form with which users interact. It includes check boxes, text areas, radio buttons, and so on. You use the `form` object to post data to a server. It has the following format:

```
<form name="formName" id="formName" target="windowName"
    action="serverURL" method="get|post" enctype="encodingType"
    [onsubmit="handlerText"]>
</form>
```

The `windowName` entry is where form responses go. If you use this, the server responses are sent to a different window—another window, a frame, or a frame literal (such as _top). The `serverURL` is the location where the information from the form goes when it's posted. The `get|post` (get or post) commands specify how the information is sent to the server. With `get`, which is the default, the information is appended to the receiving URL. With `post`, the form sends the information in a data body that the server handles. The `encodingType` entry is the MIME encoding of the data sent. This defaults to `application/x-www-form-urlencoded`; you can also use `multipart/form-data`.

Here's the format for using the object's properties and methods:

```
formName.propertyName
formName.methodName(parameters)
forms[index].propertyName
forms[index].methodName(parameters)
```

The `formName` entry is the value of the `name` attribute and the `id` attribute of the form. The `propertyName` and `methodName` entries indicate one of the properties of `form` listed in Table MR3.6. The `index` entry is an integer representing the `form` object within the array at the position indicated by the integer. The first and third statements above are equivalent, as are the second and fourth statements—statements one and two use the `form` object and statements three and four refer to the `forms` array.

TABLE MR3.6: THE PROPERTIES OF THE `form` OBJECT

PROPERTY	WHAT IT DOES/IS
action	Server URL
elements	Array of the elements in the form
encoding	enctype attribute
length	Number of elements on the form (a property of the `forms` array)
method	How the information is processed (get or post)
name	Name of the form
target	Window where form responses go

The `form` object uses the `reset` and `submit` methods and the `onreset` and `onsubmit` event handlers, and is a property of the `document` object.

EXAMPLE

```
<script type="text/javascript" language="javascript">
    <!--
        function welcome() {
            document.write("Thanks for joining us, " +
                membername + "!") }
    -->
</script>
...
<form name="members" id="members">
    <p>Please enter your name and e-mail address below.</p>
    <b>Name:</b>
    <input type="text" name="membername" size="40" /><br />
    <b>E-mail address:</b>
    <input type="text" name="email" size="40" />
    <input type="button" name="button1" value="Join now!"
        onclick="welcome()">
</form>
```

In this example, users enter their name and e-mail address. When a user clicks the button, the `welcome` function is called and a message with the name is displayed on the page.

frame

The frame object is a window within a window and has its own URL. A page can contain a series of frames. There's also a frames array that lists all the frames in your code. The frame object has the following format:

```
<frameset rows="rowHeightList" cols="columnWidthList"
   [onload="handlerText"] [onunload="handlerText"]>
   [<frame src="locationOrURL" name="frameName"
      id="frameName" />]
   [<noframes>
      // HTML and XHTML elements and so on for browsers
      // that do not support frames
   </noframes>]
</frameset>
```

The rowHeightList entry is a comma-separated list of values that sets the row heights of the frame. The default unit of measure is pixels. The columnWidthList is a comma-separated list of values that sets the column widths of the frame. The default unit of measure is pixels.

The locationOrURL entry is the location of the document to be displayed in the frame. This URL cannot include an anchor name (that is, there can be no #somewhere at the end of the URL). The location object describes the URL components. The frameName entry is the target for links.

To use the object's properties, follow this format:

```
[windowReference.]frameName.propertyName
[windowReference.]frames[index].propertyName
window.propertyName
self.propertyName
parent.propertyName
```

The windowReference entry is a variable from the window object definition or one of the synonyms: top or parent. The frameName entry is the value of the name and of the id attribute in the frame element. The index entry is an integer representing a frame object in the array, and the propertyName entry is one of the properties listed in Table MR3.7.

TABLE MR3.7: THE PROPERTIES OF THE **frame** OBJECT

PROPERTY	WHAT IT IS
frames	Array, or list, of frames in the document
name	name attribute (as assigned in the frame element)
id	id attribute (as assigned in the frame element)
length	Integer that reflects the number of child frames within this frame
parent	Window or frame that contains this frame
self	Current frame
window	Current frame

To use the object's array, follow this format:

```
[frameReference.]frames[index]
[frameReference.]frames.length
[windowReference.]frames[index]
[windowReference.]frames.length
```

The `frames` array has a `length` property that reflects the number of child frames within a frame. The `frame` object uses the `clearTimeout` and `setTimeout` methods.

The `frame` object does not use event handlers. Although the `onload` and `onunload` event handlers appear within the `frameset` element, they are event handlers for the `window` object. The `frame` object is a property of the `window` object; the `frames` array is a property of both `frame` and `window`.

EXAMPLE

This code sets up framed windows. The frameset comes after the `head` element and replaces the `body` element.

```
<!DOCTYPE html PUBLIC "-//W3C/DTD XHTML 1.0 Frameset//EN"
    "http://www.w3.org/TR/xhtml1/DTD/xhtml1-frameset.dtd">
<html xmlns="http://www.w3.org/1999/xhtml">
<head>
    <title>Central Zoo: Front Entrance</title>
</head>
<frameset cols="40%, 60%" onload="alert('We\'re in!')">
    <frame name="frame1" id="frame1" src="mainframe.html" />
    <frame name="frame2" id="frame2" src="littleframe.html" />
</frameset>
</html>
```

In this example, the page is set up to include two frames. When the frameset page loads, an alert box with the text "We're in!" will appear.

hidden

The `hidden` object represents an HTML or XHTML `hidden` element. The `hidden` object contains a text object that is suppressed (that is, not displayed) on a form. This object is used to pass information when the form is submitted. Although the user cannot change the value directly, the developer (you) can control the contents, changing it programmatically. You create a `hidden` object by using the `input` element with a `type` attribute with the value `hidden`. The `hidden` object has the following format:

```
<input type="hidden" name="hiddenName" [value="textValue"] />
```

The `hiddenName` entry is the name of the object, which allows you to access the object using the `name` property. The `textValue` entry is the initial value for the object.

The `hidden` object uses three properties—`name`, `type`, and `value`. These reflect the object name, type, and contents. The `hidden` object does not use any methods or event handlers; it's a property of the `form` object.

EXAMPLE

```
<form name="form1" id="form1">
    <input type="hidden" name="hiddenPass" />
    <input type="text" name="password" value="" size="5" />
    <input type="button" name="test" value="Test"
        onclick="document.form1.hiddenPass.value=document.form1.
        password.value; alert(document.form1.hiddenPass.value)" />
</form>
```

This example reads in a password from a text object and stores it in the hidden object. As a test of the form, we've included a line that displays the hidden object in an alert, which is not something you would normally do.

history

The history object contains the list of URLs visited; this information is available in the history list of the browser. The history object has the following format:

```
history.length
history.methodName(parameters)
```

The length entry is an integer representing a position in the history list. The methodName entry is one of the methods listed below.

The history object uses the length property. There are three methods for the history object: back, forward, and go; each of these navigates through the history list. The history object does not use event handlers; it's a property of the document object.

EXAMPLE

```
if (score < 65) { history.go(-2); }
```

The if statement checks the score against a satisfactory performance measure of 65. If the student scores less than 65 on the test, the browser goes back to the beginning of the lesson, two pages earlier.

```
<input type="button" name="reviewButton" value="Look Again!"
    onclick="history.back()" />
```

The reviewButton button performs the same function as the browser's back button.

link

A link object includes the text and images that contain the information for a hypertext jump. A link object is also an anchor object if it has a name attribute. When the jump is complete, the starting page location is stored in the destination document's referrer property. The link object has the following format:

```
<a href="locationOrURL" [name="anchorName"] [id="anchorName"]
    [target="windowName"] [onclick="handlerText"]
    [onmouseover="handlerText"]>
    linkText</a>
```

The `locationOrURL` entry is the destination address. The `anchorName` entry is the current location within the jump-from page. The `windowName` is the window that the link is loaded into, if different from the current window. This can be an existing window, a frame, or a synonym such as `_top` or `_self`.

You can also define a link using the `link` method of the `string` object.

To use a link's properties, follow this format:

```
document.links[index].propertyName
```

The `index` entry is an integer representing the `link` object in the `links` array.

To use the `links` array, follow this format:

```
document.links[index]
document.links.length
```

You can read the `links` array, but you cannot write values to it.

Table MR3.8 lists the properties of the `link` object.

TABLE MR3.8: THE PROPERTIES OF THE `link` OBJECT

PROPERTY	WHAT IT IS
hash	Anchor name in the URL
host	`hostname:port` portion of the URL
hostname	Host and domain name, or IP address, of the network host
href	Entire URL
pathname	URL-pathname (directory structure/location) part of the URL
port	Communication port on the server
protocol	Type of URL (for example, `http` or `ftp`)
search	Page name (for example, `index.html`)
target	target attribute

The `links` array uses the `length` property. The `link` object does not use any methods. The `link` object uses the `onclick`, `onmouseover`, and `onmouseout` event handlers. The `link` object is a property of the `document` object.

EXAMPLE

```
<script type="text/javascript" language="javascript">
    var there="http://www.example.com/";
</script>
...
<form name="form1" id="form1">
    <b>Choose a document, then click "Take me there!" below.</b>
    <br />
```

```
<input type="radio" name="destination" value="Overview"
   onclick="there = 'http://www.example.com/intro.html'" />
Overview of JavaScripting<br />
<input type="radio" name="destination" value="howto"
   onclick="there = 'http://www.example.com/script.html'" />
Learn to Make a Script<br />
<input type="radio" name="destination" value="reference"
   onclick="there = 'http://www.example.com/jref.html'" />
JavaScript Reference Information<br />
<p><a href="" onclick="this.href = there"
   onmouseover="self.status = there; return true; ">
   <b>Take me there!</b>
</a></p>
</form>
```

In this example, a form gives users access to the set of chapters. They can select a chapter/destination or go to the default destination.

location

The `location` object contains information about the current URL. It contains a series of properties that describe each part of the URL. A URL has the following structure:

```
protocol://hostname:port pathname search hash
```

The `protocol` specifies the type of URL (for example, `http` or `ftp`). The `hostname` contains the host and domain name, or IP address, of the network host. The `port` specifies the communication port on the server (not all addresses use this). The `pathname` is the directory structure/location on the server. The `search` value is the query string and is preceded by a question mark. The `hash` value is preceded by the hash mark (#) and indicates a target anchor on the page.

Here are some common protocol types:

about	http
file	javascript
ftp	mailto
gopher	news

The `location` object has the following format:

```
[windowReference.]location.propertyName
```

The `location` object uses the same properties as the `link` object, as shown in Table MR3.5 earlier. However, unlike the `link` object, which represents a link in a document, the `location` object can be used to change the URL (as in the example that follows), either to a new page or to a different location on the same page. The `location` object uses the `reload` (reload current document) and `replace` (replace current document) methods, but does not use event handlers; it's a property of the `document` object.

EXAMPLE

```
window.location.href=
    "http://www.hotscripts.com/JavaScript/index.html";
```

In this example, the URL of the current page is set to a JavaScript resources home page.

```
parent.frame3.location.href=
    "http://www.hotscripts.com/JavaScript/index.html";
```

This example opens the resources page in frame 3.

```
<script type="text/javascript" language="javascript">
    var takeLesson = "";
    document.write("Welcome to " + document.location +
        ". Not ever done!");
</script>
```

This example displays a message at the top of the page that welcomes users to the current location.

Math

This is a built-in object that includes a large set of methods and properties for mathematic constants and operations. An example of a constant is π (pi), which is referenced as `Math.PI`. If you're using a series of expressions, you can use the `with` construct. In general, the `Math` object has the following format:

```
varName = Math.propertyName [expression];
varName = Math.method();
```

The actual format will vary with the property in use. Check the property entries for the exact syntax. The `Math` object uses the following properties, each of which is described in the "Properties" section:

E	LOG10E
LN2	PI
LN10	SQRT1_2
LOG2E	SQRT2

The `Math` object uses the following methods, each of which is described in the "Methods and Functions" section:

abs	atan	cos	log	pow	sin
acos	atan2	exp	max	random	sqrt
asin	ceil	floor	min	round	tan

The `Math` object uses no event handlers because it's a built-in object. It's not a property of anything. See the entries for individual properties and methods for examples.

navigator

Use this object to determine a user's version of a browser. It has the following format:

```
navigator.propertyName
```

The navigator object uses the javaEnabled method to test whether Java is enabled in the browser, and it contains the properties shown in Table MR3.9. It does not use any event handlers. It's a property of the window object.

TABLE MR3.9: THE PROPERTIES OF THE navigator OBJECT

PROPERTY	WHAT IT IS
AppCodeName	Internal code name of the browser
AppName	External name of the browser
AppVersion	Version number of the browser
Platform	Operating system on which the browser is running
UserAgent	User-agent header in HTTP requests

EXAMPLE

```
var userBrowser = navigator.appName + " " +
    navigator.appVersion;
```

The values for the navigator properties appName and appVersion are in a variable called userBrowser. You can use this later to test the browser's suitability for the functionality available on your page.

password

The password object is a text field that conceals its value and displays asterisks in place of typed characters. A password object is part of a form and must be defined within a form element. You create a password object by using the input element with a type attribute with the value password. This object has the following format:

```
<input type="password" name="passwordName" [value="textValue"]
    size="integer" />
```

The passwordName entry is the name of the object. The textValue entry is a default value for the password, and size is the length of the password field.

To use the password properties and methods, follow this format:

```
passwordName.propertyName
passwordName.methodName(parameters)
formName.elements[index].propertyName
formName.elements[index].methodName(parameters)
```

The first and third statements are equivalents, as are the second and fourth statements. The `pass-wordName` entry is the value of the `name` attribute in the `password` object. The `formName` entry is the form container or an element in the `forms` array.

The `propertyName` is one of three properties: `defaultValue` is the `value` attribute, `name` is the `name` attribute, and `value` is the current contents of the `password` object's field. `methodName` is `focus`, `blur`, or `select`.

The `password` object does not use event handlers. It's a property of the `form` object.

EXAMPLE

```
<input type="password" name="password" size="8"
    value="password.defaultValue" />
```

This is useful if the user has already visited the site and created a password or if you have assigned passwords to users.

radio

A radio button forces a single selection from a set of options. Similar to the check box, it's a part of a form; unlike the check box, however, only one radio button can be selected from the set. The `radio` object has the following format:

```
<input type="radio" name="radioName" value="buttonValue"
    [checked="checked"] [onclick="handlerText"] />textToDisplay
```

The `radioName` entry is the name of the object. This offers you one method for addressing the `radio` object in your script. The `buttonValue` entry is the value that is returned to the server when the button is selected. The default is On. You can access this value using the `radio.value` property. The `checked` attribute sets the button to selected, and `textToDisplay` is the label displayed next to the radio button.

The radio button uses the `blur`, `click`, and `focus` methods and the properties shown in Table MR3.10.

TABLE MR3.10: THE PROPERTIES OF THE **radio** OBJECT

PROPERTY	WHAT IT DOES/IS
`checked="checked"`	Lets you set the selection through your script (rather than user interaction); good for situations in which one choice automatically determines several others
`defaultChecked`	The settings for the checked attribute
`length`	The number of radio buttons in the object
`name`	The name attribute (`radioName` above)
`value`	The `value` attribute (`buttonValue` above)

The `radio` object uses the `onblur`, `onclick`, and `onfocus` event handlers, and it's a property of the `form` object.

EXAMPLE

```
<script type="text/javascript" language="javascript">
var there="http://www.example.com/";
function checkThis() { confirm("Thanks for registering"); }
function welcome() {
    alert("Welcome! You can register through this page.
    For future reference, this page is ' + document.location); }
</script>
...
<body onload="welcome()">
// This loads a message that includes the page address through
// the document.location from the welcome function.
<form name="form1" id="form1" onsubmit="checkThis()">
// The form tag includes the onsubmit event handler and
// the form includes a submit button.
<b>Choose a document, then click "Take me there" below.</b>
<br />
<input type="radio" name="destination" value="Overview"
    onclick="there = 'http://www.example.com/intro.html'" />
Overview of JavaScripting<br />
// This is a typical radio button.
// These buttons all have the same name: destination.
// In this example, all the values reflect the destination/text
// display when the user makes a selection; the destination is
// stored in the variable *there*.
<input type="radio" name="destination" value="HowTo"
    onclick="there = 'http://www.example.com/script.html'" />
Learn to Make a Script<br />
<input type="radio" name="destination" value="Reference"
    onclick="there = 'http://www.example.com/jref.html'" />
JavaScript Reference Information<br />
<p><a href="" onclick="this.href = there"
        onmouseover="self.status = there; return true;">
    <b>Take me there!</b>
</a></p>
// This link includes the information to make the jump to
// a page, depending on the selection made above - using the
// variable *there* following this is another set of selections
// for a different mode. These radio buttons pick a lesson and
// use the submit button to run a function - in this case, the
// function just displays a message; ideally the function would
// process the information and display a message.
<p><input type="text" name="whoIs" value="user"
    size="15" /></p>
<p><input type="radio" name="lesson" value="Lesson 1"
    checked="checked" onclick="takeLesson = 'lesson1.htm'" />
    Lesson 1: Getting Started</p>
<p><input type="radio" name="lesson" value="Lesson 2"
    onclick="takeLesson = 'lesson2.htm'" />
```

```
    Lesson 2: Concepts and Operations</p>
<p><input type="radio" name="lesson" value="Lesson 3"
    onclick="takeLesson = 'lesson3.htm'" />
    Lesson 3: Projects</p>
<p><input type="reset" value="Defaults" name="resetToBasic" />
    </p>
<p><input type="submit" value="Send it in!"
    name="submit_form1" /></p>
<hr />
</form>
…</body>
```

This example creates two groups of radio buttons that set up the destination for the link/jump for the user or the course selections. Users identify the kind of information they want (as in Getting Started, Concepts And Operations, Projects, and so on) and the lesson they want (selected from the list of radio buttons). The `reset` statement clears any changes the user may have made and resets the form to Getting Started. The `submit` statement sends the selections to be processed according to the instructions (not seen) for the form.

reset

This object is a reset button on a form. It clears the form fields of any user interaction/entries and resets their values to the default. You create a `reset` object by using the `input` element with a `type` attribute set to the value `reset`. The `onclick` event handler cannot be canceled. Once the `reset` object is clicked, the form is reset, and all user entries are lost. The `reset` object has the following format:

```
<input type="reset" name="resetName" value="buttonText"
    [onclick="handlerText"] />
```

The `resetName` entry is the name of the object. It allows you to access the object within your script. The `buttonText` entry is the label for the button.

To use the reset properties and methods, follow this format:

```
resetName.propertyName
resetName.methodName(parameters)
formName.elements[index].propertyName
formName.elements[index].methodName(parameters)
```

The first and third statements are equivalents, as are the second and fourth.

The `reset` object has two properties—name and `value` (described earlier in Table MR3.10). It uses the `blur`, `click`, and `focus` methods and the `onblur`, `onclick`, and `onfocus` event handlers. The `reset` object is a property of the `form` object.

EXAMPLE

```
<input type="reset" name="clearForm" value="Start Over" />
```

This simple example should appear on all your forms. This statement places a reset button (this one says Start Over) that clears the current form when it's clicked.

For another example of a `reset` object, see the example in the "radio" section.

select

The `select` object presents the user with a drop-down list of preset choices. It contains an `options` array. The `select` object is created with an HTML or XHTML `select` element, and is part of a form. The `select` object has the following format:

```
<select name="selectName" [size="integer"] [multiple="multiple"]
    [onblur="handlerText"] [onchange="handlerText"]
    [onfocus="handlerText"]>
    <option value="optionValue" [selected="selected"]>
    textToDisplay</option>
    [… <option>textToDisplay</option>]
</select>
```

The `selectName` entry is the name of the object; the `select` object contains the list. The `multiple` entry indicates that the object accepts multiple selections—such as check boxes. If the list is not set to `multiple`, it's like a radio object and only one choice is available. The `option` entry is a selection element in the list, and `optionValue` is the value returned to the system when the option is selected. The `selected` entry indicates that the option is the default value for the list, and `textToDisplay` is the text shown in the list.

To select the object's properties and methods, follow this format:

```
selectName.propertyName
selectName.methodName(parameters)
formName.elements[index].propertyName
formName.elements[index].methodName(parameters)
```

To use an option's properties, follow this format:

```
selectName.options[index1].propertyName
formName.elements[index2].options[index1].propertyName
```

The `index1` entry is an integer representing the sequence of options in the list (the first option in the sequence is 0), and `index2` is an integer representing the element in the form.

To use the `options` array, follow this format:

```
selectName.options
selectName.options[index]
selectName.options.length
```

The `selectName` entry is the value of the `name` attribute in the `select` object. The `index` entry is an integer representing an option in the `select` object, and `length` is the number of options in the `select` object.

The elements in the `options` array are read-only. You can get the number of options from the list, but you cannot change the values in the list.

The `select` object uses the properties shown in Table MR3.11. The `options` array uses the properties listed in Table MR3.12.

TABLE MR3.11: THE PROPERTIES OF THE **select** OBJECT	
PROPERTY	**WHAT IT IS**
length	Number of options
name	name attribute
options	Array of the option elements
selectedIndex	Position of the selected option in the list (or the first of multiple options)

TABLE MR3.12: THE PROPERTIES OF THE **options** ARRAY	
PROPERTY	**WHAT IT IS**
defaultSelected	selected attribute indicating which option is the default selection for the list
index	Position of the option in the list (the list begins at zero)
length	Number of options
name	name attribute
selected="selected"	Lets you select an option from your script, rather than from user input
selectedIndex	Position of the selected option in the list
text	textToDisplay for the option list item
value	value attribute

The select object uses the blur and focus methods and the onblur, onchange, and onfocus event handlers. The select object is a property of form. The options array is a property of select.

EXAMPLE

```
<select name="lesson_list">
   <option selected="selected">Introduction</option>
   <option>Installation</option>
   <option>Setting up an account</option>
   <option>Creating a document</option>
   <option>Filing a document</option>
   <option>Recovering a filed document</option>
   <option>Sending a document to the printer</option>
</select>
```

The form contains a list of chapters in a book, from which the user can select a single item.

string

A string object is a series of characters, such as a name, a phrase, or other information. It has the following format:

```
stringName.propertyName
stringName.methodName(parameters)
```

The stringName entry is the variable name (that owns the string). The length entry is the size of the string. This is a character count and includes spaces and special characters. The methodName entry is one of the methods listed below.

The string object has a single property, length, which is the number of characters in the string. The string object uses the following methods:

anchor	fromcharcode	small
big	indexof	split
blink	italics	strike
bold	lastindexof	sub
charAt	link	substr
charCodeAt	match	substring
concat	replace	sup
fixed	search	toLowerCase
fontcolor	slice	toUpperCase
fontsize		

Some of these methods will look familiar, as they deal with the format of the text in the string object.

Because it's a built-in object, the string object does not use event handlers. It's not a property of anything.

EXAMPLE

```
var user_id = new string();
user_id = getUserText.value;
user_id.toUpperCase();
```

This simple example takes the contents of the text field getUserText and assigns it to a newly created string variable called user_id. The last statement shifts the contents of the variable to uppercase.

submit

This object is a button on a form that starts the processing of the form. The submission is controlled by the form's action property. You create a submit object by using the input element with a type attribute with the value submit. The submit object has the following format:

```
<input type="submit" name="submitName" value="buttonText"
    [onclick="handlerText"] />
```

To use the submit object's properties and methods, follow this format:

```
submitName.propertyName
submitName.methodName(parameters)
formName.elements[index].propertyName
formName.elements[index].methodName(parameters)
```

The submit object uses two properties—name and value. It uses the blur, click, and focus methods, and the onblur, onclick, and onfocus event handlers. The submit object is a property of the form object.

EXAMPLE

For an example of a submit object, see the example in the "radio" section.

text

The text object is a field on the form used to collect information from the user. The user can type short string sequences, such as a word, a phrase, or numbers, into the text object. You create a text object by using the input element with a type attribute with the value text. The text object has the following format:

```
<input type="text" name="textName" value="textValue"
   size="integer" [onblur="handlerText"]
   [onchange="handlerText"] [onfocus="handlerText"]
   [onselect="handlerText"] />
```

The textName entry is the variable name for the object. The textValue entry is the initial value for the text object, and size is the length of the box on the page.

To use the text object's properties and methods, follow this format:

```
textName.propertyName
textName.methodName(parameters)
formName.elements[index].propertyName
formName.elements[index].methodName(properties)
```

The text object has the three properties: defaultValue is the default value setting; name is the name attribute; and value is the current contents of the text object.

The text object uses three methods—focus, blur, and select—and it uses the onblur, onchange, onfocus, and onselect event handlers. The text object is a property of the form object.

EXAMPLE

```
var userProfile="user";
<input type="text" name="usertype" value="user" size="15"
   onchange="userProfile=this.value" />
<input type="text" name="userGroup" value="" size="32"
   onchange="userProfile+=this.value" />
```

These statements create a user profile by getting the text entries the user makes in the text objects' fields. The first statement sets the default for the variable userProfile. The next two statements change this variable only if the user changes the contents of the fields.

textarea

Like the text object, the textarea object offers a way for users to enter textual data. The textarea object is a multiline field, whereas the text object is a single line. The textarea object must also be defined within a form element. If you want the text to wrap properly within the textarea object, verify the version of the browser. The Windows platform uses a slightly different new-line code (Unix uses \n, Windows uses \r\n, and Macintosh uses \n). If you use the appVersion property, you can set the new-line character correctly.

You can dynamically update the textarea object by setting the value property. The textarea object has the following format:

```
<textarea name="textareaName" rows="integer" cols="integer"
    [onblur="handlerText"] [onchange="handlerText"]
    [onfocus="handlerText"] [onselect="handlerText"]>
    textToDisplay</textarea>
```

The textareaName entry is the name of the object.

To use the properties and methods of the textarea object, follow this format:

```
textareaName.propertyName
textareaName.methodName(parameters)
formName.elements[index].propertyName
formName.elements[index].methodName(parameters)
```

The textarea object uses three properties—defaultValue, name, and value—and three methods: focus, blur, and select. It uses the onblur, onchange, onfocus, and onselect event handlers. The textarea object is a property of the form object.

EXAMPLE

```
<p>Decribe the FOLD function and give three examples of what
    you can do with the FOLD function:</p>
<textarea name="foldEssay" rows="5" cols="65"
    onchange="question3Essay = this.value"></textarea>
```

This example gives the user a field in which to answer an essay question; the answer is stored in the variable question3Essay.

window

The window object is the topmost object for JavaScript's document, location, and history objects. The self and window properties are synonymous and refer to the current window. The keyword top refers to the uppermost window in the hierarchy, and parent refers to a window that contains one or more framesets. Because of its unique position, you do not have to address the properties of window in the same fashion as other objects: close() is the same as window.close() and self.close().

The window object uses event handlers, but the calls to these handlers are put in the body and frameset elements. It has the following format:

```
windowVar = window.open("URL", "windowName" [,"windowFeatures"]);
```

The windowVar entry is the name of a new window, and windowName is the target attribute of the form and a elements.

To use a window's properties and methods, follow this format:

```
window.propertyName
window.methodName(parameters)
self.propertyName
self.methodName(parameters)
top.propertyName
top.methodName(parameters)
parent.propertyName
parent.methodName(parameters)
windowVar.propertyName
windowVar.methodName(parameters)
propertyName methodName(parameters)
```

To define the `onload` or `onunload` event handlers, include the statement in the `body` *or* `frameset` elements.

```
<body …
    [onload="handlerText"]
    [onunload="handlerText"]>
    …
</body>

<frameset …
    [onload="handlerText"]
    [onunload="handlerText"]>
    …
</frameset>
```

The `window` object contains the properties shown in Table MR3.13.

TABLE MR3.13: THE PROPERTIES OF THE `window` OBJECT

PROPERTY	WHAT IT IS
defaultStatus	Default message for the window's status bar
frames	List (array) of the window's child frames
length	Number of frames in a parent window
name	name attribute
parent	Synonym for `windowName` where the window contains a frameset
self	Synonym for the current `windowName`
status	Priority or transient message for the status bar
top	Synonym for the topmost browser window
window	Synonym for the current `windowName`

The window object also uses these methods:

alert	moveBy	resizeTo
blur	moveTo	scroll
clearInterval	open	scrollBy
clearTimeout	print	scrollTo
close	prompt	setInterval
confirm	resizeBy	setTimeout
focus		

The window object uses two event handlers: onload and onunload. It's not a property of anything.

EXAMPLE

```
<script type="text/javascript" language="javascript">
    function checkThis() {
        windowReply = window.open("reginfo.html", "answerWindow",
            "scrollbars = yes, width = 100, height = 200");
        document.form1.submit();
        confirm("Thanks for registering");
        self.close();
    }
</script>
```

This example opens a window with the registration information.

Methods and Functions

You use methods and functions to manipulate containers, which are objects. If you think of the browser as a stage, the actors and the sets are objects; the lines spoken and the actions taken (according to the script) are the methods and functions applied to the objects.

This section is an alphabetical listing of the available JavaScript methods and functions. Each entry describes a single method or function, includes syntax information and (where appropriate) examples, and identifies the object that the method or function belongs to or affects.

abs

The abs method belongs to the Math object and returns the absolute value (an unsigned number). It has the following syntax:

```
Math.abs(number)
```

The number entry is any numeric expression or a property of an object.

EXAMPLE

```
var myNumber = -49
document.write(Math.abs(myNumber));
```

acos

The `acos` method belongs to the `Math` object and returns the arccosine of a number in radians. It has the following syntax:

```
Math.acos(number)
```

The `number` entry is any numeric expression or a property of an object.

EXAMPLE

```
var myNumber = 45;
document.write(Math.acos(myNumber));
```

alert

The `alert` method belongs to the `window` object and displays a small dialog box with a message string and an OK button. The `alert` method is most commonly used for displaying error messages when a user's input to a form element is invalid. It has the following syntax:

```
window.alert("message")
```

The `message` is any string expression or a property of an object.

EXAMPLE

```
window.alert("Welcome to my homepage.");
```

This example displays an alert box when the browser executes the code. You can also use an `alert` method with the `onload` event handler in the `body` element so the alert box will display as the page is initially being loaded.

```
<body onload="window.alert('Welcome! You can register through
    this page. For future reference, this page is ' +
    document.location)">...</body>
```

This loads a message that includes the page address through the `document.location`.

anchor

The `anchor` method belongs to the `string` object and generates an anchor for a hypertext target in a document. Use the `anchor` method with the `write` or `writeln` method. It has the following syntax:

```
text.anchor(nameAttribute)
```

The `text` and `nameAttribute` entries are any string or property of an object.

EXAMPLE
```
var intro = "Welcome to the JavaScript Tutorial!";
tocWindow = window.open("" ,"displayWindow");
tocWindow.document.write(intro.anchor("contents_anchor"));
for (x = 0; x < 5; x++) {
  switch(x) {
    case[1]: if (c1 != "true") {
      tocWindow.document.write(
        c1 + c1.anchor("overviewtoC");  }
      break;
    case[2]: if (c2 != "true") {
      tocWindow.document.write(
        c2 + c2.anchor("ObjectstoC");  }
      break;
    case[3]: if (c3 != "true") {
      tocWindow.document.write(
        c3 + c3.anchor("structuretoC");  }
      break;  }  }
```

asin

The asin method belongs to the Math object and returns the arcsine of a number in radians. It has the following syntax:

```
Math.asin(number)
```

The number entry is any numeric expression or a property of an object.

EXAMPLE
```
var myNumber = 190;
document.write(Math.asin(myNumber));
```

atan

The atan method belongs to the Math object and returns the arctangent of the number in radians. It has the following syntax:

```
Math.atan(number)
```

The number entry is any numeric expression or a property of an object.

EXAMPLE
```
var myNumber = 155;
document.write(Math.atan(myNumber));
```

atan2

The `atan2` method belongs to the `Math` object and computes the angle (in radians) between the x axis and the position represented by the x and y coordinates, which are passed as parameters. It has the following syntax:

```
Math.atan2(x,y)
```

The number entries (x,y) are the x and y coordinates of the point.

EXAMPLE

```
var x = 45;
var y = 90;
document.write(Math.atan2(x,y));
```

back

The `back` method belongs to the `history` object and uses the history list to return to the previous document. You can use this method to give users an alternative to the browser's back button. It has the following syntax:

```
history.back()
```

EXAMPLE

```
<p><input type="button" value="Take Me Back!"
     onclick="history.back()" />
   <input type="button" value="Let's Keep Going!"
     onclick="history.forward()" /></p>
```

This code puts two buttons beside each other on a line. The first button goes back to the last document; the second button is useful if the user has already moved back in the history list and is ready to go forward again.

big

The `big` method belongs to the `string` object and displays the associated string as a large font (as if the text were tagged with a `big` element). It has the following syntax:

```
stringName.big()
```

The `stringName` is any string expression or a property of an object.

EXAMPLE

```
<script type="text/javascript" language="javascript">
   var welcome = "Welcome to our flashy new digs!";
   confirm(welcome);
   // This opens a small box with the text and an OK button.
   document.write(welcome.big());
   alert("That's All Folks!");
   self.close();
</script>
```

blink

The blink method belongs to the string object and displays the associated string blinking, as if the text were tagged with a blink element. It has the following syntax:

```
stringName.blink()
```

The stringName entry is any string expression or a property of an object.

EXAMPLE

```
<script type="text/javascript" language="javascript">
   var welcome = "Welcome to our flashy new digs!";
   confirm(welcome);
   // This opens a small box with the text and an OK button.
   document.write(welcome.blink());
   alert("That's All Folks!");
   self.close();
</script>
```

blur

The blur method belongs to the password, select, text, textarea, and window objects and is the programmatic way to move the focus off a form object such as a text object. It has the following syntax:

```
password.blur()
selectName.blur()
textName.blur()
textareaName.blur()
window.blur()
```

The password entry is either the name of a password object or an element in the elements array. The selectName entry is either the name of a select object or an element in the elements array. The textName entry is either the name of a text object or an element in the elements array. The textareaName entry is either the name of a textarea object or an element in the elements array. The window entry is the name of the top-level browser window specified by the window object.

EXAMPLE

```
<script type="text/javascript" language="javascript">
   var userPass = "" ;
   var userName = "" ;
   var formulate = new window();
   // Set up the variables to be used later
   formulate.window.open();
   // Open a window for the form
   document.formulate.userPass.focus();
   var timer = setTimeout(
      "document.formulate.userPass.blur()", 8000);
   // Put the focus onto the password box
```

```
      // for 8 secs, then blur
      clearTimeout(timer);
      document.formulate.userName.focus();
      timer = setTimeout(
         "document.formulate.userName.blur()", 30000);
      // Clear the timeout, put the focus on the username box for
      // 30 secs, then blur
      document.formulate.userAuth.click();
      // Force a selection in the userAuth check box
      clearTimeout(timer);
      msgWindow.window.close();
      // Clear the timeout variable and close the window
   </script>
   …
   <form name="formulate" id="formulate">
      <input type="password" name="userPass" size="5" />
         tell us your secret
      <input type="text" name="userName" value="Bob's your uncle"
         size="15" />
      <input type="checkbox" name="userAuth" value="Validate Me" />
         authorize us to check this stuff out!
   </form>
```

bold

The bold method belongs to the string object and displays the associated string as bold—as if the text were tagged with the b element. It has the following syntax:

```
stringName.bold()
```

The stringName is any string expression or a property of an object.

EXAMPLE

```
<script type="text/javascript" language="javascript">
   var welcome = "Welcome to our flashy new digs!";
   confirm(welcome);
   // This opens a small box with the text and an OK button.
   document.write(welcome.bold());
   alert("That's All Folks!");
   self.close();
</script>
```

ceil

The ceil method belongs to the Math object and returns the nearest integer that is equal to or greater than the given number. It has the following syntax:

```
Math.ceil(number)
```

The number entry is any numeric expression or a property of an object.

```
var myNumber = 4.7;
document.write(Math.ceil(myNumber));
```

This returns the integer nearest the number (greater or equal).

charAt

The charAt method belongs to the string object and returns the character found at the given index in the string. It has the following syntax:

```
stringName.charAt(index)
```

The stringName is any numeric expression or a property of an object.

EXAMPLE

```
<script type="text/javascript" language="javascript">
    var welcome = "Welcome to our flashy new digs!";
    confirm(welcome);
    for (var place = 0; place < welcome.length; place++) {
        document.write(welcome.charAt(place) + "<br />");   }
    // This for loop displays each letter on its own line.
    alert("That's All Folks!");
    self.close();
</script>
```

charCodeAt

The charCodeAt method belongs to the string object and returns a number that represents the Unicode encoding of the character found at the given index in the string. The first character in a string is at the position numbered 0. It has the following syntax:

```
stringName.charCodeAt (index)
```

The stringName entry is any numeric expression or a property of an object.

EXAMPLE

```
var myText = wobble;
document.write(myText.charCodeAt(5));
```

This example would display the Unicode encoding for the character at the fifth position in the string myText (the letter e), which is 0066.

clear

The clear method belongs to the document object and empties the contents of the document window. It has the following syntax:

```
document.clear()
```

EXAMPLE
```
alert("That's All Folks!");
self.clear();
```

A box appears, with the message "That's All Folks!" and an OK button. The next line clears the document from the browser window.

clearInterval

The `clearInterval` method belongs to the `frame` and `window` objects and cancels an interval set with the `setInterval` method. It has the following syntax:

```
clearInterval (intervalID)
```

The `intervalID` entry is the name of the value returned by a previous call to `setInterval`.

EXAMPLE
```
<head>
<script type="text/javascript" language="javascript">
    function reminder() {
        window.alert("Don't forget to enter our contest!") }
    function setReminder() {
        var myReminder = window.setInterval("reminder()",8000); }
</script>
…</head>
<body onload="setReminder();">…
<script type="text/javascript" language="javascript">
    function noway() {
        clearInterval(myReminder); }
</script>
<form>
    <input type="button" value="pleasestop" name="stopmessage"
        onclick="return noway()" />
</form>
…</body>
```

In this example, as soon as the page loads, an alert box with the message "Don't forget to enter our contest!" will be displayed every eight seconds. The message will stop displaying when the "pleasestop" button is clicked, which calls the `noway` function.

clearTimeout

The `clearTimeout` method belongs to the `frame` and `window` objects and resets the variable for the `setTimeout` method. It has the following syntax:

```
clearTimeout(timeoutID)
```

The `timeoutID` entry is the name of the value returned by a previous call to `setTimeout`.

EXAMPLE

```
<head>
<script type="text/javascript" language="javascript">
   var myTimer;
   function timesup() {
      myTimer = setTimeout("window.alert('It's time!') ",3000);
   }
</script>
...</head>
<body onload="timesup()">...
<script type="text/javascript" language="javascript">
   function stopit() {
      clearTimeout(myTimer); }
</script>
<form>
   <input type="button" value="stop" name="stoptimer"
      onclick="return stopit()" />
</form>
...</body>
```

In this example, a timer is started when the pages loads. An alert message will be displayed unless the button labeled "stop" is clicked before three seconds have elapsed. Clicking the button calls the stopit function, which clears the timer.

click

The click method belongs to the button, checkbox, radio, reset, and submit objects and simulates, programmatically, the user's click on a form object. The click method, however, does not invoke the onclick event handler. It has the following syntax:

```
password.click()
selectName.click()
textName.click()
textareaName.click()
```

The password entry is either the name of a password object or an element in the elements array. The selectName entry is either the name of a select object or an element in the elements array. The textName entry is either the name of a text object or an element in the elements array. The textareaName is either the name of a textarea object or an element in the elements array.

EXAMPLE

```
<script type="text/javascript" language="javascript">
   likes.elements[0].click();
   //Forces a selection in the icecream check box
</script>
...
<form name="likes" id="likes">
   <input type="checkbox" name="icecream" value="vanilla" />
   vanilla
</form>
```

In this example, the vanilla check box is checked through the use of the `click` method. However, you could get the same result by using `checked="checked"` within the `input` element.

close (document Object)

This `close` method belongs to the `document` object and closes the output stream to the specified document. It has the following syntax:

```
document.close()
```

EXAMPLE

```
<script type="text/javascript" language="javascript">
    function openWin() {
        myWin= open("" ,"displayWindow",
            "width = 250, height = 300, status = no, toolbar = no,
            menubar = no");
        myWin.document.open();
        myWin.document.write("<html><head><title>My New Window");
        myWin.document.write("</title></head><body>");
        myWin.document.write("<p><font size='5'
            face='arial,helvetica'>");
        myWin.document.write("See how easy it is to create ");
        myWin.document.write("a new window using Javascript! ");
        myWin.document.write("</font></p></body></html>");
        myWin.document.close();   }
</script>
...
<form name="popup" id="popup">
    <input type=button value="New Window" onClick="openWin()"
        name="button" />
</form>
```

In this example, a pop-up window is created when the button labeled "New Window" is clicked. The `myWin.document.close` statement closes input to this pop-up window and returns the flow to the original document.

close (window Object)

This `close` method belongs to the `window` object and closes the active window. It has the following syntax:

```
windowReference.close()
```

A window can also close with the following syntax:

```
self.close()
close()
```

The `windowReference` is any valid means of identifying a window object.

EXAMPLE

```
<script type="text/javascript" language="javascript">
   var welcome = "Welcome to our flashy new digs!";
   confirm(welcome);
   // This opens a small box with the text and an OK button.
   for (var place = 0; place < welcome.length; place++) {
      document.write(welcome.charAt(place) + "<br />");
   }
   // This for loop puts out each letter on its own line.
   alert("That's All Folks!");
   self.close();
</script>
```

A box appears, with the message "That's All Folks!" and an OK button. The next line clears the document from the browser window.

concat

The concat method belongs to the string object; it concatenates the strings supplied and returns the joined strings. It has the following syntax:

```
stringName.concat(value, ...)
```

The values are one or more strings to be added to the end of stringName. If a value is not a string, the concat method converts it to a string. The stringName is any numeric expression or a property of an object.

EXAMPLE

```
<script  type="text/javascript" language="javascript">
   var myMsg = "Hello";
   var usrName = prompt("Please enter your name", " ");
   var myString;
   document.write(myMsg + " " + usrName + "<br>");
   myString = myMsg.concat("",usrName);
   document.write(myString);
</script>
```

In this example, the string myMsg ("Hello") is joined to the string usrName, which the user enters in response to the prompt. Each document.write statement displays the same output.

confirm

The confirm method belongs to the window object and displays a small dialog box with the message string and two buttons, OK and Cancel. It has the following syntax:

```
confirm("message")
```

The message entry is a string expression or a property of an object.

EXAMPLE

```
<script type="text/javascript" language="javascript">
    function checkThis() {
        windowReply=window.open("reginfo.html", "answerWindow",
            "scrollbars = yes, width = 100, height = 200");
        document.form1.submit();
        confirm("Thanks for registering");
        self.close();

    }
</script>
...

<form name="form1" id="form1" onsubmit="checkThis()">
// The form element includes the onsubmit event handler
// and the form includes a submit button.
// Following this is a set of selections.
// These radio buttons pick a lesson and use the submit
// button to run a function - in this case, the function
// just displays a message; ideally the function would
// process the information and display a message.
    <p><input type="text" name="whoIs" value="user" size="15" />
        </p>
    <p><input type="radio" name="lesson" value="Lesson 1"
        checked="checked" onclick="takeLesson = 'lesson1.htm'" />
        Lesson 1: Getting Started</p>
    <p><input type="radio" name="lesson" value="Lesson 2"
        onclick="takeLesson = 'lesson2.htm'" />
        Lesson 2: Concepts and Operations</p>
    <p><input type="radio" name="lesson" value="Lesson 3"
        onclick="takeLesson = 'lesson3.htm'" />
        Lesson 3: Projects</p>
    <p><input type="reset" value="Defaults" name="resetToBasic" />
        <input type="submit" value="Send it in!"
            name="submit_form1" /></p>
    <hr />
</form>
```

This example displays the confirmation message when the user clicks the Submit button.

COS

The cos method belongs to the Math object returns the cosine of the number. It has the following syntax:

```
Math.cos(number)
```

The number entry is any numeric expression or a property of an object.

```
<script type="text/javascript" language="javascript">
   function tryMe(baseVal) {
      var baseVal = Math.random();
      showMe = window.open("" );
      with (Math) {
         showMe.document.write(cos(baseVal) + "<br />");
         showMe.document.write(abs(cos(baseVal))+ "<br />");
         // Return the cosine of the number
         showMe.alert("Close \'er up now, skip?");
         showMe.close();  }  }
</script>
```

escape

The escape function returns the ASCII encoded value for the given string. It has the following syntax:

```
escape("string")
```

The string entry is a nonalphanumeric string that represents a reserved or unprintable character from the ISO Latin-1 character set. For example, escape(%26) returns &.

eval

The eval function runs a JavaScript expression, statement, function, or sequence of statements. The expression can include variables and object properties. It has the following syntax:

```
eval("string")
```

The string entry is a JavaScript expression, statement, function, or sequence of statements.

exp

The exp method belongs to the Math object and returns the value equal to Euler's constant (e, the base of natural logarithms—approximately 2.718) raised to the power of the given number. It has the following syntax:

```
Math.exp(number)
```

The number entry is any numeric expression or a property of an object.

EXAMPLE

```
<script type="text/javascript" language="javascript">
function tryMe(baseVal) {
   var baseVal = Math.random();
   showMe = window.open("" );
   with (Math) {
      showMe.document.write(exp(baseVal) + "<br />");
      showMe.document.write(abs(exp(baseVal)) + "<br />");
      // Return Euler's constant (e) to the power of the
      // number given
```

```
        showMe.alert("Close \'er up now, skip?");
        showMe.close();  }  }
    </script>
```

fixed

The `fixed` method belongs to the `string` object and displays the associated string in a fixed width (monospaced) font, as if the text were tagged with a `tt` element. It has the following syntax:

```
    stringName.fixed()
```

The `stringName` is any string expression or a property of an object.

EXAMPLE

```
    <script type="text/javascript" language="javascript">
        var welcome = "Welcome to our flashy new digs!";
        confirm(welcome);
        // This opens a small box with the text and an OK button.
        document.write(welcome.fixed());
        alert("That's All Folks!");
        self.close();
    </script>
```

floor

The `floor` method belongs to the `Math` object and returns the nearest integer that is equal to or less than the given number. It has the following syntax:

```
    Math.floor(number)
```

The `number` entry is any numeric expression or a property of an object.

EXAMPLE

```
    with (Math) {
        msgWindow.document.write(random());
        // Generate a random number
        msgWindow.document.write(floor(random() * baseVal));
        // Return the integer nearest the number (less or equal)
    }
```

focus

The `focus` method belongs to the `password`, `select`, `text`, `textarea`, and `window` objects and allows you to programmatically move the focus to a `form` object or browser window. This simulates the user's moving the cursor to the object. It has the following syntax:

```
    password.focus()
    selectName.focus()
    textName.focus()
    textareaName.focus()
    window.focus()
```

The `password` entry is either the name of a `password` object or an element in the `elements` array. The `selectName` entry is either the name of a `select` object or an element in the `elements` array. The `textName` is either the name of a `text` object or an element in the `elements` array. The `textareaName` is either the name of a `textarea` object or an element in the `elements` array. The `window` is the top-level browser window specified by the `window` object.

For an example of the `focus` method, see the "blur" section.

fontcolor

The `fontcolor` method belongs to the `string` object and displays the associated string in the given color as if the text were tagged with a `font` element with a `color` attribute. It has the following syntax:

```
stringName.fontcolor(colorKeyword)
```

The `stringName` entry is any string expression or a property of an object.

EXAMPLE

```
<script type="text/javascript" language="javascript">
    var welcome = "Welcome to our flashy new digs!";
    confirm(welcome);
    // This opens a small box with the text and an OK button.
    document.write(welcome.fontcolor("crimson") + "<br />");
    document.write(welcome.fontsize(8) + "<br />");
    // Some more text attributes, and these take arguments.
    alert("That's All Folks!");
    self.close();
</script>
```

fontsize

The `fontsize` method belongs to the `string` object and displays the associated string at the given size as if the text were tagged with a `font` element with a `size` attribute. It has the following syntax:

```
stringName.fontsize(size)
```

The `stringName` is any string expression or a property of an object.

EXAMPLE

```
<script type="text/javascript" language="javascript">
    var welcome = "Welcome to our flashy new digs!";
    confirm(welcome);
    // This opens a small box with the text and an OK button.
    document.write(welcome.fontcolor("crimson") + "<br />");
    document.write(welcome.fontsize(8) + "<br />");
    // Some more text attributes, and these take arguments.
    alert("That's All Folks!");
    self.close();
</script>
```

forward

The forward method belongs to the history object and uses the history list to recall a previously viewed document that the user has left via the Back button or the back method. You can use this method to give users an alternative to the browser's Forward button. You can also use history.go(1) method to perform this action. It has the following syntax:

```
history.forward()
```

EXAMPLE
```
<p><input type="button" value="Take Me Back!"
     onclick="history.back()" />
  <input type="button" value="Let's Keep Going!"
     onclick="history.forward()" /></p>
```

This code puts two buttons beside each other on a line. The first button goes back to the last document. The second button is useful if the user has already moved back in the history list and is ready to go forward again.

getDate

The getDate method belongs to the date object and returns the day of the month (0–31) for the given date. It has the following syntax:

```
dateObjectName.getDate()
```

The datObjectName entry is any date object or a property of an object.

EXAMPLE
```
<script type="text/javascript" language="javascript">
   function callMe() {
      var who = 1;
      var docMod = document.lastModified;
      switch (who) { // this switch has two streams
         case(1) :
            alert(docMod);
            chrono = new Date();
            alert(chrono.getDate());
            alert(chrono + " already?!");
            who++;
            break;
         case(2) :
            docMod = "" ;
            docMod.setDay(1);
            docMod.setMonth(6);
            docMod.setDate(30);
            docMod.setYear(2001);
            docMod.setTime(11, 59, 59);
            document.write(chrono.fontcolor("darkmagenta") +
               "<br />");
```

```
                        who++;
                        break;
                    }
                alert("That's All Folks!");
                self.close();
            }
    </script>
    ...
    <form>
        <input type="button" value="click here" name="button1"
            onclick="callMe()" />
    </form>
```

The getDate method returns local time; for Universal Coordinated Time (UTC time), use getUTCDate.

getDay

The getDay method belongs to the date object and returns the day of the week (0–6) for the given date. It has the following syntax:

```
dateObjectName.getDay()
```

The dateObjectName entry is any date object or a property of an object.

EXAMPLE

```
<script type="text/javascript" language="javascript">
    function callMe() {
        var who = 1;
        var docMod = document.lastModified;
        switch (who) { // this switch has two streams
            case(1) :
                alert(docMod);
                chrono = new Date();
                alert(chrono.getDay());
                alert(chrono + " already?!");
                who++;
                break;
            case(2) :
                docMod = "" ;
                docMod.setDay(1);
                docMod.setMonth(6);
                docMod.setDate(30);
                docMod.setYear(2001);
                docMod.setTime(11, 59, 59);
                document.write(chrono.fontcolor("darkmagenta") +
                    "<br />");
                who++;
                break;
        }
```

```
        alert("That's All Folks!");
        self.close();
    }
</script>
```

The getDay method returns local time; for Universal Coordinated Time (UTC time), use getUTCDay.

getFullYear

The getFullYear method belongs to the date object and returns all four digits of the year of the given date. It has the following syntax:

```
dateObjectName.getFullYear()
```

The dateObjectName entry is any date object or a property of an object.

EXAMPLE

```
<script type="text/javascript" language="javascript">
    function callMe() {
        var docMod = document.lastModified;
        alert(docMod);
        chrono = new Date();
        alert(chrono.getFullYear());
        alert(chrono + " already?!");
        alert("That's All Folks!");
        self.close();  }
</script>
```

The getFullYear method returns local time; for Universal Coordinated Time (UTC time), use getUTCFullYear.

getHours

The getHours method belongs to the date object and returns the hour (0–23) of the given date. It has the following syntax:

```
dateObjectName.getHours()
```

The datObjectName entry is any date object or a property of an object.

EXAMPLE

```
<script type="text/javascript" language="javascript">
    function callMe() {
        var docMod = document.lastModified;
        alert(docMod);
        chrono = new Date();
        alert(chrono.getHours());
        alert(chrono + " already?!");
        alert("That's All Folks!");
        self.close();  }
</script>
```

The getHours method returns local time; for Universal Coordinated Time (UTC time), use getUTCHours.

getMilliseconds

The getMilliseconds method belongs to the **date** object and returns the milliseconds (0–999) of the given date. It has the following syntax:

```
dateObjectName.getMilliseconds()
```

The datObjectName entry is any **date** object or a property of an object.

EXAMPLE

```
<script type="text/javascript" language="javascript">
   function callMe() {
       var docMod = document.lastModified;
       alert(docMod);
       chrono = new Date();
       alert(chrono.getMilliseconds());
       alert(chrono + " already?!");
       alert("That's All Folks!")
       self.close();  }
</script>
```

The getMilliseconds method returns local time; for Universal Coordinated Time (UTC time), use getUTCMilliseconds.

getMinutes

The getMinutes method belongs to the **date** object and returns the minutes (0–59) for the given date. It has the following syntax:

```
dateObjectName.getMinutes()
```

The dateObjectName entry is any **date** object or a property of an object.

EXAMPLE

```
<script type="text/javascript" language="javascript">
   function callMe() {
       var docMod = document.lastModified;
       alert(docMod);
       chrono = new Date();
       alert(chrono.getMinutes());
       alert(chrono + " already?!");
       alert("That's All Folks!");
       self.close();  }
</script>
```

The getMinutes method returns local time; for Universal Coordinated Time (UTC time), use getUTCMinutes.

getMonth

The getMonth method belongs to the date object and returns the month (0–11) of the given date. It has the following syntax:

```
dateObjectName.getMonth()
```

The dateObjectName entry is any date object or a property of an object.

EXAMPLE

```
<script type="text/javascript" language="javascript">
    function callMe() {
        var docMod = document.lastModified;
        alert(docMod);
        chrono = new Date();
        alert(chrono.getMonth());
        alert(chrono + " already?!");
        alert("That's All Folks!");
        self.close();  }
</script>
```

The getMonth method returns local time; for Universal Coordinated Time (UTC time), use getUTCMonth.

getSeconds

The getSeconds method belongs to the date object and returns the seconds (0–59) of the given date. It has the following syntax:

```
dateObjectName.getSeconds()
```

The datObjectName entry is any date object or a property of an object.

EXAMPLE

```
<script type="text/javascript" language="javascript">
    function callMe() {
        var docMod = document.lastModified;
        alert(docMod);
        chrono = new Date();
        alert(chrono.getSeconds());
        alert(chrono + " already?!");
        alert("That's All Folks!");
        self.close();  }
</script>
```

The getSeconds method returns local time; for Universal Coordinated Time (UTC time), use getUTCSeconds.

getTime

The getTime method belongs to the date object and returns the time (number of milliseconds since January 1, 1970 00:00:00, also known as the *epoch*) for the given date. It has the following syntax:

```
dateObjectName.getTime()
```

The dateObjectName entry is any date object or a property of an object.

EXAMPLE

```
<script type="text/javascript" language="javascript">
    function callMe() {
        var docMod = document.lastModified;
        alert(docMod);
        chrono = new Date();
        alert(chrono.getHours());
        alert(chrono + " already?!");
        alert("That's All Folks!");
        self.close();  }
</script>
```

getTimezoneOffset

The getTimezoneOffset method belongs to the date object and returns the difference between local time and Universal Coordinated Time (UTC) or GMT in minutes. It has the following syntax:

```
dateObjectName.getTimezoneOffset()
```

The dateObjectName entry is any date object or a property of an object.

EXAMPLE

```
<script type="text/javascript" language="javascript">
    function callMe() {
        var docMod = document.lastModified;
        alert(docMod);
        chrono = new Date();
        alert(chrono.get.timezoneOffset());
        alert(chrono);
        alert("That's All Folks!");
        self.close();  }
</script>
```

getYear

The getYear method belongs to the date object and returns the last two digits of the year of the given date. It has the following syntax:

```
dateObjectName.getYear()
```

The dateObjectName entry is any date object or a property of an object.

EXAMPLE

```
<script type="text/javascript" language="javascript">
    function callMe() {
        var docMod = document.lastModified;
        alert(docMod);
        chrono = new Date();
        alert(chrono.getYear());
        alert(chrono + " already?!");
        alert("That's All Folks!");
        self.close();  }
</script>
```

For Y2K (and beyond) compliance, use `getFullYear` instead, to remove any ambiguity about which century a specific year really falls in.

go

The `go` method belongs to the `history` object and uses the history list to recall a previously viewed document. You can use this method to give users an alternative to the browser's Back and Forward buttons. You can also use the `back` and `forward` methods. The `go` method has the following syntax:

```
history.go(number)
```

The `number` entry is a positive or negative integer. A positive integer moves the user forward, and a negative integer moves the user back.

EXAMPLE

```
<p><input type="button" value="Take Me Back!"
    onclick="history.back()" />
  <input type="button" value="Let's Keep Going!"
    onclick="history.forward()" /></p>
```

This code places two buttons beside each other on a line. The first button goes back to the last document. The second button is useful if the user has already moved back in the history list and is ready to go forward again.

Using the `go` method, these lines would appear like this:

```
<p><input type="button" value="Take Me Back!"
    onclick="history.go(-1)" />
  <input type="button" value="Let's Keep Going!"
    onclick="history.go(1)" /></p>
```

indexOf

The `indexOf` method belongs to the `string` object and returns the position of the first occurrence of the search value starting from the position given. It has the following syntax:

```
stringName.indexOf("searchValue" [, fromIndex])
```

The `stringName` entry is any string or object property. The `searchValue` is a string from within `stringName`. The `fromIndex` entry is the starting position for the search; the default is zero (first position).

EXAMPLE

```
var champion = "We are the champions! We are the champions!";
champion.indexOf("are");
chamption.lastIndexOf("are");
```

This example returns the number 3 for the `indexOf` statement and 25 for the `lastIndexOf` statement.

isFinite

The `isFinite` function determines whether the number evaluated is finite. It has the following syntax:

```
isFinite(testValue)
```

This example returns true for finite numbers and false for infinite.

isNaN

The `isNaN` function determines whether the value given is a number. It has the following syntax:

```
isNaN(testValue)
```

EXAMPLE

```
floatValue = parseFloat(toFloat);
if isNaN(floatValue) { not Float(); }
else { isFloat(); }
```

This example generates the value and then evaluates it.

italics

The `italics` method belongs to the `string` object and displays the associated string as italics or oblique as if the text were tagged with the i element. It has the following syntax:

```
stringName.italics()
```

The `stringName` entry is any string expression or a property of an object.

EXAMPLE

```
<script type="text/javascript" language="javascript">
   var welcome = "Welcome to our flashy new digs!";
   confirm(welcome);
   // This opens a small box with the text and an OK button.
   document.write(welcome.italics() + "<br />");
   alert("That's All Folks!");
   self.close();
</script>
```

lastIndexOf

The `lastIndexOf` method belongs to the `string` object and returns the position of the last occurrence of the search value starting from the position given. It has the following syntax:

```
stringName.lastIndexOf("searchValue" [, fromIndex])
```

The `stringName` entry is any string or object property. The `searchValue` entry is a string from within `stringName`. The `fromIndex` entry is the starting position for the search; the default is zero (first position).

EXAMPLE

```
var champion="We are the champions! We are the champions!";
champion.indexOf("are");
chamption.lastIndexOf("are");
```

This example returns the number 3 for the `indexOf` statement and 25 for the `lastIndexOf` statement.

link

The `link` method belongs to the `anchor` object and creates a jump to a URL. It has the following syntax:

```
linkText.link(hrefAttribute)
```

The `linkText` entry is a string or property that is used as the label for the link. The `hrefAttribute` entry is a valid URL for the destination.

EXAMPLE

```
var c1="JavaScripting Overview";
var c2="JavaScript Objects";
var c3="JavaScript Constructs";
...
document.write(c1.link(
    "http://www.example.com/Courses/js_overview.html");
document.write(c2.link(
    "http://www.example.com/Courses/js_objects.html");
document.write(c3.link(
    "http://www.example.com/Courses/js_constructs.html");
```

You can use this example to build the table of contents for a dynamically selected course by including a selection form and a `switch` statement.

log

The `log` method belongs to the `Math` object and returns the natural logarithm (base e) of the given number. It has the following syntax:

```
Math.log(number)
```

The `number` entry is any numeric expression or a property of an object.

EXAMPLE
```
with (Math) {
    msgWindow.document.write(random());
    // Generate a random number
    msgWindow.document.write(log(baseVal));
    // Return the natural logarithm (base of e) of the number
}
```

match

The `match` method belongs to the `string` object and is used to match a regular expression against a string. It has the following syntax:

```
stringName.match(regExp)
```

The `stringName` is any string expression or a property of an object. The `regExp` entry is a regular expression. A *regular expression* is an object that defines a group of characters. The `match` method searches a string for one or more matches of the regular expression and returns an array containing the results of the match.

max

The `max` method belongs to the `Math` object and returns the higher of two given numbers. It has the following syntax:

```
Math.max(number1, number2)
```

The `number1` and `number2` entries are any numeric expression or a property of an object.

EXAMPLE
```
with (Math) {
    msgWindow.document.write(random());
    // Generate a random number
    msgWindow.document.write(max(baseVal, (random() * 3)));
    // Return the higher of the two values
}
```

min

The `min` method belongs to the `Math` object and returns the lower of two given numbers. It has the following syntax:

```
Math.min(number1, number2)
```

The `number1` and `number2` entries are any numeric expression or a property of an object.

EXAMPLE
```
with (Math) {
    msgWindow.document.write(random());
    // Generate a random number
    msgWindow.document.write(min(baseVal, (random()*3)));
    // Return the lower of the two values
}
```

moveBy

The `moveBy` method belongs to the `window` object and moves the window to the position specified by px and py. It has the following syntax:

```
window.moveBy(px, py)
```

The `px` entry is the number of pixels to move the window to the right, and the `py` entry is the number of pixels to move the window down.

moveTo

The `moveTo` method belongs to the `window` object and moves the window to an absolute position. It has the following syntax:

```
window.moveTo(x,y)
```

The `x` entry is the *x*-coordinate of the new window position and the `y` entry is the *y*-coordinate of the new window position. The upper-left corner of the window is moved to the position specified by x and y.

open (document Object)

The `open` method for documents belongs to the `document` object and opens an output destination for the `write` and `writeln` statements. It has the following syntax:

```
document.open()
document.open(["mimeType"])
```

If the mime type is `"text/html"`, you can use the first form of this statement—`"text/html"` is the default and does not have to be specified. If you want to use a different MIME type, use the second form of this statement with one of the following:

```
text/plain
image/gif
image/jpeg
image/x-bitmap
plugIn
```

For an example of the `open` (`document` object) method, see the "close (document Object)" section.

open (window Object)

The `open` method for `window` objects belongs to the `window` object and allows you to set up and open an instance of a browser window for displaying information. It has the following syntax:

```
windowVar=window.open("URL", "windowName" [,"windowsFeatures"])
```

The `windowVar` entry is the name of the new window, and `URL` is the location of the document to be loaded into the new window. The `windowName` entry is used in the `target` attribute of the `form` and a elements. The windowsFeatures entry is a comma-separated list that can contain one or more of the following:

```
toolbar[=yes|no] | [=1|0]
location[=yes|no] | [=1|0]
directories[=yes|no] | [=1|0]
status[=yes|no] | [=1|0]
menubar[=yes|no] | [=1|0]
scrollbars[=yes|no] | [=1|0]
resizable[=yes|no] | [=1|0]
width=pixels
height=pixels
```

EXAMPLE

```
<script type="text/javascript" language="javascript">
    var userPass = "" ;
    var userName = "" ;
    var formulate =  new window();
    // Set up the variables to be used later
    formulate.window.open('http://www.example.com'
        'titlebar = no,menubar = no,scrollbars = no');
    // Open a window for the form
    document.formulate.userPass.focus();
    var timer = setTimeout(
        "document.formulate.userPass.blur()", 8000);
    // Put the focus onto the the password box for 8 secs
    clearTimeout(timer);
    document.formulate.userName.focus();
    timer = setTimeout(
        "document.formulate.userName.blur()", 30000);
    // Clear the timeout, put the focus on the username box
    // for 30 secs
    document.formulate.userAuth.click();
    // Force a selection in the userAuth check box
    clearTimeout(timer);
    msgWindow.window.close();
    // Clear the timeout variable and close the window
</script>
...
<form name="formulate" id="formulate">
    <input type="password" name="userPass" size="5" />
        tell us your secret
    <input type="text" name="userName" value="Bob's your uncle"
        size="15" />
    <input type="checkbox" name="userAuth" value="Validate Me" />
        authorize us to check this stuff out!
</form>
```

parse

The `parse` method belongs to the `date` object and returns the number of milliseconds between a given date string and January 1, 1970 00:00:00, local time. It has the following syntax:

```
Date.parse(dateString)
```

The `dateString` entry is a date or object property.

EXAMPLE

```
checkValue = Date.parse("1, 1, 99");
if isNaN(checkValue) { notGood(); }
else { isGood(); }
```

This example generates the value and then evaluates it.

parseFloat

The `parseFloat` function determines whether a value is a number and returns a floating-point number for a string. It has the following syntax:

```
parseFloat(string)
```

The `string` entry is a string or object property.

EXAMPLE

```
toFloat = "3.14";
floatValue = parseFloat(toFloat);
if isNaN(floatValue) { not Float(); }
else { isFloat(); }
```

This example generates the value and then evaluates it.

parseInt

The `parseInt` function determines whether a value is a number and returns an integer value of the given radix or base. It has the following syntax:

```
parseInt(string[, radix])
```

The `string` entry is a string or an object property, and the `radix` is an integer.

EXAMPLE

```
document.write(parseInt("F", 16));
// The 16 indicates that the F is a hexidecimal number (base 16)
document.write(parseInt("1111", 2));
document.write(parseInt ("0xF"));
```

These examples return the same value, 15.

pow

The pow method belongs to the Math object and returns the first number raised to the power of the second number. It has the following syntax:

```
Math.pow(base, exponent)
```

The base and exponent entries are any numeric expression or a property of an object.

EXAMPLE

```
with (Math) {
    msgWindow.document.write(random());
    // Generate a random number
    msgWindow.document.write(pow(baseVal, random()));
    // Raise the first number to the power of the second number
}
```

print

The print method belongs to the window object and prints the current document. It has the following syntax:

```
window.print()
```

The print method prints the document as if the user had clicked the browser's Print button.

prompt

The prompt method belongs to the window object and displays a dialog box with a message and an input field. Even though prompt is a window method, you do not have to include the windowReference in the statement. The prompt method has the following syntax:

```
prompt(message[, inputDefault])
```

The message entry is a text string or an object property, and inputDefault is a string, an integer, or an object property.

EXAMPLE

```
<script  type="text/javascript" language="javascript">
    var myMsg = "Hello";
    var usrName = prompt("Please enter your name", " ");
    var myString = myMsg + " " + usrName;
    document.write(myString);
</script>
```

In this example, the string myMsg ("Hello") is joined to the string usrName, which the user enters in response to the prompt.

random

The random method belongs to the Math object and generates a random number between 0 and 1. It has the following syntax:

```
Math.random()
```

EXAMPLE

```
<script type="text/javascript" language="javascript">
    function tryMe(baseVal) {
        var baseVal = Math.random();
        showMe = window.open("" );
        with (Math) {
            var firstOne = (random());
            var secondOne = (abs(random()));
            showMe.document.write(firstOne + "<br />")
            showMe.document.write(secondOne + "<br />")  }  }
</script>
```

replace

The replace method belongs to the string object; it does a find and replace operation on string. It has the following syntax:

```
stringName.replace(regExp, replacementString)
```

The stringName is any string expression or a property of an object. The regExp entry is a regular expression, and replacementString is a string that specifies the replacement text for regExp. A *regular expression* is an object that defines a group of characters.

EXAMPLE

```
<script type="text/javascript" language="javascript">
    function replace1 () {
        var myString;
        myString = "I feel cold."
        document.write(myString + "<br />");
        myString=myString.replace("cold"," hot");
        document.write(myString);  }
</script>
...
<body onload="replace1()">...</body>
```

In this example, the string "cold" is replaced by the string "hot".

resizeBy

The `resizeBy` method belongs to the `window` object and resizes a window by a specified amount. It has the following syntax:

```
window.resizeBy(pw,ph)
```

The `pw` entry is the increase (in number of pixels) in the width of the window, and the `ph` entry is the increase (in number of pixels) in the height of the window.

EXAMPLE

```html
<script type="text/javascript" language="javascript">
    function openWin() {
        myWin = open("" ,"displayWindow", "width = 250,
            height = 300, status = no, toolbar = no,
            menubar = no");
        myWin.document.open();
        myWin.document.write("<html><head><title>My New Window");
        myWin.document.write("</title></head><body>");
        myWin.document.write("<p><font size='5'
            face='arial,helvetica'>");
        myWin.document.write("See how easy it is to create ");
        myWin.document.write("a new window using Javascript!");
        myWin.document.write("</font></p></body></html>");
        myWin.resizeBy(50,50);
        myWin.document.close();  }
</script>
...
<form name="popup" id="popup">
    <input type=button value="New Window" onClick="openWin()"
        name="button" />
</form>
```

In this example, the pop-up window increases by 50 pixels in width and 50 pixels in height as it displays.

resizeTo

The `resizeTo` method belongs to the `window` object and resizes a window to a specified size. It has the following syntax:

```
window.resizeTo(w,h)
```

The `w` entry is the new width of the window in pixels, and the `h` entry is the new height of the window in pixels.

EXAMPLE

```html
<script type="text/javascript" language="javascript">
    function openWin() {
        myWin= open("" ,"displayWindow", "width = 250,
```

```
        height = 300, status = no, toolbar = no,
        menubar = no");
    myWin.document.open();
    myWin.document.write("<html><head><title>My New Window");
    myWin.document.write("</title></head><body>");
    myWin.document.write("<p><font size='2'
        face='arial,helvetica'>");
    myWin.document.write("See how easy it is to create ");
    myWin.document.write("a new window using Javascript!");
    myWin.document.write("</font></p></body></html>");
    myWin.resizeTo(150,150);
    myWin.document.close();  }
</script>
...
<form name="popup" id="popup">
    <input type=button value="New Window" onClick="openWin()"
        name="button" />
</form>
```

In this example, the pop-up window resizes to 150 pixels in width and 150 pixels in height as it displays.

round

The round method belongs to the Math object and returns the value of the number given to the nearest integer. It has the following syntax:

```
Math.round(number)
```

The number entry is any numeric expression or a property of an object.

EXAMPLE

```
<script type="text/javascript" language="javascript">
    function tryMe(baseVal) {
        var baseVal=Math.random();
        showMe = window.open("" );
        with (Math) {
            var firstOne = (random());
            var secondOne = (abs(random()));
            showMe.document.write(firstOne + "<br />");
            showMe.document.write(secondOne + "<br />");
            // Generate a random number
            showMe.document.write(round(baseVal * random()) +
                "<br />");
            showMe.document.write(abs(round(baseVal * random())) +
                "<br />");
            //Rounds number to the nearest integer
            showMe.alert("Close \'er up now, skip?");
            showMe.close();  }  }
</script>
```

scrollBy

The `scrollBy` method belongs to the `window` object and scrolls a document by a specified amount. It has the following syntax:

```
window.scrollBy(px,py)
```

The `px` entry is the number of pixels the document is scrolled to the right, and the `py` entry is the number of pixels the document is scrolled down.

EXAMPLE

```
<head>
<script type="text/javascript" language="javascript">
   function changeposition(x,y) {
      window.scrollBy(x,y);  }
</script>
...</head>
<body bgcolor="teal">
<table width="350" bgcolor="red">
   <tr><td> </td></tr>
</table>
<form name="scroll" id="scroll">
   <input type="button" value="Scroll Right"
      onClick="scroll(50,0)" />
</form>
...</body>
```

In this example, when the button labeled "Scroll Right" is clicked, the document scrolls 50 pixels to the right from its current position. For the `scrollBy` method to work in the browser window, though, the window must have scroll bars—that is, the window must be sized so that it requires scroll bars to display.

scrollTo

The `scrollTo` method belongs to the `window` object and scrolls a document to a specified position. It has the following syntax:

```
window.scrollTo(x,y)
```

The `x` entry is the `x`-coordinate of the new position, and the `y` entry is the `y`-coordinate of the new position. The document is scrolled within the window so that `x` and `y` are the coordinates of the upper-left corner of the window. This method has the same result as the `scroll` method but is preferred over that method because it has a more descriptive name.

EXAMPLE

```
<head>
<script type="text/javascript" language="javascript">
   function changeposition(x,y) {
      window.scrollTo(x,y);  }
```

```
</script>
...</head>
<body bgcolor="teal">
<table width="350" bgcolor="red">
   <tr><td> </td></tr>
</table>
<form name="scroll" id="scroll">
   <input type="button" value="Change" onClick="scroll(500,0) " />
</form>
...</body>
```

In this example, when the button labeled "Change" is clicked, the document scrolls to the position (500,0), which is 500 pixels to the right of the upper-left corner of the document (0,0). For the scrollTo method to work in the browser window, though, the window must have scroll bars—that is, the window must be sized so that it requires scroll bars to display.

search

The search method belongs to the string object and searches a string for the position of the first character of a specified substring. It has the following syntax:

```
stringName.search(regExp)
```

The stringName is any string expression or a property of an object. The regExp entry is a regular expression. A *regular expression* is an object that defines a group of characters. The search method returns the position of the start of the first substring that matches regExp.

EXAMPLE

```
<script type="text/javascript" language="javascript">
   function search1() {
      var myString;
      myString = "I feel cold."
      var myExp = /cold/;
      myString.search(myExp);
      alert(myString.search(myExp));   }
</script>
...
<form>
   <input type="button" name="search" value="Search"
      onclick="search1()" />
</form>
```

In this example, when the button labeled "Search" is clicked, an alert box displays with the message "7". This is the position of the first character of our search string, cold.

select

Like the focus and blur methods, the select method performs an action programmatically. It belongs to the password, text, and textarea objects. The select method selects the input area of a given password, text, or text area form object. It has the following syntax:

```
passwordName.select()
textName.select()
textareaName.select()
```

The passwordName entry is the name attribute of the password object. The textName entry is the name attribute of the text object, and textareaName is the name attribute of the textarea object.

EXAMPLE

```
<script type="text/javascript" language="javascript">
    var userPass = "" ;
    var userName = "" ;
    var formulate =  new window();
    // Set up the variables to be used later
    formulate.window.open();
    // Open a window for the form
    document.formulate.userPass.select();
    var timer = setTimeout(
        "document.formulate.userPass.blur()", 8000);
    // Select the password box
    // for 8 secs, then blur
    clearTimeout(timer);
    document.formulate.userName.select();
    timer = setTimeout(
        "document.formulate.userName.blur()", 30000);
    // Clear the timeout, select the username box
    // for 30 secs, then blur
    document.formulate.userAuth.click();
    // Force a selection in the userAuth check box
    clearTimeout(timer);
    msgWindow.window.close();
    // Clear the timeout variable and close the window
</script>
...
<form name="formulate" id="formulate">
    <input type="password" name="userPass" size="5" />
        tell us your secret
    <input type="text" name="userName" value="Bob's your uncle"
        size="15" />
    <input type="checkbox" name="userAuth" value="Validate Me" />
        authorize us to check this stuff out!
</form>
```

setDate

The `setDate` method belongs to the `date` object and sets the day of the month for a given date. It has the following syntax:

```
dateObjectName.setDate(dayValue)
```

The `dateObjectName` entry is any `date` object or a property of an object. The `dayValue` is an integer between 1 and 31 or a property of an object representing the month.

EXAMPLE

```
<script type="text/javascript" language="javascript">
    function callMe() {
        var docMod = "" ;
        docMod.setDay(1);
        docMod.setMonth(6);
        docMod.setDate(30);
        docMod.setYear(2001);
        docMod.setTime(11, 59, 59);
        alert(docMod);
        alert("That's All Folks!");
        self.close();  }
</script>
```

The `setDate` method uses local time; for Universal Coordinated Time (UTC time), use `setUTCDate`.

setFullYear

The `setFullYear` method belongs to the `date` object and sets the year for a given date. It has the following syntax:

```
dateObjectName.setFullYear(yearValue)
```

The `dateObjectName` entry is any `date` object or a property of an object. The `yearValue` entry is a four-digit integer or a property of an object representing the year.

EXAMPLE

```
var docMod = "" ;docMod.setDay(1);
docMod.setMonth(12);
docMod.setDate(31);
docMod.setFullYear(2001);
docMod.setTime(23, 59, 59);
alert(docMod);
alert("That's All Folks!");
```

The `setFullYear` method uses local time; for Universal Coordinated Time (UTC time), use `setUTCFullYear`.

setHours

The setHours method belongs to the date object and sets the hour of the day for a given date. It has the following syntax:

```
dateObjectName.setHours(hoursValue)
```

The dateObjectName entry is any date object or a property of an object. The hoursValue entry is an integer between 0 and 23 or a property of an object representing the hour.

EXAMPLE

```
<script type="text/javascript" language="javascript">
   function callMe() {
      var docMod = "" ;
      docMod.setDay(1);
      docMod.setMonth(6);
      docMod.setDate(30);
      docMod.setYear(2001);
      docMod.setHours(11);
      docMod.setMinutes(59);
      docMod.setSeconds(59);
      alert(docMod);
      alert("That's All Folks!");
      self.close();  }
</script>
```

The setHours method uses local time; for Universal Coordinated Time (UTC time), use setUTCHours.

setInterval

The setInterval method belongs to the window object and periodically executes specified code at a fixed interval. It has the following syntax:

```
window.setInterval(code,interval)
window.setInterval(function,interval,values...)
```

The code entry specifies a string of JavaScript code. The interval entry is an integer that gives the interval in milliseconds between executions of the code. The function entry is a JavaScript function, and the values entries are parameters for this function.

The setInterval method is similar to the setTimeout method. The setInterval method periodically executes code at a given interval. The setTimeout method defers the code execution for a specified interval, but does not repeatedly execute the code.

For an example of the setInterval and clearInterval methods, see the "clearInterval" section.

setMilliseconds

The setMilliseconds method belongs to the date object and sets the milliseconds of the second of the minute for a given date. It has the following syntax:

```
dateObjectName.setMilliseconds(millisecondsValue)
```

The dateObjectName entry is any date object or a property of an object. The millisecondValue entry is an integer in the range 0–999 or a property of an object representing the milliseconds.

EXAMPLE
```
function callMe() {
    var docMod = "" ;
    docMod.setDay(1);
    docMod.setMonth(6);
    docMod.setDate(30);
    docMod.setYear(2001);
    docMod.setHours(11);
    docMod.setMinutes(59);
    docMod.setSeconds(59);
    docMod.setMilliseconds(59);
    alert(docMod);
    alert("That's All Folks!");
    self.close();   }
```

The setMilliseconds method uses local time; for Universal Coordinated Time (UTC time), use setUTCMilliseconds.

setMinutes

The setMinutes method belongs to the date object and sets the minutes of the hour for a given date. It has the following syntax:

```
dateObjectName.setMinutes(minuteValue)
```

The dateObjectName entry is any date object or a property of an object. The minuteValue entry is an integer between 0 and 59 or a property of an object representing the minute.

EXAMPLE
```
<script type="text/javascript" language="javascript">
    function callMe() {
        var docMod = "" ;
        docMod.setDay(1);
        docMod.setMonth(6);
        docMod.setDate(30);
        docMod.setYear(2001);
        docMod.setHours(11);
        docMod.setMinutes(59);
        docMod.setSeconds(59);
        alert(docMod);
        alert("That's All Folks!");
        self.close();   }
</script>
```

The setMinutes method uses local time; for Universal Coordinated Time (UTC time), use setUTCMinutes.

setMonth

The `setMonth` method belongs to the `date` object and sets the month of the year for a given date. It has the following syntax:

```
dateObjectName.setMonth(monthValue)
```

The `dateObjectName` entry is any `date` object or a property of an object. The `monthValue` is an integer between 0 and 11 or a property of an object representing the month.

EXAMPLE

```
<script type="text/javascript" language="javascript">
    function callMe() {
        var docMod = "" ;
        docMod.setDay(1);
        docMod.setMonth(6);
        docMod.setDate(30);
        docMod.setYear(2001);
        docMod.setHours(11);
        docMod.setMinutes(59);
        docMod.setSeconds(59);
        alert(docMod);
        alert("That's All Folks!");
        self.close();  }
</script>
```

The `setMonth` method uses local time; for Universal Coordinated Time (UTC time), use setUTCMonth.

setSeconds

The `setSeconds` method belongs to the `date` object and sets the seconds of the minute for a given date. It has the following syntax:

```
dateObjectName.setSeconds(secondsValue)
```

The `dateObjectName` entry is any `date` object or a property of an object. The `secondsValue` entry is an integer between 0 and 59 or a property of an object representing the seconds.

EXAMPLE

```
<script type="text/javascript" language="javascript">
    function callMe() {
        var docMod = "" ;
        docMod.setDay(1);
        docMod.setMonth(6);
        docMod.setDate(30);
        docMod.setYear(2001);
        docMod.setHours(11);
```

```
        docMod.setMinutes(59);
        docMod.setSeconds(59);
        alert(docMod);
        alert("That's All Folks!");
        self.close();   }
    </script>
```

The setSeconds method uses local time; for Universal Coordinated Time (UTC time), use setUTCSeconds.

setTime

The setTime method belongs to the date object and sets the number of milliseconds since January 1, 1970 00:00:00. It has the following syntax:

```
dateObjectName.setTime(timeValue)
```

The dateObjectName entry is any date object or a property of an object. The timeValue entry is an integer or a property of an object representing the number of milliseconds since the epoch.

EXAMPLE
```
<script type="text/javascript" language="javascript">
    function callMe() {
        var docMod = "" ;
        docMod.setDay(1);
        docMod.setMonth(6);
        docMod.setDate(30);
        docMod.setYear(2001);
        docMod.setTime(11, 59, 59);
        alert(docMod);
        alert("That's All Folks!");
        self.close();   }
</script>
```

setTimeout

The setTimeout method belongs to the frame and window objects and evaluates an expression after the set number of milliseconds have passed. It has the following syntax:

```
timeoutID = setTimeout(expression, msec)
```

The timeoutID entry is the identifier for the timeout variable; it's used later by the clearTimeout method. The expression entry is a string or a property of an object. The msec entry is a numeric value, a numeric string, or an object property representing the number of millisecond units for the timeout.

For an example of the setTimeout and the clearTimeout methods, see the "clearTimeout" section.

setYear

The setYear method belongs to the date object and sets the year for a given date. It has the following syntax:

```
dateObjectName.setYear(yearValue)
```

The dateObjectName entry is any date object or a property of an object. The yearValue entry is a four-digit integer or a property of an object representing the year.

The setYear method is deprecated in JavaScript 1.2 in favor of the setFullYear method.

EXAMPLE

```
<script type="text/javascript" language="javascript">
    function callMe() {
        var docMod = "" ;
        docMod.setDay(1);
        docMod.setMonth(6);
        docMod.setDate(30);
        docMod.setYear(2001);
        docMod.setTime(11, 59, 59);
        alert(docMod);
        alert("That's All Folks!");
        self.close();  }
</script>
```

sin

The sin method belongs to the Math object and returns the sine of the given number. It has the following syntax:

```
Math.sin(number)
```

The number entry is any numeric expression or a property of an object.

EXAMPLE

```
<script type="text/javascript" language="javascript">
    function tryMe(baseVal) {
        var baseVal = Math.random();
        showMe = window.open("" );
        with (Math) {
            showMe.document.write(sin(random()) + "<br />");
            showMe.alert("Close \'er [up now, skip?");
            showMe.close();  }  }
</script>
```

slice

The slice method belongs to the string object and extracts a slice, or substring, from a string. It has the following syntax:

```
stringName.slice(index1, index2)
```

The `stringName` entry is any string expression or a property of an object. The `index1` entry is an integer representing the starting position of the substring within the string; this can be any integer from zero to `stringName.length-1`. The `index2` entry is an integer representing the ending position of the substring within the string; this can be any integer larger than `index1`, from zero to `stringName.length-1`. If either `index1` or `index2` is a negative number, the position is measured from the end of the string.

The `slice` method returns a substring containing all the characters from and including the character at `index1`, and up to but *not* including the character at `index2`.

EXAMPLE

```
<script type="text/javascript" language="javascript">
    function slice1(){
        var myString;
        myString = "JavaScriptReference"
        myString = myString.slice(0,10);
        alert([myString]);   }
</script>
…
<form>
    <input type="button" name="slice" value="Slice"
        onclick="slice1()" />
</form>
```

In this example, when the user clicks the button labeled "Slice", an alert box displays with the message "JavaScriptReference". This is the array `myString`, created by slicing the string `myString` from character 0 up to but not including character 10.

small

The `small` method belongs to the `string` object and displays the associated string using a smaller font, as if the text were tagged with a `small` element. It has the following syntax:

```
stringName.small()
```

The `stringName` entry is any string expression or a property of an object.

EXAMPLE

```
<script type="text/javascript" language="javascript">
    var welcome = "Welcome to our flashy new digs! ";
    confirm(welcome);
    // This opens a small box with the text and an OK button.
    document.write(welcome.small() + "<br />");
    alert("That's All Folks!");
    self.close();
</script>
```

split

The `split` method belongs to the `string` object and breaks a string into substrings. It has the following syntax:

```
stringName.split(boundary)
```

The `stringName` entry is any string expression or a property of an object. The `boundary` entry is the character or characters that JavaScript uses to decide where to split the string. The substrings that are created by the `split` method are put into an array created by this method.

EXAMPLE

```
<script type="text/javascript" language="javascript">
    function split1(){
        var myString;
        myString = "JavaScript Reference"
        myString = myString.split("" );
        alert([myString]);   }
</script>
...
<form>
    <input type="button" name="split" value="Split"
        onclick="split1()" />
</form>...
```

In this example, when the user clicks the button labeled "Split", an alert box displays the `myString` array. Because we used the empty string (`""`) as our boundary entry, the `myString` array is a set of every letter in `myString` as a separate array element.

sqrt

The `sqrt` method belongs to the `Math` object and returns the square root of the given number. It has the following syntax:

```
Math.sqrt(number)
```

The `number` is any nonnegative numeric expression or a property of an object.

EXAMPLE

```
<script type="text/javascript" language="javascript">
    function tryMe(baseVal) {
        var baseVal=Math.random();
        showMe = window.open("" );
        with (Math) {
            showMe.document.write(sqrt(baseVal) + "<br />");
            showMe.document.write(abs(sqrt(baseVal)) + "<br />");
            // Return the square root of the number
            showMe.alert("Close \'er up now, skip?");
            showMe.close();   }   }
</script>
```

strike

The strike method belongs to the string object and displays the associated string with strikethrough. It has the following syntax:

```
stringName.strike()
```

The stringName entry is any string expression or a property of an object.

EXAMPLE

```
<script type="text/javascript" language="javascript">
    var welcome = "Welcome to our flashy new digs!";
    confirm(welcome);
    // This opens a small box with the text and an OK button.
    document.write(welcome.strike() + "<br />");
    alert("That's All Folks!");
    self.close();
</script>
```

sub

The sub method belongs to the string object and displays the associated string subscripted to the rest of the text. It has the following syntax:

```
stringName.sub()
```

The stringName entry is any string expression or a property of an object.

EXAMPLE

```
<script type="text/javascript" language="javascript">
    var welcome = "Welcome to our flashy new digs!";
    confirm(welcome);
    // This opens a small box with the text and an OK button.
    document.write(welcome.sub() + "<br />");
    alert("That's All Folks!");
    self.close();
</script>
```

submit

The submit method belongs to the form object and submits a form. It has the following syntax:

```
formName.submit()
```

The formName entry is the name of a form or an element in the forms array.

EXAMPLE

```
<head>
<script type="text/javascript" language="javascript">
    function checkThis() {
```

```
        document.form1.submit();
        confirm("Thanks for registering");
        self.close();
    }
</script>
…</head>
<body onload="window.alert('Welcome! You can register through
    this page. For future reference, this page is ' +
    document.location)">
<form name="form1" id="form1">
    <p><input type="text" name="whoIs" value="user" size="15" />
        </p>
    <p><input type="radio" name="lesson" value="Lesson 1"
        checked="checked" onclick="takeLesson='lesson1.htm'" />
        Lesson 1: Getting Started</p>
    <p><input type="radio" name="lesson" value="Lesson 2"
        onclick="takeLesson='lesson2.htm'" />
        Lesson 2: Concepts and Operations</p>
    <p><input type="radio" name="lesson" value="Lesson 3"
        onclick="takeLesson='lesson3.htm'" />
        Lesson 3: Projects</p>
    <p><input type="reset" value="Defaults"
        name="resetToBasic" />
        <input type="submit" value="Send it in!"
        name="submit_form1" onclick="checkThis()" /></p>
    <hr />
</form>
…</body>
```

substr

The substr method belongs to the string object and returns a portion of a given string. It has the following syntax:

```
stringName.substr(index1, length)
```

The stringName entry is the string or an object property. The index1 entry is an integer representing the starting position of the substring within the string; this can be any integer from zero to stringName.length-1. The length entry is an integer representing the number of characters in the substring.

EXAMPLE

```
var champion="We are the champions! We are the champions!";
document.write(champion.substr(11,9));
document.write(champion.substr(13,3));
```

This example returns champions and amp.

substring

The substring method belongs to the string object and returns a portion of a given string. It has the following syntax:

```
stringName.substring(index1, index2)
```

The stringName entry is the string or an object property. The index1 entry is an integer representing the starting position of the substring within the string; this can be any integer from zero to stringName.length-1. The index2 entry is an integer representing the ending position of the substring within the string; this can be any integer larger than index1 from zero to stringName.length-1.

EXAMPLE

```
var champion="We are the champions! We are the champions!";
document.write(champion.substring(11,19));
document.write(champion.substring(13,15));
```

This example returns champions and amp. In contrast to the slice method, the substring method includes the final character specified.

sup

The sup method belongs to the string object and displays the associated string as a superscript to the surrounding text. It has the following syntax:

```
stringName.sup()
```

The stringName entry is any string expression or a property of an object.

EXAMPLE

```
<script type="text/javascript" language="javascript">
   var super = "Superscripted Term";
   confirm(super);
   // This opens a small box with the text and an OK button.
   document.write("Here is a " + super.sup() + "<br />");
   alert("That's All Folks!");
   self.close();
</script>
```

tan

The tan method belongs to the Math object and returns the tangent of the given number. It has the following syntax:

```
Math.tan(number)
```

The number entry is any numeric expression or a property of an object that represents the size of an angle in radians.

EXAMPLE

```
<script type="text/javascript" language="javascript">
   function updateAnswers(objAcos, objCos, objSin, objAtan,
      objTan) {
//
// This function receives information from the form below.
// The form has a series of text input boxes that result in
// the variables listed in the function call above.
// The function generates the correct value for the trig
// function and then compares the correct answer to the
// student's answer.
// If the answer is correct, the answer appears in a text box.
// If the answer is incorrect, the text Try Again! appears.
//
      var wrong = "Try Again!";
      var trueAcos = Math.acos(0.5);
      if (objAcos == trueAcos) {
         document.TrigTest.user_acos.value = objAcos; }
      else document.TrigTest.user_acos.value = wrong;

      var trueCos = Math.cos(0.5);
      if (objCos == trueCos) {
         document.TrigTest.user_cos.value = objCos; }
      else document.TrigTest.user_cos.value = wrong;

      var trueSin = Math.sin(0.5);
      if (objSin == trueSin) {
         document.TrigTest.user_sin.value = objSin; }
      else document.TrigTest.user_sin.value = wrong;

      var trueAtan = Math.atan(0.5;)
      if (objAtan == trueAtan) {
         document.TrigTest.user_atan.value = objAtan; }
      else document.TrigTest.user_atan.value = wrong;

      var trueTan = Math.tan(0.5);
      if (objTan == trueTan) {
         document.TrigTest.user_tan.value = objTan; }
      else document.TrigTest.user_tan.value = wrong;

   }
</script>
...
<form name="TrigTest" id="TrigTest">
   <p><center>Find the arc cosine (in radians) of .5.</center>
      </p>
   <input type="text" name="enterArcCosine" value="0" size="10"
```

```
            onblur="updateAnswers(this,
            document.TrigTest.enterCosine.value,
            document.TrigTest.enterSine.value,
            document.TrigTest.enterArcTangent.value,
            document.TrigTest.enterTangent.value)" />
    <p><center>Find the cosine (in radians) of .5.</center></p>
    <input type="text" name="enterCosine" value="0" size="10"
            onblur="updateAnswers(
            document.TrigTest.enterArcCosine.value,
            this, document.TrigTest.enterSine.value,
            document.TrigTest.enterArcTangent.value,
            document.TrigTest.enterTangent.value)" />
    <p><center>Find the sine (in radians) of .5.</center></p>
    <input type="text" name="enterSine" value="0" size="10"
            onblur="updateAnswers(
            document.TrigTest.enterArcCosine.value,
            document.TrigTest.enterCosine.value, this,
            document.TrigTest.enterArcTangent.value,
            document.TrigTest.enterTangent.value)" />
    <p><center>Find the arc tangent (in radians) of .5.</center>
        </p>
    <input type="text" name="enterArcTangent" value="0" size="10"
            onblur="updateAnswers(
            document.TrigTest.enterArcCosine.value,
            document.TrigTest.enterCosine.value,
            document.TrigTest.enterSine.value, this,
            document.TrigTest.enterTangent.value)" />
    <p><center>Find the tangent (in radians) of .5.</center></p>
    <input type="text" name="enterTangent" value="0" size="10"
            onblur="updateAnswers(
            document.TrigTest.enterArcCosine.value,
            document.TrigTest.enterCosine.value,
            document.TrigTest.enterSine.value,
            document.TrigTest.enterArcTan.value, this)" />
    <p>Results:</p>
    <p>arcCosine:<input type="text" name="user_acos" value=""
        size="10" /></p>
    <p>cosine:<input type="text" name="user_cos" value=""
        size="10" /></p>
    <p>sine:<input type="text" name="user_sin" value=""
        size="10" /></p>
    <p>arcTangent:<input type="text" name="user_atan" value=""
        size="10" /></p>
    <p>tangent:<input type="text" name="user_tan" value=""
        size="10" /></p>
</form>
```

toLocaleString

The toLocaleString method belongs to the date object and converts a date to a string, using the local conventions. It's generally more reliable to use the getMonth, getDay, and other such date methods to get the information if you plan to manipulate it at all. The toLocaleString method has the following syntax:

```
dataObjectName.toLocaleString()
```

The dateObjectName entry is any date object or a property of an object.

EXAMPLE

```
function (showDate) {
    var docMod = "" ;
    docMod.setDay(1);
    docMod.setMonth(6);
    docMod.setDate(30);
    docMod.setYear(2001);
    docMod.setTime(11, 59, 59);
    docMod.toLocaleString();
    document.write(docMod.fontcolor("darkmagenta") + "<br />");
    docMod.toUTCString();
    document.write(docMod.fontcolor("darkmagenta") + "<br />") }
```

This converts the contents of the date variable docMod first to local time and then to UTC time before printing out each value.

Older versions of browsers support toGMTString rather than toUTCString.

toLowerCase

The toLowerCase method belongs to the string object and converts the contents of a text string to all lowercase letters. It has the following syntax:

```
stringName.toLowerCase()
```

The stringName entry is any string expression or a property of an object.

EXAMPLE

```
<script type="text/javascript" language="javascript">
function upAndDown() {
    confirm(document.WhoAreYou.nameInfo.value.toUpperCase());
    confirm(document.WhoAreYou.FavFoodGroup.value.toLowerCase());
}
</script>
...
<form name="WhoAreYou" id="WhoAreYou">
    <input type="text" name="nameInfo" value="" size="30"
        maxlength="30" />
    <input type="text" name="FavFoodGroup" size="15" />
    <input type="submit" name="getGoing" value="Yumm!"
        onclick="upAndDown()" />
</form>
```

toUpperCase

The `toUpperCase` method belongs to the `string` object and converts the contents of a text string to all uppercase letters. It has the following syntax:

```
stringName.toUpperCase()
```

The `stringName` is any string expression or a property of an object.

EXAMPLE

```
<script type="text/javascript" language="javascript">
function upAndDown() {
   confirm(document.WhoAreYou.nameInfo.value.toUpperCase());
   confirm(document.WhoAreYou.FavFoodGroup.value.toLowerCase());
}
</script>
...
<form name="WhoAreYou" id="WhoAreYou">
   <input type="text" name="nameInfo" value="" size="30"
      maxlength="30" />
   <input type="text" name="FavFoodGroup" size="15" />
   <input type="submit" name="getGoing" value="Yumm!"
      onclick="upAndDown()" />
</form>
```

toUTCString

The `toUTCString` method belongs to the `date` object and converts a date to a string, using the international UTC conventions. The exact format varies according to the user's platform. It's generally more reliable to use the `getMonth`, `getDay`, and other such `date` methods to get the information if you plan to manipulate it at all. The `toUTCString` method has the following syntax:

```
dataObjectName.toUTCString()
```

The `dateObjectName` is any `date` object or a property of an object.

EXAMPLE

```
function (showDate) {
   var docMod = "" ;
   docMod.setDay(1);
   docMod.setMonth(6);
   docMod.setDate(30);
   docMod.setYear(2001);
   docMod.setTime(11, 59, 59);
   docMod.toLocaleString();
   document.write(docMod.fontcolor("darkmagenta") + "<br />");
   docMod.toUTCString();
   document.write(docMod.fontcolor("darkmagenta"))+ "<br />"   }
```

This converts the contents of the date variable `docMod` first to local time and then to UTC time before displaying each value.

Older versions of browsers support `toGMTString` rather than `toUTCString`.

unescape

Like the escape function, the unescape function converts an ASCII value. The unescape function takes the integer or hexadecimal value of the character and returns the ASCII character. Like the escape method, it's a built-in JavaScript method, and is not a method of any object. It has the following syntax:

```
unescape("string")
```

The string entry is either an integer ("%integer") or a hexadecimal value ("xx").

UTC

The UTC method belongs to the date object and returns the number of milliseconds between the contents of a date object and the epoch (January 1, 1970 00:00:00, Universal Coordinated Time [GMT]). It has the following syntax:

```
Date.UTC(year, month, day[, hrs][, min][, sec] )
```

The year entry is a two-digit or four-digit representation of a year (2000–2999). The month entry is a number between zero (January) and 11 (December) representing the month of the year. The day entry is a number between 1 and 31 representing the day of the month. The hrs entry is a two-digit number between 0 (midnight) and 23 (11 PM) representing the hour of the day. The min entry is a two-digit number between 0 and 59 representing the minute of the hour, and sec is a two-digit number between 0 and 59 representing the seconds.

EXAMPLE

```
var myDate = new Date(Date.UTC(2002, 7, 1, 7, 30, 0));
```

In this example, you create a new date object using a UTC specification. The UTC string for this date (August 1, 2002, 7:30 AM) is 1 Aug 2001 07:30:00 UTC (if our time zone is UTC zone 0, or London/Greenwich—otherwise, a time zone offset will convert the UTC time for the local time zone). The value of the variable myDate will be the number of milliseconds from January 1, 1970, to our date and time.

valueOf

The valueOf method belongs to the date object and returns the time (the number of milliseconds since January 1, 1970 00:00:00) for the given date. It has the following syntax:

```
dateObjectName.valueOf()
```

The dateObjectName entry is any date object or a property of an object. The value returned is the same as that returned by the getTime method of the date object.

EXAMPLE

```
<script type="text/javascript" language="javascript">
    function callMe() {
        Xmas01 = new Date("December 25, 2001 23:15:00");
```

```
        weekday = Xmas01.valueOf();
        confirm(weekday);
        var docMod = document.lastModified;
        alert(docMod);
        chrono = new Date();
        alert(chrono.getHours());
        alert(chrono + " already?!");
        alert("That's All Folks!");
        self.close();  }
  </script>
```

write

The write method belongs to the document object and sends expressions to the document as encoded strings. It has the following syntax:

```
write(expression1 [, expression2] […, expressionN])
```

The expression1 through expressionN entries are any JavaScript expression or a property of an object.

EXAMPLE

```
<script type="text/javascript" language="javascript">
    var welcome = "Welcome to our flashy new digs!";
    confirm(welcome);
    // This opens a small box with the text and an OK button.
    document.write(welcome.small() + "<br />");
    document.write(welcome.big()+"<br />");
    document.write(welcome.blink()+"<br />");
    document.write(welcome.bold()+"<br />");
    document.write("<br />")
    document.write(welcome.fixed()+"<br />");
    // These write out the contents of welcome using
    // various text attributes.
</script>
```

writeln

Like the write method, the writeln method belongs to the document object and sends expressions to the document as encoded strings. The writeln method generates a newline character (hard return) at the end of the written string. HTML and XHTML ignore the newline character except within elements such as pre. The writeln method has the following syntax:

```
writeln(expression1 [, expression2] […, expressionN])
```

The expression1 through expressionN entries are any JavaScript expression or a property of an object.

EXAMPLE

```
<script type="text/javascript" language="javascript">
    var welcome = "Welcome to our flashy new digs!";
    confirm(welcome);
    // This opens a small box with the text and an OK button.
    document.writeln(welcome.small());
    document.writeln(welcome.big());
    document.writeln(welcome.blink());
    document.writeln(welcome.bold());
    document.writeln(welcome.fixed() + "<br />");
    // These write out the contents of welcome using
    // various text attributes.
</script>
```

Event Handlers

When users interact with your Web page through JavaScript scripts, you need event handlers to recognize the event and communicate back to your script. Event handlers help manage the interaction between your users and your JavaScript objects by providing the information in the user response to the JavaScript for later use.

This section is an alphabetical listing of the available JavaScript event handlers. Each entry describes a single event handler, includes examples, and identifies the objects for which the event handler works. The syntax for these event handlers can be seen in the corresponding object listings.

onblur

A `blur` event occurs when the focus moves from one object to another on the page. The object that was in focus loses focus and is blurred. The `onblur` event handler works for the `select`, `text`, and `textarea` objects.

EXAMPLE

```
onblur="document.login.submit()";
```

When the user leaves the field, the system submits the information for logging into the next page.

onchange

A `change` event occurs when the user alters the contents of an object and then moves the focus from the object. Use the `onchange` event handler to validate the information submitted by users. The `onchange` event handler works for the `select`, `text`, and `textarea` objects.

EXAMPLE

```
onchange="testName(this.value)";
```

This example sends the contents of the field to the `testName` function when the user changes information and leaves the field.

onclick

A `click` event occurs when the user clicks an object on the page with the mouse. This event could lead to a selection or a change or could launch a piece of JavaScript code.

The `onclick` event handler works for the `document`, `button`, `checkbox`, `radio`, `link`, `reset`, and `submit` objects. It has been updated to *not* act if the event handler returns false when it's employed by a `checkbox`, `radio`, `submit`, or `reset` object.

EXAMPLE

```
onclick="compute(this.form)";
```

When the user clicks the object, the script runs the `compute` function and sends the form contents.

ondblclick

A `dblclick` event occurs when the user clicks twice very quickly on an object on the page.

It works for the `document`, `area` (in an image map), and `link` objects.

EXAMPLE

```
<a href="seeMyFamily.html" ondblclick="this.href = 'theFastTour'">
```

This example loads a different page if the user double-clicks a link.

ondragdrop

A `dragdrop` event occurs when the user drops an object, such as a file, onto the browser window.

The `ondragdrop` event handler works for the `window` object.

EXAMPLE

```
ondragdrop="send(newInfo)";
```

This passes the dropped object to a function called `send`. This could be preformatted data that the user can mail to you by dropping the file onto the Web page.

onfocus

The focus on a page is selected when the user either tabs to or clicks a field or an object on the page. Selecting within a field does not create a `focus` event; rather, it generates a `select` event. The `onfocus` event handler works for the `select`, `text`, and `textarea` objects.

EXAMPLE

```
onfocus="msgWindow.document.write('Tell me what you want!') ";
```

When the user clicks in the field object, the script writes out the phrase "Tell me what you want!"

onkeydown

A keydown event occurs as the user presses a keyboard key. This event precedes the keypress event. The onkeydown event handler works for the document, image, link, and textarea objects.

EXAMPLE

```
onkeydown="msgWindow.document.write('Tell me what you want!')";
```

When the user presses the key, the script writes out the phrase "Tell me what you want!"

onkeypress

A keypress event occurs when the user presses or holds a keyboard key. You can use this in combination with the fromCharCode and charCodeAt methods to determine which key was pressed. This is useful for operations where you prompt the user to press Y for yes and any other key for no.

The onkeypress event handler works for the document, image, link, and textarea objects.

EXAMPLE

```
onkeypress="msgWindow.document.write('Tell me what you want!') ";
```

When the user presses the key, the script writes out the phrase "Tell me what you want!"

onkeyup

A keyup event occurs when the user releases the keyboard key. You can use this to clear the results of the onkeypress or onkeydown event handlers.

The onkeyup event handler works for the document, image, link, and textarea objects.

EXAMPLE

```
onkeyup="msgWindow.document.write('Tell me what you want!')";
```

When the user releases the key, the script writes out the phrase "Tell me what you want!"

onload

A load event occurs when the browser receives all the page information, including framesets, and displays it. Locate the onload event handler inside the body or frameset elements. The onload event handler works for the window object.

EXAMPLE

```
<body onload="window.alert('Current as of ' +
    document.lastModified + '!')">
```

This example opens an alert window after the page is loaded and displays a message that includes the lastModified property. This gives the user the document's modification date.

onmousedown

A `mousedown` event occurs when the user presses one of the mouse buttons. You can use the event properties to determine which button was pressed.

The `onmousedown` event handler works for the `button`, `document`, and `link` objects.

EXAMPLE

```
onmousedown="msgWindow.document.write
   ('Tell me what you want!')";
```

When the user presses the mouse button, the script writes out the phrase "Tell me what you want!"

onmousemove

A `mousemove` event occurs when the user moves the mouse over any point on the page. This event handler does not work for any particular object, but it can be invoked if an object requests the event.

EXAMPLE

```
onmousemove="msgWindow.document.write
   ('Tell me what you want!')";
```

When the user moves the mouse, the script writes out the phrase "Tell me what you want!"

onmouseout

A `mouseout` event occurs when the user moves the mouse pointer off an object on the page. The `onmouseout` event handler defines what should happen when the user removes the mouse pointer from an object, such as a link.

The `onmouseout` event handler works for the `area`, `layer`, and `link` objects.

EXAMPLE

```
<a href="myFamily.html" onmouseout="alert
   ('Hey, we've got great pics down this way, come back!')">
Meet My Family</a>
```

When the user's mouse moves off the Meet My Family link, an alert box appears with the message "Hey, we've got great pics down this way, come back!"

onmouseover

A `mouseover` event occurs when the user passes the mouse pointer over an object on the page. You must return `True` within the `onmouseover` event handler if you want to set the `status` or `defaultStatus` property.

The `onmouseover` event handler works for the `area`, `layer`, and `link` objects. The `area` object is a type of `link` object that defines an area of an image as an image map. The `layer` object is part of the `document` object's `layers` array property, and is referenced by `id` or index value.

EXAMPLE

```
onmouseover="window.status="Come on in!"; return true";
```

When the user's mouse pointer passes over the object, the message "Come on in!" appears in the status line. You can also change the image in place, highlighting image links on the page.

```
<a href="intropage.html"
    onmouseover="document.pic1.src='images/jumpwild.jpg'"
    onmouseout="document.pic1.src='images/jump.jpg'"
    onclick="return true"></a>
```

In this example, the page displays the image `jump.jpg`, which is linked to the page `intropage`. When the user passes the mouse pointer over the image but does not click, the image changes to `jumpwild.jpg`. When the user clicks the image to jump, the return value of `True` is set by the `onclick` event handler before the jump is made.

onmouseup

A `mouseup` event occurs when the user releases the mouse button. The `onmouseup` event handler works for the `button`, `document`, and `link` objects.

EXAMPLE

```
<a href="myFamily.html" onmouseup="alert
    ('Hey, we've got great pics down this way, come back!')">
Meet My Family</a>
```

When the user's mouse button moves back up while over the Meet My Family link, an alert box appears with the message "Hey, we've got great pics down this way, come back!"

onmove

A `move` event occurs when the user or a browser-driven script moves a window or a frame.
The `onmove` event handler works for the `window` and `frame` objects.

EXAMPLE

```
onmove="window.status='Come on in!'";
```

When the window moves, the message "Come on in!" appears in the status line.

onselect

A `select` event occurs when the user highlights text inside a `text` or `textarea` field (the `onselect` event handler works for the `text` and `textarea` objects).

EXAMPLE

```
onselect="document.bgColor=blue";
```

The background color of the document changes to blue when the user selects text from the field.

onresize

A `resize` event occurs when the user or a browser-driven script changes the size of the window or frame.

The `onresize` event handler works for the `window` and `frame` objects.

EXAMPLE

```
onresize="window.status='Stop that!'";
```

When the window is resized, the message "Stop that!" appears in the status line.

onreset

Use the `onreset` event handler to act when the form is reset; it works for the `form` object.

EXAMPLE

```
<body>
<form name="form1" id="form1"
    onreset="alert('Please try again!')" … >
    <input type="text" name="newInTown" value="" size="100"
        maxlength="25" />
    <input type="Reset" name="Reset" value="Reset" />
</form>
```

This example prints a "Please try again!" alert box when the user resets the form.

onsubmit

When the document consists of one or more forms, use the `onsubmit` event handler to validate the contents of the form. This event handler works for the `form` object.

EXAMPLE

```
<script type="text/javascript" language="javascript">
    function hotelGuys (checksOut) {
        if (checksOut == "false") {
            alert("Please fill in all fields.");  }
        else {
            document.forms[0].submit();
            alert("We came here Jasper");  }  }
</script>
…
<form name="form1" id="form1"
    onsubmit="hotelGuys(checksOut = 'true')">
    <input type="text" name="newInTown" value="" size="100"
        maxlength="25" />
    <input type="submit" name="register" value="" />
</form>
```

This example uses an `if`/`else` statement either to request more information from the user or to submit the form. Normally, you wouldn't set the state in the call. You would call another function that would test the entries, and that function would then call `hotelGuys`.

onunload

Like the `load` event, the `unload` event occurs when the browser leaves a page. One good use for the `onunload` event handler is to clear any function variables you may have set into motion with the `onload` or other event handlers. The `onunload` event handler works for the `window` object.

EXAMPLE

```
<body onload="CountOn(4)" onunload="ClearCount()">…</body>
```

A counter starts when the page begins loading. You can use this to display a splash screen for a limited time. When the user leaves the page, the counter is reset to zero by the `ClearCount` function.

Properties

Properties affect objects. Unlike methods and functions, which do something within an object, properties assign attributes, such as appearance or size.

This section is an alphabetical listing of the JavaScript properties. Each entry describes a single property, includes syntax information and (typically) examples, and identifies which object the property affects.

action

The `action` property is part of the `form` object and contains the URL to which the `form` is submitted. You can set this property at any time. It has the following syntax:

```
formName.action=formActionText
```

The `formName` entry is either the form or an element from the `forms` array.

EXAMPLE

```
document.lesson3.action=http://www.example.com/L3results.htm
```

This example loads the URL `http://www.example.com/L3results.htm` into the `action` property for the form `lesson3`.

alinkColor

The `alinkColor` property is part of the `document` object and sets the color for an active link. Once the layout of the Web page is complete, this becomes a read-only property of the `document` object, so you cannot change the `alinkColor` property. The color is expressed in RGB hexadecimal (three sets of double hex digits) or as one of the color keywords. Place the code that sets this property before the `body` element, and do not use the `alink` attribute in the `body` element. The `alinkColor` property has the following syntax:

```
document.alinkColor="colorLiteral"
document.alinkColor="colorRGB"
```

EXAMPLE

```
document.alinkColor="green"
document.alinkColor="008000"
```

The two statements are equivalent. The first statement sets the `alinkColor` using the keyword green, which is 008000 in hex.

anchors

The `anchors` property is part of the `anchor` object and is the array of objects listing the named anchors in the source. The array lists the anchors in the order in which they appear in the document. The `anchors` property has the following syntax:

```
document.anchors[index]
document.anchors.length
```

The `index` entry is an integer that represents the anchor's position in the list; `length` returns the number of items in the array.

EXAMPLE
```
var visitor = document.anchors.length;
document.write("There are " + visitor +
    " links to other pages…can you visit them all?");
```

The script stores the number of anchors in the variable `visitor` and uses that in a statement written out for the user.

appCodeName

The `appCodeName` property is a read-only part of the `navigator` object. It has the following syntax:

```
navigator.appCodeName
```

EXAMPLE
```
var whoAreYou = navigator.appCodeName;
if(whoAreYou = "Mozilla") {
    document.write("Good job, carry on!");  }
```

This example gets the code name of the browser and, if it's Mozilla, writes a note to the user.

appName

The `appName` property is a read-only part of the `navigator` object. It has the following syntax:

```
navigator.appName
```

EXAMPLE
```
var whoAreYou = navigator.appName;
document.write("Hey! Good thing you're using " +
    whoAreYou + "!");
```

This example puts the application name into the variable `whoAreYou` and includes it in a statement displayed for the user.

appVersion

The appVersion property is a read-only part of the navigator object. It has the following syntax:

```
navigator.appVersion
```

The version is in the following format:

```
releaseNumber (platform; country)
```

EXAMPLE

```
document.write("You're checking us out with " +
    navigator.appVersion + ".");
```

This statement displays a result similar to this:

```
You're checking us out with 2.0 (Win95, I).
```

bgColor

The bgColor property is part of the document object and reflects the bgcolor attribute of the body element, but it can be changed at any time. The default for bgColor is in the user's browser preferences. The bgColor property has the following syntax:

```
document.bgColor="colorLiteral"
document.bgColor="colorRGB"
```

EXAMPLE

```
document.bgColor="darkblue"
document.bgColor="00008B"
```

These statements are equivalent. Both set the background color to dark blue—one through the keyword, and the other through the hex value for the color.

checked

The checked property is a Boolean value representing the state of a radio or checkbox object. True or 1 is checked; false or 0 is cleared. The checked property has the following syntax:

```
checkboxName.checked
radioName[index].checked
```

The checkboxName entry is the name attribute of a checkbox object. The radioName entry is the name attribute of a radio object. The index entry represents the radio button with the radio object.

EXAMPLE

```
<input type="radio" name="courseOption1" value="courseOption"
    checked="checked" onclick="techComm.checked = '1'" />
```

This example sets the checkbox for the techComm value of courseOption1 to checked when the user selects the courseOption1 radio button.

cookie

A cookie is information stored by the browser. The `cookie` property is part of a document object that you can read using the `substring`, `charAt`, `indexOf`, and `lastIndexOf` methods. You can also write information to a cookie. The `cookie` property has the following syntax:

```
document.cookie
```

EXAMPLE

```
document.cookie="expires in " + counter + " days";
```

This example assigns the string that reads "expires in *n* days"; *n* is the number of days remaining and is set with `counter`.

defaultChecked

The `defaultChecked` property is part of the `checkbox` and `radio` objects. It indicates the default state (checked or not checked) of a check box or radio button. You can read or set the property at any time. The `defaultChecked` property has the following syntax:

```
checkboxName.defaultChecked
radioName.[index].defaultChecked
```

EXAMPLE

```
document.chartForm.dataFocus[i].defaultChecked = true;
```

The statement sets the radio button at position i in the array to the default for the `dataFocus` group of buttons.

defaultSelected

This property is similar to the `defaultChecked` property; it indicates whether the option in a `select` object is the default selection. Only `multiple select` objects can have more than a single item selected. The `defaultSelected` property is part of the `options` array and has the following syntax:

```
selectName.options[index].defaultSelected
```

The `selectName` entry refers to the `select` object either by the `name` attribute or as an element within an array. The `index` entry is an integer representing an option in a `select` object.

EXAMPLE

```
<script type="text/javascript" language="javascript">
function backAgain () {
   alert(document.javajive.lessonList.length);
   for (var a = 0; a < document.javajive.lessonList.length;
      a++) {
      if (document.javajive.lessonList.options[a].
         defaultSelected == true) {
         document.javajive.lessonList.options[a].selected=true;
      } } }
```

```
</script>
...
<form name="javajive" id="javajive" onsubmit="backAgain ()">
    <select name="lessonList">
        <option selected="selected">Introduction</option>
        <option>Installation</option>
        <option>Setting up an account</option>
        <option>Creating a document</option>
        <option>Filing a document</option>
        <option>Recovering a filed document</option>
        <option>Sending a document to the printer</option>
    </select>
    <input type="submit" name="getchathere" value="Submit" />
</form>
```

In this example, the form contains a list of chapters in a book, from which the user can select a single item. The backAgain function cycles through the list of options to find the ones that should be selected by default and then resets the default.

defaultStatus

This property is part of the window object and contains the default message displayed in the status bar. You can set the defaultStatus property at any time. If you plan to use the status bar for an onmouseOver event handler statement, you must return True. The defaultStatus property has the following syntax:

```
windowReference.defaultStatus
```

The windowReference entry is one of the available window identifiers (such as self).

EXAMPLE

```
window.defaultStatus="Finish the modules in less than a week!";
```

The default contents for the status bar display are set to a phrase that complements the purpose of the site.

defaultValue

This property is part of the hidden, password, text, and textarea objects. It contains the default information for a password, text, or textarea object. If the object is a password, the initial value is null, regardless of the defaultValue. For a text object, the defaultValue reflects the value attribute. For textarea objects, it's the contents of the object found between the textarea tags.

If you set defaultValue through a script, it overrides the initial value. The immediate display value of the object is not changed when you modify the defaultValue through your script; if you later run a function that resets the defaults, your change appears.

The defaultValue property has the following syntax:

```
passwordName.defaultValue
textName.defaultValue
textareaName.defaultValue
```

EXAMPLE

```
document.javajive.lessonLeader.defaultValue="e. e. cummings";
…
<input type="reset" name="resetScoreCard"
    value="Reset the Scores" />
```

A line in your script changes the default value of the `lessonLeader text` object, and later in the script, the default values are reset. When this second line is executed, the contents of the `lessonLeader` text object is updated with "e. e. cummings".

E

This read-only `Math` property is approximately 2.718, which is Euler's constant, the base of natural logarithms. It's part of the `Math` object and has the following syntax:

```
Math.E
```

EXAMPLE

```
document.write("The base of natural logarithms is Euler's
    constant, which is: " + Math.E);
```

This statement displays the phrase followed by the value stored in the `E` property.

elements

The `elements` property is an array of the items in a form such as `checkbox`, `radio`, and `text` objects. These items are listed in the array in the order in which they occur. It has the following syntax:

```
document.form.elements[indexentry]
document.form.elements.length
document.forms[indexentry].elements[indexentry]
```

The `form` entry is a `form` object, `elements` is the array of items contained in the form, and `forms` is the array of all forms on the page. The `indexentry` entry is an integer representing the position of an element within an array, or the name of an array element.

EXAMPLE

```
var button1 = document.forms['form1'].elements['goNow'];
```

In this example, a variable named `button1` has been created to represent the button named `goNow` in the form named `form1`. If `form1` is the first form on the page and `goNow` is the third element in the form, the code could also be written as:

```
var button1 = document.forms[0].elements[2];
```

encoding

The `encoding` property is part of the `form` object and contains the MIME-encoding format information for the form. You can set the `encoding` property at any time; the initial value is the `enctype` attribute of the `form` element. The various encoding types may require specific values; check the specifications for the encoding type. The `encoding` property has the following syntax:

```
formName.encoding
```

EXAMPLE

```
function formEncode() { return document.javajive.encoding; }
```

The `formEncode` function gets the MIME-encoding information from the form.

fgColor

This property is part of the `document` object and specifies the foreground color of the text. You can express the color using one of the color keywords or the hexadecimal RGB value. This property uses the browser preference settings as its initial value. You can change this value by either setting the `color` attribute of the `font` element or by using the `fontcolor` method. The `fgColor` property has the following syntax:

```
document.fgColor
```

EXAMPLE

```
document.fgColor="darkred";
document.fgColor="8B0000";
```

These two statements are equivalent. The first uses the color keyword, and the second uses the hexadecimal RGB value for the same color.

forms

The `forms` property is an array that lists the objects in a form, in the order in which they occur in the code.

frames

The `frames` property is an array that lists the child frames within a frame.

hash

The `hash` property is part of the URL, and it identifies an anchor on the destination page. It's part of the `link` and `location` objects and has the following syntax:

```
location.hash
```

(See the examples for the `anchor` object and the `href` property.)

host

The `host` property is part of the URL and it identifies the `hostname:port` for the page. This property is a concatenation of the `hostname` and `port` properties. You can set the `host` property; it's better to set the `href` property, however, if you want to change a location. The `host` property is part of the `link` and `location` objects and has the following syntax:

```
links[index].host
location.host
```

(See the examples for the `link` and `location` objects.)

hostname

The hostname property is part of the URL and identifies the host server by its name or IP address. If the port property is null, the hostname and host properties are the same. The hostname property is part of the link and location objects and has the following syntax:

```
links[index].hostname
location.hostname
```

(See the examples for the link and location objects.)

href

The href property is part of the link and location objects and contains the full URL. The protocol, host, port, pathname, search, and hash properties are substrings within the href property, which has the following syntax:

```
links[index].href location.href
```

EXAMPLE

```
<script type="text/javascript" language="javascript">
var question1="false";
var question2="false";
var question3="false";
var question4="false";
var question5="false";
var question6="false";
var question7="false";
function roundTheClock() {
   for (var x = 0; x < 6; x++) {
      switch(x) {
         case(1): if (question1 != "true") {
           win1 = new window.open (answer1.location.href); }
           break;
         case(2): if (question2 != "true") {
           win2 = new window.open (answer2.location.href); }
           break;
         case(3): if (question3 != "true") {
           win3 = new window.open (answer3.location.href); }
           break;
         case(4): if (question4 != "true") {
           win4 = new window.open (answer4.location.href); }
           break;
         case(5): if (question5 != "true") {
           win5 = new window.open (answer5.location.href); }
           break;
```

```
            case(6): if (question6 != "true") {
              win6 = new window.open (answer6.location.href); }
              break;
            case(7): if (question7 != "true") {
              win7 = new window.open (answer7.location.href); }
              break;  }  }  }
</script>
```

In this example, the loop opens a series of windows containing the answers to questions that the user answered incorrectly.

index

The `index` property is part of the `options` array. It's an integer value that gives the position of an object within the `options` array of a `select` object. The `index` property has the following syntax:

```
selectName.options[indexValue].index
```

The `selectName` entry is the name of the `select` object or element in the `elements` array. The `indexValue` entry is an integer representing the `option` in a `select` object.

EXAMPLE

```
for (var x = 0; x < document.jivejingle.courseSelect.length;
    x++) {
    document.write(
        document.jivejingle.courseSelect.options[x].index);  }
```

This example displays the contents of the list of `courseSelect`.

Infinity

The `Infinity` property (primitive value) represents a positive infinite `value.lastModified`

The `lastModified` property is part of the `document` object. It's a read-only date string indicating when the document was last changed or updated and has the following syntax:

```
document.lastModified
```

EXAMPLE

```
<script type="text/javascript" language="javascript">
document.write(
    "Welcome, this course description is current as of " +
    document.lastModified);
</script>
```

This script keeps the date current without manual intervention.

length

The `length` property works with objects and arrays; you can use it to get the number of elements within the object or array. It has the following syntax:

Statement	Returns the Number Of
`formName.length`	Elements on a form
`frameReference.length`	Frames within a frame
`History.length`	Entries in the `history` object
`radioName.length`	Buttons within a `radio` object
`select.Name.length`	Objects in a `select` list object
`stringName.length`	Character spaces in a `string`
`windowReference.length`	Frames in a parent window
`anchors.length`	Entries in the stated array
`elements.length`	Entries in the stated array
`forms.length`	Entries in the stated array
`frameReference.frames.length`	Entries in the stated array
`windowReference.frames.length`	Entries in the stated array
`links.length`	Entries in the stated array
`selectName.options.length`	Entries in the stated array

The `length` property is found in the following objects and arrays:

Objects	Arrays
frame	anchors
history	elements
radio	forms
select	frames
string	links
window	options

EXAMPLE

```
var visitor = document.anchors.length document.write(
    "There are " + visitor +
    " links to other pages…can you visit them all?");
```

In this example, the script stores the number of anchors in the variable `visitor` and uses that in a statement displayed to the user.

linkColor

The `linkColor` property is part of the `document` object. It contains the setting for the inactive and unused links in a document. This property reflects the setting in the `body` element of a document. After the layout, this is a read-only property. To set this property in a script, place the code before the `body` element, and do not use the `link` attribute in the `body` element. The `linkColor` property has the following syntax:

```
document.linkColor
```

EXAMPLE

```
document.write("The " + document.linkColor +
    " jumps are places you've never been!");
```

This statement displays the link color for the user.

links

The `links` property is an array of document links listed in source order.

LN2

The `LN2` property is part of the built-in `Math` object. It's a read-only constant that represents the natural logarithm of 2 (approximately 0.693) and has the following syntax:

```
Math.LN2
```

EXAMPLE

```
document.write("Bob says your chances of winning are: " +
    longShot + " in " + longShot / Math.LN2 + ".");
```

This example computes a value and displays the results in a statement for the user.

LN10

The `LN10` property is part of the built-in `Math` object. It's a read-only constant that represents the natural logarithm of 10 (approximately 2.302) and has the following syntax:

```
Math.LN10
```

EXAMPLE

```
document.write("Bob says your chances of winning are: " +
    longShot + " in " + longShot * Math.LN10 + ".");
```

This example computes a value and displays the results in a statement for the user.

location

The `location` property is part of the `document` object. It contains the complete URL of the document. Unlike with the `location` object, you cannot change the document's `location` property. The `location` property has the following syntax:

```
document.location
```

EXAMPLE

```
<script type="text/javascript" language="javascript">
    var there="http://www.example.com/";
    var takeLesson="";
    function weAre() {
        self.status = 'Welcome, this is ' + document.location +
        '. Our site is NEVER done!';  }
    function checkThis() { alert("Thanks for registering"); }
</script>
…<body onload="window.alert('Welcome!'); weAre()">…</body>
```

This displays a notice to the user, including the document's location, in the status line of the window.

LOG2E

The LOG2E property is part of the built-in Math object. It's a read-only constant that represents the base 2 logarithm of E (approximately 1.442). It has the following syntax:

```
Math.LOG2E
```

EXAMPLE

```
document.write("Bob says your chances of winning are: " +
    longShot + " in " + longShot * Math.LOG2E + ".");
```

This example computes a value and displays the results in a statement for the user.

LOG10E

The LOG10E property is part of the built-in Math object. It's a read-only constant that represents the base 10 logarithm of E (approximately 0.434). It has the following syntax:

MATH.LOG10EEXAMPLE

```
document.write("Bob says your chances of winning are: " +
    longShot + " in " + longShot / Math.LOG10E + ".");
```

This example computes a value and displays the results in a statement for the user.

method

The method property is part of the form object. It indicates how a form is sent to the server when it's submitted. This reflects the contents of the method attribute of the form element. This property contains either get or post. You can set this property at any time. The method property has the following syntax:

```
formName.method
```

EXAMPLE

```
if (document.javajive.method == "get") {
    document.write("The server will get your answers now."); }
else {
    document.write(
        "Your answers will be posted to the server now."); }
```

This example displays different text depending on the method.

name

This property is used to identify the objects and elements contained by a number of objects and arrays. For window objects, this is a read-only property; you can set the name of other objects.

In a window object, the name reflects the windowName attribute. In other objects, it reflects the name attribute. The name property is the same for all radio buttons in a radio object.

The name property differs from the label used for the button, reset, and submit objects. The name property is not displayed; it's an internal, programmatic reference.

If a frame object contains several elements or objects with the same name, the browser creates an array using the name and listing the objects as they occur in the frame source.

The name property has the following syntax for window objects:

```
windowReference.name
window.Reference.frames.name
```

The name property has the following syntax for other objects:

```
objectName.name
frameReference.name
frameReference.frames.name
radioName[index].name
selectName.options.name
```

For a select object, objectName.name and selectName.options.name produce the same result. For a frame object, objectName.name, frameReference.name, and frameReference.frames.name produce the same result.

EXAMPLE

```
newWindow = window.open("http://www.webwonders.net/test1.htm");
function whatYouBuilt () {
    for (var counter = 0, counter < document.elements.length,
        counter++) {
        msgWindow.document.write(
            document.sample.elements[counter].name + "<br />");
    }  }
```

In this example, the function loops through the loaded document and displays a list of the elements.

The name property is found in the options array and in the following objects:

button	hidden	reset	text
checkbox	password	select	Textarea
frame	radio	submit	window

NaN

The NaN property determines whether the value given is a number. Use the isNaN method to check the (Boolean) value of NaN.

options

The options property is an array that contains a list of the options in a select object.

parent

The parent property is one of the synonyms available for referencing a window that contains the current frame. This is a read-only property for the window and frame objects. You can use this property when referencing one frame from another within a window or parent frame. It has the following syntax:

```
parent.propertyName
parent.methodName
top.frameName
top.frames[index]
```

The propertyName entry is the defaultStatus, status, length, name, or parent property. This could also be the length, name, or parent property when the reference is from a parent to a frame. The methodName entry is any method associated with the window object. (See the window object entry for more information about the available methods.) The frameName and frames[index] entries reference individual frames by either their name value or their position in an array of frames.

EXAMPLE

```
<input type="button" name="doItButton" value="Make it so!"
  onclick="parent.frames[1].document.bgColor=colorChoice" />
```

This example is part of the frame object example. In this statement, the background color of the sibling (index value 1, or the second element in the frames array) of the current frame is set to the user's color choice.

pathname

The pathname property is part of the link and location objects. It's the portion of the URL that indicates the directory location for the page on the server. You can set the pathname property at any time, but if you need to change the document pathname, it's safer to use the href property. The pathname property has the following syntax:

```
location.pathname
```

(See the examples for the location object.)

PI

The PI property is part of the built-in Math object. It's a read-only constant that represents the ratio of circle circumference to diameter (approximately 3.14). The PI property has the following syntax:

MATH.PIEXAMPLE

```
document.write("Bob says your chances of winning are: " +
    longShot + " in " + longShot * Math.PI + ".");
```

This example computes a value and displays the results in a statement for the user.

port

The port property is part of the link and location objects. It's the port element in the URL and identifies the port, if any, used on the server. If this property is null, the host and hostname properties are the same. The port property has the following syntax:

```
location.port
```

(See the example for the location object.)

protocol

The protocol property is part of the link and location objects. It's part of the URL and uses the following protocols:

Protocol	Description
file	Accesses a local file system
ftp	Uses FTP (File Transfer Protocol)
gopher	Uses the gopher protocol
http	Uses HTTP (Hypertext Transfer Protocol)
mailto	Uses SMTP (Simple Mail Transfer Protocol)
news	Uses NNTP (Network News Transfer Protocol)
snews	Uses the secure NNTP protocol
https	Uses the secure HTTP protocol
telnet	Uses the telnet protocol
tn3270	Uses the 3270 telnet protocol

The port property has the following syntax:

```
location.protocol
```

(See the examples for the link and location objects.)

referrer

The `referrer` property is part of the `document` object. It's a read-only property of the `document` object that contains the originating document URL when a user jumps from an originating document to a destination document. The `referrer` property has the following syntax:

```
document.referrer
```

EXAMPLE

```
document.write("Welcome, I see you joined us from " +
   document.referrer + ". How's the weather back there?");
```

This statement displays a message for the user that includes the location URL of the original document.

search

The `search` property is found in the `link` and `location` objects. It's part of the URL; although you can change this property at any time, it's best to use the `href` property to change `location` attributes. The `search` property has the following syntax:

```
location.search
```

EXAMPLE

```
newWindow = window.open
   ("http://www.example.com/Look/scripts?qt=property=elements");
with (document) {
   write("The href property is " +
      newWindow.location.href + "<br />");
   write("The protocol property is " +
      newWindow.location.protocol + "<br />");
   write(vThe host property is " +
      newWindow.location.host + "<br />");
   write("The host name is " +
      newWindow.location.hostName + "<br />");
   write("The port property is " +
      newWindow.location.port + "<br />");
   write("The pathname property is" +
      newWindow.location.pathname + "<br />");
   write("The search property is " +
      newWindow.location.search + "<br />");
   write("The hash property is " +
      newWindow.location.hash + "<br />");
   close();   }
```

which displays the following:

```
The href property is http://www.example.com/Look/scripts?qt=
property=elements
The protocol property is http:
The host property is www.example.com
```

```
The host name is www.example.com
The port property is
The pathname property is /Look/scripts
The search property is ?qt=property=elements
The hash property is
```

selected

The `selected` property is part of the `options` array. It contains a Boolean value that indicates whether the `option` in a `select` object is currently selected. For selected options, this property is `True`. You can set this property programmatically. It has the following syntax:

```
selectName.options[index].selected
```

EXAMPLE
```
for (x = document.saleForm.buyTheseThings.length; x > 0; x--) {
  if (document.saleForm.buyTheseThings.options[x].selected =
     "true") {
     document.saleForm.buyTheseThings.options[x].selected =
     "false"; }
  else {
     document.saleForm.buyTheseThings.options[x].selected =
     "true"; }  }
```

In this example, the `for` loop traverses the list of options altering the selections. The result is an inversion of the user's selections.

selectedIndex

The `selectedIndex` property is part of the `select` object and the `options` array. It contains information about the order in which a `select` object was defined. You can set the `selectedIndex` property at any time, and the displayed information is updated. The `selectedIndex` property works well with `select` objects that are not `multiple select` objects. It has the following syntax:

```
selectName.selectedIndex
selectName.options.selectedIndex
```

EXAMPLE
```
function whatSelection () {
   return document.saleForm.giveAwayOptions.selectedIndex; }
```

This simple function brings back the selection from the list of options.

self

The `self` property is part of the `window` object. This property is a synonym for the current window or `frame` object. Use this read-only property to help keep your code clear. It has the following syntax:

```
self.propertyName
self.methodName
```

EXAMPLE

```
self.javatest.whichIsFunction.index[x];
document.javatest.whichIsFunction.index[x];
```

These two statements are equivalent.

SQRT1_2

The SQRT1_2 property is part of the built-in Math object. It's a read-only constant that represents the inverse of the square root of 2 (approximately 0.707). It has the following syntax:

```
Math.SQRT1_2
```

EXAMPLE

```
document.write("Bob says your chances of winning are: " +
    longShot + " in " + longShot / Math.SQRT1_2 + ".");
```

This example computes a value and displays the results in a statement for the user.

SQRT2

The SQRT2 property is part of the built-in Math object. It's a read-only constant that represents the square root of 2 (approximately 1.414). It has the following syntax:

```
Math.SQRT2
```

EXAMPLE

```
document.write("Bob says your chances of winning are: " +
    longShot + " in " + longShot * Math.SQRT2 + ".");
```

This example computes a value and displays the results in a statement for the user.

status

The status property is part of the window object. It contains a priority or transient message that is displayed in the status bar of the window. It has the following syntax:

```
windowReference.status
```

EXAMPLE

```
self.status = "Welcome to our little home away from home!";
```

This example puts the message onto the window's status line.

target

The target property is part of the form, link, and location objects. For the link and location objects, the target property contains the window name for a jump. It works slightly differently for the form object: it contains the destination for form submissions. Although you can set the target property at any time, it cannot assume the value of an expression or a variable (meaning you can't build those fancy statements such as `document.write`). The `target` property has the following syntax:

```
formName.target
linkName.target
```

EXAMPLE

```
self.status("When you submit your request, the information
   will appear in " + self.buyTheseThings.target + ".");
```

This statement displays a message in the window status bar telling users where their selections will appear. This is useful if you want to confirm the request before displaying the information.

text

The `text` property is part of the `options` array. It's the displayed value in an options list. If you change the `text` property for an option list, the display character, initially set in the `option` element, does not change, but the internal information does change. The `text` property has the following syntax:

```
selectName.options[index].text
```

EXAMPLE

```
for (x = 0; x < self.javajive.pickMe.length; x++) {
   if (self.javajive.pickMe.option[x].select == true) {
      document.write(self.javajive.pickMe.option[x].text); } }
```

This example tests to see whether the option has been selected; if it has, it displays the option text. If you change the `text` property programmatically, the resulting list is different from the list of options the user sees and selects from.

title

The `title` property is part of the `document` object. It reflects the value of the `title` element, and you cannot change this value. The `title` property has the following syntax:

```
document.title
```

EXAMPLE

```
self.status(self.title);
```

top

The `top` property is part of the `window` object. It's a read-only synonym for the topmost window and has the following syntax:

```
top.propertyName
top.methodName
top.frameName
top.frames[index]
```

The `propertyName` entry is `defaultStatus`, `status`, or `length`. The `methodName` entry is any `window` method. The `frameName` and `frames[index]` entries are frame references for frames within the window.

EXAMPLE

```
top.close();
```

This closes the topmost window.

```
for (x = 0, x < top.length, x++) {
    top.frame[x].close(); }
```

This closes all the frames on a page.

undefined

The `undefined` property (primitive value) is the value of a variable that has not been assigned a specific value.

userAgent

The `userAgent` property is part of the `navigator` object. It's part of the HTTP information. Servers use this property to identify the client browser. The `userAgent` property has the following syntax:

```
navigator.userAgent
```

EXAMPLE

```
document.write("You're using " + navigator.userAgent + ".");
```

This displays the browser information, as in:

```
You're using Mozilla/4.0 (compatible; MSIE 5.5; Windows 98).
```

value

The `value` property differs for the various objects. In all cases, it reflects the `value` attribute of the object.

For `hidden`, `password`, `text`, and `textarea` objects or for an item in the `options` array, you can programmatically change the property. If you change it for the `text` and `textarea` objects, the display updates immediately. If you change it for the `password` object, security could give you some pause. If you evaluate your changes, you'll get the current value back; if a user changes it, security will not pass the changes. For the `options` array, the `value` attribute is not displayed but is an internal representation.

For the `button`, `reset`, and `submit` objects, the `value` property is a read-only reflection of the text on the face of the button.

For `checkbox` and `radio` objects, the `value` property is returned to the server when the check box or radio button is selected. It's not the value of the selection; it's simply On or Off.

The `value` property has the following syntax:

```
objectName.value
radioName[index].value
selectName.options.[index].value
```

(For examples of the `value` property, see the appropriate object entry.)
The `value` property is part of the `options` array and of the following objects:

button	password	Submit
checkbox	radio	Text
hidden	reset	Textarea

vLinkColor

The `vLinkColor` is a part of the `document` object. It contains the color settings for the links on the page that have been visited. To set this value programmatically, place your script before the `body` element; once the layout has been done, this becomes a read-only property. If you do set the property in a script, do not use the `vlink` attribute of the `body` element. To set the color, use either the color keyword or a hexadecimal RGB number (three double digits). The `vLinkColor` has the following syntax:

```
document.vLinkColor="colorLiteral"
document.vLinkColor="colorRGB"
```

EXAMPLE

```
document.vlinkColor="red"
document.vlinkColor="ff0000"
```

The two statements are equivalent. The first statement sets the `vlinkColor` using the keyword `red`, which is `ff0000` in hex.

window

The `window` property is part of the `frame` and `window` objects. It's a synonym for the current window. Although you can use the `window` property to refer to the current frame, it's better to use the `self` property in that situation. This property is read-only and has the following syntax:

```
window.propertyName
window.methodName(parameters)
```

EXAMPLE

```
window.status="Welcome to our humble home away from home!";
```

This example displays the message in the status bar.

HTML and XHTML Special Characters

HTML AND XHTML DOCUMENTS include only a limited set of plain-text characters—alphanumeric characters (letters and numbers) and some punctuation characters. You'll probably find that these plain-text characters will meet most of your needs. Occasionally, though, you will need to use other characters—such as a tilde (~), the copyright symbol (©), or even some of the special characters that normally delimit HTML or XHTML markup (such as < or >). You can include these and other special characters just by using a bit of code to define them, as we'll describe in this reference.

TIP You might refer to the following chapters as you're reading this section:

Chapter 2 (as you develop basic HTML or XHTML)

Chapter 20 (to validate your use of special characters)

As you'll see, including special characters is straightforward and similar to including the HTML or XHTML code you've been applying throughout this book. Rather than using angle brackets and letters as you do for HTML and XHTML markup, however, you'll use a short string of code to represent one special character. For example, to include a copyright symbol in your document, you would type

```
&#169;
```

So a sample line of code might look like this:

```
<p>Site Copyright &#169; 1997-2002 RayComm, Inc.</p>
```

A Web browser would display:

```
Site Copyright © 1997-2002 RayComm, Inc.
```

TIP *If you type in a special symbol and the symbol doesn't appear (or appear correctly) in the browser, check to make sure that you included the semicolon (;) at the end. It's easy to leave off that final tidbit when typing in the character string.*

TIP *Many of the character entities also have an equivalent mnemonic version that might be easier to remember and use. For example, rather than using ©, you could use © for a copyright symbol. However, test carefully in a variety of browsers, because support for the mnemonic versions isn't complete or predictable.*

Next, we'll look at types of special characters, list the character strings, and discuss character sets.

HTML and XHTML Entities

In the specialized language associated with HTML and XHTML (and other markup languages, including XML and SGML), the strings that produce special characters when interpreted and rendered by a Web browser are called *entities*. Entities come in two forms:

Mnemonic entities   Such an entity refers to a character by some name. For example, the mnemonic entity for a quotation mark is ", and the mnemonic entity for the left angle bracket, < (also known as the less-than symbol), is <.

Numeric entities   Such an entity refers to a character using a numeric code. The numeric entity that represents the quotation mark is ", and the numeric entity that represents the left angle bracket is <.

These entities are often necessary to alert browsers that you want to use a character as plain text, not as markup, computer data, or programming instructions. For example, the left angle bracket (<) denotes the beginning of a markup element, so if you just type <, browsers will assume that what follows is markup. If you have text that must be surrounded by angle brackets when viewed by users (like <this>), you signal it by typing <this>.

Entities always begin with an ampersand (&) and end with a semicolon (;):

◆ Mnemonic entities use names between those two bracketing characters, as in ".

◆ Numeric entities follow the opening ampersand with a pound sign (#) before the numeric code and also end with a semicolon, as in ©.

Entity Reference

Tables MR4.1 and MR4.2 show many of the more common entities and how to use them in HTML or XHTML. As a rule, give these a try first, and only resort to the DTD and official specifications if these entities do not meet your needs (be sure to test in various browsers, of course).

The characters in Table MR4.2 were included in HTML 2 and HTML 3.2 and are also included in the current HTML specification. Most browsers should display these characters, based on either the mnemonic or numeric representation.

TABLE MR4.1: STANDARD HTML CHARACTERS

SYMBOL	MNEMONIC REPRESENTATION	NUMERIC REPRESENTATION	DESCRIPTION
			No-break space
¡	&iexcl;	&#161;	Inverted exclamation mark
¢	&cent;	&#162;	Cent
£	&pound;	&#163;	Pound sterling
	&curren;	&#164;	General currency
¥	&yen;	&#165;	Yen
¦	&brvbar;	&#166;	Broken (vertical) bar
§	&sect;	&#167;	Section
¨	&uml;	&#168;	Umlaut (diaeresis)
©	&copy;	&#169;	Copyright sign
ª	&ordf;	&#170;	Ordinal indicator, feminine
«	&laquo;	&#171;	Angle quotation mark, left
¬	&not;	&#172;	Not
	&shy;	&#173;	Soft hyphen
®	&reg;	&#174;	Registered
¯	&macr;	&#175;	Macron
°	&deg;	&#176;	Degree
±	&plusmn;	&#177;	Plus-or-minus
²	&sup2;	&#178;	Superscript two
³	&sup3;	&#179;	Superscript three
´	&acute;	&#180;	Acute accent
µ	&micro;	&#181;	Micro
¶	&para;	&#182;	Pilcrow (paragraph)
·	&middot;	&#183;	Middle dot
¸	&cedil;	&#184;	Cedilla
¹	&sup1;	&#185;	Superscript one
¼	&frac14;	&#188;	Fraction one-quarter
º	&ordm;	&#186;	Ordinal indicator, masculine

Continued on next page

TABLE MR4.1: STANDARD HTML CHARACTERS *(continued)*

SYMBOL	MNEMONIC REPRESENTATION	NUMERIC REPRESENTATION	DESCRIPTION
»	&raquo;	&#187;	Angle quotation mark, right
½	&frac12;	&#189;	Fraction one-half
¾	&frac34;	&#190;	Fraction three-quarters
¿	&iquest;	&#191;	Inverted question mark
À	&Agrave;	&#192;	Uppercase A, grave accent
Á	&Aacute;	&#193;	Uppercase A, acute accent
Â	&Acirc;	&#194;	Uppercase A, circumflex
Ã	&Atilde;	&#195;	Uppercase A, tilde
Ä	&Auml;	&#196;	Uppercase A, diaeresis or umlaut mark
Å	&Aring;	&#197;	Uppercase A, angstrom
Æ	&AElig;	&#198;	Uppercase AE diphthong (ligature)
Ç	&Ccedil;	&#199;	Uppercase C, cedilla
È	&Egrave;	&#200;	Uppercase E, grave accent
É	&Eacute;	&#201;	Uppercase E, acute accent
Ê	&Ecirc;	&#202;	Uppercase E, circumflex
Ë	&Euml;	&#203;	Uppercase E, umlaut (diaeresis)
Ì	&Igrave;	&#204;	Uppercase I, grave accent
Í	&Iacute;	&#205;	Uppercase I, acute accent
Î	&Icirc;	&#206;	Uppercase I, circumflex
Ï	&Iuml;	&#207;	Uppercase I, umlaut (diaresis)
Ð	&ETH;	&#208;	Uppercase Eth, Icelandic
Ñ	&Ntilde;	&#209;	Uppercase N, tilde
Ò	&Ograve;	&#210;	Uppercase O, grave accent
Ó	&Oacute;	&#211;	Uppercase O, acute accent
Ô	&Ocirc;	&#212;	Uppercase O, circumflex
Õ	&Otilde;	&#213;	Uppercase O, tilde
Ö	&Ouml;	&#214;	Uppercase O, umlaut (diaresis)
×	&times;	&#215;	Multiplication

Continued on next page

TABLE MR4.1: STANDARD HTML CHARACTERS *(continued)*

SYMBOL	MNEMONIC REPRESENTATION	NUMERIC REPRESENTATION	DESCRIPTION
Ø	&Oslash;	&#216;	Uppercase O, slash
Ù	&Ugrave;	&#217;	Uppercase U, grave accent
Ú	&Uacute;	&#218;	Uppercase U, acute accent
Û	&Ucirc;	&#219;	Uppercase U, circumflex
Ü	&Uuml;	&#220;	Uppercase U, umlaut (diaresis)
Ý	&Yacute;	&#221;	Uppercase Y, acute accent
þ	&THORN;	&#222;	Uppercase THORN, Icelandic
ß	&szlig;	&#223;	Small sharp s, German
à	&agrave;	&#224;	Lowercase a, grave accent
á	&aacute;	&#225;	Lowercase a, acute accent
â	&acirc;	&#226;	Lowercase a, circumflex
ã	&atilde;	&#227;	Lowercase a, tilde
ä	&auml;	&#228;	Lowercase a, umlaut (diaresis)
å	&aring;	&#229;	Lowercase a, angstrom
æ	&aelig;	&#230;	Lowercase ae diphthong (ligature)
ç	&ccedil;	&#231;	Lowercase c, cedilla
è	&egrave;	&#232;	Lowercase e, grave accent
é	&eacute;	&#233;	Lowercase e, acute accent
ê	&ecirc;	&#234;	Lowercase e, circumflex
ë	&euml;	&#235;	Lowercase e, umlaut (diaresis)
ì	&igrave;	&#236;	Lowercase i, grave accent
í	&iacute;	&#237;	Lowercase i, acute accent
î	&icirc;	&#238;	Lowercase i, circumflex
ï	&iuml;	&#239;	Lowercase i, umlaut (diaresis)
ð	&eth;	&#240;	Lowercase eth, Icelandic
ñ	&ntilde;	&#241;	Lowercase n, tilde
ò	&ograve;	&#242;	Lowercase o, grave accent
ó	&oacute;	&#243;	Lowercase o, acute accent

Continued on next page

TABLE MR4.1: STANDARD HTML CHARACTERS *(continued)*

SYMBOL	MNEMONIC REPRESENTATION	NUMERIC REPRESENTATION	DESCRIPTION
ô	&ocirc;	&#244;	Lowercase o, circumflex
õ	&otilde;	&#245;	Lowercase o, tilde
ö	&ouml;	&#246;	Lowercase o, umlaut (diaresis)
÷	&divide;	&#247;	Division
ø	&oslash;	&#248;	Lowercase o, slash
ù	&ugrave;	&#249;	Lowercase u, grave accent
ú	&uacute;	&#250;	Lowercase u, acute accent
û	&ucirc;	&#251;	Lowercase u, circumflex
ü	&uuml;	&#252;	Lowercase u, umlaut (diaresis)
ý	&yacute;	&#253;	Lowercase y, acute accent
þ	&thorn;	&#254;	Lowercase thorn, Icelandic
ÿ	&yuml;	&#255;	Lowercase y, umlaut(diaresis)

Portions © International Organization for Standardization 1986: Permission to copy in any form is granted for use with conforming SGML systems and applications as defined in ISO 8879, provided this notice is included in all copies.

TABLE MR4.2: EXTENDED HTML AND XHTML CHARACTERS

SYMBOL	MNEMONIC REPRESENTATION	NUMERIC REPRESENTATION	DESCRIPTION
Œ	&OElig;	&#338;	Latin uppercase ligature Œ
œ	&oelig;	&#339;	Latin lowercase ligature œ
Š	&Scaron;	&#352;	Latin uppercase S with caron
š	&scaron;	&#353;	Latin lowercase s with caron
Ÿ	&Yuml;	&#376;	Latin uppercase Y with umlaut
ƒ	&fnof;	&#402;	Latin lowercase f with hook
ˆ	&circ;	&#710;	Modifier letter circumflex
˜	&tilde;	&#732;	Small tilde
Α	&Alpha;	&#913;	Greek uppercase alpha
Β	&Beta;	&#914;	Greek uppercase beta

Continued on next page

TABLE MR4.2: EXTENDED HTML AND XHTML CHARACTERS *(continued)*

SYMBOL	MNEMONIC REPRESENTATION	NUMERIC REPRESENTATION	DESCRIPTION
Γ	&Gamma;	&#915;	Greek uppercase gamma
Δ	&Delta;	&#916;	Greek uppercase delta
Ε	&Epsilon;	&#917;	Greek uppercase epsilon
Ζ	&Zeta;	&#918;	Greek uppercase zeta
Η	&Eta;	&#919;	Greek uppercase eta
Θ	&Theta;	&#920;	Greek uppercase theta
Ι	&Iota;	&#921;	Greek uppercase iota
Κ	&Kappa;	&#922;	Greek uppercase kappa
Λ	&Lambda;	&#923;	Greek uppercase lambda
Μ	&Mu;	&#924;	Greek uppercase mu
Ν	&Nu;	&#925;	Greek uppercase nu
Ξ	&Xi;	&#926;	Greek uppercase xi
Ο	&Omicron;	&#927;	Greek uppercase omicron
Π	&Pi;	&#928;	Greek uppercase pi
Ρ	&Rho;	&#929;	Greek uppercase rho
Σ	&Sigma;	&#931;	Greek uppercase sigma
Τ	&Tau;	&#932;	Greek uppercase tau
Υ	&Upsilon;	&#933;	Greek uppercase upsilon
Φ	&Phi;	&#934;	Greek uppercase phi
Χ	&Chi;	&#935;	Greek uppercase chi
Ψ	&Psi;	&#936;	Greek uppercase psi
Ω	&Omega;	&#937;	Greek uppercase omega
α	&alpha;	&#945;	Greek lowercase alpha
β	&beta;	&#946;	Greek lowercase beta
λ	&gamma;	&#947;	Greek lowercase gamma
δ	&delta;	&#948;	Greek lowercase delta
ε	&epsilon;	&#949;	Greek lowercase epsilon
ζ	&zeta;	&#950;	Greek lowercase zeta

Continued on next page

TABLE MR4.2: EXTENDED HTML AND XHTML CHARACTERS *(continued)*

SYMBOL	MNEMONIC REPRESENTATION	NUMERIC REPRESENTATION	DESCRIPTION
η	&eta;	&#951;	Greek lowercase eta
ϑ	&theta;	&#952;	Greek lowercase theta
ι	&iota;	&#953;	Greek lowercase iota
κ	&kappa;	&#954;	Greek lowercase kappa
λ	&lambda;	&#955;	Greek lowercase lambda
μ	&mu;	&#956;	Greek lowercase mu
ν	&nu;	&#957;	Greek lowercase nu
ξ	&xi;	&#958;	Greek lowercase xi
ο	&omicron;	&#959;	Greek lowercase omicron
π	&pi;	&#960;	Greek lowercase pi
ρ	&rho;	&#961;	Greek lowercase rho
ς	&sigmaf;	&#962;	Greek lowercase final sigma
σ	&sigma;	&#963;	Greek lowercase sigma
τ	&tau;	&#964;	Greek lowercase tau
υ	&upsilon;	&#965;	Greek lowercase upsilon
φ	&phi;	&#966;	Greek lowercase phi
χ	&chi;	&#967;	Greek lowercase chi
ψ	&psi;	&#968;	Greek lowercase psi
ω	&omega;	&#969;	Greek lowercase omega
θ	&thetasym;	&#977;	Greek lowercase theta symbol
ϒ	&upsih;	&#978;	Greek upsilon with hook symbol
π	&piv;	&#982;	Greek pi
			En space
			Em space
			Thin space
–	&ndash;	&#8211;	En dash
—	&mdash;	&#8212;	Em dash
‘	&lsquo;	&#8216;	left single quotation mark

Continued on next page

TABLE MR4.2: EXTENDED HTML AND XHTML CHARACTERS *(continued)*

SYMBOL	MNEMONIC REPRESENTATION	NUMERIC REPRESENTATION	DESCRIPTION
'	&rsquo;	&#8217;	right single quotation mark
‚	&sbquo;	&#8218;	Single low-9 quotation mark
"	&ldquo;	&#8220;	Left double quotation mark
"	&rdquo;	&#8221;	Right double quotation mark
„	&bdquo;	&#8222;	double low-9 quotation mark
†	&dagger;	&#8224;	Dagger
‡	&Dagger;	&#8225;	Double dagger
•	&bull;	&#8226;	Bullet (black small circle)
…	&hellip;	&#8230;	Horizontal ellipsis (three-dot leader)
‰	&permil;	&#8240;	Per mille sign
′	&prime;	&#8242;	Prime (minutes or feet)
″	&Prime;	&#8243;	Double prime (seconds or inches)
‹	&lsaquo;	&#8249;	Single left-pointing angle quotation mark
›	&rsaquo;	&#8250;	Single right-pointing angle quotation mark
—	&oline;	&#8254;	Overline (spacing overscore)
/	&frasl;	&#8260;	Fraction slash
ℑ	&image;	&#8465;	Blackletter Uppercase I (imaginary part)
℘	&weierp;	&#8472;	Script Uppercase P (power set or Weierstrass p)
ℜ	&real;	&#8476;	Blackletter Uppercase R (real part symbol)
™	&trade;	&#8482;	Trademark
ℵ	&alefsym;	&#8501;	Alef (first transfinite cardinal)
←	&larr;	&#8592;	left arrow
↑	&uarr;	&#8593;	Up arrow
→	&rarr;	&#8594;	Right arrow
↓	&darr;	&#8595;	Down arrow
↔	&harr;	&#8596;	Left-right arrow

Continued on next page

TABLE MR4.2: EXTENDED HTML AND XHTML CHARACTERS *(continued)*

SYMBOL	MNEMONIC REPRESENTATION	NUMERIC REPRESENTATION	DESCRIPTION
↵	&crarr;	&#8629;	Down arrow with corner Left (carriage return)
⇐	&lArr;	&#8656;	Left double arrow
⇑	&uArr;	&#8657;	Up double arrow
⇒	&rArr;	&#8658;	Right double arrow
⇓	&dArr;	&#8659;	Down double arrow
⇔	&hArr;	&#8660;	Left-right double arrow
∀	&forall;	&#8704;	For all
∂	&part;	&#8706;	Partial differential
∃	&exist;	&#8707;	There exists
∅	&empty;	&#8709;	Empty set (null set or diameter)
∇	&nabla;	&#8711;	Nabla (backward difference)
∈	&isin;	&#8712;	Element of
∉	&notin;	&#8713;	Not an element of
∋	&ni;	&#8715;	Contains as member
∏	&prod;	&#8719;	n-ary product (product sign)
Σ	&sum;	&#8721;	N-ary sumation
-	&minus;	&#8722;	Minus
∗	&lowast;	&#8727;	Asterisk operator
√	&radic;	&#8730;	Square root (radical)
∝	&prop;	&#8733;	Proportional to
∞	&infin;	&#8734;	Infinity
∠	&ang;	&#8736;	Angle
∩	&cap;	&#8745;	Intersection (cap)
∪	&cup;	&#8746;	Union (cup)
∫	&int;	&#8747;	Integral
∴	&there4;	&#8756;	Therefore
~	&sim;	&#8764;	Tilde operator (varies with or similar to)
≈	&cong;	&#8773;	Approximately equal to

Continued on next page

TABLE MR4.2: EXTENDED HTML AND XHTML CHARACTERS *(continued)*

SYMBOL	MNEMONIC REPRESENTATION	NUMERIC REPRESENTATION	DESCRIPTION
≅	&asymp;	&#8776;	Almost equal to(asymptotic to)
≠	&ne;	&#8800;	Not equal to
	&equiv;	&#8801;	Identical to
≤	&le;	&#8804;	Less-than or equal to
≥	&ge;	&#8805;	Greater-than or equal to
⊂	&sub;	&#8834;	Subset of
⊃	&sup;	&#8835;	Superset of
⊄	&nsub;	&#8836;	Not a subset of
⊅	&sube;	&#8838;	Subset of or equal to
⊇	&supe;	&#8839;	Superset of or equal to
⊕	&oplus;	&#8853;	Circled plus (direct sum)
⊗	&otimes;	&#8855;	Circled times (vector product)
∧	&and;	&#8869;	Logical and (wedge)
⊥	&perp;	&#8869;	Up tack (orthogonal to or perpendicular)
∨	&or;	&#8870;	Logical or (vee)
·	&sdot;	&#8901;	Dot operator
	&lceil;	&#8968;	Left ceiling (apl upstile)
⌉	&rceil;	&#8969;	Right ceiling
⌊	&lfloor;	&#8970;	Left floor (apl downstile)
⌋	&rfloor;	&#8971;	Right floor
⟨	&lang;	&#9001;	Left-pointing angle bracket
⟩	&rang;	&#9002;	Right-pointing angle bracket
◊	&loz;	&#9674;	lozenge
♠	&spades;	&#9824;	Spade
♣	&clubs;	&#9827;	Club (shamrock)
♥	&hearts;	&#9829;	Heart (valentine)
♦	&diams;	&#9830;	Diamond

HTML, XHTML, and Character Sets

Your Web server, computer, and browser all use a defined *character set*, which is the collection of letters, numbers, and symbols that can be displayed. For English and other Western languages, for example, the default character set is called ISO-8859-1, also known as ISO-Latin-1. For the vast majority of HTML and XHTML documents you develop, you won't need to change this character set.

In rare instances, you may need to specify alternative character sets, either within the HTML or XHTML documents or on the Web server. For example, you may change the character set if you're developing documents for users who require a different character set (say, Russian-language readers).

Taking ISO-8859-1 as the example, this name breaks down as follows:

◆ *ISO* is the International Organization for Standardization.

◆ *8859* uniquely identifies the standard by number.

◆ *Latin* indicates that this standard is based on the Roman alphabet and is thus familiar to speakers of Western languages.

◆ The final number 1 indicates that this is the first variant for this character set definition.

NOTE *ISO does represent the International Organization for Standardization, but it is obviously not an acronym. The organization chose ISO because it derives from the Greek isos, which means equal. You can read the full explanation at* www.iso.ch/iso/en/aboutiso/introduction/whatisISO.html.

Table MR4.3 documents all of the variants of the ISO-8859 character sets and indicates which alphabets they support.

TABLE MR4.3: ISO 8859 CHARACTER SETS

CHARSET	SCRIPT	LANGUAGES
ISO-8859-1	Latin-1	ASCII plus most Western European languages, including Albanian, Afrikaans, Basque, Catalan, Danish, Dutch, English, Faroese, Finnish, Flemish, Galician, German, Icelandic, Irish, Italian, Norwegian, Portuguese, Scottish, Spanish, and Swedish. Omits certain Dutch, French, and German characters.
ISO-8859-2	Latin-2	ASCII plus most Central European languages, including Czech, English, German, Hungarian, Polish, Romanian, Croatian, Slovak, Slovene, and Serbian.
ISO-8859-3	Latin-3	ASCII plus characters required for English, Esperanto, German, Maltese, and Galician.
ISO-8859-4	Latin-4	ASCII plus most Baltic languages, including Latvian, Lithuanian, German, Greenlandic, and Lappish; now superseded by ISO-Latin-6.
ISO-8859-5		ASCII plus Cyrillic characters for Slavic languages, including Byelorussian, Bulgarian, Macedonian, Russian, Serbian, and Ukrainian.
ISO-8859-6		ASCII plus Arabic characters.
ISO-8859-7		ASCII plus Greek characters.

Continued on next page

TABLE MR4.3: ISO 8859 CHARACTER SETS *(continued)*

CHARSET	SCRIPT	LANGUAGES
ISO-8859-8		ASCII plus Hebrew.
ISO-8859-9	Latin-5	Latin-1 except that some Turkish symbols replace Icelandic ones.
ISO-8859-10	Latin-6	ASCII plus most Nordic languages, including Latvian, Lithuanian, Inuit, non-Skolt Sami, and Icelandic.
ISO-8859-11		ASCII plus Thai.
ISO-8859-12	Latin-7	ASCII plus Celtic.
ISO-8859-13	Latin-8	ASCII plus the Baltic Rim characters.
ISO-8859-14	Latin-9	ASCII plus Sami (Finnish).
ISO-8859-15	Latin-10	Variation on Latin-1 that includes euro currency sign, plus extra accented Finnish and French characters.

Note that the foundation for all these character sets is the set of ASCII characters familiar to computer users everywhere. *ASCII* stands for American Standard Code for Information Interchange, and for the purposes of this discussion, should be considered to consist of uppercase Roman alphabetic characters (A–Z), lowercase Roman alphabetic characters (a–z), numbers (0–9), and common punctuation marks. The ASCII character set uses 8-bit codes—that is, numeric values between 0 and 255. The ISO-8859 character sets use only 7-bit, or lower-order ASCII characters—those numbered from 0 to 127. Thus, higher-order ASCII characters—those numbered from 128 to 255—are not supported in the ISO-8859 character sets.

WARNING *If you're familiar with numeric ASCII codes for higher-order ASCII characters, you'll have to do some research to identify either character or numeric entities that work with HTML and XHTML to represent those characters. Also be forewarned that the numeric codes you have to use to represent those characters will not be the same as the ASCII codes you're probably used to.*

All characters that HTML or XHTML support are defined as part of the appropriate Document Type Declarations (DTDs). For HTML 4.01, take a look at `www.w3.org/TR/html401/sgml/entities.html` for the official definition.

These declarations for XHTML are divided into three different sets, and may be downloaded from the following W3C Web pages. All these files end with an `.ent` extension, but they are plain-text files and you may view them inside any text editor or word processor. Please note that we got strange results from Notepad but had no problems with other plain-text editors and Microsoft Word.

Latin-1   `www.w3.org/TR/xhtml1/DTD/xhtml-lat1.ent`

Special characters   `www.w3.org/TR/xhtml1/DTD/xhtml-special.ent`

Symbols   `www.w3.org/TR/xhtml1/DTD/xhtml-symbol.ent`

Readers who download and examine these files will notice several key items of information relevant to using character and numeric entities with XHTML:

- Character codes included also reference the ISO-8879 and ISO-10646 standards.

- Numeric codes go well beyond the range of 0–255 associated with ISO-8859 codes—in fact, that's where ISO-8879 and ISO-10646 come into play.

- ISO-10646 is nearly synonymous with the Unicode character set, which treats ISO-8859 and ISO-8879 as subsets of itself, and uses up to 16 bits for numeric character codes. (Numeric entities typically fall in the range of 0–65,535; 65,535 is equal to $2^{16}-1$, or the biggest integer that a 16-bit number can represent.)

In fact, the Unicode character set encompasses an incredibly broad range of character and numeric entities, along with nearly every written alphabet known to humankind. As such, it provides the broadest possible definition for characters that might appear in an XML or XHTML document. Just remember that if you want to use any characters outside those defined in ISO-Latin-1 in any XHTML documents you create, you must be sure to include the appropriate entity definitions in a DTD or schema that you invoke as part of your document. As long as you follow this guideline, you can take full advantage of what Unicode has to offer. For more information about Unicode, and a complete listing of Unicode characters, visit that organization's Web site at www.unicode.org.

Color Codes

USING EITHER CASCADING STYLE SHEETS (CSS), deprecated HTML, or XHTML elements, you can define the display of almost any element on your Web page—page backgrounds, table cell backgrounds, text color, link color, and so on. Although users can define browser preferences to override your color selections, they generally don't do so because most Web pages are not developed to support that option. As a result, most users find that setting their own color preferences isn't worth the effort and, instead, will see the colors you define for page elements.

You can define colors in two ways:

Hexadecimal value   A "hex" number defines the red, green, and blue (RGB) components of a color. A hexadecimal number is signaled by a pound sign (#) followed by six digits. The first two digits are for the red component, the next two digits define the amount of green in the color, and the last two digits are for the blue component. The hex code ff indicates the maximum possible value of a component. If you want red, green, or blue to be "turned off" or not represented, you use 00. For example, #0000ff means no red or green at all and the maximum possible amount of blue.

Color name   You can also use one of the standard 16 color names that are predefined—for example, red. These are listed in Table MR5.1 along with their corresponding hexadecimal values.

TABLE MR5.1: STANDARD COLORS

STANDARD COLOR NAME	HEXADECIMAL VALUE
aqua	#00ffff
black	#000000
blue	#0000ff
fuchsia	#ff00ff
gray	#808080
green	#008000
lime	#00ff00
maroon	#800000
navy	#000080
olive	#808000
purple	#800080
red	#ff0000
silver	#c0c0c0
teal	#008080
yellow	#ffff00
white	#ffffff

TIP *Many designers misspell* gray *and use an* e *instead of* a. *If you use* grey, *the browser will display the color green because that is the closest spelling. So be careful when using* gray.

Luckily, as designers, we're not limited to just those 16 colors. Many browsers support hundreds of color names, and you can always use hexadecimal values. Keep in mind, though, that some users have systems that can only display 256 colors. In this case, the browser either uses an existing color that is close to the color you define, or the browser dithers the color using available colors. See the section "Choosing Suitable Colors," in Chapter 4, "Including Images," for more information.

Table MR5.2 includes all 216 "safe" colors (256 colors minus the 40 that most systems reserve for other uses) that consistently look good in virtually all situations, including in backgrounds and in broad expanses of color. Although you don't have to choose from just these 216 colors—most systems these days can display millions of colors—you should consider doing so to ensure that the colors display as you intend them to on all of your potential users' systems. If you've selected a color that is close to one of these safe colors, consider changing the color to one that's safe.

TABLE MR5.2: THE 216 SAFE COLOR CODES

#000000	#000033	#000066	#000099	#0000CC	#0000FF
#003300	#003333	#003366	#003399	#0033CC	#0033FF
#006600	#006633	#006666	#006699	#0066CC	#0066FF
#009900	#009933	#009966	#009999	#0099CC	#0099FF
#00CC00	#00CC33	#00CC66	#00CC99	#00CCCC	#00CCFF
#00FF00	#00FF33	#00FF66	#00FF99	#00FFCC	#00FFFF
#330000	#330033	#330066	#330099	#3300CC	#3300FF
#333300	#333333	#333366	#333399	#3333CC	#3333FF
#336600	#336633	#336666	#336699	#3366CC	#3366FF
#339900	#339933	#339966	#339999	#3399CC	#3399FF
#33CC00	#33CC33	#33CC66	#33CC99	#33CCCC	#33CCFF
#33FF00	#33FF33	#33FF66	#33FF99	#33FFCC	#33FFFF
#660000	#660033	#660066	#660099	#6600CC	#6600FF
#663300	#663333	#663366	#663399	#6633CC	#6633FF
#666600	#666633	#666666	#666699	#6666CC	#6666FF
#669900	#669933	#669966	#669999	#6699CC	#6699FF
#66CC00	#66CC33	#66CC66	#66CC99	#66CCCC	#66CCFF
#66FF00	#66FF33	#66FF66	#66FF99	#66FFCC	#66FFFF
#990000	#990033	#990066	#990099	#9900CC	#9900FF
#993300	#993333	#993366	#993399	#9933CC	#9933FF
#996600	#996633	#996666	#996699	#9966CC	#9966FF
#999900	#999933	#999966	#999999	#9999CC	#9999FF
#99CC00	#99CC33	#99CC66	#99CC99	#99CCCC	#99CCFF
#99FF00	#99FF33	#99FF66	#99FF99	#99FFCC	#99FFFF
#CC0000	#CC0033	#CC0066	#CC0099	#CC00CC	#CC00FF
#CC3300	#CC3333	#CC3366	#CC3399	#CC33CC	#CC33FF
#CC6600	#CC6633	#CC6666	#CC6699	#CC66CC	#CC66FF
#CC9900	#CC9933	#CC9966	#CC9999	#CC99CC	#CC99FF
#CCCC00	#CCCC33	#CCCC66	#CCCC99	#CCCCCC	#CCCCFF
#CCFF00	#CCFF33	#CCFF66	#CCFF99	#CCFFCC	#CCFFFF
#FF0000	#FF0033	#FF0066	#FF0099	#FF00CC	#FF00FF
#FF3300	#FF3333	#FF3366	#FF3399	#FF33CC	#FF33FF
#FF6600	#FF6633	#FF6666	#FF6699	#FF66CC	#FF66FF
#FF9900	#FF9933	#FF9966	#FF9999	#FF99CC	#FF99FF
#FFCC00	#FFCC33	#FFCC66	#FFCC99	#FFCCCC	#FFCCFF
#FFFF00	#FFFF33	#FFFF66	#FFFF99	#FFFFCC	#FFFFFF

Of course, you may find it difficult to choose colors for your Web site using just these RGB numbers or general color names. Actually *seeing* the colors displayed on a computer system can certainly help. The following Web sites contain a variety of useful color information, from color charts to interesting articles, and even some great interactive color pickers and decimal/hexadecimal converters:

Clear Ink's Palette Man:

`www.paletteman.com`

HyperSolutions' RGB color chart:

`www.hypersolutions.org/rgb.html`

Tucow's HTML color chart:

`http://look.html.tucows.com/designer/colorhexchart.html`

VisiBone's Webmaster's Color Library:

`www.visibone.com/colorlab/`

Webmonkey's color chart:

`http://hotwired.lycos.com/webmonkey/reference/color_codes/`

Index

Note to the Reader: Throughout this index **boldfaced** page numbers indicate primary discussions of a topic. *Italicized* page numbers indicate illustrations.